ENGLISH ROMANTIC POETS

E. P. 6

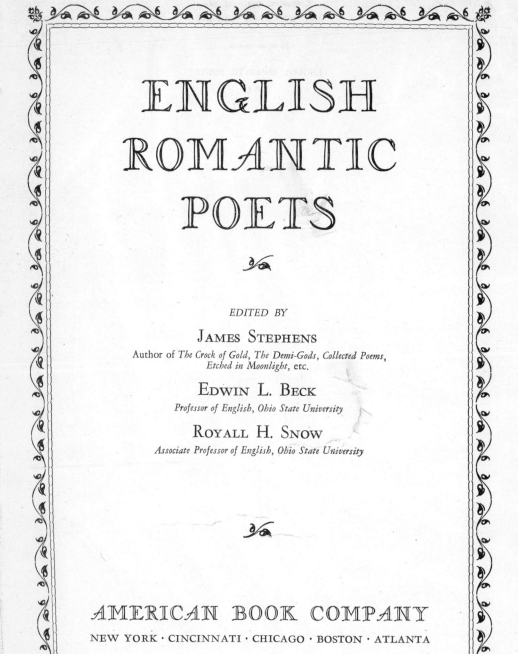

ENGLISH ROMANTIC POETS

EDITED BY

JAMES STEPHENS
Author of *The Crock of Gold, The Demi-Gods, Collected Poems, Etched in Moonlight,* etc.

EDWIN L. BECK
Professor of English, Ohio State University

ROYALL H. SNOW
Associate Professor of English, Ohio State University

AMERICAN BOOK COMPANY
NEW YORK · CINCINNATI · CHICAGO · BOSTON · ATLANTA

PREFACE

A WORD might be said about the principle of selection and arrangement of the material in this book. The quantity and the nature of the prose included represents something of a novelty in textbook procedure. Material about the poets has been excluded to allow space for the prose material which the poets wrote about poetry in general, and about themselves in particular. Poets are human beings as well as literary phenomena and, while the effort has been made to include all the more important literary pronouncements of the five major poets, space has been found to illustrate their vagaries and impulses as men. There is space for Keats to exclaim, "that thrush is a fine fellow," as well as to explain that "poetry should surprise by a fine excess."

A glance at the table of contents will explain what is meant, but attention is called especially to the personal letters of Wordsworth, Shelley, Byron, and Keats here printed. It has seemed to the editors that such material is more important to sound teaching than critical and historical matter. The facsimile reproductions of manuscript material constitute another intimate and real approach to the writers and their methods of workmanship. The descriptive caption with each illustration will serve as a general identification. For fuller information about the illustrations the reader should refer to the transcriptions of the manuscript texts and accompanying notes in Appendix I, page 795.

The poetry included is ample enough to allow for divergence of opinion and give the instructor some latitude of choice. The editors have faced that dragon which all textbook anthology editors face—the question of how much space to allow poems of little value in themselves but of interest as illustrating a tendency or a step in development. Enough of such material, in the case of the five major poets, has been included, so that the instructor may find examples convenient to his hand. *The Idiot Boy,* for example, more talked about than read, is here included. But the purely historical has emphatically been considered subordinate in the selection of this text. Space first went to what the selection of time has established, and the editors feel, again allowing for inevitable differences of opinion, that this text includes most of the established "best" of the five major poets of the period.

No effort was made to include in the section devoted to secondary figures all the rhymesters of minor historical interest. Landor, Scott, and Moore are well represented. The rest (and the group is comprehensive) are there because they also deserve to be included on the basis of intrinsic merit. There are major poets and minor in this imperfect world. The major establish their position by sustained power. The minor establish their right to a position in an anthology by occasional poems as good as those of the majors. Only such as could establish this right have been included, and therefore this textbook is advanced as a rather fair summary of the best in this period.

The date given at the end of each poem is the date of composition, unless otherwise noted. In a few cases among the secondary figures where it was difficult to ascribe a date with any certainty of accuracy, dates have been omitted. The order of arrangement of poems is chronological, except that where no great distortion was involved longer poems were shifted to the end, and shorter pieces grouped ahead of them. In the section devoted to secondary figures, the poets are arranged alphabetically.

In the preparation of the "Bibliographies and Notes" the editors are necessarily under great obligations to those who have preceded them in the study of the poets included in this collection. The Oxford University Press, New York, and the Delegates of the Clarendon Press, Oxford, England, have very kindly allowed the use of extended quotations from Benjamin P. Kurtz's *The Pursuit of Death*, C. D. Thorpe's *The Mind of John Keats*, M. R. Ridley's *Keats' Craftsmanship*, and J. Middleton Murry's *Studies in Keats* and *Countries of the Mind*. The quotations from John Livingston Lowes' *The Road to Xanadu* and Amy Lowell's *John Keats* are used by permission of Houghton Mifflin Company. The sources of quotations from other critics, biographers, and research workers are specifically indicated in connection with each quoted passage. The editors cannot emphasize too highly their indebtedness to Tom B. Haber, Ph.D., of Ohio State University, for the selection and annotation of the items making up the bibliography which precedes the notes on each individual poet.

J. S.

E. L. B.

R. H. S.

CONTENTS

PAGE

The Poets and Poetry of the Nineteenth Century: an Estimate . . By James Stephens   xix

WILLIAM WORDSWORTH (1770–1850)

Introductory Note   1
Lines Left upon a Seat in a Yew Tree   7
Margaret: or the Ruined Cottage   7
Lines Written in Early Spring   14
A Whirl-Blast from behind the Hill   14
Animal Tranquillity and Decay   15
To My Sister   15
Simon Lee, the Old Huntsman   15
We Are Seven   16
There Was a Boy   17
Expostulation and Reply   18
The Tables Turned   18
The Idiot Boy   18
Lines, Composed a Few Miles above Tintern Abbey   24
The Old Cumberland Beggar   25
Strange Fits of Passion Have I Known   28
She Dwelt among the Untrodden Ways   28
I Travelled among Unknown Men   28
Three Years She Grew in Sun and Shower   28
A Slumber Did My Spirit Seal   29
Nutting   29
Matthew   30
The Two April Mornings   30
The Fountain   31
Ruth   32
Lucy Gray   35
The Simplon Pass   35
To M. H. ("Our walk was far among the ancient trees")   36
It Was an April Morning   36
There Is an Eminence   37
When, to the Attractions of the Busy World   37
The Brothers   38
Michael   44
The Sparrow's Nest   50
The Affliction of Margaret ——   50
My Heart Leaps Up   51
To a Butterfly   51
To the Small Celandine   52
To the Daisy ("In youth from rock to rock I went")   52
To the Same Flower ("With little here to do or see")   53
To the Daisy ("Bright flower! whose home is everywhere") . . .   54
To the Cuckoo   54
Resolution and Independence   55
It Is a Beauteous Evening   57
Where Lies the Land   57
With How Sad Steps   57

	PAGE
Composed upon Westminster Bridge	57
Written in London	57
London, 1802	58
It Is Not To Be Thought Of	58
On the Extinction of the Venetian Republic	58
To Toussaint L'Ouverture	58
Composed in the Valley near Dover	58
September, 1802. Near Dover	59
Composed by the Sea-Side, near Calais	59
The Green Linnet	59
The Solitary Reaper	60
To a Highland Girl	60
Yew-Trees	61
At the Grave of Burns	61
Yarrow Unvisited	62
Stepping Westward	63
Ode: Intimations of Immortality from Recollections of Early Childhood	63
French Revolution	66
I Wandered Lonely as a Cloud	66
She Was a Phantom of Delight	67
To a Young Lady	67
Character of the Happy Warrior	67
Ode to Duty	68
Elegiac Stanzas	69
Nuns Fret Not	70
To Sleep	70
The World Is too Much with Us	70
Personal Talk	70
Yes, It Was the Mountain Echo	71
Song at the Feast of Brougham Castle	71
Two Voices Are There	73
Composed by the Side of Grasmere Lake	74
Feelings of the Tyrolese	74
Surprised by Joy	74
Yarrow Visited	74
Laodamia	75
Composed upon an Evening of Extraordinary Splendour and Beauty	79
To —— ("O dearer far than light and life are dear")	79
To a Skylark	80
Scorn Not the Sonnet	80
Why Art Thou Silent	80
Most Sweet It Is with Unuplifted Eyes	80
Serving No Haughty Muse	81
A Poet!—He Hath Put His Heart to School	81
From The Prelude	
Book I Introduction—Childhood and School-Time (lines 1–646)	81
" II School-Time (lines 376–471)	89
" IV Summer Vacation (lines 137–190)	90
" V Books (lines 1–49)	90
" VI Cambridge and the Alps (lines 592–608)	91
" VII Residence in London (lines 619–6 8)	91
" VIII Retrospect—Love of Nature Leading to Love of Man (lines 215– 38)	92
" IX Residence in France (lines 390–416)	92
" X Residence in France (lines 154–190)	92
" XI France (lines 392–423)	93
" XII Imagination and Taste (lines 93–121, 151–173, 248–261, 295–335)	93

PAGE

Book XIII   Imagination and Taste (lines 1–39)   95
  "   XIV   Conclusion (lines 40–118, 162–187)   95
From The Excursion
  Prospectus (lines 1–107)   96
  Book   II   The Solitary (lines 696–724)   99
    "   IV   Despondency Corrected (lines 332–350)   99
    "   VII   The Churchyard among the Mountains (lines 482–515)   99
    " VIII   The Parsonage (lines 231–282)   100
Preface to Lyrical Ballads   101
Selections from Wordsworth's Letters
     I   To John Wilson (Christopher North)—The Influence of Natural Objects;
             The Idiot Boy   112
    II   To Sir Walter Scott—Dryden as a Poet   116
   III   To Sir George Beaumont—The Language of Poetry   116
    IV   To Lady Beaumont—The Destiny of His Poems   117
     V   To Henry Reed—The Impressions Made by His Poems   118
    VI   To Bernard Barton—The Pure Source of His Inspiration   119
   VII   To Edward Moxon—The Seduction of Verse   119
  VIII   To Lieutenant-General Sir William M. Gomm—Poetry a Great Art . .   119
    IX   To W. R. Hamilton—Criticising a Friend's Verses   121
     X   To the Rev. Robert Montgomery—Every Writer His Own Best Critic   121
    XI   To Alexander Dyce—A Poetess of Genius   121
   XII   To Alexander Dyce—The Greatness of English Drama   121
  XIII   To W. R. Hamilton—The Hard Art of Poetry   122
   XIV   To Edward Moxon—His Poetry Goes Begging   122
    XV   To the Rev. Alexander Dyce—The Sonnet   122
   XVI   To the Rev. Alexander Dyce—On Dyce's Collection of Sonnets . . .   123
  XVII   To Sir George Beaumont—Taste in Natural Beauty   123
 XVIII   To Sir George Beaumont—Man's Treatment of Scenery   124
   XIX   To Sir George Beaumont—The Painter Reynolds   125
    XX   To the Rev. Christopher Wordsworth—Education of Man   125
   XXI   To Mr. Mathews—Disapproval of Monarchical Governments   125
  XXII   To L—— —On His Political Opinions   125
 XXIII   To the Bishop of Llandaff—On the Extraordinary Avowal of His Political
             Principles   126
  XXIV   To Robert Southey—The Nature of Tyranny   137
   XXV   To Professor Henry Reed—Philosophy at Boston   137
  XXVI   To the Right Hon. the Earl De La Warr—Declining the Laureateship .   137
 XXVII   To Lady F. Bentinck—Reason for Declining the Laureateship   138
XXVIII   To the Right Hon. the Earl De La Warr—Accepting the Laureateship .   138
  XXIX   To Professor Henry Reed—The Queen's Reception to the Laureate . .   138
   XXX   Extracts from Conversations with His Nephew, Christopher Wordsworth   139

SAMUEL TAYLOR COLERIDGE (1772–1834)

Introductory Note   141
To the Rev. W. L. Bowles   145
The Eolian Harp   145
From Religious Musings (lines 28–45, 395–419)   147
This Lime-Tree Bower My Prison   147
The Rime of the Ancient Mariner   149
Christabel   164
Frost at Midnight   173
France: An Ode   174
Lewti   175
Fears in Solitude   176

PAGE

The Nightingale 179
The Ballad of the Dark Ladié 181
Kubla Khan 182
Love 183
Dejection: An Ode 184
Hymn before Sun-rise, in the Vale of Chamouni 186
Answer to a Child's Question 187
The Exchange 188
The Pains of Sleep. 188
To William Wordsworth 188
Glycine's Song 190
From Limbo (lines 11–38) 190
The Knight's Tomb 190
Youth and Age. 191
Work without Hope 191
Song 191
Song, *ex improviso* 193
Epitaph 193
From Biographia Literaria
  Chapter IV (part) 193
    "   XIV (complete) 195
    "   XVII (complete) 199
    "   XVIII (complete) 205
    "   XIX (part) 215
    "   XX (part) 216
    "   XXII (complete) 217

GEORGE GORDON, LORD BYRON (1788–1824)

Introductory Note. 233
Stanzas for Music ("Bright be the place of thy soul!") 238
When We Two Parted 238
Well! Thou Art Happy 238
Maid of Athens, Ere We Part 239
And Thou Art Dead, As Young and Fair. 239
Lines to a Lady Weeping 240
She Walks in Beauty 240
Oh! Snatch'd Away in Beauty's Bloom. 240
When Coldness Wraps This Suffering Clay 240
The Destruction of Sennacherib 242
Stanzas for Music ("There be none of Beauty's daughters") 242
Fare Thee Well 242
Stanzas to Augusta ("When all around grew drear and dark") 243
Stanzas to Augusta ("Though the day of my destiny's over") 244
Epistle to Augusta 244
So, We'll Go No More a Roving 246
To Thomas Moore 246
Stanzas Written on the Road between Florence and Pisa 246
On This Day I Complete My Thirty-sixth Year 247
From Childe Harold's Pilgrimage
  Canto the Third (complete) 247
  Canto the Fourth
    Refuge in Venice (stanzas i–x) 266
    On Rome (stanzas lxxviii–lxxxix) 268
    Bitter Meditation (stanzas cxxi–cxxxviii) 269
    The Ocean (stanzas clxxvii–clxxxvi) 272

		PAGE
Manfred: A Dramatic Poem		274
From Don Juan		
Fragment		292
Dedication		292
Canto the First (complete)		295
Canto the Second (complete)		321
Canto the Third		
The Isles of Greece		348
Ave Maria (stanzas ci–cix)		349
The Vision of Judgment		350
Extracts from a Diary of Lord Byron, 1821		363
On Artificiality and Pope		370
Selections from the Letters of Lord Byron		
I	To Francis Hodgson	372
II	To His Mother.	373
III	To His Mother.	375
IV	To Francis Hodgson	376
V	To Scrope Davies.	376
VI	To R. C. Dallas	376
VII	To R. C. Dallas	377
VIII	To Lady Caroline Lamb	378
IX	To Lady Caroline Lamb	378
X	To Lord Holland	379
XI	To Lady Melbourne	379
XII	To W. Gifford, Esq.	380
XIII	To Miss Milbanke.	380
XIV	To Miss Milbanke.	381
XV	To Thomas Moore	382
XVI	To Thomas Moore	383
XVII	To Miss Milbanke	383
XVIII	To Lady Melbourne	384
XIX	To Thomas Moore	384
XX	To Leigh Hunt	385
XXI	To Thomas Moore	386
XXII	To Lady Byron	387
XXIII	To the Hon. Augusta Leigh	387
XXIV	To Thomas Moore	388
XXV	To Thomas Moore	389
XXVI	To John Murray	391
XXVII	To Thomas Moore	392
XXVIII	To Thomas Moore	392
XXIX	To Lady Byron	393
XXX	To John Murray	393
XXXI	To Douglas Kinnaird	396
XXXII	To John Murray	397
XXXIII	To John Murray	398
XXXIV	To the Countess Guiccioli	399
XXXV	To Thomas Moore	399
XXXVI	To John Murray	399
XXXVII	To Percy Bysshe Shelley	400
XXXVIII	To Thomas Moore	401
XXXIX	To John Murray	401
XL	To John Murray	402
XLI	To John Murray	402
XLII	To Thomas Moore	404
XLIII	To John Murray	405

PAGE

XLIV   To Lady ——— 405
XLV   To Thomas Moore 405
XLVI   To the Earl of Blessington 406
XLVII To the Hon. Douglas Kinnaird 406
XLVIII To Lieut.-Colonel Napier 407
XLIX   To the Hon. Augusta Leigh 407
L   To Thomas Moore 408

PERCY BYSSHE SHELLEY (1792–1822)

Introductory Note 409
To Wordsworth 415
Hymn to Intellectual Beauty 415
To Constantia, Singing 416
A Fragment: To Music 417
Ozymandias 417
From the Revolt of Islam: Dedication 417
Lines Written among the Euganean Hills 421
Stanzas Written in Dejection, Near Naples 425
Sonnet ("Lift not the painted veil which those who live") . . 426
Song to the Men of England 426
Ode to the West Wind 426
The Indian Serenade 427
Love's Philosophy 428
The Sensitive Plant 428
The Cloud 432
To a Skylark 433
To ——— ("I fear thy kisses, gentle maiden") 435
Hymn of Pan 435
The Two Spirits: An Allegory 435
The World's Wanderers 436
Time Long Past 436
To Night 436
To ——— 438
Song 438
Mutability 439
A Lament 439
To ——— ("One word is too often profaned") 439
To ——— ("When passion's trance is overpast") 439
Music 439
Fragment: "When Soft Winds and Sunny Skies" 440
From Hellas: Chorus 440
Lines: "When the Lamp Is Shattered" 440
To Jane: The Invitation 441
With a Guitar, to Jane 441
A Dirge 442
Alastor, or, The Spirit of Solitude 444
Prometheus Unbound 453
Epipsychidion 490
Adonais 497
The Triumph of Life 506
Stanzas — April, 1814 514
A Defence of Poetry 515
Selections from the Letters of Shelley
    I   To Thomas Jefferson Hogg 531
    II To Thomas Jefferson Hogg 532

PAGE

III To Thomas Jefferson Hogg 533
IV To Elizabeth Hitchener 533
V To Elizabeth Hitchener 534
VI To William Godwin 535
VII To William Godwin 536
VIII To Thomas Jefferson Hogg 538
IX To Leigh Hunt 538
X To Charles and James Ollier 539
XI To Leigh Hunt 541
XII To Charles and James Ollier 542
XIII To John Keats 543
XIV To the Editor of *The Quarterly Review* 543
XV To Charles Ollier 544
XVI To the Editor of *The Examiner* 545
XVII To Thomas Love Peacock 545
XVIII To John Gisborne 546
XIX To Horace Smith 547
XX To John Gisborne 548

JOHN KEATS (1795–1821)

Introductory Note 551
Bibliographical List of Keats's Volumes 555
Imitation of Spenser 557
Sonnets (1816–1817)
    I O Solitude! If I Must with You Dwell 557
    II How Many Bards Gild the Lapses of Time! 557
    III To One Who Has Been Long in City Pent 557
    IV On First Looking into Chapman's Homer 558
    V Addressed to Haydon 558
    VI Keen, Fitful Gusts Are Whisp'ring Here and There . . . 558
    VII Happy Is England! I Could Be Content 558
    VIII To G. A. W. 558
    IX On the Grasshopper and Cricket 559
    X After Dark Vapours Have Oppress'd Our Plains 559
    XI To Leigh Hunt, Esq. 559
    XII On Seeing the Elgin Marbles 559
    XIII On the Sea 559
    XIV On a Picture of Leander 560
Specimen of an Induction to a Poem 560
I Stood Tip-toe upon a Little Hill 561
From Sleep and Poetry (lines 53–154, 181–247) 564
From Endymion
    Book I
        Credo (lines 1–62) 566
        Endymion's Vision (lines 538–712) 567
        Wherein Lies Happiness (lines 769–857) 569
    Book II
        Induction (lines 1–43) 570
        Adonis in Slumber (lines 387–427) 570
    Book III
        Address to the Moon (lines 142–187) 571
    Book IV
        The Indian Maid (lines 98–181) 572
        Encounter with Sleep (lines 362–408) 573
        Loss of the Mortal Maiden (lines 496–512) 574

PAGE

Endymion Chooses Mortal Love (lines 615–721) 574
Conclusion: the Decision of the Gods (lines 969–1003) 575
Stanzas 576
Isabella; or the Pot of Basil 576
Lines on the Mermaid Tavern 583
Meg Merrilies 583
Ode ("Bards of Passion and of Mirth") 584
Sonnets (1818–1819)
   I   When I Have Fears That I May Cease to Be 584
  II   Bright Star, Would I Were Steadfast as Thou Art 584
 III   Why Did I Laugh To-night? No Voice Will Tell 585
 IV   On Fame ("Fame, like a wayward Girl, will still be coy") 585
  V   On Fame ("How fever'd is the man, who cannot look"). 585
 VI   On the Sonnet 585
 VII   To Fanny. 585
The Eve of St. Agnes. 586
The Eve of St. Mark 591
La Belle Dame sans Merci 592
Ode to Psyche 593
Ode on a Grecian Urn 594
Ode on Melancholy 595
Ode to a Nightingale 595
To Autumn 597
Lamia 598
Hyperion. 606
Selections from the Letters of John Keats
   I   To John Hamilton Reynolds 617
  II   To Leigh Hunt 617
 III   To Benjamin Bailey 618
 IV   To Benjamin Bailey 620
  V   To Benjamin Bailey 620
 VI   To George and Thomas Keats 622
 VII   To George and Thomas Keats 623
VIII   To George and Thomas Keats 623
 IX   To John Taylor 624
  X   To John Hamilton Reynolds 624
 XI   To John Taylor 625
 XII   To Benjamin Robert Haydon 626
XIII   To John Hamilton Reynolds 626
XIV   To John Taylor 627
XV   To John Hamilton Reynolds 628
XVI   To Fanny Keats 629
XVII   To John Hamilton Reynolds 631
XVIII   To James Augustus Hessey 632
XIX   To George and Georgiana Keats 632
XX   To Richard Woodhouse 634
XXI   To George and Georgiana Keats. 635
XXII   To George and Georgiana Keats. 638
XXIII   To George and Georgiana Keats. 639
XXIV   To George and Georgiana Keats. 640
XXV   To George and Georgiana Keats. 641
XXVI   To Benjamin Robert Haydon 643
XXVII   To Benjamin Robert Haydon 643
XXVIII   To Fanny Keats 644
XXIX   To Fanny Brawne 644
XXX   To Fanny Brawne 645

PAGE

XXXI To Charles Wentworth Dilke 646
XXXII To John Taylor 647
XXXIII To Benjamin Bailey 647
XXXIV To George and Georgiana Keats. 648
XXXV To Charles Armitage Brown 650
XXXVI To Georgiana Augusta Keats 651
XXXVII To James Rice 652
XXXVIII To Fanny Brawne 653
XXXIX To Fanny Brawne 653
XL To Fanny Brawne 653
XLI To Fanny Brawne 653
XLII To Fanny Brawne 653
XLIII To Fanny Brawne 654
XLIV To Benjamin Robert Haydon 654
XLV To Fanny Brawne 655
XLVI To Percy Bysshe Shelley 655
XLVII To Charles Armitage Brown 656

THOMAS LOVELL BEDDOES (1803–1849)

Introductory Note 657
How Many Times Do I Love Thee, Dear? 658
Strew Not Earth with Empty Stars 658
Songs from Death's Jest-Book
I The Swallow Leaves Her Nest 658
II If Thou Wilt Ease Thine Heart 658
III Old Adam, the Carrion Crow 659
IV We Do Lie beneath the Grass 659
Scene from Death's Jest-Book 659
Fragments Intended for the Dramas
I Subterranean City 661
II Dream of Dying. 661
III Insignificance of the World 661
IV A Beautiful Night 661
V A Lofty Mind 661
Silenus in Proteus 662
Dream-Pedlary 662
Song Translated from the German of Walther von der Vogelweide 662
The Phantom-Wooer 663
Dirge for a Young Maiden 663
Dirge ("To her couch of evening rest") 663
Song on the Water 663
Song of the Stygian Naiades 663
Lyrical Fragments
I Lines Written at Geneva 664
II Stanzas from the Ivory Gate. 664
III Threnody 665

THOMAS CAMPBELL (1777–1844)

Introductory Note 665
The Harper 666
Ye Mariners of England 666
Hohenlinden 666
Lochiel's Warning 668
Battle of the Baltic 669

PAGE

Lord Ullin's Daughter 670
To the Rainbow 671
Song: To the Evening Star 671
To Mary Sinclair, with a Volume of His Poems 672
The Dead Eagle 672

JOHN CLARE (1793–1864)

Introductory Note 673
Approach of Spring 674
Noon 674
Recollections after an Evening Walk 675
The Wood-Cutter's Night Song 676
Solitude 677
From Summer Images 681
The Swallow 681
Young Jenny 682
The Dying Child 682

HARTLEY COLERIDGE (1796–1849)

Introductory Note 683
Song: She Is Not Fair 683
"Multum Dilexit" 683
Sonnet: Long Time a Child 683

ALLAN CUNNINGHAM (1784–1842)

Introductory Note 684
A Wet Sheet and a Flowing Sea 684

ROBERT STEPHEN HAWKER (1803–1875)

Introductory Note 684
The Song of the Western Men 685

FELICIA DOROTHEA HEMANS (1793–1835)

Introductory Note 685
The Landing of the Pilgrim Fathers in New England 685
The Palm Tree 686
Come to Me, Gentle Sleep! 686
Evening Song of the Weary 687

THOMAS HOOD (1799–1845)

Introductory Note 687
The Last Man 688
Faithless Sally Brown 690
The Mermaid of Margate 691
Faithless Nelly Gray 694
From Hero and Leander 695
Fair Ines 695
Ode: Autumn 695
Ballad 696
Ruth 697

PAGE

I Remember, I Remember 697
Song 697
Silence 697
The Dream of Eugene Aram, the Murderer 698
Domestic Asides; or, Truth in Parentheses 700
Sally Simpkin's Lament 701
Epicurean Reminiscences of a Sentimentalist 701
French and English 702
Pair'd, *not* Match'd 703
The Song of the Shirt 703
The Bridge of Sighs 704
The Lay of the Labourer 706
Stanzas 707

LEIGH HUNT (1784–1859)

Introductory Note 707
From The Story of Rimini 708
The Poets 710
Written under the Engraving of a Portrait of Rafael 712
To the Grasshopper and the Cricket. 712
The Prayer in the Bower 712
Abou Ben Adhem 712
Rondeau 714
Dirge for an Infant 714
On the Death of His Son Vincent 714

CHARLES LAMB (1775–1834)

Introductory Note 714
The Old Familiar Faces 717
Hester 718

WALTER SAVAGE LANDOR (1775–1864)

Introductory Note 718
Rose Aylmer 719
Regeneration 719
Fiesolan Idyl. 722
To Corinth 722
The Death of Artemidora 723
From the Hellenics
    I   On the Hellenics 723
    II Iphigeneia and Agamemnon 723
    III The Hamadryad 724
Lyrics and Epigrams
    I   Mild Is the Parting Year 728
    II   In Clementina's Artless Mien 728
    III Pursuits! Alas, I Now Have None 728
    IV   Proud Word You Never Spoke 728
    V   Little You Think 728
    VI   Dull Is My Verse 728
    VII The Day Returns 730
    VIII Twenty Years Hence 730
    IX   I Cannot Tell 730
    X   The Maid I Love 730

PAGE

    XI   Mother, I Cannot Mind My Wheel 730
   XII   One Year Ago 730
  XIII   Yes, I Write Verses 730
   XIV   Why, Why Repine 731
    XV   I Know Not Whether I Am Proud 731
   XVI   Ye Little Household Gods 731
  XVII   Alas, How Soon the Hours 731
 XVIII   To Robert Browning 731
   XIX   I Strove with None 732
    XX   A Provident and Wakeful Fear 732
   XXI   God Scatters Beauty 732
  XXII   Death Stands above Me 732
 XXIII   So Then, I Feel Not Deeply 732
  XXIV   To Youth. 732
   XXV   To Age 734
  XXVI   To My Ninth Decade 734

JAMES (CLARENCE) MANGAN (1803–1849)

Introductory Note 734
Dark Rosaleen 735
O'Hussey's Ode to the Maguire 737
Kathaleen Ny-Houlahan 740
Siberia 740
Shapes and Signs 741

THOMAS MOORE (1779–1852)

Introductory Note 741
From Irish Melodies
    O' Breathe Not His Name 742
    The Harp that Once Through Tara's Halls 742
    Rich and Rare Were the Gems She Wore 742
    The Meeting of the Waters 743
    How Dear to Me This Hour 743
    Let Erin Remember the Days of Old 743
    The Song of Fionnuala 743
    Believe Me, If All Those Endearing Young Charms 744
    After the Battle 744
    She Is Far from the Land 744
    'Tis the Last Rose of Summer 744
    The Minstrel Boy 745
    The Time I've Lost in Wooing 745
    Come, Rest in This Bosom 745
    Dear Harp of My Country 745
    I Wish I Was by That Dim Lake 746
From National Airs
    Oft, in the Stilly Night 746
    Hark! The Vesper Hymn Is Stealing 746
From Ballads, Songs, Miscellaneous Poems, etc.
    Child's Song 747

WILLIAM MOTHERWELL (1797–1835)

Introductory Note 747
Bonnie George Campbell 747

THOMAS LOVE PEACOCK (1785–1866)

Introductory Note 747
The Grave of Love 748
For the Slender Beech and the Sapling Oak 748
Though I Be Now a Gray, Gray Friar 748
The War-Song of Dinas Vawr 748

WINTHROP MACKWORTH PRAED (1802–1839)

Introductory Note 750
To —— ("We met but in one giddy dance") 751
Peace Be Thine 751
Love at a Rout 751
Remember Me 752
How Am I Like Her? 752
The Vicar 753
The Belle of the Ball-Room 754
The Talented Man 755
Latin Hymn to the Virgin 756
The Newly-Wedded 756

SAMUEL ROGERS (1763–1855)

Introductory Note 757
A Wish 759

SIR WALTER SCOTT (1771–1832)

Introductory Note 759
From The Lay of the Last Minstrel
   I   Sweet Teviot 761
  II   Breathes There the Man 761
 III   Song of Albert Graeme 762
 IV   Harold's Song 762
From Marmion
   I   The Shepherd 763
  II   Lochinvar 763
 III   Christmas 764
 IV   The Battle 765
From The Lady of the Lake
   I   Harp of the North 770
  II   Soldier, Rest 770
 III   The Fiery Cross 770
 IV   Coronach 772
  V   The Heath This Night Must Be My Bed 773
 VI   The Toils Are Pitched 773
From Rokeby
   I   Brignall Banks 773
  II   Allen-a-Dale 775
 III   The Cypress Wreath 775
 IV   Ballad 776
Songs and Ballads
   I   William and Helen 776
  II   The Maid of Neidpath 779
 III   Lullaby of an Infant Chief 780

                                                                    PAGE
   IV   Jock of Hazeldean   780
    V   Sound the Clarion   780
   VI   Proud Maisie   780
  VII   Bonny Dundee   781

ROBERT SOUTHEY (1774–1843)

   Introductory Note   782
   Sonnet   783
   The Battle of Blenheim   783
   The Holly-Tree   785
   Written Immediately after Reading the Speech of Robert Emmet . .   785
   My Days among the Dead Are Past   786
   Imitated from the Persian   787
   Prelude   787
   From A Vision of Judgement: The Absolvers   787

HENRY KIRKE WHITE (1785–1806)

   Introductory Note   789
   Description of a Summer's Eve   790
   Verses   790
   A Pastoral Song   790
   Fragment   791

CHARLES WOLFE (1791–1823)

   Introductory Note   791
   The Burial of Sir John Moore at Corunna   791

APPENDIX

     I   The Illustrations   795
    II   Bibliographies and Notes   807
   III   Index of Authors, Titles, and First Lines of Poetry   965

THE POETS AND POETRY OF THE NINETEENTH CENTURY

AN ESTIMATE

IN ATTEMPTING to review the literature of the Nineteenth Century we find that there is, as at the back of the mind, an uneasy reflection or system of reflections. We have passed from that mode, is one such reflection. There is no means of returning to it, is another. We do not wish to do so, nor is there any reason for such returning, are yet others.

Such a passing from the mode may enable us to regard its production with another closeness, another serenity than those which were previously possible— or it may not. The epoch is so nigh to us in time it should not seem withdrawn, or of peculiar difficulty or distinction. We do find distinction and difficulty; for, truly, that epoch is sundered from us by a change that is wider and deeper than has ever before intervened between two generations.

The change that has come between the Nineteenth and Twentieth Centuries is radical; and is, progressively, sundering: it is operative in every department of Life and Letters, and is still to operate. Something is finished, and something has begun. Within the space of thirty recent years a world has come into being; and, that it might come into being, a world has been obliterated.

The Nineteenth Century bequest of prose and verse stands in danger, and one wonders if the fate that has befallen one of these two may not, by the mere logic of epidemic, extend to the other.

Nineteenth Century prose is not now *in danger* of forgetfulness—it is, already, more than partially forgotten. Reputations which, only three decades ago, were in every cultivated person's memory, and ready upon every cultivated person's lips, are still, though fadingly, in the memory, but are no longer upon the lip. The idea of Scott or Dickens or Thackeray is no longer urgent in any youthful mind. Lamb or Carlyle, Macaulay or Hazlitt or Ruskin inspires no man's enthusiasm. Only the Brontë sisters (perhaps Jane Austen and Trollope) retain devotees, and can still evoke a literary and personal curiosity in the reader or the critic. The remainder of that enormous prose literature has gone down the wind.

Thirty years ago it was inconceivable that disaster could possibly overtake this literature. Each of these writers was stayed and stablished as by or upon a hill. Each rested in the confidence that English literature and history and tradition could and would secure him against any possible calamity, and that only a veritable world-cataclysm could possibly disturb him.

In the recent thirty years we have outlived a dozen world-cataclysms, by the side of which the tramplings of a Bonaparte seem only as the aimless skirmishings of a child. The economic, the social, the cultural, the political and moral spheres of mankind have been so harassed and transformed that today no "value" inheres for us that was stable and functioning only thirty years ago.

If a great prose literature and the sanctions upon which it is founded can be thus summarily dismissed, shall the parallel poetical literature submit to the same fate? Or is it true that poetry is of another mode, another matter, another integrity than prose? That its being is independent of scientific, or moral, or philosophical values, and its nature set elsewhere than in social contingencies?

There is an inner vitality in fine poetry which, historically, has preserved it from the disintegration to which prose is subject; and the work of a Shelley or a Wordsworth must be examined with another preoccupation, and from another level, than those we should find suitable in the case of a Thackeray or a Carlyle.

The intention of an Anthology is not, primarily, critical. The effort of the compiler should be to gather so much representative matter from each author that a judgment can thereupon be formed as to the field and the worth of that particular person. Judgment upon a writer can be truly final; it can cover every ground; for the writer, whether deliberately or not, does deliver himself to his reader and critic more completely than any other artist or human being can possibly manage. The writer is known to his critic socially, morally, psychologically, and, even, spiritually. If the writer be also an artist there is no possible disguise that he can use. There is no possible evasion by which he can retire himself from critical examination. He is given in the piece and in the lump, and the critic can finally "place" him as unerringly as a botanist "places" a plant.

A Selection, however, is other than an Anthology and should have as its base a severely critical intention; and in a Selection only work that exhibits the author at his best may be included.

At this date an Anthology of Nineteenth Century poetry must attempt to be selective also. Much water has flowed under the bridges since this poetry was composed; the "values" incident to that period are established, or are so comprehended that criticism can report upon them. The problems which beset those writers, in an economic, a cultural, or a technical sense, are largely removed from us as problems; are entirely removed from us as competitive and challenging production; and the personages represented have submitted to a large general criticism, which (though the final word has not yet been said) permits a just estimate to be formed as to the weight and variety of talent they have bequeathed to us.

This bequest is (or was) our inheritance. It has (however we exclaim against this) largely fashioned our culture and our technique; and only on the condition that we find this inheritance unsatisfying or limiting can we consciously depart from it, and apply ourselves to the discovery of other means than those they used, and to the ascertaining of other values than those which contented and exercised our predecessors. Put broadly, "value" is that which we wish to consider as immutable.

Mere lapse of time does not constitute or bring into being a "new" generation. Whatever time seems engaged, the old generation is yet in being while economic and technical facts remain unchanged. That is a new generation which, of necessity, professes dissatisfaction with and challenges the basic or working values of the preceding age. Such a dissatisfaction is now in being, and to justify this is a chief reason why criticism should be extreme on all that is extended to us from the immediate past.

Every "new" generation must revaluate the values; and to do this it must seek for another definition of that in which value inheres. Wherever and whenever a new definition is made, a new epoch is in being. In every generation, the sole means we have of evaluating it lies in the definitions which it advanced on those matters which were, for it, of fruitful importance. Definition is moral, or scientific, or economic. There is no artistic or philosophic definition of one's own time, for these are seeking a timeless truth.

Every story is situated in time: no poem is. Every story is sociological: no poem is. Every story is incomplete: no poem is. Therefore prose values are at the mercy of the next day: poetic values are only at the mercy of the language.

Definition is the epoch in its youth. It is that posited upon which the age will work as upon a guiding rule: and it seems certain that until such redefinition is attempted, no restabilization of values is possible for our generation, and there is no possibility of a regeneration of the debilitated art and culture, which are "ours" because we have inherited them, and are not ours because we cannot add to their growth: for if anything seems certain it is that we will not add much to the poetic epoch that began with Shakespeare and ended with Tennyson. The reason it cannot be added to is because it is completed.

An attempt at definition is worth making. We are at sea. But we are not at sea in a desert. A world of hitherto unrevealed variety and abundance is about us, and is uncharted. The economic of, the art of, the philosophy of paucity and the mean do not now express man, his capability, or his quest; and, until our definition of that which is basic to value is brought into conformity with our facts of superabundance and potential freedom, we shall get nowhere, and engage in nothing to its, and our own, extreme.

When examining poetry in the fashion which makes an Anthology, one cannot avoid considering that some poets wear better than others, and that there are many poets who have been forgotten, and who may, or may not, be again remembered.

When examined in this fashion, certain writers such as Tennyson, Byron, and Swinburne, are seen more clearly because of the rest they have had. Each of these has, now for quite a period, gone out of public appreciation; and critical curiosity is often exercised in the query as to whether these forgotten poets can or cannot come back. To every writer this going out, or being sent to Coventry, comes. The poet is forgotten, but while such forgetfulness may be temporary, it can be final. This critic would suggest that of these three only Byron can "come back."

Two periods of public neglect come to every fine writer. The first is during his own lifetime, and is indicated, is almost explained, in the jest attributed (I think) to Balzac — "Yes, Victor Hugo is a great man: let's not talk about him."

The public must think in this fashion about their great men. To be abundantly available carries also an idea of being too available. At a point in their days our Tennysons and Hardys, our Welleses and Chestertons and Shaws, do inordinately clutter our ways: they are stamping around all of our corners: they lie, each like a sack of wet sand, upon our own struggling production; so that, in mere self-defense, we laughingly detest them; and get to our own businesses by forgetting them.

If their talents are real they "come back," but an interim of at least ten years has to be lived through by every artist, during which, if he be remembered, he is reviled; and if he be merely considered unmentionable he may cultivate his modesty, or his *choux*, as best he may. This is his Squaw Winter; and, if he live through it, he comes to an Indian Summer in which appreciation and affection are given to him from every quarter; and are given with as beautiful an unreason as they were before unreasonably withheld.

Again, upon the day following the day of his death, the artist follows the man into silence and the void; and in that oblivion he will rest for nigh on forty years ere he be again discovered (if he is to be rediscovered), or finally and utterly forgotten if his talent be one that invokes the poppy, whereupon he may sleep happily ever after.

A question that frequently arises is—what is subject matter? Not merely the subject matter of a particular poem or poet, but of poetry itself? And the answer to this will be as we see poetry in a romantic, a psychological, or a metaphysical mode.

Action in diversity is man's subject romantically. Man is man's subject psychologically. That which we call divinity is man's subject finally. Perhaps the word divinity can only mean Creator.

More closely, the mind of man, perpetually dwelling upon itself; perpetually astonished and delighted and affrighted at its own infinity; endlessly discovering, discarding, and recreating all that it can hope or imagine, or (which is the same thing) desire, is the subject matter for the poet.

That we divided this Desire-Area into fields of action, passion, and thought, and by the powerful brooding which we call poetry, indicate these again as not disparate but as harmonious and unified, is the poetic subject and problem and resolution.

To identify a something as a completion—as beautiful, powerful, sufficing, and enduring—is that which the poet, even unconsciously, seeks to do. The unconscious will to do this we call inspiration: the attainment of it is creation.

Action and passion seem to change; seem to take on new and consequently exciting aspects as the Time in which they are manifested seems to revolve, discovering other subjects for, and other powers of our desire-nature. These, outworn, moving to occultation and repair: those others coming anew to manifestation; and, so, freshening, heartening, the incoming generation which, but for this superficial change, must have lacked in vitality and in courage.

The notation of these changes also is the poet's work; but now more as psychological observer than as creator; more as metrical historian than poet; more, perhaps, as minor than major. No man can stand on tiptoe all the time, and it is rare that a poet can sustain this subtle-intense for more than few and separated instants in any poem. Shakespeare, Milton, Shelley, Wordsworth, these could, even lengthily, endure that strain and lift. None others could so sustain it.

The matter that is basic in minor poetry is other than this. Psychological or even metaphysical considerations need not be entirely absent from this work—a lethargic philosophy is indeed abundantly to be found in it—but, in general, the fundamental fact of this poetry is a sensuous one.

It might be advanced that minor poetry has properly no subject. That it is a tale in which the achievement or the thwarting of desire at its simplest is perpetually narrated; and that, however sophisticated or elegant it be, a curious poetic or metrical form of the peasant mind is continually manifested in it.

A prolonged sensuous preoccupation comes at last to a sheerly pessimistic utterance (or to that which is exactly the same thing, a foolishly optimistic one). This preoccupation and this utterance is the minor mode. Thought matures in a way that sense does not; for the latter by usage is used up, where the former by usage is used upwards. Every new sense-exploit is a nail in the coffin of sense; every new thought is a reincarnation to the thinker. So sense must fall to limitation and despair, and must imagine Death as that it really aspires to. They call it Love.

When we read a quantity of the lesser minor poetry of this period we are amused, and finally astonished, by the abundant daydream upon the theme called Love; and the equally abundant preoccupation with the theme called Death. These two (with a third exceedingly curious matter called Humor) are points of repair for, are cardinal to, the minor poets; and when they have nothing to say (an endemic condition outside of the major mode) they can, and do, find something to say about the thing called Love, or the thing called Death: or they abandon both of these in that total artistic despair which is called Humor.

There is no logical opposition to the binding together of these, at first sight, dissimilar themes. Love and birth and death are in sure connection: they *are* the sensual or peasant theme; and no man needs to be astonished by the fact that if he will write Love, and (in the Blakeian phrase) persist in his folly, he must write Death thereafter, or be (that which a poet should not be, and which all modern poets are) a discontinuous writer. A discontinuous writer is one who has not led his matter to its extreme: so love must go to sadness, humor to tenderness, thought to ecstasy.

The marvel is that a legion of writers were able to indite a myriad of poems on this love-motif, and could face their own collected volumes afterwards without being violently sickened by them.

Even more remarkable, however, is the mighty appetite which the Nineteenth Century displayed for the absurd and more than plebeian sensuality, called Love. Poetic license is a real thing—it means that a poet may tell his truth—but the poet has no license to write rubbish about rubbish: for it is, surely, to rubbish that these indefatigable love-mongers have turned the thing they seemed to adore, and which, like everything else, is adorable.

Whether we will it or not, the mind insists upon forming categories. It is almost instinctive with us to put things into order, and to put all those we know, or know of, into the degrees and precedences which we consider to be their due. But it is rare, indeed, that one criticizes immediately in this fashion, or at all upon one's own account. Before the critic comes to an examination of the artist who preceded him, an important critical work has already been done, and it is quite impossible that he should dismiss precedent criticism and employ his own practical intelligence freely upon new artistic statement. We can only instantly criticize that which is slightly inferior to us.

Before we come to criticize, a very large part of the critical work must have been done. Time is the Judge, and each succeeding Time adds but a little to the growing knowledge that it inherited. At last, when the thing called knowledge is completed, there remains but to make the judgment which is implicit in that knowledge, and this finding we consider as the final, though temperamental, statement of the critic. It is astonishing that this temperamental agreement is ever arrived at, but it is more wonderful to consider that it is always come to, and that it is never at fault. In the interval, however, every person making such temperamental statements must be closely watched, and, whenever it is possible, rigorously disagreed with.

If the present writer considers that certain poets, once accounted of great moment, have gravely diminished, and are worthy of no wider than anthological estimation, that is his temperamental conclusion. If it be thought that Tennyson had neither the matter nor the mode that could assure long life to his work, or that Meredith or Swinburne or Francis Thompson or Gerard Hopkins stand in danger when considered in the whole of their work, and as only commendable in anthologies, that statement must be considered as temperamental to the present writer, and it is, consequently, as proper to be disagreed with as of being accepted, until further examination assists the judgment to one view or the other.

Prime criticism is largely of a technique. Interim criticism is mainly of the matter which the poet feels competent to, and, so, eager to handle: but what final criticism is of, no man can say. The great poets arrive at their own titanic tensions in a subject matter which permits the extreme of energy to be deployed: which permits to, by demanding from, the poetic imagination an almost unobstructed freedom: which permits an infinite to be posited as the norm; which permits infinity, whether of matter or desire or thought, to be suggested as given, and in being, and as the essence or essential of all that is to be considered: for that "poet" who is not writing of infinity is merely current and of the market.

This is so of the greater, it is not so of the lesser craftsmen. These work in a mode which does not posit or demand freedom, and from which infinity is not deducible. They must work, that is, on the earth, for the earth; in the mind, for the mind: and their subject matter is always one which can be regarded as having a psychological rather than a spiritual importance. It is this which makes the true distinction between the major and the minor modes.

There may be, in the poetry of any generation, several major poets, but among these there is always one to be discerned as prime to them all. So, in their times, Chaucer, Shakespeare, Milton are names by the side of which all others, contemporary, are recognized as subordinate to the great one.

Such supremacy is seen to exist, spiritually, in a superior imaginative vitality; and, technically, in a more effortless handling of weightier matter than others can achieve. The matter of such a poet appears to be more definitely his; and seems, indeed, so ingested and absorbed that, however abundantly it has already been used, it can yet be considered as especially his own. We can speak of Spenserian, Shakespearian and Miltonic matter. No other poetic names can be placed before the term "matter" in this possessive and exclusive way. We cannot speak of a Wordsworthian or Shelleyan or a Keatsian matter; for the first three are of the major mode, and after them all others, howsoever great, are minor, and are to be recognised not by a matter, but by a mode.

The technique which he uses in the manifestation of this work is (apparently) as natural to the great poet as is his own being. Such a technique is always seen as an original thing: it has been liberated by, but has not been inherited from, previous experiments; and it is not capable of being used by another than that person. That which we call "originality" refers always to a technique: it can never refer to subject, for this is impersonal and universal.

It is less by his subject than by his technique that one fine artist is distinguishable from another; as it is by the indistinguishable level of their technique that the *lesser* minor poets are seen to be all of a family, and almost all of a piece. You shall easily find among these lesser poets forty, or four hundred, examples of verse, any one of which might as easily have been written by anyone else out of a score of such-weight versifiers; but the workmanship of the larger poets is so individual that it can never be reproduced, or forged, or even parodied.

Technique is exactly as rare as poetry is: it is a mystery, but it is not mysterious.

It is immediately apperceptible; it cannot be defined although it can be pointed to. Matter, poetical or other, is the common human property, but a technique is the man who uses it; and this quality is the creative instrument, and is practically indistinguishable from the created thing.

We speak loosely when we speak of a "technical" education. There is certainly a somewhat which is impartible, and the imparting of which is the means whereby human effort is seen as continuous and cohering. But this, which is so impartible, is an alphabet: it is the indispensable groundwork: it can, in every art or craft, be compassed by whosoever has a memory: but, so compassed, it is to be forgotten, and that "technique" brought to being which is the being of the artist, and which justifies (what would otherwise be an impertinence) the artist's claim that he can impart to us something on those subjects upon which we are as accurately instructed as he is.

He imparts that matter plus himself, and, consequently, plus everyone else who is of his nature and tempo; for it is always to be remembered that conversation (and especially a cultural or artistic conversation) is between equals; and that as the reader and the writer are of intellectual and imaginative identity, so only is the writer's intention received to the limit of reception; otherwise it is partially received, or it is even not received.

Instruction, whether "technical" or other, cannot perform magic. The person who appreciates poetry does so by a natural aptitude, and is a poet: this bent is greatly assisted by instruction; but he or she who is not naturally thus receptive will never appreciate poetry in the final sense in which the poet intended it.

This does not suggest that a technique of appreciation should not be contrived and employed. The artist is by no means a solitary in this world, and the matter for astonishment is less that so few receive him, as that so many do.

It is unfortunate that criticism and creative critical curiosity should have been so completely devoted to the artist, and that what Buddhism calls "skilful means" should not have been more curiously contrived for the working looker-at and listener-to for whom all that strange labor was undertaken and completed. Whether, beyond mere memorizing, a technique of instruction towards appreciation of poetry, towards appreciation of art in general, has been evolved, I do not know. Efforts, certainly, to achieve this appreciation have been and are continually being made.

In the case of the art of painting a general rule could be suggested. It is that for an even exaggeratedly large period of his tuition, the scholar should not be permitted to see any bad pictures. The contrary to this is the rule for all of us. All the pictures that we see during the impressionable age, and most of those which throng upon us in after life, are examples of poor art; and are often examples of the art of painting at actually its most commonplace manifestation. The young person to whom only good work had been made available would receive, at last, an education in taste; and even if such an one's native power could never be assisted to the extreme of final appreciation, he or she would instinctively not admire bad work. Nor is this merely a negative result: there would ensue upon such a general instruction some abatement of the torrent of poverty-stricken, or unimaginative art with which we are deluged; and, in a world that is populous with charlatans, there would be some room for the artist.

A training in the appreciation of poetry is even more difficult to contrive. There is no way by which the approach of trivial verse can be hindered from the student. Every anthology, even, contains quantities of mediocre work; for, be it only from egoism, almost every poet has as zealously garnered his poor verse as he has carefully preserved his good: and many a critic has considered that the poet is not completely seen unless his bad work is considered as well as his good.

There is almost no poet, however great, whose poetic remnant is not made inordinately bulky by the inclusion of thoroughly unworthy material; and this is so frequently the case that one is compelled to wonder if normal critical intelligence does not at moments actually desert those artists; or even if it had ever formed a conscious part of their intellectual equipment. The student must marvel at the mind which could sit to and complete, say, the *Paradise Regained*, and many another work, and may conceive that these were minds so inordinately elevated that they were entirely removed from, were transcendent to the plane in which dullness can be experienced or even imagined. Coming upon other work of the same poets he again is astonished, being confronted with a vivacity and power and tact that seem superhuman; and he will ask in bewilderment, Did they know when their work was good and when it was bad? And he must be told that very often they did not know.

The counsel to invent or contrive a technique of appreciation is a counsel of perfection. Perfect teaching lies with the teacher, and has daily to be improvised by him: so, as knowledge and enthusiasm are in his control, he will meet with the occasional success that the artist meets with, and will be glad that success is, at least, occasional. At the end, say, of every hundred years, there should be an universal solemn destruction by fire and dynamite of all the bad, the incomplete, the experimental work of the previous era: culture would then cease to be business, and begin to be life; the worker would commence to look closely at his work, and criticism would begin to be the advised, the disciplinary, the drastic overlord which it now is not. There must be poor art as long as there is poor criticism, but no longer.

What is wrong with art? This—that there is no criticism of which it stands in righteous terror. And if it be further asked, What is wrong with criticism?—for something indeed is sadly to be mourned for in that also—it is, that criticism should never be appreciative: that criticism should always be harsh and destructive; that criticism should be removed from the poem or picture, and should directly advise and, where necessary, insult the poet and the painter and the musician who has the hardihood to confront it: but so long as our criticism is lisped by youngsters from school, so long will it be impossible to create a technique of teaching where artistic appreciation will be the vulgar fact which it should centuries ago have become. There are matters about which no young person knows anything: art is one of them. Everything else is another.

There is a point at which criticism has no validity; and reaching this point, the critic is enforced to become that which, ex officio, should be uncongenial to him. To this point the critic's work has been interim, supplementary, advisory; but here he becomes (if he can manage it) the eulogist, and needs no longer to seek definition by way of analysis. Here he makes his final statement, and his final statement can no longer be scientific, but temperamental. When true excellence is attained the critic has no work to do; for it is impossible to define excellence, or to indicate by what means it is arrived at. It is purely for this moment that all critical apparatus has been invented; and it is at this moment that he finds it, not useless—for knowledge when it has been removed from the surfaces must be operative in the depths—but unable to do another work than the one it was trained for; and here he becomes merely a pleased person, who discusses his pleasure as naïvely as we all discuss pleasure only. We are not naïve about death and calamity, but satisfaction makes us children again. Children shout, on their occasions, meaninglessly but significantly; and so, but as significantly, do all eulogists.

All that which is temporary or interim, which can be considered as a middle term, is amenable to fairly close analysis or criticism. We can say why such an one (being a poor poet) is bad; and can asseverate, almost to a gram, the extent and value of that person's mental and technical and, even, imaginative equipment. Given, that the greater includes the less, criticism does actually encompass and reveal all that can be considered as within this middle term. In the entire range of the second-rate (the term being used qualificatively and not abusively) the critic has real authority, and can counsel fruitfully or condemn justly or praise wittingly—this, because the persons and matters considered submit to definition; and are, consequently, inferior to the critic. Superiority consists mainly in the ability to define and classify that which is presented.

It is at the point where instruction ends that art begins; and only at that point where art begins does technique begin. The intention of the artist is by no means to instruct, nor (despite Wordsworth and Coleridge) does the artist seek to entertain. He seeks to satisfy.

Properly, there is no artistic "message." In everything whatever, whether as substance or quality or intention, we all know as much as the artist does; but to *know* and to *see* are, temporarily, two things; and it is in this revealing, in a carrying deeper and yet deeper into consciousness, and so into fullness of knowledge, that the artist is in his art. He subtly, or powerfully, or harmoniously makes more and more manifest that which at first seemed to be quite adequately manifested:

for he reveals that the matter dwelt upon was not so completely apprehended as we had thought; and, communing with him, we discover that we have reserves of perception which, but for him, would have lain undisturbed or even unsuspected; reserves of powerful-acceptance, and realization, which, but for him, might have been carried unused to the grave. Thus, and by him, life is made more abundant, and knowledge is brought more closely to the consciousness from which it now seems so irreparably sundered: for, though we say with the lip that "knowledge is power," we know in the heart that it is not so. Knowledge reveals: it does nothing else. Power is of and from the Gods.

Between the poet and his competent reader, identity is more firmly established than even between the lover and his beloved, for here such truth as can be uttered has been uttered beyond question, and has been as unquestionably received. Having created, he imparts! It is not so: that imparting is the very act and fact of creating, and such receiving on the reader's part is the same creative deed. Between the good poet and the good reader there is no distinction of greater or less: he who "gets" Shakespeare, or Milton, or Shelley, gets what they had; he may be certain that what they gave was of their best; and that their best and his are identical.

It is easy enough to indicate what it is that we call Classical, but it is not so easy to state at what fountain (other than a purely national one) the Classical writer refreshes himself. Classicism is less referable to a specific culture than to a specific epoch. It may even be that the term is incapable of just definition except internationally.

It is only as by chance that the names of Spenser, Shakespeare, and Milton are borne to us as the fine fruits of the epochs they worked in: they are scarcely men: they are states of consciousness: their matter is during, and so their names endure, and are representative or symbolic (not solely of themselves, but) with singular completeness of the epochs which nurtured and engrossed them. Shakespeare, *qua* poet, is the total, advised, conscious Elizabethan England which was about him: Shakespeare, the man, is personally almost unconveyed by this poetry. Without that Elizabethan England he would yet, by essential, indescribable virtue, be a great poet, but he would not be the greatness we know; nor would his matter and its accompanying technique resemble those we are acquainted with.

Time (What is time? For man it is much more environment than duration.) produces, dictates, or permits (or refuses as in our day) that which we call subject; which in turn discloses the technique which is within its mode, for matter carries an appropriate technique with it. But while matter is timeless, technique is the date stamped upon it; and the epoch which gives or permits subjects of a certain emotional and intellectual elevation and a certain spare and lucid handling of them to its artists is a Classical one, while that other, which gives or permits or condones other certain subjects and their appropriate control, is Romantic. As his period and environment, so is the poet (not purely as poet, but as poet-conditioned), and his subject is perpetually that dimension or climate of the human spirit in which he finds himself, as at home; and by virtue of which he can achieve an intimate utterance, apparently upon himself, but actually upon every person of his time of a posited caste, or culture, and upon those actions which are the work of that specific caste. All art wills to be aristocratic.

There is no Classical or Romantic poet in his own right—for the artist who will live by his own right is always a poet *manqué*—but there is always the artist whose subject and technique are given and governed by his time; and whose virtue is that he is capable of being especially energized by time and subject, and can, in that vitality, control his matter almost as by instinct.

For critical and examining purposes, the artists of any particular century are conveniently divisible into hierarchies of major and minor workers, even though the term "major" be only used as a temporary and relative description. The workers of the Nineteenth Century can be so tabled. This period is curiously rich in remarkable, if thwarted and thwarting personalities; but even more singular is the abundance and variety of talents which these personalities display.

A Classical period and tradition imposes so (apparently) narrowing a discipline on its superior minds that the consequent artistic production can almost be conceived as of a single cultural contexture. An impatient examination of such a time may lead to the conclusion that what has been gained in quality has been lost in variety; and, for the world in general, this latter poverty, with the narrowing of enthusiasm which every lack entails, cannot be compensated for by any magnificence thus qualified.

The major poets of the Nineteenth Century in order of birth are: Wordsworth, Coleridge, Byron, Shelley, Keats, Tennyson, Browning, Arnold, and Swinburne.

It is already a question as to whether all of these poets are properly to be included under the term "major"; but, whatever their lapses from the highest poetic excellence may be, there is no doubt that Coleridge, Wordsworth, Shelley, and Keats are, by the assent of time, to be recognized as superior to all others of their period: and superior to all those who have since created poetry to the date of this writing.

It is certain that the highest achievements of these four poets cannot be held to rival the greatest work of their predecessors, Chaucer, Spenser, Shakespeare, and Milton. It may be that a Classical mode or training, however narrow and narrowing it seems to be, does permit an extension of the spirit, an unifying of the whole being, which the Romantic mode does not call for and cannot, therefore, elicit. This may be so; but Shakespeare has yet to be accounted for; the English language and psychology has still to be reckoned with; and a more profound criticism embarked upon ere this claim can be stated as proven, and to be relied upon.

When the Romantic mind may move as at its own will, and be disciplined by no other asceticism than its own desires evolve, it will proceed as fancy inclines rather than to a direction which the intense and guarded spirit dictates. Variety is truly a blessing, and lacking it life would degenerate into boredom; but a variety which is too abundant and too available must lead, first, to a decentralization of the mind that plays in it; and second, to a congestion of desire (which desire is for many of us the only mind we ever use), and will thus lead to a lack of control, and so, of direction; and to his being lost among the trees who had expected to be a master of the wood.

The effect of this artistic and intellectual decentralization is not apparent to the writers at the moment immersed in their own excitements and labors: it is posterity that pays, and the sense that we have inherited a debilitated art by reason of Romantic handling is one that is urgent in all the artists of the present day. Our discontent, however, is not properly, because not entirely, attributable to this cause.

In the Classical mode a consciously directed discipline is maintained by the artist upon his subject. This discipline or gravity can be conceived of as a good in itself; and, seemingly, can be relied upon to achieve that elevation of spirit and utterance which is finally the poetic aim. It is as though one said, "Only control and parsimony are certain good." Once, indeed, that was a rule, not only of art, but of life. The Romantic artist, however, is much at the mercy of his subject; or is not incontestably master of it; and he can only arrive at the great utterance, which he also seeks, not so much by a rapt distillation of the matter, as by the addition to, or the imposition upon it, of a moral or a philosophical value.

Value must be, but when value can be defined, its being is endangered: it has been brought to subjection, almost to domesticity, and that quality which is the soul of poetry, that sense of magic or infinity which illumines and delights, may be foregone by mere limitation: for poetry is not comprehended, but realized; and it ceases to be gnomic at its peril.

A remarkable fact about the poetry of the Nineteenth Century is the diversity of subject matter and of human temperament which is to be found in that poetry and those poets. When we consider the names that are salient, we note at once that personalities and ideas are not only of singular abundance but are more diverse than is evident in any other literary period. The names Coleridge and Wordsworth have no essential connection with each other, and have no connection with the names Shelley and Keats. These, again, are at as singular a remove from such other names as Byron, or Tennyson, or Swinburne, or Browning; as are those from Thompson, Beddoes, Meredith, Dowson, Hardy, or Hopkins. It is not that there is the difference of a school or of a technique. The difference is personal to the writers, and is so extreme that the Nineteenth Century is notable for a temperamental variety and a psychological richness which is unparalleled in literary annals.

Additional to this, the tale of the minor writers is as singularly rich; and the

work an
brethren.

Only
order of
work for
of the mi
vitalized,
their grea
the period
minor poe
escapes the

The ca
cally; but t
explicable a
from it—af
worth (or c
willingly or symp
by sympathy w
essence of any

Everythin
worth: and,
stand the N
clue we may
dependency.

It is not e

No poet
Wordswo
that he is
vanced a
qualifica
he is to

He i
counted
to that
Englis!
This i

W
sible t
askar

I
erly,
sub-

poets: and th separated, or even segregated, from Wordsworth
But, in truth red and aloof from every other poet whatever. This
identity and only among the greatest: Chaucer, Spenser, Shakespeare, Milto ilarly ungregarious and unique. It would seem tha
such cannot other poets than these, and that to be recognized as
fundamentall uninfluencing, is a prime quality of genius.

It is not helley and Keats are the most beloved of all the poets
in the great ly of genius, and that there is almost no poetic lapse
which is not eir readers, who are also their lovers. They are no
beloved bec young and were poets, nor even because they died
young. They use their poetry is lovely; and because it is so in
a fashion w them alone; and which can be thought of as
angelic.

With Bla m and evade comparison with even a poetic standard;
and the quest ng greater or less great than another is one that does
not arise.

Beyond ed writers they can be thought of as original; as especially or e owed; and as the imparters of a poesy more limpidly
and simply sa be found elsewhere. They have been identified with,
or as, their c way that no other poet except Blake has ever been;
and howeve ves be examined, that identification is not imperiled,
and they are estion as every other great artist has been, and should
be: for, trul e artist is, the greater and graver are the questions
that should

It can be re massive and realistic poetry than theirs has been
written; it ca at a more authentic muse than theirs has been in existance. They b poesy as by divine right: they need to don no learned
sock when th ort in their own realms: and their very lapses are yet
lapses within the lapses of all others are into prose.

But while uch in their work that is matter for marvel, that is incapable of an sion than that they gave, there remains much which
criticism (if t other than these) would consider deplorable.

It is not en helley should be a poet as by divine right, and should be
that in a sense ther poet has ever been. Work has to be done; searching
has to be don s are not available in order to be evaded, they are even to
be sought for vast amount of his work (like many another of his lesser
brothers—and gravamen of critical disapproval of the entire Romantic
mode) Shelley lways seek the hardest matter, nor the hardest way: nor
was Keats pre s when he wrote cautioning Shelley to "load every rift
with ore." Sh was instinctively pleased, and, consequently, somewhat
halted by, for ly attained harmonies. And at moments when sobriety of
utterance was f only to offset or prepare for the greater moments which

no other asceticism than its own desires evolve, it will proceed as fancy inclines rather than to a direction which the intense and guarded spirit dictates. Variety is truly a blessing, and lacking it life would degenerate into boredom; but a variety which is too abundant and too available must lead, first, to a decentralization of the mind that plays in it; and second, to a congestion of desire (which desire is for many of us the only mind we ever use), and will thus lead to a lack of control, and so, of direction; and to his being lost among the trees who had expected to be a master of the wood.

The effect of this artistic and intellectual decentralization is not apparent to the writers at the moment immersed in their own excitements and labors: it is posterity that pays, and the sense that we have inherited a debilitated art by reason of Romantic handling is one that is urgent in all the artists of the present day. Our discontent, however, is not properly, because not entirely, attributable to this cause.

In the Classical mode a consciously directed discipline is maintained by the artist upon his subject. This discipline or gravity can be conceived of as a good in itself; and, seemingly, can be relied upon to achieve that elevation of spirit and utterance which is finally the poetic aim. It is as though one said, "Only control and parsimony are certain good." Once, indeed, that was a rule, not only of art, but of life. The Romantic artist, however, is much at the mercy of his subject; or is not incontestably master of it; and he can only arrive at the great utterance, which he also seeks, not so much by a rapt distillation of the matter, as by the addition to, or the imposition upon it, of a moral or a philosophical value.

Value must be, but when value can be defined, its being is endangered: it has been brought to subjection, almost to domesticity, and that quality which is the soul of poetry, that sense of magic or infinity which illumines and delights, may be foregone by mere limitation: for poetry is not comprehended, but realized; and it ceases to be gnomic at its peril.

A remarkable fact about the poetry of the Nineteenth Century is the diversity of subject matter and of human temperament which is to be found in that poetry and those poets. When we consider the names that are salient, we note at once that personalities and ideas are not only of singular abundance but are more diverse than is evident in any other literary period. The names Coleridge and Wordsworth have no essential connection with each other, and have no connection with the names Shelley and Keats. These, again, are at as singular a remove from such other names as Byron, or Tennyson, or Swinburne, or Browning; as are those from Thompson, Beddoes, Meredith, Dowson, Hardy, or Hopkins. It is not that there is the difference of a school or of a technique. The difference is personal to the writers, and is so extreme that the Nineteenth Century is notable for a temperamental variety and a psychological richness which is unparalleled in literary annals.

Additional to this, the tale of the minor writers is as singularly rich; and the work and quality of work of these latter are as varied as are those of their greater brethren.

Only four of the poets in this century are considered as belonging to the highest order of poetry. The others are significant, each according to his power, and their work forms a body of great social, historical, and psychological importance. Many of the minor writers also are intellectually so aware, and emotionally so highly vitalized, that their best work does not fall very far from the grave excellence of their greater contemporaries. Indeed, so abundant and varied is this production, the period might be referred to as the Century of, or, even, the Paradise of the minor poet; for (excepting Shakespeare) no poet of the Romantic mode quite escapes the attribution of minor.

The cases of Shelley and Keats are curious, both psychologically and artistically; but the problems raised by these men, or by their work, are explicable; as is explicable all that has aroused affection, and the interest which unfailingly depends from it—affection is interest: it is almost nothing else. So, also, the case of Wordsworth (or of Coleridge) is curious, but these are not so easily, because not so willingly or sympathetically explained. For any explanation which is not governed by sympathy will leave out of account all those imponderables which are the essence of any human quality or action requiring to be explained.

Everything is forgiven to Shelley or Keats, nothing is forgiven to Wordsworth: and, yet, thoroughly to understand Wordsworth is thoroughly to understand the Nineteenth Century. Wordsworth is the Nineteenth Century; and any clue we may gain about him is a key to the entire Romantic mode, and its Victorian dependency.

It is not easy to be completely sympathetic to Wordsworth.

No poet has been so extravagantly praised or so extravagantly blamed as Wordsworth was, and is. It is instantly said, not only that he is a great poet, but that he is properly among the greatest: and yet this statement is not so much advanced as permitted; and, quick upon the admission, there come reservations and qualifications so many, so pregnant, that one might be forgiven for wondering if he is to be considered a poet at all.

He is a poet, indeed, and after the names of Shakespeare and Milton have been counted no other name than that of Wordsworth can be put forward as the third to that great twain; and as the fifth, in order of merit, in the great hierarchy of English genius—Shakespeare, Milton, Spenser, Chaucer, Wordsworth, Blake. This is the order of the great poets.

We can understand why Shelley and Keats are beloved; it should not be impossible to discover why we lout low to Wordsworth, and at the same instant eye him askance!

In his strength he is almost divine; but his weakness is not merely, and properly, polar to this, it is not that his weakness is "human, too human," it is almost sub-human; and, while the noddings of Homer are occasional, and can be reverenced, the noddings of Wordsworth are not occasional, nor as by accident, and are not reverential at all: (it is mainly as he nods that we find a wherewithal to judge the great man).

One imagines that perhaps Wordsworth was born out of time: that the talent which he shows is not the complete talent upon which he could have drawn: that an area of his being lay in occultation, and—which is ill in a poet—was unsuspected by and unsought by him: one accuses him of being unadventurous: he did not rise, and go, and get: he sat, and remembered, and obtained, as by a charity: one imagines that a dimension of being or cogitation analogous to those in which Shelley or Keats were so at home should also have been his innocent habitation; and that (as every philosophy is fundamentally a dubiety) he should less have plunged himself into memory, and a reflection upon this, than into his own living life; and that he should have uttered his place and being in actuality rather than to reduce these to a theory, a problem, and a dubitation.

Splendor is his, but certitude is not his in all security.

It is of the essence of poetry that the statement made shall be unshakeable in its certainty. This certainty may be of a matter that is high or low, but, in whatever statement, if certainty be lacking poetry is lacking: and this, more than any other lack, saps at the reader and the writer, and makes creation queasy. The immediate weakness of Wordsworthian poetry is that almost every statement which it makes is amenable to definition—to limitation, that is; and it is, consequently, not absolutely redeemed from prose-thought. The true poetic-statement is impervious to definition, and admits no further meditation than that from which it arose.

That poet is in uncertainty who needs and seeks a philosophic basis for work— the being of whose art lies in quite another than the philosophic world. Wordsworth considered that poetry, which is an art, should be a way of life; and that the closer it could be carried to sheer or mere living, the more it—which is not rational—would be brought to rationality. He conceived that poetry could be ennobled by vulgarizing its vocabulary—whose vocabulary is curious and pondered and ceaselessly selective: that it could be energized by forcing it to consider the peasant—the law of whose being is that it must only consider the hero: that if he could succeed in anchoring it immovably to the earth it would the more effortlessly and aërially disport in the heavens. He felt that he must conciliate poetically those "lower" orders which were then assaulting a weakening aristocracy: and he considered as a good democrat (and a good democrat cannot also be a good poet) that a moral value was not only the equal of a metaphysical or poetic one, but that it could be carried as far, and made to fare not worse. The Wordsworthian betrayal of poetry is singular, is signal, is complete—but the cause for wonder lies not here: the cause for wonder and exultation lies in the fact that poetry did not betray Wordsworth.

Although Shelley and Keats are in every respect dissimilar, yet they are bracketed together in popular and even in learned estimation, almost as twin poets: and they are sharply separated, or even segregated, from Wordsworth. But, in truth, they are sundered and aloof from every other poet whatever. This identity and solitude is found only among the greatest: Chaucer, Spenser, Shakespeare, Milton, Blake are similarly ungregarious and unique. It would seem that such cannot be stated of any other poets than these, and that to be recognized as fundamentally solitary, and uninfluencing, is a prime quality of genius.

It is not by chance that Shelley and Keats are the most beloved of all the poets in the great English hierarchy of genius, and that there is almost no poetic lapse which is not forgivable by their readers, who are also their lovers. They are not beloved because they were young and were poets, nor even because they died young. They are loved because their poetry is lovely; and because it is so in a fashion which pertains to them alone, and which can be thought of as angelic.

With Blake, they stand from and evade comparison with even a poetic standard; and the question as to their being greater or less great than another is one that does not arise.

Beyond all natively-talented writers they can be thought of as original; as especially or even uniquely endowed; and as the imparters of a poesy more limpidly and simply satisfying than can be found elsewhere. They have been identified with, or as, their own poetry, in a way that no other poet except Blake has ever been; and however their personal lives be examined, that identification is not imperiled, and they are not put to the question as every other great artist has been, and should be: for, truly, the greater the artist is, the greater and graver are the questions that should be asked of him.

It can be said that a more massive and realistic poetry than theirs has been written; it cannot be held that a more authentic muse than theirs has been in existance. They breathe the air of poesy as by divine right: they need to don no learned sock when they would disport in their own realms: and their very lapses are yet lapses within poetry where the lapses of all others are into prose.

But while there is so much in their work that is matter for marvel, that is incapable of another expression than that they gave, there remains much which criticism (if the poets were other than these) would consider deplorable.

It is not enough that Shelley should be a poet as by divine right, and should be that in a sense which no other poet has ever been. Work has to be done; searching has to be done; difficulties are not available in order to be evaded, they are even to be sought for; and in a vast amount of his work (like many another of his lesser brothers—and this is the gravamen of critical disapproval of the entire Romantic mode) Shelley did not always seek the hardest matter, nor the hardest way: nor was Keats presumptuous when he wrote cautioning Shelley to "load every rift with ore." Shelley's ear was instinctively pleased, and, consequently, somewhat halted by, for him, easily attained harmonies. And at moments when sobriety of utterance was needed, if only to offset or prepare for the greater moments which were to come, his ear did not dismiss a rhythm from his matter which can justly be termed habitual and rhetorical.

There is no doubt that in the case of Shelley an easy poetic music was, almost always, subconsciously, at his command (as it was at the command of, say, Scott or Byron), and had these poets been of the austere temper that one will conceive the great poet to be, they should not have been so simply and naïvely contented with the instant product of their gift, so that the accusation of rhetoric, of virtuosity for its own sake, is an accusation which can be brought very easily against these men: and much of the feeling which we have for and against the amateur stays with us in considering them. The feeling we have for the amateur is that he is doing "all this" for love. The feeling we have against him is that he is, finally, not serious about all this.

Something of a like disapproving criticism may be brought in the case of Keats. He too, particularly (and excusably) in his early work had scattered his talent, and so diffused it that his matter also became diffuse. He recovered quickly enough from this diffusion, and in the great Odes, and practically in all his subsequent work, he does show a firmer grasp of his matter. All his best work, however, is of relatively short breath, and the doubt as to knowledge of his objective, which comes to us on reading *Endymion*, is not entirely absent while we are considering the *Hyperion*. Even though this latter large fragment is one of the most remarkable and indeed magnificent pieces of work done in that century, one has an uneasy sense that in the myth of *Hyperion* Keats knew as little whither his story must wend as he did in the *Endymion* of his youth. Something of the quality of the improviser is sensed, actually as from verse to verse, in every work of this poet; and, whether in music or poetry, the gift of improvisation, while wonderful, is not satisfying. Artistically and intellectually this quality is a grace only to the dramatist and the wit.

It is possible that, had he lived, Keats might not have increased in poetic stature. He lacked consecutiveness and the longer breath. He was moving towards a Miltonic technique and away from his own original, perhaps narrow, talent; and it may be that we only remove from that which is already forsaking us. Like Wordsworth, like all the finer men of that time, he had an interest, amounting to an obsession, in the philosophical consideration of life. This, while it is singularly rare in our prose literature (where it is most urgently needed), does often lie as a deadening weight upon English poetry: and it may be that in his case a theory of God and man and beauty could have hardened into a true obstacle against the poetry which was in him, and which gave promise of being the greatest single contribution to poetry that the age could hope for.

The poet must surmount, as before said, his very culture and his very self; and one questions if a talent so fine-drawn, so at the mercy of the moment as that of Keats's, was capable of the descent into anonymity, of that liberating self-forgetfulness which can remove the poet from the accustomed and memorial to that dimension of being-in-rapture wherein the greatest poetry is conceived. The man must be as large, nay, he must be larger than his subject, and whether Keats was or was not the Titan he dreamed of we shall never know. Like the scenes depicted upon his own Grecian Urn, he remains for us in imperishable adolescence, and it must suffice to assert that the presence of one talent such as his would make any century illustrious.

The same uncertainty-at-the-core which we discover with so much surprise in Wordsworth is even more evident in the work of Tennyson.

This uncertainty is evident as a major fact in the mentality of the entire period, which should less be known as the Victorian than as the Sceptical Age. Both of these writers seemed able to work for long periods without that mystical urge which we call, in however unknown a tongue, inspiration—i.e.: the description of everything whatever as infinity. It is certain that to Wordsworth, in his greater poems, inspiration did frequently come and that it could transfuse an actually lethargic subject matter so that it became vivid, and splendid, and endless. This inspiration is not now evident in the greater portion of Tennyson's work; and, because of the lack of it, it is possible that our time will judge his poetry more severely than did his own day. Speaking of his work *in general*, it could be said that he is the worst "great" poet that ever lived. And again *in general*, that his is the only example of "vulgarity" in poetry that our language has known.

It is not enough to write wittingly, or with certainty, that partial thing which is the desire-nature of one's time. The work of poetry is to transcend the fact of the day; to transcend, it may be, every fact, and to bring the chosen matter into another dimension of thought, into even another dimension of emotion, than those in which it seemed to be born and active. Every statement of fact belongs to prose. It might be further said that every consecutive operation belongs to prose, and that poetry will only handle with reluctance any matter which is founded on a definite logic or ground: for it has an ability to so change the internal vibration even of emotion, that the emotion, as disclosed by poetry, has not upon its reader the effect which normally we know of, and which logically or psychologically is connected with or to be expected from that well known emotion. In prose heroism makes one proud; in verse it makes one weep. In prose again sadness makes one sad: in verse it makes one happy. These and many other such transformations are perpetually occurring in poetry: and these transformations are poetry.

To the artist it can easily be that every fact-in-itself is hideous, and that every emotion is obscene; and for the purpose of his art these facts and emotions, which (being his apparent subject) are inescapable, must be transformed from the domain in which they lie and do their everyday work to another in which they develop another result than that which is ordinarily to be expected of them.

"Æ" (George Russell) once said that poetry is written on the Mount of Transfiguration, and in saying this he made one of the most fruitful critical generalizations of our day. Unless, at some point in a poem, this transformation of matter, or transfiguration of values, takes place, the work which is being done is temporary, and is merely a note in poetic form on the mode of thinking and feeling of the day in which the work was composed. The great poets make this transformation in every poem which we recognize as great. And if in the work of Tennyson we look beyond the temporary utterance for that more highly vitalized significance which we call transformation, it is but rarely found, so that he can often appear more as an adept of poetry than a poet.

A point comes, in regarding poetry or music or painting, when we grow impatient of the work done by the *virtuosi*. In music this is readily visible, and we can see a person much more interested in his own technique than he is in music; and quite complacently giving his audience matter which is musically insignificant, under the theory that the wizardry of his technique can make up for any musical deficiency whatever.

The same virtuosity is displayed by many poets of this period. It must have seemed to such that any subject is a good subject, so adequate and satisfying did they feel their technical equipment to be: and their generation, being all technicians, were prepared, perhaps, to be more interested in the rhetoric of poetry than in poetry itself, as they were prepared to be more absorbed in the bowing of Paganini than in the music which Paganini might have produced.

There is a great danger in the virtuoso's approach to his subject, for the virtuoso is always a profoundly ignorant person. The danger is that the matter tends to be absorbed in the mode; and the recipient is nourished on necromancy. Only a matter of essentially low vitality can submit to this hypnosis, and it is soon discernible that though the passage seems purple it is shoddy. To find shoddy masquerading in the purple is artistically that which, ethically, we term vice: and it was at one time of the period we are now discussing the especial vice of English literature. In fact, every virtuoso becomes an artistic egoist, and is always writing as it were, about what he can do, which even at its best is still only the possible, rather than seeking to do that more, which is the impossible.

For the impossible is poetry. Theoretically, it cannot be done. Actually, it is done; but it is not done by any trick that we can call virtuosity. It is done by a subtle transformation of the subject matter into a something which is not other but is yet transcendent to itself; and it is done by no other means. No technical expedient can give that quality to a commonplace matter (for all matter is commonplace) which we call originality. That which we call originality is the transformation of values from the prose world to the poetic world, and the "artist" poets are generally incapable of this powerful, or subtle, effort.

Possibly the greatest and most to be mourned for failure in the annals of English poetry is that of Matthew Arnold. The work that he succeeded in doing is of great importance, even of great beauty; and one marvels that, with so complete a technique and with such internal resources as Arnold had, he was unable to lift himself beyond himself.

A poetic failure is wrongly judged if it be attributed to lack of knowledge or to lack of industry. It is more to the fact that the will of the poet fails to surmount both his nature and his culture (the latter in especial) that one should look in accounting for such a failure. Somehow, if the finality which we call poetry is to be arrived at, the poet's entire knowledge, and actually his entire personality, must be so surpassed as to be practically forgotten. It is easier to forget one's self (whom in truth one has never known) than it is to dismiss the knowledge and philosophy which one has so laboriously acquired, and yet this dismissal is fundamentally necessary for the artist, and cannot be dispensed with. Personal and cultural forgetfulness is necessary, for all personal poetry is minor poetry: and all didactic poetry is prose.

It is likely that the dissatisfaction which we continually discover in reviewing work of such great men as Coleridge, Wordsworth, and Arnold is due mainly to the fact that they are unable to agree to, or to endure, a total immersion of self in the matter they are working upon, and an attendant knowledge of and cogitation only of that. And so, too often, the final extension of being which is demanded from the poet could not be arrived at because the poets in question, on the occasions in question, were unable to dismiss themselves and their cultures summarily and completely. The Self-Ego and, in especial, the Knowledge-Ego were always getting in their way.

Something of this inability to lift beyond the norm and into an imaginative realm; to rely on invention rather than on creation, is at all times sensed in the Arnold poetry. Something of the same spiritual winglessness is continually to be sensed even in all Romantic poetry. It is the poetry of the winged heel, but not of the winged shoulder. It is indeed not "pedestrian," but that prose ill does gloom upon and threaten it.

A diminution of power, the power of complete absorption in self-forgetfulness, had come upon the greater poets of this period, and however they strove to make up the surmounting loss by virtuosity or by variety or by the substitution of philosophical or psychological for poetic values, such loss is sensed when the greatest of this verse is compared with the finest poetry of the two preceding centuries.

The case of Swinburne, another who was conceived as one of the giants of his generation, is even more curious than is that of Tennyson.

(Tennyson appears as of a richer nature than Swinburne. It is mere appearance, for Tennyson was not richly endowed; and the considerations which could interest him seemed, by being more abundant, to be more varied than those which caught the Swinburnian attention.)

At first and while we are young, feats, whether of strength or of technique, astonish us, and perhaps in terms of sheer technical agility there has not been in the history of literature one so singularly equipped as Swinburne was. It did seem that he could handle any matter that came to his pen. One can remember the astonishment (and astonishment is, while we are young, indistinguishable from delight) that came upon the first acquaintance with poems such as *Hertha, Faustine,* and the numerous other poems of that *genre* in Swinburne, and one can recollect also that when maturity came, a dissatisfaction came also, and a sense that this poet was one who nourished his readers upon innutritious fare.

To be pure, even as an athlete, is quite a considerable something, but it is not enough to make surrender that intangible quality which we call poetry. Power, not purity, is the master in every art.

Theoretically Swinburne, like Shelley, should have been, or could have been, a more important poet than time now reveals him to be. That quality of transformation into a more subtle medium does seem to be one which he could have attained. The fact that he did not, or but rarely attained it, reflects properly no censure upon Tennyson, in whose case one sees a poet doing what he could, and giving what he had, but in Swinburne one uneasily conjectures that here is a poet who never pulled his weight, and one surmises in him, as in many another excessively active person, a fundamental, a spiritual laziness, that would be busy at, but would not be busy upon.

After the intense appreciation of Swinburnian virtuosity is over, one finds that the occasions upon which he diligently applied himself to a work are rare. Occasionally he does arrive at an apparently complete utterance of his matter—an utterance, that is, of a completion which few of his contemporaries achieved; and it is particularly strange in grave poetry to discover that complete utterance can also be completely pessimistic utterance. The following lines are famous:

> From too much love of living,
>> From hope and fear set free,
> We thank with brief thanksgiving
>> Whatever gods may be
> That no life lives forever;
> That dead men rise up never;
> That even the weariest river
>> Winds somewhere safe to sea.

This statement is completely expressed, but the reader is left with the conviction that such a completion of utterance is also a completion of emptiness; and that, contrary to what we consider the fundamental statement of poetry, which is not a pessimism as in Swinburne, or an optimism as in Tennyson—but truth—the poets in these cases are not telling the truth, but are very completely uttering complete nonsense.

Only once did Swinburne direct himself to a matter of final gravity. In the elegy on the death of Baudelaire, entitled *"Ave Atque Vale,"* he measured himself against a large task, and he drew this poem so close to true poetic value that its insecurity must be mourned for.

This poem does not "come" as the famous elegies of the past had come, and (for it is by his failures that we see how and upon what an eminence the poet is to be criticized) in the failure of this work one sees the fundamental inability of Swinburnian treatment to handle values other than those which can be expressed in a term of speed, or pace.

An instinct for speed, for pace, for the internal poise and rhythm of subject matter, is an invaluable part of poetic equipment; and a lack of or an uncertainty as to those (such as is evident in most didactic poetry) has halted and brought to impotence much sound work: but these also must be transcended, and the condition known as intensity come to. It is to this lack that the great failures of the fine English poets must be attributed, and it is as finally lacking in intensity that important writers such as Arnold, Tennyson, and Swinburne must be criticized. Of these three, of course, Arnold is easily the first.

To the rule that psychological and narrative matter are debilitating to the poet there are (if they be exceptions) three strange exceptions—Chaucer, Shakespeare, and Browning. Coupling these names does not intend that there is any similarity between the work of these poets. Shakespeare's human studies are of extremely great psychological importance; nevertheless, the tale he tells and the values he attributes are lifted by sheer mastery into an art, an area, as magical, as indefinable as is that of Blake or Shelley at their most gnomic and unknown.

Browning shares with Shakespeare a continuous and sympathetic interest in the world of action and emotion and humanity. There is much more of Emotion than Passion in Browning; and much more of Passion than Emotion in Shakespeare. Indeed in the great poets it may be held that the quality called Emotion is never present in their works, being too plebeian for such wide or rapid or intense usage, and that the place of this is invariably taken by that which we call Passion. Like Shakespeare, Browning gives the impression of being inexhaustible. He is of the few poets of whom it can be said that when one has collected an extensive selection of his verse, there remains as much again to be gathered; and that the remnant is of practically as high value as was the material already taken. There has been no poet who so squarely and securely stood upon his ground; but in his case, as in the case of every important Nineteenth Century poet, Time has not yet made its final appraisement. There is much in his art which one can think of as petulance, as fantasy (for, contrary to a widely accepted idea, poetry is rarely fantastic, and is never petulant), and one is still in doubt as to the position he will finally occupy, as one is still doubtful of the position that will at last be adjudged to Blake or to Gerard Hopkins.

Before all poetry which exhibits itself as a feat the critic must stand in some dubiety, and until Time resolves the matter the critic will admit that in the case of Browning and of Blake and of Coleridge the last word has not been said. It is easy to assert of a certain poet, in this case Browning, that he is earth-bound; that psychological curiosity is a prose but not a poetical virtue; that he has not succeeded in transcending his knowledge; that to *épater* the philosopher is, artistically, as inadmissible as to *épater* the bourgeois—he still remains astonishing; and a virtuosity of this order almost absolves itself from any criticism whatever. One can only make the interim and temporary statement that this man is so remarkable as to be marvelous, and that criticism has not yet been able to establish his complete value.

In all of these poets, something of the taint of virtuosity for its own sake can be found. Thus it is with a feeling of relief that one comes to a poetry which makes no display, which is grounded in (though that be only) an emotional reality, and which is urgently needing and seeking a confidant.

Real matter is abundantly found among the greatest, but there are poets in whom real matter is scarcely discernible at all, and who are so immersed in as to be immured in their own talents. Such a poet is Swinburne, or even Browning, in whom psychological and narrative interest tends to shadow the poetic. While the Brontë sisters need not be considered as of the ranks of the great poets, and can even, if one be rigorous in the matter, be thought of as scarcely belonging to poetry at all, yet, by reason of an earnest entering into the matter upon which they were working, two of these sisters, Emily and Anne, have contributed, though it be only a note, a poetry which is singular, and which, by force of a poignantly meditated emotion, has attained that profundity of utterance which is original and is truth.

Emily Brontë has made significant to others an emotion which was purely personal to herself, and she has come at times to a completion of statement which lifts her purely personal utterance far from the merely personal. Her trouble has been so held and communicated that it is impossible to read her poems without being (that which we too seldom are) sorry for somebody other than ourselves. This is a true feat, and, no matter though the rank of poet could be denied to her, she has succeeded in doing that which many an acclaimed poet never attains to: a perfection of imparting which is one of the curiosities, if it be no other, of this literature.

Even in the case of Anne Brontë, although it be only in four or five poems, a something of that same urgent earnestness and significance is also come to.

Charlotte Brontë is quite distinct in this consideration from her two sisters. In her case it is prose that matters, and although, from the record of her prose writings, readers would consider that she had feelings and capacities beyond, and had suffered or imagined beyond the range of her sisters, the poetic tale, as told by them and by her, consigns her, on these grounds, to a considerably lower place. It could finally be said of Charlotte Brontë's poetry that it is valueless, while in the case of her sisters, though the amount be limited, it is yet so good that one is inclined to give them precedence over their great and wonderful sister.

It will be observed that in this survey reference has only been made to those authors who may be considered as the most significant poets of the century: and that the writer has dwelt with more emphasis on the weakness of these writers than on their strength.

The work of eulogy upon these great men has been abundantly done; and it is time that attention should be directed to the negative, the undecided, the extravagant and wasteful aspects of this production.

Such a situating of attention is the more needed if it can be considered (as the writer considers) that the official Classical and Romantic modes of poetry have reached their term: and that our day warrants the assumption that new values must be identified, and that a new method must be evolved for dealing with them.

There is no lack of talent amongst us today, and, perhaps, there is no lack of energy. On this latter we are uninformed, and no man's speculation is better than another's on the point. We must attend until Time discloses the possession or the absence of this central quality.

That something is lacking to us is evident, and is grievous. What is lacking now, and has been lacking since the death of Tennyson, is subject matter.

Today, whether it be for poetry or for prose, for painting or for music, there is no artistic-subject: and in consequence, no demand upon and no production of the graver artistic-energy. It may be; it almost assuredly is, that our predecessors have plundered and exhausted our fields; and that even the instrument of production, technique, has been so diligently overused by them that it, too, comes blunt and inapt to our needs, and will work no more.

That long poetic odyssey which may conveniently be referred to as the Shakespearian adventure, was completed in Tennyson: for, though an art may become trivial and yet recover, it cannot descend to vulgarity and be quicked again. In vulgarity it comes to its earth, and will be buried there.

No further adventure is possible under an Elizabethan ensign, and after more than three hundred years of conquest and splendor, we may bid that poetry adieu.

Passed for Press

James Stephen

WILLIAM WORDSWORTH

[April 7, 1770–April 23, 1850]

WILLIAM WORDSWORTH, second of the five children of John Wordsworth, an attorney, and his wife Anne, was born at Cockermouth, a little Cumberland village on the northern edge of the Lake District and near the Derwent, "the fairest of all rivers." In 1776 and 1777 Wordsworth, along with Mary Hutchinson, whom he was to marry in 1802, attended the infant school of Anne Birkett at Penrith, the Anne Birkett of whom he wrote thirty years later that she "did not affect to make theologians, or logicians, but she taught to read, and she practised the memory."

Upon the death of his mother in 1778 young Wordsworth was sent to the grammar school at Hawkshead, a small town in one of the most beautiful parts of the Lake District. Here he remained until he was sixteen, living in the cottage of a village dame, Anne Tyson, the "good creature" of *The Prelude*, upon whose grave

The thoughts of gratitude shall fall like dew.

Here too he came to love the Reverend William Taylor, headmaster of Hawkshead, who died the year Wordsworth left the school, and whom he recalls affectionately as "an honored teacher of his youth, a faithful guide, a lover of the poets." The beauty of the lakes and the mountains of the Hawkshead country, through which he freely wandered during his schoolboy days, made the deep impressions upon his sensibilities which he describes in the first books of *The Prelude*.

At the close of his Hawkshead school days in 1787, Wordsworth's uncles, to whose guardianship he had been entrusted upon the death of his father in 1783, sent him to St. John's College, Cambridge. Here he read much in classical authors, studied Italian, learned a little French and Spanish, and played a part in the social pleasures of the University. His interest in college studies was not engrossing, however, and although he received the degree B.A. in January, 1791, the greatest stimulation his mind experienced during his college days came from the trips and walking tours he took in the long vacation periods. Much of his first vacation, 1788, he spent among the lakes in the Hawkshead region, and in the autumn of this year he made his first visit to London. The next summer he spent in wandering through the beautiful shires of Derby and York, with his sister Dorothy and her good friend Mary Hutchinson. His first visit to continental Europe came in the long vacation of 1790, when he and one of his college friends went on a walking tour in France, Switzerland, and the Italian lake country.

After receiving his degree, Wordsworth lived for several months in London. Quitting London in May (1791), he went to the home of Robert Jones, the Welsh friend who had been his companion on his European trip, and with him walked for some weeks through the northern part of Wales. By September he was in Cambridge, from which place he announced, somewhat curtly, to friends and relatives who urged him to go into orders and take a curacy at Harwick, that he was not of age for ordination. In November he was in France, intent on getting a better knowledge of the French language than his college years had given him, and thrilled, no doubt, as an imaginative young man might well have been, at the thought that the Revolution was the beginning of a new age of liberty and happiness for the world.

Arriving at Orleans in early December, Wordsworth carried with him as a souvenir a stone from the late-ruined Bastile, a selection not at all difficult to understand when one remembers

I

the enthusiasm he was soon to have for the Revolution. This enthusiasm did not fully waken until Captain Beaupuy of the Republican army pointed out to him a half-starved French girl leading a heifer and knitting, and said of the sight, "It is against *that* we are fighting." Wordsworth was deeply moved, and the instinctive belief which he had in the people and in their ability to make the laws under which they were to live, developed into the social and political creed which was to rise and fall within him during the next six years. It was this stay in France which forced Nature to yield first place to Man in Wordsworth's affections and imagination.

Another significant experience that came to Wordsworth at the time of his first stay in France was his falling in love with Annette Vallon, daughter of a surgeon at Blois. The Vallon family was strongly Catholic and Royalist, but Annette, even though she did not share Wordsworth's ideas of republicanism, was apparently not greatly troubled by them. Anyway she did not let them stand in the way of her love for him, and in December, 1792, she gave birth to a daughter, to which Wordsworth gave the name Caroline Wordsworth. There is no doubt that Wordsworth's love for Annette was as deep as hers for him and that he was sincere in his promise to marry her. He was entirely dependent upon his uncles, however, and just as he and Annette had agreed that he should return to England and get their consent to his marriage, the uncles, alarmed at his revolutionary sympathies, summoned him to England forthwith. Wordsworth left France and did not see Annette again for ten years.

It is easy for the reader who measures Wordsworth by the man he had become at forty-five to think of him as a stern, cold person, incapable of ardent partisanship, sensitive, perhaps, in his understanding of nature, but above human passions and enthusiasms. That he had not always been the sober, steady being of his later years, however, is clearly shown by his ardent assumption of the cause of the Revolutionists and by his passionate devotion to Annette Vallon. This is shown too by the deep anxiety and perplexity which seized upon him soon after his return to England and which became markedly intensified when, in February, 1793, England declared war against France.

Even before the year was over, however, a change began to come over the young Revolutionist. He still believed in the theory of the Revolution, though his belief gradually faded when he saw that it was becoming a war of conquest and that its leaders were unfaithful to the principles to which he had been so strongly devoted. When Robespierre went to the guillotine in July, 1794, he rejoiced, doubtless feeling even then, as he wrote afterwards in *The Prelude*, that the madness of the leaders stood "declared and visible." Even so, it was not until 1798 and 1799, when with his sister Dorothy and Coleridge he spent six months abroad, that his "republican ardor evanesced, and with it his resentment towards England as the foe of France."

Wordsworth was greatly aided in passing through this emotional crisis by his sister Dorothy, with whom he had settled at Racedown, Dorset, in October, 1795. Dorothy Wordsworth—"Wordsworth's exquisite sister," John Keats called her—was a woman who possessed an instinctive power of interpreting landscape and who could express her interpretation in words and phrases of great charm. The growing intimacy between Wordsworth and Coleridge, who had first met in 1795, led the Wordsworths to visit Coleridge at his Nether Stowey cottage for two weeks in July, 1797. On this visit Coleridge, who had already said that he was "a little man" in Wordsworth's presence, was moved both by the unmistakable genius of the youthful poet and by the charm of his sister Dorothy whose taste, he said, "bends, protrudes, and draws in at subtlest beauties and most recondite faults." So pleased were the three at the warmth of friendship discovered on this visit that the Wordsworths moved the very same month to Alfoxden, a spacious house in the midst of beautiful grounds and within three miles of the Coleridge cottage.

Dorothy Wordsworth kept a journal of the Alfoxden days, almost every entry of which is both significant for its penetration into human feelings or for its fine sensitiveness to nature, and memorable in its expression. This is the beginning of the Alfoxden journal:

20 Jan.—The green paths down the hillsides are channels for streams. The young wheat is streaked by silver lines of water running between the ridges, the sheep are gathered together on the slopes. After the wet dark days, the country seems more populous. It peoples itself in the sunbeams.

Egged on by the constant solicitude of one who could express her deep understanding of man and nature in words and phrases "like notes or chords of music," and stimulated by the strange genius of Coleridge, Wordsworth's mind soon cleared of the dark thoughts of the Revolution, and from it gradually disappeared, we may believe, all traces of regret that he had not been able to marry Annette Vallon. The emotional crisis over, there came a period of great poetic activity.

To this period belongs the volume *Lyrical Ballads* (1798), the joint work of Wordsworth and Coleridge, the first poem in the book being Coleridge's *Ancient Mariner* and the last Wordsworth's *Tintern Abbey*. Each of the two poets had his own particular part to do in the book, and each left an interesting account of what he believed those parts to be. In his *Biographia Literaria* Coleridge wrote: "It was agreed that my endeavors should be directed to persons and characters supernatural, or at least romantic, yet so as to transfer from our inward nature a human interest and a semblance of truth sufficient to procure for these shadows of the imagination that willing suspension of disbelief for the moment which constitutes poetic faith. Mr. Wordsworth was to give the charm of novelty to things of everyday life by awakening the mind's attention to the loveliness and wonders of the world before us."

For the second edition of *Lyrical Ballads*, which appeared in 1800, Wordsworth wrote the famous Preface in which he set forth his theory of the subject and the style of poetry. He preferred "incidents and situations from common life" as the subject matter of poetry, and hence he chose to write of "humble and rustic life . . . because in that condition the essential passions of the heart find a better soil." A little study of his poems will show that he was faithful to this declaration, since "humble and rustic life" is the subject of most of them.

As to the style of poetry, Wordsworth liked a "selection of language really used by men." Humble and rustic life is the best choice in this matter also, since men in this life "are less under restraint, and speak a plainer and more emphatic language . . . and convey their feelings and notions in simple and unelaborated expressions." There are many of Wordsworth's poems in which he is faithful to this declaration of what the language of poetry should be, some, indeed, in which he is all too faithful to it; but in his greatest work he frequently uses language the beauty and fitness of which is unmatched by anything in the vocabulary of the ordinary rustic. Coleridge, who saw the inconsistency between Wordsworth's theory and his use of poetic language, pointed out that only the most unusual rustic could say,

> The sounding cataract
> Haunted me like a passion.

Yet Wordsworth's language in his finest poetry is often marked, like this, by striking beauty and nobility.

The "bitter winter" of 1798 and 1799, which Wordsworth and his sister Dorothy spent in Goslar, near the Hartz forest, Germany, was a period of unhappiness, or perhaps, unrest, for the poet, and he longed for English companionship and for the sight of English fields and woodlands. His poetic activity continued, however, and he composed *Nutting, Ruth, The Poet's Epitaph*, fragments of *The Prelude*, and the fine group of Lucy poems. In May, 1799, the brother and sister went to visit Thomas and Mary Hutchinson at Sockburn-on-Tees. In October Coleridge and Cottle, the Bristol publisher of the *Lyrical Ballads*, arrived at Sockburn, and the three, accompanied by Wordsworth's brother John, went at once on a walking tour through the Lake Country. On this tour Wordsworth kept on the lookout for a place in which to live. At Grasmere he saw Dove Cottage, a little house which greatly attracted him, and which, in late December, he and his sister Dorothy made their home.

The year 1800 was a busy one at the little Grasmere cottage. John Wordsworth, the beloved brother who later died in shipwreck, lived almost the entire year there, and Mary Hutchinson was twice a visitor at the cottage. Coleridge came, with his wife and son Hartley, and the two poets prepared the second edition of *Lyrical Ballads*, this time in two volumes. Wordsworth worked on *The Recluse*, finished the first two books of *The Prelude*, and composed *The Brothers*, *Michael*, *Hart-Leap Well*, and many other poems. His creative activity continued at full height throughout the year, but the following year was almost entirely barren of poetic accomplishment.

In 1802 began his second period of creative activity, a period which continued throughout the following year though with somewhat declining energy as the year went on. Thirty-nine of the poems published in 1807 in *Poems in Two Volumes* were composed in this period, among them such favorites as *My Heart Leaps Up*, *The Solitary Reaper*, and a number of poems expressing the poet's love of certain English birds and flowers and places.

The month of August, 1802, Wordsworth and his sister spent in Calais, France, where Annette Vallon, whom he had not seen in ten years, had agreed to meet them, with his daughter Caroline. Apparently the relations between Wordsworth and Annette on this occasion were simple and cordial and unmarked by any show of the affection of ten years gone. Descriptive of this visit Dorothy Wordsworth wrote in her journal:

"We found Annette and Caroline chez Madame Avril dans la rue de la Tête d'Or . . . We walked by the seashore almost every evening, with Annette and Caroline, or William and I alone."

In one of the poet's most beautiful sonnets, *It is a Beauteous Evening*, the "Dear Child! Dear Girl!" of the sestet is his French daughter and not, as many readers have believed, his sister Dorothy. Soon after his return from Calais, Wordsworth married Mary Hutchinson, to whom he had been betrothed for some time, and took her to the little cottage at Grasmere.

Dove Cottage, which was Wordsworth's home from the close of 1800 to 1808, except for the period between October 1806 and August 1807, is more closely associated with him by lovers of his poetry than is Rydal Mount, the beautifully situated dwelling place two miles from Grasmere, where he spent his years from 1813 to the end. At the Cottage, encouraged by the constant sympathy of his sister and by the inspiring friendship of Coleridge, he composed most of his noblest and most beautiful poetry. Indeed, the years following his life at the Cottage were productive of but few poems great in spirit, however great they may have been in number. He wrote much poetry after the year 1807, but the bulk of it is markedly out of proportion to its excellence. His second, third, and last periods of great poetic activity, falling within the years from 1802 to 1807, came when he was a resident of Dove Cottage, or in the case of the last, of Coleorton; and his residence there was rather a temporary absence from the Cottage than a real removal. Roughly measured, the years of great poetry reached only from 1797 to 1807.

By 1808 there were three children in the Wordsworth household, and Dove Cottage proving too small, the poet moved his family to Allan Bank, a new house upon which the workmen were still busy. Here he lived for three years, annoyed by smoky chimneys and by the unfinished newness of the place, working at *The Excursion* and doing some prose essays or tracts but composing no poetry of real significance.

In 1811 the Wordsworth family, now numbering five children, moved to the rectory, near the little Grasmere church. The deaths of two of the children soon after made the rectory a place of sorrow to the parents, and in 1813 they made their final move, to Rydal Mount. The same year Wordsworth was appointed stamp distributor for Westmoreland county, an appointment which was worth £400 a year and which did not place upon him a heavy burden of work. His appointment to this position, which he held until he was seventy-two years old, is sure proof that there was no longer any trace of the fiery radicalism in him which had made of his youth a period of unrest and doubt. Indeed by 1804, as one can see by reading the eleventh book of *The Prelude*, he had become a convinced conservative.

Wordsworth's life at Rydal Mount has been called a "model of domesticity." His sister and his wife were in constant attendance upon him, solicitous for his welfare and over-careful, perhaps, to preserve every bit of verse he wrote. He had numerous visitors, to whom he liked to read from his own poems and to make comments, often unfavorable, upon the work of contemporary poets. He became a great traveller, his tours taking him to Switzerland, Italy, France, and other continental countries, to Scotland several times, to Ireland, and to many localities in his own England. He spent much time in careful correction and revision of his poems, new editions of which came out from time to time, and he occasionally felt, especially in the composition of some of his sonnets, the strong stir of the old creative impulse. When he resigned the stamp distributorship in 1842, he was given a pension of £300 a year. The next year, following the death of Southey, he was made Poet Laureate. There were seven years of the Laureateship, and then April 23 (the day of Shakespeare's birth and death), 1850, the "good old steel-gray figure" died and was laid to rest in Grasmere churchyard.

Wordsworth was never a thoroughly popular poet. *Poems in Two Volumes*, which he published in 1807, was savagely attacked by Jeffrey in the *Edinburgh Review*, but Wordsworth, little disturbed by the attack, wrote to a friend: "I merely think of the pure, absolute, honest ignorance in which all worldlings of every rank and situation must be enveloped, with respect to the thoughts, feelings, and images on which the life of my poems depends." De Quincey in a burst of enthusiasm said of him that up to 1820 his name was trampled under foot, from 1820 to 1830 it was militant, and from 1830 to 1835 triumphant. Doubtless this is exaggeration, but it is true that the detractors of Wordsworth gradually gave way and that he slowly rose to a position of high approval among his countrymen. Certainly his name is well up in the list of great English poets.

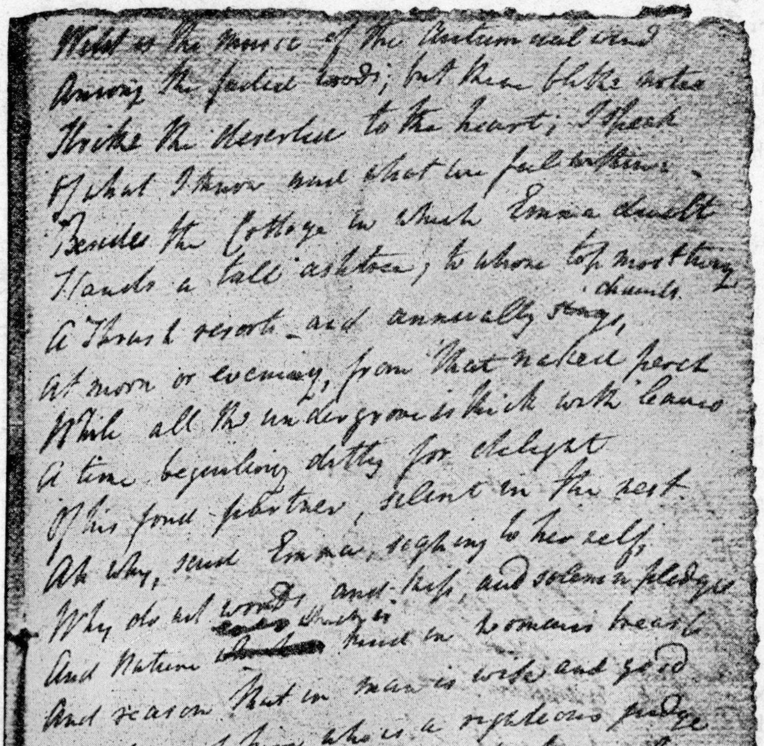

A Page from Wordsworth's MS of *The Excursion*. (See Appendix I.)

LINES

Left upon a Seat in a Yew tree, which stands
near the lake of Esthwaite, on a desolate part
of the shore, commanding a beautiful prospect.

Nay, Traveller! rest. This lonely Yew tree
 stands
Far from all human dwelling: what if here
No sparkling rivulet spread the verdant herb?
What if the bee love not these barren boughs?
Yet, if the wind breathe soft, the curling waves,
That break against the shore, shall lull thy
 mind
By one soft impulse saved from vacancy.
—————————————Who he was
That piled these stones and with the mossy sod
First covered, and here taught this aged
 Tree   10
With its dark arms to form a circling bower,
I well remember.—He was one who owned
No common soul. In youth by science nursed,
And led by nature into a wild scene
Of lofty hopes, he to the world went forth
A favoured Being, knowing no desire
Which genius did not hallow; 'gainst the taint
Of dissolute tongues, and jealousy, and hate,
And scorn,—against all enemies prepared,
All but neglect. The world, for so it thought,
Owed him no service; wherefore he at once 21
With indignation turned himself away,
And with the food of pride sustained his soul
In solitude.—Stranger! these gloomy boughs
Had charms for him; and here he loved to sit,
His only visitants a straggling sheep,
The stone-chat, or the glancing sandpiper:
And on these barren rocks, with fern and
 heath,
And juniper and thistle, sprinkled o'er,
Fixing his downcast eye, he many an hour 30
A morbid pleasure nourished, tracing here
An emblem of his own unfruitful life:
And, lifting up his head, he then would gaze
On the more distant scene,—how lovely 'tis
Thou seest,—and he would gaze till it became
Far lovelier, and his heart could not sustain
The beauty, still more beauteous! Nor, that
 time,
When nature had subdued him to herself,
Would he forget those Beings to whose minds
Warm from the labours of benevolence 40
The world, and human life, appeared a scene

Of kindred loveliness: then he would sigh,
Inly disturbed, to think that others felt
What he must never feel: and so, lost Man!
On visionary views would fancy feed,
Till his eye streamed with tears. In this deep
 vale
He died,—this seat his only monument.

If Thou be one whose heart the holy forms
Of young imagination have kept pure,
Stranger! henceforth be warned; and know
 that pride,   50
Howe'er disguised in its own majesty,
Is littleness; that he who feels contempt
For any living thing, hath faculties
Which he has never used; that thought with
 him
Is in its infancy. The man whose eye
Is ever on himself doth look on one,
The least of Nature's works, one who might
 move
The wise man to that scorn which wisdom
 holds
Unlawful, ever. O be wiser, Thou!
Instructed that true knowledge leads to love;
True dignity abides with him alone 61
Who, in the silent hour of inward thought,
Can still suspect, and still revere himself,
In lowliness of heart.

1795

MARGARET: OR THE RUINED COTTAGE

'Twas summer, and the sun had mounted
 high:
Southward the landscape indistinctly glared
Through a pale steam; but all the northern
 downs,
In clearest air ascending, showed far off
A surface dappled o'er with shadows flung
From brooding clouds; shadows that lay in
 spots
Determined and unmoved, with steady beams
Of bright and pleasant sunshine interposed;
To him most pleasant who on soft cool moss
Extends his careless limbs along the front 10
Of some huge cave, whose rocky ceiling casts
A twilight of its own, an ample shade,
Where the wren warbles, while the dreaming
 man,
Half conscious of the soothing melody,

With side-long eye looks out upon the scene,
By power of that impending covert, thrown
To finer distance. Mine was at that hour
Far other lot, yet with good hope that soon
Under a shade as grateful I should find
Rest, and be welcomed there to livelier joy. 20
Across a bare wide Common I was toiling
With languid steps that by the slippery turf
Were baffled; nor could my weak arm disperse
The host of insects gathering round my face,
And ever with me as I paced along.

Upon that open moorland stood a grove,
The wished-for port to which my course was
    bound.
Thither I came, and there, amid the gloom
Spread by a brotherhood of lofty elms,
Appeared a roofless Hut; four naked walls 30
That stared upon each other!—I looked round,
And to my wish and to my hope espied
The Friend I sought; a Man of reverend age,
But stout and hale, for travel unimpaired.
There was he seen upon the cottage-bench,
Recumbent in the shade, as if asleep;
An iron-pointed staff lay at his side.

*   *   *

    ... Supine the Wanderer lay,
His eyes as if in drowsiness half shut,
The shadows of the breezy elms above 40
Dappling his face. He had not heard the sound
Of my approaching steps, and in the shade
Unnoticed did I stand some minutes' space.
At length I hailed him, seeing that his hat
Was moist with water-drops, as if the brim
Had newly scooped a running stream. He rose,
And ere our lively greeting into peace
Had settled, "'Tis," said I, "a burning day:
My lips are parched with thirst, but you, it
    seems,
Have somewhere found relief." He, at the
    word, 50
Pointing towards a sweet-briar, bade me climb
The fence where that aspiring shrub looked out
Upon the public way. It was a plot
Of garden ground run wild, its matted weeds
Marked with the steps of those, whom, as
    they passed,
The gooseberry trees that shot in long lank
    slips,
Or currants, hanging from their leafless stems,

In scanty strings, had tempted to o'erleap
The broken wall. I looked around, and there,
Where two tall hedge-rows of thick alder
    boughs 60
Joined in a cold damp nook, espied a well
Shrouded with willow-flowers and plumy fern.
My thirst I slaked, and, from the cheerless spot
Withdrawing, straightway to the shade re-
    turned
Where sate the old Man on the cottage-bench;
And, while, beside him, with uncovered head,
I yet was standing, freely to respire,
And cool my temples in the fanning air,
Thus did he speak. "I see around me here
Things which you cannot see: we die, my
    Friend, 70
Nor we alone, but that which each man loved
And prized in his peculiar nook of earth
Dies with him, or is changed; and very soon
Even of the good is no memorial left.
—The Poets, in their elegies and songs
Lamenting the departed, call the groves,
They call upon the hills and streams to mourn,
And senseless rocks; nor idly; for they speak,
In these their invocations, with a voice
Obedient to the strong creative power 80
Of human passion. Sympathies there are
More tranquil, yet perhaps of kindred birth,
That steal upon the meditative mind,
And grow with thought. Beside yon spring I
    stood,
And eyed its waters till we seemed to feel
One sadness, they and I. For them a bond
Of brotherhood is broken: time has been
When, every day, the touch of human hand
Dislodged the natural sleep that binds them up
In mortal stillness; and they ministered 90
To human comfort. Stooping down to drink
Upon the slimy foot-stone I espied
The useless fragment of a wooden bowl,
Green with the moss of years, and subject
    only
To the soft handling of the elements:
There let it lie—how foolish are such thoughts!
Forgive them;—never—never did my steps
Approach this door but she who dwelt within
A daughter's welcome gave me, and I loved
    her
As my own child. Oh, Sir! the good die first,
And they whose hearts are dry as summer
    dust   101

Burn to the socket. Many a passenger
Hath blessed poor Margaret for her gentle
    looks,
When she upheld the cool refreshment drawn
From that forsaken spring; and no one came
But he was welcome; no one went away
But that it seemed she loved him. She is dead,
The light extinguished of her lonely hut,
The hut itself abandoned to decay,
And she forgotten in the quiet grave.   110

    "I speak," continued he, "of One whose
        stock
Of virtues bloomed beneath this lowly roof.
She was a Woman of a steady mind,
Tender and deep in her excess of love;
Not speaking much, pleased rather with the
    joy
Of her own thoughts: by some especial care
Her temper had been framed, as if to make
A Being, who by adding love to peace
Might live on earth a life of happiness.
Her wedded Partner lacked not on his side 120
The humble worth that satisfied her heart:
Frugal, affectionate, sober, and withal
Keenly industrious. She with pride would tell
That he was often seated at his loom,
In summer, ere the mower was abroad
Among the dewy grass,—in early spring,
Ere the last star had vanished.—They who
    passed
At evening, from behind the garden fence
Might hear his busy spade, which he would
    ply,
After his daily work, until the light   130
Had failed, and every leaf and flower were lost
In the dark hedges. So their days were spent
In peace and comfort; and a pretty boy
Was their best hope, next to the God in
    heaven.

    "Not twenty years ago, but you I think
Can scarcely bear it now in mind, there came
Two blighting seasons, when the fields were
    left
With half a harvest. It pleased Heaven to add
A worse affliction in the plague of war:
This happy Land was stricken to the heart! 140
A Wanderer then among the cottages,
I, with my freight of winter raiment, saw
The hardships of that season: many rich

Sank down, as in a dream, among the poor;
And of the poor did many cease to be,
And their place knew them not. Meanwhile,
    abridged
Of daily comforts, gladly reconciled
To numerous self-denials, Margaret
Went struggling on through those calamitous
    years
With cheerful hope, until the second au-
    tumn,   150
When her life's Helpmate on a sick-bed lay,
Smitten with perilous fever. In disease
He lingered long; and, when his strength re-
    turned,
He found the little he had stored, to meet
The hour of accident or crippling age,
Was all consumed. A second infant now
Was added to the troubles of a time
Laden, for them and all of their degree,
With care and sorrow: shoals of artisans
From ill-requited labour turned adrift   160
Sought daily bread from public charity,
They, and their wives and children—happier
    far
Could they have lived as do the little birds
That peck along the hedge-rows, or the kite
That makes her dwelling on the mountain
    rocks!

    "A sad reverse it was for him who long
Had filled with plenty, and possessed in peace,
This lonely Cottage. At the door he stood,
And whistled many a snatch of merry tunes.
That had no mirth in them; or with his knife
Carved uncouth figures on the heads of
    sticks—   171
Then, not less idly, sought, through every
    nook
In house or garden, any casual work
Of use or ornament; and with a strange,
Amusing, yet uneasy, novelty,
He mingled, where he might, the various tasks
Of summer, autumn, winter, and of spring.
But this endured not; his good humour soon
Became a weight in which no pleasure was:
And poverty brought on a petted mood   180
And a sore temper: day by day he drooped,
And he would leave his work—and to the
    town
Would turn without an errand his slack steps;
Or wander here and there among the fields

One while he would speak lightly of his babes,
And with a cruel tongue: at other times
He tossed them with a false unnatural joy:
And 'twas a rueful thing to see the looks
Of the poor innocent children. 'Every smile,'
Said Margaret to me, here beneath these trees,
'Made my heart bleed.' ''

      At this the Wanderer paused; 191
And, looking up to those enormous elms,
He said, "'Tis now the hour of deepest noon.
At this still season of repose and peace,
This hour when all things which are not at rest
Are cheerful; while this multitude of flies
With tuneful hum is filling all the air;
Why should a tear be on an old Man's cheek?
Why should we thus, with an untoward mind,
And in the weakness of humanity, 200
From natural wisdom turn our hearts away;
To natural comfort shut our eyes and ears;
And, feeding on disquiet, thus disturb
The calm of nature with our restless thoughts?"

HE spake with somewhat of a solemn tone:
But, when he ended, there was in his face
Such easy cheerfulness, a look so mild,
That for a little time it stole away
All recollection; and that simple tale 209
Passed from my mind like a forgotten sound.
A while on trivial things we held discourse,
To me soon tasteless. In my own despite,
I thought of that poor Woman as of one
Whom I had known and loved. He had re-hearsed
Her homely tale with such familiar power,
With such an active countenance, an eye
So busy, that the things of which he spake
Seemed present; and, attention now relaxed,
A heart-felt chilliness crept along my veins.
I rose; and, having left the breezy shade, 220
Stood drinking comfort from the warmer sun,
That had not cheered me long—ere, looking round
Upon that tranquil Ruin, I returned,
And begged of the old Man that, for my sake,
He would resume his story.

          He replied,
"It were a wantonness, and would demand
Severe reproof, if we were men whose hearts
Could hold vain dalliance with the misery
Even of the dead; contented thence to draw
A momentary pleasure, never marked 230
By reason, barren of all future good.
But we have known that there is often found
In mournful thoughts, and always might be found,
A power to virtue friendly; were't not so,
I am a dreamer among men, indeed
An idle dreamer! 'Tis a common tale,
An ordinary sorrow of man's life,
A tale of silent suffering, hardly clothed
In bodily form.—But without further bidding
I will proceed.

        While thus it fared with them,
To whom this cottage, till those hapless years, 241
Had been a blessèd home, it was my chance
To travel in a country far remote;
And when these lofty elms once more ap-peared
What pleasant expectations lured me on
O'er the flat Common!—With quick step I reached
The threshold, lifted with light hand the latch;
But, when I entered, Margaret looked at me
A little while; then turned her head away
Speechless,—and, sitting down upon a chair,
Wept bitterly. I wist not what to do, 251
Nor how to speak to her. Poor Wretch! at last
She rose from off her seat, and then,—O Sir!
I cannot *tell* how she pronounced my name:—
With fervent love, and with a face of grief
Unutterably helpless, and a look
That seemed to cling upon me, she enquired
If I had seen her husband. As she spake
A strange surprise and fear came to my heart,
Nor had I power to answer ere she told
That he had disappeared—not two months gone. 261
He left his house: two wretched days had past,
And on the third, as wistfully she raised
Her head from off her pillow, to look forth,
Like one in trouble, for returning light,
Within her chamber-casement she espied
A folded paper, lying as if placed
To meet her waking eyes. This tremblingly
She opened—found no writing, but beheld
Pieces of money carefully enclosed, 270
Silver and gold. 'I shuddered at the sight,'
Said Margaret, 'for I knew it was his hand

That must have placed it there; and ere that
    day
Was ended, that long anxious day, I learned,
From one who by my husband had been sent
With the sad news, that he had joined a troop
Of soldiers, going to a distant land.
—He left me thus—he could not gather heart
To take a farewell of me; for he feared
That I should follow with my babes, and
    sink   280
Beneath the misery of that wandering life.'

"This tale did Margaret tell with many tears:
And, when she ended, I had little power
To give her comfort, and was glad to take
Such words of hope from her own mouth as
    served
To cheer us both. But long we had not talked
Ere we built up a pile of better thoughts,
And with a brighter eye she looked around
As if she had been shedding tears of joy.
We parted.—'Twas the time of early spring;
I left her busy with her garden tools;   291
And well remember, o'er that fence she looked,
And, while I paced along the foot-way path,
Called out, and sent a blessing after me,
With tender cheerfulness, and with a voice
That seemed the very sound of happy thoughts.

"I roved o'er many a hill and many a dale,
With my accustomed load; in heat and cold,
Through many a wood and many an open
    ground,
In sunshine and in shade, in wet and fair,   300
Drooping or blithe of heart, as might befall;
My best companions now the driving winds,
And now the 'trotting brooks' and whispering
    trees,
And now the music of my own sad steps,
With many a short-lived thought that passed
    between,
And disappeared.
                I journeyed back this way,
When, in the warmth of midsummer, the wheat
Was yellow; and the soft and bladed grass,
Springing afresh, had o'er the hay-field spread
Its tender verdure. At the door arrived,   310
I found that she was absent. In the shade,
Where now we sit, I waited her return.
Her cottage, then a cheerful object, wore
Its customary look,—only, it seemed,

The honeysuckle, crowding round the porch,
Hung down in heavier tufts; and that bright
    weed,
The yellow stone-crop, suffered to take root
Along the window's edge, profusely grew
Blinding the lower panes. I turned aside,
And strolled into her garden. It appeared   320
To lag behind the season, and had lost
Its pride of neatness. Daisy-flowers and thrift
Had broken their trim border-lines, and
    straggled
O'er paths they used to deck: carnations, once
Prized for surpassing beauty, and no less
For the peculiar pains they had required,
Declined their languid heads, wanting support.
The cumbrous bind-weed, with its wreaths and
    bells,   *neg. of garden*
Had twined about her two small rows of peas,
And dragged them to the earth.
                    Ere this an hour
Was wasted.—Back I turned my restless
    steps;   331
A stranger passed; and, guessing whom I
    sought,
He said that she was used to ramble far.—
The sun was sinking in the west; and now
I sate with sad impatience. From within
Her solitary infant cried aloud;
Then, like a blast that dies away self-stilled,
The voice was silent. From the bench I rose;
But neither could divert nor soothe my
    thoughts.   339
The spot, though fair, was very desolate—
The longer I remained, more desolate:
And, looking round me, now I first observed
The corner stones, on either side the porch,
With dull red stains discoloured, and stuck
    o'er
With tufts and hairs of wool, as if the sheep,
That fed upon the Common, thither came
Familiarly, and found a couching-place
Even at her threshold. Deeper shadows fell
From these tall elms; the cottage-clock struck
    eight;—
I turned, and saw her distant a few steps.   350
Her face was pale and thin—her figure, too,
Was changed. As she unlocked the door, she
    said,
'It grieves me you have waited here so long,
But, in good truth, I've wandered much of
    late;

And, sometimes—to my shame I speak—have
    need
Of my best prayers to bring me back again.'
While on the board she spread our evening
    meal,
She told me—interrupting not the work
Which gave employment to her listless
    hands—
That she had parted with her elder child; 360
To a kind master on a distant farm
Now happily apprenticed.—'I perceive
You look at me, and you have cause; to-day
I have been travelling far; and many days
About the fields I wander, knowing this
Only, that what I seek I cannot find;
And so I waste my time: for I am changed;
And to myself,' said she, 'have done much
    wrong
And to this helpless infant. I have slept
Weeping, and weeping have I waked; my
    tears   370
Have flowed as if my body were not such
As others are; and I could never die.
But I am now in mind and in my heart
More easy; and I hope,' said she, 'that God
Will give me patience to endure the things
Which I behold at home.'
               It would have grieved
Your very soul to see her. Sir, I feel
The story linger in my heart; I fear
'Tis long and tedious; but my spirit clings
To that poor Woman:—so familiarly   380
Do I perceive her manner, and her look,
And presence; and so deeply do I feel
Her goodness, that, not seldom, in my walks
A momentary trance comes over me;
And to myself I seem to muse on One
By sorrow laid asleep; or borne away,
A human being destined to awake
To human life, or something very near
To human life, when he shall come again
For whom she suffered. Yes, it would have
    grieved   390
Your very soul to see her: evermore
Her eyelids drooped, her eyes downward were
    cast;
And, when she at her table gave me food,
She did not look at me. Her voice was low,
Her body was subdued. In every act
Pertaining to her house-affairs, appeared
The careless stillness of a thinking mind

Self-occupied; to which all outward things
Are like an idle matter. Still she sighed,
But yet no motion of the breast was seen,
No heaving of the heart. While by the fire 401
We sate together, sighs came on my ear,
I knew not how, and hardly whence they
    came.

"Ere my departure, to her care I gave,
For her son's use, some tokens of regard,
Which with a look of welcome she received;
And I exhorted her to place her trust
In God's good love, and seek his help by
    prayer.
I took my staff, and, when I kissed her babe,
The tears stood in her eyes. I left her then 410
With the best hope and comfort I could give:
She thanked me for my wish;—but for my
    hope
It seemed she did not thank me.
                    I returned,
And took my rounds along this road again
When on its sunny bank the primrose flower
Peeped forth, to give an earnest of the Spring.
I found her sad and drooping: she had learned
No tidings of her husband; if he lived,
She knew not that he lived; if he were dead,
She knew not he was dead. She seemed the
    same   420
In person and appearance; but her house
Bespake a sleepy hand of negligence;
The floor was neither dry nor neat, the hearth
Was comfortless, and her small lot of books,
Which, in the cottage-window, heretofore
Had been piled up against the corner panes
In seemly order, now, with straggling leaves
Lay scattered here and there, open or shut,
As they had chanced to fall. Her infant Babe
Had from its mother caught the trick of grief,
And sighed among its playthings. I with-
    drew,   431
And once again entering the garden saw,
More plainly still, that poverty and grief
Were now come nearer to her: weeds defaced
The hardened soil, and knots of withered grass:
No ridges there appeared of clear black mould,
No winter greenness; of her herbs and flowers,
It seemed the better part were gnawed away
Or trampled into earth; a chain of straw,
Which had been twined about the slender stem
Of a young apple-tree, lay at its root;   441

The bark was nibbled round by truant sheep.
—Margaret stood near, her infant in her arms,
And, noting that my eye was on the tree,
She said, 'I fear it will be dead and gone
Ere Robert come again.' When to the House
We had returned together, she enquired
If I had any hope:—but for her babe
And for her little orphan boy, she said,
She had no wish to live, that she must die   450
Of sorrow. Yet I saw the idle loom
Still in its place; his Sunday garments hung
Upon the self-same nail; his very staff
Stood undisturbed behind the door.
                                    And when,
In bleak December, I retraced this way,
She told me that her little babe was dead,
And she was left alone. She now, released
From her maternal cares, had taken up
The employment common through these
        wilds, and gained,
By spinning hemp, a pittance for herself;   460
And for this end had hired a neighbour's boy
To give her needful help. That very time
Most willingly she put her work aside,
And walked with me along the miry road,
Heedless how far; and, in such piteous sort
That any heart had ached to hear her, begged
That, wheresoe'er I went, I still would ask
For him whom she had lost. We parted then—
Our final parting; for from that time forth
Did many seasons pass ere I returned   470
Into this tract again.
                        Nine tedious years;
From their first separation, nine long years,
She lingered in unquiet widowhood;
A Wife and Widow. Needs must it have
        been
A sore heart-wasting! I have heard, my Friend,
That in yon arbour oftentimes she sate
Alone, through half the vacant sabbath day;
And, if a dog passed by, she still would quit
The shade, and look abroad. On this old bench
For hours she sate; and evermore her eye   480
Was busy in the distance, shaping things
That made her heart beat quick. You see that
        path,
Now faint,—the grass has crept o'er its grey
        line;
There, to and fro, she paced through many a
        day
Of the warm summer, from a belt of hemp

That girt her waist, spinning the long-drawn
        thread
With backward steps. Yet ever as there passed
A man whose garments showed the soldier's
        red,
Or crippled mendicant in soldier's garb,
The little child who sate to turn the wheel
Ceased from his task; and she with faltering
        voice   491
Made many a fond enquiry; and when they,
Whose presence gave no comfort, were gone
        by,
Her heart was still more sad. And by yon gate,
That bars the traveller's road, she often stood,
And when a stranger horseman came, the
        latch
Would lift, and in his face look wistfully:
Most happy, if, from aught discovered there
Of tender feeling, she might dare repeat
The same sad question. Meanwhile her poor
        Hut   500
Sank to decay; for he was gone, whose hand,
At the first nipping of October frost,
Closed up each chink, and with fresh bands of
        straw
Chequered the green-grown thatch. And so
        she lived
Through the long winter, reckless and alone;
Until her house by frost, and thaw, and rain,
Was sapped; and while she slept, the nightly
        damps
Did chill her breast; and in the stormy day
Her tattered clothes were ruffled by the wind,
Even at the side of her own fire. Yet still   510
She loved this wretched spot, nor would for
        worlds
Have parted hence; and still that length of
        road,
And this rude bench, one torturing hope en-
        deared,
Fast rooted at her heart: and here, my Friend,—
In sickness she remained; and here she died;
Last human tenant of these ruined walls!"

    The old Man ceased: he saw that I was
        moved;
From that low bench, rising instinctively
I turned aside in weakness, nor had power
To thank him for the tale which he had
        told.   520
I stood, and leaning o'er the garden wall

Reviewed that Woman's sufferings; and it
  seemed
To comfort me while with a brother's love
I blessed her in the impotence of grief.
Then towards the cottage I returned; and
  traced
Fondly, though with an interest more mild,
That secret spirit of humanity
Which, 'mid the calm oblivious tendencies
Of nature, 'mid her plants, and weeds, and
  flowers,
And silent overgrowings, still survived.   530
The old Man, noting this, resumed, and said,
"My Friend! enough to sorrow you have given,
The purposes of wisdom ask no more:
Nor more would she have craved as due to One
Who, in her worst distress, had ofttimes felt
The unbounded might of prayer; and learned,
  with soul
Fixed on the Cross, that consolation springs,
From sources deeper far than deepest pain,
For the meek Sufferer. Why then should we
  read   539
The forms of things with an unworthy eye?
She sleeps in the calm earth, and peace is here.
I well remember that those very plumes,
Those weeds, and the high spear-grass on that
  wall,
By mist and silent rain-drops silvered o'er,
As once I passed, into my heart conveyed
So still an image of tranquillity,
So calm and still, and looked so beautiful
Amid the uneasy thoughts which filled my
  mind,
That what we feel of sorrow and despair   549
From ruin and from change, and all the grief
That passing shows of Being leave behind,
Appeared an idle dream, that could maintain,
Nowhere, dominion o'er the enlightened spirit
Whose meditative sympathies repose
Upon the breast of Faith. I turned away,
And walked along my road in happiness."

He ceased. Ere long the sun declining shot
A slant and mellow radiance, which began
To fall upon us, while, beneath the trees,   559
We sate on that low bench: and now we felt,
Admonished thus, the sweet hour coming on.
A linnet warbled from those lofty elms,
A thrush sang loud, and other melodies,
At distance heard, peopled the milder air.

The old Man rose, and, with a sprightly mien
Of hopeful preparation, grasped his staff;
Together casting then a farewell look
Upon those silent walls, we left the shade;
And, ere the stars were visible, had reached
A village-inn,—our evening resting-place. 560
1795–1798

LINES WRITTEN IN EARLY SPRING

I HEARD a thousand blended notes,
While in a grove I sate reclined,
In that sweet mood when pleasant thoughts
Bring sad thoughts to the mind.

To her fair works did Nature link
The human soul that through me ran;
And much it grieved my heart to think
What man has made of man.

Through primrose tufts, in that green bower,
The periwinkle trailed its wreaths;   10
And 'tis my faith that every flower
Enjoys the air it breathes.

The birds around me hopped and played,
Their thoughts I cannot measure:—
But the least motion which they made,
It seemed a thrill of pleasure.

The budding twigs spread out their fan,
To catch the breezy air;
And I must think, do all I can,
That there was pleasure there.   20

If this belief from heaven be sent,
If such be Nature's holy plan,
Have I not reason to lament
What man has made of man?
1798

A WHIRL–BLAST FROM BEHIND THE HILL

A WHIRL-BLAST from behind the hill
Rushed o'er the wood with startling sound;
Then—all at once the air was still,
And showers of hailstones pattered round.
Where leafless oaks towered high above,
I sat within an undergrove
Of tallest hollies, tall and green;
A fairer bower was never seen.

From year to year the spacious floor
With withered leaves is covered o'er, 10
And all the year the bower is green.
But see! where'er the hailstones drop
The withered leaves all skip and hop;
There's not a breeze—no breath of air—
Yet here, and there, and every where
Along the floor, beneath the shade
By those embowering hollies made,
The leaves in myriads jump and spring,
As if with pipes and music rare
Some Robin Good-fellow were there, 20
And all those leaves, in festive glee,
Were dancing to the minstrelsy.

1798

ANIMAL TRANQUILLITY AND DECAY

THE little hedgerow birds,
That peck along the road, regard him not.
He travels on, and in his face, his step,
His gait, is one expression: every limb,
His look and bending figure, all bespeak
A man who does not move with pain, but
  moves
With thought.—He is insensibly subdued
To settled quiet: he is one by whom
All effort seems forgotten; one to whom
Long patience hath such mild composure
  given, 10
That patience now doth seem a thing of which
He hath no need. He is by nature led
To peace so perfect that the young behold
With envy, what the Old Man hardly feels.

1798

TO MY SISTER

IT is the first mild day of March:
Each minute sweeter than before,
The redbreast sings from the tall larch
That stands beside our door.

There is a blessing in the air,
Which seems a sense of joy to yield
To the bare trees, and mountains bare,
And grass in the green field.

My sister! ('tis a wish of mine)
Now that our morning meal is done, 10
Make haste, your morning task resign;
Come forth and feel the sun.

Edward will come with you;—and, pray,
Put on with speed your woodland dress;
And bring no book: for this one day
We'll give to idleness.

No joyless forms shall regulate
Our living calendar:
We from to-day, my Friend, will date
The opening of the year. 20

Love, now a universal birth,
From heart to heart is stealing,
From earth to man, from man to earth:
—It is the hour of feeling.

One moment now may give us more
Than years of toiling reason:
Our minds shall drink at every pore
The spirit of the season.

Some silent laws our hearts will make,
Which they shall long obey: 30
We for the year to come may take
Our temper from to-day.

And from the blessed power that rolls
About, below, above,
We'll frame the measure of our souls:
They shall be tuned to love.

Then come, my Sister! come, I pray,
With speed put on your woodland dress;
And bring no book: for this one day
We'll give to idleness. 40

1798 *meter makes it unnecessary*

SIMON LEE

THE OLD HUNTSMAN; WITH AN INCIDENT
IN WHICH HE WAS CONCERNED

IN the sweet shire of Cardigan,
Not far from pleasant Ivor-hall,
An old Man dwells, a little man,—
'Tis said he once was tall.
Full five-and-thirty years he lived
A running huntsman merry;
And still the centre of his cheek
Is red as a ripe cherry.

No man like him the horn could sound,
And hill and valley rang with glee 10
When Echo bandied, round and round,
The halloo of Simon Lee.

In those proud days, he little cared
For husbandry or tillage;
To blither tasks did Simon rouse
The sleepers of the village.

He all the country could outrun,
Could leave both man and horse behind;
And often, ere the chase was done,
He reeled, and was stone-blind.   20
And still there's something in the world
At which his heart rejoices;
For when the chiming hounds are out,
He dearly loves their voices!

milton

But, oh the heavy change!—bereft
Of health, strength, friends, and kindred, see!
Old Simon to the world is left
In liveried poverty.
His Master's dead,—and no one now
Dwells in the Hall of Ivor;   30
Men, dogs, and horses, all are dead;
He is the sole survivor.

And he is lean and he is sick;
His body, dwindled and awry,
Rests upon ankles swoln and thick;
His legs are thin and dry.
One prop he has, and only one,
His wife, an aged woman,
Lives with him, near the waterfall,
Upon the village Common.   40

Beside their moss-grown hut of clay,
Not twenty paces from the door,
A scrap of land they have, but they
Are poorest of the poor.
This scrap of land he from the heath
Enclosed when he was stronger;
But what to them avails the land
Which he can till no longer?

Oft, working by her Husband's side,
Ruth does what Simon cannot do;   50
For she, with scanty cause for pride,
Is stouter of the two.
And, though you with your utmost skill
From labour could not wean them,
'Tis little, very little—all
That they can do between them.

Few months of life has he in store
As he to you will tell,
For still, the more he works, the more
Do his weak ankles swell.   60

My gentle Reader, I perceive
How patiently you've waited,
And now I fear that you expect
Some tale will be related.

O Reader! had you in your mind
Such stores as silent thought can bring,
O gentle Reader! you would find
A tale in every thing.
What more I have to say is short,
And you must kindly take it: 70
It is no tale; but, should you think,
Perhaps a tale you'll make it.

One summer-day I chanced to see
This old Man doing all he could
To unearth the root of an old tree,
A stump of rotten wood.
The mattock tottered in his hand;
So vain was his endeavour,
That at the root of the old tree
He might have worked for ever.   80

"You're overtasked, good Simon Lee,
Give me your tool," to him I said;
And at the word right gladly he
Received my proffered aid.
I struck, and with a single blow
The tangled root I severed,
At which the poor old Man so long
And vainly had endeavoured.

The tears into his eyes were brought,
And thanks and praises seemed to run   90
So fast out of his heart, I thought
They never would have done.
—I've heard of hearts unkind, kind deeds
With coldness still returning;
Alas! the gratitude of men
Hath oftener left me mourning.

1798

WE ARE SEVEN

——A simple Child,
That lightly draws its breath,
And feels its life in every limb,
What should it know of death?

I met a little cottage Girl:
She was eight years old, she said;
Her hair was thick with many a curl
That clustered round her head.

She had a rustic, woodland air,
And she was wildly clad: 10
Her eyes were fair, and very fair;
—Her beauty made me glad.

"Sisters and brothers, little maid,
How many may you be?"
"How many? Seven in all," she said,
And wondering looked at me.

"And where are they? I pray you tell."
She answered, "Seven are we;
And two of us at Conway dwell,
And two are gone to sea.   20

"Two of us in the church-yard lie,
My sister and my brother;
And, in the church-yard cottage, I
Dwell near them with my mother."

"You say that two at Conway dwell,
And two are gone to sea,
Yet ye are seven! pray you tell,
Sweet Maid, how this may be."

Then did the little Maid reply,
"Seven boys and girls are we;   30
Two of us in the church-yard lie,
Beneath the church-yard tree."

"You run about, my little Maid,
Your limbs they are alive;
If two are in the church-yard laid,
Then ye are only five."

"Their graves are green, they may be seen,"
The little Maid replied,
"Twelve steps or more from my mother's
    door,
And they are side by side.   40

"My stockings there I often knit,
My kerchief there I hem;
And there upon the ground I sit,
And sing a song to them.

"And often after sun-set, Sir,
When it is light and fair,
I take my little porringer,
And eat my supper there.

"The first that died was sister Jane;
In bed she moaning lay,   50
Till God released her of her pain;
And then she went away.

"So in the church-yard she was laid;
And, when the grass was dry,
Together round her grave we played,
My brother John and I.

"And when the ground was white with snow,
And I could run and slide,
My brother John was forced to go,
And he lies by her side."   60

"How many are you, then," said I,
"If they two are in heaven?"
Quick was the little Maid's reply,
"O Master! we are seven."

"But they are dead; those two are dead!
Their spirits are in heaven!"
'Twas throwing words away; for still
The little Maid would have her will,
And said, "Nay, we are seven!"
1798

THERE WAS A BOY

THERE was a Boy; ye knew him well, ye cliffs
And islands of Winander!—many a time,
At evening, when the earliest stars began
To move along the edges of the hills,
Rising or setting, would he stand alone,
Beneath the trees, or by the glimmering lake;
And there, with fingers interwoven, both
    hands
Pressed closely palm to palm and to his mouth
Uplifted, he, as through an instrument,
Blew mimic hootings to the silent owls,   10
That they might answer him.—And they
    would shout
Across the watery vale, and shout again,
Responsive to his call,—with quivering peals,
And long halloos, and screams, and echoes
    loud
Redoubled and redoubled; concourse wild
Of jocund din! And, when there came a
    pause
Of silence such as baffled his best skill:
Then sometimes, in that silence, while he
    hung
Listening, a gentle shock of mild surprise
Has carried far into his heart the voice   20
Of mountain-torrents; or the visible scene
Would enter unawares into his mind
With all its solemn imagery, its rocks,

Its woods, and that uncertain heaven received
Into the bosom of the steady lake.
  This boy was taken from his mates, and died
In childhood, ere he was full twelve years old.
Pre-eminent in beauty is the vale
Where he was born and bred: the churchyard
    hangs
Upon a slope above the village-school;   30
And through that churchyard when my way
    has led
On summer-evenings, I believe that there
A long half-hour together I have stood
Mute—looking at the grave in which he lies!
1798

EXPOSTULATION AND REPLY

"Why, William, on that old grey stone,
Thus for the length of half a day,
Why, William, sit you thus alone,
And dream your time away?

"Where are your books?—that light be-
    queathed
To Beings else forlorn and blind!
Up! up! and drink the spirit breathed
From dead men to their kind.

"You look round on your Mother Earth,
As if she for no purpose bore you;   10
As if you were her first-born birth,
And none had lived before you!"

One morning thus, by Esthwaite lake,
When life was sweet, I knew not why,
To me my good friend Matthew spake,
And thus I made reply:

"The eye—it cannot choose but see;
We cannot bid the ear be still;
Our bodies feel, where'er they be,
Against or with our will.   20

"Nor less I deem that there are Powers
Which of themselves our minds impress;
That we can feed this mind of ours
In a wise passiveness.

"Think you, 'mid all this mighty sum
Of things for ever speaking,
That nothing of itself will come,
But we must still be seeking?

"—Then ask not wherefore, here, alone,
Conversing as I may,   30
I sit upon this old grey stone,
And dream my time away."
1798

THE TABLES TURNED

AN EVENING SCENE ON THE SAME SUBJECT

Up! up! my Friend, and quit your books;
Or surely you'll grow double:
Up! up! my Friend, and clear your looks;
Why all this toil and trouble?

The sun, above the mountain's head,
A freshening lustre mellow
Through all the long green fields has spread,
His first sweet evening yellow.

Books! 'tis a dull and endless strife:
Come, hear the woodland linnet,   10
How sweet his music! on my life,
There's more of wisdom in it.

And hark! how blithe the throstle sings!
He, too, is no mean preacher:
Come forth into the light of things,
Let Nature be your Teacher.

She has a world of ready wealth,
Our minds and hearts to bless—
Spontaneous wisdom breathed by health,
Truth breathed by cheerfulness.   20

One impulse from a vernal wood
May teach you more of man,
Of moral evil and of good,
Than all the sages can.

Sweet is the lore which Nature brings;
Our meddling intellect
Mis-shapes the beauteous forms of things:—
We murder to dissect.

Enough of Science and of Art;
Close up those barren leaves;   30
Come forth, and bring with you a heart
That watches and receives.
1798

THE IDIOT BOY

'Tis eight o'clock,—a clear March night,
The moon is up,—the sky is blue,
The owlet, in the moonlight air,
Shouts from nobody knows where;

He lengthens out his lonely shout,
Halloo! halloo! a long halloo!

—Why bustle thus about your door,
What means this bustle, Betty Foy?
Why are you in this mighty fret?
And why on horseback have you set　10
Him whom you love, your Idiot Boy?

Scarcely a soul is out of bed;
Good Betty, put him down again;
His lips with joy they burr at you;
But, Betty! what has he to do
With stirrup, saddle, or with rein?

But Betty's bent on her intent;
For her good neighbour Susan Gale,
Old Susan, she who dwells alone,
Is sick, and makes a piteous moan,　20
As if her very life would fail.

There's not a house within a mile,
No hand to help them in distress;
Old Susan lies a-bed in pain,
And sorely puzzled are the twain,
For what she ails they cannot guess.

And Betty's husband's at the wood,
Where by the week he doth abide,
A woodman in the distant vale;
There's none to help poor Susan Gale;　30
What must be done? what will betide?

And Betty from the lane has fetched
Her Pony, that is mild and good;
Whether he be in joy or pain,
Feeding at will along the lane,
Or bringing fagots from the wood.

And he is all in travelling trim,—
And, by the moonlight, Betty Foy
Has on the well-girt saddle set
(The like was never heard of yet)　40
Him whom she loves, her Idiot Boy.

And he must post without delay
Across the bridge and through the dale,
And by the church, and o'er the down,
To bring a Doctor from the town,
Or she will die, old Susan Gale.

There is no need of boot or spur,
There is no need of whip or wand;

For Johnny has his holly-bough,
And with a *hurly-burly* now　50
He shakes the green bough in his hand.

And Betty o'er and o'er has told
The Boy, who is her best delight,
Both what to follow, what to shun,
What do, and what to leave undone,
How turn to left, and how to right.

And Betty's most especial charge,
Was, "Johnny! Johnny! mind that you
Come home again, nor stop at all,—
Come home again, whate'er befall,　60
My Johnny, do, I pray you, do."

To this did Johnny answer make,
Both with his head and with his hand,
And proudly shook the bridle too;
And then! his words were not a few,
Which Betty well could understand.

And now that Johnny is just going,
Though Betty's in a mighty flurry,
She gently pats the Pony's side,
On which her Idiot Boy must ride,　70
And seems no longer in a hurry.

But when the Pony moved his legs,
Oh! then for the poor Idiot Boy!
For joy he cannot hold the bridle,
For joy his head and heels are idle,
He's idle all for very joy.

And, while the Pony moves his legs,
In Johnny's left hand you may see
The green bough motionless and dead:
The Moon that shines above his head　80
Is not more still and mute than he.

His heart it was so full of glee
That, till full fifty yards were gone,
He quite forgot his holly whip,
And all his skill in horsemanship:
Oh! happy, happy, happy John.

And while the Mother, at the door,
Stands fixed, her face with joy o'erflows,
Proud of herself, and proud of him,
She sees him in his travelling trim,　90
How quietly her Johnny goes.

The silence of her Idiot Boy,
What hopes it sends to Betty's heart!
He's at the guide-post—he turns right;
She watches till he's out of sight,
And Betty will not then depart.

Burr, burr—now Johnny's lips they burr,
As loud as any mill, or near it;
Meek as a lamb the Pony moves,
And Johnny makes the noise he loves,　　100
And Betty listens, glad to hear it.

Away she hies to Susan Gale:
Her Messenger's in merry tune;
The owlets hoot, the owlets curr,
And Johnny's lips they burr, burr, burr,
As on he goes beneath the moon.

His steed and he right well agree;
For of this Pony there's a rumour
That, should he lose his eyes and ears,
And should he live a thousand years,　　110
He never will be out of humour.

But then he is a horse that thinks!
And, when he thinks, his pace is slack;
Now, though he knows poor Johnny well,
Yet, for his life, he cannot tell
What he has got upon his back.

So through the moonlight lanes they go,
And far into the moonlight dale,
And by the church, and o'er the down,
To bring a Doctor from the town,　　120
To comfort poor old Susan Gale.

And Betty, now at Susan's side,
Is in the middle of her story,
What speedy help her Boy will bring,
With many a most diverting thing,
Of Johnny's wit, and Johnny's glory.

And Betty, still at Susan's side,
By this time is not quite so flurried:
Demure with porringer and plate
She sits, as if in Susan's fate　　130
Her life and soul were buried.

But Betty, poor good woman! she,
You plainly in her face may read it,
Could lend out of that moment's store
Five years of happiness or more
To any that might need it.

But yet I guess that now and then
With Betty all was not so well;
And to the road she turns her ears,
And thence full many a sound she hears,　　140
Which she to Susan will not tell.

Poor Susan moans, poor Susan groans;
"As sure as there's a moon in heaven,"
Cries Betty, "he'll be back again;
They'll both be here—'tis almost ten—
Both will be here before eleven."

Poor Susan moans, poor Susan groans;
The clock gives warning for eleven;
'Tis on the stroke—"He must be near,"
Quoth Betty, "and will soon be here,　　150
As sure as there's a moon in heaven."

The clock is on the stroke of twelve,
And Johnny is not yet in sight:
—The Moon's in heaven, as Betty sees,
But Betty is not quite at ease;
And Susan has a dreadful night.

And Betty, half an hour ago,
On Johnny vile reflections cast:
"A little idle sauntering Thing!"
With other names, an endless string;　　160
But now that time is gone and past.

And Betty's drooping at the heart,
That happy time all past and gone,
"How can it be he is so late?
The Doctor, he has made him wait;
Susan! they'll both be here anon."

And Susan's growing worse and worse,
And Betty's in a sad *quandary;*
And then there's nobody to say
If she must go, or she must stay!　　170
—She's in a sad *quandary.*

The clock is on the stroke of one;
But neither Doctor nor his Guide
Appears along the moonlight road;
There's neither horse nor man abroad,
And Betty's still at Susan's side.

And Susan now begins to fear
Of sad mischances not a few,
That Johnny may perhaps be drowned;
Or lost, perhaps, and never found;　　180
Which they must both for ever rue.

She prefaced half a hint of this
With, "God forbid it should be true!"
At the first word that Susan said
Cried Betty, rising from the bed,
"Susan, I'd gladly stay with you.

"I must be gone, I must away:
Consider, Johnny's but half-wise;
Susan, we must take care of him,
If he is hurt in life or limb"—   190
"Oh God forbid!" poor Susan cries.

"What can I do?" says Betty, going,
"What can I do to ease your pain?
Good Susan tell me, and I'll stay;
I fear you're in a deadful way,
But I shall soon be back again."

"Nay, Betty, go! good Betty, go!
There's nothing that can ease my pain."
Then off she hies; but with a prayer,
That God poor Susan's life would spare,   200
Till she comes back again.

So, through the moonlight lane she goes,
And far into the moonlight dale;
And how she ran, and how she walked,
And all that to herself she talked,
Would surely be a tedious tale.

In high and low, above, below,
In great and small, in round and square,
In tree and tower was Johnny seen,
In bush and brake, in black and green;   210
'Twas Johnny, Johnny, everywhere.

And while she crossed the bridge, there came
A thought with which her heart is sore—
Johnny perhaps his horse forsook,
To hunt the moon within the brook,
And never will be heard of more.

Now is she high upon the down,
Alone amid a prospect wide;
There's neither Johnny nor his Horse
Among the fern or in the gorse;   220
There's neither Doctor nor his Guide.

"Oh saints! what is become of him?
Perhaps he's climbed into an oak,
Where he will stay till he is dead;
Or sadly he has been misled,
And joined the wandering gipsy-folk.

"Or him that wicked Pony's carried
To the dark cave, the goblin's hall;
Or in the castle he's pursuing
Among the ghosts his own undoing;   230
Or playing with the waterfall."

At poor old Susan then she railed,
While to the town she posts away;
"If Susan had not been so ill,
Alas! I should have had him still,
My Johnny, till my dying day."

Poor Betty, in this sad distemper,
The Doctor's self could hardly spare:
Unworthy things she talked, and wild;
Even he, of cattle the most mild,   240
The Pony had his share.

But now she's fairly in the town,
And to the Doctor's door she hies;
'Tis silence all on every side;
The town so long, the town so wide,
Is silent as the skies.

And now she's at the Doctor's door,
She lifts the knocker, rap, rap, rap;
The Doctor at the casement shows
His glimmering eyes that peep and doze!   250
And one hand rubs his old night-cap.

"Oh, Doctor! Doctor! where's my Johnny?"
"I'm here, what is't you want with me?"
"Oh Sir! you know I'm Betty Foy,
And I have lost my poor dear Boy,
You know him—him you often see;

"He's not so wise as some folks be:"
"The devil take his wisdom!" said
The Doctor, looking somewhat grim,
"What, Woman! should I know of him?"
And, grumbling, he went back to bed!   261

"O woe is me! O woe is me!
Here will I die; here will I die;
I thought to find my lost one here,
But he is neither far nor near,
Oh! what a wretched Mother I!"

She stops, she stands, she looks about;
Which way to turn she cannot tell.
Poor Betty! it would ease her pain
If she had heart to knock again;   270
—The clock strikes three—a dismal knell!

Then up along the town she hies,
No wonder if her senses fail;
This piteous news so much it shocked her,
She quite forgot to send the Doctor,
To comfort poor old Susan Gale.

And now she's high upon the down,
And she can see a mile of road:
"O cruel! I'm almost threescore;
Such night as this was ne'er before,   280
There's not a single soul abroad."

She listens, but she cannot hear
The foot of horse, the voice of man;
The streams with softest sound are flowing,
The grass you almost hear it growing,
You hear it now, if e'er you can.

The owlets through the long blue night
Are shouting to each other still:
Fond lovers! yet not quite hob nob,
They lengthen out the tremulous sob,   290
That echoes far from hill to hill.

Poor Betty now has lost all hope,
Her thoughts are bent on deadly sin,
A green-grown pond she just has past,
And from the brink she hurries fast,
Lest she should drown herself therein.

And now she sits her down and weeps;
Such tears she never shed before;
"Oh dear, dear Pony! my sweet joy!
Oh carry back my Idiot Boy!   300
And we will ne'er o'erload thee more."

A thought is come into her head:
The Pony he is mild and good,
And we have always used him well;
Perhaps he's gone along the dell,
And carried Johnny to the wood.

Then up she springs as if on wings;
She thinks no more of deadly sin;
If Betty fifty ponds should see,
The last of all her thoughts would be   310
To drown herself therein.

Oh Reader! now that I might tell
What Johnny and his Horse are doing!
What they've been doing all this time,
Oh could I put it into rhyme,
A most delightful tale pursuing!

Perhaps, and no unlikely thought!
He with his Pony now doth roam
The cliffs and peaks so high that are,
To lay his hands upon a star,   320
And in his pocket bring it home.

Perhaps he's turned himself about,
His face unto his horse's tail,
And, still and mute, in wonder lost,
All silent as a horseman-ghost,
He travels slowly down the vale.

And now, perhaps, is hunting sheep,
A fierce and dreadful hunter he;
Yon valley, now so trim and green,
In five months' time, should he be seen,   330
A desert wilderness will be!

Perhaps, with head and heels on fire,
And like the very soul of evil,
He's galloping away, away,
And so will gallop on for aye,
The bane of all that dread the devil!

I to the Muses have been bound
These fourteen years, by strong indentures:
O gentle Muses! let me tell
But half of what to him befell;   340
He surely met with strange adventures.

O gentle Muses! is this kind?
Why will ye thus my suit repel?
Why of your further aid bereave me?
And can ye thus unfriended leave me;
Ye Muses! whom I love so well?

Who's yon, that, near the waterfall,
Which thunders down with headlong force,
Beneath the moon, yet shining fair,
As careless as if nothing were,   350
Sits upright on a feeding horse?

Unto his horse—there feeding free,
He seems, I think, the rein to give;
Of moon or stars he takes no heed;
Of such we in romances read:
—'Tis Johnny! Johnny! as I live.

And that's the very Pony, too!
Where is she, where is Betty Foy?
She hardly can sustain her fears;
The roaring waterfall she hears,   360
And cannot find her Idiot Boy.

Your Pony's worth his weight in gold:
Then calm your terrors, Betty Foy!
She's coming from among the trees,
And now all full in view she sees
Him whom she loves, her Idiot Boy.

And Betty sees the Pony too:
Why stand you thus, good Betty Foy?
It is no goblin, 'tis no ghost,
'Tis he whom you so long have lost,   370
He whom you love, your Idiot Boy.

She looks again—her arms are up—
She screams—she cannot move for joy;
She darts, as with a torrent's force,
She almost has o'erturned the Horse,
And fast she holds her Idiot Boy.

And Johnny burrs, and laughs aloud;
Whether in cunning or in joy
I cannot tell; but, while he laughs,
Betty a drunken pleasure quaffs   380
To hear again her Idiot Boy.

And now she's at the Pony's tail,
And now is at the Pony's head,—
On that side now, and now on this;
And, almost stifled with her bliss,
A few sad tears does Betty shed.

She kisses o'er and o'er again
Him whom she loves, her Idiot Boy;
She's happy here, is happy there,
She is uneasy everywhere;   390
Her limbs are all alive with joy.

She pats the Pony, where or when
She knows not, happy Betty Foy!
The little Pony glad may be,
But he is milder far than she,
You hardly can perceive his joy.

"Oh! Johnny, never mind the Doctor;
You've done your best, and that is all:"
She took the reins, when this was said,
And gently turned the Pony's head   400
From the loud waterfall.

By this the stars were almost gone,
The moon was setting on the hill,
So pale you scarcely looked at her:
The little birds began to stir,
Though yet their tongues were still.

The Pony, Betty, and her Boy,
Wind slowly through the woody dale;
And who is she, betimes abroad,
That hobbles up the steep rough road?   410
Who is it, but old Susan Gale?

Long time lay Susan lost in thought;
And many dreadful fears beset her,
Both for her Messenger and Nurse;
And, as her mind grew worse and worse,
Her body—it grew better.

She turned, she tossed herself in bed,
On all sides doubts and terrors met her;
Point after point did she discuss;
And, while her mind was fighting thus,   420
Her body still grew better.

"Alas! what is become of them?
These fears can never be endured;
I'll to the wood."—The word scarce said,
Did Susan rise up from her bed,
As if by magic cured.

Away she goes up hill and down,
And to the wood at length is come;
She spies her Friends, she shouts a greeting;
Oh me! it is a merry meeting   430
As ever was in Christendom.

The owls have hardly sung their last,
While our four travellers homeward wend;
The owls have hooted all night long,
And with the owls began my song,
And with the owls must end.

For, while they all were travelling home,
Cried Betty, "Tell us, Johnny, do,
Where all this long night you have been,
What you have heard, what you have seen:
And, Johnny, mind you tell us true."   441

Now Johnny all night long had heard
The owls in tuneful concert strive;
No doubt too he the moon had seen;
For in the moonlight he had been
From eight o'clock till five.

And thus, to Betty's question, he
Made answer, like a traveller bold,
(His very words I give to you,)
"The cocks did crow to-whoo, to-whoo,   450
And the sun did shine so cold!"

—Thus answered Johnny in his glory,
And that was all his travel's story.

1798

LINES

COMPOSED A FEW MILES ABOVE TINTERN ABBEY,
ON REVISITING THE BANKS OF THE WYE
DURING A TOUR. JULY 13, 1798.

FIVE years have past; five summers, with the
    length
Of five long winters! and again I hear
These waters, rolling from their mountain-
    springs
With a soft inland murmur.—Once again
Do I behold these steep and lofty cliffs,
That on a wild secluded scene impress
Thoughts of more deep seclusion; and connect
The landscape with the quiet of the sky.
The day is come when I again repose
Here, under this dark sycamore, and view 10
These plots of cottage-ground, these orchard-
    tufts,
Which at this season, with their unripe fruits,
Are clad in one green hue, and lose themselves
'Mid groves and copses. Once again I see
These hedge-rows, hardly hedge-rows, little
    lines
Of sportive wood run wild: these pastoral
    farms,
Green to the very door; and wreaths of smoke
Sent up, in silence, from among the trees!
With some uncertain notice, as might seem
Of vagrant dwellers in the houseless woods,
Or of some Hermit's cave, where by his fire 21
The Hermit sits alone.

                    These beauteous forms,
Through a long absence, have not been to me
As is a landscape to a blind man's eye:
But oft, in lonely rooms, and 'mid the din
Of towns and cities, I have owed to them,
In hours of weariness, sensations sweet,
Felt in the blood, and felt along the heart;
And passing even into my purer mind,
With tranquil restoration:—feelings too 30
Of unremembered pleasure: such, perhaps,
As have no slight or trivial influence
On that best portion of a good man's life,
His little, nameless, unremembered, acts
Of kindness and of love. Nor less, I trust,
To them I may have owed another gift,

Of aspect more sublime; that blessed mood,
In which the burthen of the mystery,
In which the heavy and the weary weight
Of all this unintelligible world,   40
Is lightened:—that serene and blessed mood,
In which the affections gently lead us on,—
Until, the breath of this corporeal frame
And even the motion of our human blood
Almost suspended, we are laid asleep
In body, and become a living soul:
While with an eye made quiet by the power
Of harmony, and the deep power of joy,
We see into the life of things.

                          If this
Be but a vain belief, yet, oh! how oft—   50
In darkness and amid the many shapes
Of joyless daylight; when the fretful stir
Unprofitable, and the fever of the world,
Have hung upon the beatings of my heart—
How oft, in spirit, have I turned to thee,
O sylvan Wye! thou wanderer thro' the woods,
How often has my spirit turned to thee!

    And now, with gleams of half-extinguished
        thought,
With many recognitions dim and faint,
And somewhat of a sad perplexity,   60
The picture of the mind revives again:
While here I stand, not only with the sense
Of present pleasure, but with pleasing thoughts
That in this moment there is life and food
For future years. And so I dare to hope,
Though changed, no doubt, from what I was
        when first
I came among these hills; when like a roe
I bounded o'er the mountains, by the sides
Of the deep rivers, and the lonely streams,
Wherever nature led: more like a man   70
Flying from something that he dreads than
    one
Who sought the thing he loved. For nature
    then
(The coarser pleasures of my boyish days,
And their glad animal movements all gone by)
To me was all in all.—I cannot paint
What then I was. The sounding cataract
Haunted me like a passion: the tall rock,
The mountain, and the deep and gloomy
    wood,
Their colours and their forms, were then to me
An appetite; a feeling and a love,   80

That had no need of a remoter charm,
By thought supplied, nor any interest
Unborrowed from the eye.—That time is past,
And all its aching joys are now no more,
And all its dizzy raptures. Not for this
Faint I, nor mourn nor murmur; other gifts
Have followed; for such loss, I would believe,
Abundant recompense. For I have learned
To look on nature, not as in the hour
Of thoughtless youth; but hearing often-
    times   90
The still, sad music of humanity,
Nor harsh nor grating, though of ample power
To chasten and subdue. And I have felt
A presence that disturbs me with the joy
Of elevated thoughts; a sense sublime
Of something far more deeply interfused,
Whose dwelling is the light of setting suns,
And the round ocean and the living air,
And the blue sky, and in the mind of man:
A motion and a spirit, that impels   100
All thinking things, all objects of all thought,
And rolls through all things. Therefore am I
    still
A lover of the meadows and the woods,
And mountains; and of all that we behold
From this green earth; of all the mighty world
Of eye, and ear,—both what they half create,
And what perceive; well pleased to recognise
In nature and the language of the sense
The anchor of my purest thoughts, the nurse,
The guide, the guardian of my heart, and
    soul   110
Of all my moral being.
                Nor perchance,
If I were not thus taught, should I the more
Suffer my genial spirits to decay:
For thou art with me here upon the banks
Of this fair river; thou my dearest Friend,
My dear, dear Friend; and in thy voice I catch
The language of my former heart, and read
My former pleasures in the shooting lights
Of thy wild eyes. Oh! yet a little while
May I behold in thee what I was once,   120
My dear, dear Sister! and this prayer I make,
Knowing that Nature never did betray
The heart that loved her; 'tis her privilege,
Through all the years of this our life, to lead
From joy to joy: for she can so inform
The mind that is within us, so impress
With quietness and beauty, and so feed

With lofty thoughts, that neither evil tongues,
Rash judgments, nor the sneers of selfish men,
Nor greetings where no kindness is, nor all
The dreary intercourse of daily life,   131
Shall e'er prevail against us, or disturb
Our cheerful faith, that all which we behold
Is full of blessings. Therefore let the moon
Shine on thee in thy solitary walk;
And let the misty mountain-winds be free
To blow against thee: and, in after years,
When these wild ecstasies shall be matured
Into a sober pleasure; when thy mind
Shall be a mansion for all lovely forms,   140
Thy memory be as a dwelling-place
For all sweet sounds and harmonies; oh! then,
If solitude, or fear, or pain, or grief,
Should be thy portion, with what healing
    thoughts
Of tender joy wilt thou remember me,
And these my exhortations! Nor, perchance—
If I should be where I no more can hear
Thy voice, nor catch from thy wild eyes these
    gleams
Of past existence—wilt thou then forget
That on the banks of this delightful stream
We stood together; and that I, so long   151
A worshipper of Nature, hither came
Unwearied in that service: rather say
With warmer love—oh! with far deeper zeal
Of holier love. Nor wilt thou then forget
That after many wanderings, many years
Of absence, these steep woods and lofty cliffs,
And this green pastoral landscape, were to me
More dear, both for themselves and for thy
    sake!

1798

THE OLD CUMBERLAND BEGGAR

I saw an aged Beggar in my walk;
And he was seated, by the highway side,
On a low structure of rude masonry
Built at the foot of a huge hill, that they
Who lead their horses down the steep rough
    road
May thence remount at ease. The aged Man
Had placed his staff across the broad smooth
    stone
That overlays the pile; and, from a bag
All white with flour, the dole of village dames,
He drew his scraps and fragments, one by
    one;   10

And scanned them with a fixed and serious
   look
Of idle computation. In the sun,
Upon the second step of that small pile,
Surrounded by those wild unpeopled hills,
He sat, and ate his food in solitude:
And ever, scattered from his palsied hand,
That, still attempting to prevent the waste,
Was baffled still, the crumbs in little showers
Fell on the ground; and the small mountain
   birds,
Not venturing yet to peck their destined
   meal,   20
Approached within the length of half his staff.

   Him from my childhood have I known;
   and then
He was so old, he seems not older now;
He travels on, a solitary Man,
So helpless in appearance, that for him
The sauntering Horseman throws not with a
   slack
And careless hand his alms upon the ground,
But stops,—that he may safely lodge the coin
Within the old Man's hat; nor quits him so,
But still, when he has given his horse the
   rein,   30
Watches the aged Beggar with a look
Sidelong, and half-reverted. She who tends
The toll-gate, when in summer at her door
She turns her wheel, if on the road she sees
The aged Beggar coming, quits her work,
And lifts the latch for him that he may pass.
The post-boy, when his rattling wheels o'er-
   take
The aged Beggar in the woody lane,
Shouts to him from behind; and, if thus warned
The old man does not change his course, the
   boy   40
Turns with less noisy wheels to the roadside,
And passes gently by, without a curse
Upon his lips or anger at his heart.

   He travels on, a solitary Man;
His age has no companion. On the ground
His eyes are turned, and, as he moves along,
They move along the ground; and, evermore,
Instead of common and habitual sight
Of fields with rural works, of hill and dale,
And the blue sky, one little span of earth   50
Is all his prospect. Thus, from day to day,

Bow-bent, his eyes for ever on the ground,
He plies his weary journey; seeing still,
And seldom knowing that he sees, some straw,
Some scattered leaf, or marks which, in one
   track,
The nails of cart or chariot-wheel have left
Impressed on the white road,—in the same line,
At distance still the same. Poor Traveler!
His staff trails with him; scarcely do his feet
Disturb the summer dust; he is so still   60
In look and motion, that the cottage curs,
Ere he has passed the door, will turn away,
Weary of barking at him. Boys and girls,
The vacant and the busy, maids and youths,
And urchins newly breeched—all pass him by:
Him even the slow-paced waggon leaves be-
   hind.

   But deem not this Man useless.—Statesmen!
   ye
Who are so restless in your wisdom, ye
Who have a broom still ready in your hands
To rid the world of nuisances; ye proud,   70
Heart-swoln, while in your pride ye contem-
   plate
Your talents, power, or wisdom, deem him
   not
A burthen of the earth! 'Tis Nature's law
That none, the meanest of created things,
Of forms created the most vile and brute,
The dullest or most noxious, should exist
Divorced from good—a spirit and pulse of
   good,
A life and soul, to every mode of being
Inseparably linked. Then be assured   79
That least of all can aught—that ever owned
The heaven-regarding eye and front sublime
Which man is born to—sink, howe'er de-
   pressed,
So low as to be scorned without a sin;
Without offence to God cast out of view;
Like the dry remnant of a garden-flower
Whose seeds are shed, or as an implement
Worn out and worthless. While from door to
   door,
This old Man creeps, the villagers in him
Behold a record which together binds
Past deeds and offices of charity,   90
Else unremembered, and so keeps alive
The kindly mood in hearts which lapse of
   years,

And that half-wisdom half-experience gives,
Make slow to feel, and by sure steps resign
To selfishness and cold oblivious cares.
Among the farms and solitary huts,
Hamlets and thinly-scattered villages,
Where'er the aged Beggar takes his rounds,
The mild necessity of use compels
To acts of love; and habit does the work 100
Of reason; yet prepares that after-joy
Which reason cherishes. And thus the soul,
By that sweet taste of pleasure unpursued,
Doth find herself insensibly disposed
To virtue and true goodness.
                                        Some there are,
By their good works exalted, lofty minds,
And meditative, authors of delight
And happiness, which to the end of time
Will live, and spread, and kindle: even such
    minds
In childhood, from this solitary Being,   110
Or from like wanderer, haply have received
(A thing more precious far than all that books
Or the solicitudes of love can do!)
That first mild touch of sympathy and thought,
In which they found their kindred with a
    world
Where want and sorrow were. The easy man
Who sits at his own door,—and, like the pear
That overhangs his head from the green wall,
Feeds in the sunshine; the robust and young,
The prosperous and unthinking, they who
    live   120
Sheltered, and flourish in a little grove
Of their own kindred;—all behold in him
A silent monitor, which on their minds
Must needs impress a transitory thought
Of self-congratulation, to the heart
Of each recalling his peculiar boons,
His charters and exemptions; and, perchance,
Though he to no one give the fortitude
And circumspection needful to preserve
His present blessings, and to husband up 130
The respite of the season, he, at least,
And 'tis no vulgar service, makes them felt.

    Yet further.———Many, I believe, there
        are
Who live a life of virtuous decency,
Men who can hear the Decalogue and feel
No self-reproach; who of the moral law
Established in the land where they abide

Are strict observers; and not negligent
In acts of love to those with whom they dwell,
Their kindred, and the children of their
    blood.   140
Praise be to such, and to their slumbers peace!
—But of the poor man ask, the abject poor;
Go, and demand of him, if there be here
In this cold abstinence from evil deeds,
And these inevitable charities,
Wherewith to satisfy the human soul?
No—man is dear to man; the poorest poor
Long for some moments in a weary life
When they can know and feel that they have
    been,
Themselves, the fathers and the dealers-out 150
Of some small blessings; have been kind to
    such
As needed kindness, for this single cause,
That we have all of us one human heart.
—Such pleasure is to one kind Being known,
My neighbour, when with punctual care, each
    week,
Duly as Friday comes, though pressed herself
By her own wants, she from her store of meal
Takes one unsparing handful for the scrip
Of this old Mendicant, and, from her door
Returning with exhilarated heart,   160
Sits by her fire, and builds her hope in heaven.

    Then let him pass, a blessing on his head!
And while in that vast solitude to which
The tide of things has borne him, he appears
To breathe and live but for himself alone,
Unblamed, uninjured, let him bear about
The good which the benignant law of Heaven
Has hung around him: and, while life is his,
Still let him prompt the unlettered villagers
To tender offices and pensive thoughts.   170
—Then let him pass, a blessing on his head!
And, long as he can wander, let him breathe
The freshness of the valleys; let his blood
Struggle with frosty air and winter snows;
And let the chartered wind that sweeps the
    heath
Beat his grey locks against his withered face.
Reverence the hope whose vital anxiousness
Gives the last human interest to his heart.
May never HOUSE, misnamed of INDUSTRY,
Make him a captive!—for that pent-up din,
Those life-consuming sounds that clog the
    air,   181

Be his the natural silence of old age!
Let him be free of mountain solitudes;
And have around him, whether heard or
    not,
The pleasant melody of woodland birds.
Few are his pleasures: if his eyes have now
Been doomed so long to settle upon earth
That not without some effort they behold
The countenance of the horizontal sun,
Rising or setting, let the light at least   190
Find a free entrance to their languid orbs,
And let him, *where* and *when* he will, sit down
Beneath the trees, or on a grassy bank
Of highway side, and with the little birds
Share his chance-gathered meal; and, finally,
As in the eye of Nature he has lived,
So in the eye of Nature let him die!

1797

STRANGE FITS OF PASSION
HAVE I KNOWN

STRANGE fits of passion have I known:
And I will dare to tell,
But in the Lover's ear alone,
What once to me befell.

When she I loved looked every day
Fresh as a rose in June,
I to her cottage bent my way,
Beneath an evening-moon.

Upon the moon I fixed my eye,
All over the wide lea;   10
With quickening pace my horse drew nigh
Those paths so dear to me.

And now we reached the orchard-plot;
And, as we climbed the hill,
The sinking moon to Lucy's cot
Came near, and nearer still.

In one of those sweet dreams I slept,
Kind Nature's gentlest boon!
And all the while my eyes I kept
On the descending moon.   20

My horse moved on; hoof after hoof
He raised, and never stopped:
When down behind the cottage roof,
At once, the bright moon dropped.

What fond and wayward thoughts will slide
Into a Lover's head!

"O mercy!" to myself I cried,
"If Lucy should be dead!"

1799

SHE DWELT AMONG THE
UNTRODDEN WAYS

SHE dwelt among the untrodden ways
    Beside the springs of Dove,
A Maid whom there were none to praise
    And very few to love:

A violet by a mossy stone
    Half hidden from the eye!
—Fair as a star, when only one
    Is shining in the sky.

She lived unknown, and few could know
    When Lucy ceased to be;   10
But she is in her grave, and, oh,
    The difference to me!

1799

I TRAVELLED AMONG UNKNOWN
MEN

I TRAVELLED among unknown men,
    In lands beyond the sea;
Nor, England! did I know till then
    What love I bore to thee.

'Tis past, that melancholy dream!
    Nor will I quit thy shore
A second time; for still I seem
    To love thee more and more.

Among thy mountains did I feel
    The joy of my desire;   10
And she I cherished turned her wheel
    Beside an English fire.

Thy mornings showed, thy nights concealed,
    The bowers where Lucy played;
And thine too is the last green field
    That Lucy's eyes surveyed.

1799

THREE YEARS SHE GREW IN
SUN AND SHOWER

THREE years she grew in sun and shower,
Then Nature said, "A lovelier flower
    On earth was never sown;

This Child I to myself will take;
She shall be mine, and I will make
A Lady of my own.

"Myself will to my darling be
Both law and impulse: and with me
The Girl, in rock and plain,
In earth and heaven, in glade and bower,   10
Shall feel an overseeing power
To kindle or restrain.

"She shall be sportive as the fawn
That wild with glee across the lawn
Or up the mountain springs;
And hers shall be the breathing balm,
And hers the silence and the calm
Of mute insensate things.

"The floating clouds their state shall lend
To her; for her the willow bend;   20
Nor shall she fail to see
Even in the motions of the Storm
Grace that shall mould the Maiden's form
By silent sympathy.

"The stars of midnight shall be dear *clear expression*
To her; and she shall lean her ear
In many a secret place
Where rivulets dance their wayward round,
And beauty born of murmuring sound
Shall pass into her face.   30

"And vital feelings of delight
Shall rear her form to stately height, *Shelley used this*
Her virgin bosom swell;
Such thoughts to Lucy I will give
While she and I together live
Here in this happy dell."

Thus Nature spake—The work was done—
How soon my Lucy's race was run!
She died, and left to me
This heath, this calm, and quiet scene;   40
The memory of what has been,
And never more will be.

1799

A SLUMBER DID MY SPIRIT SEAL

A SLUMBER did my spirit seal;
    I had no human fears:
She seemed a thing that could not feel
    The touch of earthly years.

only one that doesn't mention Lucy's name

No motion has she now, no force;
    She neither hears nor sees;
Rolled round in earth's diurnal course,
    With rocks, and stones, and trees.

1799

NUTTING

——————————It seems a day
(I speak of one from many singled out),
One of those heavenly days that cannot die;
When, in the eagerness of boyish hope,
I left our cottage-threshold, sallying forth
With a huge wallet o'er my shoulders slung,
A nutting-crook in hand; and turned my steps
Tow'rd some far-distant wood, a Figure *clothes*
    quaint,
Tricked out in proud disguise of cast-off weeds
Which for that service had been husbanded,
By exhortation of my frugal Dame—   11
Motley accoutrement, of power to smile
At thorns, and brakes, and brambles,—and in
    truth
More ragged than need was! O'er pathless
    rocks,
Through beds of matted fern, and tangled
    thickets,
Forcing my way, I came to one dear nook
Unvisited, where not a broken bough
Drooped with its withered leaves, ungracious
    sign
Of devastation; but the hazels rose
Tall and erect, with tempting clusters hung,
A virgin scene!—A little while I stood,   21
Breathing with such suppression of the heart
As joy delights in; and with wise restraint
Voluptuous, fearless of a rival, eyed
The banquet;—or beneath the trees I sate
Among the flowers, and with the flowers I
    played;
A temper known to those who, after long
And weary expectation, have been blest
With sudden happiness beyond all hope.
Perhaps it was a bower beneath whose leaves
The violets of five seasons re-appear   31
And fade, unseen by any human eye;
Where fairy water-breaks do murmur on
For ever; and I saw the sparkling foam,
And—with my cheek on one of those green
    stones
That, fleeced with moss, under the shady trees,

Lay round me, scattered like a flock of sheep—
I heard the murmur and the murmuring sound,
In that sweet mood when pleasure loves to
    pay
Tribute to ease; and, of its joy secure,   40
The heart luxuriates with indifferent things,
Wasting its kindliness on stocks and stones,
And on the vacant air. Then up I rose,
And dragged to earth both branch and bough,
    with crash
And merciless ravage: and the shady nook
Of hazels, and the green and mossy bower,
Deformed and sullied, patiently gave up
Their quiet being: and unless I now
Confound my present feelings with the past,
Ere from the mutilated bower I turned   50
Exulting, rich beyond the wealth of kings,
I felt a sense of pain when I beheld
The silent trees, and saw the intruding sky.—
Then, dearest Maiden, move along these
    shades
In gentleness of heart; with gentle hand
Touch—for there is a spirit in the woods.
1799

MATTHEW

If Nature, for a favourite child,
In thee hath tempered so her clay,
That every hour thy heart runs wild,
Yet never once doth go astray,

Read o'er these lines; and then review
This tablet, that thus humbly rears
In such diversity of hue
Its history of two hundred years.

—When through this little wreck of fame,
Cipher and syllable! thine eye   10
Has travelled down to Matthew's name,
Pause with no common sympathy.

And if a sleeping tear should wake,
Then be it neither checked nor stayed:
For Matthew a request I make
Which for himself he had not made.

Poor Matthew, all his frolics o'er,
Is silent as a standing pool;
Far from the chimney's merry roar,
And murmur of the village school.   20

The sighs which Matthew heaved were sighs
Of one tired out with fun and madness;
The tears which came to Matthew's eyes
Were tears of light, the dew of gladness.

Yet sometimes, when the secret cup
Of still and serious thought went round,
It seemed as if he drank it up—
He felt with spirit so profound.

—Thou soul of God's best earthly mould!
Thou happy Soul! and can it be   30
That these two words of glittering gold
Are all that must remain of thee?
1799

THE TWO APRIL MORNINGS

We walked along, while bright and red
Uprose the morning sun;
And Matthew stopped, he looked, and said,
"The will of God be done!"

A village schoolmaster was he,
With hair of glittering grey;
As blithe a man as you could see
On a spring holiday.

And on that morning, through the grass,
And by the steaming rills,   10
We travelled merrily, to pass
A day among the hills.

"Our work," said I, "was well begun,
Then from thy breast what thought,
Beneath so beautiful a sun,
So sad a sigh has brought?"

A second time did Matthew stop;
And fixing still his eye
Upon the eastern mountain-top,
To me he made reply: 20

"Yon cloud with that long purple cleft
Brings fresh into my mind
A day like this which I have left
Full thirty years behind.

"And just above yon slope of corn
Such colours, and no other,
Were in the sky, that April morn,
Of this the very brother.

"With rod and line I sued the sport
Which that sweet season gave, 30
And, to the churchyard come, stopped short
Beside my daughter's grave.

"Nine summers had she scarcely seen,
The pride of all the vale;
And then she sang;—she would have been
A very nightingale.

"Six feet in earth my Emma lay;
And yet I loved her more,
For so it seemed, than till that day
I e'er had loved before. 40

"And, turning from her grave, I met,
Beside the churchyard yew,
A blooming Girl, whose hair was wet
With points of morning dew.

"A basket on her head she bare;
Her brow was smooth and white:
To see a child so very fair,
It was a pure delight!

"No fountain from its rocky cave
E'er tripped with foot so free; 50
She seemed as happy as a wave
That dances on the sea.

"There came from me a sigh of pain
Which I could ill confine;
I looked at her, and looked again:
And did not wish her mine!"

Matthew is in his grave, yet now,
Methinks, I see him stand,
As at that moment, with a bough
Of wilding in his hand. 60

1799

THE FOUNTAIN

A CONVERSATION

WE talked with open heart, and tongue
Affectionate and true,
A pair of friends, though I was young,
And Matthew seventy-two.

We lay beneath a spreading oak,
Beside a mossy seat;
And from the turf a fountain broke,
And gurgled at our feet.

"Now, Matthew!" said I, "let us match
This water's pleasant tune 10
With some old border-song, or catch
That suits a summer's noon;

"Or of the church-clock and the chimes
Sing here beneath the shade,
That half-mad thing of witty rhymes
Which you last April made!"

In silence Matthew lay, and eyed
The spring beneath the tree;
And thus the dear old Man replied,
The grey-haired man of glee: 20

"No check, no stay, this Streamlet fears;
How merrily it goes!
'Twill murmur on a thousand years,
And flow as now it flows.

"And here, on this delightful day,
I cannot choose but think
How oft, a vigorous man, I lay
Beside this fountain's brink.

"My eyes are dim with childish tears,
My heart is idly stirred, 30
For the same sound is in my ears
Which in those days I heard.

"Thus fares it still in our decay:
And yet the wiser mind
Mourns less for what age takes away
Than what it leaves behind.

"The blackbird amid leafy trees,
The lark above the hill,
Let loose their carols when they please,
Are quiet when they will. 40

"With Nature never do they wage
A foolish strife; they see
A happy youth, and their old age
Is beautiful and free:

"But we are pressed by heavy laws;
And often, glad no more,
We wear a face of joy, because
We have been glad of yore.

"If there be one who need bemoan
His kindred laid in earth, 50
The household hearts that were his own;
It is the man of mirth.

"My days, my Friend, are almost gone,
My life has been approved,
And many love me! but by none
Am I enough beloved."

"Now both himself and me he wrongs,
The man who thus complains!
I live and sing my idle songs
Upon these happy plains;   60

"And, Matthew, for thy children dead
I'll be a son to thee!"
At this he grasped my hand, and said,
"Alas! that cannot be."

We rose up from the fountain-side;
And down the smooth descent
Of the green sheep-track did we glide;
And through the wood we went;

And, ere we came to Leonard's rock,
He sang those witty rhymes   70
About the crazy old church-clock,
And the bewildered chimes.

1799

RUTH

When Ruth was left half desolate,
Her Father took another Mate;
And Ruth, not seven years old,
A slighted child, at her own will
Went wandering over dale and hill,
In thoughtless freedom, bold.

And she had made a pipe of straw,
And music from that pipe could draw
Like sounds of winds and floods;
Had built a bower upon the green,   10
As if she from her birth had been
An infant of the woods.

Beneath her father's roof, alone
She seemed to live; her thoughts her own;
Herself her own delight;
Pleased with herself, nor sad, nor gay;
And, passing thus the live-long day,
She grew to woman's height.

There came a Youth from Georgia's shore—
A military casque he wore,   20
With splendid feathers drest;

He brought them from the Cherokees;
The feathers nodded in the breeze,
And made a gallant crest.

From Indian blood you deem him sprung:
But no! he spake the English tongue,
And bore a soldier's name;
And, when America was free
From battle and from jeopardy,
He 'cross the ocean came.   30

With hues of genius on his cheek
In finest tones the Youth could speak:
—While he was yet a boy,
The moon, the glory of the sun,
And streams that murmur as they run,
Had been his dearest joy.

He was a lovely Youth! I guess
The panther in the wilderness
Was not so fair as he;
And, when he chose to sport and play,   40
No dolphin ever was so gay
Upon the tropic sea.

Among the Indians he had fought,
And with him many tales he brought
Of pleasure and of fear;
Such tales as told to any maid
By such a Youth, in the green shade,
Were perilous to hear.

He told of girls—a happy rout!
Who quit their fold with dance and shout,
Their pleasant Indian town,   51
To gather strawberries all day long;
Returning with a choral song
When daylight is gone down.

He spake of plants that hourly change
Their blossoms, through a boundless range
Of intermingling hues;
With budding, fading, faded flowers
They stand the wonder of the bowers
From morn to evening dews.   60

He told of the magnolia, spread
High as a cloud, high over head!
The cypress and her spire;
—Of flowers that with one scarlet gleam
Cover a hundred leagues, and seem
To set the hills on fire.

The Youth of green savannahs spake,
And many an endless, endless lake,
With all its fairy crowds
Of islands, that together lie   70
As quietly as spots of sky
Among the evening clouds.

"How pleasant," then he said, "it were
A fisher or a hunter there,
In sunshine or in shade
To wander with an easy mind;
And build a household fire, and find
A home in every glade!

"What days and what bright years! Ah me!
Our life were life indeed, with thee   80
So passed in quiet bliss,
And all the while," said he, "to know
That we were in a world of woe,
On such an earth as this!"

And then he sometimes interwove
Fond thoughts about a father's love:
"For there," said he, "are spun
Around the heart such tender ties,
That our own children to our eyes
Are dearer than the sun.   90

"Sweet Ruth! and could you go with me
My helpmate in the woods to be,
Our shed at night to rear;
Or run, my own adopted bride,
A sylvan huntress at my side,
And drive the flying deer!

"Beloved Ruth!"—No more he said.
The wakeful Ruth at midnight shed
A solitary tear:
She thought again—and did agree   100
With him to sail across the sea,
And drive the flying deer.

"And now, as fitting is and right,
We in the church our faith will plight,
A husband and a wife."
Even so they did; and I may say
That to sweet Ruth that happy day
Was more than human life.

Through dream and vision did she sink,
Delighted all the while to think   110
That on those lonesome floods,

And green savannahs, she should share
His board with lawful joy, and bear
His name in the wild woods.

But, as you have before been told,
This Stripling, sportive, gay, and bold,
And, with his dancing crest,
So beautiful, through savage lands
Had roamed about, with vagrant bands
Of Indians in the West.   120

The wind, the tempest roaring high,
The tumult of a tropic sky,
Might well be dangerous food
For him, a Youth to whom was given
So much of earth—so much of heaven,
And such impetuous blood.

Whatever in those climes he found
Irregular in sight or sound
Did to his mind impart
A kindred impulse, seemed allied   130
To his own powers, and justified
The workings of his heart.

Nor less, to feed voluptuous thought,
The beauteous forms of nature wrought,
Fair trees and gorgeous flowers;
The breezes their own languor lent;
The stars had feelings, which they sent
Into those favoured bowers.

Yet, in his worst pursuits I ween
That sometimes there did intervene   140
Pure hopes of high intent:
For passions linked to forms so fair
And stately needs must have their share
Of noble sentiment.

But ill he lived, much evil saw,
With men to whom no better law
Nor better life was known;
Deliberately, and undeceived,
Those wild men's vices he received,
And gave them back his own.   150

His genius and his moral frame
Were thus impaired, and he became
The slave of low desires:
A Man who without self-control
Would seek what the degraded soul
Unworthily admires.

And yet he with no feigned delight
Had wooed the Maiden, day and night
Had loved her, night and morn:
What could he less than love a Maid   160
Whose heart with so much nature played?
So kind and so forlorn!

Sometimes, most earnestly, he said,
"O Ruth! I have been worse than dead;
False thoughts, thoughts bold and vain,
Encompassed me on every side
When I, in confidence and pride,
Had crossed the Atlantic main.

"Before me shone a glorious world—
Fresh as a banner bright, unfurled   170
To music suddenly:
I looked upon those hills and plains,
And seemed as if let loose from chains,
To live at liberty.

"No more of this; for now, by thee
Dear Ruth! more happily set free
With nobler zeal I burn;
My soul from darkness is released,
Like the whole sky when to the east
The morning doth return."   180

Full soon that better mind was gone:
No hope, no wish remained, not one,—
They stirred him now no more;
New objects did new pleasure give,
And once again he wished to live
As lawless as before.

Meanwhile, as thus with him it fared,
They for the voyage were prepared,
And went to the sea-shore,
But, when they thither came, the Youth   190
Deserted his poor Bride, and Ruth
Could never find him more.

God help thee, Ruth!—Such pains she had,
That she in half a year was mad,
And in a prison housed;
And there, with many a doleful song
Made of wild words, her cup of wrong
She fearfully caroused.

Yet sometimes milder hours she knew,
Nor wanted sun, nor rain, nor dew,   200
Nor pastimes of the May;

—They all were with her in her cell;
And a clear brook with cheerful knell
Did o'er the pebbles play.

When Ruth three seasons thus had lain,
There came a respite to her pain;
She from her prison fled;
But of the Vagrant none took thought;
And where it liked her best she sought
Her shelter and her bread.   210

Among the fields she breathed again:
The master-current of her brain
Ran permanent and free;
And, coming to the Banks of Tone,
There did she rest; and dwell alone
Under the greenwood tree.

The engines of her pain, the tools
That shaped her sorrow, rocks and pools,
And airs that gently stir
The vernal leaves—she loved them still;   220
Nor ever taxed them with the ill
Which had been done to her.

A Barn her *winter* bed supplies;
But, till the warmth of summer skies
And summer days is gone,
(And all do in this tale agree)
She sleeps beneath the greenwood tree,
And other home hath none.

An innocent life, yet far astray!
And Ruth will, long before her day,   230
Be broken down and old:
Sore aches she needs must have! but less
Of mind than body's wretchedness,
From damp, and rain, and cold.

If she is prest by want of food,
She from her dwelling in the wood
Repairs to a road-side;
And there she begs at one steep place
Where up and down with easy pace
The horsemen-travellers ride.   240

That oaten pipe of hers is mute,
Or thrown away; but with a flute
Her loneliness she cheers:
This flute, made of a hemlock stalk,
At evening in his homeward walk
The Quantock woodman hears.

I, too, have passed her on the hills
Setting her little water-mills
By spouts and fountains wild—
Such small machinery as she turned   250
Ere she had wept, ere she had mourned,
A young and happy Child!

Farewell! and when thy days are told,
Ill-fated Ruth, in hallowed mould
Thy corpse shall buried be,
For thee a funeral bell shall ring,
And all the congregation sing
A Christian psalm for thee.

1799

common measure

LUCY GRAY

OR, SOLITUDE

does not belong to Lucy poem

OFT I had heard of Lucy Gray:
And, when I crossed the wild,
I chanced to see at break of day
The solitary child.

No mate, no comrade Lucy knew;
She dwelt on a wide moor,
—The sweetest thing that ever grew
Beside a human door!

ostent-ment anim

You yet may spy the fawn at play,
The hare upon the green;   10
But the sweet face of Lucy Gray
Will never more be seen.

"To-night will be a stormy night—
You to the town must go;
And take a lantern, Child, to light
Your mother through the snow."

"That, Father! will I gladly do:
'Tis scarcely afternoon—
The minster-clock has just struck two,
And yonder is the moon!"   20

At this the Father raised his hook,
And snapped a faggot-band;
He plied his work;—and Lucy took
The lantern in her hand.

Not blither is the mountain roe:
With many a wanton stroke
Her feet disperse the powdery snow,
That rises up like smoke.

The storm came on before its time:
She wandered up and down;   30
And many a hill did Lucy climb:
But never reached the town.

The wretched parents all that night
Went shouting far and wide;
But there was neither sound nor sight
To serve them for a guide.

At day-break on a hill they stood
That overlooked the moor;
And thence they saw the bridge of wood,
A furlong from their door.   40

They wept—and, turning homeward, cried,
"In heaven we all shall meet;"
—When in the snow the mother spied
The print of Lucy's feet.

Then downwards from the steep hill's edge
They tracked the footmarks small;
And through the broken hawthorn hedge,
And by the long stone-wall;

And then an open field they crossed:
The marks were still the same;   50
They tracked them on, nor ever lost;
And to the bridge they came.

They followed from the snowy bank
Those footmarks, one by one,
Into the middle of the plank;
And further there were none!

—Yet some maintain that to this day
She is a living child;
That you may see sweet Lucy Gray
Upon the lonesome wild.   60

O'er rough and smooth she trips along,
And never looks behind;
And sings a solitary song
That whistles in the wind.

1799

THE SIMPLON PASS

————————BROOK and road
Were fellow-travellers in this gloomy Pass,
And with them did we journey several hours
At a slow step. The immeasurable height
Of woods decaying, never to be decayed,
The stationary blasts of waterfalls,

And in the narrow rent, at every turn,
Winds thwarting winds bewildered and for-
lorn,
The torrents shooting from the clear blue sky,
The rocks that muttered close upon our ears,
Black drizzling crags that spake by the way-
side   11
As if a voice were in them, the sick sight
And giddy prospect of the raving stream,
The unfettered clouds and region of the heav-
ens,
Tumult and peace, the darkness and the
light—
Were all like workings of one mind, the
features
Of the same face, blossoms upon one tree,
Characters of the great Apocalypse,
The types and symbols of Eternity,   19
Of first, and last, and midst, and without end.

1799

TO M. H.

Our walk was far among the ancient trees:
There was no road, nor any woodman's path;
But a thick umbrage—checking the wild
growth
Of weed and sapling, along soft green turf
Beneath the branches—of itself had made
A track, that brought us to a slip of lawn,
And a small bed of water in the woods.
All round this pool both flocks and herds
might drink
On its firm margin, even as from a well,
Or some stone-basin which the herdsman's
hand   10
Had shaped for their refreshment; nor did sun,
Or wind from any quarter, ever come,
But as a blessing to this calm recess,
This glade of water and this one green field.
The spot was made by Nature for herself;
The travellers know it not, and 'twill remain
Unknown to them; but it is beautiful;
And if a man should plant his cottage near,
Should sleep beneath the shelter of its trees,
And blend its waters with his daily meal, 20
He would so love it, that in his death-hour
Its image would survive among his thoughts:
And therefore, my sweet Mary, this still Nook,
With all its beeches, we have named from You!

1799

IT WAS AN APRIL MORNING

It was an April morning: fresh and clear
The Rivulet, delighting in its strength,
Ran with a young man's speed; and yet the
voice
Of waters which the winter had supplied
Was softened down into a vernal tone.
The spirit of enjoyment and desire,
And hopes and wishes, from all living things
Went circling, like a multitude of sounds.
The budding groves seemed eager to urge on
The steps of June; as if their various hues
Were only hindrances that stood between 11
Them and their object: but, meanwhile, pre-
vailed
Such an entire contentment in the air
That every naked ash, and tardy tree
Yet leafless, showed as if the countenance
With which it looked on this delightful day
Were native to the summer.—Up the brook
I roamed in the confusion of my heart,
Alive to all things and forgetting all.
At length I to a sudden turning came   20
In this continuous glen, where down a rock
The Stream, so ardent in its course before,
Sent forth such sallies of glad sound, that all
Which I till then had heard appeared the voice
Of common pleasure: beast and bird, the lamb,
The shepherd's dog, the linnet and the thrush,
Vied with this waterfall, and made a song
Which, while I listened, seemed like the wild
growth
Or like some natural produce of the air,
That could not cease to be. Green leaves were
here;   30
But 'twas the foliage of the rocks—the birch,
The yew, the holly, and the bright green thorn,
With hanging islands of resplendent furze:
And on a summit, distant a short space,
By any who should look beyond the dell
A single mountain-cottage might be seen.
I gazed and gazed, and to myself I said,
"Our thoughts at least are ours; and this wild
nook,
My Emma, I will dedicate to thee."
——Soon did the spot become my other
home,   40
My dwelling, and my out-of-doors abode.
And of the Shepherds who have seen me there,
To whom I sometimes in our idle talk

Have told this fancy, two or three, perhaps,
Years after we are gone and in our graves,
When they have cause to speak of this wild
    place,
May call it by the name of EMMA'S DELL.
1800

THERE IS AN EMINENCE

THERE is an Eminence,—of these our hills
The last that parleys with the setting sun;
We can behold it from our orchard seat;
And, when at evening we pursue our walk
Along the public way, this Peak, so high
Above us, and so distant in its height,
Is visible; and often seems to send
Its own deep quiet to restore our hearts.
The meteors make of it a favourite haunt:
The star of Jove, so beautiful and large   10
In the mid heavens, is never half so fair
As when he shines above it. 'Tis in truth
The loneliest place we have among the clouds.
And She who dwells with me, whom I have
    loved
With such communion that no place on earth
Can ever be a solitude to me,
Hath to this lonely Summit given my Name.
1800

WHEN, TO THE ATTRACTIONS OF THE BUSY WORLD

WHEN, to the attractions of the busy world
Preferring studious leisure, I had chosen
A habitation in this peaceful Vale,
Sharp season followed of continual storm
In deepest winter; and, from week to week,
Pathway, and lane, and public road, were
    clogged
With frequent showers of snow. Upon a hill,
At a short distance from my cottage, stands
A stately Fir-grove, whither I was wont
To hasten, for I found, beneath the roof   10
Of that perennial shade, a cloistral place
Of refuge, with an unincumbered floor.
Here, in safe covert, on the shallow snow,
And sometimes on a speck of visible earth,
The redbreast near me hopped; nor was I
    loth
To sympathize with vulgar coppice birds
That, for protection from the nipping blast,

Hither repaired.—A single beech-tree grew
Within this grove of firs! and, on the fork
Of that one beech, appeared a thrush's nest;
A last year's nest, conspicuously built   21
At such small elevation from the ground
As gave sure sign that they, who in that house
Of nature and of love had made their home
Amid the fir-trees, all the summer long
Dwelt in a tranquil spot. And oftentimes
A few sheep, stragglers from some mountain-
    flock,
Would watch my motions with suspicious
    stare,
From the remotest outskirts of the grove,—
Some nook where they had made their final
    stand,   30
Huddling together from two fears—the fear
Of me and of the storm. Full many an hour
Here did I lose. But in this grove the trees
Had been so thickly planted and had thriven
In such perplexed and intricate array,
That vainly did I seek beneath their stems
A length of open space, where to and fro
My feet might move without concern or care;
And, baffled thus, though earth from day to
    day   39
Was fettered, and the air by storm disturbed,
I ceased the shelter to frequent,—and prized,
Less than I wished to prize, that calm recess.

The snows dissolved, and genial Spring re-
    turned
To clothe the fields with verdure. Other haunts
Meanwhile were mine; till one bright April
    day,
By chance retiring from the glare of noon
To this forsaken covert, there I found
A hoary pathway traced between the trees,
And winding on with such an easy line
Along a natural opening, that I stood   50
Much wondering how I could have sought in
    vain
For what was now so obvious. To abide,
For an allotted interval of ease,
Under my cottage-roof, had gladly come
From the wild sea a cherished Visitant;
And with the sight of this same path—begun,
Begun and ended, in the shady grove,
Pleasant conviction flashed upon my mind
That, to this opportune recess allured,
He had surveyed it with a finer eye,   60

A heart more wakeful; and had worn the track
By pacing here, unwearied and alone,
In that habitual restlessness of foot
That haunts the Sailor, measuring o'er and o'er
His short domain upon the vessel's deck,
While she pursues her course through the
    dreary sea.

    When thou hadst quitted Esthwaite's pleas-
    ant shore,
And taken thy first leave of those green hills
And rocks that were the play-ground of thy
    youth,
Year followed year, my Brother! and we two,
Conversing not, knew little in what mould 71
Each other's mind was fashioned; and at
    length,
When once again we met in Grasmere Vale,
Between us there was little other bond
Than common feelings of fraternal love.
But thou, a School-boy, to the sea hadst
    carried
Undying recollections; Nature there
Was with thee; she, who loved us both, she
    still
Was with thee; and even so didst thou become
A *silent* Poet; from the solitude   80
Of the vast sea didst bring a watchful heart
Still couchant, an inevitable ear,
And an eye practised like a blind man's touch.
—Back to the joyless Ocean thou art gone;
Nor from this vestige of thy musing hours
Could I withhold thy honoured name,—and
    now
I love the fir-grove with a perfect love.
Thither do I withdraw when cloudless suns
Shine hot, or wind blows troublesome and
    strong;
And there I sit at evening, when the steep 90
Of Silver-how, and Grasmere's peaceful lake
And one green island, gleam between the stems
Of the dark firs, a visionary scene!
And while I gaze upon the spectacle
Of clouded splendour, on this dream-like sight
Of solemn loveliness, I think on thee,
My Brother, and on all which thou hast lost.
Nor seldom, if I rightly guess, while Thou,
Muttering the verses which I muttered first
Among the mountains, through the midnight
    watch   100
Art pacing thoughtfully the vessel's deck

In some far region, here, while o'er my head,
At every impulse of the moving breeze,
The fir-grove murmurs with a sea-like sound,
Alone I tread this path;—for aught I know,
Timing my steps to thine; and, with a store
Of undistinguishable sympathies,
Mingling most earnest wishes for the day
When we, and others whom we love, shall
    meet   109
A second time, in Grasmere's happy Vale.
1800–1802

THE BROTHERS

"THESE Tourists, heaven preserve us! needs
    must live
A profitable life: some glance along,
Rapid and gay, as if the earth were air,
And they were butterflies to wheel about
Long as the summer lasted: some, as wise,
Perched on the forehead of a jutting crag,
Pencil in hand and book upon the knee,
Will look and scribble, scribble on and look,
Until a man might travel twelve stout miles,
Or reap an acre of his neighbour's corn.   10
But, for that moping Son of Idleness,
Why can he tarry *yonder?*—In our church-yard
Is neither epitaph nor monument,
Tombstone nor name—only the turf we tread
And a few natural graves."

                To Jane, his wife,
Thus spake the homely Priest of Ennerdale.
It was a July evening; and he sate
Upon the long stone-seat beneath the eaves
Of his old cottage,—as it chanced, that day,
Employed in winter's work. Upon the stone
His wife sate near him, teasing matted wool, 21
While, from the twin cards toothed with glit-
    tering wire,
He fed the spindle of his youngest child,
Who, in the open air, with due accord
Of busy hands and back-and-forward steps,
Her large round wheel was turning. Towards
    the field
In which the Parish Chapel stood alone,
Girt round with a bare ring of mossy wall,
While half an hour went by, the Priest had sent
Many a long look of wonder: and at last,   30
Risen from his seat, beside the snow-white
    ridge

Of carded wool which the old man had piled
He laid his implements with gentle care,
Each in the other locked; and down the path,
That from his cottage to the church-yard led,
He took his way, impatient to accost
The Stranger, whom he saw still lingering
    there.

'Twas one well known to him in former days,
A Shepherd-lad; who ere his sixteenth year
Had left that calling, tempted to entrust   40
His expectations to the fickle winds
And perilous waters; with the mariners
A fellow-mariner; and so had fared
Through twenty seasons; but he had been
    reared
Among the mountains, and he in his heart
Was half a shepherd on the stormy seas.
Oft in the piping shrouds had Leonard heard
The tones of waterfalls, and inland sounds
Of caves and trees:—and when the regular
    wind
Between the tropics filled the steady sail,   50
And blew with the same breath through days
    and weeks,
Lengthening invisibly its weary line
Along the cloudless Main, he, in those hours
Of tiresome indolence, would often hang
Over the vessel's side, and gaze and gaze;
And, while the broad blue wave and sparkling
    foam
Flashed round him images and hues that
    wrought
In union with the employment of his heart,
He, thus by feverish passion overcome,
Even with the organs of his bodily eye,   60
Below him, in the bosom of the deep,
Saw mountains; saw the forms of sheep that
    grazed
On verdant hills—with dwellings among trees,
And shepherds clad in the same country grey
Which he himself had worn.

                And now, at last,
From perils manifold, with some small wealth
Acquired by traffic 'mid the Indian Isles,
To his paternal home he is returned,
With a determined purpose to resume
The life he had lived there; both for the
    sake   70
Of many darling pleasures, and the love

Which to an only brother he has borne
In all his hardships, since that happy time
When, whether it blew foul or fair, they two
Were brother-shepherds on their native hills,
—They were the last of all their race: and now,
When Leonard had approached his home, his
    heart
Failed in him; and, not venturing to enquire
Tidings of one so long and dearly loved,
He to the solitary church-yard turned;   80
That, as he knew in what particular spot
His family were laid, he thence might learn
If still his Brother lived, or to the file
Another grave was added.—He had found
Another grave,—near which a full half-hour
He had remained; but, as he gazed, there grew
Such a confusion in his memory,
That he began to doubt; and even to hope
That he had seen this heap of turf before,—
That it was not another grave; but one   90
He had forgotten. He had lost his path,
As up the vale, that afternoon, he walked
Through fields which once had been well
    known to him:
And oh what joy this recollection now
Sent to his heart! he lifted up his eyes,
And, looking round, imagined that he saw
Strange alteration wrought on every side
Among the woods and fields, and that the
    rocks,
And everlasting hills themselves were changed.

    By this the Priest, who down the field had
    come,   100
Unseen by Leonard, at the church-yard gate
Stopped short,—and thence, at leisure, limb
    by limb
Perused him with a gay complacency.
Ay, thought the Vicar, smiling to himself,
'Tis one of those who needs must leave the
    path
Of the world's business to go wild alone:
His arms have a perpetual holiday;
The happy man will creep about the fields,
Following his fancies by the hour, to bring
Tears down his cheek, or solitary smiles   110
Into his face, until the setting sun
Write fool upon his forehead.—Planted thus
Beneath a shed that over-arched the gate
Of this rude church-yard, till the stars ap-
    peared

The good Man might have communed with
   himself,
But that the Stranger, who had left the grave,
Approached; he recognised the Priest at once,
And, after greetings interchanged, and given
By Leonard to the Vicar as to one
Unknown to him, this dialogue ensued.   120
   Leonard.   You live, Sir, in these dales, a
      quiet life:
Your years make up one peaceful family;
And who would grieve and fret, if, welcome
   come
And welcome gone, they are so like each other,
They cannot be remembered? Scarce a funeral
Comes to this church-yard once in eighteen
   months;
And yet, some changes must take place among
   you:
And you, who dwell here, even among these
   rocks,
Can trace the finger of mortality,
And see, that with our threescore years and
   ten   130
We are not all that perish.——I remember,
(For many years ago I passed this road)
There was a foot-way all along the fields
By the brook-side——'tis gone——and that dark
   cleft!
To me it does not seem to wear the face
Which then it had!
   Priest.   Nay, Sir, for aught I know,
That chasm is much the same——
   Leonard.   But, surely, yonder——
   Priest.   Ay, there, indeed, your memory is
      a friend
That does not play you false.——On that tall
   pike
(It is the loneliest place of all these hills) 140
There were two springs which bubbled side
   by side,
As if they had been made that they might be
Companions for each other: the huge crag
Was rent with lightning——one hath disap-
   peared;
The other, left behind, is flowing still.
For accidents and changes such as these,
We want not store of them;——a water-spout
Will bring down half a mountain; what a feast
For folks that wander up and down like you,
To see an acre's breadth of that wide cliff 150
One roaring cataract! a sharp May-storm

Will come with loads of January snow,
And in one night send twenty score of sheep
To feed the ravens; or a shepherd dies
By some untoward death among the rocks:
The ice breaks up and sweeps away a bridge;
A wood is felled:——and then for our own
   homes!
A child is born or christened, a field ploughed,
A daughter sent to service, a web spun,
The old house-clock is decked with a new
   face;   160
And hence, so far from wanting facts or dates
To chronicle the time, we all have here
A pair of diaries,——one serving, Sir,
For the whole dale, and one for each fire-
   side——
Yours was a stranger's judgment: for histo-
   rians,
Commend me to these valleys!
   Leonard.   Yet your Church-yard
Seems, if such freedom may be used with you,
To say that you are heedless of the past:
An orphan could not find his mother's grave:
Here's neither head nor foot-stone, plate of
   brass,   170
Cross-bones nor skull,——type of our earthly
   state
Nor emblem of our hopes: the dead man's
   home
Is but a fellow to that pasture-field.
   Priest. Why, there, Sir, is a thought that's
      new to me!
The stone-cutters, 'tis true, might beg their
   bread
If every English church-yard were like ours;
Yet your conclusion wanders from the truth:
We have no need of names and epitaphs;
We talk about the dead by our fire-sides.
And then, for our immortal part! *we* want 180
No symbols, Sir, to tell us that plain tale:
The thought of death sits easy on the man
Who has been born and dies among the
   mountains.
   Leonard. Your Dalesmen, then, do in each
      other's thoughts
Possess a kind of second life: no doubt
You, Sir, could help me to the history
Of half these graves?
   Priest.   For eight-score winters past,
With what I've witnessed, and with what
      I've heard,

Perhaps I might; and, on a winter-evening,
If you were seated at my chimney's nook, 190
By turning o'er these hillocks one by one,
We two could travel, Sir, through a strange
    round;
Yet all in the broad highway of the world.
Now there's a grave—your foot is half upon
    it,—
It looks just like the rest; and yet that man
Died broken-hearted.
    Leonard.   'Tis a common case.
We'll take another: who is he that lies
Beneath yon ridge, the last of those three
    graves?
It touches on that piece of native rock
Left in the church-yard wall.
    Priest.   That's Walter Ewbank. 200
He had as white a head and fresh a cheek
As ever were produced by youth and age
Engendering in the blood of hale four-score.
Through five long generations had the heart
Of Walter's forefathers o'erflowed the bounds
Of their inheritance, that single cottage—
You see it yonder! and those few green fields.
They toiled and wrought, and still, from sire
    to son,
Each struggled, and each yielded as before
A little—yet a little,—and old Walter, 210
They left to him the family heart, and land
With other burthens than the crop it bore.
Year after year the old man still kept up
A cheerful mind,—and buffeted with bond,
Interest, and mortgages; at last he sank,
And went into his grave before his time.
Poor Walter! whether it was care that spurred
    him
God only knows, but to the very last
He had the lightest foot in Ennerdale:
His pace was never that of an old man: 220
I almost see him tripping down the path
With his two grandsons after him:—but you,
Unless our Landlord be your host tonight,
Have far to travel,—and on these rough paths
Even in the longest day of midsummer—
    Leonard. But those two Orphans!
    Priest.   Orphans!—Such they were—
Yet not while Walter lived:—for, though
    their parents
Lay buried side by side as now they lie,
The old man was a father to the boys,
Two fathers in one father: and if tears, 230

Shed when he talked of them where they were
    not,
And hauntings from the infirmity of love,
Are aught of what makes up a mother's heart,
This old Man, in the day of his old age,
Was half a mother to them.—If you weep, Sir,
To hear a stranger talking about strangers,
Heaven bless you when you are among your
    kindred!
Ay—you may turn that way—it is a grave
Which will bear looking at.
    Leonard.   These boys—I hope
They loved this good old Man?—
    Priest.   They did—and truly: 240
But that was what we almost overlooked,
They were such darlings of each other. Yes,
Though from the cradle they had lived with
    Walter,
The only kinsman near them, and though he
Inclined to both by reason of his age,
With a more fond, familiar, tenderness;
They, notwithstanding, had much love to
    spare,
And it all went into each other's hearts.
Leonard, the elder by just eighteen months,
Was two years taller: 'twas a joy to see,
To hear, to meet them!—From their house
    the school   251
Is distant three short miles, and in the time
Of storm and thaw, when every water-course
And unbridged stream, such as you may have
    noticed
Crossing our roads at every hundred steps,
Was swoln into a noisy rivulet,
Would Leonard then, when elder boys re-
    mained
At home, go staggering through the slippery
    fords,
Bearing his brother on his back. I have seen
    him,
On windy days, in one of those stray
    brooks,   260
Ay, more than once I have seen him, mid-leg
    deep,
Their two books lying both on a dry stone,
Upon the hither side: and once I said,
As I remember, looking round these rocks
And hills on which we all of us were born,
That God who made the great book of the
    world
Would bless such piety—

Leonard.   It may be then—
Priest. Never did worthier lads break Eng-
    lish bread;
The very brightest Sunday Autumn saw,
With all its mealy clusters of ripe nuts,   270
Could never keep those boys away from
    church,
Or tempt them to an hour of sabbath breach.
Leonard and James! I warrant, every corner
Among these rocks, and every hollow place
That venturous foot could reach, to one or
    both
Was known as well as to the flowers that grow
    there.
Like roe-bucks they went bounding o'er the
    hills;
They played like two young ravens on the
    crags:
Then they could write, ay, and speak too, as
    well
As many of their betters—and for Leonard!
The very night before he went away,   281
In my own house I put into his hand
A Bible, and I'd wager house and field
That, if he be alive, he has it yet.
    Leonard. It seems, these Brothers have not
        lived to be
A comfort to each other—
    Priest.   That they might
Live to such end is what both old and young
In this our valley all of us have wished,
And what, for my part, I have often prayed:
But Leonard—
    Leonard.   Then James still is left among
        you!   290
    Priest. 'Tis of the elder brother I am speak-
        ing:
They had an uncle;—he was at that time
A thriving man, and trafficked on the seas:
And, but for that same uncle, to this hour
Leonard had never handled rope or shroud:
For the boy loved the life which we lead here;
And though of unripe years, a stripling only,
His soul was knit to this his native soil.
But, as I said, old Walter was too weak
To strive with such a torrent; when he died,
The estate and house were sold; and all their
    sheep,   301
A pretty flock, and which, for aught I know,
Had clothed the Ewbanks for a thousand
    years:—

Well—all was gone, and they were destitute,
And Leonard, chiefly for his Brother's sake,
Resolved to try his fortune on the seas.
Twelve years are past since we had tidings
    from him.
If there were one among us who had heard
That Leonard Ewbank was come home again,
From the Great Gavel, down by Leeza's
    banks,   310
And down the Enna, far as Egremont,
The day would be a joyous festival;
And those two bells of ours, which there you
    see—
Hanging in the open air—but, O good Sir!
This is sad talk—they'll never sound for
    him—
Living or dead.—When last we heard of
    him,
He was in slavery among the Moors
Upon the Barbary coast.—'Twas not a little
That would bring down his spirit; and no
    doubt,
Before it ended in his death, the Youth 320
Was sadly crossed.—Poor Leonard! when we
    parted,
He took me by the hand, and said to me,
If e'er he should grow rich, he would return,
To live in peace upon his father's land,
And lay his bones among us.
    Leonard.   If that day
Should come, 'twould needs be a glad day
    for him;
He would himself, no doubt, be happy then
As any that should meet him—
    Priest.   Happy! Sir—
    Leonard. You said his kindred all were in
        their graves,
And that he had one Brother—
    Priest.   That is but 330
A fellow-tale of sorrow. From his youth
James, though not sickly, yet was delicate;
And Leonard being always by his side
Had done so many offices about him,
That, though he was not of a timid nature,
Yet still the spirit of a mountain-boy
In him was somewhat checked; and, when his
    Brother
Was gone to sea, and he was left alone,
The little colour that he had was soon
Stolen from his cheek; he drooped, and pined,
    and pined—   340

Leonard. But these are all the graves of full-
grown men!

Priest. Ay, Sir, that passed away: we took
him to us;

He was the child of all the dale—he lived

Three months with one, and six months with
another;

And wanted neither food, nor clothes, nor
love:

And many, many happy days were his.

But, whether blithe or sad, 'tis my belief

His absent Brother still was at his heart.

And, when he dwelt beneath our roof, we
found   349

(A practice till this time unknown to him)

That often, rising from his bed at night,

He in his sleep would walk about, and sleeping

He sought his brother Leonard.—You are
moved!

Forgive me, Sir: before I spoke to you,

I judged you most unkindly.

   Leonard.   But this Youth,

How did he die at last?

   Priest.   One sweet May-morning,

(It will be twelve years since when Spring
returns)

He had gone forth among the new-dropped
lambs,

With two or three companions, whom their
course

Of occupation led from height to height 360

Under a cloudless sun—till he, at length,

Through weariness, or, haply, to indulge

The humour of the moment, lagged behind.

You see yon precipice;—it wears the shape

Of a vast building made of many crags;

And in the midst is one particular rock

That rises like a column from the vale,

Whence by our shepherds it is called THE
PILLAR.

Upon its aëry summit crowned with heath,

The loiterer, not unnoticed by his comrades,   370

Lay stretched at ease; but, passing by the place

On their return, they found that he was gone.

No ill was feared; till one of them by chance

Entering, when evening was far spent, the
house

Which at that time was James's home, there
learned

That nobody had seen him all that day:

The morning came, and still he was unheard of:

The neighbours were alarmed, and to the
brook

Some hastened; some ran to the lake: ere noon

They found him at the foot of that same rock

Dead, and with mangled limbs. The third day
after   381

I buried him, poor Youth, and there he lies!

   Leonard. And that then *is* his grave!—Before his death

You say that he saw many happy years?

   Priest. Ay, that he did—

   Leonard. And all went well with him?—

   Priest. If he had one, the Youth had twenty
homes.

   Leonard. And you believe, then, that his
mind was easy?—

   Priest. Yes, long before he died, he found
that time

Is a true friend to sorrow; and, unless

His thoughts were turned on Leonard's
luckless fortune,   390

He talked about him with a cheerful love.

   Leonard. He could not come to an unhal-
lowed end!

   Priest. Nay, God forbid!—You recollect
I mentioned

A habit which disquietude and grief

Had brought upon him; and we all conjectured

That, as the day was warm, he had lain down

On the soft heath,—and, waiting for his comrades,

He there had fallen asleep; that in his sleep

He to the margin of the precipice

Had walked, and from the summit had fallen
headlong: 400

And so no doubt he perished. When the Youth

Fell, in his hand he must have grasped, we
think,

His shepherd's staff; for on that Pillar of rock

It had been caught mid-way; and there for
years

It hung;—and mouldered there.

               The Priest here ended—

The Stranger would have thanked him, but
he felt

A gushing from his heart, that took away

The power of speech. Both left the spot in
silence;

And Leonard, when they reached the church-
yard gate,
As the Priest lifted up the latch, turned
round,—   410
And, looking at the grave, he said, "My
Brother!"
The Vicar did not hear the words: and now
He pointed towards his dwelling-place, en-
treating
That Leonard would partake his homely fare:
The other thanked him with an earnest voice;
But added, that, the evening being calm,
He would pursue his journey. So they parted.

It was not long ere Leonard reached a grove
That overhung the road: he there stopped
short,
And, sitting down beneath the trees, re-
viewed   420
All that the Priest had said: his early years
Were with him:—his long absence, cherished
hopes,
And thoughts which had been his an hour
before,
All pressed on him with such a weight, that
now,
This vale, where he had been so happy,
seemed
A place in which he could not bear to live:
So he relinquished all his purposes.
He travelled back to Egremont: and thence,
That night, he wrote a letter to the Priest,
Reminding him of what had passed between
them;   430
And adding, with a hope to be forgiven,
That it was from the weakness of his heart
He had not dared to tell him who he was.
This done, he went on shipboard, and is now
A seaman, a grey-headed Mariner.

1800

MICHAEL
A PASTORAL POEM

IF from the public way you turn your steps
Up the tumultuous brook of Green-head
Ghyll,
You will suppose that with an upright path
Your feet must struggle; in such bold ascent
The pastoral mountains front you, face to face.
But, courage! for around that boisterous brook

The mountains have all opened out them-
selves,
And made a hidden valley of their own.
No habitation can be seen; but they
Who journey thither find themselves alone 10
With a few sheep, with rocks and stones, and
kites
That overhead are sailing in the sky.
It is in truth an utter solitude;
Nor should I have made mention of this Dell
But for one object which you might pass by,
Might see and notice not. Beside the brook
Appears a straggling heap of unhewn stones!
And to that simple object appertains
A story—unenriched with strange events,
Yet not unfit, I deem, for the fireside,   20
Or for the summer shade. It was the first
Of those domestic tales that spake to me
Of Shepherds, dwellers in the valleys, men
Whom I already loved;—not verily
For their own sakes, but for the fields and hills
Where was their occupation and abode.
And hence this Tale, while I was yet a Boy
Careless of books, yet having felt the power
Of Nature, by the gentle agency
Of natural objects, led me on to feel   30
For passions that were not my own, and
think
(At random and imperfectly indeed)
On man, the heart of man, and human life.
Therefore, although it be a history
Homely and rude, I will relate the same
For the delight of a few natural hearts;
And, with yet fonder feeling, for the sake
Of youthful Poets, who among these hills
Will be my second self when I am gone.

Upon the forest-side in Grasmere Vale 40
There dwelt a Shepherd, Michael was his
name;
An old man, stout of heart, and strong of limb.
His bodily frame had been from youth to age
Of an unusual strength: his mind was keen,
Intense, and frugal, apt for all affairs,
And in his shepherd's calling he was prompt
And watchful more than ordinary men.
Hence had he learned the meaning of all
winds,
Of blasts of every tone; and oftentimes,
When others heeded not, He heard the
South   50

Make subterraneous music, like the noise
Of bagpipers on distant Highland hills.
The Shepherd, at such warning, of his flock
Bethought him, and he to himself would say,
"The winds are now devising work for me!"
And, truly, at all times, the storm, that drives
The traveller to a shelter, summoned him
Up to the mountains: he had been alone
Amid the heart of many thousand mists,
That came to him, and left him, on the heights.   60
So lived he till his eightieth year was past.
And grossly that man errs, who should suppose
That the green valleys, and the streams and rocks,
Were things indifferent to the Shepherd's thoughts.
Fields, where with cheerful spirits he had breathed
The common air; hills, which with vigorous step
He had so often climbed; which had impressed
So many incidents upon his mind
Of hardship, skill or courage, joy or fear;
Which, like a book, preserved the memory 70
Of the dumb animals, whom he had saved,
Had fed or sheltered, linking to such acts
The certainty of honourable gain;
Those fields, those hills—what could they less? had laid
Strong hold on his affections, were to him
A pleasurable feeling of blind love,
The pleasure which there is in life itself.

His days had not been passed in singleness.
His Helpmate was a comely matron, old—
Though younger than himself full twenty years.   80
She was a woman of a stirring life,
Whose heart was in her house: two wheels she had
Of antique form; this large, for spinning wool;
That small, for flax; and, if one wheel had rest,
It was because the other was at work.
The Pair had but one inmate in their house,
An only Child, who had been born to them
When Michael, telling o'er his years, began
To deem that he was old,—in shepherd's phrase,
With one foot in the grave. This only Son, 90

With two brave sheep-dogs tried in many a storm,
The one of an inestimable worth,
Made all their household. I may truly say,
That they were as a proverb in the vale
For endless industry. When day was gone,
And from their occupations out of doors
The Son and Father were come home, even then,
Their labour did not cease; unless when all
Turned to the cleanly supper-board, and there,
Each with a mess of pottage and skimmed milk,   100
Sat round the basket piled with oaten cakes,
And their plain home-made cheese. Yet when the meal
Was ended, Luke (for so the Son was named)
And his old Father both betook themselves
To such convenient work as might employ
Their hands by the fire-side; perhaps to card
Wool for the Housewife's spindle, or repair
Some injury done to sickle, flail, or scythe,
Or other implement of house or field.

Down from the ceiling, by the chimney's edge,   110
That in our ancient uncouth country style
With huge and black projection overbrowed
Large space beneath, as duly as the light
Of day grew dim the Housewife hung a lamp;
An aged utensil, which had performed
Service beyond all others of its kind.
Early at evening did it burn—and late,
Surviving comrade of uncounted hours,
Which, going by from year to year, had found,
And left, the couple neither gay perhaps 120
Nor cheerful, yet with objects and with hopes,
Living a life of eager industry.
And now, when Luke had reached his eighteenth year,
There by the light of this old lamp they sate,
Father and Son, while far into the night
The Housewife plied her own peculiar work,
Making the cottage through the silent hours
Murmur as with the sound of summer flies.
This light was famous in its neighbourhood,
And was a public symbol of the life 130
That thrifty Pair had lived. For, as it chanced,
Their cottage on a plot of rising ground

Stood single, with large prospect, north and
    south,
High into Easedale, up to Dunmail-Raise,
And westward to the village near the lake;
And from this constant light, so regular,
And so far seen, the House itself, by all
Who dwelt within the limits of the vale,
Both old and young, was named THE EVE-
    NING STAR.

    Thus living on through such a length of
    years,   140
The Shepherd, if he loved himself, must needs
Have loved his Helpmate; but to Michael's
    heart
This son of his old age was yet more dear—
Less from instinctive tenderness, the same
Fond spirit that blindly works in the blood of
    all—
Than that a child, more than all other gifts
That earth can offer to declining man,
Brings hope with it, and forward-looking
    thoughts,
And stirrings of inquietude, when they
By tendency of nature needs must fail.   150
Exceeding was the love he bare to him,
His heart and his heart's joy! For oftentimes
Old Michael, while he was a babe in arms,
Had done him female service, not alone
For pastime and delight, as is the use
Of fathers, but with patient mind enforced
To acts of tenderness; and he had rocked
His cradle, as with a woman's gentle hand.

    And in a later time, ere yet the Boy
Had put on boy's attire, did Michael love, 160
Albeit of a stern unbending mind,
To have the Young-one in his sight, when he
Wrought in the field, or on his shepherd's
    stool
Sate with a fettered sheep before him stretched
Under the large old oak, that near his door
Stood single, and, from matchless depth of
    shade,
Chosen for the Shearer's covert from the
    sun,
Thence in our rustic dialect was called
The CLIPPING TREE, a name which yet it
    bears.
There, while they two were sitting in the
    shade,   170

With others round them, earnest all and
    blithe,
Would Michael exercise his heart with
    looks
Of fond correction and reproof bestowed
Upon the Child, if he disturbed the sheep
By catching at their legs, or with his shouts
Scared them, while they lay still beneath the
    shears.

    And when by Heaven's good grace the
    boy grew up
A healthy Lad, and carried in his cheek
Two steady roses that were five years old;
Then Michael from a winter coppice cut   180
With his own hand a sapling, which he
    hooped
With iron, making it throughout in all
Due requisites a perfect shepherd's staff,
And gave it to the Boy; wherewith equipt
He as a watchman oftentimes was placed
At gate or gap, to stem or turn the flock;
And, to his office prematurely called,
There stood the urchin, as you will divine,
Something between a hindrance and a help;
And for this cause not always, I believe,   190
Receiving from his Father hire of praise;
Though nought was left undone which staff,
    or voice,
Or looks, or threatening gestures, could per-
    form.

    But soon as Luke, full ten years old, could
    stand
Against the mountain blasts; and to the
    heights,
Not fearing toil, nor length of weary ways,
He with his Father daily went, and they
Were as companions, why should I relate
That objects which the Shepherd loved before
Were dearer now? that from the Boy there
    came   200
Feelings and emanations—things which were
Light to the sun and music to the wind;
And that the old Man's heart seemed born
    again?

    Thus in his Father's sight the Boy grew up:
And now, when he had reached his eight-
    eenth year,
He was his comfort and his daily hope.

While in this sort the simple household
    lived
From day to day, to Michael's ear there came
Distressful tidings. Long before the time
Of which I speak, the Shepherd had been
    bound   210
In surety for his brother's son, a man
Of an industrious life, and ample means;
But unforeseen misfortunes suddenly
Had prest upon him; and old Michael now
Was summoned to discharge the forfeiture,
A grievous penalty, but little less
Than half his substance. This unlooked-for
    claim,
At the first hearing, for a moment took
More hope out of his life than he supposed
That any old man ever could have lost.   220
As soon as he had armed himself with strength
To look his trouble in the face, it seemed
The Shepherd's sole resource to sell at once
A portion of his patrimonial fields.
Such was his first resolve; he thought again,
And his heart failed him. "Isabel," said he,
Two evenings after he had heard the news,
"I have been toiling more than seventy years,
And in the open sunshine of God's love
Have we all lived; yet, if these fields of ours 230
Should pass into a stranger's hand, I think
That I could not lie quiet in my grave.
Our lot is a hard lot; the sun himself
Has scarcely been more diligent than I;
And I have lived to be a fool at last
To my own family. An evil man
That was, and made an evil choice, if he
Were false to us; and, if he were not false,
There are ten thousand to whom loss like this
Had been no sorrow. I forgive him;—but 240
'Twere better to be dumb than to talk thus.

"When I began, my purpose was to speak
Of remedies and of a cheerful hope.
Our Luke shall leave us, Isabel; the land
Shall not go from us, and it shall be free;
He shall possess it, free as is the wind
That passes over it. We have, thou know'st,
Another kinsman—he will be our friend
In this distress. He is a prosperous man,
Thriving in trade—and Luke to him shall
    go,   250
And with his kinsman's help and his own thrift
He quickly will repair this loss, and then

He may return to us. If here he stay,
What can be done? Where every one is poor,
What can be gained?"
                At this the old Man paused,
And Isabel sat silent, for her mind
Was busy, looking back into past times.
There's Richard Bateman, thought she to her-
    self,
He was a parish-boy—at the church-door
They made a gathering for him, shillings,
    pence,   260
And halfpennies, wherewith the neighbours
    bought
A basket, which they filled with pedlar's
    wares;
And, with this basket on his arm, the lad
Went up to London, found a master there,
Who, out of many, chose the trusty boy
To go and overlook his merchandise
Beyond the seas; where he grew wondrous
    rich,
And left estates and monies to the poor,
And, at his birth-place, built a chapel floored
With marble, which he sent from foreign
    lands.   270
These thoughts, and many others of like
    sort,
Passed quickly through the mind of Isabel,
And her face brightened. The old Man was
    glad,
And thus resumed:—"Well, Isabel! this
    scheme
These two days has been meat and drink
    to me.
Far more than we have lost is left us yet.
—We have enough—I wish indeed that I
Were younger;—but this hope is a good hope.
Make ready Luke's best garments, of the best
Buy for him more, and let us send him forth
To-morrow, or the next day, or to-night: 281
—If he *could* go, the Boy should go to-
    night."

    Here Michael ceased, and to the fields went
    forth
With a light heart. The Housewife for five
    days
Was restless morn and night, and all day long
Wrought on with her best fingers to prepare
Things needful for the journey of her son.
But Isabel was glad when Sunday came

To stop her in her work: for, when she lay
By Michael's side, she through the last two
    nights   290
Heard him, how he was troubled in his sleep:
And when they rose at morning she could see
That all his hopes were gone. That day at
    noon
She said to Luke, while they two by them-
    selves
Were sitting at the door, "Thou must not go:
We have no other Child but thee to lose,
None to remember—do not go away,
For if thou leave thy Father he will die."
The Youth made answer with a jocund voice;
And Isabel, when she had told her fears,   300
Recovered heart. That evening her best fare
Did she bring forth, and all together sat
Like happy people round a Christmas fire.

    With daylight Isabel resumed her work;
And all the ensuing week the house appeared
As cheerful as a grove in Spring: at length
The expected letter from their kinsman came,
With kind assurances that he would do
His utmost for the welfare of the Boy;
To which, requests were added, that forth-
    with   310
He might be sent to him. Ten times or more
The letter was read over; Isabel
Went forth to show it to the neighbours
    round;
Nor was there at that time on English land
A prouder heart than Luke's. When Isabel
Had to her house returned, the old Man said,
"He shall depart to-morrow." To this word
The Housewife answered, talking much of
    things
Which, if at such short notice he should go,
Would surely be forgotten. But at length
She gave consent, and Michael was at ease. 321

    Near the tumultuous brook of Greenhead
    Ghyll,
In that deep valley, Michael had designed
To build a Sheep-fold; and, before he heard
The tidings of his melancholy loss,
For this same purpose he had gathered up
A heap of stones, which by the streamlet's edge
Lay thrown together, ready for the work.
With Luke that evening thitherward he
    walked:

And soon as they had reached the place he
    stopped,   330
And thus the old Man spake to him:—
    "My son,
To-morrow thou wilt leave me: with full
    heart
I look upon thee, for thou art the same
That wert a promise to me ere thy birth,
And all thy life hast been my daily joy.
I will relate to thee some little part
Of our two histories; 'twill do thee good
When thou art from me, even if I should
    touch
On things thou canst not know of.——After
    thou
First cam'st into the world—as oft befalls 340
To new-born infants—thou didst sleep away
Two days, and blessings from thy Father's
    tongue
Then fell upon thee. Day by day passed on,
And still I loved thee with increasing love.
Never to living ear came sweeter sounds
Than when I heard thee by our own fire-side
First uttering, without words, a natural tune;
While thou, a feeding babe, didst in thy joy
Sing at thy Mother's breast. Month followed
    month,
And in the open fields my life was passed
And on the mountains; else I think that
    thou   351
Hadst been brought up upon thy Father's
    knees.
But we were playmates, Luke: among these
    hills,
As well thou knowest, in us the old and young
Have played together, nor with me didst thou
Lack any pleasure which a boy can know."
Luke had a manly heart; but at these words
He sobbed aloud. The old Man grasped his
    hand,
And said, "Nay, do not take it so—I see
That these are things of which I need not
    speak.   360
—Even to the utmost I have been to thee
A kind and a good Father: and herein
I but repay a gift which I myself
Received at others' hands; for, though now old
Beyond the common life of man, I still
Remember them who loved me in my youth.
Both of them sleep together: here they lived,
As all their Forefathers had done; and, when

At length their time was come, they were not
 loth
To give their bodies to the family mould.
I wished that thou shouldst live the life they
 lived,   371
But 'tis a long time to look back, my Son,
And see so little gain from threescore years.
These fields were burthened when they came
 to me;
Till I was forty years of age, not more
Than half of my inheritance was mine.
I toiled and toiled; God blessed me in my work,
And till these three weeks past the land was
 free.
—It looks as if it never could endure
Another Master. Heaven forgive me, Luke, 380
If I judge ill for thee, but it seems good
That thou shouldst go."
    At this the old Man paused;
Then, pointing to the stones near which they
 stood,
Thus, after a short silence, he resumed:
"This was a work for us; and now, my Son,
It is a work for me. But, lay one stone—
Here, lay it for me, Luke, with thine own
 hands.
Nay, Boy, be of good hope;—we both may
 live
To see a better day. At eighty-four
I still am strong and hale;—do thou thy
 part;   390
I will do mine.—I will begin again
With many tasks that were resigned to thee:
Up to the heights, and in among the storms,
Will I without thee go again, and do
All works which I was wont to do alone,
Before I knew thy face.—Heaven bless thee,
 . Boy!
Thy heart these two weeks has been beating
 fast
With many hopes; it should be so—yes—
 yes—
I knew that thou couldst never have a wish
To leave me, Luke: thou hast been bound
 to me   400
Only by links of love: when thou art gone,
What will be left to us!—But I forget
My purposes. Lay now the corner-stone,
As I requested; and hereafter, Luke,
When thou art gone away, should evil men
Be thy companions, think of me, my Son,

And of this moment; hither turn thy thoughts,
And God will strengthen thee: amid all fear
And all temptation, Luke, I pray that thou
May'st bear in mind the life thy Fathers
 lived,   410
Who, being innocent, did for that cause
Bestir them in good deeds. Now, fare thee
 well—
When thou return'st, thou in this place wilt
 see
A work which is not here: a covenant
'Twill be between us; but, whatever fate
Befall thee, I shall love thee to the last,
And bear thy memory with me to the grave."

  The Shepherd ended here; and Luke stooped
 down,
And, as his Father had requested, laid
The first stone of the Sheep-fold. At the
 sight   420
The old Man's grief broke from him; to his
 heart
He pressed his Son, he kissèd him and wept;
And to the house together they returned.
—Hushed was that House in peace, or seeming
 peace,
Ere the night fell:—with morrow's dawn the
 Boy
Began his journey, and, when he had reached
The public way, he put on a bold face;
And all the neighbours, as he passed their
 doors,
Came forth with wishes and with farewell
 prayers,
That followed him till he was out of sight. 430

  A good report did from their Kinsman
 come,
Of Luke and his well-doing: and the Boy
Wrote loving letters, full of wondrous news,
Which, as the Housewife phrased it, were
 throughout
"The prettiest letters that were ever seen."
Both parents read them with rejoicing hearts.
So, many months passed on: and once again
The Shepherd went about his daily work
With confident and cheerful thoughts; and
 now
Sometimes when he could find a leisure
 hour   440
He to that valley took his way, and there

Wrought at the Sheep-fold. Meantime Luke
    began
To slacken in his duty; and, at length,
He in the dissolute city gave himself
To evil courses: ignominy and shame
Fell on him, so that he was driven at last
To seek a hiding-place beyond the seas.

    There is a comfort in the strength of love;
'Twill make a thing endurable, which else
Would overset the brain, or break the heart:
I have conversed with more than one who well
Remember the old Man, and what he was 452
Years after he had heard this heavy news.
His bodily frame had been from youth to age
Of an unusual strength. Among the rocks
He went, and still looked up to sun and cloud,
And listened to the wind; and, as before,
Performed all kinds of labour for his sheep,
And for the land, his small inheritance.
And to that hollow dell from time to time 460
Did he repair, to build the Fold of which
His flock had need. 'Tis not forgotten yet
The pity which was then in every heart
For the old Man—and 'tis believed by all
That many and many a day he thither went,
And never lifted up a single stone.

    There, by the Sheep-fold, sometimes was he
    seen
Sitting alone, or with his faithful Dog,
Then old, beside him, lying at his feet.
The length of full seven years, from time to
    time, 470
He at the building of this Sheep-fold wrought,
And left the work unfinished when he died.
Three years, or little more, did Isabel
Survive her Husband: at her death the estate
Was sold, and went into a stranger's hand.
The cottage which was named the EVENING
    STAR
Is gone—the ploughshare has been through
    the ground
On which it stood; great changes have been
    wrought
In all the neighbourhood:—yet the oak is left
That grew beside their door; and the remains
Of the unfinished Sheep-fold may be seen
Beside the boisterous brook of Greenhead
    Ghyll. 482

1800

THE SPARROW'S NEST

BEHOLD, within the leafy shade,
Those bright blue eggs together laid!
On me the chance-discovered sight
Gleamed like a vision of delight.
I started—seeming to espy
The home and sheltered bed,
The Sparrow's dwelling, which, hard by
My Father's house, in wet or dry
My sister Emmeline and I
    Together visited. 10

She looked at it and seemed to fear it;
Dreading, tho' wishing, to be near it:
Such heart was in her, being then
A little Prattler among men.
The Blessing of my later years
Was with me when a boy:
She gave me eyes, she gave me ears;
And humble cares, and delicate fears;
A heart, the fountain of sweet tears;
    And love, and thought, and joy. 20

1801

THE AFFLICTION OF MARGARET ——

Parental love

I

WHERE art thou, my beloved Son,
Where art thou, worse to me than dead?
Oh find me, prosperous or undone!
Or, if the grave be now thy bed,
Why am I ignorant of the same
That I may rest; and neither blame
Nor sorrow may attend thy name?

II

Seven years, alas! to have received
No tidings of an only child;
To have despaired, have hoped, believed, 10
And been for evermore beguiled;
Sometimes with thoughts of very bliss!
I catch at them, and then I miss;
Was ever darkness like to this?

III

He was among the prime in worth,
An object beauteous to behold;
Well born, well bred; I sent him forth
Ingenuous, innocent, and bold:

If things ensued that wanted grace,
As hath been said, they were not base; 20
And never blush was on my face.

IV

Ah! little doth the young-one dream,
When full of play and childish cares,
What power is in his wildest scream,
Heard by his mother unawares!
He knows it not, he cannot guess:
Years to a mother bring distress;
But do not make her love the less.

V

Neglect me! no, I suffered long
From that ill thought; and, being blind, 30
Said, "Pride shall help me in my wrong:
Kind mother have I been, as kind
As ever breathed:" and that is true;
I've wet my path with tears like dew,
Weeping for him when no one knew.

VI

My Son, if thou be humbled, poor,
Hopeless of honour and of gain,
Oh! do not dread thy mother's door:
Think not of me with grief and pain:
I now can see with better eyes; 40
And worldly grandeur I despise,
And fortune with her gifts and lies.

VII

Alas! the fowls of heaven have wings,
And blasts of heaven will aid their flight;
They mount—how short a voyage brings
The wanderers back to their delight!
Chains tie us down by land and sea;
And wishes, vain as mine, may be
All that is left to comfort thee.

VIII

Perhaps some dungeon hears thee groan, 50
Maimed, mangled by inhuman men;
Or thou upon a desert thrown
Inheritest the lion's den;
Or hast been summoned to the deep,
Thou, thou and all thy mates, to keep
An incommunicable sleep.

IX

I look for ghosts; but none will force
Their way to me: 'tis falsely said
That there was ever intercourse
Between the living and the dead; 60

For, surely, then I should have sight
Of him I wait for day and night,
With love and longings infinite.

X

My apprehensions come in crowds;
I dread the rustling of the grass;
The very shadows of the clouds
Have power to shake me as they pass:
I question things and do not find
One that will answer to my mind;
And all the world appears unkind. 70

XI

Beyond participation lie
My troubles, and beyond relief:
If any chance to heave a sigh,
They pity me, and not my grief.
Then come to me, my Son, or send
Some tidings that my woes may end;
I have no other earthly friend!

? 1801

MY HEART LEAPS UP

My heart leaps up when I behold
    A rainbow in the sky:
So was it when my life began;
So is it now I am a man;
So be it when I shall grow old,
    Or let me die!
The Child is father of the Man;
And I could wish my days to be
Bound each to each by natural piety.

1802

TO A BUTTERFLY

Stay near me—do not take thy flight!
A little longer stay in sight!
Much converse do I find in thee,
Historian of my infancy!
Float near me; do not yet depart!
Dead times revive in thee:
Thou bring'st, gay creature as thou art!
A solemn image to my heart,
My father's family!

Oh! pleasant, pleasant were the days, 10
The time, when in our childish plays,
My sister Emmeline and I
Together chased the butterfly!

A very hunter did I rush
Upon the prey;—with leaps and springs
I followed on from brake to bush;
But she, God love her! feared to brush
The dust from off its wings.

1802

TO THE SMALL CELANDINE

PANSIES, lilies, kingcups, daisies,
Let them live upon their praises;
Long as there's a sun that sets,
Primroses will have their glory;
Long as there are violets,
They will have a place in story:
There's a flower that shall be mine,
'Tis the little Celandine.

Eyes of some men travel far
For the finding of a star;   10
Up and down the heavens they go,
Men that keep a mighty rout!
I'm as great as they, I trow,
Since the day I found thee out,
Little Flower—I'll make a stir,
Like a sage astronomer.

Modest, yet withal an Elf
Bold, and lavish of thyself;
Since we needs must first have met
I have seen thee, high and low,   20
Thirty years or more, and yet
'Twas a face I did not know;
Thou hast now, go where I may,
Fifty greetings in a day.

Ere a leaf is on a bush,
In the time before the thrush
Has a thought about her nest,
Thou wilt come with half a call,
Spreading out thy glossy breast
Like a careless Prodigal;   30
Telling tales about the sun,
When we've little warmth, or none.

Poets, vain men in their mood!
Travel with the multitude:
Never heed them; I aver
That they all are wanton wooers;
But the thrifty cottager,
Who stirs little out of doors,
Joys to spy thee near her home;
Spring is coming, Thou art come!   40

Comfort have thou of thy merit,
Kindly, unassuming Spirit!
Careless of thy neighbourhood,
Thou dost show thy pleasant face
On the moor, and in the wood,
In the lane;—there's not a place,
Howsoever mean it be,
But 'tis good enough for thee.

Ill befall the yellow flowers,
Children of the flaring hours!   50
Buttercups, that will be seen,
Whether we will see or no;
Others, too, of lofty mien;
They have done as worldlings do,
Taken praise that should be thine,
Little, humble Celandine.

Prophet of delight and mirth,
Ill-requited upon earth;
Herald of a mighty band,
Of a joyous train ensuing,   60
Serving at my heart's command,
Tasks that are no tasks renewing,
I will sing, as doth behove,
Hymns in praise of what I love!

1802

TO THE DAISY

"Her divine skill taught me this,
That from every thing I saw
I could some instruction draw,
And raise pleasure to the height
Through the meanest object's sight.
By the murmur of a spring,
Or the least bough's rustelling;
By a Daisy whose leaves spread
Shut when Titan goes to bed;
Or a shady bush or tree;
She could more infuse in me
Than all Nature's beauties can
In some other wiser man."

G. WITHER

IN youth from rock to rock I went,
From hill to hill in discontent
Of pleasure high and turbulent,
    Most pleased when most uneasy;
But now my own delights I make,—
My thirst at every rill can slake,
And gladly Nature's love partake
    Of Thee, sweet Daisy!

Thee Winter in the garland wears
That thinly decks his few grey hairs;   10
Spring parts the clouds with softest airs,
   That she may sun thee;
Whole Summer-fields are thine by right;
And Autumn, melancholy Wight!
Doth in thy crimson head delight
   When rains are on thee.

In shoals and bands, a morrice train,
Thou greet'st the traveller in the lane;
Pleased at his greeting thee again;
   Yet nothing daunted,   20
Nor grieved if thou be set at nought:
And oft alone in nooks remote
We meet thee, like a pleasant thought,
   When such are wanted.

Be violets in their secret mews
The flowers the wanton Zephyrs choose;
Proud be the rose, with rains and dews
   Her head impearling,
Thou liv'st with less ambitious aim,
Yet hast not gone without thy fame;   30
Thou art indeed by many a claim
   The Poet's darling.

If to a rock from rains he fly,
Or, some bright day of April sky,
Imprisoned by hot sunshine lie
   Near the green holly,
And wearily at length should fare;
He needs but look about, and there
Thou art!—a friend at hand, to scare
   His melancholy.   40

A hundred times, by rock or bower,
Ere thus I have lain couched an hour,
Have I derived from thy sweet power
   Some apprehension;
Some steady love; some brief delight;
Some memory that had taken flight;
Some chime of fancy wrong or right;
   Or stray invention.

If stately passions in me burn,
And one chance look to Thee should turn,   50
I drink out of an humbler urn
   A lowlier pleasure;
The homely sympathy that heeds
The common life our nature breeds;
A wisdom fitted to the needs
   Of hearts at leisure.

Fresh-smitten by the morning ray,
When thou art up, alert and gay,
Then, cheerful Flower! my spirits play
   With kindred gladness: 60
And when, at dusk, by dews opprest
Thou sink'st, the image of thy rest
Hath often eased my pensive breast
   Of careful sadness.

And all day long I number yet,
All seasons through, another debt,
Which I, wherever thou art met,
   To thee am owing;
An instinct call it, a blind sense;
A happy, genial influence,   70
Coming one knows not how, nor whence,
   Nor whither going.

Child of the Year! that round dost run
Thy pleasant course,—when day's begun
As ready to salute the sun
   As lark or leveret,
Thy long-lost praise thou shalt regain;
Nor be less dear to future men
Than in old time;—thou not in vain
   Art Nature's favourite.   80

1802

TO THE SAME FLOWER

WITH little here to do or see
Of things that in the great world be,
Daisy! again I talk to thee,
   For thou art worthy,
Thou unassuming Common-place
Of Nature, with that homely face,
And yet with something of a grace
   Which love makes for thee!

Oft on the dappled turf at ease
I sit, and play with similes,   10
Loose types of things through all degrees,
   Thoughts of thy raising:
And many a fond and idle name
I give to thee, for praise or blame,
As is the humour of the game,
   While I am gazing.

A nun demure of lowly port;
Or sprightly maiden, of Love's court,
In thy simplicity the sport
   Of all temptations;   20

A queen in crown of rubies drest;
A starveling in a scanty vest;
Are all, as seems to suit thee best,
    Thy appellations.

A little Cyclops with one eye
Staring to threaten and defy,
That thought comes next—and instantly
    The freak is over,
The shape will vanish—and behold
A silver shield with boss of gold,   30
That spreads itself, some faery bold
    In fight to cover!

I see thee glittering from afar—
And then thou art a pretty star;
Not quite so fair as many are
    In heaven above thee!
Yet like a star, with glittering crest,
Self-poised in air thou seem'st to rest;—
May peace come never to his nest,
    Whom shall reprove thee!   40

Bright *Flower!* for by that name at last,
When all my reveries are past,
I call thee, and to that cleave fast,
    Sweet silent creature!
That breath'st with me in sun and air,
Do thou, as thou art wont, repair
My heart with gladness, and a share
    Of thy meek nature!

1802

TO THE DAISY

BRIGHT Flower! whose home is everywhere,
Bold in maternal Nature's care,
And all the long year through the heir
    Of joy and sorrow;
Methinks that there abides in thee
Some concord with humanity,
Given to no other flower I see
    The forest thorough!

Is it that Man is soon deprest?
A thoughtless Thing! who, once unblest,   10
Does little on his memory rest,
    Or on his reason,
And Thou wouldst teach him how to find
A shelter under every wind,
A hope for times that are unkind
    And every season?

Thou wander'st the wide world about,
Unchecked by pride or scrupulous doubt,
With friends to greet thee, or without,
    Yet pleased and willing;   20
Meek, yielding to the occasion's call,
And all things suffering from all.
Thy function apostolical
    In peace fulfilling.

1802

TO THE CUCKOO

O BLITHE New-comer! I have heard,
I hear thee and rejoice.
O Cuckoo! shall I call thee Bird,
Or but a wandering Voice?

While I am lying on the grass
Thy twofold shout I hear;
From hill to hill it seems to pass
At once far off, and near.

Though babbling only to the Vale,
Of sunshine and of flowers,   10
Thou bringest unto me a tale
Of visionary hours.

Thrice welcome, darling of the Spring!
Even yet thou art to me
No bird, but an invisible thing,
A voice, a mystery;

The same whom in my schoolboy days
I listened to; that Cry
Which made me look a thousand ways
In bush, and tree, and sky.   20

To seek thee did I often rove
Through woods and on the green;
And thou wert still a hope, a love;
Still longed for, never seen.

And I can listen to thee yet;
Can lie upon the plain
And listen, till I do beget
That golden time again.

O blessèd Bird! the earth we pace
Again appears to be   30
An unsubstantial, faery place;
That is fit home for Thee!

1802

RESOLUTION AND INDEPENDENCE

[handwritten: rime royal]

I

THERE was a roaring in the wind all night;
The rain came heavily and fell in floods;
But now the sun is rising calm and bright;
The birds are singing in the distant woods;
Over his own sweet voice the Stock-dove
broods;
The Jay makes answer as the Magpie chatters;
And all the air is filled with pleasant noise of
waters.

II

All things that love the sun are out of doors;
The sky rejoices in the morning's birth;
The grass is bright with rain-drops;—on the
moors   10
The hare is running races in her mirth;
And with her feet she from the plashy earth
Raises a mist; that, glittering in the sun,
Runs with her all the way, wherever she doth
run.

III

I was a Traveller then upon the moor;
I saw the hare that raced about with joy;
I heard the woods and distant waters roar;
Or heard them not, as happy as a boy:
The pleasant season did my heart employ:
My old remembrances went from me wholly;
And all the ways of men, so vain and melan-
choly.   21

IV

But, as it sometimes chanceth, from the might
Of joy in minds that can no further go,
As high as we have mounted in delight
In our dejection do we sink as low;
To me that morning did it happen so;
And fears and fancies thick upon me came;
Dim sadness—and blind thoughts, I knew
not, nor could name.

[handwritten: says same in lines written early spring]

V

I heard the sky-lark warbling in the sky;
And I bethought me of the playful hare: 30
Even such a happy Child of earth am I;
Even as these blissful creatures do I fare;
Far from the world I walk, and from all care;
But there may come another day to me—
Solitude, pain of heart, distress, and poverty.

VI

My whole life I have lived in pleasant thought,
As if life's business were a summer mood;
As if all needful things would come unsought
To genial faith, still rich in genial good;
But how can he expect that others should   40
Build for him, sow for him, and at his call
Love him, who for himself will take no heed
at all?

VII

I thought of Chatterton, the marvellous Boy,
The sleepless Soul that perished in his pride;
Of Him who walked in glory and in joy
Following his plough, along the mountain-
side: *[handwritten: Burns]*
By our own spirits are we deified:
We Poets in our youth begin in gladness;
But thereof come in the end despondency and
madness.

VIII

Now, whether it were by peculiar grace,   50
A leading from above, a something given,
Yet it befell that, in this lonely place,
When I with these untoward thoughts had
striven,
Beside a pool bare to the eye of heaven
I saw a Man before me unawares:
The oldest man he seemed that ever wore grey
hairs.

IX

As a huge stone is sometimes seen to lie
Couched on the bald top of an eminence;
Wonder to all who do the same espy,
By what means it could thither come, and
whence;   60
So that it seems a thing endued with sense:
Like a sea-beast crawled forth, that on a shelf
Of rock or sand reposeth, there to sun itself;

[handwritten marginalia: however in const.]

X

Such seemed this Man, not all alive nor dead,
Nor all asleep—in his extreme old age:
His body was bent double, feet and head
Coming together in life's pilgrimage;
As if some dire constraint of pain, or rage
Of sickness felt by him in times long past,
A more than human weight upon his frame
had cast.   70

XI

Himself he propped, limbs, body, and pale
    face,
Upon a long grey staff of shaven wood:
And, still as I drew near with gentle pace,
Upon the margin of that moorish flood
Motionless as a cloud the old Man stood,
That heareth not the loud winds when they
    call;
And moveth all together, if it move at all.

XII

At length, himself unsettling, he the pond
Stirred with his staff, and fixedly did look
Upon the muddy water, which he conned,
As if he had been reading in a book: 81
And now a stranger's privilege I took;
And, drawing to his side, to him did say,
"This morning gives us promise of a glorious
    day."

XIII

A gentle answer did the old Man make,
In courteous speech which forth he slowly
    drew:
And him with further words I thus bespake,
"What occupation do you there pursue?
This is a lonesome place for one like you."
Ere he replied, a flash of mild surprise   90
Broke from the sable orbs of his yet-vivid eyes.

XIV

His words came feebly, from a feeble chest,
But each in solemn order followed each,
With something of a lofty utterance drest—
Choice word and measured phrase, above the
    reach
Of ordinary men; a stately speech;
Such as grave Livers do in Scotland use,
Religious men, who give to God and man
    their dues.

XV

He told, that to these waters he had come
To gather leeches, being old and poor: 100
Employment hazardous and wearisome!
And he had many hardships to endure:
From pond to pond he roamed, from moor to
    moor;
Housing, with God's good help, by choice or
    chance;
And in this way he gained an honest main-
    tenance.

XVI

The old Man still stood talking by my side;
But now his voice to me was like a stream
Scarce heard; nor word from word could I
    divide;
And the whole body of the Man did seem
Like one whom I had met with in a dream;   110
Or like a man from some far region sent,
To give me human strength, by apt ad-
    monishment.

XVII

My former thoughts returned: the fear that
    kills;
And hope that is unwilling to be fed;
Cold, pain, and labour, and all fleshly ills;
And mighty Poets in their misery dead.
—Perplexed, and longing to be comforted,
My question eagerly did I renew,
"How is it that you live, and what is it you
    do?"

XVIII

He with a smile did then his words repeat;
And said that, gathering leeches, far and wide
He travelled; stirring thus about his feet   122
The waters of the pools where they abide.
"Once I could meet with them on every side;
But they have dwindled long by slow decay;
Yet still I persevere, and find them where I
    may."

XIX

While he was talking thus, the lonely place,
The old Man's shape, and speech—all troubled
    me:
In my mind's eye I seemed to see him pace
About the weary moors continually,   130
Wandering about alone and silently.
While I these thoughts within myself pur-
    sued,
He, having made a pause, the same discourse
    renewed.

XX

And soon with this he other matter blended,
Cheerfully uttered, with demeanour kind,
But stately in the main; and, when he ended,
I could have laughed myself to scorn to find
In that decrepit Man so firm a mind.
"God," said I, "be my help and stay secure;
I'll think of the Leech-gatherer on the lonely
    moor!"   140

1802

IT IS A BEAUTEOUS EVENING

IT is a beauteous evening, calm and free,
The holy time is quiet as a Nun
Breathless with adoration; the broad sun
Is sinking down in its tranquillity;
The gentleness of heaven broods o'er the Sea:
Listen! the mighty Being is awake,
And doth with his eternal motion make
A sound like thunder—everlastingly.
Dear Child! dear Girl! that walkest with me
   here, *daughter - Jr.*
If thou appear untouched by solemn thought,
Thy nature is not therefore less divine: 11
Thou liest in Abraham's bosom all the year;
And worshipp'st at the Temple's inner shrine,
God being with thee when we know it not.
1802

WHERE LIES THE LAND

WHERE lies the Land to which yon Ship must
   go?
Fresh as a lark mounting at break of day,
Festively she puts forth in trim array;
Is she for tropic suns, or polar snow?
What boots the enquiry?—Neither friend nor
   foe
She cares for; let her travel where she may,
She finds familiar names, a beaten way
Ever before her, and a wind to blow.
Yet still I ask, what haven is her mark?
And, almost as it was when ships were rare, 10
(From time to time, like Pilgrims, here and
   there
Crossing the waters) doubt, and something
   dark,
Of the old Sea some reverential fear,
Is with me at thy farewell, joyous Bark!
? Pub. 1807

WITH HOW SAD STEPS

WITH how sad steps, O Moon, thou climb'st
   the sky,
"How silently, and with how wan a face!"
Where art thou? Thou so often seen on high
Running among the clouds a Wood-nymph's
   race!
Unhappy Nuns, whose common breath's a sigh
Which they would stifle, move at such a pace!

The northern Wind, to call thee to the chase,
Must blow to-night his bugle horn. Had I
The power of Merlin, Goddess! this should be:
And all the stars, fast as the clouds were
   riven,   10
Should sally forth, to keep thee company,
Hurrying and sparkling through the clear blue
   heaven;
But, Cynthia! should to thee the palm be given,
Queen both for beauty and for majesty.
1802

COMPOSED UPON WESTMINSTER
BRIDGE, SEPTEMBER 3, 1802

EARTH has not anything to show more fair:
Dull would he be of soul who could pass by
A sight so touching in its majesty:
This City now doth, like a garment, wear
The beauty of the morning; silent, bare,
Ships, towers, domes, theatres, and temples lie
Open unto the fields, and to the sky;
All bright and glittering in the smokeless air.
Never did sun more beautifully steep
In his first splendour, valley, rock, or hill; 10
Ne'er saw I, never felt, a calm so deep!
The river glideth at his own sweet will:
Dear God! the very houses seem asleep;
And all that mighty heart is lying still!
1802

WRITTEN IN LONDON,
SEPTEMBER, 1802

O FRIEND! I know not which way I must look
For comfort, being, as I am, opprest,
To think that now our life is only drest
For show; mean handy-work of craftsman,
   cook,
Or groom!—We must run glittering like a
   brook
In the open sunshine, or we are unblest:
The wealthiest man among us is the best:
No grandeur now in nature or in book
Delights us. Rapine, avarice, expense,
This is idolatry; and these we adore: 10
Plain living and high thinking are no more:
The homely beauty of the good old cause
Is gone; our peace, our fearful innocence,
And pure religion breathing household laws.
1802

LONDON, 1802

MILTON! thou shouldst be living at this hour:
England hath need of thee: she is a fen
Of stagnant waters: altar, sword, and pen,
Fireside, the heroic wealth of hall and bower,
Have forfeited their ancient English dower
Of inward happiness. We are selfish men;
Oh! raise us up, return to us again;
And give us manners, virtue, freedom, power.
Thy soul was like a Star, and dwelt apart;
Thou hadst a voice whose sound was like the
     sea: 10
Pure as the naked heavens, majestic, free,
So didst thou travel on life's common way,
In cheerful godliness; and yet thy heart
The lowliest duties on herself did lay.

1802

IT IS NOT TO BE THOUGHT OF

IT is not to be thought of that the Flood
Of British freedom, which, to the open sea
Of the world's praise, from dark antiquity
Hath flowed, "with pomp of waters, unwith-
     stood,"
Roused though it be full often to a mood
Which spurns the check of salutary bands,
That this most famous Stream in bogs and
     sands
Should perish; and to evil and to good
Be lost for ever. In our halls is hung
Armoury of the invincible Knights of old: 10
We must be free or die, who speak the tongue
That Shakespeare spake; the faith and morals
     hold
Which Milton held.—In every thing we are
     sprung
Of Earth's first blood, have titles manifold.

1802 or 1803

ON THE EXTINCTION OF THE
VENETIAN REPUBLIC

ONCE did She hold the gorgeous east in fee;
And was the safeguard of the west: the worth
Of Venice did not fall below her birth,
Venice, the eldest Child of Liberty.
She was a maiden City, bright and free;
No guile seduced, no force could violate;
And, when she took unto herself a Mate,

She must espouse the everlasting Sea.
And what if she had seen those glories fade,
Those titles vanish, and that strength decay; 10
Yet shall some tribute of regret be paid
When her long life hath reached its final day:
Men are we, and must grieve when even the
     Shade
Of that which once was great is passed away.

1802

TO TOUSSAINT L'OUVERTURE

TOUSSAINT, the most unhappy man of men!
Whether the whistling Rustic tend his plough
Within thy hearing, or thy head be now
Pillowed in some deep dungeon's earless
     den;—
O miserable Chieftain! where and when
Wilt thou find patience! Yet die not; do
     thou
Wear rather in thy bonds a cheerful brow:
Though fallen thyself, never to rise again,
Live, and take comfort. Thou hast left behind
Powers that will work for thee; air, earth, and
     skies;   10
There's not a breathing of the common
     wind
That will forget thee; thou hast great allies;
Thy friends are exultations, agonies,
And love, and man's unconquerable mind.

1802

COMPOSED IN THE VALLEY NEAR
DOVER ON THE DAY OF
LANDING

HERE, on our native soil, we breathe once
     more.
The cock that crows, the smoke that curls,
     that sound
Of bells;—those boys who in yon meadow-
     ground
In white-sleeved shirts are playing; and the
     roar
Of the waves breaking on the chalky shore;—
All, all are English. Oft have I looked round
With joy in Kent's green vales; but never
     found
Myself so satisfied in heart before.
Europe is yet in bonds; but let that pass,

Thought for another moment. Thou art
      free,   10
My Country! and 'tis joy enough and pride
For one hour's perfect bliss, to tread the
      grass
Of England once again, and hear and see,
With such a dear Companion at my side.

1802

SEPTEMBER, 1802. NEAR DOVER

INLAND, within a hollow vale, I stood;
And saw, while sea was calm and air was
      clear,
The coast of France—the coast of France how
      near!
Drawn almost into frightful neighbourhood.
I shrunk; for verily the barrier flood
Was like a lake, or river bright and fair,
A span of waters; yet what power is there!
What mightiness for evil and for good!
Even so doth God protect us if we be
Virtuous and wise. Winds blow, and waters
      roll,   10
Strength to the brave, and Power, and Deity;
Yet in themselves are nothing! One decree
Spake laws to *them*, and said that by the
      soul
Only, the Nations shall be great and free.

1802

COMPOSED BY THE SEA-SIDE, NEAR CALAIS, AUGUST, 1802

FAIR Star of evening, Splendour of the west,
Star of my Country! — on the horizon's
      brink
Thou hangest, stooping, as might seem, to
      sink
On England's bosom; yet well pleased to
      rest,
Meanwhile, and be to her a glorious crest
Conspicuous to the Nations. Thou, I think,
Shouldst be my Country's emblem; and
      shouldst wink,
Bright Star! with laughter on her banners,
      drest
In thy fresh beauty. There! that dusky spot
Beneath thee, that is England; there she lies. 10
Blessings be on you both! one hope, one lot,

One life, one glory!—I, with many a fear
For my dear Country, many heartfelt sighs,
Among men who do not love her, linger here.

1802

THE GREEN LINNET

BENEATH these fruit-tree boughs that shed
Their snow-white blossoms on my head,
With brightest sunshine round me spread
      Of spring's unclouded weather,
In this sequestered nook how sweet
To sit upon my orchard-seat!
And birds and flowers once more to greet,
      My last year's friends together.

One have I marked, the happiest guest
In all this covert of the blest: 10
Hail to Thee, far above the rest
      In joy of voice and pinion!
Thou, Linnet! in thy green array,
Presiding Spirit here to-day,
Dost lead the revels of the May;
      And this is thy dominion.

While birds, and butterflies, and flowers,
Make all one band of paramours,
Thou, ranging up and down the bowers,
      Art sole in thy employment: 20
A Life, a Presence like the Air,
Scattering thy gladness without care,
Too blest with any one to pair;
      Thyself thy own enjoyment.

Amid yon tuft of hazel trees,
That twinkle to the gusty breeze,
Behold him perched in ecstasies,
      Yet seeming still to hover;
There! where the flutter of his wings
Upon his back and body flings   30
Shadows and sunny glimmerings,
      That cover him all over.

My dazzled sight he oft deceives,
A Brother of the dancing leaves;
Then flits, and from the cottage eaves
      Pours forth his song in gushes;
As if by that exulting strain
He mocked and treated with disdain
The voiceless Form he chose to feign,
      While fluttering in the bushes.   40

1803

THE SOLITARY REAPER

BEHOLD her, single in the field,
Yon solitary Highland Lass!
Reaping and singing by herself;
Stop here, or gently pass!
Alone she cuts and binds the grain,
And sings a melancholy strain;
O listen! for the Vale profound
Is overflowing with the sound.

No Nightingale did ever chaunt
More welcome notes to weary bands   10
Of travellers in some shady haunt,
Among Arabian sands:
A voice so thrilling ne'er was heard
In spring-time from the Cuckoo-bird,
Breaking the silence of the seas
Among the farthest Hebrides.

Will no one tell me what she sings?—
Perhaps the plaintive numbers flow
For old, unhappy, far-off things,
And battles long ago: 20
Or is it some more humble lay,
Familiar matter of to-day?
Some natural sorrow, loss, or pain,
That has been, and may be again?

Whate'er the theme, the Maiden sang
As if her song could have no ending;
I saw her singing at her work,
And o'er the sickle bending;—
I listened, motionless and still;
And, as I mounted up the hill,   30
The music in my heart I bore,
Long after it was heard no more.

1803

TO A HIGHLAND GIRL

AT INVERSNEYDE, UPON LOCH LOMOND

SWEET Highland Girl, a very shower
Of beauty is thy earthly dower!
Twice seven consenting years have shed
Their utmost bounty on thy head:
And these grey rocks; that household
     lawn;
Those trees, a veil just half withdrawn;
This fall of water that doth make
A murmur near the silent lake;

This little bay; a quiet road
That holds in shelter thy Abode—   10
In truth together do ye seem
Like something fashioned in a dream;
Such Forms as from their covert peep
When earthly cares are laid asleep!
But, O fair Creature! in the light
Of common day, so heavenly bright,
I bless Thee, Vision as thou art,
I bless thee with a human heart;
God shield thee to thy latest years!
Thee, neither know I, nor thy peers;   20
And yet my eyes are filled with tears.

With earnest feeling I shall pray
For thee when I am far away:
For never saw I mien, or face,
In which more plainly I could trace
Benignity and home-bred sense
Ripening in perfect innocence.
Here scattered, like a random seed,
Remote from men, Thou dost not need
The embarrassed look of shy distress,   30
And maidenly shamefacedness:
Thou wear'st upon thy forehead clear
The freedom of a Mountaineer:
A face with gladness overspread!
Soft smiles, by human kindness bred!
And seemliness complete, that sways
Thy courtesies, about thee plays;
With no restraint, but such as springs
From quick and eager visitings
Of thoughts that lie beyond the reach   40
Of thy few words of English speech:
A bondage sweetly brooked, a strife
That gives thy gestures grace and life!
So have I, not unmoved in mind,
Seen birds of tempest-loving kind—
Thus beating up against the wind.

What hand but would a garland cull
For thee who art so beautiful?
O happy pleasure! here to dwell
Beside thee in some heathy dell;   50
Adopt your homely ways, and dress,
A Shepherd, thou a Shepherdess!
But I could frame a wish for thee
More like a grave reality:
Thou art to me but as a wave
Of the wild sea; and I would have
Some claim upon thee, if I could,
Though but of common neighbourhood.

What joy to hear thee, and to see!
Thy elder Brother I would be,   60
Thy Father—anything to thee!

Now thanks to Heaven! that of its grace
Hath led me to this lonely place.
Joy have I had; and going hence
I bear away my recompense.
In spots like these it is we prize
Our Memory, feel that she hath eyes:
Then, why should I be loth to stir?
I feel this place was made for her;
To give new pleasure like the past,   70
Continued long as life shall last.
Nor am I loth, though pleased at heart,
Sweet Highland Girl! from thee to part;
For I, methinks, till I grow old,
As fair before me shall behold,
As I do now, the cabin small,
The lake, the bay, the waterfall;
And Thee, the Spirit of them all!

1803

YEW–TREES

THERE is a Yew-tree, pride of Lorton Vale,
Which to this day stands single, in the midst
Of its own darkness, as it stood of yore:
Not loth to furnish weapons for the bands
Of Umfraville or Percy ere they marched
To Scotland's heaths; or those that crossed the
sea
And drew their sounding bows at Azincour,
Perhaps at earlier Crecy, or Poictiers.
Of vast circumference and gloom profound
This solitary Tree! a living thing   10
Produced too slowly ever to decay;
Of form and aspect too magnificent
To be destroyed. But worthier still of note
Are those fraternal Four of Borrowdale,
Joined in one solemn and capacious grove;
Huge trunks! and each particular trunk a
growth
Of intertwisted fibres serpentine
Up-coiling, and inveterately convolved;
Nor uninformed with Phantasy, and looks
That threaten the profane; a pillared shade, 20
Upon whose grassless floor of red-brown hue,
By sheddings from the pining umbrage
tinged
Perennially—beneath whose sable roof

Of boughs, as if for festal purpose decked
With unrejoicing berries—ghostly Shapes
May meet at noontide; Fear and trembling
Hope,
Silence and Foresight; Death the Skeleton
And Time the Shadow;—there to celebrate,
As in a natural temple scattered o'er
With altars undisturbed of mossy stone,   30
United worship; or in mute repose
To lie, and listen to the mountain flood
Murmuring from Glaramara's inmost caves.

1803

AT THE GRAVE OF BURNS
1803
SEVEN YEARS AFTER HIS DEATH

I SHIVER, Spirit fierce and bold,
At thought of what I now behold:
As vapours breathed from dungeons cold
Strike pleasure dead,
So sadness comes from out the mould
Where Burns is laid.

And have I then thy bones so near,
And thou forbidden to appear?
As if it were thyself that's here
I shrink with pain;   10
And both my wishes and my fear
Alike are vain.

Off weight—nor press on weight!—away
Dark thoughts!—they came, but not to stay;
With chastened feelings would I pay
The tribute due
To him, and aught that hides his clay
From mortal view.

Fresh as the flower, whose modest worth
He sang, his genius "glinted" forth,   20
Rose like a star that touching earth,
For so it seems,
Doth glorify its humble birth
With matchless beams.

The piercing eye, the thoughtful brow,
The struggling heart, where be they now?—
Full soon the Aspirant of the plough,
The prompt, the brave,
Slept, with the obscurest, in the low
And silent grave.   30

I mourned with thousands, but as one
More deeply grieved, for He was gone
Whose light I hailed when first it shone,
    And showed my youth
How Verse may build a princely throne
    On humble truth.

Alas! where'er the current tends,
Regret pursues and with it blends,—
Huge Criffel's hoary top ascends
    By Skiddaw seen,—   40
Neighbours we were, and loving friends
    We might have been;

True friends though diversely inclined;
But heart with heart and mind with mind,
Where the main fibres are entwined,
    Through Nature's skill,
May even by contraries be joined
    More closely still.

The tear will start, and let it flow;
Thou "poor Inhabitant below,"   50
At this dread moment—even so—
    Might we together
Have sate and talked where gowans blow,
    Or on wild heather.

What treasures would have then been placed
Within my reach; of knowledge graced
By fancy what a rich repast!
    But why go on?—
Oh! spare to sweep, thou mournful blast,
    His grave grass-grown.   60

There, too, a Son, his joy and pride,
(Not three weeks past the Stripling died,)
Lies gathered to his Father's side,
    Soul-moving sight!
Yet one to which is not denied
    Some sad delight.

For *he* is safe, a quiet bed
Hath early found among the dead,
Harboured where none can be misled,
    Wronged, or distrest;   70
And surely here it may be said
    That such are blest.

And oh for Thee, by pitying grace
Checked oft-times in a devious race,
May He, who halloweth the place
    Where Man is laid,
Receive thy Spirit in the embrace
    For which it prayed!

Sighing I turned away; but ere
Night fell I heard, or seemed to hear,   80
Music that sorrow comes not near,
    A ritual hymn,
Chanted in love that casts out fear
    By Seraphim.

1803

YARROW UNVISITED

FROM Stirling castle we had seen
The mazy Forth unravelled;
Had trod the banks of Clyde, and Tay,
And with the Tweed had travelled;
And when we came to Clovenford,
Then said my "*winsome Marrow*,"
"Whate'er betide, we'll turn aside,
And see the Braes of Yarrow."

"Let Yarrow folk, *frae* Selkirk town,
Who have been buying, selling,   10
Go back to Yarrow, 'tis their own;
Each maiden to her dwelling!
On Yarrow's banks let herons feed,
Hares couch, and rabbits burrow!
But we will downward with the Tweed,
Nor turn aside to Yarrow.

"There's Galla Water, Leader Haughs,
Both lying right before us;
And Dryborough, where with chiming Tweed
The lintwhites sing in chorus;   20
There's pleasant Tiviot-dale, a land
Made blithe with plough and harrow:
Why throw away a needful day
To go in search of Yarrow?

"What's Yarrow but a river bare,
That glides the dark hills under?
There are a thousand such elsewhere
As worthy of your wonder."
—Strange words they seemed of slight and
    scorn;
My True-love sighed for sorrow;   30
And looked me in the face, to think
I thus could speak of Yarrow!

"Oh! green," said I, "are Yarrow's holms,
And sweet is Yarrow flowing!
Fair hangs the apple frae the rock,
But we will leave it growing.

O'er hilly path, and open Strath,
We'll wander Scotland thorough;
But, though so near, we will not turn
Into the dale of Yarrow.   40

"Let beeves and home-bred kine partake
The sweets of Burn-mill meadow;
The swan on still St. Mary's Lake
Float double, swan and shadow!
We will not see them; will not go,
To-day, nor yet to-morrow;
Enough if in our hearts we know
There's such a place as Yarrow.

"Be Yarrow stream unseen, unknown!
It must, or we shall rue it: 50
We have a vision of our own;
Ah! why should we undo it?
The treasured dreams of times long past,
We'll keep them, winsome Marrow!
For when we're there, although 'tis fair,
'Twill be another Yarrow!

"If Care with freezing years should come,
And wandering seem but folly,—
Should we be loth to stir from home,
And yet be melancholy;   60
Should life be dull, and spirits low,
'Twill soothe us in our sorrow,
That earth hath something yet to show,
The bonny holms of Yarrow!"

1803

STEPPING WESTWARD

While my Fellow-traveller and I were walking by the side of Loch Ketterine, one fine evening after sunset, in our road to a Hut where, in the course of our Tour, we had been hospitably entertained some weeks before, we met, in one of the loneliest parts of that solitary region, two well-dressed Women, one of whom said to us, by way of greeting, "What, you are stepping westward?" (*Wordsworth's note.*)

"*What*, you are stepping *westward?*"—
     "*Yea*."
—'Twould be a *wildish* destiny,
If we, who thus together roam
In a strange Land, and far from home,
Were in this place the guests of Chance:
Yet who would stop, or fear to advance,
Though home or shelter he had none,
With such a sky to lead him on?

The dewy ground was dark and cold;
Behind, all gloomy to behold;   10
And stepping westward seemed to be
A kind of *heavenly* destiny:
I liked the greeting; 'twas a sound
Of something without place or bound;
And seemed to give me spiritual right
To travel through that region bright.

The voice was soft, and she who spake
Was walking by her native lake:
The salutation had to me
The very sound of courtesy: 20
Its power was felt; and while my eye
Was fixed upon the glowing Sky,
The echo of the voice enwrought
A human sweetness with the thought
Of travelling through the world that lay
Before me in my endless way.

1803

ODE

INTIMATIONS OF IMMORTALITY FROM RECOLLECTIONS OF EARLY CHILDHOOD

The Child is father of the Man;
And I could wish my days to be
Bound each to each by natural piety.

I

THERE was a time when meadow, grove, and
     stream,
The earth, and every common sight,
     To me did seem
     Apparelled in celestial light,
The glory and the freshness of a dream.
It is not now as it hath been of yore;—
     Turn wheresoe'er I may,
     By night or day,
The things which I have seen I now can see no
     more.

II

     The Rainbow comes and goes,   10
     And lovely is the Rose,
     The Moon doth with delight
Look round her when the heavens are bare,
     Waters on a starry night
     Are beautiful and fair;
The sunshine is a glorious birth;
     But yet I know, where'er I go,
That there hath past away a glory from the
     earth.

III

Now, while the birds thus sing a joyous song,
   And while the young lambs bound   20
     As to the tabor's sound,
To me alone there came a thought of grief:
A timely utterance gave that thought relief,
     And I again am strong:
The cataracts blow their trumpets from the
     steep;
No more shall grief of mine the season wrong;
I hear the Echoes through the mountains
     throng,
The Winds come to me from the fields of sleep,
     And all the earth is gay;
       Land and sea   30
       Give themselves up to jollity,
       And with the heart of May
       Doth every Beast keep holiday;—
        Thou Child of Joy,
Shout round me, let me hear thy shouts, thou
     happy Shepherd-boy!

IV

Ye blessèd Creatures, I have heard the call
   Ye to each other make; I see
The heavens laugh with you in your jubilee;
     My heart is at your festival,
     My head hath its coronal,   40
The fulness of your bliss, I feel—I feel it all.
     Oh evil day! if I were sullen
     While Earth herself is adorning,
      This sweet May-morning,
     And the Children are culling
       On every side,
     In a thousand valleys far and wide,
     Fresh flowers; while the sun shines
      warm,
And the Babe leaps up on his Mother's arm:—
     I hear, I hear, with joy I hear!   50
     —But there's a Tree, of many, one,
A single Field which I have looked upon,
Both of them speak of something that is gone:
     The Pansy at my feet
     Doth the same tale repeat:
Whither is fled the visionary gleam?
Where is it now, the glory and the dream?

V

Our birth is but a sleep and a forgetting:
The Soul that rises with us, our life's Star,
     Hath had elsewhere its setting,   60
     And cometh from afar:

     Not in entire forgetfulness,
     And not in utter nakedness,
But trailing clouds of glory do we come
     From God, who is our home:
Heaven lies about us in our infancy!
Shades of the prison-house begin to close
     Upon the growing Boy,
But He beholds the light, and whence it flows,
     He sees it in his joy;   70
The Youth, who daily farther from the east
     Must travel, still is Nature's Priest,
     And by the vision splendid
     Is on his way attended;
At length the Man perceives it die away,
And fade into the light of common day.

VI

Earth fills her lap with pleasures of her own;
Yearnings she hath in her own natural kind,
And, even with something of a Mother's mind,
     And no unworthy aim,   80
     The homely Nurse doth all she can
To make her Foster-child, her Inmate Man,
     Forget the glories he hath known,
And that imperial palace whence he came.

VII

Behold the Child among his new-born blisses,
A six years' Darling of a pigmy size!
See, where 'mid work of his own hand he lies,
Fretted by sallies of his mother's kisses,
With light upon him from his father's eyes!
See, at his feet, some little plan or chart,   90
Some fragment from his dream of human life,
Shaped by himself with newly-learned art;
     A wedding or a festival,
     A mourning or a funeral;
      And this hath now his heart,
     And unto this he frames his song:
      Then will he fit his tongue
To dialogues of business, love, or strife;
     But it will not be long
     Ere this be thrown aside,   100
     And with new joy and pride
The little Actor cons another part;
Filling from time to time his "humorous
     stage"
With all the Persons, down to palsied Age,
That Life brings with her in her equipage;
     As if his whole vocation
     Were endless imitation.

VIII

Thou, whose exterior semblance doth belie
   Thy Soul's immensity;
Thou best Philosopher, who yet dost keep 110
Thy heritage, thou Eye among the blind,
That, deaf and silent, read'st the eternal deep,
Haunted for ever by the eternal mind,—
   Mighty Prophet! Seer blest!
   On whom those truths do rest,
Which we are toiling all our lives to find,
In darkness lost, the darkness of the grave;
Thou, over whom thy Immortality
Broods like the Day, a Master o'er a Slave,
A Presence which is not to be put by;   120
   [To whom the grave
Is but a lonely bed without the sense or sight
   Of day or the warm light,
A place of thought where we in waiting lie;]
Thou little Child, yet glorious in the might
Of heaven-born freedom on thy being's
   height,
Why with such earnest pains dost thou pro-
   voke
The years to bring the inevitable yoke,
Thus blindly with thy blessedness at strife?
Full soon thy Soul shall have her earthly
   freight,   130
And custom lie upon thee with a weight,
Heavy as frost, and deep almost as life!

IX

   O joy! that in our embers
   Is something that doth live,
   That nature yet remembers
   What was so fugitive!
The thought of our past years in me doth breed
Perpetual benediction: not indeed
For that which is most worthy to be blest;
Delight and liberty, the simple creed   140
Of Childhood, whether busy or at rest,
With new-fledged hope still fluttering in his
   breast:—
   Not for these I raise
   The song of thanks and praise;
  But for those obstinate questionings
  Of sense and outward things,
  Fallings from us, vanishings;
  Blank misgivings of a Creature
Moving about in worlds not realised,
High instincts before which our mortal Na-
   ture   150

Did tremble like a guilty Thing surprised:
   But for those first affections,
   Those shadowy recollections,
  Which, be they what they may,
Are yet the fountain-light of all our day,
Are yet a master-light of all our seeing;
  Uphold us, cherish, and have power to make
Our noisy years seem moments in the being
Of the eternal Silence: truths that wake,
   To perish never: 160
Which neither listlessness, nor mad endeavour,
   Nor Man nor Boy,
Nor all that is at enmity with joy,
Can utterly abolish or destroy!
  Hence in a season of calm weather
   Though inland far we be,
Our Souls have sight of that immortal sea
   Which brought us hither,
   Can in a moment travel thither,
And see the Children sport upon the shore, 170
And hear the mighty waters rolling evermore.

X

Then sing, ye Birds, sing, sing a joyous song!
   And let the young Lambs bound
   As to the tabor's sound!
We in thought will join your throng,
   Ye that pipe and ye that play,
   Ye that through your hearts today
   Feel the gladness of the May!
What though the radiance which was once so
   bright
Be now for ever taken from my sight,   180
  Though nothing can bring back the hour
Of splendour in the grass, of glory in the
   flower;
   We will grieve not, rather find
   Strength in what remains behind;
   In the primal sympathy
   Which having been must ever be;
   In the soothing thoughts that spring
   Out of human suffering;
   In the faith that looks through death,
In years that bring the philosophic mind.

XI

And O, ye Fountains, Meadows, Hills, and
   Groves,   191
Forebode not any severing of our loves!
Yet in my heart of hearts I feel your might;
I only have relinquished one delight
To live beneath your more habitual sway.

I love the Brooks which down their channels
    fret,
Even more than when I tripped lightly as they;
The innocent brightness of a new-born Day
        Is lovely yet;   199
The Clouds that gather round the setting sun
Do take a sober colouring from an eye
That hath kept watch o'er man's mortality;
Another race hath been, and other palms are
    won.
Thanks to the human heart by which we live,
Thanks to its tenderness, its joys, and fears,
To me the meanest flower that blows can give
Thoughts that do often lie too deep for tears.

1803–1806

FRENCH REVOLUTION

AS IT APPEARED TO ENTHUSIASTS AT ITS COMMENCEMENT

OH! pleasant exercise of hope and joy!
For mighty were the auxiliars which then
    stood
Upon our side, we who were strong in love!
Bliss was it in that dawn to be alive, .
But to be young was very heaven!—Oh!
    times,
In which the meagre, stale, forbidding ways
Of custom, law, and statute, took at once
The attraction of a country in romance!
When Reason seemed the most to assert her
    rights,
When most intent on making of herself   10
A prime Enchantress—to assist the work
Which then was going forward in her name!
Not favoured spots alone, but the whole earth,
The beauty wore of promise, that which sets
(As at some moment might not be unfelt
Among the bowers of paradise itself)
The budding rose above the rose full blown.
What temper at the prospect did not wake
To happiness unthought of? The inert
Were roused, and lively natures rapt away! 20
They who had fed their childhood upon
    dreams,
The playfellows of fancy, who had made
All powers of swiftness, subtilty, and strength
Their ministers,—who in lordly wise had
    stirred
Among the grandest objects of the sense,

And dealt with whatsoever they found there
As if they had within some lurking right
To wield it;—they, too, who, of gentle mood,
Had watched all gentle motions, and to these
Had fitted their own thoughts, schemers more
    mild,   30
And in the region of their peaceful selves;—
Now was it that both found, the meek and
    lofty
Did both find, helpers to their heart's desire,
And stuff at hand, plastic as they could
    wish;
Were called upon to exercise their skill,
Not in Utopia, subterranean fields,
Or some secreted island, Heaven knows where!
But in the very world, which is the world
Of all of us,—the place where in the end
We find our happiness, or not at all!   40

1804

I WANDERED LONELY AS A CLOUD ✷

I WANDERED lonely as a cloud
That floats on high o'er vales and hills,
When all at once I saw a crowd,
A host, of golden daffodils;
Beside the lake, beneath the trees,
Fluttering and dancing in the breeze.

Continuous as the stars that shine
And twinkle on the milky way,
They stretched in never-ending line
Along the margin of a bay: 10
Ten thousand saw I at a glance,
Tossing their heads in sprightly dance.

The waves beside them danced; but they
Out-did the sparkling waves in glee:
A poet could not but be gay,
In such a jocund company:
I gazed—and gazed—but little thought
What wealth the show to me had brought:

For oft, when on my couch I lie
In vacant or in pensive mood,   20
They flash upon that inward eye
Which is the bliss of solitude;
And then my heart with pleasure fills,
And dances with the daffodils.

1804

SHE WAS A PHANTOM OF DELIGHT

She was a Phantom of delight
When first she gleamed upon my sight,
A lovely Apparition, sent
To be a moment's ornament;
Her eyes as stars of Twilight fair;
Like Twilight's, too, her dusky hair;
But all things else about her drawn
From May-time and the cheerful Dawn;
A dancing Shape, an Image gay,
To haunt, to startle, and way-lay.   10

I saw her upon nearer view,
A Spirit, yet a Woman too!
Her household motions light and free,
And steps of virgin-liberty;
A countenance in which did meet
Sweet records, promises as sweet;
A Creature not too bright or good
For human nature's daily food;
For transient sorrows, simple wiles,
Praise, blame, love, kisses, tears, and smiles. 20

And now I see with eye serene
The very pulse of the machine;
A Being breathing thoughtful breath,
A Traveller between life and death;
The reason firm, the temperate will,
Endurance, foresight, strength, and skill;
A perfect Woman, nobly planned,
To warn, to comfort, and command;
And yet a Spirit still, and bright
With something of angelic light.   30

1804

TO A YOUNG LADY

WHO HAD BEEN REPROACHED FOR TAKING
LONG WALKS IN THE COUNTRY

Dear Child of Nature, let them rail!
—There is a nest in a green dale,
A harbour and a hold;
Where thou, a Wife and Friend, shalt see
Thy own heart-stirring days, and be
A light to young and old.

There, healthy as a shepherd boy,
And treading among flowers of joy
Which at no season fade,

Thou, while thy babes around thee cling, 10
Shalt show us how divine a thing
A Woman may be made.

Thy thoughts and feelings shall not die,
Nor leave thee, when grey hairs are nigh,
A melancholy slave;
But an old age serene and bright,
And lovely as a Lapland night,
Shall lead thee to thy grave.

1805

CHARACTER OF THE HAPPY WARRIOR

Who is the happy Warrior? Who is he
That every man in arms should wish to be?
—It is the generous Spirit, who, when brought
Among the tasks of real life, hath wrought
Upon the plan that pleased his boyish thought:
Whose high endeavours are an inward light
That makes the path before him always bright:
Who, with a natural instinct to discern
What knowledge can perform, is diligent to
     learn;
Abides by this resolve, and stops not there,   10
But makes his moral being his prime care;
Who, doomed to go in company with Pain,
And Fear, and Bloodshed, miserable train!
Turns his necessity to glorious gain;
In face of these doth exercise a power
Which is our human nature's highest dower;
Controls them and subdues, transmutes, be-
     reaves
Of their bad influence, and their good receives:
By objects, which might force the soul to abate
Her feeling, rendered more compassionate;   20
Is placable—because occasions rise
So often that demand such sacrifice;
More skilful in self-knowledge, even more
     pure,
As tempted more; more able to endure,
As more exposed to suffering and distress;
Thence, also, more alive to tenderness.
—'Tis he whose law is reason; who depends
Upon that law as on the best of friends;
Whence, in a state where men are tempted still
To evil for a guard against worse ill,   30
And what in quality or act is best
Doth seldom on a right foundation rest,
He labours good on good to fix, and owes
To virtue every triumph that he knows:

—Who, if he rise to station of command,
Rises by open means; and there will stand
On honourable terms, or else retire,
And in himself possess his own desire;
Who comprehends his trust, and to the same
Keeps faithful with a singleness of aim;   40
And therefore does not stoop, nor lie in wait
For wealth, or honours, or for worldly state;
Whom they must follow; on whose head must
    fall,
Like showers of manna, if they come at all:
Whose powers shed round him in the common
    strife,
Or mild concerns of ordinary life,
A constant influence, a peculiar grace;
But who, if he be called upon to face
Some awful moment to which Heaven has
    joined
Great issues, good or bad for human kind, 50
Is happy as a Lover; and attired
With sudden brightness, like a Man inspired;
And, through the heat of conflict, keeps the law
In calmness made, and sees what he foresaw;
Or if an unexpected call succeed,
Come when it will, is equal to the need:
—He who, though thus endued as with a sense
And faculty for storm and turbulence,
Is yet a Soul whose master-bias leans
To homefelt pleasures and to gentle scenes; 60
Sweet images! which, wheresoe'er he be,
Are at his heart; and such fidelity
It is his darling passion to approve;
More brave for this, that he hath much to
    love:——
'Tis, finally, the Man, who, lifted high,
Conspicuous object in a Nation's eye,
Or left unthought-of in obscurity,—
Who, with a toward or untoward lot,
Prosperous or adverse, to his wish or not—
Plays, in the many games of life, that one 70
Where what he most doth value must be won:
Whom neither shape of danger can dismay,
Nor thought of tender happiness betray;
Who, not content that former worth stand
    fast,
Looks forward, persevering to the last,
From well to better, daily self-surpast:
Who, whether praise of him must walk the
    earth
For ever, and to noble deeds give birth,
Or he must fall, to sleep without his fame,

And leave a dead unprofitable name—   80
Finds comfort in himself and in his cause;
And, while the mortal mist is gathering, draws
His breath in confidence of Heaven's applause:
This is the happy Warrior; this is He
That every Man in arms should wish to be.

1805 or 1806

ODE TO DUTY

" Jam non consilio bonus, sed more eò perductus,
ut non tantum rectè facere possim, sed nisi rectè
facere non possim." [1]

Stern Daughter of the Voice of God!
O Duty! if that name thou love
Who art a light to guide, a rod
To check the erring, and reprove;
Thou, who art victory and law
When empty terrors overawe;
From vain temptations dost set free;
And calm'st the weary strife of frail humanity

There are who ask not if thine eye
Be on them; who, in love and truth,   10
Where no misgiving is, rely
Upon the genial sense of youth:
Glad Hearts! without reproach or blot;
Who do thy work, and know it not:
Oh! if through confidence misplaced
They fail, thy saving arms, dread Power!
    around them cast.

Serene will be our days and bright,
And happy will our nature be,
When love is an unerring light,
And joy its own security.   20
And they a blissful course may hold
Even now, who, not unwisely bold,
Live in the spirit of this creed;
Yet seek thy firm support, according to their
    need.

I, loving freedom, and untried;
No sport of every random gust,
Yet being to myself a guide,
Too blindly have reposed my trust:
And oft, when in my heart was heard
Thy timely mandate, I deferred   30

[1] "Now I am urged on, not by good resolution,
but rather by custom; so that it is not that I
am able to do right, but that I am not able to
do wrong."

The task, in smoother walks to stray;
But thee I now would serve more strictly, if I
   may.

Through no disturbance of my soul,
Or strong compunction in me wrought,
I supplicate for thy control;
But in the quietness of thought:
Me this unchartered freedom tires;
I feel the weight of chance-desires:
My hopes no more must change their name,
I long for a repose that ever is the same.   40

[Yet not the less would I throughout
Still act according to the voice
Of my own wish; and feel past doubt
That my submissiveness was choice:
Not seeking in the school of pride
For "precepts over dignified,"
Denial and restraint I prize
No farther than they breed a second Will more
   wise.]

Stern Lawgiver! yet thou dost wear
The Godhead's most benignant grace;
Nor know we anything so fair
As is the smile upon thy face:
Flowers laugh before thee on their beds
And fragrance in thy footing treads;
Thou dost preserve the stars from wrong;
And the most ancient heavens, through Thee,
   are fresh and strong.

To humbler functions, awful Power!
I call thee: I myself commend   50
Unto thy guidance from this hour;
Oh, let my weakness have an end!
Give unto me, made lowly wise,
The spirit of self-sacrifice;
The confidence of reason give;
And in the light of truth thy Bondman let me
   live!

1805

ELEGIAC STANZAS

SUGGESTED BY A PICTURE OF PEELE CASTLE, IN
A STORM, PAINTED BY SIR GEORGE BEAUMONT

I WAS thy neighbour once, thou rugged Pile!
Four summer weeks I dwelt in sight of thee:
I saw thee every day; and all the while
Thy Form was sleeping on a glassy sea.

So pure the sky, so quiet was the air!
So like, so very like, was day to day!
Whene'er I looked, thy Image still was there;
It trembled, but it never passed away.

How perfect was the calm! it seemed no sleep;
No mood, which season takes away, or brings:
I could have fancied that the mighty Deep   11
Was even the gentlest of all gentle Things.

Ah! THEN, if mine had been the Painter's hand,
To express what then I saw; and add the gleam,
The light that never was, on sea or land,
The consecration, and the Poet's dream;

I would have planted thee, thou hoary Pile
Amid a world how different from this!
Beside a sea that could not cease to smile;
On tranquil land, beneath a sky of bliss.   20

Thou shouldst have seemed a treasure-house
   divine
Of peaceful years; a chronicle of heaven;—
Of all the sunbeams that did ever shine
The very sweetest had to thee been given.

A Picture had it been of lasting ease,
Elysian quiet, without toil or strife;
No motion but the moving tide, a breeze,
Or merely silent Nature's breathing life.

Such, in the fond illusion of my heart,
Such Picture would I at that time have
   made: 30
And seen the soul of truth in every part,
A steadfast peace that might not be betrayed.

So once it would have been,—'tis so no more;
I have submitted to a new control:
A power is gone, which nothing can restore;
A deep distress hath humanised my Soul.

Not for a moment could I now behold
A smiling sea, and be what I have been:
The feeling of my loss will ne'er be old;
This, which I know, I speak with mind
   serene.   40

Then, Beaumont, Friend! who would have
   been the Friend,
If he had lived, of Him whom I deplore,
This work of thine I blame not, but commend;
This sea in anger, and that dismal shore.

O 'tis a passionate Work!—yet wise and well,
Well chosen is the spirit that is here;
That Hulk which labours in the deadly swell,
This rueful sky, this pageantry of fear!

And this huge Castle, standing here sublime,
I love to see the look with which it braves, 50
Cased in the unfeeling armour of old time,
The lightning, the fierce wind, and trampling
　　waves.

Farewell, farewell the heart that lives alone,
Housed in a dream, at distance from the Kind!
Such happiness, wherever it be known,
Is to be pitied; for 'tis surely blind.

But welcome fortitude, and patient cheer,
And frequent sights of what is to be borne!
Such sights, or worse, as are before me here.—
Not without hope we suffer and we mourn. 60
1805

NUNS FRET NOT

NUNS fret not at their convent's narrow room;
And hermits are contented with their cells;
And students with their pensive citadels;
Maids at the wheel, the weaver at his loom,
Sit blithe and happy; bees that soar for bloom,
High as the highest Peak of Furness-fells,
Will murmur by the hour in foxglove bells:
In truth the prison, unto which we doom
Ourselves, no prison is: and hence for me,
In sundry moods, 'twas pastime to be bound 10
Within the Sonnet's scanty plot of ground;
Pleased if some Souls (for such there needs
　　must be)
Who have felt the weight of too much liberty,
Should find brief solace there, as I have found.
1806

TO SLEEP

A FLOCK of sheep that leisurely pass by,
One after one; the sound of rain, and bees
Murmuring; the fall of rivers, winds and seas,
Smooth fields, white sheets of water, and pure
　　sky;
I have thought of all by turns, and yet do lie
Sleepless! and soon the small birds' melodies
Must hear, first uttered from my orchard trees;
And the first cuckoo's melancholy cry.
Even thus last night, and two nights more, I
　　lay

And could not win thee, Sleep! by any
　　stealth: 10
So do not let me wear to-night away:
Without Thee what is all the morning's
　　wealth?
Come, blessed barrier between day and day,
Dear mother of fresh thoughts and joyous
　　health!
1806

THE WORLD IS TOO MUCH
WITH US

THE world is too much with us; late and soon,
Getting and spending, we lay waste our
　　powers:
Little we see in Nature that is ours;
We have given our hearts away, a sordid boon!
This Sea that bares her bosom to the moon;
The winds that will be howling at all hours,
And are up-gathered now like sleeping
　　flowers;
For this, for everything, we are out of tune;
It moves us not.—Great God! I'd rather be
A Pagan suckled in a creed outworn; 10
So might I, standing on this pleasant lea,
Have glimpses that would make me less for-
　　lorn;
Have sight of Proteus rising from the sea;
Or hear old Triton blow his wreathèd horn.
1806

PERSONAL TALK

I

I AM not One who much or oft delight
To season my fireside with personal talk,—
Of friends, who live within an easy walk,
Or neighbours, daily, weekly, in my sight:
And, for my chance-acquaintance, ladies
　　bright,
Sons, mothers, maidens withering on the stalk,
These all wear out of me, like Forms with
　　chalk
Painted on rich men's floors, for one feast-
　　night.
Better than such discourse doth silence long,
Long, barren silence, square with my desire; 10
To sit without emotion, hope, or aim,
In the loved presence of my cottage-fire,
And listen to the flapping of the flame,
Or kettle whispering its faint under-song.

II

"Yet life," you say, "is life; we have seen and
    see,
And with a living pleasure we describe;
And fits of sprightly malice do but bribe
The languid mind into activity.
Sound sense, and love itself, and mirth and
    glee
Are fostered by the comment and the gibe." 20
Even be it so: yet still among your tribe,
Our daily world's true Worldlings, rank not
    me!
Children are blest, and powerful; their world
    lies
More justly balanced; partly at their feet,
And part far from them:—sweetest melodies
Are those that are by distance made more
    sweet;
Whose mind is but the mind of his own eyes,
He is a Slave; the meanest we can meet!

III

Wings have we,—and as far as we can go
We may find pleasure: wilderness and
    wood,   30
Blank ocean and mere sky, support that mood
Which with the lofty sanctifies the low.
Dreams, books, are each a world; and books,
    we know,
Are a substantial world, both pure and good:
Round these, with tendrils strong as flesh and
    blood,
Our pastime and our happiness will grow.
There find I personal themes, a plenteous store,
Matter wherein right voluble I am,
To which I listen with a ready ear;
Two shall be named, pre-eminently dear,— *Othello*
The gentle Lady married to the Moor;   41
And heavenly Una with her milk-white Lamb. *Fairy Queen. Spencer*

IV

Nor can I not believe but that hereby
Great gains are mine; for thus I live remote
From evil-speaking; rancour, never sought,
Comes to me not; malignant truth, or lie.
Hence have I genial seasons, hence have I
Smooth passions, smooth discourse, and joy-
    ous thought:
And thus from day to day my little boat
Rocks in its harbour, lodging peaceably.   50
Blessings be with them—and eternal praise,

Who gave us nobler loves, and nobler cares—
The Poets, who on earth have made us heirs
Of truth and pure delight by heavenly lays!
Oh! might my name be numbered among
    theirs,
Then gladly would I end my mortal days.

1806

YES, IT WAS THE MOUNTAIN ECHO

Yes, it was the mountain Echo,
Solitary, clear, profound,
Answering to the shouting Cuckoo,
Giving to her sound for sound!

Unsolicited reply
To a babbling wanderer sent;
Like her ordinary cry,
Like—but oh, how different!

Hears not also mortal Life?
Hear not we, unthinking Creatures!   10
Slaves of folly, love, or strife—
Voices of two different natures?

Have not *we* too?—yes, we have
Answers, and we know not whence;
Echoes from beyond the grave,
Recognised intelligence!

Such rebounds our inward ear
Catches sometimes from afar—
Listen, ponder, hold them dear;
For of God,—of God they are.   20

1806

SONG AT THE FEAST OF BROUGHAM CASTLE

UPON THE RESTORATION OF LORD CLIFFORD,
THE SHEPHERD, TO THE ESTATES AND
HONOURS OF HIS ANCESTORS

High in the breathless Hall the Minstrel sate,
And Emont's murmur mingled with the
    Song.—
The words of ancient time I thus translate,
A festal strain that hath been silent long:—

"From town to town, from tower to tower,
The red rose is a gladsome flower.
Her thirty years of winter past,
The red rose is revived at last;
She lifts her head for endless spring,
For everlasting blossoming: 10

Both roses flourish, red and white:
In love and sisterly delight
The two that were at strife are blended,
And all old troubles now are ended.—
Joy! joy to both! but most to her
Who is the flower of Lancaster!
Behold her how She smiles to-day
On this great throng, this bright array!
Fair greeting doth she send to all
From every corner of the hall;   20
But chiefly from above the board
Where sits in state our rightful Lord,
A Clifford to his own restored!

   "They came with banner, spear, and
     shield;
And it was proved in Bosworth-field.
Not long the Avenger was withstood—
Earth helped him with the cry of blood:
St. George was for us, and the might
Of blessed Angels crowned the right.
Loud voice the Land has uttered forth,   30
We loudest in the faithful north:
Our fields rejoice, our mountains ring,
Our streams proclaim a welcoming;
Our strong-abodes and castles see
The glory of their loyalty.

   "How glad is Skipton at this hour—
Though lonely, a deserted Tower;
Knight, squire, and yeoman, page and
     groom:
We have them at the feast of Brough'm.
How glad Pendragon—though the sleep   40
Of years be on her!—She shall reap
A taste of this great pleasure, viewing
As in a dream her own renewing.
Rejoiced is Brough, right glad, I deem,
Beside her little humble stream;
And she that keepeth watch and ward
Her statelier Eden's course to guard;
They both are happy at this hour,
Though each is but a lonely Tower:—
But here is perfect joy and pride   50
For one fair House by Emont's side,
This day, distinguished without peer,
To see her Master and to cheer—
Him, and his Lady-mother dear!

   "Oh! it was a time forlorn
When the fatherless was born—
Give her wings that she may fly,

Or she sees her infant die!
Swords that are with slaughter wild
Hunt the Mother and the Child.   80
Who will take them from the light?
—Yonder is a man in sight—
Yonder is a house—but where?
No, they must not enter there.
To the caves, and to the brooks,
To the clouds of heaven she looks;
She is speechless, but her eyes
Pray in ghostly agonies.
Blissful Mary, Mother mild,
Maid and Mother undefiled,   70
Save a Mother and her Child!

   "Now Who is he that bounds with joy
On Carrock's side, a Shepherd-boy?
No thoughts hath he but thoughts that
     pass
Light as the wind along the grass.
Can this be He who hither came
In secret, like a smothered flame?
O'er whom such thankful tears were shed
For shelter, and a poor man's bread!
God loves the Child; and God hath willed 80
That those dear words should be fulfilled,
The Lady's words, when forced away
The last she to her Babe did say:
'My own, my own, thy Fellow-guest
I may not be; but rest thee, rest,
For lowly shepherd's life is best!'

   "Alas! when evil men are strong
No life is good, no pleasure long.
The Boy must part from Mosedale's groves,
And leave Blencathara's rugged coves,   90
And quit the flowers that summer brings
To Glenderamakin's lofty springs;
Must vanish, and his careless cheer
Be turned to heaviness and fear.
—Give Sir Lancelot Threlkeld praise!
Hear it, good man, old in days!
Thou tree of covert and of rest
For this young Bird that is distrest;
Among thy branches safe he lay,
And he was free to sport and play,   100
When falcons were abroad for prey.

   "A recreant harp, that sings of fear
And heaviness in Clifford's ear!
I said, when evil men are strong,
No life is good, no pleasure long,

A weak and cowardly untruth!
Our Clifford was a happy Youth,
And thankful through a weary time,
That brought him up to manhood's prime.
—Again he wanders forth at will,   110
And tends a flock from hill to hill:
His garb is humble; ne'er was seen
Such garb with such a noble mien;
Among the shepherd-grooms no mate
Hath he, a Child of strength and state!
Yet lacks not friends for simple glee,
Nor yet for higher sympathy.
To his side the fallow-deer
Came, and rested without fear;
The eagle, lord of land and sea,   120
Stooped down to pay him fealty;
And both the undying fish that swim
Through Bowscale-tarn did wait on him;
The pair were servants of his eye
In their immortality;
And glancing, gleaming, dark or bright,
Moved to and fro, for his delight.
He knew the rocks which Angels haunt
Upon the mountains visitant;
He hath kenned them taking wing: 130
And into caves where Faeries sing
He hath entered; and been told
By Voices how men lived of old.
Among the heavens his eye can see
The face of thing that is to be;
And, if that men report him right,
His tongue could whisper words of might.
—Now another day is come,
Fitter hope, and nobler doom;
He hath thrown aside his crook,   140
And hath buried deep his book;
Armour rusting in his halls
On the blood of Clifford calls;—
'Quell the Scot,' exclaims the Lance—
Bear me to the heart of France,
Is the longing of the Shield—
Tell thy name, thou trembling Field;
Field of death, where'er thou be,
Groan thou with our victory!
Happy day, and mighty hour,   150
When our Shepherd in his power,
Mailed and horsed, with lance and sword,
To his ancestors restored
Like a re-appearing Star,
Like a glory from afar,
First shall head the flock of war!"

Alas! the impassioned minstrel did not
    know
How, by Heaven's grace, this Clifford's heart
    was framed:
How he, long forced in humble walks to go,
Was softened into feeling, soothed, and
    tamed.   160

Love had he found in huts where poor men
    lie;
His daily teachers had been woods and rills,
The silence that is in the starry sky,
The sleep that is among the lonely hills.

In him the savage virtue of the Race,
Revenge, and all ferocious thoughts were
    dead:
Nor did he change; but kept in lofty place
The wisdom which adversity had bred.

Glad were the vales, and every cottage-hearth;
The Shepherd-lord was honoured more and
    more;   170
And, ages after he was laid in earth,
"The good Lord Clifford" was the name he
    bore.

1807

Parody by Stevens

TWO VOICES ARE THERE

Two Voices are there; one is of the sea,
One of the mountains; each a mighty Voice:
In both from age to age thou didst rejoice,
They were thy chosen music, Liberty!
There came a Tyrant, and with holy glee
Thou fought'st against him; but hast vainly
    striven:
Thou from thy Alpine holds at length art
    driven,
Where not a torrent murmurs heard by thee.
Of one deep bliss thine ear hath been bereft:
Then cleave, O cleave to that which still is
    left;   10
For, high-souled Maid, what sorrow would it
    be
That Mountain floods should thunder as
    before,
And Ocean bellow from his rocky shore,
And neither awful Voice be heard by thee!

1807

COMPOSED BY THE SIDE OF GRAS–MERE LAKE

CLOUDS, lingering yet, extend in solid bars
Through the grey west; and lo! these waters, steeled
By breezeless air to smoothest polish, yield
A vivid repetition of the stars;
Jove, Venus, and the ruddy crest of Mars
Amid his fellows beauteously revealed
At happy distance from earth's groaning field,
Where ruthless mortals wage incessant wars.
Is it a mirror?—or the nether Sphere
Opening to view the abyss in which she feeds   10
Her own calm fires?—But list! a voice is near;
Great Pan himself low-whispering through the reeds,
"Be thankful, thou; for, if unholy deeds
Ravage the world, tranquillity is here!"
1807

FEELINGS OF THE TYROLESE

THE Land we from our fathers had in trust,
And to our children will transmit, or die;
This is our maxim, this our piety;
And God and Nature say that it is just.
That which we *would* perform in arms—we must!
We read the dictate in the infant's eye;
In the wife's smile; and in the placid sky;
And, at our feet, amid the silent dust
Of them that were before us.—Sing aloud
Old songs, the precious music of the heart!   10
Give, herds and flocks, your voices to the wind!
While we go forth, a self-devoted crowd,
With weapons grasped in fearless hands, to assert
Our virtue, and to vindicate mankind.
1809

SURPRISED BY JOY

SURPRISED by joy—impatient as the Wind
I turned to share the transport—Oh! with whom
But Thee, deep buried in the silent tomb,

That spot which no vicissitude can find?
Love, faithful love, recalled thee to my mind—
But how could I forget thee? Through what power,
Even for the least division of an hour,
Have I been so beguiled as to be blind
To my most grievous loss!—That thought's return
Was the worst pang that sorrow ever bore,   10
Save one, one only, when I stood forlorn,
Knowing my heart's best treasure was no more;
That neither present time, nor years unborn
Could to my sight that heavenly face restore.
After June, 1812

YARROW VISITED

SEPTEMBER, 1814

AND is this—Yarrow?—*This* the Stream
Of which my fancy cherished,
So faithfully, a waking dream?
An image that hath perished!
O that some Minstrel's harp were near,
To utter notes of gladness,
And chase this silence from the air,
That fills my heart with sadness!

Yet why?—a silvery current flows
With uncontrolled meanderings;   10
Nor have these eyes by greener hills
Been soothed, in all my wanderings.
And, through her depths, Saint Mary's Lake
Is visibly delighted;
For not a feature of those hills
Is in the mirror slighted.

A blue sky bends o'er Yarrow Vale,
Save where that pearly whiteness
Is round the rising sun diffused,
A tender hazy brightness;   20
Mild dawn of promise! that excludes
All profitless dejection;
Though not unwilling here to admit
A pensive recollection.

Where was it that the famous Flower
Of Yarrow Vale lay bleeding?
His bed perchance was yon smooth mound
On which the herd is feeding:

And haply from this crystal pool,
Now peaceful as the morning, 30
The Water-wraith ascended thrice—
And gave his doleful warning.

Delicious is the Lay that sings
The haunts of happy Lovers,
The path that leads them to the grove,
The leafy grove that covers:
And Pity sanctifies the Verse
That paints, by strength of sorrow,
The unconquerable strength of love;
Bear witness, rueful Yarrow! 40

But thou, that didst appear so fair
To fond imagination,
Dost rival in the light of day
Her delicate creation:
Meek loveliness is round thee spread,
A softness still and holy;
The grace of forest charms decayed,
And pastoral melancholy.

That region left, the vale unfolds
Rich groves of lofty stature, 50
With Yarrow winding through the pomp
Of cultivated nature;
And, rising from those lofty groves,
Behold a Ruin hoary!
The shattered front of Newark's Towers,
Renowned in Border story.

Fair scenes for childhood's opening bloom,
For sportive youth to stray in;
For manhood to enjoy his strength;
And age to wear away in! 60
Yon cottage seems a bower of bliss,
A covert for protection
Of tender thoughts, that nestle there—
The brood of chaste affection.

How sweet, on this autumnal day,
The wild-wood fruits to gather,
And on my True-love's forehead plant
A crest of blooming heather!
And what if I enwreathed my own!
'Twere no offence to reason; 70
The sober Hills thus deck their brows
To meet the wintry season.

I see—but not by sight alone,
Loved Yarrow, have I won thee;
A ray of fancy still survives—
Her sunshine plays upon thee!

Thy ever-youthful waters keep
A course of lively pleasure;
And gladsome notes my lips can breathe,
Accordant to the measure. 80

The vapours linger round the Heights,
They melt, and soon must vanish;
One hour is theirs, nor more is mine—
Sad thought, which I would banish,
But that I know, where'er I go,
Thy genuine image, Yarrow!
Will dwell with me—to heighten joy,
And cheer my mind in sorrow.

1814

LAODAMIA

"WITH sacrifice before the rising morn
Vows have I made by fruitless hope inspired;
And from the infernal Gods, 'mid shades forlorn
Of night, my slaughtered Lord have I required:
Celestial pity I again implore;—
Restore him to my sight—great Jove, restore!"

So speaking, and by fervent love endowed
With faith, the Suppliant heavenward lifts her hands;
While, like the sun emerging from a cloud,
Her countenance brightens—and her eye expands; 10
Her bosom heaves and spreads, her stature grows;
And she expects the issue in repose.

O terror! what hath she perceived?—O joy!
What doth she look on?—whom doth she behold?
Her Hero slain upon the beach of Troy?
His vital presence? his corporeal mould?
It is—if sense deceive her not—'tis He!
And a God leads him, wingèd Mercury!

Mild Hermes spake—and touched her with his wand
That calms all fear; "Such grace hath crowned thy prayer, 20
Laodamía! that at Jove's command
Thy Husband walks the paths of upper air:
He comes to tarry with thee three hours' space;
Accept the gift, behold him face to face!"

Forth sprang the impassioned Queen her Lord
    to clasp;
Again that consummation she essayed;
But unsubstantial Form eludes her grasp
As often as that eager grasp was made.
The Phantom parts—but parts to re-unite,
And re-assume his place before her sight.   30

"Protesiláus, lo! thy guide is gone!
Confirm, I pray, the vision with thy voice:
This is our palace,—yonder is thy throne;
Speak, and the floor thou tread'st on will
    rejoice.
Not to appal me have the gods bestowed
This precious boon; and blest a sad abode."

"Great Jove, Laodamía! doth not leave
His gifts imperfect:—Spectre though I be,
I am not sent to scare thee or deceive;
But in reward of thy fidelity.   40
And something also did my worth obtain;
For fearless virtue bringeth boundless gain.

"Thou knowest, the Delphic oracle foretold
That the first Greek who touched the Trojan
    strand
Should die; but me the threat could not with-
    hold:
A generous cause a victim did demand;
And forth I leapt upon the sandy plain;
A self-devoted chief—by Hector slain."

"Supreme of Heroes—bravest, noblest, best!
Thy matchless courage I bewail no more,   50
Which then, when tens of thousands were
    deprest
By doubt, propelled thee to the fatal shore;
Thou found'st—and I forgive thee—here
    thou art—
A nobler counsellor than my poor heart.

"But thou, though capable of sternest deed,
Wert kind as resolute, and good as brave;
And he, whose power restores thee, hath de-
    creed
Thou shouldst elude the malice of the grave:
Redundant are thy locks, thy lips as fair   59
As when their breath enriched Thessalian air.

"No Spectre greets me,—no vain Shadow this;
Come, blooming Hero, place thee by my side!
Give, on this well-known couch, one nuptial
    kiss

To me, this day, a second time thy bride!"
Jove frowned in heaven: the conscious Parcæ
    threw
Upon those roseate lips a Stygian hue.

"This visage tells thee that my doom is past:
Nor should the change be mourned, even if
    the joys
Of sense were able to return as fast
And surely as they vanish. Earth destroys 70
Those raptures duly—Erebus disdains:
Calm pleasures there abide—majestic pains.

"Be taught, O faithful Consort, to control
Rebellious passion: for the Gods approve
The depth, and not the tumult, of the soul;
A fervent, not ungovernable, love.
Thy transports moderate; and meekly mourn
When I depart, for brief is my sojourn—"

"Ah wherefore?—Did not Hercules by force
Wrest from the guardian Monster of the
    tomb   80
Alcestis, a reanimated corse,
Given back to dwell on earth in vernal bloom?
Medea's spells dispersed the weight of years,
And Æson stood a youth 'mid youthful peers.

"The Gods to us are merciful—and they
Yet further may relent: for mightier far
Than strength of nerve and sinew, or the
    sway
Of magic potent over sun and star,
Is love, though oft to agony distrest,
And though his favourite seat be feeble
    woman's breast.   90

"But if thou goest, I follow—" "Peace!" he
    said,—
She looked upon him and was calmed and
    cheered;
The ghastly colour from his lips had fled;
In his deportment, shape, and mien, appeared
Elysian beauty, melancholy grace,
Brought from a pensive though a happy place.

He spake of love, such love as Spirits feel
In worlds whose course is equable and pure;
No fears to beat away—no strife to heal—
The past unsighed for, and the future sure; 100
Spake of heroic arts in graver mood
Revived, with finer harmony pursued;

Of all that is most beauteous—imaged there
In happier beauty; more pellucid streams,
An ampler ether, a diviner air,
And fields invested with purpureal gleams;
Climes which the sun, who sheds the brightest
    day
Earth knows, is all unworthy to survey.

Yet there the Soul shall enter which hath
    earned
That privilege by virtue.—"Ill," said he,   110
"The end of man's existence I discerned,
Who from ignoble games and revelry
Could draw, when we had parted, vain de-
    light,
While tears were thy best pastime, day and
    night;

"And while my youthful peers before my
    eyes
(Each hero following his peculiar bent)
Prepared themselves for glorious enterprise
By martial sports,—or, seated in the tent,
Chieftains and kings in council were detained;
What time the fleet at Aulis lay enchained.

"The wished-for wind was given:—I then
    revolved   121
The oracle, upon the silent sea;
And, if no worthier led the way, resolved
That, of a thousand vessels, mine should be
The foremost prow in pressing to the strand,—
Mine the first blood that tinged the Trojan
    sand.

"Yet bitter, oft-times bitter, was the pang
When of thy loss I thought, belovèd Wife!
On thee too fondly did my memory hang,
And on the joys we shared in mortal life,—
The paths which we had trod—these foun-
    tains, flowers;   131
My new-planned cities, and unfinished
    towers.

"But should suspense permit the Foe to
    cry,
'Behold they tremble!—haughty their array,
Yet of their number no one dares to die?'
In soul I swept the indignity away:
Old frailties then recurred:—but lofty thought,
In act embodied, my deliverance wrought.

"And Thou, though strong in love, art all
    too weak
In reason, in self-government too slow; 140
I counsel thee by fortitude to seek
Our blest re-union in the shades below.
The invisible world with thee hath sym-
    pathised;
Be thy affections raised and solemnised.

"Learn, by a mortal yearning, to ascend—
Seeking a higher object. Love was given,
Encouraged, sanctioned, chiefly for that end;
For this the passion to excess was driven—
That self might be annulled: her bondage
    prove
The fetters of a dream opposed to love."—

Aloud she shrieked! for Hermes reappears! 151
Round the dear Shade she would have clung
        —'tis vain:
The hours are past—too brief had they been
    years;
And him no mortal effort can detain:
Swift, toward the realms that know not
    earthly day,
He through the portal takes his silent way,
And on the palace-floor a lifeless corse she
    lay.

Thus, all in vain exhorted and reproved,
She perished; and, as for a wilful crime,   159
By the just Gods whom no weak pity moved,
Was doomed to wear out her appointed time,
Apart from happy Ghosts, that gather flowers
Of blissful quiet 'mid unfading bowers.

—Yet tears to human suffering are due;
And mortal hopes defeated and o'erthrown
Are mourned by man, and not by man
    alone,
As fondly he believes.—Upon the side
Of Hellespont (such faith was entertained)
A knot of spiry trees for ages grew
From out the tomb of him for whom she
    died;   170
And ever, when such stature they had gained
That Ilium's walls were subject to their
    view,
The trees' tall summits withered at the sight;
A constant interchange of growth and blight!

1814

Edith May Southey
from
Wm Wordsworth

THE

WAGGONER,

𝔞 𝔓oem.

TO WHICH ARE ADDED,

SONNETS.

BY

WILLIAM WORDSWORTH.

" What's in a NAME ?"

" Brutus will start a Spirit as soon as Cæsar !"

LONDON:

Printed by Strahan and Spottiswoode, Printers-Street ;

FOR LONGMAN, HURST, REES, ORME, AND BROWN,

PATERNOSTER-ROW.

1819.

Title-page of a Presentation Copy of *The Waggoner*.
(See Appendix I.)

COMPOSED UPON AN EVENING OF EXTRAORDINARY SPLENDOUR AND BEAUTY

I

Had this effulgence disappeared
With flying haste, I might have sent,
Among the speechless clouds, a look
Of blank astonishment;
But 'tis endued with power to stay,
And sanctify one closing day,
That frail Mortality may see—
What is?—ah no, but what *can* be!
Time was when field and watery cove
With modulated echoes rang,   10
While choirs of fervent Angels sang
Their vespers in the grove;
Or, crowning, star-like, each some sovereign
     height,
Warbled, for heaven above and earth below,
Strains suitable to both.—Such holy rite,
Methinks, if audibly repeated now
From hill or valley, could not move
Sublimer transport, purer love,
Than doth this silent spectacle—the gleam—
The shadow—and the peace supreme!   20

II

No sound is uttered,—but a deep
And solemn harmony pervades
The hollow vale from steep to steep,
And penetrates the glades.
Far-distant images draw nigh,
Called forth by wondrous potency
Of beamy radiance, that imbues
Whate'er it strikes with gem-like hues!
In vision exquisitely clear,
Herds range along the mountain side;   30
And glistening antlers are descried;
And gilded flocks appear.
Thine is the tranquil hour, purpureal Eve!
But long as god-like wish, or hope divine,
Informs my spirit, ne'er can I believe
That this magnificence is wholly thine!
—From worlds not quickened by the sun
A portion of the gift is won;
An intermingling of Heaven's pomp is spread
On ground which British shepherds tread! 40

III

And if there be whom broken ties
Afflict, or injuries assail,

Yon hazy ridges to their eyes
Present a glorious scale,
Climbing suffused with sunny air,
To stop—no record hath told where!
And tempting Fancy to ascend,
And with immortal Spirits blend!
—Wings at my shoulders seem to play;
But, rooted here, I stand and gaze   50
On those bright steps that heavenward raise
Their practicable way.
Come forth, ye drooping old men, look
     abroad,
And see to what fair countries ye are bound!
And if some traveller, weary of his road,
Hath slept since noon-tide on the grassy
     ground,
Ye Genii! to his covert speed;
And wake him with such gentle heed
As may attune his soul to meet the dower
Bestowed on this transcendent hour!   60

IV

Such hues from their celestial Urn
Were wont to stream before mine eye,
Where'er it wandered in the morn
Of blissful infancy.
This glimpse of glory, why renewed?
Nay, rather speak with gratitude;
For, if a vestige of those gleams
Survived, 'twas only in my dreams.
Dread Power! whom peace and calmness serve
No less than Nature's threatening voice,   70
If aught unworthy be my choice,
From Thee if I would swerve;
Oh, let Thy grace remind me of the light
Full early lost, and fruitlessly deplored;
Which, at this moment, on my waking sight
Appears to shine, by miracle restored;
My soul, though yet confined to earth,
Rejoices in a second birth!
—'Tis past, the visionary splendour fades;
And night approaches with her shades.   80
1818

TO——

O dearer far than light and life are dear,
Full oft our human foresight I deplore;
Trembling, through my unworthiness, with
     fear
That friends, by death disjoined, may meet
     no more!

Misgivings, hard to vanquish or control,
Mix with the day, and cross the hour of rest;
While all the future, for thy purer soul,
With "sober certainties" of love is blest.

That sigh of thine, not meant for human ear,
Tells that these words thy humbleness offend;
Yet bear me up—else faltering in the rear   11
Of a steep march: support me to the end.

Peace settles where the intellect is meek,
And Love is dutiful in thought and deed;
Through Thee communion with that Love
     I seek:
The faith Heaven strengthens where *he*
     moulds the Creed.

1824

TO A SKYLARK

ETHEREAL minstrel! pilgrim of the sky !
Dost thou despise the earth where cares
     abound?
Or, while the wings aspire, are heart and eye
Both with thy nest upon the dewy ground?
Thy nest which thou canst drop into at will,
Those quivering wings composed, that music
     still!

Leave to the nightingale her shady wood;
A privacy of glorious light is thine;
Whence thou dost pour upon the world a
     flood
Of harmony, with instinct more divine;   10
Type of the wise who soar, but never roam;
True to the kindred points of Heaven and
     Home!

1825

SCORN NOT THE SONNET

SCORN not the Sonnet; Critic, you have
     frowned,
Mindless of its just honours; with this key
Shakespeare unlocked his heart; the melody
Of this small lute gave ease to Petrarch's
     wound;
A thousand times this pipe did Tasso sound;
With it Camöens soothed an exile's grief;
The Sonnet glittered a gay myrtle leaf
Amid the cypress with which Dante crowned

His visionary brow: a glow-worm lamp,
It cheered mild Spenser, called from Faery-
     land   10
To struggle through dark ways; and when a
     damp
Fell round the path of Milton, in his hand
The Thing became a trumpet; whence he
     blew
Soul-animating strains—alas, too few!

1827

WHY ART THOU SILENT

WHY art thou silent! Is thy love a plant
Of such weak fibre that the treacherous air
Of absence withers what was once so fair?
Is there no debt to pay, no boon to grant?
Yet have my thoughts for thee been vig-
     ilant—
Bound to thy service with unceasing care,
The mind's least generous wish a mendicant
For nought but what thy happiness could
     spare.
Speak—though this soft warm heart, once
     free to hold
A thousand tender pleasures, thine and mine,
Be left more desolate, more dreary cold   11
Than a forsaken bird's-nest filled with snow
'Mid its own bush of leafless eglantine—
Speak, that my torturing doubts their end
     may know!

1832 or 1833

MOST SWEET IT IS WITH UNUP-
LIFTED EYES

MOST sweet it is with unuplifted eyes
To pace the ground, if path be there or
     none,
While a fair region round the traveller lies
Which he forbears again to look upon;
Pleased rather with some soft ideal scene,
The work of Fancy, or some happy tone
Of meditation, slipping in between
The beauty coming and the beauty gone.
If Thought and Love desert us, from that
     day
Let us break off all commerce with the
     Muse: 10

With Thought and Love companions of our
    way,
Whate'er the senses take or may refuse,
The Mind's internal heaven shall shed her dews
Of inspiration on the humblest lay.

1833

SERVING NO HAUGHTY MUSE

VALEDICTORY SONNET

Closing the Volume of Sonnets published in 1838.

SERVING no haughty Muse, my hands have here
Disposed some cultured Flowerets (drawn
    from spots
Where they bloomed singly, or in scattered
    knots,)
Each kind in several beds of one parterre;
Both to allure the casual Loiterer,
And that, so placed, my Nurslings may re-
    quite
Studious regard with opportune delight,
Nor be unthanked, unless I fondly err.
But metaphor dismissed, and thanks apart,
Reader, farewell! My last words let them be—
If in this book Fancy and Truth agree;   11
If simple Nature trained by careful Art
Through It have won a passage to thy heart;
Grant me thy love, I crave no other fee!

1838

A POET!—HE HATH PUT HIS HEART TO SCHOOL

A POET!—He hath put his heart to school,
Nor dares to move unpropped upon the staff
Which Art hath lodged within his hand—
    must laugh
By precept only, and shed tears by rule.
Thy Art be Nature; the live current quaff,
And let the groveller sip his stagnant pool,
In fear that else, when Critics grave and cool
Have killed him, Scorn should write his epi-
    taph.
How does the Meadow-flower its bloom un-
    fold?
Because the lovely little flower is free   10
Down to its root, and, in that freedom, bold;
And so the grandeur of the Forest-tree
Comes not by casting in a formal mould,
But from its *own* divine vitality.

1842

From THE PRELUDE

INTRODUCTION—CHILDHOOD AND SCHOOL-TIME

BOOK I (COMPLETE)

OH THERE is blessing in this gentle breeze,
A visitant that while it fans my cheek
Doth seem half-conscious of the joy it brings
From the green fields, and from yon azure sky.
Whate'er its mission, the soft breeze can come
To none more grateful than to me; escaped
From the vast city, where I long had pined
A discontented sojourner: now free,
Free as a bird to settle where I will.   9
What dwelling shall receive me? in what vale
Shall be my harbour? underneath what grove
Shall I take up my home? and what clear
    stream
Shall with its murmur lull me into rest?
The earth is all before me. With a heart
Joyous, nor scared at its own liberty,
I look about; and should the chosen guide
Be nothing better than a wandering cloud,
I cannot miss my way. I breathe again!
Trances of thought and mountings of the
    mind
Come fast upon me: it is shaken off,   20
That burthen of my own unnatural self,
The heavy weight of many a weary day
Not mine, and such as were not made for me.
Long months of peace (if such bold word ac-
    cord
With any promises of human life),
Long months of ease and undisturbed delight
Are mine in prospect; whither shall I turn,
By road or pathway, or through trackless field,
Up hill or down, or shall some floating thing
Upon the river point me out my course? 30

Dear Liberty! Yet what would it avail
But for a gift that consecrates the joy?
For I, methought, while the sweet breath of
    heaven
Was blowing on my body, felt within
A correspondent breeze, that gently moved
With quickening virtue, but is now become
A tempest, a redundant energy,
Vexing its own creation. Thanks to both,
And their congenial powers, that, while they
    join

In breaking up a long-continued frost,   40
Bring with them vernal promises, the hope
Of active days urged on by flying hours,—
Days of sweet leisure, taxed with patient
        thought
Abstruse, nor wanting punctual service high,
Matins and vespers of harmonious verse!

    Thus far, O Friend! did I, not used to make
A present joy the matter of a song,
Pour forth that day my soul in measured
        strains
That would not be forgotten, and are here
Recorded: to the open fields I told   50
A prophecy: poetic numbers came
Spontaneously to clothe in priestly robe
A renovated spirit singled out,
Such hope was mine, for holy services.
My own voice cheered me, and, far more, the
        mind's
Internal echo of the imperfect sound;
To both I listened, drawing from them both
A cheerful confidence in things to come.

    Content and not unwilling now to give
A respite to this passion, I paced on   60
With brisk and eager steps; and came, at
        length,
To a green shady place, where down I sate
Beneath a tree, slackening my thoughts by
        choice,
And settling into gentler happiness.
'Twas autumn, and a clear and placid day,
With warmth, as much as needed, from a sun
Two hours declined towards the west; a day
With silver clouds, and sunshine on the grass,
And in the sheltered and the sheltering grove
A perfect stillness. Many were the thoughts 70
Encouraged and dismissed, till choice was
        made
Of a known Vale, whither my feet should
        turn,
Nor rest till they had reached the very door
Of the one cottage which methought I saw.
No picture of mere memory ever looked
So fair; and while upon the fancied scene
I gazed with growing love, a higher power
Than Fancy gave assurance of some work
Of glory there forthwith to be begun,
Perhaps too there performed. Thus long I
        mused,   80

Nor e'er lost sight of what I mused upon,
Save when, amid the stately grove of oaks,
Now here, now there, an acorn, from its cup
Dislodged, through sere leaves rustled, or
        at once
To the bare earth dropped with a startling
        sound.
From that soft couch I rose not, till the sun
Had almost touched the horizon; casting then
A backward glance upon the curling cloud
Of city smoke, by distance ruralised;
Keen as a Truant or a Fugitive,   90
But as a Pilgrim resolute, I took,
Even with the chance equipment of that hour,
The road that pointed toward the chosen Vale.
It was a splendid evening, and my soul
Once more made trial of her strength, nor
        lacked
Æolian visitations; but the harp
Was soon defrauded, and the banded host
Of harmony dispersed in straggling sounds,
And lastly utter silence! "Be it so;
Why think of anything but present good?" 100
So, like a home-bound labourer, I pursued
My way beneath the mellowing sun, that shed
Mild influence; nor left in me one wish
Again to bend the Sabbath of that time
To a servile yoke. What need of many words?
A pleasant loitering journey, through three
        days
Continued, brought me to my hermitage.
I spare to tell of what ensued, the life
In common things—the endless store of
        things,
Rare, or at least so seeming, every day   110
Found all about me in one neighbourhood—
The self-congratulation, and, from morn
To night, unbroken cheerfulness serene.
But speedily an earnest longing rose
To brace myself to some determined aim,
Reading or thinking; either to lay up
New stores, or rescue from decay the old
By timely interference: and therewith
Came hopes still higher, that with outward
        life
I might endue some airy phantasies   120
That had been floating loose about for years,
And to such beings temperately deal forth
The many feelings that oppressed my heart.
That hope hath been discouraged; welcome
        light

Dawns from the east, but dawns to disappear
And mock me with a sky that ripens not
Into a steady morning: if my mind,
Remembering the bold promise of the past,
Would gladly grapple with some noble theme,
Vain is her wish; where'er she turns she finds
Impediments from day to day renewed.   131

And now it would content me to yield up
Those lofty hopes awhile, for present gifts
Of humbler industry. But, oh, dear Friend!
The Poet, gentle creature as he is,
Hath, like the Lover, his unruly times;
His fits when he is neither sick nor well,
Though no distress be near him but his own
Unmanageable thoughts: his mind, best
    pleased
While she as duteous as the mother dove   140
Sits brooding, lives not always to that end,
But like the innocent bird, hath goadings on
That drive her as in trouble through the
    groves;
With me is now such passion, to be blamed
No otherwise than as it lasts too long.

When, as becomes a man who would pre-
    pare
For such an arduous work, I through myself
Make rigorous inquisition, the report
Is often cheering; for I neither seem
To lack that first great gift, the vital soul, 150
Nor general Truths, which are themselves a
    sort
Of Elements and Agents, Under-powers,
Subordinate helpers of the living mind:
Nor am I naked of external things,
Forms, images, nor numerous other aids
Of less regard, though won perhaps with toil
And needful to build up a Poet's praise.
Time, place, and manners do I seek, and these
Are found in plenteous store, but nowhere
    such
As may be singled out with steady choice; 160
No little band of yet remembered names
Whom I, in perfect confidence, might hope
To summon back from lonesome banish-
    ment,
And make them dwellers in the hearts of men
Now living, or to live in future years.
Sometimes the ambitious Power of choice,
    mistaking

Proud spring-tide swellings for a regular sea,
Will settle on some British theme, some old
Romantic tale by Milton left unsung;
More often turning to some gentle place   170
Within the groves of Chivalry, I pipe
To shepherd swains, or seated harp in hand,
Amid reposing knights by a river side
Or fountain, listen to the grave reports
Of dire enchantments faced and overcome
By the strong mind, and tales of warlike feats,
Where spear encountered spear, and sword
    with sword
Fought, as if conscious of the blazonry
That the shield bore, so glorious was the strife;
Whence inspiration for a song that winds   180
Through ever-changing scenes of votive quest
Wrongs to redress, harmonious tribute paid
To patient courage and unblemished truth,
To firm devotion, zeal unquenchable,
And Christian meekness hallowing faithful
    loves.
Sometimes, more sternly moved, I would
    relate
How vanquished Mithridates northward
    passed,
And, hidden in the cloud of years, became
Odin, the Father of a race by whom
Perished the Roman Empire: how the friends
And followers of Sertorius, out of Spain   191
Flying, found shelter in the Fortunate Isles,
And left their usages, their arts and laws,
To disappear by a slow gradual death,
To dwindle and to perish one by one,
Starved in those narrow bounds: but not the
    soul
Of Liberty, which fifteen hundred years
Survived, and, when the European came
With skill and power that might not be with-
    stood,
Did, like a pestilence, maintain its hold   200
And wasted down by glorious death that race
Of natural heroes: or I would record
How, in tyrannic times, some high-souled
    man,
Unnamed among the chronicles of kings,
Suffered in silence for Truth's sake; or tell,
How that one Frenchman,[1] through continued
    force

[1] Dominique de Gourgues, who in 1567 sailed to Florida to avenge the massacre of the French by the Spaniards.—Ed. of 1850.

Of meditation on the inhuman deeds
Of those who conquered first the Indian
    Isles,
Went single in his ministry across
The Ocean; not to comfort the oppressed, 210
But, like a thirsty wind, to roam about
Withering the Oppressor: how Gustavus
    sought
Help at his need in Dalecarlia's mines:
How Wallace fought for Scotland; left the
    name
Of Wallace to be found, like a wild flower,
All over his dear Country; left the deeds
Of Wallace, like a family of Ghosts,
To people the steep rocks and river banks,
Her natural sanctuaries, with a local soul
Of independence and stern liberty.   220
Sometimes it suits me better to invent
A tale from my own heart, more near akin
To my own passions and habitual thoughts;
Some variegated story, in the main
Lofty, but the unsubstantial structure melts
Before the very sun that brightens it,
Mist into air dissolving! Then a wish,
My last and favourite aspiration, mounts
With yearning toward some philosophic song
Of Truth that cherishes our daily life;   230
With meditations passionate from deep
Recesses in man's heart, immortal verse
Thoughtfully fitted to the Orphean lyre;
But from this awful burthen I full soon
Take refuge and beguile myself with trust
That mellower years will bring a riper mind
And clearer insight. Thus my days are past
In contradiction; with no skill to part
Vague longing, haply bred by want of power,
From paramount impulse not to be with-
    stood,   240
A timorous capacity from prudence,
From circumspection, infinite delay.
Humility and modest awe themselves
Betray me, serving often for a cloak
To a more subtle selfishness; that now
Locks every function up in blank reserve,
Now dupes me, trusting to an anxious eye
That with intrusive restlessness beats off
Simplicity and self-presented truth.
Ah! better far than this, to stray about   250
Voluptuously through fields and rural walks,
And ask no record of the hours, resigned
To vacant musing, unreproved neglect

Of all things, and deliberate holiday.
Far better never to have heard the name
Of zeal and just ambition, than to live
Baffled and plagued by a mind that every
    hour
Turns recreant to her task; takes heart again,
Then feels immediately some hollow thought
Hang like an interdict upon her hopes.   260
This is my lot; for either still I find
Some imperfection in the chosen theme,
Or see of absolute accomplishment
Much wanting, so much wanting, in myself,
That I recoil and droop, and seek repose
In listlessness from vain perplexity,
Unprofitably travelling toward the grave,
Like a false steward who hath much received
And renders nothing back.
                          Was it for this
That one, the fairest of all rivers, loved   270
To blend his murmurs with my nurse's song,
And, from his alder shades and rocky falls,
And from his fords and shallows, sent a voice
That flowed along my dreams? For this,
    didst thou,
O Derwent! winding among grassy holms
Where I was looking on, a babe in arms,
Make ceaseless music that composed my
    thoughts
To more than infant softness, giving me
Amid the fretful dwellings of mankind
A foretaste, a dim earnest, of the calm   280
That Nature breathes among the hills and
    groves.

    When he had left the mountains and re-
    ceived
On his smooth breast the shadow of those
    towers
That yet survive, a shattered monument
Of feudal sway, the bright blue river passed
Along the margin of our terrace walk;
A tempting playmate whom we dearly loved.
Oh, many a time have I, a five years' child,
In a small mill-race severed from his stream,
Made one long bathing of a summer's day; 290
Basked in the sun, and plunged and basked
    again
Alternate, all a summer's day, or scoured
The sandy fields, leaping through flowery
    groves
Of yellow ragwort; or when rock and hill,

The woods, and distant Skiddaw's lofty
    height,
Were bronzed with deepest radiance, stood
    alone
Beneath the sky, as if I had been born
On Indian plains, and from my mother's hut
Had run abroad in wantonness, to sport,
A naked savage, in the thunder shower.   300

Fair seed-time had my soul, and I grew up
Fostered alike by beauty and by fear:
Much favoured in my birthplace, and no less
In that belovèd Vale to which erelong
We were transplanted—there were we let
    loose
For sports of wider range. Ere I had told
Ten birth-days, when among the mountain-
    slopes
Frost, and the breath of frosty wind, had
    snapped
The last autumnal crocus, 'twas my joy
With store of springes o'er my shoulder
    hung   310
To range the open heights where woodcocks
    run
Among the smooth green turf. Through half
    the night,
Scudding away from snare to snare, I plied
That anxious visitation;—moon and stars
Were shining o'er my head. I was alone,
And seemed to be a trouble to the peace
That dwelt among them. Sometimes it befell
In these night wanderings, that a strong desire
O'erpowered my better reason, and the bird
Which was the captive of another's toil   320
Became my prey; and when the deed was done
I heard among the solitary hills
Low breathings coming after me, and sounds
Of undistinguishable motion, steps
Almost as silent as the turf they trod.

    Nor less when spring had warmed the cul-
        tured Vale
Moved we as plunderers where the mother-
    bird
Had in high places built her lodge; though
    mean
Our object and inglorious, yet the end
Was not ignoble. Oh! when I have hung 330
Above the raven's nest, by knots of grass
And half-inch fissures in the slippery rock

But ill sustained, and almost (so it seemed)
Suspended by the blast that blew amain,
Shouldering the naked crag, oh, at that time
While on the perilous ridge I hung alone,
With what strange utterance did the loud dry
    wind
Blow through my ear! the sky seemed not a
    sky
Of earth—and with what motion moved the
    clouds!

    Dust as we are, the immortal spirit grows
Like harmony in music; there is a dark   341
Inscrutable workmanship that reconciles
Discordant elements, makes them cling to-
    gether
In one society. How strange that all
The terrors, pains, and early miseries,
Regrets, vexations, lassitudes interfused
Within my mind, should e'er have borne a
    part,
And that a needful part, in making up
The calm existence that is mine when I
Am worthy of myself! Praise to the end! 350
Thanks to the means which Nature deigned to
    employ;
Whether her fearless visitings, or those
That came with soft alarm, like hurtless light
Opening the peaceful clouds; or she may use
Severer interventions, ministry
More palpable, as best might suit her aim.

    One summer evening (led by her) I found
A little boat tied to a willow tree
Within a rocky cave, its usual home.
Straight I unloosed her chain, and stepping
    in   360
Pushed from the shore. It was an act of stealth
And troubled pleasure, nor without the voice
Of mountain-echoes did my boat move on;
Leaving behind her still, on either side,
Small circles glittering idly in the moon,
Until they melted all into one track
Of sparkling light. But now, like one who
    rows,
Proud of his skill, to reach a chosen point
With an unswerving line, I fixed my view
Upon the summit of a craggy ridge,   370
The horizon's utmost boundary; far above
Was nothing but the stars and the grey sky.
She was an elfin pinnace; lustily

I dipped my oars into the silent lake,
And, as I rose upon the stroke, my boat
Went heaving through the water like a swan;
When, from behind that craggy steep till then
The horizon's bound, a huge peak, black and huge,
As if with voluntary power instinct   379
Upreared its head. I struck and struck again,
And growing still in stature the grim shape
Towered up between me and the stars, and still,
For so it seemed, with purpose of its own
And measured motion like a living thing,
Strode after me. With trembling oars I turned,
And through the silent water stole my way
Back to the covert of the willow tree;
There in her mooring-place I left my bark,—
And through the meadows homeward went, in grave
And serious mood; but after I had seen   390
That spectacle, for many days, my brain
Worked with a dim and undetermined sense
Of unknown modes of being; o'er my thoughts
There hung a darkness, call it solitude
Or blank desertion. No familiar shapes
Remained, no pleasant images of trees,
Of sea or sky, no colours of green fields;
But huge and mighty forms, that do not live
Like living men, moved slowly through the mind
By day, and were a trouble to my dreams.

Wisdom and Spirit of the universe!   401
Thou Soul that art the eternity of thought,
That givest to forms and images a breath
And everlasting motion, not in vain
By day or star-light thus from my first dawn
Of childhood didst thou intertwine for me
The passions that build up our human soul;
Not with the mean and vulgar works of man,
But with high objects, with enduring things—
With life and nature—purifying thus   410
The elements of feeling and of thought,
And sanctifying, by such discipline,
Both pain and fear, until we recognise
A grandeur in the beatings of the heart.
Nor was this fellowship vouchsafed to me
With stinted kindness. In November days,

When vapours rolling down the valley made
A lonely scene more lonesome, among woods,
At noon and 'mid the calm of summer nights,
When, by the margin of the trembling lake,
Beneath the gloomy hills homeward I went
In solitude, such intercourse was mine;   422
Mine was it in the fields both day and night,
And by the waters, all the summer long.

And in the frosty season, when the sun
Was set, and visible for many a mile
The cottage windows blazed through twilight gloom,
I heeded not their summons: happy time
It was indeed for all of us—for me
It was a time of rapture! Clear and loud   430
The village clock tolled six,—I wheeled about,
Proud and exulting like an untired horse
That cares not for his home. All shod with steel,
We hissed along the polished ice in games
Confederate, imitative of the chase
And woodland pleasures,—the resounding horn,
The pack loud chiming, and the hunted hare.
So through the darkness and the cold we flew,
And not a voice was idle; with the din
Smitten, the precipices rang aloud;   440
The leafless trees and every icy crag
Tinkled like iron; while far distant hills
Into the tumult sent an alien sound
Of melancholy not unnoticed, while the stars
Eastward were sparkling clear, and in the west
The orange sky of evening died away.
Not seldom from the uproar I retired
Into a silent bay, or sportively
Glanced sideway, leaving the tumultuous throng,
To cut across the reflex of a star   450
That fled, and, flying still before me, gleamed
Upon the glassy plain; and oftentimes,
When we had given our bodies to the wind,
And all the shadowy banks on either side
Came sweeping through the darkness, spinning still
The rapid line of motion, then at once
Have I, reclining back upon my heels,
Stopped short; yet still the solitary cliffs
Wheeled by me—even as if the earth had rolled

With visible motion her diurnal round! 460
Behind me did they stretch in solemn train,
Feebler and feebler, and I stood and watched
Till all was tranquil as a dreamless sleep.⟩

Ye Presences of Nature in the sky
And on the earth! Ye Visions of the hills!
And Souls of lonely places! can I think
A vulgar hope was yours when ye employed
Such ministry, when ye through many a year
Haunting me thus among my boyish sports,
On caves and trees, upon the woods and
    hills,   470
Impressed upon all forms the characters
Of danger or desire; and thus did make
The surface of the universal earth
With triumph and delight, with hope and
    fear,
Work like a sea?
                    Not uselessly employed,
Might I pursue this theme through every
    change
Of exercise and play, to which the year
Did summon us in his delightful round.

We were a noisy crew; the sun in heaven
Beheld not vales more beautiful than ours; 480
Nor saw a band in happiness and joy
Richer, or worthier of the ground they trod.
I could record with no reluctant voice
The woods of autumn, and their hazel bowers
With milk-white clusters hung; the rod and
    line,
True symbol of hope's foolishness, whose
    strong
And unreproved enchantment led us on
By rocks and pools shut out from every star,
All the green summer, to forlorn cascades
Among the windings hid of mountain
    brooks.   490
—Unfading recollections! at this hour
The heart is almost mine with which I felt,
From some hill-top on sunny afternoons,
The paper kite high among fleecy clouds
Pull at her rein like an impetuous courser;
Or, from the meadows sent on gusty days,
Beheld her breast the wind, then suddenly
Dashed headlong, and rejected by the storm.

Ye lowly cottages wherein we dwelt,
A ministration of your own was yours;   500
Can I forget you, being as you were

So beautiful among the pleasant fields
In which ye stood? or can I here forget
The plain and seemly countenance with which
Ye dealt out your plain comforts? Yet had ye
Delights and exultations of your own.
Eager and never weary we pursued
Our home-amusements by the warm peat-fire
At evening, when with pencil, and smooth
    slate
In square divisions parcelled out and all   510
With crosses and with cyphers scribbled
    o'er,
We schemed and puzzled, head opposed to
    head
In strife too humble to be named in verse:
Or round the naked table, snow-white deal,
Cherry or maple, sate in close array,
And to the combat, Loo or Whist, led on
A thick-ribbed army; not, as in the world,
Neglected and ungratefully thrown by
Even for the very service they had wrought,
But husbanded through many a long cam-
    paign.   520
Uncouth assemblage was it, where no few
Had changed their functions; some, plebeian
    cards
Which Fate, beyond the promise of their
    birth,
Had dignified, and called to represent
The persons of departed potentates.
Oh, with what echoes on the board they fell!
Ironic diamonds,—clubs, hearts, diamonds,
    spades,
A congregation piteously akin!
Cheap matter offered they to boyish wit,
Those sooty knaves, precipitated down   530
With scoffs and taunts, like Vulcan out of
    heaven:
The paramount ace, a moon in her eclipse,
Queens gleaming through their splendour's
    last decay,
And monarchs surly at the wrongs sustained
By royal visages. Meanwhile abroad
Incessant rain was falling, or the frost
Raged bitterly, with keen and silent tooth;
And, interrupting oft that eager game,
From under Esthwaite's splitting fields of ice
The pent-up air, struggling to free itself, 540
Gave out to meadow-grounds and hills a loud
Protracted yelling, like the noise of wolves
Howling in troops along the Bothnic Main.

Nor, sedulous as I have been to trace
How Nature by extrinsic passion first
Peopled the mind with forms sublime or fair,
And made me love them, may I here omit
How other pleasures have been mine, and
    joys
Of subtler origin; how I have felt,
Not seldom even in that tempestuous time,
Those hallowed and pure motions of the
    sense   551
Which seem, in their simplicity, to own
An intellectual charm; that calm delight
Which, if I err not, surely must belong
To those first-born affinities that fit
Our new existence to existing things,
And, in our dawn of being, constitute
The bond of union between life and joy.

Yes, I remember when the changeful earth,
And twice five summers on my mind had
    stamped   560
The faces of the moving year, even then
I held unconscious intercourse with beauty
Old as creation, drinking in a pure
Organic pleasure from the silver wreaths
Of curling mist, or from the level plain
Of waters coloured by impending clouds.

The sands of Westmoreland, the creeks and
    bays
Of Cumbria's rocky limits, they can tell
How, when the Sea threw off his evening
    shade
And to the shepherd's hut on distant hills
Sent welcome notice of the rising moon, 571
How I have stood, to fancies such as these
A stranger, linking with the spectacle
No conscious memory of a kindred sight,
And bringing with me no peculiar sense
Of quietness or peace; yet have I stood,
Even while mine eye hath moved o'er many
    a league
Of shining water, gathering as it seemed,
Through every hair-breadth in that field of
    light,
New pleasure like a bee among the flowers. 580

Thus oft amid those fits of vulgar joy
Which, through all seasons, on a child's
    pursuits
Are prompt attendants, 'mid that giddy bliss

Which, like a tempest, works along the blood
And is forgotten; even then I felt
Gleams like the flashing of a shield;—the earth
And common face of Nature spake to me
Rememberable things; sometimes, 'tis true,
By chance collisions and quaint accidents
(Like those ill-sorted unions, work sup-
    posed   590
Of evil-minded fairies), yet not vain
Nor profitless, if haply they impressed
Collateral objects and appearances,
Albeit lifeless then, and doomed to sleep
Until maturer seasons called them forth
To impregnate and to elevate the mind.
—And if the vulgar joy by its own weight
Wearied itself out of the memory,
The scenes which were a witness of that joy
Remained in their substantial lineaments 600
Depicted on the brain, and to the eye
Were visible, a daily sight; and thus
By the impressive discipline of fear,
By pleasure and repeated happiness,
So frequently repeated, and by force
Of obscure feelings representative
Of things forgotten, these same scenes so
    bright,
So beautiful, so majestic in themselves,
Though yet the day was distant, did become
Habitually dear, and all their forms   610
And changeful colours by invisible links
Were fastened to the affections.
                                  I began
My story early—not misled, I trust,
By an infirmity of love for days
Disowned by memory—ere the breath of
    spring
Planting my snowdrops among winter snows:
Nor will it seem to thee, O Friend! so prompt
In sympathy, that I have lengthened out
With fond and feeble tongue a tedious tale.
Meanwhile, my hope has been, that I might
    fetch   620
Invigorating thoughts from former years;
Might fix the wavering balance of my mind,
And haply meet reproaches too, whose power
May spur me on, in manhood now mature,
To honourable toil. Yet should these hopes
Prove vain, and thus should neither I be taught
To understand myself, nor thou to know
With better knowledge how the heart was
    framed

Of him thou lovest; need I dread from thee
Harsh judgments, if the song be loth to quit
Those recollected hours that have the charm
Of visionary things, those lovely forms   632
And sweet sensations that throw back our life,
And almost make remotest infancy
A visible scene, on which the sun is shining?

   One end at least hath been attained; my
     mind
Hath been revived, and if this genial mood
Desert me not, forthwith shall be brought
   down
Through later years the story of my life. 639
The road lies plain before me;—'tis a theme
Single and of determined bounds; and hence
I choose it rather at this time, than work
Of ampler or more varied argument,
Where I might be discomfited and lost:
And certain hopes are with me, that to thee
This labour will be welcome, honoured Friend!

SCHOOL–TIME

BOOK II (LINES 376–471)

       Nor should this, perchance,
Pass unrecorded, that I still had loved
The exercise and produce of a toil,
Than analytic industry to me
More pleasing, and whose character I deem
Is more poetic as resembling more   381
Creative agency. The song would speak
Of that interminable building reared
By observation of affinities
In objects where no brotherhood exists
To passive minds. My seventeenth year was
   come;
And, whether from this habit rooted now
So deeply in my mind, or from excess
In the great social principle of life
Coercing all things into sympathy,   390
To unorganic natures were transferred
My own enjoyments; or the power of truth
Coming in revelation, did converse
With things that really are; I, at this time,
Saw blessings spread around me like a sea.
Thus while the days flew by, and years passed
   on,
From Nature and her overflowing soul
I had received so much, that all my thoughts
Were steeped in feeling; I was only then

Contented, when with bliss ineffable   400
I felt the sentiment of Being spread
O'er all that moves and all that seemeth still;
O'er all that, lost beyond the reach of thought
And human knowledge, to the human eye
Invisible, yet liveth to the heart;
O'er all that leaps and runs, and shouts and
   sings,
Or beats the gladsome air; o'er all that glides
Beneath the wave, yea, in the wave itself,
And mighty depth of waters. Wonder not
If high the transport, great the joy I felt   410
Communing in this sort through earth and
   heaven
With every form of creature, as it looked
Towards the Uncreated with a countenance
Of adoration, with an eye of love.
One song they sang, and it was audible,
Most audible, then, when the fleshly ear,
O'ercome by humblest prelude of that strain,
Forgot her functions, and slept undisturbed.

   If this be error, and another faith
Find easier access to the pious mind,   420
Yet were I grossly destitute of all
Those human sentiments that make this earth
So dear, if I should fail with grateful voice
To speak of you, ye mountains, and ye lakes
And sounding cataracts, ye mists and winds
That dwell among the hills where I was born.
If in my youth I have been pure in heart,
If, mingling with the world, I am content
With my own modest pleasures, and have lived
With God and Nature communing, removed
From little enmities and low desires,   431
The gift is yours; if in these times of fear
This melancholy waste of hopes o'erthrown,
If, 'mid indifference and apathy,
And wicked exultation when good men
On every side fall off, we know not how,
To selfishness, disguised in gentle names
Of peace and quiet and domestic love,
Yet mingled not unwillingly with sneers
On visionary minds; if, in this time   440
Of dereliction and dismay, I yet
Despair not of our nature, but retain
A more than Roman confidence, a faith
That fails not, in all sorrow my support,
The blessing of my life; the gift is yours,
Ye winds and sounding cataracts! 'tis yours,
Ye mountains! thine, O Nature! Thou hast fed

My lofty speculations; and in thee,
For this uneasy heart of ours, I find
A never-failing principle of joy   450
And purest passion.
             Thou, my Friend! wert reared
In the great city, 'mid far other scenes;
But we, by different roads, at length have
    gained
The self-same bourne. And for this cause to
    thee
I speak, unapprehensive of contempt,
The insinuated scoff of coward tongues,
And all that silent language which so oft
In conversation between man and man
Blots from the human countenance all trace
Of beauty and of love. For thou hast sought
The truth in solitude, and, since the days 461
That gave thee liberty, full long desired,
To serve in Nature's temple, thou hast been
The most assiduous of her ministers;
In many things my brother, chiefly here
In this our deep devotion.
                Fare thee well!
Health and the quiet of a healthful mind
Attend thee! seeking oft the haunts of men,
And yet more often living with thyself,
And for thyself, so haply shall thy days   470
Be many, and a blessing to mankind.

SUMMER VACATION
BOOK IV (LINES 137–190)

           ... When first I made
Once more the circuit of our little lake,
If ever happiness hath lodged with man,
That day consummate happiness was mine, 140
Wide-spreading, steady, calm, contemplative.
The sun was set, or setting, when I left
Our cottage door, and evening soon brought on
A sober hour, not winning or serene,
For cold and raw the air was, and untuned;
But as a face we love is sweetest then
When sorrow damps it, or, whatever look
It chance to wear, is sweetest if the heart
Have fulness in herself; even so with me
It fared that evening. Gently did my soul 150
Put off her veil, and, self-transmuted, stood
Naked, as in the presence of her God.
While on I walked, a comfort seemed to touch
A heart that had not been disconsolate:

Strength came where weakness was not known
    to be,
At least not felt; and restoration came
Like an intruder knocking at the door
Of unacknowledged weariness. I took
The balance, and with firm hand weighed my-
    self.   159
—Of that external scene which round me lay,
Little, in this abstraction, did I see;
Remembered less; but I had inward hopes
And swellings of the spirit, was rapt and
    soothed,
Conversed with promises, had glimmering
    views
How life pervades the undecaying mind;
How the immortal soul with God-like power
Informs, creates, and thaws the deepest sleep
That time can lay upon her; how on earth
Man, if he do but live within the light
Of high endeavours, daily spreads abroad 170
His being armed with strength that cannot fail.
Nor was there want of milder thoughts, of love,
Of innocence, and holiday repose;
And more than pastoral quiet, 'mid the stir
Of boldest projects, and a peaceful end
At last, or glorious, by endurance won.
Thus musing, in a wood I sate me down
Alone, continuing there to muse: the slopes
And heights meanwhile were slowly over-
    spread   179
With darkness, and before a rippling breeze
The long lake lengthened out its hoary line,
And in the sheltered coppice where I sate,
Around me from among the hazel leaves,
Now here, now there, moved by the straggling
    wind,
Came ever and anon a breath-like sound,
Quick as the pantings of the faithful dog,
The off and on companion of my walk;
And such, at times, believing them to be, 188
I turned my head to look if he were there;
Then into solemn thought I passed once more.

BOOKS
BOOK V (LINES 1–49)

WHEN Contemplation, like the night-calm felt
Through earth and sky, spreads widely, and
    sends deep
Into the soul its tranquillising power,

Even then I sometimes grieve for thee, O Man,
Earth's paramount Creature! not so much for woes
That thou endurest; heavy though that weight be,
Cloud-like it mounts, or touched with light divine
Doth melt away; but for those palms achieved,
Through length of time, by patient exercise
Of study and hard thought; there, there, it is
That sadness finds its fuel. Hitherto,   11
In progress through this Verse, my mind hath looked
Upon the speaking face of earth and heaven
As her prime teacher, intercourse with man
Established by the sovereign Intellect,
Who through that bodily image hath diffused,
As might appear to the eye of fleeting time,
A deathless spirit. Thou also, man! hast wrought,
For commerce of thy nature with herself,
Things that aspire to unconquerable life;   26
And yet we feel—we cannot choose but feel—
That they must perish. Tremblings of the heart
It gives, to think that our immortal being
No more shall need such garments; and yet man,
As long as he shall be the child of earth,
Might almost "weep to have" what he may lose,
Nor be himself extinguished, but survive,
Abject, depressed, forlorn, disconsolate.
A thought is with me sometimes, and I say,—
Should the whole frame of earth by inward throes   30
Be wrenched, or fire come down from far to scorch
Her pleasant habitations, and dry up
Old Ocean, in his bed left singed and bare,
Yet would the living Presence still subsist
Victorious, and composure would ensue,
And kindlings like the morning—presage sure
Of day returning and of life revived.
But all the meditations of mankind,
Yea, all the adamantine holds of truth
By reason built, or passion, which itself   40
Is highest reason in a soul sublime;
The consecrated works of Bard and Sage,
Sensuous or intellectual, wrought by men,
Twin labourers and heirs of the same hopes;
Where would they be? Oh! why hath not the Mind

Some element to stamp her image on
In nature somewhat nearer to her own?
Why, gifted with such powers to send abroad
Her spirit, must it lodge in shrines so frail?

CAMBRIDGE AND THE ALPS
BOOK VI (LINES 592–608)

Imagination—here the Power so called
Through sad incompetence of human speech,
That awful Power rose from the mind's abyss
Like an unfathered vapour that enwraps,
At once, some lonely traveller. I was lost;
Halted without an effort to break through;
But to my conscious soul I now can say—
"I recognise thy glory:" in such strength
Of usurpation, when the light of sense   600
Goes out, but with a flash that has revealed
The invisible world, doth greatness make abode,
There harbours; whether we be young or old,
Our destiny, our being's heart and home,
Is with infinitude, and only there;
With hope it is, hope that can never die,
Effort, and expectation, and desire,
And something evermore about to be.

RESIDENCE IN LONDON
BOOK VII (LINES 619–649)

As the black storm upon the mountain-top
Sets off the sunbeam in the valley, so   620
That huge fermenting mass of humankind
Serves as a solemn background, or relief,
To single forms and objects, whence they draw,
For feeling and contemplative regard,
More than inherent liveliness and power.
How oft, amid those overflowing streets,
Have I gone forward with the crowd, and said
Unto myself, "The face of every one
That passes by me is a mystery!"
Thus have I looked, nor ceased to look, oppressed   630
By thoughts of what and whither, when and how,
Until the shapes before my eyes became
A second-sight procession, such as glides
Over still mountains, or appears in dreams;
And once, far-travelled in such mood, beyond

The reach of common indication, lost
Amid the moving pageant, I was smitten
Abruptly, with the view (a sight not rare)
Of a blind Beggar, who, with upright face,
Stood, propped against a wall, upon his chest
Wearing a written paper, to explain   641
His story, whence he came, and who he was.
Caught by the spectacle my mind turned round
As with the might of waters; an apt type
This label seemed of the utmost we can know,
Both of ourselves and of the universe;
And, on the shape of that unmoving man,
His steadfast face and sightless eyes, I gazed,
As if admonished from another world.

RETROSPECT—LOVE OF NATURE LEADING TO LOVE OF MAN

BOOK VIII (LINES 215–238)

                    . . . Yet, hail to you
Moors, mountains, headlands, and ye hollow
          vales,
Ye long deep channels for the Atlantic's voice,
Powers of my native region! Ye that seize
The heart with firmer grasp! Your snows and
          streams
Ungovernable, and your terrifying winds,   220
That howl so dismally for him who treads
Companionless your awful solitudes!
There, 'tis the shepherd's task the winter long
To wait upon the storms: of their approach
Sagacious, into sheltering coves he drives
His flock, and thither from the homestead
          bears
A toilsome burden up the craggy ways,
And deals it out, their regular nourishment
Strewn on the frozen snow. And when the
          spring
Looks out, and all the pastures dance with
          lambs,   230
And when the flock, with warmer weather,
          climbs
Higher and higher, him his office leads
To watch their goings, whatsoever track
The wanderers choose. For this he quits his
          home
At day-spring, and no sooner doth the sun
Begin to strike him with a fire-like heat,
Than he lies down upon some shining rock,
And breakfasts with his dog. . . .

RESIDENCE IN FRANCE

BOOK IX (LINES 390–416)

   Oh, sweet it is, in academic groves,   390
Or such retirement, Friend! as we have known
In the green dales beside our Rotha's stream,
Greta, or Derwent, or some nameless rill,
To ruminate, with interchange of talk,
On rational liberty, and hope in man,
Justice and peace. But far more sweet such
          toil—
Toil, say I, for it leads to thoughts abstruse—
If nature then be standing on the brink
Of some great trial, and we hear the voice
Of one devoted,—one whom circumstance
Hath called upon to embody his deep sense
In action, give it outwardly a shape,   402
And that of benediction, to the world.
Then doubt is not, and truth is more than
          truth,—
A hope it is, and a desire; a creed
Of zeal, by an authority Divine
Sanctioned, of danger, difficulty, or death.
Such conversation, under Attic shades,
Did Dion hold with Plato; ripened thus
For a deliverer's glorious task,—and such   410
He, on that ministry already bound,
Held with Eudemus and Timonides,
Surrounded by adventurers in arms,
When those two vessels with their daring
          freight,
For the Sicilian Tyrant's overthrow,
Sailed from Zacynthus. . . .

RESIDENCE IN FRANCE

BOOK X (LINES 154–190)

                    . . . I revolved,
How much the destiny of Man had still
Hung upon single persons; that there was,
Transcendent to all local patrimony,
One nature, as there is one sun in heaven;
That objects, even as they are great, thereby
Do come within the reach of humblest eyes;
That Man is only weak through his mistrust
And want of hope where evidence divine 162
Proclaims to him that hope should be most
          sure;
Nor did the inexperience of my youth
Preclude conviction, that a spirit strong

In hope, and trained to noble aspirations,
A spirit thoroughly faithful to itself,
Is for Society's unreasoning herd
A domineering instinct, serves at once
For way and guide, a fluent receptacle   170
That gathers up each petty straggling rill
And vein of water, glad to be rolled on
In safe obedience; that a mind, whose rest
Is where it ought to be, in self-restraint,
In circumspection and simplicity,
Falls rarely in entire discomfiture
Below its aim, or meets with, from without,
A treachery that foils it or defeats;
And, lastly, if the means on human will,
Frail human will, dependent should betray 180
Him who too boldly trusted them, I felt
That 'mid the loud distractions of the world
A sovereign voice subsists within the soul,
Arbiter undisturbed of right and wrong,
Of life and death, in majesty severe
Enjoining, as may best promote the aims
Of truth and justice, either sacrifice,
From whatsoever region of our cares
Or our infirm affections Nature pleads,
Earnest and blind, against the stern decree.   190

FRANCE

BOOK XI (LINES 392–423)

But indignation works where hope is not,
And thou, O Friend! wilt be refreshed. There
    is
One great society alone on earth:
The noble Living and the noble Dead.

Thine be such converse strong and sanative
A ladder for thy spirit to reascend
To health and joy and pure contentedness;
To me the grief confined, that thou art gone
From this last spot of earth, where Freedom
    now   400
Stands single in her only sanctuary;
A lonely wanderer art gone, by pain
Compelled and sickness, at this latter day,
This sorrowful reverse for all mankind.
I feel for thee, must utter what I feel:
The sympathies erewhile in part discharged,
Gather afresh, and will have vent again:
My own delights do scarcely seem to me
My own delights; the lordly Alps themselves,

Those rosy peaks, from which the Morning
    looks   410
Abroad on many nations, are no more
For me that image of pure gladsomeness
Which they were wont to be. Through kin-
    dred scenes,
For purpose, at a time, how different!
Thou tak'st thy way, carrying the heart and
    soul
That Nature gives to Poets, now by thought
Matured, and in the summer of their strength.
Oh! wrap him in your shades, ye giant woods,
On Etna's side; and thou, O flowery field
Of Enna! is there not some nook of thine, 420
From the first playtime of the infant world
Kept sacred to restorative delight,
When from afar invoked by anxious love?

IMAGINATION AND TASTE, HOW IMPAIRED AND RESTORED

BOOK XII (LINES 93–121, 151–173, 248–261, 295–335)

O Soul of Nature! excellent and fair!
That didst rejoice with me, with whom I, too,
Rejoiced through early youth, before the
    winds
And roaring waters, and in lights and shades
That marched and countermarched about the
    hills
In glorious apparition, Powers on whom
I daily waited, now all eye and now
All ear; but never long without the heart 100
Employed, and man's unfolding intellect:
O Soul of Nature! that, by laws divine
Sustained and governed, still dost overflow
With an impassioned life, what feeble ones
Walk on this earth! how feeble have I been
When thou wert in thy strength! Nor this
    through stroke
Of human suffering, such as justifies
Remissness and inaptitude of mind,
But through presumption; even in pleasure
    pleased
Unworthily, disliking here, and there   110
Liking; by rules of mimic art transferred
To things above all art; but more,—for this,
Although a strong infection of the age,
Was never much my habit—giving way
To a comparison of scene with scene,

Bent overmuch on superficial things,
Pampering myself with meagre novelties
Of colour and proportion; to the moods
Of time and season, to the moral power,
The affections and the spirit of the place, 120
Insensible. . . .

      * * *

      . . . And yet I knew a maid,
A young enthusiast, who escaped these bonds;
Her eye was not the mistress of her heart;
Far less did rules prescribed by passive taste,
Or barren intermeddling subtleties,
Perplex her mind; but, wise as women are
When genial circumstance hath favoured them,
She welcomed what was given, and craved no
    more;
Whate'er the scene presented to her view
That was the best, to that she was attuned 160
By her benign simplicity of life,
And through a perfect happiness of soul,
Whose variegated feelings were in this
Sisters, that they were each some new delight.
Birds in the bower, and lambs in the green
    field,
Could they have known her, would have
    loved; methought
Her very presence such a sweetness breathed,
That flowers, and trees, and even the silent
    hills,
And everything she looked on, should have
    had
An intimation how she bore herself   170
Towards them and to all creatures. God de-
    lights
In such a being; for, her common thoughts
Are piety, her life is gratitude.

      * * *
               [I] . . . saw
A naked pool that lay beneath the hills,
The beacon on the summit, and, more near,
A girl, who bore a pitcher on her head,   251
And seemed with difficult steps to force her
    way
Against the blowing wind. It was, in truth,
An ordinary sight; but I should need
Colours and words that are unknown to man,
To paint the visionary dreariness
Which, while I looked all round for my lost
    guide,
Invested moorland waste, and naked pool,
The beacon crowning the lone eminence,

The female and her garments vexed and
    tossed   260
By the strong wind. . . .

      * * *

      . . . Uncertain on which road to fix
My expectation, thither I repaired,
Scout-like, and gained the summit; 'twas a day
Tempestuous, dark, and wild, and on the
    grass
I sate half-sheltered by a naked wall;
Upon my right hand couched a single sheep,
Upon my left a blasted hawthorn stood;   301
With those companions at my side, I watched,
Straining my eyes intensely, as the mist
Gave intermitting prospect of the copse
And plain beneath. Ere we to school re-
    turned,—
That dreary time,—ere we had been ten days
Sojourners in my father's house, he died,
And I and my three brothers, orphans then,
Followed his body to the grave. The event,
With all the sorrow that it brought, appeared
A chastisement; and when I called to mind   311
That day so lately past, when from the crag
I looked in such anxiety of hope;
With trite reflections of morality,
Yet in the deepest passion, I bowed low
To God, Who thus corrected my desires;
And, afterwards, the wind and sleety rain,
And all the business of the elements;
The single sheep, and the one blasted tree,
And the bleak music from that old stone
    wall,   320
The noise of wood and water, and the mist
That on the line of each of those two roads
Advanced in such indisputable shapes;
All these were kindred spectacles and sounds
To which I oft repaired, and thence would
    drink,
As at a fountain; and on winter nights,
Down to this very time, when storm and rain
Beat on my roof, or, haply, at noon-day,
While in a grove I walk, whose lofty trees,
Laden with summer's thickest foliage, rock
In a strong wind, some working of the
    spirit,   331
Some inward agitations thence are brought,
Whate'er their office, whether to beguile
Thoughts over busy in the course they took,
Or animate an hour of vacant ease.

IMAGINATION AND TASTE, HOW IMPAIRED AND RESTORED

(CONCLUDED)

BOOK XIII (LINES 1–39)

FROM Nature doth emotion come, and
   moods
Of calmness equally are Nature's gift:
This is her glory; these two attributes
Are sister horns that constitute her strength.
Hence Genius, born to thrive by inter-
   change
Of peace and excitation, finds in her
His best and purest friend; from her receives
That energy by which he seeks the truth,
From her that happy stillness of the mind
Which fits him to receive it when unsought. 10

   Such benefit the humblest intellects
Partake of, each in their degree; 'tis mine
To speak, what I myself have known and
   felt;
Smooth task! for words find easy way, inspired
By gratitude, and confidence in truth.
Long time in search of knowledge did I
   range
The field of human life, in heart and mind
Benighted; but, the dawn beginning now
To re-appear, 'twas proved that not in vain
I had been taught to reverence a Power   20
That is the visible quality and shape
And image of right reason; that matures
Her processes by steadfast laws; gives birth
To no impatient or fallacious hopes,
No heat of passion or excessive zeal,
No vain conceits; provokes to no quick
   turns
Of self-applauding intellect; but trains
To meekness, and exalts by humble faith;
Holds up before the mind intoxicate
With present objects, and the busy dance 30
Of things that pass away, a temperate show
Of objects that endure; and by this course
Disposes her, when over-fondly set
On throwing off incumbrances, to seek
In man, and in the frame of social life,
Whate'er there is desirable and good
Of kindred permanence, unchanged in form
And function, or, through strict vicissitude
Of life and death, revolving.

CONCLUSION

BOOK XIV (LINES 40–118, 162–187)

The Moon hung naked in a firmament   40
Of azure without cloud, and at my feet
Rested a silent sea of hoary mist.
A hundred hills their dusky backs upheaved
All over this still ocean; and beyond,
Far, far beyond, the solid vapours stretched,
In headlands, tongues, and promontory shapes,
Into the main Atlantic, that appeared
To dwindle, and give up his majesty,
Usurped upon far as the sight could reach.
Not so the ethereal vault; encroachment
   none   50
Was there, nor loss; only the inferior stars
Had disappeared, or shed a fainter light
In the clear presence of the full-orbed Moon,
Who, from her sovereign elevation, gazed
Upon the billowy ocean, as it lay
All meek and silent, save that through a rift—
Not distant from the shore whereon we stood,
A fixed, abysmal, gloomy, breathing-place—
Mounted the roar of waters, torrents, streams
Innumerable, roaring with one voice!   60
Heard over earth and sea, and, in that hour,
For so it seemed, felt by the starry heavens.

   When into air had partially dissolved
That vision, given to spirits of the night
And three chance human wanderers, in calm
   thought
Reflected, it appeared to me the type
Of a majestic intellect, its acts
And its possessions, what it has and craves,
What in itself it is, and would become.
There I beheld the emblem of a mind   70
That feeds upon infinity, that broods
Over the dark abyss, intent to hear
Its voices issuing forth to silent light
In one continuous stream; a mind sustained
By recognitions of transcendent power,
In sense conducting to ideal form,
In soul of more than mortal privilege.
One function, above all, of such a mind
Had Nature shadowed there, by putting forth,
'Mid circumstances awful and sublime,   80
That mutual domination which she loves
To exert upon the face of outward things,
So moulded, joined, abstracted, so endowed
With interchangeable supremacy,

That men, least sensitive, see, hear, perceive,
And cannot choose but feel. The power, which all
Acknowledge when thus moved, which Nature thus
To bodily sense exhibits, is the express
Resemblance of that glorious faculty
That higher minds bear with them as their own.   90
This is the very spirit in which they deal
With the whole compass of the universe:
They from their native selves can send abroad
Kindred mutations; for themselves create
A like existence; and, whene'er it dawns
Created for them, catch it, or are caught
By its inevitable mastery,
Like angels stopped upon the wing by sound
Of harmony from Heaven's remotest spheres.
Them the enduring and the transient both   100
Serve to exalt; they build up greatest things
From least suggestions; ever on the watch,
Willing to work and to be wrought upon,
They need not extraordinary calls
To rouse them; in a world of life they live,
By sensible impressions not enthralled,
But by their quickening impulse made more prompt
To hold fit converse with the spiritual world,
And with the generations of mankind
Spread over time, past, present, and to come,
Age after age, till Time shall be no more.   111
Such minds are truly from the Deity,
For they are Powers; and hence the highest bliss
That flesh can know is theirs—the consciousness
Of Whom they are, habitually infused
Through every image and through every thought,
And all affections by communion raised
From earth to heaven, from human to divine.

*   *   *

                    . . . To fear and love,
To love as prime and chief, for there fear ends,
Be this ascribed; to early intercourse,
In presence of sublime or beautiful forms,
With the adverse principles of pain and joy—
Evil as one is rashly named by men
Who know not what they speak. By love subsists

All lasting grandeur, by pervading love;   169
That gone, we are as dust.—Behold the fields
In balmy spring-time full of rising flowers
And joyous creatures; see that pair, the lamb
And the lamb's mother, and their tender ways
Shall touch thee to the heart; thou callest this love,
And not inaptly so, for love it is,
Far as it carries thee. In some green bower
Rest, and be not alone, but have thou there
The One who is thy choice of all the world:
There linger, listening, gazing, with delight
Impassioned, but delight how pitiable!   180
Unless this love by a still higher love
Be hallowed, love that breathes not without awe;
Love that adores, but on the knees of prayer,
By heaven inspired; that frees from chains the soul,
Lifted, in union with the purest, best,
Of earth-born passions, on the wings of praise
Bearing a tribute to the Almighty's Throne.

From THE EXCURSION
PROSPECTUS

ON Man, on Nature, and on Human Life,
Musing in solitude, I oft perceive
Fair trains of imagery before me rise,
Accompanied by feelings of delight
Pure, or with no unpleasing sadness mixed;
And I am conscious of affecting thoughts
And dear remembrances, whose presence soothes
Or elevates the Mind, intent to weigh
The good and evil of our mortal state.
—To these emotions, whencesoe'er they come,   10
Whether from breath of outward circumstance,
Or from the Soul—an impulse to herself—
I would give utterance in numerous verse.
Of Truth, of Grandeur, Beauty, Love, and Hope,
And melancholy Fear subdued by Faith;
Of blessèd consolations in distress;
Of moral strength, and intellectual Power;
Of joy in widest commonalty spread;
Of the individual Mind that keeps her own
Inviolate retirement, subject there   20
To Conscience only, and the law supreme

To Mrs Lees
with best wishes
William Wordsworth

Ambleside
16th March 1837

THE EXCURSION.

Presentation Copy of Wordsworth's *The Excursion.*
(See Appendix I.)

Of that Intelligence which governs all—
I sing:—'fit audience let me find though few!'

  So prayed, more gaining than he asked, the
    Bard—
In holiest mood. Urania, I shall need
Thy guidance, or a greater Muse, if such
Descend to earth or dwell in highest heaven!
For I must tread on shadowy ground, must
    sink
Deep—and, aloft ascending, breathe in worlds
To which the heaven of heavens is but a veil.
All strength—all terror, single or in bands, 31
That ever was put forth in personal form—
Jehovah—with his thunder, and the choir
Of shouting Angels, and the empyreal
    thrones—
I pass them unalarmed. Not Chaos, not
The darkest pit of lowest Erebus,
Nor aught of blinder vacancy, scooped out
By help of dreams—can breed such fear and
    awe
As fall upon us often when we look
Into our Minds, into the Mind of Man— 40
My haunt, and the main region of my song.
—Beauty—a living Presence of the earth,
Surpassing the most fair ideal Forms
Which craft of delicate Spirits hath composed
From earth's materials—waits upon my steps;
Pitches her tents before me as I move,
An hourly neighbour. Paradise, and groves
Elysian, Fortunate Fields—like those of old
Sought in the Atlantic Main—why should
    they be
A history only of departed things,   50
Or a mere fiction of what never was?
For the discerning intellect of Man,
When wedded to this goodly universe
In love and holy passion, shall find these
A simple produce of the common day.
—I, long before the blissful hour arrives,
Would chant, in lonely peace, the spousal verse
Of this great consummation:—and, by words
Which speak of nothing more than what we
    are,
Would I arouse the sensual from their sleep 60
Of Death, and win the vacant and the vain
To noble raptures; while my voice proclaims
How exquisitely the individual Mind
(And the progressive powers perhaps no less
Of the whole species) to the external World

Is fitted:—and how exquisitely, too—
Theme this but little heard of among men—
The external World is fitted to the Mind;
And the creation (by no lower name
Can it be called) which they with blended
    might   70
Accomplish:—this is our high argument.
—Such grateful haunts foregoing, if I oft
Must turn elsewhere—to travel near the
    tribes
And fellowships of men, and see ill sights
Of madding passions mutually inflamed;
Must hear Humanity in fields and groves
Pipe solitary anguish; or must hang
Brooding above the fierce confederate storm
Of sorrow, barricadoed evermore   79
Within the walls of cities—may these sounds
Have their authentic comment; that even
    these
Hearing, I be not downcast or forlorn!—
Descend, prophetic Spirit! that inspir'st
The human Soul of universal earth,
Dreaming on things to come; and dost pos-
    sess
A metropolitan temple in the hearts
Of mighty Poets: upon me bestow
A gift of genuine insight; that my Song
With star-like virtue in its place may shine,
Shedding benignant influence, and secure, 90
Itself, from all malevolent effect
Of those mutations that extend their sway
Throughout the nether sphere!—And if with
    this
I mix more lowly matter; with the thing
Contemplated, describe the Mind and Man
Contemplating; and who, and what he was—
The transitory Being that beheld
This Vision; when and where, and how he
    lived;—
Be not this labour useless. If such theme
May sort with highest objects, then—dread
    Power!   100
Whose gracious favour is the primal source
Of all illumination,—may my Life
Express the image of a better time,
More wise desires, and simpler manners;—
    nurse
My Heart in genuine freedom:—all pure
    thoughts
Be with me;—so shall thy unfailing love
Guide, and support, and cheer me to the end!

THE SOLITARY

BOOK II (LINES 696–724)

". . . —Many are the notes
Which, in his tuneful course, the wind draws
    forth
From rocks, woods, caverns, heaths, and
    dashing shores;
And well those lofty brethren bear their part
In the wild concert—chiefly when the
    storm   700
Rides high; then all the upper air they fill
With roaring sound, that ceases not to flow,
Like smoke, along the level of the blast,
In mighty current; theirs, too, is the song
Of stream and headlong flood that seldom
    fails;
And, in the grim and breathless hour of noon,
Methinks that I have heard them echo back
The thunder's greeting. Nor have nature's
    laws
Left them ungifted with a power to yield
Music of finer tone; a harmony,   710
So do I call it, though it be the hand
Of silence, though there be no voice;—the
    clouds,
The mist, the shadows, light of golden suns,
Motions of moonlight, all come thither—
    touch,
And have an answer—thither come, and shape
A language not unwelcome to sick hearts
And idle spirits:—there the sun himself,
At the calm close of summer's longest day,
Rests his substantial orb;—between those
    heights
And on the top of either pinnacle,   720
More keenly than elsewhere in night's blue
    vault,
Sparkle the stars, as of their station proud.
Thoughts are not busier in the mind of man
Than the mute agents stirring there. . . ."

DESPONDENCY CORRECTED

BOOK IV (LINES 332–350)

"Happy is he who lives to understand,
Not human nature only, but explores
All natures,—to the end that he may find
The law that governs each; and where begins
The union, the partition where, that makes
Kind and degree, among all visible Beings;
The constitutions, powers, and faculties,
Which they inherit,—cannot step beyond,—
And cannot fall beneath; that do assign   340
To every class its station and its office,
Through all the mighty commonwealth of
    things;
Up from the creeping plant to sovereign Man.
Such converse, if directed by a meek,
Sincere, and humble spirit, teaches love:
For knowledge is delight; and such delight
Breeds love: yet, suited as it rather is
To thought and to the climbing intellect,
It teaches less to love, than to adore;
If that be not indeed the highest love!"   350

THE CHURCHYARD AMONG THE MOUNTAINS

BOOK VII (LINES 482–515)

"Soul-cheering Light, most bountiful of
    things!
Guide of our way, mysterious comforter!
Whose sacred influence, spread through earth
    and heaven,
We all too thanklessly participate,
Thy gifts were utterly withheld from him
Whose place of rest is near yon ivied porch.
Yet, of the wild brooks ask if he complained;
Ask of the channelled rivers if they held
A safer, easier, more determined, course.   490
What terror doth it strike into the mind
To think of one, blind and alone, advancing
Straight toward some precipice's airy brink!
But, timely warned, *He* would have stayed his
    steps,
Protected, say enlightened, by his ear;
And on the very edge of vacancy
Not more endangered than a man whose eye
Beholds the gulf beneath.—No floweret
    blooms
Throughout the lofty range of these rough
    hills,
Nor in the woods, that could from him con-
    ceal   500
Its birthplace; none whose figure did not live
Upon his touch. The bowels of the earth
Enriched with knowledge his industrious
    mind;
The ocean paid him tribute from the stores

Lodged in her bosom; and, by science led,
His genius mounted to the plains of heaven.
—Methinks I see him—how his eye-balls
    rolled,
Beneath his ample brow, in darkness paired,—
But each instinct with spirit; and the frame
Of the whole countenance alive with thought,
Fancy, and understanding; while the voice
Discoursed of natural or moral truth   512
With eloquence, and such authentic power,
That, in his presence, humbler knowledge
    stood
Abashed, and tender pity overawed."

THE PARSONAGE

BOOK VIII (LINES 231–282)

When from the Wanderer's lips these words
    had fallen,
I said, "And, did in truth those vaunted Arts
Possess such privilege, how could we escape
Sadness and keen regret, we who revere,
And would preserve as things above all price,
The old domestic morals of the land,
Her simple manners, and the stable worth
That dignified and cheered a low estate?
Oh! where is now the character of peace,
Sobriety, and order, and chaste love,   240
And honest dealing, and untainted speech,
And pure good-will, and hospitable cheer;
That made the very thought of country-life
A thought of refuge, for a mind detained
Reluctantly amid the bustling crowd?
Where now the beauty of the sabbath kept
With conscientious reverence, as a day
By the almighty Lawgiver pronounced
Holy and blest? and where the winning grace
Of all the lighter ornaments attached   250
To time and season, as the year rolled round?"

"Fled!" was the Wanderer's passionate
    response,
"Fled utterly! or only to be traced
In a few fortunate retreats like this;
Which I behold with trembling, when I
    think
What lamentable change, a year—a month—
May bring; that brook converting as it runs
Into an instrument of deadly bane
For those, who, yet untempted to forsake
The simple occupations of their sires,   260
Drink the pure water of its innocent stream
With lip almost as pure.—Domestic bliss
(Or call it comfort, by a humbler name,)
How art thou blighted for the poor Man's
    heart!
Lo! in such neighbourhood, from morn to
    eve,
The habitations empty! or perchance
The Mother left alone,—no helping hand
To rock the cradle of her peevish babe;
No daughters round her, busy at the wheel,
Or in dispatch of each day's little growth 270
Of household occupation; no nice arts
Of needle-work; no bustle at the fire,
Where once the dinner was prepared with
    pride;
Nothing to speed the day, or cheer the
    mind;
Nothing to praise, to teach, or to command!

"The Father, if perchance he still retain
His old employments, goes to field or wood,
No longer led or followed by the Sons;
Idlers perchance they were,—but in *his* sight;
Breathing fresh air, and treading the green
    earth;   280
Till their short holiday of childhood ceased,
Ne'er to return! . . ."

PREFACE

TO THE SECOND EDITION (1800) OF SEVERAL
OF THE FOREGOING POEMS, PUBLISHED,
WITH AN ADDITIONAL VOLUME, UNDER
THE TITLE OF "LYRICAL BALLADS"

THE first Volume of these Poems has already been submitted to general perusal. It was published, as an experiment, which, I hoped, might be of some use to ascertain, how far, by fitting 10 to metrical arrangement a selection of the real language of men in a state of vivid sensation, that sort of pleasure and that quantity of pleasure may be imparted, which a Poet may rationally endeavour to impart.

I had formed no very inaccurate estimate of the probable effect of those Poems: I flattered myself that they who should be pleased with them would read them with more than common pleasure: and, on the other hand, I was 20 well aware, that by those who should dislike them, they would be read with more than common dislike. The result has differed from my expectation in this only, that a greater number have been pleased than I ventured to hope I 25 should please.

Several of my Friends are anxious for the success of these Poems, from a belief, that, if the views with which they were composed 30 were indeed realised, a class of Poetry would be produced, well adapted to interest mankind permanently, and not unimportant in the quality, and in the multiplicity of its moral relations: and on this account they have ad-35 vised me to prefix a systematic defence of the theory upon which the Poems were written. But I was unwilling to undertake the task, knowing that on this occasion the Reader would look coldly upon my arguments, since 40 I might be suspected of having been principally influenced by the selfish and foolish hope of *reasoning* him into an approbation of these particular Poems: and I was still more unwilling to undertake the task, because, ade-45 quately to display the opinions, and fully to enforce the arguments, would require a space wholly disproportionate to a preface. For, to treat the subject with the clearness and coherence of which it is susceptible, it would be 50 necessary to give a full account of the present state of the public taste in this country, and to determine how far this taste is healthy or depraved; which, again, could not be determined, without pointing out in what manner 5 language and the human mind act and re-act on each other, and without retracing the revolutions, not of literature alone, but likewise of society itself. I have therefore altogether declined to enter regularly upon this 10 defence; yet I am sensible, that there would be something like impropriety in abruptly obtruding upon the Public, without a few words of introduction, Poems so materially different from those upon which general approbation is 15 at present bestowed.

It is supposed, that by the act of writing in verse an Author makes a formal engagement that he will gratify certain known habits of association; that he not only thus apprises the 20 Reader that certain classes of ideas and expressions will be found in his book, but that others will be carefully excluded. This exponent or symbol held forth by metrical language must in different eras of literature have excited very 25 different expectations: for example, in the age of Catullus, Terence, and Lucretius, and that of Statius or Claudian; and in our own country, in the age of Shakespeare and Beaumont and Fletcher, and that of Donne and Cowley, or 30 Dryden, or Pope. I will not take upon me to determine the exact import of the promise which, by the act of writing in verse, an Author in the present day makes to his reader: but it will undoubtedly appear to many per-35 sons that I have not fulfilled the terms of an engagement thus voluntarily contracted. They who have been accustomed to the gaudiness and inane phraseology of many modern writers, if they persist in reading this book to its con-40 clusion, will, no doubt, frequently have to struggle with feelings of strangeness and awkwardness: they will look round for poetry, and will be induced to inquire by what species of courtesy these attempts can be permitted 45 to assume that title. I hope therefore the reader will not censure me for attempting to state what I have proposed to myself to perform; and also (as far as the limits of a preface will permit) to explain some of the chief reasons 50 which have determined me in the choice of my purpose: that at least he may be spared any unpleasant feeling of disappointment, and that I myself may be protected from one of the most dishonourable accusations which can be brought against an Author; namely, that of an indolence which prevents him from endeavouring to ascertain what is his duty, or, when his duty is ascertained, prevents him from performing it.

The principal object, then, proposed in these Poems was to choose incidents and situations from common life, and to relate or describe them, throughout, as far as was possible in a selection of language really used by men, and, at the same time, to throw over them a certain colouring of imagination, whereby ordinary things should be presented to the mind in an unusual aspect; and, further, and above all, to make these incidents and situations interesting by tracing in them, truly though not ostentatiously, the primary laws of our nature: chiefly, as far as regards the manner in which we associate ideas in a state of excitement. Humble and rustic life was generally chosen, because, in that condition, the essential passions of the heart find a better soil in which they can attain their maturity, are less under restraint, and speak a plainer and more emphatic language; because in that condition of life our elementary feelings coexist in a state of greater simplicity, and, consequently, may be more accurately contemplated, and more forcibly communicated; because the manners of rural life germinate from those elementary feelings, and, from the necessary character of rural occupations, are more easily comprehended, and are more durable; and, lastly, because in that condition the passions of men are incorporated with the beautiful and permanent forms of nature. The language, too, of these men has been adopted (purified indeed from what appear to be its real defects, from all lasting and rational causes of dislike or disgust) because such men hourly communicate with the best objects from which the best part of language is originally derived; and because, from their rank in society and the sameness and narrow circle of their intercourse, being less under the influence of social vanity, they convey their feelings and notions in simple and unelaborated expressions. Accordingly, such a language, arising out of repeated experience and regular feelings, is a more permanent, and a far more philosophical language, than that which is frequently substituted for it by Poets, who think that they are conferring honour upon themselves and their art, in proportion as they separate themselves from the sympathies of men, and indulge in arbitrary and capricious habits of expression, in order to furnish food for fickle tastes, and fickle appetites, of their own creation.[1]

I cannot, however, be insensible to the present outcry against the triviality and meanness, both of thought and language, which some of my contemporaries have occasionally introduced into their metrical compositions; and I acknowledge that this defect, where it exists, is more dishonourable to the Writer's own character than false refinement or arbitrary innovation, though I should contend at the same time, that it is far less pernicious in the sum of its consequences. From such verses the Poems in these volumes will be found distinguished at least by one mark of difference, that each of them has a worthy *purpose*. Not that I always began to write with a distinct purpose formally conceived; but habits of meditation have, I trust, so prompted and regulated my feelings, that my descriptions of such objects as strongly excite those feelings, will be found to carry along with them a *purpose*. If this opinion be erroneous, I can have little right to the name of a Poet. For all good poetry is the spontaneous overflow of powerful feelings: and though this be true, Poems to which any value can be attached were never produced on any variety of subjects but by a man who, being possessed of more than usual organic sensibility, had also thought long and deeply. For our continued influxes of feeling are modified and directed by our thoughts, which are indeed the representatives of all our past feelings; and, as by contemplating the relation of these general representatives to each other, we discover what is really important to men, so, by the repetition and continuance of this act, our feelings will be connected with important subjects, till at length, if we be

---

[1] It is worth while here to observe, that the affecting parts of Chaucer are almost always expressed in language pure and universally intelligible even to this day.

originally possessed of much sensibility, such habits of mind will be produced, that, by obeying blindly and mechanically the impulses of those habits, we shall describe objects, and utter sentiments, of such a nature, and in such connection with each other, that the understanding of the Reader must necessarily be in some degree enlightened, and his affections strengthened and purified.

It has been said that each of these poems has a purpose. Another circumstance must be mentioned which distinguishes these Poems from the popular Poetry of the day; it is this, that the feeling therein developed gives importance to the action and situation, and not the action and situation to the feeling.

A sense of false modesty shall not prevent me from asserting, that the Reader's attention is pointed to this mark of distinction, far less for the sake of these particular Poems than from the general importance of the subject. The subject is indeed important! For the human mind is capable of being excited without the application of gross and violent stimulants; and he must have a very faint perception of its beauty and dignity who does not know this, and who does not further know, that one being is elevated above another, in proportion as he possesses this capability. It has therefore appeared to me, that to endeavour to produce or enlarge this capability is one of the best services in which, at any period, a Writer can be engaged; but this service, excellent at all times, is especially so at the present day. For a multitude of causes, unknown to former times, are now acting with a combined force to blunt the discriminating powers of the mind, and, unfitting it for all voluntary exertion, to reduce it to a state of almost savage torpor. The most effective of these causes are the great national events which are daily taking place, and the increasing accumulation of men in cities, where the uniformity of their occupations produces a craving for extraordinary incident, which the rapid communication of intelligence hourly gratifies. To this tendency of life and manners the literature and theatrical exhibitions of the country have conformed themselves. The invaluable works of our elder writers, I had almost said the works of Shakespeare and Milton, are driven into neglect by frantic novels, sickly and stupid German Tragedies, and deluges of idle and extravagant stories in verse.—When I think upon this degrading thirst after outrageous stimulation, I am almost ashamed to have spoken of the feeble endeavour made in these volumes to counteract it; and, reflecting upon the magnitude of the general evil, I should be oppressed with no dishonourable melancholy, had I not a deep impression of certain inherent and indestructible qualities of the human mind, and likewise of certain powers in the great and permanent objects that act upon it, which are equally inherent and indestructible; and were there not added to this impression a belief, that the time is approaching when the evil will be systematically opposed, by men of greater powers, and with far more distinguished success.

Having dwelt thus long on the subjects and aim of these Poems, I shall request the Reader's permission to apprise him of a few circumstances relating to their *style*, in order, among other reasons, that he may not censure me for not having performed what I never attempted. The Reader will find that personifications of abstract ideas rarely occur in these volumes; and are utterly rejected, as an ordinary device to elevate the style, and raise it above prose. My purpose was to imitate, and, as far as possible, to adopt the very language of men; and assuredly such personifications do not make any natural or regular part of that language. They are, indeed, a figure of speech occasionally prompted by passion, and I have made use of them as such; but have endeavoured utterly to reject them as a mechanical device of style, or as a family language which Writers in metre seem to lay claim to by prescription. I have wished to keep the Reader in the company of flesh and blood, persuaded that by so doing I shall interest him. Others who pursue a different track will interest him likewise; I do not interfere with their claim, but wish to prefer a claim of my own. There will also be found in these volumes little of what is usually called poetic diction; as much pains has been taken to avoid it as is ordinarily taken to produce it; this has been done for the reason already alleged, to bring my language near to the language of men; and further, because the pleasure which I have proposed to myself to impart, is of a kind very different from that which is supposed by many persons to be the proper object of poetry. Without being culpably particular, I do not know how to give my Reader a more exact notion of the style in which it was my wish and intention to write, than by informing him that I have at all times endeavoured to look steadily at my subject; consequently, there is I hope in these Poems little falsehood of description, and my ideas are expressed in language fitted to their respective importance. Something must have been gained by this practice, as it is friendly to one property of all good poetry, namely, good sense: but it has necessarily cut me off from a large portion of phrases and figures of speech which from father to son have long been regarded as the common inheritance of Poets. I have also thought it expedient to restrict myself still further, having abstained from the use of many expressions, in themselves proper and beautiful, but which have been foolishly repeated by bad Poets, till such feelings of disgust are connected with them as it is scarcely possible by any art of association to overpower.

If in a poem there should be found a series of lines, or even a single line, in which the language, though naturally arranged, and according to the strict laws of metre, does not differ from that of prose, there is a numerous class of critics, who, when they stumble upon these prosaisms, as they call them, imagine that they have made a notable discovery, and exult over the Poet as over a man ignorant of his own profession. Now these men would establish a canon of criticism which the Reader will conclude he must utterly reject, if he wishes to be pleased with these volumes. And it would be a most easy task to prove to him, that not only the language of a large portion of every good poem, even of the most elevated character, must necessarily, except with reference to the metre, in no respect differ from that of good prose, but likewise that some of the most interesting parts of the best poems will be found to be strictly the language of prose when prose is well written. The truth of this assertion might be demonstrated by innumerable passages from almost all the poetical writings, even of Milton himself. To illustrate the subject in a general manner, I will here adduce a short composition of Gray, who was at the head of those who, by their reasonings, have attempted to widen the space of separation betwixt Prose and Metrical composition, and was more than any other man curiously elaborate in the structure of his own poetic diction.

In vain to me the smiling mornings shine,
And reddening Phoebus lifts his golden fire:
The birds in vain their amorous descant join,
Or cheerful fields resume their green attire.
These ears, alas! for other notes repine;
A different object do these eyes require;
My lonely anguish melts no heart but mine,
And in my breast the imperfect joys expire;
Yet morning smiles the busy race to cheer,
And new-born pleasure brings to happier men;
The fields to all their wonted tribute bear;
To warm their little loves the birds complain.
I fruitless mourn to him that cannot hear,
And weep the more because I weep in vain.

It will easily be perceived, that the only part of this Sonnet which is of any value is the lines printed in Italics; it is equally obvious, that, except in the rhyme, and in the use of the single word "fruitless" for fruitlessly, which is so far a defect, the language of these lines does in no respect differ from that of prose.

By the foregoing quotation it has been shown that the language of Prose may yet be well adapted to Poetry; and it was previously asserted, that a large portion of the language of every good poem can in no respect differ from that of good Prose. We will go further. It may be safely affirmed, that there neither is, nor can be, any *essential* difference between the language of prose and metrical composition. We are fond of tracing the resemblance between Poetry and Painting, and, accordingly, we call them Sisters: but where shall we find bonds of connection sufficiently strict to typify the affinity betwixt metrical and prose composition? They both speak by and to the same organs; the bodies in which both of them are clothed may be said to be of the same substance, their affections are kindred, and almost identical, not necessarily differing even in degree; Poetry [1] sheds no tears "such as Angels

---

[1] I here use the word "Poetry" (though against my own judgment) as opposed to the word Prose, and synonymous with metrical composition. But

weep," but natural and human tears; she can boast of no celestial ichor that distinguishes her vital juices from those of prose; the same human blood circulates through the veins of them both.

If it be affirmed that rhyme and metrical arrangement of themselves constitute a distinction which overturns what has just been said on the strict affinity of metrical language with that of prose, and paves the way for other artificial distinctions which the mind voluntarily admits, I answer that the language of such Poetry as is here recommended is, as far as is possible, a selection of the language really spoken by men; that this selection, wherever it is made with true taste and feeling, will of itself form a distinction far greater than would at first be imagined, and will entirely separate the composition from the vulgarity and meanness of ordinary life; and, if metre be superadded thereto, I believe that a dissimilitude will be produced altogether sufficient for the gratification of a rational mind. What other distinction would we have? Whence is it to come? And where is it to exist? Not, surely, where the Poet speaks through the mouths of his characters: it cannot be necessary here, either for elevation of style, or any of its supposed ornaments: for, if the Poet's subject be judiciously chosen, it will naturally, and upon fit occasion, lead him to passions the language of which, if selected truly and judiciously, must necessarily be dignified and variegated, and alive with metaphors and figures. I forbear to speak of an incongruity which would shock the intelligent Reader, should the Poet interweave any foreign splendour of his own with that which the passion naturally suggests: it is sufficient to say that such addition is unnecessary. And, surely, it is more probable that those passages, which with propriety abound with metaphors and figures, will have their due effect, if, upon other occasions where

much confusion has been introduced into criticism by this contradistinction of Poetry and Prose, instead of the more philosophical one of Poetry and Matter of Fact, or Science. The only strict antithesis to Prose is Metre; nor is this, in truth, a *strict* antithesis, because lines and passages of metre so naturally occur in writing prose, that it would be scarcely possible to avoid them, even were it desirable.

the passions are of a milder character, the style also be subdued and temperate.

But, as the pleasure which I hope to give by the Poems now presented to the Reader must depend entirely on just notions upon this subject, and, as it is in itself of high importance to our taste and moral feelings, I cannot content myself with these detached remarks. And if, in what I am about to say, it shall appear to some that my labour is unnecessary, and that I am like a man fighting a battle without enemies, such persons may be reminded, that, whatever be the language outwardly holden by men, a practical faith in the opinions which I am wishing to establish is almost unknown. If my conclusions are admitted, and carried as far as they must be carried if admitted at all, our judgments concerning the works of the greatest Poets both ancient and modern will be far different from what they are at present, both when we praise, and when we censure: and our moral feelings influencing and influenced by these judgments will, I believe, be corrected and purified.

Taking up the subject, then, upon general grounds, let me ask, what is meant by the word Poet? What is a Poet? To whom does he address himself? And what language is to be expected from him?—He is a man speaking to men: a man, it is true, endowed with more lively sensibility, more enthusiasm and tenderness, who has a greater knowledge of human nature, and a more comprehensive soul, than are supposed to be common among mankind; a man pleased with his own passions and volitions, and who rejoices more than other men in the spirit of life that is in him; delighting to contemplate similar volitions and passions as manifested in the goings-on of the Universe, and habitually impelled to create them where he does not find them. To these qualities he has added a disposition to be affected more than other men by absent things as if they were present; an ability of conjuring up in himself passions, which are indeed far from being the same as those produced by real events, yet (especially in those parts of the general sympathy which are pleasing and delightful) do more nearly resemble the passions produced by real events, than anything which, from the motions of their own minds merely, other men are accustomed to feel in themselves:—whence, and from practice, he has acquired a greater readiness and power in expressing what he thinks and feels, and especially those thoughts and feelings which, by his own choice, or from the structure of his own mind, arise in him without immediate external excitement.

But whatever portion of this faculty we may suppose even the greatest Poet to possess, there cannot be a doubt that the language which it will suggest to him, must often, in liveliness and truth, fall short of that which is uttered by men in real life, under the actual pressure of those passions, certain shadows of which the Poet thus produces, or feels to be produced, in himself.

However exalted a notion we would wish to cherish of the character of a Poet, it is obvious, that while he describes and imitates passions, his employment is in some degree mechanical, compared with the freedom and power of real and substantial action and suffering. So that it will be the wish of the Poet to bring his feelings near to those of the persons whose feelings he describes, nay, for short spaces of time, perhaps, to let himself slip into an entire delusion, and even confound and identify his own feelings with theirs; modifying only the language which is thus suggested to him by a consideration that he describes for a particular purpose, that of giving pleasure. Here, then, he will apply the principle of selection which has been already insisted upon. He will depend upon this for removing what would otherwise be painful or disgusting in the passion; he will feel that there is no necessity to trick out or to elevate nature: and, the more industriously he applies this principle, the deeper will be his faith that no words, which *his* fancy or imagination can suggest, will be to be compared with those which are the emanations of reality and truth.

But it may be said by those who do not object to the general spirit of these remarks, that, as it is impossible for the Poet to produce upon all occasions language as exquisitely fitted for the passion as that which the real passion itself suggests, it is proper that he should consider himself as in the situation of a translator, who does not scruple to substitute excellencies of another kind for those which are unattainable by him; and endeavours occasionally to surpass his original, in order to make some amends for the general inferiority to which he feels that he must submit. But this would be to encourage idleness and unmanly despair. Further, it is the language of men who speak of what they do not understand; who talk of Poetry as of a matter of amusement and idle pleasure; who will converse with us as gravely about a *taste* for Poetry, as they express it, as if it were a thing as indifferent as a taste for rope-dancing, or Frontiniac or Sherry. Aristotle, I have been told, has said, that Poetry is the most philosophic of all writing: it is so: its object is truth, not individual and local, but general, and operative; not standing upon external testimony, but carried alive into the heart by passion; truth which is its own testimony, which gives competence and confidence to the tribunal to which it appeals, and receives them from the same tribunal. Poetry is the image of man and nature. The obstacles which stand in the way of the fidelity of the Biographer and Historian, and of their consequent utility, are incalculably greater than those which are to be encountered by the Poet who comprehends the dignity of his art. The Poet writes under one restriction only, namely, the necessity of giving immediate pleasure to a human Being possessed of that information which may be expected from him, not as a lawyer, a physician, a mariner, an astronomer, or a natural philosopher, but as a Man. Except this one restriction, there is no object standing between the Poet and the image of things; between this, and the Biographer and Historian, there are a thousand.

Nor let this necessity of producing immediate pleasure be considered as a degradation of the Poet's art. It is far otherwise. It is an acknowledgment of the beauty of the universe, an acknowledgment the more sincere, because not formal, but indirect; it is a task light and easy to him who looks at the world in the spirit of love: further, it is a homage paid to the native and naked dignity of man, to the grand elementary principle of pleasure, by which he knows, and feels, and lives, and moves. We have no sympathy but what is propagated by pleasure: I would not be misunderstood; but wherever we sympathise with pain, it will be found that the sympathy is produced and carried on by subtle combinations with pleasure. We have no knowledge, that is, no general principles drawn from the contemplation of particular facts, but what has been built up by pleasure, and exists in us by pleasure alone. The Man of science, the Chemist and Mathematician, whatever difficulties and disgusts they may have had to struggle with, know and feel this. However painful may be the objects with which the Anatomist's knowledge is connected, he feels that his knowledge is pleasure; and where he has no pleasure he has no knowledge. What then does the Poet? He considers man and the objects that surround him as acting and re-acting upon each other, so as to produce an infinite complexity of pain and pleasure; he considers man in his own nature and in his ordinary life as contemplating this with a certain quantity of immediate knowledge, with certain convictions, intuitions, and deductions, which from habit acquire the quality of intuitions; he considers him as looking upon this complex scene of ideas and sensations, and finding everywhere objects that immediately excite in him sympathies which, from the necessities of his nature, are accompanied by an overbalance of enjoyment.

To this knowledge which all men carry about with them, and to these sympathies in which, without any other discipline than that of our daily life, we are fitted to take delight, the Poet principally directs his attention. He considers man and nature as essentially adapted to each other, and the mind of man as naturally the mirror of the fairest and most interesting properties of nature. And thus the Poet, prompted by this feeling of pleasure, which accompanies him through the whole course of his studies, converses with general nature, with affections akin to those, which, through labour and length of time, the Man of science has raised up in himself, by conversing with those particular parts of nature which are the objects of his studies. The knowledge both of the Poet and the Man of science is pleasure; but the knowledge of the one cleaves to us as a necessary part of our existence, our natural and unalienable inheritance; the other is a personal and individual acquisition, slow to come to us, and by no habitual and direct sympathy connecting us with our fellow-beings. The Man of science seeks truth as a remote and unknown benefactor; he cherishes and loves it in his solitude: the Poet, singing a song in which all human beings join with him, rejoices in the presence of truth as our visible friend and hourly companion. Poetry is the breath and finer spirit of all knowledge; it is the impassioned expression which is in the countenance of all Science. Emphatically may it be said of the Poet, as Shakespeare hath said of man, "that he looks before and after." He is the rock of defence for human nature; an upholder and preserver, carrying everywhere with him relationship and love. In spite of difference of soil and climate, of language and manners, of laws and customs: in spite of things silently gone out of mind, and things violently destroyed; the Poet binds together by passion and knowledge the vast empire of human society, as it is spread over the whole earth, and over all time. The objects of the Poet's thoughts are everywhere; though the eyes and senses of man are, it is true, his favourite guides, yet he will follow wheresoever he can find an atmosphere of sensation in which to move his wings. Poetry is the first and last of all knowledge—it is as immortal as the heart of man. If the labours of Men of science should ever create any material revolution, direct or indirect, in our condition, and in the impressions which we habitually receive, the Poet will sleep then no more than at present; he will be ready to follow the steps of the Man of science, not only in those general indirect effects, but he will be at his side, carrying sensation into the midst of the objects of the science itself. The remotest discoveries of the Chemist, the Botanist, or Mineralogist, will be as proper objects of the Poet's art as any upon which it can be employed, if the time should ever come when these things shall be familiar to us, and the relations under which they are contemplated by the followers of these respective sciences shall be manifestly and palpably material to us as enjoying and suffering beings. If the time should ever come when what is now called science, thus familiarised to men, shall be ready to put on, as it were, a form of flesh and blood, the Poet will lend his divine spirit to aid the transfiguration, and will welcome the Being thus produced, as a dear and genuine inmate of the household of man. —It is not, then, to be supposed that any one, who holds that sublime notion of Poetry which I have attempted to convey, will break in upon the sanctity and truth of his pictures by transitory and accidental ornaments, and endeavour to excite admiration of himself by arts, the necessity of which must manifestly depend upon the assumed meanness of his subject.

What has been thus far said applies to Poetry in general; but especially to those parts of composition where the Poet speaks through the mouths of his characters; and upon this point it appears to authorise the conclusion that there are few persons of good sense, who would not allow that the dramatic parts of composition are defective, in proportion as they deviate from the real language of nature, and are coloured by a diction of the Poet's own, either peculiar to him as an individual Poet or belonging simply to Poets in general; to a body of men who, from the circumstance of their compositions being in metre, it is expected will employ a particular language.

It is not, then, in the dramatic parts of composition that we look for this distinction of language; but still it may be proper and necessary where the Poet speaks to us in his own person and character. To this I answer by referring the Reader to the description before given of a Poet. Among the qualities there enumerated as principally conducing to form a Poet, is implied nothing differing in kind from other men, but only in degree. The sum of what was said is, that the Poet is chiefly distinguished from other men by a greater promptness to think and feel without immediate external excitement, and a greater power in expressing such thoughts and feelings as are produced in him in that manner. But these passions and thoughts and feelings are the general passions and thoughts and feelings of men. And with what are they connected? Undoubtedly with our moral sentiments and animal sensations, and with the causes which excite these; with the operations of the elements, and the appearances of the visible universe; with storm and sunshine, with the revolutions of the seasons, with cold and heat, with loss of friends and kindred, with injuries and resentments, gratitude and hope, with fear and sorrow. These, and the like, are the sensations and objects which the Poet describes, as they are the sensations of other men, and the objects which interest them. The Poet thinks and feels in the spirit of human passions. How, then, can his language differ in any material degree from that of all other men who feel vividly and see clearly? It might be *proved* that it is impossible. But supposing that this were not the case, the Poet might then be allowed to use a peculiar language when expressing his feelings for his own gratification, or that of men like himself. But Poets do not write for Poets alone, but for men. Unless therefore we are advocates for that admiration which subsists upon ignorance, and that pleasure which arises from hearing what we do not understand, the Poet must descend from this supposed height; and, in order to excite rational sympathy, he must express himself as other men express themselves. To this it may be added, that while he is only selecting from the real language of men, or, which amounts to the same thing, composing accurately in the spirit of such selection, he is treading upon safe ground, and we know what we are to expect from him. Our feelings are the same with respect to metre; for, as it may be proper to remind the Reader, the distinction of metre is regular and uniform, and not, like that which is produced by what is usually called POETIC DICTION, arbitrary, and subject to infinite caprices upon which no calculation whatever can be made. In the one case, the Reader is utterly at the mercy of the Poet, respecting what imagery or diction he may choose to connect with the passion; whereas, in the other, the metre obeys certain laws, to which the Poet and Reader both willingly submit because they are certain, and because no interference is made by them with the passion, but such as the concurring testimony of ages has shown to heighten and improve the pleasure which co-exists with it.

It will now be proper to answer an obvious question, namely, Why, professing these opinions, have I written in verse? To this, in addition to such answer as is included in what has been already said, I reply, in the first place, Because, however I may have restricted myself, there is still left open to me what confessedly constitutes the most valuable object of all writing, whether in prose or verse; the great and universal passions of men, the most general and interesting of their occupations, and the entire world of nature before me—to supply endless combinations of forms and imagery. Now, supposing for a moment that whatever is interesting in these objects may be as vividly described in prose, why should I be condemned for attempting to superadd to such description the charm which, by the consent of all nations, is acknowledged to exist in metrical language? To this, by such as are yet unconvinced, it may be answered that a very small part of the pleasure given by Poetry depends upon the metre, and that it is injudicious to write in metre, unless it be accompanied with the other artificial distinctions of style with which metre is usually accompanied, and that, by such deviation, more will be lost from the shock which will thereby be given to the Reader's associations than will be counterbalanced by any pleasure which he can derive from the general power of numbers. In answer to those who still contend for the necessity of accompanying metre with certain appropriate colours of style in order to the accomplishment of its appropriate end, and who also, in my opinion, greatly underrate the power of metre in itself, it might, perhaps, as far as relates to these Volumes, have been almost sufficient to observe, that poems are extant, written upon more humble subjects, and in a still more naked and simple style, which have continued to give pleasure from generation to generation. Now, if nakedness and simplicity be a defect, the fact here mentioned affords a strong presumption that poems somewhat less naked and simple are capable of affording pleasure at the present day; and, what I wished *chiefly* to attempt, at present, was to justify myself for having written under the impression of this belief.

But various causes might be pointed out why, when the style is manly, and the subject of some importance, words metrically arranged will long continue to impart such a pleasure to mankind as he who proves the extent of that pleasure will be desirous to impart. The end of Poetry is to produce excitement in co-existence with an overbalance of pleasure; but, by the supposition, excitement is an unusual and irregular state of the mind; ideas and feelings do not, in that state, succeed each other in accustomed order. If the words, however, by which this excitement is produced be in themselves powerful, or the images and feelings have an undue proportion of pain connected with them, there is some danger that the excitement may be carried beyond its proper bounds. Now the co-presence of something regular, something to which the mind has been accustomed in various moods and in a less excited state, cannot but have great efficacy in tempering and restraining the passion by an intertexture of ordinary feeling, and of feeling not strictly and necessarily connected with the passion. This is unquestionably true; and hence, though the opinion will at first appear paradoxical, from the tendency of metre to divest language, in a certain degree, of its reality, and thus to throw a sort of half-consciousness of unsubstantial existence over the whole composition, there can be little doubt but that more pathetic situations and sentiments, that is, those which have a greater proportion of pain connected with them, may be endured in metrical composition, especially in rhyme, than in prose. The metre of the old ballads is very artless; yet they contain many passages which would illustrate this opinion; and, I hope, if the following Poems be attentively perused, similar instances will be found in them. This opinion may be further illustrated by appealing to the Reader's own experience of the reluctance with which he comes to the re-perusal of the distressful parts of "Clarissa Harlowe," or the "Gamester;" while Shakespeare's writings, in the most pathetic scenes, never act upon us, as pathetic, beyond the bounds of pleasure—an effect which, in a much greater degree than might at first be imagined, is to be ascribed to small, but continual and regular impulses of pleasurable surprise from the metrical arrangement.— On the other hand (what it must be allowed will much more frequently happen) if the Poet's words should be incommensurate with the passion, and inadequate to raise the Reader to a height of desirable excitement, then, (unless the Poet's choice of his metre has been grossly injudicious) in the feelings of pleasure which the Reader has been accustomed to connect with metre in general, and in the feeling, whether cheerful or melancholy, which he has been accustomed to connect with that particular movement of metre, there will be found something which will greatly contribute to impart passion to the words, and to effect the complex end which the Poet proposes to himself.

If I had undertaken a SYSTEMATIC defence of the theory here maintained, it would have been my duty to develope the various causes upon which the pleasure received from metrical language depends. Among the chief of these causes is to be reckoned a principle which must be well known to those who have made any of the Arts the object of accurate reflection; namely, the pleasure which the mind derives from the perception of similitude in dissimilitude. This principle is the great spring of the activity of our minds, and their chief feeder. From this principle the direction of the sexual appetite, and all the passions connected with it, take their origin: it is the life of our ordinary conversation; and upon the accuracy with which similitude in dissimilitude, and dissimilitude in similitude are perceived, depend our taste and our moral feelings. It would not be a useless employment to apply this principle to the consideration of metre, and to show that metre is hence enabled to afford much pleasure, and to point out in what manner that pleasure is produced. But my limits will not permit me to enter upon this subject, and I must content myself with a general summary.

I have said that poetry is the spontaneous overflow of powerful feelings: it takes its origin from emotion recollected in tranquillity: the emotion is contemplated till, by a species of reaction, the tranquillity gradually disappears, and an emotion, kindred to that which was before the subject of contemplation, is gradually produced, and does itself actually exist in the mind. In this mood successful composition generally begins, and in a mood similar to this it is carried on; but the emotion, of whatever kind, and in whatever degree, from various causes, is qualified by various pleasures, so that in describing any passions whatsoever, which are voluntarily described, the mind will, upon the whole, be in a state of enjoyment. If Nature be thus cautious to preserve in a state of enjoyment a being so employed, the Poet ought to profit by the lesson held forth to him, and ought especially to take care, that, whatever passions he communicates to his Reader, those passions, if his Reader's mind be sound and vigorous, should always be accompanied with an overbalance of pleasure. Now the music of harmonious metrical language, the sense of difficulty overcome, and the blind association of pleasure which has been previously received from works of rhyme or metre of the same or similar construction, an indistinct perception perpetually renewed of language closely resembling that of real life, and yet, in the circumstance of metre, differing from it so widely—all these imperceptibly make up a complex feeling of delight, which is of the most important use in tempering the painful feeling always found intermingled with powerful descriptions of the deeper passions. This effect is always produced in pathetic and impassioned poetry; while, in lighter compositions, the ease and gracefulness with which the Poet manages his numbers are themselves confessedly a principal source of the gratification of the Reader. All that it is *necessary* to say, however, upon this subject, may be effected by affirming, what few persons will deny, that, of two descriptions, either of passions, manners, or characters, each of them equally well executed, the one in prose and the other in verse, the verse will be read a hundred times where the prose is read once.

Having thus explained a few of my reasons for writing in verse, and why I have chosen subjects from common life, and endeavoured to bring my language near to the real language of men, if I have been too minute in pleading my own cause, I have at the same time been treating a subject of general interest; and for this reason a few words shall be added with reference solely to these particular poems, and to some defects which will probably be found in them. I am sensible that my associations must have sometimes been particular instead of general, and that, consequently, giving to things a false importance, I may have sometimes written upon unworthy subjects; but I am less apprehensive on this account, than that my language may frequently have suffered from those arbitrary connections of feelings and ideas with particular words and phrases, from which no man can altogether protect himself. Hence I have no doubt, that, in some instances, feelings, even of the ludicrous, may be given to my Readers by expressions which appeared to me tender and pathetic. Such faulty expressions, were I convinced they were faulty at present, and that they must necessarily continue to be so, I would willingly take all reasonable pains to correct. But it is dangerous to make these alterations on the simple authority of a few individuals, or even of certain classes of men; for where the understanding of an Author is not convinced, or his feelings altered, this cannot be done without great injury to himself: for his own feelings are his stay and support; and, if he set them aside in one instance, he may be induced to repeat this act till his mind shall lose all confidence in itself, and become utterly debilitated. To this it may be added, that the critic ought never to forget that he is himself exposed to the same errors as the Poet, and, perhaps, in a much greater degree: for there can be no presumption in saying of most readers, that it is not probable they will be so well acquainted with the various stages of meaning through which words have passed, or with the fickleness or stability of the relations of particular ideas to each other; and, above all, since they are so much less interested in the subject, they may decide lightly and carelessly.

Long as the Reader has been detained, I hope he will permit him to caution him against a mode of false criticism which has been applied to Poetry, in which the language closely resembles that of life and nature. Such verses have been triumphed over in parodies, of which Dr. Johnson's stanza is a fair specimen:—

> I put my hat upon my head
> And walked into the Strand,
> And there I met another man
> Whose hat was in his hand.

Immediately under these lines let us place one of the most justly-admired stanzas of the "Babes in the Wood,"

> These pretty Babes with hand in hand
> Went wandering up and down;
> But never more they saw the Man
> Approaching from the Town.

In both these stanzas the words, and the order of the words, in no respect differ from the most unimpassioned conversation. There are words in both, for example, "the Strand," and "the Town," connected with none but the most familiar ideas; yet the one stanza we admit as admirable, and the other as a fair example of the superlatively contemptible. Whence arises this difference? Not from the metre, not from the language, not from the order of the words; but the *matter* expressed in Dr. Johnson's stanza is contemptible. The proper method of treating trivial and simple verses, to which Dr. Johnson's stanza would be a fair parallelism, is not to say, this is a bad kind of poetry, or, this is not poetry; but, this wants sense; it is neither interesting in itself, nor can *lead* to anything interesting; the images neither originate in that sane state of feeling which arises out of thought, nor can excite thought or feeling in the Reader. This is the only sensible manner of dealing with such verses. Why trouble yourself about the species till you have previously decided upon the genus? Why take pains to prove that an ape is not a Newton, when it is self-evident that he is not a man?

One request I must make of my reader, which is, that in judging these Poems he would decide by his own feelings genuinely, and not by reflection upon what will probably be the judgment of others. How common is it to hear a person say, I myself do not object to this style of composition, or this or that expression, but, to such and such classes of people it will appear mean or ludicrous! This mode of criticism, so destructive of all sound unadulterated judgment, is almost universal: let the Reader then abide, independently, by his own feelings, and, if he finds himself affected, let him not suffer such conjectures to interfere with his pleasure.

If an Author, by any single composition, has impressed us with respect for his talents, it is useful to consider this as affording a presumption, that on other occasions where we have been displeased, he, nevertheless, may not have written ill or absurdly; and further, to give him so much credit for this one composition as may induce us to review what has displeased us, with more care than we should otherwise have bestowed upon it. This is not only an act of justice, but, in our decisions upon poetry especially, may conduce, in a high degree, to the improvement of our own taste; for an *accurate* taste in poetry, and in all the other arts, as Sir Joshua Reynolds has observed, is an *acquired* talent, which can only be produced by thought and a long-continued intercourse with the best models of composition. This is mentioned, not with so ridiculous a purpose as to prevent the most inexperienced Reader from judging for himself, (I have already said that I wish him to judge for himself;) but merely to temper the rashness of decision, and to suggest, that, if Poetry be a subject on which much time has not been bestowed, the judgment may be erroneous; and that, in many cases, it necessarily will be so.

Nothing would, I know, have so effectually contributed to further the end which I have in view, as to have shown of what kind the pleasure is, and how that pleasure is produced, which is confessedly produced by metrical composition essentially different from that which I have here endeavoured to recommend: for the Reader will say that he has been pleased by such composition; and what more can be done for him? The power of any art is limited; and he will suspect, that, if it be proposed to furnish him with new friends, that can be only upon condition of his abandoning his old friends. Besides, as I have said, the Reader is himself conscious of the pleasure which he has received from such composition, composition to which he has peculiarly attached the endearing name of Poetry; and all men feel an habitual gratitude, and something of an honourable bigotry, for the objects which have long continued to please them: we not only wish to be pleased, but to be pleased in that particular way in which we have been accustomed to be pleased. There is in these feelings enough to resist a host of arguments; and I should be the less able to combat them successfully, as I am willing to allow, that, in order entirely to enjoy the Poetry which I am recommending, it would be necessary to give

up much of what is ordinarily enjoyed. But, would my limits have permitted me to point out how this pleasure is produced, many obstacles might have been removed, and the Reader assisted in perceiving that the powers of language are not so limited as he may suppose; and that it is possible for poetry to give other enjoyments, of a purer, more lasting, and more exquisite nature. This part of the subject has not been altogether neglected, but it has not been so much my present aim to prove, that the interest excited by some other kinds of poetry is less vivid, and less worthy of the nobler powers of the mind, as to offer reasons for presuming, that if my purpose were fulfilled, a species of poetry would be produced, which is genuine poetry; in its nature well adapted to interest mankind permanently, and likewise important in the multiplicity and quality of its moral relations.

From what has been said, and from a perusal of the Poems, the Reader will be able clearly to perceive the object which I had in view: he will determine how far it has been attained; and, what is a much more important question, whether it be worth attaining: and upon the decision of these two questions will rest my claim to the approbation of the Public.

SELECTIONS FROM WORDSWORTH'S LETTERS

I To John Wilson (Christopher North)

(1) THE INFLUENCE OF NATURAL OBJECTS
(2) *THE IDIOT BOY*

1802

My dear Sir,

Had it not been for a very amiable modesty, you could not have imagined that your letters could give me any offence. It was on many accounts highly grateful to me. I was pleased to find that I had given so much pleasure to an ingenuous and able mind, and I further considered the enjoyment which you had had from my Poems as an earnest that others might be delighted with them in the same or a like manner. It is plain from your letter that the pleasure which I have given you has not been blind or unthinking; you have studied the poems, and prove that you have entered into the spirit of them. They have not given you a cheap or vulgar pleasure; therefore I feel that you are entitled to my kindest thanks for having done some violence to your natural diffidence in the communication which you have made to me.

There is scarcely any part of your letter that does not deserve particular notice; but partly from some constitutional infirmities, and partly from certain habits of mind, I do not write any letters unless upon business, not even to my dearest friends. Except during absence from my own family I have not written five letters of friendship during the last five years. I have mentioned this in order that I may retain your good opinion, should my letter be less minute than you are entitled to expect. You seem to be desirous of my opinion on the influence of natural objects in forming the character of Nations. This cannot be understood without first considering their influence upon men in general, first, with reference to such objects as are common to all countries; and, next, such as belong exclusively to any particular country, or in a greater degree to it than to another. Now it is manifest that no human being can be so besotted and debased by oppression, penury, or any other evil which unhumanises man, as to be utterly insensible to the colours, forms, or smell of flowers, the [voices] and motions of birds and beasts, the appearances of the sky and heavenly bodies, the general warmth of a fine day, the terror and uncomfortableness of a storm, etc. etc. How dead soever many full-grown men may outwardly seem to these things, all are more or less affected by them; and in childhood, in the first practice and exercise of their senses, they must have been not the nourishers merely, but often the fathers of their passions. There cannot be a doubt that in tracts of country where images of danger, melancholy, grandeur, or loveliness, softness, and ease prevail, they will make themselves felt powerfully in forming the characters of the people, so as to produce uniformity or national character where the nation is small and is not made up of men who, inhabiting different soils, climates, etc., by their civil usages and relations, materially interfere with each other. It was so formerly, no doubt, in the Highlands of Scotland; but we cannot perhaps observe much of it in our own island at the present day, because, even in the most sequestered places, by manufactures, traffic, religion, law, interchange of inhabitants, etc., distinctions are done away, which would otherwise have been strong and obvious. This complex state of society does not, however, prevent the characters of individuals from frequently receiving a strong bias, not merely from the impressions of general nature, but also from local objects and images. But it seems that to produce these effects, in the degree in which we frequently find them to be produced, there must be a peculiar sensibility of original organisation combining with moral accidents, as is exhibited in *The Brothers* and in *Ruth;* I mean, to produce this in a marked degree; not that I believe that any man was ever brought up in the country without loving it, especially in his better moments, or in a district of particular grandeur or beauty without feeling some stronger attachment to it on that account than he would otherwise have felt. I include, you will observe, in these considerations, the influence of climate, changes in the atmosphere and elements, and the labours and occupations which particular districts require.

You begin what you say upon the *Idiot Boy*, with this observation, that nothing is a fit subject for poetry which does not please. But here follows a question, Does not please whom? Some have little knowledge of natural imagery of any kind, and, of course, little relish for it; some are disgusted with the very mention of the words pastoral poetry, sheep or shepherds; some cannot tolerate a poem with a ghost or any supernatural agency in it; others would shrink from an animated description of the pleasures of love, as from a thing carnal and libidinous; some cannot bear to see delicate and refined feelings ascribed to men in low conditions in society, because their vanity and self-love tell them that these belong only to themselves, and men like themselves in dress, station, and way of life; others are disgusted with the naked language of some of the most interesting passions of men, because it is either indelicate, or gross, or vulgar; as many fine ladies could not bear certain expressions in *The Mother* and *The Thorn*, and, as in the instance of Adam Smith, who, we are told, could not endure the ballad of *Clym of the Clough*, because the author had not written like a gentleman. Then there are professional and national prejudices for evermore. Some take no interest in the description of a particular passion or quality, as love of solitariness, we will say, genial activity of fancy, love of nature, religion, and so forth, because they have little or nothing of it in themselves; and so on without end. I return then to [the] question, please whom? or what? I answer, human nature as it has been [and ever] will be. But where are we to find the best measure of this? I answer, [from with]in; by stripping our own hearts naked, and by looking out of ourselves to-[wards men] who lead the simplest lives, and those most according to nature; men who have never known false refinements, wayward and artificial desires, false criticisms, effeminate habits of thinking and feeling, or who, having known these things, have outgrown them. This latter class is the most to be depended upon, but it is very small in number. People in our rank in life are perpetually falling into one sad mistake, namely, that of supposing that human nature and the persons they associate with are one and the same thing. Whom do we generally associate with? Gentlemen, persons of fortune, professional men, ladies, persons who can afford to buy, or can easily procure books of half-a-guinea price, hot-pressed, and printed upon superfine paper. These persons are, it is true, a part of human nature, but we err lamentably if we suppose them to be fair representatives of the vast mass of human existence. And yet few ever consider books but with reference to their power of pleasing these persons and men of a higher rank; few descend lower, among cottages and fields, and among children. A man must have done this habitually before his judgment upon *The Idiot Boy* would be in any way decisive with me. I know I have done this myself habitually; I wrote the poem with exceeding delight and pleasure, and whenever I read it I read it with pleasure. You have given me praise for having reflected faithfully in my Poems the feelings of human nature. I would fain hope that I have done so. But a great Poet ought to do more than this; he ought, to a certain degree, to rectify men's feelings, to give them new compositions of feeling, to render their feelings more sane, pure, and permanent, in short, more consonant to nature, that is, to eternal nature, and the great moving spirit of things. He ought to travel before men occasionally as well as at their sides. I may illustrate this by a reference to natural objects. What false notions have prevailed from generation to generation of the true character of the Nightingale. As far as my Friend's Poem in the *Lyrical Ballads* is read, it will contribute greatly to rectify these. You will recollect a passage in Cowper, where, speaking of rural sounds, he says,

> And even the boding Owl
> That hails the rising moon has charms for me.

Cowper was passionately fond of natural objects, yet you see he mentions it as a marvelous thing that he could connect pleasure with the cry of the owl. In the same poem he speaks in the same manner of that beautiful plant, the gorse; making in some degree an amiable boast of his loving it, 'unsightly' and unsmooth as it is. There are many aversions of this kind, which, though they have some foundation in nature, have yet so slight a one, that, though they may have prevailed hundreds of years, a philosopher will look upon them as accidents. So with respect to many moral feelings, either of love or dislike. What excessive admiration was paid in former times to personal prowess and military success; it is so with the latter even at the present day, but surely not nearly so much as heretofore. So with regard to birth, and innumerable other modes of sentiment, civil and religious. But you will be inclined to ask by this time how all this applies to *The Idiot Boy*. To this I can only say that the loathing and disgust which many people have at the sight of an idiot is a feeling which, though having some foundation in human nature, is not necessarily attached to it in any virtuous degree, but is owing in a great measure to a false delicacy, and, if I may say it without rudeness, a certain want of comprehensiveness of thinking and feeling. Persons in the lower classes of society have little or nothing of this: if an idiot is born in a poor man's house, it must be taken care of, and cannot be boarded out, as it would be by gentlefolks, or sent to a public or private receptacle for such unfortunate beings. [Poor people], seeing frequently among their neighbours such objects, easily [forget] whatever there is of natural disgust about them, and have [therefore] a sane state, so that without pain or suffering they [perform] their duties towards them. I could with pleasure pursue this subject, but I must now strictly adopt the plan which I proposed to myself when I began to write this letter, namely, that of setting down a few hints or memorandums, which you will think of for my sake.

I have often applied to idiots, in my own mind, that sublime expression of scripture that their "life is hidden with God." They are worshipped, probably from a feeling of this sort, in several parts of the East. Among the Alps, where they are numerous, they are considered, I believe, as a blessing to the family to which they belong. I have, indeed, often looked upon the conduct of fathers and mothers of the lower classes of society towards idiots as the great triumph of the human heart. It is there that we see the strength, disinterestedness, and grandeur of love; nor have I ever been able to contemplate an object that calls out so many excellent and virtuous sentiments without finding it hallowed thereby, and having something in me which bears down before it, like a deluge, every feeble sensation of disgust and aversion.

There are, in my opinion, several important mistakes in the latter part of your letter which I could have wished to notice; but I find myself much fatigued. These refer both to the Boy and the Mother. I must content myself simply with observing that it is probable that the principal cause of your dislike to this particular poem lies in the word Idiot. If there had been any such word in our language, to which we had attached passion, as lack-wit, half-wit, witless, etc., I should have certainly employed it in preference; but there is no such word. Observe (this is entirely in reference to this particular poem), my "Idiot" is not one of those who cannot articulate, and such as are usually disgusting in their persons:

Whether in cunning or in joy,
And then his words were not a few, etc.

See also the last speech at the end of the poem. The "Boy" whom I had in my mind was by no means disgusting in his appearance, quite the contrary; and I have known several with imperfect faculties, who are handsome in their persons and features. There is one, at present, within a mile of my own house, who is remarkably so, though [he has something] of a stare and vacancy in his countenance. A friend of mine, knowing that some persons had a dislike to the poem, such as you have expressed, advised me to add a stanza, describing the person of the Boy [so as] to entirely separate him in the imaginations of my readers from that class of idiots who are disgusting in their persons; but the narration in the poem is so rapid and impassioned, that I could not find a place in which to insert the stanza without checking the progress of it, and [so leaving] a deadness upon the feeling. This poem has, I know, frequently produced the same effect as it did upon you and your friends; but there are many also to whom it affords exquisite delight, and who, indeed, prefer it to any other of my poems. This proves that the feelings there delineated are such as men may sympathize with. This is enough for my purpose. It is not enough for me as a Poet, to delineate merely such feelings as all men do sympathize with; but it is also highly desirable to add to these others, such as all men may sympathize with, and such as there is reason to believe they would be better and more moral beings if they did sympathize with.

I conclude with regret, because I have not said one half of [what I intended] to say; but I am sure you will deem my excuse sufficient, [when I] inform you that my head aches violently, and I am in other respects unwell. I must, however, again give you my warmest thanks for your kind letter. I shall be happy to hear from you again: and do not think it unreasonable that I should request a letter from you, when I feel that the answer which I may make to it will not perhaps be above three or four lines. This I mention to you with frankness, and you will not take it ill after what I have before said of my remissness in writing letters.

II To Sir Walter Scott

DRYDEN AS A POET

November 7, 1805

I was much pleased to hear of your engagement with Dryden; not that he is, as a poet, any great favourite of mine. I admire his talents and genius highly, but his is not a poetical genius. The only qualities I can find in Dryden that are essentially poetical are a certain ardor and impetuosity of mind, with an excellent ear. It may seem strange that I do not add to this, great command of language; that he certainly has, and of such language too, as it is most desirable that a poet should possess, or rather, that he should not be without. But it is not language that is, in the highest sense of the word, poetical, being neither of the imagination nor of the passions; I mean the amiable, the ennobling, or the intense passions. I do not mean to say that there is nothing of this in Dryden, but as little, I think, as is possible, considering how much he has written. You will easily understand my meaning, when I refer to his versification of *Palamon and Arcite*, as contrasted with the language of Chaucer. Dryden had neither a tender heart nor a lofty sense of moral dignity. Whenever his language is poetically impassioned, it is mostly upon unpleasing subjects, such as the follies, vices, and crimes of classes of men, or of individuals. That his cannot be the language of imagination must have necessarily followed from this; that there is not a single image from nature in the whole body of his works; and in his translation from Virgil, whenever Virgil can be fairly said to have his eye upon his object, Dryden always spoils the passage.

III To Sir George Beaumont

THE LANGUAGE OF POETRY

(c. 1807)

My dear Sir George,

I am quite delighted to hear of your picture for Peter Bell; I was much pleased with the sketch, and I have no doubt that the picture will surpass it as far as a picture ought to do. I long much to see it. I should approve of any engraver approved by you. But remember that no poem of mine will ever be popular; and I am afraid that the sale of Peter would not carry the expense of the engraving, and that the poem, in the estimation of the public, would be a weight upon the print. I say not this in modest disparagement of the poem, but in sorrow for the sickly taste of the public in verse. The people would love the poem of Peter Bell, but the public (a very different being) will never love it. Thanks for dear Lady B's transcript from your friend's letter; it is written with candor, but I must say a word or two not in praise of it. "Instances of what I mean," says your friend, "are to be found in a poem on a Daisy" (by the bye, it is on *the* Daisy, a mighty difference!) "and on Daffodils reflected in the Water." Is this accurately transcribed by Lady Beaumont? If it be, what shall we think of criticism or judgment founded upon, and exemplified by, a poem which must have been so inattentively perused? My language is precise; and, therefore, it would be false modesty to charge myself with blame.

> . . . Beneath the trees,
> Ten thousand dancing in the breeze.
> The waves beside them danced, but they
> Outdid the sparkling waves in glee.

Can expression be more distinct? And let me ask your friend how it is possible for flowers to be reflected in water when there are waves? They may, indeed, in still water; but the very object of my poem is the trouble or agitation, both of the flowers and the water. I must needs respect the understanding of every one honored by your friendship; but sincerity compels me to say that my poems must be more nearly looked at, before they can give rise to any remarks of much value, even from the strongest minds. With respect to this individual poem, Lady B. will recollect how Mrs. Fermor expressed herself upon it. A letter also was sent to me, addressed to a friend of mine, and by him communicated to me, in which this identical poem was singled out for fervent approbation. What then shall we say? Why, let the poet first consult his own heart, as I have done, and leave the rest to posterity—to, I hope, an improving posterity. The fact is, the English public are at this moment in the same state of mind with respect to my poems, if small things may be compared with great, as the French are in respect to Shakespeare, and not the French alone, but almost the whole Continent. In short, in your friend's letter, I am condemned for the very thing for which I ought to have been praised, viz., that I have not written down to the level of superficial observers and unthinking minds. Every great poet is a teacher: I wish either to be considered as a teacher, or as nothing. . . .

IV To Lady Beaumont

THE DESTINY OF HIS POEMS

Coleorton, 21 May, 1807

My dear Lady Beaumont,

Though I am to see you so soon, I cannot but write a word or two, to thank you for the interest you take in my poems, as evinced by your solicitude about their immediate reception. I write partly to thank you for this, and to express the pleasure it has given me, and partly to remove any uneasiness from your mind which the disappointments you sometimes meet with in this labor of love, may occasion. I see that you have many battles to fight for me—more than, in the ardor and confidence of your pure and elevated mind, you had even thought of being summoned to; but be assured that this opposition is nothing more than what I distinctly foresaw that you and my other friends would have to encounter. I say this, not to give myself credit for an eye of prophecy, but to allay any vexatious thoughts on my account which this opposition may have produced in you.

It is impossible that any expectations can be lower than mine concerning the immediate effect of this little work upon what is called the public. I do not here take into consideration the envy and malevolence, and all the bad passions which always stand in the way of a work of any merit from a living poet; but merely think of the pure, absolute, honest ignorance in which all worldlings of every rank and situation must be enveloped, with respect to the thoughts, feelings and images on which the life of my poems depends. The things which I have taken, whether from within or without, what have they to do with routs, dinners, morning calls, hurry from door to door, from street to street, on foot or in car-

riage; with Mr. Pitt or Mr. Fox, Mr. Paul or Sir Francis Burdett, the Westminster election or the borough of Honiton? In a word—for I cannot stop to make my way through the 5 hurry of images that present themselves to me —what have they to do with the endless talking about things nobody cares anything for except as far as their own vanity is concerned, and this with persons they care nothing for 10 but as their vanity or *selfishness* is concerned? —what have they to do (to say all at once) with a life without love? In such a life there can be no thought; for we have no thought (save thoughts of pain) but as far as we have 15 love and admiration.

It is an awful truth, that there neither is, nor can be, any genuine enjoyment of poetry among nineteen out of twenty of those persons who live, or wish to live, in the broad light of 20 the world—among those who either are, or are striving to make themselves, people of consideration in society. This is a truth, and an awful one, because to be incapable of a feeling of poetry, in my sense of the word, is 25 to be without love of human nature and reverence for God.

Upon this I shall insist elsewhere; at present let me confine myself to my object, which is to make you, my dear friend, as easy-hearted 30 as myself with respect to these poems. Trouble not yourself upon their present reception; of what moment is that compared with what I trust is their destiny?—to console the afflicted; to add sunshine to daylight, by making the 35 happy happier; to teach the young and the gracious of every age to see, to think, and feel, and therefore to become more actively and securely virtuous; this is their office, which I trust they will faithfully perform, long after 40 we (that is, all that is mortal of us) are mouldered in our graves. I am well aware how far it would seem to many I overrate my own exertions, when I speak in this way, in direct connexion with the volume I have just made 45 public.

I am not, however, afraid of such censure, insignificant as probably the majority of those poems would appear to very respectable persons. I do not mean London wits and witlings, 50 for these have too many foul passions about them to be respectable, even if they had more intellect than the benign laws of Providence will allow to such a heartless existence as theirs is; but grave, kindly-natured, worthy persons, who would be pleased if they could. I hope that these volumes are not without some rec-ommendations, even for readers of this class: but their imagination has slept; and the voice which is the voice of my poetry, without imagination, cannot be heard. . . .

My letter (as this second sheet, which I am 10 obliged to take, admonishes me) is growing to an enormous length; and yet, saving that I have expressed my calm confidence that these poems will live, I have said nothing which has a particular application to the object of it, 15 which was to remove all disquiet from your mind on account of the condemnation they may at present incur from that portion of my contemporaries who are called the public. I am sure, my dear Lady Beaumont, if you attach 20 any importance to it, it can only be from an apprehension that it may affect me, upon which I have already set you at ease; or from a fear that this present blame is ominous of their future or final destiny. If this be the case, your 25 tenderness for me betrays you. Be assured that the decision of these persons has nothing to do with the question; they are altogether in-competent judges. These people, in the sense-less hurry of their idle lives, do not read books, 30 they merely snatch a glance at them, that they may talk about them. And even if this were not so, never forget what, I believe, was ob-served to you by Coleridge, that every great and original writer, in proportion as he is 35 great or original, must himself create the taste by which he is to be relished; he must teach the art by which he is to be seen; this, in a certain degree, even to all persons, however wise and pure may be their lives, and however 40 unvitiated their taste. But for those who dip into books in order to give an opinion of them, or talk about them to take up an opinion— for this multitude of unhappy and misguided, and misguiding beings, an entire regeneration 45 must be produced; and if this be possible, it must be a work of time. To conclude, my ears are stone-dead to this idle buzz, and my flesh as insensible as iron to these petty stings; and after what I have said, I am sure yours will 50

be the same. I doubt not that you will share with me an invincible confidence that my writings (and among them these little poems) will co-operate with the benign tendencies in human nature and society, wherever found; 5 and that they will in their degree be efficacious in making men wiser, better, and happier. Farewell. I will not apologize for this letter, though its length demands an apology. . . .

V To Henry Reed

THE IMPRESSION MADE BY HIS POEMS

Rydal Mount, Dec. 23, 1839

My dear Sir,

The year is upon the point of expiring; and a letter of yours, dated May 7th, though not received till late in June (for I was moving about all last spring and part of the summer), remains unacknowledged. I have also to thank 20 you for the acceptable present of the two volumes which reached me some time after-wards.

*   *   *

Your letters are naturally turned upon the impression which my poems have made, and the estimation they are held, or likely to be held in, through the vast country to which you belong. I wish I could feel as lively as 30 you do upon this subject, or even upon the general destiny of those works. Pray do not be long surprised at this declaration. There is a difference of more than the length of your life, I believe, between our ages. I am stand-ing on the brink of that vast ocean I must sail so soon; I must speedily lose sight of the shore; and I could not once have conceived how little I now am troubled by the thought of how long or short a time they who remain on that 40 shore may have sight of me. The other day I chanced to be looking over a MS. poem, be-longing to the year 1803, though not actually composed till many years afterwards. It was suggested by visiting the neighborhood of 45 Dumfries, in which Burns had resided, and where he died; it concluded thus:

Sweet Mercy to the gates of heaven
This minstrel led, his sins forgiven;
The rueful conflict, the heart riven
  With vain endeavor,

And memory of earth's bitter leaven
Effaced forever.

Here the verses closed; but I instantly added,
the other day,

But why to him confine the prayer,
When kindred thoughts and yearnings bear
On the frail heart the purest share
With all that live?
The best of what we do and are,
Just God, forgive!

The more I reflect upon this last exclamation, the more I feel (and perhaps it may in some degree be the same with you) justified in attaching comparatively small importance to any literary monument that I may be enabled to leave behind. It is well, however, I am convinced, that men think otherwise in the earlier part of their lives; and why it is so, is a point I need not touch upon in writing to you. . . .

VI To Bernard Barton

THE PURE SOURCE OF HIS INSPIRATION

Jan. 12, 1816

It is always a satisfaction to me to learn that I have given pleasure upon rational grounds; and I have nothing to object to your poetical panegyric but the occasion which called it forth. An admirer of my works, zealous as you have declared yourself to be, condescends too much when he gives way to an impulse proceeding from the ——, or indeed from any other Review. The writers in these publications, while they prosecute their inglorious employment, cannot be supposed to be in a state of mind very favorable for being affected by the finer influences of a thing so pure as genuine poetry; and as to the instance which has incited you to offer me this tribute of your gratitude, though I have not seen it, I doubt not but that it is a splenetic effusion of the conductor of that Review, who has taken a perpetual retainer from his own incapacity to plead against my claims to public approbation.

* * *

It pleases, though it does not surprise me, to learn that, having been affected early in life by my verse, you have returned again to your old loves after some little infidelities, which you were shamed into by commerce with the scribbling and chattering part of the world. I have heard of many who, upon their first acquaintance with my poetry, have had much to get over before they could thoroughly relish it; but never of one who, having once learned to enjoy it, had ceased to value it or survived his admiration. This is as good an external assurance as I can desire that my inspiration is from a pure source, and that my principles of composition are trustworthy.

VII To Edward Moxon

THE SEDUCTION OF VERSE

Dec. 8, 1826

. . . I always feel some apprehension for the destiny of those who in youth addict themselves to the composition of verse. It is a very seducing employment, and, though begun in disinterested love of the Muses, is too apt to connect itself with self-love, and the disquieting passions which follow in the train of that our natural infirmity. Fix your eyes upon acquiring independence by honorable business, and let the Muses come after rather than go before. Such lines as the latter of this couplet,

Where lovely woman, chaste as heaven above,
Shines in the golden virtues of her love,

and many other passages in your poem, give proof of no commonplace sensibility. I am therefore the more earnest that you should guard yourself against this temptation.

VIII To Lt.-Gen. Sir William M. Gomm

POETRY A GREAT ART

Rydal Mount, April 16, 1834

. . . Poetry is infinitely more of an art than the world is disposed to believe. Nor is this any dishonor to it; both for the reason that the poetic faculty is not rarely bestowed, and for this cause, also, that men would not be disposed to ascribe so much to inspiration, if they did not feel how near and dear to them poetry is.

Reduced Facsimile of a Statement about an Agreement with Moxon the Publisher. In Wordsworth's Handwriting. (See Appendix I.)

IX To W. R. Hamilton

CRITICISING A FRIEND'S VERSES

Sept. 24, 1827

The logical faculty has infinitely more to do with poetry than the young and the inexperi- 5 enced, whether writer or critic, ever dreams of. Indeed, as the materials upon which that faculty is exercised in poetry are so subtle, so plastic, so complex, the application of it requires an adroitness which can proceed from nothing 10 but practice, a discernment which emotion is so far from bestowing that at first it is ever in the way of it. Here I must stop: only let me advert to two lines:

But shall despondence therefore blench my brow,
Or pining sorrow sickly ardor o'er.

These are two of the worst lines in mere expression. "Blench" is perhaps miswritten for "blanch;" if not, I don't understand the word. 20 *Blench* signifies to flinch. If "blanch" be the word, the next ought to be "hair." You can't here use brow for the hair upon it, because a white brow or forehead is a beautiful characteristic of youth. "Sickly ardor o'er" was at first 25 reading to me unintelligible. I took "sickly" to be an adjective joined with "ardor," whereas you mean it as a portion of a verb, from Shakespeare, "Sicklied o'er with the pale cast of thought." But the separation of the parts or 30 decomposition of the word, as here done, is not to be endured.

Let me now come to your sister's verses, for which I thank you. They are surprisingly vigorous for a female pen, but occasionally too 35 rugged, and especially for such a subject; they have also the same faults in expression as your own, but not, I think, in quite an equal degree. Much is to be hoped from feelings so strong, and from a mind thus disposed. I should have 40 entered into particulars with these also, had I seen you after they came into my hands. Your sister is, no doubt, aware that in her poem she has trodden the same ground as Gray, in his *Ode upon a Distant Prospect of Eton College.* 45 What he has been contented to treat in the abstract, she has represented in particular, and with admirable spirit. But again, my dear Sir, let me exhort you (and do you exhort your sister) to deal little with modern writers, but fix your attention almost exclusively upon those who have stood the test of time. . . .

X To the Rev. Robert Montgomery

EVERY WRITER HIS OWN BEST CRITIC

Feb. 1835

I cannot conclude without one word of literary advice, which I hope you will deem my advanced age entitles me to give. Do not, my 10 dear Sir, be anxious about any individual's opinion concerning your writings, however highly you may think of his genius or rate his judgment. Be a severe critic to yourself; and depend upon it, no person's decision upon the 15 merit of your works will bear comparison in point of value with your own. You must be conscious from what feeling they have flowed, and how far they may or may not be allowed to claim, on that account, permanent respect; 20 and, above all, I would remind you, with a view to tranquillise and steady your mind, that no man takes the trouble of surveying and pondering another's writings with a hundredth part of the care which an author of sense and 25 genius will have bestowed upon his own. Add to this reflection another, which I press upon you, as it has supported me through life, viz., that Posterity will settle all accounts justly, and that works which deserve to last will last; 30 and, if undeserving this fate, the sooner they perish the better.

XI To Alexander Dyce

A POETESS OF GENIUS

Oct. 16, 1829

. . . There is one poetess to whose writings I am especially partial, the Countess of Winchelsea. I have perused her poems frequently, 40 and should be happy to name such passages as I think most characteristic of her genius, and most fit to be selected.

XII To Alexander Dyce

THE GREATNESS OF ENGLISH DRAMA

May, 1830

. . . The poetic genius of England, with the exception of Chaucer, Spenser, Milton, Dryden, Pope, and a very few more, is to be sought in her drama.

XIII To W. R. Hamilton

THE HARD ART OF POETRY

Nov. 22, 1831

. . . The composition of verse is infinitely more of an art than men are prepared to believe; and absolute success in it depends upon innumerable minutiae, which it grieves me you should stoop to acquire a knowledge of. Milton talks of "pouring easy his unpremeditated verse." It would be harsh, untrue, and odious, to say there is anything like cant in this; but it is not true to the letter, and tends to mislead. I could point out to you five hundred passages in Milton upon which labor has been bestowed, and twice five hundred more to which additional labor would have been serviceable. Not that I regret the absence of such labor, because no poem contains more proofs of skill acquired by practice.

XIV To Edward Moxon

HIS POETRY GOES BEGGING

Aug. 1833

* * *

There does not appear to be much genuine relish for poetical publications in Cumberland, if I may judge from the fact of not a copy of my poems having been sold there by one of the leading booksellers, though Cumberland is my native county. Byron and Scott are, I am persuaded, the only popular writers in that line,—perhaps the word ought rather to be that they are fashionable writers.

XV To the Rev. Alexander Dyce

THE SONNET

1833

* * *

You propose to give specimens of the best sonnet-writers in our language. May I ask if by this be meant a selection of the best sonnets, best both as to kind and degree? A sonnet may be excellent in its kind, but that kind of very inferior interest to one of a higher order, though not perhaps in every minute particular quite so well executed, and from the pen of a writer of inferior genius. It should seem that the best rule to follow would be, first, to pitch upon the sonnets which are best both in kind and perfectness of execution, and, next, those which, although of a humbler quality, are admirable for the finish and happiness of the execution; taking care to exclude all those which have not one or other of these recommendations, however striking they might be, as characteristic of the age in which the author lived, or some peculiarity of his manner. The 10th sonnet of Donne, beginning "Death, be not proud," is so eminently characteristic of his manner, and at the same time so weighty in the thought, and vigorous in the expression, that I would entreat you to insert it, though to modern taste it may be repulsive, quaint, and labored. There are two sonnets of Russell, which, in all probability, you may have noticed, "Could, then, the babes," and the one upon Philoctetes, the last six lines of which are first-rate. Southey's *Sonnet to Winter* pleases me much; but, above all, among modern writers, that of Sir Egerton Brydges, upon *Echo and Silence*. Miss Williams's *Sonnet upon Twilight* is pleasing; that upon *Hope* of great merit.

Do you mean to have a short preface upon the construction of the sonnet? Though I have written so many, I have scarcely made up my own mind upon the subject. It should seem that the sonnet, like every other legitimate composition, ought to have a beginning, a middle, and an end; in other words, to consist of three parts, like the three propositions of a syllogism, if such an illustration may be used. But the frame of meter adopted by the Italians does not accord with this view; and, as adhered to by them, it seems to be, if not arbitrary, best fitted to a division of the sense into two parts, of eight and six lines each. Milton, however, has not submitted to this; in the better half of his sonnets the sense does not close with the rhyme at the eighth line, but overflows into the second portion of the meter. Now, it has struck me, that this is not done merely to gratify the ear by variety and freedom of sound, but also to aid in giving that pervading sense of intense unity in which the excellence of the sonnet has always seemed to me mainly to consist. Instead of looking at this composition as a piece of architecture, making a whole out of three parts, I have been much in the habit of preferring the image of an orbicular body,—a sphere, or a dew-drop. All this will appear to you a little fanciful; and I am well aware that a sonnet will often be found excellent, where the beginning, the middle, and the end are distinctly marked, and also where it is distinctly separated into two parts, to which, as I before observed, the strict Italian model, as they write it, is favourable. Of this last construction of sonnet, Russell's upon *Philoctetes* is a fine specimen; the first eight lines give the hardship of the case, the six last the consolation, or the per-contra.

XVI To the Rev. Alexander Dyce

ON DYCE'S COLLECTION OF SONNETS

Dec. 4, 1833

* * *

The selection of sonnets appears to me to be very judicious. If I were inclined to make an exception, it would be in the single case of the sonnet of Coleridge upon Schiller, which is too much of a rant for my taste. The one by him upon Linley's music is much superior in execution; indeed, as a strain of feeling, and for unity of effect, it is very happily done. I was glad to see Mr. Southey's *Sonnet to Winter.* A lyrical poem of my own, upon the disasters of the French army in Russia, has so striking a resemblance to it, in contemplating winter under two aspects, that, in justice to Mr. Southey, who preceded me, I ought to have acknowledged it in a note; and I shall do so upon some future occasion.

How do you come on with Skelton? And is there any prospect of a new edition of your *Specimens of British Poetesses?* If I could get at the original works of the elder poetesses, such as the Duchess of Newcastle, Mrs. Behn, Orinda, etc., I should be happy to assist you with my judgment in such a publication, which, I think, might be made still more interesting than this first edition, especially if more matter were crowded into a page. The two volumes of *Poems by Eminent Ladies,* Helen Maria Williams's *Works,* Mrs. Smith's *Sonnets,* and Lady Winchelsea's *Poems,* form the scanty materials which I possess for assisting such a publication.

It is a remarkable thing, th___ ballads, perhaps, of modern ____ *Robin Grey* and the *Lament* ____ *the Scots at Flodden-field,* a____ pens of females.

XVII To Sir George Beaumont

TASTE IN NATURAL BEAUTY

October 17, 1805

... So that Nature had greatly the advantage in those days, when what has been called English gardening was unheard of. This is now beginning to be perceived, and we are setting out to travel backwards. Painters and poets have had the credit of being reckoned the fathers of English gardening; they will also have, hereafter, the better praise of being fathers of a better taste. It was a misconception of the meaning and principles of poets and painters which gave countenance to the modern system of gardening, which is now, I hope, on the decline; in other words, we are submitting to the rule which you at present are guided by, that of having our houses belonging to the country, which will of course lead us back to the simplicity of Nature. And leaving your own individual sentiments and present work out of the question, what good can come of any other guide, under any circumstances? We have, indeed, distinctions of rank, hereditary legislators, and large landed proprietors; but from numberless causes the state of society is so much altered, that nothing of that lofty or imposing interest, formerly attached to large property in land, can now exist; none of the poetic pride, and pomp, and circumstance; nor anything that can be considered as making amends for violation done to the holiness of Nature.

* * *

I know nothing which to me would be so pleasing or affecting as to be able to say when I am in the midst of a large estate—This man is not the victim of his condition; he is not the spoiled child of worldly grandeur; the thought of himself does not take the lead in his enjoyments; he is, when he ought to be, lowly-minded, and has human feeling; he has a true relish of simplicity, and therefore stands the best chance of being happy; at least, without there is no happiness, because there can be no true sense of the bounty and beauty of the creation, or insight into the constitution of the human mind. Let a man of wealth and influence show, by the appearance of the country in his neighbourhood, that he treads in the steps of the good sense of the age, and occasionally goes foremost; let him give countenance to improvements in agriculture, steering clear of the pedantry of it, and showing that its grossest utilities will connect themselves harmoniously with the more intellectual arts, and even thrive the best under such connection; let him do his utmost to be surrounded with tenants living comfortably, which will bring always with it the best of all graces that a country can have—flourishing fields and happy-looking houses; and, in that part of his estate devoted to park and pleasure-ground, let him keep himself as much out of sight as possible; let Nature be all in all, taking care that everything done by man shall be in the way of being adopted by her. If people choose that a great mansion should be the chief figure in a country, let this kind of keeping prevail through the picture, and true taste will find no fault.

* * *

All just and solid pleasure in natural objects rests upon two pillars, God and Man. Laying out grounds, as it is called, may be considered as a liberal art, in some sort like poetry and painting; and its object, like that of all the liberal arts, is, or ought to be, to move the affections under the control of good sense; that is, those of the best and wisest: but, speaking with more precision, it is to assist Nature in moving the affections, and, surely, as I have said, the affections of those who have the deepest perception of the beauty of Nature; who have the most valuable feelings, that is, the most permanent, the most independent, the most ennobling, connected with Nature and human life. No liberal art aims merely at the gratification of an individual or a class: the painter or poet is degraded in proportion as he does so; the true servants of the Arts pay homage to the human kind as impersonated in unwarped and enlightened minds. If this be so when we are merely putting together words or colors, how much more ought

the feeling to prevail when we are in the midst of the realities of things; of the beauty and harmony, of the joy and happiness of living creatures; of men and children, of birds and beasts, of hills and streams, and trees and flowers; with the changes of night and day, evening and morning, summer and winter; and all their unwearied actions and energies, as benign in the spirit that animates them as they are beautiful and grand in that form and clothing which is given to them for the delight of our senses!

* * *

In a word, if I were disposed to write a sermon (and this is something like one) upon the subject of taste in natural beauty, I should take for my text the little pathway in Lowther woods, and all which I had to say would begin and end in the human heart, as under the direction of the Divine Nature, conferring value on the objects of the senses, and pointing out what is valuable in them.

XVIII To Sir George Beaumont
MAN'S TREATMENT OF SCENERY
August 28, 1811

* * *

A man by little and little becomes so delicate and fastidious with respect to forms in scenery, where he has a power to exercise a control over them, that if they do not exactly please him in all moods and every point of view, his power becomes his law; he banishes one, and then rids himself of another; impoverishing and monotonising landscapes, which, if not originally distinguished by the bounty of nature, must be ill able to spare the inspiring varieties which Art, and the occupations and wants of life in a country left more to itself, never fail to produce. This relish of humanity Foxley wants, and is therefore to me, in spite of all its recommendations, a melancholy spot, —I mean that part of it which the owner keeps to himself, and has taken so much pains with. I heard the other day of two artists who thus expressed themselves upon the subject of a scene among our lakes: "Plague upon those vile enclosures!" said one; "they spoil every thing." "Oh," said the other, "I never *see* them." Glover was the name of this last. Now, for my part, I should not wish to be either of these gentlemen; but to have in my own mind the power of turning to advantage, wherever it is possible, every object of art and nature as they appear before me. . . .

XIX To Sir George Beaumont

THE PAINTER REYNOLDS

Grasmere, Aug. 30, (?) 1804

* * *

When I ventured to express my regret at Sir Joshua Reynolds giving so much of his time to portrait painting and to his friends, I did not mean to recommend absolute solitude 10 and seclusion from the world as an advantage to him or anybody else. I think it a great evil; and indeed, in the case of a painter, frequent intercourse with the living world seems absolutely necessary to keep the mind in health 15 and vigour. I spoke, in some respects, in compliment to Sir Joshua Reynolds, feeling deeply, as I do, the power of his genius, and loving passionately the labours of genius in every way in which I am capable of comprehending them. 20 Mr. Malone, in the account prefixed to the *Discourses*, tells us that Sir Joshua generally passed the time from eleven till four every day in portrait painting. This it was that grieved me, as a sacrifice of great things to 25 little ones. . . .

XX To the Rev. Christopher Wordsworth

EDUCATION OF MAN

April 27, 1830

. . . The more I reflect upon the subject, the more I am convinced that positive instruction, even of a religious character, is much over- 35 rated. The education of man, and above all of a Christian, is the education of duty, which is most forcibly taught by the business and concerns of life, of which, even for children, especially the children of the poor, book learn- 40 ing is but a small part. There is an officious disposition on the part of the upper and middle classes to precipitate the tendency of the people towards intellectual culture in a manner subversive of their own happiness, and dangerous 45 to the peace of society. It is mournful to observe of how little avail are lessons of piety taught at school, if household attentions and obligations be neglected in consequence of the time taken up in school tuition, and if the head 5 be stuffed with vanity from the gentlemanliness of the employment of reading.

XXI To William Mathews

DISAPPROVAL OF MONARCHICAL GOVERNMENTS

June, [1794]

. . . I disapprove of monarchical and aristocratical governments, however modified. Hereditary distinctions, and privileged orders of every species, I think, must necessarily counteract the progress of human improvement. Hence it follows, that I am not among the admirers of the British constitution. I conceive that a more excellent system of civil policy might be established among us; yet in my ardour to attain the goal, I do not forget the nature of the ground where the race is to be run. The destruction of those institutions which I condemn, appears to me to be hastening on too rapidly. I recoil from the bare idea of a revolution. I am a determined enemy to every species of violence. I see no connection, but what the obstinacy of pride and ignorance renders necessary, between justice and the sword, between reason and bonds. I deplore the miserable condition of the French, and think that we can only be guarded from the same scourge by the undaunted efforts of 30 good men. . . . I severely condemn all inflammatory address to the passions of men. I know that the multitude walk in darkness. I would put into each man's hands a lantern, to guide him, and not have him to set out upon his 35 journey depending for illumination on abortive flashes of lightning, or the coruscations of transitory meteors.

XXII To L——

ON HIS POLITICAL OPINIONS

Rydal Mount, Dec. 4, 1821

My dear L——

Your letter ought to have been much earlier 45 acknowledged, and would have been so, had I not been sure you would ascribe my silence to its true cause, viz. procrastination, and not to indifference to your kind attention. There is another feeling which both urged and indisposed me to write to you,—I mean the allusion which, in so friendly a manner, you make to a supposed change in my political opinions. To the scribblers in pamphlets and periodical publications who have heaped so much obloquy upon myself and my friends Coleridge and Southey, I have not condescended to reply, nor ever shall; but to you, my candid and enlightened friend, I will say a few words on this subject, which, if we have the good fortune to meet again, as I hope we may, will probably be further dwelt upon.

I should think that I had lived to little purpose if my notions on the subject of government had undergone no modification: my youth must, in that case, have been without enthusiasm, and my manhood endued with small capability of profiting by reflection. If I were addressing those who have dealt so liberally with the words renegade, apostate, etc., I should retort the charge upon them, and say, you have been deluded by places and persons, while I have stuck to principles. I abandoned France and her rulers when they abandoned the struggle for liberty, gave themselves up to tyranny, and endeavored to enslave the world. I disapproved of the war against France at its commencement, thinking, which was, perhaps, an error, that it might have been avoided; but after Buonaparte had violated the independence of Switzerland, my heart turned against him and against the nation that could submit to be the instrument of such an outrage. Here it was that I parted, in feeling, from the Whigs, and to a certain degree united with their adversaries, who were free from the delusion (such I must ever regard it) of Mr. Fox and his party, that a safe and honorable peace was practicable with the French nation, and that an ambitious conqueror like Buonaparte could be softened down into a commercial rival.

In a determination, therefore, to aim at the overthrow of that inordinate ambition by war, I sided with the ministry, not from general approbation of their conduct, but as men who thought right on this essential point. How deeply this question interested me will be plain to any one who will take the trouble of reading my political sonnets, and the tract occasioned by the Convention of Cintra, in which are sufficient evidences of my dissatisfaction with the mode of conducting the war, and a prophetic display of the course which it would take if carried on upon the principles of justice, and with due respect for the feelings of the oppressed nations.

This is enough for foreign politics, as influencing my attachments.

XXIII To the Bishop of Llandaff on the Extraordinary Avowal of His Political Principles, contained in the Appendix to his late Sermon.

1793

My Lord,

Reputation may not improperly be termed the moral life of man. Alluding to our natural existence, Addison, in a sublime allegory well known to your Lordship, has represented us as crossing an immense bridge, from whose surface from a variety of causes we disappear one after another, and are seen no more. Every one who enters upon public life has such a bridge to pass. Some slip through at the very commencement of their career from thoughtlessness, others pursue their course a little longer, till, misled by the phantoms of avarice and ambition, they fall victims to their delusion. Your Lordship was either seen, or supposed to be seen, continuing your way for a long time unseduced and undismayed; but those who now look for you will look in vain, and it is feared you have at last fallen, through one of the numerous trap-doors, into the tide of contempt, to be swept down to the ocean of oblivion.

It is not my intention to be illiberal; these latter expressions have been forced from me by indignation. Your Lordship has given a proof that even religious controversy may be conducted without asperity; I hope I shall profit by your example. At the same time, with a spirit which you may not approve— for it is a republican spirit—I shall not preclude myself from any truths, however severe, which I may think beneficial to the cause which I have undertaken to defend. You will not, then, be surprised when I inform you that it is only the name of its author which has induced me to notice an Appendix to a Sermon which you have lately given to the world, with a hope that it may have some effect in calming a perturbation which, you say, has been excited in the minds of the lower orders of the community. While, with a servility which has prejudiced many people against religion itself, the ministers of the Church of England have appeared as writers upon public measures only to be the advocates of slavery civil and religious, your Lordship stood almost alone as the defender of truth and political charity. The names of levelling prelate, bishop of the Dissenters, which were intended as a dishonour to your character, were looked upon by your friends—perhaps by yourself—as an acknowledgment of your possessing an enlarged and philosophical mind; and, like the generals in a neighbour-country, if it had been equally becoming your profession, you might have adopted, as an honourable title, a denomination intended as a stigma.

On opening your Appendix, your admirers will naturally expect to find an impartial statement of the grievances which harass this Nation, and a sagacious inquiry into the proper modes of redress. They will be disappointed. Sensible how large a portion of mankind receive opinions upon authority, I am apprehensive lest the doctrines which they will there find should derive a weight from your name to which they are by no means intrinsically entitled. I will therefore examine what you have advanced, from a hope of being able to do away any impression left on the minds of such as may be liable to confound with argument a strong prepossession for your Lordship's talents, experience, and virtues.

Before I take notice of what you appear to have laid down as principles, it may not be improper to advert to some incidental opinions found at the commencement of your political confession of faith.

At a period big with the fate of the human race I am sorry that you attach so much importance to the personal sufferings of the late royal martyr, and that an anxiety for the issue of the present convulsions should not have prevented you from joining in the idle cry of modish lamentation which has resounded from the Court to the cottage. You wish it to be supposed you are one of those who are unpersuaded of the guilt of Louis XVI. If you had attended to the history of the French Revolution as minutely as its importance demands, so far from stopping to bewail his death, you would rather have regretted that the blind fondness of his people had placed a human being in that monstrous situation which rendered him unaccountable before a human tribunal. A bishop (M. Grégoire), a man of philosophy and humanity as distinguished as your Lordship, declared at the opening of the National Convention—and twenty-five millions of men were convinced of the truth of the assertion—that there was not a citizen on the tenth of August who, if he could have dragged before the eyes of Louis the corpse of one of his murdered brothers, might not have exclaimed to him: "Tyran, voilà ton ouvrage." Think of this, and you will not want consolation under any depression your spirits may feel at the contrast exhibited by Louis on the most splendid throne of the universe, and Louis alone in the tower of the Temple or on the scaffold. But there is a class of men who received the news of the late execution with much more heartfelt sorrow than that which you, among such a multitude, so officiously express. The passion of pity is one which, above all others, a Christian teacher should be cautious of cherishing the abuse when, under the influence of reason, it is regulated by the disproportion of the pain suffered to the guilt incurred. It is from the passion thus directed that the men of whom I have just spoken are afflicted by the catastrophe of the fallen monarch. They are sorry that the prejudice and weakness of mankind have made it necessary to force an individual into an unnatural situation, which requires more than human talents and human virtues, and at the same time precludes him from attaining even a moderate knowledge of common life, and from feeling a particular share in the interests of mankind. But, above all, these men lament that any combination of circumstances should have rendered it necessary or advisable to veil for a moment the statues of the laws, and that by such emergency the cause of twenty-five millions of people, I may say of the whole human race, should have been so materially injured. Any other sorrow for the death of Louis is irrational and weak.

In France royalty is no more. The person of the last anointed is no more also; and I flatter myself I am not alone, even in this kingdom, when I wish that it may please the Almighty neither by the hands of His priests nor His nobles (I allude to a striking passage of Racine) to raise his posterity to the rank of his ancestors, and reillume the torch of extinguished David. [Here Wordsworth appends a quotation from "Athalie," Act I, sc. 2.]

You say: "I fly with terror and abhorrence even from the altar of Liberty, when I see it stained with the blood of the aged, of the innocent, of the defenceless sex, of the ministers of religion, and of the faithful adherents of a fallen monarch." What! have you so little knowledge of the nature of man as to be ignorant that a time of revolution is not the season of true Liberty? Alas, the obstinacy and perversion of man is such that she is too often obliged to borrow the very arms of Despotism to overthrow him, and, in order to reign in peace, must establish herself by violence. She deplores such stern necessity, but the safety of the people, her supreme law, is her consolation. This apparent contradiction between the principles of liberty and the march of revolutions; this spirit of jealousy, of severity, of disquietude, of vexation, indispensable from a state of war between the oppressors and oppressed, must of necessity confuse the ideas of morality, and contract the benign exertion of the best affections of the human heart. Political virtues are developed at the expense of moral ones; and the sweet emotions of compassion, evidently dangerous when traitors are to be punished, are too often altogether smothered. But is this a sufficient reason to reprobate a conclusion from which is to spring a fairer order of things? It is the province of education to rectify the erroneous notions which a habit of oppression, and even of resistance, may have created, and to soften this ferocity of character, proceeding from a necessary suspension of the mild and social virtues; it belongs to her to create a race of men who, truly free, will look upon their fathers as only enfranchised.

I proceed to the sorrow you express for the fate of the French priesthood. The measure by which that body was immediately stripped of part of its possessions, and a more equal distribution enjoined of the rest, does not meet with your Lordship's approbation. You do not question the right of the Nation over ecclesiastical wealth; you have voluntarily abandoned a ground which you were conscious was altogether untenable. Having allowed this right, can you question the propriety of exerting it at that particular period? The urgencies of the State were such as required the immediate application of a remedy. Even the clergy were conscious of such necessity; and aware, from the immunities they had long enjoyed, that the people would insist upon their bearing some share of the burden, offered of themselves a considerable portion of their superfluities. The Assembly was true to justice, and refused to compromise the interest of the Nation by accepting as a satisfaction the insidious offerings of compulsive charity. They enforced their right. They took from the clergy a large share of their wealth, and applied it to the alleviation of the national misery. Experience shows daily the wise employment of the ample provision which yet remains to them. While you reflect on the vast diminution which some men's fortunes must have undergone, your sorrow for these individuals will be diminished by recollecting the unworthy motives which induced the bulk of them to undertake the office, and the scandalous arts which enabled so many to attain the rank and enormous wealth which it has seemed necessary to annex to the charge of a Christian pastor. You will rather look upon it as a signal act of justice that they should thus unexpectedly be stripped of the rewards of their vices and their crimes. If you should lament the sad reverse by which the hero of the necklace (Prince de Rohan) has been divested of about 1,300,000 livres of annual revenue, you may find some consolation that a part of this prodigious mass of riches is gone to preserve from famine some thousands of curés, who were pining in villages unobserved by Courts.

I now proceed to principles. Your Lordship very properly asserts that "the liberty of man in a state of society consists in his being subject to no law but the law enacted by the general will of the society to which he belongs." You approve of the object which the French had in view when, in the infancy of the Revolution, they were attempting to destroy arbitrary power, and to erect a temple to Liberty on its remains. It is with surprise, then, that I find you afterwards presuming to dictate to the world a servile adoption of the British constitution. It is with indignation I perceive you "reprobate" a people for having imagined happiness and liberty more likely to flourish in the open field of a Republic than under the shade of Monarchy. You are therefore guilty of a most glaring contradiction. Twenty-five millions of Frenchmen have felt that they could have no security for their liberties under any modification of monarchical power. They have in consequence unanimously chosen a Republic. You cannot but observe that they have only exercised that right in which, by your own confession, liberty essentially resides.

As to your arguments, by which you pretend to justify your anathemas of a Republic— if arguments they may be called—they are so concise, that I cannot but transcribe them. "I dislike a Republic for this reason, because of all forms of government, scarcely excepting the most despotic, I think a Republic the most oppressive to the bulk of the people; they are deceived in it with a show of liberty, but they live in it under the most odious of all tyrannies —the tyranny of their equals."

This passage is a singular proof of that fatality by which the advocates of error furnish weapons for their own destruction: while it is merely assertion in respect to a justification of your aversion to Republicanism, a strong argument may be drawn from it in its favour. Mr. Burke, in a philosophic lamentation over the extinction of chivalry, told us that in those times vice lost half its evil by losing all its grossness. Infatuated moralist! Your Lordship excites compassion as labouring under the same delusion. Slavery is a bitter and a poisonous draught. We have but one conclusion under it, that a Nation may dash the cup to the ground when she pleases. Do not imagine that by taking from its bitterness you weaken its deadly quality; no, by rendering it more palatable you contribute to its power of destruction. We submit without repining to the chastisements of Providence, aware that we are creatures, that opposition is vain and remonstrance impossible. But when redress is in our own power and resistance is rational, we suffer with the same humility from beings like ourselves, because we are taught from infancy that we were born in a state of inferiority to our oppressors, that they were sent into the world to scourge, and we to be scourged. Accordingly we see the bulk of mankind, actuated by these fatal prejudices, even more ready to lay themselves under the feet of the great than the great are to trample upon them. Now taking for granted, that in Republics men live under the tyranny of what you call their equals, the circumstance of this being the most odious of all tyrannies is what a Republican would boast of; as soon as tyranny becomes odious, the principal step is made towards its destruction. Reflecting on the degraded state of the mass of mankind, a philosopher will lament that oppression is not odious to them, that the iron, while it eats the soul, is not felt to enter into it. "Tout homme né dans l'esclavage naît pour l'esclavage, rien n'est plus certain; les esclaves perdent tout dans leurs fers, jusqu'au désir d'en sortir; ils aiment leur servitude, comme les compagnons d'Ulysse aimaient leur abrutissement."

I return to the quotation in which you reprobate Republicanism. Relying upon the temper of the times, you have surely thought little argument necessary to contest what few will be hardy enough to support; the strongest of auxiliaries, imprisonment and the pillory, has left your arm little to perform. But the happiness of mankind is so closely connected with this subject, that I cannot suffer such considerations to deter me from throwing out a few hints, which may lead to a conclusion that a Republic legitimately constructed contains less of an oppressive principle than any other form of government.

Your Lordship will scarcely question that much of human misery, that the great evils which desolate States, proceed from the governors' having an interest distinct from that of the governed. It should seem a natural deduction, that whatever has a tendency to identify the two must also in the same degree promote the general welfare. As the magnitude of almost all States prevents the possibility of their enjoying a pure democracy, philosophers—from a wish, as far as is in their power, to make the governors and the governed one—will turn their thoughts to the system of universal representation, and will annex an equal importance to the suffrage of every individual. Jealous of giving up no more of the authority of the people than is necessary, they will be solicitous of finding out some method by which the office of their delegates may be confined as much as is practicable to the proposing and deliberating upon laws rather than to enacting them; reserving to the people the power of finally inscribing them in the national code. Unless this is attended to, as soon as a people has chosen representatives, it no longer has a political existence, except as it is understood to retain the privilege of annihilating the trust when it shall think proper, and of resuming its original power. Sensible that at the moment of election an interest distinct from that of the general body is created, an enlightened legislator will endeavour by every possible method to diminish the operation of such interest. The first and most natural mode that presents itself is that of shortening the regular duration of this trust, in order that the man who has betrayed it may soon be superseded by a more worthy successor. But this is not enough; aware of the possibility of imposition, and of the natural tendency of power to corrupt the heart of man, a sensible Republican will think it essential that the office of legislator be not intrusted to the same man for a succession of years. He will also be induced to this wise restraint by the grand principle of identification; he will be more sure of the virtue of the legislator by knowing that, in the capacity of private citizen, to-morrow he must either smart under the oppression or bless the justice of the law which he has enacted to-day.

Perhaps in the very outset of this inquiry the principle on which I proceed will be questioned, and I shall be told that the people are not the proper judges of their own welfare. But because under every government of mod-ern times, till the foundation of the American Republic, the bulk of mankind have appeared incapable of discerning their true interests, no conclusion can be drawn against my principle. At this moment have we not daily the strongest proofs of the success with which, in what you call the best of all monarchical governments, the popular mind may be debauched? Left to the quiet exercise of their own judgment, do you think that the people would have thought it necessary to set fire to the house of the philosophic Priestley, and to hunt down his life like that of a traitor or a parricide? that, deprived almost of the necessaries of existence by the burden of their taxes, they would cry out, as with one voice, for a war from which not a single ray of consolation can visit them to compensate for the additional keenness with which they are about to smart under the scourge of labour, of cold, and of hunger?

Appearing, as I do, the advocate of Republicanism, let me not be misunderstood. I am well aware from the abuse of the executive power in States, that there is not a single European nation but what affords a melancholy proof that if, at this moment, the original authority of the people should be restored, all that could be expected from such restoration would in the beginning be but change of tyranny. Considering the nature of a Republic in reference to the present condition of Europe, your Lordship stops here; but a philosopher will extend his views much farther; having dried up the source from which flows the corruption of the public opinion, he will be sensible that the stream will go on gradually refining itself. I must add also that the coercive power is of necessity so strong in all the old governments, that a people could not at first make an abuse of that liberty which a legitimate Republic supposes. The animal just released from its stall will exhaust the overflow of its spirits in a round of wanton vagaries; but it will soon return to itself, and enjoy its freedom in moderate and regular delight.

But, to resume the subject of universal representation, I ought to have mentioned before that in the choice of its representatives a people will not immorally hold out wealth as a criterion of integrity, nor lay down as a fundamental rule, that to be qualified for the trying duties of legislation a citizen should be possessed of a certain fixed property. Virtues, talents, and acquirements are all that it will look for.

Having destroyed every external object of delusion, let us now see what makes the supposition necessary that the people will mislead themselves. Your Lordship respects "peasants and mechanics when they intrude not themselves into concerns for which their education has not fitted them."

Setting aside the idea of a peasant or mechanic being a legislator, what vast education is requisite to enable him to judge amongst his neighbours which is most qualified by his industry and integrity to be intrusted with the care of the interests of himself and of his fellow-citizens? But leaving this ground, as governments formed on such a plan proceed in a plain and open manner, their administration would require much less of what is called talents and experience, that is, of disciplined treachery and hoary Machiavelism; and at the same time, as it would no longer be their interest to keep the mass of the nation in ignorance, a moderate portion of useful knowledge would be universally disseminated. If your Lordship has travelled in the democratic cantons of Switzerland, you must have seen the herdsmen with the staff in one hand and the book in the other. In the constituent Assembly of France was found a peasant whose sagacity was as distinguished as his integrity, whose blunt honesty overawed and baffled the refinements of hypocritical patriots. The people of Paris followed him with acclamations, and the name of Père Gérard will long be mentioned with admiration and respect through the eighty-three departments.

From these hints, if pursued further, might be demonstrated the expediency of the whole people "intruding themselves" on the office of legislation, and the wisdom of putting into force what they may claim as a right. But government is divided into two parts—the legislative and executive. The executive power you would lodge in the hands of an individual. Before we inquire into the propriety of this measure, it will be necessary to state the proper objects of the executive power in governments where the principle of universal representation is admitted. With regard to that portion of this power which is exerted in the application of the laws, it may be observed that much of it would be superseded. As laws, being but the expression of the general will, would be enacted only from an almost universal conviction of their utility, any resistance to such laws, any desire of eluding them, must proceed from a few refractory individuals. As far, then, as relates to the internal administration of the country, a Republic has a manifest advantage over a Monarchy, inasmuch as less force is requisite to compel obedience to its laws.

From the judicial tribunals of our own country, though we labour under a variety of partial and oppressive laws, we have an evident proof of the nullity of regal interference, as the king's name is confessedly a mere fiction, and justice is known to be most equitably administered when the judges are least dependent on the crown.

I have spoken of laws partial and oppressive; our penal code is so crowded with disproportioned penalties and indiscriminate severity that a conscientious man would sacrifice, in many instances, his respect for the laws to the common feelings of humanity; and there must be a strange vice in that legislation from which can proceed laws in whose execution a man cannot be instrumental without forfeiting his self-esteem and incurring the contempt of his fellow-citizens.

But to return from this digression; with regard to the other branches of the executive government, which relate rather to original measures than to administering the law, it may be observed that the power exercised in conducting them is distinguished by almost imperceptible shades from the legislative, and that all such as admit of open discussion and of the delay attendant on public deliberations are properly the province of the representative assembly. If this observation be duly attended to, it will appear that this part of the executive power will be extremely circumscribed, will be stripped almost entirely of a deliberative capacity, and will be reduced to a mere hand or instrument. As a Republican government would leave this power to a select body destitute of the means of corruption, and whom the people, continually contributing, could at all times bring to account or dismiss, will it not necessarily ensue that a body so selected and supported would perform their simple functions with greater efficacy and fidelity than the complicated concerns of royalty can be expected to meet with in the councils of princes; of men who from their wealth and interest have forced themselves into trust; and of statesmen, whose constant object is to exalt themselves by laying pitfalls for their colleagues and for their country.

I shall pursue this subject no further; but adopting your Lordship's method of argument, instead of continuing to demonstrate the superiority of a Republican executive government, I will repeat some of the objections which have been often made to monarchy, and have not been answered.

My first objection to regal government is its instability, proceeding from a variety of causes. Where monarchy is found in its greatest intensity, as in Morocco and Turkey, this observation is illustrated in a very pointed manner, and indeed is more or less striking as governments are more or less despotic. The reason is obvious: as the monarch is the chooser of his ministers, and as his own passions and caprice are in general the sole guides of his conduct, these ministers, instead of pursuing directly the one grand object of national welfare, will make it their chief study to vary their measures according to his humours. But a minister may be refractory: his successor will naturally run headlong into plans totally the reverse of the former system; for if he treads in the same path, he is well aware that a similar fate will attend him. This observation will apply to each succession of kings, who, from vanity and a desire of distinction, will in general studiously avoid any step which may lead to a suspicion that they are so spiritless as to imitate their predecessor. That a similar instability is not incident to Republics is evident from their very constitution.

As from the nature of monarchy, particularly of hereditary monarchy, there must always be a vast disproportion between the duties to be performed and the powers that are to perform them; and as the measures of government, far from gaining additional vigour, are, on the contrary, enfeebled by being intrusted to one hand, what arguments can be used for allowing to the will of a single being a weight which, as history shows, will subvert that of the whole body politic? And this brings me to my grand objection to monarchy, which is drawn from THE ETERNAL NATURE OF MAN. The office of king is a trial to which human virtue is not equal. Pure and universal representation, by which alone liberty can be secured, cannot, I think, exist together with monarchy. It seems madness to expect a manifestation of the general will, at the same time that we allow to a particular will that weight which it must obtain in all governments that can with any propriety be called monarchical. They must war with each other till one of them is extinguished. It was so in France and . . .

I shall not pursue this topic further, but, as you are a teacher of purity of morals, I cannot but remind you of that atmosphere of corruption without which it should seem that courts cannot exist.

You seem anxious to explain what ought to be understood by the equality of men in a state of civil society; but your Lordship's success has not answered your trouble. If you had looked in the articles of the Rights of Man, you would have found your efforts superseded: "Equality, without which liberty cannot exist, is to be met with in perfection in that State in which no distinctions are admitted but such as have evidently for their object the general good;" "The end of government cannot be attained without authorising some members of the society to command, and of course without imposing on the rest the necessity of obedience."

Here, then, is an inevitable inequality, which may be denominated that of power. In order to render this as small as possible, a legislator will be careful not to give greater force to such authority than is essential to its due execution. Government is at best but a necessary evil. Compelled to place themselves in a state of subordination, men will obviously endeavour to prevent the abuse of that superiority to which they submit; accordingly they will cautiously avoid whatever may lead those in whom it is acknowledged to suppose they hold it as a right. Nothing will more effectually contribute to this than that the person in whom authority has been lodged should occasionally descend to the level of private citizen; he will learn from it a wholesome lesson, and the people will be less liable to confound the person with the power. On this principle hereditary authority will be prescribed; and on another also—that in such a system as that of hereditary authority, no security can be had for talents adequate to the discharge of the office, and consequently the people can only feel the mortification of being humbled without having protected themselves.

Another distinction will arise amongst mankind, which, though it may be easily modified by government, exists independent of it; I mean the distinction of wealth, which always will attend superior talents and industry. It cannot be denied that the security of individual property is one of the strongest and most natural motives to induce men to bow their necks to the yoke of civil government. In order to attain this end of security to property, a legislator will proceed with impartiality. He should not suppose that, when he has insured to their proprietors the possession of lands and movables against the depredation of the necessitous, nothing remains to be done. The history of all ages has demonstrated that wealth not only can secure itself, but includes even an oppressive principle. Aware of this, and that the extremes of poverty and riches have a necessary tendency to corrupt the human heart, he will banish from his code all laws such as the unnatural monster of primogeniture, such as encourage associations against labour in the form of corporate bodies, and indeed all that monopolising system of legislation, whose baleful influence is shown in the depopulation of the country and in the necessity which reduces the sad relicks to owe their very existence to the ostentatious bounty of their oppressors. If it is true in common life, it is still more true in governments, that we should be just before we are generous; but our legislators seem to have forgotten or despised this homely maxim. They have unjustly left unprotected that most important part of property, not less real because it has no material existence, that which ought to enable the labourer to provide food for himself and his family. I appeal to innumerable statutes, whose constant and professed object it is to lower the price of labour, to compel the workman to be content with arbitrary wages, evidently too small from the necessity of legal enforcement of the acceptance of them. Even from the astonishing amount of the sums raised for the support of one description of the poor may be concluded the extent and greatness of that oppression, whose effects have rendered it possible for the few to afford so much, and have shown us that such a multitude of our brothers exist in even helpless indigence. Your Lordship tells us that the science of civil government has received all the perfection of which it is capable. For my part, I am more enthusiastic. The sorrow I feel from the contemplation of this melancholy picture is not unconsoled by a comfortable hope that the class of wretches called mendicants will not much longer shock the feelings of humanity; that the miseries entailed upon the marriage of those who are not rich will no longer tempt the bulk of mankind to fly to that promiscuous intercourse to which they are impelled by the instincts of nature and the dreadful satisfaction of escaping the prospect of infants, sad fruit of such intercourse, whom they are unable to support. If these flattering prospects be ever realised, it must be owing to some wise and salutary regulations counteracting that inequality among mankind which proceeds from the present fixed disproportion of their possessions.

I am not an advocate for the agrarian law nor for sumptuary regulations, but I contend that the people amongst whom the law of primogeniture exists, and among whom corporate bodies are encouraged, and immense salaries annexed to useless and indeed hereditary offices, is oppressed by an inequality in the distribution of wealth which does not necessarily attend men in a state of civil society.

Thus far we have considered inequalities inseparable from civil society. But other arbitrary distinctions exist among mankind, either from choice or usurpation. I allude to titles, to stars, ribbons, and garters, and other badges of fictitious superiority. Your Lordship will not question the grand principle on which this inquiry set out; I look upon it, then, as my duty to try the propriety of these distinctions by that criterion, and think it will be no difficult task to prove that these separations among mankind are absurd, impolitic, and immoral. Considering hereditary nobility as a reward for services rendered to the State—and it is to my charity that you owe the permission of taking up the question on this ground—what services can a man render to the State adequate to such a compensation that the making of laws, upon which the happiness of millions is to depend, shall be lodged in him and his posterity, however depraved may be their principles, however contemptible their understandings?

But here I may be accused of sophistry; I ought to subtract every idea of power from such distinction, though from the weakness of mankind it is impossible to disconnect them. What services then, can a man render to society to compensate for the outrage done to the dignity of our nature when we bind ourselves to address him and his posterity with humiliating circumlocutions, calling him most noble, most honourable, most high, most august, serene, excellent, eminent, and so forth; when it is more than probable that such unnatural flattery will but generate vices which ought to consign him to neglect and solitude, or make him the perpetual object of the finger of scorn? And does not experience justify the observation, that where titles—a thing very rare—have been conferred as the rewards of merit, those to whom they have descended, far from being thereby animated to imitate their ancestor, have presumed upon that lustre which they supposed thrown round them, and, prodigally relying on such resources, lavished what alone was their own, their personal reputation?

It would be happy if this delusion were confined to themselves; but, alas, the world is weak enough to grant the indulgence which they assume. Vice, which is forgiven in one character, will soon cease to meet with sternness of rebuke when found in others. Even at first she will entreat pardon with confidence, assured that ere long she will be charitably supposed to stand in no need of it.

But let me ask you seriously, from the mode in which these distinctions are originally conferred, is it not almost necessary that, far from being the rewards of services rendered to the State, they should usually be the recompense of an industrious sacrifice of the general welfare to the particular aggrandisement of that power by which they are bestowed? Let us even alter their source, and consider them as proceeding from the Nation itself, and deprived of that hereditary quality; even here I should proscribe them, and for the most evident reason—that a man's past services are no sufficient security for his future character; he who to-day merits the civic wreath may to-morrow deserve the Tarpeian rock. Besides, where respect is not perverted, where the world is not taught to reverence men without regarding their conduct, the esteem of mankind will have a very different value, and, when a proper independence is secured, will be regarded as a sufficient recompense for services however important, and will be a much surer guarantee of the continuance of such virtues as may deserve it.

I have another strong objection to nobility, which is that it has a necessary tendency to dishonour labour, a prejudice which extends far beyond its own circle; that it binds down whole ranks of men to idleness, while it gives the enjoyment of a reward which exceeds the hopes of the most active exertions of human industry. The languid tedium of this noble repose must be dissipated, and gaming, with the tricking manoeuvres of the horse-race, afford occupation to hours which it would be happy for mankind had they been totally unemployed.

Reflecting on the corruption of the public manners, does your Lordship shudder at the prostitution which miserably deluges our streets? You may find the cause in our aristocratical prejudices. Are you disgusted with the hypocrisy and sycophancy of our intercourse in private life? You may find the cause in the necessity of dissimulation which we have established by regulations which oblige us to address as our superiors, indeed as our masters, men whom we cannot but internally despise. Do you lament that such large portions of mankind should stoop to occupations unworthy the dignity of their nature? You may find in the pride and luxury thought necessary to nobility how such servile arts are encouraged. Besides, where the most honourable of the Land do not blush to accept such offices as groom of the bedchamber, master of the hounds, lords in waiting, captain of the honourable band of gentlemen-pensioners, is it astonishing that the bulk of the people should not ask of an occupation, what is it? but what may be gained by it?

If the long equestrian train of equipage should make your Lordship sigh for the poor who are pining in hunger, you will find that little is thought of snatching the bread from their mouths to eke out the "necessary splendour" of nobility.

I have not time to pursue this subject further, but am so strongly impressed with the baleful influence of aristocracy and nobility upon human happiness and virtue, that if, as I am persuaded, monarchy cannot exist without such supporters, I think that reason sufficient for the preference I have given to the Republican system.

It is with reluctance that I quit the subjects I have just touched upon; but the nature of this Address does not permit me to continue the discussion. I proceed to what more immediately relates to this Kingdom at the present crisis.

You ask with triumphant confidence, to what other law are the people of England subject than the general will of the society to which they belong? Is your Lordship to be told that acquiescence is not choice, and that obedience is not freedom? If there is a single man in Great Britain who has no suffrage in the election of a representative, the will of the society of which he is a member is not generally expressed; he is a Helot in that society. You answer the question, so confidently put, in this singular manner: "The King, we are all justly persuaded, has not the inclination—and we all know that, if he had the inclination, he has not the power—to substitute his will in the place of law. The House of Lords has no such power. The House of Commons has no such power." This passage, so artfully and unconstitutionally framed to agree with the delusions of the moment, cannot deceive a thinking reader. The expression of your full persuasion of the upright intentions of the King can only be the language of flattery. You are not to be told that it is constitutionally a maxim not to attribute to the person of the King the measures and misconduct of government. Had you chosen to speak, as you ought to have done, openly and explicitly, you must have expressed your just persuasion and implicit confidence in the integrity, moderation, and wisdom of his Majesty's ministers. Have you forgot the avowed ministerial maxim of Sir Robert Walpole? Are you ignorant of the overwhelming corruption of the present day?

You seem unconscious of the absurdity of separating what is inseparable even in imagination. Would it have been any consolation to the miserable Romans under the second triumvirate to have been asked insultingly, Is it Octavius, is it Anthony, or is it Lepidus that has caused this bitterness of affliction? and when the answer could not be returned with certainty, to have been reproached that their sufferings were imaginary? The fact is that the King *and* Lords *and* Commons, by what is termed the omnipotence of Parliament, have constitutionally the right of enacting whatever laws they please in defiance of the petitions or remonstrances of the nation. They have the power of doubling our enormous debt of 240 million, and *may* pursue measures which could never be supposed the emanation of the general will without concluding that people stripped of reason, of sentiment, and even of that first instinct which prompts them to preserve their own existence.

I congratulate your Lordship upon your enthusiastic fondness for the judicial proceedings of this country. I am happy to find you have passed through life without having your fleece torn from your back in the thorny labyrinth of litigation. But you have not lived always in colleges, and must have passed by some victims, whom it cannot be supposed, without a reflection on your heart, that you have forgotten. Here I am reminded of what I have said on the subject of representation—to be qualified for the office of the legislation you should have felt like the bulk of mankind; their sorrows should be familiar to you, of which, if you are ignorant, how can you redress them? As a member of the assembly which, from a confidence in its experience, sagacity, and wisdom, the constitution has invested with the supreme appellant jurisdiction to determine the most doubtful points of an intricate jurisprudence, your Lordship cannot, I presume, be ignorant of the consuming expense of our never-ending process, the verbosity of unintelligible statutes, and the perpetual contrariety in our judicial decisions.

"The greatest freedom that can be enjoyed by man in a state of civil society, the greatest security that can be given with respect to the protection of his character, property, personal liberty, limb, and life, is afforded to every individual by our present constitution."

"Let it never be forgotten by ourselves, and let us impress the observation upon the hearts of our children, that we are in possession of both (liberty and equality), of as much of both as can be consistent with the end for which civil society was introduced among mankind."

Many of my readers will hardly believe me when I inform them that these passages are copied verbatim from your Appendix. Mr. Burke roused the indignation of all ranks of men when, by a refinement in cruelty superior to that which in the East yokes the living to the dead, he strove to persuade us that we and our posterity to the end of time were riveted to a constitution by the indissoluble compact of —a dead parchment, and were bound to cherish a corse at the bosom when reason might call aloud that it should be entombed. Your Lordship aims at the same detestable object by means more criminal, because more dangerous and insidious. Attempting to lull the people of England into a belief that any inquiries directed towards the nature of liberty and equality can in no other way lead to their happiness than by convincing them that they have already arrived at perfection in the science of government, what is your object but to exclude them for ever from the most fruitful field of human knowledge? Besides, it is another cause to execrate this doctrine that the consequence of such fatal delusion would be that they must entirely draw off their attention, not only from the government, but from their governors; that the stream of public vigilance, far from clearing and enriching the prospect of society, would by its stagnation consign it to barren-

ness, and by its putrefaction infect it with death. You have aimed an arrow at liberty and philosophy, the eyes of the human race; why, like the inveterate enemy of Philip, in putting your name to the shaft, did you not declare openly its destination?

As a teacher of religion, your Lordship cannot be ignorant of a class of breaches of duty which may be denominated faults of omission. You profess to give your opinions upon the present turbulent crisis, expressing a wish that they may have some effect in tranquillising the minds of the people. Whence comes it, then, that the two grand causes in this working of the popular mind are passed over in silence? Your Lordship's conduct may bring to mind the story of a company of strolling comedians, who gave out the play of Hamlet as the performance of the evening. The audience were not a little surprised to be told, on the drawing up of the curtain, that from circumstances of particular convenience it was hoped that they would dispense with the omission of the character of—Hamlet! But to be serious—for the subject is serious in the extreme—from your silence respecting the general call for a PARLIAMENTARY REFORM, supported by your assertion that we at present enjoy as great a portion of liberty and equality as is consistent with civil society, what can be supposed but that you are a determined enemy to the redress of what the people of England call and feel to be grievances?

From your omitting to speak upon the war, and your general disapprobation of French measures and French principles, expressed particularly at this moment, we are necessarily led also to conclude that you have no wish to dispel an infatuation which is now giving up to the sword so large a portion of the poor, and consigning the rest to the more slow and more painful consumption of want. I could excuse your silence on this point, as it would ill become an English bishop at the close of the eighteenth century to make the pulpit the vehicle of exhortations which would have disgraced the incendiary of the Crusades, the hermit Peter. But you have deprived yourself of the plea of decorum by giving no opinion on the REFORM OF THE LEGISLATURE. As undoubtedly you have some secret reason for the reservation of your sentiments on this latter head, I cannot but apply the same reason to the former. Upon what principle is your conduct to be explained? In some parts of England it is quaintly said, when a drunken man is seen reeling towards his home, that he has business on both sides of the road. Observing your Lordship's tortuous path, the spectators will be far from insinuating that you have partaken of Mr. Burke's intoxicating bowl; they will content themselves, shaking their heads as you stagger along, with remarking that you have business on both sides of the road.

The friends of Liberty congratulate themselves upon the odium under which they are at present labouring, as the causes which have produced it have obliged so many of her false adherents to disclaim with officious earnestness any desire to promote her interests; nor are they disheartened by the diminution which their body is supposed already to have sustained. Conscious that an enemy lurking in our ranks is ten times more formidable than when drawn out against us, that the unblushing aristocracy of a Maury or a Cazalès is far less dangerous than the insidious mask of patriotism assumed by a La Fayette or a Mirabeau, we thank you for your desertion. Political convulsions have been said particularly to call forth concealed abilities, but it has been seldom observed how vast is their consumption of them. Reflecting upon the fate of the greatest portion of the members of the constituent and legislative assemblies, we must necessarily be struck with a prodigious annihilation of human talents. Aware that this necessity is attached to a struggle for Liberty, we are the less sorry that we can expect no advantage from the mental endowments of your Lordship. Besides the names which I— [Here the manuscript breaks off.]

XXIV To Robert Southey, Esq.

THE NATURE OF TYRANNY

1827

. . . I did not notice a single sentiment or opinion that I could have wished away but one —where you support the notion that, if the Duke of Wellington had not lived and commanded, Buonaparte must have continued the master of Europe. I do not object to this from any dislike I have to the Duke, but from a conviction—I trust, a philosophic one—that Providence would not allow the upsetting of so diabolical a system as Buonaparte's to depend upon the existence of any individual. Justly was it observed by Lord Wellesley, that Buonaparte was of an order of minds that created for themselves great reverses. He might have gone further, and said that it is of the nature of tyranny to work to its own destruction.

XXV To Professor Henry Reed

PHILOSOPHY AT BOSTON

1841

. . . Do you know Miss Peabody of Boston? She has just sent me, with the highest eulogy, certain essays of Mr. Emerson. Our [? Carlyle] and he appear to be what the French used to call *esprits forts*, though the French idols showed their spirit after a somewhat different fashion. Our two present Philosophes, who have taken a language which they suppose to be English for their vehicle, are verily *par nobile fratrum*, and it is a pity that the weakness of our age has not left them exclusively to this appropriate reward——mutual admiration. Where is the thing which now passes for philosophy at Boston to stop?

XXVI To the Right Hon. Earl De La Warr, Lord Chamberlain

DECLINING THE LAUREATESHIP

Rydal Mount, Ambleside, April 1, 1843

My Lord,

The recommendation made by your Lordship to the Queen, and graciously approved by her Majesty, that the vacant office of Poet Laureate should be offered to me, affords me high gratification. Sincerely am I sensible of this honour; and let me be permitted to add, that the being deemed worthy to succeed my lamented and revered friend, Mr. Southey, enhances the pleasure I receive upon this occasion.

The appointment, I feel, however, imposes duties which, far advanced in life as I am, I cannot venture to undertake, and therefore must beg leave to decline the acceptance of an offer that I shall always remember with no unbecoming pride.

Her Majesty will not, I trust, disapprove of a determination forced upon me by reflections which it is impossible for me to set aside.

Deeply feeling the distinction conferred upon me, and grateful for the terms in which your Lordship has made the communication.

XXVII To Lady F. Bentinck

REASON FOR DECLINING THE LAUREATESHIP

1843

The Lord Chamberlain, in terms the most honourable, has, with the Queen's approbation, offered me the vacant Laureateship. Had I been several years younger I should have accepted the office with pride and pleasure; but on Friday I shall enter, God willing, my 74th year, and on account of so advanced an age I begged permission to decline it, not venturing to undertake its duties. For though, as you are aware, the formal task-work of New Year and Birthday Odes was abolished when the appointment was given to Mr. Southey, he still considered himself obliged in conscience to produce, and did produce, verses, some of very great merit, upon important public occasions. He failed to do so upon the Queen's Coronation, and I know that this omission caused him no little uneasiness. The same might happen to myself upon some important occasion, and I should be uneasy under the possibility; I hope, therefore, that neither you nor Lord Lonsdale, nor any of my friends, will blame me for what I have done.

XXVIII To the Right Hon. the Earl De La Warr

ACCEPTING THE LAUREATESHIP

Rydal Mount, Ambleside, April 4, 1843
My Lord,

Being assured by your Lordship's letter and by one from Sir Robert Peel, both received this day, that the appointment to the Laureateship is to be considered merely honorary, the apprehensions which at first compelled me to decline accepting the offer of that appointment are entirely removed.

Sir Robert Peel has also done me the honour of uniting his wish with that which your Lordship has urged in a manner most gratifying to my feelings; so that, under these circumstances, and sanctioned as the recommendation has been by Her Majesty's gracious approval, it is with unalloyed pleasure that I accept this high distinction.

XXIX To Professor Henry Reed

THE QUEEN'S RECEPTION TO THE LAUREATE

July 1, 1845

I took the journey to London solely to pay my respects to the Queen upon my appointment to the Laureateship upon the decease of my friend Mr. Southey. The weather was very cold, and I caught an inflammation in one of my eyes, which rendered my stay in the south very uncomfortable. I nevertheless did, in respect to the object of my journey, all that was required. The reception given me by the Queen at her ball was most gracious. Mrs. Everett, the wife of your minister, among many others, was a witness to it, without knowing who I was. It moved her to the shedding of tears. This effect was in part produced, I suppose, by American habits of feeling, as pertaining to a republican government. To see a greyhaired man of seventy-five years of age kneeling down in a large assembly to kiss the hand of a young woman is a sight for which institutions essentially democratic do not prepare a spectator of either sex, and must naturally place the opinions upon which a republic is founded, and the sentiments which support it, in strong contrast with a government based and upheld as ours is. I am not, therefore, surprised that Mrs. Everett was moved, as she herself described to persons of my acquaintance, among others to Mr. Rogers the poet.

* * *

I saw Tennyson several times when I was in London. He is decidedly the first of our living poets, and I hope will live to give the world still better things. You will be pleased to hear that he expressed in the strongest terms his gratitude to my writings. To this I was far from indifferent, though persuaded that he is not much in sympathy with what I should myself most value in my attempts, viz., the spirituality with which I have endeavored to invest the material universe, and the moral relations under which I have wished to exhibit its most ordinary appearances.

XXX Extracts from Conversations with His Nephew, Christopher Wordsworth

When I began to give myself up to the profession of a poet for life, I was impressed with a conviction, that there were four English poets whom I must have continually before me as examples—Chaucer, Shakespeare, Spenser, and Milton. These I must study, and equal if I could; and I need not think of the rest.

* * *

I have been charged by some with disparaging Pope and Dryden. This is not so. I have committed much of both to memory. As far as Pope goes, he succeeds; but his Homer is not Homer, but Pope.

* * *

I cannot account for Shakespeare's low estimate of his own writings, except from the sublimity, the superhumanity, of his genius. They were infinitely below his conception of what they might have been, and ought to have been.

* * *

1827.—T. Moore has great natural genius; but he is too lavish of brilliant ornament. His poems smell of the perfumer's and milliner's shops. He is not content with a ring and a bracelet, but he must have rings in the ears, rings on the nose—rings everywhere.

* * *

Byron seems to me deficient in feeling. Professor Wilson, I think, used to say that *Beppo* was his best poem; because all his faults were there brought to a height. I never read the *English Bards* through. His critical prognostications have, for the most part, proved erroneous.

* * *

. . . I can say without vanity, that I have bestowed great pains on my style, full as much as any of my contemporaries have done on theirs. I yield to none in love for my art. I, therefore, labour at it with reverence, affection,

and industry. My main endeavour, as to style, has been that my poems should be written in pure intelligible English. Lord Byron has spoken severely of my compositions. However faulty they may be, I do not think that I ever could have prevailed upon myself to print such lines as he has done; for instance,

I stood at Venice on the Bridge of Sighs,
A palace and a prison on each hand.

Some person ought to write a critical review, analyzing Lord Byron's language, in order to guard others against imitating him in these respects.

* * *

Shelley is one of the best artists of us all: I mean in workmanship of style.

* * *

In my Ode on the "Intimations of Immortality in Childhood," I do not profess to give a literal representation of the state of the affections and of the moral being in childhood. I record my own feelings at that time—my absolute spirituality, my "all-soulness," if I may so speak. At that time I could not believe that I should lie down quietly in the grave, and that my body would moulder into dust.

* * *

Scientific men are often too fond of aiming to be men of the world. They crave too much for titles, and stars, and ribbons. If Bacon had dwelt only in the court of Nature, and cared less for that of James the First, he would have been a greater man, and a happier one too.

* * *

S——, in the work you mentioned to me, confounds imagery and imagination. Sensible objects really existing, and felt to exist, are imagery; and they may form the materials of a descriptive poem, where objects are delineated as they are. Imagination is a subjective term; it deals with objects not as they are, but as they appear to the mind of the poet.

The imagination is that intellectual lens through the medium of which the poetical observer sees the objects of his observation, modified both in form and colour; or it is that inventive dresser of dramatic tableaux, by which the persons of the play are invested with new drapery, or placed in new attitudes; or it is that chemical faculty by which elements of the most different nature and distant origin are blended together into one harmonious and homogeneous whole.

* * *

Walter Scott is not a careful composer. He allows himself many liberties, which betray a want of respect for his reader. For instance, he is too fond of inversions; i.e. he often places the verb before the substantive, and the accusative before the verb. W. Scott quoted, as from me,

> The swan on *sweet* St. Mary's lake
> Floats double, swan and shadow,

instead of *still;* thus obscuring my idea, and betraying his own uncritical principles of composition.

SAMUEL TAYLOR COLERIDGE
[October 21, 1772–July 25, 1834]

SAMUEL TAYLOR COLERIDGE was the thirteenth and youngest child of the vicar of Ottery St. Mary in Devon. His father died when he was nine and Coleridge was sent to Christ's Hospital where he remained for nine years without seeing his family. The school was a good one, though, after Ottery St. Mary, a dreary place. The headmaster at the time, the Rev. Boyer, was notable for the soundness of his common-sense and the irrationality of his floggings, particularly the latter. Coleridge's expanding mind, however, gained perhaps more from his chance reading than from his regular schooling, for he read prodigiously. And he loved to expound to the other schoolboys the ideas he had gathered. Plato and the neo-platonists with their conception of a world transcending the world of matter and their conception of beauty as a shining through of spiritual reality in material forms—it was such writers that fired Coleridge's youthful imagination, and he turned away from such studies as history, which dealt with facts, as insipid beside abstract speculation.

It was with philosophic talk that Coleridge held his schoolfellows spellbound. Lamb has left a picture of the "inspired charity boy" already talking "in deep and sweet intonations," and even as a youth revealing what was to be one of his most marked powers—his eloquence. He went on talking the remainder of his life. Many years later Hazlitt declared, "He may be said to have lived on the sound of his own voice," and to understand Coleridge one must understand his tendency to dissipate his abilities in talk rather than bring them to the focus of accomplishment. Of the nature of his talk there are mixed reports. As a preacher, Hazlitt reports him launching into his subject "like an eagle dallying with the wind," and his talk was much the same. The splendor of the momentary effect was undeniable, but it was evaporative and evasive talk, and the bewildered listener had difficulty afterwards in remembering the substance.

At the university (Coleridge entered Jesus College, Cambridge, in 1791) he continued to talk, professing democratic principles in the undergraduate debates and earning the reputation of a radical. His political opinion had two phases—desire for reform in England with consequent opposition to the policies of Pitt, and enthusiasm for the *theory* of the French Revolution. Before he left Christ's Hospital he had written an *Ode on the Destruction of the Bastile* and as late as December 1796, in the *Ode to the Departing Year,* he was prophesying disaster to the England of Pitt "doom'd to fall, enslaved and vile." Later he revised the line to read, "Not yet enslaved, not wholly vile."

He won a scholarship in his first year at the university and, although he failed for another later, his scholarship was of recognized brilliance. Finally, however, in a fit of discouragement over some debts, he quietly left the university and, although he hated the military, enlisted in the army. And, for some Coleridgean reason, although he disliked horses, he selected the cavalry in which to enlist. His service in the Dragoons, under the assumed name of Silas Titus Comberback, was unhappy (among other difficulties was the problem of staying on top of his horse) and fortunately brief. His brothers bought his discharge and he returned to Cambridge. But Coleridge had had his first lesson in his utter incapacity to deal with a more realistic world than that of the abstract ideas he loved.

Coleridge took no degree, and it was a fantastic scheme which lured him away from the university. Southey, whom he met at Oxford in June 1794, was proposing that a colony of educated men and women should withdraw from the world to some spot where a few hours daily work would provide them with the simple necessities of life, leaving the rest of their time free for high intellectual converse. Coleridge's imagination took fire: he foresaw in the second generation a combination of "the innocence of the patriarchal age with the knowledge and genuine refinements of European culture" and in the colony itself a model for the regeneration of society. For months Coleridge's eloquence expended itself upon Pantisocracy, as the scheme was called. The twelve gentlemen, however, who were to found the colony required twelve wives. Two of the Pantisocrats were engaged to sisters and, slightly to his own surprise, Coleridge found himself symmetrically engaged to a third sister. A fourth girl of the family, feeling perhaps that there had been enough of a good thing, declined a fourth Pantisocrat.

Late in 1794 Coleridge finally left Cambridge. In October 1795 he married Sarah Fricker. They went to a flower-surrounded cottage by the sea at Clevedon, and Coleridge was truly happy on what was really a prolonged honeymoon. Not since Coleridge had left Ottery St. Mary at the age of nine, had he had any touch of home life or domestic intimacy at all. Now he found himself among flowers with a bride. His practical preparations, however, may be judged from the urgent letter his publisher received two days after the Coleridges reached Clevedon, requesting that the following articles, among others, be forwarded, ". . . two ventilators; two glasses for the wash-hand stand; one small tin teakettle; one pair of candlesticks; one carpet brush; a pair of slippers; a cheese toaster; two large tin spoons; a bible; a keg of porter; coffee; raisins; currants; catsup; . . ."

Difficulties, however, arose. The publisher, Cottle of Bristol, was offering Coleridge a guinea for each hundred lines. But, faced with the necessity of producing, Coleridge found himself helpless. The schedule of the practical world was paralyzing to him and, dismayed, he wrote little. Pantisocracy also collapsed about this time for lack of funds and from the defection of Southey.

Coleridge roused himself. He would publish a magazine—*The Watchman* (1796)—"that all might know the truth, and that the truth might make them free." He tried hard for subscribers and his friends helped him, so that the magazine was launched with over a thousand subscribers. No one liked the first issue. Nearly half his subscribers actively disliked the second and canceled subscriptions. With the tenth issue the magazine suspended. Friends had to pay the debts of the magazine and Coleridge, in despair at the failure of his real effort to support himself in a cash-and-carry world, took laudanum to relieve his distress of mind.

Coleridge in a letter of this period drew a keen self-portrait which is worth reprinting in detail. He writes, "Your portrait of yourself interested me. As to me, my face, unless when animated by immediate eloquence, expresses great sloth, and great, indeed, almost idiotic good nature. 'Tis a mere carcass of a face; fat, flabby, and expressive chiefly of inexpression. Yet I am told that my eyes, eyebrows, and forehead are physiognomically good; 'tis a good shape enough if measured, but my gait is awkward, and the walk of the whole man indicates *indolence capable of energies*. I am, and ever have been, a great reader, and have read almost everything—a library cormorant. I am *deep* in all out of the way books, whether of the monkish times, or of the puritanical era. I have read and digested most of the historical writers; but I do not *like* history. Metaphysics and poetry and 'facts of mind,' that is, accounts of all the strange phantasms that ever possessed 'your philosophy'; dreamers, from Thoth the Egyptian to Taylor the English pagan, are my darling studies. In short, I seldom read except to amuse myself, and I am almost always reading. Of useful knowledge, I am a so-so chemist, and I love chemistry. All else is *blank;* but I *will* be (please God) an horticulturalist and a farmer. I compose very little, and I absolutely hate composition, and such is my dislike that even a sense of duty is sometimes too weak to overpower it.

"I cannot breathe through my nose, so my mouth, with sensual thick lips, is almost always open. In conversation I am impassioned, and oppose what I deem error with an eagerness which is often mistaken for personal asperity; but I am ever so swallowed up in the *thing* that I perfectly forget my *opponent*. Such am I."

In the financial and emotional emergency which followed the collapse of *The Watchman*, Thomas Poole—a hard-headed merchant who had resisted Coleridge's eloquence on the subject of Pantisocracy but had gained a lively appreciation of his genius—took a cottage for him at Nether Stowey. Coleridge, bent on winning his living from the soil, attacked the place earnestly with a spade as a preparation toward raising vegetables. In July 1797, however, Wordsworth and his sister Dorothy moved to Alfoxden to be near the poet Coleridge, and vegetables were promptly forgotten. The association of Wordsworth and Coleridge was one of the most fruitful in the history of English literature. Up to this date neither poet had written anything upon which sceptical posterity would have wasted much time. But in a season both poets reached full poetic maturity and, although Wordsworth afterward equalled the quality of the work he produced in this and the following year, neither poet ever surpassed it.

Two more dissimilar personalities never had higher admiration for opposites, and probably in this combination of admiration and contrast lay the magic of the contact. It is easy to think of Coleridge with his brilliance of speech and his range of metaphysical speculation dominating the group—an irritant to Wordsworth's rather sluggish self-assurance. On the other hand, "the Gods approve the depth and not the tumult of the soul," and about the silent Wordsworth, more than two years Coleridge's senior and already tempered by experiences more real than any Coleridge had ever faced, there was a sense of reserve power and serenity.

The close association ended in the summer of 1798 and by the end of 1798 Coleridge had completed most of the work upon which his fame rests. *The Ancient Mariner*, *Christabel* (Part I), *Kubla Khan*, *Frost at Midnight*, *Fears in Solitude*, *France: An Ode*, all belong to this period. The last two, and especially *France: An Ode*, reveal his revulsion of feeling toward the French Revolution and the emergence of the political conservative that Coleridge was to be for the remainder of his days. In such poems as *The Ancient Mariner*, *Christabel*, and *Kubla Khan*, Coleridge achieved the magic which was his, and his alone. Another product of this season was the *Lyrical Ballads*, published by Wordsworth and Coleridge together in September 1798. The great *Preface*, written by Wordsworth for a later edition—that of 1800—deals only with Wordsworth's own theories, and Coleridge's contribution to the volume was small in quantity—only four poems. One of them, however, was *The Ancient Mariner*. His contribution to the discussions which led up to the book is another matter and was undoubtedly of the highest importance. Coleridge's statement of the purpose of the book is given in the *Biographia Literaria* (Chap. XIV).

The story of Coleridge the poet practically comes to an end with the writing of *Dejection: An Ode* (April 1802). After the brief flare-up of his genius, a change had come over him, and a reading of the fourth and sixth stanzas of that ode will show that he was aware of it. Afterwards he was to write little poetry of value. Opium obviously was one of the causes of the collapse of his power. He had taken it in 1796 after the failure of *The Watchman*. There is no sign that the habit had grown dangerously on him during the period of his association with Wordsworth, but he occasionally took the drug. *Kubla Khan* was actually composed during an opium dream and has a dream's splendor and irrationality. *The Ancient Mariner* is not a dream poem, as Professor Lowes has pointed out in *The Road to Xanadu*, but is the work of a conscious artist in control of his materials. How far, however, the drug, sensitizing Coleridge's faculties, contributed to the peculiar magic of this poem and *Christabel*, it would be hard to decide. *Dejection: An Ode* belongs to a period (1801–3) when he was living at Keswick, where he had settled on his return from a trip to Germany. The brilliance of his talk was unbroken, but poetry was dead in him. *The Pains of Sleep* (Sept. 1803), written less than eighteen months after *Dejection*, shows how the opium habit had brought suffering on him. From a trip to Malta (1804–6), Coleridge returned completely in the grip of the habit, and in the years which followed, he sank into a state of pitiful physical and spiritual prostration.

There is no need to trace the extent of that collapse. Nor is there any need to trace in detail activities which belong to the critic and philosopher rather than the poet. *The Watchman* was not Coleridge's only journalistic venture. In 1799 he contributed to *The Morning Post* and a dozen years later to *The Courier*. In the winter of 1809–10 he again edited a magazine of his own—*The Friend*—whose "main object . . . was to establish the philosophical distinction between the Reason and the Understanding" and which quite reasonably suffered a more disastrous fate than *The Watchman*. Always a great talker, he tried to capitalize on his ability by giving public lectures. As early as 1795, in the Pantisocracy days, he had lectured on politics. In 1808 he gave a series of lectures on Poetry and the Fine Arts which failed because of his exhausted physical condition. In the winter of 1811–12, showing a flash of his real brilliance, he gave his great lectures on Shakespeare and Milton. In 1818 he lectured again. But throughout the period, 1806–1816, he was handicapped by the physical prostration his drug habit had brought him to.

Finally, however, Coleridge put himself under the medical care of Dr. Gilman, with whom he lived from 1816 to 1834, and by a terrible effort brought his habit under control; he never broke it. The *Biographia Literaria* (1817) was the first and most important product of this period of restored ability. It is a strange and brilliant medley of philosophy and criticism. Coleridge turned more and more toward abstruse speculation. The old magic was still in his voice, and he spent the last years of his life thinking and talking metaphysics and theology.

"Coleridge," says Carlyle, "sat on the brow of Highgate Hill in those years, looking down on London and its smoke tumult like a sage escaped from the inanity of life's battle, attracting towards him the thoughts of innumerable brave souls still engaged there. . . . The practical intellects of the world did not much heed him, or carelessly reckoned him a metaphysical dreamer; but to the rising spirits of the young generation he had this dusky sublime character, and sat there as a kind of Magus, girt in mystery and enigma."

TO THE REV. W. L. BOWLES

[SECOND VERSION]

MY heart has thank'd thee, BOWLES! for those
    soft strains
    Whose sadness soothes me, like the mur-
      muring
    Of wild-bees in the sunny showers of spring!
For hence not callous to the mourner's pains

Through Youth's gay prime and thornless
    paths I went:
    And when the mightier Throes of mind
      began,
    And drove me forth, a thought-bewilder'd
      man,
Their mild and manliest melancholy lent

A mingled charm, such as the pang consign'd
    To slumber, though the big tear it renew'd;
    Bidding a strange mysterious PLEASURE
      brood   11
Over the wavy and tumultuous mind,

As the great SPIRIT erst with plastic sweep
Mov'd on the darkness of the unform'd deep.
Pub. 1796

THE EOLIAN HARP

COMPOSED AT CLEVEDON, SOMERSETSHIRE

MY pensive Sara! thy soft cheek reclined
Thus on mine arm, most soothing sweet it is
To sit beside our Cot, our Cot o'ergrown
With white-flower'd Jasmin, and the broad-
    leav'd Myrtle,
(Meet emblems they of Innocence and Love!)
And watch the clouds, that late were rich
    with light,
Slow saddening round, and mark the star of eve
Serenely brilliant (such should Wisdom be)
Shine opposite! How exquisite the scents
Snatch'd from yon bean-field! and the world
    so hush'd!   10
The stilly murmur of the distant Sea
Tells us of silence.
                And that simplest Lute,
Placed length-ways in the clasping casement,
    hark!
How by the desultory breeze caress'd,

Like some coy maid half yielding to her lover,
It pours such sweet upbraiding, as must needs
Tempt to repeat the wrong! And now, its
    strings
Boldlier swept, the long sequacious notes
Over delicious surges sink and rise,
Such a soft floating witchery of sound   20
As twilight Elfins make, when they at eve
Voyage on gentle gales from Fairy-Land,
Where Melodies round honey-dropping
    flowers,
Footless and wild, like birds of Paradise,
Nor pause, nor perch, hovering on untam'd
    wing!
O! the one Life within us and abroad,
Which meets all motion and becomes its soul,
A light in sound, a sound-like power in light,
Rhythm in all thought, and joyance every
    where—
Methinks, it should have been impossible 30
Not to love all things in a world so fill'd;
Where the breeze warbles, and the mute still
    air
Is Music slumbering on her instrument.

    And thus, my Love! as on the midway slope
Of yonder hill I stretch my limbs at noon,
Whilst through my half-clos'd eye-lids I be-
    hold
The sunbeams dance, like diamonds, on the
    main,
And tranquil muse upon tranquillity;
Full many a thought uncall'd and undetain'd,
And many idle flitting phantasies,   40
Traverse my indolent and passive brain,
As wild and various as the random gales
That swell and flutter on this subject Lute!

    And what if all of animated nature
Be but organic Harps diversely fram'd,
That tremble into thought, as o'er them sweeps
Plastic and vast, one intellectual breeze,
At once the Soul of each, and God of all?

    But thy more serious eye a mild reproof
Darts, O belovéd Woman! nor such thoughts
Dim and unhallow'd dost thou not reject, 51
And biddest me walk humbly with my God.
Meek Daughter in the family of Christ!
Well hast thou said and holily disprais'd
These shapings of the unregenerate mind;

15

By livid fount, or roar of blazing stream,

~~Cyber Night thunder of a subphur'd mayer~~ *of*

If ever to her idless dragon eyes,

O ALBION! thy predestin'd ruins rise,

The Fiend-hag on her perilous couch doth leap,

Mutt'ring distemper'd triumph in her charmed sleep.

Away, my soul, away!

In vain, in vain, the birds of warning sing—

And hark! I hear the famin'd brood of prey

Lank

Flap their ~~dark~~ pennons on the groaning wind!   *Lank*

Away, my soul, away!

I unpartaking of the evil thing,

With daily prayer/ and daily toil/   *of of,*

Soliciting for food my scanty soil,

Have wail'd my country with a loud lament.

Now I recenter my immortal mind

I suspect, almost suspect, that the word "dark" was intentionally substituted for "lank" — if so, 'twas the most tasteless thing thou ever didst. dear Joseph! —

A Page of Coleridge's Corrected Copy for the 1797 Edition of the *Poems*.
(See Appendix I.)

Bubbles that glitter as they rise and break
On vain Philosophy's aye-babbling spring.
For never guiltless may I speak of him,
The Incomprehensible! save when with awe
I praise him, and with Faith that inly *feels;* 60
Who with his saving mercies healéd me,
A sinful and most miserable man,
Wilder'd and dark, and gave me to possess
Peace, and this Cot, and thee, heart-honour'd
    Maid!

1795

From RELIGIOUS MUSINGS

      . . . Lovely was the death
Of Him whose life was Love! Holy with power
He on the thought-benighted Sceptic beamed
Manifest Godhead, melting into day   31
What floating mists of dark idolatry
Broke and misshaped the omnipresent Sire:
And first by Fear uncharmed the drowséd
    Soul.
Till of its nobler nature it 'gan feel
Dim recollections; and thence soared to Hope.
Strong to believe whate'er of mystic good
The Eternal dooms for His immortal sons.
From Hope and firmer Faith to perfect Love
Attracted and absorbed: and centered there 40
God only to behold, and know, and feel,
Till by exclusive consciousness of God
All self-annihilated it shall make
God its Identity: God all in all!
We and our Father one! . . .

        Believe thou, O my soul,
Life is a vision shadowy of Truth;
And vice, and anguish, and the wormy grave,
Shapes of a dream! The veiling clouds retire,
And lo! the Throne of the redeeming God
Forth flashing unimaginable day   400
Wraps in one blaze earth, heaven, and deepest
    hell.

Contemplant Spirits! ye that hovèr o'er
With untired gaze the immeasurable fount
Ebullient with creative Deity!
And ye of plastic power, that interfused
Roll through the grosser and material mass
In organizing surge! Holies of God!
(And what if Monads of the infinite mind?)
I haply journeying my immortal course

Shall sometime join your mystic choir! Till
    then   410
I discipline my young and novice thought
In ministeries of heart-stirring song,
And aye on Meditation's heaven-ward wing
Soaring aloft I breathe the empyreal air
Of Love, omnific, omnipresent Love,
Whose day-spring rises glorious in my soul
As the great Sun, when he his influence
Sheds on the frost-bound waters—The glad
    stream
Flows to the ray and warbles as it flows.

1794–1796

THIS LIME–TREE BOWER MY PRISON

[ADDRESSED TO CHARLES LAMB, OF THE INDIA HOUSE, LONDON]

In the June of 1797 some long-expected friends paid a visit to the author's cottage; and on the morning of their arrival, he met with an accident, which disabled him from walking during the whole time of their stay. One evening, when they had left him for a few hours, he composed the following lines in the garden-bower. (*Coleridge's note.*)

WELL, they are gone, and here must I remain,
This lime-tree bower my prison! I have lost
Beauties and feelings, such as would have been
Most sweet to my remembrance even when age
Had dimm'd mine eyes to blindness! They,
    meanwhile,
Friends, whom I never more may meet again,
On springy heath, along the hill-top edge,
Wander in gladness, and wind down, per-
    chance,
To that still roaring dell, of which I told;
The roaring dell, o'erwooded, narrow, deep, 10
And only speckled by the mid-day sun;
Where its slim trunk the ash from rock to rock
Flings arching like a bridge;—that branchless
    ash,
Unsunn'd and damp, whose few poor yellow
    leaves
Ne'er tremble in the gale, yet tremble still,
Fann'd by the water-fall! and there my friends
Behold the dark green file of long lank weeds,
That all at once (a most fantastic sight!)
Still nod and drip beneath the dripping edge
Of the blue clay-stone.

          Now, my friends emerge 20
Beneath the wide wide Heaven—and view
    again
The many-steepled tract magnificent
Of hilly fields and meadows, and the sea,
With some fair bark, perhaps, whose sails light
    up
The slip of smooth clear blue betwixt two
    Isles
Of purple shadow! Yes! they wander on
In gladness all; but thou, methinks, most glad,
My gentle-hearted Charles! for thou hast
    pined
And hunger'd after Nature, many a year,
In the great City pent, winning thy way   30
With sad yet patient soul, through evil and
    pain
And strange calamity! Ah! slowly sink
Behind the western ridge, thou glorious Sun!
Shine in the slant beams of the sinking orb,
Ye purple heath-flowers! richlier burn, ye
    clouds!
Live in the yellow light, ye distant groves!
And kindle, thou blue Ocean! So my friend
Struck with deep joy may stand, as I have
    stood,
Silent with swimming sense; yea, gazing round
On the wide landscape, gaze till all doth seem
Less gross than bodily; and of such hues   41
As veil the Almighty Spirit, when yet he makes
Spirits perceive his presence.

              A delight
Comes sudden on my heart, and I am glad
As I myself were there! Nor in this bower,
This little lime-tree bower, have I not mark'd

Much that has sooth'd me. Pale beneath the
    blaze
Hung the transparent foliage; and I watch'd
Some broad and sunny leaf, and lov'd to see
The shadow of the leaf and stem above   50
Dappling its sunshine! And that walnut-tree
Was richly ting'd, and a deep radiance lay
Full on the ancient ivy, which usurps
Those fronting elms, and now, with blackest
    mass
Makes their dark branches gleam a lighter hue
Through the late twilight: and though now the
    bat
Wheels silent by, and not a swallow twitters,
Yet still the solitary humble-bee
Sings in the bean-flower! Henceforth I shall
    know
That Nature ne'er deserts the wise and pure; 60
No plot so narrow, be but Nature there,
No waste so vacant, but may well employ
Each faculty of sense, and keep the heart
Awake to Love and Beauty! and sometimes
'Tis well to be bereft of promis'd good,
That we may lift the soul, and contemplate
With lively joy the joys we cannot share.
My gentle-hearted Charles! when the last rook
Beat its straight path along the dusky air
Homewards, I blest it! deeming its black wing
(Now a dim speck, now vanishing in light) 71
Had cross'd the mighty Orb's dilated glory,
While thou stood'st gazing; or, when all was
    still,
Flew creeking o'er thy head, and had a charm
For thee, my gentle-hearted Charles, to whom
No sound is dissonant which tells of Life.

1797

THE RIME OF THE ANCIENT MARINER

wondering Jew

IN SEVEN PARTS

ARGUMENT

How a Ship, having first sailed to the Equator, was driven by Storms to the cold Country towards the South Pole; how the Ancient Mariner cruelly and in contempt of the laws of hospitality killed a Sea-bird and how he was followed by many and strange Judgements: and in what manner he came back to his own Country.

PART I

An ancient Mariner meeteth three Gallants bidden to a wedding-feast, and detaineth one.

IT is an ancient Mariner,
And he stoppeth one of three.
'By thy long grey beard and glittering eye,
Now wherefore stopp'st thou me?

The Bridegroom's doors are opened wide,
And I am next of kin;
The guests are met, the feast is set:
May'st hear the merry din.'

He holds him with his skinny hand,
'There was a ship,' quoth he.   10
'Hold off! unhand me, grey-beard loon!'
Eftsoons his hand dropt he.

The Wedding-Guest is spellbound by the eye of the old seafaring man, and constrained to hear his tale.

He holds him with his glittering eye—
The Wedding-Guest stood still,
And listens like a three years' child:
The Mariner hath his will.

The Wedding-Guest sat on a stone:
He cannot choose but hear;
And thus spake on that ancient man,
The bright-eyed Mariner.   20

'The ship was cheered, the harbour cleared,
Merrily did we drop
Below the kirk, below the hill,
Below the lighthouse top.

The Mariner tells how the ship sailed southward with a good wind and fair weather, till it reached the line.

The Sun came up upon the left,
Out of the sea came he!
And he shone bright, and on the right
Went down into the sea.

Higher and higher every day,
Till over the mast at noon—'   *contrast*   30
The Wedding-Guest here beat his breast,
For he heard the loud bassoon.

The Wedding-
Guest heareth the
bridal music; but
the Mariner con-
tinueth his tale.

The bride hath paced into the hall,
Red as a rose is she;
Nodding their heads before her goes
The merry minstrelsy.

The Wedding-Guest he beat his breast,
Yet he cannot choose but hear;
And thus spake on that ancient man,
The bright-eyed Mariner.   40

The ship driven by
a storm toward the
south pole.

'And now the STORM-BLAST came, and he
Was tyrannous and strong:
He struck with his o'ertaking wings,
And chased us south along.

With sloping masts and dipping prow,
As who pursued with yell and blow
Still treads the shadow of his foe,
And forward bends his head,
The ship drove fast, loud roared the blast,
And southward aye we fled.   50

And now there came both mist and snow,
And it grew wondrous cold:
And ice, mast-high, came floating by,
As green as emerald.

The land of ice,
and of fearful
sounds where no
living thing was
to be seen.

And through the drifts the snowy clifts
Did send a dismal sheen:
Nor shapes of men nor beasts we ken—
The ice was all between.

The ice was here, the ice was there,
The ice was all around: 60
It cracked and growled, and roared and howled,
Like noises in a swound!

Till a great sea-
bird, called the
Albatross, came
through the snow-
fog, and was re-
ceived with great
joy and hospi-
tality.

At length did cross an Albatross,
Thorough the fog it came;
As if it had been a Christian soul,
We hailed it in God's name.

It ate the food it ne'er had eat,
And round and round it flew.
The ice did split with a thunder-fit;
The helmsman steered us through!   70

And lo! the Albatross proveth
a bird of good omen, and fol-
loweth the ship as it returned
northward through fog and
floating ice.

And a good south wind sprung up behind;
The Albatross did follow,
And every day, for food or play,
Came to the mariner's hollo!

In mist or cloud, on mast or shroud,
It perched for vespers nine;
Whiles all the night, through fog-smoke white,
Glimmered the white Moon-shine.'

<table>
<tr><td>The ancient Mariner inhospitably killeth the pious bird of good omen.</td></tr>
</table>

'God save thee, ancient Mariner!
From the fiends, that plague thee thus!—
Why look'st thou so?'—With my cross-bow
I shot the ALBATROSS.

PART II

The Sun now rose upon the right:
Out of the sea came he,
Still hid in mist, and on the left
Went down into the sea.

And the good south wind still blew behind,
But no sweet bird did follow,
Nor any day for food or play
Came to the mariners' hollo!

His shipmates cry out against the ancient Mariner, for killing the bird of good luck.

And I had done a hellish thing,
And it would work 'em woe:
For all averred, I had killed the bird
That made the breeze to blow.
Ah wretch! said they, the bird to slay,
That made the breeze to blow!

But when the fog cleared off, they justify the same, and thus make themselves accomplices in the crime.

Nor dim nor red, like God's own head,
The glorious Sun uprist:
Then all averred, I had killed the bird
That brought the fog and mist.
'Twas right, said they, such birds to slay,
That bring the fog and mist.

The fair breeze continues; the ship enters the Pacific Ocean, and sails northward, even till it reaches the Line.

The fair breeze blew, the white foam flew,
The furrow followed free;
We were the first that ever burst
Into that silent sea.

The ship hath been suddenly becalmed.

Down dropt the breeze, the sails dropt down,
'Twas sad as sad could be;
And we did speak only to break
The silence of the sea!

All in a hot and copper sky,
The bloody Sun, at noon,
Right up above the mast did stand,
No bigger than the Moon.

Day after day, day after day,
We stuck, nor breath nor motion;
As idle as a painted ship
Upon a painted ocean.

And the Albatross
begins to be
avenged.

Water, water, every where,
And all the boards did shrink;   120
Water, water, every where,
Nor any drop to drink.

The very deep did rot: O Christ!
That ever this should be!
Yea, slimy things did crawl with legs
Upon the slimy sea.

About, about, in reel and rout
The death-fires danced at night;
The water, like a witch's oils,
Burnt green, and blue and white.   130

A Spirit had followed them; one
of the invisible inhabitants of this
planet, neither departed souls nor
angels; concerning whom the
learned Jew, Josephus, and
the Platonic Constantinopolitan,
Michael Psellus, may be consulted. They are very numerous,
and there is no climate or element
without one or more.

And some in dreams assuréd were
Of the Spirit that plagued us so;
Nine fathom deep he had followed us
From the land of mist and snow.

And every tongue, through utter drought,
Was withered at the root;
We could not speak, no more than if
We had been choked with soot.

The shipmates, in their sore distress, would fain throw the whole
guilt on the ancient Mariner: in
sign whereof they hang the dead
sea-bird round his neck.

Ah! well a-day! what evil looks
Had I from old and young!   140
Instead of the cross, the Albatross
About my neck was hung.

PART III

There passed a weary time. Each throat
Was parched, and glazed each eye.
A weary time! a weary time!
How glazed each weary eye,
When looking westward, I beheld
A something in the sky.

The ancient Mar-
iner beholdeth a
sign in the ele-
ment afar off.

At first it seemed a little speck,
And then it seemed a mist;   150
It moved and moved, and took at last
A certain shape, I wist.

A speck, a mist, a shape, I wist!
And still it neared and neared:
As if it dodged a water-sprite,
It plunged and tacked and veered.

At its nearer ap-
proach, it seemeth
him to be a ship;
and at a dear ran-
som he freeth his
speech from the
bonds of thirst.

With throats unslaked, with black lips baked,
We could nor laugh nor wail;
Through utter drought all dumb we stood!
I bit my arm, I sucked the blood,   160
And cried, A sail, a sail!

With throats unslaked, with black lips baked,
Agape they heard me call:

A flash of joy;

Gramercy! they for joy did grin,
And all at one their breath drew in,
As they were drinking all.

And horror fol-
lows. For can it
be a ship that
comes onward
without wind or
tide?

See! see! (I cried) she tacks no more!
Hither to work us weal;
Without a breeze, without a tide,
She steadies with upright keel!   170

The western wave was all a-flame.
The day was well nigh done!
Almost upon the western wave
Rested the broad bright Sun;
When that strange shape drove suddenly
Betwixt us and the Sun.

It seemeth him
but the skeleton
of a ship.

And straight the Sun was flecked with bars,
(Heaven's Mother send us grace!)
As if through a dungeon-grate he peered
With broad and burning face.   180

Alas! (thought I, and my heart beat loud)
How fast she nears and nears!
Are those *her* sails that glance in the Sun,
Like restless gossameres?

And its ribs are seen
as bars on the face of
the setting Sun.

Are those *her* ribs through which the Sun
Did peer, as through a grate?

The Spectre-Woman
and her Death-mate,
and no other on board
the skeleton ship.

And is that Woman all her crew?
Is that a DEATH? and are there two?
Is DEATH that woman's mate?

Like vessel, like
crew!

Her lips were red, *her* looks were free,   190
Her locks were yellow as gold:
Her skin was as white as leprosy,
The Night-mare LIFE-IN-DEATH was she,
Who thicks man's blood with cold.

Death and Life-
in-Death have
diced for the ship's
crew, and she (the
latter) winneth the
ancient Mariner.

The naked hulk alongside came,
And the twain were casting dice;
'The game is done! I've won! I've won!'
Quoth she, and whistles thrice.

No twilight within
the courts of the
Sun.

The Sun's rim dips; the stars rush out:
At one stride comes the dark;   200
With far-heard whisper, o'er the sea,
Off shot the spectre-bark.

At the rising of
the Moon,

We listened and looked sideways up!
Fear at my heart, as at a cup,
My life-blood seemed to sip!
The stars were dim, and thick the night,
The steersman's face by his lamp gleamed white;
From the sails the dew did drip—
Till clomb above the eastern bar
The hornéd Moon, with one bright star   210
Within the nether tip.

One after another,

One after one, by the star-dogged Moon,
Too quick for groan or sigh,
Each turned his face with a ghastly pang,
And cursed me with his eye.

His shipmates
drop down dead.

Four times fifty living men,
(And I heard nor sigh nor groan)
With heavy thump, a lifeless lump,
They dropped down one by one.

But Life-in-Death
begins her work on
the ancient Mar-
iner.

The souls did from their bodies fly,—   220
They fled to bliss or woe!
And every soul, it passed me by,
Like the whizz of my cross-bow!

Part IV

The Wedding-
Guest feareth that
a Spirit is talking
to him;

'I fear thee, ancient Mariner!
I fear thy skinny hand!
And thou art long, and lank, and brown,
As is the ribbed sea-sand.

But the ancient
Mariner assureth
him of his bodily
life, and proceed-
eth to relate his
horrible penance.

I fear thee and thy glittering eye,
And thy skinny hand, so brown.'—
Fear not, fear not, thou Wedding-Guest!   230
This body dropt not down.

Alone, alone, all, all alone,
Alone on a wide wide sea!
And never a saint took pity on
My soul in agony.

He despiseth the
creatures of the
calm,

The many men, so beautiful!
And they all dead did lie:
And a thousand thousand slimy things
Lived on; and so did I.

And envieth that
they should live,
and so many lie
dead.

I looked upon the rotting sea,   240
And drew my eyes away;
I looked upon the rotting deck,
And there the dead men lay.

I looked to heaven, and tried to pray;
But or ever a prayer had gusht,
A wicked whisper came, and made
My heart as dry as dust.

I closed my lids, and kept them close,
And the balls like pulses beat;
For the sky and the sea, and the sea and the sky   250
Lay like a load on my weary eye,
And the dead were at my feet.

But the curse
liveth for him in
the eye of the dead
men.

The cold sweat melted from their limbs,
Nor rot nor reek did they:
The look with which they looked on me
Had never passed away.

An orphan's curse would drag to hell
A spirit from on high;
But oh! more horrible than that
Is the curse in a dead man's eye!   260
Seven days, seven nights, I saw that curse,
And yet I could not die.

In his loneliness and fixedness
he yearneth towards the journeying Moon, and the stars
that still sojourn, yet still move
onward; and every where the
blue sky belongs to them, and is
their appointed rest, and their
native country and their own
natural homes, which they enter
unannounced, as lords that are
certainly expected and yet there
is a silent joy at their arrival.

The moving Moon went up the sky,
And no where did abide:
Softly she was going up,
And a star or two beside—

Her beams bemocked the sultry main,
Like April hoar-frost spread;
But where the ship's huge shadow lay,
The charméd water burnt alway   270
A still and awful red.

By the light of the
Moon he be-
holdeth God's
creatures of the
great calm.

Beyond the shadow of the ship,
I watched the water-snakes:
They moved in tracks of shining white,
And when they reared, the elfish light
Fell off in hoary flakes.

Within the shadow of the ship
I watched their rich attire:
Blue, glossy green, and velvet black,
They coiled and swam; and every track   280
Was a flash of golden fire.

Their beauty and
their happiness.

He blesseth them
in his heart.

O happy living things! no tongue
Their beauty might declare:
A spring of love gushed from my heart,
And I blessed them unaware:
Sure my kind saint took pity on me,
And I blessed them unaware.

The spell begins
to break.

The self-same moment I could pray;
And from my neck so free
The Albatross fell off, and sank   290
Like lead into the sea.

Part V

Oh sleep! it is a gentle thing,
Beloved from pole to pole!
To Mary Queen the praise be given!
She sent the gentle sleep from Heaven,
That slid into my soul.

By grace of the
holy Mother, the
ancient Mariner is
refreshed with
rain.

The silly buckets on the deck,
That had so long remained,
I dreamt that they were filled with dew;
And when I awoke, it rained.   300

My lips were wet, my throat was cold,
My garments all were dank;
Sure I had drunken in my dreams,
And still my body drank.

I moved, and could not feel my limbs:
I was so light—almost
I thought that I had died in sleep,
And was a blessèd ghost.

He heareth sounds
and seeth strange
sights and commo-
tions in the sky and
the element.

And soon I heard a roaring wind:
It did not come anear;   310
But with its sound it shook the sails,
That were so thin and sere.

The upper air burst into life!
And a hundred fire-flags sheen,
To and fro they were hurried about!
And to and fro, and in and out,
The wan stars danced between.

And the coming wind did roar more loud,
And the sails did sigh like sedge;
And the rain poured down from one black cloud;   320
The Moon was at its edge.

The thick black cloud was cleft, and still
The Moon was at its side:
Like waters shot from some high crag,
The lightning fell with never a jag,
A river steep and wide.

The loud wind never reached the ship,
Yet now the ship moved on!
Beneath the lightning and the Moon
The dead men gave a groan. 330

They groaned, they stirred, they all uprose,
Nor spake, nor moved their eyes;
It had been strange, even in a dream,
To have seen those dead men rise.

The helmsman steered, the ship moved on;
Yet never a breeze up-blew;
The mariners all 'gan work the ropes,
Where they were wont to do;
They raised their limbs like lifeless tools—
We were a ghastly crew. 340

The body of my brother's son
Stood by me, knee to knee:
The body and I pulled at one rope,
But he said nought to me.

'I fear thee, ancient Mariner!'
Be calm, thou Wedding-Guest!
'Twas not those souls that fled in pain,
Which to their corses came again,
But a troop of spirits blest:

For when it dawned—they dropped their arms, 350
And clustered round the mast;
Sweet sounds rose slowly through their mouths,
And from their bodies passed.

Around, around, flew each sweet sound,
Then darted to the Sun;
Slowly the sounds came back again,
Now mixed, now one by one.

Sometimes a-dropping from the sky
I hear the sky-lark sing;
Sometimes all little birds that are, 360
How they seemed to fill the sea and air
With their sweet jargoning!

The bodies of the ship's crew are inspired, and the ship moves on;

But not by the souls of the men, nor by dæmons of earth or middle air, but by a blessed troop of angelic spirits, sent down by the invocation of the guardian saint.

And now 'twas like all instruments,
Now like a lonely flute;
And now it is an angel's song,
That makes the heavens be mute.

It ceased; yet still the sails made on
A pleasant noise till noon,
A noise like of a hidden brook
In the leafy month of June,   370
That to the sleeping woods all night
Singeth a quiet tune.

Till noon we quietly sailed on,
Yet never a breeze did breathe:
Slowly and smoothly went the ship,
Moved onward from beneath.

The lonesome
Spirit from the
south-pole carries
on the ship as far
as the Line, in
obedience to the
angelic troop, but
still requireth ven-
geance.

Under the keel nine fathom deep,
From the land of mist and snow,
The spirit slid: and it was he
That made the ship to go.   380
The sails at noon left off their tune,
And the ship stood still also.

The Sun, right up above the mast,
Had fixed her to the ocean:
But in a minute she 'gan stir,
With a short uneasy motion—
Backwards and forwards half her length
With a short uneasy motion.

Then like a pawing horse let go,
She made a sudden bound: 390
It flung the blood into my head,
And I fell down in a swound.

The Polar Spirit's
fellow-dæmons, the
invisible inhabit-
ants of the ele-
ment, take part in
his wrong; and two
of them relate, one
to the other, that
penance long and
heavy for the an-
cient Mariner hath
been accorded to
the Polar Spirit,
who returneth
southward.

How long in that same fit I lay,
I have not to declare;
But ere my living life returned,
I heard and in my soul discerned
Two voices in the air.

'Is it he?' quoth one, 'Is this the man?
By him who died on cross,
With his cruel bow he laid full low   400
The harmless Albatross.

The spirit who bideth by himself
In the land of mist and snow,
He loved the bird that loved the man
Who shot him with his bow.'

The other was a softer voice,
As soft as honey-dew:
Quoth he, 'The man hath penance done,
And penance more will do.'

PART VI

FIRST VOICE

'But tell me, tell me! speak again,   410
Thy soft response renewing—
What makes that ship drive on so fast?
What is the ocean doing?'

SECOND VOICE

'Still as a slave before his lord,
The ocean hath no blast·
His great bright eye most silently
Up to the Moon is cast--

If he may know which way to go;
For she guides him smooth or grim.
See, brother, see! how graciously   420
She looketh down on him.'

FIRST VOICE

'But why drives on that ship so fast,
Without or wave or wind?'

SECOND VOICE

'The air is cut away before,
And closes from behind.

Fly, brother, fly! more high, more high!
Or we shall be belated:
For slow and slow that ship will go,
When the Mariner's trance is abated.'

The Mariner hath been cast into a trance; for the angelic power causeth the vessel to drive northward faster than human life could endure.

I woke, and we were sailing on   430
As in a gentle weather:
'Twas night, calm night, the moon was high;
The dead men stood together.

The supernatural motion is retarded; the Mariner awakes, and his penance begins anew.

All stood together on the deck,
For a charnel-dungeon fitter:
All fixed on me their stony eyes,
That in the Moon did glitter.

The pang, the curse, with which they died,
Had never passed away:
I could not draw my eyes from theirs,   440
Nor turn them up to pray.

The curse is finally
expiated.

And now this spell was snapt: once more
I viewed the ocean green,
And looked far forth, yet little saw
Of what had else been seen—

Like one, that on a lonesome road
Doth walk in fear and dread,
And having once turned round walks on,
And turns no more his head;
Because he knows, a frightful fiend   450
Doth close behind him tread.

But soon there breathed a wind on me,
Nor sound nor motion made:
Its path was not upon the sea,
In ripple or in shade.

It raised my hair, it fanned my cheek
Like a meadow-gale of spring—
It mingled strangely with my fears,
Yet it felt like a welcoming.

Swiftly, swiftly flew the ship,   460
Yet she sailed softly too:
Sweetly, sweetly blew the breeze—
On me alone it blew.

And the ancient
Mariner beholdeth
his native country.

Oh! dream of joy! is this indeed
The light-house top I see?
Is this the hill? is this the kirk?
Is this mine own countree?

We drifted o'er the harbour-bar,
And I with sobs did pray—
O let me be awake, my God!   470
Or let me sleep alway.

The harbour-bay was clear as glass,
So smoothly it was strewn!
And on the bay the moonlight lay,
And the shadow of the Moon.

The rock shone bright, the kirk no less,
That stands above the rock:
The moonlight steeped in silentness
The steady weathercock.

And the bay was white with silent light,   480

The angelic spirits
leave the dead
bodies,

Till rising from the same,
Full many shapes, that shadows were,
In crimson colours came.

And appear in
their own forms
of light.

A little distance from the prow
Those crimson shadows were:
I turned my eyes upon the deck—
Oh, Christ! what saw I there!

Each corse lay flat, lifeless and flat,
And, by the holy rood!
A man all light, a seraph-man,   490
On every corse there stood.

This seraph-band, each waved his hand:
It was a heavenly sight!
They stood as signals to the land,
Each one a lovely light;

This seraph-band, each waved his hand,
No voice did they impart—
No voice; but oh! the silence sank
Like music on my heart.

But soon I heard the dash of oars,   500
I heard the Pilot's cheer;
My head was turned perforce away
And I saw a boat appear.

The Pilot and the Pilot's boy,
I heard them coming fast:
Dear Lord in Heaven! it was a joy
The dead men could not blast.

I saw a third—I heard his voice:
It is the Hermit good!
He singeth loud his godly hymns   510
That he makes in the wood.
He'll shrieve my soul, he'll wash away
The Albatross's blood.

PART VII

The Hermit of the
Wood,

This Hermit good lives in that wood
Which slopes down to the sea.
How loudly his sweet voice he rears!
He loves to talk with marineres
That come from a far countree.

He kneels at morn, and noon, and eve—
He hath a cushion plump: 520
It is the moss that wholly hides
The rotted old oak-stump.

The skiff-boat neared: I heard them talk,
'Why, this is strange, I trow!
Where are those lights so many and fair,
That signal made but now?'

Approacheth the
ship with wonder.

'Strange, by my faith!' the Hermit said—
'And they answered not our cheer!
The planks looked warped! and see those sails,
How thin they are and sere!   530
I never saw aught like to them,
Unless perchance it were

Brown skeletons of leaves that lag
My forest-brook along;
When the ivy-tod is heavy with snow,
And the owlet whoops to the wolf below,
That eats the she-wolf's young.'

'Dear Lord! it hath a fiendish look—
(The Pilot made reply)
I am a-feared'—'Push on, push on!'   540
Said the Hermit cheerily.

The boat came closer to the ship,
But I nor spake nor stirred;
The boat came close beneath the ship,
And straight a sound was heard.

The ship suddenly
sinketh.

Under the water it rumbled on,
Still louder and more dread:
It reached the ship, it split the bay;
The ship went down like lead.

The ancient Mar-
iner is saved in
the Pilot's boat.

Stunned by that loud and dreadful sound,   550
Which sky and ocean smote,
Like one that hath been seven days drowned
My body lay afloat;
But swift as dreams, myself I found
Within the Pilot's boat.

Upon the whirl, where sank the ship,
The boat spun round and round;
And all was still, save that the hill
Was telling of the sound.

I moved my lips—the Pilot shrieked   560
And fell down in a fit;
The holy Hermit raised his eyes,
And prayed where he did sit.

I took the oars: the Pilot's boy,
Who now doth crazy go,
Laughed loud and long, and all the while
His eyes went to and fro.
'Ha! ha!' quoth he, 'full plain I see,
The Devil knows how to row.'

And now, all in my own countree,   570
I stood on the firm land!
The Hermit stepped forth from the boat,
And scarcely he could stand.

The ancient Mar-
iner earnestly en-
treateth the Hermit
to shrieve him; and
the penance of life
falls on him.

'O shrieve me, shrieve me, holy man!'
The Hermit crossed his brow.
'Say quick,' quoth he, 'I bid thee say—
What manner of man art thou?'

Forthwith this frame of mine was wrenched
With a woful agony,
Which forced me to begin my tale;   580
And then it left me free.

And ever and anon
throughout his fu-
ture life an agony
constraineth him
to travel from land
to land;

Since then, at an uncertain hour,
That agony returns:
And till my ghastly tale is told,
This heart within me burns.

I pass, like night, from land to land;
I have strange power of speech;
That moment that his face I see,
I know the man that must hear me:
To him my tale I teach.   590

What loud uproar bursts from that door!
The wedding-guests are there:
But in the garden-bower the bride
And bride-maids singing are:
And hark the little vesper bell,
Which biddeth me to prayer!

O Wedding-Guest! this soul hath been
Alone on a wide wide sea:
So lonely 'twas, that God himself
Scarce seeméd there to be.   600

O sweeter than the marriage-feast,
'Tis sweeter far to me,
To walk together to the kirk
With a goodly company!—

To walk together to the kirk,
And all together pray,
While each to his great Father bends,
Old men, and babes, and loving friends
And youths and maidens gay!

And to teach, by
his own example,
love and reverence
to all things that
God made and
loveth.

Farewell, farewell! but this I tell   610
To thee, thou Wedding-Guest!
He prayeth well, who loveth well
Both man and bird and beast.

He prayeth best, who loveth best
All things both great and small;
For the dear God who loveth us,
He made and loveth all.

The Mariner, whose eye is bright,
Whose beard with age is hoar,
Is gone: and now the Wedding-Guest   620
Turned from the bridegroom's door.

He went like one that hath been stunned,
And is of sense forlorn:
A sadder and a wiser man,
He rose the morrow morn.

1797–1798

CHRISTABEL[1]

PART I

'Tis the middle of night by the castle clock,
And the owls have awakened the crowing
        cock;
Tu—whit!——Tu—whoo!
And hark, again! the crowing cock,
How drowsily it crew.

Sir Leoline, the Baron rich,
Hath a toothless mastiff bitch;
From her kennel beneath the rock
She maketh answer to the clock,
Four for the quarters, and twelve for the
        hour;   10
Ever and aye, by shine and shower,
Sixteen short howls, not over loud;
Some say, she sees my lady's shroud.

[1] The two parts of *Christabel* were published
together in 1816. Composition dates are given at
the end of each part.

Is the night chilly and dark?
The night is chilly, but not dark.
The thin gray cloud is spread on high,
It covers but not hides the sky.
The moon is behind, and at the full;
And yet she looks both small and dull.
The night is chill, the cloud is gray: 20
'Tis a month before the month of May,
And the Spring comes slowly up this way.

The lovely lady, Christabel,
Whom her father loves so well,
What makes her in the wood so late,
A furlong from the castle gate?
She had dreams all yesternight
Of her own betrothéd knight;
And she in the midnight wood will pray
For the weal of her lover that's far away.   30

She stole along, she nothing spoke,
The sighs she heaved were soft and low,
And naught was green upon the oak

But moss and rarest mistletoe:
She kneels beneath the huge oak tree,
And in silence prayeth she.

The lady sprang up suddenly,
The lovely lady, Christabel!
It moaned as near, as near can be,
But what it is she cannot tell.—   40
On the other side it seems to be,
Of the huge, broad-breasted, old oak tree.

The night is chill; the forest bare;
Is it the wind that moaneth bleak?
There is not wind enough in the air
To move away the ringlet curl
From the lovely lady's cheek—
There is not wind enough to twirl
The one red leaf, the last of its clan,
That dances as often as dance it can,   50
Hanging so light, and hanging so high,
On the topmost twig that looks up at the sky.

Hush, beating heart of Christabel!
Jesu, Maria, shield her well!
She folded her arms beneath her cloak,
And stole to the other side of the oak.
      What sees she there?

There she sees a damsel bright,
Drest in a silken robe of white,
That shadowy in the moonlight shone: 60
The neck that made that white robe wan,
Her stately neck, and arms were bare;
Her blue-veined feet unsandal'd were,
And wildly glittered here and there
The gems entangled in her hair.
I guess, 'twas frightful there to see
A lady so richly clad as she—
Beautiful exceedingly!

Mary mother, save me now!
(Said Christabel,) And who art thou?   70

The lady strange made answer meet,
And her voice was faint and sweet:—
Have pity on my sore distress,
I scarce can speak for weariness:
Stretch forth thy hand, and have no fear!
Said Christabel, How camest thou here?
And the lady, whose voice was faint and sweet,
Did thus pursue her answer meet:—

My sire is of a noble line,
And my name is Geraldine: 80
Five warriors seized me yestermorn,
Me, even me, a maid forlorn:
They choked my cries with force and fright,
And tied me on a palfrey white.
The palfrey was as fleet as wind,
And they rode furiously behind.
They spurred amain, their steeds were white:
And once we crossed the shade of night.
As sure as Heaven shall rescue me,
I have no thought what men they be;   90
Nor do I know how long it is
(For I have lain entranced I wis)
Since one, the tallest of the five,
Took me from the palfrey's back,
A weary woman, scarce alive.
Some muttered words his comrades spoke:
He placed me underneath this oak;
He swore they would return with haste;
Whither they went I cannot tell—
I thought I heard, some minutes past,   100
Sounds as of a castle bell.
Stretch forth thy hand (thus ended she),
And help a wretched maid to flee.

Then Christabel stretched forth her hand,
And comforted fair Geraldine:
O well, bright dame! may you command
The service of Sir Leoline;
And gladly our stout chivalry
Will he send forth and friends withal
To guide and guard you safe and free   110
Home to your noble father's hall.

She rose: and forth with steps they passed
That strove to be, and were not, fast.
Her gracious stars the lady blest,
And thus spake on sweet Christabel:
All our household are at rest,
The hall as silent as the cell;
Sir Leoline is weak in health,
And may not well awakened be,
But we will move as if in stealth,   120
And I beseech your courtesy,
This night, to share your couch with me.

They crossed the moat, and Christabel
Took the key that fitted well;
A little door she opened straight,
All in the middle of the gate;

The gate that was ironed within and without,
Where an army in battle array had marched
 out.
The lady sank, belike through pain,
And Christabel with might and main   130
Lifted her up, a weary weight,
Over the threshold of the gate:
Then the lady rose again,
And moved, as she were not in pain.

So free from danger, free from fear,
They crossed the court: right glad they were.
And Christabel devoutly cried
To the lady by her side,
Praise we the Virgin all divine
Who hath rescued thee from thy distress! 140
Alas, alas! said Geraldine,
I cannot speak for weariness.
So free from danger, free from fear,
They crossed the court: right glad they were.

Outside her kennel, the mastiff old
Lay fast asleep, in moonshine cold.
The mastiff old did not awake,
Yet she an angry moan did make!
And what can ail the mastiff bitch?
Never till now she uttered yell   150
Beneath the eye of Christabel.
Perhaps it is the owlet's scritch:
For what can ail the mastiff bitch?

They passed the hall, that echoes still,
Pass as lightly as you will!
The brands were flat, the brands were dying,
Amid their own white ashes lying;
But when the lady passed, there came
A tongue of light, a fit of flame;
And Christabel saw the lady's eye,   160
And nothing else saw she thereby,
Save the boss of the shield of Sir Leoline
 tall,
Which hung in a murky old niche in the wall.
O softly tread, said Christabel,
My father seldom sleepeth well.

Sweet Christabel her feet doth bare,
And jealous of the listening air
They steal their way from stair to stair,
Now in glimmer, and now in gloom,
And now they pass the Baron's room,   170
As still as death, with stifled breath!

And now have reached her chamber door,
And now doth Geraldine press down
The rushes of the chamber floor.

The moon shines dim in the open air,
And not a moonbeam enters here.
But they without its light can see
The chamber carved so curiously,
Carved with figures strange and sweet,
All made out of the carver's brain,   180
For a lady's chamber meet:
The lamp with twofold silver chain
Is fastened to an angel's feet.

The silver lamp burns dead and dim;
But Christabel the lamp will trim.
She trimmed the lamp, and made it bright,
And left it swinging to and fro,
While Geraldine, in wretched plight,
Sank down upon the floor below.

O weary lady, Geraldine,   190
I pray you, drink this cordial wine!
It is a wine of virtuous powers;
My mother made it of wild flowers.

And will your mother pity me,
Who am a maiden most forlorn?
Christabel answered—Woe is me!
She died the hour that I was born.
I have heard the grey-haired friar tell
How on her death-bed she did say,
That she should hear the castle-bell   200
Strike twelve upon my wedding-day.
O mother dear! that thou wert here!
I would, said Geraldine, she were!

But soon with altered voice, said she—
'Off, wandering mother! Peak and pine!
I have power to bid thee flee.'
Alas! what ails poor Geraldine?
Why stares she with unsettled eye?
Can she the bodiless dead espy?
And why with hollow voice cries she,   210
'Off, woman, off! this hour is mine—
Though thou her guardian spirit be,
Off, woman, off! 'tis given to me.'

Then Christabel knelt by the lady's side,
And raised to heaven her eyes so blue—

Alas! said she, this ghastly ride—
Dear lady! it hath wildered you!
The lady wiped her moist cold brow,
And faintly said, ''tis over now!;

Again the wild-flower wine she drank: 220
Her fair large eyes 'gan glitter bright,
And from the floor whereon she sank,
The lofty lady stood upright:
She was most beautiful to see,
Like a lady of a far countrée.

And thus the lofty lady spake—
'All they who live in the upper sky,
Do love you, holy Christabel!
And you love them, and for their sake
And for the good which me befel, 230
Even I in my degree will try,
Fair maiden, to requite you well.
But now unrobe yourself; for I
Must pray, ere yet in bed I lie.'

Quoth Christabel, So let it be!
And as the lady bade, did she.
Her gentle limbs did she undress,
And lay down in her loveliness.

But through her brain of weal and woe
So many thoughts moved to and fro, 240
That vain it were her lids to close;
So half-way from the bed she rose,
And on her elbow did recline
To look at the lady Geraldine.

Beneath the lamp the lady bowed,
And slowly rolled her eyes around;
Then drawing in her breath aloud,
Like one that shuddered, she unbound
The cincture from beneath her breast:
Her silken robe, and inner vest, 250
Dropt to her feet, and full in view,
Behold! her bosom and half her side——
A sight to dream of, not to tell!
O shield her! shield sweet Christabel!

Yet Geraldine nor speaks nor stirs;
Ah! what a stricken look was hers!
Deep from within she seems half-way
To lift some weight with sick assay,
And eyes the maid and seeks delay;
Then suddenly, as one defied, 260

Collects herself in scorn and pride,
And lay down by the Maiden's side!—
And in her arms the maid she took,
Ah wel-a-day!
And with low voice and doleful look
These words did say:
'In the touch of this bosom there worketh a
spell,
Which is lord of thy utterance, Christabel!
Thou knowest to-night, and wilt know to-
morrow,
This mark of my shame, this seal of my sorrow;
But vainly thou warrest, 271
For this is alone in
Thy power to declare,
That in the dim forest
Thou heard'st a low moaning,
And found'st a bright lady, surpassingly
fair;
And didst bring her home with thee in love
and in charity,
To shield her and shelter her from the damp
air.'

1797

The Conclusion to Part I

It was a lovely sight to see
The lady Christabel, when she 280
Was praying at the old oak tree.
Amid the jaggéd shadows
Of mossy leafless boughs,
Kneeling in the moonlight,
To make her gentle vows;
Her slender palms together prest,
Heaving sometimes on her breast;
Her face resigned to bliss or bale—
Her face, oh call it fair not pale,
And both blue eyes more bright than clear,
Each about to have a tear. 291

With open eyes (ah woe is me!)
Asleep, and dreaming fearfully,
Fearfully dreaming, yet, I wis,
Dreaming that alone, which is—
O sorrow and shame! Can this be she,
The lady, who knelt at the old oak tree?
And lo! the worker of these harms,
That holds the maiden in her arms,
Seems to slumber still and mild, 300
As a mother with her child.

A star hath set, a star hath risen,
O Geraldine! since arms of thine
Have been the lovely lady's prison.
O Geraldine! one hour was thine—
Thou'st had thy will! By tairn and rill,
The night-birds all that hour were still.
But now they are jubilant anew,   308
From cliff and tower, tu—whoo! tu—whoo!
Tu—whoo! tu—whoo! from wood and fell!

And see! the lady Christabel
Gathers herself from out her trance;
Her limbs relax, her countenance
Grows sad and soft; the smooth thin lids
Close o'er her eyes; and tears she sheds—
Large tears that leave the lashes bright!
And oft the while she seems to smile
As infants at a sudden light!

Yea, she doth smile, and she doth weep,
Like a youthful hermitess,   320
Beauteous in a wilderness,
Who, praying always, prays in sleep.
And, if she move unquietly,
Perchance, 'tis but the blood so free
Comes back and tingles in her feet.
No doubt, she hath a vision sweet.
What if her guardian spirit 'twere,
What if she knew her mother near?
But this she knows, in joys and woes,
That saints will aid if men will call: 330
For the blue sky bends over all!

1797

PART II

Each matin bell, the Baron saith,
Knells us back to a world of death.
These words Sir Leoline first said,
When he rose and found his lady dead:
These words Sir Leoline will say
Many a morn to his dying day!

And hence the custom and law began
That still at dawn the sacristan,
Who duly pulls the heavy bell,   340
Five and forty beads must tell
Between each stroke—a warning knell,
Which not a soul can choose but hear
From Bratha Head to Wyndermere.

Saith Bracy the bard, So let it knell!
And let the drowsy sacristan
Still count as slowly as he can!
There is no lack of such, I ween,
As well fill up the space between.
In Langdale Pike and Witch's Lair,   350
And Dungeon-ghyll so foully rent,
With ropes of rock and bells of air
Three sinful sextons' ghosts are pent,
Who all give back, one after t'other,
The death-note to their living brother;
And oft too, by the knell offended,
Just as their one! two! three! is ended,
The devil mocks the doleful tale
With a merry peal from Borodale.

The air is still! through mist and cloud   360
That merry peal comes ringing loud;
And Geraldine shakes off her dread,
And rises lightly from the bed;
Puts on her silken vestments white,
And tricks her hair in lovely plight,
And nothing doubting of her spell
Awakens the lady Christabel.
'Sleep you, sweet lady Christabel?
I trust that you have rested well.'

And Christabel awoke and spied   370
The same who lay down by her side—
O rather say, the same whom she
Raised up beneath the old oak tree!
Nay, fairer yet! and yet more fair!
For she belike hath drunken deep
Of all the blessedness of sleep!
And while she spake, her looks, her air
Such gentle thankfulness declare,
That (so it seemed) her girded vests
Grew tight beneath her heaving breasts.   380
'Sure I have sinn'd!' said Christabel,
'Now heaven be praised if all be well!'
And in low faltering tones, yet sweet,
Did she the lofty lady greet
With such perplexity of mind
As dreams too lively leave behind.

So quickly she rose, and quickly arrayed
Her maiden limbs, and having prayed
That He, who on the cross did groan,
Might wash away her sins unknown,   390
She forthwith led fair Geraldine
To meet her sire, Sir Leoline.

The lovely maid and the lady tall
Are pacing both into the hall,
And pacing on through page and groom,
Enter the Baron's presence-room.

The Baron rose, and while he prest
His gentle daughter to his breast,
With cheerful wonder in his eyes
The lady Geraldine espies,   400
And gave such welcome to the same,
As might beseem so bright a dame!

But when he heard the lady's tale,
And when she told her father's name,
Why waxed Sir Leoline so pale,
Murmuring o'er the name again,
Lord Roland de Vaux of Tryermaine?

Alas! they had been friends in youth;
But whispering tongues can poison truth;
And constancy lives in realms above;   410
And life is thorny; and youth is vain;
And to be wroth with one we love
Doth work like madness in the brain.
And thus it chanced, as I divine,
With Roland and Sir Leoline.
Each spake words of high disdain
And insult to his heart's best brother:
They parted—ne'er to meet again!
But never either found another
To free the hollow heart from paining—   420
They stood aloof, the scars remaining,
Like cliffs which had been rent asunder;
A dreary sea now flows between;—
But neither heat, nor frost, nor thunder,
Shall wholly do away, I ween,
The marks of that which once hath been.

Sir Leoline, a moment's space,
Stood gazing on the damsel's face:
And the youthful Lord of Tryermaine
Came back upon his heart again.   430

O then the Baron forgot his age,
His noble heart swelled high with rage;
He swore by the wounds in Jesu's side
He would proclaim it far and wide,
With trump and solemn heraldry,
That they, who thus had wronged the dame,
Were base as spotted infamy!   *irony*
'And if they dare deny the same,

My herald shall appoint a week,
And let the recreant traitors seek   440
My tourney court—that there and then
I may dislodge their reptile souls   *irony*
From the bodies and forms of men!'
He spake: his eye in lightning rolls!
For the lady was ruthlessly seized; and he
          kenned
In the beautiful lady the child of his friend!

And now the tears were on his face,
And fondly in his arms he took
Fair Geraldine, who met the embrace,
Prolonging it with joyous look.   450
Which when she viewed, a vision fell
Upon the soul of Christabel,
The vision of fear, the touch and pain!
She shrunk and shuddered, and saw again—
(Ah, woe is me! Was it for thee,
Thou gentle maid! such sights to see?)

Again she saw that bosom old,
Again she felt that bosom cold,
And drew in her breath with a hissing sound:
Whereat the Knight turned wildly round, 460
And nothing saw, but his own sweet maid
With eyes upraised, as one that prayed.

The touch, the sight, had passed away,
And in its stead that vision blest,
Which comforted her after-rest
While in the lady's arms she lay,
Had put a rapture in her breast,
And on her lips and o'er her eyes
Spread smiles like light!
          With new surprise,
'What ails then my belovéd child?'   470
The Baron said—His daughter mild
Made answer, 'All will yet be well!'
I ween, she had no power to tell
Aught else: so mighty was the spell.

Yet he, who saw this Geraldine,
Had deemed her sure a thing divine:
Such sorrow with such grace she blended,
As if she feared she had offended
Sweet Christabel, that gentle maid!
And with such lowly tones she prayed   480
She might be sent without delay
Home to her father's mansion.

                'Nay!
Nay, by my soul!' said Leoline.
'Ho! Bracy the bard, the charge be thine!
Go thou, with music sweet and loud,
And take two steeds with trappings proud,
And take the youth whom thou lov'st best
To bear thy harp, and learn thy song,
And clothe you both in solemn vest,
And over the mountains haste along,   490
Lest wandering folk, that are abroad,
Detain you on the valley road.

'And when he has crossed the Irthing flood,
My merry bard! he hastes, he hastes
Up Knorren Moor, through Halegarth Wood,
And reaches soon that castle good
Which stands and threatens Scotland's wastes.

'Bard Bracy! bard Bracy! your horses are fleet,
Ye must ride up the hall, your music so sweet,
More loud than your horses' echoing feet!   500
And loud and loud to Lord Roland call,
Thy daughter is safe in Langdale hall!
Thy beautiful daughter is safe and free—
Sir Leoline greets thee thus through me!
He bids thee come without delay
With all thy numerous array
And take thy lovely daughter home:
And he will meet thee on the way
With all his numerous array
White with their panting palfreys' foam: 510
And, by mine honour! I will say,
That I repent me of the day
When I spake words of fierce disdain
To Roland de Vaux of Tryermaine!—
—For since that evil hour hath flown,
Many a summer's sun hath shone;
Yet ne'er found I a friend again
Like Roland de Vaux of Tryermaine.'

The lady fell, and clasped his knees,
Her face upraised, her eyes o'erflowing;   520
And Bracy replied, with faltering voice,
His gracious Hail on all bestowing!—
'Thy words, thou sire of Christabel,
Are sweeter than my harp can tell;
Yet might I gain a boon of thee,
This day my journey should not be,
So strange a dream hath come to me,
That I had vowed with music loud
To clear yon wood from thing unblest,
Warned by a vision in my rest!   530

For in my sleep I saw that dove,
That gentle bird, whom thou dost love,
And call'st by thy own daughter's name—
Sir Leoline! I saw the same
Fluttering, and uttering fearful moan,
Among the green herbs in the forest alone.
Which when I saw and when I heard,
I wonder'd what might ail the bird;
For nothing near it could I see,
Save the grass and green herbs underneath the
     old tree.   540

'And in my dream methought I went
To search out what might there be found;
And what the sweet bird's trouble meant,
That thus lay fluttering on the ground.
I went and peered, and could descry
No cause for her distressful cry;
But yet for her dear lady's sake
I stooped, methought, the dove to take,
When lo! I saw a bright green snake
Coiled around its wings and neck.   550
Green as the herbs on which it couched,
Close by the dove's its head it crouched;
And with the dove it heaves and stirs,
Swelling its neck as she swelled hers!
I woke; it was the midnight hour,
The clock was echoing in the tower;
But though my slumber was gone by,
This dream it would not pass away—
It seems to live upon my eye!
And thence I vowed this self-same day   560
With music strong and saintly song
To wander through the forest bare,
Lest aught unholy loiter there.'

Thus Bracy said: the Baron, the while,
Half-listening heard him with a smile;
Then turned to Lady Geraldine,
His eyes made up of wonder and love;
And said in courtly accents fine,
'Sweet maid, Lord Roland's beauteous dove,
With arms more strong than harp or song,   570
Thy sire and I will crush the snake!'
He kissed her forehead as he spake,
And Geraldine in maiden wise
Casting down her large bright eyes,
With blushing cheek and courtesy fine
She turned her from Sir Leoline;
Softly gathering up her train,
That o'er her right arm fell again;

And folded her arms across her chest,
And couched her head upon her breast,   580
And looked askance at Christabel——.
Jesu, Maria, shield her well!

A snake's small eye blinks dull and shy;
And the lady's eyes they shrunk in her head,
Each shrunk up to a serpent's eye,
And with somewhat of malice, and more of
        dread,
At Christabel she looked askance!—
One moment—and the sight was fled!
But Christabel in dizzy trance
Stumbling on the unsteady ground   590
Shuddered aloud, with a hissing sound;
And Geraldine again turned round,
And like a thing, that sought relief,
Full of wonder and full of grief,
She rolled her large bright eyes divine
Wildly on Sir Leoline.

The maid, alas! her thoughts are gone,
She nothing sees—no sight but one!
The maid, devoid of guile and sin,
I know not how, in fearful wise,   600
So deeply had she drunken in
That look, those shrunken serpent eyes,
That all her features were resigned
To this sole image in her mind:
And passively did imitate
That look of dull and treacherous hate!
And thus she stood, in dizzy trance,
Still picturing that look askance
With forced unconscious sympathy
Full before her father's view——   610
As far as such a look could be
In eyes so innocent and blue!

And when the trance was o'er, the maid
Paused awhile, and inly prayed:
Then falling at the Baron's feet,
'By my mother's soul do I entreat
That thou this woman send away!'
She said: and more she could not say:
For what she knew she could not tell,
O'er-mastered by the mighty spell.   620

Why is thy cheek so wan and wild,
Sir Leoline? Thy only child
Lies at thy feet, thy joy, thy pride,
So fair, so innocent, so mild;

The same, for whom thy lady died!
O by the pangs of her dear mother
Think thou no evil of thy child!
For her, and thee, and for no other,
She prayed the moment ere she died:
Prayed that the babe for whom she died,   630
Might prove her dear lord's joy and pride!
    That prayer her deadly pangs beguiled,
        Sir Leoline!
    And wouldst thou wrong thy only child,
        Her child and thine?

Within the Baron's heart and brain
If thoughts, like these, had any share,
They only swelled his rage and pain,
And did but work confusion there.
His heart was cleft with pain and rage,   640
His cheeks they quivered, his eyes were wild,
Dishonoured thus in his old age;
Dishonoured by his only child,
And all his hospitality
To the wronged daughter of his friend
By more than woman's jealousy
Brought thus to a disgraceful end—
He rolled his eye with stern regard
Upon the gentle minstrel bard,
And said in tones abrupt, austere—   650
'Why, Bracy! dost thou loiter here?
I bade thee hence!' The bard obeyed;
And turning from his own sweet maid,
The agéd knight, Sir Leoline,
Led forth the lady Geraldine!

1800

THE CONCLUSION TO PART II

A little child, a limber elf,
Singing, dancing to itself,
A fairy thing with red round cheeks,
That always finds, and never seeks,
Makes such a vision to the sight   660
As fills a father's eyes with light;
And pleasures flow in so thick and fast
Upon his heart, that he at last
Must needs express his love's excess
With words of unmeant bitterness.
Perhaps 'tis pretty to force together
Thoughts so all unlike each other;
To mutter and mock a broken charm,
To dally with wrong that does no harm.
Perhaps 'tis tender too and pretty   670

Told every woe, for which thy breast might smart,

Neglect and grinning Scorn, and Want combin'd.

Recoiling back thou sent'st the friend of Pain

To roll a tide of Death through every freezing vein.

⸻

O Spirit blest!

Whether the ~~eternal~~ throne around

Amidst the blaze of Cherubim

Thou pourest forth the grateful hymn,

Or soaring through the vast domain

Enrapturst angels with thy strain.

Grant me, like thee, the lyre to sound,

Like thee, with fire divine to glow;

But, ah! when rage the Waves of Woe,

Grant me with firmer breast t' oppose their hate,

And soar beyond the Storm with upright eye elate.

S. T. Coleridge 1790

Some Lines from One of Coleridge's Poems, with Signature. (See Appendix I.)

At each wild word to feel within
A sweet recoil of love and pity.
And what, if in a world of sin
(O sorrow and shame should this be true!)
Such giddiness of heart and brain   ·
Comes seldom save from rage and pain,
So talks as it's most used to do.

1801

FROST AT MIDNIGHT

THE Frost performs its secret ministry,
Unhelped by any wind. The owlet's cry
Came loud—and hark, again! loud as before.
The inmates of my cottage, all at rest,
Have left me to that solitude, which suits
Abstruser musings: save that at my side
My cradled infant slumbers peacefully.
'Tis calm indeed! so calm, that it disturbs
And vexes meditation with its strange
And extreme silentness. Sea, hill, and wood, 10
This populous village! Sea, and hill, and
    wood,
With all the numberless goings-on of life,
Inaudible as dreams! the thin blue flame
Lies on my low-burnt fire, and quivers not;
Only that film, which fluttered on the grate,
Still flutters there, the sole unquiet thing.
Methinks, its motion in this hush of nature
Gives it dim sympathies with me who live,
Making it a companionable form,
Whose puny flaps and freaks the idling Spirit
By its own moods interprets, every where 21
Echo or mirror seeking of itself,
And makes a toy of Thought.

                    But O! how oft,
How oft, at school, with most believing mind,
Presageful, have I gazed upon the bars,
To watch that fluttering *stranger!* and as oft
With unclosed lids, already had I dreamt
Of my sweet birth-place, and the old church-
    tower,
Whose bells, the poor man's only music, rang
From morn to evening, all the hot Fair-day, 30
So sweetly, that they stirred and haunted me
With a wild pleasure, falling on mine ear
Most like articulate sounds of things to
    come!
So gazed I, till the soothing things, I dreamt,

Lulled me to sleep, and sleep prolonged my
    dreams!
And so I brooded all the following morn,
Awed by the stern preceptor's face, mine eye
Fixed with mock study on my swimming
    book:
Save if the door half opened, and I snatched
A hasty glance, and still my heart leaped up,
For still I hoped to see the *stranger's* face, 41
Townsman, or aunt, or sister more beloved,
My play-mate when we both were clothed
    alike!

Dear Babe, that sleepest cradled by my side
Whose gentle breathings, heard in this deep
    calm,
Fill up the interspersèd vacancies
And momentary pauses of the thought!
My babe so beautiful! it thrills my heart
With tender gladness, thus to look at thee,
And think that thou shalt learn far other
    lore
And in far other scenes! For I was reared 51
In the great city, pent 'mid cloisters dim,
And saw nought lovely but the sky and stars.
But *thou*, my babe! shalt wander like a breeze
By lakes and sandy shores, beneath the crags
Of ancient mountain, and beneath the clouds,
Which image in their bulk both lakes and
    shores
And mountain crags: so shalt thou see and
    hear
The lovely shapes and sounds intelligible
Of that eternal language, which thy God   60
Utters, who from eternity doth teach
Himself in all, and all things in himself.
Great universal Teacher! he shall mould
Thy spirit, and by giving make it ask.

Therefore all seasons shall be sweet to thee,
Whether the summer clothe the general earth
With greenness, or the redbreast sit and sing
Betwixt the tufts of snow on the bare branch
Of mossy apple-tree, while the nigh thatch
Smokes in the sun-thaw; whether the eave-
    drops fall   70
Heard only in the trances of the blast,
Or if the secret ministry of frost
Shall hang them up in silent icicles,
Quietly shining to the quiet Moon.

February, 1798

FRANCE: AN ODE

I

Ye Clouds! that far above me float and
  pause,
  Whose pathless march no mortal may con-
  troul!
Ye Ocean-Waves! that, wheresoe'er ye roll,
Yield homage only to eternal laws!
Ye Woods! that listen to the night-birds sing-
  ing,
  Midway the smooth and perilous slope re-
  clined,
Save when your own imperious branches
  swinging,
  Have made a solemn music of the wind!
Where, like a man beloved of God,
Through glooms, which never woodman trod,
  How oft, pursuing fancies holy,   11
My moonlight way o'er flowering weeds I
  wound,
  Inspired, beyond the guess of folly,
By each rude shape and wild unconquerable
  sound!
O ye loud Waves! and O ye Forests high!
  And O ye Clouds that far above me soared!
Thou rising Sun! thou blue rejoicing Sky!
  Yea, every thing that is and will be free!
Bear witness for me, wheresoe'er ye be,
With what deep worship I have still adored
  The spirit of divinest Liberty.   21

II

When France in wrath her giant-limbs up-
  reared,
  And with that oath, which smote air, earth,
  and sea,
  Stamped her strong foot and said she would
  be free,
Bear witness for me, how I hoped and feared!
With what a joy my lofty gratulation
  Unawed I sang, amid a slavish band:
And when to whelm the disenchanted nation,
  Like fiends embattled by a wizard's wand,
  The Monarchs marched in evil day,   30
  And Britain joined the dire array;
Though dear her shores and circling ocean,
Though many friendships, many youthful loves
  Had swoln the patriot emotion
And flung a magic light o'er all her hills and
  groves;

Yet still my voice, unaltered, sang defeat
  To all that braved the tyrant-quelling lance,
And shame too long delayed and vain retreat!
For ne'er, O Liberty! with partial aim
I dimmed thy light or damped thy holy flame;
  But blessed the pæans of delivered France,
And hung my head and wept at Britain's
  name.   42

III

'And what,' I said, 'though Blasphemy's loud
  scream
  With that sweet music of deliverance strove!
  Though all the fierce and drunken passions
  wove
A dance more wild than e'er was maniac's
  dream!
  Ye storms, that round the dawning East as-
  sembled,
The Sun was rising, though yet hid his light!'
  And when, to soothe my soul, that hoped
  and trembled,
The dissonance ceased, and all seemed calm
  and bright;   50
  When France her front deep-scarr'd and
  gory
Concealed with clustering wreaths of glory;
  When, insupportably advancing,
Her arm made mockery of the warrior's
  ramp;
  While timid looks of fury glancing,
Domestic treason, crushed beneath her fatal
  stamp,
Writhed like a wounded dragon in his gore;
  Then I reproached my fears that would not
  flee;
'And soon,' I said, 'shall Wisdom teach her
  lore
In the low huts of them that toil and groan! 60
And, conquering by her happiness alone,
  Shall France compel the nations to be free,
Till Love and Joy look round, and call the
  Earth their own.'

IV

Forgive me, Freedom! O forgive those dreams!
  I hear thy voice, I hear thy loud lament,
  From bleak Helvetia's icy caverns sent—
I hear thy groans upon her blood-stained
  streams!
  Heroes, that for your peaceful country per-
  ished,

And ye that, fleeing, spot your mountain-
        snows
    With bleeding wounds; forgive me, that I
        cherished   70
One thought that ever blessed your cruel foes!
    To scatter rage, and traitorous guilt,
    Where Peace her jealous home had built;
        A patriot-race to disinherit
Of all that made their stormy wilds so dear;
        And with inexpiable spirit
To taint the bloodless freedom of the moun-
        taineer—
    O France, that mockest Heaven, adulterous,
        blind,
    And patriot only in pernicious toils!
Are these thy boasts, Champion of human
        kind?   80
    To mix with Kings in the low lust of sway,
Yell in the hunt, and share the murderous prey;
To insult the shrine of Liberty with spoils
    From freemen torn; to tempt and to betray?

                    V

    The Sensual and the Dark rebel in vain,
    Slaves by their own compulsion! In mad
        game
    They burst their manacles and wear the name
    Of Freedom, graven on a heavier chain!
O Liberty! with profitless endeavour
Have I pursued thee, many a weary hour; 90
    But thou nor swell'st the victor's strain, nor
        ever
Didst breathe thy soul in forms of human
        power.
    Alike from all, howe'er they praise thee,
    (Nor prayer, nor boastful name delays thee)
        Alike from Priestcraft's harpy minions,
    And factious Blasphemy's obscener slaves,
        Thou speedest on thy subtle pinions,
    The guide of homeless winds, and playmate of
        the waves!
And there I felt thee!—on that sea-cliff's verge,
    Whose pines, scarce travelled by the breeze
        above,   100
Had made one murmur with the distant surge!
Yes, while I stood and gazed, my temples bare,
And shot my being through earth, sea, and air,
    Possessing all things with intensest love,
        O Liberty! my spirit felt thee there.
    1798

LEWTI

OR THE CIRCASSIAN LOVE-CHAUNT

AT midnight by the stream I roved,
To forget the form I loved.
Image of Lewti! from my mind
Depart; for Lewti is not kind.

The Moon was high, the moonlight gleam
    And the shadow of a star
Heaved upon Tamaha's stream;
    But the rock shone brighter far,
The rock half sheltered from my view
By pendent boughs of tressy yew.—   10
So shines my Lewti's forehead fair,
Gleaming through her sable hair.
Image of Lewti! from my mind
Depart; for Lewti is not kind.

I saw a cloud of palest hue,
    Onward to the moon it passed;
Still brighter and more bright it grew,
With floating colours not a few,
    Till it reached the moon at last:
Then the cloud was wholly bright,   20
With a rich and amber light!
And so with many a hope I seek,
    And with such joy I find my Lewti;
And even so my pale wan cheek
    Drinks in as deep a flush of beauty!
Nay, treacherous image! leave my mind,
If Lewti never will be kind.

The little cloud—it floats away,
    Away it goes; away so soon!
Alas! it has no power to stay: 30
Its hues are dim, its hues are grey—
    Away it passes from the moon!

How mournfully it seems to fly,
    Ever fading more and more,
To joyless regions of the sky—
    And now 'tis whiter than before!
As white as my poor cheek will be,
    When, Lewti! on my couch I lie,
A dying man for love of thee.
Nay, treacherous image! leave my mind— 40
And yet, thou didst not look unkind.

I saw a vapour in the sky,
Thin, and white, and very high;
I ne'er beheld so thin a cloud:

Perhaps the breezes that can fly
  Now below and now above,
Have snatched aloft the lawny shroud
  Of Lady fair—that died for love.
For maids, as well as youths, have perished
From fruitless love too fondly cherished.   50
Nay, treacherous image! leave my mind—
For Lewti never will be kind.

Hush! my heedless feet from under
  Slip the crumbling banks for ever:
Like echoes to a distant thunder,
  They plunge into the gentle river.
The river-swans have heard my tread,
And startle from their reedy bed.
O beauteous birds! methinks ye measure
  Your movements to some heavenly tune! 60
O beauteous birds! 'tis such a pleasure
  To see you move beneath the moon,
I would it were your true delight
To sleep by day and wake all night.

I know the place where Lewti lies,
When silent night has closed her eyes:
  It is a breezy jasmine-bower,
The nightingale sings o'er her head:
  Voice of the Night! had I the power
That leafy labyrinth to thread,   70
And creep, like thee, with soundless tread,
I then might view her bosom white
Heaving lovely to my sight,
As these two swans together heave
On the gently-swelling wave.

Oh! that she saw me in a dream,
  And dreamt that I had died for care;
All pale and wasted I would seem,
  Yet fair withal, as spirits are!
I'd die indeed, if I might see   80
Her bosom heave, and heave for me!
Soothe, gentle image! soothe my mind!
To-morrow Lewti may be kind.

? 1798 Pub. 1798

FEARS IN SOLITUDE

WRITTEN IN APRIL, 1798, BEGIN WITH
ALARM OF AN INVASION

A GREEN and silent spot, amid the hills,
A small and silent dell! O'er stiller place
No singing sky-lark ever poised himself.

The hills are heathy, save that swelling slope,
Which hath a gay and gorgeous covering on,
All golden with the never-bloomless furze,
Which now blooms most profusely: but the
  dell,
Bathed by the mist, is fresh and delicate
As vernal corn-field, or the unripe flax,
When, through its half-transparent stalks, at
  eve,   10
The level sunshine glimmers with green light.
Oh! 'tis a quiet spirit-healing nook!
Which all, methinks, would love; but chiefly
  he,
The humble man, who, in his youthful years,
Knew just so much of folly, as had made
His early manhood more securely wise!
Here he might lie on fern or withered heath,
While from the singing lark (that sings un-
  seen
The minstrelsy that solitude loves best),
And from the sun, and from the breezy air, 20
Sweet influences trembled o'er his frame;
And he, with many feelings, many thoughts,
Made up a meditative joy, and found
Religious meanings in the forms of Nature!
And so, his senses gradually wrapt
In a half sleep, he dreams of better worlds,
And dreaming hears thee still, O singing lark,
That singest like an angel in the clouds!

  My God! it is a melancholy thing   29
For such a man, who would full fain preserve
His soul in calmness, yet perforce must feel
For all his human brethren—O my God!
It weighs upon the heart, that he must think
What uproar and what strife may now be
  stirring
This way or that way o'er these silent hills—
Invasion, and the thunder and the shout,
And all the crash of onset; fear and rage,
And undetermined conflict—even now,
Even now, perchance, and in his native isle:
Carnage and groans beneath this blessed sun!
We have offended, Oh! my countrymen!   41
We have offended very grievously,
And been most tyrannous. From east to west
A groan of accusation pierces Heaven!
The wretched plead against us; multitudes
Countless and vehement, the sons of God,
Our brethren! Like a cloud that travels on,
Steamed up from Cairo's swamps of pestilence,

Even so, my countrymen! have we gone forth
And borne to distant tribes slavery and pangs,
And, deadlier far, our vices, whose deep
    taint   51
With slow perdition murders the whole man,
His body and his soul! Meanwhile, at home,
All individual dignity and power
Engulfed in Courts, Committees, Institutions,
Associations and Societies,
A vain, speech-mouthing, speech-reporting
    Guild,
One Benefit-Club for mutual flattery,
We have drunk up, demure as at a grace,
Pollutions from the brimming cup of wealth;
Contemptuous of all honourable rule,   61
Yet bartering freedom and the poor man's life
For gold, as at a market! The sweet words
Of Christian promise, words that even yet
Might stem destruction, were they wisely
    preached,
Are muttered o'er by men, whose tones pro-
    claim
How flat and wearisome they feel their trade:
Rank scoffers some, but most too indolent
To deem them falsehoods or to know their
    truth.
Oh! blasphemous! the Book of Life is made 70
A superstitious instrument, on which
We gabble o'er the oaths we mean to break;
For all must swear—all and in every place,
College and wharf, council and justice-court;
All, all must swear, the briber and the bribed,
Merchant and lawyer, senator and priest,
The rich, the poor, the old man and the young;
All, all make up one scheme of perjury,
That faith doth reel; the very name of God
Sounds like a juggler's charm; and, bold with
    joy,   80
Forth from his dark and lonely hiding-place,
(Portentous sight!) the owlet Atheism,
Sailing on obscene wings athwart the noon,
Drops his blue-fringéd lids, and holds them
    close,
And hooting at the glorious sun in Heaven,
Cries out, "Where is it?"

                  Thankless too for peace,
(Peace long preserved by fleets and perilous
    seas)
Secure from actual warfare, we have loved
To swell the war-whoop, passionate for war!

Alas! for ages ignorant of all   90
Its ghastlier workings, (famine or blue plague,
Battle, or siege, or flight through wintry
    snows,)
We, this whole people, have been clamorous
For war and bloodshed; animating sports,
The which we pay for as a thing to talk of,
Spectators and not combatants! No guess
Anticipative of a wrong unfelt,
No speculation on contingency,
However dim and vague, too vague and dim
To yield a justifying cause; and forth,   100
(Stuffed out with big preamble, holy names,
And adjurations of the God in Heaven,)
We send our mandates for the certain death
Of thousands and ten thousands! Boys and
    girls,
And women, that would groan to see a child
Pull off an insect's leg, all read of war,
The best amusement for our morning meal!
The poor wretch, who has learnt his only
    prayers
From curses, who knows scarcely words
    enough
To ask a blessing from his Heavenly Father,
Becomes a fluent phraseman, absolute   111
And technical in victories and defeats,
And all our dainty terms for fratricide;
Terms which we trundle smoothly o'er our
    tongues
Like mere abstractions, empty sounds to which
We join no feeling and attach no form!
As if the soldier died without a wound;
As if the fibres of this godlike frame
Were gored without a pang; as if the wretch,
Who fell in battle, doing bloody deeds,   120
Passed off to Heaven, translated and not killed;
As though he had no wife to pine for him,
No God to judge him! Therefore, evil days
Are coming on us, O my countrymen!
And what if all-avenging Providence,
Strong and retributive, should make us know
The meaning of our words, force us to feel
The desolation and the agony
Of our fierce doings?

                  Spare us yet awhile,
Father and God! O! spare us yet awhile!   130
Oh! let not English women drag their flight
Fainting beneath the burthen of their babes,
Of the sweet infants, that but yesterday

Laughed at the breast! Sons, brothers, hus-
   bands, all
Who ever gazed with fondness on the forms
Which grew up with you round the same fire-
   side,
And all who ever heard the sabbath-bells
Without the infidel's scorn, make yourselves
   pure!
Stand forth! be men! repel an impious foe,
Impious and false, a light yet cruel race,   140
Who laugh away all virtue, mingling mirth
With deeds of murder; and still promising
Freedom, themselves too sensual to be free,
Poison life's amities, and cheat the heart
Of faith and quiet hope, and all that soothes,
And all that lifts the spirit! Stand we forth;
Render them back upon the insulted ocean,
And let them toss as idly on its waves
As the vile sea-weed, which some mountain-
   blast
Swept from our shores! And oh! may we re-
   turn   150
Not with a drunken triumph, but with fear,
Repenting of the wrongs with which we
   stung
So fierce a foe to frenzy!

                 I have told,
O Britons! O my brethren! I have told
Most bitter truth, but without bitterness.
Nor deem my zeal or factious or mistimed;
For never can true courage dwell with them,
Who, playing tricks with conscience, dare not
   look
At their own vices. We have been too long
Dupes of a deep delusion! Some, belike,   160
Groaning with restless enmity, expect
All change from change of constituted power;
As if a Government had been a robe,
On which our vice and wretchedness were
   tagged
Like fancy-points and fringes, with the robe
Pulled off at pleasure. Fondly these attach
A radical causation to a few
Poor drudges of chastising Providence,
Who borrow all their hues and qualities
From our own folly and rank wickedness,   170
Which gave them birth and nursed them.
                Others, meanwhile,
Dote with a mad idolatry; and all
Who will not fall before their images,

And yield them worship, they are enemies
Even of their country!

            Such have I been deemed.—
But, O dear Britain! O my Mother Isle!
Needs must thou prove a name most dear and
   holy
To me, a son, a brother, and a friend,
A husband, and a father! who revere
All bonds of natural love, and find them all   180
Within the limits of thy rocky shores.
O native Britain! O my Mother Isle!
How shouldst thou prove aught else but dear
   and holy
To me, who from thy lakes and mountain-
   hills,
Thy clouds, thy quiet dales, thy rocks and
   seas,
Have drunk in all my intellectual life,
All sweet sensations, all ennobling thoughts,
All adoration of the God in nature,
All lovely and all honourable things,
Whatever makes this mortal spirit feel   190
The joy and greatness of its future being?
There lives nor form nor feeling in my soul
Unborrowed from my country! O divine
And beauteous island! thou hast been my sole
And most magnificent temple, in the which
I walk with awe, and sing my stately songs,
Loving the God that made me!—

                  May my fears,
My filial fears, be vain! and may the vaunts
And menace of the vengeful enemy
Pass like the gust, that roared and died away
In the distant tree: which heard, and only
   heard   201
In this low dell, bowed not the delicate grass.

   But now the gentle dew-fall sends abroad
The fruit-like perfume of the golden furze:
The light has left the summit of the hill,
Though still a sunny gleam lies beautiful,
Aslant the ivied beacon. Now farewell,
Farewell, awhile, O soft and silent spot!
On the green sheep-track, up the heathy hill,
Homeward I wind my way; and lo! recalled
From bodings that have well-nigh wearied
   me,   211
I find myself upon the brow, and pause
Startled! And after lonely sojourning

In such a quiet and surrounded nook,
This burst of prospect, here the shadowy main,
Dim-tinted, there the mighty majesty
Of that huge amphitheatre of rich
And elmy fields, seems like society—
Conversing with the mind, and giving it
A livelier impulse and a dance of thought! 220
And now, belovéd Stowey! I behold
Thy church-tower, and, methinks, the four
    huge elms
Clustering, which mark the mansion of my
    friend;
And close behind them, hidden from my view,
Is my own lowly cottage, where my babe
And my babe's mother dwell in peace! With
    light
And quickened footsteps thitherward I tend,
Remembering thee, O green and silent dell!
And grateful, that by nature's quietness
And solitary musings, all my heart   230
Is softened, and made worthy to indulge
Love, and the thoughts that yearn for human
    kind.

NETHER STOWEY, April 20, 1798

THE NIGHTINGALE

A CONVERSATION POEM, APRIL, 1798

No cloud, no relique of the sunken day
Distinguishes the West, no long thin slip
Of sullen light, no obscure trembling hues.
Come, we will rest on this old mossy bridge!
You see the glimmer of the stream beneath,
But hear no murmuring: it flows silently,
O'er its soft bed of verdure. All is still,
A balmy night! and though the stars be dim,
Yet let us think upon the vernal showers   9
That gladden the green earth, and we shall find
A pleasure in the dimness of the stars.
And hark! the Nightingale begins its song,
"Most musical, most melancholy" bird!
A melancholy bird? Oh! idle thought!
In Nature there is nothing melancholy.
But some night-wandering man whose heart
    was pierced
With the remembrance of a grievous wrong,
Or slow distemper, or neglected love,
(And so, poor wretch! filled all things with
    himself,
And made all gentle sounds tell back the tale

Of his own sorrow) he, and such as he,   21
First named these notes a melancholy strain.
And many a poet echoes the conceit;
Poet who hath been building up the rhyme
When he had better far have stretched his
    limbs
Beside a brook in mossy forest-dell,
By sun or moon-light, to the influxes
Of shapes and sounds and shifting elements
Surrendering his whole spirit, of his song
And of his fame forgetful! so his fame   30
Should share in Nature's immortality,
A venerable thing! and so his song
Should make all Nature lovelier, and itself
Be loved like Nature! But 'twill not be so;
And youths and maidens most poetical,
Who lose the deepening twilights of the spring
In ball-rooms and hot theatres, they still
Full of meek sympathy must heave their sighs
O'er Philomela's pity-pleading strains.

My Friend, and thou, our Sister! we have
    learnt   40
A different lore: we may not thus profane
Nature's sweet voices, always full of love
And joyance! 'Tis the merry Nightingale
That crowds, and hurries, and precipitates
With fast thick warble his delicious notes,
As he were fearful that an April night
Would be too short for him to utter forth
His love-chant, and disburthen his full soul
Of all its music!

            And I know a grove
Of large extent, hard by a castle huge,   50
Which the great lord inhabits not; and so
This grove is wild with tangling underwood,
And the trim walks are broken up, and grass,
Thin grass and king-cups grow within the
    paths.
But never elsewhere in one place I knew
So many nightingales; and far and near,
In wood and thicket, over the wide grove,
They answer and provoke each other's song,
With skirmish and capricious passagings,
And murmurs musical and swift jug jug,   60
And one low piping sound more sweet than
    all—
Stirring the air with such a harmony,
That should you close your eyes, you might
    almost

The Raven (Coleridge)

Beneath a goodly old Oak-tree
There was of swine a large company.
They were making a rude repast
Grunting as they crunch'd the mast.
Then they trotted away, for the wind grew high:
One acorn they left & no more mote you spy.
But soon came a Raven, who lik'd not such folly:
He belong'd, I believe, to the Witch Melancholy!
Blacker was he than blackest jet,
Flew low in the rain, his feathers were wet.
He pick'd up the acorn & buried it strait
By the side of a River both deep and great.
Where then did the Raven go?
He went high and low:
Over hill, over dale did the black Raven go.
Many Autumns, many Springs
Travell'd he on wandering wings:
Many Summers, many Winters —
I can't tell half his adventures!

Reduced Facsimile of the First Page of the MS of Coleridge's *The Raven*. (See Appendix I.)

Forget it was not day! On moonlight bushes,
Whose dewy leaflets are but half-disclosed,
You may perchance behold them on the twigs,
Their bright, bright eyes, their eyes both
    bright and full,
Glistening, while many a glow-worm in the
    shade
Lights up her love-torch.

                A most gentle Maid,
Who dwelleth in her hospitable home   70
Hard by the castle, and at latest eve
(Even like a Lady vowed and dedicate
To something more than Nature in the grove)
Glides through the pathways; she knows all
    their notes,
That gentle Maid! and oft, a moment's space,
What time the moon was lost behind a cloud,
Hath heard a pause of silence; till the moon
Emerging, hath awakened earth and sky
With one sensation, and those wakeful birds
Have all burst forth in choral minstrelsy, 80
As if some sudden gale had swept at once
A hundred airy harps! And she hath watched
Many a nightingale perch giddily
On blossomy twig still swinging from the
    breeze,
And to that motion tune his wanton song
Like tipsy Joy that reels with tossing head.

Farewell, O Warbler! till to-morrow eve,
And you, my friends! farewell, a short fare-
    well!
We have been loitering long and pleasantly,
And now for our dear homes.—That strain
    again!   90
Full fain it would delay me! My dear babe,
Who, capable of no articulate sound,
Mars all things with his imitative lisp,
How he would place his hand beside his ear,
His little hand, the small forefinger up,
And bid us listen! And I deem it wise
To make him Nature's play-mate. He knows
    well
The evening-star; and once, when he awoke
In most distressful mood (some inward pain
Had made up that strange thing, an infant's
    dream—)   100
I hurried with him to our orchard-plot,
And he beheld the moon, and, hushed at once,
Suspends his sobs, and laughs most silently,

While his fair eyes, that swam with undropped
    tears,
Did glitter in the yellow moon-beam! Well!—
It is a father's tale: But if that Heaven
Should give me life, his childhood shall grow
    up
Familiar with these songs, that with the night
He may associate joy.—Once more, farewell,
Sweet Nightingale! once more, my friends!
    farewell.   110
1798

THE BALLAD OF THE DARK
LADIÉ

A FRAGMENT

BENEATH yon birch with silver bark,
And boughs so pendulous and fair,
The brook falls scatter'd down the rock:
    And all is mossy there!

And there upon the moss she sits,
The Dark Ladié in silent pain;
The heavy tear is in her eye,
    And drops and swells again.

Three times she sends her little page
Up the castled mountain's breast,   10
If he might find the Knight that wears
    The Griffin for his crest.

The sun was sloping down the sky,
And she had linger'd there all day,
Counting moments, dreaming fears—
    Oh wherefore can he stay?

She hears a rustling o'er the brook,
She sees far off a swinging bough!
"'Tis He! 'Tis my betrothéd Knight!
    Lord Falkland, it is Thou!"   20

She springs, she clasps him round the neck,
She sobs a thousand hopes and fears,
Her kisses glowing on his cheeks
    She quenches with her tears.

         *   *   *

"My friends with rude ungentle words
They scoff and bid me fly to thee!
O give me shelter in thy breast!
    O shield and shelter me!

"My Henry, I have given thee much,
I gave what I can ne'er recall,   30
I gave my heart, I gave my peace,
    O Heaven! I gave thee all."

The Knight made answer to the Maid,
While to his heart he held her hand,
"Nine castles hath my noble sire,
    None statelier in the land.

"The fairest one shall be my love's,
The fairest castle of the nine!
Wait only till the stars peep out,
    The fairest shall be thine: 40

"Wait only till the hand of eve
Hath wholly closed yon western bars,
And through the dark we two will steal
    Beneath the twinkling stars!"—

"The dark? the dark? No! not the dark?
The twinkling stars? How, Henry? How?"
O God! 'twas in the eye of noon
    He pledged his sacred vow!

And in the eye of noon my love
Shall lead me from my mother's door,   50
Sweet boys and girls all clothed in white
    Strewing flowers before:

But first the nodding minstrels go
With music meet for lordly bowers,
The children next in snow-white vests.
    Strewing buds and flowers!

And then my love and I shall pace,
My jet black hair in pearly braids,
Between our comely bachelors
    And blushing bridal maids.   60

*   *   *

1798

KUBLA KHAN:

OR, A VISION IN A DREAM. A FRAGMENT

THE following fragment is here published at
the request of a poet of great and deserved
celebrity, and, as far as the Author's own opinions are concerned, rather as a psychological
curiosity, than on the ground of any supposed
poetic merits.

In the summer of the year 1797 [error for

1798], the Author, then in ill health, had retired to a lonely farm-house between Porlock and Linton, on the Exmoor confines of
Somerset and Devonshire. In consequence of
a slight indisposition, an anodyne had been
prescribed, from the effects of which he fell
asleep in his chair at the moment that he was
reading the following sentence, or words of
the same substance, in 'Purchas's Pilgrimage':
'Here the Khan Kubla commanded a palace
to be built, and a stately garden thereunto.
And thus ten miles of fertile ground were
inclosed with a wall.' The Author continued
for about three hours in a profound sleep,
at least of the external senses, during which
time he has the most vivid confidence, that
he could not have composed less than from
two to three hundred lines; if that indeed can
be called composition in which all the images
rose up before him as *things*, with a parallel
production of the correspondent expressions,
without any sensation or consciousness of
effort. On awaking he appeared to himself to
have a distinct recollection of the whole, and
taking his pen, ink, and paper, instantly and
eagerly wrote down the lines that are here
preserved. At this moment he was unfortunately called out by a person on business from
Porlock, and detained by him above an hour,
and on his return to his room, found, to his no
small surprise and mortification, that though he
still retained some vague and dim recollection
of the general purport of the vision, yet, with
the exception of some eight or ten scattered
lines and images, all the rest had passed away
like the images on the surface of a stream
into which a stone has been cast, but, alas!
without the after restoration of the latter! . . .
    Yet from the still surviving recollections in
his mind, the Author has frequently purposed
to finish for himself what had been originally,
as it were, given to him. Σαμερον αδιον ασω:[1]
but the tomorrow is yet to come.

    In Xanadu did Kubla Khan
    A stately pleasure-dome decree:
    Where Alph, the sacred river, ran
    Through caverns measureless to man
        Down to a sunless sea.

[1] "I shall sing sweeter tomorrow."

So twice five miles of fertile ground
With walls and towers were girdled round:
And there were gardens bright with sinuous rills,
Where blossomed many an incense-bearing tree;
And here were forests ancient as the hills,   10
Enfolding sunny spots of greenery.

But oh! that deep romantic chasm which slanted
Down the green hill athwart a cedarn cover!
A savage place! as holy and enchanted
As e'er beneath a waning moon was haunted
By woman wailing for her demon-lover!
And from this chasm, with ceaseless turmoil seething,
As if this earth in fast thick pants were breathing,
A mighty fountain momently was forced:
Amid whose swift half-intermitted burst   20
Huge fragments vaulted like rebounding hail,
Or chaffy grain beneath the thresher's flail:
And 'mid these dancing rocks at once and ever
It flung up momently the sacred river.
Five miles meandering with a mazy motion
Through wood and dale the sacred river ran,
Then reached the caverns measureless to man,
And sank in tumult to a lifeless ocean:
And 'mid this tumult Kubla heard from far
Ancestral voices prophesying war!   30

The shadow of the dome of pleasure
Floated midway on the waves;
Where was heard the mingled measure
From the fountain and the caves.
It was a miracle of rare device,
A sunny pleasure-dome with caves of ice!

A damsel with a dulcimer
In a vision once I saw:
It was an Abyssinian maid,
And on her dulcimer she played,   40
Singing of Mount Abora.
Could I revive within me
Her symphony and song,
To such a deep delight 'twould win me,
That with music loud and long,
I would build that dome in air,
That sunny dome! those caves of ice!
And all who heard should see them there,

And all should cry, Beware! Beware!
His flashing eyes, his floating hair!   50
Weave a circle round him thrice,
And close your eyes with holy dread,
For he on honey-dew hath fed,
And drunk the milk of Paradise.

1798

LOVE

ALL thoughts, all passions, all delights,
Whatever stirs this mortal frame,
All are but ministers of Love,
    And feed his sacred flame.

Oft in my waking dreams do I
Live o'er again that happy hour,
When midway on the mount I lay,
    Beside the ruined tower.

The moonshine, stealing o'er the scene
Had blended with the lights of eve;   10
And she was there, my hope, my joy,
    My own dear Genevieve!

She leant against the arméd man,
The statue of the arméd knight;
She stood and listened to my lay,
    Amid the lingering light.

Few sorrows hath she of her own,
My hope! my joy! my Genevieve!
She loves me best, whene'er I sing
    The songs that make her grieve.   20

I played a soft and doleful air,
I sang an old and moving story—
An old rude song, that suited well
    That ruin wild and hoary.

She listened with a flitting blush,
With downcast eyes and modest grace;
For well she knew, I could not choose
    But gaze upon her face.

I told her of the Knight that wore
Upon his shield a burning brand;   30
And that for ten long years he wooed
    The Lady of the Land.

I told her how he pined: and ah!
The deep, the low, the pleading tone
With which I sang another's love,
    Interpreted my own.

She listened with a flitting blush,
With downcast eyes, and modest grace;
And she forgave me, that I gazed
    Too fondly on her face!   40

But when I told the cruel scorn
That crazed that bold and lovely Knight,
And that he crossed the mountain-woods,
    Nor rested day nor night;

That sometimes from the savage den,
And sometimes from the darksome shade,
And sometimes starting up at once
    In green and sunny glade,—

There came and looked him in the face
An angel beautiful and bright;   50
And that he knew it was a Fiend,
    This miserable Knight!

And that unknowing what he did,
He leaped amid a murderous band,
And saved from outrage worse than death
    The Lady of the Land!

And how she wept, and clasped his knees;
And how she tended him in vain—
And ever strove to expiate
    The scorn that crazed his brain;—   60

And that she nursed him in a cave;
And how his madness went away,
When on the yellow forest-leaves
    A dying man he lay;—

His dying words—but when I reached
That tenderest strain of all the ditty,
My faultering voice and pausing harp
    Disturbed her soul with pity!

All impulses of soul and sense
Had thrilled my guileless Genevieve;   70
The music and the doleful tale,
    The rich and balmy eve;

And hopes, and fears that kindle hope,
An undistinguishable throng,
And gentle wishes long subdued,
    Subdued and cherished long!

She wept with pity and delight,
She blushed with love, and virgin-shame;
And like the murmur of a dream,
    I heard her breathe my name.   80

Her bosom heaved—she stepped aside,
As conscious of my look she stepped—
Then suddenly, with timorous eye
    She fled to me and wept.

She half enclosed me with her arms,
She pressed me with a meek embrace;
And bending back her head, looked up,
    And gazed upon my face.

'Twas partly love, and partly fear,
And partly 'twas a bashful art,   90
That I might rather feel, than see,
    The swelling of her heart.

I calmed her fears, and she was calm,
And told her love with virgin pride;
And so I won my Genevieve,
    My bright and beauteous Bride.

1799

DEJECTION: AN ODE

[WRITTEN APRIL 4, 1802]

    Late, late yestreen I saw the new Moon,
    With the old Moon in her arms;
    And I fear, I fear, my Master dear!
    We shall have a deadly storm.
        Ballad of Sir Patrick Spence

I

WELL! If the Bard was weather-wise, who
    made
  The grand old ballad of Sir Patrick Spence,
  This night, so tranquil now, will not go
    hence
Unroused by winds, that ply a busier trade
Than those which mould yon cloud in lazy
    flakes,
Or the dull sobbing draft, that moans and
    rakes
Upon the strings of this Æolian lute,
    Which better far were mute.
  For lo! the New-moon winter-bright!
  And overspread with phantom light,   10
  (With swimming phantom light o'erspread
  But rimmed and circled by a silver thread)
I see the old Moon in her lap, foretelling
  The coming-on of rain and squally blast.
And oh! that even now the gust were swelling,
  And the slant night-shower driving loud
    and fast!

Those sounds which oft have raised me, whilst
    they awed,
    And sent my soul abroad,
Might now perhaps their wonted impulse give,
Might startle this dull pain, and make it move
    and live!   20

II

A grief without a pang, void, dark, and drear,
  A stifled, drowsy, unimpassioned grief,
  Which finds no natural outlet, no relief,
    In word, or sigh, or tear—
O Lady! in this wan and heartless mood,
To other thoughts by yonder throstle woo'd,
  All this long eve, so balmy and serene,
Have I been gazing on the western sky,
  And its peculiar tint of yellow green:
And still I gaze—and with how blank an
    eye!   30
And those thin clouds above, in flakes and
    bars,
That give away their motion to the stars;
Those stars, that glide behind them or be-
    tween,
Now sparkling, now bedimmed, but always
    seen:
Yon crescent Moon, as fixed as if it grew
In its own cloudless, starless lake of blue;
I see them all so excellently fair,
I see, not feel, how beautiful they are!

III

  My genial spirits fail;
  And what can these avail   40
To lift the smothering weight from off my
    breast?
  It were a vain endeavour,
  Though I should gaze for ever
On that green light that lingers in the west:
I may not hope from outward forms to win
The passion and the life, whose fountains are
    within.

IV

O Lady! we receive but what we give,
And in our life alone does Nature live:
Ours is her wedding garment, ours her shroud!
  And would we aught behold, of higher
    worth,   50
Than that inanimate cold world allowed
To the poor loveless ever-anxious crowd,

Ah! from the soul itself must issue forth
A light, a glory, a fair luminous cloud
    Enveloping the Earth—
And from the soul itself must there be sent
  A sweet and potent voice, of its own birth,
Of all sweet sounds the life and element!

V

O pure of heart! thou need'st not ask of
    me
What this strong music in the soul may be! 60
What, and wherein it doth exist,
This light, this glory, this fair luminous mist,
This beautiful and beauty-making power.
  Joy, virtuous Lady! Joy that ne'er was
    given,
Save to the pure, and in their purest hour,
Life, and Life's effluence, cloud at once and
    shower,
Joy, Lady! is the spirit and the power,
Which wedding Nature to us gives in dower
  A new Earth and new Heaven,
Undreamt of by the sensual and the proud—
Joy is the sweet voice, Joy the luminous
    cloud—   71
    We in ourselves rejoice!
And thence flows all that charms or ear or
    sight,
  All melodies the echoes of that voice,
All colours a suffusion from that light.

VI

There was a time when, though my path was
    rough,
  This joy within me dallied with distress,
And all misfortunes were but as the stuff
  Whence Fancy made me dreams of happi-
    ness:
For hope grew round me, like the twining
    vine,   80
And fruits, and foliage, not my own, seemed
    mine.
But now afflictions bow me down to earth:
Nor care I that they rob me of my mirth;
  But oh! each visitation
Suspends what nature gave me at my birth,
  My shaping spirit of Imagination.
For not to think of what I needs must feel,
  But to be still and patient, all I can;
And haply by abstruse research to steal
  From my own nature all the natural man—

This was my sole resource, my only plan: 91
Till that which suits a part infects the whole,
And now is almost grown the habit of my
    soul.

VII

Hence, viper thoughts, that coil around my
    mind,
    Reality's dark dream!
I turn from you, and listen to the wind,
    Which long has raved unnoticed. What a
    scream
Of agony by torture lengthened out
That lute sent forth! Thou Wind, that rav'st
    without,
    Bare crag, or mountain-tairn, or blasted
    tree,   100
Or pine-grove whither woodman never clomb,
Or lonely house, long held the witches' home,
    Methinks were fitter instruments for thee,
Mad Lutanist! who in this month of showers,
Of dark-brown gardens, and of peeping flow-
    ers,
Mak'st Devils' yule, with worse than wintry
    song,
The blossoms, buds, and timorous leaves
    among.
    Thou Actor, perfect in all tragic sounds!
Thou mighty Poet, e'en to frenzy bold!
    What tell'st thou now about?   110
    'Tis of the rushing of an host in rout,
    With groans, of trampled men, with smart-
    ing wounds—
At once they groan with pain, and shudder
    with the cold!
But hush! there is a pause of deepest silence!
    And all that noise, as of a rushing crowd,
With groans, and tremulous shudderings—all
    is over—
    It tells another tale, with sounds less deep
    and loud!
    A tale of less affright,
    And tempered with delight,
As Otway's self had framed the tender lay,—
    'Tis of a little child   121
    Upon a lonesome wild,
Not far from home, but she hath lost her
    way:
And now moans low in bitter grief and fear,
And now screams loud, and hopes to make her
    mother hear.

VIII

'Tis midnight, but small thoughts have I of
    sleep:
Full seldom may my friend such vigils keep!
Visit her, gentle Sleep! with wings of healing,
    And may this storm be but a mountain-
    birth,
May all the stars hang bright above her dwell-
    ing,   130
    Silent as though they watched the sleeping
    Earth!
      With light heart may she rise,
      Gay fancy, cheerful eyes,
    Joy lift her spirit, joy attune her voice;
To her may all things live, from pole to pole,
Their life the eddying of her living soul!
    O simple spirit, guided from above,
Dear Lady! friend devoutest of my choice,
Thus mayest thou ever, evermore rejoice.

1802

HYMN BEFORE SUN–RISE, IN THE VALE OF CHAMOUNI

Besides the Rivers, Arve and Arveiron, which
have their sources in the foot of Mont Blanc, five
conspicuous torrents rush down its sides; and
within a few paces of the Glaciers, the Gentiana
Major grows in immense numbers, with its "flowers of loveliest blue."

HAST thou a charm to stay the morning-star
In his steep course? So long he seems to pause
On thy bald awful head, O sovran BLANC,
The Arve and Arveiron at thy base
Rave ceaselessly; but thou, most awful Form!
Risest from forth thy silent sea of pines,
How silently! Around thee and above
Deep is the air and dark, substantial, black,
An ebon mass: methinks thou piercest it,
As with a wedge! But when I look again,   10
It is thine own calm home, thy crystal shrine,
Thy habitation from eternity!
O dread and silent Mount! I gazed upon
    thee,
Till thou, still present to the bodily sense,
Didst vanish from my thought: entranced in
    prayer
I worshipped the Invisible alone.

Yet, like some sweet beguiling melody,
So sweet, we know not we are listening to it,

Thou, the meanwhile, wast blending with my
    Thought,
Yea, with my Life and Life's own secret joy:
Till the dilating Soul, enrapt, transfused,   21
Into the mighty vision passing—there
As in her natural form, swelled vast to Heaven!

    Awake, my soul! not only passive praise
Thou owest! not alone these swelling tears,
Mute thanks and secret ecstasy! Awake,
Voice of sweet song! Awake, my heart, awake!
Green vales and icy cliffs, all join my Hymn.

    Thou first and chief, sole sovereign of the
    Vale!
O struggling with the darkness all the night, 30
And visited all night by troops of stars,
Or when they climb the sky or when they sink:
Companion of the morning-star at dawn,
Thyself Earth's rosy star, and of the dawn
Co-herald: wake, O wake, and utter praise!
Who sank thy sunless pillars deep in Earth?
Who filled thy countenance with rosy light?
Who made thee parent of perpetual streams?

    And you, ye five wild torrents fiercely glad!
Who called you forth from night and utter
    death,   40
From dark and icy caverns called you forth,
Down those precipitous, black, jaggéd rocks,
For ever shattered and the same for ever?
Who gave you your invulnerable life,
Your strength, your speed, your fury, and
    your joy,
Unceasing thunder and eternal foam?
And who commanded (and the silence came),
Here let the billows stiffen, and have rest?

    Ye Ice-falls! ye that from the mountain's
    brow
Adown enormous ravines slope amain—   50
Torrents, methinks, that heard a mighty voice,
And stopped at once amid their maddest
    plunge!
Motionless torrents! silent cataracts!
Who made you glorious as the Gates of
    Heaven
Beneath the keen full moon? Who bade the sun
Clothe you with rainbows? Who, with living
    flowers
Of loveliest blue, spread garlands at your
    feet?—

God! let the torrents, like a shout of nations,
Answer! and let the ice-plains echo, God!
God! sing ye meadow-streams with gladsome
    voice!   60
Ye pine-groves, with your soft and soul-like
    sounds!
And they too have a voice, yon piles of snow,
And in their perilous fall shall thunder, God!

    Ye living flowers that skirt the eternal frost!
Ye wild goats sporting round the eagle's nest!
Ye eagles, play-mates of the mountain-storm!
Ye lightnings, the dread arrows of the clouds!
Ye signs and wonders of the element!
Utter forth God, and fill the hills with praise!

    Thou too, hoar Mount! with thy sky-point-
    ing peaks,   70
Oft from whose feet the avalanche, unheard,
Shoots downward, glittering through the pure
    serene
Into the depth of clouds, that veil thy breast—
Thou too again, stupendous Mountain! thou
That as I raise my head, awhile bowed low
In adoration, upward from thy base
Slow travelling with dim eyes suffused with
    tears,
Solemnly seemest, like a vapoury cloud,
To rise before me—Rise, O ever rise,
Rise like a cloud of incense from the Earth! 80
Thou kingly Spirit throned among the hills,
Thou dread ambassador from Earth to Heaven,
Great Hierarch! tell thou the silent sky,
And tell the stars, and tell yon rising sun
Earth, with her thousand voices, praises God.
  1802

ANSWER TO A CHILD'S
QUESTION

Do you ask what the birds say? The Sparrow,
    the Dove,
The Linnet and Thrush say, 'I love and I love!'
In the winter they're silent—the wind is so
    strong;
What it says, I don't know, but it sings a loud
    song.
But green leaves, and blossoms, and sunny
    warm weather,
And singing, and loving—all come back to-
    gether.

But the Lark is so brimful of gladness and love,
The green fields below him, the blue sky
    above,
That he sings, and he sings; and for ever sings
    he—
'I love my Love, and my Love loves me!' 10
1802

THE EXCHANGE

WE pledged our hearts, my love and I,—
    I in my arms the maiden clasping;
I could not guess the reason why,
    But, oh! I trembled like an aspen.

Her father's love she bade me gain;
    I went, but shook like any reed!
I strove to act the man—in vain!
    We had exchanged our hearts indeed.
1804

THE PAINS OF SLEEP

ERE on my bed my limbs I lay,
It hath not been my use to pray
With moving lips or bended knees;
But silently, by slow degrees,
My spirit I to Love compose,
In humble trust mine eye-lids close,
With reverential resignation,
No wish conceived, no thought exprest,
Only a sense of supplication;
A sense o'er all my soul imprest 10
That I am weak, yet not unblest,
Since in me, round me, every where
Eternal Strength and Wisdom are.

But yester-night I prayed aloud
In anguish and in agony,
Up-starting from the fiendish crowd
Of shapes and thoughts that tortured me:
A lurid light, a trampling throng,
Sense of intolerable wrong,
And whom I scorned, those only strong! 20
Thirst of revenge, the powerless will
Still baffled, and yet burning still!
Desire with loathing strangely mixed
On wild or hateful objects fixed.
Fantastic passions! maddening brawl!
And shame and terror over all!
Deeds to be hid which were not hid,

Which all confused I could not know
Whether I suffered, or I did:
For all seemed guilt, remorse or woe, 30
My own or others still the same
Life-stifling fear, soul-stifling shame.

So two nights passed: the night's dismay
Saddened and stunned the coming day.
Sleep, the wide blessing, seemed to me
Distemper's worst calamity.
The third night, when my own loud scream
Had waked me from the fiendish dream,
O'ercome with sufferings strange and wild,
I wept as I had been a child; 40
And having thus by tears subdued
My anguish to a milder mood,
Such punishments, I said, were due
To natures deepliest stained with sin,—
For aye entempesting anew
The unfathomable hell within,
The horror of their deeds to view,
To know and loathe, yet wish and do!
Such griefs with such men well agree,
But wherefore, wherefore fall on me? 50
To be beloved is all I need,
And whom I love, I love indeed.
1803

TO WILLIAM WORDSWORTH

COMPOSED ON THE NIGHT AFTER HIS RECITA-
TION OF A POEM ON THE GROWTH OF AN
INDIVIDUAL MIND

FRIEND of the wise! and Teacher of the Good!
Into my heart have I received that Lay
More than historic, that prophetic Lay
Wherein (high theme by thee first sung aright)
Of the foundations and the building up
Of a Human Spirit thou hast dared to tell
What may be told, to the understanding mind
Revealable; and what within the mind
By vital breathings secret as the soul
Of vernal growth, oft quickens in the heart
Thoughts all too deep for words!—

               Theme hard as high! 11
Of smiles spontaneous, and mysterious fears
(The first-born they of Reason and twin-birth),
Of tides obedient to external force,
And currents self-determined, as might seem,
Or by some inner Power; of moments awful,

Now in thy inner life, and now abroad,
When power streamed from thee, and thy
    soul received
The light reflected, as a light bestowed—
Of fancies fair, and milder hours of youth, 20
Hyblean murmurs of poetic thought
Industrious in its joy, in vales and glens
Native or outland, lakes and famous hills!
Or on the lonely high-road, when the stars
Were rising; or by secret mountain-streams,
The guides and the companions of thy way!

Of more than Fancy, of the Social Sense
Distending wide, and man beloved as man,
Where France in all her towns lay vibrating
Like some becalméd bark beneath the burst
Of Heaven's immediate thunder, when no
    cloud   31
Is visible, or shadow on the main.
For thou wert there, thine own brows gar-
    landed,
Amid the tremor of a realm aglow,
Amid a mighty nation jubilant,
When from the general heart of human kind
Hope sprang forth like a full-born Deity!
——Of that dear Hope afflicted and struck
    down,
So summoned homeward, thenceforth calm
    and sure
From the dread watch-tower of man's ab-
    solute self,   40
With light unwaning on her eyes, to look
Far on—herself a glory to behold,
The Angel of the vision! Then (last strain)
Of Duty, chosen Laws controlling choice,
Action and joy!—An Orphic song indeed,
A song divine of high and passionate thoughts
To their own music chaunted!

            O great Bard!
Ere yet that last strain dying awed the air,
With stedfast eye I viewed thee in the choir
Of ever-enduring men. The truly great   50
Have all one age, and from one visible space
Shed influence! They, both in power and act,
Are permanent, and Time is not with them,
Save as it worketh for them, they in it.
Nor less a sacred Roll, than those of old,
And to be placed, as they, with gradual fame
Among the archives of mankind, thy work
Makes audible a linkéd lay of Truth,

Of Truth profound a sweet continuous lay,
Not learnt, but native, her own natural notes!
Ah! as I listened with a heart forlorn,   61
The pulses of my being beat anew:
And even as Life returns upon the drowned,
Life's joy rekindling roused a throng of pains—
Keen pangs of Love, awakening as a babe
Turbulent, with an outcry in the heart;
And fears self-willed, that shunned the eye of
    Hope;
And Hope that scarce would know itself from
    Fear;
Sense of past Youth, and Manhood come in
    vain,
And Genius given, and Knowledge won in
    vain;   70
And all which I had culled in wood-walks wild,
And all which patient toil had reared, and all,
Commune with thee had opened out—but
    flowers
Strewed on my corse, and borne upon my bier
In the same coffin, for the self-same grave!

   That way no more! and ill beseems it me,
Who came a welcomer in herald's guise,
Singing of Glory, and Futurity,
To wander back on such unhealthful road,
Plucking the poisons of self-harm! And ill 80
Such intertwine beseems triumphal wreaths
Strew'd before thy advancing!

            Nor do thou,
Sage Bard! impair the memory of that hour
Of thy communion with my nobler mind
By pity or grief, already felt too long!
Nor let my words import more blame than
    needs.
The tumult rose and ceased: for Peace is nigh
Where Wisdom's voice has found a listening
    heart.
Amid the howl of more than wintry storms,
The Halcyon hears the voice of vernal hours
Already on the wing.

          Eve following eve, 91
Dear tranquil time, when the sweet sense of
    Home
Is sweetest! moments for their own sake hailed
And more desired, more precious, for thy
    song,
In silence listening, like a devout child,

My soul lay passive, by thy various strain
Driven as in surges now beneath the stars,
With momentary stars of my own birth,
Fair constellated foam, still darting off
Into the darkness; now a tranquil sea,   100
Outspread and bright, yet swelling to the
    moon.

And when—O Friend! my comforter and
    guide!
Strong in thyself, and powerful to give
    strength!—
Thy long sustainéd Song finally closed,
And thy deep voice had ceased—yet thou thy-
    self
Wert still before my eyes, and round us both
That happy vision of belovéd faces—
Scarce conscious, and yet conscious of its close
I sate, my being blended in one thought   109
(Thought was it? or aspiration? or resolve?)
Absorbed, yet hanging still upon the sound—
And when I rose, I found myself in prayer.

January, 1807

GLYCINE'S SONG

(From *Zapolya*)

A SUNNY shaft did I behold,
    From sky to earth it slanted:
And poised therein a bird so bold—
    Sweet bird, thou wert enchanted!

He sank, he rose, he twinkled, he trolled
    Within that shaft of sunny mist;
His eyes of fire, his beak of gold,
    All else of amethyst!

And thus he sang: "Adieu! adieu!
    Love's dreams prove seldom true.   10
The blossoms they make no delay:
The sparkling dew-drops will not stay.
    Sweet month of May,
      We must away;
        Far, far away!
          Today! today!"

1815

From LIMBO

*   *   *

'Tis a strange place, this Limbo!—not a Place,
Yet name it so;—where Time and weary Space

Fettered from flight, with night-mare sense of
    fleeing,
Strive for their last crepuscular half-being;—
Lank Space, and scytheless Time with branny
    hands
Barren and soundless as the measuring sands,
Not mark'd by flit of Shades,—unmeaning
    they
As moonlight on the dial of the day!
But that is lovely—looks like Human Time,—
An Old Man with a steady look sublime,   20
That stops his earthly task to watch the skies;
But he is blind—a Statue hath such eyes;—
Yet having moonward turn'd his face by
    chance,
Gazes the orb with moon-like countenance,
With scant white hairs, with foretop bald and
    high,
He gazes still,—his eyeless face all eye;—
As 'twere an organ full of silent sight,
His whole face seemeth to rejoice in light!
Lip touching lip, all moveless, bust and limb—
He seems to gaze at that which seems to gaze
    on him!   30
    No such sweet sights doth Limbo den im-
    mure,
Wall'd round, and made a spirit-jail secure,
By the mere horror of blank Naught-at-all,
Whose circumambience doth these ghosts en-
    thral.
A lurid thought is growthless, dull Privation,
Yet that is but a Purgatory curse;
Hell knows a fear far worse,
A fear—a future state;—'tis positive Negation!

1817

THE KNIGHT'S TOMB

WHERE is the grave of Sir Arthur O'Kellyn?
Where may the grave of that good man be?—
By the side of a spring, on the breast of Hel-
    vellyn,
Under the twigs of a young birch tree!
The oak that in summer was sweet to hear,
And rustled its leaves in the fall of the year,
And whistled and roared in the winter alone,
Is gone,—and the birch in its stead is grown.—
The Knight's bones are dust,
And his good sword rust;—   10
His soul is with the saints, I trust.

? 1817

YOUTH AND AGE[1]

VERSE, a breeze mid blossoms straying,
Where Hope clung feeding, like a bee—
Both were mine! Life went a-maying
    With Nature, Hope, and Poesy,
        When I was young!

When I was young?—Ah, woful When!
Ah! for the change 'twixt Now and Then!
This breathing house not built with hands,
This body that does me grievous wrong,
O'er aery cliffs and glittering sands,   10
How lightly then it flashed along:—
Like those trim skiffs, unknown of yore,
On winding lakes and rivers wide,
That ask no aid of sail or oar,
That fear no spite of wind or tide!
Nought cared this body for wind or weather
When Youth and I lived in't together.

Flowers are lovely; Love is flower-like;
Friendship is a sheltering tree;
O! the joys, that came down shower-like,   20
Of Friendship, Love, and Liberty,
        Ere I was old!

Ere I was old? Ah woful Ere,
Which tells me, Youth's no longer here!
O Youth! for years so many and sweet,
'Tis known, that Thou and I were one,
I'll think it but a fond conceit—
It cannot be that Thou art gone!
Thy vesper-bell hath not yet toll'd:—
And thou wert aye a masker bold!   30
What strange disguise hast now put on,
To make believe, that thou art gone?
I see these locks in silvery slips,
This drooping gait, this altered size:
But Spring-tide blossoms on thy lips,
And tears take sunshine from thine eyes!
Life is but thought: so think I will
That Youth and I are house-mates still.

Dew-drops are the gems of morning,
But the tears of mournful eve!   40
Where no hope is, life's a warning

[1] The first 38 lines of this poem were written in 1823 and published independently in 1828.

That only serves to make us grieve,
        When we are old:
That only serves to make us grieve
With oft and tedious taking-leave,
Like some poor nigh-related guest,
That may not rudely be dismist;
Yet hath outstay'd his welcome while,
And tells the jest without the smile.

1823–1832

WORK WITHOUT HOPE

LINES COMPOSED 21ST FEBRUARY 1825

ALL Nature seems at work. Slugs leave their
    lair—
The bees are stirring—birds are on the
    wing—
And Winter slumbering in the open air,
Wears on his smiling face a dream of Spring!
And I the while, the sole unbusy thing,
Nor honey make, nor pair, nor build, nor
    sing.

  Yet well I ken the banks where amaranths
    blow,
Have traced the fount whence streams of
    nectar flow.
Bloom, O ye amaranths! bloom for whom ye
    may,
For me ye bloom not! Glide, rich streams,
    away!   10
With lips unbrightened, wreathless brow, I
    stroll:
And would you learn the spells that drowse
    my soul?
Work without Hope draws nectar in a sieve,
And Hope without an object cannot live.

1825

SONG

THOUGH veiled in spires of myrtle-wreath,
Love is a sword which cuts its sheath,
And through the clefts itself has made,
We spy the flashes of the blade!

But through the clefts itself has made
We likewise see Love's flashing blade,
By rust consumed, or snapt in twain;
And only hilt and stump remain.

? 1825

Verse, a breeze, mid blossoms straying,
Where Hope clings feeding like a bee,
Both were mine! Life went a maying
With Nature, Hope, and Poesy.
   When I was young!
When I was young? ah, woful when!
Ah, for the change 'twixt now and then!
This house of clay not built with hands,
This body that does me grievous wrong;
O'er hill and dale and sounding sands,
How lightly then it flash'd along;
Like those trim boats, unknown of yore,
On winding lakes and rivers wide,
That ask no aid of sail or oar,
That fear no spite of wind or tide;—
Nought cared this body for wind or weather,
When Youth and I lived in't together.
Flowers are lovely; Love is flower-like;
Friendship is a sheltering tree;
O the joys that come down shower-like
Of beauty, truth, and Liberty.
    Ere I was old!
Ere I was old! Ah, woful ere,
Which tells me Youth's no longer here!
O youth for years so many and sweet,
'Tis known that thou and I were one,
I'll think it but a false conceit,
It cannot be that thou art gone!
Thy vesper bell hath not yet toll'd;
And thou wert aye a masker bold,
What strange disguise hast now put on,
To make believe that thou art gone?
I see these locks in silvery slips,
This drooping gait, this alter'd size;
But spring-tide blossoms on thy lips,
And tears take sunshine from thine eyes.
Life is but thought, so think I will
That youth and I are house-mates still.

           S. T. C.

A Part of Coleridge's *Youth and Age*. (See Appendix I.)

SONG, *ex improviso*

ON HEARING A SONG IN PRAISE OF A LADY'S BEAUTY

'TIS not the lily-brow I prize,
Nor roseate cheeks, nor sunny eyes,
　　Enough of lilies and of roses!
A thousand-fold more dear to me
The gentle look that Love discloses,—
　　The look that Love alone can see!

Keepsake, 1830

EPITAPH

STOP, Christian passer-by!—Stop, child of God,
And read with gentle breast. Beneath this sod
A poet lies, or that which once seem'd he.
O, lift one thought in prayer for S. T. C.;
That he who many a year with toil of breath
Found death in life, may here find life in death!
Mercy for praise—to be forgiven for fame
He ask'd, and hoped, through Christ. Do thou
　　the same!

9th November, 1833

From BIOGRAPHIA LITERARIA
1817
CHAPTER IV

The Lyrical Ballads with the Preface—Mr. Wordsworth's earlier poems—On fancy and imagination—The investigation of the distinction important to the Fine Arts.

I have wandered far from the object in view, but as I fancied to myself readers who would respect the feelings that had tempted me from the main road; so I dare calculate on not a few, who will warmly sympathize with them. At present it will be sufficient for my purpose, if I have proved, that Mr. Southey's writings no more than my own furnished the original occasion to this fiction of a new school of poetry, and to the clamours against its supposed founders and proselytes.

As little do I believe that Mr. Wordsworth's *Lyrical Ballads* were in themselves the cause. I speak exclusively of the two volumes so entitled. A careful and repeated examination of these confirms me in the belief, that the omission of less than a hundred lines would have precluded nine-tenths of the criticism on this work. I hazard this declaration, however, on the supposition, that the reader has taken it up, as he would have done any other collection of poems purporting to derive their subjects or interests from the incidents of domestic or ordinary life, intermingled with higher strains of meditation which the poet utters in his own person and character; with the proviso, that these poems were perused without knowledge of, or reference to, the author's peculiar opinions, and that the reader had not had his attention previously directed to those peculiarities. In that case, as actually happened with Mr. Southey's earlier works, the lines and passages which might have offended the general taste, would have been considered as mere inequalities, and attributed to inattention, not to perversity of judgment. The men of business who had passed their lives chiefly in cities, and who might therefore be expected to derive the highest pleasure from acute notices of men and manners conveyed in easy, yet correct and pointed language; and all those who, reading but little poetry, are most stimulated with that species of it, which seems most distant from prose, would probably have passed by the volumes altogether. Others more catholic in their taste, and yet habituated to be most pleased when most excited, would have contented themselves with deciding, that the author had been successful in proportion to the elevation of his style and subject. Not a few, perhaps, might, by their admiration of the "Lines written near Tintern Abbey," on revisiting the Wye, those "Left upon a Yew Tree Seat," "The Old Cumberland Beggar," and "Ruth," have been gradually led to peruse with kindred feeling "The Brothers," the "Hart-leap Well," and whatever other poems in that collection may be described as holding a middle place between those written in the highest and those in the humblest style; as for instance between the "Tintern Abbey," and "The Thorn," or "Simon Lee." Should their taste submit to no further change, and still remain unreconciled to the colloquial phrases, or the imitations of them, that are, more or less, scattered through the class last mentioned; yet even from the small number of the latter, they would have deemed them but an inconsiderable subtraction from the merit of the whole work; or, what is sometimes not unpleasing in the publication of a new writer, as serving to ascertain the natural tendency, and consequently the proper direction of the author's genius.

In the critical remarks, therefore, prefixed and annexed to the *Lyrical Ballads*, I believe, we may safely rest, as the true origin of the unexampled opposition which Mr. Wordsworth's writings have been since doomed to encounter. The humbler passages in the poems themselves were dwelt on and cited to justify the rejection of the theory. What in and for themselves would have been either forgotten or forgiven as imperfections, or at least comparative failures, provoked direct hostility when announced as intentional, as the result of choice after full deliberation. Thus the poems, admitted by all as excellent, joined with those which had pleased the far greater number, though they formed two-thirds of the whole work, instead of being deemed (as in all right they should have been, even if we take for granted that the reader judged aright) an atonement for the few exceptions, gave wind and fuel to the animosity against both the poems and the poet. In all perplexity there is a portion of fear, which predisposes the mind to anger. Not able to deny that the author possessed both genius and a powerful intellect, they felt *very positive*,—but yet were not *quite certain* that he might not be in the right, and they themselves in the wrong; an unquiet state of mind, which seeks alleviation by quarrelling with the occasion of it, and by wondering at the perverseness of the man, who had written a long and argumentative essay to persuade them, that

Fair is foul, and foul is fair;

in other words, that they had been all their lives admiring without judgment, and were now about to censure without reason.

That this conjecture is not wide from the mark, I am induced to believe from the noticeable fact, which I can state on my own knowledge, that the same general censure has been grounded by almost every different person on some different poem. Among those, whose candour and judgment I estimate highly, I distinctly remember six who expressed their objections to the *Lyrical Ballads* almost in the same words, and altogether to the same purport, at the same time admitting, that several of the poems had given them great pleasure; and, strange as it might seem, the composition which one cited as execrable, another quoted as his favourite. I am indeed convinced in my own mind, that could the same experiment have been tried with these volumes, as was made in the well known story of the picture, the result would have been the same; the parts which had been covered by black spots on the one day, would be found equally *albo lapide notatæ*[1] on the succeeding.

However this may be, it was assuredly hard and unjust to fix the attention on a few separate and insulated poems with as much aversion, as if they had been so many plague-spots on the whole work, instead of passing them over in silence, as so much blank paper, or leaves of a bookseller's catalogue; especially, as no one pretended to have found in them any immorality or indelicacy; and the poems, therefore, at the worst, could only be regarded as so many light or inferior coins in a rouleau of gold, not as so much alloy in a weight of bullion. A friend whose talents I hold in the highest respect, but whose judgment and strong sound sense I have had almost continued occasion to revere, making the usual complaints to me concerning both the style and subjects of Mr. Wordsworth's minor poems; I admitted that there were some few of the tales and incidents, in which I could not myself find a sufficient cause for their having been recorded in metre. I mentioned "Alice Fell" as an instance; "Nay," replied my friend with more than usual quickness of manner, "I cannot agree with you there!—that, I own, does seem to me a remarkably pleasing poem." In the *Lyrical Ballads*, (for my experience does not enable me to extend the remark equally unqualified to the two subsequent volumes,) I have heard at different times, and from different individuals, every single poem extolled

[1] "Marked by white stone"; a sign of good omen, much as we say "a red-letter day."

and reprobated, with the exception of those of loftier kind, which as was before observed, seem to have won universal praise. This fact of itself would have made me diffident in my censures, had not a still stronger ground been furnished by the strange contrast of the heat and long continuance of the opposition, with the nature of the faults stated as justifying it. The seductive faults, the *dulcia vitia* of Cowley, Marini, or Darwin might reasonably be 10 thought capable of corrupting the public judgment for half a century, and require a twenty years war, campaign after campaign, in order to dethrone the usurper and re-establish the legitimate taste. But that a downright 15 simpleness, under the affectation of simplicity, prosaic words in feeble metre, silly thoughts in childish phrases, and a preference of mean, degrading, or at best trivial associations and characters, should succeed in forming a school 20 of imitators, a company of almost religious admirers, and this too among young men of ardent minds, liberal education, and not

——with academic laurels unbestowed;

and that this bare and bald counterfeit of poetry, which is characterized as below criticism, should for nearly twenty years have wellnigh engrossed criticism, as the main, if not the only, butt of review, magazine, pamphlet, 30 poem, and paragraph; this is indeed matter of wonder. . . .

I was in my twenty-fourth year, when I had the happiness of knowing Mr. Wordsworth personally, and while memory lasts, I shall 35 hardly forget the sudden effect produced on my mind, by his recitation of a manuscript poem, which still remains unpublished, but of which the stanza and tone of style were the same as those of "The Female Vagrant," as 40 originally printed in the first volume of the *Lyrical Ballads.* . . .

It was not however the freedom from false taste, whether as to common defects, or to those more properly his own, which made so 45 unusual an impression on my feelings immediately, and subsequently on my judgment. It was the union of deep feeling with profound thought; the fine balance of truth in observing, with the imaginative faculty in 50 modifying, the objects observed; and above all

the original gift of spreading the tone, the atmosphere, and with it the depth and height of the ideal world around forms, incidents, and situations, of which, for the common view, 5 custom had bedimmed all the lustre, had dried up the sparkle and the dew drops. . . .

CHAPTER XIV

Occasion of the Lyrical Ballads, and the objects originally proposed—Preface to the second edition —The ensuing controversy, its causes and acrimony—Philosophic definitions of a Poem and Poetry with scholia.

During the first year that Mr. Wordsworth and I were neighbours, our conversations 15 turned frequently on the two cardinal points of poetry, the power of exciting the sympathy of the reader by a faithful adherence to the truth of nature, and the power of giving the interest of novelty by the modifying colours 20 of imagination. The sudden charm, which accidents of light and shade, which moon-light or sunset diffused over a known and familiar landscape, appeared to represent the prac- 25 ticability of combining both. These are the poetry of nature. The thought suggested itself—(to which of us I do not recollect)—that a series of poems might be composed of two sorts. In the one, the incidents and agents were 30 to be, in part at least, supernatural; and the excellence aimed at was to consist in the interesting of the affections by the dramatic truth of such emotions, as would naturally accompany such situations, supposing them real. And real 35 in this sense they have been to every human being who, from whatever source of delusion, has at any time believed himself under supernatural agency. For the second class, subjects were to be chosen from ordinary life; the characters and incidents were to be such as will be 40 found in every village and its vicinity, where there is a meditative and feeling mind to seek after them, or to notice them, when they present themselves.

In this idea originated the plan of the LYR- 45 ICAL BALLADS; in which it was agreed, that my endeavours should be directed to persons and characters supernatural, or at least romantic; yet so as to transfer from our inward 50 nature a human interest and a semblance of truth sufficient to procure for these shadows of imagination that willing suspension of disbelief for the moment, which constitutes poetic faith. Mr. Wordsworth, on the other hand, was to propose to himself as his object, to give the charm of novelty to things of every day, and to excite a feeling analogous to the supernatural, by awakening the mind's attention to the lethargy of custom, and directing it to the loveliness and the wonders of the world before us; an inexhaustible treasure, but for which, in consequence of the film of familiarity and selfish solicitude, we have eyes, yet see not, ears that hear not, and hearts that neither feel nor understand.

With this view I wrote THE ANCIENT MARINER, and was preparing among other poems, THE DARK LADIE, and the CHRISTABEL, in which I should have more nearly realized my ideal, than I had done in my first attempt. But Mr. Wordsworth's industry had proved so much more successful, and the number of his poems so much greater, that my compositions, instead of forming a balance, appeared rather an interpolation of heterogeneous matter. Mr. Wordsworth added two or three poems written in his own character, in the impassioned, lofty, and sustained diction, which is characteristic of his genius. In this form the LYRICAL BALLADS were published; and were presented by him, as an experiment, whether subjects, which from their nature rejected the usual ornaments and extra-colloquial style of poems in general, might not be so managed in the language of ordinary life as to produce the pleasurable interest, which it is the peculiar business of poetry to impart. To the second edition he added a preface of considerable length; in which, notwithstanding some passages of apparently a contrary import, he was understood to contend for the extension of this style to poetry of all kinds, and to reject as vicious and indefensible all phrases and forms of speech that were not included in what he (unfortunately, I think, adopting an equivocal expression) called the language of real life. From this preface, prefixed to poems in which it was impossible to deny the presence of original genius, however mistaken its direction might be deemed, arose the whole long-continued controversy. For from the conjunction of perceived power with supposed

heresy I explain the inveteracy and in some instances, I grieve to say, the acrimonious passions, with which the controversy has been conducted by the assailants.

Had Mr. Wordsworth's poems been the silly, the childish things, which they were for a long time described as being: had they been really distinguished from the compositions of other poets merely by meanness of language and inanity of thought; had they indeed contained nothing more than what is found in the parodies and pretended imitations of them; they must have sunk at once, a dead weight, into the slough of oblivion, and have dragged the preface along with them. But year after year increased the number of Mr. Wordsworth's admirers. They were found too not in the lower classes of the reading public, but chiefly among young men of strong sensibility and meditative minds; and their admiration (inflamed perhaps in some degree by opposition) was distinguished by its intensity, I might almost say, by its religious fervour. These facts, and the intellectual energy of the author, which was more or less consciously felt, where it was outwardly and even boisterously denied, meeting with sentiments of aversion to his opinions, and of alarm at their consequences, produced an eddy of criticism, which would of itself have borne up the poems by the violence with which it whirled them round and round. With many parts of this preface in the sense attributed to them and which the words undoubtedly seem to authorize, I never concurred; but on the contrary objected to them as erroneous in principle, and as contradictory (in appearance at least) both to other parts of the same preface, and to the author's own practice in the greater part of the poems themselves. Mr. Wordsworth in his recent collection has, I find, degraded this prefatory disquisition to the end of his second volume, to be read or not at the reader's choice. But he has not, as far as I can discover, announced any change in his poetic creed. At all events, considering it as the source of a controversy, in which I have been honoured more than I deserve by the frequent conjunction of my name with his, I think it expedient to declare once for all, in what points I coincide with the opinions supported in that preface, and in what points I altogether differ. But in order to render myself intelligible I must previously, in as few words as possible, explain my views, first, of a Poem; and secondly, of Poetry itself, in kind, and in essence.

The office of philosophical disquisition consists in just distinction; while it is the privilege of the philosopher to preserve himself constantly aware, that distinction is not division. In order to obtain adequate notions of any truth, we must intellectually separate its distinguishable parts; and this is the technical process of philosophy. But having so done, we must then restore them in our conceptions to the unity, in which they actually co-exist; and this is the result of philosophy. A poem contains the same elements as a prose composition; the difference therefore must consist in a different combination of them, in consequence of a different object being proposed. According to the difference of the object will be the difference of the combination. It is possible, that the object may be merely to facilitate the recollection of any given facts or observations by artificial arrangement; and the composition will be a poem, merely because it is distinguished from prose by metre, or by rhyme, or by both conjointly. In this, the lowest sense, a man might attribute the name of a poem to the well-known enumeration of the days in the several months:

> Thirty days hath September,
> April, June, and November, &c.

and others of the same class and purpose. And as a particular pleasure is found in anticipating the recurrence of sounds and quantities, all compositions that have this charm superadded, whatever be their contents, *may* be entitled poems.

So much for the superficial form. A difference of object and contents supplies an additional ground of distinction. The immediate purpose may be the communication of truths; either of truth absolute and demonstrable, as in works of science; or of facts experienced and recorded, as in history. Pleasure, and that of the highest and most permanent kind, may result from the attainment of the end; but it is not itself the immediate end. In other works

the communication of pleasure may be the immediate purpose; and though truth, either moral or intellectual, ought to be the ultimate end, yet this will distinguish the character of the author, not the class to which the work belongs. Blest indeed is that state of society, in which the immediate purpose would be baffled by the perversion of the proper ultimate end; in which no charm of diction or imagery could exempt the BATHYLLUS even of an Anacreon, or the ALEXIS of Virgil, from disgust and aversion!

But the communication of pleasure may be the immediate object of a work not metrically composed; and that object may have been in a high degree attained, as in novels and romances. Would then the mere superaddition of metre, with or without rhyme, entitle these to the name of poems? The answer is, that nothing can permanently please, which does not contain in itself the reason why it is so, and not otherwise. If metre be superadded, all other parts must be made consonant with it. They must be such, as to justify the perpetual and distinct attention to each part, which an exact correspondent recurrence of accent and sound are calculated to excite. The final definition then, so deduced, may be thus worded. A poem is that species of composition, which is opposed to works of science, by proposing for its *immediate* object pleasure, not truth; and from all other species—(having *this* object in common with it)—it is discriminated by proposing to itself such delight from the *whole*, as is compatible with a distinct gratification from each component *part*.

Controversy is not seldom excited in consequence of the disputants attaching each a different meaning to the same word; and in few instances has this been more striking, than in disputes concerning the present subject. If a man chooses to call every composition a poem, which is rhyme, or measure, or both, I must leave his opinion uncontroverted. The distinction is at least competent to characterize the writer's intention. If it were subjoined, that the whole is likewise entertaining or affecting, as a tale, or as a series of interesting reflections, I of course admit this as another fit ingredient of a poem, and an additional merit. But if the definition sought for be that of a *legitimate* poem, I answer, it must be one, the parts of which mutually support and explain each other; all in their proportion harmonizing with, and supporting the purpose and known influences of metrical arrangement. The philosophic critics of all ages coincide with the ultimate judgment of all countries, in equally denying the praises of a just poem, on the one hand, to a series of striking lines or distiches, each of which, absorbing the whole attention of the reader to itself, becomes disjoined from its context, and forms a separate whole, instead of a harmonizing part; and on the other hand, to an unsustained composition, from which the reader collects rapidly the general result unattracted by the component parts. The reader should be carried forward, not merely or chiefly by the mechanical impulse of curiosity, or by a restless desire to arrive at the final solution; but by the pleasureable activity of mind excited by the attractions of the journey itself. Like the motion of a serpent, which the Egyptians made the emblem of intellectual power; or like the path of sound through the air;—at every step he pauses and half recedes, and from the retrogressive movement collects the force which again carries him onward. *Præcipitandus est liber spiritus*,[1] says Petronius most happily. The epithet, *liber*, here balances the preceding verb; and it is not easy to conceive more meaning condensed in fewer words.

But if this should be admitted as a satisfactory character of a poem, we have still to seek for a definition of poetry. The writings of Plato, and Jeremy Taylor, and Burnet's Theory of the Earth, furnish undeniable proofs that poetry of the highest kind may exist without metre, and even without the contradistinguishing objects of a poem. The first chapter of Isaiah—(indeed a very large portion of the whole book)—is poetry in the most emphatic sense; yet it would be not less irrational than strange to assert, that pleasure, and not truth was the immediate object of the prophet. In short, whatever specific import we attach to the word, Poetry, there will be found involved in it, as a necessary consequence, that a poem of any length neither can be, nor ought to be, all poetry. Yet if an harmonious whole is to be produced, the remaining parts must be preserved in keeping with the poetry; and this can be no otherwise effected than by such a studied selection and artificial arrangement, as will partake of one, though not a peculiar property of poetry. And this again can be no other than the property of exciting a more continuous and equal attention than the language of prose aims at, whether colloquial or written.

My own conclusions on the nature of poetry, in the strictest use of the word, have been in part anticipated in some of the remarks on the Fancy and Imagination in the early part of this work. What is poetry?—is so nearly the same question with, what is a poet?—that the answer to the one is involved in the solution of the other. For it is a distinction resulting from the poetic genius itself, which sustains and modifies the images, thoughts, and emotions of the poet's own mind.

The poet, described in ideal perfection, brings the whole soul of man into activity, with the subordination of its faculties to each other according to their relative worth and dignity. He diffuses a tone and spirit of unity, that blends, and (as it were) *fuses*, each into each, by that synthetic and magical power, to which I would exclusively appropriate the name of Imagination. This power, first put in action by the will and understanding, and retained under their irremissive, though gentle and unnoticed, control, *laxis effertur habenis*,[1] reveals itself in the balance or reconcilement of opposite or discordant qualities: of sameness, with difference; of the general with the concrete; the idea with the image; the individual with the representative; the sense of novelty and freshness with old and familiar objects; a more than usual state of emotion with more than usual order; judgment ever awake and steady self-possession with enthusiasm and feeling profound or vehement; and while it blends and harmonizes the natural and the artificial, still subordinates art to nature; the manner to the matter; and our admiration of the poet to our sympathy with the poetry. Doubtless, as Sir John Davies observes of the soul—(and his words may with slight alteration be applied, and even more appropriately, to the poetic Imagination)—

---

[1] "The free spirit must be impelled forward."

[1] "Carried along with loose reins."

Doubtless this could not be, but that she turns
   Bodies to *spirit* by sublimation strange,
As fire converts to fire the things it burns,
   As we our food into our nature change.

From their gross matter she abstracts *their* forms,
   And draws a kind of quintessence from things;
Which to her proper nature she transforms
   To bear them light on her celestial wings.

Thus does she, when from *individual states*
   She doth abstract the universal kinds;
Which then re-clothed in divers names and fates
   Steal access through the senses to our minds.

Finally Good Sense is the Body of poetic genius, Fancy its Drapery, Motion its Life, and Imagination the Soul that is everywhere, and in each; and forms all into one graceful and intelligent whole.

CHAPTER XVII

Examination of the tenets peculiar to Mr. Wordsworth—Rustic life (above all, low and rustic life) especially unfavourable to the formation of a human diction—The best parts of language the product of philosophers, not of clowns or shepherds—Poetry essentially ideal and generic—The language of Milton as much the language of real life, yea, incomparably more so than that of the cottager.

As far then as Mr. Wordsworth in his preface contended, and most ably contended, for a reformation in our poetic diction, as far as he has evinced the truth of passion, and the dramatic propriety of those figures and metaphors in the original poets, which, stripped of their justifying reasons, and converted into mere artifices of connection or ornament, constitute the characteristic falsity in the poetic style of the moderns; and as far as he has, with equal acuteness and clearness, pointed out the process by which this change was effected, and the resemblances between that state into which the reader's mind is thrown by the pleasurable confusion of thought from an unaccustomed train of words and images; and that state which is induced by the natural language of impassioned feeling; he undertook a useful task, and deserves all praise, both for the attempt and for the execution. The provocations to this remonstrance in behalf of truth and nature were still of perpetual recurrence before and after the publication of this preface. I cannot likewise but add, that the comparison of such poems of merit, as have been given to the public within the last ten or twelve years, with the majority of those produced previously to the appearance of that preface, leave no doubt on my mind, that Mr. Wordsworth is fully justified in believing his efforts to have been by no means ineffectual. Not only in the verses of those who have professed their admiration of his genius, but even of those who have distinguished themselves by hostility to his theory, and depreciation of his writings, are the impressions of his principles plainly visible. It is possible, that with these principles others may have been blended, which are not equally evident; and some which are unsteady and subvertible from the narrowness or imperfection of their basis. But it is more than possible, that these errors of defect or exaggeration, by kindling and feeding the controversy, may have conduced not only to the wider propagation of the accompanying truths, but that, by their frequent presentation to the mind in an excited state, they may have won for them a more permanent and practical result. A man will borrow a part from his opponent the more easily, if he feels himself justified in continuing to reject a part. While there remain important points in which he can still feel himself in the right, in which he still finds firm footing for continued resistance, he will gradually adopt those opinions, which were the least remote from his own convictions, as not less congruous with his own theory than with that which he reprobates. In like manner with a kind of instinctive prudence, he will abandon by little and little his weakest posts, till at length he seems to forget that they had ever belonged to him, or affects to consider them at most as accidental and "petty annexments," the removal of which leaves the citadel unhurt and unendangered.

My own differences from certain supposed parts of Mr. Wordsworth's theory ground themselves on the assumption, that his words had been rightly interpreted, as purporting that the proper diction for poetry in general consists altogether in a language taken, with due exceptions, from the mouths of men in real life, a language which actually constitutes the natural conversation of men under the influence of natural feelings. My objection is, first, that in any sense this rule is applicable only to certain classes of poetry; secondly, that even to these classes it is not applicable, except in such a sense, as hath never by any one (as far as I know or have read,) been denied or doubted; and lastly, that as far as, and in that degree in which it is practicable, it is yet as a rule useless, if not injurious, and therefore either need not, or ought not to be practised. The poet informs his reader, that he had generally chosen low and rustic life; but not as low and rustic, or in order to repeat that pleasure of doubtful moral effect, which persons of elevated rank and of superior refinement oftentimes derive from a happy imitation of the rude unpolished manners and discourse of their inferiors. For the pleasure so derived may be traced to three exciting causes. The first is the naturalness, in fact, of the things represented. The second is the apparent naturalness of the representation, as raised and qualified by an imperceptible infusion of the author's own knowledge and talent, which infusion does, indeed, constitute it an imitation as distinguished from a mere copy. The third cause may be found in the reader's conscious feeling of his superiority awakened by the contrast presented to him; even as for the same purpose the kings and great barons of yore retained, sometimes actual clowns and fools, but more frequently shrewd and witty fellows in that character. These, however, were not Mr. Wordsworth's objects. *He* chose low and rustic life, "because in that condition the essential passions of the heart find a better soil, in which they can attain their maturity, are less under restraint, and speak a plainer and more emphatic language; because in that condition of life our elementary feelings coexist in a state of greater simplicity, and consequently may be more accurately contemplated, and more forcibly communicated; because the manners of rural life germinate from those elementary feelings; and from the necessary character of rural occupations are more easily comprehended, and are more durable; and lastly, because in that condition the passions of men are incorporated with the beautiful and permanent forms of nature."

Now it is clear to me, that in the most interesting of the poems, in which the author is more or less dramatic, as THE BROTHERS, MICHAEL, RUTH, THE MAD MOTHER, and others, the persons introduced are by no means taken from low or rustic life in the common acceptation of those words! and it is not less clear, that the sentiments and language, as far as they can be conceived to have been really transferred from the minds and conversation of such persons, are attributable to causes and circumstances not necessarily connected with "their occupations and abode." The thoughts, feelings, language, and manners of the shepherd-farmers in the vales of Cumberland and Westmoreland, as far as they are actually adopted in those poems, may be accounted for from causes, which will and do produce the same results in every state of life, whether in town or country. As the two principal I rank that independence, which raises a man above servitude, or daily toil for the profit of others, yet not above the necessity of industry and a frugal simplicity of domestic life; and the accompanying unambitious, but solid and religious, education, which has rendered few books familiar, but the Bible, and the Liturgy or Hymn book. To this latter cause, indeed, which is so far accidental, that it is the blessing of particular countries and a particular age, not the product of particular places or employments, the poet owes the show of probability, that his personages might really feel, think, and talk with any tolerable resemblance to his representation. It is an excellent remark of Dr. Henry More's, that "a man of confined education, but of good parts, by constant reading of the Bible will naturally form a more winning and commanding rhetoric than those that are learned: the intermixture of tongues and of artificial phrases debasing *their* style."

It is, moreover, to be considerd that to the formation of healthy feelings, and a reflecting mind, negations involve impediments not less formidable than sophistication and vicious intermixture. I am convinced, that for the human soul to prosper in rustic life a certain vantage-ground is prerequisite. It is not every man that is likely to be improved by a country life or by country labours. Education, or original sensibility, or both, must pre-exist, if the changes, forms, and incidents of nature are to prove a sufficient stimulant. And where these are not sufficient, the mind contracts and hardens by want of stimulants: and the man becomes selfish, sensual, gross, and hard-hearted. Let the management of the Poor Laws in Liverpool, Manchester, or Bristol be compared with the ordinary dispensation of the poor rates in agricultural villages, where the farmers are the overseers and guardians of the poor. If my own experience have not been particularly unfortunate, as well as that of the many respectable country clergymen with whom I have conversed on the subject, the result would engender more than scepticism concerning the desirable influences of low and rustic life in and for itself. Whatever may be concluded on the other side, from the stronger local attachments and enterprising spirit of the Swiss, and other mountaineers, applies to a particular mode of pastoral life, under forms of property that permit and beget manners truly republican, not to rustic life in general, or to the absence of artificial cultivation. On the contrary the mountaineers, whose manners have been so often eulogized, are in general better educated and greater readers than men of equal rank elsewhere. But where this is not the case, as among the peasantry of North Wales, the ancient mountains, with all their terrors and all their glories, are pictures to the blind, and music to the deaf.

I should not have entered so much into detail upon this passage, but here seems to be the point, to which all the lines of difference converge as to their source and centre;—I mean, as far as, and in whatever respect, my poetic creed *does* differ from the doctrines promulgated in this preface. I adopt with full faith, the principle of Aristotle, that poetry, as poetry, is essentially ideal, that it avoids and excludes all accident; that its apparent individualities of rank, character, or occupation must be representative of a class; and that the persons of poetry must be clothed with generic attributes, with the common attributes of the class: not with such as one gifted individual might possibly possess, but such as from his situation it is most probable beforehand that he would possess. If my premises are right and my deductions legitimate, it follows that there can be no poetic medium

between the swains of Theocritus and those of an imaginary golden age.

The characters of the vicar and the shepherd-mariner in the poem of THE BROTHERS, and that of the shepherd of Green-head Ghyll in the MICHAEL, have all the verisimilitude and representative quality, that the purposes of poetry can require. They are persons of a known and abiding class, and their manners and sentiments the natural product of circumstances common to the class. Take Michael for instance:

An old man stout of heart, and strong of limb.
His bodily frame had been from youth to age
Of an unusual strength: his mind was keen,
Intense, and frugal, apt for all affairs,
And in his shepherd's calling he was prompt
And watchful more than ordinary men.
Hence he had learned the meaning of all winds.
Of blasts of every tone; and oftentimes
When others heeded not, He heard the South
Make subterraneous music, like the noise
Of bagpipers on distant Highland hills.
The Shepherd, at such warning, of his flock
Bethought him, and he to himself would say,
'The winds are now devising work for me!'
And truly, at all times, the storm, that drives
The traveller to a shelter, summoned him
Up to the mountains: he had been alone
Amid the heart of many thousand mists,
That came to him and left him on the heights.
So lived he, until his eightieth year was past.
And grossly that man errs, who should suppose
That the green valleys, and the streams and rocks,
Were things indifferent to the Shepherd's thoughts.
Fields, where with cheerful spirits he had breathed
The common air; the hills, which he so oft
Had climbed with vigorous steps; which had impressed
So many incidents upon his mind
Of hardship, skill or courage, joy or fear;
Which, like a book, preserved the memory
Of the dumb animals, whom he had saved,
Had fed or sheltered, linking to such acts,
So grateful in themselves, the certainty
Of honourable gain; these fields, these hills
Which were his living Being, even more
Than his own blood—what could they less? had laid
Strong hold on his affections, were to him
A pleasurable feeling of blind love,
The pleasure which there is in life itself.

On the other hand, in the poems which are pitched in a lower key, as the HARRY GILL, and THE IDIOT BOY, the feelings are those of human nature in general; though the poet has judiciously laid the scene in the country, in order to place himself in the vicinity of interesting images, without the necessity of ascribing a sentimental perception of their beauty to the persons of his drama. In THE IDIOT BOY, indeed, the mother's character is not so much the real and native product of a "situation where the essential passions of the heart find a better soil, in which they can attain their maturity and speak a plainer and more emphatic language," as it is an impersonation of an instinct abandoned by judgment. Hence the two following charges seem to me not wholly groundless: at least, they are the only plausible objections, which I have heard to that fine poem. The one is, that the author has not, in the poem itself, taken sufficient care to preclude from the reader's fancy the disgusting images of ordinary morbid idiocy, which yet it was by no means his intention to represent. He was even by the "burr, burr, burr," uncounteracted by any preceding description of the boy's beauty, assisted in recalling them. The other is, that the idiocy of the boy is so evenly balanced by the folly of the mother, as to present to the general reader rather a laughable burlesque on the blindness of anile dotage, than an analytic display of maternal affection in its ordinary workings.

In THE THORN, the poet himself acknowledges in a note the necessity of an introductory poem, in which he should have portrayed the character of the person from whom the words of the poem are supposed to proceed: a superstitious man moderately imaginative, of slow faculties and deep feelings, "a captain of a small trading vessel, for example, who, being past the middle age of life, had retired upon an annuity, or small independent income, to some village or country town of which he was not a native, or in which he had not been accustomed to live. Such men having nothing to do become credulous and talkative from indolence." But in a poem, still more in a lyric poem—and the Nurse in ROMEO AND JULIET alone prevents me from extending the remark even to dramatic poetry, if indeed even the Nurse can be deemed altogether a case in point—it is not possible to imitate truly a dull and garrulous discourser, without repeating the effects of dullness and garrulity. However this may be, I dare assert, that the parts—(and these form the far larger portion of the whole) —which might as well or still better have proceeded from the poet's own imagination, and have been spoken in his own character, are those which have given, and which will continue to give, universal delight; and that the passages exclusively appropriate to the supposed narrator, such as the last couplet of the third stanza; the seven last lines of the tenth; and the five following stanzas, with the exception of the four admirable lines at the commencement of the fourteenth, are felt by many unprejudiced and unsophisticated hearts, as sudden and unpleasant sinkings from the height to which the poet had previously lifted them, and to which he again re-elevates both himself and his reader.

If then I am compelled to doubt the theory, by which the choice of characters was to be directed, not only a priori, from grounds of reason, but both from the few instances in which the poet himself need be supposed to have been governed by it, and from the comparative inferiority of those instances; still more must I hesitate in my assent to the sentence which immediately follows the former citation; and which I can neither admit as particular fact, nor as general rule. "The language, too, of these men has been adopted (purified indeed from what appear to be its real defects, from all lasting and rational causes of dislike or disgust) because such men hourly communicate with the best objects from which the best part of language is originally derived; and because, from their rank in society and the sameness and narrow circle of their intercourse, being less under the action of social vanity, they convey their feelings and notions in simple and unelaborated expressions." To this I reply; that a rustic's language, purified from all provincialism and grossness, and so far reconstructed as to be made consistent with the rules of grammar— (which are in essence no other than the laws of universal logic, applied to psychological materials)—will not differ from the language of any other man of common sense, however learned or refined he may be, except as far as the notions, which the rustic has to convey, are fewer and more indiscriminate. This will become still clearer, if we add the consideration

—(equally important though less obvious)— that the rustic, from the more imperfect development of his faculties, and from the lower state of their cultivation, aims almost solely to convey insulated facts, either those of his scanty experience or his traditional belief; while the educated man chiefly seeks to discover and express those connections of things, or those relative bearings of fact to fact, from which some more or less general law is deducible. For facts are valuable to a wise man, chiefly as they lead to the discovery of the indwelling law, which is the true being of things, the sole solution of their modes of existence, and in the knowledge of which consists our dignity and our power.

As little can I agree with the assertion, that from the objects with which the rustic hourly communicates the best part of language is formed. For first, if to communicate with an object implies such an acquaintance with it, as renders it capable of being discriminately reflected on, the distinct knowledge of an uneducated rustic would furnish a very scanty vocabulary. The few things and modes of action requisite for his bodily conveniences would alone be individualized; while all the rest of nature would be expressed by a small number of confused general terms. Secondly, I deny that the words and combinations of words derived from the objects, with which the rustic is familiar, whether with distinct or confused knowledge, can be justly said to form the best part of language. It is more than probable, that many classes of the brute creation possess discriminating sounds, by which they can convey to each other notices of such objects as concern their food, shelter, or safety. Yet we hesitate to call the aggregate of such sounds a language, otherwise than metaphorically. The best part of human language, properly so called, is derived from reflection on the acts of the mind itself. It is formed by a voluntary appropriation of fixed symbols to internal acts, to processes and results of imagination, the greater part of which have no place in the consciousness of uneducated man; though in civilized society, by imitation and passive remembrance of what they hear from their religious instructors and other superiors,

the most uneducated share in the harvest which they neither sowed, nor reaped. If the history of the phrases in hourly currency among our peasants were traced, a person not previously aware of the fact would be surprised at finding so large a number, which three or four centuries ago were the exclusive property of the universities and the schools; and, at the commencement of the Reformation, had been transferred from the school to the pulpit, and thus gradually passed into common life. The extreme difficulty, and often the impossibility, of finding words for the simplest moral and intellectual processes of the languages of uncivilized tribes has proved perhaps the weightiest obstacle to the progress of our most zealous and adroit missionaries. Yet these tribes are surrounded by the same nature as our peasants are; but in still more impressive forms; and they are, moreover, obliged to particularize many more of them. When, therefore, Mr. Wordsworth adds, "accordingly, such a language"—(meaning, as before, the language of rustic life purified from provincialism)—"arising out of repeated experience and regular feelings, is a more permanent, and a far more philosophical language, than that which is frequently substituted for it by Poets, who think that they are conferring honour upon themselves and their art in proportion as they indulge in arbitrary and capricious habits of expression;" it may be answered, that the language, which he has in view, can be attributed to rustics with no greater right, than the style of Hooker or Bacon to Tom Brown or Sir Roger L'Estrange. Doubtless, if what is peculiar to each were omitted in each, the result must needs be the same. Further, that the poet, who uses an illogical diction, or a style fitted to excite only the low and changeable pleasure of wonder by means of groundless novelty, substitutes a language of folly and vanity, not for that of the rustic, but for that of good sense and natural feeling.

Here let me be permitted to remind the reader, that the positions, which I controvert, are contained in the sentences—"a selection of the real language of men;"—"the language of these men" (that is, men in low and rustic life) "has been adopted; I have proposed to myself to imitate, and, as far as is possible, to adopt the very language of men."

"Between the language of prose and that of metrical composition, there neither is, nor can be, any *essential difference:*" it is against these exclusively that my opposition is directed.

I object, in the very first instance, to an equivocation in the use of the word "real." Every man's language varies, according to the extent of his knowledge, the activity of his faculties, and the depth or quickness of his feelings. Every man's language has, first, its individualities; secondly, the common properties of the class to which he belongs; and thirdly, words and phrases of universal use. The language of Hooker, Bacon, Bishop Taylor, and Burke differs from the common language of the learned class only by the superior number and novelty of the thoughts and relations which they had to convey. The language of Algernon Sidney differs not at all from that, which every well-educated gentleman would wish to write, and (with due allowances for the undeliberateness, and less connected train, of thinking natural and proper to conversation) such as he would wish to talk. Neither one nor the other differ half as much from the general language of cultivated society, as the language of Mr. Wordsworth's homeliest composition differs from that of a common peasant. For "real" therefore, we must substitute ordinary, or *lingua communis*. And this, we have proved, is no more to be found in the phraseology of low and rustic life than in that of any other class. Omit the peculiarities of each and the result of course must be common to all. And assuredly the omissions and changes to be made in the language of rustics, before it could be transferred to any species of poem, except the drama or other professed imitation, are at least as numerous and weighty, as would be required in adapting to the same purpose the ordinary language of tradesmen and manufacturers. Not to mention, that the language so highly extolled by Mr. Wordsworth varies in every county, nay in every village, according to the accidental character of the clergyman, the existence or non-existence of schools; or even, perhaps, as the exciseman, publican, and barber happen to be, or not to be, zealous politicians, and readers of the weekly newspaper *pro bono publico.* Anterior to cultivation the *lingua communis* of every country, as Dante has well observed, exists every where in parts, and no where as a whole.

Neither is the case rendered at all more tenable by the addition of the words, "in a state of excitement." For the nature of a man's words, where he is strongly affected by joy, grief, or anger, must necessarily depend on the number and quality of the general truths, conceptions and images, and of the words expressing them, with which his mind had been previously stored. For the property of passion is not to create; but to set in increased activity. At least, whatever new connections of thought or images, or—(which is equally, if not more than equally, the appropriate effect of strong excitement)—whatever generalizations of truth or experience the heat of passion may produce; yet the terms of their conveyance must have pre-existed in his former conversations, and are only collected and crowded together by the unusual stimulation. It is indeed very possible to adopt in a poem the unmeaning repetitions, habitual phrases, and other blank counters, which an unfurnished or confused understanding interposes at short intervals, in order to keep hold of his subject, which is still slipping from him, and to give him time for recollection; or, in mere aid of vacancy, as in the scanty companies of a country stage the same player pops backwards and forwards, in order to prevent the appearance of empty spaces, in the procession of Macbeth, or Henry VIII. But what assistance to the poet, or ornament to the poem, these can supply, I am at a loss to conjecture. Nothing assuredly can differ either in origin or in mode more widely from the apparent tautologies of intense and turbulent feeling, in which the passion is greater and of longer endurance than to be exhausted or satisfied by a single representation of the image or incident exciting it. Such repetitions I admit to be a beauty of the highest kind; as illustrated by Mr. Wordsworth himself from the song of Deborah. *At her feet he bowed, he fell, he lay down: at her feet he bowed, he fell: where he bowed, there he fell down dead.* Judges v. 27.

CHAPTER XVIII

Language of metrical composition, why and wherein essentially different from that of prose—Origin and elements of metre—Its necessary consequences, and the conditions thereby imposed on the metrical writer in the choice of his diction.

I CONCLUDE, therefore, that the attempt is impracticable; and that, were it not impracticable, it would still be useless. For the very power of making the selection implies the previous possession of the language selected. Or where can the poet have lived? And by what rules could he direct his choice, which would not have enabled him to select and arrange his words by the light of his own judgment? We do not adopt the language of a class by the mere adoption of such words exclusively, as that class would use, or at least understand; but likewise by following the order, in which the words of such men are wont to succeed each other. Now this order, in the intercourse of uneducated men, is distinguished from the diction of their superiors in knowledge and power, by the greater disjunction and separation in the component parts of that, whatever it be, which they wish to communicate. There is a want of that prospectiveness of mind, that surview, which enables a man to foresee the whole of what he is to convey, appertaining to any one point; and by this means so to subordinate and arrange the different parts according to their relative importance, as to convey it at once, and as an organized whole.

Now I will take the first stanza, on which I have chanced to open, in the Lyrical Ballads. It is one the most simple and the least peculiar in its language.

"In distant countries have I been,
And yet I have not often seen
A healthy man, a man full grown,
Weep in the public roads, alone.
But such a one, on English ground,
And in the broad highway, I met;
Along the broad highway he came,
His cheeks with tears were wet:
Sturdy he seemed, though he was sad;
And in his arms a lamb he had."

The words here are doubtless such as are current in all ranks of life; and of course not less so in the hamlet and cottage than in the shop, manufactory, college, or palace. But is this the *order*, in which the rustic would have placed the words? I am grievously deceived, if the following less compact mode of commencing the same tale be not a far more faithful copy. "I have been in a many parts, far and near, and I don't know that I ever saw before a man crying by himself in the public road; a grown man I mean, that was neither sick nor hurt," etc., etc. But when I turn to the following stanza in The Thorn:

"At all times of the day and night
This wretched woman thither goes;
And she is known to every star,
And every wind that blows:
And there, beside the Thorn, she sits,
When the blue day-light's in the skies,
And when the whirlwind's on the hill,
Or frosty air is keen and still,
And to herself she cries,
Oh misery! Oh misery!
Oh woe is me! O misery!"

and compare this with the language of ordinary men; or with that which I can conceive at all likely to proceed, in real life, from such a narrator, as is supposed in the note to the poem; compare it either in the succession of the images or of the sentences; I am reminded of the sublime prayer and hymn of praise, which Milton, in opposition to an established liturgy, presents as a fair specimen of common extemporary devotion, and such as we might expect to hear from every self-inspired minister of a conventicle! And I reflect with delight, how little a mere theory, though of his own workmanship, interferes with the processes of genuine imagination in a man of true poetic genius, who possesses, as Mr. Wordsworth, if ever man did, most assuredly does possess,

"The Vision and the Faculty divine."

One point then alone remains, but that the most important; its examination having been, indeed, my chief inducement for the preceding inquisition. "There neither is nor can be any essential difference between the language of prose and metrical composition." Such is Mr. Wordsworth's assertion. Now prose itself, at least in all argumentative and consecutive works, differs, and ought to differ, from the language of conversation; even as reading ought to differ from talking. Unless therefore the difference denied be that of the mere words, as materials common to all styles of writing, and not of the style itself in the universally admitted sense of the term, it might be naturally presumed that there must exist a still greater between the ordonnance of poetic composition and that of prose, than is expected to distinguish prose from ordinary conversation.

There are not, indeed, examples wanting in the history of literature, of apparent paradoxes that have summoned the public wonder as new and startling truths, but which, on examination, have shrunk into tame and harmless truisms; as the eyes of a cat, seen in the dark, have been mistaken for flames of fire. But Mr. Wordsworth is among the last men, to whom a delusion of this kind would be attributed by anyone, who had enjoyed the slightest opportunity of understanding his mind and character. Where an objection has been anticipated by such an author as natural, his answer to it must needs be interpreted in some sense which either is, or has been, or is capable of being controverted. My object then must be to discover some other meaning for the term "essential difference" in this place, exclusive of the indistinction and community of the words themselves. For whether there ought to exist a class of words in the English, in any degree resembling the poetic dialect of the Greek and Italian, is a question of very subordinate importance. The number of such words would be small indeed, in our language; and even in the Italian and Greek, they consist not so much of different words, as of slight differences in the forms of declining and conjugating the same words; forms, doubtless, which having been, at some period more or less remote, the common grammatic flexions of some tribe or province, had been accidentally appropriated to poetry by the general admiration of certain master intellects, the first established lights of inspiration, to whom that dialect happened to be native.

Essence, in its primary signification, means the principle of individuation, the inmost principle of the possibility of any thing, as that particular thing. It is equivalent to the idea of a thing, whenever we use the word, idea, with philosophic precision. Existence, on the other hand, is distinguished from essence, by the superinduction of reality. Thus we speak of the essence, and essential properties of a circle; but we do not therefore assert, that any thing, which really exists, is mathematically circular. Thus too, without any tautology we contend for the existence of the Supreme Being; that is, for a reality correspondent to the idea. There is, next, a secondary use of the word essence, in which it signifies the point or ground of contra-distinction between two modifications of the same substance or subject. Thus we should be allowed to say, that the style of architecture of Westminster Abbey is essentially different from that of St. Paul, even though both had been built with blocks cut into the same form, and from the same quarry. Only in this latter sense of the term must it have been denied by Mr. Wordsworth (for in this sense alone is it affirmed by the general opinion) that the language of poetry (that is the formal construction, or architecture, of the words and phrases) is essentially different from that of prose. Now the burden of the proof lies with the oppugner, not with the supporters of the common belief. Mr. Wordsworth, in consequence, assigns as the proof of his position, "that not only the language of a large portion of every good poem, even of the most elevated character, must necessarily, except with reference to the metre, in no respect differ from that of good prose, but likewise that some of the most interesting parts of the best poems will be found to be strictly the language of prose, when prose is well written. The truth of this assertion might be demonstrated by innumerable passages from almost all the poetical writings, even of Milton himself." He then quotes Gray's sonnet—

"In vain to me the smiling mornings shine,
And reddening Phœbus lifts his golden fire;
The birds in vain their amorous descant join,
Or cheerful fields resume their green attire.
These ears, alas! for other notes repine;
A different object do these eyes require;
My lonely anguish melts no heart but mine;
And in my breast the imperfect joys expire.
Yet morning smiles the busy race to cheer,
And new-born pleasure brings to happier men;
The fields to all their wonted tribute bear;
To warm their little loves the birds complain:
I fruitless mourn to him that cannot hear,
And weep the more, because I weep in vain."

and adds the following remark:—"It will easily be perceived, that the only part of this Sonnet which is of any value, is the lines printed in italics; it is equally obvious, that, except in the rhyme, and in the use of the single word 'fruitless' for fruitlessly, which is so far a defect, the language of these lines does in no respect differ from that of prose."

An idealist defending his system by the fact, that when asleep we often believe ourselves awake, was well answered by his plain neighbour, "Ah, but when awake do we ever believe ourselves asleep?" Things identical must be convertible. The preceding passage seems to rest on a similar sophism. For the question is not, whether there may not occur in prose an order of words, which would be equally proper in a poem; nor whether there are not beautiful lines and sentences of frequent occurrence in good poems, which would be equally becoming as well as beautiful in good prose; for neither the one nor the other has ever been either denied or doubted by any one. The true question must be, whether there are not modes of expression, a construction, and an order of sentences, which are in their fit and natural place in a serious prose composition, but would be disproportionate and heterogeneous in metrical poetry; and, *vice versa*, whether in the language of a serious poem there may not be an arrangement both of words and sentences, and a use and selection of (what are called) figures of speech, both as to their kind, their frequency, and their occasions, which on a subject of equal weight would be vicious and alien in correct and manly prose. I contend, that in both cases this unfitness of each for the place of the other frequently will and ought to exist.

And first from the origin of metre. This I would trace to the balance in the mind effected by that spontaneous effort which strives to hold in check the workings of passion. It might be easily explained likewise in what manner this salutary antagonism is assisted by the very state, which it counteracts; and how this balance of antagonists became organized into metre (in the usual acceptation of that term), by a supervening act of the will and judgment, consciously and for the foreseen purpose of pleasure. Assuming these principles, as the *data* of our argument, we deduce from them two legitimate conditions, which the critic is entitled to expect in every metrical work. First, that, as the elements of metre owe their existence to a state of increased excitement, so the metre itself should be accompanied by the natural language of excitement. Secondly, that as these elements are formed into metre artificially, by a voluntary act, with the design and for the purpose of blending delight with emotion, so the traces of present volition should throughout the metrical language be proportionately discernible. Now these two conditions must be reconciled and co-present. There must be not only a partnership, but a union; an interpenetration of passion and of will, of spontaneous impulse and of voluntary purpose. Again, this union can be manifested only in a frequency of forms and figures of speech, (originally the offspring of passion, but now the adopted children of power), greater than would be desired or endured, where the emotion is not voluntarily encouraged and kept up for the sake of that pleasure, which such emotion, so tempered and mastered by the will, is found capable of communicating. It not only dictates, but of itself tends to produce a more frequent employment of picturesque and vivifying language, than would be natural in any other case, in which there did not exist, as there does in the present, a previous and well understood, though tacit, compact between the poet and his reader, that the latter is entitled to expect, and the former bound to supply this species and degree of pleasurable excitement. We may in some measure apply to this union the answer of Polixenes, in the Winter's Tale, to Perdita's neglect of the streaked gilliflowers, because she had heard it said,

"There is an art, which, in their piedness, shares
With great creating nature.
Pol.   Say there be;
Yet nature is made better by no mean,
But nature makes that mean; so, o'er that art,
Which, you say, adds to nature, is an art,
That nature makes. You see, sweet maid, we
    marry
A gentler scion to the wildest stock;
And make conceive a bark of baser kind
By bud of nobler race. This is an art,
Which does mend nature,—change it rather; but
The art itself is nature,"

Secondly, I argue from the effects of metre. As far as metre acts in and for itself, it tends to increase the vivacity and susceptibility both of the general feelings and of the attention. This effect it produces by the continued excitement of surprise, and by the quick reciprocations of curiosity still gratified and still re-excited, which are too slight indeed to be at any one moment objects of distinct consciousness, yet become considerable in their aggregate influence. As a medicated atmosphere, or as wine during animated conversation, they act powerfully, though themselves unnoticed. Where, therefore, correspondent food and appropriate matter are not provided for the attention and feelings thus roused there must needs be a disappointment felt; like that of leaping in the dark from the last step of a stair-case, when we had prepared our muscles for a leap of three or four.

The discussion on the powers of metre in the preface is highly ingenious and touches at all points on truth. But I cannot find any statement of its powers considered abstractly and separately. On the contrary Mr. Wordsworth seems always to estimate metre by the powers, which it exerts during, (and, as I think, in consequence of), its combination with other elements of poetry. Thus the previous difficulty is left unanswered, what the elements are, with which it must be combined, in order to produce its own effects to any pleasurable purpose. Double and tri-syllable rhymes, indeed, form a lower species of wit, and, attended to exclusively for their own sake, may become a source of momentary amusement; as in poor Smart's distich to the Welsh Squire who had promised him a hare:

"Tell me, thou son of great Cadwallader!
  Hast sent the hare? or hast thou swallow'd her?"

But for any poetic purposes, metre resembles, (if the aptness of the simile may excuse its meanness), yeast, worthless or disagreeable by itself, but giving vivacity and spirit to the liquor with which it is proportionally combined.

The reference to THE CHILDREN IN THE WOOD by no means satisfies my judgment. We all willingly throw ourselves back for awhile into the feelings of our childhood. This ballad, therefore, we read under such recollections of our own childish feelings, as would equally endear to us poems, which Mr. Wordsworth himself would regard as faulty in the opposite extreme of gaudy and technical ornament. Before the invention of printing, and in a still greater degree, before the introduction of writing, metre, especially alliterative metre, (whether alliterative at the beginning of the words, as in PIERCE PLOUMAN, or at the end, as in rhymes,) possessed an independent value as assisting the recollection, and consequently the preservation, of any series of truths or incidents. But I am not convinced by the collation of facts, that THE CHILDREN IN THE WOOD owes either its preservation, or its popularity, to its metrical form. Mr. Marshal's repository affords a number of tales in prose inferior in pathos and general merit, some of as old a date, and many as widely popular. TOM HICKATHRIFT, JACK THE GIANT-KILLER, GOODY TWO-SHOES, and LITTLE RED RIDING-HOOD are formidable rivals. And that they have continued in prose, cannot be fairly explained by the assumption, that the comparative meanness of their thoughts and images precluded even the humblest forms of metre. The scene of GOODY TWO-SHOES in the church is perfectly susceptible of metrical narration; and, among the Θαύματα θαυμαστότατα[1] even of the present age, I do not recollect a more astonishing image than that of the "whole rookery, that flew out of the giant's beard," scared by the tremendous voice, with which this monster answered the challenge of the heroic TOM HICKATHRIFT!

If from these we turn to compositions universally, and independently of all early associations, beloved and admired; would the MARIA, THE MONK, or THE POOR MAN'S ASS of Sterne, be read with more delight, or have a better chance of immortality, had they without any change in the diction been composed in rhyme, than in their present state? If I am not grossly mistaken, the general reply would be in the negative. Nay, I will confess, that, in Mr. Wordsworth's own volumes, the ANECDOTE FOR FATHERS, SIMON LEE, ALICE FELL, BEGGARS, and THE SAILOR'S MOTHER, notwithstanding the beauties which are to be

[1] "Most marvellous marvels."

found in each of them where the poet interposes the music of his own thoughts, would have been more delightful to me in prose, told and managed, as by Mr. Wordsworth they would have been, in a moral essay or pedestrian tour.

Metre in itself is simply a stimulant of the attention, and therefore excites the question: Why is the attention to be thus stimulated? Now the question cannot be answered by the pleasure of the metre itself: for this we have shown to be conditional, and dependent on the appropriateness of the thoughts and expressions, to which the metrical form is superadded. Neither can I conceive any other answer that can be rationally given, short of this: I write in metre, because I am about to use a language different from that of prose. Besides, where the language is not such, how interesting soever the reflections are, that are capable of being drawn by a philosophic mind from the thoughts or incidents of the poem, the metre itself must often become feeble. Take the last three stanzas of THE SAILOR'S MOTHER, for instance. If I could for a moment abstract from the effect produced on the author's feelings, as a man, by the incident at the time of its real occurrence, I would dare appeal to his own judgment, whether in the metre itself he found a sufficient reason for *their* being written *metrically?*

And, thus continuing, she said,.
"I had a Son, who many a day
Sailed on the seas; but he is dead;
In Denmark he was cast away;
And I have travelled far as Hull to see
What clothes he might have left, or other property.

The Bird and Cage they both were his:
'Twas my Son's Bird; and neat and trim
He kept it: many voyages
This Singing-bird hath gone with him;
When last he sailed he left the Bird behind;
As it might be, perhaps, from bodings of his mind.

He to a Fellow-lodger's care
Had left it, to be watched and fed,
Till he came back again; and there
I found it when my Son was dead;
And now, God help me for my little wit!
I trail it with me, Sir! he took so much delight
  in it."

If disproportioning the emphasis we read these stanzas so as to make the rhymes percep-

tible, even tri-syllable rhymes could scarcely produce an equal sense of oddity and strangeness, as we feel here in finding *rhymes at all* in sentences so exclusively colloquial. I would further ask whether, but for that visionary state, into which the figure of the woman and the susceptibility of his own genius had placed the poet's imagination,—(a state, which spreads its influence and colouring over all, that co-exists with the exciting cause, and in which

"The simplest, and the most familiar things
  Gain a strange power of spreading awe around
    them,")

I would ask the poet whether he would not have felt an abrupt downfall in these verses from the preceding stanza?

"The ancient spirit is not dead;
  Old times, thought I, are breathing there;
  Proud was I that my country bred
  Such strength, a dignity so fair:
  She begged an alms, like one in poor estate;
  I looked at her again, nor did my pride abate."

It must not be omitted, and is besides worthy of notice, that those stanzas furnish the only fair instance that I have been able to discover in all Mr. Wordsworth's writings, of an actual adoption, or true imitation, of *the real and very language of low and rustic life*, freed from provincialisms.

Thirdly, I deduce the position from all the causes elsewhere assigned, which render metre the proper form of poetry, and poetry imperfect and defective without metre. Metre, therefore, having been connected with poetry most often and by a peculiar fitness, whatever else is combined with metre must, though it be not itself essentially poetic, have nevertheless some property in common with poetry, as an *intermedium* of affinity, a sort, (if I may dare borrow a well-known phrase from technical chemistry), of *mordaunt* between it and the super-added metre. Now poetry, Mr. Wordsworth truly affirms, does always imply passion: which word must be here understood in its most general sense, as an excited state of the feelings and faculties. And as every passion has its proper pulse, so will it likewise have its characteristic modes of expression. But where there exists that degree of genius and talent which entitles a writer to aim at the honours of a poet, the very act of poetic composition itself is, and is allowed to imply and to produce, an unusual state of excitement, which of course justifies and demands a correspondent difference of language, as truly, though not perhaps in as marked a degree, as the excitement of love, fear, rage, or jealousy. The vividness of the descriptions or declamations in Donne or Dryden, is as much and as often derived from the force and fervour of the describer, as from the reflections, forms or incidents, which constitute their subject and materials. The wheels take fire from the mere rapidity of their motion. To what extent, and under what modifications, this may be admitted to act, I shall attempt to define in an after remark on Mr. Wordsworth's reply to this objection, or rather on his objection to this reply, as already anticipated in his preface.

Fourthly, and as intimately connected with this, if not the same argument in a more general form, I adduce the high spiritual instinct of the human being impelling us to seek unity by harmonious adjustment, and thus establishing the principle that *all* the parts of an organized whole must be assimilated to the more *important* and *essential* parts. This and the preceding arguments may be strengthened by the reflection, that the composition of a poem is among the imitative arts; and that imitation, as opposed to copying, consists either in the interfusion of the same throughout the radically different, or of the different throughout a base radically the same. .

Lastly, I appeal to the practice of the best poets, of all countries and in all ages, as authorizing the opinion, (deduced from all the foregoing,) that in every import of the word essential, which would not here involve a mere truism, there may be, is, and ought to be an *essential* difference between the language of prose and of metrical composition.

In Mr. Wordsworth's criticism of Gray's Sonnet, the reader's sympathy with his praise or blame of the different parts is taken for granted rather perhaps too easily. He has not, at least, attempted to win or compel it by argumentative analysis. In my conception at least, the lines rejected as of no value do, with the exception of the two first, differ as much

and as little from the language of common life, as those which he has printed in italics as possessing genuine excellence. Of the five lines thus honourably distinguished, two of them differ from prose even more widely, than the lines which either precede or follow, in the position of the words.

"A different object do these eyes require;
My lonely anguish melts no heart but mine;
And in my breast the imperfect joys expire."

But were it otherwise, what would this prove, but a truth, of which no man ever doubted?—*videlicet*, that there are sentences, which would be equally in their place both in verse and prose. Assuredly it does not prove the point, which alone requires proof; namely, that there are not passages, which would suit the one and not suit the other. The first line of this sonnet is distinguished from the ordinary language of men by the epithet to morning. For we will set aside, at present, the consideration, that the particular word "smiling" is hackneyed, and, as it involves a sort of personification, not quite congruous with the common and material attribute of "*shining*." And, doubtless, this adjunction of epithets for the purpose of additional description, where no particular attention is demanded for the quality of the thing, would be noticed as giving a poetic cast to a man's conversation. Should the sportsman exclaim, "Come boys! the rosy morning calls you up:"—he will be supposed to have some song in his head. But no one suspects this, when he says, "A wet morning shall not confine us to our beds." This then is either a defect in poetry, or it is not. Whoever should decide in the affirmative, I would request him to re-peruse any one poem, of any confessedly great poet from Homer to Milton, or from Æschylus to Shakespeare; and to strike out, (in thought I mean), every instance of this kind. If the number of these fancied erasures did not startle him; or if he continued to deem the work improved by their total omission; he must advance reasons of no ordinary strength and evidence, reasons grounded in the essence of human nature. Otherwise, I should not hesitate to consider him as a man not so much proof against all authority, as dead to it.

The second line,

"And reddening Phœbus lifts his golden fire;—"

has indeed almost as many faults as words. But then it is a bad line, not because the language is distinct from that of prose; but because it conveys incongruous images; because it con- 5 founds the cause and the effect, the real thing with the personified representative of the thing; in short, because it differs from the language of good sense! That the "Phœbus" is hackneyed, and a school-boy image, is an accidental fault, 10 dependent on the age in which the author wrote, and not deduced from the nature of the thing. That it is part of an exploded mythology, is an objection more deeply grounded. Yet when the torch of ancient learning was re- 15 kindled, so cheering were its beams, that our eldest poets, cut off by Christianity from all accredited machinery, and deprived of all acknowledged guardians and symbols of the great objects of nature, were naturally induced 20 to adopt, as a poetic language, those fabulous personages, those forms of the supernatural in nature, which had given them such dear delight in the poems of their great masters. Nay, even at this day what scholar of genial 25 taste will not so far sympathize with them, as to read with pleasure in Petrarch, Chaucer, or Spenser, what he would perhaps condemn as puerile in a modern poet?

I remember no poet, whose writings would 30 safelier stand the test of Mr. Wordsworth's theory, than Spenser. Yet will Mr. Wordsworth say, that the style of the following stanza is either undistinguished from prose, and the language of ordinary life? Or that it is vicious, 35 and that the stanzas are *blots* in THE FAERY QUEEN?

"By this the northern wagoner had set
   His sevenfold teme behind the stedfast starre,
   That was in ocean waves yet never wet,
   But firme is fixt and sendeth light from farre
   To all that in the wild deep wandering arre:
   And chearfull chaunticlere with his note shrill
   Had warned once that Phœbus' fiery carre
   In hast was climbing up the easterne hill,
   Full envious that night so long his roome did fill."

"At last the golden orientall gate
   Of greatest heaven gan to open fayre,
   And Phœbus fresh, as brydegrome to his mate,
   Came dauncing forth, shaking his deawie hayre,

And hurl'd his glist'ring beams through gloomy ayre:
   Which when the wakeful elfe perceived, streightway
   He started up, and did him selfe prepare
   In sun-bright armes and battailous array;
   For with that pagan proud he combat will that day."

On the contrary to how many passages, both in hymn books and in blank verse poems, could I, (were it not invidious), direct the reader's attention, the style of which is most 10 unpoetic, because, and only because, it is the style of prose? He will not suppose me capable of having in my mind such verses, as

"I put my hat upon my head
   And walk'd into the Strand;
   And there I met another man,
   Whose hat was in his hand."

To such specimens it would indeed be a fair and full reply, that these lines are not bad, because they are unpoetic; but because they 20 are empty of all sense and feeling; and that it were an idle attempt to prove that "an ape is not a Newton, when it is self-evident that he is not a man." But the sense shall be good and weighty, the language correct and dignified, 25 the subject interesting and treated with feeling; and yet the style shall, notwithstanding all these merits, be justly blamable as prosaic, and solely because the words and the order of the words would find their appropriate place in 30 prose, but are not suitable to metrical composition. The CIVIL WARS of Daniel is an instructive, and even interesting work; but take the following stanzas, (and from the hundred instances which abound I might probably have 35 selected others far more striking):

"And to the end we may with better ease
   Discern the true discourse, vouchsafe to shew
   What were the times foregoing near to these,
   That these we may with better profit know.
   Tell how the world fell into this disease;
   And how so great distemperature did grow;
   So shall we see with what degrees it came;
   How things at full do soon wax out of frame."

"Ten kings had from the Norman Conqu'ror reign'd
   With intermix'd and variable fate,
   When England to her greatest height attain'd
   Of power, dominion, glory, wealth, and state;
   After it had with much ado sustain'd
   The violence of princes, with debate

For titles and the often mutinies
Of nobles for their ancient liberties."

"For first, the Norman, conqu'ring all by might,
By might was forc'd to keep what he had got;
Mixing our customs and the form of right
With foreign constitutions, he had brought;
Mast'ring the mighty, humbling the poorer wight,
By all severest means that could be wrought;
And, making the succession doubtful, rent
His new-got state, and left it turbulent."

Will it be contended on the one side, that
these lines are mean and senseless? Or on the
other, that they are not prosaic, and for *that*
reason unpoetic? This poet's well-merited epithet is that of the "well-languaged Daniel;" [15]
but likewise, and by the consent of his contemporaries no less than of all succeeding
critics, "the prosaic Daniel." Yet those, who
thus designate this wise and amiable writer
from the frequent incorrespondency of his [20]
diction to his metre in the majority of his
compositions, not only deem them valuable
and interesting on other accounts; but willingly admit, that there are to be found throughout his poems, and especially in his EPISTLES [25]
and in his HYMEN'S TRIUMPH, many and exquisite specimens of that style which, as the
neutral ground of prose and verse, is common
to both. A fine and almost faultless extract,
eminent as for other beauties, so for its per- [30]
fection in this species of diction, may be seen
in Lamb's DRAMATIC SPECIMENS, a work of
various interest from the nature of the selections themselves,—(all from the plays of
Shakespeare's contemporaries),—and deriving [35]
a high additional value from the notes, which
are full of just and original criticism, expressed
with all the freshness of originality.

Among the possible effects of practical adherence to a theory, that aims to identify the [40]
style of prose and verse,—(if it does not indeed
claim for the latter a yet nearer resemblance to
the average style of men in the *vivâ voce* intercourse of real life)—we might anticipate the
following as not the least likely to occur. It [45]
will happen, as I have indeed before observed,
that the metre itself, the sole acknowledged
difference, will occasionally become metre to
the eye only. The existence of *prosaisms*, and
that they detract from the merit of a poem, [50]
must at length be conceded, when a number

of successive lines can be rendered, even to
the most delicate ear, unrecognizable as verse,
or as having even been intended for verse,
by simply transcribing them as prose; when [5]
if the poem be in blank verse, this can be
effected without any alteration, or at most by
merely restoring one or two words to their
proper places, from which they have been
transplanted[1] for no assignable cause or reason [10]
but that of the author's convenience; but if it
be in rhyme, by the mere exchange of the
final word of each line for some other of the
same meaning, equally appropriate, dignified
and euphonic.

[1] As the ingenious gentleman under the influence of the Tragic Muse contrived to dislocate,
"I wish you a good morning, Sir! Thank you, Sir,
and I wish you the same," into two blank-verse
heroics:—

To you a morning good, good Sir! I wish.
You, Sir! I thank: to you the same wish I.

In those parts of Mr. Wordsworth's works which
I have thoroughly studied, I find fewer instances
in which this would be practicable than I have met
in many poems, where an approximation of prose
has been sedulously and on system guarded against.
Indeed excepting the stanzas already quoted from
THE SAILOR'S MOTHER, I can recollect but one instance: that is to say, a short passage of four or five
lines in THE BROTHERS, that model of English pastoral, which I never yet read with unclouded eye.—
"James, pointing to its summit, over which they
had all purposed to return together, informed them
that he would wait for them there. They parted,
and his comrades passed that way some two hours
after, but they did not find him at the appointed
place, a *circumstance of which they took no heed:*
but one of them, going by chance into the house,
which at this time was James's house, learnt *there,*
that nobody had seen him all that day." The only
change which has been made is in the position of the
little word *there* in two instances, the position in
the original being clearly such as is not adopted
in ordinary conversation. The other words printed
in italics were so marked because, though good
and genuine English, they are not the phraseology
of common conversation either in the word put
in apposition, or in the connection by the genitive
pronoun. Men in general would have said, "but
that was a circumstance they paid no attention
to, or took no notice of;" and the language is,
on the theory of the preface, justified only by the
narrator's being the Vicar. Yet if any ear *could*
suspect, that these sentences were ever printed as
metre, on those very words alone could the suspicion have been grounded.

The answer or objection in the preface to the anticipated remark "that metre paves the way to other distinctions," is contained in the following words. "The distinction of rhyme and metre is regular and uniform, and not, like that produced by (what is usually called) poetic diction, arbitrary, and subject to infinite caprices, upon which no calculation whatever can be made. In the one case the reader is utterly at the mercy of the poet respecting what imagery or diction he may choose to connect with the passion." But is this a *poet*, of whom a poet is speaking? No surely! rather of a fool or madman: or at best of a vain or ignorant phantast! And might not brains so wild and so deficient make just the same havoc with rhymes and metres, as they are supposed to effect with modes and figures of speech? How is the reader at the mercy of such men? If he continue to read their nonsense, is it not his own fault? The ultimate end of criticism is much more to establish the principles of writing, than to furnish rules how to pass judgment on what has been written by others; if indeed it were possible that the two could be separated. But if it be asked, by what principles the poet is to regulate his own style, if he do not adhere closely to the sort and order of words which he hears in the market, wake, high-road, or plough-field? I reply; by principles, the ignorance or neglect of which would convict him of being no poet, but a silly or presumptuous usurper of the name. By the principles of grammar, logic, psychology. In one word by such a knowledge of the facts, material and spiritual, that most appertain to his art, as, if it have been governed and applied by good sense, and rendered instinctive by habit, becomes the representative and reward of our past conscious reasonings, insights, and conclusions, and acquires the name of Taste. By what *rule* that does not leave the reader at the poet's mercy, and the poet at his own, is the latter to distinguish between the language suitable to suppressed, and the language, which is characteristic of indulged, anger? Or between that of rage and that of jealousy? Is it obtained by wandering about in search of angry or jealous people in uncultivated society, in order to copy their words? Or not far rather by the power of imagination proceeding upon

the *all in each* of human nature? By meditation, rather than by observation? And by the latter in consequence only of the former? As eyes, for which the former has pre-determined their field of vision, and to which, as to *its* organ, it communicates a microscopic power? There is not, I firmly believe, a man now living, who has, from his own inward experience, a clearer intuition, than Mr. Wordsworth himself, that the last mentioned are the true sources of *genial* discrimination. Through the same process and by the same creative agency will the poet distinguish the degree and kind of the excitement produced by the very act of poetic composition. As intuitively will he know, what differences of style it at once inspires and justifies; what intermixture of conscious volition is natural to that state; and in what instances such figures and colours of speech degenerate into mere creatures of an arbitrary purpose, cold technical artifices of ornament or connection. For, even as truth is its own light and evidence, discovering at once itself and falsehood, so is it the prerogative of poetic genius to distinguish by parental instinct its proper offspring from the changelings, which the gnomes of vanity or the fairies of fashion may have laid in its cradle or called by its names. Could a rule be given from without, poetry would cease to be poetry, and sink into a mechanical art. It would be μόρφωσις, not ποίησις.[1] The rules of the Imagination are themselves the very powers of growth and production. The words to which they are reducible, present only the outlines and external appearance of the fruit. A deceptive counterfeit of the superficial form and colours may be elaborated; but the marble peach feels cold and heavy, and children only put it to their mouths. We find no difficulty in admitting as excellent, and the legitimate language of poetic fervour self-impassioned, Donne's apostrophe to the Sun in the second stanza of his PROGRESS OF THE SOUL.

"Thee, eye of heaven! this great Soul envies not;
By thy male force is all, we have, begot.
In the first East thou now beginn'st to shine,
Suck'st early balm and island spices there,
And wilt anon in thy loose-rein'd career
At Tagus, Po, Seine, Thames, and Danow dine,
And see at night this western world of mine:

[1] "A mere shaping, not a creation."

Yet hast thou not more nations seen than she,
Who before thee one day began to be,
And, thy frail light being quench'd, shall long,
    long outlive thee."

Or the next stanza but one:

"Great Destiny, the commissary of God,
That hast mark'd out a path and period
For every thing! Who, where we offspring took,
Our ways and ends see'st at one instant: thou
Knot of all causes! Thou, whose changeless brow
Ne'er smiles nor frowns! O! vouchsafe thou to
    look,
And shew my story in thy eternal book," etc.

As little difficulty do we find in excluding
from the honours of unaffected warmth and
elevation the madness prepense of pseudo-
poesy, or the startling hysteric of weakness
over-exerting itself, which bursts on the unprepared reader in sundry odes and apostro-
phes to abstract terms. Such are the Odes to
Jealousy, to Hope, to Oblivion, and the like, 10
in Dodsley's collection and the magazines of
that day, which seldom fail to remind me of
an Oxford copy of verses on the two SUTTONS,
commencing with

    "Inoculation, heavenly maid! descend!"

It is not to be denied that men of undoubted 15
talents, and even poets of true, though not of
first-rate, genius, have from a mistaken theory
deluded both themselves and others in the
opposite extreme. I once read to a company
of sensible and well-educated women the in- 20
troductory period of Cowley's preface to his
"Pindaric Odes," written in imitation of the
style and manner of the odes of Pindar. "If,"
(says Cowley), "a man should undertake to
translate Pindar, word for word, it would be 25
thought that one madman had translated another: as may appear, when he, that understands
not the original, reads the verbal traduction of
him into Latin prose, than which nothing
seems more raving." I then proceeded with 30
his own free version of the second Olympic,
composed for the charitable purpose of *ration-
alizing* the Theban Eagle.

"Queen of all harmonious things,
  Dancing words and speaking strings,
What god, what hero, wilt thou sing?
What happy man to equal glories bring? 35
Begin, begin thy noble choice,
And let the hills around reflect the image of thy
  voice

Pisa does to Jove belong,
Jove and Pisa claim thy song.
The fair first-fruits of war, th' Olympic games,
Alcides, offer'd up to Jove;
Alcides, too, thy strings may move,
But, oh! what man to join with these can worthy
    prove?
Join Theron boldly to their sacred names;
Theron the next honour claims;
Theron to no man gives place,
Is first in Pisa's and in Virtue's race;
Theron there, and he alone,
Ev'n his own swift forefathers has outgone."

One of the company exclaimed, with the
full assent of the rest, that if the original were
madder than this, it must be incurably mad.
I then translated the ode from the Greek, and 5
as nearly as possible, word for word; and the
impression was, that in the general movement
of the periods, in the form of the connections
and transitions, and in the sober majesty of
lofty sense, it appeared to them to approach 10
more nearly, than any other poetry they had
heard, to the style of our Bible, in the prophetic
books. The first strophe will suffice as a specimen:

"Ye harp-controlling hymns! (or) ye hymns the
    sovereigns of harps!
What God? what Hero?
What Man shall we celebrate?
Truly Pisa indeed is of Jove,
But the Olympiad (or the Olympic games) did
    Hercules establish,
The first-fruits of the spoils of war.
But Theron for the four-horsed car,
That bore victory to him,
It behoves us now to voice aloud:
The Just, the Hospitable,
The Bulwark of Agrigentum,
Of renowned fathers
The Flower, even him
Who preserves his native city erect and safe."

But are such rhetorical caprices condemnable only for their deviation from the language
of real life? and are they by no other means to
be precluded, but by the rejection of all distinctions between prose and verse, save that
of metre? Surely good sense, and a moderate
insight into the constitution of the human
mind, would be amply sufficient to prove, that
such language and such combinations are the
native product neither of the fancy nor of the
imagination; that their operation consists in
the excitement of surprise by the juxta-position

and *apparent* reconciliation of widely different or incompatible things. As when, for instance, the hills are made to reflect the image of a *voice*. Surely, no unusual taste is requisite to see clearly, that this compulsory juxta-position is not produced by the presentation of impressive or delightful forms to the inward vision, nor by any sympathy with the modifying powers with which the genius of the poet had united and inspirited all the objects of his thought; that it is therefore a species of *wit*, a pure work of the *will*, and implies a leisure and self-possession both of thought and of feeling, incompatible with the steady fervour of a mind possessed and filled with the grandeur of its subject. To sum up the whole in one sentence. When a poem, or a part of a poem, shall be adduced, which is evidently vicious in the figures and centexture of its style, yet for the condemnation of which no reason can be assigned, except that it differs from the style in which men actually converse, then, and not till then, can I hold this theory to be either plausible, or practicable, or capable of furnishing either rule, guidance, or precaution, that might not, more easily and more safely, as well as more naturally, have been deduced in the author's own mind from considerations of grammar, logic, and the truth and nature of things, confirmed by the authority of works, whose fame is not of one country nor of one age.

CHAPTER XIX

Continuation—Concerning the real object which, it is probable, Mr. Wordsworth had before him in his critical preface—Elucidation and application of this.

It might appear from some passages in the former part of Mr. Wordsworth's preface, that he meant to confine his theory of style, and the necessity of a close accordance with the actual language of men, to those particular subjects from low and rustic life, which by way of experiment he had purposed to naturalize as a new species in our English poetry. But from the train of argument that follows; from the reference to Milton; and from the spirit of his critique on Gray's sonnet; those sentences appear to have been rather courtesies

of modesty, than actual limitations of his system. Yet so groundless does this system appear on a close examination; and so strange and overwhelming in its consequences, that I cannot, and I do not, believe that the poet did ever himself adopt it in the unqualified sense, in which his expressions have been understood by others, and which, indeed, according to all the common laws of interpretation they seem to bear. What then did he mean? I apprehend, that in the clear perception, not unaccompanied with disgust or contempt, of the gaudy affectations of a style which passed current with too many for poetic diction, (though in truth it had as little pretensions to poetry, as to logic or common sense,) he narrowed his view for the time; and feeling a justifiable preference for the language of nature and of good sense, even in its humblest and least ornamented forms, he suffered himself to express, in terms at once too large and too exclusive, his predilection for a style the most remote possible from the false and showy splendour which he wished to explode. It is possible, that this predilection, at first merely comparative, deviated for a time into direct partiality. But the real object which he had in view, was, I doubt not, a species of excellence which had been long before most happily characterized by the judicious and amiable Garve, whose works are so justly beloved and esteemed by the Germans, in his remarks on Gellert, from which the following is literally translated. "The talent, that is required in order to make excellent verses, is perhaps greater than the philosopher is ready to admit, or would find it in his power to acquire: the talent to seek only the apt expression of the thought, and yet to find at the same time with it the rhyme and the metre. Gellert possessed this happy gift, if ever any one of our poets possessed it; and nothing perhaps contributed more to the great and universal impression which his fables made on their first publication, or conduces more to their continued popularity. It was a strange and curious phænomenon, and such as in Germany had been previously unheard of, to read verses in which everything was expressed just as one would wish to talk, and yet all dignified, attractive, and interesting; and all at the same time perfectly correct as to the measure of the syllables and the rhyme. It is certain, that poetry when it has attained this excellence makes a far greater impression than prose. So much so indeed, that even the grati-fication which the very rhymes afford, be- 5 comes then no longer a contemptible or trifling gratification."

However novel this phænomenon may have been in Germany at the time of Gellert, it is by no means new, nor yet of recent existence 10 in our language. Spite of the licentiousness with which Spenser occasionally compels the orthography of his words into a subservience to his rhymes, the whole FAERY QUEEN is an almost continued instance of this beauty. Wal- 15 ler's song GO, LOVELY ROSE, is doubtless familiar to most of my readers; but if I had happened to have had by me the Poems of Cotton, more but far less deservedly celebrated as the author of the VIRGIL TRAVESTIED, I 20 should have indulged myself, and I think have gratified many, who are not acquainted with his serious works, by selecting some admirable specimens of this style. There are not a few poems in that volume, replete with every ex- 25 cellence of thought, image, and passion, which we expect or desire in the poetry of the milder muse; and yet so worded, that the reader sees no one reason either in the selection or the order of the words, why he might not have 30 said the very same in an appropriate conversa-tion, and cannot conceive how indeed he could have expressed such thoughts otherwise with-out loss or injury to his meaning.

But in truth our language is, and from the 35 first dawn of poetry ever has been, particularly rich in compositions distinguished by this excellence. The final e, which is now mute, in Chaucer's age was either sounded or dropt indifferently. We ourselves still use either "be- 40 loved" or "belov'd" according as the rhyme, or measure, or the purpose of more or less solemnity may require. Let the reader then only adopt the pronunciation of the poet and of the court, at which he lived, both with 45 respect to the final e and to the accentuation of the last syllable; I would then venture to ask, what even in the colloquial language of elegant and unaffected women, (who are the peculiar mistresses of "pure English and undefiled,") 50 what could we hear more natural, or seemingly

more unstudied, than the following stanzas from Chaucer's TROILUS AND CRESEIDE.

"And after this forth to the gate he wente,
Ther as Creseide out rode a ful gode paas,
And up and doun there made he many' a wente,
And to himselfe ful oft he said, Alas!
Fro hennis rode my blisse and my solas:
As wouldè blisful God now for his joie,
I might her sene agen come in to Troie!
    And to the yondir hil I gan her gide,
Alas! and there I toke of her my leve:
And yond I saw her to her fathir ride;
For sorow of whiche mine hert shall to-cleve;
And hithir home I came whan it was eve,
And here I dwel, out-cast from allè joie,
And shal, til I maie sene her efte in Troie.
    "And of himselfe imaginid he ofte
To ben defaitid, pale and woxin lesse
Than he was wonte, and that men saidin softe,
What may it be? who can the sothè gesse,
Why Troilus hath al this hevinesse?
And al this n' as but his melancolie,
That he had of himselfe suche fantasie.
    Anothir time imaginin he would
That every wight, that past him by the wey,
Had of him routhe, and that thei saien should,
I am right sory, Troilus wol dey!
And thus he drove a daie yet forth or twey,
As ye have herde: suche life gan he to lede
As he that stode betwixin hope and drede:
    For which him likid in his songis shewe
Th' encheson of his wo as he best might,
And made a songe of wordis but a fewe,
Somwhat his woful hertè for to light,
And whan he was from every mann'is sight
With softé voice he of his lady dere,
That absent was, gan sing as ye may here:

* * *

    This song, when he thus songin had, ful sone
He fil agen into his sighis olde:
And every night, as was his wonte to done;
He stodè the bright moonè to beholde
And all his sorowe to the moone he tolde,
And said: I wis, whan thou art hornid newe,
I shall be glad, if al the world be trewe!"

Another exquisite master of this species of style, where the scholar and the poet supplies the material, but the perfect well-bred gentle-man the expressions and the arrangement, is George Herbert. . . .

CHAPTER XX

The former subject continued—The neutral style, or that common to Prose and Poetry, exemplified by specimens from Chaucer, Herbert, and others.

. . . The words themselves in the foregoing extracts [from some of Wordsworth's poems], are, no doubt, sufficiently common for the greater part.—But in what poem are they not so, if we except a few misadventurous attempts to translate the arts and sciences into verse? In The Excursion the number of polysyllabic (or what the common people call, *dictionary*) words is more than usually great. And so must it needs be, in proportion to the number and variety of an author's conceptions, and his solicitude to express them with precision.—But are those words *in those places* commonly employed in real life to express the same thought or outward thing? Are they the style used in the ordinary intercourse of spoken words? No! nor are the modes of connections; and still less the breaks and transitions. Would any but a poet—at least could any one without being conscious that he had expressed himself with noticeable vivacity—have described a bird singing loud by, "The thrush is *busy* in the wood?"—or have spoken of boys with a string of club-moss round their rusty hats, as the boys *"with their green coronal?"*—or have translated a beautiful May-day into *"Both earth and sky keep jubilee?"*—or have brought all the different marks and circumstances of a sea-loch before the mind, as the actions of a living and acting power? Or have represented the reflection of the sky in the water, as *"That uncertain heaven received into the bosom of the steady lake?"* Even the grammatical construction is not unfrequently peculiar; as "The wind, the tempest roaring high, the tumult of a tropic sky, might well be *dangerous food to him*, a youth to whom was given, &c." There is a peculiarity in the frequent use of the ἀσυνάρτητον (that is, the omission of the connective particle before the last of several words, or several sentences used grammatically as single words, all being in the same case and governing or governed by the same verb) and not less in the construction of words by apposition (*"to him, a youth"*). In short, were there excluded from Mr. Wordsworth's poetic compositions all, that a literal adherence to the theory of his preface *would* exclude, two thirds at least of the marked beauties of his poetry must be erased. For a far greater number of lines would be sacrificed than in any other recent poet; because the pleasure received from Wordsworth's poems being less

derived either from excitement of curiosity or the rapid flow of narration, the *striking* passages form a larger proportion of their value. I do not adduce it as a fair criterion of comparative excellence, nor do I even think it such; but merely as matter of fact. I affirm, that from no contemporary writer could so many lines be quoted, without reference to the poem in which they are found, for their own independent weight or beauty. From the sphere of my own experience I can bring to my recollection three persons of no every-day powers and acquirements, who had read the poems of others with more and more unallayed pleasure, and had thought more highly of their authors, as poets; who yet have confessed to me, that from no modern work had so many passages started up anew in their minds at different times, and as different occasions had awakened a meditative mood.

CHAPTER XXII

The characteristic defects of Wordsworth's poetry, with the principles from which the judgment, that they are defects, is deduced—Their proportion to the beauties—For the greatest part characteristic of his theory only.

If Mr. Wordsworth have set forth principles of poetry which his arguments are insufficient to support, let him and those who have adopted his sentiments be set right by the confutation of those arguments, and by the substitution of more philosophical principles. And still let the due credit be given to the portion and importance of the truths, which are blended with his theory; truths, the too exclusive attention to which had occasioned its errors, by tempting him to carry those truths beyond their proper limits. If his mistaken theory have at all influenced his poetic compositions, let the effects be pointed out, and the instances given. But let it likewise be shown, how far the influence has acted; whether diffusively, or only by starts; whether the number and importance of the poems and passages thus infected be great or trifling compared with the sound portion; and, lastly, whether they are inwoven into the texture of his works, or are loose and separable. The result of such a trial would evince beyond a doubt, what it is high time to announce decisively and aloud, that the supposed characteristics of Mr. Wordsworth's poetry, whether admired or reprobated; whether they are simplicity or simpleness; faithful adherence to essential nature, or wilful selections from human nature of its meanest forms and under the least attractive associations; are as little the real characteristics of his poetry at large, as of his genius and the constitution of his 10 mind.

In a comparatively small number of poems he chose to try an experiment; and this experiment we will suppose to have failed. Yet even in these poems it is impossible not to perceive 15 that the natural tendency of the poet's mind is to great objects and elevated conceptions. The poem entitled FIDELITY is for the greater part written in language, as unraised and naked as any perhaps in the two volumes. Yet take 20 the following stanza and compare it with the preceding stanzas of the same poem.

> "There sometimes doth a leaping fish
> Send through the tarn a lonely cheer;
> The crags repeat the raven's croak,
> In symphony austere;
> Thither the rainbow comes—the cloud—
> And mists that spread the flying shroud;
> And sun-beams; and the sounding blast,
> That, if it could, would hurry past;
> But that enormous barrier holds it fast."

Or compare the four last lines of the concluding stanza with the former half.

> "Yes, proof was plain that, since the day
> On which the Traveller thus had died,
> The Dog had watched about the spot,
> Or by his Master's side:
> *How nourish'd here through such long time*
> *He knows, who gave that love sublime,—*
> *And gave that strength of feeling, great*
> *Above all human estimate!"*

Can any candid and intelligent mind hesitate in determining, which of these best represents the tendency and native character of the poet's genius? Will he not decide that the one was 45 written because the poet *would* so write, and the other because he could not so entirely repress the force and grandeur of his mind, but that he must in some part or other of every composition write otherwise? In short, that 50 his only disease is the being out of his element;

like the swan, that, having amused himself, for a while, with crushing the weeds on the river's bank, soon returns to his own majestic movements on its reflecting and sustaining 5 surface. Let it be observed that I am here supposing the imagined judge, to whom I appeal, to have already decided against the poet's theory, as far as it is different from the principles of the art, generally acknowledged. 10

I cannot here enter into a detailed examination of Mr. Wordsworth's works; but I will attempt to give the main results of my own judgment, after an acquaintance of many years, and repeated perusals. And though, to appreciate the defects of a great mind it is necessary to understand previously its characteristic excellences, yet I have already expressed myself with sufficient fulness, to preclude most of the ill effects that might arise from my pursuing a contrary arrangement. I will therefore 20 commence with what I deem the prominent *defects* of his poems hitherto published.

The first characteristic, though only occasional defect, which I appear to myself to find 25 in these poems is the *inconstancy* of the style. Under this name I refer to the sudden and unprepared transitions from lines or sentences of peculiar felicity—(at all events striking and original)—to a style, not only unimpassioned 30 but undistinguished. He sinks too often and too abruptly to that style, which I should place in the second division of language, dividing it into the three species; first, that which is peculiar to poetry; second, that which is only 35 proper in prose; and third, the neutral or common to both. There have been works, such as Cowley's Essay on Cromwell, in which prose and verse are intermixed (not as in the Consolation of Boetius, or the ARGENIS of Barclay, 40 by the insertion of poems supposed to have been spoken or composed on occasions previously related in prose, but) the poet passing from one to the other, as the nature of the thoughts or his own feelings dictated. Yet this 45 mode of composition does not satisfy a cultivated taste. There is something unpleasant in the being thus obliged to alternate states of feeling so dissimilar, and this too in a species of writing, the pleasure from which is in part 50 derived from the preparation and previous expectation of the reader. A portion of that awkwardness is felt which hangs upon the introduction of songs in our modern comic operas; and to prevent which the judicious Metastasio (as to whose exquisite taste there can be no hesitation, whatever doubts may be entertained as to his poetic genius) uniformly placed the *aria* at the end of the scene, at the same time that he almost always raises and impassions the style of the recitative immediately preceding. Even in real life, the difference is great and evident between words used as the arbitrary marks of thought, our smooth market-coin of intercourse, with the image and superscription worn out by currency; and those which convey pictures either borrowed from one outward object to enliven and particularize some other; or used allegorically to body forth the inward state of the person speaking; or such as are at least the exponents of his peculiar turn and unusual extent of faculty. So much so indeed, that in the social circles of private life we often find a striking use of the latter put a stop to the general flow of conversation, and by the excitement arising from concentred attention produce a sort of damp and interruption for some minutes after. But in the perusal of works of literary art, we prepare ourselves for such language; and the business of the writer, like that of a painter whose subject requires unusual splendour and prominence, is so to raise the lower and neutral tints, that what in a different style would be the commanding colours, are here used as the means of that gentle *degradation* requisite in order to produce the effect of a whole. Where this is not achieved in a poem, the metre merely reminds the reader of his claims in order to disappoint them; and where this defect occurs frequently, his feelings are alternately startled by anticlimax and hyperclimax.

I refer the reader to the exquisite stanzas cited for another purpose from THE BLIND HIGHLAND BOY; and then annex, as being in my opinion instances of this *disharmony* in style, the two following:

"And one, the rarest, was a shell,
  Which he, poor child, had studied well:
  The shell of a green turtle, thin
  And hollow;—you might sit therein,
    It was so wide, and deep."

"Our Highland Boy oft visited
  The house which held this prize; and, led
  By choice or chance, did thither come
  One day, when no one was at home,
    And found the door unbarred."

Or page 172, vol. I.

" 'Tis gone forgotten, *let me do
  My best.* There was a smile or two—
  I can remember them, I see
  The smiles worth all the world to me.
  Dear Baby! I must lay thee down:
  Thou troublest me with strange alarms;
  Smiles hast thou, sweet ones of thine own;
  I cannot keep thee in my arms;
  For they confound me: *as it is,*
  I have forgot those smiles of his!"

Or page 269, vol. I.

"Thou hast a nest, for thy love and thy rest
  And though little troubled with sloth
  Drunken lark! thou would'st be loth
  To be such a traveller as I.
    Happy, happy liver!
  *With a soul as strong as a mountain river
  Pouring out praise to th'Almighty giver,*
  Joy and jollity be with us both!
  Hearing thee or else some other,
    As merry a brother
  I on the earth will go plodding on
  By myself cheerfully till the day is done."

The incongruity, which I appear to find in this passage, is that of the two noble lines in italics with the preceding and following. So vol. II, page 30.

"Close by a Pond, upon the further side,
  He stood alone; a minute's space I guess,
  I watch'd him, he continuing motionless:
  To the Pool's further margin then I drew;
  He being all the while before me full in view."

Compare this with the repetition of the same image, in the next stanza but two.

"And, still as I drew near with gentle pace,
  Beside the little pond or moorish flood
  Motionless as a Cloud the Old Man stood,
  That heareth not the loud winds when they call;
  And moveth altogether, if it move at all."

Or lastly, the second of the three following stanzas, compared both with the first and the third.

"My former thoughts returned; the fear that kills,
  And hope that is unwilling to be fed;
  Cold, pain, and labour, and all fleshly ills;
  And mighty Poets in their misery dead.

But now, perplex'd by what the Old Man had
    said,
My question eagerly did I renew,
'How is it that you live, and what is it you do?'

He with a smile did then his words repeat;
And said, that gathering Leeches far and wide
He travell'd; stirring thus about his feet
The waters of the Ponds where they abide.
'Once I could meet with them on every side;
'But they have dwindled long by slow decay;
'Yet still I persevere, and find them where I may.'

While he was talking thus, the lonely place,
The Old Man's shape, and speech, all troubled me
In my mind's eye I seemed to see him pace
About the weary moors continually,
Wandering about alone and silently."

Indeed this fine poem is especially characteristic of the author. There is scarce a defect or
excellence in his writings of which it would
not present a specimen. But it would be unjust
not to repeat that this defect is only occasional.
From a careful reperusal of the two volumes
of poems, I doubt whether the objectionable
passages would amount in the whole to one
hundred lines; not the eighth part of the number of pages. In THE EXCURSION the feeling
of incongruity is seldom excited by the diction
of any passage considered in itself, but by the
sudden superiority of some other passage
forming the context.

The second defect I can generalize with
tolerable accuracy, if the reader will pardon
an uncouth and new-coined word. There is,
I should say, not seldom a *matter-of-factness*
in certain poems. This may be divided into,
first, a laborious minuteness and fidelity in the
representation of objects, and their positions,
as they appeared to the poet himself; secondly,
the insertion of accidental circumstances, in
order to the full explanation of his living characters, their dispositions and actions; which
circumstances might be necessary to establish
the probability of a statement in real life, where
nothing is taken for granted by the hearer; but
appear superfluous in poetry, where the reader
is willing to believe for his own sake. To this
accidentality I object, as contravening the essence of poetry, which Aristotle pronounces to
be σπουδαιότατον καὶ φιλοσοφώτατον γένος,[1]

[1] "A most serious and philosophic kind of activity."

the most intense, weighty and philosophical
product of human art; adding, as the reason,
that it is the most catholic and abstract. The
following passage from Davenant's prefatory
letter to Hobbes well expresses this truth.
"When I considered the actions which I meant
to describe, (those inferring the persons), I was
again persuaded rather to choose those of a
former age, than the present; and in a century
so far removed, as might preserve me from
their improper examinations, who know not
the requisites of a poem, nor how much pleasure they lose, (and even the pleasures of heroic
poesy are not unprofitable), who take away
the liberty of a poet, and fetter his feet in the
shackles of an historian. For why should a
poet doubt in story to mend the intrigues of
fortune by more delightful conveyances of
probable fictions, because austere historians
have entered into bond to truth? An obligation, which were in poets as foolish and unnecessary, as is the bondage of false martyrs,
who live in chains for a mistaken opinion.
*But by this I would imply, that truth, narrative
and past, is the idol of historians, (who worship
a dead thing), and truth operative, and by
effects continually alive, is the mistress of poets,
who hath not her existence in matter, but in
reason.*"

For this minute accuracy in the painting
of local imagery, the lines in THE EXCURSION,
pp. 96, 97, and 98, may be taken, if not as a
striking instance, yet as an illustration of my
meaning. It must be some strong motive—
(as, for instance, that the description was necessary to the intelligibility of the tale)—which
could induce me to describe in a number of
verses what a draughtsman could present to
the eye with incomparably greater satisfaction
by half a dozen strokes of his pencil, or the
painter with as many touches of his brush.
Such descriptions too often occasion in the
mind of a reader, who is determined to understand his author, a feeling of labour, not very
dissimilar to that, with which he would construct a diagram, line by line, for a long geo-
metrical proposition. It seems to be like taking
the pieces of a dissected map out of its box.
We first look at one part, and then at another,
then join and dove-tail them; and when the
successive acts of attention have been com-

pleted, there is a retrogressive effort of mind to behold it as a whole. The poet should paint to the imagination, not to the fancy; and I know no happier case to exemplify the distinction between these two faculties. Masterpieces of the former mode of poetic painting abound in the writings of Milton, for example:

"The fig-tree; not that kind for fruit renown'd,
But such as at this day, to Indians known,
In Malabar or Decan spreads her arms
Branching so broad and long, that in the ground
The bended twigs take root, *and daughters grow
About the mother tree, a pillar'd shade
High over-arch'd and* ECHOING WALKS BETWEEN:
*There oft the Indian herdsman, shunning heat,
Shelters in cool, and tends his pasturing herds
At hoop-holes cut through thickest shade:*"

This is creation rather than painting, or if painting, yet such, and with such co-presence of the whole picture flashed at once upon the eye, as the sun paints in a camera obscura. But the poet must likewise understand and command what Bacon calls the *vestigia communia* of the senses, the latency of all in each, and more especially as by a magical *penna duplex*, the excitement of vision by sound and the exponents of sound. Thus, "The echoing walks between," may be almost said to reverse the fable in tradition of the head of Memnon, in the Egyptian statue. Such may be deservedly entitled the *creative words* in the world of imagination.

The second division respects an apparent minute adherence to *matter-of-fact* in character and incidents; *a biographical* attention to probability, and an *anxiety* of explanation and retrospect. Under this head I shall deliver, with no feigned diffidence, the results of my best reflection on the great point of controversy between Mr. Wordsworth and his objectors; namely, on *the choice of his characters.* I have already declared, and, I trust justified, my utter dissent from the mode of argument which his critics have hitherto employed. To *their* question,—"Why did you choose such a character, or a character from such a rank of life?"—the poet might in my opinion fairly retort: why with the conception of my character did you make wilful choice of mean or ludicrous associations not furnished by me,

but supplied from your own sickly and fastidious feelings? How was it, indeed, probable, that such arguments could have any weight with an author, whose plan, whose guiding principle, and main object it was to attack and subdue that state of association, which leads us to place the chief value on those things on which man differs from man, and to forget or disregard the high dignities, which belong to Human Nature, the sense and the feeling, which may be, and ought to be, found in all ranks? The feelings with which, as Christians, we contemplate a mixed congregation rising or kneeling before their common Maker, Mr. Wordsworth would have us entertain at all times, as men, and as readers; and by the excitement of this lofty, yet prideless impartiality in poetry, he might hope to have encouraged its continuance in real life. The praise of good men be his! In real life, and, I trust, even in my imagination, I honour a virtuous and wise man, without reference to the presence or absence of artificial advantages. Whether in the person of an armed baron, a laurelled bard, or of an old Pedlar, or still older Leech-gatherer, the same qualities of head and heart must claim the same reverence. And even in poetry I am not conscious, that I have ever suffered my feelings to be disturbed or offended by any thoughts or images, which the poet himself has not presented.

But yet I object, nevertheless, and for the following reasons. First, because the object in view, as an *immediate* object, belongs to the moral philosopher, and would be pursued, not only more appropriately, but in my opinion with far greater probability of success, in sermons or moral essays, than in an elevated poem. It seems, indeed, to destroy the main fundamental distinction, not only between a poem and prose, but even between philosophy and works of fiction, inasmuch as it proposes *truth* for its immediate object, instead of *pleasure.* Now till the blessed time shall come, when truth itself shall be pleasure, and both shall be so united, as to be distinguishable in words only, not in feeling, it will remain the poet's office to proceed upon that state of association, which actually exists as general; instead of attempting first to make it what it ought to be, and then to let the pleasure follow. But here is unfortunately a small *hysteron-proteron*.[1] For the communication of pleasure is the introductory means by which alone the poet must expect to moralize his readers. Secondly: though I were to admit, for a moment, *this* argument to be groundless: yet how is the moral effect to be produced, by merely attaching the name of some low profession to powers which are *least* likely, and to qualities which are assuredly not *more* likely, to be found in it? The Poet, speaking in his own person, may at once delight and improve us by sentiments, which teach us the independence of goodness, of wisdom, and even of genius, on the favours of fortune. And having made a due reverence before the throne of Antonine, he may bow with equal awe before Epictetus among his fellow-slaves—

—————————————"and rejoice
In the plain presence of his dignity."

Who is not at once delighted and improved, when the Poet Wordsworth himself exclaims,

"Oh! many are the Poets that are sown
　By Nature; men endowed with highest gifts
　The vision and the faculty divine,
　Yet wanting the accomplishment of verse,
　Nor having e'er, as life advanced, been led
　By circumstance to take unto the height
　The measure of themselves, these favoured Be
　　ings,
　All but a scattered few, live out their time,
　Husbanding that which they possess within,
　And go to the grave, unthought of. Strongest
　　minds
　Are often those of whom the noisy world
　Hears least."

To use a colloquial phrase, such sentiments, in such language, do one's heart good; though I for my part, have not the fullest faith in the truth of the observation. On the contrary I believe the instances to be exceedingly rare; and should feel almost as strong an objection to introduce such a character in a poetic fiction, as a pair of black swans on a lake, in a fancy landscape. When I think how many, and how much better books than Homer, or even than Herodotus, Pindar or Æschylus, could have read, are in the power of almost every man, in a country where almost every man is in-

structed to read and write; and how restless, how difficultly hidden, the powers of genius are; and yet find even in situations the most favourable, according to Mr. Wordsworth, for the formation of a pure and poetic language; in situations which ensure familiarity with the grandest objects of the imagination; but one Burns, among the shepherds of Scotland, and not a single poet of humble life among those of English lakes and mountains; I conclude, that Poetic Genius is not only a very delicate but a very rare plant.

But be this as it may, the feelings with which,

"I think of Chatterton, the marvellous Boy,
　The sleepless Soul, that perished in his pride;
　Of Burns, who walk'd in glory and in joy
　Behind his plough, upon the mountain-side"—

are widely different from those with which I should read a *poem*, where the author, having occasion for the character of a poet and a philosopher in the fable of his narration, had chosen to make him a chimney-sweeper; and then, in order to remove all doubts on the subject, had *invented* an account of his birth, parentage and education, with all the strange and fortunate accidents which had concurred in making him at once poet, philosopher, and sweep! Nothing, but biography, can justify this. If it be admissible even in a novel, it must be one in the manner of De Foe's, that were meant to pass for histories, not in the manner of Fielding's: in THE LIFE OF MOLL FLANDERS, or COLONEL JACK, not in a TOM JONES, or even a JOSEPH ANDREWS. Much less then can it be legitimately introduced in a poem, the characters of which, amid the strongest individualization, must still remain representative. The precepts of Horace, on this point, are grounded on the nature both of poetry and of the human mind. They are not more peremptory, than wise and prudent. For in the first place a deviation from them perplexes the reader's feelings, and all the circumstances which are feigned in order to make such accidents less improbable, divide and disquiet his faith, rather than aid and support it. Spite of all attempts, the fiction will appear, and unfortunately not as fictitious but as false. The reader not only knows, that the sentiments and language are the poet's own, and his own too in his artificial

---

[1] "The latter first"; i.e., here the cart has been put before the horse.

character, as poet; but by the fruitless endeavours to make him think the contrary, he is not even suffered to forget it. The effect is similar to that produced by an Epic Poet, when the fable and the characters are *derived* from Scripture history, as in THE MESSIAH OF KLOPSTOCK, or in CUMBERLAND'S CALVARY; and not merely *suggested* by it as in the PARADISE LOST of Milton. That illusion, contra-distinguished from delusion, that negative faith, which simply permits the images presented to work by their own force, without either denial or affirmation of their real existence by the judgment, is rendered impossible by their immediate neighbourhood to words and facts of known and absolute truth. A faith, which transcends even historic belief, must absolutely *put out* this mere poetic *analogon* of faith, as the summer sun is said to extinguish our household fires, when it shines full upon them. What would otherwise have been yielded to as pleasing fiction, is repelled as revolting falsehood. The effect produced in this latter case by the solemn belief of the reader, is in a less degree brought about in the instances, to which I have been objecting, by the baffled attempts of the author to *make* him believe.

Add to all the foregoing the seeming uselessness both of the project and of the anecdotes from which it is to derive support. Is there one word, for instance, attributed to the pedlar in THE EXCURSION, characteristic of a *Pedlar?* One sentiment, that might not more plausibly, even without the aid of any previous explanation, have proceeded from any wise and beneficent old man, of a rank or profession in which the language of learning and refinement are natural and to be expected? Need the rank have been at all particularized, where nothing follows which the knowledge of that rank is to explain or illustrate? When on the contrary this information renders the man's language, feelings, sentiments, and information a riddle, which must itself be solved by episodes of anecdote? Finally when this, and this alone, could have induced a genuine Poet to inweave in a poem of the loftiest style, and on subjects the loftiest and of most universal interest, such minute matters of fact, (not unlike those furnished for the obituary of a magazine by the friends of some obscure "ornament of society lately deceased" in some obscure town,) as

"Among the hills of Athol he was born:
There, on a small hereditary Farm,
An unproductive slip of rugged ground,
His Father dwelt; and died in poverty;
While He, whose lowly fortune I retrace,
The youngest of three sons, was yet a babe,
A little One—unconscious of their loss.
But ere he had outgrown his infant days
His widowed Mother, for a second Mate,
Espoused the teacher of the Village School;
Who on her offspring zealously bestowed
Needful instruction."

"From his sixth year, the Boy of whom I speak,
In summer tended cattle on the Hills;
But, through the inclement and the perilous days
Of long-continuing winter, he repaired
To his Step-father's School,"—&c.

For all the admirable passages interposed in this narration, might, with trifling alterations, have been far more appropriately, and with far greater verisimilitude, told of a poet in the character of a poet; and without incurring another defect which I shall now mention, and a sufficient illustration of which will have been here anticipated.

Third; an undue predilection for the *dramatic* form in certain poems, from which one or other of two evils result. Either the thoughts and diction are different from that of the poet, and then there arises an incongruity of style; or they are the same and indistinguishable, and then it presents a species of ventriloquism, where two are represented as talking, while in truth one man only speaks.

The fourth class of defects is closely connected with the former; but yet are such as arise likewise from an intensity of feeling disproportionate to such knowledge and value of the objects described, as can be fairly anticipated of men in general, even of the most cultivated classes; and with which therefore few only, and those few particularly circumstanced, can be supposed to sympathize: In this class, I comprise occasional prolixity, repetition, and an eddying, instead of progression, of thought. As instances, see pages 27, 28, and 62 of the Poems, Vol. I. and the first eighty lines of the VIth Book of THE EXCURSION.

Fifth and last; thoughts and images too great for the subject. This is an approximation to what might be called mental bombast, as distinguished from verbal: for, as in the latter there is a disproportion of the expressions to the thoughts so in this there is a disproportion of thought to the circumstance and occasion. This, by the bye, is a fault of which none but a man of genius is capable. It is the awkwardness and strength of Hercules with the distaff of Omphale.

It is a well-known fact, that bright colours in motion both make and leave the strongest impressions on the eye. Nothing is more likely too, than that a vivid image or visual *spectrum*, thus originated, may become the link of association in recalling the feelings and images that had accompanied the original impression. But if we describe this in such lines, as

> "They flash upon that inward eye,
> Which is the bliss of solitude!"

in what words shall we describe the joy of retrospection, when the images and virtuous actions of a whole well-spent life, pass before that conscience which is indeed the *inward* eye: which is indeed "*the bliss of solitude?*" Assuredly we seem to sink most abruptly, not to say burlesquely, and almost as in a medley, from this couplet to—

> "And then my heart with pleasure fills,
> And dances with the *daffodils*."
>
> Vol. I. p. 328.

The second instance is from Vol. II. page 12, where the poet having gone out for a day's tour of pleasure, meets early in the morning with a knot of Gipsies, who had pitched their blanket-tents and straw-beds, together with their children and asses, in some field by the road-side. At the close of the day on his return our tourist found them in the same place. "Twelve hours," says he,

> "Twelve hours, twelve bounteous hours are gone, while I
> Have been a traveller under open sky,
> Much witnessing of change and cheer,
> Yet as I left I find them here!"

Whereat the poet, without seeming to reflect that the poor tawny wanderers might probably have been tramping for weeks together through road and lane, over moor and mountain, and consequently must have been right glad to rest themselves, their children and cattle, for one whole day; and overlooking the obvious truth, that such repose might be quite as necessary for them, as a walk of the same continuance was pleasing or healthful for the more fortunate poet; expresses his indignation in a series of lines, the diction and imagery of which would have been rather above, than below the mark, had they been applied to the immense empire of China improgressive for thirty centuries:

> "The weary Sun betook himself to rest:—
> —Then issued Vesper from the fulgent west,
> Outshining, like a visible God,
> The glorious path in which he trod.
> And now, ascending, after one dark hour,
> And one night's diminution of her power,
> Behold the mighty Moon! this way
> She looks, as if at them—but they
> Regard not her:—oh, better wrong and strife,
> Better vain deeds or evil than such life!
> The silent Heavens have goings on:
> The stars have tasks!—but *these* have none!"

The last instance of this defect, (for I know no other than these already cited) is from the Ode, page 351, Vol. II., where, speaking of a child; "a six years' Darling of a pigmy size," he thus addresses him:

> "Thou best Philosopher, who yet dost keep
> Thy heritage, thou Eye among the blind,
> That, deaf and silent, read'st the eternal deep,
> Haunted for ever by the Eternal Mind,—
> Mighty Prophet! Seer blest!
> On whom those truths do rest,
> Which we are toiling all our lives to find!
> Thou, over whom thy Immortality
> Broods like the Day, a Master o'er a Slave,
> A Present which is not to be put by!"

Now here, not to stop at the daring spirit of metaphor which connects the epithets "deaf and silent," with the apostrophized *eye:* or (if we are to refer it to the preceding word, "Philosopher"), the faulty and equivocal syntax of the passage; and without examining the propriety of making a "Master *brood* o'er a Slave," or "the *Day*" brood *at all;* we will merely ask, what does all this mean? In what sense is a child of that age a *Philosopher?* In what sense does he *read* "the eternal deep?" In what sense is he declared to be "*for ever haunted*" by the Supreme Being? or so inspired as to deserve the splendid titles of a *Mighty Prophet*, a *blessed Seer?* By reflection? by knowledge? by conscious intuition? or by *any* form or modification of consciousness? These would be tidings indeed; but such as would pre-suppose an immediate revelation to the inspired communicator, and require miracles to authenticate his inspiration. Children at this age give us no such information of themselves; and at what time were we dipped in the Lethe, which has produced such utter oblivion of a state so godlike? There are many of us that still possess some remembrances, more or less distinct, respecting themselves at six years old; pity that the worthless straws only should float, while treasures, compared with which all the mines of Golconda and Mexico were but straws, should be absorbed by some unknown gulf into some unknown abyss.

But if this be too wild and exorbitant to be suspected as having been the poet's meaning; if these mysterious gifts, faculties, and operations, are not accompanied with consciousness; who else is conscious of them? or how can it be called the child, if it be no part of the child's conscious being? For aught I know, the thinking Spirit within me may be *substantially* one with the principle of life, and of vital operation. For aught I know, it might be employed as a secondary agent in the marvellous organization and organic movements of my body. But, surely, it would be strange language to say, that *I* construct my *heart!* or that *I* propel the finer influences through my *nerves?* or that *I* compress my brain, and draw the curtains of sleep round my own eyes! Spinoza and Behmen were, on different systems, both Pantheists; and among the ancients there were philosophers, teachers of the EN KAI ΠAN,[1] who not only taught that God was All, but that this All constituted God. Yet not even these would confound the *part, as* a part, with the whole, *as* the whole. Nay, in no system is the distinction between the individual and God, between the Modification, and the one only Substance, more sharply drawn, than in that of Spinoza. Jacobi indeed relates of Lessing, that, after a conversation with him at the house of the Poet, Gleim, (the Tyrtæus and Anacreon of the German Parnassus,) in which conversation Lessing had avowed privately to Jacobi his reluctance to admit any *personal* existence of the Supreme Being, or the *possibility* of personality except in a finite Intellect, and while they were sitting at table, a shower of rain came on unexpectedly. Gleim expressed his regret at the circumstance, because they had meant to drink their wine in the garden: upon which Lessing in one of his half-earnest, half-joking moods, nodded to Jacobi, and said, "It is *I*, perhaps, that am doing *that*," i.e., *raining!*—and Jacobi answered, "or perhaps I;" Gleim contented himself with staring at them both, without asking for any explanation.

So with regard to this passage. In what sense can the magnificent attributes, above quoted, be appropriated to a *child*, which would not make them equally suitable to a *bee*, or a *dog*, or a *field of corn:* or even to a ship, or to the wind and waves that propel it? The omnipresent Spirit works equally in them, as in the child; and the child is equally unconscious of it as they. It cannot surely be, that the four lines, immediately following, are to contain the explanation?

"To whom the grave
Is but a lonely bed without the sense or sight
Of day or the warm light,
A place of thought where we in waiting lie;"—

Surely, it cannot be that this wonder-rousing apostrophe is but a comment on the little poem, "We are Seven?"—that the whole meaning of the passage is reducible to the assertion, that a child, who by the bye at six years old would have been better instructed in most Christian families, has no other notion of death than that of lying in a dark, cold place? And still, I hope, not as in a *place of thought!* not the frightful notion of lying *awake* in his grave! The analogy between death and sleep is too simple, too natural, to render so horrid a belief possible for children; even had they not been in the habit, as all Christian children are, of hearing the latter term used to express the former. But if the child's belief be only, that "he is not dead, but sleepeth:" wherein does it differ from that of his father and mother or any other adult and instructed person? To form an idea of a thing's becoming nothing;

_____
[1] "One and all."

or of nothing becoming a thing; is impossible to all finite beings alike, of whatever age, and however educated or uneducated. Thus it is with splendid paradoxes in general. If the words are taken in the common sense, they convey an absurdity; and if, in contempt of dictionaries and custom, they are so interpreted as to avoid the absurdity, the meaning dwindles into some bald truism. Thus you must at once understand the words *contrary* to their common import, in order to arrive at any *sense;* and *according* to their common import, if you are to receive from them any feeling of *sublimity* or *admiration.*

Though the instances of this defect in Mr. Wordsworth's poems are so few, that for themselves it would have been scarcely just to attract the reader's attention toward them; yet I have dwelt on it, and perhaps the more for this very reason. For being so very few, they cannot sensibly detract from the reputation of an author, who is even characterized by the number of profound truths in his writings, which will stand the severest analysis; and yet few as they are, they are exactly those passages which his *blind* admirers would be most likely, and best able, to imitate. But Wordsworth, where he is indeed Wordsworth, may be mimicked by copyists, he may be plundered by plagiarists; but he cannot be imitated, except by those who are not born to be imitators. For without his depth of feeling and his imaginative power his *sense* would want its vital warmth and peculiarity; and without his strong sense, his *mysticism* would become *sickly*— mere fog, and dimness!

To these defects which, as appears by the extracts, are only occasional, I may oppose, with far less fear of encountering the dissent of any candid and intelligent reader, the following (for the most part correspondent) excellencies. First, an austere purity of language both grammatically and logically; in short a perfect appropriateness of the words to the meaning. Of how high value I deem this, and how particularly estimable I hold the example at the present day, has been already stated: and in part too the reasons on which I ground both the moral and intellectual importance of habituating ourselves to a strict accuracy of expression. It is noticeable, how limited an acquaintance with the masterpieces of art will suffice to form a correct and even a sensitive taste, where none but masterpieces have been seen and admired: while on the other hand, the most correct notions, and the widest acquaintance with the works of excellence of all ages and countries, will not perfectly secure us against the contagious familiarity with the far more numerous offspring of tastelessness or of a perverted taste. If this be the case, as it notoriously is, with the arts of music and painting, much more difficult will it be, to avoid the infection of multiplied and daily examples in the practice of an art, which uses words, and words only, as its instruments. In poetry, in which every line, every phrase, may pass the ordeal of deliberation and deliberate choice, it is possible, and barely possible, to attain that *ultimatum* which I have ventured to propose as the infallible test of a blameless style; namely: its *untranslatableness* in words of the same language without injury to the meaning. Be it observed, however, that I include in the *meaning* of a word not only its correspondent object, but likewise all the associations which it recalls. For language is framed to convey not the object alone, but likewise the character, mood and intentions of the person who is representing it. In poetry it *is* practicable to preserve the diction uncorrupted by the affectations and misappropriations, which promiscuous authorship, and reading not promiscuous only because it is disproportionally most conversant with the compositions of the day, have rendered general. Yet even to the poet, composing in his own province, it is an arduous work: and as the result and pledge of a watchful good sense, of fine and luminous distinction, and of complete self-possession, may justly claim all the honour which belongs to an attainment equally difficult and valuable, and the more valuable for being rare. It is at *all* times the proper food of the understanding; but in an age of corrupt eloquence it is both food and antidote.

In prose I doubt whether it be even possible to preserve our style wholly unalloyed by the vicious phraseology which meets us everywhere, from the sermon to the newspaper, from the harangue of the legislator to the speech from the convivial chair, announcing a *toast* or sentiment. Our chains rattle, even while we are complaining of them. The poems of Boetius rise high in our estimation when we compare them with those of his contemporaries, as Sidonius Apollinaris, and others. They might even be referred to a purer age, but that the prose, in which they are set, as jewels in a crown of lead or iron, betrays the true age of the writer. Much however may be effected by education. I believe not only from grounds of reason, but from having in great measure assured myself of the fact by actual though limited experience, that, to a youth led from his first boyhood to investigate the meaning of every·word and the reason of its choice and position, logic presents itself as an old acquaintance under new names.

On some future occasion, more especially demanding such disquisition, I shall attempt to prove the close connection between veracity and habits of mental accuracy; the beneficial after-effects of verbal precision in the preclusion of fanaticism, which masters the feelings more especially by indistinct watch-words; and to display the advantages which language alone, at least which language with incomparably greater ease and certainty than any other means, presents to the instructor of impressing modes of intellectual energy so constantly, so imperceptibly, and as it were by such elements and atoms, as to secure in due time the formation of a second nature. When we reflect, that the cultivation of the judgment is a positive command of the moral law, since the reason can give the *principle* alone, and the conscience bears witness only to the *motive*, while the application and effects must depend on the judgment: when we consider, that the greater part of our success and comfort in life depends on distinguishing the similar from the same, that which is peculiar in each thing from that which it has in common with others, so as still to select the most probable, instead of the merely possible or positively unfit, we shall learn to value earnestly and with a practical seriousness a mean, already prepared for us by nature and society, of teaching the young mind to think well and wisely by the same unremembered process and with the same never forgotten results, as those by which it is taught to speak and converse. Now how much warmer the interest is, how much more genial the feelings of reality and practicability, and thence how much stronger the impulses to imitation are, which a *contemporary* writer, and especially a contemporary *poet*, excites in youth and commencing manhood, has been treated of in the earlier pages of these sketches. I have only to add, that all the praise which is due to the exertion of such influence for a purpose so important, joined with that which must be claimed for the infrequency of the same excellence in the same perfection, belongs in full right to Mr. Wordsworth. I am far however from denying that we have poets whose *general* style possesses the same excellence, as Mr. Moore, Lord Byron, Mr. Bowles, and, in all his later and more important works, our laurel-honouring Laureate. But there are none, in whose works I do not appear to myself to find *more* exceptions, than in those of Wordsworth. Quotations or specimens would here be wholly out of place, and must be left for the critic who doubts and would invalidate the justice of this eulogy so applied.

The second characteristic excellence of Mr. Wordsworth's work is: a correspondent weight and sanity of the Thoughts and Sentiments,—won, not from books; but—from the poet's own meditative observation. They are *fresh* and have the dew upon them. His muse, at least when in her strength of wing, and when she hovers aloft in her proper element,

> Makes audible a linked lay of truth,
> Of truth profound a sweet continuous lay,
> Not learnt, but native, her own natural notes!

Even throughout his smaller poems there is scarcely one, which is not rendered valuable by some just and original reflection.

See page 25, vol. II.: or the two following passages in one of his humblest compositions.

> "O Reader! had you in your mind
> Such stores as silent thought can bring,
> O gentle Reader! you would find
> A tale in every thing;"

and

> "I've heard of hearts unkind, kind deeds
> With coldness still returning;
> Alas! the gratitude of men
> Has oftener left *me* mourning;"

or in a still higher strain the six beautiful quatrains, page 134.

"Thus fares it still in our decay:
And yet the wiser mind
Mourns less for what age takes away
Than what it leaves behind.

The Blackbird in the summer trees,
The Lark upon the hill,
Let loose their carols when they please,
Are quiet when they will.

With Nature never do *they* wage
A foolish strife; they see
A happy youth, and their old age
Is beautiful and free!

But we are pressed by heavy laws;
And often glad no more,
We wear a face of joy, because
We have been glad of yore.

If there is one, who need bemoan,
His kindred laid in earth,
The household hearts that were his own.
It is the man of mirth.

My days, my Friend, are almost gone,
My life has been approved,
And many love me; but by none
Am I enough beloved;"

or the sonnet on Buonaparte, page 202, vol. II.
or finally (for a volume would scarce suffice to
exhaust the instances,) the last stanza of the
poem on the withered Celandine, vol. II.
p. 312.

"To be a Prodigal's Favorite—then, worse truth,
A Miser's Pensioner—behold our lot!
O Man! that from thy fair and shining youth
Age might but take the things Youth needed
    not."

Both in respect of this and of the former
excellence, Mr. Wordsworth strikingly resembles Samuel Daniel, one of the golden
writers of our golden Elizabethan age, now
most causelessly neglected: Samuel Daniel,
whose diction bears no mark of time, no distinction of age which has been, and as long
as our language shall last, will be so far the
language of the to-day and for ever, as that
it is more intelligible to us, than the transitory
fashions of our own particular age. A similar
praise is due to his sentiments. No frequency
of perusal can deprive them of their freshness.
For though they are brought into the full daylight of every reader's comprehension; yet are
they drawn up from depths which few in any
age are privileged to visit, into which few in
any age have courage or inclination to de-

scend. If Mr. Wordsworth is not equally with
Daniel alike intelligible to all readers of
average understanding in all passages of his
works, the comparative difficulty does not
arise from the greater impurity of the ore, but
from the nature and uses of the metal. A poem
is not necessarily obscure, because it does not
aim to be popular. It is enough, if a work be
perspicuous to those for whom it is written,
and

"Fit audience find, though few."

To the "Ode on the Intimations of Immortality from Recollections of early Childhood" the poet might have prefixed the lines
which Dante addresses to one of his own
Canzoni—

"Canzone, i' credo, che saranno radi
Color, che tua ragione intendan bene,
Tanto lor sei faticoso ed alto."

"O lyric song, there will be few, I think,
Who may thy import understand aright:
Thou art for *them* so arduous and so high!"

But the ode was intended for such readers
only as had been accustomed to watch the flux
and reflux of their inmost nature, to venture at
times into the twilight realms of consciousness, and to feel a deep interest in modes of
inmost being, to which they know that the
attributes of time and space are inapplicable
and alien, but which yet can not be conveyed,
save in symbols of time and space. For such
readers the sense is sufficiently plain, and
they will be as little disposed to charge Mr.
Wordsworth with believing the Platonic pre-
existence in the ordinary interpretation of the
words, as I am to believe, that Plato himself
ever meant or taught it.

Πολλά μοι ὑπ’ ἀγκῶ-
νος ὠκέα βέλη
ἔνδον ἐντι φαρέτρας
φωνᾶντα συνετοῖσιν· ἐς
δὲ τὸ πᾶν ἑρμηνέων
χατίζει. σοφὸς ὁ πολ-
λὰ εἰδὼς φυᾷ·
μαθόντες δὲ λάβροι
παγγλωσσίᾳ, κόρακες ὥς,
ἄκραντα γαρύετον
Διὸς πρὸς ὄρνιχα θεῖον.[1]

[1] "Many swift arrows beneath my arm are
within my quiver, arrows that have a voice only

Third (and wherein he soars far above Daniel) the sinewy strength and originality of single lines and paragraphs: the frequent *curiosa felicitas* of his diction, of which I need not here give specimens, having anticipated them in a preceding page. This beauty, and as eminently characteristic of Wordsworth's poetry, his rudest assailants have felt themselves compelled to acknowledge and admire.

Fourth; the perfect truth of nature in his images and descriptions as taken immediately from nature, and proving a long and genial intimacy with the very spirit which gives the physiognomic expression to all the works of nature. Like a green field reflected in a calm and perfectly transparent lake, the image is distinguished from the reality only by its greater softness and lustre. Like the moisture or the polish on a pebble, genius neither distorts nor false-colours its objects; but on the contrary brings out many a vein and many a tint, which escape the eye of common observation, thus raising to the rank of gems what had been often kicked away by the hurrying foot of the traveller on the dusty high road of custom.

Let me refer to the whole description of skating, vol. I. page 42 to 47, especially to the lines

"So through the darkness and the cold we flew,
    And not a voice was idle: with the din
    Meanwhile the precipices rang aloud;
    The leafless trees and every icy crag
    Tinkled like iron; while the distant hills
    Into the tumult sent an alien sound
    Of melancholy, not unnoticed, while the stars,
    Eastward, were sparkling clear, and in the west
    The orange sky of evening died away."

Or to the poem on THE GREEN LINNET, vol. I. page 244. What can be more accurate yet more lovely than the two concluding stanzas?

    "Upon yon tuft of hazel trees,
        That twinkle to the gusty breeze,
        Behold him perched in ecstasies,
            Yet seeming still to hover;

There! where the flutter of his wings
Upon his back and body flings
Shadows and sunny glimmerings,
    That cover him all over.

While thus before my eyes he gleams,
A Brother of the Leaves he seems;
When in a moment forth he teems
    His little song in gushes:
As if it pleased him to disdain
And mock the Form which he did feign
While he was dancing with the train
    Of Leaves among the bushes."

Or the description of the blue-cap, and of the noontide silence, page 284; or the poem to the cuckoo, page 299; or, lastly, though I might multiply the references to ten times the number, to the poem, so completely Wordsworth's, commencing

"Three years she grew in sun and shower"—

Fifth: a meditative pathos, a union of deep and subtle thought with sensibility; a sympathy with man as man; the sympathy indeed of a contemplator, rather than a fellow-sufferer or co-mate, (*spectator, haud particeps*) but of a contemplator, from whose view no difference of rank conceals the sameness of the nature; no injuries of wind or weather, or toil, or even of ignorance, wholly disguise the human face divine. The superscription and the image of the Creator still remain legible to *him* under the dark lines, with which guilt or calamity had cancelled or cross-barred it. Here the Man and the Poet lose and find themselves in each other, the one as glorified, the latter as substantiated. In this mild and philosophic pathos, Wordsworth appears to me without a compeer. Such as he *is:* so he *writes.* See vol. I. page 134 to 136, or that most affecting composition, THE AFFLICTION OF MARGARET —— OF ——, page 165 to 168, which no mother, and, if I may judge by my own experience, no parent can read without a tear. Or turn to that genuine lyric, in the former edition, entitled, THE MAD MOTHER, page 174 to 178, of which I cannot refrain from quoting two of the stanzas, both of them for their pathos, and the former for the fine transition in the two concluding lines of the stanza, so expressive of that deranged state, in which, from the increased sensibility, the sufferer's attention is abruptly drawn off by every trifle,

---

for the wise; for the general world there is need of interpreters. Wise is the man who knows much by gift of Nature; but the obstreperous and wordy, after learning something, like crows, sing ineffectual nonsense in the presence of the divine bird of Zeus."

Pindar, *Olymp.* II. 149–159.

and in the same instant plucked back again by the one despotic thought, bringing home with it, by the blending, *fusing* power of Imagination and Passion, the alien object to which it had been so abruptly diverted, no 5 longer an alien but an ally and an inmate.

"Suck, little babe, oh suck again!
　It cools my blood; it cools my brain;
　Thy lips, I feel them, baby! they
　Draw from my heart the pain away.
　Oh! press me with thy little hand;
　It loosens something at my chest:
　About that tight and deadly band
　I feel thy little fingers prest.
　The breeze I see is in the tree!
　It comes to cool my babe and me."

"Thy father cares not for my breast,
　'Tis thine, sweet baby, there to rest;
　'Tis all thine own!—and if its hue
　Be changed, that was so fair to view,
　'Tis fair enough for thee, my dove!
　My beauty, little child, is flown,
　But thou wilt live with me in love;
　And what if my poor cheek be brown?
　'Tis well for me, thou canst not see
　How pale and wan it else would be."

Last, and pre-eminently, I challenge for this poet the gift of Imagination in the highest and strictest sense of the word. In the play of 10 *fancy*, Wordsworth, to my feelings, is not always graceful, and sometimes recondite. The *likeness* is occasionally too strange, or demands too peculiar a point of view, or is such as appears the creature of predetermined 15 research, rather than spontaneous presentation. Indeed his fancy seldom displays itself, as mere and unmodified fancy. But in imaginative power, he stands nearest of all modern writers to Shakespeare and Milton; and yet in 20 a kind perfectly unborrowed and his own. To employ his own words, which are at once an instance and an illustration, he does indeed to all thoughts and to all objects—

"———————add the gleam,
　The light that never was, on sea or land,
　The consecration, and the Poet's dream."

I shall select a few examples as most ob- 25 viously manifesting this faculty; but if I should ever be fortunate enough to render my analysis of Imagination, its origin and characters, thoroughly intelligible to the reader, he will scarcely open on a page of this 30 poet's works without recognising, more or less, the presence and the influences of this faculty.

From the poem on the YEW TREES, vol. I. page 303, 304.

"But worthier still of note
Are those fraternal Four of Borrowdale,
Joined in one solemn and capacious grove;
Huge trunks!—and each particular trunk a growth
Of intertwisted fibres serpentine
Up-coiling, and inveterately convolved;
Not uninformed with phantasy, and looks
That threaten the profane;—a pillared shade,
Upon whose grassless floor of red-brown hue,
By sheddings from the pinal umbrage tinged
Perennially—beneath whose sable roof
Of boughs, as if for festal purpose, decked
With unrejoicing berries—ghostly shapes
May meet at noontide; FEAR and trembling HOPE,
SILENCE and FORESIGHT; DEATH, the Skeleton,
And TIME, the Shadow; there to celebrate,
As in a natural temple scattered o'er
With altars undisturbed of mossy stone,
United worship; or in mute repose
To lie, and listen to the mountain flood
Murmuring from Glazamara's inmost caves."

The effect of the old man's figure in the poem of RESOLUTION AND INDEPENDENCE, vol. II. page 33.

"While he was talking thus, the lonely place,
　The Old Man's shape, and speech, all troubled me:
　In my mind's eye I seemed to see him pace
　About the weary moors continually,
　Wandering about alone and silently."

Or the 8th, 9th, 19th, 26th, 31st, and 33rd, in the collection of miscellaneous sonnets— the sonnet on the subjugation of Switzerland, page 210, or the last ode, from which I especially select the two following stanzas or paragraphs, page 349 to 350.

"Our birth is but a sleep and a forgetting:
　The Soul that rises with us, our life's Star,
　Hath had elsewhere its setting,
　　And cometh from afar.
Not in entire forgetfulness,
And not in utter nakedness,
But trailing clouds of glory do we come
From God, who is our home:
Heaven lies about us in our infancy!
Shades of the prison-house begin to close
　Upon the growing Boy;
But He beholds the light, and whence it flows,
　He sees it in his joy!
The Youth who daily further from the East
Must travel, still is Nature's Priest,

And by the vision splendid
Is on his way attended;
At length the Man perceives it die away,
And fade into the light of common day."

And page 352 to 354 of the same ode.

"O joy! that in our embers
Is something that doth live,
That nature yet remembers
What was so fugitive!
The thought of our past years in me doth
   breed
Perpetual benedictions: not indeed
For that which is most worthy to be blest;
Delight and liberty, the simple creed
Of Childhood, whether busy or at rest,
With new-fledged hope still fluttering in his
   breast:—
Not for these I raise
The song of thanks and praise;
But for those obstinate questionings
Of sense and outward things,
Fallings from us, vanishings;
Blank misgivings of a Creature
Moving about in worlds not realized,
High instincts, before which our mortal Nature
Did tremble like a guilty Thing surprised!
But for those first affections,
Those shadowy recollections,
Which, be they what they may,
Are yet the fountain light of all our day,
Are yet a master light of all our seeing;
Uphold us—cherish—and have power to make
Our noisy years seem moments in the being
Of the eternal Silence; truths that wake
   To perish never;
Which neither listlessness, nor mad endeavour,
Nor Man nor Boy,
Nor all that is at enmity with joy,
Can utterly abolish or destroy!
Hence, in a season of calm weather,
Though inland far we be,
Our Souls have sight of that immortal sea
Which brought us hither;
Can in a moment travel thither,—
And see the children sport upon the shore,
And hear the mighty waters rolling evermore."

And since it would be unfair to conclude with an extract, which, though highly characteristic, must yet, from the nature of the thoughts and the subject, be interesting or perhaps intelligible, to but a limited number of readers; I will add, from the poet's last published work, a passage equally Wordsworthian; of the beauty of which, and of the imaginative power displayed therein, there can be but one opinion, and one feeling. See White Doe, page 5.

"Fast the church-yard fills;—anon
Look again and they all are gone;
The cluster round the porch, and the folk
Who sate in the shade of the Prior's Oak!
And scarcely have they disappeared
Ere the prelusive hymn is heard;—
With one consent the people rejoice,
Filling the church with a lofty voice!
They sing a service which they feel:
For 'tis the sun-rise now of zeal;
And faith and hope are in their prime
In great Eliza's golden time."

"A moment ends the fervent din,
And all is hushed, without and within;
For though the priest, more tranquilly,
Recites the holy liturgy,
The only voice which you can hear
Is the river murmuring near.
—When soft!—the dusky trees between,
And down the path through the open green,
Where is no living thing to be seen;
And through yon gateway, where is found,
Beneath the arch with ivy bound,
Free entrance to the church-yard ground—
And right across the verdant sod,
Towards the very house of God;
Comes gliding in with lovely gleam,
Comes gliding in serene and slow,
Soft and silent as a dream,
A solitary Doe!
White she is as lily of June,
And beauteous as the silver moon
When out of sight the clouds are driven
And she is left alone in heaven!
Or like a ship some gentle day
In sunshine sailing far away—
A glittering ship that hath the plain
Of ocean for her own domain."

*   *   *

"What harmonious pensive changes
Wait upon her as she ranges
Round and through this Pile of state
Overthrown and desolate!
Now a step or two her way
Is through space of open day,
Where the enamoured sunny light
Brightens her that was so bright;
Now doth a delicate shadow fall,
Falls upon her like a breath,
From some lofty arch or wall,
As she passes underneath."

The following analogy will, I am apprehensive, appear dim and fantastic, but in reading Bartram's Travels I could not help transcribing the following lines as a sort of allegory, or connected simile and metaphor of Wordsworth's intellect and genius.—"The soil is a deep, rich, dark mould, on a deep stratum of tenacious clay; and that on a foundation of rocks, which often break through both strata, lifting their backs above the surface. The trees which chiefly grow here are the gigantic, black oak; magnolia grandiflora; fraximus excelsior; platane; and a few stately tulip trees." What Mr. Wordsworth *will* produce, it is not for me to prophesy: but I could pronounce with the liveliest convictions what he is capable of producing. It is the FIRST GENUINE PHILOSOPHIC POEM.

The preceding criticism will not, I am aware, avail to overcome the prejudices of those, who have made it a business to attack and ridicule Mr. Wordsworth's compositions.

Truth and prudence might be imaged as concentric circles. The poet may perhaps have passed beyond the latter, but he has confined himself far within the bounds of the former, in designating these critics, as "too petulant to be passive to a genuine poet, and too feeble to grapple with him; . . . men of palsied imaginations, in whose minds all healthy action is languid; . . . who, therefore, feed as the many direct them, or with the many are greedy after vicious provocatives."

So much for the detractors from Wordsworth's merits. On the other hand, much as I might wish for their fuller sympathy, I dare not flatter myself, that the freedom with which I have declared my opinions concerning both his theory and his defects, most of which are more or less connected with his theory, either as cause or effect, will be satisfactory or pleasing to *all* the poet's admirers and advocates. More indiscriminate than mine their admiration may be: deeper and more sincere it cannot

be. But I have advanced no opinion either for praise or censure, other than as texts introductory to the reasons which compel me to form it. Above all, I was fully convinced that such a criticism was not only wanted; but that, if executed with adequate ability, it must conduce, in no mean degree, to Mr. Wordsworth's *reputation*. His *fame* belongs to another age, and can neither be accelerated nor retarded. How small the proportion of the defects are to the beauties, I have repeatedly declared; and that no one of them originates in deficiency of poetic genius. Had they been more and greater, I should still, as a friend to his literary character in the present age, consider an analytic display of them as *pure gain;* if only it removed, as surely to all reflecting minds even the foregoing analysis must have removed, the strange mistake, so slightly grounded, yet so widely and industriously propagated, of Mr. Wordsworth's turn for *simplicity!* I am not half as much irritated by hearing his enemies abuse him for vulgarity of style, subject, and conception, as I am disgusted with the gilded side of the same meaning, as displayed by some affected admirers, with whom he is, forsooth, a "sweet, simple poet!" and *so* natural, that little master Charles and his younger sister are *so* charmed with them, that they play at "Goody Blake," or at "Johnny and Betty Foy!"

Were the collection of poems, published with these biographical sketches, important enough, (which I am not vain enough to believe,) to deserve such a distinction; *even as I have done, so would I be done unto. . . .*

GEORGE GORDON, LORD BYRON

[January 22, 1788–April 19, 1824]

A FEW months before his marriage Byron wrote his fiancée that he hoped he was "not very ill-natured *off the stage*," and the italics are Byron's own. The difficulty in judging Byron lies in the fact that he was so seldom off the stage. Circumstances made a dramatic figure of him, and vanity, at least at first, impelled him to play up to situations. Few men have had more theatrical careers, and certainly Byron was the most notorious, although perhaps not the most noteworthy, man of letters of his century.

Providence, as if wishing to contribute a prologue, provided a suitable set of ancestors. Byron's grandfather was "foul-weather Jack"—an admiral who seemed never to sail without encountering a hurricane. Byron's father was a handsome spendthrift who married and squandered the fortunes of two heiresses. The great-uncle from whom Byron inherited the title was known as the "wicked lord"—a title acquired when he killed a kinsman in a quarrel over nothing. Providence, having seen to it that the boy should grow up incredibly handsome and magnetic, saw to it that he should be born lame, and supplied him with a mother who alternately caressed him and flung the andirons at him, and once called him "a lame brat." "I was born so, mother," was his white-faced answer. The mother, without the assistance of Providence, disposed of the boy's guardian, who fled from his duties, resolving never again to encounter "that woman," and thereby removed any chance of wise dealing with the child. Providence, meanwhile, disposed of various heirs to the title (Byron at his birth had not been expected to inherit) and at the age of ten made him George Gordon, sixth Lord Byron. Thereafter Providence felt, with some justice, that the further creation of drama could be left to Byron himself.

He went through Harrow and he went through Cambridge. At Cambridge he published *Hours of Idleness* (1807) and when, the following year, the *Edinburgh Review*, delighted with the opportunity to attack bad poetry and a presumptuous young lord at the same time, attacked it, Byron, who was at work on a satire on English Bards, angrily enlarged his subject and in 1809 published *English Bards and Scotch Reviewers*—an effective fighting book. Without waiting to see its effect, he departed on a two-year trip (July 1809–July 1811) to the Near East. There was a girl in Cadiz who asked for his heart and his large yellow diamond ring. There was one in Malta who got the diamond. He was in a shipwreck, nearly died of a fever, was the guest of a Pacha, visited the ruins of Troy, swam the Hellespont, rescued at the point of a pistol a girl who was about to be drowned sewed up in a sack, and came home, looking, as a consequence of the fever, pale and romantic. He brought back the mss. of the first two cantos of *Childe Harold*. Byron himself did not think them very good, but a friend (R. C. Dallas) persuaded him to publish them. Their success was emphatic. On the tenth of March 1812 Byron awoke and found himself famous. The curtain was up on the Byron drama.

For a brief time Byron was the sensation of London society. It is easy to see why. He was reckless, handsome, and magnetic. He was a traveller with the glamour of far lands about him. He was a lord. He was a poet whose melancholy had stirred a nation, the great suffering soul which cried out for sympathy. And sympathy he was given in lavish measure, particularly by the feminine half of society. One society beauty, Lady Caroline Lamb, who had been anxious to meet him, turned on her heel, without waiting his introduction, and went home to write in her diary, "mad, bad, and dangerous to know." A little later, however, she was writing, "That beautiful pale face is my fate." Such was the effect he produced.

Byron was the creature of his time and, at least in these first days of his triumph, no worse than his time. He was shaped by it rather than the shaper of it. But to every thing Byron did there was a touch of drama, of the conspicuous, so that when the final crash came and he went into exile he bore across Europe "the pageant of his bleeding heart"—and all Europe watched.

But after the publication of the first two cantos of *Childe Harold* and in spite of his whirl of society, Byron continued to write and to triumph. *The Giaour* (1813), *The Bride of Abydos* (1813), *The Corsair* (1814), *Lara* (1814), appeared, and *The Corsair* sold the unprecedented number of 10,000 copies on the day of publication. But there was a new and dangerous quality in his triumph. The Byron fever had been abating, but the public were reading scandal and personal allusion into his works, and it was partly because of this that interest in him remained feverish. And to the second edition of *The Corsair* he added, among six short pieces, the *Lines to a Lady Weeping* which, because they were a reflection on the Prince Regent, provoked a perfect storm of anti-Byron hysteria in the Tory press. These *Lines* had previously appeared anonymously and created a disturbance. It was characteristic of Byron that he should re-print them over his signature and re-create the storm.

Byron had been thinking of marrying and settling down "if any one will have me," and in September 1814 he became engaged to Anne Isabella Milbanke. Of her he had once written to Caroline Lamb, "I should like her more, if she were less perfect," but he had nevertheless proposed (in 1812) to Miss Milbanke within a few months of that judgment—and been rejected. She accepted his second proposal, and they were married in December 1814. Whether Byron ever really loved her is doubtful. What happened inside their tormented household, no one really knows. Certainly the beginning was not auspicious. A wax taper had been left burning in their room and late on the wedding night Byron awoke suddenly to find the room filled with its red glare. "My God," Byron exclaimed, "I am in hell!" His young wife was awake to hear him.

A year later Lady Byron, taking her baby girl with her, went, apparently for a brief visit, to her parents. A few weeks later her father informed Byron that Lady Byron would not return to him. The suddenness of the act undoubtedly stunned Byron. The cause of it he always professed not to know, and he angrily blamed his wife's female relatives. Certainly no explanation was ever publicly advanced during his lifetime. But almost equally certainly he did know what would be the cause alleged, and did not choose to force the issue to the courts. This does not necessarily prove him guilty.

But the storm burst. The accumulated venom of jealousy, distrust, and hatred which had been gathering against him during his mockingly triumphant career was released. He had mocked the Tories. He had mocked the middle classes. He had let scandal gather as it might. Ready to fight at the slightest honorable attaint of his personal honor (and fighting in those days was with deadly weapons), he had allowed gossips to brew their scandal, snuffling in corners, and they had brewed a broth for him to boil in. The very fact that Lady Byron advanced no public explanation did him the greatest possible damage which could have been done. In default of any plain charge, any rumor *might* be true. And through London rumor ran like fire through dry straw.

In January 1816 Lady Byron had gone to her parents. In February Byron first heard from her father. On April 21 he signed a deed of amicable separation. And on April 24 he left London. His friends in the late days had kept him from the theatres lest there be public disturbances. Feeling was, indeed, so high that there was a real risk his public appearance might cause a riot. He had been compared in the press to most of the known villains of recorded history. On the morning of his departure, his coachman sat with drawn pistols in the perilous interval he waited for Byron to come out of the house. But in Dover the passageways of the inn where he stopped were cluttered with ladies, disguised as chambermaids, striving for a last glimpse of "Byron," and when he went to the boat, the two sides of his path were lined by a crowd jeering. His friends Hobhouse and Scrope Davies braved the storm to see him off at Dover, and Hobhouse came home to write in his journal, "God bless him for a gallant spirit and a kind one." So departed Byron from England.

And became suddenly a great poet! The English speaking world had *thought* him a poet, whereas, in fact, he had been merely a conspicuous personality. Exiled, he stopped on his way to Switzerland to compose on the actual field of Waterloo a gorgeous stanza for a new canto of *Childe Harold*. In Switzerland he encountered the Shelleys and Claire Clairmont who had accompanied them. The two poets became friends and there were several months of companionship, during which Byron was writing steadily. It was Shelley who took back to England the ms. of the third canto of *Childe Harold* (published 1816) which made trash of all the poetry Byron had written before. Against the impact of the new Byron practically nothing of the Byron of the Fever survives. The triumphant *Corsair* is unread. *The Bride of Abydos* is stale scandal. The original cantos of *Childe Harold* are anæmic beside the later work. Only some of the shorter lyrical pieces of the early days remain alive.

From Switzerland, Byron went to Venice, which remained his headquarters for several years (1816–1819). It was at Venice that Byron sank to his lowest. Despite his pride and angry defiance of the world, he was obviously unnerved by disgrace and exile, and he flung himself into debauchery, scandalizing even Venice, a city which was not easily scandalized. But the power of his poetry, however, continued. The fourth canto of *Childe Harold* (finished December, 1817) was written in Venice, after a trip to Florence and Rome. So was *Manfred* (published 1817) and *Don Juan* was begun there in 1818. This is not bad production from a man busy scandalizing a scandalous city, and it is only a part of the poetic production. And from Venice also began that torrent of letters with which the lonely exile showered his friends—letters which alone place Byron among the great writers.

They are truly great letters. And the most striking qualities about them are their flashing wit and unquenchable zest for life. Coming from a man who as a poet, up to this time, had revealed himself solely as a master of misanthropy and despair, they present an apparent paradox. The explanation is simple enough. The theatrical, misanthropic Byron was perfectly sincere but he was only part of Byron. Another part and quality of Byron had as yet found expression only in talk and in the letters. It was the quality which bound men to him with hoops of steel and brought the conservative Hobhouse and the wittily drunken gambler Scrope Davies to brave the hostility of England and come down to Dover to see him off; that had led Lady Jersey in the dark days of 1816 to give a great reception in his honor in a desperate effort to turn the social tide. There is no inconsistency here. It is simply that Byron, like a diamond, had many facets. No one accuses a diamond of insincerity because it flashes now red, now blue to the sunlight.

At Venice in 1818 Byron had begun *Don Juan*, and by 1819, having put the worst of his excesses behind him, he was writing apace. And also he had fallen in love. To the young Countess Guiccioli he remained faithful the remainder of his life. He was angry with her; he was bored with her; he felt extremely silly as he set about learning the punctilios of the Italian code for such an affair; but escape her he did not. Abandoning Venice, he followed her to Ravenna (December 1819). And when she left Ravenna, he spluttered and cursed and wrote Moore, "I am in all the sweat, dust, and blasphemy of an universal packing . . . As I could not say, with Hamlet, 'Get thee to a nunnery,' I am preparing to follow. It is awful work, this love . . ." And follow her to Pisa he did in October 1821.

Meanwhile his poetic energy was prodigious. *Sardanapalus, Marino Faliero, The Two Foscari* (none of which are in his best vein), *The Vision of Judgment* (one of his best pieces), and *Cain* (one of his most sensational), were a part of his production. And the cantos of *Don Juan* flowed from his pen. The first cantos·had been sent from Venice, and early in 1819 he heard that a council of such trusted friends as Hobhouse, Davies, Kinnaird, and Moore had, appalled, voted for the poem's suppression. "I tell you it *is* poetry" wrote Byron angrily. And then he wrote again defending *Don Juan* as a "human poem." Published the first two cantos were in 1819 but anonymously (Byron at first omitted the Dedication as he would not hit his enemy Southey "in the dark") and so anonymously that even the publisher Murray omitted his name from the title page. The uproar which followed in England was terrific.

England, of course, received *Don Juan* in fragments with an insulting fragment as a cocktail. Posterity receives the book as a whole and without the cayenne of personal feeling. Nevertheless it is still necessary to remember that "books are for those who can read them," that this book is a whole, and that its greatness lies in no single part—its greatness lies in the magnificently vital fusion of varied elements. *Don Juan*, after a Dedication which insults the poet laureate and a double handful of important poets, swings into risqué bedroom farce of the most gallic type, gaily told, and then, at the opening of the second canto, goes slap-stick in the best manner of the early custard-pie-throwing motion picture, when the young lover simultaneously tries to read a love letter and grows actively seasick. Shipwreck, the brutal ferocities of starvation, death, and cannibalism in an open boat follow, savagely told. And then the young hero, the sole survivor, awakens into one of the purest and most beautiful romances the English language possesses. This is high praise and it can be said without risk of challenge from even Byron's worst enemies. So the poem begins. Through the whole runs the mocking and satirical comment of disillusioned genius. For the first time all the facets of the Byron diamond had caught the sun at once, and for the first time he wrote poetry which was as good literature as his prose letters.

The last phase of Byron's life was his expedition to Greece, and it was the perfect end for the great Byron drama. The Greeks had revolted from Turkey, and the Greek Committee (a group of Englishmen in London, sympathetic with the cause) elected Byron to membership in the Spring of 1823. He accepted the responsibility and prepared to go to Greece to assist on the field while the Committee acted in London.

The charge has been made that Byron's liberalism was a matter of words—that he was "on the stage" and merely making gestures. Dramatize he undoubtedly did—or rather the world dramatized him. He could not even be sincere without someone putting a press notice about it in the papers. But it should be noted that far back in 1812, before the first cantos of *Childe Harold* were out and he was famous, he made his maiden speech in the House of Lords and he made it in behalf of the working men and in defiance of the Lords' majority, and he ended by stating that even if the majority got the law it was trying to pass, the law couldn't be enforced unless there were "twelve butchers for a jury, and a Jeffreys for a judge." That was taking a political stand firmly when his own career was yet to make. In Italy, at Ravenna, Byron is supposed to have become a member of the revolutionary society of the Carbonari. In any case, when a republican revolt against Austrian tyranny became possible, he certainly bought guns and ammunition for the "patriots" and, when the possession of guns became personally dangerous, the "patriots" equally certainly returned them to him and left him to take the consequences should there be a police raid. Byron, indeed, talked about the "poetry of politics," but he supplied guns at Ravenna. And in Greece, aware that, having had the fever before he would die of another attack, and aware that Missolonghi was a fever trap, Byron nevertheless went to Missolonghi when he was needed there. And at Missolonghi he died. This seems sincere.

Byron could not even die without sensationalism. He sailed for Greece on Friday the thirteenth (July, 1823), and calm, then storm checked him. "Where shall we be, this day year," he asked. And that day a year hence his body was being carried to the tomb. He paused in a Greek island under British protection until he could get news of conditions and where he was needed. Then he made a dash for Missolonghi. Byronically, Turkish cruisers appeared. A ship was lost (later recovered), another piled up on rocks in a narrow channel. But the Byron group finally reached Missolonghi entire (January 5, 1824). Then there was quarrelling and faction—and rain, rain, rain in a fever trap and Lord Byron, the spoiled darling, sleeping on a mat. There was incompetence, there was treachery, there was murder, there was mutiny. And Byron, failing in health, somehow kept things going. What he touched went right. But instantly something else went wrong and he had to turn to it. He was almost dying when the Suliotes (his personal troops whom he most trusted and into whose tribe he had been accepted as a blood brother on his first Near Eastern Trip) revolted for more pay, and he staggered up from his bed to subdue them. In his sector of duty he kept the revolution alive. He died on April 19, 1824 and on the night of his death a great thunderstorm broke and there was a wild flaring of lightning over his body.

Greece asked for that body to bury it in one of the most beautiful temples surviving from her golden age. England refused it burial space in Westminster Abbey. In England it was carried north by road, and on the road it passed the carriage of Lady Caroline Lamb (who did not know what body was passing), to be buried in the village church of Hucknall Torkard—near Newstead Abbey.

STANZAS FOR MUSIC

I

BRIGHT be the place of thy soul!
  No lovelier spirit than thine
E'er burst from its mortal control,
  In the orbs of the blessed to shine.
On earth thou wert all but divine,
  As thy soul shall immortally be;
And our sorrow may cease to repine
  When we know that thy God is with thee.

II

Light be the turf of thy tomb!
  May its verdure like emeralds be!   10
There should not be the shadow of gloom
  In aught that reminds us of thee.
Young flowers and an evergreen tree
  May spring from the spot of thy rest:
But nor cypress nor yew let us see;
  For why should we mourn for the blest?

1808

WHEN WE TWO PARTED

WHEN we two parted
  In silence and tears,
Half broken-hearted
  To sever for years,
Pale grew thy cheek and cold,
  Colder thy kiss;
Truly that hour foretold
  Sorrow to this.

The dew of the morning
  Sunk chill on my brow—   10
It felt like the warning
  Of what I feel now.
Thy vows are all broken,
  And light is thy fame:
I hear thy name spoken,
  And share in its shame.

They name thee before me,
  A knell to mine ear;
A shudder comes o'er me—
  Why wert thou so dear?   20
They know not I knew thee,
  Who knew thee too well:—
Long, long shall I rue thee,
  Too deeply to tell.

In secret we met—
  In silence I grieve,
That thy heart could forget,
  Thy spirit deceive.
If I should meet thee
  After long years,   30
How should I greet thee?—
  With silence and tears.

? 1808

WELL! THOU ART HAPPY

WELL! thou art happy, and I feel
  That I should thus be happy too;
For still my heart regards thy weal
  Warmly, as it was wont to do.

Thy husband's blest—and 'twill impart
  Some pangs to view his happier lot:
But let them pass—Oh! how my heart
  Would hate him if he loved thee not!

When late I saw thy favourite child,
  I thought my jealous heart would break: 10
But when the unconscious infant smiled,
  I kiss'd it for its mother's sake.

I kiss'd it,—and repress'd my sighs
  Its father in its face to see;
But then it had its mother's eyes,
  And they were all to love and me.

Mary, adieu! I must away:
  While thou art blest I'll not repine;
But near thee I can never stay;
  My heart would soon again be thine.   20

I deem'd that time, I deem'd that pride,
  Had quench'd at length my boyish flame;
Nor knew, till seated by thy side,
  My heart in all,—save hope,—the same.

Yet was I calm: I knew the time
  My breast would thrill before thy look;
But now to tremble were a crime—
  We met,—and not a nerve was shook.

I saw thee gaze upon my face,
  Yet meet with no confusion there: 30
One only feeling could'st thou trace;
  The sullen calmness of despair.

Away! away! my early dream
  Remembrance never must awake:
Oh! where is Lethe's fabled stream?
  My foolish heart, be still, or break.

November 2, 1808

MAID OF ATHENS, ERE WE PART

Ζώη μοῦ, σᾶς ἀγαπῶ.[1]

MAID of Athens, ere we part,
  Give, oh give me back my heart!
Or, since that has left my breast,
  Keep it now, and take the rest!
Hear my vow before I go,
  Ζώη μοῦ, σᾶς ἀγαπῶ.

By those tresses unconfined,
  Woo'd by each Ægean wind;
By those lids whose jetty fringe
  Kiss thy soft cheeks' blooming tinge; 10
By those wild eyes like the roe,
  Ζώη μοῦ, σᾶς ἀγαπῶ.

By that lip I long to taste;
  By that zone-encircled waist;
By all the token-flowers that tell
  What words can never speak so well;
By love's alternate joy and woe,
  Ζώη μοῦ, σᾶς ἀγαπῶ.

Maid of Athens! I am gone:
  Think of me, sweet! when alone. 20
Though I fly to Istambol,
  Athens holds my heart and soul:
Can I cease to love thee? No!
  Ζώη μοῦ, σᾶς ἀγαπῶ.

Athens, 1810

AND THOU ART DEAD, AS YOUNG AND FAIR

"Heu, quanto minus est cum reliquis versari
quam tui meminisse!"[2]

AND thou art dead, as young and fair
  As aught of mortal birth;
And form so soft, and charms so rare,
  Too soon return'd to Earth!

[1] "My life, I love you."
[2] "Alas, how barren it is to be engaged with those
left living, rather than to be mindful of you!"

Though Earth received them in her bed
And o'er the spot the crowd may tread
  In carelessness or mirth,
There is an eye which could not brook
A moment on that grave to look.

I will not ask where thou liest low, 10
  Nor gaze upon the spot;
There flowers or weeds at will may grow,
  So I behold them not:
It is enough for me to prove
That what I loved, and long must love,
  Like common earth can rot;
To me there needs no stone to tell,
'Tis Nothing that I loved so well.

Yet did I love thee to the last
  As fervently as thou, 20
Who didst not change through all the past,
  And canst not alter now.
The love where Death has set his seal,
Nor age can chill, nor rival steal,
  Nor falsehood disavow:
And, what were worse, thou canst not see
Or wrong, or change, or fault in me.

The better days of life were ours;
  The worst can be but mine:
The sun that cheers, the storm that lowers, 30
  Shall never more be thine.
The silence of that dreamless sleep
I envy now too much to weep;
  Nor need I to repine,
That all those charms have pass'd away;
I might have watch'd through long decay.

The flower in ripen'd bloom unmatch'd
  Must fall the earliest prey;
Though by no hand untimely snatch'd,
  The leaves must drop away: 40
And yet it were a greater grief
To watch it withering, leaf by leaf,
  Than see it pluck'd to-day;
Since earthly eye but ill can bear
To trace the change to foul from fair.

I know not if I could have borne
  To see thy beauties fade;
The night that follow'd such a morn
  Had worn a deeper shade:

Thy day without a cloud hath pass'd,   50
And thou wert lovely to the last;
  Extinguish'd, not decay'd;
As stars that shoot along the sky
Shine brightest as they fall from high.

As once I wept, if I could weep,
  My tears might well be shed,
To think I was not near to keep
  One vigil o'er thy bed;
To gaze, how fondly! on thy face,
To fold thee in a faint embrace,   60
  Uphold thy drooping head;
And show that love, however vain,
Nor thou nor I can feel again.

Yet how much less it were to gain,
  Though thou hast left me free,
The loveliest things that still remain,
  Than thus remember thee!
The all of thine that cannot die
Through dark and dread Eternity
  Returns again to me,   70
And more thy buried love endears
Than aught except its living years.

February, 1812

LINES TO A LADY WEEPING

WEEP, daughter of a royal line,
  A Sire's disgrace, a realm's decay;
Ah! happy if each tear of thine
  Could wash a father's fault away!

Weep—for thy tears are Virtue's tears—
  Auspicious to these suffering isles;
And be each drop in future years
  Repaid thee by thy people's smiles!

March, 1812

SHE WALKS IN BEAUTY

SHE walks in beauty, like the night
  Of cloudless climes and starry skies;
And all that's best of dark and bright
  Meet in her aspect and her eyes:
Thus mellow'd to that tender light
  Which heaven to gaudy day denies.

One shade the more, one ray the less,
  Had half impair'd the nameless grace

Which waves in every raven tress,
  Or softly lightens o'er her face;   10
Where thoughts serenely sweet express
  How pure, how dear their dwelling-place.

And on that cheek, and o'er that brow,
  So soft, so calm, yet eloquent,
The smiles that win, the tints that glow,
  But tell of days in goodness spent,
A mind at peace with all below,
  A heart whose love is innocent!

1814

OH! SNATCH'D AWAY IN BEAUTY'S BLOOM

OH! snatch'd away in beauty's bloom,
On thee shall press no ponderous tomb;
  But on thy turf shall roses rear
  Their leaves, the earliest of the year;
And the wild cypress wave in tender gloom:

And oft by yon blue gushing stream
  Shall Sorrow lean her drooping head,
And feed deep thought with many a dream,
  And lingering pause and lightly tread;
  Fond wretch! as if her step disturb'd the
    dead!   10

Away! we know that tears are vain,
  That death nor heeds nor hears distress:
Will this unteach us to complain?
  Or make one mourner weep the less?
And thou—who tell'st me to forget,
Thy looks are wan, thine eyes are wet.

1814–15

WHEN COLDNESS WRAPS THIS SUFFERING CLAY

WHEN coldness wraps this suffering clay,
  Ah! whither strays the immortal mind?
It cannot die, it cannot stay,
  But leaves its darken'd dust behind.
Then, unembodied, doth it trace
  By steps each planet's heavenly way?
Or fill at once the realms of space,
  A thing of eyes, that all survey?

Eternal, boundless, undecay'd,
  A thought unseen, but seeing all,   10
All, all in earth or skies display'd,
  Shall it survey, shall it recall:

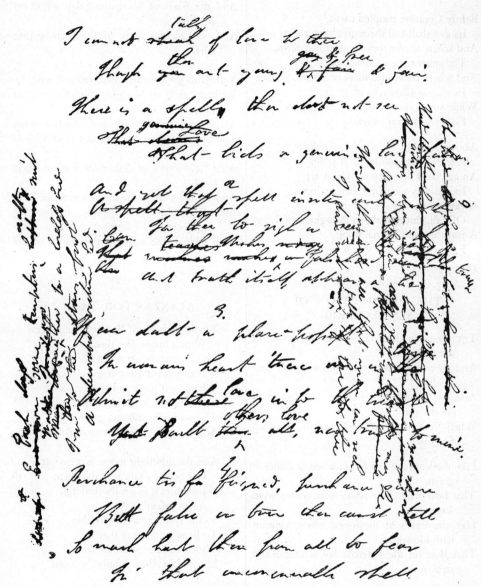

Six Stanzas of Byron's MS of *Love and Gold*. (See Appendix I.)

Each fainter trace that memory holds
  So darkly of departed years,
In one broad glance the soul beholds,
  And all, that was, at once appears.

Before Creation peopled earth,
  Its eye shall roll through chaos back;
And where the furthest heaven had birth,
  The spirit trace its rising track.   20
And where the future mars or makes,
  Its glance dilate o'er all to be,
While sun is quench'd or system breaks,
  Fix'd in its own eternity.

Above or Love, Hope, Hate, or Fear,
  It lives all passionless and pure:
An age shall fleet like earthly year;
  Its years as moments shall endure.
Away, away, without a wing,
  O'er all, through all, its thought shall fly, 30
A nameless and eternal thing,
  Forgetting what it was to die.

1814-15

THE DESTRUCTION OF
SENNACHERIB

THE Assyrian came down like the wolf on
  the fold,
And his cohorts were gleaming in purple and
  gold;
And the sheen of their spears was like stars
  on the sea,
When the blue wave rolls nightly on deep
  Galilee.

Like the leaves of the forest when Summer is
  green,
That host with their banners at sunset were
  seen:
Like the leaves of the forest when Autumn
  hath blown,
That host on the morrow lay wither'd and
  strown.

For the Angel of Death spread his wings on
  the blast,   9
And breathed in the face of the foe as he pass'd;
And the eyes of the sleepers wax'd deadly
  and chill,
And their hearts but once heaved, and for
  ever grew still!

And there lay the steed with his nostril all
  wide,
But through it there roll'd not the breath of
  his pride;
And the foam of his gasping lay white on
  the turf,
And cold as the spray of the rock-beating
  surf.

And there lay the rider distorted and pale,
With the dew on his brow, and the rust on
  his mail:
And the tents were all silent, the banner alone,
The lances unlifted, the trumpet unblown. 20

And the widows of Ashur are loud in their
  wail,
And the idols are broke in the temple of Baal;
And the might of the Gentile, unsmote by
  the sword,
Hath melted like snow in the glance of the
  Lord!

1815

STANZAS FOR MUSIC

THERE be none of Beauty's daughters
  With a magic like thee;
And like music on the waters
  Is thy sweet voice to me:
When, as if its sound were causing
The charmed ocean's pausing,
The waves lie still and gleaming,
And the lull'd winds seem dreaming:

And the midnight moon is weaving
  Her bright chain o'er the deep;   10
Whose breast is gently heaving,
  As an infant's asleep:
So the spirit bows before thee,
To listen and adore thee;
With a full but soft emotion,
Like the swell of Summer's ocean.

1816

FARE THEE WELL

FARE thee well! and if for ever,
  Still for ever, fare thee well:
Even though unforgiving, never
  'Gainst thee shall my heart rebel.

Would that breast were bared before thee
    Where thy head so oft hath lain,
While that placid sleep came o'er thee
    Which thou ne'er canst know again:

Would that breast, by thee glanced over,
    Every inmost thought could show!   10
Then thou wouldst at last discover
    'Twas not well to spurn it so.

Though the world for this commend thee—
    Though it smile upon the blow,
Even its praises must offend thee,
    Founded on another's woe:

Though my many faults defaced me,
    Could no other arm be found,
Than the one which once embraced me,
    To inflict a cureless wound?   20

Yet, oh yet, thyself deceive not;
    Love may sink by slow decay,
But by sudden wrench, believe not
    Hearts can thus be torn away:

Still thine own its life retaineth,
    Still must mine, though bleeding, beat;
And the undying thought which paineth
    Is—that we no more may meet.

These are words of deeper sorrow
    Than the wail above the dead;   30
Both shall live, but every morrow
    Wake us from a widow'd bed.

And when thou wouldst solace gather,
    When our child's first accents flow,
Wilt thou teach her to say "Father!"
    Though his care she must forego?

When her little hands shall press thee,
    When her lip to thine is press'd,
Think of him whose prayer shall bless thee,
    Think of him thy love had bless'd!   40

Should her lineaments resemble
    Those thou never more may'st see,
Then thy heart will softly tremble
    With a pulse yet true to me.

All my faults perchance thou knowest,
    All my madness none can know;
All my hopes, where'er thou goest,
    Wither, yet with *thee* they go.

Every feeling hath been shaken;
    Pride, which not a world could bow,   50
Bows to thee—by thee forsaken,
    Even my soul forsakes me now:

But 'tis done—all words are idle—
    Words from me are vainer still;
But the thoughts we cannot bridle
    Force their way without the will.

Fare thee well! thus disunited,
    Torn from every nearer tie,
Sear'd in heart, and lone, and blighted,
    More than this I scarce can die.   60

March 17, 1816

STANZAS TO AUGUSTA

When all around grew drear and dark,
    And reason half withheld her ray—
And hope but shed a dying spark
    Which more misled my lonely way;

In that deep midnight of the mind,
    And that internal strife of heart,
When dreading to be deem'd too kind,
    The weak despair—the cold depart;

When fortune changed—and love fled far,
    And hatred's shafts flew thick and fast,   10
Thou wert the solitary star
    Which rose and set not to the last.

Oh! blest be thine unbroken light!
    That watch'd me as a seraph's eye,
And stood between me and the night,
    For ever shining sweetly nigh.

And when the cloud upon us came,
    Which strove to blacken o'er thy ray—
Then purer spread its gentle flame,
    And dash'd the darkness all away.   20

Still may thy spirit dwell on mine,
    And teach it what to brave or brook—
There's more in one soft word of thine
    Than in the world's defied rebuke.

Thou stood'st, as stands a lovely tree,
    That still unbroke, though gently bent,
Still waves with fond fidelity
    Its boughs above a monument.

The winds might rend—the skies might pour,
  But there thou wert—and still wouldst be
Devoted in the stormiest hour   31
  To shed thy weeping leaves o'er me.

But thou and thine shall know no blight,
  Whatever fate on me may fall;
For heaven in sunshine will requite
  The kind—and thee the most of all.

Then let the ties of baffled love
  Be broken—thine will never break;
Thy heart can feel—but will not move;
  Thy soul, though soft, will never shake. 40

And thee, when all was lost beside,
  Were found and still are fix'd in thee;—
And bearing still a breast so tried,
  Earth is no desert—ev'n to me.
1816

STANZAS TO AUGUSTA

Though the day of my destiny's over,
  And the star of my fate hath declined,
Thy soft heart refused to discover
  The faults which so many could find;
Though thy soul with my grief was ac-
    quainted,
  It shrunk not to share it with me,
And the love which my spirit hath painted
  It never hath found but in *thee*.

Then when nature around me is smiling,
  The last smile which answers to mine, 10
I do not believe it beguiling,
  Because it reminds me of thine;
And when winds are at war with the ocean,
  As the breasts I believed in with me,
If their billows excite an emotion,
  It is that they bear me from *thee*.

Though the rock of my last hope is shiver'd,
  And its fragments are sunk in the wave,
Though I feel that my soul is deliver'd
  To pain—it shall not be its slave.   20
There is many a pang to pursue me:
  They may crush, but they shall not con-
    temn;
They may torture, but shall not subdue me;
  'Tis of *thee* that I think—not of them.

Though human, thou didst not deceive me,
  Though woman, thou didst not forsake,
Though loved, thou forborest to grieve me,
  Though slander'd thou never couldst shake;
Though trusted, thou didst not disclaim me,
  Though parted, it was not to fly,   30
Though watchful, 'twas not to defame me,
  Nor, mute, that the world might belie.

Yet I blame not the world, nor despise it,
  Nor the war of the many with one;
If my soul was not fitted to prize it,
  'Twas folly not sooner to shun:
And if dearly that error hath cost me,
  And more than I once could foresee,
I have found that, whatever it lost me,
  It could not deprive me of *thee*.   40

From the wreck of the past, which hath
    perish'd,
  Thus much I at least may recall,
It hath taught me that what I most cherish'd
  Deserved to be dearest of all:
In the desert a fountain is springing,
  In the wide waste there still is a tree,
And a bird in the solitude singing,
  Which speaks to my spirit of *thee*.
July 24, 1816

EPISTLE TO AUGUSTA

My sister! my sweet sister! if a name
Dearer and purer were, it should be thine;
Mountains and seas divide us, but I claim
No tears, but tenderness to answer mine:
Go where I will, to me thou art the same—
A loved regret which I would not resign.
There yet are two things in my destiny,—
A world to roam through, and a home with
    thee.

The first were nothing—had I still the last,
  It were the haven of my happiness;   10
But other claims and other ties thou hast,
  And mine is not the wish to make them less.
A strange doom is thy father's son's, and
    past
Recalling, as it lies beyond redress;
Reversed for him our grandsire's fate of
    yore,—
He had no rest at sea, nor I on shore.

If my inheritance of storms hath been
In other elements, and on the rocks
Of perils, overlook'd or unforeseen,   19
I have sustain'd my share of worldly shocks,
The fault was mine; nor do I seek to screen
My errors with defensive paradox;
I have been cunning in mine overthrow,
The careful pilot of my proper woe.

Mine were my faults, and mine be their
     reward.
My whole life was a contest, since the day
That gave me being, gave me that which
     marr'd
The gift,—a fate, or will, that walk'd
     astray;
And I at times have found the struggle
     hard,
And thought of shaking off my bonds of
     clay: 30
But now I fain would for a time survive,
If but to see what next can well arrive.

Kingdoms and empires in my little day
I have outlived, and yet I am not old;
And when I look on this, the petty spray
Of my own years of trouble, which have
     roll'd
Like a wild bay of breakers, melts away:
Something—I know not what—does still
     uphold
A spirit of slight patience;—not in vain,
Even for its own sake, do we purchase pain. 40

Perhaps the workings of defiance stir
Within me—or perhaps a cold despair,
Brought on when ills habitually recur,—
Perhaps a kinder clime, or purer air,
(For even to this may change of soul refer,
And with light armour we may learn to
     bear,)
Have taught me a strange quiet, which
     was not
The chief companion of a calmer lot.

I feel almost at times as I have felt
In happy childhood; trees, and flowers,
     and brooks,   50
Which do remember me of where I dwelt
Ere my young mind was sacrificed to
     books,

Come as of yore upon me, and can melt
My heart with recognition of their looks;
And even at moments I could think I see
Some living thing to love—but none like thee.

Here are the Alpine landscapes which
     create
A fund for contemplation;—to admire
Is a brief feeling of a trivial date;
But something worthier do such scenes
     inspire: 60
Here to be lonely is not desolate,
For much I view which I could most desire,
And, above all, a lake I can behold
Lovelier, not dearer, than our own of old.

Oh that thou wert but with me!—but I
     grow
The fool of my own wishes, and forget
The solitude which I have vaunted so
Has lost its praise in this but one regret;
There may be others which I less may
     show;—
I am not of the plaintive mood, and yet
I feel an ebb in my philosophy,   71
And the tide rising in my alter'd eye.

I did remind thee of our own dear Lake,
By the old Hall which may be mine no more.
Leman's is fair; but think not I forsake
The sweet remembrance of a dearer shore:
Sad havoc Time must with my memory
     make,
Ere *that* or *thou* can fade these eyes before;
Though, like all things which I have loved,
     they are
Resign'd for ever, or divided far.   80

The world is all before me; I but ask
Of Nature that with which she will com-
     ply—
It is but in her summer's sun to bask,
To mingle with the quiet of her sky,
To see her gentle face without a mask,
And never gaze on it with apathy.
She was my early friend, and now shall be
My sister—till I look again on thee.

I can reduce all feelings but this one;   89
And that I would not;—for at length I see
Such scenes as those wherein my life begun.
The earliest—even the only paths for me—

Had I but sooner learnt the crowd to shun,
I had been better than I now can be;
The passions which have torn me would
    have slept;
I had not suffer'd, and *thou* hadst not wept.

With false Ambition what had I to do?
Little with Love, and least of all with
    Fame;
And yet they came unsought, and with me
    grew,
And made me all which they can make—a
    name.   100
Yet this was not the end I did pursue;
Surely I once beheld a nobler aim.
But all is over—I am one the more
To baffled millions which have gone before.

And for the future, this world's future may
From me demand but little of my care;
I have outlived myself by many a day;
Having survived so many things that were;
My years have been no slumber, but the
    prey
Of ceaseless vigils; for I had the share   110
Of life which might have fill'd a century,
Before its fourth in time had pass'd me by.

And for the remnant which may be to come
I am content; and for the past I feel
Not thankless,—for within the crowded
    sum
Of struggles, happiness at times would
    steal,
And for the present, I would not benumb
My feelings further.—Nor shall I conceal
That with all this I still can look around,
And worship Nature with a thought profound.

For thee, my own sweet sister, in thy heart
I know myself secure, as thou in mine;   122
We were and are—I am, even as thou art—
Beings who ne'er each other can resign;
It is the same, together or apart,
From life's commencement to its slow de-
    cline
We are entwined—let death come slow or
    fast,
The tie which bound the first endures the last!
1816

SO, WE'LL GO NO MORE A ROVING

So, we'll go no more a roving
    So late into the night,
Though the heart be still as loving,
    And the moon be still as bright.

For the sword outwears its sheath,
    And the soul wears out the breast,
And the heart must pause to breathe,
    And love itself have rest.

Though the night was made for loving,
    And the day returns too soon,   10
Yet we'll go no more a roving
    By the light of the moon.

1817

TO THOMAS MOORE

MY boat is on the shore,
    And my bark is on the sea;
But, before I go, Tom Moore,
    Here's a double health to thee!

Here's a sigh to those who love me,
    And a smile to those who hate;
And, whatever sky's above me,
    Here's a heart for every fate.

Though the ocean roar around me,
    Yet it still shall bear me on;   10
Though a desert should surround me,
    It hath springs that may be won.

Were't the last drop in the well,
    As I gasp'd upon the brink,
Ere my fainting spirit fell,
    'Tis to thee that I would drink.

With that water, as this wine,
    The libation I would pour
Should be—peace with thine and mine,
    And a health to thee, Tom Moore.   20

July, 1817

STANZAS WRITTEN ON THE ROAD BETWEEN FLORENCE AND PISA

OH, talk not to me of a name great in story;
The days of our youth are the days of our
    glory;

And the myrtle and ivy of sweet two-and-
 twenty
Are worth all your laurels, though ever so
 plenty.

What are garlands and crowns to the brow
 that is wrinkled?
'Tis but as a dead-flower with May-dew be-
 sprinkled.
Then away with all such from the head that
 is hoary!
What care I for the wreaths that can *only* give
 glory!

Oh FAME!—if I e'er took delight in thy praises,
'Twas less for the sake of thy high-sounding
 phrases,   10
Than to see the bright eyes of the dear one
 discover,
She thought that I was not unworthy to love
 her.

There chiefly I sought thee, *there* only I found
 thee;
Her glance was the best of the rays that surround thee;
When it sparkled o'er aught that was bright
 in my story,
I knew it was love, and I felt it was glory.

November, 1821

ON THIS DAY I COMPLETE MY THIRTY–SIXTH YEAR

MISSOLONGHI, Jan. 22, 1824.

'TIS time this heart should be unmoved,
 Since others it hath ceased to move:
Yet, though I cannot be beloved,
 Still let me love!

My days are in the yellow leaf;
 The flowers and fruits of love are gone;
The worm, the canker, and the grief
 Are mine alone!

The fire that on my bosom preys
 Is lone as some volcanic isle;   10
No torch is kindled at its blaze—
 A funeral pile.

The hope, the fear, the jealous care,
 The exalted portion of the pain

And power of love, I cannot share,
 But wear the chain.

But 'tis not *thus*—and 'tis not *here*—
 Such thoughts should shake my soul, nor
 now,
Where glory decks the hero's bier,
 Or binds his brow.   20

The sword, the banner, and the field,
 Glory and Greece, around me see!
The Spartan, borne upon his shield,
 Was not more free.

Awake! (not Greece—she *is* awake!)
 Awake, my spirit! Think through *whom*
Thy life-blood tracks its parent lake,
 And then strike home!

Tread those reviving passions down,
 Unworthy manhood!—unto thee   30
Indifferent should the smile or frown
 Of beauty be.

If thou regrett'st thy youth, *why live?*
 The land of honourable death
Is here:—up to the field, and give
 Away thy breath!

Seek out—less often sought than found—
 A soldier's grave, for thee the best;
Then look around, and choose thy ground,
 And take thy rest.   40

CHILDE HAROLD'S PILGRIMAGE

CANTO THE THIRD

I

Is thy face like thy mother's, my fair child!
ADA! sole daughter of my house and heart?
When last I saw thy young blue eyes they
 smiled,
And then we parted,—not as now we part,
But with a hope.—
                    Awaking with a start,
The waters heave around me; and on high
The winds lift up their voices: I depart,
Whither I know not; but the hour's gone by,
When Albion's lessening shores could grieve
 or glad mine eye.

II

Once more upon the waters! yet once
    more!   10
And the waves bound beneath me as a steed
That knows his rider. Welcome to their
    roar!
Swift be their guidance, wheresoe'er it lead!
Though the strain'd mast should quiver as a
    reed,
And the rent canvas fluttering strew the gale,
Still must I on; for I am as a weed,
Flung from the rock, on Ocean's foam to
    sail
Where'er the surge may sweep, the tempest's
    breath prevail.

III

In my youth's summer I did sing of One,
The wandering outlaw of his own dark
    mind;   20
Again I seize the theme, then but begun,
And bear it with me, as the rushing wind
Bears the cloud onwards: in that Tale I find
The furrows of long thought, and dried-up
    tears,
Which, ebbing, leave a sterile track behind,
O'er which all heavily the journeying years
Plod the last sands of life,—where not a flower
    appears.

IV

Since my young days of passion—joy, or
    pain,
Perchance my heart and harp have lost a
    string,
And both may jar: it may be, that in vain 30
I would essay as I have sung to sing.
Yet, though a dreary strain, to this I cling;
So that it wean me from the weary dream
Of selfish grief or gladness—so it fling
Forgetfulness around me—it shall seem
To me, though to none else, a not ungrateful
    theme.

V

He, who grown aged in this world of woe,
In deeds, not years, piercing the depths of
    life,
So that no wonder waits him; nor below
Can love or sorrow, fame, ambition, strife,
Cut to his heart again with the keen knife 41

Of silent, sharp endurance: he can tell
Why thought seeks refuge in lone caves, yet
    rife
With airy images, and shapes which dwell
Still unimpair'd, though old, in the soul's
    haunted cell.

VI

'Tis to create, and in creating live
A being more intense that we endow
With form our fancy, gaining as we give
The life we image, even as I do now.
What am I? Nothing: but not so art thou, 50
Soul of my thought! with whom I traverse
    earth,
Invisible but gazing, as I glow
Mix'd with thy spirit, blended with thy
    birth,
And feeling still with thee in my crush'd feel-
    ings' dearth.

VII

Yet must I think less wildly:—I *have*
    thought
Too long and darkly, till my brain became,
In its own eddy boiling and o'erwrought,
A whirling gulf of phantasy and flame:
And thus, untaught in youth my heart to
    tame,
My springs of life were poison'd. 'Tis too
    late!   60
Yet am I changed; though still enough the
    same
In strength to bear what time cannot abate,
And feed on bitter fruits without accusing
    Fate.

VIII

Something too much of this:—but now 'tis
    past,
And the spell closes with its silent seal.
Long absent HAROLD re-appears at last;
He of the breast which fain no more would
    feel,
Wrung with the wounds which kill not,
    but ne'er heal;
Yet Time, who changes all, had alter'd him
In soul and aspect as in age: years steal 70
Fire from the mind as vigour from the limb;
And life's enchanted cup but sparkles near the
    brim.

Let such approach this consecrated land—
And pass in peace along the magic waste
But spare its relics—let no wanton hand
Deface the scenes already how defaced!
Not for such purpose were these altars placed
Revere the remnant nations once revered—
So may our country's name be undisgraced!
So mayst thou prosper where thy youth was reared
By every honest joy of love & life endeared!—

For thee, who thus in too protracted song
Hast soothed thine idlesse with inglorious lays,
Soon shall thy voice be lost amid the throng
Of louder minstrels of these later days,
To these reign this strife for fading Bays

A Page from Byron's *Childe Harold's Pilgrimage*. (See Appendix I.)

IX

His had been quaff'd too quickly, and he
found
The dregs were wormwood; but he fill'd
again,
And from a purer fount, on holier ground,
And deem'd its spring perpetual; but in vain!
Still round him clung invisibly a chain
Which gall'd for ever, fettering though un-
seen,
And heavy though it clank'd not; worn with
pain,
Which pined although it spoke not, and
grew keen, 80
Entering with every step he took through
many a scene.

X

Secure in guarded coldness, he had mix'd
Again in fancied safety with his kind,
And deem'd his spirit now so firmly fix'd
And sheath'd with an invulnerable mind,
That, if no joy, no sorrow lurk'd behind;
And he, as one, might 'midst the many
stand
Unheeded, searching through the crowd to
find
Fit speculation; such as in strange land
He found in wonder-works of God and Na-
ture's hand. 90

XI

But who can view the ripen'd rose, nor seek
To wear it? who can curiously behold
The smoothness and the sheen of beauty's
cheek,
Nor feel the heart can never all grow old?
Who can contemplate Fame through clouds
unfold
The star which rises o'er her steep, nor
climb?
Harold, once more within the vortex, roll'd
On with the giddy circle, chasing Time,
Yet with a nobler aim than in youth's fond
prime.

XII

But soon he knew himself the most unfit 100
Of men to herd with Man; with whom he
held
Little in common; untaught to submit

His thoughts to others, though his soul was
quell'd
In youth by his own thoughts; still uncom-
pell'd,
He would not yield dominion of his mind
To spirits against whom his own rebell'd;
Proud though in desolation; which could
find
A life within itself, to breathe without mankind.

XIII

Where rose the mountains, there to him
were friends;
Where roll'd the ocean, thereon was his
home; 110
Where a blue sky, and glowing clime, ex-
tends,
He had the passion and the power to roam;
The desert, forest, cavern, breaker's foam,
Were unto him companionship; they spake
A mutual language, clearer than the tome
Of his land's tongue, which he would oft
forsake
For Nature's pages glass'd by sunbeams on the
lake.

XIV

Like the Chaldean, he could watch the stars,
Till he had peopled them with beings bright
As their own beams; and earth, and earth-
born jars, 120
And human frailties, were forgotten quite:
Could he have kept his spirit to that flight
He had been happy; but this clay will sink
Its spark immortal, envying it the light
To which it mounts, as if to break the link
That keeps us from yon heaven which woos
us to its brink.

XV

But in Man's dwellings he became a thing
Restless and worn, and stern and wearisome,
Droop'd as a wild-born falcon with clipt
wing,
To whom the boundless air alone were
home: 130
Then came his fit again, which to o'ercome,
As eagerly the barr'd-up bird will beat
His breast and beak against his wiry dome
Till the blood tinge his plumage, so the heat
Of his impeded soul would through his bosom
eat.

XVI

Self-exiled Harold wanders forth again,
With nought of hope left, but with less of
gloom;
The very knowledge that he lived in vain,
That all was over on this side the tomb,
Had made Despair a smilingness assume, 140
Which, though 'twere wild,—as on the
plunder'd wreck
When mariners would madly meet their
doom
With draughts intemperate on the sinking
deck,—
Did yet inspire a cheer, which he forbore to
check.

XVII

Stop!—for thy tread is on an Empire's dust!
An Earthquake's spoil is sepulchred below!
Is the spot mark'd with no colossal bust?
Nor column trophied for triumphal show?
None; but the moral's truth tells simpler so,
As the ground was before, thus let it be;—
How that red rain hath made the harvest
grow!   151
And is this all the world has gain'd by thee,
Thou first and last of fields! king-making
Victory?

XVIII

And Harold stands upon this place of skulls,
The grave of France, the deadly Waterloo!
How in an hour the power which gave an-
nuls
Its gifts, transferring fame as fleeting too!
In "pride of place" here last the eagle flew,
Then tore with bloody talon the rent plain,
Pierced by the shaft of banded nations
through;   160
Ambition's life and labours all were vain;
He wears the shatter'd links of the world's
broken chain.

XIX

Fit retribution! Gaul may champ the bit
And foam in fetters;—but is Earth more
free?
Did nations combat to make *One* submit;
Or league to teach all kings true sover-
eignty?
What! shall reviving Thraldom again be

servitude

The patch'd-up idol of enlighten'd days?
Shall we, who struck the Lion down, shall
we
Pay the Wolf homage? proffering lowly
gaze   170
And servile knees to thrones? No; *prove* before
ye praise!

XX

If not, o'er one fallen despot boast no more!
In vain fair cheeks were furrow'd with hot
tears
For Europe's flowers long rooted up before
The trampler of her vineyards; in vain years
Of death, depopulation, bondage, fears,
Have all been borne, and broken by the
accord
Of roused-up millions; all that most endears
Glory, is when the myrtle wreathes a sword
Such as Harmodius drew on Athens' tyrant
lord.   *delivered Athens from*   180
Hyppias + Hypparster

XXI

There was a sound of revelry by night,
And Belgium's capital had gather'd then
Her Beauty and her Chivalry, and bright
The lamps shone o'er fair women and brave
men;
A thousand hearts beat happily; and when
Music arose with its voluptuous swell,
Soft eyes look'd love to eyes which spake
again,
And all went merry as a marriage bell;
But hush! hark! a deep sound strikes like a
rising knell!   *Becky Sharp*
Ball at Brussel
by Lady de Ros

XXII

Did ye not hear it?—No; 'twas but the
wind,   190
Or the car rattling o'er the stony street;
On with the dance! let joy be unconfined;
No sleep till morn, when Youth and Pleas-
ure meet
To chase the glowing Hours with flying
feet—
But hark!—that heavy sound breaks in once
more,
As if the clouds its echo would repeat;
And nearer, clearer, deadlier than before!
Arm! Arm! it is—it is—the cannon's opening
roar!

famous account of
Waterloo

XXIII

Within a window'd niche of that high hall
Sate Brunswick's fated chieftain; he did
    hear   200
That sound the first amidst the festival,
And caught its tone with Death's prophetic
    ear;
And when they smiled because he deem'd
    it near,
His heart more truly knew that peal too well
Which stretch'd his father on a bloody
    bier,
And roused the vengeance blood alone
    could quell;
He rush'd into the field, and, foremost fight-
    ing, fell.

XXIV

Ah! then and there was hurrying to and
    fro,
And gathering tears, and tremblings of dis-
    tress,
And cheeks all pale, which but an hour
    ago   210
Blush'd at the praise of their own loveliness;
And there were sudden partings, such as
    press
The life from out young hearts, and choking
    sighs
Which ne'er might be repeated; who could
    guess
If ever more should meet those mutual eyes,
Since upon night so sweet such awful morn
    could rise!

XXV

And there was mounting in hot haste: the
    steed,
The mustering squadron, and the clattering
    car,
Went pouring forward with impetuous
    speed,
And swiftly forming in the ranks of war; 220
And the deep thunder peal on peal afar;
And near, the beat of the alarming drum
Roused up the soldier ere the morning
    star;
While throng'd the citizens with terror
    dumb,
Or whispering, with white lips—"The foe!
    they come! they come!"

XXVI

And wild and high the "Cameron's gather-
    ing" rose!
The war-note of Lochiel, which Albyn's
    hills
Have heard, and heard, too, have her Saxon
    foes:—
How in the noon of night that pibroch
    thrills,
Savage and shrill! But with the breath which
    fills   230
Their mountain-pipe, so fill the mountain-
    eers
With the fierce native daring which in-
    stils
The stirring memory of a thousand years,
And Evan's, Donald's fame rings in each
    clansman's ears!

XXVII

And Ardennes waves above them her green
    leaves,
Dewy with nature's tear-drops as they
    pass,
Grieving, if aught inanimate e'er grieves,
Over the unreturning brave,—alas!
Ere evening to be trodden like the grass
Which now beneath them, but above shall
    grow   240
In its next verdure, when this fiery mass
Of living valour, rolling on the foe
And burning with high hope shall moulder
    cold and low.

XXVIII

Last noon beheld them full of lusty life,
Last eve in Beauty's circle proudly gay,
The midnight brought the signal-sound of
    strife,
The morn the marshalling in arms,—the
    day
Battle's magnificently stern array!
The thunder-clouds close o'er it, which
    when rent
The earth is cover'd thick with other
    clay,
Which her own clay shall cover, heap'd and
    pent,   251
Rider and horse,—friend, foe,—in one red
    burial blent!

XXIX

Their praise is hymn'd by loftier harps than
    mine:
Yet one I would select from that proud
    throng,
Partly because they blend me with his line,
And partly that I did his sire some wrong,
And partly that bright names will hallow
    song;
And his was of the bravest, and when
    shower'd
The death-bolts deadliest the thinn'd files
    along,
Even where the thickest of war's tempest
    lower'd,   260
They reach'd no nobler breast than thine,
    young gallant Howard!

XXX

There have been tears and breaking hearts
    for thee,
And mine were nothing had I such to give;
But when I stood beneath the fresh green
    tree,
Which living waves where thou didst cease
    to live,
And saw around me the wide field revive
With fruits and fertile promise, and the
    Spring
Came forth her work of gladness to con-
    trive,
With all her reckless birds upon the wing,
I turn'd from all she brought to those she could
    not bring.   270

XXXI

I turn'd to thee, to thousands, of whom
    each
And one as all a ghastly gap did make
In his own kind and kindred, whom to
    teach
Forgetfulness were mercy for their sake;
The Archangel's trump, not Glory's, must
    awake
Those whom they thirst for; though the
    sound of Fame
May for a moment soothe, it cannot slake
The fever of vain longing, and the name
So honour'd but assumes a stronger, bitterer
    claim.

XXXII

They mourn, but smile at length; and, smil-
    ing, mourn: 280
The tree will wither long before it fall;
The hull drives on, though mast and sail
    be torn;
The roof-tree sinks, but moulders on the
    hall
In massy hoariness; the ruin'd wall
Stands when its wind-worn battlements are
    gone;
The bars survive the captive they enthral;
The day drags through, though storms keep
    out the sun;
And thus the heart will break, yet brokenly
    live on:

XXXIII

Even as a broken mirror, which the glass
In every fragment multiplies; and makes   290
A thousand images of one that was,
The same, and still the more, the more it
    breaks;
And thus the heart will do which not for-
    sakes,
Living in shatter'd guise; and still, and cold,
And bloodless, with its sleepless sorrow
    aches,
Yet withers on till all without is old,
Showing no visible sign, for such things are
    untold.

XXXIV

There is a very life in our despair,
Vitality of poison,—a quick root
Which feeds these deadly branches; for it
    were   300
As nothing did we die; but Life will suit
Itself to Sorrow's most detested fruit,
Like to the apples on the Dead Sea's shore,
All ashes to the taste: Did man compute
Existence by enjoyment, and count o'er
Such hours 'gainst years of life,—say, would
    he name threescore?

XXXV

The Psalmist number'd out the years of
    man:
They are enough; and if thy tale be *true*,
Thou, who didst grudge him even that fleet-
    ing span,

More than enough, thou fatal Waterloo! 310
Millions of tongues record thee, and anew
Their children's lips shall echo them, and
  say—
"Here, where the sword united nations drew,
Our countrymen were warring on that day!"
And this is much, and all which will not
  pass away.

XXXVI

There sunk the greatest, nor the worst of
  men,
Whose spirit, antithetically mixt,
One moment of the mightiest, and again
On little objects with like firmness fixt;
Extreme in all things! hadst thou been be-
  twixt, 320
Thy throne had still been thine, or never
  been;
For daring made thy rise as fall: thou seek'st
Even now to re-assume the imperial mien,
And shake again the world, the Thunderer
  of the scene!

XXXVII

Conqueror and captive of the earth art thou!
She trembles at thee still, and thy wild name
Was ne'er more bruited in men's minds than
  now
That thou art nothing, save the jest of Fame,
Who woo'd thee once, thy vassal, and became
The flatterer of thy fierceness, till thou wert
A god unto thyself; nor less the same 331
To the astounded kingdoms all inert,
Who deem'd thee for a time whate'er thou
  didst assert.

XXXVIII

Oh, more or less than man—in high or low,
Battling with nations, flying from the field;
Now making monarchs' necks thy footstool,
  now
More than thy meanest soldier taught to
  yield;
An empire thou couldst crush, command,
  rebuild,
But govern not thy pettiest passion, nor,
However deeply in men's spirits skill'd, 340
Look through thine own, nor curb the lust
  of war,
Nor learn that tempted Fate will leave the
  loftiest star.

XXXIX

Yet well thy soul hath brook'd the turning
  tide
With that untaught innate philosophy,
Which, be it wisdom, coldness, or deep
  pride,
Is gall and wormwood to an enemy.
When the whole host of hatred stood hard
  by,
To watch and mock thee shrinking, thou
  hast smiled
With a sedate and all-enduring eye;—
When Fortune fled her spoil'd and favourite
  child, 350
He stood unbow'd beneath the ills upon him
  piled.

XL

Sager than in thy fortunes; for in them
Ambition steel'd thee on too far to show
That just habitual scorn, which could con-
  temn
Men and their thoughts; 'twas wise to feel,
  not so
To wear it ever on thy lip and brow,
And spurn the instruments thou wert to
  use
Till they were turn'd unto thine overthrow:
'Tis but a worthless world to win or lose;
So hath it proved to thee, and all such lot
  who choose. 360

XLI

If, like a tower upon a headland rock,
Thou hadst been made to stand or fall alone,
Such scorn of man had help'd to brave the
  shock;
But men's thoughts were the steps which
  paved thy throne,
Their admiration thy best weapon shone;
The part of Philip's son was thine, not then
(Unless aside thy purple had been thrown)
Like stern Diogenes to mock at men;
For sceptred cynics earth were far too wide a
  den.

XLII

But quiet to quick bosoms is a hell, 370
And *there* hath been thy bane; there is a fire
And motion of the soul which will not dwell
In its own narrow being, but aspire
Beyond the fitting medium of desire;

And, but once kindled, quenchless ever-
    more,
Preys upon high adventure, nor can tire
Of aught but rest; a fever at the core,
Fatal to him who bears, to all who ever bore.

XLIII

This makes the madmen who have made
    men mad
By their contagion; Conquerors and Kings,
Founders of sects and systems, to whom
    add   381
Sophists, Bards, Statesmen, all unquiet
    things
Which stir too strongly the soul's secret
    springs,
And are themselves the fools to those they
    fool;
Envied, yet how unenviable! what stings
Are theirs! One breast laid open were a
    school
Which would unteach mankind the lust to
    shine or rule:

XLIV

Their breath is agitation, and their life
A storm whereon they ride, to sink at last,
And yet so nursed and bigoted to strife, 390
That should their days, surviving perils
    past,
Melt to calm twilight, they feel overcast
With sorrow and supineness, and so die;
Even as a flame unfed, which runs to waste
With its own flickering, or a sword laid
    by,
Which eats into itself, and rusts ingloriously.

XLV

He who ascends to mountain-tops, shall
    find
The loftiest peaks most wrapt in clouds and
    snow;
He who surpasses or subdues mankind, 399
Must look down on the hate of those below.
Though high *above* the sun of glory glow,
And far *beneath* the earth and ocean spread,
Round him are icy rocks, and loudly blow
Contending tempests on his naked head,
And thus reward the toils which to those sum-
    mits led.

XLVI

Away with these! true Wisdom's world will
    be
Within its own creation, or in thine,
Maternal Nature! for who teems like thee,
Thus on the banks of thy majestic Rhine?
There Harold gazes on a work divine, 410
A blending of all beauties; streams and dells,
Fruit, foliage, crag, wood, cornfield, moun-
    tain, vine,
And chiefless castles breathing stern fare-
    wells
From gray but leafy walls, where Ruin greenly
    dwells.

XLVII

And there they stand, as stands a lofty mind,
Worn, but unstooping to the baser crowd,
All tenantless, save to the crannying wind,
Or holding dark communion with the
    crowd.
There was a day when they were young and
    proud;   419
Banners on high, and battles pass'd below;
But they who fought are in a bloody shroud,
And those which waved are shredless dust
    ere now,
And the bleak battlements shall bear no future
    blow.

XLVIII

Beneath those battlements, within those
    walls,
Power dwelt amidst her passions; in proud
    state
Each robber chief upheld his armed halls,
Doing his evil will, nor less elate
Than mightier heroes of a longer date.
What want these outlaws conquerors should
    have
But history's purchased page to call them
    great?   430
A wider space, an ornamented grave?
Their hopes were not less warm, their souls
    were full as brave.

XLIX

In their baronial feuds and single fields,
What deeds of prowess unrecorded died!
And Love, which lent a blazon to their
    shields,

With emblems well devised by amorous
    pride,
Through all the mail of iron hearts would
    glide;
But still their flame was fierceness, and drew
    on
Keen contest and destruction near allied,
And many a tower for some fair mischief
    won,   440
Saw the discolour'd Rhine beneath its ruin run.

L

But Thou, exulting and abounding river!
Making thy waves a blessing as they flow
Through banks whose beauty would endure
    for ever
Could man but leave thy bright creation so,
Nor its fair promise from the surface mow
With the sharp scythe of conflict,—then
    to see
Thy valley of sweet waters, were to know
Earth paved like Heaven; and to seem such
    to me,
Even now what wants thy stream?—that it
    should Lethe be.   450

LI

A thousand battles have assail'd thy banks,
But these and half their fame have pass'd
    away,
And Slaughter heap'd on high his weltering
    ranks;
Their very graves are gone, and what are
    they?
Thy tide wash'd down the blood of yesterday,
And all was stainless, and on thy clear
    stream
Glass'd, with its dancing light, the sunny
    ray;
But o'er the blacken'd memory's blighting
    dream
Thy waves would vainly roll, all sweeping as
    they seem.

LII

Thus Harold inly said, and pass'd along, 460
Yet not insensible to all which here
Awoke the jocund birds to early song
In glens which might have made even exile
    dear:
Though on his brow were graven lines
    austere,

And tranquil sternness, which had ta'en the
    place
Of feelings fierier far but less severe,
Joy was not always absent from his face,
But o'er it in such scenes would steal with
    transient trace.

LIII

Nor was all love shut from him, though his
    days
Of passion had consumed themselves to
    dust.   470
It is in vain that we would coldly gaze
On such as smile upon us; the heart must
Leap kindly back to kindness, though dis-
    gust
Hath wean'd it from all worldlings: thus he
    felt,
For there was soft remembrance, and sweet
    trust
In one fond breast, to which his own would
    melt,
And in its tenderer hour on that his bosom
    dwelt.

LIV

And he had learn'd to love,—I know not
    why,
For this in such as him seems strange of
    mood,—
The helpless looks of blooming infancy, 480
Even in its earliest nurture; what subdued,
To change like this, a mind so far imbued
With scorn of man, it little boots to know;
But thus it was; and though in solitude
Small power the nipp'd affections have to
    grow,
In him this glow'd when all beside had ceased
    to glow.

LV

And there was one soft breast, as hath been
    said,
Which unto his was bound by stronger ties
Than the church links withal; and, though
    unwed,   489
That love was pure, and, far above disguise,
Had stood the test of mortal enmities
Still undivided, and cemented more
By peril, dreaded most in female eyes;
But this was firm, and from a foreign shore
Well to that heart might his these absent greet-
    ings pour!

1

The castled crag of Drachenfels
Frowns o'er the wide and winding Rhine,
Whose breast of waters broadly swells
Between the banks which bear the vine,
And hills all rich with blossom'd trees, 500
And fields which promise corn and wine,
And scatter'd cities crowning these,
Whose far white walls along them shine,
Have strew'd a scene, which I should see
With double joy wert *thou* with me.

2

And peasant girls, with deep blue eyes,
And hands which offer early flowers,
Walk smiling o'er this paradise;
Above, the frequent feudal towers
Through green leaves lift their walls of gray;   510
And many a rock which steeply lowers,
And noble arch in proud decay,
Look o'er this vale of vintage-bowers;
But one thing want these banks of Rhine,—
Thy gentle hand to clasp in mine!

3

I send the lilies given to me;
Though long before thy hand they touch,
I know that they must wither'd be,
But yet reject them not as such;
For I have cherish'd them as dear, 520
Because they yet may meet thine eye,
And guide thy soul to mine even here,
When thou behold'st them drooping nigh,
And know'st them gather'd by the Rhine,
And offer'd from my heart to thine!

4

The river nobly foams and flows,
The charm of this enchanted ground,
And all its thousand turns disclose
Some fresher beauty varying round:
The haughtiest breast its wish might bound   530
Through life to dwell delighted here;
Nor could on earth a spot be found
To nature and to me so dear,
Could thy dear eyes in following mine
Still sweeten more these banks of Rhine!

LVI

By Coblentz, on a rise of gentle ground,
There is a small and simple pyramid,
Crowning the summit of the verdant mound;
Beneath its base are heroes' ashes hid,
Our enemy's—but let not that forbid 540
Honour to Marceau! o'er whose early tomb
Tears, big tears, gush'd from the rough soldier's lid,
Lamenting and yet envying such a doom,
Falling for France, whose rights he battled to resume.

LVII

Brief, brave, and glorious was his young career,—
His mourners were two hosts, his friends and foes;
And fitly may the stranger lingering here
Pray for his gallant spirit's bright repose;
For he was Freedom's champion, one of those,   549
The few in number, who had not o'erstept
The charter to chastise which she bestows
On such as wield her weapons; he had kept
The whiteness of his soul, and thus men o'er him wept.

LVIII

Here Ehrenbreitstein, with her shatter'd wall
Black with the miner's blast, upon her height
Yet shows of what she was, when shell and ball
Rebounding idly on her strength did light:
A tower of victory! from whence the flight
Of baffled foes was watch'd along the plain:
But Peace destroy'd what War could never blight,   560
And laid those proud roofs bare to Summer's rain—
On which the iron shower for years had pour'd in vain.

LIX

Adieu to thee, fair Rhine! How long delighted
The stranger fain would linger on his way!
Thine is a scene alike where souls united
Or lonely Contemplation thus might stray;
And could the ceaseless vultures cease to prey

On self-condemning bosoms, it were here,
Where Nature, nor too sombre nor too gay,
Wild but not rude, awful yet not austere, 570
Is to the mellow Earth as Autumn to the year.

LX

Adieu to thee again! a vain adieu!
There can be no farewell to scene like thine;
The mind is colour'd by thy every hue;
And if reluctantly the eyes resign
Their cherish'd gaze upon thee, lovely
    Rhine!
'Tis with the thankful heart of parting
    praise;
More mighty spots may rise, more glaring
    shine,
But none unite in one attaching maze
The brilliant, fair, and soft,—the glories of
    old days. 580

LXI

The negligently grand, the fruitful bloom
Of coming ripeness, the white city's sheen,
The rolling stream, the precipice's gloom,
The forest's growth, and Gothic walls be-
    tween,
The wild rocks shaped as they had turrets
    been,
In mockery of man's art; and these withal
A race of faces happy as the scene,
Whose fertile bounties here extend to all,
Still springing o'er thy banks, though Empires
    near them fall.

LXII

But these recede. Above me are the Alps,
The palaces of Nature, whose vast walls 591
Have pinnacled in clouds their snowy scalps,
And throned Eternity in icy halls
Of cold sublimity, where forms and falls
The avalanche—the thunderbolt of snow!
All that expands the spirit, yet appals,
Gather around these summits, as to show
How Earth may pierce to Heaven, yet leave
    vain man below.

LXIII

But ere these matchless heights I dare to
    scan,
There is a spot should not be pass'd in
    vain,— 600

Morat! the proud, the patriot field! where
    man
May gaze on ghastly trophies of the slain,
Nor blush for those who conquer'd on that
    plain;
Here Burgundy bequeath'd his tombless
    host,
A bony heap, through ages to remain,
Themselves their monument;—the Stygian
    coast
Unsepulchred they roam'd, and shriek'd each
    wandering ghost.

LXIV

While Waterloo with Cannæ's carnage
    vies,
Morat and Marathon twin names shall stand;
They were true Glory's stainless victories,
Won by the unambitious heart and hand
Of a proud, brotherly, and civic band, 612
All unbought champions in no princely
    cause
Of vice-entail'd Corruption; they no land
Doom'd to bewail the blasphemy of laws
Making kings' rights divine, by some Draconic
    clause.

LXV

By a lone wall a lonelier column rears
A gray and grief-worn aspect of old days;
'Tis the last remnant of the wreck of years,
And looks as with the wild-bewilder'd gaze
Of one to stone converted by amaze, 621
Yet still with consciousness; and there it
    stands
Making a marvel that it not decays,
When the coeval pride of human hands,
Levell'd Adventicum, hath strew'd her sub-
    ject lands.

LXVI

And there—oh! sweet and sacred be the
    name!—
Julia—the daughter, the devoted—gave
Her youth to Heaven; her heart, beneath a
    claim
Nearest to Heaven's, broke o'er a father's
    grave.
Justice is sworn 'gainst tears, and hers would
    crave 630
The life she lived in; but the judge was just,

And then she died on him she could not
  save.
Their tomb was simple, and without a
  bust,
And held within their urn one mind, one heart,
  one dust.

LXVII

But these are deeds which should not pass
  away,
And names that must not wither, though the
  earth
Forgets her empires with a just decay,
The enslavers and the enslaved, their death
  and birth;
The high, the mountain-majesty of worth
Should be, and shall, survivor of its woe, 640
And from its immortality look forth
In the sun's face, like yonder Alpine snow,
Imperishably pure beyond all things below.

LXVIII

Lake Leman woos me with its crystal face,
The mirror where the stars and mountains
  view
The stillness of their aspect in each trace
Its clear depth yields of their far height and
  hue:
There is too much of man here, to look
  through
With a fit mind the might which I behold;
But soon in me shall Loneliness renew 650
Thoughts hid, but not less cherish'd than of
  old,
Ere mingling with the herd had penn'd me in
  their fold.

LXIX

To fly from, need not be to hate, man-
  kind:
All are not fit with them to stir and toil,
Nor is it discontent to keep the mind
Deep in its fountain, lest it overboil
In the hot throng, where we become the
  spoil
Of our infection, till too late and long
We may deplore and struggle with the coil,
In wretched interchange of wrong for
  wrong   660
Midst a contentious world, striving where
  none are strong.

LXX

There, in a moment we may plunge our years
In fatal penitence, and in the blight
Of our own soul turn all our blood to tears,
And colour things to come with hues of
  Night;
The race of life becomes a hopeless flight
To those that walk in darkness: on the sea
The boldest steer but where their ports
  invite;
But there are wanderers o'er Eternity
Whose bark drives on and on, and anchor'd
  ne'er shall be.   670

LXXI

Is it not better, then, to be alone,
And love Earth only for its earthly sake?
By the blue rushing of the arrowy Rhone,
Or the pure bosom of its nursing lake,
Which feeds it as a mother who doth make
A fair but froward infant her own care,
Kissing its cries away as these awake;—
Is it not better thus our lives to wear,
Than join the crushing crowd, doom'd to
  inflict or bear?

LXXII

I live not in myself, but I become   680
Portion of that around me; and to me
High mountains are a feeling, but the hum
Of human cities torture: I can see
Nothing to loathe in nature, save to be
A link reluctant in a fleshly chain,
Class'd among creatures, when the soul can
  flee,
And with the sky, the peak, the heaving plain
Of ocean, or the stars, mingle, and not in vain.

LXXIII

And thus I am absorb'd, and this is life:
I look upon the peopled desert past,   690
As on a place of agony and strife,
Where, for some sin, to sorrow I was cast,
To act and suffer, but remount at last
With a fresh pinion; which I feel to spring,
Though young, yet waxing vigorous as the
  blast
Which it would cope with, on delighted
  wing,
Spurning the clay-cold bonds which round
  our being cling.

LXXIV

And when, at length, the mind shall be all
    free
From what it hates in this degraded form,
Reft of its carnal life, save what shall be 700
Existent happier in the fly and worm,—
When elements to elements conform,
And dust is as it should be, shall I not
Feel all I see, less dazzling, but more
    warm?
The bodiless thought? the Spirit of each
    spot?
Of which, even now, I share at times the im-
    mortal lot?

LXXV

Are not the mountains, waves, and skies,
    a part
Of me and of my soul, as I of them?
Is not the love of these deep in my heart
With a pure passion? should I not con-
    temn   710
All objects, if compared with these? and
    stem
A tide of suffering, rather than forego
Such feelings for the hard and worldly
    phlegm
Of those whose eyes are only turn'd below,
Gazing upon the ground, with thoughts which
    dare not glow?

LXXVI

But this is not my theme; and I return
To that which is immediate, and require
Those who find contemplation in the urn,
To look on One, whose dust was once all
    fire,
A native of the land where I respire 720
The clear air for a while—a passing guest,
Where he became a being,—whose desire
Was to be glorious; 'twas a foolish quest,
The which to gain and keep, he sacrificed all
    rest.

LXXVII

Here the self-torturing sophist, wild Rous-
    seau,
The apostle of affliction, he who threw
Enchantment over passion, and from woe
Wrung overwhelming eloquence, first drew
The breath which made him wretched; yet
    he knew

How to make madness beautiful, and cast
O'er erring deeds and thoughts a heavenly
    hue   731
Of words, like sunbeams, dazzling as they
    past
The eyes, which o'er them shed tears feelingly
    and fast.

LXXVIII

His love was passion's essence:—as a tree
On fire by lightning, with ethereal flame
Kindled he was, and blasted; for to be
Thus, and enamour'd, were in him the same.
But his was not the love of living dame,
Nor of the dead who rise upon our dreams,
But of ideal beauty, which became 740
In him existence, and o'erflowing teems
Along his burning page, distemper'd though
    it seems.

LXXIX

This breathed itself to life in Julie, *this*
Invested her with all that's wild and sweet;
This hallow'd, too, the memorable kiss
Which every morn his fever'd lip would
    greet,
From hers, who but with friendship his
    would meet;
But to that gentle touch through brain and
    breast
Flash'd the thrill'd spirit's love-devouring
    heat;   749
In that absorbing sigh perchance more blest
Than vulgar minds may be with all they seek
    possest.

LXXX

His life was one long war with self-sought
    foes,
Or friends by him self-banish'd; for his
    mind
Had grown Suspicion's sanctuary, and
    chose,
For its own cruel sacrifice, the kind,
'Gainst whom he raged with fury strange
    and blind.
But he was phrensied,—wherefore, who
    may know?
Since cause might be which skill could never
    find;
But he was phrensied by disease or woe,
To that worst pitch of all, which wears a
    reasoning show.   760

LXXXI

For then he was inspired, and from him
  came,
As from the Pythian's mystic cave of yore,
Those oracles which set the world in flame,
Nor ceased to burn till kingdoms were no
  more:
Did he not this for France? which lay before
Bow'd to the inborn tyranny of years?
Broken and trembling to the yoke she bore,
Till by the voice of him and his compeers
Roused up to too much wrath, which follows
  o'ergrown fears?

LXXXII

They made themselves a fearful monument!
The wreck of old opinions—things which
  grew,   771
Breathed from the birth of time: the veil
  they rent,
And what behind it lay, all earth shall view.
But good with ill they also overthrew,
Leaving but ruins, wherewith to rebuild
Upon the same foundation, and renew
Dungeons and thrones, which the same hour
  refill'd,
As heretofore, because ambition was self-
  will'd.

LXXXIII

But this will not endure, nor be endured!
Mankind have felt their strength, and made
  it felt.   780
They might have used it better, but, allured
By their new vigour, sternly have they dealt
On one another; pity ceased to melt
With her once natural charities. But they,
Who in oppression's darkness caved had
  dwelt,
They were not eagles, nourish'd with the
  day;
What marvel then, at times, if they mistook
  their prey?

LXXXIV

What deep wounds ever closed without a
  scar?
The heart's bleed longest, and but heal to
  wear
That which disfigures it; and they who
  war   790

With their own hopes, and have been vanquish'd, bear
Silence, but not submission: in his lair
Fix'd Passion holds his breath, until the
  hour
Which shall atone for years; none need
  despair:
It came, it cometh, and will come,—the
  power
To punish or forgive—in *one* we shall be
  slower.

LXXXV

Clear, placid Leman! thy contrasted lake,
With the wild world I dwelt in, is a thing
Which warns me, with its stillness, to for-
  sake
Earth's troubled waters for a purer spring.
This quiet sail is as a noiseless wing   801
To waft me from distraction; once I loved
Torn ocean's roar, but thy soft murmuring
Sounds sweet as if a Sister's voice reproved,
That I with stern delights should e'er have
  been so moved.

LXXXVI

It is the hush of night, and all between
Thy margin and the mountains, dusk, yet
  clear,
Mellow'd and mingling, yet distinctly seen,
Save darken'd Jura, whose capt heights ap-
  pear
Precipitously steep; and drawing near,   810
There breathes a living fragrance from the
  shore,
Of flowers yet fresh with childhood; on the
  ear
Drops the light drip of the suspended oar,
Or chirps the grasshopper one good-night
  carol more;

LXXXVII

He is an evening reveller, who makes
His life an infancy, and sings his fill;
At intervals, some bird from out the brakes
Starts into voice a moment, then is still.
There seems a floating whisper on the hill,
But that is fancy, for the starlight dews 820
All silently their tears of love instil,
Weeping themselves away, till they infuse
Deep into nature's breast the spirit of her hues.

LXXXVIII

Ye stars! which are the poetry of heaven!
If in your bright leaves we would read the
   fate
Of men and empires,—'tis to be forgiven,
That in our aspirations to be great,
Our destinies o'erleap their mortal state,
And claim a kindred with you; for ye are
A beauty and a mystery, and create   830
In us such love and reverence from afar,
That fortune, fame, power, life, have named
   themselves a star.

LXXXIX

All heaven and earth are still—though not
   in sleep,
But breathless, as we grow when feeling
   most;
And silent, as we stand in thoughts too
   deep:—
All heaven and earth are still: From the
   high host
Of stars, to the lull'd lake and mountain-
   coast,
All is concenter'd in a life intense,
Where not a beam, nor air, nor leaf is lost,
But hath a part of being, and a sense   840
Of that which is of all Creator and defence.

XC

Then stirs the feeling infinite, so felt
In solitude, where we are *least* alone;
A truth, which through our being then doth
   melt,
And purifies from self: it is a tone,
The soul and source of music, which makes
   known
Eternal harmony, and sheds a charm
Like to the fabled Cytherea's zone,
Binding all things with beauty;—'twould
   disarm
The spectre Death, had he substantial power
   to harm.   850

XCI

Not vainly did the early Persian make
His altar the high places, and the peak
Of earth-o'ergazing mountains, and thus
   take
A fit and unwall'd temple, there to seek
The Spirit, in whose honour shrines are
   weak,
Uprear'd of human hands. Come, and com-
   pare
Columns and idol-dwellings, Goth or Greek,
With Nature's realms of worship, earth and
   air,
Nor fix on fond abodes to circumscribe thy
   pray'r!

XCII

The sky is changed!—and such a change!
   Oh night,   860
And storm, and darkness, ye are wondrous
   strong,
Yet lovely in your strength, as is the light
Of a dark eye in woman! Far along,
From peak to peak, the rattling crags among
Leaps the live thunder! Not from one lone
   cloud,
But every mountain now hath found a
   tongue,
And Jura answers, through her misty shroud,
Back to the joyous Alps, who call to her aloud!

XCIII

And this is in the night:—Most glorious
   night!
Thou wert not sent for slumber! let me
   be   870
A sharer in thy fierce and far delight,—
A portion of the tempest and of thee!
How the lit lake shines, a phosphoric sea,
And the big rain comes dancing to the
   earth!
And now again 'tis black,—and now, the
   glee
Of the loud hills shakes with its mountain-
   mirth,
As if they did rejoice o'er a young earthquake's
   birth.

XCIV

Now, where the swift Rhone cleaves his way
   between
Heights which appear as lovers who have
   parted
In hate, whose mining depths so intervene,   880
That they can meet no more, though broken-
   hearted;

Though in their souls, which thus each other thwarted,
Love was the very root of the fond rage
Which blighted their life's bloom, and then departed:
Itself expired, but leaving them an age
Of years all winters,—war within themselves to wage.

XCV

Now, where the quick Rhone thus hath cleft his way,
The mightiest of the storms hath ta'en his stand:
For here, not one, but many, make their play,
And fling their thunder-bolts from hand to hand,   890
Flashing and cast around; of all the band,
The brightest through these parted hills hath fork'd
His lightnings,—as if he did understand,
That in such gaps as desolation work'd,
There the hot shaft should blast whatever therein lurk'd.

XCVI

Sky, mountains, river, winds, lake, lightnings! ye!
With night, and clouds, and thunder, and a soul
To make these felt and feeling, well may be
Things that have made me watchful; the far roll
Of your departing voices, is the knoll   900
Of what in me is sleepless,—if I rest.
But where of ye, O tempests! is the goal?
Are ye like those within the human breast?
Or do ye find, at length, like eagles, some high nest?

XCVII

Could I embody and unbosom now
That which is most within me,—could I wreak
My thoughts upon expression, and thus throw
Soul, heart, mind, passions, feelings, strong or weak,
All that I would have sought, and all I seek,

Bear, know, feel, and yet breathe—into *one* word,   910
And that one word were Lightning, I would speak;
But as it is, I live and die unheard,
With a most voiceless thought, sheathing it as a sword.

XCVIII

The morn is up again, the dewy morn,
With breath all incense, and with cheek all bloom,
Laughing the clouds away with playful scorn,
And living as if earth contain'd no tomb,—
And glowing into day: we may resume
The march of our existence: and thus I,
Still on thy shores, fair Leman! may find room   920
And food for meditation, nor pass by
Much, that may give us pause, if ponder'd fittingly.

XCIX

Clarens! sweet Clarens, birthplace of deep Love!
Thine air is the young breath of passionate thought;
Thy trees take root in Love; the snows above
The very Glaciers have his colours caught,
And sun-set into rose-hues sees them wrought
By rays which sleep there lovingly: the rocks,
The permanent crags, tell here of Love, who sought
In them a refuge from the worldly shocks,
Which stir and sting the soul with hope that woos, then mocks.   931

C

Clarens! by heavenly feet thy paths are trod,—
Undying Love's, who here ascends a throne
To which the steps are mountains; where the god
Is a pervading life and light,—so shown
Not on those summits solely, nor alone
In the still cave and forest; o'er the flower
His eye is sparkling, and his breath hath blown,

His soft and summer breath, whose tender
    power
Passes the strength of storms in their most
    desolate hour.   940

CI

All things are here of *him;* from the black
    pines,
Which are his shade on high, and the loud
    roar
Of torrents, where he listeneth, to the
    vines
Which slope his green path downward to
    the shore,
Where the bow'd waters meet him, and
    adore,
Kissing his feet with murmurs; and the
    wood,
The covert of old trees, with trunks all
    hoar,
But light leaves, young as joy, stands
    where it stood,
Offering to him, and his, a populous solitude.

CII

A populous solitude of bees and birds, 950
And fairy-form'd and many-colour'd things,
Who worship him with notes more sweet
    than words,
And innocently open their glad wings,
Fearless and full of life: the gush of springs,
And fall of lofty fountains, and the bend
Of stirring branches, and the bud which
    brings
The swiftest thought of beauty, here extend,
Mingling, and made by Love, unto one mighty
    end.

CIII

He who hath loved not, here would learn
    that lore,
And make his heart a spirit; he who knows
That tender mystery, will love the more; 961
For this is Love's recess, where vain men's
    woes,
And the world's waste, have driven him far
    from those,
For 'tis his nature to advance or die;
He stands not still, but or decays, or grows
Into a boundless blessing, which may vie
With the immortal lights, in its eternity!

CIV

'Twas not for fiction chose Rousseau this
    spot,
Peopling it with affections; but he found
It was the scene which Passion must
    allot   970
To the mind's purified beings; 'twas the
    ground
Where early Love his Psyche's zone un-
    bound,
And hallow'd it with loveliness: 'tis lone,
And wonderful, and deep, and hath a
    sound,
And sense, and sight of sweetness; here the
    Rhone
Hath spread himself a couch, the Alps have
    rear'd a throne.

CV

Lausanne! and Ferney! ye have been the
    abodes
Of names which unto you bequeath'd a
    name;
Mortals, who sought and found, by danger-
    ous roads,
A path to perpetuity of fame: 980
They were gigantic minds, and their steep
    aim
Was, Titan-like, on daring doubts to pile
Thoughts which should call down thunder,
    and the flame
Of Heaven again assail'd, if Heaven the
    while
On man and man's research could deign do
    more than smile.

CVI

The one was fire and fickleness, a child
Most mutable in wishes, but in mind
A wit as various,—gay, grave, sage, or
    wild,—
Historian, bard, philosopher, combined;
He multiplied himself among mankind, 990
The Proteus of their talents: But his own
Breathed most in ridicule,—which, as the
    wind,
Blew where it listed, laying all things
    prone,—
Now to o'erthrow a fool, and now to shake
    a throne.

CVII *Gibbon*

The other, deep and slow, exhausting thought,
And hiving wisdom with each studious year,
In meditation dwelt, with learning wrought,
And shaped his weapon with an edge severe,
Sapping a solemn creed with solemn sneer; 1000
The lord of irony,—that master-spell,
Which stung his foes to wrath, which grew from fear,
And doom'd him to the zealot's ready Hell,
Which answers to all doubts so eloquently well.

CVIII

Yet, peace be with their ashes,—for by them,
If merited, the penalty is paid;
It is not ours to judge,—far less condemn;
The hour must come when such things shall be made
Known unto all, or hope and dread allay'd
By slumber, on one pillow, in the dust,
Which, thus much we are sure, must lie decay'd; 1010
And when it shall revive, as is our trust,
'Twill be to be forgiven, or suffer what is just.

CIX

But let me quit man's works, again to read
His Maker's, spread around me, and suspend
This page, which from my reveries I feed,
Until it seems prolonging without end.
The clouds above me to the white Alps tend,
And I must pierce them, and survey what-e'er
May be permitted, as my steps I bend
To their most great and growing region, where 1020
The earth to her embrace compels the powers of air.

CX

Italia! too, Italia! looking on thee,
Full flashes on the soul the light of ages,
Since the fierce Carthaginian almost won thee,
To the last halo of the chiefs and sages
Who glorify thy consecrated pages;
Thou wert the throne and grave of empires; still,
The fount at which the panting mind assuages

Her thirst of knowledge, quaffing there her fill,
Flows from the eternal source of Rome's imperial hill. 1030

CXI

Thus far have I proceeded in a theme
Renew'd with no kind auspices:—to feel *learned lesson*
We are not what we have been, and to deem
We are not what we should be, and to steel
The heart against itself; and to conceal,
With a proud caution, love, or hate, or aught,—
Passion or feeling, purpose, grief or zeal,—
Which is the tyrant spirit of our thought,
Is a stern task of soul:—No matter,—it is taught.

CXII

And for these words, thus woven into song,
It may be that they are a harmless wile,—
The colouring of the scenes which fleet along, 1042
Which I would seize, in passing, to beguile
My breast, or that of others, for a while.
Fame is the thirst of youth, but I am not
So young as to regard men's frown or smile,
As loss or guerdon of a glorious lot; *reward*
I stood and stand alone,—remember'd or forgot.

CXIII

I have not loved the world, nor the world me;
I have not flatter'd its rank breath, nor bow'd 1050
To its idolatries a patient knee,
Nor coin'd my cheek to smiles, nor cried aloud
In worship of an echo; in the crowd
They could not deem me one of such; I stood
Among them, but not of them; in a shroud
Of thoughts which were not their thoughts, and still could,
Had I not filled my mind, which thus itself subdued.

CXIV

I have not loved the world, nor the world me,—
But let us part fair foes; I do believe,
Though I have found them not, that there may be 1060

Words which are things, hopes which will
not deceive,
And virtues which are merciful, nor weave
Snares for the failing; I would also deem
O'er others' griefs that some sincerely
grieve;
That two, or one, are almost what they
seem,
That goodness is no name, and happiness no
dream.

CXV

My daughter! with thy name this song
begun;
My daughter! with thy name thus much
shall end;
I see thee not, I hear thee not, but none
Can be so wrapt in thee; thou art the
friend   1070
To whom the shadows of far years extend:
Albeit my brow thou never shouldst behold,
My voice shall with thy future visions blend,
And reach into thy heart, when mine is cold,
A token and a tone, even from thy father's
mould.

CXVI

To aid thy mind's development, to watch
Thy dawn of little joys, to sit and see
Almost thy very growth, to view thee catch
Knowledge of objects,—wonders yet to
thee!
To hold thee lightly on a gentle knee, 1080
And print on thy soft cheek a parent's
kiss,—
This, it should seem, was not reserved for
me;
Yet this was in my nature: as it is,
I know not what is there, yet something like
to this.

CXVII

Yet, though dull Hate as duty should be
taught,
I know that thou wilt love me; though my
name
Should be shut from thee, as a spell still
fraught
With desolation, and a broken claim:
Though the grave closed between us,—
'twere the same,
I know that thou wilt love me; though to
drain   1090

My blood from out thy being were an aim,
And an attainment,—all would be in vain,—
Still thou wouldst love me, still that more
than life retain.

CXVIII

The child of love, though born in bitterness,
And nurtured in convulsion. Of thy sire
These were the elements, and thine no less.
As yet such are around thee, but thy fire
Shall be more temper'd, and thy hope far
higher.
Sweet be thy cradled slumbers! O'er the sea
And from the mountains where I now re-
spire,   1100
Fain would I waft such blessing upon thee,
As, with a sigh, I deem thou might'st have
been to me.

1816

From CANTO THE FOURTH

REFUGE IN VENICE

I

I stood in Venice, on the Bridge of Sighs;
A palace and a prison on each hand:
I saw from out the wave her structures rise
As from the stroke of the enchanter's
wand:
A thousand years their cloudy wings ex-
pand
Around me, and a dying Glory smiles
O'er the far times, when many a subject land
Look'd to the winged Lion's marble piles,
Where Venice sate in state, throned on her
hundred isles!

II

She looks a sea Cybele, fresh from ocean,
Rising with her tiara of proud towers   11
At airy distance, with majestic motion,
A ruler of the waters and their powers:
And such she was;—her daughters had
their dowers
From spoils of nations, and the exhaustless
East
Pour'd in her lap all gems in sparkling
showers.
In purple was she robed, and of her feast
Monarchs partook, and deem'd their dignity
increased.

III

In Venice Tasso's echoes are no more,
And silent rows the songless gondolier; 20
Her palaces are crumbling to the shore,
And music meets not always now the ear:
Those days are gone—but Beauty still is
here.
States fall, arts fade—but Nature doth not
die,
Nor yet forget how Venice once was dear,
The pleasant place of all festivity,
The revel of the earth, the masque of Italy!

IV

But unto us she hath a spell beyond
Her name in story, and her long array
Of mighty shadows, whose dim forms
despond   30
Above the dogeless city's vanish'd sway;
Ours is a trophy which will not decay
With the Rialto; Shylock and the Moor,
And Pierre, cannot be swept or worn
away—
The keystones of the arch! though all were
o'er,
For us repeopled were the solitary shore.

V

The beings of the mind are not of clay;
Essentially immortal, they create
And multiply in us a brighter ray
And more beloved existence: that which
Fate   40
Prohibits to dull life, in this our state
Of mortal bondage, by these spirits
supplied,
First exiles, then replaces what we hate;
Watering the heart whose early flowers
have died,
And with a fresher growth replenishing the
void.

VI

Such is the refuge of our youth and age,
The first from Hope, the last from Vacancy;
And this worn feeling peoples many a
page,
And, may be, that which grows beneath
mine eye:
Yet there are things whose strong reality 50

Outshines our fairy-land; in shape and
hues
More beautiful than our fantastic sky,
And the strange constellations which the
Muse
O'er her wild universe is skilful to diffuse:

VII

I saw or dream'd of such,—but let them
go,—
They came like truth, and disappear'd like
dreams;
And whatsoe'er they were—are now but
so: ·
I could replace them if I would; still teems
My mind with many a form which aptly
seems
Such as I sought for, and at moments
found;   60
Let these too go—for waking Reason deems
Such overweening phantasies unsound,
And other voices speak, and other sights sur-
round.

VIII

I've taught me other tongues, and in
strange eyes
Have made me not a stranger; to the mind
Which is itself, no changes bring surprise;
Nor is it harsh to make, nor hard to find
A country with—ay, or without mankind;
Yet was I born where men are proud to
be,—
Not without cause; and should I leave be-
hind   70
The inviolate island of the sage and free,
And seek me out a home by a remoter sea,

IX

Perhaps I loved it well: and should I lay
My ashes in a soil which is not mine,
My spirit shall resume it—if we may
Unbodied choose a sanctuary. I twine
My hopes of being remember'd in my line
With my land's language: if too fond and
far
These aspirations in their scope incline,—
If my fame should be, as my fortunes are,
Of hasty growth and blight, and dull Ob-
livion bar   81

X

My name from out the temple where the
  dead
Are honour'd by the nations—let it be—
And light the laurels on a loftier head!
And be the Spartan's epitaph on me—
"Sparta hath many a worthier son than he."
Meantime I seek no sympathies, nor need;
The thorns which I have reap'd are of the
  tree
I planted: they have torn me, and I bleed:
I should have known what fruit would spring
  from such a seed.   90

*   *   *

ON ROME

LXXVIII

Oh Rome! my country! city of the soul!
The orphans of the heart must turn to thee,
Lone mother of dead empires! and control
In their shut breasts their petty misery.
What are our woes and sufferance? Come
  and see
The cypress, hear the owl, and plod your way
O'er steps of broken thrones and temples,
  Ye!   560
Whose agonies are evils of a day—
A world is at our feet as fragile as our clay.

LXXIX

The Niobe of nations! there she stands,
Childless and crownless, in her voiceless
  woe;
An empty urn within her wither'd hands,
Whose holy dust was scatter'd long ago;
The Scipios' tomb contains no ashes now;
The very sepulchres lie tenantless
Of their heroic dwellers: dost thou flow,
Old Tiber! through a marble wilderness? 570
Rise, with thy yellow waves, and mantle her
  distress.

LXXX

The Goth, the Christian, Time, War,
  Flood, and Fire,
Have dealt upon the seven-hill'd city's pride;
She saw her glories star by star expire,
And up the steep barbarian monarchs ride,
Where the car climb'd the Capitol; far and
  wide

Temple and tower went down, nor left a
  site:
Chaos of ruins! who shall trace the void,
O'er the dim fragments cast a lunar light,
And say, "here was, or is," where all is
  doubly night?   580

LXXXI

The double night of ages, and of her,
Night's daughter, Ignorance, hath wrapt
  and wrap
All round us: we but feel our way to err:
The ocean hath its chart, the stars their
  map,
And Knowledge spreads them on her ample
  lap;
But Rome is as the desert, where we steer
Stumbling o'er recollections; now we clap
Our hands, and cry "Eureka!" it is clear—
When but some false mirage of ruin rises near.

LXXXII

Alas! the lofty city! and alas!   590
The trebly hundred triumphs! and the day
When Brutus made the dagger's edge sur-
  pass
The conqueror's sword in bearing fame
  away!
Alas, for Tully's voice, and Virgil's lay,
And Livy's pictured page!—but these shall
  be
Her resurrection; all beside—decay.
Alas, for Earth, for never shall we see
That brightness in her eye she bore when
  Rome was free!

LXXXIII

Oh thou, whose chariot roll'd on Fortune's
  wheel,   599
Triumphant Sylla! Thou, who didst subdue
Thy country's foes ere thou wouldst pause
  to feel
The wrath of thy own wrongs, or reap the
  due
Of hoarded vengeance till thine eagles flew
O'er prostrate Asia;—thou, who with thy
  frown
Annihilated senates—Roman, too,
With all thy vices, for thou didst lay down
With an atoning smile a more than earthly
  crown—

LXXXIV

The dictatorial wreath—couldst thou divine
To what would one day dwindle that which
    made 609
Thee more than mortal? and that so supine
By aught than Romans Rome should thus
    be laid?
She who was named Eternal, and array'd
Her warriors but to conquer—she who
    veil'd
Earth with her haughty shadow, and dis-
    play'd,
Until the o'er-canopied horizon fail'd,
Her rushing wings—Oh! she who was Al-
    mighty hail'd!

LXXXV

Sylla was first of victors; but our own,
The sagest of usurpers, Cromwell!—he
Too swept off senates while he hew'd the
    throne
Down to a block—immortal rebel! See 620
What crimes it costs to be a moment free,
And famous through all ages! but beneath
His fate the moral lurks of destiny;
His day of double victory and death
Beheld him win two realms, and, happier
    yield his breath.

LXXXVI

The third of the same moon whose former
    course
Had all but crown'd him, on the self-same
    day
Deposed him gently from his throne of
    force,
And laid him with the earth's preceding clay.
And show'd not Fortune thus how fame and
    sway, 630
And all we deem delightful, and consume
Our souls to compass through each arduous
    way,
Are in her eyes less happy than the tomb?
Were they but so in man's, how different were
    his doom!

LXXXVII

And thou, dread statue! yet existent in
The austerest form of naked majesty,
Thou who beheldest, 'mid the assassins' din,
At thy bathed base the bloody Cæsar lie,
Folding his robe in dying dignity,

An offering to thine altar from the queen
Of gods and men, great Nemesis! did he die,
And thou, too, perish, Pompey? have ye
    been 642
Victors of countless kings, or puppets of a
    scene?

LXXXVIII

And thou, the thunder-stricken nurse of
    Rome!
She-wolf! whose brazen-imaged dugs im-
    part
The milk of conquest yet within the dome
Where, as a monument of antique art,
Thou standest:—Mother of the mighty
    heart,
Which the great founder suck'd from thy
    wild teat,
Scorch'd by the Roman Jove's ethereal
    dart, 650
And thy limbs black with lightning—dost
    thou yet
Guard thine immortal cubs, nor thy fond
    charge forget?

LXXXIX

Thou dost; but all thy foster-babes are
    dead—
The men of iron: and the world hath rear'd
Cities from out their sepulchres: men bled
In imitation of the things they fear'd,
And fought and conquer'd, and the same
    course steer'd,
At apish distance; but as yet none have,
Nor could, the same supremacy have
    near'd,
Save one vain man, who is not in the
    grave, 660
But, vanquish'd by himself, to his own slaves
    a slave—

* * *

BITTER MEDITATION

CXXI

Oh Love! no habitant of earth thou art—
An unseen seraph, we believe in thee,—
A faith whose martyrs are the broken
    heart,—
But never yet hath seen, nor e'er shall see
The naked eye, thy form, as it should be;

The mind hath made thee, as it peopled
    heaven,
Even with its own desiring phantasy,
And to a thought such shape and image
    given,
As haunts the unquench'd soul—parch'd,
    wearied, wrung, and riven.

CXXII

Of its own beauty is the mind diseased, 1090
And fevers into false creation:—where,
Where are the forms the sculptor's soul
    hath seiz'd?
In him alone. Can Nature show so fair?
Where are the charms and virtues which
    we dare
Conceive in boyhood and pursue as men,
The unreach'd Paradise of our despair,
Which o'er-informs the pencil and the pen,
And overpowers the page where it would
    bloom again?

CXXIII

Who loves, raves—'tis youth's frenzy—but
    the cure   1099
Is bitterer still, as charm by charm unwinds
Which robed our idols, and we see too sure
Nor worth nor beauty dwells from out the
    mind's
Ideal shape of such; yet still it binds
The fatal spell, and still it draws us on,
Reaping the whirlwind from the oft-sown
    winds;
The stubborn heart, its alchemy begun,
Seems ever near the prize—wealthiest when
    most undone.

CXXIV

We wither from our youth, we gasp away—
Sick—sick; unfound the boon, unslaked the
    thirst,   1109
Though to the last, in verge of our decay,
Some phantom lures, such as we sought at
    first—
But all too late,—so are we doubly curst.
Love, fame, ambition, avarice—'tis the
    same,
Each idle, and all ill, and none the worst—
For all are meteors with a different name,
And Death the sable smoke where vanishes
    the flame.

CXXV

Few—none—find what they love or could
    have loved,
Though accident, blind contact, and the
    strong
Necessity of loving, have removed
Antipathies—but to recur, ere long,   1120
Envenom'd with irrevocable wrong;
And Circumstance, that unspiritual god
And miscreator, makes and helps along
Our coming evils with a crutch-like rod,
Whose touch turns Hope to dust,—the dust
    we all have trod.

CXXVI

Our life is a false nature: 'tis not in
The harmony of things,—this hard decree,
This uneradicable taint of sin,
This boundless upas, this all-blasting tree,
Whose root is earth, whose leaves and
    branches be   1130
The skies which rain their plagues on men
    like dew—
Disease, death, bondage—all the woes we
    see,
And worse, the woes we see not—which
    throb through
The immedicable soul, with heart-aches ever
    new.

CXXVII

Yet let us ponder boldly—'tis a base
Abandonment of reason to resign
Our right of thought—our last and only
    place
Of refuge; this, at least, shall still be mine:
Though from our birth the faculty divine
Is chain'd and tortured—cabin'd, cribb'd,
    confined,   1140
And bred in darkness, lest the truth should
    shine
Too brightly on the unprepared mind,
The beam pours in, for time and skill will
    couch the blind.

CXXVIII

Arches on arches! as it were that Rome,
Collecting the chief trophies of her line,
Would build up all her triumphs in one
    dome,
Her Coliseum stands; the moonbeams shine
As 'twere its natural torches, for divine

Should be the light which streams here to
illume
This long-explored but still exhaustless
mine   1150
Of contemplation; and the azure gloom
Of an Italian night, where the deep skies
assume

CXXIX

Hues which have words, and speak to ye
of heaven,
Floats o'er this vast and wondrous monu-
ment,
And shadows forth its glory. There is given
Unto the things of earth, which Time hath
bent,
A spirit's feeling, and where he hath leant
His hand, but broke his scythe, there is a
power
And magic in the ruin'd battlement,
For which the palace of the present hour
Must yield its pomp, and wait till ages are its
dower.   1161

CXXX

Oh Time! the beautifier of the dead,
Adorner of the ruin, comforter
And only healer when the heart hath bled;
Time! the corrector where our judgments
err,
The test of truth, love—sole philosopher,
For all beside are sophists—from thy thrift,
Which never loses though it doth defer—
Time, the avenger! unto thee I lift
My hands, and eyes, and heart, and crave of
thee a gift: 1170

CXXXI

Amidst this wreck, where thou hast made a
shrine
And temple more divinely desolate,
Among thy mightier offerings here are
mine,
Ruins of years, though few, yet full of fate:
If thou hast ever seen me too elate,
Hear me not; but if calmly I have borne
Good, and reserved my pride against the
hate
Which shall not whelm me, let me not have
worn
This iron in my soul in vain—shall *they* not
mourn?   1179

CXXXII

And thou, who never yet of human wrong
Left the unbalanced scale, great Nemesis!
Here, where the ancient paid thee homage
long—
Thou who didst call the Furies from the
abyss,
And round Orestes bade them howl and
hiss
For that unnatural retribution—just,
Had it but been from hands less near—in
this
Thy former realm, I call thee from the
dust!
Dost thou not hear my heart?—Awake! thou
shalt, and must.

CXXXIII

It is not that I may not have incurr'd
For my ancestral faults or mine the wound
I bleed withal, and, had it been conferr'd
With a just weapon, it had flow'd unbound;
But now my blood shall not sink in the
ground;   1193
To thee I do devote it—*thou* shalt take
The vengeance, which shall yet be sought
and found,
Which if *I* have not taken for the sake——
But let that pass—I sleep, but thou shalt yet
awake.

CXXXIV

And if my voice break forth, 'tis not that
now
I shrink from what is suffer'd: let him speak
Who hath beheld decline upon my brow,
Or seen my mind's convulsion leave it
weak;   1201
But in this page a record will I seek.
Not in the air shall these my words dis-
perse,
Though I be ashes; a far hour shall wreak
The deep prophetic fulness of this verse,
And pile on human heads the mountain of my
curse!

CXXXV

That curse shall be Forgiveness.—Have I
not—
Hear me, my mother Earth! behold it,
Heaven!
Have I not had to wrestle with my lot?

Have I not suffer'd things to be forgiven?
Have I not had my brain sear'd, my heart
   riven,   1211
Hopes sapp'd, name blighted, Life's life
   lied away?
And only not to desperation driven,
Because not altogether of such clay
As rots into the souls of those whom I survey.

CXXXVI

From mighty wrongs to petty perfidy
Have I not seen what human things could
   do?
From the loud roar of foaming calumny
To the small whisper of the as paltry few,
And subtler venom of the reptile crew,
The Janus glance of whose significant eye,
Learning to lie with silence, would *seem*
   true,   1222
And without utterance, save the shrug or
   sigh,
Deal round to happy fools its speechless
   obloquy.

CXXXVII

But I have lived, and have not lived in
   vain:
My mind may lose its force, my blood its
   fire,
And my frame perish even in conquering
   pain;
But there is that within me which shall tire
Torture and Time, and breathe when I ex-
   pire;
Something unearthly, which they deem not
   of,   1230
Like the remember'd tone of a mute lyre,
Shall on their soften'd spirits sink, and
   move
In hearts all rocky now the late remorse of
   love.

CXXXVIII

The seal is set.—Now welcome, thou dread
   power!
Nameless, yet thus omnipotent, which here
Walk'st in the shadow of the midnight
   hour
With a deep awe, yet all distinct from fear;
Thy haunts are ever where the dead walls
   rear

Their ivy mantles, and the solemn scene
Derives from thee a sense so deep and
   clear   1240
That we become a part of what has been,
And grow unto the spot, all-seeing but unseen.

* * *

THE OCEAN

CLXXVII

Oh! that the Desert were my dwelling-
   place,
With one fair Spirit for my minister,
That I might all forget the human race,
And, hating no one, love but only her!
Ye elements!—in whose ennobling stir
I feel myself exalted—Can ye not   1590
Accord me such a being? Do I err
In deeming such inhabit many a spot?
Though with them to converse can rarely be
   our lot.

CLXXVIII

There is a pleasure in the pathless woods,
There is a rapture on the lonely shore,
There is society, where none intrudes,
By the deep Sea, and music in its roar:
I love not Man the less, but Nature more,
From these our interviews, in which I
   steal
From all I may be, or have been before, 1600
To mingle with the Universe, and feel
What I can ne'er express, yet cannot all con-
   ceal.

CLXXIX

Roll on, thou deep and dark blue Ocean—
   roll!
Ten thousand fleets sweep over thee in
   vain;
Man marks the earth with ruin—his control
Stops with the shore; upon the watery
   plain
The wrecks are all thy deed, nor doth re-
   main
A shadow of man's ravage, save his own,
When, for a moment, like a drop of rain,
He sinks into thy depths with bubbling
   groan,   1610
Without a grave, unknell'd, uncoffin'd, and
   unknown.

CLXXX

His steps are not upon thy paths,—thy
fields
Are not a spoil for him,—thou dost arise
And shake him from thee; the vile strength
he wields
For earth's destruction thou dost all despise,
Spurning him from thy bosom to the skies,
And send'st him, shivering in thy playful
spray
And howling, to his Gods, where haply lies
His petty hope in some near port or bay,
And dashest him again to earth:—there let
him lay.   1620

CLXXXI

The armaments which thunderstrike the
walls
Of rock-built cities, bidding nations quake,
And monarchs tremble in their capitals,
The oak leviathans, whose huge ribs make
Their clay creator the vain title take
Of lord of thee, and arbiter of war—
These are thy toys, and, as the snowy
flake,
They melt into thy yeast of waves, which
mar
Alike the Armada's pride or spoils of Tra-
falgar.

CLXXXII

Thy shores are empires, changed in all
save thee—   1630
Assyria, Greece, Rome, Carthage, what are
they?
Thy waters wash'd them power while they
were free,
And many a tyrant since; their shores obey
The stranger, slave, or savage; their decay
Has dried up realms to deserts:—not so
thou;—
Unchangeable, save to thy wild waves' play,
Time writes no wrinkle on thine azure brow:
Such as creation's dawn beheld, thou rollest
now.

CLXXXIII

Thou glorious mirror, where the Almighty's form
Glasses itself in tempests; in all time, — 1640
Calm or convulsed, in breeze, or gale, or
storm,

Icing the pole, or in the torrid clime
Dark-heaving—boundless, endless, and sub-
lime,
The image of eternity, the throne
Of the Invisible; even from out thy slime
The monsters of the deep are made; each
zone
Obeys thee; thou goest forth, dread, fathom-
less, alone.

CLXXXIV

And I have loved thee, Ocean! and my joy
Of youthful sports was on thy breast to be
Borne, like thy bubbles, onward: from a
boy   1650
I wanton'd with thy breakers—they to me
Were a delight; and if the freshening sea
Made them a terror—'twas a pleasing
fear,
For I was as it were a child of thee,
And trusted to thy billows far and near,
And laid my hand upon thy mane—as I do
here.

CLXXXV

My task is done, my song hath ceased, my
theme
Has died into an echo; it is fit
The spell should break of this protracted
dream.
The torch shall be extinguish'd which hath
lit   1660
My midnight lamp—and what is writ, is
writ;
Would it were worthier! but I am not now
That which I have been—and my visions
flit
Less palpably before me—and the glow
Which in my spirit dwelt is fluttering, faint,
and low.

CLXXXVI

Farewell! a word that must be, and hath
been—
A sound which makes us linger;—yet—
farewell!
Ye! who have traced the Pilgrim to the
scene
Which is his last, if in your memories
dwell
A thought which once was his, if on ye
swell   1670

A single recollection, not in vain
He wore his sandal-shoon and scallop-shell;
Farewell! with *him* alone may rest the pain,
If such there were—with *you*, the moral of
  his strain.

1817

MANFRED: A DRAMATIC POEM

"There are more things in heaven and earth,
  Horatio,
Than are dreamt of in your philosophy."

DRAMATIS PERSONÆ

Manfred	Witch of the Alps
Chamois Hunter	Arimanes
Abbot of St. Maurice	Nemesis
Manuel	The Destinies
Herman	Spirits, &c.

The Scene of the Drama is amongst the Higher Alps—partly in the Castle of Manfred, and partly in the Mountains.

ACT I

SCENE I—Manfred *alone.—Scene, a Gothic Gallery.—Time, Midnight*

Man. The lamp must be replenish'd, but
  even then
It will not burn so long as I must watch:
My slumbers—if I slumber—are not sleep,
But a continuance of enduring thought,
Which then I can resist not: in my heart
There is a vigil, and these eyes but close
To look within; and yet I live, and bear
The aspect and the form of breathing men.
But grief should be the instructor of the wise;
Sorrow is knowledge: they who know the
  most   10
Must mourn the deepest o'er the fatal truth,
The Tree of Knowledge is not that of Life.
Philosophy and science, and the springs
Of wonder, and the wisdom of the world,
I have essay'd, and in my mind there is
A power to make these subject to itself—
But they avail not: I have done men good,
And I have met with good even among men—
But this avail'd not: I have had my foes,
And none have baffled, many fallen before
  me—   20

But this avail'd not:—Good, or evil, life,
Powers, passions, all I see in other beings,
Have been to me as rain unto the sands,
Since that all-nameless hour. I have no dread,
And feel the curse to have no natural fear,
Nor fluttering throb, that beats with hopes or
  wishes,
Or lurking love of something on the earth.
Now to my task.—
           Mysterious agency!
Ye spirits of the unbounded Universe!
Whom I have sought in darkness and in
  light—   30
Ye, who do compass earth about, and dwell
In subtler essence—ye, to whom the tops
Of mountains inaccessible are haunts,
And earth's and ocean's caves familiar
  things—
I call upon ye by the written charm
Which gives me power upon you—Rise!
  Appear!   [*A pause.*
They come not yet.—Now by the voice of him
Who is the first among you—by this sign,
Which makes you tremble—by the claims of
  him   39
Who is undying,—Rise! Appear!——Appear!
         [*A pause.*
If it be so—Spirits of earth and air,
Ye shall not thus elude me: by a power,
Deeper than all yet urged, a tyrant-spell,
Which had its birthplace in a star condemn'd,
The burning wreck of a demolish'd world,
A wandering hell in the eternal space;
By the strong curse which is upon my soul,
The thought which is within me and around me,
I do compel ye to my will—Appear!
  [*A star is seen at the darker end of the gallery: it is stationary; and a voice is heard singing.*

First Spirit

Mortal! to thy bidding bow'd,   50
From my mansion in the cloud,
Which the breath of twilight builds,
And the summer's sunset gilds
With the azure and vermilion,
Which is mix'd for my pavilion;
Though thy quest may be forbidden,
On a star-beam I have ridden:
To thine adjuration bow'd,
Mortal—be thy wish avow'd!

Voice of the SECOND SPIRIT

Mont Blanc is the monarch of mountains; 60
  They crown'd him long ago
On a throne of rocks, in a robe of clouds,
  With a diadem of snow.
Around his waist are forests braced,
  The Avalanche in his hand;
But ere it fall, that thundering ball
  Must pause for my command.
The Glacier's cold and restless mass
  Moves onward day by day;
But I am he who bids it pass, 70
  Or with its ice delay.
I am the spirit of the place,
  Could make the mountain bow
And quiver to his cavern'd base—
  And what with me wouldst *Thou?*

Voice of the THIRD SPIRIT

  In the blue depth of the waters,
    Where the wave hath no strife,
  Where the wind is a stranger,
    And the sea-snake hath life,
  Where the Mermaid is decking 80
    Her green hair with shells,
  Like the storm on the surface
    Came the sound of thy spells;
  O'er my calm Hall of Coral
    The deep echo roll'd—
  To the Spirit of Ocean
    Thy wishes unfold!

FOURTH SPIRIT

Where the slumbering earthquake
  Lies pillow'd on fire,
And the lakes of bitumen 90
  Rise boilingly higher;
Where the roots of the Andes
  Strike deep in the earth,
As their summits to heaven
  Shoot soaringly forth;
I have quitted my birthplace,
  Thy bidding to bide—
Thy spell hath subdued me,
  Thy will be my guide!

FIFTH SPIRIT

I am the Rider of the wind, 100
  The Stirrer of the storm;
The hurricane I left behind
  Is yet with lightning warm;

To speed to thee, o'er shore and sea
  I swept upon the blast:
The fleet I met sail'd well, and yet
  'Twill sink ere night be past.

SIXTH SPIRIT

My dwelling is the shadow of the night,
Why doth thy magic torture me with light?

SEVENTH SPIRIT

The star which rules thy destiny 110
Was ruled, ere earth began, by me:
It was a world as fresh and fair
As e'er revolved round sun in air;
Its course was free and regular,
Space bosom'd not a lovelier star.
The hour arrived—and it became
A wandering mass of shapeless flame,
A pathless comet, and a curse,
The menace of the universe;
Still rolling on with innate force,
Without a sphere, without a course, 120
A bright deformity on high,
The monster of the upper sky!
And thou! beneath its influence born—
Thou worm! whom I obey and scorn—
Forced by a power (which is not thine,
And lent thee but to make thee mine)
For this brief moment to descend,
Where these weak spirits round thee bend
And parley with a thing like thee— 130
What wouldst thou, Child of Clay! with me?

The SEVEN SPIRITS

Earth, ocean, air, night, mountains, winds,
  thy star,
  Are at thy beck and bidding, Child of Clay!
Before thee at thy quest their spirits are—
  What wouldst thou with us, son of mor-
    tals—say?
Man. Forgetfulness——
First Spirit. Of what—of whom—and why?
Man. Of that which is within me; read it
    there—
Ye know it, and I cannot utter it.
  Spirit. We can but give thee that which
    we possess:
Ask of us subjects, sovereignty, the power 140
O'er earth—the whole, or portion—or a sign
Which shall control the elements, whereof

We are the dominators,—each and all,
These shall be thine.
    Man.   Oblivion, self-oblivion!
Can ye not wring from out the hidden realms
Ye offer so profusely what I ask?
    Spirit. It is not in our essence, in our skill;
But—thou may'st die.
    Man.   Will death bestow it on me?
    Spirit. We are immortal, and do not for-
    get;
We are eternal; and to us the past   150
Is, as the future, present. Art thou answer'd?
    Man. Ye mock me—but the power which
    brought ye here
Hath made you mine. Slaves, scoff not at my
    will!
The mind, the spirit, the Promethean spark,
The lightning of my being, is as bright,
Pervading, and far darting as your own,
And shall not yield to yours, though coop'd
    in clay!
Answer, or I will teach you what I am.
    Spirit. We answer as we answer'd; our
    reply   159
Is even in thine own words.
    Man.   Why say ye so?
    Spirit. If, as thou say'st, thine essence be
    as ours,
We have replied in telling thee, the thing
Mortals call death hath nought to do with us.
    Man. I then have call'd ye from your
    realms in vain;
Ye cannot, or ye will not, aid me.
    Spirit.   Say,
What we possess we offer; it is thine:
Bethink ere thou dismiss us; ask again;
Kingdom, and sway, and strength, and length
    of days——
    Man. Accursed! what have I to do with
    days?   169
They are too long already.—Hence—begone!
    Spirit. Yet pause: being here, our will
    would do thee service;
Bethink thee, is there then no other gift
Which we can make not worthless in thine
    eyes?
    Man. No, none: yet stay—one moment,
    ere we part,
I would behold ye face to face. I hear
Your voices, sweet and melancholy sounds,
As music on the waters; and I see

The steady aspect of a clear large star;
But nothing more. Approach me as ye are,
Or one, or all, in your accustom'd forms. 180
    Spirit. We have no forms, beyond the ele-
    ments
Of which we are the mind and principle:
But choose a form—in that we will appear.
    Man. I have no choice; there is no form on
    earth
Hideous or beautiful to me. Let him,
Who is most powerful of ye, take such aspect
As unto him may seem most fitting—Come!
    Seventh Spirit (*appearing in the shape of
    a beautiful female figure*). Behold!
    Man. Oh God! if it be thus, and *thou*
Art not a madness and a mockery,
I yet might be most happy, I will clasp
    thee,   190
And we again will be——
                          The figure vanishes.
                       My heart is crush'd!
                      [*Manfred falls senseless.*

(*A voice is heard in the incantation which
    follows*)

When the moon is on the wave,
    And the glow-worm in the grass,
And the meteor on the grave,
    And the wisp on the morass;
When the falling stars are shooting,
And the answer'd owls are hooting,
And the silent leaves are still
In the shadow of the hill,
Shall my soul be upon thine,   200
With a power and with a sign.

Though thy slumber may be deep,
Yet thy spirit shall not sleep;
There are shades which will not vanish,
There are thoughts thou canst not banish;
By a power to thee unknown,
Thou canst never be alone;
Thou art wrapt as with a shroud,
Thou art gather'd in a cloud;
And for ever shalt thou dwell   210
In the spirit of this spell.

Though thou seest me not pass by,
Thou shalt feel me with thine eye
As a thing that, though unseen,
Must be near thee, and hath been;

And when in that secret dread
Thou hast turn'd around thy head,
Thou shalt marvel I am not
As thy shadow on the spot,
And the power which thou dost feel 220
Shall be what thou must conceal.

And a magic voice and verse
Hath baptized thee with a curse;
And a spirit of the air
Hath begirt thee with a snare;
In the wind there is a voice
Shall forbid thee to rejoice;
And to thee shall night deny
All the quiet of her sky;
And the day shall have a sun, 230
Which shall make thee wish it done.

From thy false tears I did distil
An essence which hath strength to kill;
From thy own heart I then did wring
The black blood in its blackest spring;
From thy own smile I snatch'd the snake,
For there it coil'd as in a brake;
From thy own lip I drew the charm
Which gave all these their chiefest harm;
In proving every poison known, 240
I found the strongest was thine own.

By thy cold breast and serpent smile,
By thy unfathom'd gulfs of guile,
By that most seeming virtuous eye,
By thy shut soul's hypocrisy;
By the perfection of thine art
Which pass'd for human thine own heart;
By thy delight in others' pain,
And by thy brotherhood of Cain,
I call upon thee! and compel 250
Thyself to be thy proper Hell!

And on thy head I pour the vial
Which doth devote thee to this trial;
Nor to slumber, nor to die,
Shall be in thy destiny;
Though thy death shall still seem near
To thy wish, but as a fear;
Lo! the spell now works around thee,
And the clankless chain hath bound thee;
O'er thy heart and brain together 260
Hath the word been pass'd—now wither!

SCENE II

The Mountain of the Jungfrau.—Time, Morn-
*ing.—*MANFRED *alone upon the Cliffs.*

Man. The spirits I have raised abandon me,
The spells which I have studied baffle me,
The remedy I reck'd of tortured me;
I lean no more on superhuman aid;
It hath no power upon the past, and for
The future, till the past be gulf'd in darkness,
It is not of my search.—My mother Earth!
And thou fresh breaking Day, and you, ye
    Mountains,
Why are ye beautiful? I cannot love ye.
And thou, the bright eye of the universe, 10
That openest over all, and unto all
Art a delight—thou shin'st not on my heart.
And you, ye crags, upon whose extreme edge
I stand, and on the torrent's brink beneath
Behold the tall pines dwindled as to shrubs
In dizziness of distance; when a leap,
A stir, a motion, even a breath, would bring
My breast upon its rocky bosom's bed
To rest for ever—wherefore do I pause?
I feel the impulse—yet I do not plunge; 20
I see the peril—yet do not recede;
And my brain reels—and yet my foot is firm:
There is a power upon me which withholds,
And makes it my fatality to live,—
If it be life to wear within myself
This barrenness of spirit, and to be
My own soul's sepulchre, for I have ceased
To justify my deeds unto myself—
The last infirmity of evil. Ay,
Thou winged and cloud-cleaving minister, 30
                    [*An eagle passes.*
Whose happy flight is highest into heaven,
Well may'st thou swoop so near me—I
    should be
Thy prey, and gorge thine eaglets; thou art
    gone
Where the eye cannot follow thee; but thine
Yet pierces downward, onward, or above,
With a pervading vision.—Beautiful!
How beautiful is all this visible world!
How glorious in its action and itself!
But we, who name ourselves its sovereigns,
    we,
Half dust, half deity, alike unfit 40
To sink or soar, with our mix'd essence make
A conflict of its elements, and breathe

The breath of degradation and of pride,
Contending with low wants and lofty will,
Till our mortality predominates,
And men are—what they name not to them-
     selves,
And trust not to each other. Hark! the note,
                    [*The Shepherd's pipe in the
                              distance is heard.*
The natural music of the mountain reed——
For here the patriarchal days are not
A pastoral fable—pipes in the liberal air,   50
Mix'd with the sweet bells of the sauntering
     herd;
My soul would drink those echoes. Oh, that
     I were
The viewless spirit of a lovely sound,
A living voice, a breathing harmony,
A bodiless enjoyment—born and dying
With the blest tone which made me!

Enter from below a CHAMOIS HUNTER

Chamois Hunter.   Even so
This way the chamois leapt: her nimble feet
Have baffled me; my gains to-day will scarce
Repay my break-neck travail.—What is here?
Who seems not of my trade, and yet hath
     reach'd   60
A height which none even of our moun-
     taineers,
Save our best hunters, may attain: his garb
Is goodly, his mien manly, and his air
Proud as a free-born peasant's, at this dis-
     tance:
I will approach him nearer.
     Man. (*not perceiving the other*). To be
          thus—
Grey-hair'd with anguish, like these blasted
     pines,
Wrecks of a single winter, barkless, branch-
     less,
A blighted trunk upon a cursed root,
Which but supplies a feeling to decay—
And to be thus, eternally but thus,   70
Having been otherwise! Now furrow'd o'er
With wrinkles, plough'd by moments,—not
     by years,—
And hours, all tortured into ages—hours
Which I outlive!—Ye toppling crags of ice!
Ye avalanches, whom a breath draws down
In mountainous o'erwhelming, come and
     crush me!

I hear ye momently above, beneath,
Crash with a frequent conflict; but ye pass,
And only fall on things that still would live,
On the young flourishing forest, or the hut
And hamlet of the harmless villager.   81
     C. Hun. The mists begin to rise from up the
          valley;
I'll warn him to descend, or he may chance
To lose at once his way and life together.
     Man. The mists boil up around the glaciers;
          clouds
Rise curling fast beneath me, white and sul-
     phury,
Like foam from the roused ocean of deep
     Hell,
Whose every wave breaks on a living shore,
Heap'd with the damn'd like pebbles.—I am
     giddy.
     C. Hun. I must approach him cautiously;
          if near,   90
A sudden step will startle him, and he
Seems tottering already.
     Man.   Mountains have fallen,
Leaving a gap in the clouds, and with the
     shock
Rocking their Alpine brethren; filling up
The ripe green valleys with destruction's
     splinters;
Damming the rivers with a sudden dash,
Which crush'd the waters into mist and made
Their fountains find another channel—thus,
Thus, in its old age, did Mount Rosenberg—
Why stood I not beneath it?
     C. Hun.   Friend! have a care,
Your next step may be fatal!—for the love 101
Of him who made you, stand not on that
     brink!
     Man. (*not hearing him*). Such would have
          been for me a fitting tomb;
My bones had then been quiet in their depth;
They had not then been strewn upon the rocks
For the wind's pastime—as thus—thus they
     shall be—
In this one plunge.—Farewell, ye opening
     heavens!
Look not upon me thus reproachfully—
You were not meant for me—Earth! take these
     atoms!
     [*As* MANFRED *is in act to spring from the
     cliff, the* CHAMOIS HUNTER *seizes and
     retains him with a sudden grasp.*

C. Hun. Hold, madman!—though aweary
of thy life,
Stain not our pure vales with thy guilty
blood: 111
Away with me——I will not quit my hold.
  Man. I am most sick at heart—nay, grasp
  me not—
I am all feebleness—the mountains whirl
Spinning around me——I grow blind——
  What art thou?
    C. Hun. I'll answer that anon. Away with
    me—
The clouds grow thicker—there—now lean
on me—
Place your foot here—here, take this staff,
and cling
A moment to that shrub—now give me your
hand,
And hold fast by my girdle—softly—well—
The Chalet will be gain'd within an hour: 121
Come on, we'll quickly find a surer footing,
And something like a pathway, which the
torrent
Hath wash'd since winter.—Come, 'tis
bravely done—
You should have been a hunter.—Follow
me.
    [*As they descend the rocks with
    difficulty, the scene closes.*

ACT II

SCENE I.—*A Cottage amongst the Bernese
Alps*

MANFRED *and the* CHAMOIS HUNTER

C. Hun. No, no—yet pause—thou must
not yet go forth:
Thy mind and body are alike unfit
To trust each other, for some hours, at least;
When thou art better, I will be thy guide—
But whither?
  Man. It imports not: I do know
My route full well, and need no further
guidance.
    C. Hun. Thy garb and gait bespeak thee of
    high lineage—
One of the many chiefs, whose castled crags
Look o'er the lower valleys—which of these
May call thee lord? I only know their portals;

My way of life leads me but rarely down 11
To bask by the huge hearths of those old
halls,
Carousing with the vassals; but the paths,
Which step from out our mountains to their
doors,
I know from childhood—which of these is
thine?
  Man. No matter.
    C. Hun. Well, sir, pardon me the
    question,
And be of better cheer. Come, taste my wine;
'Tis of an ancient vintage; many a day
'T has thaw'd my veins among our glaciers,
now
Let it do thus for thine—Come, pledge me
fairly. 20
  Man. Away, away! there's blood upon the
  brim!
Will it then never—never sink in the earth?
    C. Hun. What dost thou mean? thy senses
    wander from thee.
    Man. I say 'tis blood—my blood! the pure
    warm stream
Which ran in the veins of my fathers, and in
ours
When we were in our youth, and had one
heart,
And loved each other as we should not love,
And this was shed: but still it rises up,
Colouring the clouds, that shut me out from
heaven,
Where thou art not—and I shall never be. 30
    C. Hun. Man of strange words, and some
    half-maddening sin,
Which makes thee people vacancy, whate'er
Thy dread and sufferance be, there's comfort
yet—
The aid of holy men, and heavenly patience—
    Man. Patience and patience! Hence—that
    word was made
For brutes of burthen, not for birds of prey;
Preach it to mortals of a dust like thine,—
I am not of thine order.
    C. Hun. Thanks to heaven!
I would not be of thine for the free fame
Of William Tell; but whatsoe'er thine ill, 40
It must be borne, and these wild starts are
useless.
  Man. Do I not bear it?—Look on me—I
  live.

C. Hun. This is convulsion, and no healthful life.

Man. I tell thee, man! I have lived many
years,

Many long years, but they are nothing now
To those which I must number: ages—ages—
Space and eternity—and consciousness,
With the fierce thirst of death—and still un-
slaked!

C. Hun. Why, on thy brow the seal of
middle age
Hath scarce been set; I am thine elder far. 50

Man. Think'st thou existence doth depend
on time?

It doth; but actions are our epochs: mine
Have made my days and nights imperishable,
Endless, and all alike, as sands on the shore,
Innumerable atoms; and one desert,
Barren and cold, on which the wild waves
break,
But nothing rests, save carcasses and wrecks,
Rocks, and the salt-surf weeds of bitterness.

C. Hun. Alas! he's mad—but yet I must
not leave him.

Man. I would I were—for then the things
I see   60
Would be but a distemper'd dream.

C. Hun.   What is it
That thou dost see, or think thou look'st
upon?

Man. Myself, and thee—a peasant of the
Alps—
Thy humble virtues, hospitable home,
And spirit patient, pious, proud, and free;
Thy self-respect, grafted on innocent thoughts;
Thy days of health, and nights of sleep; thy
toils,
By danger dignified, yet guiltless; hopes
Of cheerful old age and a quiet grave,
With cross and garland over its green turf, 70
And thy grandchildren's love for epitaph;
This do I see—and then I look within—
It matters not—my soul was scorch'd already!

C. Hun. And wouldst thou then exchange
thy lot for mine?

Man. No, friend! I would not wrong thee,
nor exchange
My lot with living being: I can bear—
However wretchedly, 'tis still to bear—
In life what others could not brook to dream,
But perish in their slumber.

C. Hun.   And with this—
This cautious feeling for another's pain, 80
Canst thou be black with evil?—say not so.
Can one of gentle thoughts have wreak'd
revenge
Upon his enemies?

Man.   Oh! no, no, no!
My injuries came down on those who loved
me—
On those whom I best loved: I never quell'd
An enemy, save in my just defence—
But my embrace was fatal.

C. Hun.   Heaven give thee rest!
And penitence restore thee to thyself;
My prayers shall be for thee.

Man.   I need them not—
But can endure thy pity. I depart— 90
'Tis time—farewell!—Here's gold, and thanks
for thee—
No words—it is thy due.—Follow me not—
I know my path—the mountain peril's past:
And once again I charge thee, follow not!

[*Exit* MANFRED.

SCENE II

A lower Valley in the Alps.—A Cataract.

Enter MANFRED

It is not noon—the sunbow's rays still arch
The torrent with the many hues of heaven,
And roll the sheeted silver's waving column
O'er the crag's headlong perpendicular,
And fling its lines of foaming light along,
And to and fro, like the pale courser's tail,
The Giant steed, to be bestrode by Death,
As told in the Apocalypse. No eyes
But mine now drink this sight of loveliness;
I should be sole in this sweet solitude, 10
And with the Spirit of the place divide
The homage of these waters.—I will call her.

[MANFRED *takes some of the water into
the palm of his hand, and flings it
into the air, muttering the adjuration.
After a pause, the* WITCH OF THE
ALPS *rises beneath the arch of the
sunbow of the torrent.*

Beautiful Spirit! with thy hair of light,
And dazzling eyes of glory, in whose form
The charms of earth's least mortal daughters
grow
To an unearthly stature, in an essence

Of purer elements; while the hues of youth,—
Carnation'd like a sleeping infant's cheek,
Rock'd by the beating of her mother's heart,
Or the rose tints, which summer's twilight
　leaves　　　　　　　　　　　　　20
Upon the lofty glacier's virgin snow,
The blush of earth embracing with her
　heaven,—
Tinge thy celestial aspect, and make tame
The beauties of the sunbow which bends o'er
　thee.
Beautiful Spirit! in thy calm clear brow,
Wherein is glass'd serenity of soul,
Which of itself shows immortality,
I read that thou wilt pardon to a Son
Of Earth, whom the abstruser powers permit
At times to commune with them—if that he
Avail him of his spells—to call thee thus,　31
And gaze on thee a moment.
Witch.　　　　　　　　Son of Earth!
I know thee, and the powers which give thee
　power;
I know thee for a man of many thoughts,
And deeds of good and ill, extreme in both,
Fatal and fated in thy sufferings.
I have expected this—what wouldst thou with
　me?
Man. To look upon thy beauty—nothing
　further.
The face of the earth hath madden'd me, and I
Take refuge in her mysteries, and pierce　40
To the abodes of those who govern her—
But they can nothing aid me. I have sought
From them what they could not bestow, and
　now
I search no further.
Witch.　　　　　What could be the quest
Which is not in the power of the most power-
　ful,
The rulers of the invisible?
Man.　　　　　：A boon;
But why should I repeat it? 'twere in vain.
Witch. I know not that; let thy lips utter it.
Man. Well, though it torture me, 'tis but
　the same;
My pang shall find a voice. From my youth
　upwards　　　　　　　　　　50
My spirit walk'd not with the souls of men,
Nor look'd upon the earth with human eyes;
The thirst of their ambition was not mine,
The aim of their existence was not mine;

My joys, my griefs, my passions, and my
　powers,
Made me a stranger; though I wore the form,
I had no sympathy with breathing flesh,
Nor midst the creatures of clay that girded me
Was there but one who—but of her anon.
I said with men, and with the thoughts of
　men,　　　　　　　　　　　60
I held but slight communion; but instead,
My joy was in the wilderness,—to breathe
The difficult air of the iced mountain's top,
Where the birds dare not build, nor insect's
　wing
Flit o'er the herbless granite; or to plunge
Into the torrent, and to roll along
On the swift whirl of the new breaking wave
Of river-stream, or ocean, in their flow.
In these my early strength exulted; or
To follow through the night the moving
　moon,　　　　　　　　　　　70
The stars and their development; or catch
The dazzling lightnings till my eyes grew
　dim;
Or to look, list'ning, on the scatter'd leaves,
While Autumn winds were at their evening
　song.
These were my pastimes, and to be alone;
For if the beings, of whom I was one,—
Hating to be so,—cross'd me in my path,
I felt myself degraded back to them,
And was all clay again. And then I dived,
In my lone wanderings, to the caves of death,
Searching its cause in its effect; and drew　81
From wither'd bones, and skulls, and heap'd
　up dust,
Conclusions most forbidden. Then I pass'd
The nights of years in sciences untaught,
Save in the old time; and with time and toil,
And terrible ordeal, and such penance
As in itself hath power upon the air,
And spirits that do compass air and earth,
Space, and the peopled infinite, I made
Mine eyes familiar with Eternity,　　　90
Such as, before me, did the Magi, and
He who from out their fountain dwellings
　raised
Eros and Anteros, at Gadara,
As I do thee;—and with my knowledge grew
The thirst of knowledge, and the power and
　joy
Of this most bright intelligence, until—

Witch. Proceed.

Man. Oh! I but thus prolong'd my words,
Boasting these idle attributes, because
As I approach the core of my heart's grief—
But to my task. I have not named to thee 100
Father or mother, mistress, friend, or being,
With whom I wore the chain of human ties;
If I had such, they seem'd not such to me;
Yet there was one—

Witch. Spare not thyself—proceed.

Man. She was like me in lineaments; her eyes,
Her hair, her features, all, to the very tone
Even of her voice, they said were like to mine;
But soften'd all, and temper'd into beauty:
She had the same lone thoughts and wanderings,
The quest of hidden knowledge, and a mind
To comprehend the universe: nor these 111
Alone, but with them gentler powers than mine,
Pity, and smiles, and tears—which I had not;
And tenderness—but that I had for her;
Humility—and that I never had.
Her faults were mine—her virtues were her own—
I loved her, and destroy'd her!

Witch. With thy hand?

Man. Not with my hand, but heart, which broke her heart;
It gazed on mine, and wither'd. I have shed
Blood, but not hers—and yet her blood was shed; 120
I saw—and could not stanch it.

Witch. And for this—
A being of the race thou dost despise,
The order, which thine own would rise above,
Mingling with us and ours,—thou dost forego
The gifts of our great knowledge, and shrink'st back
To recreant mortality——Away!

Man. Daughter of Air! I tell thee, since that hour—
But words are breath—look on me in my sleep,
Or watch my watchings—Come and sit by me!
My solitude is solitude no more, 130
But peopled with the Furies;—I have gnash'd
My teeth in darkness till returning morn,
Then cursed myself till sunset;—I have pray'd
For madness as a blessing—'tis denied me.
I have affronted death—but in the war
Of elements the waters shrunk from me,
And fatal things pass'd harmless; the cold hand
Of an all-pitiless demon held me back,
Back by a single hair, which would not break.
In fantasy, imagination, all 140
The affluence of my soul—which one day was
A Crœsus in creation—I plunged deep,
But, like an ebbing wave, it dash'd me back
Into the gulf of my unfathom'd thought,
I plunged amidst mankind—Forgetfulness
I sought in all, save where 'tis to be found,
And that I have to learn; my sciences,
My long-pursued and superhuman art,
Is mortal here: I dwell in my despair—
And live—and live for ever.

Witch. It may be 150
That I can aid thee.

Man. To do this thy power
Must wake the dead, or lay me low with them.
Do so—in any shape—in any hour—
With any torture—so it be the last.

Witch. That is not in my province; but if thou
Wilt swear obedience to my will, and do
My bidding, it may help thee to thy wishes.

Man. I will not swear—Obey! and whom? the spirits
Whose presence I command, and be the slave
Of those who served me—Never!

Witch. Is this all? 160
Hast thou no gentler answer?—Yet bethink thee,
And pause ere thou rejectest.

Man. I have said it.

Witch. Enough! I may retire then—say!

Man. Retire!

[*The* WITCH *disappears.*

Man. (*alone*). We are the fools of time and terror: Days
Steal on us, and steal from us; yet we live,
Loathing our life, and dreading still to die.
In all the days of this detested yoke—
This vital weight upon the struggling heart,
Which sinks with sorrow, or beats quick with pain,
Or joy that ends in agony or faintness— 170

In all the days of past and future, for
In life there is no present, we can number
How few—how less than few—wherein the
    soul
Forbears to pant for death, and yet draws
    back
As from a stream in winter, though the chill
Be but a moment's. I have one resource
Still in my science—I can call the dead,
And ask them what it is we dread to be:
The sternest answer can but be the Grave,
And that is nothing. If they answer not— 180
The buried Prophet answered to the Hag
Of Endor; and the Spartan Monarch drew
From the Byzantine maid's unsleeping spirit
An answer and his destiny—he slew
That which he loved, unknowing what he
    slew,
And died unpardon'd—though he call'd in aid
The Phyxian Jove, and in Phigalia roused
The Arcadian Evocators to compel
The indignant shadow to depose her wrath,
Or fix her term of vengeance—she replied 190
In words of dubious import, but fulfill'd.
If I had never lived, that which I love
Had still been living; had I never loved,
That which I love would still be beautiful,
Happy and giving happiness. What is she?
What is she now?—a sufferer for my sins—
A thing I dare not think upon—or nothing.
Within few hours I shall not call in vain—
Yet in this hour I dread the thing I dare:
Until this hour I never shrunk to gaze 200
On spirit, good or evil—now I tremble,
And feel a strange cold thaw upon my heart.
But I can act even what I most abhor,
And champion human fears.—The night ap-
    proaches.   [*Exit.*

SCENE III

The Summit of the Jungfrau Mountain

Enter FIRST DESTINY

The moon is rising broad, and round, and
    bright;
And here on snows, where never human foot
Of common mortal trod, we nightly tread,
And leave no traces: o'er the savage sea,
The glassy ocean of the mountain ice,
We skim its rugged breakers, which put on
The aspect of a tumbling tempest's foam,
Frozen in a moment—a dead whirlpool's
    image:
And this most steep fantastic pinnacle,
The fretwork of some earthquake—where the
    clouds   10
Pause to repose themselves in passing by—
Is sacred to our revels, or our vigils;
Here do I wait my sisters, on our way
To the Hall of Arimanes, for to-night
Is our great festival—'tis strange they come
    not.

    A Voice without, singing

    The Captive Usurper,
      Hurl'd down from the throne,
    Lay buried in torpor,
      Forgotten and lone;
    I broke through his slumbers,   20
      I shiver'd his chain,
    I leagued him with numbers—
      He's Tyrant again!
With the blood of a million he'll answer my
    care,
With a nation's destruction—his flight and
    despair.

    Second Voice, without

The ship sail'd on, the ship sail'd fast,
But I left not a sail, and I left not a mast;
There is not a plank of the hull or the deck,
And there is not a wretch to lament o'er his
    wreck;
Save one, whom I held, as he swam, by the
    hair,   30
And he was a subject well worthy my care;
A traitor on land, and a pirate at sea—
But I saved him to wreak further havoc for
    me!

    FIRST DESTINY, *answering*

    The city lies sleeping;
      The morn, to deplore it,
    May dawn on it weeping:
      Sullenly, slowly,
    The black plague flew o'er it—
      Thousands lie lowly;
    Tens of thousands shall perish;   40
      The living shall fly from
    The sick they should cherish;
      But nothing can vanquish
    The touch that they die from.
      Sorrow and anguish,

And evil and dread,
   Envelope a nation;
The blest are the dead,
Who see not the sight
   Of their own desolation;   50
This work of a night—
This wreck of a realm—this deed of my
  doing—
For ages I've done, and shall still be renewing!

Enter the SECOND *and* THIRD DESTINIES

The Three

Our hands contain the hearts of men,
   Our footsteps are their graves;
We only give to take again
   The spirits of our slaves!

First Des. Welcome!—Where's Nemesis?
Second Des.   At some great work;
But what I know not, for my hands were full.
Third Des. Behold she cometh.

Enter NEMESIS

First Des.   Say, where hast thou been? 60
My sisters and thyself are slow to-night.
  Nem. I was detain'd repairing shatter'd
  thrones,
Marrying fools, restoring dynasties,
Avenging men upon their enemies,
And making them repent their own revenge;
Goading the wise to madness; from the dull
Shaping out oracles to rule the world
Afresh, for they were waxing out of date,
And mortals dared to ponder for themselves,
To weigh kings in the balance, and to speak 70
Of freedom, the forbidden fruit.—Away!
We have outstay'd the hour—mount we our
  clouds!   [*Exeunt.*

SCENE IV

*The Hall of Arimanes—Arimanes on his
Throne, a Globe of Fire, surrounded by
the Spirits.*

Hymn of the SPIRITS

Hail to our Master!—Prince of Earth and Air!
  Who walks the clouds and waters—in his
  hand
The sceptre of the elements, which tear
  Themselves to chaos at his high command!
He breatheth—and a tempest shakes the sea;

He speaketh—and the clouds reply in thun-
  der;
He gazeth—from his glance the sunbeams
  flee;
He moveth—earthquakes rend the world
  asunder.
Beneath his footsteps the volcanoes rise;
  His shadow is the Pestilence; his path   10
The comets herald through the crackling
  skies;
  And planets turn to ashes at his wrath.
To him War offers daily sacrifice;
  To him Death pays his tribute; Life is his,
With all its infinite of agonies—
  And his the spirit of whatever is!

Enter the DESTINIES *and* NEMESIS

First Des. Glory to Arimanes! on the earth
His power increaseth—both my sisters did
His bidding, nor did I neglect my duty!
  Second Des. Glory to Arimanes! we who
  bow   20
The necks of men, bow down before his
  throne!
  Third Des. Glory to Arimanes! we await
His nod!
  Nem. Sovereign of Sovereigns! we are thine,
And all that liveth, more or less, is ours,
And most things wholly so; still to increase
Our power, increasing thine, demands our
  care,
And we are vigilant. Thy late commands
Have been fulfill'd to the utmost.

Enter MANFRED

  A Spirit.   What is here?
A mortal!—Thou most rash and fatal wretch,
Bow down and worship!
  Second Spirit.   I do know the man— 30
A Magian of great power, and fearful skill!
  Third Spirit. Bow down and worship,
  slave!—
What, know'st thou not
Thine and our Sovereign?—Tremble, and
  obey!
  All the Spirits. Prostrate thyself, and thy
  condemned clay,
Child of the Earth! or dread the worst.
  Man.   I know it;
And yet ye see I kneel not.
  Fourth Spirit.   'Twill be taught thee.

Man. 'Tis taught already;—many a night
on the earth,
On the bare ground, have I bow'd down my
face,
And strew'd my head with ashes; I have
known
The fulness of humiliation, for   40
I sunk before my vain despair, and knelt
To my own desolation.
 Fifth Spirit.   Dost thou dare
Refuse to Arimanes on his throne
What the whole earth accords, beholding not
The terror of his glory?—Crouch, I say.
 Man. Bid *him* bow down to that which is
above him,
The overruling Infinite—the Maker
Who made him not for worship—let him
kneel,
And we will kneel together.
 The Spirits.   Crush the worm!
Tear him in pieces!—
 First Des. Hence! avaunt!—he's mine. 50
Prince of the Powers invisible! This man
Is of no common order, as his port
And presence here denote; his sufferings
Have been of an immortal nature, like
Our own; his knowledge, and his powers and
will,
As far as is compatible with clay,
Which clogs the ethereal essence, have been
such
As clay hath seldom borne; his aspirations
Have been beyond the dwellers of the earth,
And they have only taught him what we
know—   60
That knowledge is not happiness, and science
But an exchange of ignorance for that
Which is another kind of ignorance.
This is not all—the passions, attributes
Of earth and heaven, from which no power,
nor being,
Nor breath from the worm upwards is exempt,
Have pierced his heart, and in their conse-
quence
Made him a thing which I, who pity not,
Yet pardon those who pity. He is mine,
And thine, it may be; be it so, or not,   70
No other Spirit in this region hath
A soul like his—or power upon his soul.
 Nem. What doth he here then?
 First Des.   Let him answer that.

Man. Ye know what I have known; and
without power
I could not be amongst ye: but there are
Powers deeper still beyond—I come in quest
Of such, to answer unto what I seek.
 Nem. What wouldst thou?
 Man.   Thou canst not reply to me.
Call up the dead—my question is for them. 79
 Nem. Great Arimanes, doth thy will avouch
The wishes of this mortal?
 Ari.   Yea.
 Nem.   Whom wouldst thou
Uncharnel?
 Man. One without a tomb—call up
Astarte.

NEMESIS

 Shadow! or Spirit!
  Whatever thou art,
 Which still doth inherit
  The whole or a part
 Of the form of thy birth,
  Of the mould of thy clay,
 Which return'd to the earth,   90
  Re-appear to the day!
 Bear what thou borest,
  The heart and the form,
 And the aspect thou worest
  Redeem from the worm.
Appear!—Appear!—Appear!
Who sent thee there requires thee here!
  [*The Phantom of* ASTARTE *rises and
   stands in the midst.*

Man. Can this be death? there's bloom upon
her cheek;
But now I see it is no living hue,
But a strange hectic—like the unnatural red
Which Autumn plants upon the perish'd leaf.
It is the same! Oh, God! that I should dread 101
To look upon the same—Astarte!—No,
I cannot speak to her—but bid her speak—
Forgive me or condemn me.

NEMESIS

 By the power which hath broken
  The grave which enthrall'd thee,
 Speak to him who hath spoken,
  Or those who have call'd thee!

 Man.   She is silent,
And in that silence I am more than answer'd.

Nem. My power extends no further. Prince
of Air!   111
It rests with thee alone—command her voice.
Ari. Spirit—obey this sceptre!
Nem.   Silent still!
She is not of our order, but belongs
To the other powers. Mortal! thy quest is vain,
And we are baffled also.
Man.   Hear me, hear me—
Astarte! my beloved! speak to me:
I have so much endured—so much endure—
Look on me! the grave hath not changed thee
more
Than I am changed for thee. Thou lovedst
me   120
Too much, as I loved thee: we were not made
To torture thus each other, though it were
The deadliest sin to love as we have loved.
Say that thou loath'st me not—that I do bear
This punishment for both—that thou wilt be
One of the blessed—and that I shall die;
For hitherto all hateful things conspire
To bind me in existence—in a life
Which makes me shrink from immortality—
A future like the past. I cannot rest.   130
I know not what I ask, nor what I seek:
I feel but what thou art, and what I am;
And I would hear yet once before I perish
The voice which was my music—Speak to
me!
For I have call'd on thee in the still night,
Startled the slumbering birds from the hush'd
boughs,
And woke the mountain wolves, and made
the caves
Acquainted with thy vainly echoed name,
Which answer'd me—many things answer'd
me—
Spirits and men—but thou wert silent all.   140
Yet speak to me! I have outwatch'd the stars,
And gazed o'er heaven in vain in search of
thee.
Speak to me! I have wander'd o'er the earth,
And never found thy likeness—Speak to me!
Look on the fiends around—they feel for me:
I fear them not, and feel for thee alone—
Speak to me! though it be in wrath;—but
say—
I reck not what—but let me hear thee once—
This once—once more!
Phantom of Astarte.   Manfred!

Man.   Say on, say on—
I live but in the sound—it is thy voice!   150
Phan. Manfred! To-morrow ends thine
earthly ills.
Farewell!
Man. Yet one word more—am I forgiven?
Phan. Farewell!
Man.   Say, shall we meet again?
Phan. Farewell!
Man. One word for mercy! Say, thou lovest
me.
Phan. Manfred!
                [*The Spirit of* ASTARTE *disappears.*
Nem. She's gone, and will not be recall'd;
Her words will be fulfill'd. Return to the
earth.
A Spirit. He is convulsed.—This is to be a
mortal
And seek the things beyond mortality.
Another Spirit. Yet, see, he mastereth him-
self, and makes
His torture tributary to his will.   160
Had he been one of us, he would have made
An awful spirit.
Nem.   Hast thou further question
Of our great sovereign, or his worshippers?
Man. None.
Nem.   Then for a time farewell.
Man. We meet then! Where? On the
earth?—
Even as thou wilt: and for the grace accorded
I now depart a debtor. Fare ye well!
                          [*Exit* MANFRED.
(*Scene closes.*)

ACT III

SCENE I.—*A Hall in the Castle of Manfred.*

MANFRED *and* HERMAN

Man. What is the hour?
Her.   It wants but one till sunset,
And promises a lovely twilight.
Man.   Say,
Are all things so disposed of in the tower
As I directed?
Her.   All, my lord, are ready:
Here is the key and casket.
Man.   It is well:
Thou may'st retire.   [*Exit* HERMAN.

Man. (alone). There is a calm upon me—
Inexplicable stillness! which till now
Did not belong to what I knew of life.
If that I did not know philosophy
To be of all our vanities the motliest, 10
The merest word that ever fool'd the ear
From out the schoolman's jargon, I should
  deem
The golden secret, the sought "Kalon," found,
And seated in my soul. It will not last,
But it is well to have known it, though but
  once:
It hath enlarged my thoughts with a new
  sense,
And I within my tablets would note down
That there is such a feeling. Who is there?

Re-enter HERMAN

Her. My lord, the abbot of St. Maurice
  craves
To greet your presence.

Enter the ABBOT OF ST. MAURICE

Abbot.   Peace be with Count Manfred! 20
Man. Thanks, holy father! welcome to these
  walls;
Thy presence honours them, and blesseth
  those
Who dwell within them.
Abbot.   Would it were so, Count!—
But I would fain confer with thee alone.
Man. Herman, retire.—What would my
  reverend guest?
Abbot. Thus, without prelude:—Age and
  zeal, my office,
And good intent, must plead my privilege;
Our near, though not acquainted neighbour-
  hood,
May also be my herald. Rumours strange,
And of unholy nature, are abroad, 30
And busy with thy name; a noble name
For centuries: may he who bears it now
Transmit it unimpair'd!
Man.   Proceed,—I listen.
Abbot. 'Tis said thou holdest converse with
  the things
Which are forbidden to the search of man;
That with the dwellers of the dark abodes,
The many evil and unheavenly spirits
Which walk the valley of the shade of death,
Thou communest. I know that with mankind,

Thy fellows in creation, thou dost rarely 40
Exchange thy thoughts, and that thy solitude
Is as an anchorite's, were it but holy.
Man. And what are they who do avouch
  these things?
Abbot. My pious brethren—the scared peas-
  antry—
Even thy own vassals—who do look on thee
With most unquiet eyes. Thy life's in peril.
Man. Take it.
Abbot.   I come to save, and not destroy:
I would not pry into thy secret soul;
But if these things be sooth, there still is time
For penitence and pity: reconcile thee 50
With the true church, and through the church
  to heaven.
Man. I hear thee. This is my reply: whate'er
I may have been, or am, doth rest between
Heaven and myself. I shall not choose a mortal
To be my mediator. Have I sinn'd
Against your ordinances? prove and punish!
Abbot. My son! I did not speak of punish-
  ment,
But penitence and pardon;—with thyself
The choice of such remains—and for the last,
Our institutions and our strong belief 60
Have given me power to smooth the path from
  sin
To higher hope and better thoughts; the first
I leave to heaven,—"Vengeance is mine
  alone!"
So saith the Lord, and with all humbleness
His servant echoes back the awful word.
Man. Old man! there is no power in holy
  men,
Nor charm in prayer, nor purifying form
Of penitence, nor outward look, nor fast,
Nor agony—nor, greater than all these,
The innate tortures of that deep despair, 70
Which is remorse without the fear of hell,
But all in all sufficient to itself
Would make a hell of heaven—can exorcise
From out the unbounded spirit the quick
  sense
Of its own sins, wrongs, sufferance, and re-
  venge
Upon itself; there is no future pang
Can deal that justice on the self-condemn'd
He deals on his own soul.
Abbot.   All this is well;
For this will pass away, and be succeeded

By an auspicious hope, which shall look up 80
With calm assurance to that blessed place,
Which all who seek may win, whatever be
Their earthly errors, so they be atoned:
And the commencement of atonement is
The sense of its necessity. Say on—
And all our church can teach thee shall be
   taught;
And all we can absolve thee shall be pardon'd.
   Man. When Rome's sixth emperor was
   near his last,
The victim of a self-inflicted wound,
To shun the torments of a public death   90
From senates once his slaves, a certain soldier,
With show of loyal pity, would have stanch'd
The gushing throat with his officious robe;
The dying Roman thrust him back, and said—
Some empire still in his expiring glance—
"It is too late—is this fidelity?"
   Abbot. And what of this?
   Man.   I answer with the Roman—
"It is too late!"
   Abbot.   It never can be so,
To reconcile thyself with thy own soul,
And thy own soul with heaven. Hast thou no
   hope?   100
'Tis strange—even those who do despair
   above,
Yet shape themselves some fantasy on earth,
To which frail twig they cling, like drowning
   men.
   Man. Ay—father! I have had those earthly
   visions,
And noble aspirations in my youth,
To make my own the mind of other men,
The enlightener of nations; and to rise
I knew not whither—it might be to fall;
But fall, even as the mountain-cataract,
Which having leapt from its more dazzling
   height,   110
Even in the foaming strength of its abyss,
(Which casts up misty columns that become
Clouds raining from the re-ascended skies,)
Lies low but mighty still.—But this is past,
My thoughts mistook themselves.
   Abbot.   And wherefore so?
   Man. I could not tame my nature down;
   for he
Must serve who fain would sway; and soothe,
   and sue,
And watch all time, and pry into all place,

And be a living lie, who would become
A mighty thing amongst the mean, and such
The mass are; I disdain'd to mingle with   121
A herd, though to be leader—and of wolves.
The lion is alone, and so am I.
   Abbot. And why not live and act with other
   men?
   Man. Because my nature was averse from
   life;
And yet not cruel; for I would not make,
But find a desolation. Like the wind,
The red-hot breath of the most lone simoom,
Which dwells but in the desert, and sweeps
   o'er
The barren sands which bear no shrubs to
   blast,   130
And revels o'er their wild and arid waves,
And seeketh not, so that it is not sought,
But being met is deadly,—such hath been
The course of my existence; but there came
Things in my path which are no more.
   Abbot.   Alas!
I 'gin to fear that thou art past all aid
From me and from my calling; yet so young,
I still would—
   Man.   Look on me! there is an order
Of mortals on the earth, who do become
Old in their youth, and die ere middle age,   140
Without the violence of warlike death;
Some perishing of pleasure, some of study,
Some worn with toil, some of mere weariness,
Some of disease, and some insanity,
And some of wither'd or of broken hearts;
For this last is a malady which slays
More than are number'd in the lists of Fate,
Taking all shapes, and bearing many names.
Look upon me! for even of all these things
Have I partaken; and of all these things,   150
One were enough; then wonder not that I
Am what I am, but that I ever was,
Or having been, that I am still on earth.
   Abbot. Yet, hear me still——
   Man.   Old man! I do respect
Thine order, and revere thine years; I deem
Thy purpose pious, but it is in vain:
Think me not churlish; I would spare thyself,
Far more than me, in shunning at this time
All further colloquy—and so—farewell.
                    [*Exit* MANFRED.
   Abbot. This should have been a noble crea-
   ture: he   160

Hath all the energy which would have made
A goodly frame of glorious elements,
Had they been wisely mingled; as it is,
It is an awful chaos—light and darkness,
And mind and dust, and passions and pure
    thoughts
Mix'd, and contending without end or order,—
All dormant or destructive: he will perish,
And yet he must not; I will try once more.
For such are worth redemption; and my duty
Is to dare all things for a righteous end.   170
I'll follow him—but cautiously, though surely.
                                        [*Exit* ABBOT.

SCENE II

Another Chamber

MANFRED *and* HERMAN

Her. My lord, you bade me wait on you at
    sunset:
He sinks behind the mountain.
Man.   Doth he so?
I will look on him. [MANFRED *advances to the*
                    Window of the Hall.
                    Glorious Orb! the idol
Of early nature, and the vigorous race
Of undiseased mankind, the giant sons
Of the embrace of angels, with a sex
More beautiful than they, which did draw down
The erring spirits who can ne'er return.—
Most glorious orb! that wert a worship, ere
The mystery of thy making was reveal'd!   10
Thou earliest minister of the Almighty,
Which gladden'd, on their mountain tops, the
    hearts
Of the Chaldean shepherds, till they pour'd
Themselves in orisons! Thou material God!
And representative of the Unknown—
Who chose thee for his shadow! Thou chief
    star!
Centre of many stars! which mak'st our earth
Endurable, and temperest the hues
And hearts of all who walk within thy rays!
Sire of the seasons! Monarch of the climes,   20
And those who dwell in them! for near or far,
Our inborn spirits have a tint of thee
Even as our outward aspects;—thou dost rise,
And shine, and set in glory. Fare thee well!
I ne'er shall see thee more. As my first glance
Of love and wonder was for thee, then take
My latest look; thou wilt not beam on one

To whom the gifts of life and warmth have been
Of a more fatal nature. He is gone:
I follow.   [*Exit* MANFRED.   30

SCENE III

*The Mountains—The Castle of Manfred at
some distance—A Terrace before a Tower—
Time, Twilight.*

HERMAN, MANUEL, *and other Dependents of*
MANFRED

Her. 'Tis strange enough; night after night,
    for years,
He hath pursued long vigils in this tower,
Without a witness. I have been within it,—
So have we all been oft-times; but from it,
Or its contents, it were impossible
To draw conclusions absolute, of aught
His studies tend to. To be sure, there is
One chamber where none enter: I would give
The fee of what I have to come these three
    years,
To pore upon its mysteries.
Manuel.   'Twere dangerous,   10
Content thyself with what thou know'st al-
    ready.
Her. Ah! Manuel! thou art elderly and
    wise,
And couldst say much; thou hast dwelt within
    the castle—
How many years is't?
Manuel.   Ere Count Manfred's birth,
I served his father, whom he nought re-
    sembles.
Her. There be more sons in like predica-
    ment.
But wherein do they differ?
Manuel.   I speak not
Of features or of form, but mind and habits;
Count Sigismund was proud, but gay and
    free,—
A warrior and a reveller; he dwelt not   20
With books and solitude, nor made the night
A gloomy vigil, but a festal time,
Merrier than day; he did not walk the rocks
And forests like a wolf, nor turn aside
From men and their delights.
Her.   Beshrew the hour,
But those were jocund times! I would that such
Would visit the old walls again; they look
As if they had forgotten them.

Manuel.   These walls
Must change their chieftain first. Oh! I have
          seen
Some strange things in them, Herman.
     Her.   Come, be friendly; 30
Relate me some to while away our watch:
I've heard thee darkly speak of an event
Which happen'd hereabouts, by this same
          tower.
     Manuel. That was a night indeed! I do re-
          member
'Twas twilight, as it may be now, and such
Another evening;—yon red cloud, which rests
On Eigher's pinnacle, so rested then,—
So like that it might be the same; the wind
Was faint and gusty, and the mountain
          snows
Began to glitter with the climbing moon; 40
Count Manfred was, as now, within his
          tower,—
How occupied, we knew not, but with him
The sole companion of his wanderings
And watchings—her, whom of all earthly
          things
That lived, the only thing he seem'd to love,—
As he, indeed, by blood was bound to do,
The lady Astarte, his—
                    Hush! who comes here?

Enter the ABBOT

Abbot. Where is your master?
     Her.   Yonder in the tower.
Abbot. I must speak with him.
     Manuel.   'Tis impossible;
He is most private, and must not be thus 50
Intruded on.
     Abbot.   Upon myself I take
The forfeit of my fault, if fault there be—
But I must see him.
     Her.   Thou hast seen him once
This eve already.
     Abbot.   Herman! I command thee,
Knock, and apprize the Count of my approach.
     Her. We dare not.
     Abbot.   Then it seems I must be herald
Of my own purpose.
     Manuel.   Reverend father, stop—
I pray you pause.
     Abbot.   Why so?
     Manuel.   But step this way,
And I will tell you further.   [*Exeunt.*

SCENE IV

Interior of the Tower

MANFRED *alone.*

The stars are forth, the moon above the tops
Of the snow-shining mountains.—Beautiful!
I linger yet with Nature, for the Night
Hath been to me a more familiar face
Than that of man; and in her starry shade
Of dim and solitary loveliness,
I learn'd the language of another world.
I do remember me, that in my youth,
When I was wandering,—upon such a night
I stood within the Coliseum's wall,   10
'Midst the chief relics of almighty Rome;
The trees which grew along the broken arches
Waved dark in the blue midnight, and the
          stars
Shone through the rents of ruin; from afar
The watch-dog bay'd beyond the Tiber; and
More near from out the Cæsars' palace came
The owl's long cry, and, interruptedly,
Of distant sentinels the fitful song
Begun and died upon the gentle wind.   19
Some cypresses beyond the time-worn breach
Appear'd to skirt the horizon, yet they stood
Within a bowshot. Where the Cæsars dwelt,
And dwell the tuneless birds of night, amidst
A grove which springs through levell'd battle-
          ments,
And twines its roots with the imperial hearths,
Ivy usurps the laurel's place of growth;
But the gladiators' bloody Circus stands,
A noble wreck in ruinous perfection,
While Cæsar's chambers, and the Augustan
          halls,
Grovel on earth in indistinct decay.   30
And thou didst shine, thou rolling moon, upon
All this, and cast a wide and tender light,
Which soften'd down the hoar austerity
Of rugged desolation, and fill'd up,
As 'twere anew, the gaps of centuries;
Leaving that beautiful which still was so,
And making that which was not, till the place
Became religion, and the heart ran o'er
With silent worship of the great of old,—   39
The dead but sceptred sovereigns, who still rule
Our spirits from their urns.
                    'Twas such a night!
'Tis strange that I recall it at this time;

But I have found our thoughts take wildest
flight
Even at the moment when they should array
Themselves in pensive order.

Enter the ABBOT

Abbot. My good lord!
I crave a second grace for this approach;
But yet let not my humble zeal offend
By its abruptness—all it hath of ill
Recoils on me; its good in the effect
May light upon your head—could I say
heart— 50
Could I touch *that*, with words or prayers,
I should
Recall a noble spirit which hath wander'd;
But is not yet all lost.
Man. Thou know'st me not;
My days are number'd, and my deeds re-
corded:
Retire, or 'twill be dangerous—Away!
Abbot. Thou dost not mean to menace me?
Man. Not I;
I simply tell thee peril is at hand,
And would preserve thee.
Abbot. What dost thou mean?
Man. Look there!
What dost thou see?
Abbot. Nothing.
Man. Look there I say,
And stedfastly;—now tell me what thou
seest? 60
Abbot. That which should shake me, but I
fear it not:
I see a dusk and awful figure rise,
Like an infernal god, from out the earth;
His face wrapt in a mantle, and his form
Robed as with angry clouds: he stands be-
tween
Thyself and me—but I do fear him not.
Man. Thou hast no cause—he shall not
harm thee—but
His sight may shock thine old limbs into palsy.
I say to thee—Retire!
Abbot. And I reply—
Never—till I have battled with this fiend:— 70
What doth he here?
Man. Why—ay—what doth he here?
I did not send for him,—he is unbidden.
Abbot. Alas! lost mortal! what with guests
like these

Hast thou to do? I tremble for thy sake:
Why doth he gaze on thee, and thou on him?
Ah! he unveils his aspect: on his brow
The thunder-scars are graven: from his eye
Glares forth the immortality of hell—
Avaunt!—
Man. Pronounce—what is thy mission?
Spirit. Come!
Abbot. What art thou, unknown being? an-
swer!—speak! 80
Spirit. The genius of this mortal.—Come!
'tis time.
Man. I am prepared for all things, but deny
The power which summons me. Who sent
thee here?
Spirit. Thou'lt know anon—Come! come!
Man. I have commanded
Things of an essence greater far than thine,
And striven with thy masters. Get thee hence!
Spirit. Mortal! thine hour is come—Away!
I say.
Man. I knew, and know my hour is come
but not
To render up my soul to such as thee:
Away! I'll die as I have lived—alone. 90
Spirit. Then I must summon up my breth-
ren.—Rise!
[*Other Spirits rise up.*
Abbot. Avaunt! ye evil ones!—Avaunt! I
say;
Ye have no power where piety hath power,
And I do charge ye in the name——
Spirit. Old man!
We know ourselves, our mission, and thine
order;
Waste not thy holy words on idle uses,
It were in vain: this man is forfeited.
Once more I summon him—Away! Away!
Man. I do defy ye,—though I feel my soul
Is ebbing from me, yet I do defy ye; 100
Nor will I hence, while I have earthly breath
To breathe my scorn upon ye—earthly
strength
To wrestle, though with spirits; what ye take
Shall be ta'en limb by limb.
Spirit. Reluctant mortal!
Is this the Magian who would so pervade
The world invisible, and make himself
Almost our equal? Can it be that thou
Art thus in love with life? the very life
Which made thee wretched!

Man.   Thou false fiend, thou liest!
My life is in its last hour,—*that* I know,   110
Nor would redeem a moment of that hour;
I do not combat against death, but thee
And thy surrounding angels; my past power,
Was purchased by no compact with thy crew,
But by superior science—penance, daring,
And length of watching, strength of mind,
    and skill
In knowledge of our fathers—when the earth
Saw men and spirits walking side by side,
And gave ye no supremacy: I stand
Upon my strength—I do defy—deny—   120
Spurn back, and scorn ye!—
  Spirit.   But thy many crimes
Have made thee———
  Man.   What are they to such as thee?
Must crimes be punish'd but by other crimes,
And greater criminals?—Back to thy hell!
Thou hast no power upon me, *that* I feel;
Thou never shalt possess me, *that* I know:
What I have done is done; I bear within
A torture which could nothing gain from thine:
The mind which is immortal makes itself
Requital for its good or evil thoughts,—   130
Is its own origin of ill and end
And its own place and time: its innate sense,
When stripp'd of this mortality, derives
No colour from the fleeting things without,
But is absorb'd in sufferance or in joy,
Born from the knowledge of its own desert.
Thou didst not tempt me, and thou couldst
    not tempt me;
I have not been thy dupe, nor am thy prey—
But was my own destroyer, and will be   139
My own hereafter.—Back, ye baffled fiends!—
The hand of death is on me—but not yours!
        [*The Demons disappear.*
  Abbot. Alas! how pale thou art—thy lips
    are white—
And thy breast heaves—and in thy gasping
    throat
The accents rattle: Give thy prayers to
    heaven—
Pray—albeit but in thought,—but die not
    thus.
  Man. 'Tis over—my dull eyes can fix thee
    not;
But all things swim around me, and the earth
Heaves as it were beneath me. Fare thee well!
Give me thy hand.

  Abbot.   Cold—cold—even to the heart—
But yet one prayer—Alas! how fares it with
    thee?   150
  Man. Old man! 'tis not so difficult to die.
                      [MANFRED *expires.*
  Abbot. He's gone—his soul hath ta'en its
    earthless flight;
Whither? I dread to think—but he is gone.

1816–1817

DON JUAN

"Difficile est propriè communia dicere."
                      —HORACE.

"Dost thou think, because thou art virtuous,
there shall be no more cakes and ale? Yes, by
Saint Anne, and ginger shall be hot i' the mouth,
too!"—SHAKESPEARE, *Twelfth Night, or What
You Will.*

FRAGMENT

On the back of the Poet's MS. of Canto I

I WOULD to heaven that I were so much clay,
    As I am blood, bone, marrow, passion,
        feeling—
Because at least the past were pass'd away—
    And for the future—(but I write this reeling,
Having got drunk exceedingly to-day,
    So that I seem to stand upon the ceiling)
I say—the future is a serious matter—
And so—for God's sake—hock and soda-
    water!

DEDICATION

I

BOB SOUTHEY! You're a poet—Poet-laureate,
    And representative of all the race;
Although 'tis true that you turn'd out a Tory
    at
Last,—yours has lately been a common case;
And now, my Epic Renegade! what are ye at?
    With all the Lakers, in and out of place?
A nest of tuneful persons, to my eye
Like "four and twenty Blackbirds in a pye;

II

"Which pye being open'd they began to sing"
    (This old song and new simile holds good),
"A dainty dish to set before the King,"   11
    Or Regent, who admires such kind of
        food;—
And Coleridge, too, has lately taken wing,

A Stanza from Byron's *Don Juan*. (See Appendix I.)

But like a hawk encumber'd with his hood,—
Explaining metaphysics to the nation—
I wish he would explain his Explanation.

III

You, Bob! are rather insolent, you know,
  At being disappointed in your wish
To supersede all warblers here below,
  And be the only Blackbird in the dish;   20
And then you overstrain yourself, or so,
  And tumble downward like the flying fish
Gasping on deck, because you soar too high,
    Bob,
And fall, for lack of moisture quite a-dry, Bob!

IV

And Wordsworth, in a rather long "Excur-
    sion"
  (I think the quarto holds five hundred
    pages),
Has given a sample from the vasty version
  Of his new system to perplex the sages;
'Tis poetry—at least by his assertion,
  And may appear so when the dog-star
    rages—   30
And he who understands it would be able
To add a story to the Tower of Babel.

V

You—Gentlemen! by dint of long seclusion
  From better company, have kept your own
At Keswick, and, through still continued fusion
  Of one another's minds, at last have grown
To deem as a most logical conclusion,
  That Poesy has wreaths for you alone:
There is a narrowness in such a notion,
Which makes me wish you'd change your
    lakes for ocean.   40

VI

I would not imitate the petty thought,
  Nor coin my self-love to so base a vice,
For all the glory your conversion brought,
  Since gold alone should not have been its
    price.
You have your salary: was't for that you
    wrought?
  And Wordsworth has his place in the Excise.
You're shabby fellows—true—but poets still,
And duly seated on the immortal hill.

VII

Your bays may hide the baldness of your
    brows—
  Perhaps some virtuous blushes;—let them
    go—   50
To you I envy neither fruit nor boughs—
  And for the fame you would engross be-
    low,
The field is universal, and allows
  Scope to all such as feel the inherent
    glow:
Scott, Rogers, Campbell, Moore, and Crabbe,
    will try
'Gainst you the question with posterity.

VIII

For me, who, wandering with pedestrian
    Muses,
  Contend not with you on the winged steed,
I wish your fate may yield ye, when she
    chooses,
  The fame you envy, and the skill you
    need;   60
And recollect a poet nothing loses
  In giving to his brethren their full meed
Of merit, and complaint of present days
Is not the certain path to future praise.

IX

He that reserves his laurels for posterity
  (Who does not often claim the bright re-
    version)
Has generally no great crop to spare it, he
  Being only injured by his own assertion;
And although here and there some glorious
    rarity
  Arise like Titan from the sea's immersion,
The major part of such appellants go   71
To—God knows where—for no one else can
    know.

X

If, fallen in evil days on evil tongues,
  Milton appealed to the Avenger, Time,
If Time, the Avenger, execrates his wrongs,
  And makes the word "Miltonic" mean
    "*sublime*,"
He deign'd not to belie his soul in songs,
  Nor turn his very talent to a crime;
He did not loathe the Sire to laud the Son,
But closed the tyrant-hater he begun.   80

XI

Think'st thou, could he—the blind Old Man—
   arise,
   Like Samuel from the grave, to freeze once
     more
The blood of monarchs with his prophecies,
   Or be alive again—again all hoar
With time and trials, and those helpless eyes,
   And heartless daughters—worn—and pale
    —and poor;
Would *he* adore a sultan? *he* obey
The intellectual eunuch Castlereagh?

XII

Cold-blooded, smooth-faced, placid miscreant!
   Dabbling its sleek young hands in Erin's
    gore,   90
And thus for wider carnage taught to pant,
   Transferr'd to gorge upon a sister shore,
The vulgarest tool that Tyranny could want,
   With just enough of talent, and no more,
To lengthen fetters by another fix'd,
And offer poison long already mix'd.

XIII

An orator of such set trash of phrase
   Ineffably—legitimately vile,
That even its grossest flatterers dare not
   praise,
   Nor foes—all nations—condescend to smile;
Not even a sprightly blunder's spark can
   blaze   101
From that Ixion grindstone's ceaseless toil,
That turns and turns to give the world a
   notion
Of endless torments and perpetual motion.

XIV

A bungler even in its disgusting trade,
   And botching, patching, leaving still be-
   hind
Something of which its masters are afraid,
   States to be curb'd, and thoughts to be
   confined,
Conspiracy or Congress to be made—
   Cobbling at manacles for all mankind— 110
A tinkering slave-maker, who mends old
   chains,
With God and man's abhorrence for its
   gains.

XV

If we may judge of matter by the mind,
   Emasculated to the marrow *It*
Hath but two objects, how to serve, and
   bind,
   Deeming the chain it wears even men may
   fit,
Eutropius of its many masters,—blind
   To worth as freedom, wisdom as to wit.
Fearless—because *no* feeling dwells in ice,
Its very courage stagnates to a vice.   120

XVI

Where shall I turn me not to *view* its bonds,
   For I will never *feel* them;—Italy!
Thy late reviving Roman soul desponds
   Beneath the lie this State-thing breathed o'er
   thee—
Thy clanking chain, and Erin's yet green
   wounds,
   Have voices—tongues to cry aloud for
   me.
Europe has slaves, allies, kings, armies still,
And Southey lives to sing them very ill.

XVII

Meantime, Sir Laureate, I proceed to dedicate,
   In honest simple verse, this song to you. 130
And, if in flattering strains I do not predicate,
   'Tis that I still retain my "buff and blue;"
My politics as yet are all to educate:
   Apostasy's so fashionable, too,
To keep *one* creed's a task grown quite Her-
   culean:
Is it not so, my Tory, Ultra-Julian?

VENICE, September 16, 1818

CANTO THE FIRST

I

I WANT a hero: an uncommon want,
   When every year and month sends forth a
   new one,
Till, after cloying the gazettes with cant,
   The age discovers he is not the true one:
Of such as these I should not care to vaunt,
   I'll therefore take our ancient friend Don
   Juan—
We all have seen him, in the pantomime,
Sent to the devil somewhat ere his time.

II

Vernon, the butcher Cumberland, Wolfe,
 Hawke,
 Prince Ferdinand, Granby, Burgoyne, Kep-
  pel, Howe,   10
Evil and good, have had their tithe of talk,
 And fill'd their sign-posts then, like Welles-
  ley now;
Each in their turn like Banquo's monarchs
 stalk,
 Followers of fame, "nine farrow" of that
  sow:
France, too, had Buonaparté and Dumourier
Recorded in the Moniteur and Courier.

III

Barnave, Brissot, Condorcet, Mirabeau,
 Pétion, Clootz, Danton, Marat, La Fayette,
Were French, and famous people, as we know;
 And there were others, scarce forgotten
  yet,   20
Joubert, Hoche, Marceau, Lannes, Desaix,
 Moreau,
 With many of the military set,
Exceedingly remarkable at times,
But not at all adapted to my rhymes.

IV

Nelson was once Britannia's god of war,
 And still should be so, but the tide is
  turn'd;
There's no more to be said of Trafalgar,
 'Tis with our hero quietly inurn'd;
Because the army's grown more popular,
 At which the naval people are concern'd; 39
Besides, the prince is all for the land-service,
Forgetting Duncan, Nelson, Howe, and Jervis.

V

Brave men were living before Agamemnon
 And since, exceeding valorous and sage,
A good deal like him too, though quite the
  same none;
 But then they shone not on the poet's page,
And so have been forgotten:—I condemn
  none,
 But can't find any in the present age
Fit for my poem (that is, for my new one);
So, as I said, I'll take my friend Don Juan. 40

VI

Most epic poets plunge "in medias res"
 (Horace makes this the heroic turnpike
  road),
And then your hero tells, whene'er you please,
 What went before—by way of episode,
While seated after dinner at his ease,
 Beside his mistress in some soft abode,
Palace, or garden, paradise, or cavern,
Which serves the happy couple for a tavern.

VII

That is the usual method, but not mine—
 My way is to begin with the beginning; 50
The regularity of my design
 Forbids all wandering as the worst of sin-
  ning,
And therefore I shall open with a line
 (Although it cost me half an hour in spin-
  ning)
Narrating somewhat of Don Juan's father,
And also of his mother, if you'd rather.

VIII

In Seville was he born, a pleasant city,
 Famous for oranges and women—he
Who has not seen it will be much to pity,
 So says the proverb—and I quite agree; 60
Of all the Spanish towns is none more pretty,
 Cadiz, perhaps—but that you soon may
  see:—
Don Juan's parents lived beside the river,
A noble stream, and call'd the Guadalquivir.

IX

His father's name was Jóse—*Don*, of course,
 A true Hidalgo, free from every stain
Of Moor or Hebrew blood, he traced his source
 Through the most Gothic gentlemen of
  Spain;
A better cavalier ne'er mounted horse,
 Or, being mounted, e'er got down again, 70
Than Jóse, who begot our hero, who
Begot—but that's to come——Well, to re-
  new:

X

His mother was a learned lady, famed
 For every branch of every science known—
In every Christian language ever named,
 With virtues equall'd by her wit alone:

She made the cleverest people quite ashamed,
  And even the good with inward envy
    groan,
Finding themselves so very much exceeded
In their own way by all the things that she
  did.   80

XI

Her memory was a mine: she knew by heart
  All Calderon and greater part of Lopé,
So that if any actor miss'd his part
  She could have served him for the prompt-
    er's copy;
For her Feinagle's were an useless art,
  And he himself obliged to shut up shop—he
Could never make a memory so fine as
That which adorn'd the brain of Donna Inez.

XII

Her favourite science was the mathematical,
  Her noblest virtue was her magnanimity; 90
Her wit (she sometimes tried at wit) was Attic
  all,
  Her serious sayings darken'd to sublimity;
In short, in all things she was fairly what I
  call
A prodigy—her morning dress was dimity,
  Her evening silk, or, in the summer, muslin,
And other stuffs, with which I won't stay
  puzzling.

XIII

She knew the Latin—that is, "the Lord's
  prayer,"
  And Greek—the alphabet—I'm nearly sure;
She read some French romances here and
  there,
  Although her mode of speaking was not
    pure;   100
For native Spanish she had no great care,
  At least her conversation was obscure;
Her thoughts were theorems, her words a
  problem,
As if she deem'd that mystery would ennoble
  'em.

XIV

She liked the English and the Hebrew tongue,
  And said there was analogy between 'em;
She proved it somehow out of sacred song,
  But I must leave the proofs to those who've
    seen 'em,

But this I heard her say, and can't be wrong,
  And all may think which way their judg-
    ments lean 'em,   110
"'Tis strange—the Hebrew noun which means
  'I am,'
The English always use to govern d—n."

XV

Some women use their tongues—she *look'd* a
  lecture,
  Each eye a sermon, and her brow a homily,
An all-in-all sufficient self-director,
  Like the lamented late Sir Samuel Romilly,
The Law's expounder, and the State's cor-
  rector,
  Whose suicide was almost an anomaly—
One sad example more, that "All is vanity,"—
(The jury brought their verdict in "In-
  sanity.")   120

XVI

In short, she was a walking calculation,
  Miss Edgeworth's novels stepping from
    their covers,
Or Mrs. Trimmer's books on education,
  Or "Cœlebs' Wife" set out in quest of
    lovers,
Morality's prim personification,
  In which not Envy's self a flaw discovers;
To others' share let "female errors fall,"
For she had not even one—the worst of all.

XVII

Oh! she was perfect past all parallel—
  Of any modern female saint's comparison;
So far above the cunning powers of hell, 131
  Her guardian angel had given up his gar-
    rison;
Even her minutest motions went as well
  As those of the best time-piece made by
    Harrison:
In virtues nothing earthly could surpass her,
Save thine "incomparable oil," Macassar!

XVIII

Perfect she was, but as perfection is
  Insipid in this naughty world of ours,
Where our first parents never learn'd to kiss
  Till they were exiled from their earlier
    bowers,   140

Where all was peace, and innocence, and bliss
  (I wonder how they got through the twelve
    hours),
Don Jóse, like a lineal son of Eve,
Went plucking various fruit without her leave.

XIX

He was a mortal of the careless kind,
  With no great love for learning, or the
    learn'd,
Who chose to go where'er he had a mind,
  And never dream'd his lady was concern'd;
The world, as usual, wickedly inclined
  To see a kingdom or a house o'erturn'd, 150
Whisper'd he had a mistress, some said *two*,
But for domestic quarrels *one* will do.

XX

Now Donna Inez had, with all her merit,
  A great opinion of her own good qualities;
Neglect, indeed, requires a saint to bear it,
  And such, indeed, she was in her moralities;
But then she had a devil of a spirit,
  And sometimes mix'd up fancies with reali-
    ties,
And let few opportunities escape
Of getting her liege lord into a scrape.   160

XXI

This was an easy matter with a man
  Oft in the wrong, and never on his guard;
And even the wisest, do the best they can,
  Have moments, hours, and days, so un-
    prepared,
That you might "brain them with their lady's
    fan;"
  And sometimes ladies hit exceeding hard,
And fans turn into falchions in fair hands,
And why and wherefore no one understands.

XXII

'Tis pity learned virgins ever wed
  With persons of no sort of education,   170
Or gentlemen, who, though well born and
    bred,
  Grow tired of scientific conversation;
I don't choose to say much upon this head,
  I'm a plain man, and in a single station,
But—Oh! ye lords of ladies intellectual,
Inform us truly, have they not hen-peck'd you
    all?

XXIII

Don Jóse and his lady quarrell'd—*why*,
  Not any of the many could divine,
Though several thousand people chose to try,
  'Twas surely no concern of theirs nor
    mine;   180
I loathe that low vice—curiosity;
  But if there's anything in which I shine,
'Tis in arranging all my friends' affairs,
Not having, of my own, domestic cares.

XXIV

And so I interfered, and with the best
  Intentions, but their treatment was not kind;
I think the foolish people were possess'd,
  For neither of them could I ever find,
Although their porter afterwards confess'd—
  But that's no matter, and the worst's be-
    hind,   190
For little Juan o'er me threw, down stairs,
A pail of housemaid's water unawares.

XXV

A little curly-headed, good-for-nothing,
  And mischief-making monkey from his
    birth;
His parents ne'er agreed except in doting
  Upon the most unquiet imp on earth;
Instead of quarrelling, had they been but
    both in
  Their senses, they'd have sent young master
    forth
To school, or had him soundly whipp'd at
    home,   199
To teach him manners for the time to come.

XXVI

Don Jóse and the Donna Inez led
  For some time an unhappy sort of life,
Wishing each other, not divorced, but dead;
  They lived respectably as man and wife,
Their conduct was exceedingly well-bred,
  And gave no outward signs of inward strife,
Until at length the smother'd fire broke out,
And put the business past all kind of doubt.

XXVII

For Inez call'd some druggists and physicians,
  And tried to prove her loving lord was *mad*,
But as he had some lucid intermissions,   211
  She next decided he was only *bad;*

Yet when they ask'd her for her depositions,
  No sort of explanation could be had,
Save that her duty both to man and God
Required this conduct—which seem'd very
    odd.

XXVIII

She kept a journal, where his faults were noted,
  And open'd certain trunks of books and
    letters,
All which might, if occasion served, be quoted;
  And then she had all Seville for abettors, 220
Besides her good old grandmother (who
    doted);
  The hearers of her case became repeaters,
Then advocates, inquisitors, and judges,
Some for amusement, others for old grudges.

XXIX

And then this best and meekest woman bore
  With such serenity her husband's woes,
Just as the Spartan ladies did of yore,
  Who saw their spouses kill'd, and nobly
    chose
Never to say a word about them more—
  Calmly she heard each calumny that rose,
And saw *his* agonies with such sublimity, 231
That all the world exclaim'd, "What mag-
    nanimity!"

XXX

No doubt this patience, when the world is
    damning us,
  Is philosophic in our former friends;
'Tis also pleasant to be deem'd magnanimous,
  The more so in obtaining our own ends;
And what the lawyers call a "*malus animus*"
  Conduct like this by no means compre-
    hends:
Revenge in person's certainly no virtue,
But then 'tis not *my* fault, if *others* hurt
    you.   240

XXXI

And if our quarrels should rip up old stories,
  And help them with a lie or two additional,
I'm not to blame, as you well know—no
    more is
  Any one else—they were become tradi-
    tional;
Besides, their resurrection aids our glories
  By contrast, which is what we just were
    wishing all:

And science profits by this resurrection—
  Dead scandals form good subjects for dis-
    section.

XXXII

Their friends had tried at reconciliation,
  Then their relations, who made matters
    worse,   250
('Twere hard to tell upon a like occasion
  To whom it may be best to have recourse—
I can't say much for friend or yet relation):
  The lawyers did their utmost for divorce,
But scarce a fee was paid on either side
Before, unluckily, Don Jóse died.

XXXIII

He died: and most unluckily, because,
  According to all hints I could collect
From counsel learned in those kinds of laws
  (Although their talk's obscure and circum-
    spect),   260
His death contrived to spoil a charming cause;
  A thousand pities also with respect
To public feeling, which on this occasion
Was manifested in a great sensation.

XXXIV

But ah! he died; and buried with him lay
  The public feeling and the lawyers' fees:
His house was sold, his servants sent away,
  A Jew took one of his two mistresses,
A priest the other—at least so they say:
  I ask'd the doctors after his disease— 270
He died of the slow fever called the tertian,
And left his widow to her own aversion.

XXXV

Yet Jóse was an honourable man,
  That I must say, who knew him very well;
Therefore his frailties I'll no further scan,
  Indeed there were not many more to tell:
And if his passions now and then outran
  Discretion, and were not so peaceable
As Numa's (who was also named Pompilius),
He had been ill brought up, and was born
    bilious.   280

XXXVI

Whate'er might be his worthlessness or worth,
  Poor fellow! he had many things to wound
    him,

Let's own—since it can do no good on earth—
  It was a trying moment that which found
    him
Standing alone beside his desolate hearth,
  Where all his household gods lay shiver'd
    round him:
No choice was left his feelings or his pride,
Save death or Doctors' Commons—so he
  died.

XXXVII

Dying intestate, Juan was sole heir
  To a chancery suit, and messuages and
    lands, 290
Which, with a long minority and care,
  Promised to turn out well in proper hands:
Inez became sole guardian, which was fair,
  And answer'd but to nature's just demands;
An only son left with an only mother
Is brought up much more wisely than an-
  other.

XXXVIII

Sagest of women, even of widows, she
  Resolved that Juan should be quite a para-
    gon,
And worthy of the noblest pedigree:
  (His sire was of Castile, his dam from
    Aragon). 300
Then for accomplishments of chivalry,
  In case our lord the king should go to war
    again,
He learn'd the arts of riding, fencing, gunnery,
And how to scale a fortress—or a nunnery.

XXXIX

But that which Donna Inez most desired,
  And saw into herself each day before all
The learned tutors whom for him she hired,
  Was, that his breeding should be strictly
    moral:
Much into all his studies she inquired, 309
  And so they were submitted first to her, all,
Arts, sciences, no branch was made a mystery
To Juan's eyes, excepting natural history.

XL

The languages, especially the dead,
  The sciences, and most of all the abstruse,
The arts, at least all such as could be said
  To be the most remote from common use,

In all these he was much and deeply read:
  But not a page of anything that's loose,
Or hints continuation of the species,
  Was ever suffer'd, lest he should grow vi-
    cious. 320

XLI

His classic studies made a little puzzle,
  Because of filthy loves of gods and god-
    desses,
Who in the earlier ages raised a bustle,
  But never put on pantaloons or bodices;
His reverend tutors had at times a tussle,
  And for their Æneids, Iliads, and Odysseys,
Were forced to make an odd sort of apology,
For Donna Inez dreaded the Mythology.

XLII

Ovid's a rake, as half his verses show him,
  Anacreon's morals are a still worse sample,
Catullus scarcely has a decent poem, 331
  I don't think Sappho's Ode a good example,
Although Longinus tells us there is no hymn
  Where the sublime soars forth on wings
    more ample;
But Virgil's songs are pure, except that horrid
  one
Beginning with "Formosum Pastor Corydon."

XLIII

Lucretius' irreligion is too strong
  For early stomachs, to prove wholesome
    food;
I can't help thinking Juvenal was wrong,
  Although no doubt his real intent was
    good,
For speaking out so plainly in his song, 341
  So much indeed as to be downright rude;
And then what proper person can be partial
To all those nauseous epigrams of Martial?

XLIV

Juan was taught from out the best edition,
  Expurgated by learned men, who place,
Judiciously, from out the schoolboy's vision,
  The grosser parts; but, fearful to deface
Too much their modest bard by this omis-
  sion,
  And pitying sore his mutilated case, 350
They only add them all in an appendix,
Which saves, in fact, the trouble of an index;

XLV

For there we have them all "at one fell
  swoop,"
  Instead of being scatter'd through the pages;
They stand forth marshall'd in a handsome
  troop,
  To meet the ingenuous youth of future ages,
Till some less rigid editor shall stoop
  To call them back into their separate cages,
Instead of standing staring all together,   359
Like garden gods—and not so decent either.

XLVI

The Missal too (it was the family Missal)
  Was ornamented in a sort of way
Which ancient mass-books often are, and this
  all
  Kinds of grotesques illumined; and how
  they,
Who saw those figures on the margin kiss all,
  Could turn their optics to the text and pray,
Is more than I know—But Don Juan's mother
Kept this herself, and gave her son another.

XLVII

Sermons he read, and lectures he endured,
  And homilies, and lives of all the saints; 370
To Jerome and to Chrysostom inured,
  He did not take such studies for restraints;
But how faith is acquired, and then insured,
  So well not one of the aforesaid paints
As Saint Augustine in his fine Confessions,
Which makes the reader envy his transgres-
  sions.

XLVIII

This, too, was a seal'd book to little Juan—
  I can't but say that his mamma was right,
If such an education was the true one.
  She scarcely trusted him from out her sight;
Her maids were old, and if she took a new
  one, 381
  You might be sure she was a perfect fright,
She did this during even her husband's life—
I recommend as much to every wife.

XLIX

Young Juan wax'd in godliness and grace;
  At six a charming child, and at eleven
With all the promise of as fine a face
  As e'er to man's maturer growth was given.

He studied steadily and grew apace,
  And seem'd, at least, in the right road to
  heaven, 390
For half his days were pass'd at church, the
  other
Between his tutors, confessor, and mother.

L

At six, I said, he was a charming child,
  At twelve he was a fine, but quiet boy;
Although in infancy a little wild,
  They tamed him down amongst them: to
  destroy
His natural spirit not in vain they toil'd, 397
  At least it seem'd so; and his mother's joy
Was to declare how sage, and still, and steady,
Her young philosopher was grown already.

LI

I had my doubts, perhaps I have them still,
  But what I say is neither here nor there:
I knew his father well, and have some skill
  In character—but it would not be fair
From sire to son to augur good or ill:
  He and his wife were an ill sorted pair—
But scandal's my aversion—I protest
Against all evil speaking, even in jest.

LII

For my part I say nothing—nothing—but
  This I will say—my reasons are my own—
That if I had an only son to put 411
  To school (as God be praised that I have
  none),
'Tis not with Donna Inez I would shut
  Him up to learn his catechism alone,
No—no—I'd send him out betimes to college,
For there it was I pick'd up my own knowl-
  edge.

LIII

For there one learns—'tis not for me to boast,
  Though I acquired—but I pass over *that*,
As well as all the Greek I since have lost:
  I say that there's the place—but *"Verbum
  sat,"* 420
I think I pick'd up too, as well as most,
  Knowledge of matters—but no matter
  what—
I never married—but, I think, I know
That sons should not be educated so.

LIV

Young Juan now was sixteen years of age,
  Tall, handsome, slender, but well knit: he
    seem'd
Active, though not so sprightly, as a page;
  And everybody but his mother deem'd
Him almost man; but she flew in a rage
  And bit her lips (for else she might have
    scream'd)   430
If any said so, for to be precocious
Was in her eyes a thing the most atrocious.

LV

Amongst her numerous acquaintance, all
  Selected for discretion and devotion,
There was the Donna Julia, whom to call
  Pretty were but to give a feeble notion
Of many charms in her as natural
  As sweetness to the flower, or salt to ocean,
Her zone to Venus, or his bow to Cupid,
(But this last simile is trite and stupid).   440

LVI

The darkness of her Oriental eye
  Accorded with her Moorish origin;
(Her blood was not all Spanish, by the by;
  In Spain, you know, this is a sort of sin).
When proud Granada fell, and, forced to fly,
  Boabdil wept, of Donna Julia's kin
Some went to Africa, some stay'd in Spain,
Her great great grandmamma chose to re-
  main.

LVII

She married (I forget the pedigree)
  With an Hidalgo, who transmitted down
His blood less noble than such blood should
  be;   451
  At such alliances his sires would frown,
In that point so precise in each degree
  That they bred *in and in*, as might be shown,
Marrying their cousins—nay, their aunts, and
  nieces,
Which always spoils the breed, if it increases.

LVIII

This heathenish cross restored the breed again,
  Ruin'd its blood, but much improved its
    flesh;
For from a root the ugliest in old Spain
  Sprung up a branch as beautiful as fresh;

The sons no more were short, the daughters
  plain: 461
  But there's a rumour which I fain would
    hush,
'Tis said that Donna Julia's grandmamma
Produced her Don more heirs at love than
  law.

LIX

However this might be, the race went on
  Improving still through every generation,
Until it centred in an only son,
  Who left an only daughter: my narration
May have suggested that this single one
  Could be but Julia (whom on this occa-
    sion   470
I shall have much to speak about), and she
Was married, charming, chaste, and twenty-
  three.

LX

Her eye (I'm very fond of handsome eyes)
  Was large and dark, suppressing half its
    fire
Until she spoke, then through its soft disguise
  Flash'd an expression more of pride than
    ire,
And love than either; and there would arise
  A something in them which was not desire,
But would have been, perhaps, but for the soul
Which struggled through and chasten'd down
  the whole.   480

LXI

Her glossy hair was cluster'd o'er a brow
  Bright with intelligence, and fair, and
    smooth;
Her eyebrow's shape was like the aërial bow,
  Her cheek all purple with the beam of
    youth,
Mounting, at times, to a transparent glow,
  As if her veins ran lightning; she, in sooth,
Possess'd an air and grace by no means com-
  mon:
Her stature tall—I hate a dumpy woman.

LXII

Wedded she was some years, and to a man
  Of fifty, and such husbands are in plenty; 490
And yet, I think, instead of such a ONE
  'Twere better to have TWO of five-and-
  twenty,

Especially in countries near the sun:
　And now I think on 't, "mi vien in mente,"
Ladies even of the most uneasy virtue
Prefer a spouse whose age is short of thirty.

LXIII

'Tis a sad thing, I cannot choose but say,
　And all the fault of that indecent sun,
Who cannot leave alone our helpless clay,
　But will keep baking, broiling, burning on,
That howsoever people fast and pray,　　501
　The flesh is frail, and so the soul undone:
What men call gallantry, and gods adultery,
Is much more common where the climate's
　　sultry.

LXIV

Happy the nations of the moral North!
　Where all is virtue, and the winter season
Sends sin, without a rag on, shivering forth
　('Twas snow that brought St. Anthony to
　　reason);
Where juries cast up what a wife is worth,
　By laying whate'er sum, in mulct, they
　　please on　　　　　　　　　510
The lover, who must pay a handsome price,
Because it is a marketable vice.

LXV

Alfonso was the name of Julia's lord,
　A man well looking for his years, and who
Was neither much beloved nor yet abhorr'd:
　They lived together as most people do,
Suffering each other's foibles by accord,
　And not exactly either *one* or *two;*
Yet he was jealous, though he did not show it,
For jealousy dislikes the world to know it. 520

LXVI

Julia was—yet I never could see why—
　With Donna Inez quite a favourite friend;
Between their tastes there was small sympathy,
　For not a line had Julia ever penn'd:
Some people whisper (but, no doubt, they lie,
　For malice still imputes some private end)
That Inez had, ere Don Alfonso's marriage,
Forgot with him her very prudent carriage;

LXVII

And that still keeping up the old connexion,
　Which time had lately render'd much more
　　chaste,　　　　　　　　530

She took his lady also in affection,
　And certainly this course was much the
　　best:
She flatter'd Julia with her sage protection,
　And complimented Don Alfonso's taste;
And if she could not (who can?) silence
　　scandal,
At least she left it a more slender handle.

LXVIII

I can't tell whether Julia saw the affair
　With other people's eyes, or if her own
Discoveries made, but none could be aware
　Of this, at least no symptom e'er was
　　shown;
Perhaps she did not know, or did not care, 541
　Indifferent from the first, or callous grown:
I'm really puzzled what to think or say,
She kept her counsel in so close a way.

LXIX

Juan she saw, and, as a pretty child,
　Caress'd him often—such a thing might be
Quite innocently done, and harmless styled,
　When she had twenty years, and thirteen
　　he;
But I am not so sure I should have smiled
　When he was sixteen, Julia twenty-three;
These few short years make wondrous altera-
　　tions,　　　　　　　　551
Particularly amongst sun-burnt nations.

LXX

Whate'er the cause might be, they had be-
　　come
　Changed; for the dame grew distant, the
　　youth shy,
Their looks cast down, their greetings almost
　　dumb,
　And much embarrassment in either eye;
There surely will be little doubt with some
　That Donna Julia knew the reason why,
But as for Juan, he had no more notion
Than he who never saw the sea or ocean. 560

LXXI

Yet Julia's very coldness still was kind,
　And tremulously gentle her small hand
Withdrew itself from his, but left behind
　A little pressure, thrilling, and so bland

And slight, so very slight, that to the mind
   'Twas but a doubt; but ne'er magician's
     wand
Wrought change with all Armida's fairy art
   Like what this light touch left on Juan's
     heart.

LXXII

And if she met him, though she smiled no
     more,
   She look'd a sadness sweeter than her
     smile,   570
As if her heart had deeper thoughts in store
   She must not own, but cherish'd more the
     while
For that compression in its burning core;
   Even innocence itself has many a wile,
And will not dare to trust itself with truth,
And love is taught hypocrisy from youth.

LXXIII

But passion most dissembles, yet betrays
   Even by its darkness; as the blackest sky
Foretells the heaviest tempest, it displays
   Its workings through the vainly guarded
     eye,   580
And in whatever aspect it arrays
   Itself, 'tis still the same hypocrisy:
Coldness or anger, even disdain or hate,
Are masks it often wears, and still too late.

LXXIV

Then there were sighs, the deeper for suppres-
     sion,
   And stolen glances, sweeter for the theft,
And burning blushes, though for no trans-
     gression,
   Tremblings when met, and restlessness
     when left;
All these are little preludes to possession,
   Of which young passion cannot be bereft,
And merely tend to show how greatly love
     is   591
Embarrass'd at first starting with a novice.

LXXV

Poor Julia's heart was in an awkward state;
   She felt it going, and resolved to make
The noblest efforts for herself and mate,
   For honour's, pride's, religion's, virtue's
     sake.

Her resolutions were most truly great,
   And almost might have made a Tarquin
     quake:
She pray'd the Virgin Mary for her grace,
As being the best judge of a lady's case.   600

LXXVI

She vow'd she never would see Juan more,
   And next day paid a visit to his mother,
And look'd extremely at the opening door,
   Which, by the Virgin's grace, let in another;
Grateful she was, and yet a little sore—
   Again it opens, it can be no other,
'Tis surely Juan now—No! I'm afraid
That night the Virgin was no further pray'd.

LXXVII

She now determined that a virtuous woman
   Should rather face and overcome tempta-
     tion,   610
That flight was base and dastardly, and no
     man
   Should ever give her heart the least sensa-
     tion;
That is to say, a thought beyond the common
   Preference, that we must feel upon occasion,
For people who are pleasanter than others,
But then they only seem so many brothers.

LXXVIII

And even if by chance—and who can tell?
   The devil's so very sly—she should discover
That all within was not so very well,
   And, if still free, that such or such a lover
Might please perhaps, a virtuous wife can
     quell   621
   Such thoughts, and be the better when
     they're over;
And if the man should ask, 'tis but denial:
I recommend young ladies to make trial.

LXXIX

And then there are such things as love divine,
   Bright and immaculate, unmix'd and pure,
Such as the angels think so very fine,
   And matrons, who would be no less secure,
Platonic, perfect, "just such love as mine:"
   Thus Julia said—and thought so, to be
     sure;   630
And so I'd have her think, were I the man
On whom her reveries celestial ran.

LXXX

Such love is innocent, and may exist
  Between young persons without any dan-
    ger:
A hand may first, and then a lip be kist;
  For my part, to such doings I'm a stranger,
But *hear* these freedoms form the utmost
    list
  Of all o'er which such love may be a ranger:
If people go beyond, 'tis quite a crime,
But not my fault—I tell them all in time. 640

LXXXI

Love, then, but love within its proper limits
  Was Julia's innocent determination
In young Don Juan's favour, and to him its
  Exertion might be useful on occasion;
And, lighted at too pure a shrine to dim its
  Ethereal lustre, with what sweet persua-
    sion
He might be taught, by love and her to-
    gether—
I really don't know what, nor Julia either.

LXXXII

Fraught with this fine intention, and well
    fenced
  In mail of proof—her purity of soul,   650
She, for the future of her strength con-
    vinced,
  And that her honour was a rock, or mole,
Exceeding sagely from that hour dispensed
  With any kind of troublesome control;
But whether Julia to the task was equal
Is that which must be mention'd in the sequel.

LXXXIII

Her plan she deem'd both innocent and
    feasible,
  And, surely, with a stripling of sixteen
Not scandal's fangs could fix on much that's
    seizable,
  Or if they did so, satisfied to mean   660
Nothing but what was good, her breast was
    peaceable,
  A quiet conscience makes one so serene!
Christians have burnt each other, quite per-
    suaded
That all the Apostles would have done as
    they did.

LXXXIV

And if in the mean time her husband died,
  But Heaven forbid that such a thought
    should cross
Her brain, though in a dream! (and then she
    sigh'd)
  Never could she survive that common loss;
But just suppose that moment should betide,
  I only say suppose it—*inter nos*.   670
(This should be *entre nous*, for Julia thought
In French, but then the rhyme would go for
    nought.)

LXXXV

I only say, suppose this supposition:
  Juan being then grown up to man's estate
Would fully suit a widow of condition,
  Even seven years hence it would not be
    too late;
And in the interim (to pursue this vision)
  The mischief, after all, could not be great,
For he would learn the rudiments of love,
I mean the seraph way of those above.   680

LXXXVI

So much for Julia. Now we'll turn to Juan.
  Poor little fellow! he had no idea
Of his own case, and never hit the true one;
  In feelings quick as Ovid's Miss Medea,
He puzzled over what he found a new one,
  But not as yet imagined it could be a
Thing quite in course, and not at all alarming,
Which, with a little patience, might grow
    charming.

LXXXVII

Silent and pensive, idle, restless, slow,
  His home deserted for the lonely wood, 690
Tormented with a wound he could not know,
  His, like all deep grief, plunged in solitude:
I'm fond myself of solitude or so,
  But then, I beg it may be understood,
By solitude I mean a Sultan's, not
A hermit's, with a haram for a grot.

LXXXVIII

"Oh Love! in such a wilderness as this,
  Where transport and security entwine,
Here is the empire of thy perfect bliss,
  And here thou art a god indeed divine." 700

The bard I quote from does not sing amiss,
  With the exception of the second line,
For that same twining "transport and se-
  curity"
Are twisted to a phrase of some obscurity.

LXXXIX

The poet meant, no doubt, and thus appeals
  To the good sense and senses of mankind,
The very thing which everybody feels,
  As all have found on trial, or may find,
That no one likes to be disturb'd at meals
  Or love.—I won't say more about "en-
    twined"   710
Or "transport," as we knew all that before,
But beg "Security" will bolt the door.

XC

Young Juan wander'd by the glassy brooks,
  Thinking unutterable things; he threw
Himself at length within the leafy nooks
  Where the wild branch of the cork forest
    grew;
There poets find materials for their books,
  And every now and then we read them
    through,
So that their plan and prosody are eligible,
Unless, like Wordsworth, they prove unin-
  telligible.   720

XCI

He, Juan (and not Wordsworth), so pursued
  His self-communion with his own high soul,
Until his mighty heart, in its great mood,
  Had mitigated part, though not the whole
Of its disease; he did the best he could
  With things not very subject to control,
And turn'd, without perceiving his condition,
Like Coleridge, into a metaphysician.

XCII

He thought about himself, and the whole earth,
  Of man the wonderful, and of the stars, 730
And how the deuce they ever could have birth;
  And then he thought of earthquakes, and
    of wars,
How many miles the moon might have in girth,
  Of air-balloons, and of the many bars
To perfect knowledge of the boundless
  skies;—
And then he thought of Donna Julia's eyes.

XCIII

In thoughts like these true wisdom may dis-
  cern
  Longings sublime, and aspirations high,
Which some are born with, but the most part
  learn
  To plague themselves withal, they know
    not why: 740
'Twas strange that one so young should thus
  concern
  His brain about the action of the sky;
If *you* think 'twas philosophy that this did,
I can't help thinking puberty assisted.

XCIV

He pored upon the leaves, and on the flowers,
  And heard a voice in all the winds; and
    then
He thought of wood-nymphs and immortal
  bowers,
  And how the goddesses came down to
    men:
He miss'd the pathway, he forgot the hours,
  And when he look'd upon his watch again,
He found how much old Time had been a
  winner—   751
He also found that he had lost his dinner.

XCV

Sometimes he turn'd to gaze upon his book,
  Boscan, or Garcilasso;—by the wind
Even as the page is rustled while we look,
  So by the poesy of his own mind
Over the mystic leaf his soul was shook,
  As if 'twere one whereon magicians bind
Their spells, and give them to the passing
  gale   759
According to some good old woman's tale.

XCVI

Thus would he while his lonely hours away
  Dissatisfied, nor knowing what he wanted;
Nor glowing reverie, nor poet's lay,
  Could yield his spirit that for which it
    panted,
A bosom whereon he his head might lay,
  And hear the heart beat with the love it
    granted,
With——several other things, which I forget,
Or which, at least, I need not mention yet.

XCVII

Those lonely walks, and lengthening reveries,
  Could not escape the gentle Julia's eyes; 770
She saw that Juan was not at his ease;
  But that which chiefly may, and must sur-
    prise,
Is, that the Donna Inez did not tease
  Her only son with question or surmise;
Whether it was she did not see, or would
    not,
Or, like all very clever people, could not.

XCVIII

This may seem strange, but yet 'tis very
    common;
  For instance—gentlemen, whose ladies take
Leave to o'erstep the written rights of woman,
  And break the——Which commandment
    is't they break? 780
(I have forgot the number, and think no man
  Should rashly quote, for fear of a mistake.)
I say, when these same gentlemen are jealous,
They make some blunder, which their ladies
    tell us.

XCIX

A real husband always is suspicious,
  But still no less suspects in the wrong
    place,
Jealous of some one who had no such wishes,
  Or pandering blindly to his own disgrace,
By harbouring some dear friend extremely
    vicious;
  The last indeed's infallibly the case: 790
And when the spouse and friend are gone off
    wholly,
He wonders at their vice, and not his folly.

C

Thus parents also are at times short-sighted;
  Though watchful as the lynx, they ne'er
    discover,
The while the wicked world beholds de-
    lighted,
  Young Hopeful's mistress, or Miss Fanny's
    lover,
Till some confounded escapade has blighted
  The plan of twenty years, and all is over;
And then the mother cries, the father swears,
And wonders why the devil he got heirs. 800

CI

But Inez was so anxious, and so clear
  Of sight, that I must think, on this occasion,
She had some other motive much more near
  For leaving Juan to this new temptation,
But what that motive was, I shan't say here;
  Perhaps to finish Juan's education,
Perhaps to open Don Alfonso's eyes,
In case he thought his wife too great a prize.

CII

It was upon a day, a summer's day;—
  Summer's indeed a very dangerous sea-
    son, 810
And so is spring about the end of May;
  The sun, no doubt, is the prevailing reason;
But whatsoe'er the cause is, one may say,
  And stand convicted of more truth than
    treason,
That there are months which nature grows
    more merry in,—
March has its hares, and May must have its
    heroine. *adult time*

CIII

'Twas on a summer's day—the sixth of
    June:—
  I like to be particular in dates,
Not only of the age, and year, but moon;
  They are a sort of post-house, where the
    Fates 820
Change horses, making history change its
    tune,
  Then spur away o'er empires and o'er
    states,
Leaving at last not much besides chronology,
Excepting the post-obits of theology.

CIV

'Twas on the sixth of June, about the hour
  Of half-past six—perhaps still nearer
    seven—
When Julia sate within as pretty a bower
  As e'er held houri in that heathenish
    heaven
Described by Mahomet, and Anacreon Moore, *translations*
  To whom the lyre and laurels have been
    given, 830
With all the trophies of triumphant song—
He won them well, and may he wear them
    long!

CV

She sate, but not alone; I know not well
　How this same interview had taken place,
And even if I knew, I should not tell—
　People should hold their tongues in any
　　case;
No matter how or why the thing befell,
　But there were she and Juan, face to face—
When two such faces are so, 'twould be wise,
But very difficult, to shut their eyes.　　840

CVI

How beautiful she look'd! her conscious heart
　Glow'd in her cheek, and yet she felt no
　　wrong.
Oh Love! how perfect is thy mystic art,
　Strengthening the weak, and trampling on
　　the strong!
How self-deceitful is the sagest part
　Of mortals whom thy lure hath led along!—
The precipice she stood on was immense,
So was her creed in her own innocence.

CVII

She thought of her own strength, and Juan's
　　youth,
　And of the folly of all prudish fears,　　850
Victorious virtue, and domestic truth,
　And then of Don Alfonso's fifty years:
I wish these last had not occurr'd, in sooth,
　Because that number rarely much endears,
And through all climes, the snowy and the
　　sunny,
Sounds ill in love, whate'er it may in money.

CVIII

When people say, "I've told you *fifty* times,"
　They mean to scold, and very often do;
When poets say, "I've written *fifty* rhymes,"
　They make you dread that they'll recite
　　them too;　　860
In gangs of *fifty*, thieves commit their crimes;
　At *fifty* love for love is rare, 'tis true,
But then, no doubt, it equally as true is,
A good deal may be bought for *fifty* Louis.

CIX

Julia had honour, virtue, truth, and love
　For Don Alfonso; and she inly swore,
By all the vows below to powers above,
　She never would disgrace the ring she wore,

Nor leave a wish which wisdom might re-
　　prove;
　And while she ponder'd this, besides much
　　more,　　870
One hand on Juan's carelessly was thrown,
Quite by mistake—she thought it was her
　　own;

CX

Unconsciously she lean'd upon the other,
　Which play'd within the tangles of her
　　hair;
And to contend with thoughts she could not
　　smother
　She seem'd, by the distraction of her air.
'Twas surely very wrong in Juan's mother
　To leave together this imprudent pair,
She who for many years had watch'd her son
　　so—
I'm very certain *mine* would not have done
　　so.　　880

CXI

The hand which still held Juan's, by degrees
　Gently, but palpably confirm'd its grasp,
As if it said, "Detain me, if you please;"
　Yet there's no doubt she only meant to
　　clasp
His fingers with a pure Platonic squeeze;
　She would have shrunk as from a toad, or
　　asp,
Had she imagined such a thing could rouse
A feeling dangerous to a prudent spouse.

CXII

I cannot know what Juan thought of this,
　But what he did, is much what you would
　　do;　　890
His young lip thank'd it with a grateful kiss,
　And then, abash'd at its own joy, withdrew
In deep despair, lest he had done amiss,—
　Love is so very timid when 'tis new:
She blush'd, and frown'd not, but she strove
　　to speak,
And held her tongue, her voice was grown so
　　weak.

CXIII

The sun set, and up rose the yellow moon:
　The devil's in the moon for mischief; they
Who call'd her CHASTE, methinks, began too
　　soon
　Their nomenclature; there is not a day, 900

The longest, not the twenty-first of June,
  Sees half the business in a wicked way,
On which three single hours of moonshine
    smile—
And then she looks so modest all the while.

CXIV

There is a dangerous silence in that hour,
  A stillness, which leaves room for the full soul
To open all itself, without the power
  Of calling wholly back its self-control;
The silver light which, hallowing tree and
    tower,
  Sheds beauty and deep softness o'er the
    whole,   910
Breathes also to the heart, and o'er it throws
A loving languor, which is not repose.

CXV

And Julia sate with Juan, half embraced
  And half retiring from the glowing arm,
Which trembled like the bosom where 'twas
    placed;
  Yet still she must have thought there was
    no harm,
Or else 'twere easy to withdraw her waist;
  But then the situation had its charm,
And then——God knows what next—I can't
    go on;
I'm almost sorry that I e'er begun.   920

CXVI

Oh Plato! Plato! you have paved the way,
  With your confounded fantasies, to more
Immoral conduct by the fancied sway
  Your system feigns o'er the controlless core
Of human hearts, than all the long array
  Of poets and romancers:—You're a bore,
A charlatan, a coxcomb—and have been,
At best, no better than a go-between.

CXVII

And Julia's voice was lost, except in sighs,
  Until too late for useful conversation; 930
The tears were gushing from her gentle eyes,
  I wish, indeed, they had not had occasion;
But who, alas! can love, and then be wise?
  Not that remorse did not oppose temptation;
A little still she strove, and much repented,
And whispering "I will ne'er consent"—
consented.

CXVIII

'Tis said that Xerxes offer'd a reward
  To those who could invent him a new
    pleasure;
Methinks the requisition's rather hard,
  And must have cost his majesty a treasure:
For my part, I'm a moderate-minded bard 941
  Fond of a little love (which I call leisure);
I care not for new pleasures, as the old
Are quite enough for me, so they but hold.

CXIX

Oh Pleasure! you're indeed a pleasant thing,
  Although one must be damn'd for you, no
    doubt:
I make a resolution every spring
  Of reformation, ere the year run out,
But somehow, this my vestal vow takes wing,
  Yet still, I trust, it may be kept through-
    out: 950
I'm very sorry, very much ashamed,
And mean, next winter, to be quite reclaim'd.

CXX

Here my chaste Muse a liberty must take—
  Start not! still chaster reader—she'll be nice
    hence-
Forward, and there is no great cause to quake;
  This liberty is a poetic licence,
Which some irregularity may make
  In the design, and as I have a high sense
Of Aristotle and the Rules, 'tis fit
To beg his pardon when I err a bit.   960

CXXI

This licence is to hope the reader will
  Suppose from June the sixth (the fatal day
Without whose epoch my poetic skill
  For want of facts would all be thrown
    away),
But keeping Julia and Don Juan still
  In sight, that several months have pass'd;
    we'll say
'Twas in November, but I'm not so sure
About the day—the era's more obscure.

CXXII

We'll talk of that anon.—'Tis sweet to hear
  At midnight on the blue and moonlit deep
The song and oar of Adria's gondolier,   971
  By distance mellow'd, o'er the waters sweep;

'Tis sweet to see the evening star appear;
  'Tis sweet to listen as the night-winds creep
From leaf to leaf; 'tis sweet to view on high
The rainbow, based on ocean, span the sky.

CXXIII

'Tis sweet to hear the watch-dog's honest bark
  Bay deep-mouth'd welcome as we draw near
    home;
'Tis sweet to know there is an eye will mark
  Our coming, and look brighter when we
    come;   980
'Tis sweet to be awaken'd by the lark,
  Or lull'd by falling waters; sweet the hum
Of bees, the voice of girls, the song of birds,
The lisp of children, and their earliest words.

CXXIV

Sweet is the vintage, when the showering
    grapes
  In Bacchanal profusion reel to earth,
Purple and gushing; sweet are our escapes
  From civic revelry to rural mirth;
Sweet to the miser are his glittering heaps,
  Sweet to the father is his first-born's birth,
Sweet is revenge—especially to women,   991
Pillage to soldiers, prize-money to seamen.

CXXV

Sweet is a legacy, and passing sweet
  The unexpected death of some old lady
Or gentleman of seventy years complete,
  Who've made "us youth" wait too—too
    long already
For an estate, or cash, or country seat,
  Still breaking, but with stamina so steady
That all the Israelites are fit to mob its
Next owner for their double-damn'd post-
    obits.   1000

CXXVI

'Tis sweet to win, no matter how, one's laurels,
  By blood or ink; 'tis sweet to put an end
To strife; 'tis sometimes sweet to have our
    quarrels,
  Particularly with a tiresome friend:
Sweet is old wine in bottles, ale in barrels;
  Dear is the helpless creature we defend
Against the world; and dear the schoolboy
    spot
We ne'er forget, though there we are forgot.

CXXVII

But sweeter still than this, than these, than
    all,
  Is first and passionate love—it stands
    alone,   1010
Like Adam's recollection of his fall;
  The tree of knowledge has been pluck'd—
    all's known—
And life yields nothing further to recall
  Worthy of this ambrosial sin, so shown,
No doubt in fable, as the unforgiven
Fire which Prometheus filch'd for us from
    heaven.

CXXVIII

Man's a strange animal, and makes strange
    use
  Of his own nature, and the various arts,
And likes particularly to produce
  Some new experiment to show his parts; 1020
This is the age of oddities let loose,
  Where different talents find their different
    marts;
You'd best begin with truth, and when you've
    lost your
Labour, there's a sure market for imposture.

CXXIX

What opposite discoveries we have seen!
  (Signs of true genius, and of empty pock-
    ets.)
One makes new noses, one a guillotine,
  One breaks your bones, one sets them in
    their sockets;
But vaccination certainly has been   1029
  A kind antithesis to Congreve's rockets,
With which the Doctor paid off an old pox,
By borrowing a new one from an ox.

CXXX

Bread has been made (indifferent) from pota-
    toes;
  And galvanism has set some corpses grin-
    ning,
But has not answer'd like the apparatus
  Of the Humane Society's beginning,
By which men are unsuffocated gratis:
  What wondrous new machines have late
    been spinning!
I said the small pox has gone out of late;
Perhaps it may be follow'd by the great. 1040

CXXXI

'Tis said the great came from America;
   Perhaps it may set out on its return,—
The population there so spreads, they say
   'Tis grown high time to thin it in its
     turn,
With war, or plague, or famine, any way,
   So that civilisation they may learn;
And which in ravage the more loathsome evil
     is—
Their real lues, or our pseudo-syphilis?

CXXXII

This is the patent age of new inventions
   For killing bodies, and for saving souls, 1050
All propagated with the best intentions;
   Sir Humphrey Davy's lantern, by which
     coals
Are safely mined for in the mode he men-
     tions,
   Tombuctoo travels, voyages to the Poles,
Are ways to benefit mankind, as true,
Perhaps, as shooting them at Waterloo.

CXXXIII

Man's a phenomenon, one knows not what,
   And wonderful beyond all wondrous meas-
     ure;
'Tis pity though, in this sublime world, that
   Pleasure's a sin, and sometimes sin's a pleas-
     ure;   1060
Few mortals know what end they will be at,
   But whether glory, power, or love, or treas-
     ure,
The path is through perplexing ways, and
     when
The goal is gain'd, we die, you know—and
     then——

CXXXIV

What then?—I do not know, no more do
     you—
   And so good night.—Return we to our
     story:
'Twas in November, when fine days are few,
   And the far mountains wax a little hoary,
And clap a white cape on their mantles blue;
   And the sea dashes round the promontory,
And the loud breaker boils against the rock,
And sober suns must set at five o'clock. 1072

CXXXV

'Twas, as the watchmen say, a cloudy night;
   No moon, no stars, the wind was low or loud
By gusts, and many a sparkling hearth was
     bright
   With the piled wood, round which the
     family crowd;
There's something cheerful in that sort of
     light,
   Even as a summer sky's without a cloud:
I'm fond of fire, and crickets, and all that,
A lobster salad, and champagne, and chat. 1080

CXXXVI

'Twas midnight—Donna Julia was in bed,
   Sleeping, most probably,—when at her
     door
Arose a clatter might awake the dead,
   If they had never been awoke before,
And that they have been so we all have read,
   And are to be so, at the least, once more;—
The door was fasten'd, but with voice and fist
First knocks were heard, then "Madam—
     Madam—hist!

CXXXVII

"For God's sake, Madam—Madam—here's
     my master,
   With more than half the city at his back—
Was ever heard of such a curst disaster! 1091
   'Tis not my fault—I kept good watch—
     Alack!
Do pray undo the bolt a little faster—
   They're on the stair just now, and in a crack
Will all be here; perhaps he yet may fly—
Surely the window's not so *very* high!"

CXXXVIII

By this time Don Alfonso was arrived,
   With torches, friends, and servants in great
     number;
The major part of them had long been wived,
   And therefore paused not to disturb the
     slumber   1100
Of any wicked woman, who contrived
   By stealth her husband's temples to encum-
     ber:
Examples of this kind are so contagious,
Were *one* not punish'd, *all* would be outra-
     geous.

CXXXIX

I can't tell how, or why, or what suspicion
  Could enter into Don Alfonso's head;
But for a cavalier of his condition
  It surely was exceedingly ill-bred,
Without a word of previous admonition,
  To hold a levee round his lady's bed, 1110
And summon lackeys, arm'd with fire and
    sword,
  To prove himself the thing he most abhorr'd.

CXL

Poor Donna Julia! starting as from sleep
  (Mind—that I do not say—she had not
    slept),
Began at once to scream, and yawn, and weep;
  Her maid, Antonia, who was an adept,
Contrived to fling the bed-clothes in a heap,
  As if she had just now from out them
    crept:
I can't tell why she should take all this trouble
To prove her mistress had been sleeping
    double. 1120

CXLI

But Julia mistress, and Antonia maid,
  Appear'd like two poor harmless women,
    who
Of goblins, but still more of men afraid,
  Had thought one man might be deterr'd by
    two,
And therefore side by side were gently laid,
  Until the hours of absence should run
    through,
And truant husband should return, and say,
"My dear, I was the first who came away."

CXLII

Now Julia found at length a voice, and cried,
  "In heaven's name, Don Alfonso, what d'ye
    mean? 1130
Has madness seized you? would that I had
    died
  Ere such a monster's victim I had been!
What may this midnight violence betide,
  A sudden fit of drunkenness or spleen?
Dare you suspect me, whom the thought
    would kill?
Search, then, the room!"—Alfonso said, "I
    will."

CXLIII

He search'd, *they* search'd, and rummaged
    everywhere,
  Closet and clothes-press, chest and window-
    seat,
And found much linen, lace, and several pair
  Of stockings, slippers, brushes, combs, com-
    plete, 1140
With other articles of ladies fair,
  To keep them beautiful, or leave them neat:
Arras they prick'd and curtains with their
    swords,
And wounded several shutters, and some
    boards.

CXLIV

Under the bed they search'd, and there they
    found—
  No matter what—it was not that they
    sought;
They open'd windows, gazing if the ground
  Had signs or footmarks, but the earth said
    nought;
And then they stared each other's faces round:
  'Tis odd, not one of all these seekers
    thought, 1150
And seems to me almost a sort of blunder,
Of looking *in* the bed as well as under.

CXLV

During this inquisition Julia's tongue
  Was not asleep—"Yes, search and search,"
    she cried,
"Insult on insult heap, and wrong on wrong!
  It was for this that I became a bride!
For this in silence I have suffer'd long
  A husband like Alfonso at my side;
But now I'll bear no more, nor here remain,
If there be law or lawyers in all Spain. 1160

CXLVI

"Yes, Don Alfonso! husband now no more,
  If ever you indeed deserved the name,
Is't worthy of your years?—you have three-
    score—
  Fifty, or sixty, it is all the same—
Is't wise or fitting, causeless to explore
  For facts against a virtuous woman's fame?
Ungrateful, perjured, barbarous Don Alfonso,
How dare you think your lady would go on
    so?

CXLVII

"Is it for this I have disdain'd to hold
  The common privileges of my sex? 1170
That I have chosen a confessor so old
  And deaf, that any other it would vex,
And never once he has had cause to scold,
  But found my very innocence perplex
So much, he always doubted I was married—
How sorry you will be when I've miscarried!

CXLVIII

"Was it for this that no Cortejo e'er
  I yet have chosen from out the youth of
    Seville?
Is it for this I scarce went anywhere,
  Except to bull-fights, mass, play, rout, and
    revel? 1180
Is it for this, whate'er my suitors were,
  I favour'd none—nay, was almost uncivil?
Is it for this that General Count O'Reilly,
Who took Algiers, declares I used him vilely?

CXLIX

"Did not the Italian Musico Cazzani
  Sing at my heart six months at least in vain?
Did not his countryman, Count Corniani,
  Call me the only virtuous wife in Spain?
Were there not also Russians, English, many?
  The Count Strongstroganoff I put in pain,
And Lord Mount Coffeehouse, the Irish peer,
Who kill'd himself for love (with wine) last
    year. 1192

CL

"Have I not had two bishops at my feet?
  The Duke of Ichar, and Don Fernan Nunez?
And is it thus a faithful wife you treat?
  I wonder in what quarter now the moon is:
I praise your vast forbearance not to beat
  Me also, since the time so opportune is—
Oh, valiant man! with sword drawn and cock'd
    trigger, 1199
Now, tell me, don't you cut a pretty figure?

CLI

"Was it for this you took your sudden jour-
    ney,
  Under pretense of business indispensable,
With that sublime of rascals your attorney,
  Whom I see standing there, and looking
    sensible

Of having play'd the fool? though both I
    spurn, he
  Deserves the worst, his conduct's less de-
    fensible, ·
Because, no doubt, 'twas for his dirty fee,
And not from any love to you nor me.

CLII

"If he comes here to take a deposition,
  By all means let the gentleman proceed; 1210
You've made the apartment in a fit condi-
    tion:—
  There's pen and ink for you, sir, when you
    need—
Let everything be noted with precision,
  I would not you for nothing should be
    fee'd—
But as my maid's undrest, pray turn your
    spies out."
"Oh!" sobb'd Antonia, "I could tear their
    eyes out."

CLIII

"There is the closet, there the toilet, there
  The antechamber—search them under, over;
There is the sofa, there the great arm-chair,
  The chimney—which would really hold a
    lover. 1220
I wish to sleep, and beg you will take care
  And make no further noise, till you discover
The secret cavern of this lurking treasure—
And when 'tis found, let me, too, have that
    pleasure.

CLIV

"And now, Hidalgo! now that you have thrown
  Doubt upon me, confusion over all,
Pray have the courtesy to make it known
  Who is the man you search for? how d'ye
    call
Him? what's his lineage? let him but be
    shown—
  I hope he's young and handsome—is he
    tall? 1230
Tell me—and be assured, that since you stain
Mine honour thus, it shall not be in vain.

CLV

"At least, perhaps, he has not sixty years,
  At that age he would be too old for slaughter,
Or for so young a husband's jealous fears—
  (Antonia! let me have a glass of water.)

I am ashamed of having shed these tears,
  They are unworthy of my father's daughter;
My mother dream'd not in my natal hour,
That I should fall into a monster's power. 1240

CLVI

"Perhaps 'tis of Antonia you are jealous,
  You saw that she was sleeping by my side,
When you broke in upon us with your fel-
    lows;
  Look where you please—we've nothing,
    sir, to hide;
Only another time, I trust, you'll tell us,
  Or for the sake of decency abide
A moment at the door, that we may be
Drest to receive so much good company.

CLVII

"And now, sir, I have done, and say no
    more;
  The little I have said may serve to show 1250
The guileless heart in silence may grieve o'er
  The wrongs to whose exposure it is slow:—
I leave you to your conscience as before,
  'Twill one day ask you, *why* you used me
    so?
God grant you feel not then the bitterest grief!
Antonia! where's my pocket-handkerchief?"

CLVIII

She ceased, and turn'd upon her pillow; pale
  She lay, her dark eyes flashing through their
    tears,
Like skies that rain and lighten; as a veil,
  Waved and o'ershading her wan cheek,
    appears   1260
Her streaming hair; the black curls strive, but
    fail,
  To hide the glossy shoulder, which uprears
Its snow through all;—her soft lips lie apart,
And louder than her breathing beats her heart.

CLIX

The Senhor Don Alfonso stood confused;
  Antonia bustled round the ransack'd room,
And, turning up her nose, with looks abused
  Her master, and his myrmidons, of whom
Not one, except the attorney, was amused;
  He, like Achates, faithful to the tomb, 1270
So there were quarrels, cared not for the cause,
Knowing they must be settled by the laws.

CLX

With prying snub-nose, and small eyes, he
    stood,
  Following Antonia's motions here and there,
With much suspicion in his attitude;
  For reputations he had little care;
So that a suit or action were made good,
  Small pity had he for the young and fair,
And ne'er believed in negatives, till these 1279
Were proved by competent false witnesses.

CLXI

But Don Alfonso stood with downcast looks,
  And, truth to say, he made a foolish figure;
When, after searching in five hundred nooks,
  And treating a young wife with so much
    rigour,
He gain'd no point, except some self-rebukes,
  Added to those his lady with such vigour
Had pour'd upon him for the last half hour,
Quick, thick, and heavy—as a thunder-shower.

CLXII

At first he tried to hammer an excuse,   1289
  To which the sole reply was tears and sobs,
And indications of hysterics, whose
  Prologue is always certain throes, and
    throbs,
Gasps, and whatever else the owners choose:
  Alfonso saw his wife, and thought of Job's;
He saw too, in perspective, her relations,
And then he tried to muster all his patience.

CLXIII

He stood in act to speak, or rather stammer,
  But sage Antonia cut him short before
The anvil of his speech received the hammer,
  With "Pray, sir, leave the room, and say
    no more,   1300
Or madam dies."—Alfonso mutter'd, "D—n
    her."
  But nothing else, the time of words was
    o'er;
He cast a rueful look or two, and did,
He knew not wherefore, that which he was
    bid.

CLXIV

With him retired his "*posse comitatus*,"
  The attorney last, who linger'd near the door
Reluctantly, still tarrying there as late as
  Antonia let him—not a little sore

At this most strange and unexplain'd "*hiatus*"
  In Don Alfonso's facts, which just now
    wore   1310
An awkward look; as he revolved the case,
The door was fasten'd in his legal face.

CLXV

No sooner was it bolted, than—Oh shame!
  Oh sin! Oh sorrow! and Oh womankind!
How can you do such things and keep your
    fame,
  Unless this world, and t'other too, be
    blind?
Nothing so dear as an unfilch'd good name!
  But to proceed—for there is more behind:
With much heartfelt reluctance be it said,
Young Juan slipp'd, half-smother'd, from the
    bed.   1320

CLXVI

He had been hid—I don't pretend to say
  How, nor can I indeed describe the where—
Young, slender, and pack'd easily, he lay,
  No doubt, in little compass, round or
    square;
But pity him I neither must nor may
  His suffocation by that pretty pair;
'Twere better, sure, to die so, than be shut
With maudlin Clarence in his Malmsey butt.

CLXVII

And, secondly, I pity not, because
  He had no business to commit a sin, 1330
Forbid by heavenly, fined by human laws,
  At least 'twas rather early to begin;
But at sixteen the conscience rarely gnaws
  So much as when we call our old debts in
At sixty years, and draw the accompts of evil,
And find a deuced balance with the devil.

CLXVIII

Of his position I can give no notion:
  'Tis written in the Hebrew Chronicle,
How the physicians, leaving pill and potion,
  Prescribed, by way of blister, a young
    belle,   1340
When old King David's blood grew dull in
    motion,
  And that the medicine answer'd very well;
Perhaps 'twas in a different way applied,
  For David lived, but Juan nearly died.

CLXIX

What's to be done? Alfonso will be back
  The moment he has sent his fools away.
Antonia's skill was put upon the rack,
  But no device could be brought into play—
And how to parry the renew'd attack? 1349
  Besides, it wanted but few hours of day:
Antonia puzzled; Julia did not speak,
But press'd her bloodless lip to Juan's cheek.

CLXX

He turn'd his lip to hers, and with his hand
  Call'd back the tangles of her wandering
    hair;
Even then their love they could not all com-
    mand,
  And half forgot their danger and despair:
Antonia's patience now was at a stand—
  "Come, come, 'tis no time now for fooling
    there,"
She whisper'd, in great wrath—"I must de-
    posit
This pretty gentleman within the closet: 1360

CLXXI

"Pray, keep your nonsense for some luckier
    night—
  Who can have put my master in this mood?
What will become on't—I'm in such a fright,
  The devil's in the urchin, and no good—
Is this a time for giggling? this a plight?
  Why, don't you know that it may end in
    blood?
You'll lose your life, and I shall lose my place,
My mistress all, for that half-girlish face.

CLXXII

"Had it but been for a stout cavalier
  Of twenty-five or thirty—(come, make
    haste)   1370
But for a child, what piece of work is here!
  I really, madam, wonder at your taste—
(Come, sir, get in)—my master must be
    near:
  There, for the present, at the least, he's
    fast,
And if we can but till the morning keep
Our counsel—Juan, mind, you must not
    sleep)."

CLXXIII

Now, Don Alfonso entering, but alone,
  Closed the oration of the trusty maid:
She loiter'd, and he told her to be gone,
  An order somewhat sullenly obey'd;   1380
However, present remedy was none,
  And no great good seem'd answer'd if she
    staid;
Regarding both with slow and sidelong view,
She snuff'd the candle, curtsied, and withdrew.

CLXXIV

Alfonso paused a minute—then begun
  Some strange excuses for his late proceed-
    ing:
He would not justify what he had done,
  To say the best, it was extreme ill-breeding;
But there were ample reasons for it, none   1389
  Of which he specified in this his pleading:
His speech was a fine sample, on the whole,
Of rhetoric, which the learn'd call "*rigmarole*."

CLXXV

Julia said nought; though all the while there
    rose
  A ready answer, which at once enables
A matron, who her husband's foible knows,
  But a few timely words to turn the tables,
Which, if it does not silence, still must pose,—
  Even if it should comprise a pack of fables;
'Tis to retort with firmness, and when he
Suspects with *one*, do you reproach with
  three.   1400

CLXXVI

Julia, in fact, had tolerable grounds,—
  Alfonso's loves with Inez were well known;
But whether 'twas that one's own guilt con-
    founds—
  But that can't be, as has been often shown,
A lady with apologies abounds;—
  It might be that her silence sprang alone
From delicacy to Don Juan's ear,
To whom she knew his mother's fame was
  dear.

CLXXVII

There might be one more motive, which
    makes two,
  Alfonso ne'er to Juan had alluded,—   1410
Mentioned his jealousy, but never who
  Had been the happy lover, he concluded,

Conceal'd amongst his premises; 'tis true,
  His mind the more o'er this its mystery
    brooded
To speak of Inez now were, one may say,
Like throwing Juan in Alfonso's way.

CLXXVIII

A hint, in tender cases, is enough;
  Silence is best: besides there is a *tact*—
(That modern phrase appears to me sad stuff,
  But it will serve to keep my verse com-
    pact)—   1420
Which keeps, when push'd by questions rather
    rough,
  A lady always distant from the fact:
The charming creatures lie with such a grace,
There's nothing so becoming to the face.

CLXXIX

They blush, and we believe them, at least I
  Have always done so; 'tis of no great use,
In any case, attempting a reply,
  For then their eloquence grows quite pro-
    fuse;
And when at length they're out of breath,
    they sigh,
  And cast their languid eyes down, and let
    loose   1430
A tear or two, and then we make it up;
And then—and then—and then—sit down
  and sup.

CLXXX

Alfonso closed his speech, and begg'd her
    pardon,
  Which Julia half withheld, and then half
    granted,
And laid conditions, he thought very hard, on,
  Denying several little things he wanted:
He stood like Adam lingering near his garden,
  With useless penitence perplex'd and
    haunted,
Beseeching she no further would refuse,
When, lo! he stumbled o'er a pair of shoes. 1440

CLXXXI

A pair of shoes!—what then? not much, if
    they
  Are such as fit with ladies' feet, but these
(No one can tell how much I grieve to say)
  Were masculine; to see them, and to seize,

Was but a moment's act.—Ah! well-a-day!
  My teeth begin to chatter, my veins freeze—
Alfonso first examined well their fashion,
And then flew out into another passion.

CLXXXII

He left the room for his relinquish'd sword,
  And Julia instant to the closet flew.   1450
"Fly, Juan, fly! for heaven's sake—not a
    word—
  The door is open—you may yet slip through
The passage you so often have explored—
  Here is the garden-key—Fly—fly—Adieu!
Haste—haste! I hear Alfonso's hurrying feet—
Day has not broke—there's no one in the
    street."

CLXXXIII

None can say that this was not good advice,
  The only mischief was, it came too late;
Of all experience 'tis the usual price,
  A sort of income-tax laid on by fate: 1460
Juan had reach'd the room-door in a trice,
  And might have done so by the garden-
    gate,
But met Alfonso in his dressing-gown,
Who threaten'd death—so Juan knock'd him
    down.

CLXXXIV

Dire was the scuffle, and out went the light;
  Antonia cried out "Rape!" and Julia "Fire!"
But now a servant stirr'd to aid the fight.
  Alfonso, pommell'd to his heart's desire,
Swore lustily he'd be revenged this night;
  And Juan, too, blasphemed an octave
    higher;   1470
His blood was up: though young, he was a
    Tartar,
And not at all disposed to prove a martyr.

CLXXXV

Alfonso's sword had dropp'd ere he could
    draw it,
  And they continued battling hand to hand,
For Juan very luckily ne'er saw it;
  His temper not being under great command,
If at that moment he had chanced to claw it,
  Alfonso's days had not been in the land
Much longer.—Think of husbands', lovers'
    lives!
And how ye may be doubly widows—wives!

CLXXXVI

Alfonso grappled to detain the foe,   1481
  And Juan throttled him to get away,
And blood ('twas from the nose) began to
    flow;
  At last, as they more faintly wrestling
    lay,
Juan contrived to give an awkward blow,
  And then his only garment quite gave
    way;
He fled, like Joseph, leaving it; but there,
I doubt, all likeness ends between the pair.

CLXXXVII

Lights came at length, and men, and maids,
    who found
  An awkward spectacle their eyes before; 1490
Antonia in hysterics, Julia swoon'd,
  Alfonso leaning, breathless, by the door;
Some half-torn drapery scatter'd on the
    ground,
  Some blood, and several footsteps, but no
    more:
Juan the gate gain'd, turn'd the key about,
And liking not the inside, lock'd the out.

CLXXXVIII

Here ends this canto.—Need I sing, or say,
  How Juan, naked, favour'd by the night,
Who favours what she should not, found his
    way,   1499
  And reach'd his home in an unseemly plight?
The pleasant scandal which arose next day,
  The nine days' wonder which was brought
    to light,
And how Alfonso sued for a divorce,
Were in the English newspapers, of course.

CLXXXIX

If you would like to see the whole proceed-
    ings,
  The depositions and the cause at full,
The names of all the witnesses, the pleadings
  Of counsel to nonsuit, or to annul,
There's more than one edition, and the read-
    ings
  Are various, but they none of them are
    dull;   1510
The best is that in short-hand ta'en by Gurney,
Who to Madrid on purpose made a journey.

CXC

But Donna Inez, to divert the train
  Of one of the most circulating scandals
That had for centuries been known in Spain,
  At least since the retirement of the Vandals,
First vow'd (and never had she vow'd in
    vain)
  To Virgin Mary several pounds of candles;
And then, by the advice of some old ladies,
She sent her son to be shipp'd off from Ca-
    diz.   1520

CXCI

She had resolved that he should travel through
  All European climes, by land or sea,
To mend his former morals, and get new,
  Especially in France and Italy
(At least this is the thing most people do).
  Julia was sent into a convent: she
Grieved, but, perhaps, her feelings may be
    better
Shown in the following copy of her Letter:—

CXCII

"They tell me 'tis decided you depart:
  'Tis wise—'tis well, but not the less a
    pain;   1530
I have no further claim on your young heart,
  Mine is the victim, and would be again:
To love too much has been the only art
  I used;—I write in haste, and if a stain
Be on this sheet, 'tis not what it appears;
My eyeballs burn and throb, but have no tears.

CXCIII

"I loved, I love you, for this love have lost
  State, station, heaven, mankind's, my own
    esteem,
And yet cannot regret what it hath cost,   1540
  So dear is still the memory of that dream;
Yet, if I name my guilt, 'tis not to boast,
  None can deem harshlier of me than I deem:
I trace this scrawl because I cannot rest—
I've nothing to reproach or to request.

CXCIV

"Man's love is of man's life a thing apart,
  'Tis woman's whole existence; man may
    range
The court, camp, church, the vessel, and the
    mart;
  Sword, gown, gain, glory, offer in exchange

Pride, fame, ambition, to fill up his heart,
  And few there are whom these cannot es-
    trange;   1550
Men have all these resources, we but one,
To love again, and be again undone.

CXCV

"You will proceed in pleasure, and in pride,
  Beloved and loving many; all is o'er
For me on earth, except some years to hide
  My shame and sorrow deep in my heart's
    core:
These I could bear, but cannot cast aside
  The passion which still rages as before,—
And so farewell—forgive me, love me—No,
That word is idle now—but let it go.   1560

CXCVI

"My breast has been all weakness, is so yet:
  But still I think I can collect my mind;
My blood still rushes where my spirit's set,
  As roll the waves before the settled wind;
My heart is feminine, nor can forget—
  To all, except one image, madly blind;
So shakes the needle, and so stands the pole,
As vibrates my fond heart to my fix'd soul.

CXCVII

"I have no more to say, but linger still,
  And dare not set my seal upon this sheet,
And yet I may as well the task fulfil,   1571
  My misery can scarce be more complete:
I had not lived till now, could sorrow kill;
  Death shuns the wretch who fain the blow
    would meet,
And I must even survive this last adieu,
And bear with life to love and pray for you!"

CXCVIII

This note was written upon gilt-edge paper
  With a neat little crow-quill, slight and
    new;
Her small white hand could hardly reach the
    taper,
  It trembled as magnetic needles do,   1580
And yet she did not let one tear escape her;
  The seal a sun-flower; "*Elle vous suit
    partout*,"
The motto, cut upon a white cornelian;
The wax was superfine, its hue vermilion.

CXCIX

This was Don Juan's earliest scrape; but
    whether
  I shall proceed with his adventures is
Dependent on the public altogether;
  We'll see, however, what they say to this,
Their favour in an author's cap's a feather,
    And no great mischief's done by their ca-
      price;   1590
And if their approbation we experience,
Perhaps they'll have some more about a year
    hence.

CC

My poem's epic, and is meant to be
Divided in twelve books; each book containing,
With love, and war, a heavy gale at sea,
  A list of ships, and captains, and kings
    reigning,
New characters; the episodes are three:
  A panoramic view of hell's in training,
After the style of Virgil and of Homer,
So that my name of Epic's no misnomer. 1600

CCI

All these things will be specified in time,
  With strict regard to Aristotle's rules,
The *Vade Mecum* of the true sublime,
  Which makes so many poets, and some
    fools:
Prose poets like blank-verse, I'm fond of
    rhyme,
  Good workmen never quarrel with their
    tools;
I've got new mythological machinery,
And very handsome supernatural scenery.

CCII

There's only one slight difference between
  Me and my epic brethren gone before, 1610
And here the advantage is my own, I ween
  (Not that I have not several merits more,
But this will more peculiarly be seen);
  They so embellish, that 'tis quite a bore
Their labyrinth of fables to thread through,
Whereas this story's actually true.

CCIII

If any person doubt it, I appeal
  To history, tradition, and to facts, 1619
To newspapers, whose truth all know and feel,
  To plays in five, and operas in three acts;

All these confirm my statement a good deal,
  But that which more completely faith exacts
Is, that myself, and several now in Seville,
Saw Juan's last elopement with the devil.

CCIV

If ever I should condescend to prose,
  I'll write poetical commandments, which
Shall supersede beyond all doubt all those
  That went before; in these I shall enrich
My text with many things that no one knows,
  And carry precept to the highest pitch: 1630
I'll call the work "Longinus o'er a Bottle,
Or, Every Poet his *own* Aristotle."

CCV

Thou shalt believe in Milton, Dryden, Pope;
Thou shalt not set up Wordsworth, Coleridge,
    Southey;
Because the first is crazed beyond all hope,
  The second drunk, the third so quaint and
    mouthy:
With Crabbe it may be difficult to cope,
  And Campbell's Hippocrene is somewhat
    drouthy:
Thou shalt not steal from Samuel Rogers, nor
Commit—flirtation with the muse of Moore.

CCVI

Thou shalt not covet Mr. Sotheby's Muse,
  His Pegasus, nor anything that's his; 1642
Thou shalt not bear false witness like "the
    Blues"—
  (There's one, at least, is very fond of this);
Thou shalt not write, in short, but what I
    choose:
  This is true criticism, and you may kiss—
Exactly as you please, or not,—the rod;
But if you don't, I'll lay it on, by G—d!

CCVII

If any person should presume to assert
  This story is not moral, first, I pray, 1650
That they will not cry out before they're
    hurt,
  Then that they'll read it o'er again, and say
(But, doubtless, nobody will be so pert),
  That this is not a moral tale, though gay;
Besides, in Canto Twelfth, I mean to show
The very place where wicked people go.

CCVIII

If, after all, there should be some so blind
    To their own good this warning to despise,
Led by some tortuosity of mind,   1659
    Not to believe my verse and their own eyes,
And cry that they "the moral cannot find,"
    I tell him, if a clergyman, he lies;
Should captains the remark, or critics, make,
They also lie too—under a mistake.

CCIX

The public approbation I expect,
    And beg they'll take my word about the
        moral,
Which I with their amusement will connect
    (So children cutting teeth receive a coral);
Meantime they'll doubtless please to recollect
    My epical pretensions to the laurel: 1670
For fear some prudish readers should grow
        skittish,
I've bribed my grandmother's review—the
        British.

CCX

I sent it in a letter to the Editor,
    Who thank'd me duly by return of post—
I'm for a handsome article his creditor;
    Yet, if my gentle Muse he please to roast,
And break a promise after having made it her,
    Denying the receipt of what it cost,
And smear his page with gall instead of honey,
All I can say is—that he had the money. 1680

CCXI

I think that with this holy new alliance
    I may ensure the public, and defy
All other magazines of art or science,
    Daily, or monthly, or three monthly; I
Have not essay'd to multiply their clients,
    Because they tell me 'twere in vain to try,
And that the Edinburgh Review and Quarterly
Treat a dissenting author very martyrly.

CCXII

"*Non ego hoc ferrem calida juventâ*
    Consule Planco,"[1] Horace said, and so   1690
Say I; by which quotation there is meant a
    Hint that some six or seven good years ago

[1] "I should not have endured this in my passionate youth in the consulship of Plancus." (Horace, *Odes*, III, xiv, 27)

(Long ere I dreamt of dating from the Brenta)
    I was most ready to return a blow,
And would not brook at all this sort of thing
    In my hot youth—when George the Third
        was King.

CCXIII

But now at thirty years my hair is gray—
    (I wonder what it will be like at forty?
I thought of a peruke the other day—)
    My heart is not much greener; and, in
        short, I   1700
Have squander'd my whole summer while
        'twas May,
    And feel no more the spirit to retort; I
Have spent my life, both interest and principal,
And deem not, what I deem'd, my soul in-
        vincible.

CCXIV

No more—no more—Oh! never more on me
    The freshness of the heart can fall like dew,
Which out of all the lovely things we see
    Extracts emotions beautiful and new;
Hived in our bosoms like the bag o' the bee.
    Think'st thou the honey with those objects
        grew?   1710
Alas! 'twas not in them, but in thy power
To double even the sweetness of a flower.

CCXV

No more—no more—Oh! never more, my
        heart,
    Canst thou be my sole world, my universe!
Once all in all, but now a thing apart,
    Thou canst not be my blessing or my curse:
The illusion's gone for ever, and thou art
    Insensible, I trust, but none the worse,
And in thy stead I've got a deal of judgment,
Though heaven knows how it ever found a
        lodgment.   1720

CCXVI

My days of love are over; me no more
    The charms of maid, wife, and still less of
        widow,
Can make the fool of which they made be-
        fore,—
    In short, I must not lead the life I did do;
The credulous hope of mutual minds is o'er,
    The copious use of claret is forbid too,
So for a good old-gentlemanly vice,
I think I must take up with avarice.

CCXVII

Ambition was my idol, which was broken
  Before the shrines of Sorrow, and of Pleas-
    ure;   1730
And the two last have left me many a token
  O'er which reflection may be made at leisure;
Now, like Friar Bacon's brazen head, I've
    spoken,
  "Time is, Time was, Time's past:"—a
    chymic treasure
Is glittering youth, which I have spent be-
    times—
My heart in passion, and my head on rhymes.

CCXVIII

What is the end of fame? 'tis but to fill
  A certain portion of uncertain paper:
Some liken it to climbing up a hill,
  Whose summit, like all hills, is lost in
    vapour;   1740
For this men write, speak, preach, and heroes
    kill,
  And bards burn what they call their "mid-
    night taper,"
To have, when the original is dust,
A name, a wretched picture, and worse bust.

CCXIX

What are the hopes of man? Old Egypt's King
  Cheops erected the first pyramid
And largest, thinking it was just the thing
  To keep his memory whole, and mummy
    hid:
But somebody or other rummaging,
  Burglariously broke his coffin's lid.   1750
Let not a monument give you or me hopes,
Since not a pinch of dust remains of Cheops.

CCXX

But I, being fond of true philosophy,
  Say very often to myself, "Alas!
All things that have been born were born to
    die,
  And flesh (which Death mows down to
    hay) is grass;
You've pass'd your youth not so unpleasantly,
  And if you had it o'er again—'twould
    pass—
So thank your stars that matters are no worse,
And read your Bible, sir, and mind your
    purse."   1760

CCXXI

But for the present, gentle reader! and
  Still gentler purchaser! the bard—that's I—
Must, with permission, shake you by the hand,
  And so your humble servant, and good-
    bye!
We meet again, if we should understand
  Each other; and if not, I shall not try
Your patience further than by this short
    sample—
'Twere well if others follow'd my example.

CCXXII

"Go, little book, from this my solitude!
  I cast thee on the waters—go thy ways! 1770
And if, as I believe, thy vein be good,
  The world will find thee after many days."
When Southey's read, and Wordsworth un-
    derstood,
  I can't help putting in my claim to praise—
The four first rhymes are Southey's, every line:
For God's sake, reader! take them not for
    mine!
November, 1818

CANTO THE SECOND

I

OH ye! who teach the ingenuous youth of
    nations,
  Holland, France, England, Germany, or
    Spain,
I pray ye flog them upon all occasions,
  It mends their morals, never mind the pain:
The best of mothers and of educations
  In Juan's case were but employ'd in vain,
Since, in a way that's rather of the oddest, he
Became divested of his native modesty.

II

Had he but been placed at a public school,
  In the third form, or even in the fourth, 10
His daily task had kept his fancy cool,
  At least, had he been nurtured in the north.
Spain may prove an exception to the rule,
  But then exceptions always prove its
    worth—
A lad of sixteen causing a divorce
Puzzled his tutors very much, of course.

III

I can't say that it puzzles me at all,
  If all things be consider'd; first, there was
His lady-mother, mathematical,
  A——never mind;—his tutor, an old ass;
A pretty woman—(that's quite natural,   21
  Or else the thing had hardly come to pass)
A husband rather old, not much in unity
With his young wife—a time, and opportunity.

IV

Well—well; the world must turn upon its
  axis,
  And all mankind turn with it, heads or tails,
And live and die, make love and pay our
  taxes,
  And as the veering wind shifts, shift our
    sails;
The king commands us, and the doctor quacks
  us,
  The priest instructs, and so our life exhales,
A little breath, love, wine, ambition, fame, 31
Fighting, devotion, dust,—perhaps a name.

V

I said, that Juan had been sent to Cadiz—
  A pretty town, I recollect it well—
'Tis there the mart of the colonial trade is,
  (Or was, before Peru learn'd to rebel,)
And such sweet girls—I mean, such graceful
  ladies,
  Their very walk would make your bosom
    swell;
I can't describe it, though so much it strike,
Nor liken it—I never saw the like: 40

VI

An Arab horse, a stately stag, a barb
  New broke, a cameleopard, a gazelle,
No—none of these will do;—and then their
  garb,
  Their veil and petticoat—Alas! to dwell
Upon such things would very near absorb
  A canto—then their feet and ankles,—well,
Thank Heaven I've got no metaphor quite
  ready,
(And so, my sober Muse—come, let's be
  steady—

VII

Chaste Muse!—well, if you must, you must)
  —the veil
  Thrown back a moment with the glancing
    hand,   50
While the o'erpowering eye, that turns you
  pale,
  Flashes into the heart:—All sunny land
Of love! when I forget you, may I fail
  To——say my prayers—but never was
    there plann'd
A dress through which the eyes give such a
  volley,
Excepting the Venetian Fazzioli.

VIII

But to our tale: the Donna Inez sent
  Her son to Cadiz only to embark;
To stay there had not answer'd her intent,
  But why?—we leave the reader in the
    dark—   60
'Twas for a voyage the young man was
  meant,
  As if a Spanish ship were Noah's ark,
To wean him from the wickedness of earth,
And send him like a dove of promise forth.

IX

Don Juan bade his valet pack his things
  According to direction, then received
A lecture and some money: for four springs
  He was to travel; and though Inez grieved
(As every kind of parting has its stings),
  She hoped he would improve—perhaps believed: 70
A letter, too, she gave (he never read it)
Of good advice—and two or three of credit.

X

In the mean time, to pass her hours away,
  Brave Inez now set up a Sunday school
For naughty children, who would rather
  play
  (Like truant rogues) the devil, or the fool;
Infants of three years old were taught that
  day,
  Dunces were whipt, or set upon a stool:
The great success of Juan's education
Spurr'd her to teach another generation.   80

XI

Juan embark'd—the ship got under way,
　The wind was fair, the water passing rough;
A devil of a sea rolls in that bay,
　As I, who've cross'd it oft, know well
　　enough;
And, standing upon deck, the dashing spray
　Flies in one's face, and makes it weather-
　　tough:
And there he stood to take, and take again,
His first—perhaps his last—farewell of Spain.

XII

I can't but say it is an awkward sight   89
　To see one's native land receding through
The growing waters; it unmans one quite,
　Especially when life is rather new:
I recollect Great Britain's coast looks white,
　But almost every other country's blue,
When gazing on them, mystified by distance,
We enter on our nautical existence.

XIII

So Juan stood, bewilder'd on the deck:
　The wind sung, cordage strain'd, and sailors
　　swore,
And the ship creak'd, the town became a
　　speck,
　From which away so fair and fast they
　　bore.
The best of remedies is a beef-steak   100
　Against sea-sickness: try it, sir, before
You sneer, and I assure you this is true,
For I have found it answer—so may you.

XIV

Don Juan stood, and, gazing from the stern,
　Beheld his native Spain receding far:
First partings form a lesson hard to learn,
　Even nations feel this when they go to war;
There is a sort of unexprest concern,
　A kind of shock that sets one's heart ajar: 110
At leaving even the most unpleasant people
And places, one keeps looking at the steeple.

XV

But Juan had got many things to leave,
　His mother, and a mistress, and no wife,
So that he had much better cause to grieve
　Than many persons more advanced in life;

And if we now and then a sigh must heave
　At quitting even those we quit in strife,
No doubt we weep for those the heart en-
　　dears—
That is, till deeper griefs congeal our tears. 120

XVI

So Juan wept, as wept the captive Jews
　By Babel's waters, still remembering Sion:
I'd weep,—but mine is not a weeping Muse,
　And such light griefs are not a thing to die
　　on;
Young men should travel, if but to amuse
　Themselves; and the next time their servants
　　tie on
Behind their carriages their new portmanteau,
Perhaps it may be lined with this my canto.

XVII

And Juan wept, and much he sigh'd and
　　thought,
　While his salt tears dropp'd into the salt
　　sea,   130
"Sweets to the sweet;" (I like so much to
　　quote;
　You must excuse this extract,—'tis where
　　she,
The Queen of Denmark, for Ophelia brought
　Flowers to the grave;) and, sobbing often,
　　he
Reflected on his present situation,
And seriously resolved on reformation.

XVIII

"Farewell, my Spain! a long farewell!" he
　　cried,
　"Perhaps I may revisit thee no more,
But die, as many an exiled heart hath died,
　Of its own thirst to see again thy shore: 140
Farewell, where Guadalquivir's waters glide!
　Farewell, my mother! and, since all is
　　o'er,
Farewell, too, dearest Julia!—(here he drew
Her letter out again, and read it through.)

XIX

"And oh! if e'er I should forget, I swear—
　But that's impossible, and cannot be—
Sooner shall this blue ocean melt to air,
　Sooner shall earth resolve itself to sea,

Than I resign thine image, oh, my fair!
  Or think of anything, excepting thee; 150
A mind diseased no remedy can physic—
  (Here the ship gave a lurch, and he grew sea-
    sick.)

XX

"Sooner shall heaven kiss earth—(here he fell
    sicker)
  Oh, Julia! what is every other woe?—
(For God's sake let me have a glass of liquor;
  Pedro, Battista, help me down below.)
Julia, my love—(you rascal, Pedro, quicker)—
  Oh, Julia!—(this curst vessel pitches so)—
Beloved Julia, hear me still beseeching!"
(Here he grew inarticulate with retching.) 160

XXI

He felt that chilling heaviness of heart,
  Or rather stomach, which, alas! attends,
Beyond the best apothecary's art,
  The loss of love, the treachery of friends,
Or death of those we dote on, when a part
  Of us dies with them as each fond hope
    ends:
No doubt he would have been much more
    pathetic,
But the sea acted as a strong emetic.

XXII

Love's a capricious power: I've known it hold
  Out through a fever caused by its own
    heat,
But be much puzzled by a cough and cold, 171
  And find a quinsy very hard to treat;
Against all noble maladies he's bold,
  But vulgar illnesses don't like to meet,
Nor that a sneeze should interrupt his sigh,
Nor inflammations redden his blind eye.

XXIII

But worst of all is nausea, or a pain
  About the lower region of the bowels;
Love, who heroically breathes a vein,
  Shrinks from the application of hot towels,
And purgatives are dangerous to his reign, 181
  Sea-sickness death: his love was perfect,
    how else
Could Juan's passion, while the billows roar,
Resist his stomach, ne'er at sea before?

XXIV

The ship, call'd the most holy "Trinidada,"
  Was steering duly for the port Leghorn;
For there the Spanish family Moncada
  Were settled long ere Juan's sire was
    born:
They were relations, and for them he had a
  Letter of introduction, which the morn 190
Of his departure had been sent him by
His Spanish friends for those in Italy.

XXV

His suite consisted of three servants and
  A tutor, the licentiate Pedrillo,
Who several languages did understand,
  But now lay sick and speechless on his pil-
    low,
And, rocking in his hammock, long'd for
    land,
  His headache being increased by every bil-
    low;
And the waves oozing through the port-hole
    made
His berth a little damp, and him afraid. 200

XXVI

'Twas not without some reason, for the wind
  Increased at night, until it blew a gale;
And though 'twas not much to a naval mind,
  Some landsmen would have look'd a little
    pale,
For sailors are, in fact, a different kind:
  At sunset they began to take in sail,
For the sky show'd it would come on to
    blow,
And carry away, perhaps, a mast or so.

XXVII

At one o'clock the wind with sudden shift
  Threw the ship right into the trough of
    the sea, 210
Which struck her aft, and made an awkward
    rift,
  Started the stern-post, also shatter'd the
Whole of her stern-frame, and, ere she could
    lift
  Herself from out her present jeopardy,
The rudder tore away: 'twas time to sound
The pumps, and there were four feet water
    found.

XXVIII

One gang of people instantly was put
　Upon the pumps, and the remainder set
To get up part of the cargo, and what not;
　But they could not come at the leak as yet;
At last they did get at it really, but　　221
　Still their salvation was an even bet:
The water rush'd through in a way quite puzzling,
While they thrust sheets, shirts, jackets, bales of muslin,

XXIX

Into the opening; but all such ingredients
　Would have been vain, and they must have gone down,
Despite of all their efforts and expedients,
　But for the pumps: I'm glad to make them known
To all the brother tars who may have need hence,
　For fifty tons of water were upthrown　230
By them per hour, and they all had been undone,
But for the maker, Mr. Mann, of London.

XXX

As day advanced the weather seem'd to abate,
　And then the leak they reckon'd to reduce,
And keep the ship afloat, though three feet yet
　Kept two hand and one chain-pump still in use.
The wind blew fresh again: as it grew late
　A squall came on, and while some guns broke loose,
A gust—which all descriptive power transcends—
Laid with one blast the ship on her beam ends.　240

XXXI

There she lay, motionless, and seem'd upset;
　The water left the hold, and wash'd the decks,
And made a scene men do not soon forget;
　For they remember battles, fires, and wrecks,
Or any other thing that brings regret,
　Or breaks their hopes, or hearts, or heads, or necks;
Thus drownings are much talk'd of by the divers,
And swimmers, who may chance to be survivors.

XXXII

Immediately the masts were cut away,　249
　Both main and mizen: first the mizen went,
The main-mast follow'd; but the ship still lay
　Like a mere log, and baffled our intent.
Foremast and bowsprit were cut down, and they
　Eased her at last (although we never meant
To part with all till every hope was blighted),
And then with violence the old ship righted.

XXXIII

It may be easily supposed, while this
　Was going on, some people were unquiet,
That passengers would find it much amiss
　To lose their lives, as well as spoil their diet;
That even the able seaman, deeming his　261
　Days nearly o'er, might be disposed to riot,
As upon such occasions tars will ask
For grog, and sometimes drink rum from the cask.

XXXIV

There's nought, no doubt, so much the spirit calms
　As rum and true religion: thus it was,
Some plunder'd, some drank spirits, some sung psalms,
　The high wind made the treble, and as bass
The hoarse harsh waves kept time; fright cured the qualms
　Of all the luckless landsmen's sea-sick maws:
Strange sounds of wailing, blasphemy, devotion,　271
Clamour'd in chorus to the roaring ocean.

XXXV

Perhaps more mischief had been done, but for
　Our Juan, who, with sense beyond his years,
Got to the spirit-room, and stood before
　It with a pair of pistols; and their fears,
As if Death were more dreadful by his door
　Of fire than water, spite of oaths and tears,
Kept still aloof the crew, who, ere they sunk,
Thought it would be becoming to die drunk.

XXXVI

"Give us more grog," they cried, "for it will be
　All one an hour hence." Juan answer'd, "No!
'Tis true that death awaits both you and me,
　But let us die like men, not sink below　284

Like brutes:"—and thus his dangerous post
  kept he,
  And none liked to anticipate the blow;
And even Pedrillo, his most reverend tutor,
Was for some rum a disappointed suitor.

XXXVII

The good old gentleman was quite aghast,
  And made a loud and pious lamentation; 290
Repented all his sins, and made a last
  Irrevocable vow of reformation;
Nothing should tempt him more (this peril
  past)
  To quit his academic occupation,
In cloisters of the classic Salamanca,
To follow Juan's wake, like Sancho Panca.

XXXVIII

But now there came a flash of hope once more;
  Day broke, and the wind lull'd: the masts
    were gone;
The leak increased; shoals round her, but no
  shore,   299
  The vessel swam, yet still she held her own.
They tried the pumps again, and though be-
  fore
  Their desperate efforts seem'd all useless
    grown,
A glimpse of sunshine set some hands to
  bale—
The stronger pump'd, the weaker thrumm'd
  a sail.

XXXIX

Under the vessel's keel the sail was pass'd,
  And for the moment it had some effect;
But with a leak, and not a stick of mast,
  Nor rag of canvas, what could they expect?
But still 'tis best to struggle to the last,
  'Tis never too late to be wholly wreck'd: 310
And though 'tis true that man can only die
  once,
'Tis not so pleasant in the Gulf of Lyons.

XL

There winds and waves had hurl'd them, and
  from thence,
  Without their will, they carried them away;
For they were forced with steering to dispense,
  And never had as yet a quiet day

On which they might repose, or even com-
  mence
  A jurymast or rudder, or could say
The ship would swim an hour, which, by
  good luck,   319
Still swam—though not exactly like a duck.

XLI

The wind, in fact, perhaps, was rather less,
  But the ship labour'd so, they scarce could
    hope
To weather out much longer; the distress
  Was also great with which they had to
    cope
For want of water, and their solid mess
  Was scant enough: in vain the telescope
Was used—nor sail nor shore appear'd in
  sight,
Nought but the heavy sea, and coming night.

XLII

Again the weather threaten'd,—again blew
  A gale, and in the fore and after hold   330
Water appear'd; yet, though the people knew
  All this, the most were patient, and some
    bold,
Until the chains and leathers were worn
  through
  Of all our pumps:—a wreck complete she
    roll'd,
At mercy of the waves, whose mercies are
Like human beings during civil war.

XLIII

Then came the carpenter, at last, with tears
  In his rough eyes, and told the captain, he
Could do no more: he was a man in years,
  And long had voyaged through many a
    stormy sea,   340
And if he wept at length, they were not fears
  That made his eyelids as a woman's be,
But he, poor fellow, had a wife and children,
Two things for dying people quite bewilder-
  ing.

XLIV

The ship was evidently settling now
  Fast by the head; and, all distinction gone,
Some went to prayers again, and made a vow
  Of candles to their saints—but there were
    none

To pay them with; and some look'd o'er the
    bow;
    Some hoisted out the boats; and there was
      one   350
That begg'd Pedrillo for an absolution,
Who told him to be damn'd—in his confu-
    sion.

XLV

Some lash'd them in their hammocks; some
    put on
    Their best clothes, as if going to a fair;
Some cursed the day on which they saw the
    sun,
    And gnash'd their teeth, and howling, tore
      their hair;
And others went on as they had begun,
    Getting the boats out, being well aware
That a tight boat will live in a rough sea, 359
Unless with breakers close beneath her lee.

XLVI

The worst of all was, that in their condition,
    Having been several days in great distress,
'Twas difficult to get out such provision
    As now might render their long suffering
      less:
Men, even when dying, dislike inanition;
    Their stock was damaged by the weather's
      stress:
Two casks of biscuit, and a keg of butter,
Were all that could be thrown into the cutter.

XLVII

But in the long-boat they contrived to stow
    Some pounds of bread, though injured by
      the wet;   370
Water, a twenty-gallon cask or so;
    Six flasks of wine: and they contrived to
      get
A portion of their beef up from below,
    And with a piece of pork, moreover, met,
But scarce enough to serve them for a lunch-
    eon—
Then there was rum, eight gallons in a punch-
    eon.

XLVIII

The other boats, the yawl and pinnace, had
    Been stove in the beginning of the gale;
And the long-boat's condition was but bad,
    As there were but two blankets for a sail, 380

And one oar for a mast, which a young lad
    Threw in by good luck over the ship's rail;
And two boats could not hold, far less be
    stored,
To save one half the people then on board.

XLIX

'Twas twilight, and the sunless day went down
    Over the waste of waters; like a veil,
Which, if withdrawn, would but disclose the
    frown
    Of one whose hate is mask'd but to assail.
Thus to their hopeless eyes the night was
    shown,
    And grimly darkled o'er the faces pale, 390
And the dim desolate deep: twelve days had
    Fear
Been their familiar, and now Death was here.

L

Some trial had been making at a raft,
    With little hope in such a rolling sea,
A sort of thing at which one would have
    laugh'd,
    If any laughter at such times could be,
Unless with people who too much have
    quaff'd,
    And have a kind of wild and horrid glee,
Half epileptical, and half hysterical:—
Their preservation would have been a mir-
    acle.   400

LI

At half-past eight o'clock, booms, hencoops,
    spars,
    And all things, for a chance, had been cast
    loose
That still could keep afloat the struggling tars,
    For yet they strove, although of no great use:
There was no light in heaven but a few stars,
    The boats put off o'ercrowded with their
      crews;
She gave a heel, and then a lurch to port,
And, going down head foremost—sunk, in
    short.

LII

Then rose from sea to sky the wild farewell—
    Then shriek'd the timid, and stood still the
      brave—   410
Then some leap'd overboard with dreadful yell,
    As eager to anticipate their grave;

And the sea yawn'd around her like a hell,
   And down she suck'd with her the whirling
      wave,
Like one who grapples with his enemy,
And strives to strangle him before he die.

LIII

And first one universal shriek there rush'd,
   Louder than the loud ocean, like a crash
Of echoing thunder; and then all was hush'd,
   Save the wild wind and the remorseless dash
Of billows; but at intervals there gush'd,   421
   Accompanied with a convulsive splash,
A solitary shriek, the bubbling cry
Of some strong swimmer in his agony.

LIV

The boats, as stated, had got off before,
   And in them crowded several of the crew;
And yet their present hope was hardly more
   Than what it had been, for so strong it blew
There was slight chance of reaching any shore;
   And then they were too many, though so
     few—   430
Nine in the cutter, thirty in the boat,
Were counted in them when they got afloat.

LV

All the rest perish'd; near two hundred souls
   Had left their bodies; and what's worse,
     alas!
When over Catholics the ocean rolls,
   They must wait several weeks before a mass
Takes off one peck of purgatorial coals,
   Because, till people know what's come to
     pass,
They won't lay out their money on the dead—
It costs three francs for every mass that's
   said.   440

LVI

Juan got into the long-boat, and there
   Contrived to help Pedrillo to a place;
It seem'd as if they had exchanged their care,
   For Juan wore the magisterial face
Which courage gives, while poor Pedrillo's
   pair
   Of eyes were crying for their owner's case:
Battista, though (a name call'd shortly Tita),
Was lost by getting at some aqua-vita.

LVII

Pedro, his valet, too, he tried to save,
   But the same cause, conducive to his loss, 450
Left him so drunk, he jump'd into the wave,
   As o'er the cutter's edge he tried to cross,
And so he found a wine-and-watery grave;
   They could not rescue him although so
     close,
Because the sea ran higher every minute,
And for the boat—the crew kept crowding in
   it.

LVIII

A small old spaniel—which had been Don
   Jóse's,
   His father's, whom he loved, as ye may
     think,
For on such things the memory reposes
   With tenderness—stood howling on the
     brink,   460
Knowing, (dogs have such intellectual noses!)
   No doubt, the vessel was about to sink;
And Juan caught him up, and ere he stepp'd
Off threw him in, then after him he leap'd.

LIX

He also stuff'd his money where he could
   About his person, and Pedrillo's too,
Who let him do, in fact, whate'er he would,
   Not knowing what himself to say, or do,
As every rising wave his dread renew'd;
   But Juan, trusting they might still get
     through,   470
And deeming there were remedies for any
   ill,
Thus re-embark'd his tutor and his spaniel.

LX

'Twas a rough night, and blew so stiffly yet,
   That the sail was becalm'd between the
     seas,
Though on the wave's high top too much to
   set,
   They dared not take it in for all the breeze:
Each sea curl'd o'er the stern, and kept them
   wet,
   And made them bale without a moment's
     ease,
So that themselves as well as hopes were
   damp'd,
And the poor little cutter quickly swamp'd. 480

LXI

Nine souls more went in her: the long-boat
    still
  Kept above water, with an oar for mast,
Two blankets stitch'd together, answering ill
  Instead of sail, were to the oar made fast:
Though every wave roll'd menacing to fill,
  And present peril all before surpass'd,
They grieved for those who perish'd with the
    cutter,
And also for the biscuit-casks and butter.

LXII

The sun rose red and fiery, a sure sign
  Of the continuance of the gale: to run   490
Before the sea until it should grow fine,
  Was all that for the present could be
    done:
A few tea-spoonfuls of their rum and wine
  Were served out to the people, who begun
To faint, and damaged bread wet through the
    bags,
And most of them had little clothes but rags.

LXIII

They counted thirty, crowded in a space
  Which left scarce room for motion or exer-
    tion;
They did their best to modify their case,
  One half sate up, though numb'd with the
    immersion,   500
While t'other half were laid down in their
    place,
  At watch and watch; thus, shivering like
    the tertian
Ague in its cold fit, they fill'd their boat,
With nothing but the sky for a great coat.

LXIV

'Tis very certain the desire of life
  Prolongs it: this is obvious to physicians,
When patients, neither plagued with friends
    nor wife,
  Survive through very desperate conditions,
Because they still can hope, nor shines the
    knife   509
  Nor shears of Atropos before their visions:
Despair of all recovery spoils longevity,
And makes men's miseries of alarming brev-
    ity.

LXV

'Tis said that persons living on annuities
  Are longer lived than others,—God knows
    why,
Unless to plague the grantors,—yet so true
    it is,
  That some, I really think, *do* never die;
Of any creditors the worst a Jew it is,
  And *that's* their mode of furnishing sup-
    ply:
In my young days they lent me cash that
    way,
Which I found very troublesome to pay. 520

LXVI

'Tis thus with people in an open boat,
  They live upon the love of life, and bear
More than can be believed, or even thought,
  And stand like rocks the tempest's wear and
    tear;
And hardship still has been the sailor's lot,
  Since Noah's ark went cruising here and
    there;
She had a curious crew as well as cargo,
Like the first old Greek privateer, the Argo.

LXVII

But man is a carnivorous production,
  And must have meals, at least one meal a
    day;   530
He cannot live, like woodcocks, upon suction,
  But, like the shark and tiger, must have
    prey;
Although his anatomical construction
  Bears vegetables, in a grumbling way,
Your labouring people think beyond all
    question
Beef, veal, and mutton, better for digestion.

LXVIII

And thus it was with this our hapless crew;
  For on the third day there came on a calm,
And though at first their strength it might
    renew,
  And lying on their weariness like balm, 540
Lull'd them like turtles sleeping on the blue
  Of ocean, when they woke they felt a
    qualm,
And fell all ravenously on their provision,
Instead of hoarding it with due precision.

LXIX

The consequence was easily foreseen—
   They ate up all they had, and drank their
      wine,
In spite of all remonstrances, and then
   On what, in fact, next day were they to dine?
They hoped the wind would rise, these foolish
      men!
   And carry them to shore; these hopes were
      fine,   550
But as they had but one oar, and that brittle,
It would have been more wise to save their
      victual.

LXX

The fourth day came, but not a breath of air,
   And Ocean slumber'd like an unwean'd
      child:
The fifth day, and their boat lay floating there,
   The sea and sky were blue, and clear, and
      mild—
With their one oar (I wish they had had a pair)
   What could they do? and hunger's rage
      grew wild:
So Juan's spaniel, spite of his entreating,
Was kill'd, and portion'd out for present
      eating.   560

LXXI

On the sixth day they fed upon his hide,
   And Juan, who had still refused, because
The creature was his father's dog that died,
   Now feeling all the vulture in his jaws,
With some remorse received (though first
      denied)
   As a great favour one of the fore-paws,
Which he divided with Pedrillo, who
Devour'd it, longing for the other too.

LXXII

The seventh day, and no wind—the burning
      sun
   Blister'd and scorch'd, and, stagnant on the
      sea,   570
They lay like carcasses; and hope was none,
   Save in the breeze that came not: savagely
They glared upon each other—all was done,
   Water, and wine, and food,—and you
      might see
The longings of the cannibal arise
(Although they spoke not) in their wolfish
      eyes.

LXXIII

At length one whisper'd his companion, who
   Whisper'd another, and thus it went round,
And then into a hoarser murmur grew,   579
   An ominous, and wild, and desperate sound;
And when his comrade's thought each suf-
      ferer knew,
   'Twas but his own, suppress'd till now, he
      found:
And out they spoke of lots for flesh and blood,
And who should die to be his fellow's food.

LXXIV

But ere they came to this, they that day shared
   Some leathern caps, and what remain'd of
      shoes;
And then they look'd around them, and
      despair'd,
   And none to be the sacrifice would choose;
At length the lots were torn up, and prepared,
   But of materials that must shock the
      Muse—   590
Having no paper, for the want of better,
They took by force from Juan Julia's letter.

LXXV

Then lots were made, and mark'd, and mix'd,
      and handed
   In silent horror, and their distribution
Lull'd even the savage hunger which de-
      manded,
   Like the Promethean vulture, this pollu-
      tion;
None in particular had sought or plann'd it,
   'Twas nature gnaw'd them to this reso-
      lution,
By which none were permitted to be neuter—
And the lot fell on Juan's luckless tutor.   600

LXXVI

He but requested to be bled to death:
   The surgeon had his instruments, and bled
Pedrillo, and so gently ebb'd his breath,
   You hardly could perceive when he was
      dead.
He died as born, a Catholic in faith,
   Like most in the belief in which they're
      bred,
And first a little crucifix he kiss'd,
And then held out his jugular and wrist.

LXXVII

The surgeon, as there was no other fee,
  Had his first choice of morsels for his
    pains;   610
But being thirstiest at the moment, he
  Preferr'd a draught from the fast-flowing
    veins:
Part was divided, part thrown in the sea,
  And such things as the entrails and the
    brains
Regaled two sharks, who follow'd o'er the
    billow—
The sailors ate the rest of poor Pedrillo.

LXXVIII

The sailors ate him, all save three or four,
  Who were not quite so fond of animal food;
To these was added Juan, who, before
  Refusing his own spaniel, hardly could 620
Feel now his appetite increased much more;
  'Twas not to be expected that he should,
Even in extremity of their disaster,
Dine with them on his pastor and his master.

LXXIX

'Twas better that he did not; for, in fact,
  The consequence was awful in the extreme;
For they, who were most ravenous in the act,
  Went raging mad—Lord! how they did
    blaspheme!
And foam, and roll, with strange convulsions
    rack'd,
  Drinking salt-water like a mountain-
    stream;   630
Tearing, and grinning, howling, screeching,
    swearing,
And, with hyæna-laughter, died despairing.

LXXX

Their numbers were much thinn'd by this
    infliction,
  And all the rest were thin enough, Heaven
    knows:
And some of them had lost their recollection,
  Happier than they who still perceived their
    woes;
But others ponder'd on a new dissection,
  As if not warn'd sufficiently by those
Who had already perish'd, suffering madly,
For having used their appetites so sadly. 640

LXXXI

And next they thought upon the master's
    mate,
  As fattest; but he saved himself, because,
Besides being much averse from such a fate,
  There were some other reasons: the first
    was,
He had been rather indisposed of late;
  And that which chiefly proved his saving
    clause,
Was a small present made to him at Cadiz,
By general subscription of the ladies.

LXXXII

Of poor Pedrillo something still remain'd,
  But was used sparingly,—some were
    afraid,   650
And others still their appetites constrain'd,
  Or but at times a little supper made;
All except Juan, who throughout abstain'd,
  Chewing a piece of bamboo, and some lead:
At length they caught two boobies, and a
    noddy,
And then they left off eating the dead body.

LXXXIII

And if Pedrillo's fate should shocking be,
  Remember Ugolino condescends
To eat the head of his arch-enemy
  The moment after he politely ends   660
His tale: if foes be food in hell, at sea
  'Tis surely fair to dine upon our friends,
When shipwreck's short allowance grows too
    scanty,
Without being much more horrible than Dante.

LXXXIV

And the same night there fell a shower of rain,
  For which their mouths gaped, like the
    cracks of earth
When dried to summer dust; till taught by
    pain,
  Men really know not what good water's
    worth;
If you had been in Turkey or in Spain,
  Or with a famish'd boat's-crew had your
    berth,   670
Or in the desert heard the camel's bell,
You'd wish yourself where Truth is—in a
    well.

LXXXV

It pour'd down torrents, but they were no
  richer,
  Until they found a ragged piece of sheet,
Which served them as a sort of spongy
  pitcher,
  And when they deem'd its moisture was
  complete,
They wrung it out, and though a thirsty
  ditcher
  Might not have thought the scanty draught
  so sweet
As a full pot of porter, to their thinking
They ne'er till now had known the joys of
drinking.   680

LXXXVI

And their baked lips, with many a bloody
  crack,
  Suck'd in the moisture, which like nectar
  stream'd;
Their throats were ovens, their swoln tongues
  were black
  As the rich man's in hell, who vainly
  scream'd
To beg the beggar, who could not rain back
  A drop of dew, when every drop had
  seem'd
To taste of heaven—If this be true, indeed,
Some Christians have a comfortable creed.

LXXXVII

There were two fathers in this ghastly crew,
  And with them their two sons, of whom
  the one   690
Was more robust and hardy to the view,
  But he died early; and when he was
  gone,
His nearest messmate told his sire, who
  threw
  One glance at him, and said, "Heaven's will
  be done!
I can do nothing," and he saw him thrown
Into the deep without a tear or groan.

LXXXVIII

The other father had a weaklier child,
  Of a soft cheek, and aspect delicate;
But the boy bore up long, and with a mild
  And patient spirit held aloof his fate;   700

Little he said, and now and then he smiled,
  As if to win a part from off the weight
He saw increasing on his father's heart,
  With the deep deadly thought, that they
  must part.

LXXXIX

And o'er him bent his sire, and never raised
  His eyes from off his face, but wiped the
  foam
From his pale lips, and ever on him gazed,
  And when the wish'd-for shower at length
  was come,
And the boy's eyes, which the dull film half
  glazed,
  Brighten'd, and for a moment seem'd to
  roam,   710
He squeezed from out a rag some drops of rain
Into his dying child's mouth—but in vain.

XC

The boy expired—the father held the clay,
  And look'd upon it long, and when at last
Death left no doubt, and the dead burthen lay
  Stiff on his heart, and pulse and hope were
  past,
He watch'd it wistfully, until away
  'Twas borne by the rude wave wherein
  'twas cast;
Then he himself sunk down all dumb and
  shivering,
And gave no sign of life, save his limbs
  quivering.   720

XCI

Now overhead a rainbow, bursting through
  The scattering clouds, shone, spanning the
  dark sea,
Resting its bright base on the quivering blue;
  And all within its arch appear'd to be
Clearer than that without, and its wide hue
  Wax'd broad and waving, like a banner free,
Then changed like to a bow that's bent, and
  then
Forsook the dim eyes of these shipwreck'd
  men.

XCII

It changed, of course; a heavenly chameleon,
  The airy child of vapour and the sun,   730
Brought forth in purple, cradled in vermilion,
  Baptized in molten gold, and swathed in dun,

Glittering like crescents o'er a Turk's pavilion,
   And blending every colour into one,
Just like a black eye in a recent scuffle
(For sometimes we must box without the
   muffle).

XCIII

Our shipwreck'd seamen thought it a good
   omen—
   It is as well to think so, now and then;
'Twas an old custom of the Greek and Roman,
   And may become of great advantage
   when   740
Folks are discouraged; and most surely no
   men
Had greater need to nerve themselves again
Than these, and so this rainbow look'd like
   hope—
Quite a celestial kaleidoscope.

XCIV

About this time a beautiful white bird,
   Web-footed, not unlike a dove in size
And plumage (probably it might have err'd
   Upon its course), pass'd oft before their
   eyes,
And tried to perch, althought it saw and heard
   The men within the boat, and in this guise
It came and went, and flutter'd round them
   till   751
Night fell:—this seem'd a better omen still.

XCV

But in this case I also must remark,
   'Twas well this bird of promise did not
   perch,
Because the tackle of our shatter'd bark
   Was not so safe for roosting as a church;
And had it been the dove from Noah's ark,
   Returning there from her successful search,
Which in their way that moment chanced to
   fall,
They would have eat her, olive-branch and
   all.   760

XCVI

With twilight it again came on to blow,
   But not with violence; the stars shone out,
The boat made way; yet now they were so
   low,
   They knew not where nor what they were
   about;

Some fancied they saw land, and some said
   "No!"
   The frequent fog-banks gave them cause to
   doubt—
Some swore that they heard breakers, others
   guns,
And all mistook about the latter once.

XCVII

As morning broke, the light wind died away,
   When he who had the watch sung out and
   swore,   770
If 'twas not land that rose with the sun's ray,
   He wish'd that land he never might see
   more:
And the rest rubb'd their eyes, and saw a bay,
   Or thought they saw, and shaped their
   course for shore;
For shore it was, and gradually grew
Distinct, and high, and palpable to view.

XCVIII

And then of these some part burst into tears,
   And others, looking with a stupid stare,
Could not yet separate their hopes from fears,
   And seem'd as if they had no further care;
While a few pray'd—(the first time for some
   years)—   781
   And at the bottom of the boat three were
Asleep: they shook them by the hand and head,
And tried to awaken them, but found them
   dead.

XCIX

The day before, fast sleeping on the water,
   They found a turtle of the hawk's-bill kind,
And by good fortune, gliding softly, caught her,
   Which yielded a day's life, and to their
   mind
Proved even still a more nutritious matter,
   Because it left encouragement behind: 790
They thought that in such perils, more than
   chance
Had sent them this for their deliverance.

C

The land appear'd a high and rocky coast,
   And higher grew the mountains as they
   drew,
Set by a current, toward it: they were lost
   In various conjectures, for none knew

To what part of the earth they had been
    tost,
  So changeable had been the winds that
    blew;
Some thought it was Mount Ætna, some the
    highlands
Of Candia, Cyprus, Rhodes, or other is-
    lands.   800

CI

Meantime the current, with a rising gale,
  Still set them onwards to the welcome
    shore,
Like Charon's bark of spectres, dull and
    pale:
  Their living freight was now reduced to
    four,
And three dead, whom their strength could
    not avail
  To heave into the deep with those be-
    fore,
Though the two sharks still follow'd them,
    and dash'd
The spray into their faces as they splash'd.

CII

Famine, despair, cold, thirst, and heat, had
    done
  Their work on them by turns, and thinn'd
    them to   810
Such things a mother had not known her son
  Amidst the skeletons of that gaunt crew;
By night chill'd, by day scorch'd, thus one by
    one
  They perish'd, until wither'd to these
    few,
But chiefly by a species of self-slaughter,
In washing down Pedrillo with salt water.

CIII

As they drew nigh the land, which now was
    seen
  Unequal in its aspect here and there,
They felt the freshness of its growing green,
  That waved in forest-tops, and smooth'd
    the air,   820
And fell upon their glazed eyes like a screen
  From glistening waves, and skies so hot
    and bare—
Lovely seem'd any object that should sweep
Away the vast, salt, dread, eternal deep.

CIV

The shore look'd wild, without a trace of man,
  And girt by formidable waves; but they
Were mad for land, and thus their course
    they ran,
  Though right ahead the roaring breakers lay:
A reef between them also now began
  To show its boiling surf and bounding
    spray,   830
But finding no place for their landing better,
They ran the boat for shore,—and overset
    her.

CV

But in his native stream, the Guadalquivir,
  Juan to lave his youthful limbs was wont;
And having learnt to swim in that sweet
    river,
  Had often turn'd the art to some account:
A better swimmer you could scarce see ever,
  He could, perhaps, have pass'd the Helles-
    pont,
As once (a feat on which ourselves we prided)
Leander, Mr. Ekenhead, and I did.   840

CVI

So here, though faint, emaciated, and stark,
  He buoy'd his boyish limbs, and strove to
    ply
With the quick wave, and gain, ere it was dark,
  The beach which lay before him, high and
    dry:
The greatest danger here was from a shark,
  That carried off his neighbour by the
    thigh;
As for the other two, they could not swim,
So nobody arrived on shore but him.

CVII

Nor yet had he arrived but for the oar,   849
  Which, providentially for him, was wash'd
Just as his feeble arms could strike no more,
  And the hard wave o'erwhelm'd him as
    'twas dash'd
Within his grasp; he clung to it, and sore
  The waters beat while he thereto was
    lash'd;
At last, with swimming, wading, scrambling,
    he
Roll'd on the beach, half senseless, from the
    sea:

CVIII

There, breathless, with his digging nails he
    clung
Fast to the sand, lest the returning wave,
From whose reluctant roar his life he wrung,
    Should suck him back to her insatiate
    grave: 860
And there he lay, full length, where he was
    flung,
    Before the entrance of a cliff-worn cave,
With just enough of life to feel its pain,
And deem that it was saved, perhaps in vain.

CIX

With slow and staggering effort he arose,
    But sunk again upon his bleeding knee
And quivering hand; and then he look'd for
    those
    Who long had been his mates upon the sea;
But none of them appear'd to share his woes,
    Save one, a corpse, from out the famish'd
    three,   870
Who died two days before, and now had
    found
An unknown barren beach for burial-ground.

CX

And as he gazed, his dizzy brain spun fast.
    And down he sunk; and as he sunk, the sand
Swam round and round, and all his senses
    pass'd:
    He fell upon his side, and his stretch'd
    hand
Droop'd dripping on the oar (their jury-
    mast),
    And, like a wither'd lily, on the land
His slender frame and pallid aspect lay,
As fair a thing as e'er was form'd of clay. 880

CXI

How long in his damp trance young Juan lay
    He knew not, for the earth was gone for him,
And time had nothing more of night nor day
    For his congealing blood, and senses dim;
And how this heavy faintness pass'd away
    He knew not, till each painful pulse and
    limb,
And tingling vein, seem'd throbbing back to
    life,
For Death, though vanquish'd, still retired
    with strife.

CXII

His eyes he open'd, shut, again unclosed,
    For all was doubt and dizziness; he thought
He still was in the boat, and had but dozed, 891
    And felt again with his despair o'erwrought,
And wish'd it death in which he had reposed,
    And then once more his feelings back were
    brought,
And slowly by his swimming eyes was seen
A lovely female face of seventeen.

CXIII

'Twas bending close o'er his, and the small
    mouth
    Seem'd almost prying into his for breath;
And chafing him, the soft warm hand of youth
    Recall'd his answering spirits back from
    death;   900
And, bathing his chill temples, tried to soothe
    Each pulse to animation, till beneath
Its gentle touch and trembling care, a sigh
To these kind efforts made a low reply.

CXIV

Then was the cordial pour'd, and mantle flung
    Around his scarce-clad limbs; and the fair
    arm
Raised higher the faint head which o'er it
    hung;
    And her transparent cheek, all pure and
    warm,
Pillow'd his death-like forehead; then she
    wrung
    His dewy curls, long drench'd by every
    storm;   910
And watch'd with eagerness each throb that
    drew
A sigh from his heaved bosom—and hers, too.

CXV

And lifting him with care into the cave,
    The gentle girl, and her attendant,—one
Young, yet her elder, and of brow less grave,
    And more robust of figure—then begun
To kindle fire, and as the new flames gave
    Light to the rocks that roof'd them, which
    the sun
Had never seen, the maid, or whatsoe'er
She was, appear'd distinct, and tall, and
    fair.   920

CXVI

Her brow was overhung with coins of gold,
  That sparkled o'er the auburn of her hair,
Her clustering hair, whose longer locks were
    roll'd
  In braids behind; and though her stature
    were
Even of the highest for a female mould,
  They nearly reach'd her heel; and in her air
There was a something which bespoke com-
    mand,
As one who was a lady in the land.

CXVII

Her hair, I said, was auburn; but her eyes
  Were black as death, their lashes the same
    hue,   930
Of downcast length, in whose silk shadow lies
  Deepest attraction; for when to the view
Forth from its raven fringe the full glance
    flies,
  Ne'er with such force the swiftest arrow
    flew;
'Tis as the snake late coil'd, who pours his
  • length,
And hurls at once his venom and his strength.

CXVIII

Her brow was white and low, her cheek's
    pure dye
  Like twilight rosy still with the set sun;
Short upper lip—sweet lips! that make us
    sigh
  Ever to have seen such; for she was one
Fit for the model of a statuary   941
  (A race of mere impostors, when all's
    done—
I've seen much finer women, ripe and real,
Than all the nonsense of their stone ideal).

CXIX

I'll tell you why I say so, for 'tis just
  One should not rail without a decent cause:
There was an Irish lady, to whose bust
  I ne'er saw justice done, and yet she was
A frequent model; and if e'er she must
  Yield to stern Time and Nature's wrinkling
    laws,   950
They will destroy a face which mortal thought
Ne'er compass'd, nor less mortal chisel
    wrought.

CXX

And such was she, the lady of the cave:
  Her dress was very different from the
    Spanish,
Simpler, and yet of colours not so grave;
  For, as you know, the Spanish women
    banish
Bright hues when out of doors, and yet, while
    wave
  Around them (what I hope will never
    vanish)
The basquina and the mantilla, they
Seem at the same time mystical and gay.   960

CXXI

But with our damsel this was not the case:
  Her dress was many-colour'd, finely spun;
Her locks curl'd negligently round her face,
  But through them gold and gems profusely
    shone:
Her girdle sparkled, and the richest lace
  Flow'd in her veil, and many a precious
    stone
Flash'd on her little hand; but, what was
    shocking,
Her small snow feet had slippers, but no
    stocking.

CXXII

The other female's dress was not unlike,
  But of inferior materials: she   970
Had not so many ornaments to strike,
  Her hair had silver only, bound to be
Her dowry; and her veil, in form alike,
  Was coarser; and her air, though firm, less
    free;
Her hair was thicker, but less long; her eyes
As black, but quicker, and of smaller size.

CXXIII

And these two tended him, and cheer'd him
    both
  With food and raiment, and those soft
    attentions,
Which are—(as I must own)—of female
    growth,   979
  And have ten thousand delicate inventions:
They made a most superior mess of broth,
  A thing which poesy but seldom mentions,
But the best dish that e'er was cook'd since
    Homer's
Achilles order'd dinner for new comers.

CXXIV

I'll tell you who they were, this female pair, ·
  Lest they should seem princesses in disguise;
Besides, I hate all mystery, and that air   987
  Of clap-trap, which your recent poets prize;
And so, in short, the girls they really were
  They shall appear before your curious eyes,
Mistress and maid; the first was only daughter
Of an old man, who lived upon the water.

CXXV

A fisherman he had been in his youth,
  And still a sort of fisherman was he;
But other speculations were, in sooth,
  Added to his connexion with the sea,
Perhaps not so respectable, in truth:
  A little smuggling, and some piracy,
Left him, at last, the sole of many masters
Of an ill-gotten million of piastres.   1000

CXXVI

A fisher, therefore, was he,—though of men,
  Like Peter the Apostle,—and he fish'd
For wandering merchant vessels, now and
    then,
  And sometimes caught as many as he
    wish'd;
The cargoes he confiscated, and gain
  He sought in the slave-market too, and
    dish'd
Full many a morsel for that Turkish trade,
By which, no doubt, a good deal may be
    made.

CXXVII

He was a Greek, and on his isle had built
  (One of the wild and smaller Cyclades) 1010
A very handsome house from out his guilt,
  And there he lived exceedingly at ease.
Heaven knows what cash he got, or blood he
    spilt,
  A sad old fellow was he, if you please;
But this I know, it was a spacious building,
Full of barbaric carving, paint, and gilding.

CXXVIII

He had an only daughter, call'd Haidée,
  The greatest heiress of the Eastern Isles;
Besides, so very beautiful was she,   1019
  Her dowry was as nothing to her smiles:

Still in her teens, and like a lovely tree
  She grew to womanhood, and between
    whiles
Rejected several suitors, just to learn
How to accept a better in his turn.

CXXIX

And walking out upon the beach, below
  The cliff,—towards sunset, on that day she
    found,
Insensible,—not dead, but nearly so,—
  Don Juan, almost famish'd, and half
    drown'd;
But being naked, she was shock'd, you know,
  Yet deem'd herself in common pity bound,
As far as in her lay, "to take him in,   1031
A stranger" dying, with so white a skin.

CXXX

But taking him into her father's house
  Was not exactly the best way to save,
But like conveying to the cat the mouse,
  Or people in a trance into their grave;
Because the good old man had so much
    "νοῦς,"
  Unlike the honest Arab thieves so brave,
He would have hospitably cured the stranger
And sold him instantly when out of danger.

CXXXI

And therefore, with her maid, she thought it
    best   1041
  (A virgin always on her maid relies)
To place him in the cave for present rest:
  And when, at last, he open'd his black eyes,
Their charity increased about their guest;
  And their compassion grew to such a size,
It open'd half the turnpike gates to heaven—
(St. Paul says, 'tis the toll which must be
    given).

CXXXII

They made a fire,—but such a fire as they 1049
  Upon the moment could contrive with such
Materials as were cast up round the bay,—
  Some broken planks, and oars, that to the
    touch
Were nearly tinder, since so long they lay
  A mast was almost crumbled to a crutch;
But, by God's grace, here wrecks were in such
    plenty,
That there was fuel to have furnish'd twenty.

CXXXIII

He had a bed of furs, and a pelisse,
  For Haidée stripp'd her sables off to make
His couch; and, that he might be more at
  ease,
  And warm, in case by chance he should
    awake,   1060
They also gave a petticoat apiece,
  She and her maid,—and promised by day-
    break
To pay him a fresh visit, with a dish
For breakfast, of eggs, coffee, bread, and fish.

CXXXIV

And thus they left him to his lone repose:
  Juan slept like a top, or like the dead,
Who sleep at last, perhaps (God only knows),
  Just for the present; and in his lull'd head
Not even a vision of his former woes
  Throbb'd in accursed dreams, which some-
    times spread .   1070
Unwelcome visions of our former years,
Till the eye, cheated, opens thick with tears.

CXXXV

Young Juan slept all dreamless:—but the
  maid,
  Who smooth'd his pillow, as she left the
    den
Look'd back upon him, and a moment staid,
  And turn'd, believing that he call'd again.
He slumber'd; yet she thought, at least she
  said
  (The heart will slip, even as the tongue and
    pen),
He had pronounced her name—but she for-
  got
That at this moment Juan knew it not.   1080

CXXXVI

And pensive to her father's house she went,
  Enjoining silence strict to Zoe, who
Better than her knew what, in fact, she meant,
  She being wiser by a year or two:
A year or two's an age when rightly spent,
  And Zoe spent hers, as most women do,
In gaining all that useful sort of knowledge
Which is acquired in Nature's good old col-
  lege.

CXXXVII

The morn broke, and found Juan slumbering
  still   1089
  Fast in his cave, and nothing clash'd upon
His rest: the rushing of the neighbouring rill,
  And the young beams of the excluded sun,
Troubled him not, and he might sleep his fill;
  And need he had of slumber yet, for none
Had suffer'd more—his hardships were com-
    parative
To those related in my grand-dad's "Narra-
  tive."

CXXXVIII

Not so Haidée: she sadly toss'd and tumbled,
  And started from her sleep, and, turning o'er
Dream'd of a thousand wrecks, o'er which
  she stumbled,
  And handsome corpses strew'd upon the
    shore;   1100
And woke her maid so early that she grumbled,
  And call'd her father's old slaves up, who
    swore
In several oaths—Armenian, Turk, and
  Greek—
They knew not what to think of such a freak.

CXXXIX

But up she got, and up she made them get,
  With some pretence about the sun, that
    makes
Sweet skies just when he rises, or is set;
  And 'tis, no doubt, a sight to see when
    breaks
Bright Phœbus, while the mountains still are
  wet
  With mist, and every bird with him
    awakes,   1110
And night is flung off like a mourning suit
Worn for a husband,—or some other brute.

CXL

I say, the sun is a most glorious sight:
  I've seen him rise full oft, indeed of late
I have sat up on purpose all the night,
  Which hastens, as physicians say, one's fate;
And so all ye, who would be in the right
  In health and purse, begin your day to date
From daybreak, and when coffin'd at four-
  score
Engrave upon the plate, you rose at four. 1120

CXLI

And Haidée met the morning face to face;
  Her own was freshest, though a feverish
  flush
Had dyed it with the headlong blood, whose
  race
From heart to cheek is curb'd into a blush,
Like to a torrent which a mountain's base,
  That overpowers some Alpine river's rush,
Checks to a lake, whose waves in circles
  spread;
Or the Red Sea—but the sea is not red.

CXLII

And down the cliff the island virgin came,
  And near the cave her quick light footsteps
  drew,   1130
While the sun smiled on her with his first
  flame,
  And young Aurora kiss'd her lips with dew,
Taking her for a sister; just the same
  Mistake you would have made on seeing
  the two,
Although the mortal, quite as fresh and fair,
Had all the advantage, too, of not being air.

CXLIII

And when into the cavern Haidée stepp'd
  All timidly, yet rapidly, she saw
That like an infant Juan sweetly slept;
  And then she stopp'd, and stood as if in
  awe   1140
(For sleep is awful), and on tiptoe crept
  And wrapt him closer, lest the air, too raw,
Should reach his blood, then o'er him still as
  death
Bent, with hush'd lips, that drank his scarce-
  drawn breath.

CXLIV

And thus like to an angel o'er the dying
  Who die in righteousness, she lean'd; and
  there
All tranquilly the shipwreck'd boy was lying,
  As o'er him lay the calm and stirless air:
But Zoe the meantime some eggs was frying,
  Since, after all, no doubt the youthful
  pair   1150
Must breakfast, and betimes—lest they should
  ask it,
She drew out her provision from the basket.

CXLV

She knew that the best feelings must have
  victual,
  And that a shipwreck'd youth would hungry
  be;
Besides, being less in love, she yawn'd a
  little
  And felt her veins chill'd by the neigh-
  bouring sea;
And so, she cook'd their breakfast to a tittle;
  I can't say that she gave them any tea,
But there were eggs, fruit, coffee, bread, fish,
  honey,
With Scio wine,—and all for love, not money.
                                          1160

CXLVI

And Zoe, when the eggs were ready, and
  The coffee made, would fain have waken'd
  Juan;
But Haidée stopp'd her with her quick small
  hand,
  And without word, a sign her finger drew on
Her lip, which Zoe needs must understand;
  And, the first breakfast spoilt, prepared a
  new one,
Because her mistress would not let her break
That sleep which seem'd as it would ne'er
  awake.

CXLVII

For still he lay, and on his thin worn cheek
  A purple hectic play'd like dying day 1170
On the snow-tops of distant hills; the streak
  Of sufferance yet upon his forehead lay,
Where the blue veins look'd shadowy, shrunk,
  and weak;
  And his black curls were dewy with the
  spray,
Which weigh'd upon them yet, all damp and
  salt,
Mix'd with the stony vapours of the vault.

CXLVIII

And she bent o'er him, and he lay beneath,
  Hush'd as the babe upon its mother's
  breast,
Droop'd as the willow when no winds can
  breathe,
  Lull'd like the depth of ocean when at
  rest,   1180

Fair as the crowning rose of the whole wreath,
  Soft as the callow cygnet in its nest;
In short, he was a very pretty fellow,
Although his woes had turn'd him rather
  yellow.

CXLIX

He woke and gazed, and would have slept
  again,
  But the fair face which met his eyes forbade
Those eyes to close, though weariness and
  pain
  Had further sleep a further pleasure made;
For woman's face was never form'd in vain
  For Juan, so that even when he pray'd
He turn'd from grisly saints, and martyrs
  hairy,   1191
To the sweet portraits of the Virgin Mary.

CL

And thus upon his elbow he arose,
  And look'd upon the lady, in whose cheek
The pale contended with the purple rose,
  As with an effort she began to speak;
Her eyes were eloquent, her words would
  pose,
  Although she told him, in good modern
  Greek,
With an Ionian accent, low and sweet,
That he was faint, and must not talk, but
  eat.   1200

CLI

Now Juan could not understand a word,
  Being no Grecian; but he had an ear,
And her voice was the warble of a bird,
  So soft, so sweet, so delicately clear,
That finer, simpler music ne'er was heard;
  The sort of sound we echo with a tear,
Without knowing why—an overpowering
  tone,
Whence melody descends as from a throne.

CLII

And Juan gazed as one who is awoke
  By a distant organ, doubting if he be   1210
Not yet a dreamer, till the spell is broke
  By the watchman, or some such reality,
Or by one's early valet's cursed knock;
  At least it is a heavy sound to me,
Who like a morning slumber—for the night
Shows stars and women in a better light.

CLIII

And Juan, too, was help'd out from his dream,
  Or sleep, or whatsoe'er it was, by feeling
A most prodigious appetite; the steam
  Of Zoe's cookery no doubt was stealing
Upon his senses, and the kindling beam   1221
  Of the new fire, which Zoe kept up, kneel-
  ing,
To stir her viands, made him quite awake
And long for food, but chiefly a beef-steak.

CLIV

But beef is rare within these oxless isles;
  Goat's flesh there is, no doubt, and kid, and
  mutton,
And, when a holiday upon them smiles,
  A joint upon their barbarous spits they
  put on:
But this occurs but seldom, between whiles,
  For some of these are rocks with scarce a
  hut on;   1230
Others are fair and fertile, among which
This, though not large, was one of the most
  rich.

CLV

I say that beef is rare, and can't help thinking
  That the old fable of the Minotaur—
From which our modern morals, rightly
  shrinking,
  Condemn the royal lady's taste who wore
A cow's shape for a mask—was only (sinking
  The allegory) a mere type, no more,
That Pasiphae promoted breeding cattle,
To make the Cretans bloodier in battle. 1240

CLVI

For we all know that English people are
  Fed upon beef—I won't say much of beer,
Because 'tis liquor only, and being far
  From this my subject, has no business here;
We know, too, they are very fond of war,
  A pleasure—like all pleasures—rather dear;
So were the Cretans—from which I infer
That beef and battles both were owing to her.

CLVII

But to resume. The languid Juan raised
  His head upon his elbow, and he saw   1250
A sight on which he had not lately gazed,
  As all his latter meals had been quite raw,

Three or four things, for which the Lord he
    praised,
  And, feeling still the famish'd vulture gnaw,
He fell upon whate'er was offer'd, like
A priest, a shark, an alderman, or pike.

CLVIII

He ate, and he was well supplied; and she,
    Who watch'd him like a mother, would
    have fed
Him past all bounds, because she smiled to see
    Such appetite in one she had deem'd
    dead: 1260
But Zoe, being older than Haidée,
    Knew (by tradition, for she ne'er had read)
That famish'd people must be slowly nurst.
And fed by spoonfuls, else they always burst.

CLIX

And so she took the liberty to state,
    Rather by deeds than words, because the
    case
Was urgent, that the gentleman, whose fate
    Had made her mistress quit her bed to trace
The sea-shore at this hour, must leave his plate,
    Unless he wish'd to die upon the place—1270
She snatch'd it, and refused another morsel,
Saying, he had gorged enough to make a
    horse ill.

CLX

Next they—he being naked, save a tatter'd
    Pair of scarce decent trowsers—went to
    work,
And in the fire his recent rags they scatter'd,
    And dress'd him, for the present, like a
    Turk,
Or Greek—that is, although it not much
    matter'd,
    Omitting turban, slippers, pistols, dirk,—
They furnish'd him, entire, except some
    stitches,   1279
With a clean shirt, and very spacious breeches.

CLXI

And then fair Haidée tried her tongue at
    speaking,
  But not a word could Juan comprehend,
Although he listen'd so that the young Greek
    in
    Her earnestness would ne'er have made an
    end;

And, as he interrupted not, went eking
    Her speech out to her protégé and friend,
Till pausing at the last her breath to take,
She saw he did not understand Romaic.

CLXII

And then she had recourse to nods, and signs,
    And smiles, and sparkles of the speaking
    eye,   1290
And read (the only book she could) the lines
    Of his fair face, and found, by sympathy,
The answer eloquent, where the soul shines
    And darts in one quick glance a long reply;
And thus in every look she saw exprest
A world of words, and things at which she
    guess'd.

CLXIII

And now, by dint of fingers and of eyes,
    And words repeated after her, he took
A lesson in her tongue; but by surmise,
    No doubt, less of her language than her look:
As he who studies fervently the skies   1301
    Turns oftener to the stars than to his book,
Thus Juan learn'd his alpha beta better
From Haidée's glance than any graven letter.

CLXIV

'Tis pleasing to be school'd in a strange tongue
    By female lips and eyes—that is, I mean,
When both the teacher and the taught are
    young,
    As was the case, at least, where I have been;
They smile so when one's right, and when
    one's wrong
    They smile still more, and then there inter-
    vene   1310
Pressure of hands, perhaps even a chaste
    kiss;—
I learn'd the little that I know by this:

CLXV

That is, some words of Spanish, Turk, and
    Greek,
    Italian not at all, having no teachers;
Much English I cannot pretend to speak,
    Learning that language chiefly from its
    preachers,
Barrow, South, Tillotson, whom every week
    I study, also Blair, the highest reachers
Of eloquence in piety and prose—
I hate your poets, so read none of those. 1320

CLXVI

As for the ladies, I have nought to say,
  A wanderer from the British world of
    fashion,
Where I, like other "dogs, have had my day,"
  Like other men, too, may have had my
    passion—
But that, like other things, has pass'd away,
  And all her fools whom I *could* lay the lash
    on:
Foes, friends, men, women, now are nought
    to me
But dreams of what has been, no more to be.

CLXVII

Return we to Don Juan. He begun
  To hear new words, and to repeat them;
    but   1330
Some feelings, universal as the sun,
  Were such as could not in his breast be
    shut
More than within the bosom of a nun:
  He was in love,—as you would be, no
    doubt,
With a young benefactress,—so was she,
Just in the way we very often see.

CLXVIII

And every day by daybreak—rather early
  For Juan, who was somewhat fond of rest—
She came into the cave, but it was merely
  To see her bird reposing in his nest;   1340
And she would softly stir his locks so curly,
  Without disturbing her yet slumbering
    guest,
Breathing all gently o'er his cheek and mouth,
As o'er a bed of roses the sweet south.

CLXIX

And every morn his colour freshlier came,
  And every day help'd on his convalescence;
'Twas well, because health in the human
    frame
  Is pleasant, besides being true love's
    essence,
For health and idleness to passion's flame
  Are oil and gunpowder; and some good
    lessons   1350
Are also learnt from Ceres and from Bacchus,
Without whom Venus will not long attack us.

CLXX

While Venus fills the heart (without heart
    really
  Love, though good always, is not quite so
    good),
Ceres presents a plate of vermicelli,—
  For love must be sustain'd like flesh and
    blood,
While Bacchus pours out wine, or hands a
    jelly:
  Eggs, oysters, too, are amatory food;
But who is their purveyor from above
Heaven knows,—it may be Neptune, Pan, or
    Jove.   1360

CLXXI

When Juan woke he found some good things
    ready,
  A bath, a breakfast, and the finest eyes
That ever made a youthful heart less steady,
  Besides her maid's, as pretty for their size;
But I have spoken of all this already—
  And repetition's tiresome and unwise,—
Well—Juan, after bathing in the sea,
Came always back to coffee and Haidée.

CLXXII

Both were so young, and one so innocent,
  That bathing pass'd for nothing; Juan
    seem'd   1370
To her, as 'twere, the kind of being sent,
  Of whom these two years she had nightly
    dream'd,
A something to be loved, a creature meant
  To be her happiness, and whom she deem'd
To render happy: all who joy would win
Must share it,—Happiness was born a twin.

CLXXIII

It was such pleasure to behold him, such
  Enlargement of existence to partake
Nature with him, to thrill beneath his touch,
  To watch him slumbering, and to see him
    wake;   1380
To live with him for ever were too much;
  But then the thought of parting made her
    quake:
He was her own, her ocean-treasure, cast
Like a rich wreck—her first love, and her
    last.

CLXXIV

And thus a moon roll'd on, and fair Haidée
  Paid daily visits to her boy, and took
Such plentiful precautions, that still he
  Remain'd unknown within his craggy nook;
At last her father's prows put out to sea,
  For certain merchantmen upon the look,
Not as of yore to carry off an Io,   1391
But three Ragusan vessels bound for Scio.

CLXXV

Then came her freedom, for she had no
    mother,
  So that, her father being at sea, she was
Free as a married woman, or such other
  Female, as where she likes may freely pass,
Without even the encumbrance of a brother,
  The freest she that ever gazed on glass:
I speak of Christian lands in this comparison,
Where wives, at least, are seldom kept in
    garrison.   1400

CLXXVI

Now she prolong'd her visits and her talk
  (For they must talk), and he had learnt to say
So much as to propose to take a walk,—
  For little had he wander'd since the day
On which, like a young flower snapp'd from
    the stalk,
  Drooping and dewy on the beach he lay,—
And thus they walk'd out in the afternoon,
And saw the sun set opposite the moon.

CLXXVII

It was a wild and breaker-beaten coast,   1409
  With cliffs above, and a broad sandy shore,
Guarded by shoals and rocks as by an host,
  With here and there a creek, whose aspect
    wore
A better welcome to the tempest-tost;
  And rarely ceased the haughty billow's roar,
Save on the dead long summer days, which
    make
The outstretch'd ocean glitter like a lake.

CLXXVIII

And the small ripple spilt upon the beach
  Scarcely o'erpass'd the cream of your
    champagne,
When o'er the brim the sparkling bumpers
    reach,   1419
  That spring-dew of the spirit! the heart's rain!

Few things surpass old wine; and they may
    preach
  Who please,—the more because they preach
    in vain,—
Let us have wine and women, mirth and
    laughter,
Sermons and soda-water the day after.

CLXXIX

Man, being reasonable, must get drunk;
  The best of life is but intoxication:
Glory, the grape, love, gold, in these are sunk
  The hopes of all men, and of every nation;
Without their sap, how branchless were the
    trunk
  Of life's strange tree, so fruitful on occasion!
But to return,—Get very drunk; and when
You wake with headache, you shall see what
    then.   1432

CLXXX

Ring for your valet—bid him quickly bring
  Some hock and soda-water, then you'll
    know
A pleasure worthy Xerxes the great king;
  For not the blest sherbet, sublimed with
    snow,
Nor the first sparkle of the desert spring,
  Nor Burgundy in all its sunset glow,
After long travel, ennui, love, or slaughter,
Vie with that draught of hock and soda-
    water.   1440

CLXXXI

The coast—I think it was the coast that I
  Was just describing—Yes, it was the coast—
Lay at this period quiet as the sky,
  The sands untumbled, the blue waves untost,
And all was stillness, save the sea-bird's cry,
  And dolphin's leap, and little billow crost
By some low rock or shelve, that made it fret
Against the boundary it scarcely wet.

CLXXXII

And forth they wander'd, her sire being gone,
  As I have said, upon an expedition;   1450
And mother, brother, guardian, she had none,
  Save Zoe, who, although with due precision
She waited on her lady with the sun,
  Thought daily service was her only mission,
Bringing warm water, wreathing her long
    tresses,
And asking now and then for cast-off dresses.

CLXXXIII

It was the cooling hour, just when the rounded
  Red sun sinks down behind the azure hill,
Which then seems as if the whole earth it
    bounded,
    Circling all nature, hush'd, and dim, and
    still,   1460
With the far mountain-crescent half sur-
    rounded
  On one side, and the deep sea calm and chill,
Upon the other, and the rosy sky,
With one star sparkling through it like an eye.

CLXXXIV

And thus they wander'd forth, and hand in
  hand,
  Over the shining pebbles and the shells,
Glided along the smooth and harden'd sand,
  And in the worn and wild receptacles
Work'd by the storms, yet work'd as it were
  plann'd,
  In hollow halls, with sparry roofs and
  · cells,   1470
They turn'd to rest; and, each clasp'd by an
  arm,
Yielded to the deep twilight's purple charm.

CLXXXV

They look'd up to the sky, whose floating
  glow
  Spread like a rosy ocean, vast and bright;
They gazed upon the glittering sea below,
  Whence the broad moon rose circling into
  sight;
They heard the waves splash, and the wind so
  low,
  And saw each other's dark eyes darting light
Into each other—and, beholding this,
Their lips drew near, and clung into a kiss; 1480

CLXXXVI

A long, long kiss, a kiss of youth, and love,
  And beauty, all concentrating like rays
Into one focus, kindled from above;
  Such kisses as belong to early days,
Where heart, and soul, and sense, in concert
  move,
  And the blood's lava, and the pulse a blaze,
Each kiss a heart-quake,—for a kiss's strength,
I think it must be reckon'd by its length.

CLXXXVII

By length I mean duration; theirs endured
  Heaven knows how long—no doubt they
    never reckon'd;   1490
And if they had, they could not have secured
  The sum of their sensations to a second:
They had not spoken; but they felt allured,
  As if their souls and lips each other beckon'd,
Which, being join'd, like swarming bees they
  clung—
Their hearts the flowers from whence the
  honey sprung.

CLXXXVIII

They were alone, but not alone as they
  Who shut in chambers think it loneliness;
The silent ocean, and the starlight bay,
  The twilight glow, which momently grew
  less,   1500
The voiceless sands, and dropping caves, that
  lay
  Around them, made them to each other
  press,
As if there were no life beneath the sky
Save theirs, and that their life could never
  die.

CLXXXIX

They fear'd no eyes nor ears on that lone
  beach,
  They felt no terrors from the night; they
  were
All in all to each other; though their speech
  Was broken words, they *thought* a language
  there,—
And all the burning tongues the passions
  teach
  Found in one sigh the best interpreter 1510
Of nature's oracle—first love,—that all
Which Eve has left her daughters since her
  fall.

CXC

Haidée spoke not of scruples, ask'd no vows,
  Nor offer'd any; she had never heard
Of plight and promises to be a spouse,
  Or perils by a loving maid incurr'd;
She was all which pure ignorance allows,
  And flew to her young mate like a young
  bird,
And never having dreamt of falsehood, she
Had not one word to say of constancy.

CXCI

She loved, and was beloved—she adored, 1521
  And she was worshipp'd; after nature's
    fashion,
Their intense souls, into each other pour'd,
  If souls could die, had perish'd in that
    passion,—
But by degrees their senses were restored,
  Again to be o'ercome, again to dash on;
And, beating 'gainst *his* bosom, Haidée's heart
Felt as if never more to beat apart.

CXCII

Alas! they were so young, so beautiful, 1529
  So lonely, loving, helpless, and the hour
Was that in which the heart is always full,
  And, having o'er itself no further power,
Prompts deeds eternity cannot annul,
  But pays off moments in an endless shower
Of hell-fire—all prepared for people giving
Pleasure or pain to one another living.

CXCIII

Alas! for Juan and Haidée! they were
  So loving and so lovely—till then never,
Excepting our first parents, such a pair 1539
  Had run the risk of being damn'd for ever;
And Haidée, being devout as well as fair,
  Had, doubtless, heard about the Stygian
    river,
And hell and purgatory—but forgot
Just in the very crisis she should not.

CXCIV

They look upon each other, and their eyes
  Gleam in the moonlight; and her white
    arm clasps
Round Juan's head, and his around her lies
  Half buried in the tresses which it grasps;
She sits upon his knee, and drinks his sighs,
  He hers, until they end in broken gasps; 1550
And thus they form a group that's quite
    antique,
Half naked, loving, natural, and Greek.

CXCV

And when those deep and burning moments
    pass'd,
  And Juan sunk to sleep within her arms,
She slept not, but all tenderly, though fast,
  Sustain'd his head upon her bosom's
    charms;

And now and then her eye to heaven is
    cast,
  And then on the pale cheek her breast now
    warms,
Pillow'd on her o'erflowing heart, which
    pants
With all it granted, and with all it grants. 1560

CXCVI

An infant when it gazes on a light,
  A child the moment when it drains the
    breast,
A devotee when soars the Host in sight,
  An Arab with a stranger for a guest,
A sailor when the prize has struck in fight,
  A miser filling his most hoarded chest,
Feel rapture; but not such true joy are reaping
As they who watch o'er what they love while
    sleeping.

CXCVII

For there it lies so tranquil, so beloved,
  All that it hath of life with us is living; 1570
So gentle, stirless, helpless, and unmoved,
  And all unconscious of the joy 'tis giving;
All it hath felt, inflicted, pass'd, and proved,
  Hush'd into depths beyond the watcher's
    diving;
There lies the thing we love with all its errors
And all its charms, like death without its
    terrors.

CXCVIII

The lady watch'd her lover—and that hour
  Of Love's, and Night's, and Ocean's soli-
    tude,
O'erflowed her soul with their united power;
  Amidst the barren sand and rocks so
    rude   1580
She and her wave-worn love had made their
    bower,
  Where nought upon their passion could
    intrude,
And all the stars that crowded the blue
    space
Saw nothing happier than her glowing face.

CXCIX

Alas! the love of women! it is known
  To be a lovely and a fearful thing;
For all of theirs upon that die is thrown,
  And if 'tis lost, life hath no more to bring

To them but mockeries of the past alone,
 And their revenge is as the tiger's spring,1590
Deadly, and quick, and crushing; yet, as real
Torture is theirs, what they inflict they feel.

CC

They are right; for man, to man so oft unjust,
 Is always so to women; one sole bond
Awaits them, treachery is all their trust;
 Taught to conceal, their bursting hearts
  despond
Over their idol, till some wealthier lust
 Buys them in marriage—and what rests
  beyond?
A thankless husband, next a faithless lover,
Then dressing, nursing, praying, and all's
 over.   1600

CCI

Some take a lover, some take drams or prayers,
 Some mind their household, others dissi-
  pation,
Some run away, and but exchange their cares,
 Losing the advantage of a virtuous station;
Few changes e'er can better their affairs,
 Theirs being an unnatural situation,
From the dull palace to the dirty hovel:
Some play the devil, and then write a novel.

CCII

Haidée was Nature's bride, and knew not
 this:
 Haidée was Passion's child, born where
  the sun   1610
Showers triple light, and scorches even the
 kiss
 Of his gazelle-eyed daughters; she was one
Made but to love, to feel that she was his
 Who was her chosen: what was said or done
Elsewhere was nothing. She had nought to
 fear,
Hope, care, nor love beyond,—her heart beat
 here.

CCIII

And oh! that quickening of the heart, that
 beat!
 How much it costs us! yet each rising
  throb
Is in its cause as its effect so sweet,
 That Wisdom, ever on the watch to rob

Joy of its alchemy, and to repeat   1621
 Fine truths; even Conscience, too, has a
  tough job
To make us understand each good old maxim,
So good—I wonder Castlereagh don't tax
 'em.

CCIV

And now 'twas done—on the lone shore were
 plighted
 Their hearts; the stars, their nuptial torches,
  shed
Beauty upon the beautiful they lighted:
 Ocean their witness, and the cave their bed,
By their own feelings hallow'd and united,
 Their priest was Solitude, and they were
  wed: 1630
And they were happy, for to their young eyes
Each was an angel, and earth paradise.

CCV

Oh, Love! of whom great Cæsar was the suitor,
 Titus the master, Antony the slave,
Horace, Catullus, scholars, Ovid tutor,
 Sappho the sage blue-stocking, in whose
  grave
All those may leap who rather would be
 neuter—
 (Leucadia's rock still overlooks the wave)—
Oh, Love! thou art the very god of evil,
For, after all, we cannot call thee devil. 1640

CCVI

Thou mak'st the chaste connubial state pre-
 carious,
 And jestest with the brows of mightiest men:
Cæsar and Pompey, Mahomet, Belisarius,
 Have much employ'd the muse of history's
  pen:
Their lives and fortunes were extremely
 various,
 Such worthies Time will never see again;
Yet to these four in three things the same
 luck holds,
They all were heroes, conquerors, and
 cuckolds.

CCVII

Thou mak'st philosophers; there's Epicurus
 And Aristippus, a material crew!   1650
Who to immoral courses would allure us
 By theories quite practicable too;

If only from the devil they would insure us,
  How pleasant were the maxim (not quite
    new),
"Eat, drink, and love; what can the rest
    avail us?"
So said the royal sage Sardanapalus.

CCVIII

But Juan! had he quite forgotten Julia?
  And should he have forgotten her so soon?
I can't but say it seems to me most truly a
  Perplexing question; but, no doubt, the
    moon   1660
Does these things for us, and whenever
    newly a
Strong palpitation rises, 'tis her boon,
Else how the devil is it that fresh features
Have such a charm for us poor human
    creatures?

CCIX

I hate inconstancy—I loathe, detest,
  Abhor, condemn, abjure the mortal made
Of such quicksilver clay that in his breast
  No permanent foundation can be laid;
Love, constant love, has been my constant
    guest,
  And yet last night, being at a masquer-
    ade,   1670
I saw the prettiest creature, fresh from Milan,
Which gave me some sensations like a villain.

CCX

But soon Philosophy came to my aid,
  And whisper'd, "Think of every sacred
    tie!"
"I will, my dear Philosophy!" I said,
  "But then her teeth, and then, oh, Heaven!
    her eye!
I'll just inquire if she be wife or maid,
  Or neither—out of curiosity."
"Stop!" cried Philosophy, with air so Grecian
(Though she was masqued then as a fair
    Venetian);   1680

CCXI

"Stop!" so I stopp'd.—But to return: that
    which
  Men call inconstancy is nothing more
Than admiration due where nature's rich
  Profusion with young beauty covers o'er

Some favour'd object; and as in the niche
  A lovely statue we almost adore,
This sort of adoration of the real
Is but a heightening of the "beau ideal."

CCXII

'Tis the perception of the beautiful,
  A fine extension of the faculties,   1690
Platonic, universal, wonderful,
  Drawn from the stars, and filter'd through
    the skies,
Without which life would be extremely dull;
  In short, it is the use of our own eyes,
With one or two small senses added, just
To hint that flesh is form'd of fiery dust.

CCXIII

Yet 'tis a painful feeling, and unwilling,
  For surely if we always could perceive
In the same object graces quite as killing
  As when she rose upon us like an Eve, 1700
'Twould save us many a heart-ache, many a
    shilling
  (For we must get them any how, or grieve),
Whereas, if one sole lady pleased for ever,
How pleasant for the heart, as well as liver!

CCXIV

The heart is like the sky, a part of heaven,
  But changes night and day, too, like the sky;
Now o'er it clouds and thunder must be
    driven,
  And darkness and destruction as on high:
But when it hath been scorch'd, and pierced,
    and riven,   1709
  Its storms expire in water-drops; the eye
Pours forth at last the heart's blood turn'd to
    tears,
Which make the English climate of our years.

CCXV

The liver is the lazaret of bile,
  But very rarely executes its function,
For the first passion stays there such a while,
  That all the rest creep in and form a junction,
Like knots of vipers on a dunghill's soil,
  Rage, fear, hate, jealousy, revenge, com-
    punction,
So that all mischiefs spring up from this entrail,
Like earthquakes from the hidden fire call'd
    "central."   1720

CCXVI

In the mean time, without proceeding more
   In this anatomy, I've finish'd now
Two hundred and odd stanzas as before,
   That being about the number I'll allow
Each canto of the twelve, or twenty-four;
   And, laying down my pen, I make my bow,
Leaving Don Juan and Haidée to plead
For them and theirs with all who deign to
   read.

January, 1819

From CANTO III

THE ISLES OF GREECE

1

THE isles of Greece, the isles of Greece!
   Where burning Sappho loved and sung,
Where grew the arts of war and peace,
   Where Delos rose, and Phœbus sprung!
Eternal summer gilds them yet,
But all, except their sun, is set.

2

The Scian and the Teian muse,
   The hero's harp, the lover's lute,
Have found the fame your shores refuse:
   Their place of birth alone is mute   10
To sounds which echo further west
Than your sires' "Islands of the Blest."

3

The mountains look on Marathon—
   And Marathon looks on the sea;
And musing there an hour alone,
   I dream'd that Greece might still be free;
For standing on the Persians' grave,
I could not deem myself a slave.

4

A king sate on the rocky brow
   Which looks o'er sea-born Salamis;   20
And ships, by thousands, lay below,
   And men in nations;—all were his!
He counted them at break of day—
And when the sun set where were they?

5

And where are they? and where art thou,
   My country? On thy voiceless shore

The heroic lay is tuneless now—
   The heroic bosom beats no more!
And must thy lyre, so long divine,
Degenerate into hands like mine?   30

6

'Tis something, in the dearth of fame,
   Though link'd among a fetter'd race,
To feel at least a patriot's shame,
   Even as I sing, suffuse my face;
For what is left the poet here?
For Greeks a blush—for Greece a tear.

7

Must *we* but weep o'er days more blest?
   Must *we* but blush?—Our fathers bled.
Earth! render back from out thy breast
   A remnant of our Spartan dead!   40
Of the three hundred grant but three,
To make a new Thermopylæ!

8

What, silent still? and silent all?
   Ah! no;—the voices of the dead
Sound like a distant torrent's fall,
   And answer, "Let one living head,
But one arise,—we come, we come!"
'Tis but the living who are dumb.

9

In vain—in vain: strike other chords;
   Fill high the cup with Samian wine!   50
Leave battles to the Turkish hordes,
   And shed the blood of Scio's vine!
Hark! rising to the ignoble call—
How answers each bold Bacchanal!

10

You have the Pyrrhic dance as yet;
   Where is the Pyrrhic phalanx gone?
Of two such lessons, why forget
   The nobler and the manlier one?
You have the letters Cadmus gave—
Think ye he meant them for a slave?   60

11

Fill high the bowl with Samian wine!
   We will not think of themes like these!
It made Anacreon's song divine:
   He served—but served Polycrates—
A tyrant; but our masters then
Were still, at least, our countrymen.

12

The tyrant of the Chersonese
  Was freedom's best and bravest friend;
That tyrant was Miltiades!
  Oh! that the present hour would lend 70
Another despot of the kind!
Such chains as his were sure to bind.

13

Fill high the bowl with Samian wine!
  On Suli's rock, and Parga's shore,
Exists the remnant of a line
  Such as the Doric mothers bore;
And there, perhaps, some seed is sown,
The Heracleidan blood might own.

14

Trust not for freedom to the Franks—
  They have a king who buys and sells; 80
In native swords, and native ranks,
  The only hope of courage dwells:
But Turkish force, and Latin fraud,
Would break your shield, however broad.

15

Fill high the bowl with Samian wine!
  Our virgins dance beneath the shade—
I see their glorious black eyes shine;
  But gazing on each glowing maid,
My own the burning tear-drop laves, 89
To think such breasts must suckle slaves.

16

Place me on Sunium's marbled steep,
  Where nothing, save the waves and I,
May hear our mutual murmurs sweep;
  There, swan-like, let me sing and die:
A land of slaves shall ne'er be mine—
Dash down yon cup of Samian wine!

AVE MARIA

CI

T'our tale.—The feast was over, the slaves gone,
  The dwarfs and dancing girls had all retired;
The Arab lore and poet's song were done,
  And every sound of revelry expired;
The lady and her lover, left alone,
  The rosy flood of twilight's sky admired;—
Ave Maria! o'er the earth and sea,
That heavenliest hour of Heaven is worthiest
  thee!

CII

Ave Maria! blessed be the hour!
  The time, the clime, the spot, where I so
    oft 810
Have felt that moment in its fullest power
  Sink o'er the earth so beautiful and soft,
While swung the deep bell in the distant
    tower,
  Or the faint dying day-hymn stole aloft,
And not a breath crept through the rosy air,
And yet the forest leaves seem'd stirr'd with
  prayer.

CIII

Ave Maria! 'tis the hour of prayer!
  Ave Maria! 'tis the hour of love!
Ave Maria! may our spirits dare 819
  Look up to thine and to thy Son's above!
Ave Maria! oh that face so fair!
  Those downcast eyes beneath the Almighty
    dove—
What though 'tis but a pictured image strike,
That painting is no idol,—'tis too like.

CIV

Some kinder casuists are pleased to say,
  In nameless print—that I have no devo-
    tion;
But set those persons down with me to
  pray,
  And you shall see who has the properest
    notion
Of getting into heaven the shortest way;
  My altars are the mountains and the
    ocean, 830
Earth, air, stars,—all that springs from the
  great Whole,
Who hath produced, and will receive the soul.

CV

Sweet hour of twilight!—in the solitude
  Of the pine forest, and the silent shore
Which bounds Ravenna's immemorial wood,
  Rooted where once the Adrian wave flow'd
    o'er,
To where the last Cæsarean fortress stood,
  Evergreen forest! which Boccaccio's lore
And Dryden's lay made haunted ground to
  me, 839
How have I loved the twilight hour and
  thee!

CVI

The shrill cicalas, people of the pine,
  Making their summer lives one ceaseless
    song,
Were the sole echoes, save my steed's and
  mine,
  And vesper bell's that rose the boughs along;
The spectre huntsman of Onesti's line,
  His hell-dogs, and their chase, and the fair
    throng
Which learn'd from this example not to fly
From a true lover,—shadow'd my mind's
  eye.

CVII

Oh, Hesperus! thou bringest all good things—
  Home to the weary, to the hungry cheer,
To the young bird the parent's brooding
    wings,   851
  The welcome stall to the o'erlabour'd steer;
Whate'er of peace about our hearth stone
    clings,
  Whate'er our household gods protect of
    dear,
Are gather'd round us by thy look of rest;
Thou bring'st the child, too, to the mother's
  breast.

CVIII

Soft hour! which wakes the wish and melts the
  heart
  Of those who sail the seas, on the first day
When they from their sweet friends are torn
    apart;   859
  Or fills with love the pilgrim on his way
As the far bell of vesper makes him start,
  Seeming to weep the dying day's decay;
Is this a fancy which our reason scorns?
Ah! surely nothing dies but something mourns!

CIX

When Nero perish'd by the justest doom
  Which ever the destroyer yet destroy'd,
Amidst the roar of liberated Rome,
  Of nations freed, and the world overjoy'd,
Some hands unseen strew'd flowers upon his
    tomb: 869
  Perhaps the weakness of a heart not void
Of feeling for some kindness done, when
    power
Had left the wretch an uncorrupted hour.

1819–1820

THE VISION OF JUDGMENT

BY QUEVEDO REDIVIVUS

I

Saint Peter sat by the celestial gate:
  His keys were rusty, and the lock was
    dull,
So little trouble had been given of late;
  Not that the place by any means was full,
But since the Gallic era "eighty-eight"
  The devils had ta'en a longer, stronger
    pull,
And "a pull altogether," as they say
At sea—which drew most souls another
    way.

II

The angels all were singing out of tune,
  And hoarse with having little else to do, 10
Excepting to wind up the sun and moon,
  Or curb a runaway young star or two,
Or wild colt of a comet, which too soon
  Broke out of bounds o'er th' ethereal blue,
Splitting some planet with its playful tail,
As boats are sometimes by a wanton whale.

III

The guardian seraphs had retired on high,
  Finding their charges past all care below;
Terrestrial business fill'd nought in the sky
  Save the recording angel's black bureau; 20
Who found, indeed, the facts to multiply
  With such rapidity of vice and woe,
That he had stripp'd off both his wings in
    quills,
And yet was in arrear of human ills.

IV

His business so augmented of late years,
  That he was forced, against his will no
    doubt,
(Just like those cherubs, earthly ministers,)
  For some resource to turn himself about,
And claim the help of his celestial peers,
  To aid him ere he should be quite worn
    out   30
By the increased demand for his remarks:
Six angels and twelve saints were named his
  clerks.

V

This was a handsome board—at least for
    heaven;
    And yet they had even then enough to do,
So many conquerors' cars were daily driven,
    So many kingdoms fitted up anew;
Each day too slew its thousands six or seven,
    Till at the crowning carnage, Waterloo,
They threw their pens down in divine dis-
    gust—
The page was so besmear'd with blood and
    dust.   40

VI

This by the way; 'tis not mine to record
    What angels shrink from: even the very
    devil
On this occasion his own work abhorr'd,
    So surfeited with the infernal revel:
Though he himself had sharpen'd every sword,
    It almost quench'd his innate thirst of evil.
(Here Satan's sole good work deserves in-
    sertion—
'Tis, that he has both generals in reversion.)

VII

Let's skip a few short years of hollow peace,
    Which peopled earth no better, hell as
    wont,   50
And heaven none—they form the tyrant's
    lease,
    With nothing but new names subscribed
    upon 't;
'Twill one day finish: meantime they increase,
    "With seven heads and ten horns," and all
    in front,
Like Saint John's foretold beast; but ours are
    born
Less formidable in the head than horn.

VIII

In the first year of freedom's second dawn
    Died George the Third; although no tyrant,
    one
Who shielded tyrants, till each sense with-
    drawn
    Left him nor mental nor external sun: 60
A better farmer ne'er brush'd dew from lawn,
    A worse king never left a realm undone!
He died—but left his subjects still behind,
One half as mad—and t'other no less blind.

IX

He died! his death made no great stir on earth:
    His burial made some pomp; there was pro-
    fusion
Of velvet, gilding, brass, and no great dearth
    Of aught but tears—save those shed by
    collusion.
For these things may be bought at their true
    worth;
    Of elegy there was the due infusion—   70
Bought also; and the torches, cloaks, and
    banners,
Heralds, and relics of old Gothic manners,

X

Form'd a sepulchral melodrame. Of all
    The fools who flock'd to swell or see the
    show,
Who cared about the corpse? The funeral
    Made the attraction, and the black the woe.
There throbb'd not there a thought which
    pierced the pall;
    And when the gorgeous coffin was laid low,
It seem'd the mockery of hell to fold
The rottenness of eighty years in gold.   80

XI

So mix his body with the dust! It might
    Return to what it *must* far sooner, were
The natural compound left alone to fight
    Its way back into earth, and fire, and air;
But the unnatural balsams merely blight
    What nature made him at his birth, as bare
As the mere million's base unmummied clay—
Yet all his spices but prolong decay.

XII

He's dead—and upper earth with him has done;
    He's buried; save the undertaker's bill,   90
Or lapidary scrawl, the world is gone
    For him, unless he left a German will:
But where's the proctor who will ask his son?
    In whom his qualities are reigning still,
Except that household virtue, most uncom-
    mon,
Of constancy to a bad, ugly woman.

XIII

"God save the king!" It is a large economy
    In God to save the like; but if he will
Be saving, all the better; for not one am I
    Of those who think damnation better still:

I hardly know too if not quite alone am I 101
  In this small hope of bettering future ill
By circumscribing, with some slight restriction,
The eternity of hell's hot jurisdiction.

XIV

I know this is unpopular; I know
  'Tis blasphemous; I know one may be damn'd
For hoping no one else may e'er be so;
  I know my catechism; I know we're cramm'd
With the best doctrines till we quite o'erflow;
  I know that all save England's church have shamm'd, 110
And that the other twice two hundred churches
And synagogues have made a *damn'd* bad purchase.

XV

God help us all! God help me too! I am,
  God knows, as helpless as the devil can wish,
And not a whit more difficult to damn,
  Than is to bring to land a late-hook'd fish,
Or to the butcher to purvey the lamb;
  Not that I'm fit for such a noble dish,
As one day will be that immortal fry
Of almost everybody born to die. 120

XVI

Saint Peter sat by the celestial gate,
  And nodded o'er his keys; when, lo! there came
A wondrous noise he had not heard of late—
  A rushing sound of wind, and stream, and flame;
In short, a roar of things extremely great,
  Which would have made aught save a saint exclaim;
But he, with first a start and then a wink,
Said, "There's another star gone out, I think!"

XVII

But ere he could return to his repose,
  A cherub flapp'd his right wing o'er his eyes— 130
At which St. Peter yawn'd, and rubb'd his nose:
  "Saint porter," said the angel, "prithee rise!"

Waving a goodly wing, which glow'd, as glows
  An earthly peacock's tail, with heavenly dyes:
To which the saint replied, "Well, what's the matter?
  Is Lucifer come back with all this clatter?"

XVIII

"No," quoth the cherub; "George the Third is dead."
  "And who *is* George the Third?" replied the apostle:
"*What George? what Third?*" "The king of England," said
  The angel. "Well! he won't find kings to jostle 140
Him on his way; but does he wear his head?
  Because the last we saw here had a tussle,
And ne'er would have got into heaven's good graces,
Had he not flung his head in all our faces.

XIX

"He was, if I remember, king of France:
  That head of his, which could not keep a crown
On earth, yet ventured in my face to advance
  A claim to those of martyrs—like my own:
If I had had my sword, as I had once
  When I cut ears off, I had cut him down; 150
But having but my *keys*, and not my brand,
I only knock'd his head from out his hand.

XX

"And then he set up such a headless howl,
  That all the saints came out and took him in;
And there he sits by St. Paul, cheek by jowl;
  That fellow Paul—the parvenù! The skin
Of St. Bartholomew, which makes his cowl
  In heaven, and upon earth redeem'd his sin,
So as to make a martyr, never sped
Better than did this weak and wooden head. 160

XXI

"But had it come up here upon its shoulders,
  There would have been a different tale to tell:
The fellow-feeling in the saint's beholders
  Seems to have acted on them like a spell,

And so this very foolish head heaven solders
  Back on its trunk: it may be very well,
And seems the custom here to overthrow
Whatever has been wisely done below."

XXII

The angel answer'd, "Peter! do not pout:
  The king who comes has head and all
    entire,   170
And never knew much what it was about—
  He did as doth the puppet—by its wire,
And will be judged like all the rest, no doubt:
  My business and your own is not to inquire
Into such matters, but to mind our cue—
Which is to act as we are bid to do."

XXIII

While thus they spake, the angelic caravan,
  Arriving like a rush of mighty wind,
Cleaving the fields of space, as doth the swan
  Some silver stream (say Ganges, Nile, or
    Inde,   180
Or Thames, or Tweed), and 'midst them an
    old man
  With an old soul, and both extremely blind,
Halted before the gate, and in his shroud
Seated their fellow traveller on a cloud.

XXIV

But bringing up the rear of this bright host
  A Spirit of a different aspect waved
His wings, like thunder-clouds above some
    coast
  Whose barren beach with frequent wrecks
    is paved;
His brow was like the deep when tempest-
    toss'd;
  Fierce and unfathomable thoughts engraved
Eternal wrath on his immortal face,   191
And *where* he gazed a gloom pervaded space.

XXV

As he drew near, he gazed upon the gate
  Ne'er to be enter'd more by him or Sin,
With such a glance of supernatural hate,
  As made Saint Peter wish himself within;
He patter'd with his keys at a great rate,
  And sweated through his apostolic skin:
Of course his perspiration was but ichor,
Or some such other spiritual liquor.   200

XXVI

The very cherubs huddled all together,
  Like birds when soars the falcon; and they felt
A tingling to the tip of every feather,
  And form'd a circle like Orion's belt
Around their poor old charge; who scarce
    knew whither
  His guards had led him, though they gently
    dealt
With royal manes (for by many stories,
And true, we learn the angels all are Tories).

XXVII

As things were in this posture, the gate flew
  Asunder, and the flashing of its hinges 210
Flung over space an universal hue
  Of many-colour'd flame, until its tinges
Reach'd even our speck of earth, and made a new
  Aurora borealis spread its fringes
O'er the North Pole; the same seen, when ice-
    bound,
By Captain Parry's crew, in "Melville's
    Sound." *unsuccesse try to discover*

XXVIII *northwest pass*

And from the gate thrown open issued beaming
  A beautiful and mighty Thing of Light,
Radiant with glory, like a banner streaming
  Victorious from some world-o'erthrowing
    fight: 220
My poor comparisons must needs be teeming
  With earthly likenesses, for here the night
Of clay obscures our best conceptions, saving
Johanna Southcote, or Bob Southey raving.

XXIX

'Twas the archangel Michael; all men know
  The make of angels and archangels, since
There's scarce a scribbler has not one to show,
  From the fiends' leader to the angels' prince;
There also are some altar-pieces, though
  I really can't say that they much evince 230
One's inner notions of immortal spirits;
But let the connoisseurs explain *their* merits.

XXX

Michael flew forth in glory and in good;
  A goodly work of him from whom all glory
And good arise; the portal past—he stood;
  Before him the young cherubs and saints
    hoary—

(I say *young*, begging to be understood
  By looks, not years; and should be very
    sorry
To state, they were not older than St. Peter,
But merely that they seem'd a little sweeter).

XXXI

The cherubs and the saints bow'd down be-
    fore   241
  That arch-angelic hierarch, the first
Of essences angelical, who wore
  The aspect of a god; but this ne'er nursed
Pride in his heavenly bosom, in whose core
  No thought, save for his Master's service,
    durst
Intrude, however glorified and high;
He knew him but the viceroy of the sky.

XXXII

He and the sombre, silent Spirit met—
  They knew each other both for good and
    ill;   250
Such was their power, that neither could for-
    get
  His former friend and future foe; but still
There was a high, immortal, proud regret
  In either's eye, as if 'twere less their will
Than destiny to make the eternal years
Their date of war, and their "champ clos"
    the spheres.

XXXIII

But here they were in neutral space: we know
  From Job, that Satan hath the power to pay
A heavenly visit thrice a year or so;
  And that the "sons of God," like those of
    clay,   260
Must keep him company; and we might show
  From the same book, in how polite a way
The dialogue is held between the Powers
Of Good and Evil—but 'twould take up
  hours.

XXXIV

And this is not a theologic tract,
  To prove with Hebrew and with Arabic,
If Job be allegory or a fact,
  But a true narrative; and thus I pick
From out the whole but such and such an act
  As sets aside the slightest thought of trick.
'Tis every tittle true, beyond suspicion, 271
And accurate as any other vision.

XXXV

The spirits were in neutral space, before
  The gate of heaven; like eastern thresholds
    is
The place where Death's grand cause is argued
    o'er,
  And souls despatch'd to that world or to
    this;
And therefore Michael and the other wore
  A civil aspect: though they did not kiss,
Yet still between his Darkness and his Bright-
    ness
There pass'd a mutual glance of great polite-
    ness.   280

XXXVI

The Archangel bow'd, not like a modern beau,
  But with a graceful Oriental bend,
Pressing one radiant arm just where below
  The heart in good men is supposed to tend;
He turn'd as to an equal, not too low,
  But kindly; Satan met his ancient friend
With more hauteur, as might an old Castilian
Poor noble meet a mushroom rich civilian.

XXXVII

He merely bent his diabolic brow
  An instant; and then raising it, he stood 290
In act to assert his right or wrong, and show
  Cause why King George by no means could
    or should
Make out a case to be exempt from woe
  Eternal, more than other kings, endued
With better sense and hearts, whom history
  mentions,
Who long have "paved hell with their good
  intentions."

XXXVIII

Michael began: "What wouldst thou with this
  man,
  Now dead, and brought before the Lord?
    What ill
Hath he wrought since his mortal race began,
  That thou canst claim him? Speak! and do
    thy will,   300
If it be just: if in this earthly span
  He hath been greatly failing to fulfil
His duties as a king and mortal, say,
And he is thine; if not, let him have way."

XXXIX

"Michael!" replied the Prince of Air, "even
  here,
  Before the Gate of him thou servest, must
I claim my subject: and will make appear
That as he was my worshipper in dust,
So shall he be in spirit, although dear
  To thee and thine, because nor wine nor
    lust   310
Were of his weaknesses; yet on the throne
He reign'd o'er millions to serve me alone.

XL

"Look to *our* earth, or rather *mine;* it was,
  Once, more thy master's: but I triumph not
In this poor planet's conquest; nor, alas!
  Need he thou servest envy me my lot:
With all the myriads of bright worlds which
    pass
  In worship round him, he may have forgot
Yon weak creation of such paltry things:
I think few worth damnation save their
    kings,—   320

XLI

"And these but as a kind of quit-rent, to
  Assert my right as lord: and even had
I such an inclination, 'twere (as you
  Well know) superfluous; they are grown
    so bad,
That hell has nothing better left to do
  Than leave them to themselves: so much
    more mad
And evil by their own internal curse,
Heaven cannot make them better, nor I
    worse.

XLII

"Look to the earth, I said, and say again:
  When this old, blind, mad, helpless, weak,
    poor worm   330
Began in youth's first bloom and flush to
    reign,
  The world and he both wore a different
    form,
And much of earth and all the watery plain
  Of ocean call'd him king: through many a
    storm
His isles had floated on the abyss of time;
For the rough virtues chose them for their
    clime.

XLIII

"He came to his sceptre young; he leaves it
    old:
  Look to the state in which he found his
    realm,
And left it; and his annals too behold,
  How to a minion first he gave the helm; 340
How grew upon his heart a thirst for gold,
  The beggar's vice, which can but over-
    whelm
The meanest hearts; and for the rest, but
    glance
Thine eye along America and France.

XLIV

"'Tis true, he was a tool from first to last
  (I have the workmen safe); but as a tool
So let him be consumed. From out the past
  Of ages, since mankind have known the
    rule
Of monarchs—from the bloody rolls amass'd
  Of sin and slaughter—from the Cæsar's
    school,   350
Take the worst pupil; and produce a reign
More drench'd with gore, more cumber'd with
    the slain.

XLV

"He ever warr'd with freedom and the free:
  Nations as men, home subjects, foreign
    foes,
So that they utter'd the word 'Liberty!'
  Found George the Third their first oppo-
    nent. Whose
History was ever stain'd as his will be
  With national and individual woes?
I grant his household abstinence; I grant
His neutral virtues, which most monarchs
    want;   360

XLVI

"I know he was a constant consort; own
  He was a decent sire, and middling lord.
All this is much, and most upon a throne;
  As temperance, if at Apicius' board,
Is more than at an anchorite's supper shown.
  I grant him all the kindest can accord;
And this was well for him, but not for
    those
Millions who found him what oppression
    chose.

XLVII

"The New World shook him off; the Old
    yet groans   369
  Beneath what he and his prepared, if not
Completed: he leaves heirs on many thrones
To all his vices, without what begot
Compassion for him—his tame virtues; drones
  Who sleep, or despots who have now forgot
A lesson which shall be re-taught them, wake
Upon the thrones of earth; but let them quake!

XLVIII

"Five millions of the primitive, who hold
  The faith which makes ye great on earth,
    implored
A *part* of that vast *all* they held of old,— 379
  Freedom to worship—not alone your Lord,
Michael, but you, and you, Saint Peter! Cold
  Must be your souls, if you have not abhorr'd
The foe to Catholic participation
In all the license of a Christian nation.

XLIX

"True! he allow'd them to pray God; but as
  A consequence of prayer, refused the law
Which would have placed them upon the
    same base
  With those who did not hold the saints in
    awe."   388
But here Saint Peter started from his place,
  And cried, "You may the prisoner withdraw:
Ere heaven shall ope her portals to this Guelph,
While I am guard, may I be damn'd myself!

L

"Sooner will I with Cerberus exchange
  My office (and *his* is no sinecure)
Than see this royal Bedlam bigot range
  The azure fields of heaven, of that be sure!"
"Saint!" replied Satan, "you do well to avenge
  The wrongs he made your satellites endure;
And if to this exchange you should be given,
I'll try to coax *our* Cerberus up to heaven!" 400

LI

Here Michael interposed: "Good saint! and
    devil!
  Pray, not so fast; you both outrun discretion.
Saint Peter! you were wont to be more civil!
  Satan! excuse this warmth of his expression,

And condescension to the vulgar's level:
  Even saints sometimes forget themselves in
    session.
Have you got more to say?"—"No."—"If
    you please,
I'll trouble you to call your witnesses."

LII

Then Satan turn'd and waved his swarthy
    hand,
  Which stirr'd with its electric qualities 410
Clouds farther off than we can understand,
  Although we find him sometimes in our
    skies;
Infernal thunder shook both sea and land
  In all the planets, and hell's batteries
Let off the artillery, which Milton mentions
As one of Satan's most sublime inventions.

LIII

This was a signal unto such damn'd souls
  As have the privilege of their damnation
Extended far beyond the mere controls
  Of worlds past, present, or to come; no
    station   420
Is theirs particularly in the rolls
  Of hell assign'd; but where their inclination
Or business carries them in search of game,
They may range freely—being damn'd the
    same.

LIV

They're proud of this—as very well they
    may,
  It being a sort of knighthood, or gilt key
Stuck in their loins; or like to an "entré"
  Up the back stairs, or such free-masonry.
I borrow my comparisons from clay,
  Being clay myself. Let not those spirits
    be   430
Offended with such base low likenesses;
We know their posts are nobler far than these.

LV

When the great signal ran from heaven to
    hell—
  About ten million times the distance reck-
    on'd
From our sun to its earth, as we can tell
  How much time it takes up, even to a
    second,

For every ray that travels to dispel
  The fogs of London, through which, dimly
    beacon'd,
The weathercocks are gilt some thrice a year,
If that the *summer* is not too severe: 440

LVI

I say that I can tell—'twas half a minute;
  I know the solar beams take up more time
Ere, pack'd up for their journey, they begin it;
  But then their telegraph is less sublime,
And if they ran a race, they would not win it
  'Gainst Satan's couriers bound for their own
    clime.
The sun takes up some years for every ray
To reach its goal—the devil not half a day.

LVII

Upon the verge of space, about the size
  Of half-a-crown, a little speck appear'd 450
  In the Ægean, ere a squall); it near'd,
  (I've seen a something like it in the skies
And, growing bigger, took another guise;
  Like an aërial ship it tack'd, and steer'd,
Or *was* steer'd (I am doubtful of the gram-
    mar
Of the last phrase, which makes the stanza
    stammer;—

LVIII

But take your choice): and then it grew a
    cloud;
  And so it was—a cloud of witnesses.
But such a cloud! No land e'er saw a crowd
  Of locusts numerous as the heavens saw
    these;   460
They shadow'd with their myriads space; their
    loud
  And varied cries were like those of wild
    geese
(If nations may be liken'd to a goose),
And realised the phrase of "hell broke loose."

LIX

Here crash'd a sturdy oath of stout John
    Bull,
  Who damn'd away his eyes as heretofore:
There Paddy brogued "By Jasus!"—"What's
    your wull?"
  The temperate Scot exclaim'd: the French
    ghost swore

In certain terms I shan't translate in full,
  As the first coachman will; and 'midst the
    war,   470
The voice of Jonathan was heard to express,
"*Our* president is going to war, I guess."

LX

Besides there were the Spaniard, Dutch, and
    Dane;
  In short, an universal shoal of shades,
From Otaheite's isle to Salisbury Plain,
  Of all climes and professions, years and
    trades,
Ready to swear against the good king's
    reign,
  Bitter as clubs in cards are against spades:
All summon'd by this grand "subpœna," to
Try if kings mayn't be damn'd like me or
    you.   480

LXI

When Michael saw this host, he first grew
    pale,
  As angels can; next, like Italian twilight,
He turn'd all colours—as a peacock's tail,
  Or sunset streaming through a Gothic sky-
    light
In some old abbey, or a trout not stale,
  Or distant lightning on the horizon *by* night,
Or a fresh rainbow, or a grand review
Of thirty regiments in red, green, and blue.

LXII

Then he address'd himself to Satan: "Why—
  My good old friend, for such I deem you,
    though   490
Our different parties make us fight so shy,
  I ne'er mistake you for a *personal* foe;
Our difference is *political*, and I
  Trust that, whatever may occur below,
You know my great respect for you: and
    this
Makes me regret whate'er you do amiss—

LXIII

"Why, my dear Lucifer, would you abuse
  My call for witnesses? I did not mean
That you should half of earth and hell pro-
    duce;
  'Tis even superfluous, since two honest,
    clean,   500

True testimonies are enough: we lose
　Our time, nay, our eternity, between
The accusation and defence: if we
Hear both, 'twill stretch our immortality."

LXIV

Satan replied, "To me the matter is
　Indifferent, in a personal point of view:
I can have fifty better souls than this
　With far less trouble than we have gone
　　through
Already; and I merely argued his
　Late majesty of Britain's case with you 510
Upon a point of form: you may dispose
Of him; I've kings enough below, God
　knows!"

LXV

Thus spoke the Demon (late call'd "multi-
　faced"
　By multo-scribbling Southey). "Then we'll
　call
One or two persons of the myriads placed
　Around our congress, and dispense with all
The rest," quoth Michael: "Who may be so
　graced
　As to speak first? there's choice enough—
　who shall
It be?" Then Satan answer'd, "There are
　many;
But you may choose Jack Wilkes as well as
　any." 520

LXVI

A merry, cock-eyed, curious-looking sprite
　Upon the instant started from the throng,
Dress'd in a fashion now forgotten quite;
　For all the fashions of the flesh stick long
By people in the next world; where unite
　All the costumes since Adam's, right or
　wrong,
From Eve's fig-leaf down to the petticoat,
Almost as scanty, of days less remote.

LXVII

The spirit look'd around upon the crowds
　Assembled, and exclaim'd, "My friends of
　all 530
The spheres, we shall catch cold amongst these
　clouds;
　So let's to business: why this general call?

If those are freeholders I see in shrouds,
　And 'tis for an election that they bawl,
Behold a candidate with unturn'd coat!
Saint Peter, may I count upon your vote?"

LXVIII

"Sir," replied Michael, "you mistake; these
　things
　Are of a former life, and what we do
Above is more august; to judge of kings
　Is the tribunal met: so now you know." 540
"Then I presume those gentlemen with
　wings,"
　Said Wilkes, "are cherubs; and that soul
　below
Looks much like George the Third, but to my
　mind
A good deal older—Bless me! is he blind?"

LXIX

"He is what you behold him, and his doom
　Depends upon his deeds," the Angel said;
"If you have aught to arraign in him, the
　tomb
　Gives license to the humblest beggar's
　head
To lift itself against the loftiest."—"Some,"
　Said Wilkes, "don't wait to see them laid
　in lead, 550
For such a liberty—and I, for one,
Have told them what I thought beneath the
　sun."

LXX

"*Above* the sun repeat, then, what thou hast
　To urge against him," said the Archangel.
　"Why,"
Replied the spirit, "since old scores are past,
　Must I turn evidence? In faith, not I.
Besides, I beat him hollow at the last,
　With all his Lords and Commons: in the
　sky
I don't like ripping up old stories, since
His conduct was but natural in a prince. 560

LXXI

"Foolish, no doubt, and wicked, to oppress
　A poor unlucky devil without a shilling;
But then I blame the man himself much less
　Than Bute and Grafton, and shall be un-
　willing

To see him punish'd here for their excess,
  Since they were both damn'd long ago, and
    still in
Their place below: for me, I have forgiven,
And vote his 'habeas corpus' into heaven."

LXXII

"Wilkes," said the Devil, "I understand all
    this;
  You turn'd to half a courtier ere you died,
And seem to think it would not be amiss 571
  To grow a whole one on the other side
Of Charon's ferry; you forget that *his*
  Reign is concluded; whatsoe'er betide,
He won't be sovereign more: you've lost your
    labour,
For at the best he will but be your neighbour.

LXXIII

"However, I knew what to think of it,
  When I beheld you in your jesting way,
Flitting and whispering round about the spit
  Where Belial, upon duty for the day, 580
With Fox's lard was basting William Pitt,
  His pupil; I knew what to think, I say:
That fellow even in hell breeds farther ills;
  I'll have him *gagg'd*—'twas one of his own
    bills.

LXXIV

"Call Junius!" From the crowd a shadow
    stalk'd,
  And at the name there was a general
    squeeze,
So that the very ghosts no longer walk'd
  In comfort, at their own aërial ease,
But were all ramm'd, and jamm'd (but to be
    balk'd,
  As we shall see), and jostled hands and
    knees, 590
Like wind compress'd and pent within a
    bladder,
Or like a human colic, which is sadder.

LXXV

The shadow came—a tall, thin, grey-hair'd
    figure,
  That look'd as it had been a shade on earth;
Quick in its motions, with an air of vigour,
  But nought to mark its breeding or its
    birth;

Now it wax'd little, then again grew bigger,
  With now an air of gloom, or savage mirth;
But as you gazed upon its features, they
  Changed every instant—to *what*, none could
    say. 600

LXXVI

The more intently the ghosts gazed, the less
  Could they distinguish whose the features
    were;
The Devil himself seem'd puzzled even to
    guess;
  They varied like a dream—now here, now
    there;
And several people swore from out the press,
  They knew him perfectly; and one could
    swear
He was his father: upon which another
Was sure he was his mother's cousin's brother:

LXXVII

Another, that he was a duke, or knight,
  An orator, a lawyer, or a priest, 610
A nabob, a man-midwife; but the wight
  Mysterious changed his countenance at
    least
As oft as they their minds; though in full
    sight
  He stood, the puzzle only was increased;
The man was a phantasmagoria in
Himself—he was so volatile and thin.

LXXVIII

The moment that you had pronounced him
    one,
  Presto! his face changed, and he was an-
    other;
And when that change was hardly well put on,
  It varied, till I don't think his own mother
(If that he had a mother) would her son 621
  Have known, he shifted so from one to
    t'other;
Till guessing from a pleasure grew a task,
At this epistolary "Iron Mask."

LXXIX

For sometimes he like Cerberus would seem—
  "Three gentlemen at once" (as sagely says
Good Mrs. Malaprop); then you might deem
  That he was not even *one;* now many
    rays

Were flashing round him; and now a thick
   steam
  Hid him from sight—like fogs on London
    days: 630
Now Burke, now Tooke, he grew to people's
   fancies,
And certes often like Sir Philip Francis.

LXXX

I've an hypothesis—'tis quite my own;
  I never let it out till now, for fear
Of doing people harm about the throne,
  And injuring some minister or peer,
On whom the stigma might perhaps be blown;
  It is—my gentle public, lend thine ear!
'Tis, that what Junius we are wont to call
Was *really*, *truly*, nobody at all.   640

LXXXI

I don't see wherefore letters should not be
  Written without hands, since we daily view
Them written without heads; and books, we
  see,
  Are fill'd as well without the latter too:
And really till we fix on somebody
  For certain sure to claim them as his due,
Their author, like the Niger's mouth, will
  bother
The world to say if *there* be mouth or author.

LXXXII

"And who and what art thou?" the Arch-
  angel said.
  "For *that* you may consult my title-
   page,"
Replied this mighty shadow of a shade: 651
  "If I have kept my secret half an age,
I scarce shall tell it now."—"Canst thou up-
  braid,"
  Continued Michael, "George Rex, or allege
Aught further?" Junius answer'd, "You had
  better
First ask him for *his* answer to my letter:

LXXXIII

"My charges upon record will outlast
  The brass of both his epitaph and tomb."
"Repent'st thou not," said Michael, "of some
  past   659
Exaggeration? something which may doom

Thyself if false, as him if true? Thou wast
  Too bitter—is it not so?—in thy gloom
Of passion?"—"Passion!" cried the phantom
  dim,
"I loved my country, and I hated him.

LXXXIV

"What I have written, I have written: let
  The rest be on his head or mine!" So spoke
Old "Nominis Umbra"; and while speaking
  yet,
  Away he melted in celestial smoke.
Then Satan said to Michael, "Don't forget
  To call George Washington, and John
   Horne Tooke,   670
And Franklin;"—but at this time there was
  heard
A cry for room, though not a phantom stirr'd.

LXXXV

At length with jostling, elbowing, and the aid
  Of cherubim appointed to that post,
The devil Asmodeus to the circle made
  His way, and look'd as if his journey cost
Some trouble. When his burden down he laid,
  "What's this?" cried Michael; "why, 'tis
   not a ghost?"
"I know it," quoth the incubus; "but he
Shall be one, if you leave the affair to me.   680

LXXXVI

"Confound the renegado! I have sprain'd
  My left wing, he's so heavy; one would
   think
Some of his works about his neck were
  chain'd.
  But to the point; while hovering o'er the brink
Of Skiddaw (where as usual it still rain'd),
  I saw a taper, far below me, wink,
And stooping, caught this fellow at a libel—
No less on history than the Holy Bible.

LXXXVII

"The former is the devil's scripture, and
  The latter yours, good Michael: so the affair
Belongs to all of us, you understand.   691
  I snatch'd him up just as you see him there,
And brought him off for sentence out of hand:
  I've scarcely been ten minutes in the air—
At least a quarter it can hardly be:
I dare say that his wife is still at tea."

LXXXVIII

Here Satan said, "I know this man of old,
  And have expected him for some time here;
A sillier fellow you will scarce behold,
  Or more conceited in his petty sphere: 700
But surely it was not worth while to fold
  Such trash below your wing, Asmodeus
    dear:
We had the poor wretch safe (without being
    bored
With carriage) coming of his own accord.

LXXXIX

"But since he's here, let's see what he has
    done."
  "Done!" cried Asmodeus, "he anticipates
The very business you are now upon,
  And scribbles as if head clerk to the
    Fates.
Who knows to what his ribaldry may run,
  When such an ass as this, like Balaam's,
    prates?" 710
"Let's hear," quoth Michael, "what he has to
    say:
You know we're bound to that in every way."

XC

Now the bard, glad to get an audience, which
  By no means often was his case below,
Began to cough, and hawk, and hem, and
    pitch
  His voice into that awful note of woe
To all unhappy hearers within reach
  Of poets when the tide of rhyme's in
    flow;
But stuck fast with his first hexameter,
Not one of all whose gouty feet would stir. 720

XCI

But ere the spavin'd dactyls could be spurr'd
  Into recitative, in great dismay
Both cherubim and seraphim were heard
  To murmur loudly through their long ar-
    ray;
And Michael rose ere he could get a word
  Of all his founder'd verses under way,
And cried, "For God's sake stop, my friend!
    'twere best—
Non Di, non homines—you know the rest."

XCII

A general bustle spread throughout the throng,
  Which seem'd to hold all verse in detesta-
    tion; 730
The angels had of course enough of song
  When upon service; and the generation
Of ghosts had heard too much in life, not
    long
  Before, to profit by a new occasion:
The monarch, mute till then, exclaim'd,
    "What! what!
Pye come again? No more—no more of that!"

XCIII

The tumult grew; an universal cough
  Convulsed the skies, as during a debate,
When Castlereagh has been up long enough
  (Before he was first minister of state, 740
I mean—the slaves hear now); some cried
    "Off, off!"
  As at a farce; till, grown quite desperate,
The bard Saint Peter pray'd to interpose
(Himself an author) only for his prose.

XCIV

The varlet was not an ill-favour'd knave;
  A good deal like a vulture in the face,
With a hook nose and a hawk's eye, which
    gave
  A smart and sharper-looking sort of grace
To his whole aspect, which, though rather
    grave,
  Was by no means so ugly as his case; 750
But that, indeed, was hopeless as can be,
Quite a poetic felony "de se."

XCV

Then Michael blew his trump, and still'd the
    noise
  With one still greater, as is yet the mode
On earth besides; except some grumbling
    voice,
  Which now and then will make a slight
    inroad
Upon decorous silence, few will twice
  Lift up their lungs when fairly overcrow'd;
And now the bard could plead his own bad
    cause,
With all the attitudes of self-applause. 760

XCVI

He said—(I only give the heads)—he said,
  He meant no harm in scribbling; 'twas his
      way
Upon all topics; 'twas, besides, his bread,
  Of which he butter'd both sides; 'twould
      delay
Too long the assembly (he was pleased to
      dread),
  And take up rather more time than a day,
To name his works—he would but cite a
      few—
  "Wat Tyler"—"Rhymes on Blenheim"—
      "Waterloo."

XCVII

He had written praises of a regicide;
  He had written praises of all kings what-
      ever;   770
He had written for republics far and wide,
  And then against them bitterer than ever;
For pantisocracy he once had cried
  Aloud, a scheme less moral than 'twas
      clever;
Then grew a hearty anti-jacobin—
Had turn'd his coat—and would have turn'd
      his skin.

XCVIII

He had sung against all battles, and again
  In their high praise and glory; he had
      call'd
Reviewing "the ungentle craft," and then
  Become as base a critic as e'er crawl'd— 780
Fed, paid, and pamper'd by the very men
  By whom his muse and morals had been
      maul'd:
He had written much blank verse, and blanker
      prose,
And more of both than anybody knows.

XCIX

He had written Wesley's life:—here turning
      round
  To Satan, "Sir, I'm ready to write yours,
In two octavo volumes, nicely bound,
  With notes and preface, all that most allures
The pious purchaser; and there's no ground
  For fear, for I can choose my own re-
      viewers: 790
So let me have the proper documents,
  That I may add you to my other saints."

C

Satan bow'd, and was silent. "Well, if you,
  With amiable modesty, decline
My offer, what says Michael? There are few
  Whose memoirs could be render'd more
      divine.
Mine is a pen of all work; not so new
  As it was once, but I would make you
      shine
Like your own trumpet. By the way, my
      own
Has more of brass in it, and is as well blown.

CI

"But talking about trumpets, here's my Vi-
      sion!   801
  Now you shall judge, all people; yes, you
      shall
Judge with my judgment, and by my decision
  Be guided who shall enter heaven or fall.
I settle all these things by intuition,
  Times present, past, to come, heaven, hell,
      and all,
Like King Alfonso. When I thus see double,
I save the Deity some worlds of trouble."

CII

He ceased, and drew forth an MS.; and no
  Persuasion on the part of devils, saints, 810
Or angels, now could stop the torrent; so
  He read the first three lines of the con-
      tents;
But at the fourth, the whole spiritual show
  Had vanish'd, with variety of scents,
Ambrosial and sulphureous, as they sprang,
Like lightning, off from his "melodious twang."

CIII

Those grand heroics acted as a spell:
  The angels stopp'd their ears and plied their
      pinions;
The devils ran howling, deafen'd, down to
      hell;
  The ghosts fled, gibbering, for their own
      dominions—   820
(For 'tis not yet decided where they dwell,
  And I leave every man to his opinions);
Michael took refuge in his trump—but, lo!
His teeth were set on edge, he could not
      blow!

CIV

Saint Peter, who has hitherto been known
  For an impetuous saint, upraised his keys,
And at the fifth line knock'd the poet down;
  Who fell like Phaëton, but more at ease,
Into his lake, for there he did not drown;
  A different web being by the Destinies 830
Woven for the Laureate's final wreath, when-
    e'er
Reform shall happen either here or there.

CV

He first sank to the bottom—like his works,
  But soon rose to the surface—like him-
    self;
For all corrupted things are buoy'd like
    corks,
  By their own rottenness, light as an elf,

Or wisp that flits o'er a morass: he lurks,
  It may be, still, like dull books on a shelf,
In his own den, to scrawl some "Life" or
    "Vision,"
  As Welborn says—"the devil turn'd pre-
    cisian." 840

CVI

As for the rest, to come to the conclusion
  Of this true dream, the telescope is gone
Which kept my optics free from all delusion,
  And show'd me what I in my turn have
    shown;
All I saw farther, in the last confusion,
  Was, that King George slipp'd into heaven
    for one;
And when the tumult dwindled to a calm,
I left him practising the hundredth psalm.

1821

EXTRACTS FROM A DIARY OF LORD BYRON, 1821

Ravenna, January 4, 1821

"A sudden thought strikes me." Let me begin a journal once more. The last I kept was in Switzerland, in record of a tour made in the Bernese Alps, which I made to send to my sister in 1816, and I suppose that she has it still, for she wrote to me that she was pleased 10 with it. Another, and longer, I kept in 1813–1814, which I gave to Thomas Moore in the same year.

This morning I gat me up late, as usual—weather bad—bad as England—worse. The 15 snow of last week melting to the sirocco of to-day, so that there were two d—d things at once. Could not even get to ride on horseback in the forest. Stayed at home all the morning—looked at the fire—wondered when the post 20 would come. Post came at the Ave Maria, instead of half-past one o'clock, as it ought. Galignani's messengers, six in number,—a letter from Faenza, but none from England. Very sulky in consequence (for there ought to have 25 been letters), and ate in consequence a copious dinner; for when I am vexed it makes me swallow quicker—but drank very little.

I was out of spirits—read the papers—thought what *fame* was, on reading, in a case of murder, that "Mr. Wych, grocer, at Tunbridge, sold some bacon, flour, cheese, and, it is believed, some plums, to some gipsy woman 5 accused. He had on his counter (I quote faithfully) a *book*, the 'Life of *Pamela*,' which he was *tearing* for *waste* paper, etc. In the cheese was found, etc., and a *leaf of 'Pamela' wrapt round the bacon*." What would Richardson, the vainest and luckiest of *living* authors (*i.e.* while alive),—he who, with Aaron Hill, used to prophesy and chuckle over the presumed fall of Fielding (the *prose* Homer of human nature) and of Pope (the most beautiful of poets),— 15 what would he have said, could he have traced his pages from their place on the French prince's toilets (see Boswell's "Johnson") to the grocer's counter and the gipsy-murderess's bacon!

What would he have said? what can anybody 20 say, save what Solomon said long before us? After all, it is but passing from one counter to another, from the bookseller's to the other tradesman's—grocer or pastry-cook. For my part, I have met with most poetry upon trunks; 25 so that I am apt to consider the trunk-maker as the sexton of authorship.

Wrote five letters in about half an hour, short and savage, to all my rascally correspondents. Carriage came. Heard the news of three murders at Faenza and Forli—a carabinier, a smuggler, and an attorney—all last night. The two first in a quarrel, the latter by premeditation.

Three weeks ago—almost a month—the 7th it was—I picked up the commandant, mortally wounded, out of the street; he died in my house; assassins unknown, but presumed political. His brethren wrote from Rome last night to thank me for having assisted him in his last moments. Poor fellow! it was a pity; he was a good soldier, but imprudent. It was eight in the evening when they killed him. We heard the shot; my servants and I ran out, and found him expiring, with five wounds, two whereof mortal,—by slugs they seemed. I examined him, but did not go to the dissection next morning. . . .

January 5, 1821

Rose late—dull and drooping—the weather dripping and dense. Snow on the ground, and sirocco above in the sky, like yesterday. Roads up to the horse's belly, so that riding (at least for pleasure) is not very feasible. Added a postscript to my letter to Murray. Read the conclusion, for the fiftieth time (I have read all W. Scott's novels at least fifty times), of the third series of "Tales of my Landlord,"—grand work—Scotch Fielding, as well as great English poet—wonderful man! I long to get drunk with him.

Dined versus six o' clock. Forgot that there was a plum pudding (I have added, lately, *eating* to my "family of vices"), and had dined before I knew it. . . .

Hear the carriage—order pistols and greatcoat, as usual—necessary articles. Weather cold—carriage open, and inhabitants somewhat savage—rather treacherous and highly inflamed by politics. Fine fellows, though, good materials for a nation. Out of chaos God made a world, and out of high passions comes a people.

Clock strikes—going out to make love. Somewhat perilous, but not disagreeable. Memorandum—a new screen put up to-day. It is rather antique, but will do with a little repair.

Thaw continues—hopeful that riding may be practicable to-morrow. Sent the papers to All.—grand events coming. . . .

Settled that the R. will break out on the 7th or 8th of March, in which appointment I should trust, had it not been settled that it was to have broken out in October, 1820. But those Bolognese shirked the Romagnuoles. . . .

January 6, 1821

. . . At eight went out to visit. Heard a little music—like music. Talked with Count Pietro G. of the Italian comedian, Vestris, who is now at Rome—have seen him often act in Venice—a good actor—very. Somewhat of a mannerist; but excellent in broad comedy, as well as in the sentimental pathetic. He has made me frequently laugh and cry, neither of which is now a very easy matter—at least for a player to produce in me.

Thought of the state of women under the ancient Greeks—convenient enough. Present state a remnant of the barbarism of the chivalry and feudal ages—artificial and unnatural. They ought to mind home—and be well fed and clothed—but not mixed in society. Well educated, too, in religion—but to read neither poetry nor politics—nothing but books of piety and cookery. Music—drawing—dancing—also a little gardening and ploughing now and then. I have seen them mending the roads in Epirus with good success. Why not, as well as hay-making and milking?

Came home and read Mitford again, and played with my mastiff—gave him his supper. Made another reading to the epigram, but the turn the same. To-night at the theatre, there being a prince on his throne in the last scene of the comedy,—the audience laughed, and asked him for a *constitution*. This shows the state of the public mind here, as well as the assassinations. It won't do. There must be an universal republic—and there ought to be.

The crow is lame of a leg—wonder how it happened—some fool trod upon his toe, I suppose. The falcon pretty brisk—the cats large and noisy—the monkeys I have not looked to since the cold weather, as they suffer by being brought up. Horses must be gay—get a ride as soon as weather serves. Deuced muggy still—an Italian winter is a sad thing, but all the other seasons are charming.

What is the reason that I have been, all my

lifetime, more or less *ennuyé?* and that, if any-thing, I am rather less so now than I was at twenty, as far as my recollection serves? I do not know how to answer this, but presume that it is constitutional,—as well as the waking in low spirits, which I have invariably done for many years. Temperance and exercise, which I have practised at times, and for a long time together vigorously and violently, made little or no difference. Violent passions did;—when under their immediate influence—it is odd, but—I was in agitated, but *not* in de-pressed, spirits.

A dose of salts has the effect of a temporary inebriation, like light champagne, upon me. But wine and spirits make me sullen and sav-age to ferocity—silent, however, and retiring, and not quarrelsome, if not spoken to. Swim-ming also raises my spirits,—but in general they are low, and get daily lower. That is *hopeless;* for I do not think I am so much *ennuyé* as I was at nineteen. The proof is, that then I must game, or drink, or be in motion of some kind, or I was miserable. At present, I can mope in quietness; and like being alone better than any company—except the lady's whom I serve. But I feel a something, which makes me think that, if I ever reach near to old age, like Swift, "I shall die at top" first. Only I do not dread idiotism or madness so much as he did. On the contrary, I think some quieter stages of both must be preferable to much of what men think the possession of their senses.

January 7, 1821, Sunday

... The Count Pietro G. took me aside to say that the Patriots have had notice from Forli (twenty miles off) that to-night the govern-ment and its party mean to strike a stroke—that the cardinal here has had orders to make several arrests immediately, and that, in conse-quence, the Liberals are arming, and have posted patrols in the streets, to sound the alarm and give notice to fight for it.

He asked me "what should be done?" I answered, "Fight for it, rather than be taken in detail;" and offered if any of them are in immediate apprehension of arrest to receive them in my house (which is defensible), and to defend them, with my servants and them-selves (we have arms and ammunition), as long as we can,—or to try to get them away under cloud of night. On going home, I offered him the pistols which I had about me,—but he refused, but said he would come off to me in case of accidents.

It wants half an hour of midnight, and rains; —as Gibbet says, "a fine night for their enter-prise—dark as hell, and blows like the devil." If the row don't happen *now*, it must soon. I thought that their system of shooting people would soon produce a reaction—and now it seems coming. I will do what I can in the way of combat, though a little out of exercise. The cause is a good one.

Turned over and over half a score of books for the passage in question, and can't find it. Expect to hear the drum and the musketry momently (for they swear to resist, and are right),—but I hear nothing, as yet, save the plash of the rain and the gusts of the wind at intervals. Don't like to go to bed, because I hate to be waked, and would rather sit up for the row, if there is to be one.

Mended the fire—have got the arms—and a book or two, which I shall turn over. I know little of their numbers, but think the Carbonari strong enough to beat the troops, even here. With twenty men this house might be de-fended for twenty-four hours against any force to be brought against it, *now* in this place, for the same time; and, in such a time, the country would have notice, and would rise,—if ever they *will* rise, of which there is some doubt. In the meantime, I may as well read as do any-thing else, being alone.

January 8, 1821, Monday

... The truth is, that —— cares for little but his place (which is a good one), and wishes to play pretty with both parties. He has changed his mind thirty times these last three moons, to my knowledge, for he corresponds with me. But he is not a bloody fellow—only an avaricious one.

It seems that, just at this moment (as Lydia Languish says), there will be no elopement after all. I wish that I had known as much last night,—or, rather, this morning,—I should have gone to bed two hours earlier. ...

Tuesday, January 9, 1821

... Heard some music. At nine the usual visitors—news, *war*, or rumours of war. Consulted with P. G., etc. They mean to *insurrect* here, and are to honour me with a call thereupon. I shall not fall back; though I don't think them in force or heart sufficient to make much of it. But, *onward!*—it is now the time to act, and what signifies *self*, if a single spark of that which would be worthy of the past can be bequeathed unquenchedly to the future? It is not one man, nor a million, but the *spirit* of liberty which must be spread. The waves which dash upon the shore are, one by one, broken, but yet the *ocean* conquers, nevertheless. It overwhelms the Armada, it wears the rock, and, if the *Neptunians* are to be believed, it has not only destroyed, but made a world. In like manner, whatever the sacrifice of individuals, the great cause will gather strength, sweep down what is rugged, and fertilise (for *seaweed* is *manure*) what is cultivable. And so, the mere selfish calculation ought never to be made on such occasions; and, at present, it shall not be computed by me. I was never a good arithmetician of chances, and shall not commence now. ...

January 12, 1821

The weather still so humid and impracticable, that London, in its most oppressive fogs, were a summer-bower to this mist and sirocco, which has now lasted (but with one day's interval), chequered with snow or heavy rain only, since the 30th of December, 1820. It is so far lucky that I have a literary turn; but it is very tiresome not to be able to stir out, in comfort, on any horse but Pegasus, for so many days. The roads are even worse than the weather, by the long splashing, and the heavy soil, and the growth of the waters.

Read the "Poets"—English, that is to say—out of Campbell's edition. There is a good deal of taffeta in some of Tom's prefatory phrases, but his work is good as a whole. I like him best, though, in his own poetry.

Murray writes that they want to act the "Tragedy of Marino Faliero"—more fools they, it was written for the closet. I have protested against this piece of usurpation. ...

Scott is certainly the most wonderful writer of the day. His novels are a new literature in themselves, and his poetry as good as any—if not better (only on an erroneous system)—and only ceased to be so popular, because the vulgar learned were tired of hearing "Aristides called the Just," and Scott the Best, and ostracised him.

I like him, too, for his manliness of character, for the extreme pleasantness of his conversation, and his good-nature toward myself, personally. May he prosper!—for he deserves it. I know no reading to which I fall with such alacrity as a work of W. Scott's. ...

January 13, 1821, Saturday

... Dined—news come—the *Powers* mean to war with the peoples. The intelligence seems positive—let it be so—they will be beaten in the end. The king-times are fast finishing. There will be blood shed like water, and tears like mist; but the peoples will conquer in the end. I shall not live to see it, but I foresee it. ...

January 14, 1821

Turned over Seneca's tragedies. Wrote the opening lines of the intended tragedy of "Sardanapalus." Rode out some miles into the forest. Misty and rainy. Returned—dined—wrote some more of my tragedy.

Read Diodorus Siculus—turned over Seneca, and some other books. Wrote some more of the tragedy. Took a glass of grog. After having ridden hard in rainy weather, and scribbled, and scribbled again, the spirits (at least mine) need a little exhilaration, and I don't like laudanum now as I used to do. So I have mixed a glass of strong waters and single waters, which I shall now proceed to empty. Therefore and thereunto I conclude this day's diary. ...

January 15, 1821

Weather fine. Received visit. Rode out into the forest—fired pistols. Returned home—dined—dipped into a volume of Mitford's "Greece"—wrote part of a scene of "Sardanapalus." Went out—heard some music—heard some politics. More ministers from the other

Italian powers gone to Congress. War seems certain,—in that case, it will be a savage one. Talked over various important matters with one of the initiated. At ten and half returned home. 5

I have just thought of something odd. In the year 1814, Moore ("the poet," *par excellence,* and he deserves it) and I were going together, in the same carriage, to dine with Earl Grey, the Capo Politico of the remaining Whigs. 10 Murray, the magnificent (the illustrious publisher of that name), had just sent me a Java *Gazette*—I know not why, or wherefore. Pulling it out, by way of curiosity, we found it to contain a dispute (the said Java *Gazette*) on 15 Moore's merits and mine. I think, if I had been there, that I could have saved them the trouble of disputing on the subject. But, there is *fame* for you at six and twenty! Alexander had conquered India at the same age; but I doubt if 20 he was disputed about, or his conquests compared with those of Indian Bacchus, at Java.

It was a great fame to be named with Moore; greater to be compared with him; greatest— *pleasure,* at least—to be *with* him; and, surely, 25 an odd coincidence, that we should be dining together while they were quarrelling about us beyond the equinoctial line. . . .

January 21, 1821

. . . To-morrow is my birthday—that is to say, at twelve o' the clock, midnight, *i. e.* in twelve minutes, I shall have completed thirty and three years of age!—and I go to my bed 35 with a heaviness of heart at having lived so long, and to so little purpose.

It is three minutes past twelve. "'Tis the middle of night by the castle clock," and I am now thirty-three!

> Eheu, fugaces, Posthume, Posthume,
> Labuntur anni;[1]—

but I don't regret them so much for what I have done, as for what I *might* have done. 45

> Through life's road, so dim and dirty,
> I have dragged to three and thirty.
> What have these years left to me?
> Nothing—except thirty-three.

[1] "Alas, O Posthumus, Posthumus, the fleeting years slip by."

January 22, 1821

> 1821.
> Here lies
> interred in the Eternity
> of the Past,
> from whence there is no
> Resurrection
> for the Days—whatever there may be
> for the Dust—
> the Thirty-Third Year
> of an ill-spent Life,
> Which, after
> a lingering disease of many months,
> sunk into a lethargy,
> and expired,
> January 22d, 1821, A. D.
> Leaving a successor
> Inconsolable
> for the very loss which
> occasioned its
> Existence.

January 24, 1821

Returned—met some masques in the Corso —"Vive la bagatelle!"—the Germans are on the Po, the Barbarians at the gate, and their masters in council at Leybach (or whatever the 25 eructation of the sound may syllable into a human pronunciation), and lo! they dance and sing and make merry, "for to-morrow they may die." Who can say that the Arlequins are 30 not right? Like the Lady Baussiere, and my old friend Burton—I 'rode on.'

Dined—(damn this pen!)—beef tough— there is no beef in Italy worth a curse; unless a man could eat an old ox with the hide on, 35 singed in the sun.

The principal persons in the events which may occur in a few days are gone out on a *shooting party.* If it were like a *"highland* hunting," a pretext of the chase for a grand 40 reunion of counsellors and chiefs, it would be all very well. But it is nothing more or less than a real snivelling, popping, small-shot, water-hen waste of powder, ammunition, and shot, for their own special amusement: a rare 45 set of fellows for "a man to risk his neck with," as "Marishall Wells" says in the "Black Dwarf."

If they gather,—"whilk is to be doubted,"— they will not muster a thousand men. The rea- 50 son of this is that the populace are not interested,—only the higher and middle orders. I wish that the peasantry *were:* they are a fine savage race of two-legged leopards. . . .

January 25, 1821

. . . Answered Murray's letter—read—lounged. Scrawled this additional page of life's log-book. One day more is over of it and of me:—but "which is best, life or death, the gods only know," as Socrates said to his judges, on the breaking up of the tribunal. Two thousand years since that sage's declaration of ignorance have not enlightened us more upon this important point; for, according to the Christian dispensation, no one can know whether he is *sure* of salvation—even the most righteous—since a single slip of faith may throw him on his back, like a skater, while gliding smoothly to his paradise. Now, therefore, whatever the certainty of faith in the facts may be, the certainty of the individual as to his happiness or misery is no greater than it was under Jupiter.

It has been said that the immortality of the soul is a "grand peut-être"—but still it is a *grand* one. Everybody clings to it—the stupidest, and dullest, and wickedest of human bipeds is still persuaded that he is immortal.

January 26, 1821

. . . On dismounting, found Lieutenant E. just arrived from Faenza. Invited him to dine with me to-morrow. Did *not* invite him for to-day, because there was a small *turbot* (Friday, fast regularly and religiously), which I wanted to eat all myself. Ate it.

Went out—found T. as usual—music. The gentlemen, who make revolutions and are gone on a shooting, are not yet returned. They don't return till Sunday—that is to say, they have been out for five days, buffooning while the interests of a whole country are at stake, and even they themselves compromised.

It is a difficult part to play amongst such a set of assassins and blockheads—but, when the scum is skimmed off, or has boiled over, good may come of it. If this country could but be freed, what would be too great for the accomplishment of that desire? for the extinction of that Sigh of Ages? Let us hope. They have hoped these thousand years. The very revolvement of the chances may bring it—it is upon the dice. . . .

January 31, 1821
Midnight.

I have been reading Grimm's "Correspondence." He repeats frequently, in speaking of a poet, or a man of genius in any department, even in music (Gretry, for instance), that he must have "une âme qui se tourmente, un esprit violent." How far this may be true, I know not; but if it were, I should be a poet "per eccellenza;" for I have always had "une âme" which not only tormented itself but everybody else in contact with it; and an "esprit violent," which has almost left me without any "esprit" at all. As to defining what a poet *should* be, it is not worth while, for what are *they* worth? what have they done? . . .

February 2, 1821

I have been considering what can be the reason why I always wake, at a certain hour in the morning, and always in very bad spirits—I may say, in actual despair and despondency, in all respects—even of that which pleased me overnight. In about an hour or two this goes off, and I compose either to sleep again, or, at least, to quiet. In England, five years ago, I had the same kind of hypochondria, but accompanied with so violent a thirst that I have drank as many as fifteen bottles of soda-water in one night, after going to bed, and been still thirsty—calculating, however, some lost from the bursting out and effervescence and overflowing of the soda-water, in drawing the corks, or striking off the necks of the bottles from mere thirsty impatience At present, I have *not* the thirst; but the depression of spirits is no less violent.

I read in Edgeworth's "Memoirs" of something similar (except that his thirst expended itself on *small beer*) in the case of Sir F. B. Delaval;—but then he was, at least, twenty years older. What is it?—liver? In England, Le Man (the apothecary) cured me of the thirst in three days, and it had lasted as many years. I suppose that it is all hypochondria.

What I feel most growing upon me are laziness, and a disrelish more powerful than indifference. If I rouse, it is into fury. I presume that I shall end (if not earlier by accident, or some such termination) like Swift—"dying at top." I confess I do not contemplate this with so much horror as he apparently did for some years before it happened. But Swift had hardly *begun life* at the very period (thirty-three) when I feel quite an *old sort* of feel.

Oh! there is an organ playing in the street— a waltz, too! I must leave off to listen. They are playing a waltz which I have heard ten thousand times at the balls in London, between 1812 and 1815. Music is a strange thing.

February 16, 1821

Last night Il Conte P. G. sent a man with a bag full of bayonets, some muskets, and some hundreds of cartridges to my house, without apprising me, though I had seen him not half an hour before. About ten days ago, when there was to be a rising here, the Liberals and my brethren C. asked me to purchase some arms for a certain few of our ragamuffins. I did so immediately, and ordered ammunition, etc., and they were armed accordingly. Well— the rising is prevented by the Barbarians marching a week sooner than appointed; and an *order* is issued, and in force, by the government, "that all persons having arms concealed, etc., shall be liable to," etc.,—and what do my friends, the patriots, do two days afterward? Why, they throw back upon my hands, and into my house, these very arms (without a word of warning previously) with which I had furnished them at their own request, and at my own peril and expense.

It was lucky that Lega was at home to receive them. If any of the servants had (except Tita and F. and Lega), they would have betrayed it immediately. In the meantime, if they are denounced or discovered, I shall be in a scrape. . . .

February 18, 1821

. . . To-day I have had no communication with my Carbonari cronies; but, in the meantime, my lower apartments are full of their bayonets, fusils, cartridges, and what not. I suppose that they consider me as a depot, to be sacrificed, in case of accidents. It is no great matter, supposing that Italy could be liberated, who or what is sacrificed. It is a grand object— the very *poetry* of politics. Only think—a free Italy! Why, there has been nothing like it since the days of Augustus. I reckon the times of Cæsar (Julius) free; because the commotions left everybody a side to take, and the parties were pretty equal at the set-out. But, afterward, it was all prætorian and legionary business—and since!—we shall see, or, at least, some will see, what card will turn up. It is best to hope, even of the hopeless. The Dutch did more than these fellows have to do, in the Seventy Years' War.

February 24, 1821

Rode, etc., as usual. The secret intelligence arrived this morning from the frontier to the C. is as bad as possible. The *plan* has missed— the chiefs are betrayed, military, as well as civil—and the Neapolitans not only have *not* moved, but have declared to the P. government, and to the Barbarians, that they know nothing of the matter!

Thus the world goes; and thus the Italians are always lost for lack of union among themselves. What is to be done *here*, between the two fires, and cut off from the N^n. frontier, is not decided. My opinion was,—better to rise than be taken in detail; but how it will be settled now, I cannot tell. Messengers are despatched to the delegates of the other cities to learn their resolutions.

I always had an idea that it would be *bungled;* but was willing to hope, and am so still. Whatever I can do by money, means, or person, I will venture freely for their freedom; and have so repeated to them (some of the chiefs here) half an hour ago. I have two thousand five hundred scudi, better than five hundred pounds, in the house, which I offered to begin with.

February 27, 1821

. . . Yesterday wrote two notes on the "Bowles and Pope" controversy, and sent them off to Murray by the post. The old woman whom I relieved in the forest (she is ninety-four years of age) brought me two bunches of violets. "Nam vita gaudet mortua floribus." I was much pleased with the present.

An English woman would have presented a pair of worsted stockings, at least, in the month of February. Both excellent things; but the former are more elegant. The present, at this season, reminds one of Gray's stanza, omitted 5 from his "Elegy:"

"Here scatter'd oft, the *earliest* of the year,
 By hands unseen, are showers of violets found;
The redbreast loves to build and warble here,
And little footsteps lightly print the ground."

As fine a stanza as any in his "Elegy." I wonder that he could have the heart to omit it.

Last night I suffered horribly—from an indigestion, I believe. I *never* sup—that is, never 10 at home. But, last night, I was prevailed upon by the Countess Gamba's persuasion, and the strenuous example of her brother, to swallow, at supper, a quantity of boiled cockles, and to dilute them, *not* reluctantly, with some Imola 15 wine. When I came home, apprehensive of the consequences, I swallowed three or four glasses of spirits, which men (the venders) call brandy, rum, or hollands, but which gods would entitle spirits of wine, coloured or sugared. All 20 was pretty well till I got to bed, when I became somewhat swollen, and considerably vertiginous. I got out, and mixing some soda-powders, drank them off. This brought on temporary relief. I returned to bed; but grew 25 sick and sorry once and again. Took more soda-water. At last I fell into a dreary sleep. Woke, and was ill all day, till I had galloped a few miles. Query—was it the cockles, or what I took to correct them, that caused the com- 30 motion? I think both. I remarked in my illness the complete inertion, inaction, and destruction of my chief mental faculties. I tried to rouse them, and yet could not—and this is the *soul!* I should believe that it was married to 35 the body, if they did not sympathise so much with each other. If the one rose, when the other fell, it would be a sign that they longed for the natural state of divorce. But as it is, they seem to draw together like post-horses.

Let us hope the best—it is the grand possession.

[END OF THE DIARY]

ON ARTIFICIALITY AND POPE

Extracts from the "Letter to John Murray, Esq. on the Rev. W. L. Bowles's Strictures on the Life and Writings of Pope"

[These paragraphs (about one seventh of the "Letter") omit argumentative detail on special points or poems, but indicate Byron's line of thought in the quarrel. The "Letter" was dated from Ravenna Feb. 7, 1821.]

. . . The Euxine is a noble sea to look upon, and the port of Constantinople the most beautiful of harbours, and yet I cannot but think that the twenty sail of the line, some of one hundred and forty guns, rendered it more "poetical" by day in the sun, and by night perhaps still more, for the Turks illuminate their vessels-of-war in a manner the most picturesque, and yet all this is *artificial*. . . . Even an old boat, keel upwards, wrecked upon the barren sand, is a "poetical" object (and Wordsworth, who made a poem about a washing-tub and a blind boy, may tell you so as well as I), whilst a long extent of sand and unbroken water, without the boat, would be as like dull prose as any pamphlet lately published. . . .

The beautiful but barren Hymettus, the 25 whole coast of Attica, her hills and mountains, Pentelicus Anchesmus, Philopappus, etc., are in themselves poetical, and would be so if the name of Athens, of Athenians, and her very ruins, were swept from the earth. But am I to 30 be told that the "nature" of Attica would be *more* poetical without the "art" of the Acropolis? of the Temple of Theseus? and of the still all Greek and glorious monuments of her exquisitely artificial genius? Ask the traveller 35 what strikes him as most poetical, the Parthenon, or the rock on which it stands? . . .

Let us examine a little further this "babble of green fields" and of bare nature in general as 40 superior to artificial imagery, for the poetical purposes of the fine arts. In landscape painting, the great artist does not give you a literal copy of a country, but he invents and composes one. Nature, in her actual aspect, does not furnish 45 him with such existing scenes as he requires. Even where he presents you with some famous city, or celebrated scene from mountain or other nature, it must be taken from some particular point of view, and with such light, and shade, and distance, etc., as serve not only to heighten its beauties, but to shadow its deformities. The poetry of nature alone, *exactly* as she appears, is not sufficient to bear him out. The very sky of his painting is not the *portrait* of the sky of nature; it is a composition of different *skies,* observed at different times, and not the whole copied from any *particular* day. And why? Because nature is not lavish of her beauties; they are widely scattered, and occasionally displayed, to be selected with care, and gathered with difficulty.

Of sculpture I have just spoken. It is the great scope of the sculptor to heighten nature into heroic beauty, *i.e.* in plain English, to surpass his model. When Canova forms a statue, he takes a limb from one, a hand from another, a feature from a third, and a shape, it may be, from a fourth, probably at the same time improving upon all, as the Greek of old did in embodying his Venus. . . .

Art is *not* inferior to nature for poetical purposes. What makes a regiment of soldiers a more noble object of view than the same mass of mob? Their arms, their dresses, their banners, and the *art* and artificial symmetry of their position and movements. A Highlander's plaid, a Mussulman's turban, and a Roman toga, are more poetical than the tattooed or untattooed buttocks of a New Sandwich savage, although they were described by William Wordsworth himself like the "idiot in his glory."

I have seen as many mountains as most men, and more fleets than the generality of landsmen; and, to my mind, a large convoy with a few sail of the line to conduct them is as noble and as poetical a prospect as all that inanimate nature can produce. I prefer the "mast of some great ammiral," with all its tackle, to the Scotch fir or the alpine tannen; and think that *more* poetry *has been* made out of it. . . .

Mr. Bowles makes the chief part of a ship's poesy depend upon the *"wind:"* then why is a ship under sail more poetical than a hog in a high wind? The hog is all nature, the ship is all art, "coarse canvas," "blue bunting," and "tall poles"; both are violently acted upon by the wind, tossed here and there, to and fro, and yet nothing but excess of hunger could make me look upon the pig as the more poetical of the two, and then only in the shape of a griskin. . . .

To the question, "Whether the description of a game of cards [1] be as poetical, supposing the execution of the artists equal, as a description of a walk in a forest?" it may be answered that the *materials* are certainly not equal; but that "the *artist*" who has rendered the "game of cards poetical" is *by far the greater* of the two. But all this "ordering" of poets is purely arbitrary on the part of Mr. Bowles. There may or may not be, in fact, different "orders" of poetry, but the poet is always ranked according to his execution, and not according to his branch of the art. . . .

The depreciation of Pope is partly founded upon a false idea of the dignity of his order of poetry, to which he has partly contributed by the ingenuous boast:

"That not in fancy's maze he wandered long,
But *stoop'd* to truth, and moralised his song."

He should have written "rose to truth." In my mind, the highest of all poetry is ethical poetry, as the highest of all earthly objects must be moral truth. Religion does not make a part of my subject; it is something beyond human powers, and has failed in all human hands except Milton's and Dante's, and even Dante's powers are involved in his delineation of human passions, though in supernatural circumstances. What made Socrates the greatest of men? His moral truth—his ethics. What proved Jesus Christ the Son of God hardly less than his miracles? His moral precepts. And if ethics have made a philosopher the first of men, and have not been disdained as an adjunct to his Gospel by the Deity himself, are we to be told that ethical poetry, or didactic poetry, or by whatever name you term it, whose object is to make men better and wiser, is not the *very first order* of poetry; and are we to be told this too by one of the priesthood? It requires more mind, more wisdom, more

---

[1] Pope in *The Rape of the Lock* had described a game of cards, and Bowles had raised the question which Byron answers.

power, than all the "forests" that ever were "walked" for their "description," and all the epics that ever were founded upon fields of battle. The Georgics are indisputably, and, I believe, *undisputedly* even a finer poem than the Æneid. Virgil knew this; he did not order *them* to be burnt.

"The proper study of mankind is man."

It is the fashion of the day to lay great stress upon what they call "imagination" and "invention," the two commonest of qualities. An Irish peasant, with a little whiskey in his head, will imagine and invent more than would furnish forth a modern poem. If Lucretius had not been spoiled by the Epicurean system, we should have had a far superior poem to any now in existence. As mere poetry, it is the first of Latin poems. What, then, has ruined it? His ethics. Pope has not this defect; his moral is as pure as his poetry is glorious. . . .

The attempt of the poetical populace of the present day to obtain an ostracism against Pope is as easily accounted for as the Athenian's shell against Aristides; they are tired of hearing him always called "the Just." They are also fighting for life; for, if he maintains his station, they will reach their own by falling. They have raised a mosque by the side of a Grecian temple of the purest architecture; and, more barbarous than the barbarians from whose practice I have borrowed the figure, they are not contented with their own grotesque edifice, unless they destroy the prior, and purely beautiful fabric which preceded, and which shames them and theirs for ever and ever. I shall be told that amongst those I *have* been (or, it may be, still *am*) conspicuous,— true, and I am ashamed of it. I *have* been amongst the builders of this Babel, attended by a confusion of tongues, but *never* amongst the envious destroyers of the classic temple of our predecessor. I have loved and honoured the fame and name of that illustrious and unrivalled man, far more than my own paltry renown, and the trashy jingle of the crowd of "Schools" and upstarts who pretend to rival, or even surpass him. Sooner than a single leaf should be torn from his laurel, it were better that all which these men, and that I, as one of their set, have ever written, should

"Line trunks, clothe spice, or, fluttering in a row, Befringe the rails of Bedlam, or Soho!"

There are those who will believe this, and those who will not. You, sir, know how far I am sincere, and whether my opinion, not only in the short work intended for publication, and in private letters which can never be published, has or has not been the same. I look upon this as the declining age of English poetry; no regard for others, no selfish feeling, can prevent me from seeing this, and expressing the truth. There can be no worse sign for the taste of the times than the depreciation of Pope. It would be better to receive for proof Mr. Cobbett's rough but strong attack upon Shakespeare and Milton, than to allow this smooth and "candid" undermining of the reputation of the most *perfect* of our poets, and the purest of our moralists. Of his power in the *passions*, in description, in the mock heroic, I leave others to descant. I take him on his strong ground as an *ethical* poet: in the former, none excel; in the mock heroic and the ethical, none equal him; and, in my mind, the latter is the highest of all poetry, because it does that in *verse* which the greatest of men have wished to accomplish in prose. If the essence of poetry must be a *lie*, throw it to the dogs, or banish it from your republic, as Plato would have done. He who can reconcile poetry with truth and wisdom is the only true "*poet*" in its real sense, "the *maker*," "the *creator*,"—why must this mean the "liar," the "feigner," the "tale-teller?" A man may make and create better things than these. . . .

SELECTIONS FROM THE LETTERS OF LORD BYRON[1]

I TO FRANCIS HODGSON

Lisbon, July 16th, 1809

Thus far have we pursued our route, and seen all sorts of marvellous sights, palaces,

[1] Letters VIII, IX, XIII, XIV, XVII, XXII, XXIII, XXIX, XLIII, XLVIII and XLIX are from the text of E. H. Prothero's *Letters and Journals of Lord Byron*. Letters XI, XVIII, XXXI and XLVII are from Sir John Murray's

convents, etc.,—which, being to be heard in my friend Hobhouse's forthcoming Book of Travels, I shall not anticipate by smuggling any account whatsoever to you in a private and clandestine manner. I must just observe that the village of Cintra in Estremadura is the most beautiful, perhaps, in the world.

I am very happy here, because I loves oranges, and talks bad Latin to the monks, who understand it, as it is like their own,—and I goes into society (with my pocket-pistols), and I swims in the Tagus all across at once, and I rides on an ass or a mule, and swears Portuguese, and have got a diarrhoea and bites from the mosquitoes. But what of that? Comfort must not be expected by folks that go a pleasuring.

When the Portuguese are pertinacious, I say, "Carracho!"—the great oath of the grandees, that very well supplies the place of "Damme,"—and, when dissatisfied with my neighbour, I pronounce him "Ambra di merdo." With these two phrases, and a third, "Avra bouro," which signifieth "Get an ass," I am universally understood to be a person of degree and a master of languages. How merrily we lives that travellers be!—if we had food and raiment. But, in sober sadness, any thing is better than England, and I am infinitely amused with my pilgrimage as far as it has gone.

To-morrow we start to ride post near 400 miles as far as Gibraltar, where we embark for Melita and Byzantium. A letter to Malta will find me, or to be forwarded, if I am absent. Pray embrace the Drury and Dwyer and all the Ephesians you encounter. I am writing with Butler's donative pencil, which makes my bad hand worse. Excuse illegibility.

Hodgson! send me the news, and the deaths and defeats and capital crimes and the mis-

Lord Byron's Correspondence. For permission to reprint both these groups of letters, thanks are due to Charles Scribner's Sons. The greater part of the letters here given are from the text of Thomas Moore's *Letters and Journals of Lord Byron.* Very many omissions were made by Moore, and for the most part not supplied in later editions of the letters, as most of Moore's originals have disappeared. In some cases in the present text only the interesting paragraphs of a letter have been given and dots have been used to indicate omissions.

fortunes of one's friends; and let us hear of literary matters, and the controversies and the criticisms. All this will be pleasant—"Suave mari magno," etc. Talking of that, I have been 5 seasick, and sick of the sea. Adieu.

Yours faithfully, etc.

II To His Mother

Prevesa, November 12, 1809

My dear Mother,

I have now been some time in Turkey: this place is on the coast, but I have traversed the interior of the province of Albania on a visit to the Pacha. I left Malta in the Spider, a brig of war, on the 21st of September, and arrived in eight days at Prevesa. I thence have been about 150 miles, as far as Tepaleen, his Highness's country palace, where I stayed three 20 days. The name of the Pacha is *Ali,* and he is considered a man of the first abilities: he governs the whole of Albania (the ancient Illyricum), Epirus, and part of Macedonia. His son, Vely Pacha, to whom he has given me letters, 25 governs the Morea, and has great influence in Egypt; in short, he is one of the most powerful men in the Ottoman empire. When I reached Yanina, the capital, after a journey of three days over the mountains, through a country of 30 the most picturesque beauty, I found that Ali Pacha was with his army in Illyricum, besieging Ibrahim Pacha in the castle of Berat. He had heard that an Englishman of rank was in his dominions, and had left orders in Yanina 35 with the commandant to provide a house, and supply me with every kind of necessary *gratis;* and, though I have been allowed to make presents to the slaves, etc., I have not been permitted to pay for a single article of house-40 hold consumption.

I rode out on the vizier's horses, and saw the palaces of himself and grandsons: they are splendid, but too much ornamented with silk and gold. I then went over the mountains 45 through Zitza, a village with a Greek monastery (where I slept on my return), in the most beautiful situation (always excepting Cintra, in Portugal) I ever beheld. In nine days I reached Tepaleen. Our journey was much prolonged 50 by the torrents that had fallen from the mountains, and intersected the roads. I shall never forget the singular scene on entering Tepaleen at five in the afternoon, as the sun was going down. It brought to my mind (with some change of *dress*, however) Scott's description of Branksome Castle in his *Lay*, and the feudal system. The Albanians, in their dresses (the most magnificent in the world, consisting of a long *white kilt*, gold-worked cloak, crimson velvet gold-laced jacket and waistcoat, silver-mounted pistols and daggers), the Tartars with their high caps, the Turks in their vast pelisses and turbans, the soldiers and black slaves with the horses, the former in groups in an immense large open gallery in front of the palace, the latter placed in a kind of cloister below it, two hundred steeds ready caparisoned to move in a moment, couriers entering or passing out with despatches, the kettle-drums beating, boys calling the hour from the minaret of the mosque, altogether, with the singular appearance of the building itself, formed a new and delightful spectacle to a stranger. I was conducted to a very handsome apartment, and my health inquired after by the vizier's secretary, "a-la-mode Turque!"

The next day I was introduced to Ali Pacha. I was dressed in a full suit of staff uniform, with a very magnificent sabre, etc. The vizier received me in a large room paved with marble; a fountain was playing in the centre; the apartment was surrounded by scarlet ottomans. He received me standing, a wonderful compliment from a Mussulman, and made me sit down on his right hand. I have a Greek interpreter for general use, but a physician of Ali's, named Femlario, who understands Latin, acted for me on this occasion. His first question was, why, at so early an age, I left my country? —(the Turks have no idea of traveling for amusement). He then said, the English minister, Captain Leake, had told him I was of a great family, and desired his respects to my mother; which I now, in the name of Ali Pacha, present to you. He said he was certain I was a man of birth, because I had small ears, curling hair, and little white hands, and expressed himself pleased with my appearance and garb. He told me to consider him as a father whilst I was in Turkey, and said he looked on me as his son. Indeed, he treated me like a child, sending me almonds and sugared sherbet, fruit and sweetmeats, twenty times a day. He begged me to visit him often, and at night, when he was at leisure. I then, after coffee and pipes, retired for the first time. I saw him thrice afterwards. It is singular, that the Turks, who have no hereditary dignities, and few great families, except the Sultans, pay so much respect to birth; for I found my pedigree more regarded than my title. . . .

To-day I saw the remains of the town of Actium, near which Antony lost the world, in a small bay, where two frigates could hardly manœuvre: a broken wall is the sole remnant. On another part of the gulf stand the ruins of Nicopolis, built by Augustus in honour of his victory. Last night I was at a Greek marriage; but this and a thousand things more I have neither time nor space to describe.

I am going to-morrow, with a guard of fifty men, to Patras in the Morea, and thence to Athens, where I shall winter. Two days ago I was nearly lost in a Turkish ship of war, owing to the ignorance of the captain and crew, though the storm was not violent. Fletcher yelled after his wife, the Greeks called on all the saints, the Mussulmans on Alla; the captain burst into tears and ran below deck, telling us to call on God; the sails were split, the main-yard shivered, the wind blowing fresh, the night setting in, and all our chance was to make Corfu, which is in possession of the French, or (as Fletcher pathetically termed it) "a watery grave." I did what I could to console Fletcher, but finding him incorrigible, wrapped myself up in my Albanian capote (an immense cloak), and lay down on deck to wait the worst. I have learnt to philosophize in my travels, and if I had not, complaint was useless. Luckily the wind abated, and only drove us on the coast of Suli, on the main land, where we landed, and proceeded, by the help of the natives, to Prevesa again; but I shall not trust Turkish sailors in future, though the Pacha had ordered one of his own galliots to take me to Patras. I am therefore going as far as Missolonghi by land, and there have only to cross a small gulf to get to Patras.

Fletcher's next epistle will be full of marvels: we were one night lost for nine hours in the mountains in a thunder-storm, and since nearly wrecked. In both cases Fletcher was sorely bewildered, from apprehensions of famine and banditti in the first, and drowning in the second instance. His eyes were a little hurt by the lightning, or crying (I don't know which), but are now recovered. When you write, address to me at Mr. Strané's, English consul, Patras, Morea.

I could tell you I know not how many incidents that I think would amuse you, but they crowd on my mind as much as they would swell my paper, and I can neither arrange them in the one, nor put them down on the other, except in the greatest confusion. I like the Albanians much; they are not all Turks; some tribes are Christians. But their religion makes little difference in their manner or conduct. They are esteemed the best troops in the Turkish service. I lived on my route, two days at once, and three days again, in a barrack at Salora, and never found soldiers so tolerable, though I have been in the garrisons of Gibraltar and Malta, and seen Spanish, French, Sicilian, and British troops in abundance. I have had nothing stolen, and was always welcome to their provision and milk. Not a week ago an Albanian chief (every village has its chief, who is called Primate), after helping us out of the Turkish galley in her distress, feeding us, and lodging my suite, consisting of Fletcher, a Greek, two Athenians, a Greek priest, and my companion, Mr. Hobhouse, refused any compensation but a written paper stating that I was well received; and when I pressed him to accept a few sequins, "No," he replied; "I wish you to love me, not to pay me." These are his words.

It is astonishing how far money goes in this country. While I was in the capital, I had nothing to pay, by the vizier's order; but since, though I have generally had sixteen horses, and generally six or seven men, the expense has not been *half* as much as staying only three weeks in Malta, though Sir A. Ball, the governor, gave me a house for nothing, and I had only *one servant*. By the by, I expect Hanson to remit regularly; for I am not about to stay in this province for ever. Let him write to me at Mr. Strané's, English consul, Patras. The fact is, the fertility of the plains is wonderful, and specie is scarce, which makes this remarkable cheapness. I am going to Athens to study modern Greek, which differs much from the ancient, though radically similar. I have no desire to return to England, nor shall I, unless compelled by absolute want, and Hanson's neglect; but I shall not enter into Asia for a year or two, as I have much to see in Greece, and I may perhaps cross into Africa, at least the Egyptian part. Fletcher, like all Englishmen, is very much dissatisfied, though a little reconciled to the Turks by a present of eighty piastres from the vizier, which, if you consider every thing, and the value of specie here, is nearly worth ten guineas English. He has suffered nothing but from cold, heat, and vermin, which those who lie in cottages and cross mountains in a cold country must undergo, and of which I have equally partaken with himself; but he is not valiant, and is afraid of robbers and tempests. I have no one to be remembered to in England, and wish to hear nothing from it, but that you are well, and a letter or two on business from Hanson, whom you may tell to write. I will write when I can, and beg you to believe me

Your affectionate son.

III To His Mother

Smyrna, April 9, 1810

Dear Mother,—I know you will be glad to hear from me: I wish I could say I am equally delighted to write. However, there is no great loss in my scribbles, except to the portmanteau-makers, who, I suppose, will get all by and by.

Nobody but yourself asks me about my creed,—what I am, am not, etc., etc. If I were to begin *explaining*, God knows where I should leave off; so we will say no more about that, if you please.

I am no "good soul," and not an atheist, but an English gentleman, I hope, who loves his mother, mankind, and his country. I have not time to write more at present, and beg you to believe me,

Ever yours, etc.

P.S.—Are the Miss —— anxiously expecting my arrival and contributions to their gossip and *rhymes*, which are about as bad as they can be?

IV To Francis Hodgson

Patras, Morea, October 3, 1810

As I have just escaped from a physician and a fever, which confined me five days to bed, you won't expect much "allegrezza" in the ensuing letter. In this place there is an indigenous distemper, which, when the wind blows from the Gulf of Corinth (as it does five months out of six) attacks great and small, and makes woful work with visitors. Here be also two physicians, one of whom trusts to his genius (never having studied)—the other to a campaign of eighteen months against the sick of Otranto, which he made in his youth with great effect.

When I was seized with my disorder, I protested against both these assassins;—but what can a helpless, feverish, toast-and-watered poor wretch do? In spite of my teeth and tongue, the English consul, my Tartar, Albanians, dragoman, forced a physician upon me, and in three days vomited and glystered me to the last gasp. In this state I made my epitaph—take it:

> Youth, Nature, and relenting Jove,
> To keep my lamp *in* strongly strove;
> But Romanelli was so stout
> He beat all three—and *blew* it *out*.

But Nature and Jove, being piqued at my doubts, did, in fact, at last, beat Romanelli, and here I am, well but weakly, at your service.

Since I left Constantinople, I have made a tour of the Morea, and visited Vely Pacha, who paid me great honours and gave me a pretty stallion. H. is doubtless in England before even the date of this letter:—he bears a despatch from me to your bardship. He writes to me from Malta, and requests my journal, if I keep one. I have none, or he should have it; but I have replied, in a consolatory and exhortatory epistle, praying him to abate three and sixpence in the price of his next boke, seeing that half-a-guinea is a price not to be given for any thing save an opera ticket.

As for England, it is long since I have heard from it. Every one at all connected with my concerns is asleep, and you are my only correspondent, agents excepted. I have really no friends in the world; though all my old school-companions are gone forth into that world, and walk about there in monstrous disguises, in the garb of guardsmen, lawyers, parsons, fine gentlemen, and such other masquerade dresses. So, I here shake hands and cut with all these busy people, none of whom write to me. Indeed, I asked it not;—and here I am, a poor traveller and heathenish philosopher, who hath perambulated the greatest part of the Levant, and seen a great quantity of very improvable land and sea, and, after all, am no better than when I set out—Lord help me! . . .

V To Scrope Davies

Newstead Abbey, August 7, 1811

My dearest Davies,

Some curse hangs over me and mine. My mother lies a corpse in this house: one of my best friends is drowned in a ditch. What can I say, or think, or do? I received a letter from him the day before yesterday. My dear Scrope, if you can spare a moment, do come down to me—I want a friend. Matthews's last letter was written on *Friday*—on Saturday he was not. In ability, who was like Matthews? How did we all shrink before him? You do me but justice in saying, I would have risked my paltry existence to have preserved his. This very evening did I mean to write, inviting him, as I invite you, my very dear friend, to visit me. God forgive —— for his apathy! What will our poor Hobhouse feel! His letters breathe but of Matthews. Come to me, Scrope, I am almost desolate—left almost alone in the world—I had but you, and H., and M., and let me enjoy the survivors whilst I can. Poor M., in his letter of Friday, speaks of his intended contest for Cambridge, and a speedy journey to London. Write or come, but come if you can, or one or both.

Yours ever.

VI To R. C. Dallas

Newstead Abbey, Notts., August 12, 1811

Peace be with the dead! Regret cannot wake them. With a sign to the departed, let us resume the dull business of life, in the certainty that we also shall have our repose. Besides her who gave me being, I have lost more than one who made that being tolerable.—The best friend of my friend Hobhouse, Matthews, a man of the first talents, and also not the worst of my narrow circle, has perished miserably in the muddy waves of the Cam, always fatal to genius:—my poor schoolfellow, Wingfield, at Coimbra—within a month; and whilst I had heard from *all three*, but not seen *one*. Matthews wrote to me the very day before his death; and though I feel for his fate, I am still more anxious for Hobhouse, who, I very much fear, will hardly retain his senses; his letters to me since the event have been most incoherent. But let this pass; we shall all one day pass along with the rest—the world is too full of such things, and our very sorrow is selfish.

I received a letter from you, which my late occupations prevented me from duly noticing, —I hope your friends and family will long hold together. I shall be glad to hear from you, on business, on commonplace, or anything, or nothing—but death—I am already too familiar with the dead. It is strange that I look on the skulls which stand beside me (I have always had *four* in my study) without emotion, but I cannot strip the features of those I have known of their fleshy covering, even in idea, without a hideous sensation; but the worms are less ceremonious.—Surely, the Romans did well when they burned the dead.—I shall be happy to hear from you, and am, yours, etc.

VII To R. C. Dallas

Newstead, August 21, 1811

Your letter gives me credit for more acute feelings than I possess; for though I feel tolerably miserable, yet I am at the same time subject to a kind of hysterical merriment, or rather laughter without merriment, which I can neither account for nor conquer, and yet I do not feel relieved by it; but an indifferent person would think me in excellent spirits.[1]

[1] Byron refers several times to his melancholy gaiety. In 1821 he filled a notebook with "Detached Thoughts" which include the following paragraphs on the subject:

"People have wondered at the Melancholy which runs through my writings. Others have wondered at my personal gaiety; but I recollect once, after an hour, in which I had been sincerely

"We must forget these things," and have recourse to our old selfish comforts, or rather comfortable selfishness. I do not think I shall return to London immediately, and shall therefore accept freely what is offered courteously—your meditation between me and Murray. I don't think my name will answer the purpose, and you must be aware that my plaguy Satire will bring the north and south Grub Streets down upon the 'Pilgrimage';— but, nevertheless, if Murray makes a point of it, and you coincide with him, I will do it daringly; so let it be entitled, "By the Author of English Bards and Scotch Reviewers." My remarks on the Romaic, etc. once intended to accompany the "Hints from Horace," shall go along with the other, as being indeed more appropriate; also the smaller poems now in my possession, with a few selected from those published in —'s Miscellany. I have found amongst my poor mother's papers all my letters from the East, and one in particular of some length, from Albania. From this, if necessary, I can work up a note or two on that subject. As I kept no journal, the letters written on the spot are the best. But of this anon, when we have definitively arranged.

and particularly gay, and rather brilliant, in company, my wife replying to me when I said (upon her remarking my high spirits) 'and yet, Bell, I have been called and mis-called Melancholy—you must have seen how falsely, frequently.' 'No, B.,' (she answered) 'It is not so: at heart you are the most melancholy of mankind, and often when apparently gayest.'

"If I could explain at length the real causes which have contributed to increase this perhaps natural temperament of mine, this Melancholy which hath made me a bye-word, nobody would wonder; but this is impossible without doing much mischief. I do not know what other men's lives have been, but I cannot conceive anything more strange than some of the earlier parts of mine. I have written my memoirs, but omitted all the really consequential and important parts, from deference to the dead, to the living, and to those who must be both.

"I sometimes think that I should have written the whole as a lesson, but it might have proved a lesson to be learnt rather than avoided; for passion is a whirlpool, which is not to be viewed nearly without attraction from its Vortex.

"I must not go on with these reflections, or I shall be letting out some secret or other to paralyze posterity."

Has Murray shown the work to any one? He may—but I will have no traps for applause. Of course there are little things I would wish to alter, and perhaps the two stanzas of a buffooning cast on London's Sunday are as well left out. I much wish to avoid identifying Childe Harold's character with mine, and that, in sooth, is my second objection to my name appearing in the title-page. When you have made arrangements as to time, size, type, etc., favour me with a reply. I am giving you an universe of trouble, which thanks cannot atone for. I made a kind of prose apology for my scepticism at the head of the MS., which, on recollection, is so much more like an attack than a defence, that, haply, it might better be omitted:—perpend, pronounce. After all, I fear Murray will be in a scrape with the orthodox; but I cannot help it, though I wish him well through it. As for me, "I have supped full of criticism," and I don't think that the "most dismal treatise" will stir and rouse my "fell of hair" till "Birnam wood do come to Dunsinane." . . .

VIII To Lady Caroline Lamb

(Undated. Probably late March, 1812)

I never supposed you artful: we are all selfish,—nature did that for us. But even when you attempt deceit occasionally, you cannot maintain it, which is all the better; want of success will curb the tendency. Every word you utter, every line you write, proves you to be either *sincere* or a *fool*. Now as I know you are not the one, I must believe you the other.

I never knew a woman with greater or more pleasing talents, *general* as in a woman they should be, something of everything, and too much of nothing. But these are unfortunately coupled with a total want of common conduct. For instance, the *note* to your *page*—do you suppose I delivered it? or did you mean that I should? I did not, of course.

Then your heart, my poor Caro (what a little volcano!), that pours *lava* through your veins; and yet I cannot wish it a bit colder, to make a *marble slab* of, as you sometimes see (to understand my foolish metaphor) brought in vases, tables, etc., from Vesuvius, when hardened after an eruption. To drop my detestable tropes and figures, you know I have always thought you the cleverest, most agreeable, absurd, amiable, perplexing, dangerous, fascinating little being that lives now, or ought to have lived 2000 years ago. I won't talk to you of beauty; I am no judge. But our beauties cease to be so when near you, and therefore you have either some, or something better. And now, Caro, this nonsense is the first and last compliment (if it be such) I ever paid you. You have often reproached me as wanting in that respect; but others will make up the deficiency.

Come to Lord Grey's; at least do not let me keep you away. All that you so often *say*, I *feel*. Can more be said or felt? This same prudence is tiresome enough; but one *must* maintain it, or what *can* one do to be saved? Keep to it.

IX To Lady Caroline Lamb

May 1st, 1812

My dear Lady Caroline,—I have read over the few poems of Miss Milbank with attention. They display fancy, feeling, and a little practice would very soon induce facility of expression. Though I have an abhorrence of Blank Verse, I like the lines on Dermody so much that I wish they were in rhyme. The lines in the Cave of Seaham have a turn of thought which I cannot sufficiently commend, and here I am at least candid as my own opinions differ upon such subjects. The first stanza is very good indeed, and the others, with a few slight alterations, might be rendered equally excellent. The last are smooth and pretty. But these are all, has she no others? She certainly is a very extraordinary girl; who would imagine so much strength and variety of thought under that placid Countenance? It is not necessary for Miss M. to be an authoress, indeed I do not think publishing at all creditable either to men or women, and (though you will not believe me) very often feel ashamed of it myself; but I have no hesitation in saying that she has talents which, were it proper or requisite to indulge, would have led to distinction.

A friend of mine (fifty years old, and an author, but not *Rogers*) has just been here. As there is no name to the MSS. I shewed them to him, and he was much more enthusiastic in his praises than I have been. He thinks them beautiful; I shall content myself with observing that they are better, much better, than anything of Miss M.'s protegee (*sic*) Blacket. You will say as much of this to Miss M. as you think proper. I say all this very sincerely. I have no desire to be better acquainted with Miss Milbank; she is too good for a fallen spirit to know, and I should like her more if she were less perfect.[1]

Believe me, yours ever most truly.

X TO LORD HOLLAND

June 25, 1812

My dear Lord,

I must appear very ungrateful, and have, indeed, been very negligent, but till last night I was not apprized of Lady Holland's restoration, and I shall call to-morrow to have the satisfaction, I trust, of hearing that she is well. —I hope that neither politics nor gout have assailed your Lordship since I last saw you, and that you also are "as well as could be expected." The other night, at a ball, I was presented by order to our gracious Regent, who honoured me with some conversation, and professed a predilection for poetry.—I confess it was a most unexpected honour, and I thought of poor B—s's adventure, with some apprehension of a similar blunder. I have now great hope, in the event of Mr. Pye's decease, of "warbling truth at court," like Mr. Mallet of indifferent memory.—Consider, one hundred marks a year! besides the wine and the dis-

grace; but then remorse would make me drown myself in my own butt before the year's end, or the finishing of my first dithyrambic.—So that, after all, I shall not meditate our laureate's death by pen or poison.

Will you present my best respects to Lady Holland, and believe me hers and yours very sincerely.

XI TO LADY MELBOURNE

Cheltenham, September 10, 1812

Dear Lady Melbourne,—I presume you have heard and will not be sorry to hear *again* that they [2] are safely deposited in Ireland, and that the sea rolls between you and *one* of your torments; the other you see is still at your elbow. Now (if you are as sincere as I sometimes almost dream) you will not regret to hear, that I wish this to end, and it certainly shall not be renewed on my part. It is not that I love another, but loving at all is quite out of my way; I am tired of being a fool, and when I look back on the waste of time, and the destruction of all my plans last winter by this last romance, I am—what I ought to have been long ago. It is true from early habit, one must make love mechanically, as one swims. I was once very fond of both, but now as I never swim, unless I tumble into the water, I don't make love till almost obliged, though I fear *that* is not the shortest way out of the troubled waves with which in such accidents we must struggle.

But I will say no more on this topic, as I am not sure of my ground, and you can easily outwit me, as you always hitherto have done.

To-day I have had a letter from Lord Holland, wishing me to write for the opening theatre, but as all Grub Street seems engaged in the contest, I have no ambition to enter the lists, and have thrown my few ideas into the fire. I never risk *rivalry* in anything, you see the very *lowest*, as in this case, discourages me, from a sort of mixed feeling, I don't know if it be *pride*, but *you* will say it certainly is not *modesty*. I suppose your friend Twiss will be *one*. I hear there are five hundred, and I wish him success. I really think he would do it well, but few men who have any character to lose

---

[1] In his journal Byron has the following entry dated Nov. 30, 1813:

"Yesterday, a very pretty letter from Annabella, which I answered. What an odd situation and friendship is ours!—without one spark of love on either side, and produced by circumstances which in general lead to coldness on one side, and aversion on the other. She is a very superior woman, and very little spoiled, which is strange in an heiress—a girl of twenty—a peeress that is to be, in her own right—an only child, and a savante, who has always had her own way. She is a poetess—a mathematician—a metaphysician, and yet, withal, very kind, generous, and gentle, with very little pretension. Any other head would be turned with half her acquisitions, and a tenth of her advantages."

[2] Lady Caroline Lamb and her mother.

would risk it in an anonymous scramble, for the sake of their own feelings.

I have written to Lord H. to thank him and decline the chance.

Betty is performing here, I fear very ill. His figure is that of a hippopotamus, his face like the bull and mouth on the panels of a heavy coach, his arms like fins fattened out of shape, his voice the gargling of an alderman with the quinsy, and his acting altogether ought to be natural, for it certainly is like nothing that *Art* has ever yet exhibited on the stage.

Will you honour me with a line at your leisure? On the most *indifferent* subjects you please and believe me ever,

Yours very affectionately.

XII To W. Gifford, Esq.

June 18, 1813

My dear Sir,

I feel greatly at a loss how to write to you at all—still more to thank you as I ought. If you knew the veneration with which I have ever regarded you, long before I had the most distant prospect of becoming your acquaintance, literary or personal, my embarrassment would not surprise you.

Any suggestion of yours, even were it conveyed in the less tender shape of the text of the Baviad, or a Monk Mason note in Massinger, would have been obeyed; I should have endeavoured to improve myself by your censure: judge then if I should be less willing to profit by your kindness. It is not for me to bandy compliments with my elders and my betters: I receive your approbation with gratitude, and will not return my brass for your gold, by expressing more fully those sentiments of admiration, which, however sincere, would, I know, be unwelcome.

To your advice on religious topics, I shall equally attend. Perhaps the best way will be by avoiding them altogether. The already published objectionable passages have been much commented upon, but certainly have been rather strongly interpreted. I am no bigot to infidelity, and did not expect that, because I doubted the immortality of man, I should be charged with denying the existence of a God. It was the comparative insignificance of our-

selves and *our world*, when placed in comparison with the mighty whole, of which it is an atom, that first led me to imagine that our pretensions to eternity might be overrated.

This, and being early disgusted with a calvinistic Scotch school, where I was cudgelled to church for the first ten years of my life, afflicted me with this malady; for, after all, it is, I believe, a disease of the mind as much as other kinds of hypochondria.

* * *

XIII To Miss Milbanke

Sept. 26, 1813

My dear Friend,—for such you will permit me to call you—On my return to town I find some consolation for having left a number of pleasant people in your letter—the more so as I begun to doubt if I should ever receive another. You ask me some questions, and as they are about myself, you must pardon the egotism into which my answers must betray me. I am glad that you know any "good deed" that I am supposed ever to have blundered upon, simply because it proves that you have not heard me invariably ill spoken of. If true I am sufficiently rewarded by a short step towards your good opinion. You don't like my "restless" doctrines—I should be very sorry if you did; but I can't stagnate nevertheless. If I must sail let it be on the ocean no matter how stormy—any thing but a dull cruise on a land lake without ever losing sight of the same insipid shores by which it is surrounded.

"Gay" but not "content"—very true. You say I never attempt to justify myself. You are right. At times I can't and occasionally I won't defend by explanation; life is not worth having on such terms. The only attempt I ever made at defence was in a poetical point of view—and what did it end in? not an exculpation of me, but an attack on all other persons whatsoever. I should make a pretty scene indeed if I went on defending—besides, by proving myself (supposing it possible) a good sort of quiet country gentleman, to how many people should I give more pain than pleasure? Do you think accusers like one the better for being confuted? You have detected a laughter "false to the heart"—allowed—yet I have been tolerably sincere with you and I fear sometimes troublesome. To the charge of pride I suspect I must plead guilty, because when a boy and a very young one it was the constant reproach of schoolfellows and tutors. Since I grew up I have heard less about it—probably because I have now neither schoolfellow nor tutor. It was however originally defensive—for at that time my hand like Ishmael's was against every one's and every one's against mine. I now come to a subject of your inquiry which you must have perceived I always hitherto avoided—an awful one—"Religion." I was bred in Scotland among Calvinists in the first part of my life which gave me a dislike to that persuasion. Since that period I have visited the most bigotted and credulous of countries—Spain, Greece, Turkey. As a spectacle the Catholic is more fascinating than the Greek or the Moslem; but the last is the only believer who practises the precepts of his Prophet to the last chapter of his creed. My opinions are quite undecided. I may say so sincerely, since, when given over at Patras in 1810, I rejected and ejected three Priest-loads of spiritual consolation by threatening to turn Mussulman if they did not leave me in quiet. I was in great pain and looked upon death as in that respect a relief—without much regret for the past, and few speculations on the future. Indeed so indifferent was I to my bodily situation, that, tho' I was without any attendant but a young Frenchman as ill as myself, two barbarous Arnouts, and a deaf and desperate Greek Quack—and my English servant (a man with me) within two days journey—I would not allow the last to be sent for—worth all the rest as he would have been in attendance at such a time, because—I really don't know why—unless it was an indifference to which I am certainly not subject when in good health. I believe doubtless in God, and should be happy to be convinced of much more. If I do not at present place implicit faith in tradition and revelation of any human creed, I hope it is not from want of reverence for the Creator but the created, and when I see a man publishing a pamphlet to prove that Mr. Pitt is risen from the dead (as was done a week ago), perfectly positive in the truth of his assertion, I must be permitted to doubt more miracles equally well attested; but

the moral of Christianity is perfectly beautiful—and the very sublime of virtue—yet even there we find some of its finer precepts in the earlier axioms of the Greeks—particularly "do unto others as you would they should do unto you"—the forgiveness of injuries and more which I do not remember. Good night; I have sent you a long prose. I hope your answer will be equal in length—I am sure it will be more amusing—You write remarkably well—which you won't like to hear, so I shall say no more about it.

Ever yours most sincerely.

P.S.—I shall post-scribble this half sheet. When at Aston I sent you a short note for I began to feel a little nervous about the reception of my last letter. I shall be down there again next week and merely left to escape from the Doncaster Races—being very ill adapted for provincial festivities—but I shall rejoin the party when they are over. This letter was written last night after a two days journey with little rest and no refreshment (for eating on the road throws me into a fever directly); you will therefore not wonder if it is a meagre performance. When you honor me with an answer, address to London. Present my invariable respects to Sir R. and L^y Mil. and once more receive them for yourself. Good morning.

XIV To Miss Milbanke

Nov. 10, 1813

I perceive by part of your last letter that you are still inclined to believe me a gloomy personage. Those who pass so much of their time entirely alone can't be always in very high spirits; yet I don't know,—though I certainly do enjoy society to a certain extent, I never passed two hours in mixed company without wishing myself out of it again. Still I look upon myself as a facetious companion, well reputed by all the wits at whose jests I readily laugh, and whose repartees I take care never to incur by any kind of contest,—for which I feel as little qualified as I do for the more solid pursuits of demonstration.

* * *

I by no means rank poetry or poets high in the scale of intellect. This may look like affectation, but it is my real opinion. It is the lava of the imagination whose eruption prevents an earthquake. They say poets never or rarely go *mad.* Cowper and Collins are instances to the contrary (but Cowper was no poet). It is, however, to be remarked that they rarely do, but are generally so near it that I cannot help thinking rhyme is so far useful in anticipating and preventing the disorder. I prefer the talents of action—of war, or the senate, or even of science,—to all the speculations of those mere dreamers of another existence (I don't mean religiously but fancifully) and spectators of this apathy. Disgust and perhaps incapacity have rendered me now a mere spectator; but I have occasionally mixed in the active and tumultuous departments of existence, and in these alone my recollection rests with any satisfaction, though not the best parts of it.

XV To Thomas Moore

2, Albany, April 9, 1814

Viscount Althorpe is about to be married, and I have gotten his spacious bachelor apartments in Albany, to which you will, I hope, address a speedy answer to this mine epistle.

I am but just returned to town, from which you may infer that I have been out of it; and I have been boxing, for exercise, with Jackson for this last month daily. I have also been drinking, and, on one occasion, with three other friends at the Cocoa Tree, from six till four, yea, unto five in the matin. We clareted and champagned till two—then supped, and finished with a kind of regency punch composed of madeira, brandy, and *green* tea, no *real* water being admitted therein. There was a night for you!—without once quitting the table, except to ambulate home, which I did alone, and in utter contempt of a hackney-coach and my own *vis*, both of which were deemed necessary for our conveyance. And so, —I am very well, and they say it will hurt my constitution.

I have also, more or less, been breaking a few of the favourite commandments; but I mean to pull up and marry, if any one will have me. In the mean time, the other day I nearly killed myself with a collar of brawn,

which I swallowed for supper, and *in*digested for I don't know how long; but that is by the by. All this gourmandise was in honour of Lent; for I am forbidden meat all the rest of the year, but it is strictly enjoined me during your solemn fast. I have been, and am, in very tolerable love; but of that hereafter as it may be.

My dear Moore, say what you will in your preface; and quiz any thing, or any body,— me, if you like it. Oons! dost thou think me of the *old,* or rather *elderly,* school? If one can't jest with one's friends, with whom can we be facetious? You have nothing to fear from ——, whom I have not seen, being out of town when he called. He will be very correct, smooth, and all that, but I doubt whether there will be any "grace beyond the reach of art";—and, whether there is or not, how long will you be so d—d modest? As for Jeffrey, it is a very handsome thing of him to speak well of an old antagonist, —and what a mean mind dared not do. Any one will revoke praise; but—were it not partly my own case—I should say that very few have strength of mind to unsay their censure, or follow it up with praise of other things.

What think you of the review of *Levis?* It beats the Bag and my hand-grenade hollow, as an invective, and hath thrown the Court into hysterics, as I hear from very good authority. Have you heard from . . .

No more rhyme for—or rather, *from*—me. I have taken my leave of that stage, and henceforth will mountebank it no longer. I have had my day, and there's an end. The utmost I expect, or even wish, is to have it said in the Biographia Britannica, that I might perhaps have been a poet, had I gone on and amended. My great comfort is, that the temporary celebrity I have wrung from the world has been in the very teeth of all opinions and prejudices. I have flattered no ruling powers; I have never concealed a single thought that tempted me. They can't say I have truckled to the times, nor to popular topics (as Johnson, or somebody, said of Cleveland), and whatever I have gained has been at the expenditure of as much *personal* favour as possible; for I do believe never was a bard more unpopular, *quoad homo,* than myself, And now I have done;— "ludite nunc alios." Every body may be d—d, they seem fond of it, and resolved to stickle lustily for endless brimstone.

Oh—by the by, I had nearly forgot. There is a long Poem, an "Anti-Byron," coming out, to prove that I have formed a conspiracy to overthrow, by *rhyme*, all religion and government and have already made great progress! It is not very scurrilous, but serious and ethereal. I never felt myself important, till I saw and heard of my being such a little Voltaire as to induce such a production. Murray would not publish it, for which he was a fool, and so I told him; but some one else will, doubtless. "Something too much of this."

Your French scheme is good, but let it be *Italian;* all the Angles will be at Paris. Let it be Rome, Milan, Naples, Florence, Turin, Venice, or Switzerland, and "egad!" (as Bayes saith), I will connubiate and join you; and we will write a new "Inferno" in our Paradise. Pray, think of this—and I will really buy a wife and a ring, and say the ceremony, and settle near you in a summer-house upon the Arno, or the Po, or the Adriatic.

Ah! my poor little pagod, Napoleon, has walked off his pedestal. He has abdicated, they say. This would draw molten brass from the eyes of Zatanai. What! "kiss the ground before young Malcolm's feet, and then be baited by the rabble's curse!" I cannot bear such a crouching catastrophe. I must stick to Sylla, for my modern favourites don't do,—their resignations are of a different kind. All health and prosperity, my dear Moore. Excuse this lengthy letter.

Ever, etc.

P.S. The Quarterly quotes you frequently in an article on America; and every body I know asks perpetually after you and yours. When will you answer them in person?

XVI To Thomas Moore

Newstead Abbey, Sept. 20, 1814

Here's to her who long
    Hath waked the poet's sigh!
The girl who gave to song
    What gold could never buy.

—My dear Moore, I am going to be married—that is, I am accepted, and one usually hopes the rest will follow. My mother of the Gracchi (that *are* to be) *you* think too straitlaced for me, although the paragon of only children, and invested with "golden opinions of all sorts of men," and full of "most blest conditions" as Desdemona herself. Miss Milbanke is the lady, and I have her father's invitation to proceed there in my elect capacity, —which, however, I cannot do till I have settled some business in London, and got a blue coat.

She is said to be an heiress, but of that I know nothing certainly, and shall not inquire. But I do know, that she has talents and excellent qualities; and you will not deny her judgment, after having refused six suitors and taken me.

Now, if you have any thing to say against this, pray do; my mind's made up, positively fixed, determined, and therefore I will listen to reason, because now it can do no harm. Things may occur to break it off, but I will hope not. In the mean time, I tell you (a *secret,* by the by,—at least, till I know she wishes it to be public) that I have proposed and am accepted. You need not be in a hurry to wish me joy, for one mayn't be married for months. I am going to town to-morrow; but expect to be here, on my way there, within a fortnight.

If this had not happened, I should have gone to Italy. In my way down, perhaps, you will meet me at Nottingham, and come over with me here. I need not say that nothing will give me greater pleasure. I must, of course, reform thoroughly; and, seriously, if I can contribute to her happiness, I shall secure my own. She is so good a person, that—that—in short, I wish I was a better.

Ever, etc.

XVII To Miss Milbanke

(Extract.)

20 Oct., 1814

I have been so much amused with your "extracts," though I had no idea what an evil spirit I then appeared in your eyes. You were quite right however, as far as appearances, but that was not my natural character. I was just returned from a far country where everything was different, and felt bewildered and not very happy in my own, which I had left without regret and returned to without interest. I found myself, I did not very well know why, an object of curiosity which I never wished to excite—and about a poem which I had no conception was to make such a fuss. My mind and my feelings were moreover occupied with considerations which had nothing in common with the circle where I was whirling, so that no wonder I was repulsive and cold. I never could conquer my disposition to be both in a crowd from which I was always wishing myself away.

Those who know me most intimately can tell you that I am if anything too *childish*, with a greater turn for the ridiculous than for anything serious,—and, I could hope, not very ill natured *off the stage*, and, if angry, never loud. I can't say much for these qualifications, but I have such a regard for yours, that I am sure we shall be a very happy couple. I wish you had a greater passion for governing, for I don't shine in conducting myself, and am very docile with a gentle guide.

XVIII To Lady Melbourne

November 13, 1814

My dear Lady M.,—I delivered your letters, but have only mentioned ye receipt of your last to myself.

Do you know I have grave doubts if this will be a marriage now? Her disposition is the very reverse of our imaginings. She is overrun with fine feelings, scruples about herself and her disposition (I suppose, in fact, she means mine), and to crown all, is taken ill once every three days with I know not what. But the day before, and the day after, she seems well; looks and eats well, and is cheerful and confiding, and in short like any other person in good health and spirits. A few days ago she made one *scene*, not altogether out of C.'s style; it was too long and too trifling, in fact, for me to transcribe, but it did me no good. In the article of conversation, however, she has improved with a vengeance, but I don't much admire these same agitations upon slight occasions. I don't know, but I think it by no means improbable, you will see me in town soon. I can only interpret these things

one way, and merely wait to be certain, to make my obeisance and "exit singly." I hear of nothing but "feeling" from morning till night, except from Sir Ralph, with whom I go on to admiration. Lady Milbanke too is pretty well; but I am never sure of A. for a moment. The least word, and you know I rattle on through thick and thin (always, however, avoiding anything I think can offend her favourite notions), if only to prevent me from yawning. The least word, or alteration of tone, has some inference drawn from it. Sometimes we are too much alike, and then again too unlike. This comes of system, and squaring her notions to the devil knows what. For my part, I have lately had recourse to the eloquence of *action* (which Demosthenes calls the first part of oratory), and find it succeeds very well, and makes her very quiet; which gives me some hopes of the efficacy of the "calming process," so renowned in "our philosophy." In fact, and *entre nous*, it is really amusing; she is like a child in that respect, and quite caressable into kindness, and good humour; though I don't think her temper *bad* at any time, but very *self* tormenting and anxious, and romantic.

In short, it is impossible to foresee how this will end *now*, any more than two years ago; if there is a break, it shall be her doing not mine.

Ever yours most truly.

XIX To Thomas Moore

Seaham, Stockton-on-Tees, February 2, 1815

I have heard from London that you have left Chatsworth and all the women full of "entusymusy" about you, personally and poetically; and, in particular, that "When first I met thee" has been quite overwhelming in its effect. I told you it was one of the best things you ever wrote, though that dog Power wanted you to omit part of it. They are all regretting your absence at Chatsworth, according to my informant—"all the ladies quite, etc. etc. etc." Stap my vitals!

Well, now you have got home again—which I dare say is as agreeable as a "draught of cool small beer to the scorched palate of a waking sot"—now you have got home again,

I say, probably I shall hear from you. Since I wrote last, I have been transferred to my father-in-law's, with my lady and my lady's maid, etc. etc. etc. and the treaclemoon is over, and I am awake, and find myself married. My spouse and I agree to—and in—admiration. Swift says "no *wise* man ever married"; but, for a fool, I think it the most ambrosial of all possible future states. I still think one ought to marry upon *lease;* but am very sure I should renew mine at the expiration, though next term were for ninety and nine years.

I wish you would respond, for I am here "oblitusque meorum obliviscendus et illis."[1] Pray tell me what is going on in the way of intriguery, and how the w—s and rogues of the upper Beggar's Opera go on—or rather go off—in or after marriage; or who are going to break any particular commandment. Upon this dreary coast, we have nothing but county meetings and shipwrecks; and I have this day dined upon fish, which probably dined upon the crews of several colliers lost in the late gales. But I saw the sea once more in all the glories of surf and foam,—almost equal to the Bay of Biscay, and the interesting white squalls and short seas of Archipelago memory.

My papa, Sir Ralpho, hath recently made a speech at a Durham tax-meeting; and not only at Durham, but here, several times since, after dinner. He is now, I believe, speaking it to himself (I left him in the middle) over various decanters, which can neither interrupt him nor fall asleep,—as might possibly have been the case with some of his audience.

                                        Ever thine.

I must go to tea—damn tea. I wish it was Kinnaird's brandy, and with you to lecture me about it.

XX To Leigh Hunt

13, Terrace, Piccadilly, September–
                    October 30, 1815

My dear Hunt,—Many thanks for your books, of which you already know my opinion. Their external splendour should not disturb you as inappropriate—they have still more within than without. I take leave to differ with you on Wordsworth, as freely as I once agreed with you; at that time I gave him credit for a promise, which is unfulfilled. I still think his capacity warrants all you say of *it* only, but that his performances since *Lyrical Ballads* are miserably inadequate to the ability which lurks within him: there is undoubtedly much natural talent spilt over the *Excursion;* but it is rain upon rocks—where it stands and stagnates, or rain upon sands—where it falls without fertilizing. Who can understand him? Let those who do, make him intelligible. Jacob Behman, Swedenborg, and Joanna Southcote, are mere types of this arch-apostle of mystery and mysticism. But I have done,—no, I have not done, for I have two petty, and perhaps unworthy objections in small matters to make to him, which, with his pretensions to accurate observation, and fury against Pope's false translation of "the Moonlight scene in Homer," I wonder he should have fallen into;—these be they:—He says of Greece in the body of his book—that it is a land of

> "*Rivers, fertile plains*, and *sounding* shores,
> Under a cope of *variegated* sky."

The rivers are dry half the year, the plains are barren, and the shores *still* and *tideless* as the Mediterranean can make them; the sky is any-thing but variegated, being for months and months but "darkly, deeply, beautifully blue." —The next is in his notes, where he talks of our "Monuments crowded together in the busy, etc., of a large town," as compared with the "still seclusion of a Turkish cemetery in some *remote* place." This is pure stuff; for *one* monument in our churchyards there are *ten* in the Turkish, and so crowded, that you cannot walk between them; that is, divided merely by a path or road; and as to "*remote places*," men never take the trouble in a barbarous country, to carry their dead very far; they must have lived near to where they were buried. There are no cemeteries in "remote places," except such as have the cypress and the tombstone still left, where the olive and the habitation of the living have perished. . . .

These things I was struck with, as coming peculiarly in my own way; and in both of these he is wrong; yet I should have noticed neither, but for his attack on Pope for a like blunder,

[1] "My friends forgetting, by my friends forgot." (Sir Theodore Martin's translation of Horace.)

and a peevish affectation about him of despising a popularity which he will never obtain. I write in great haste, and, I doubt, not much to the purpose; but you have it hot and hot, just as it comes, and so let it go. By-the-way, both he and you go too far against Pope's "So when the moon," etc.; it is no translation, I know; but it is not such false description as asserted. I have read it on the spot; there is a burst, and a lightness, and a glow about the night in the Troad, which makes the "planets vivid," and the "pole glowing." The moon is —at least the sky is, clearness itself; and I know no more appropriate expression for the expansion of such a heaven—o'er the scene— the plain—the sky—Ida—the Hellespont— Simois—Scamander—and the Isles—than that of a "flood of glory." I am getting horribly lengthy, and must stop: to the whole of your letter "I say ditto to Mr. Burke," as the Bristol candidate cried by way of electioneering harangue. You need not speak of morbid feelings and vexations to me; I have plenty; but I must blame partly the times, and chiefly myself; but let us forget them. *I* shall be very apt to do so when I see you next. Will you come to the theatre and see our new management? You shall cut it up to your heart's content, root and branch, afterwards, if you like; but come and see it! If not, I must come and see you.

Ever yours, very truly and affectionately.

P.S.—Not a word from Moore for these two months. Pray let me have the rest of *Rimini.* You have two excellent points in that poem—originality and Italianism. I will back you as a bard against half the fellows on whom you have thrown away much good criticism and eulogy; but don't let your bookseller publish in *quarto;* it is the worst size possible for circulation. I say this on bibliopolical authority.

Again, yours ever.

XXI To Thomas Moore

March 8, 1816

I rejoice in your promotion as Chairman and Charitable Steward, etc. etc. These be dignities which await only the virtuous. But then, recollect you are *six* and *thirty* (I speak this enviously—not of your age, but the 'honour—love—obedience—troops of friends,

which accompany it), and I have eight years good to run before I arrive at such hoary perfection; by which time,—if I *am* at all,—it will probably be in a state of grace or progressing merits.

I must set you right in one point, however. The fault was *not*—no, nor even the misfortune—in my "choice" (unless in *choosing at all*) —for I do not believe—and I must say it, in the very dregs of all this bitter business—that there ever was a better, or even a brighter, a kinder, or a more amiable and agreeable being than Lady B. I never had, nor can have, any reproach to make her, while with me. Where there is blame, it belongs to myself, and, if I cannot redeem, I must bear it.

Her nearest relatives are a . . . —my circumstances have been and are in a state of great confusion—my health has been a good deal disordered, and my mind ill at ease for a considerable period. Such are the causes (I do not name then as excuses) which have frequently driven me into excess, and disqualified my temper for comfort. Something also may be attributed to the strange and desultory habits which, becoming my own master at an early age, and scrambling about, over and through the world, may have induced. I still, however, think that, if I had had a fair chance, by being placed in even a tolerable situation, I might have gone on fairly. But that seems hopeless,—and there is nothing more to be said. At present—except my health, which is better (it is odd, but agitation or contest of any kind gives a rebound to my spirits and sets me up for the time)—I have to battle with all kinds of unpleasantnesses, including private and pecuniary difficulties, etc., etc.

I believe I may have said this before to you, —but I risk repeating it. It is nothing to bear the *privations* of adversity, or, more properly, ill fortune; but my pride recoils from its *indignities*. However, I have no quarrel with that same pride, which will, I think, buckler me through every thing. If my heart could have been broken, it would have been so years ago, and by events more afflicting than these.

I agree with you (to turn from this topic to our shop) that I have written too much. The last things were, however, published very reluctantly by me, and for reasons I will explain when we meet. I know not why I have dwelt so much on the same scenes, except that I find them fading, or *confusing* (if such a word may be) in my memory, in the midst of present turbulence and pressure, and I felt anxious to stamp before the die was worn out. I now break it. With those countries, and events connected with them, all my really poetical feelings begin and end. Were I to try, I could make nothing of any other subject,—and that I have apparently exhausted. "Woe to him," says Voltaire, "who says all he could say on any subject." There are some on which, perhaps, I could have said still more: but I leave them all, and not too soon.

Do you remember the lines I sent you early last year, which you still have? I don't wish (like Mr. Fitzgerald, in the Morning Post) to claim the character of "Vates" in all its translations, but were they not a little prophetic? I mean those beginning "There's not a joy the world can," etc. etc. on which I rather pique myself as being the truest, though the most melancholy, I ever wrote.

What a scrawl have I sent you! You say nothing of yourself, except that you are a Lancasterian churchwarden, and an encourager of mendicants. When are you out? and how is your family? My child is very well and flourishing, I hear; but I must see also. I feel no disposition to resign it to the contagion of its grandmother's society, though I am unwilling to take it from the mother. It is weaned, however, and something about it must be decided.

Ever, etc.

know that some time ago I made my will in her favour and her children, because any child of ours was provided for by other and better means. This could not be prejudice to you, for we had not then differed, and even now is useless during your life by the terms of our settlements. Therefore,—be kind to her, for never has she acted or spoken towards you but as your friend. And recollect, that, though it may be an advantage to you to have lost a husband, it is sorrow to her to have the waters now, or the earth hereafter, between her and her brother. It may occur to your memory that you formerly promised me this much. I repeat it—for deep resentments have but *half* recollections. Do not deem this promise cancell'd, for it was not a vow.

I have received from Mr. Wharton a letter containing one question and two pieces of intelligence. The carriage is yours, and, as it only carried us to Halnaby, and London, and you to Kirkby, it will yet convey you many a more propitious journey.

The receipts can remain, unless you find them troublesome; if so, let them be sent to Augusta, through whom I would also receive occasional accounts of my child. My address will be left with Mrs. Leigh; the ring is of no lapidary value, but it contains the hair of a King and of an ancestor, and I wish it to be preserved to Miss Byron.

With regard to a subsequent letter from Mr. Wharton I have to observe that it is the "law's delay" not mine, and that, when the tenor of the bond is settled between him and Mr. H., I am ready to sign.

Yours truly.

XXII To Lady Byron

(Undated. Early April, 1816)

More last words—not many—and such as you will attend to; answer I do not expect, nor does it import; but you will at least hear me.— I have just parted from Augusta, almost the last being whom you have left me to part with.

Wherever I may go,—and I am going far,— you and I can never meet in this world, nor in the next. Let this content or atone.—If any accident occurs to me, be kind to Augusta; if she is then also nothing—to her children. You

XXIII To the Hon. Augusta Leigh

Diodati, Geneva,
September 8th, 1816

. . . I have been in some danger on the lake (near Meillerie), but nothing to speak of; and, as to all these "mistresses," Lord help me—I have had but one. Now don't scold; but what could I do?—a foolish girl,[1] in spite of all I could say or do, would come after me, or rather went before—for I found her here— and I have had all the plague possible to per-

[1] Claire Clairmont, Mary Shelley's half sister.

suade her to go back again; but at last she went. Now, dearest, I do most truly tell thee, that I could not help this, that I did all I could to prevent it, and have at last put an end to it. I was not in love, nor have any love left for any; but I could not exactly play the Stoic with a woman, who had scrambled eight hundred miles to unphilosophize me. Besides, I had been regaled of late with so many "two courses and a *desert*" (Alas!) of aversion, that I was fain to take a little love (if pressed particularly) by way of novelty. And now you know all that I know of that matter, and it's over. Pray write. I have heard nothing since your last, at least a month or five weeks ago. I go out very little, except into the *air*, and on journeys, and on the water, and to Copet, where Mᵉ de Staël has been particularly kind and friendly towards me, and (I hear) fought battles without number in my very indifferent cause. It has (they say) made quite as much noise on this as the other side of *La Manche*. Heaven knows why—but I seem destined to set people by the ears.

Don't hate me, but believe me, ever yours most affectionately.

XXIV To Thomas Moore

Venice, November 17, 1816

I wrote to you from Verona the other day in my progress hither, which letter I hope you will receive. Some three years ago, or it may be more, I recollect your telling me that you had received a letter from our friend Sam, dated "On board his gondola." *My* gondola is, at this present, waiting for me on the canal; but I prefer writing to you in the house, it being autumn—and rather an English autumn than otherwise. It is my intention to remain at Venice during the winter, probably, as it has always been (next to the East) the greenest island of my imagination. It has not disappointed me; though its evident decay would, perhaps, have that effect upon others. But I have been familiar with ruins too long to dislike desolation. Besides, I have fallen in love, which, next to falling into the canal (which would be of no use, as I can swim), is the best or the worst thing I could do. I have got some extremely good apartments in the house of a

"Merchant of Venice," who is a good deal occupied with business, and has a wife in her twenty-second year. Marianna (that is her name) is in her appearance altogether like an antelope. She has the large, black, oriental eyes, with the peculiar expression in them which is seen rarely among *Europeans*—even the Italians—and which many of the Turkish women give themselves by tinging the eyelid,—an art not known out of that country, I believe. This expression she has *naturally*,—and something more than this. In short, I cannot describe the effect of this kind of eye,—at least upon me. Her features are regular, and rather aquiline—mouth small—skin clear and soft, with a kind of hectic colour—forehead remarkably good: her hair is of the dark gloss, curl, and colour of Lady Jersey's: her figure is light and pretty, and she is a famous songstress —scientifically so: her natural voice (in conversation, I mean,) is very sweet; and the naïveté of the Venetian dialect is always pleasing in the mouth of a woman.

November 23

You will perceive that my description, which was proceeding with the minuteness of a passport, has been interrupted for several days. In the mean time.

* * *

December 5

Since my former dates, I do not know that I have much to add on the subject, and, luckily, nothing to take away; for I am more pleased than ever with my Venetian, and begin to feel very serious on that point—so much so, that I shall be silent.

* * *

By way of divertisement, I am studying daily, at an Armenian monastery, the Armenian language. I found that my mind wanted something craggy to break upon; and this —as the most difficult thing I could discover here for an amusement—I have chosen, to torture me into attention. It is a rich language, however, and would amply repay any one the trouble of learning it. I try, and shall go on;—but I answer for nothing, least of all for my intentions or my success. There are some very curious MSS. in the monastery, as well as books; translations also from Greek originals, now lost, and from Persian and Syriac, etc., besides works of their own people. Four years ago the French instituted an Armenian professorship. Twenty pupils presented themselves on Monday morning, full of noble ardour, ingenuous youth, and impregnable industry. They persevered, with a courage worthy of the nation and of universal conquest, till Thursday; when *fifteen* of the *twenty* succumbed to the six-and-twentieth letter of the alphabet. It is, to be sure, a Waterloo of an Alphabet—that must be said for them. But it is so like these fellows, to do by it as they did by their sovereigns—abandon both; to parody the old rhymes, "Take a thing and give a thing"—"Take a King and give a King." They are the worst of animals, except their conquerors.

I hear that H—n is your neighbour, having a living in Derbyshire. You will find him an excellent-hearted fellow, as well as one of the cleverest; a little, perhaps, too much japanned by preferment in the church and the tuition of youth, as well as inoculated with the disease of domestic felicity, besides being overrun with fine feelings about woman and *constancy* (that small change of Love, which people exact so rigidly, receive in such counterfeit coin, and repay in baser metal); but, otherwise, a very worthy man, who has lately got a pretty wife, and (I suppose) a child by this time. Pray remember me to him, and say that I know not which to envy most—his neighbourhood, him, or you.

Of Venice I shall say little. You must have seen many descriptions; and they are most of them like. It is a poetical place; and classical, to us, from Shakespeare and Otway. I have not yet sinned against it in verse, nor do I know that I shall do so, having been tuneless since I crossed the Alps, and feeling, as yet, no renewal of the *estro*. By the way, I suppose you have seen *Glenarvon*.[1] Madame de Staël lent it me to read from Copet last autumn. It seems to me that, if the authoress had written the *truth*, and nothing but the truth—the whole truth—the romance would not only have been more *romantic*, but more entertaining. As for the likeness, the picture

[1] By Lady Caroline Lamb.

can't be good—I did not sit long enough. When you have leisure, let me hear from and of you, believing me

Ever and truly yours most affectionately.

P.S. Oh! *your poem*—is it out? I hope Longman has paid his thousands: but don't you do as H— T—'s father did, who, having made money by a quarto tour, became a vinegar merchant; when, lo! his vinegar turned sweet (and be d—d to it) and ruined him. My last letter to you (from Verona) was enclosed to Murray—have you got it? Direct to me *here, poste restante*. There are no English here at present. There were several in Switzerland—some women; but, except Lady Dalrymple Hamilton, most of them as ugly as virtue—at least, those that I saw.

XXV To Thomas Moore

Venice, January 28, 1817

Your letter of the 8th is before me. The remedy for your plethora is simple—abstinence. I was obliged to have recourse to the like some years ago, I mean in point of *diet*, and, with the exception of some convivial weeks and days (it might be months, now and then), have kept to Pythagoras ever since. For all this, let me hear that you are better. You must not *indulge* in "filthy beer," nor in porter, nor eat *suppers*—the last are the devil to those who swallow dinner.

* * *

I am truly sorry to hear of your father's misfortune—cruel at any time, but doubly cruel in advanced life. However, you will, at least, have the satisfaction of doing your part by him, and, depend upon it, it will not be in vain. Fortune, to be sure, is a female, but not such a b— as the rest (always excepting your wife and my sister from such sweeping terms); for she generally has some justice in the long run. I have no spite against her, though, between her and Nemesis, I have had some sore gauntlets to run—but then I have done my best to deserve no better. But to *you*, she is a good deal in arrear, and she will come round—mind if she don't: you have the vigour of life, of independence, of talent, spirit, and character all with you. What you can do for yourself, you have done and will do; and surely there are some others in the world who would not be sorry to be of use, if you would allow them to be useful, or at least attempt it.

I think of being in England in the spring. If there is a row, by the sceptre of King Ludd, but I'll be one; and if there is none, and only a continuance of "this meek, piping time of peace," I will take a cottage a hundred yards to the south of your abode, and become your neighbour; and we will compose such canticles, and hold such dialogues as shall be the terror of the *Times* (including the newspaper of that name), and the wonder, and honour, and praise of the *Morning Chronicle* and posterity.

I rejoice to hear of your forthcoming in February—though I tremble for the "magnificence" which you attribute to the new *Childe Harold.* I am glad you like it; it is a fine indistinct piece of poetical desolation, and my favourite. I was half mad during the time of its composition, between metaphysics, mountains, lakes, love unextinguishable, thoughts unutterable, and the night-mare of my own delinquencies. I should, many a good day, have blown my brains out, but for the recollection that it would have given pleasure to my mother-in-law; and, even *then*, if I could have been certain to haunt her——but I won't dwell upon these trifling family matters.

Venice is in the *estro* of her carnival, and I have been up these last two nights at the ridotto and the opera, and all that kind of things. Now for an adventure. A few days ago a gondolier brought me a billet without a subscription, intimating a wish on the part of the writer to meet me either in gondola, or at the island of San Lazaro, or at a third rendezvous, indicated in the note. "I know the country's disposition well,"—in Venice "they do let heaven see those tricks they dare not show" etc. etc.; so, for all response, I said that neither of the three places suited me; but that I would either be at home at ten at night *alone,* or be at the ridotto at midnight, where the writer might meet me masked. At ten o'clock I was at home and alone (Marianna was gone with her husband to a conversazione), when the door of my apartment opened,

and in walked a well-looking and (for an Italian) *bionda* girl of about nineteen, who informed me that she was married to the brother of my *amorosa*, and wished to have some conversation with me. I made a decent reply, and we had some talk in Italian and Romaic (her mother being a Greek of Corfu), when, lo! in a very few minutes in marches, to my very great astonishment, Marianna S——, *in propria persona*, and, after making a most polite curtsy to her sister-in-law and to me, without a single word seizes her said sister-in-law by the hair, and bestows upon her some sixteen slaps, which would have made your ear ache only to hear their echo. I need not describe the screaming which ensued. The luckless visitor took flight. I seized Marianna, who, after several vain efforts to get away in pursuit of the enemy, fairly went into fits in my arms; and, in spite of reasoning, eau de Cologne, vinegar, half a pint of water, and God knows what other waters beside, continued so till past midnight.

After damning my servants for letting people in without apprizing me, I found that Marianna in the morning had seen her sister-in-law's gondolier on the stairs; and, suspecting that this apparition boded her no good, had either returned of her own accord, or been followed by her maids or some other spy of her people to the conversazione, from whence she returned to perpetrate this piece of pugilism. I had seen fits before, and also some small scenery of the same genus in and out of our island; but this was not all. After about an hour, in comes—who? why, Signor S——, her lord and husband, and finds me with his wife fainting upon a sofa, and all the apparatus of confusion, deshevelled hair, hats, handkerchiefs, salts, smelling bottles—and the lady as pale as ashes, without sense or motion. His first question was, "What is all this?" The lady could not reply—so I did. I told him the explanation was the easiest thing in the world; but, in the mean time, it would be as well to recover his wife—at least, her senses. This came about in due time of suspiration and respiration.

You need not be alarmed—jealousy is not the order of the day in Venice, and daggers are out of fashion, while duels, on love matters, are unknown—at least, with the husbands. But, for all this, it was an awkward affair; and though he must have known that I made love to Marianna, yet I believe he was not, till that evening, aware of the extent to which it had gone. It is very well known that almost all the married women have a lover; but it is usual to keep up the forms, as in other nations. I did not, therefore, know what the devil to say. I could not out with the truth, out of regard to her, and I did not choose to lie for my sake;—besides, the thing told itself. I thought the best way would be to let her explain it as she chose (a woman being never at a loss—the devil always sticks by them)—only determining to protect and carry her off, in case of any ferocity on the part of the Signor. I saw that he was quite calm. She went to bed, and next day—how they settled it, I know not, but settled it they did. Well—then I had to explain to Marianna about this never-to-be-sufficiently-confounded sister-in-law; which I did by swearing innocence, eternal constancy, etc. etc. . . . But the sister-in-law, very much discomposed with being treated in such wise, has (not having her own shame before her eyes) told the affair to half Venice, and the servants (who were summoned by the fight and the fainting) to the other half. But, here, nobody minds such trifles, except to be amused by them. I don't know whether you will be so, but I have scrawled a long letter out of these follies.

Believe me ever, etc.

XXVI To John Murray

Sept. 15, 1817

Dear Sir,—I enclose a sheet for correction, if ever you get to another edition. You will observe that the blunder in printing makes it appear as if the Chateau was *over* St. Gingo, instead of being on the opposite shore of the Lake, over Clarens. So, separate the paragraphs, otherwise my *to*pography will seem as inaccurate as your *ty*pography on this occasion.

The other day I wrote to convey my proposition with regard to the fourth and concluding canto. I have gone over and extended it to one hundred and fifty stanzas, which is almost as long as the two first were originally, and longer by itself than any of the smaller poems except the "Corsair." Mr. Hobhouse has made some very valuable and accurate notes of considerable length, and you may be sure that I will do for the text all that I can to finish with decency. I look upon Childe Harold as my best; and as I begun, I think of concluding with it. But I make no resolutions on that head, as I broke my former intention with regard to the "Corsair." However, I fear that I shall never do better; and yet, not being thirty years of age, for some moons to come, one ought to be progressive as far as intellect goes for many a good year. But I have had a devilish deal of tear and wear of mind and body in my time, besides having published too often and much already. God grant me some judgment to do what may be most fitting in that and every thing else, for I doubt my own exceedingly.

I have read "Lalla Rookh," but not with sufficient attention yet, for I ride about, and lounge, and ponder, and—two or three other things; so that my reading is very desultory, and not so attentive as it used to be. I am very glad to hear of its popularity, for Moore is a very noble fellow in all respects, and will enjoy it without any of the bad feelings which success—good or evil—sometimes engenders in the men of rhyme. Of the poem itself, I will tell you my opinion when I have mastered it: I say of the *poem*, for I don't like the *prose* at all, at all; and in the meantime, the "Fire-worshippers" is the best, and the "Veiled Prophet" the worst, of the volume.

With regard to poetry in general, I am convinced, the more I think of it, that he and *all* of us—Scott, Southey, Wordsworth, Moore, Campbell, I,—are all in the wrong, one as much as another; that we are upon a wrong revolutionary poetical system, or systems, not worth a damn in itself, and from which none but Rogers and Crabbe are free; and that the present and next generations will finally be of this opinion. I am the more confirmed in this by having lately gone over some of our classics, particularly *Pope*, whom I tried in this way:—I took Moore's poems and my own and some others, and went over them side by side with Pope's, and I was really astonished (I ought not to have been so) and mortified at the ineffable distance in point of sense, harmony, effect, and even *imagination*, passion, and *invention*, between the little Queen Anne's man, and us of the Lower Empire. Depend upon it, it is all Horace then, and Claudian now, among us; and if I had to begin again, I would mould myself accordingly. Crabbe's the man, but he has got a coarse and impracticable subject, and . . . [Rogers] is retired upon half-pay, and has done enough, unless he were to do as he did formerly.

XXVII   To Thomas Moore
Venice, February 2, 1818

Your letter of December 8th arrived but this day, by some delay, common but inexplicable. Your domestic calamity is very grievous, and I feel with you as much as I *dare* feel at all. Throughout life, your loss must be my loss, and your gain my gain; and, though my heart may ebb, there will always be a drop for you among the dregs.

I know how to feel with you, because (selfishness being always the substratum of our damnable clay) I am quite wrapt up in my own children. Besides my little legitimate, I have made unto myself an illegitimate since (to say nothing of one before), and I look forward to one of these as the pillar of my old age, supposing that I ever reach—which I hope I never shall—that desolating period. I have a great love for my little Ada, though perhaps she may torture me, like . . .

Your offered address will be as acceptable as you can wish. I don't much care what the wretches of the world think of me—all *that's* past. But I care a good deal what *you* think of me, and, so, say what you like. You *know* that I am not sullen; and, as to being *savage*, such things depend on circumstances. However, as to being in good humour in *your* society, there is no great merit in that, because it would be an effort, or an insanity, to be otherwise.

I don't know what Murray may have been saying or quoting. I called Crabbe and Sam the fathers of present Poesy; and said, that I thought—except them—all of *"us youth"* were on a wrong tack. But I never said that we did not sail well. Our fame will be hurt by *admiration* and *imitation*. When I say *our*, I mean *all* (Lakers included), except the postscript of the Augustans. The next generation (from the quantity and facility of imitation) will tumble and break their necks off our Pegasus, who runs away with us; but we keep the *saddle*, because we broke the rascal and can ride. But though easy to mount, he is the devil to guide; and the next fellows must go back to the riding-school and the manège, and learn to ride the "great horse."

Talking of horses, by the way, I have transported my own, four in number, to the Lido (*beach*, in English), a strip of some ten miles along the Adriatic, a mile or two from the city; so that I not only get a row in my gondola, but a spanking gallop of some miles daily along a firm and solitary beach, from the fortress to Malamocco, the which contributes considerably to my health and spirits.

I have hardly had a wink of sleep this week past. We are in the agonies of the Carnival's last days, and I must be up all night again, as well as to-morrow. I have had some curious masking adventures this Carnival, but, as they are not yet over, I shall not say on. I will work the mine of my youth to the last veins of the ore, and then—good night. I have lived, and am content.

Hobhouse went away before the Carnival began, so that he had little or no fun. Besides, it requires some time to be thoroughgoing with the Venetians; but of all this anon, in some other letter.

I must dress for the evening. There is an opera and ridotto, and I know not what, besides balls; and so, ever and ever yours.

P.S. I send this without revision, so excuse errors. I delight in the fame and fortune of Lalla, and again congratulate you on your well-merited success.

XXVIII   To Thomas Moore
Venice, September 19, 1818

. . . I have finished the first canto (a long one, of about 180 octaves) of a poem in the style and manner of "Beppo," encouraged by the good success of the same. It is called "Don Juan," and is meant to be a little quietly facetious upon every thing. But I doubt whether it is not—at least, as far as it has yet gone—too free for these very modest days. However, I shall try the experiment, anonymously; and if it don't take, it will be discontinued. It is dedicated to Southey in good, simple, savage verse, upon the Laureate's politics, and the way he got them. But the bore of copying it out is intolerable; and if I had an amanuensis he would be of no use, as my writing is so difficult to decipher.

My poem's Epic, and is meant to be
  Divided in twelve books, each book containing,
With love and war, a heavy gale at sea—
  A list of ships, and captains, and kings reigning—
New characters, etc., etc.

The above are two stanzas, which I send you as a brick of my Babel, and by which you can judge of the texture of the structure. . . .

XXIX To Lady Byron[1]

Venice, Nov. 18, 1818

Sir Samuel Romilly has cut his throat for the loss of his wife. It is now nearly three years since he became, in the face of his compact (by a retainer—previous, and, I believe, general), the advocate of the measures and the Approver of the proceedings, which deprived me of mine. I would not exactly, like Mr. Thwackum, when Philosopher Square bit his own tongue—"saddle him with a Judgement;" but

"This even-handed Justice
Commends the ingredients of our poisoned Chalice
To our own lips."

This Man little thought, when he was lacerating my heart according to law, while he was poisoning my life at its sources, aiding and abetting in the blighting, branding, and exile that was to be the result of his counsels in their indirect effects, that in less than thirty-six moons—in the pride of his triumph as the highest candidate for the representation of the Sister-City of the mightiest of Capitals—in the fullness of his professional career—in the greenness of a healthy old age—in the radiance of fame, and the complacency of self-earned riches—that a domestic affliction would lay

[1] Printed by Prothero from a draft in the Murray Mss.

him in the earth, with the meanest of malefactors, in a cross-road with the stake in his body, if the verdict of insanity did not redeem his ashes from the sentence of the laws he had lived upon by interpreting or misinterpreting, and died in violating.

This man had eight children, lately deprived of their mother: could he not live? Perhaps, previous to his annihilation, he felt a portion of what he contributed his legal mite to make me feel; but I have lived—lived to see him a Sexagenary Suicide.

It was not in vain that I invoked Nemesis in the midnight of Rome from the awfullest of her ruins.

Fare you well.

XXX To John Murray

Venice, April 6, 1819

The Second Canto of Don Juan was sent, on Saturday last, by post, in four packets, two of four, and two of three sheets each, containing in all two hundred and seventeen stanzas, octave measure. But I will permit no curtailments, except those mentioned about Castlereagh and . . . You sha'n't make *canticles* of my cantos. The poem will please, if it is lively; if it is stupid, it will fail: but I will have none of your damned cutting and slashing. If you please, you may publish *anonymously;* it will perhaps be better; but I will battle my way against them all, like a porcupine.

So you and Mr. Foscolo, etc. want me to undertake what you call a "great work?" an Epic Poem, I suppose, or some such pyramid. I'll try no such thing; I hate tasks. And then "seven or eight years!" God send us all well this day three months, let alone years. If one's years can't be better employed than in sweating poesy, a man had better be a ditcher. And works, too!—is Childe Harold nothing? You have so many "*divine*" poems, is it nothing to have written a *human* one? without any of your worn-out machinery. Why, man, I could have spun the thoughts of the four cantos of that poem into twenty, had I wanted to book-make, and its passion into as many modern tragedies. Since you want *length*, you shall have enough of *Juan*, for I'll make fifty cantos.

Jy 10th 1823.

Dear H.

It appears to me that your brother might direct his Counsel to cite from "Wat Tyler" and ask why that is not prosecuted? Always also a little from his Vision. And it would be as well to send off your Collectanea quickly that they may have time to prepare them for the Court and Courtiers. I have sent to Mrs L. for the Hereti=lix of being which — a Poem of about seven hundred and fifty lines height — the Age of Bronze — or Carmen Seculare et Annus micabilis — with this epi=graph. "Impar Congressus Achilli." It is calculated for the reading part

First Page of a Letter from Byron to Leigh Hunt. (See Appendix I.)

of the Million — being all on
politics &c &c and a review of
the Day in general — in my early
English Bards style — but a little
more stilted and somewhat too
full of "glittering of war" and
classical & historical allusions,
if not as are necessary they can
be added. — If it will do for
"the Liberal" — it and the Police
will form (in size that is) a
good half number. — But of
this you are judge. — It is in
the heroic couplet measure — which
is "an old friend with a new face."
I congratulate you on the weather

Yrs ever,
N. B.

Second Page of a Letter from Byron to Leigh Hunt. (See Appendix I.)

And Foscolo, too! Why does *he* not do something more than the Letters of Ortis, and a tragedy, and pamphlets? He has good fifteen years more at his command than I have: what has he done all that time?—proved his genius, doubtless, but not fixed its fame, nor done his utmost.

Besides, I mean to write my best work in *Italian*, and it will take me nine years more thoroughly to master the language; and then if my fancy exists, and I exist too, I will try what I *can* do *really*. As to the estimation of the English which you talk of, let them calculate what it is worth, before they insult me with their insolent condescension.

I have not written for their pleasure. If they are pleased, it is that they chose to be so; I have never flattered their opinions, nor their pride; nor will I. Neither will I make "Ladies' books" *al dilettar le femine e la plebe*. I have written from the fulness of my mind, from passion, from impulse, from many motives, but not for their "sweet voices."

I know the precise worth of popular applause, for few scribblers have had more of it; and if I chose to swerve into their paths, I could retain it, or resume it. But I neither love ye, nor fear ye; and though I buy with ye and sell with ye, I will neither eat with ye, drink with ye, nor pray with ye. They made me, without my search, a species of popular idol; they, without reason or judgment, beyond the caprice of their good pleasure, threw down the image from its pedestal: it was not broken with the fall, and they would, it seems, again replace it,—but they shall not.

You ask about my health: about the beginning of the year I was in a state of great exhaustion, attended by such debility of stomach that nothing remained upon it; and I was obliged to reform my "way of life," which was conducting me from the "yellow leaf" to the ground, with all deliberate speed. I am better in health and morals, and very much yours, etc.

P.S. I have read Hodgson's "Friends." . . . He is right in defending Pope against the bastard pelicans of the poetical winter day, who add insult to their parricide, by sucking the blood of the parent of English *real* poetry —poetry without fault—and then spurning the bosom which fed them.

XXXI To Douglas Kinnaird

Venice, April 24, 1819

Dear Douglas,—Damn *"the Vampire."* What do I know of Vampires? It must be some bookselling imposture; contradict it in a solemn paragraph.

I sent off on April 3rd the 2nd canto to *Don Juan* addressed to Murray, I hope it is arrived—by the Lord it is a Capo d'Opera, so "full of pastime and prodigality," but you shan't decimate or mutilate, no—"rather than that, come critics into the list, and champion me to the uttermost."

Nor you, nor that rugged rhinoceros Murray, have ever told me, in answer to *fifty* times the question, if he ever received the additions to Canto *first*, entitled "Julia's letter" and also some four stanzas for the beginning.

I have fallen in love, within the last month, with a Romagnuola Countess from Ravenna, the spouse of a year of Count Guiccioli, who is sixty—the girl twenty.

She is as fair as sunrise, and warm as noon, but she is young, and was not content with what she had done, unless it was to be turned to the advantage of the public, and so she made an *éclat*, which rather astonished even the Venetians, and electrified the Conversazioni of the Benzona, the Albrizzi, and the Michelli, and made her husband look embarrassed.

They have gone back to Ravenna some time, but they return in the winter. She is the queerest woman I ever met with, for in general they cost one something one way or other, whereas by an odd combination of circumstances, I have proved an expense to HER, which is not *my* custom, but an accident; however it don't matter.

She is a sort of Italian Caroline Lamb, except that she is much prettier, and not so savage. But she has the same red-hot head, the same noble disdain of public opinion, with the superstructure of all that Italy can add to such natural dispositions.

She is also of the Ravenna noblesse, educated in a convent, sacrificed to wealth, filial duty, and all that

I am damnably in love, but they are gone, for many months—and nothing but hope keeps me alive *seriously*.

Yours ever.

XXXII To John Murray

Bologna, June 7, 1819

Tell Mr. Hobhouse that I wrote to him a few days ago from Ferrara. It will therefore be idle in him or you to wait for any further answers or returns of proofs from Venice, as I have directed that no English letters be sent after me. The publication can be proceeded in without, and I am already sick of your remarks, to which I think not the least attention ought to be paid.

Tell Mr. Hobhouse that, since I wrote to him, I had availed myself of my Ferrara letters, and found the society much younger and better there than at Venice. I am very much pleased with the little the shortness of my stay permitted me to see of the Gonfaloniere Count Mosti, and his family and friends in general.

I have been picture-gazing this morning at the famous Domenichino and Guido, both of which are superlative. I afterwards went to the beautiful cemetery of Bologna, beyond the walls, and found, besides the superb burial-ground, an original of a Custode, who reminded one of the grave-digger in Hamlet. He has a collection of Capuchins' skulls, labelled on the forehead, and taking down one of them, said, "This was Brother Desiderio Berro, who died at forty—one of my best friends. I begged his head of his brethren after decease, and they gave it me. I put it in lime, and then boiled it. Here it is, teeth and all, in excellent preservation. He was the merriest, cleverest fellow I ever knew. Wherever he went, he brought joy; and whenever any one was melancholy, the sight of him was enough to make him cheerful again. He walked so actively, you might have taken him for a dancer—he joked—he laughed—oh! he was such a Frate as I never saw before, nor ever shall again!"

He told me that he had himself planted all the cypresses in the cemetery; that he had the greatest attachment to them and to his dead

people; that since 1801 they had buried fifty-three thousand persons. In showing some older monuments, there was that of a Roman girl of twenty, with a bust by Bernini. She was a princess Bartorini, dead two centuries ago; he said that, on opening her grave, they had found her hair complete, and "as yellow as gold." Some of the epitaphs at Ferrara pleased me more than the more splendid monuments at Bologna; for instance—

> "Martini Luigi
>   Implora pace."

> "Lucrezia Picini
>   Implora eterna quiete."

Can any thing be more full of pathos? Those few words say all that can be said or sought: the dead had had enough of life; all they wanted was rest, and this they *implored!* There is all the helplessness, and humble hope, and deathlike prayer, that can arise from the grave —"implora pace." I hope whoever may survive me, and shall see me put in the foreigners' burying-ground at the Lido, within the fortress by the Adriatic, will see those two words, and no more, put over me; I trust they won't think of "pickling, and bringing me home to Clod or Blunderbuss Hall." I am sure my bones would not rest in an English grave, or my clay mix with the earth of that country. I believe the thought would drive me mad on my deathbed, could I suppose that any of my friends would be base enough to convey my carcass back to your soil.—I would not even feed your worms, if I could help it.

So, as Shakespeare says of Mowbray, the banished Duke of Norfolk, who died at Venice (see Richard II), that he, after fighting

> "Against black Pagans, Turks, and Saracens,
>   And toil'd with works of war, retired himself
> To Italy, and there, at *Venice*, gave
> His body to that *pleasant* country's earth,
> And his pure soul unto his captain, Christ,
> Under whose colours he had fought so long."

Before I left Venice, I had returned to you your late, and Mr. Hobhouse's, sheets of Juan. Don't wait for further answers from me, but address yours to Venice, as usual. I know nothing of my own movements; I may return there in a few days, or not for some time. All depends on circumstances. I left Mr. Hoppner very well. My daughter Allegra was well too, and is growing pretty; her hair is growing darker, and her eyes are blue. Her temper and her ways, Mr. Hoppner says, are like mine, as well as her features: she will make, in that case, a manageable young lady.

I have never heard any thing of Ada, the little Electra of my Mycenae. . . . But there will come a day of reckoning, even if I should not live to see it. I have at least seen—[1] shivered, who was one of my assassins. When that man was doing his worst to uproot my whole family tree, branch, and blossoms— when, after taking my retainer, he went over to them—when he was bringing desolation on my hearth, and destruction on my house-hold gods—did he think that, in less than three years, a natural event—a severe do-mestic, but an expected and common calamity —would lay his carcass in a cross-road, or stamp his name in a Verdict of Lunacy! Did he (who in his sexagenary . . .) reflect or con-sider what *my* feelings must have been, when wife, and child, and sister, and name, and fame, and country, were to be my sacrifice on his legal altar—and this at a moment when my health was declining, my fortune embar-rassed, and my mind had been shaken by many kinds of disappointment—while I was yet young, and might have reformed what might be wrong in my conduct, and retrieved what was perplexing in my affairs! But he is in his grave, and . . . What a long letter I have scribbled!

Yours, etc.

P.S. Here, as in Greece, they strew flowers on the tombs. I saw a quantity of rose-leaves, and entire roses, scattered over the graves at Ferrara. It has the most pleasing effect you can imagine.

XXXIII To John Murray

Bologna, August 12, 1819

I do not know how far I may be able to reply to your letter, for I am not very well to-day. Last night I went to the representation of Alfieri's Mirra, the two last acts of which threw me into convulsions. I do not mean by

[1] Sir Samuel Romilly. See Byron's letter to Lady Byron, November 18, 1818.

that word a lady's hysterics, but the agony of reluctant tears, and the choking shudder, which I do not often undergo for fiction. This is but the second time for any thing under reality: the first was on seeing Kean's Sir Giles Overreach. The worst was, that the "Dama" in whose box I was went off in the same way, I really believe more from fright than any other sympathy—at least with the players: but she has been ill, and I have been ill, and we are all languid and pathetic this morning, with great expenditure of sal volatile. But, to return to your letter of the 23d of July.

You are right, Gifford is right, Crabbe is right, Hobhouse is right—you are all right, and I am all wrong; but do, pray, let me have that pleasure. Cut me up root and branch; quarter me in the Quarterly; send round my "disjecti membra poetæ," like those of the Levite's concubine; make me, if you will, a spectacle to men and angels; but don't ask me to alter, for I won't:—I am obstinate and lazy—and there's the truth.

But nevertheless, I will answer your friend P—, who objects to the quick succession of fun and gravity, as if in that case the gravity did not (in intention, at least,) heighten the fun. His metaphor is, that "we are never scorched and drenched at the same time." Blessings on his experience! Ask him these questions about "scorching and drenching." Did he never play at cricket, or walk a mile in hot weather? Did he never spill a dish of tea over himself in handing the cup to his charmer, to the great shame of his nankeen breeches? Did he never swim in the sea at noonday with the sun in his eyes and on his head, which all the foam of ocean could not cool? Did he never draw his foot out of too hot water, d—ning his eyes and his valet's? . . . Did he never tumble into a river or lake, fishing, and sit in his wet clothes in the boat, or on the bank, afterwards, "scorched and drenched," like a true sportsman? "Oh for breath to ut-ter!"—but make him my compliments; he is a clever fellow for all that—a very clever fellow.

You ask me for the plan of Doony Johnny; I *have* no plan; I *had* no plan; but I had or have materials; though if, like Tony Lumpkin, "I am to be snubbed so when I am in spirits," the poem will be naught, and the poet turn serious again. If it don't take, I will leave it off where it is, with all due respect to the public; but if continued, it must be in my own way. You might as well make Hamlet (or Diggory) "act mad" in a strait waistcoat as trammel my buffoonery, if I am to be a buffoon; their gestures and my thoughts would only be pitiably absurd and ludicrously constrained. Why, man, the soul of such writing is its licence; at least the *liberty* of that *licence*, if one likes—*not* that one should abuse it. It is like Trial by Jury and Peerage and Habeas Corpus—a very fine thing, but chiefly in the *reversion;* because no one wishes to be tried for the mere pleasure of proving his possession of the privilege.

But a truce with these reflections. You are too earnest and eager about a work never intended to be serious. Do you suppose that I could have any intention but to giggle and make giggle?—a playful satire, with as little poetry as could be helped, was what I meant. And as to the indecency, do, pray, read in Boswell what *Johnson*, the sullen moralist, says of *Prior* and Paulo Purgante. . . .

XXXIV To the Countess Guiccioli

Bologna, August 25, 1819

My dearest Teresa,—I have read this book in your garden;—my love, you were absent, or else I could not have read it. It is a favourite book of yours, and the writer was a friend of mine. You will not understand these English words, and *others* will not understand them,— which is the reason I have not scrawled them in Italian. But you will recognize the handwriting of him who passionately loved you, and you will divine that, over a book which was yours, he could only think of love. In that word, beautiful in all languages, but most so in yours—*Amor mio*—is comprised my existence here and hereafter. I feel I exist here, and I fear that I shall exist hereafter,—to *what* purpose you will decide; my destiny rests with you, and you are a woman, seventeen years of age, and two out of a convent. I wish that you had staid there, with all my heart,—or, at least, that I had never met you in your married state.

But all this is too late. I love you, and you love me,—at least, you *say so*, and *act* as if you *did* so, which last is a great consolation in all events. But I more than love you, and cannot cease to love you.

Think of me, sometimes, when the Alps and the ocean divide us,—but they never will, unless you *wish* it.

XXXV To Thomas Moore

Ravenna, August 31, 1820

D—n your "mezzo cammin"—you should say "the prime of life," a much more consolatory phrase. Besides, it is not correct. I was born in 1788, and consequently am but thirty-two. You are mistaken on another point. The "Sequin Box" never came into requisition, nor is it likely to do so. It were better that it had, for then a man is not *bound*, you know. As to reform, I did reform—what would you have? "Rebellion lay in his way, and he found it." I verily believe that nor you, nor any man of poetical temperament, can avoid a strong passion of some kind. It is the poetry of life. What should I have known or written, had I been a quiet, mercantile politician, or a lord in waiting? A man must travel and turmoil, or there is no existence. Besides, I only meant to be a Cavalier Servente, and had no idea it would turn out a romance, in the Anglo fashion. . . .

XXXVI To John Murray

Ravenna, February 16, 1821

In the month of March will arrive from Barcelona *Signor Curioni*, engaged for the Opera. He is an acquaintance of mine, and a gentlemanly young man, high in his profession. I must request your personal kindness and patronage in his favour. Pray introduce him to such of the theatrical people, editors of papers, and others, as may be useful to him in his profession, publicly and privately. . . .

The fifth is so far from being the last of Don Juan, that it is hardly the beginning. I meant to take him the tour of Europe, with a proper mixture of siege, battle, and adventure, and to make him finish as *Anacharsis Cloots*, in the French Revolution. To how many cantos this may extend, I know not, nor whether (even if I live) I shall complete it; but this was my notion: I meant to have made him a cavalier servente in Italy, and a cause for a divorce in England, and a sentimental "Werther-faced man" in Germany, so as to 5 show the different ridicules of the society in each of those countries, and to have displayed him gradually *gâté* and *blasé* as he grew older, as is natural. But I had not quite fixed whether to make him end in hell, or in an unhappy 10 marriage, not knowing which would be the severest: the Spanish tradition says hell; but it is probably only an allegory of the other state. You are now in possession of my notions on the subject.[1]

You say the Doge will not be popular: did I ever write for *popularity?* I defy you to show a work of mine (except a tale or two) of a popular style or complexion. It appears to me that there is room for a different style of the 20 drama; neither a servile following of the old drama, which is a grossly erroneous one, nor yet *too French*, like those who succeeded the older writers. It appears to me, that good English, and a severer approach to the rules, 25 might combine something not dishonourable to our literature. I have also attempted to make a play without love; and there are neither rings, nor mistakes, nor starts, nor outrageous ranting villains, nor melodrame in it. All this 30 will prevent its popularity, but does not persuade me that it is *therefore* faulty. Whatever faults it has will arise from deficiency in the conduct, rather than in the conception, which is simple and severe. 35

So *you epigrammatize* upon *my epigram?* I will *pay* you for *that*, mind if I don't, some day. I never let any one off in the long run (*who first begins*). Remember Sam, and see if I don't do you as good a turn. You unnatural 40 publisher! what! quiz your own authors? You are a paper cannibal! . . .

As for news, the Barbarians are marching on Naples, and if they lose a single battle, all Italy will be up. It will be like the Spanish 45 row, if they have any bottom.

[1] "Don Juan will be known by and bye, for what it is intended,—a Satire on abuses of the present states of Society, and not an eulogy of vice: it may be now and then voluptuous: I can't 50 help that." Letter to Murray, Oct. 25, 1822.

"Letters opened?"—to be sure they are, and that's the reason why I always put in my opinion of the German Austrian scoundrels. There is not an Italian who loathes them more than I do; and whatever I could do to scour Italy and the earth of their infamous oppression would be done *con amore.*

Yours, etc.

XXXVII To Percy Bysshe Shelley

Ravenna, April 26, 1821

The child continues doing well, and the accounts are regular and favourable. It is gratifying to me that you and Mrs. Shelley do not disapprove of the step which I have taken, which is merely temporary.

I am very sorry to hear what you say of Keats—is it *actually* true? I did not think criticism had been so killing. Though I differ from you essentially in your estimate of his performances, I so much abhor all unnecessary pain, that I would rather he had been seated on the highest peak of Parnassus than have perished in such a manner. Poor fellow! though with such inordinate self-love he would probably have not been very happy. I read the review of "Endymion" in the Quarterly. It was severe,—but surely not so severe as many reviews in that and other journals upon others.

I recollect the effect on me of the Edinburgh on my first poem; it was rage, and resistance, and redress—but not despondency nor despair. I grant that those are not amiable feelings; but, in this world of bustle and broil, and especially in the career of writing, a man should calculate upon his powers of *resistance* before he goes into the arena.

"Except not life from pain nor danger free,
Nor deem the doom of man reversed for thee."

You know my opinion of *that second-hand* school of poetry. You also know my high opinion of your own poetry,—because it is of *no* school. I read Cenci—but, besides that I think the *subject* essentially *un*dramatic, I am not an admirer of our old dramatists, *as models.* I deny that the English have hitherto had a drama at all. Your Cenci, however, was a work of power, and poetry. As to *my* drama, pray revenge yourself upon it, by being as free as I have been with yours.

I have not yet got your Prometheus, which I long to see. I have heard nothing of mine, and do not know that it is yet published. I have published a pamphlet on the Pope controversy, which you will not like. Had I known that Keats was dead—or that he was alive and so sensitive—I should have omitted some remarks upon his poetry, to which I was provoked by his *attack* upon *Pope*, and my disapprobation of *his own* style of writing.

You want me to undertake a great Poem—I have not the inclination nor the power. As I grow older, the indifference—*not* to life, for we love it by instinct—but to the stimuli of life, increases. Besides, this late failure of the Italians has latterly disappointed me for many reasons,—some public, some personal. My respects to Mrs. S.

Yours ever.

P.S. Could not you and I contrive to meet this summer? Could not you take a run here *alone?*

XXXVIII To Thomas Moore

Ravenna, July 5, 1821

How do you suppose that I ever would allow any thing that *could* be said on your account to weigh with *me?* I only regret that Bowles had not *said* that you were the writer of that note until afterwards, when out he comes with it, in a private letter to Murray, which Murray sends to me. D—n the controversy!

> D—n Twizzle,
> D—n the bell,
> And d—n the fool who rung it—Well!
> From all such plagues I'll quickly be deliver'd.

I have had a friend of your Mr. Irving's—a very pretty lad—a Mr. Coolidge, of Boston—only somewhat too full of poesy and "entusymusy." I was very civil to him during his few hours' stay, and talked with him much of Irving, whose writings are my delight. But I suspect that he did not take quite so much to me, from his having expected to meet a misanthropical gentleman, in wolf-skin breeches, and answering in fierce monosyllables, instead of a man of this world. I can never get people to understand that poetry is the expression of *excited passion*, and that there is no such thing as a life of passion any more than a continuous earthquake, or an eternal fever. Besides, who would ever *shave* themselves in such a state?

I have had a curious letter to-day from a girl in England (I never saw her), who says she is given over of a decline, but could not go out of the world without thanking me for the delight which my poesy for several years, etc. etc. etc. It is signed simply N. N. A. and has not a word of "cant" or preachment in it upon *any* opinions. She merely says that she is dying, and that as I had contributed so highly to her existing pleasure, she thought that she might say so, begging me to *burn* her *letter*—which, by the way, I can *not* do, as I look upon such a letter, in such circumstances, as better than a diploma from Gottingen. I once had a letter from Drontheim, in *Norway* (but not from a dying woman), in verse, on the same score of gratulation. These are the things which make one at times believe that . . ., and such fellows, are poets also, it is better to be out of the corps.

I am now in the fifth act of "Foscari," being the third tragedy in twelve months, besides *proses;* so you perceive that I am not at all idle. And are you, too, busy? I doubt that your life at Paris draws too much upon your time, which is a pity. Can't you divide your day, so as to combine both? I have had plenty of all sorts of worldly business on my hands last year,—and yet it is not so difficult to give a few hours to the *Muses*. This sentence is so like . . . that—

Ever, etc.

If we were together, I should publish both my plays (periodically) in our *joint* journal. It should be our plan to publish all our best things in that way.

XXXIX To John Murray

Ravenna, July 6, 1821

In agreement with a wish expressed by Mr. Hobhouse, it is my determination to omit the stanza upon the *horse of Semiramis* in the Fifth Canto of Don Juan. I mention this, in case you are, or intend to be, the publisher of the remaining Cantos. . . .

At the particular request of the Contessa G. I have promised *not* to continue Don Juan. You will therefore look upon these three Cantos as the last of the poem. She had read the two first in the French translation, and never ceased beseeching me to write no more of it. The reason of this is not at first obvious to a superficial observer of FOREIGN manners; but it arises from the wish of all women to exalt the sentiment of the passions, and to keep up the illusion which is their empire. Now Don Juan strips off this illusion, and laughs at that and most other things. I never knew a woman who did *not* protect *Rousseau*, nor one who did not dislike De Grammont, Gil Blas, and all the comedy of the passions, when brought out naturally. But "king's blood must keep word," as Serjeant Bothwell says....

XL To John Murray

Ravenna, August 31, 1821

I have received the Juans, which are printed so *carelessly*, especially the fifth canto, as to be disgraceful to me, and not creditable to you. It really must be *gone over again* with the *manuscript*, the errors are so gross;—words added—changed—so as to make cacophony and nonsense. You have been careless of this poem because some of your synod don't approve of it; but I tell you that it will be long before you see any thing half so good as poetry or writing. Upon what principle have you omitted the note on Bacon and Voltaire? and one of the concluding stanzas sent as an addition?—because it ended, I suppose, with—

"And do not link, two virtuous souls for life
Into that *moral centaur*, man and wife?"

Now, I must say, once for all, that I will not permit any human being to take such liberties with my writings because I am absent. I desire the omissions to be replaced (except the stanza on Semiramis)—particularly the stanza upon the Turkish marriages; and I request that the whole be carefully *gone over* with the MS.

I never saw such stuff as is printed:—Gulleyaz instead of Gu*lb*eyaz, etc. Are you aware that Gulbeyaz is a real name, and the other nonsense? I copied the *cantos* out carefully, so that there is *no* excuse, as the printer read, or at least *prints*, the MS. of the plays without error.

If you have no feeling for your own reputation, pray have some little for mine. I have read over the poem carefully, and I tell you, *it is poetry*. Your little envious knot of parson-poets may say what they please: time will show that I am not in this instance mistaken.

Desire my friend Hobhouse to correct the press, especially of the last canto, from the manuscript as it is. It is enough to drive one out of one's reason to see the infernal torture of words from the original. For instance the line—

And *pair* their rhymes as Venus yokes her doves—

is printed—

And *praise* their rhymes, etc.

Also *"precarious"* for *"precocious"*; and this line, stanza 133,

And this strong extreme effect to tire no longer.

Now do turn to the manuscript and see if I ever wrote such a *line*: it is *not verse*.

No wonder the poem should fail (which, however, it *won't*, you will see) with such things allowed to creep about it. Replace what is omitted, and correct what is so shamefully misprinted, and let the poem have fair play; and I fear nothing.

I see in the last two numbers of the Quarterly a strong itching to assail me (see the review of "The Etonian"): let it, and see if they shan't have enough of it. I do not allude to Gifford, who has always been my friend, and whom I do not consider as responsible for the articles written by others. . . .

You will publish the plays when ready. I am in such a humour about this printing of Don Juan so inaccurately that I must close this.

Yours.

P.S. I presume that you have *not* lost the *stanza* to which I allude? It was sent afterwards: look over my letters and find it.

XLI To John Murray

Ravenna, September 24, 1821

I have been thinking over our late correspondence, and wish to propose to you the following articles for our future:

1stly. That you shall write to me of yourself, of the health, wealth, and welfare of all friends; but of *me* (*quoad me*) little or nothing.

2dly. That you shall send me soda-powders, tooth-powder, tooth-brushes, or any such anti-odontalgic or chemical articles, as heretofore, "ad libitum," upon being reimbursed for the same.

3dly. That you shall *not* send me any modern, or (as they are called) *new*, publications in *English whatsoever*, save and excepting any writing, prose or verse, of (or reasonably presumed to be of) Walter Scott, Crabbe, Moore, Campbell, Rogers, Gifford, Joanna Baillie, *Irving* (the American), Hogg, Wilson (Isle of Palms man), or *any* especial *single* work of fancy which is thought to be of considerable merit; *Voyages* and *Travels*, provided that they are *neither in Greece, Spain, Asia Minor, Albania*, nor *Italy*, will be welcome. Having travelled the countries mentioned, I know that what is said of them can convey nothing farther which I desire to know about them.— No other English works whatsoever.

4thly. That you send me no periodical works whatsoever—*no* Edinburgh, Quarterly, Monthly, nor any review, magazine, or newspapers, English or foreign, of any description.

5thly. That you send me no opinions whatsoever, either *good, bad*, or *indifferent*, of yourself, or your friends, or others, concerning any work, or works, of mine, past, present, or to come.

6thly. That all negotiations in matters of business between you and me pass through the medium of the Hon. Douglas Kinnaird, my friend and trustee, or Mr. Hobhouse, as "alter ego," and tantamount to myself during my absence—or presence.

Some of these propositions may at first seem strange, but they are founded. The quantity of trash I have received as books is incalculable, and neither amused nor instructed. Reviews and magazines are at the best but ephemeral and superficial reading:—*who thinks* of the *grand article* of *last year* in any *given Review?* In the next place, if they regard myself, they tend to increase *egotism*. If favourable, I do not deny that the praise *elates*, and if unfavourable, that the abuse *irritates*. The latter may conduct me to inflict a species of satire, which would neither do good to you nor to your friends: *they* may smile *now*, and so may *you;* but if I took you all in hand, it would not be difficult to cut you up like gourds. I did as much by as powerful people at nineteen years old, and I know little as yet in three-and-thirty, which should prevent me from making all your ribs gridirons for your hearts, if such were my propensity: but it is *not;* therefore let me hear none of your provocations. If any thing occurs so very gross as to require my notice, I shall hear of it from my legal friends. For the rest, I merely request to be left in ignorance.

The same applies to opinions, *good, bad*, or *indifferent*, of persons in conversation or correspondence. These do not *interrupt*, but they *soil*, the *current* of my *mind*. I am sensitive enough, but *not* till I am *troubled;* and here I am beyond the touch of the short arms of literary England, except the few feelers of the polypus that crawl over the channels in the way of extract.

All these precautions *in* England would be useless; the libeller or the flatterer would there reach me in spite of all; but in Italy we know little of literary England, and think less, except what reaches us through some garbled and brief extract in some miserable gazette. For *two years* (excepting two or three articles cut out and sent to *you*, by the post) I never read a newspaper which was not forced upon me by some accident, and know, upon the whole, as little of England as you all do of Italy, and God knows *that* is little enough, with all your travels, etc. etc. etc. The English travellers *know Italy* as *you* know Guernsey: how much is *that?*

If any thing occurs so violently gross or personal as requires notice, Mr. Douglas Kinnaird will let me *know;* but of *praise*, I desire to hear *nothing*.

You will say, "to what tends all this?" I will answer THAT;—to keep my mind *free and unbiassed* by all paltry and personal irritabilities of praise or censure—to let my genius take its natural direction, while my feelings are like the dead, who know nothing and feel nothing of all or aught that is said or done in their regard.

If you can observe these conditions, you will spare yourself and others some pain: let me not be worked upon to rise up; for if I do, it will not be for a little. If you can*not* observe these conditions, we shall cease to be correspondents,—but not *friends*, for I shall always be yours ever and truly.

P.S. I have taken these resolutions not from any irritation against *you* or *yours*, but simply upon reflection that all reading, either praise or censure, of myself has done me harm. When I was in Switzerland and Greece, I was out of the way of hearing either, and *how I wrote there!*—In Italy I am out of the way of it too; but latterly, partly through my fault, and partly through your kindness in wishing to send me the *newest* and most periodical publications, I have had a crowd of Reviews, etc. thrust upon me, which have bored me with their jargon, of one kind or another, and taken off my attention from greater objects. You have also sent me a parcel of trash of poetry, for no reason that I can conceive, unless to provoke me to write a new "English Bards." Now *this* I wish to avoid; for if ever I *do*, it will be a strong production; and I desire peace, as long as the fools will keep their nonsense out of my way.

XLII   To Thomas Moore

Pisa, March 4, 1822

Since I wrote the enclosed, I have waited another post, and now have your answer acknowledging the arrival of the packet—a troublesome one, I fear, to you in more ways than one, both from weight external and internal. . . .

I am sorry you think Werner even *approaching* to any fitness for the stage, which, with my notions upon it, is very far from my present object. With regard to the publication, I have already explained that I have no exorbitant expectations of either fame or profit in the present instances; but wish them published because they are written, which is the common feeling of all scribblers.

With respect to "Religion," can I never convince you that *I* have no such opinions as the characters in that drama, which seems to have frightened every body? Yet *they* are nothing to the expressions in Goethe's Faust (which are ten times hardier), and not a whit more

bold than those of Milton's Satan. My ideas of a character may run away with me: like all imaginative men, I, of course, embody myself with the character while I *draw* it, but not a moment after the pen is from off the paper

I am no enemy to religion, but the contrary. As a proof, I am educating my natural daughter a strict Catholic in a convent of Romagna, for I think people can never have *enough* of religion, if they are to have any. I incline, myself, very much to the Catholic doctrines; but if I am to write a drama, I must make my characters speak as I conceive them likely to argue.

As to poor Shelley, who is another bugbear to you and the world, he is, to my knowledge, the *least* selfish and the mildest of men—a man who has made more sacrifices of his fortune and feelings for others than any I ever heard of. With his speculative opinions I have nothing in common, nor desire to have.

The truth is, my dear Moore, you live near the *stove* of society, where you are unavoidably influenced by its heat and its vapours. I did so once—and too much—and enough to give a colour to my whole future existence. As my success in society was *not* inconsiderable, I am surely not a prejudiced judge upon the subject, unless in its favour; but I think it, as now constituted, *fatal* to all great original undertakings of every kind. I never courted it *then*, when I was young and high in blood and one of its "curled darlings"; and do you think I would do so *now*, when I am living in a clearer atmosphere? One thing *only* might lead me back to it, and that is, to try once more if I could do any good in *politics;* but *not* in the petty politics I see now preying upon our miserable country.

Do not let me be misunderstood, however. If you speak your *own* opinions, they ever had, and will have, the greatest weight with *me*. But if you merely *echo* the "monde" (and it is difficult not to do so, being in its favour and its ferment), I can only regret that you should ever repeat any thing to which I cannot pay attention.

But I am prosing. The gods go with you, and as much immortality of all kinds as may suit your present and all other existence.

Yours, etc.

XLIII To John Murray

Pisa, August 3, 1822

Dear Sir,

. . . I presume you have heard that Mr. Shelley and Capt. Williams were lost on the 7th Ul^to in their passage from Leghorn to Spezia in their own open boat. You may imagine the state of their families: I never saw such a scene, nor wish to see such another.

You were all brutally mistaken about Shelley, who was, without exception, the *best* and least selfish man I ever knew. I never knew one who was not a beast in comparison.

Yours ever.

XLIV To Lady ——

Albaro, November 10, 1822

*   *   *

The Chevalier persisted in declaring himself an ill-used gentleman, and describing you as a kind of cold Calypso, who lead astray people of an amatory disposition without giving them any sort of compensation, contenting yourself, it seems, with only making *one* fool instead of two, which is the more approved method of proceeding on such occasions. For my part, I think, you are quite right; and be assured from me that a woman (as society is constituted in England) who gives any advantage to a man may expect a lover, but will sooner or later find a tyrant; and this is not the man's fault either, perhaps, but is the necessary and natural result of the circumstances of society which, in fact, tyrannize over the man equally with the woman, that is to say, if either of them have any feeling or honour.

You can write to me at your leisure and inclination. I have always laid it down as a maxim, and found it justified by experience, that a man and a woman make far better friendships than can exist between two of the same sex; but *these* with this condition, that they never have made, or are to make, love with each other. Lovers may, and, indeed, generally *are* enemies, but they never can be friends; because there must always be a spice of jealousy and a something of self in all their speculations.

Indeed, I rather look upon love altogether as a sort of hostile transaction, very necessary to make or to break matches, and keep the world going, but by no means a sinecure to the parties concerned.

Now, as my love perils are, I believe, pretty well over, and yours, by all accounts, are never to begin, we shall be the best friends imaginable, as far as both are concerned; and with this advantage, that we may both fall to loving right and left through all our acquaintance, without either sullenness or sorrow from that amiable passion which are its inseparable attendants.

Believe me, etc.

XLV To Thomas Moore

Genoa, February 20, 1823

My dear Tom,

I must again refer you to those two letters addressed to you at Passy before I read your speech in Galignani, etc., and which you do not seem to have received.

Of Hunt I see little—once a month or so, and then on his own business, generally. You may easily suppose that I know too little of Hampstead and his satellites to have much communion or community with him. My whole present relation to him arose from Shelley's unexpected wreck. You would not have had me leave him in the street with his family, would you? and as to the other plan you mention, you forget how it would *humiliate* him—that his writings should be supposed to be dead weight! Think a moment—he is perhaps the vainest man on earth, at least his own friends say so pretty loudly; and if he were in other circumstances, I might be tempted to take him down a peg; but not now, —it would be cruel. It is a cursed business; but neither the motive nor the means rest upon my conscience, and it happens that he and his brother *have* been so far benefited by the publication in a pecuniary point of view. His brother is a steady, bold fellow, such as *Prynne*, for example, and full of moral, and, I hear, physical courage.

And *you* are *really* recanting, or softening to the clergy! It will do little good for you—it is *you*, not the poem, they are at. They will say they frightened you—forbid it, Ireland! Believe me

Yours ever.

XLVI To the Earl of Blessington

April 5, 1823

My dear Lord,

How is your gout? or rather, how are you? I return the Count D'Orsay's Journal, which is a very extraordinary production, and of a most melancholy truth in all that regards high life in England. I know, or knew, personally, most of the personages and societies which he describes; and after reading his remarks have the sensation fresh upon me as if I had seen them yesterday. I would however plead in behalf of some few exceptions, which I will mention by and by. The most singular thing is, *how* he should have penetrated *not* the *fact*, but the *mystery* of the English *ennui*, at two-and-twenty. I was about the same age when I made the same discovery, in almost precisely the same circles—(for there is scarcely a person mentioned whom I did not see nightly or daily, and was acquainted more or less intimately with most of them)—but I never could have described it so well. *Il faut être Français*, to effect this.

But he ought also to have been in the country during the hunting season, with "a select party of distinguished guests," as the papers term it. He ought to have seen the gentlemen after dinner (on the hunting days), and the soirée ensuing thereupon—and the women looking as if they had hunted, or rather been hunted; and I could have wished that he had been at a dinner in town, which I recollect at Lord Cowper's—small, but select, and composed of the most amusing people. The dessert was hardly on the table, when, out of twelve, I counted *five asleep;* of that five, there were *Tierney*, Lord ——, and Lord Darnley—I forget the other two, but they were either wits or orators—perhaps poets.

My residence in the East and in Italy has made me somewhat indulgent of the siesta;—but then they set regularly about it in warm countries, and perform it in solitude (or at most in a tête-à-tête with a proper companion), and retire quietly to their rooms to get out of the sun's way for an hour or two.

Altogether, your friend's Journal is a very formidable production. Alas! our dearly beloved countrymen have only discovered that they are tired, and not that they are tiresome; and I suspect that the communication of the latter unpleasant verity will not be better received than truths usually are. I have read the whole with great attention and instruction. I am too good a patriot to say *pleasure*—at least I won't say so, whatever I may think. I showed it (I hope no breach of confidence), to a young Italian lady of rank, *très instruite* also; and who passes, or passed, for being one of three most celebrated belles in the district of Italy, where her family and connexions resided in less troublesome times as to politics (which is not Genoa, by the way), and she was delighted with it, and says that she has derived a better notion of English society from it than from all Madame de Staël's metaphysical disputations on the same subject, in her work on the Revolution. I beg that you will thank the young philosopher, and make my compliments to Lady B. and her sister.

Believe me your very obliged and faithful

N. B.

P.S. There is a rumour in letters of some disturbance or complot in the French Pyrenean army—generals suspected or dismissed, and ministers of war travelling to see what's the matter. "Marry (as David says), this hath an angry favour."

Tell Count D'Orsay that some of the names are not quite intelligible, especially of the clubs; he speaks of *Watts*—perhaps he is right, but in my time *Watier's* was the Dandy Club, of which (though no dandy) I was a member, at the time too of its greatest glory, when Brummell and Mildmay, Alvanley and Pierrepoint, gave the Dandy balls; and we (the club, that is,) got up the famous masquerade at Burlington House and Garden, for Wellington. He does not speak of the *Alfred*, which was the most *recherché* and most tiresome of any, as I know by being a member of that too.

XLVII To the Hon. Douglas Kinnaird

Genoa, May 21, 1823

My dear Douglas,—I am doing all I can to get away, but I have all kinds of obstacles thrown in my way by the "absurd woman-kind," who seems determined on sacrificing herself in every way, and preventing me from doing any good, and all without reason; for her relations, and her husband (who is moving the Pope and the Government here to get her to live with him again) and everybody, are earnest with her to return to Ravenna. She wants to go up to Greece too! forsooth, a precious place to go to at present! Of course the idea is ridiculous, as everything must there be sacrificed to seeing her out of harm's way. It is a case too, in which interest does not enter, and therefore hard to deal with; for I have no kind of control in that way, and if she makes a scene (and she has a turn that way) we shall have another romance, and tale of ill usage, and abandonment, and Lady Caro-lining, and Lady Byroning, and Glenarvoning, all cut and dry. There never was a man who gave up so much to women, and all I have gained by it has been the character of treating them harshly. However I shall do what I can, and have hopes; for her father has been re-called from his political exile; but with this proviso, that he do not return without his daughter. If I left a woman for another woman, she might have cause to complain, but really when a man merely wishes to go on a great duty, for a good cause, this selfishness on the part of the "feminie" is rather too much.

Ever yours.

XLVIII TO LIEUT.-COLONEL NAPIER

Metaxata, Sept. 9, 1823

My dear Colonel,—I return you your some-what desponding correspondent's epistle, with many thanks for that as for other and many kindnesses. I have had two from Blaquiere (dated Ancona and addrest to me at Genoa) in the old style, but more sanguine than Signor Pavone's. All this comes of what Mr. Braham pronounces "*Entusymusy*," expecting too much and starting at speed; it is lucky for me so far that, fail or not fail, I can hardly be disap-pointed, for I believed myself on a fool's er-rand from the outset, and must, therefore, like Dogberry, "spare no wisdom." I will at least linger on here or there till I see whether I *can* be of *any* service in *any* way; and if I doubt it,

it is because I do not feel confidence in my in-dividual capacity for this kind of bear-taming, and not from a disbelief in the powers of a more active or less indifferent character to be of use to them, though I feel persuaded that that person must be a military man.

But I like the Cause at least, and will stick by it while it is not degraded nor dishonoured.

You have been so kind to me (as indeed all our compatriots have been) that any additional trouble I should give you would be in the Gospel phrase—another "coal of fire" upon my head.

The first time I descend into the valley, I will call, and I hope whenever you come up this way you will look in and see how com-fortable we are under your auspices.

Ever yours.

XLIX TO THE HON. AUGUSTA LEIGH

Cephalonia, 8bre. 12, 1823

My dearest Augusta,—Your three letters on the subject of Ada's indisposition have made me very anxious to hear further of her amelio-ration. I have been subject to the same com-plaint, but not at so early an age, nor in so great a degree. Besides, it never affected my eyes but rather my hearing, and that only partially and slightly and for a short time. I had dreadful and almost periodical headaches till I was fourteen, and sometimes since; but abstinence and a habit of bathing my head in cold water every morning cured me, I think, at least I have been less molested since that period . . . Let me know how she is. I need not say how *very* anxious I am (at this dis-tance particularly) to hear of her welfare.

You ask why I came up amongst the Greeks? It was stated to me that my so doing might tend to their advantage in some measure in their present struggle for independence, both as an individual and as a member for the Com-mittee now in England. How far this may be realized I cannot pretend to anticipate, but I am willing to do what I can. They have at length found leisure to quarrel among them-selves, after repelling their other enemies, and it is no very easy part that I may have to play to avoid appearing partial to one or other of their factions. They have turned out Mavrocordato, who was the only *Washington* or *Kosciusko* kind of man amongst them, and they have not yet sent their deputies to London to treat for a loan, nor in short done themselves so much good as they might have done. I have written Mr. Hobhouse three several times with a budget of documents on the subject, from which he can extract all the present information for the Committee. I have written to their Gov.ᵗ at Tripolizza and Salamis, and am waiting for instructions *where* to proceed, for things are in such a state amongst them, that it is difficult to conjecture where one could be useful to them, if at all. However, I have some hopes that they will see their own interest sufficiently not to quarrel till they have received their national independence, and then they can fight it out among them in a domestic manner—and welcome. You may suppose that I have something to *think* of at least, for you can have no idea what an intriguing cunning unquiet generation they are, and as emissaries of all parties come to me at present, and I must act impartially, it makes me exclaim, as Julian did at his military exercises, "Oh! Plato, what a task for a Philosopher!"

However, *you* won't think much of *my philosophy;* nor do I, *entre nous.*

If you think this epistle or any part of it worth transmitting to Lady B. you can send her a copy, as I suppose . . . she cannot be altogether indifferent as to my "whereabouts" and *what*abouts.

* * *

I wish you would obtain from Lady B. some account of Ada's disposition, habits, studies, moral tendencies, and temper, as well as of her personal appearance, for except from the miniature drawn five years ago (and she is now double that age nearly) I have no idea of even her aspect. When I am advised on these points, I can form some notion of her character and what way her dispositions or indispositions ought to be treated. At *her* present age I have an idea that I had many feelings and notions which people would not believe if I stated them *now,* and therefore I may as well keep them to myself. Is she social or solitary, taciturn or talkative, fond of reading or otherwise? And what is her *tic?*—I mean her foible. Is she passionate? I hope that the Gods have made her anything save *poetical*—it is enough to have one such fool in a family. You can answer all this at your leisure: address to *Genoa* as usual, the letters will be forwarded better by my Correspondents there.

Yours ever.

L   To Thomas Moore

Cephalonia, December 27, 1823

I received a letter from you some time ago. I have been too much employed latterly to write as I could wish, and even now must write in haste.

I embark for Missolonghi to join Mavrocordato in four-and-twenty hours. The state of parties (but it were a long story) has kept me here till *now;* but now that Mavrocordato (their Washington, or their Kosciusko) is employed again, I can act with a *safe conscience.* I carry money to pay the squadron, etc., and I have influence with the Suliotes, *supposed* sufficient to keep them in harmony with some of the dissentients;—for there are plenty of differences, but trifling.

It is imagined that we shall attempt either Patras, or the castles on the Straits; and it seems, by most accounts, that the Greeks,—at any rate, the Suliotes, who are in affinity with me of "bread and salt,"—expect that I should march with them, and—be it even so! If any thing in the way of fever, fatigue, famine, or otherwise, should cut short the middle age of a brother warbler,—like Garcilasso de la Vega, Kleist, Korner, Joukoffsky (a Russian nightingale—see Bowring's Anthology), or Thersander, or,—or somebody else—but never mind—I pray you to remember me in your "smiles and wine."

I have hopes that the cause will triumph; but, whether it does or no, still "Honour must be minded as strictly as a milk diet." I trust to observe both.

Ever, etc.

PERCY BYSSHE SHELLEY
[August 4, 1792–July 8, 1822]

PERCY BYSSHE SHELLEY was the son of a worthy if conservative country gentleman whom he was to puzzle sadly before his years were ended. Sent first to Syon House Academy and later to Eton, young Shelley showed himself clearly no ordinary schoolboy. His dreamy sensitiveness and his refusal to fit into the school pattern made him an object of attack for the other boys, but the paroxysms of rage with which he would turn on his tormentors and fling at their heads the nearest available missile (even when that missile happened to be a startled smaller boy) won him some immunity. Meanwhile he devoured cheaply lurid novels of necromancers and ghosts and ruined castles and, during his holidays, terrified himself and his adoring younger sisters by spinning wild yarns at night. Later he became interested in science—or rather in its mysterious and spectacular aspects. One day an Eton master, suspecting the worst, entered Shelley's room to find him apparently half enveloped in blue flame. "What on earth are you doing?" exclaimed the master and, "Please, sir," Shelley replied, "I am raising the devil."

By the time Shelley entered Oxford in the autumn of 1810, Timothy Shelley had already had occasion to regard his eldest son with surprise, and some of the liberal political opinions the young man was expressing were disturbing to a conservative mind. As an unhappy schoolboy at Syon House Academy a vague sense of the existence of oppressed and oppressing classes had dawned in him, and he began to feel that the clash of boy and master was but an echo of a greater strife in the world outside. Then and there he resolved, "I will be wise, and just, and free, and mild, if in me lies." And as he grew older, he began to see it as an impossibility that power, with its ability to command obedience, could exist side by side with freedom and the individual's right to equality. Authority then, as such, was naturally to be hated by the wise and free. Before Shelley left Eton he was a rebel against the symbols of constraint—kings, priests, and schoolmasters—and years later he wrote as the conclusion to his great *Prometheus Unbound:*

> To defy Power, which seems omnipotent;
> To love and bear; to hope till Hope creates
> From its own wreck the thing it contemplates;
> Neither to change, nor falter, nor repent;
> This, like thy glory, Titan, is to be
> Good, great and joyous, beautiful and free;
> This is alone Life, Joy, Empire, and Victory.

And it was at Eton, where his rebelliousness took form, that Shelley also was first called Atheist. It seems that there were various rather unofficial schoolboy officers known as the Pope, the Bishop, the Mayor, the Governor, etc. The office of the Atheist was generally vacant as it took extreme daring to fill it. The gods of the Eton schoolboys were the Masters, and the Atheist was not a disbeliever (it is hard to disbelieve in the existence of a Master who perhaps flogged you yesterday) but really an anti-theist—an opposer of the gods. It was Shelley's singular success in upsetting the peace of mind of schoolmasters which first won him among his school fellows the formidable title of "Shelley the Atheist."

At Oxford Shelley struck up a friendship with Thomas Jefferson Hogg, a Scotsman whose dry humor missed none of the absurdities of his friend, and whose affection never undervalued his qualities. Shelley's interest in chemistry continued and Hogg has described Shelley's room:

"As if the young chemist, in order to analyse the mystery of creation, had endeavoured first to reconstruct the primeval chaos," there were books, boots, papers, clothes, pistols, phials, money, bags, boxes, and crucibles scattered in every place. The carpet was burned. There were bottles of soda water and bits of lemon. A blunted razor, an electrical machine, an air pump, a galvanic trough, a solar microscope, and heaps of books were about. Such was the room in the early days of Shelley's occupancy and history does not record what it later became.

And in this setting Hogg and Shelley talked or read together through the afternoons and evenings. From six till ten, Shelley would curl up before the fire (so close that Hogg was some-times terrified lest he burst into flames) and sleep; and at ten Shelley would wake and talk until two in the morning, the hour which Hogg had set as the irrevocable dead-line. The two were in sympathy in their political liberalism. And as Shelley's interest in chemistry waned somewhat his interest in philosophy grew, and the two read the sceptical materialistic philosophers of the eighteenth century, particularly Locke and Hume. Disaster came of it.

Shelley, who loved a philosophical argument, drew up an anonymous pamphlet, consisting chiefly of arguments from these philosophers, entitled *The Necessity of Atheism* and ending with the devastating Q.E.D. of the geometricians. The pamphlet was on sale in Oxford—for twenty minutes. Shelley, however, had sent it to numerous dignitaries, including a creditable number of Bishops, along with a distressed letter, signed "Jeremiah Stukely," saying that Jeremiah could find no answer to the pamphlet and needed spiritual help. Shelley's object was to start an argu-ment. Many things happened promptly and Shelley and Hogg, before the end of their first year, found themselves, in March, 1811, expelled from Oxford.

Timothy Shelley tried to deal with the situation. It seems odd that the opinions of a nineteen year old should be so volcanic in effect, but it must be remembered that the time was one of war hysteria. Timothy's formula was simple: he was a conservative member of parliament and would smooth things down, the boy would apologize to the college authorities and, because the boy was the heir to a fortune, they would accept the apology, and afterwards—well, there was plenty of money in the family purse and, if the boy chose to sow a few of the usual wild oats, Timothy wouldn't be stingy.

But Shelley would not retract and Timothy, prepared to be generous, encountered something in his son he could not understand. Shelley did not wish to sow wild oats. He wished to say what he believed. It was unthinkable to him that for the sake of personal advantage he should for-swear a principle. It remained unthinkable to him until his death. He was of the true idealists who believe ideas more real than brass. Blinded he may have been at one time or another, but he was always blinded by star-dust, never by the dust of worldly compromise. That Shelley on the particular matter, the materialistic scepticism which provoked the crisis, *was* sowing wild oats, intellectual wild oats, Timothy could not understand.

Shelley took lodgings in London—in Poland Street because it made him think of Thaddeus of Warsaw and freedom. His sisters, to whom he had preached his doctrines, sent him their pocket money on which to live. And in the society of "the disinterested, the free" of which he talked, became enrolled their schoolmate, Harriet Westbrook, the daughter of a retired coffee-house keeper. Mysterious persecutions (since explained as schoolgirl disciplines) were inflicted upon her, and Shelley counseled her to resist tyranny. She suffered for principle and for Shelley, and then turned to Shelley for help. Shelley, rather surprised, on principle posted off to Scotland with her and then, lest she suffer from his saving of her, married her against his principles (he opposed marriage). This was in August 1811 when Shelley was nineteen and Harriet sixteen.

Three years later, in July 1814, Shelley deserted Harriet and her child, and less than six years after that elopement Harriet drowned herself. Meanwhile the start of the marriage cast no grim shadows. Harriet in the new household read aloud often and long; studied excitedly; Shelley philosophized on the immediate remodeling of the world. They went to Ireland, where Shelley, intending to settle the Irish question on the principles of Brotherly Love and Universal Tolerance, printed an *Address to the Irish People*. Not immediately succeeding, Shelley returned after seven weeks (February–April 1812). Some of the printed matter he shipped back agitated a Surveyor of Customs so exceedingly that he notified without delay the Secretary of State, the Secretary of the Post Office, and the Irish Secretary. These officials were not alarmed. By August Shelley's Irish servant had been clapped into jail for posting up a Declaration of Rights which began "Government has no rights" and, although Dan Healy loyally kept his mouth shut as to the author of the Declaration, the Earls of Chichester and Sandwich (joint Postmasters-General) and the Home Secretary were considering it wise to have this strange young heir to a country squire watched. Shelley meanwhile (July 1812) had welcomed to his home Elizabeth Hitchener as the sister of his soul and a member of the enlightened. Harriet greeted her as "Portia." By December she was dismissed by both as the "Brown Demon."

Shelley and Harriet, however, were both growing up through these phantasias. Shelley was surrendering none of the essential principles on which he acted. He was deepening and widening as his juvenile flurries met rebuff. Harriet, a pretty schoolgirl, was growing toward the stage where she would think of herself as the wife of an heir, grow tired of a wandering life, and wish for a coach and four.

Early in 1813 (Feb.), before his coming of age, Shelley finished his *Queen Mab* and its notes. In his college days he had published some negligible poetry and two lurid prose romances. *Queen Mab* was Shelley's first sustained effort although he later disowned it as "villainous trash." In his notes he shows himself the opposer of institutions, laws, and governments. Men free and equal neither envy nor oppress one another. Institutions, by introducing the idea of rank, introduce the vices of society: envy, servility, greed, jealousy, etc. In institutions, then, rather than in the soul, is the source of evil, and Shelley opposed them with shrill vehemence, his opposition to priests being especially shocking to the susceptibilities of his time.

It was some time after the publication of *Queen Mab* that Shelley and Harriet began drifting apart. She could not match Shelley's growth. And the situation was strained by the eternal presence of Eliza, Harriet's beloved sister, who had come to live with them immediately after the elopement, and had remained painfully present ever since. Eliza Westbrook was not a very likeable person at best and, while Harriet clung to her, Shelley grew more and more acutely to dislike her. Meanwhile Shelley had made other friends, the Boinvilles and the philosopher Godwin from whose *Political Justice* he had taken many of his radical ideas, and whom he hailed as the master of his mind. Godwin was in financial difficulties, and Shelley, in seeking to help him, was a frequent visitor at Godwin's house in London. Harriet with her child—and Eliza— was at Bath.

In late May or June at Godwin's, Shelley met Mary, the child of Godwin's first wife Mary Wollstonecraft. Young Mary Godwin was the remarkable daughter of remarkable parents— intelligent, sensitive, courageous, good-looking. All her life she had lived in that world of ideas which was Shelley's world. The two were immediately attracted to one another. Godwin, when he perceived the danger, tried to separate them, but was helpless. At the end of July 1814 Shelley and Mary eloped to the continent. No valid defence can be offered for Shelley except that there are many Harriets and few Shelleys, and posterity profited by the sacrifice of Harriet. Shelley himself thought he was justified or posterity would not have profited.

Upon their return from the continent Mary and Shelley faced real poverty and the winter was a trying one. But with his financial affairs reduced to some order, Shelley recovered tranquility and began to devote himself to poetry. It was in 1815 that he composed *Alastor* (published 1816) and in Mary's companionship began to find the bent of his genius, but even in the finding of it there was an element of disillusion. His boyish high hopes for the immediate reform of the world were over. In poetry he was to find expression. And in *Alastor* his political ideas are set aside and he writes of the individual's quest for an ideal love.

The following year Mary and Shelley, accompanied by Mary's half sister Claire Clairmont, went again to Switzerland where they met Byron, and the two poets became friends. The story of Claire's infatuation for Byron is now well known, but Shelley knew nothing of it then and the time was one of happiness and companionship. Shelley was to have grief and shock enough on his return to England in the Autumn. Soon after their return Shelley and Mary were shocked by the suicide of Fanny Imlay—Mary's half sister, of whom both of them were very fond, and soon after this came the suicide of Harriet. Shelley's health and nerves broke under this double shock, and the closing months of 1816 were gloomy ones. "Is there no drinking of pearls," inquires Francis Thompson, "except they be dissolved in biting tears?"

Through 1817, in ill-health and distressed by the bitter chancery suit (which he lost) for the possession of Harriet's children, Shelley worked on various ambitious literary projects. *Prince Athanase* belongs to this time, *Rosalind and Helen* was begun, and *Laon and Cythna* (published as *The Revolt of Islam* in 1818) was written. In this last again he speaks as the poet-prophet in the effort to kindle "a virtuous enthusiasm for those doctrines of liberty and justice, that faith and hope in something good, which neither violence nor misrepresentation, nor prejudice, can ever wholly extinguish."

But, however high-minded Shelley may seem to posterity, his own England judged him cruelly, and in March 1818 he left England forever, a thoroughly misunderstood man—how misunderstood may be judged from his obituary in *The Gentleman's Magazine* a few years later. "We ought," wrote the editor, "as justly to regret the decease of the devil (if that were possible) as of one of his coadjutors."

In Italy, away from ever-pressing hostility and in a glorious climate, Shelley's health recovered and he came to full poetic expression. He was not, however, free from despondency and in his lyrics, beside the rapturous and ecstatic note which is to be found in some of his best known pieces, there is a parallel strain, equally marked, of melancholy, of uncertainty before the evanescence and mystery of life. Even in his *Ode to the West Wind* although it was written (1819) when Shelley's powers were at their height and although it reaches a triumphant conclusion, there is an acute sense of the weight and thorns of life.

Shelley's year of marvels was 1819. That was the year of *The Cenci*, as fine a poetic drama as the century produced, if not *the* finest, and of *Prometheus Unbound*. "The blue sky of Rome," Shelley wrote, "and the effect of the vigorous awakening of spring in that divinest climate, and the new life with which it drenches the spirits even to intoxication, were the inspiration of this drama." Which is only part of the truth. The spirit of that schoolboy, who at Syon House resolved to be "wise, and just, and free," who in *Queen Mab* asserted the integrity of the human soul and challenged institutions, the spirit which preserved that idealism through disillusion, had to come into the intoxication of the Italian spring and recover hope before the *Prometheus Unbound* could be written.

Prometheus Unbound ends in triumph, and the poet, who had begun with direct political action and failed in it, foresees victory. One wonders if Shelley had ever surrendered his hope of the actual accomplishment of a perfect world. In his mind perhaps was germinating an idea which came to expression the following year in *The Defence of Poetry*. Poets were not futile beings but active political forces. More sensitive to the currents of life than ordinary men and perceiving them more swiftly, the ideas which the poet expressed today must become the obvious policies of tomorrow. And the essay concludes with the flaming line: "Poets are the unacknowledged legislators of the world." A hundred battlefields have since belied him, but they have not soiled the poetry Shelley wrote, believing that his perfect world must come.

Through the early days of their life in Italy the Shelleys had had few friends and had lived in seclusion, but after they moved to the Pisa-Leghorn district early in 1820 a little circle began to grow up in which they could find companionship. The Gisbornes, Medwin, Trelawney, the Williamses, Prince Mavrocordato, Byron, a professor Pacchiani—the circle was large enough. It was Pacchiani who introduced the Shelleys to Emilia Viviani in late November 1820. Emilia, as Shelley saw the case, was a beautiful girl imprisoned in a convent pending marriage against her will, and instantly Shelley's sympathetic imagination went soaring. *Epipsychidion* (1821) was the poetic result. The year 1821, also, was the year in which Shelley composed *Adonais*, his great elegy for Keats, and his *Hellas*, inspired by sympathy for the Greek cause.

Epipsychidion belongs to that series of poems which begins with *Alastor*, runs, among others, through such diverse poems as *The Hymn to Intellectual Beauty*, *The Sensitive Plant*, "One word is too often profaned," and *Prometheus Unbound*, and ends with *The Triumph of Life* on which Shelley was engaged at the time of his death. The series deals with love and the individual's relationship to love in the abstract and to the loved one. The theme is equal, if not superior, in importance in Shelley's work to the theme of justice and freedom, although not so easy to summarize. It is generally discussed under the portentous heading, "Shelley and Platonism," although the theme was present in Shelley before he was much under the influence of Plato, and although when Shelley was most under Plato's influence he was also likely to be most Shelleyan. Summarizing crudely a great philosopher: Plato identified as the same the beautiful and the good. Love was a desire to be permanently identified with the beautiful (defined as the good) and permanence must mean immortality to be permanent. This permanent (immortal) identification could take place on various planes. It could be physical, leading to procreation and continuance in succeeding generations. It could be a marriage of minds and a continuance in ideas. There were thus several planes and, purified and exalted through love itself, the individual mounted, as on a ladder, to higher and higher planes of love, approaching ever closer to perception of, and identity with an abstract beauty (good) which was eternal, unproduced, indestructible—something undefined, with the breath of God in it and the splendor of the stars about it. The *Adonais*, not one of the love poems, is connected with the group, its conclusion being related to the platonic conception.

To attempt to find pure platonism in Shelley is unprofitable, because it is only fragmentarily there. Merely against this framework of thought should his great poems be thought of. Poetically and emotionally Shelley belies Plato, because the symbol of his eternal quest is usually a woman—radiant and overwhelming. Plato's love of beauty is thus reduced to its lowest plane. But Shelley is not of the sensual poets precisely because *the woman is not an object in herself but is a symbol*, a symbol of that eternal beautiful and good, toward which he is straining and hopes ever to find in the real world about him. Shelley's love poetry has intensity and fire—to the bloodlessness of the idea he adds the splendor of the flesh, to the disillusion of the flesh he adds the springtime of eternal idealism. As a poet, the poet Shelley has added to, rather than borrowed from, the poet Plato.

Emilia Viviani, although the *Epipsychidion* she inspired was a great poem, proved "a cloud instead of a Juno," and Shelley set to work on *The Triumph of Life*, which he left unfinished. He and Williams had moved their families to a villa at Lerici for the summer of 1822. But Leigh Hunt had come to Italy to edit a magazine Shelley had inspired and Byron was to contribute to, and so, in July, Shelley and Williams sailed their tricky little yacht over to Leghorn to greet Hunt. Business, visits, and gossip transacted, they sailed on July 8 for home. A storm came up. And that was the end.

On July 18th Shelley's body was found on the beach and buried with quicklime in the sand— there was fear along the coast of all bodies, because of the plague. It was the last irony which befell Shelley that, in exile lest his mind poison England, his body should be buried in quicklime lest his flesh poison Italy. . . . Efforts were made with the authorities, and on August 16th Trelawney, Hunt, and Byron saw the body exhumed and cremated on the beach. Oil, wine, and salt "made the yellow flames glisten and quiver." Byron flung himself into the water and swam out to sea. The ashes were buried at Rome.

TO WORDSWORTH

POET of Nature, thou hast wept to know
That things depart which never may return:
Childhood and youth, friendship and love's
    first glow,
Have fled like sweet dreams, leaving thee to
    mourn.
These common woes I feel. One loss is mine
Which thou too feel'st, yet I alone deplore.
Thou wert as a lone star, whose light did
    shine
On some frail bark in winter's midnight
    roar:
Thou hast like to a rock-built refuge stood
Above the blind and battling multitude: 10
In honoured poverty thy voice did weave
Songs consecrate to truth and liberty,—
Deserting these, thou leavest me to grieve,
Thus having been, that thou shouldst cease
    to be.

1815

HYMN TO INTELLECTUAL BEAUTY

I

THE awful shadow of some unseen Power
    Floats though unseen among us,—visiting
    This various world with as inconstant wing
As summer winds that creep from flower to
    flower,—
Like moonbeams that behind some piny
    mountain shower,
    It visits with inconstant glance
    Each human heart and countenance;
Like hues and harmonies of evening,—
    Like clouds in starlight widely spread,—
    Like memory of music fled,—   10
    Like aught that for its grace may be
Dear, and yet dearer for its mystery.

II

Spirit of BEAUTY, that dost consecrate
    With thine own hues all thou dost shine
        upon
    Of human thought or form,—where art
        thou gone?
Why dost thou pass away and leave our state,
This dim vast vale of tears, vacant and deso-
    late?

Ask why the sunlight not for ever
    Weaves rainbows o'er yon mountain-
        river,
Why aught should fail and fade that once is
    shown,   20
    Why fear and dream and death and birth
    Cast on the daylight of this earth
    Such gloom,—why man has such a scope
For love and hate, despondency and hope?

III

No voice from some sublimer world hath ever
    To sage or poet these responses given—
    Therefore the names of Demon, Ghost, and
        Heaven,
Remain the records of their vain endeavour,
Frail spells—whose uttered charm might not
        avail to sever,
    From all we hear and all we see,   30
    Doubt, chance, and mutability.
Thy light alone—like mist o'er mountains
        driven,
    Or music by the night-wind sent
    Through strings of some still instrument,
    Or moonlight on a midnight stream,
Gives grace and truth to life's unquiet dream.

IV

Love, Hope, and Self-esteem, like clouds
        depart
    And come, for some uncertain moment
        lent.
Man were immortal, and omnipotent,   39
Didst thou, unknown and awful as thou art,
Keep with thy glorious train firm state within
        his heart.
    Thou messenger of sympathies,
    That wax and wane in lovers' eyes—
Thou—that to human thought art nourish-
        ment,
    Like darkness to a dying flame!
    Depart not as thy shadow came,
    Depart not—lest the grave should be,
Like life and fear, a dark reality.

V

While yet a boy I sought for ghosts, and sped
    Through many a listening chamber, cave
        and ruin,   50
    And starlight wood, with fearful steps pur-
        suing

Hopes of high talk with the departed dead.
I called on poisonous names with which our
    youth is fed;
      I was not heard—I saw them not—
      When musing deeply on the lot
Of life, at that sweet time when winds are
    wooing
      All vital things that wake to bring
      News of birds and blossoming,—
    Sudden, thy shadow fell on me;
I shrieked, and clasped my hands in ecstasy! 60

VI

I vowed that I would dedicate my powers
    To thee and thine—have I not kept the vow?
    With beating heart and streaming eyes, even
      now
I call the phantoms of a thousand hours
Each from his voiceless grave: they have in
    visioned bowers
      Of studious zeal or love's delight
      Outwatched with me the envious night—
They know that never joy illumed my brow
    Unlinked with hope that thou wouldst
      free
    This world from its dark slavery,   70
    That thou—O awful LOVELINESS,
Wouldst give whate'er these words cannot
    express.

VII

The day becomes more solemn and serene
    When noon is past—there is a harmony
    In autumn, and a lustre in its sky,
Which through the summer is not heard or
    seen,
As if it could not be, as if it had not been!
    Thus let thy power, which like the truth
    Of nature on my passive youth
Descended, to my onward life supply   80
    Its calm—to one who worships thee,
    And every form containing thee,
    Whom, SPIRIT fair, thy spells did bind
To fear himself, and love all human kind.

1816

TO CONSTANTIA, SINGING

I

THUS to be lost and thus to sink and die,
    Perchance were death indeed!—Constantia,
    turn!

In thy dark eyes a power like light doth lie,
    Even though the sounds which were thy
      voice, which burn
Between thy lips, are laid to sleep;
    Within thy breath, and on thy hair, like
      odour, it is yet,
And from thy touch like fire doth leap.
    Even while I write, my burning cheeks are
      wet,
    Alas, that the torn heart can bleed, but not
      forget!

II

A breathless awe, like the swift change   10
    Unseen, but felt in youthful slumbers,
Wild, sweet, but uncommunicably strange,
    Thou breathest now in fast ascending
      numbers.
The cope of heaven seems rent and cloven
    By the enchantment of thy strain,
And on my shoulders wings are woven,
    To follow its sublime career
Beyond the mighty moons that wane
    Upon the verge of Nature's utmost sphere,
    Till the world's shadowy walls are past and
      disappear.   20

III

Her voice is hovering o'er my soul—it lingers
    O'ershadowing it with soft and lulling
      wings,
The blood and life within those snowy fingers
    Teach witchcraft to the instrumental strings.
My brain is wild, my breath comes quick—
    The blood is listening in my frame,
And thronging shadows, fast and thick,
    Fall on my overflowing eyes;
My heart is quivering like a flame;   29
    As morning dew, that in the sunbeam dies,
    I am dissolved in these consuming ecstasies.

IV

I have no life, Constantia, now, but thee
    Whilst, like the world-surrounding air, thy
      song
Flows on, and fills all things with melody.—
    Now is thy voice a tempest swift and strong,
On which, like one in trance upborne,
    Secure o'er rocks and waves I sweep,
Rejoicing like a cloud of morn.
    Now 'tis the breath of summer night,
Which when the starry waters sleep,   40

Round western isles, with incense-blos-
  soms bright,
Lingering, suspends my soul in its voluptuous flight.

1817

A FRAGMENT: TO MUSIC

SILVER key of the fountain of tears,
  Where the spirit drinks till the brain is wild;
Softest grave of a thousand fears,
  Where their mother, Care, like a drowsy
    child,
    Is laid asleep in flowers.

1817

OZYMANDIAS

I MET a traveller from an antique land
Who said: Two vast and trunkless legs of
  stone
Stand in the desert . . . Near them, on the sand,
Half sunk, a shattered visage lies, whose
  frown,
And wrinkled lip, and sneer of cold command,
Tell that its sculptor well those passions read
Which yet survive, stamped on these lifeless
  things,
The hand that mocked them, and the heart
  that fed:
And on the pedestal these words appear:
'My name is Ozymandias, king of kings: 10
Look on my works, ye Mighty, and despair!'
Nothing beside remains. Round the decay
Of that colossal wreck, boundless and bare
The lone and level sands stretch far away.

1817

From THE REVOLT OF ISLAM

DEDICATION: TO MARY —— ——

There is no danger to a man, that knows
What life and death is: there's not any law
Exceeds his knowledge; neither is it lawful
That he should stoop to any other law.
                                    CHAPMAN

I

So now my summer task is ended, Mary,
  And I return to thee, mine own heart's
    home;
  As to his Queen some victor Knight of
    Faëry,

Earning bright spoils for her enchanted
    dome;
  Nor thou disdain, that ere my fame be-
    come
A star among the stars of mortal night,
  If it indeed may cleave its natal gloom,
Its doubtful promise thus I would unite
With thy belovèd name, thou Child of love
    and light.

II

The toil which stole from thee so many an
    hour,   10
  Is ended,—and the fruit is at thy feet!
No longer where the woods to frame a
    bower
  With interlacèd branches mix and meet,
  Or where with sound like many voices
    sweet,
Waterfalls leap among wild islands green,
  Which framed for my lone boat a lone
    retreat
Of moss-grown trees and weeds, shall I be
    seen:
But beside thee, where still my heart has ever
    been.

III

Thoughts of great deeds were mine, dear
    Friends, when first
  The clouds which wrap this world from
    youth did pass.   20
I do remember well the hour which burst
  My spirit's sleep: a fresh May-dawn it was,
  When I walked forth upon the glittering
    grass,
And wept, I knew not why; until there rose
  From the near schoolhouse, voices, that,
    alas!
Were but one echo from a world of woes—
The harsh and grating strife of tyrants and of
    foes.

IV

And then I clasped my hands and looked
    around—
  —But none was near to mock my stream-
    ing eyes,
Which poured their warm drops on the
    sunny ground—   30
  So, without shame, I spake:—'I will be
    wise,

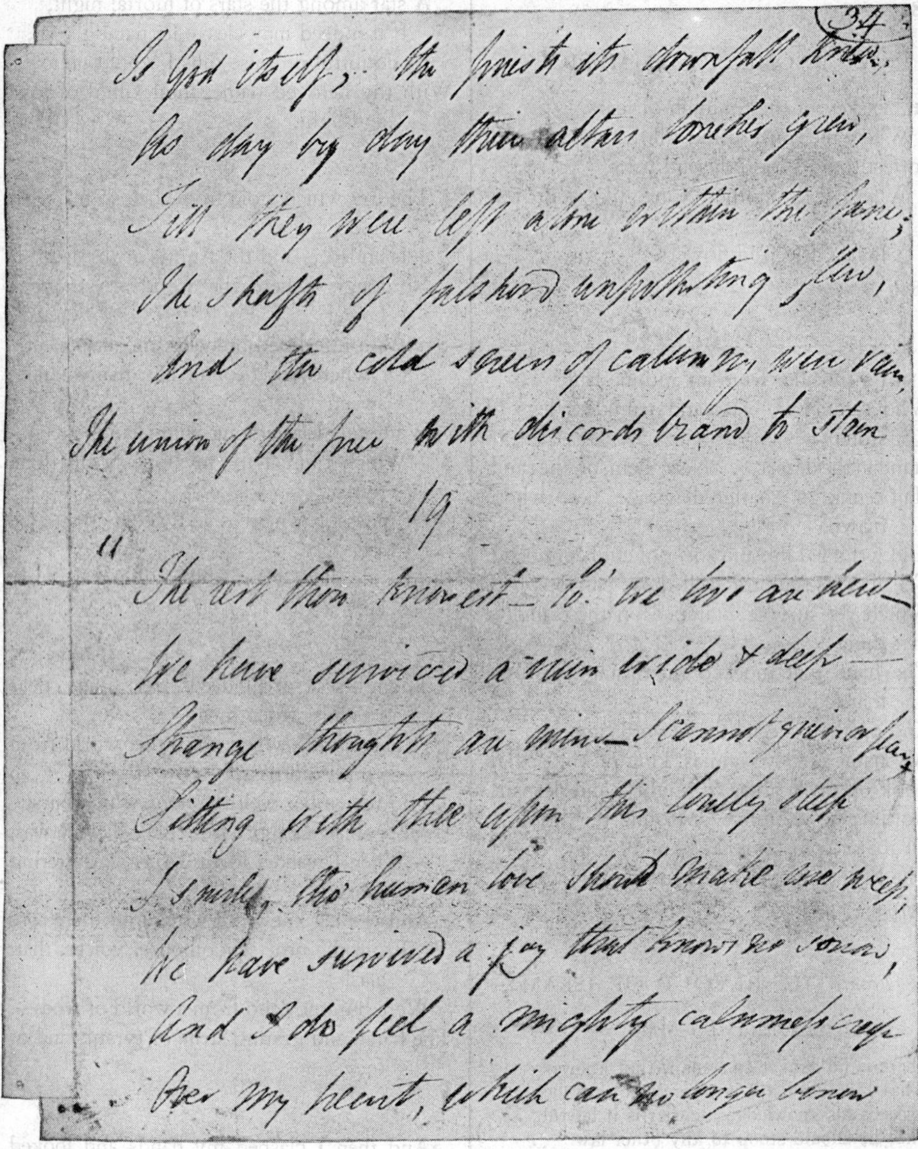

A Leaf from Shelley's MS of *The Revolt of Islam*. (See Appendix I.)

35)

Its hour from chance or change, dark children of
tomorrow.

20

We know not what will come—yet Laon,
dearest
By thee a shall be the prophetess of Love,
Her lips shall rob thee of the grace thou wearest,
To hide thy heart, and clothe thee shapes
which rove
Within the homeless future's winter grove;
For I now, sitting thus beside thee, seem
Even with thy breath & blood to live & move,
And violence & wrong are as a dream
Which rolls from steadfast truth, an unreturning stream.

21

*Leaf of the M.S. of the
"Revolt of Islam" in Shelley's
handwriting. given me by
G. H. Lewes.   W.B.S.*

Another Leaf from Shelley's MS of The Revolt of Islam. (See Appendix I.)

And just, and free, and mild, if in me lies
Such power, for I grow weary to behold
The selfish and the strong still tyrannise
Without reproach or check.' I then con-
trolled
My tears, my heart grew calm, and I was meek
and bold.

V

And from that hour did I with earnest
thought
Heap knowledge from forbidden mines of
lore,
Yet nothing that my tyrants knew or taught
I cared to learn, but from that secret
store   40
Wrought linkèd armour for my soul, be-
fore
It might walk forth to war among mankind;
Thus power and hope were strengthened
more and more
Within me, till there came upon my mind
A sense of loneliness, a thirst with which I
pined.

VI

Alas, that love should be a blight and snare
To those who seek all sympathies in
one!—
Such once I sought in vain; then black
despair,
The shadow of a starless night, was
thrown
Over the world in which I moved
alone:—   50
Yet never found I one not false to me,
Hard hearts, and cold, like weights of icy
stone
Which crushed and withered mine, that
could not be
Aught but a lifeless clod, until revived by thee.

VII

Thou Friend, whose presence on my wintry
heart
Fell, like bright Spring upon some herbless plain;
How beautiful and calm and free thou wert
In thy young wisdom, when the mortal
chain
Of Custom thou didst burst and rend in
twain,

And walked as free as light the clouds
among,   60
Which many an envious slave then
breathed in vain
From his dim dungeon, and my spirit
sprung
To meet thee from the woes which had begirt
it long!

VIII

No more alone through the world's wilder-
ness,
Although I trod the paths of high intent,
I journeyed now: no more companionless,
Where solitude is like despair, I went.—
There is the wisdom of a stern content
When Poverty can blight the just and good,
When Infamy dares mock the innocent, 70
And cherished friends turn with the multi-
tude
To trample: this was ours, and we unshaken
stood!

IX

Now has descended a serener hour,
And with inconstant fortune, friends re-
turn;
Though suffering leaves the knowledge and
the power
Which says:—Let scorn be not repaid
with scorn.
And from thy side two gentle babes are
born
To fill our home with smiles, and thus are
we
Most fortunate beneath life's beaming
morn;
And these delights, and thou, have been to
me   80
The parents of the Song I consecrate to thee.

X

Is it, that now my inexperienced fingers
But strike the prelude of a loftier strain?
Or, must the lyre on which my spirit lingers
Soon pause in silence, ne'er to sound
again,
Though it might shake the Anarch Cus-
tom's reign,
And charm the minds of men to Truth's
own sway
Holier than was Amphion's? I would fain

Reply in hope—but I am worn away,
And Death and Love are yet contending for
   their prey. 90

XI

And what art thou? I know, but dare not
   speak:
Time may interpret to his silent years.
Yet in the paleness of thy thoughtful cheek,
   And in the light thine ample forehead
   wears,
   And in thy sweetest smiles, and in thy
   tears,
And in thy gentle speech, a prophecy
   Is whispered, to subdue my fondest
   fears:
And through thine eyes, even in thy soul I
   see
A lamp of vestal fire burning internally.

XII

They say that thou wert lovely from thy
   birth, 100
   Of glorious parents, thou aspiring Child.
I wonder not—for One then left this earth
   Whose life was like a setting planet
   mild,
   Which clothed thee in the radiance un-
   defiled
Of its departing glory; still her fame
   Shines on thee, through the tempests
   dark and wild
Which shake these latter days; and thou
   canst claim
The shelter, from thy Sire, of an immortal
   name.

XIII

One voice came forth from many a mighty
   spirit,
   Which was the echo of three thousand
   years; 110
And the tumultuous world stood mute to
   hear it,
   As some lone man who in a desert hears
   The music of his home:—unwonted fears
Fell on the pale oppressors of our race,
   And Faith, and Custom, and low-
   thoughted cares,
Like thunder-stricken dragons, for a space
Left the torn human heart, their food and
   dwelling-place.

XIV

Truth's deathless voice pauses among mankind!
   If there must be no response to my cry—
If men must rise and stamp with fury
   blind 120
On his pure name who loves them,—thou
   and I,
   Sweet friend! can look from our tranquillity
Like lamps into the world's tempestuous
   night,—
   Two tranquil stars, while clouds are passing by
Which wrap them from the foundering
   seaman's sight,
That burn from year to year with unextinguished light.

1817. Published 1818

LINES WRITTEN AMONG THE EUGANEAN HILLS

MANY a green isle needs must be
In the deep wide sea of Misery,
Or the mariner, worn and wan,
Never thus could voyage on—
Day and night, and night and day,
Drifting on his dreary way,
With the solid darkness black
Closing round his vessel's track;
Whilst above the sunless sky,
Big with clouds, hangs heavily, 10
And behind the tempest fleet
Hurries on with lightning feet,
Riving sail, and cord, and plank,
Till the ship has almost drank
Death from the o'er-brimming deep;
And sinks down, down, like that sleep
When the dreamer seems to be
Weltering through eternity;
And the dim low line before
Of a dark and distant shore 20
Still recedes, as ever still
Longing with divided will,
But no power to seek or shun,
He is ever drifted on
O'er the unreposing wave
To the haven of the grave.
What, if there no friends will greet;
What, if there no heart will meet

His with love's impatient beat;
Wander wheresoe'er he may.   30
Can he dream before that day
To find refuge from distress
In friendship's smile, in love's caress?
Then 'twill wreak him little woe
Whether such there be or no:
Senseless is the breast, and cold,
Which relenting love would fold;
Bloodless are the veins and chill
Which the pulse of pain did fill;
· Every little living nerve   40
That from bitter words did swerve
Round the tortured lips and brow,
Are like sapless leaflets now
Frozen upon December's bough.

On the beach of a northern sea
Which tempests shake eternally,
As once the wretch there lay to sleep,
Lies a solitary heap,
One white skull and seven dry bones,
On the margin of the stones,   50
Where a few gray rushes stand,
Boundaries of the sea and land:
Nor is heard one voice of wail
But the sea-mews, as they sail
O'er the billows of the gale;
Or the whirlwind up and down
Howling, like a slaughtered town,
When a king in glory rides
Through the pomp of fratricides:
Those unburied bones around   60
There is many a mournful sound;
There is no lament for him,
Like a sunless vapour, dim,
Who once clothed with life and thought
What now moves nor murmurs not.

Ay, many flowering islands lie
In the waters of wide Agony:
To such a one this morn was led,
My bark by soft winds piloted:
'Mid the mountains Euganean   70
I stood listening to the paean
With which the legioned rooks did hail
The sun's uprise majestical;
Gathering round with wings all hoar,
Through the dewy mist they soar
Like grey shades, till the eastern heaven
Bursts, and then, as clouds of even,

Flecked with fire and azure, lie
In the unfathomable sky,
So their plumes of purple grain,   80
Starred with drops of golden rain,
Gleam above the sunlight woods,
As in silent multitudes
On the morning's fitful gale
Through the broken mist they sail,
And the vapours cloven and gleaming
Follow down the dark steep streaming,
Till all is bright, and clear, and still,
Round the solitary hill.

Beneath is spread like a green sea   90
The waveless plain of Lombardy,
Bounded by the vaporous air,
Islanded by cities fair;
Underneath Day's azure eyes
Ocean's nursling, Venice lies,
A peopled labyrinth of walls,
Amphitrite's destined halls,
Which her hoary sire now paves
With his blue and beaming waves.
Lo! the sun upsprings behind,   100
Broad, red, radiant, half-reclined
On the level quivering line
Of the waters crystalline;
And before that chasm of light,
As within a furnace bright,
Column, tower, and dome, and spire,
Shine like obelisks of fire,
Pointing with inconstant motion
From the altar of dark ocean
To the sapphire-tinted skies;   110
As the flames of sacrifice
From the marble shrines did rise,
As to pierce the dome of gold
Where Apollo spoke of old.

Sun-girt City, thou hast been
Ocean's child, and then his queen;
Now is come a darker day,
And thou soon must be his prey,
If the power that raised thee here
Hallow so thy watery bier.   120
A less drear ruin then than now,
With thy conquest-branded brow
Stooping to the slave of slaves
From thy throne, among the waves
Wilt thou be, when the sea-mew
Flies, as once before it flew,

O'er thine isles depopulate,
And all is in its ancient state,
Save where many a palace gate
With green sea-flowers overgrown   130
Like a rock of Ocean's own,
Topples o'er the abandoned sea
As the tides change sullenly.
The fisher on his watery way,
Wandering at the close of day,
Will spread his sail and seize his oar
Till he pass the gloomy shore,
Lest thy dead should, from their sleep
Bursting o'er the starlight deep,
Lead a rapid masque of death   140
O'er the waters of his path.

Those who alone thy towers behold
Quivering through aëreal gold,
As I now behold them here,
Would imagine not they were
Sepulchres, where human forms,
Like pollution-nourished worms,
To the corpse of greatness cling,
Murdered, and now mouldering:
But if Freedom should awake   150
In her omnipotence, and shake
From the Celtic Anarch's hold
All the keys of dungeons cold,
Where a hundred cities lie
Chained like thee, ingloriously,
Thou and all thy sister band
Might adorn this sunny land,
Twining memories of old time
With new virtues more sublime;
If not, perish thou and they!—   160
Clouds which stain truth's rising day
By her sun consumed away—
Earth can spare ye: while like flowers,
In the waste of years and hours,
From your dust new nations spring
With more kindly blossoming.

Perish—let there only be
Floating o'er thy heartless sea
As the garment of thy sky
Clothes the world immortally,   170
One remembrance, more sublime
Than the tattered pall of time,
Which scarce hides thy visage wan;—
That a tempest-cleaving Swan
Of the songs of Albion,
Driven from his ancestral streams

By the might of evil dreams,
Found a nest in thee; and Ocean
Welcomed him with such emotion
That its joy grew his, and sprung   180
From his lips like music flung
O'er a mighty thunder-fit,
Chastening terror:—what though yet
Poesy's unfailing River,
Which through Albion winds forever
Lashing with melodious wave
Many a sacred Poet's grave,
Mourn its latest nursling fled?
What though thou with all thy dead
Scarce can for this fame repay   190
Aught thine own? oh, rather say
Though thy sins and slaveries foul
Overcloud a sunlike soul?
As the ghost of Homer clings
Round Scamander's wasting springs;
As divinest Shakespeare's might
Fills Avon and the world with light
Like omniscient power which he
Imaged 'mid mortality;
As the love from Petrarch's urn,   200
Yet amid yon hills doth burn,
A quenchless lamp by which the heart
Sees things unearthly;—so thou art,
Mighty spirit—so shall be
The City that did refuge thee.

Lo, the sun floats up the sky
Like thought-wingèd Liberty,
Till the universal light
Seems to level plain and height;
From the sea a mist has spread,   210
And the beams of morn lie dead
On the towers of Venice now,
Like its glory long ago.
By the skirts of that gray cloud
Many-domèd Padua proud
Stands, a peopled solitude,
'Mid the harvest-shining plain,
Where the peasant heaps his grain
In the garner of his foe,
And the milk-white oxen slow   220
With the purple vintage strain,
Heaped upon the creaking wain,
That the brutal Celt may swill
Drunken sleep with savage will;
And the sickle to the sword
Lies unchanged, though many a lord,

Like a weed whose shade is poison,
Overgrows this region's foison,
Sheaves of whom are ripe to come
To destruction's harvest-home: 230
Men must reap the things they sow,
Force from force must ever flow,
Or worse; but 'tis a bitter woe
That love or reason cannot change
The despot's rage, the slave's revenge.
Padua, thou within whose walls
Those mute guests at festivals,
Son and Mother, Death and Sin,
Played at dice for Ezzelin,
Till Death cried, "I win, I win!"   240
And sin cursed to lose the wager,
But Death promised, to assuage her,
That he would petition for
Her to be made Vice-Emperor,
When the destined years were o'er,
Over all between the Po
And the eastern Alpine snow,
Under the mighty Austrian.
Sin smiled so as Sin only can,
And since that time, ay, long before,   250
Both have ruled from shore to shore,—
That incestuous pair, who follow
Tyrants as the sun the swallow,
As Repentance follows Crime,
And as changes follow Time.

In thine halls the lamp of learning,
Padua, now no more is burning;
Like a meteor, whose wild way
Is lost over the grave of day,
It gleams betrayed and to betray: 260
Once remotest nations came
To adore that sacred flame,
When it lit not many a hearth
On this cold and gloomy earth:
Now new fires from antique light
Spring beneath the wide world's might;
But their spark lies dead in thee,
Trampled out by Tyranny.
As the Norway woodman quells,
In the depth of piny dells,   270
One light flame among the brakes,
While the boundless forest shakes,
And its mighty trunks are torn
By the fire thus lowly born:
The spark beneath his feet is dead,
He starts to see the flames it fed

Howling through the darkened sky
With a myriad tongues victoriously,
And sinks down in fear: so thou,
O Tyranny, beholdest now   280
Light around thee, and thou hearest
The loud flames ascend, and fearest:
Grovel on the earth; ay, hide
In the dust thy purple pride!

Noon descends around me now:
'Tis the noon of autumn's glow,
When a soft and purple mist
Like a vaporous amethyst,
Or an air-dissolvèd star
Mingling light and fragrance, far   290
From the curved horizon's bound
To the point of Heaven's profound,
Fills the overflowing sky;
And the plains that silent lie
Underneath, the leaves unsodden
Where the infant Frost has trodden
With his morning-wingèd feet,
Whose bright print is gleaming yet;
And the red and golden vines,
Piercing with their trellised lines   300
The rough, dark-skirted wilderness;
The dun and bladed grass no less,
Pointing from this hoary tower
In the windless air; the flower
Glimmering at my feet; the line
Of the olive-sandalled Apennine
In the south dimly islanded;
And the Alps, whose snows are spread
High between the clouds and sun;
And of living things each one;   310
And my spirit which so long
Darkened this swift stream of song,—
Interpenetrated lie
By the glory of the sky:
Be it love, light, harmony,
Odour, or the soul of all
Which from Heaven like dew doth fall,
Or the mind which feeds this verse
Peopling the lone universe.

Noon descends, and after noon   320
Autumn's evening meets me soon,
Leading the infantine moon,
And that one star, which to her
Almost seems to minister

Half the crimson light she brings
From the sunset's radiant springs:
And the soft dreams of the morn
(Which like wingèd winds had borne
To that silent isle, which lies
Mid remembered agonies,   330
The frail bark of this lone being)
Pass, to other sufferers fleeing,
And its ancient pilot, Pain.
Sits beside the helm again.

Other flowering isles must be
In the sea of Life and Agony:
Other spirits float and flee
O'er that gulf: even now, perhaps,
On some rock the wild wave wraps,
With folded wings they waiting sit   340
For my bark, to pilot it
To some calm and blooming cove,
Where for me, and those I love,
May a windless bower be built,
Far from passion, pain, and guilt,
In a dell mid lawny hills,
Which the wild-sea murmur fills,
And soft sunshine, and the sound
Of old forests echoing round,
And the light and smell divine   350
Of all flowers that breathe and shine:
We may live so happy there,
That the Spirits of the Air,
Envying us, may even entice
To our healing Paradise
The polluting multitude;
But their rage would be subdued
By that clime divine and calm,
And the winds whose wings rain balm
On the uplifted soul, and leaves   360
Under which the bright sea heaves;
While each breathless interval
In their whisperings musical
The inspired soul supplies
With its own deep melodies,
And the love which heals all strife
Circling, like the breath of life,
All things in that sweet abode
With its own mild brotherhood:
They, not it, would change; and soon   370
Every sprite beneath the moon
Would repent its envy vain,
And the earth grow young again.

1818

STANZAS

WRITTEN IN DEJECTION, NEAR NAPLES

I

THE sun is warm, the sky is clear,
    The waves are dancing fast and bright,
Blue isles and snowy mountains wear
    The purple noon's transparent might,
    The breath of the moist earth is light,
Around its unexpanded buds;
    Like many a voice of one delight,
The winds, the birds, the ocean floods,
The City's voice itself, is soft like Solitude's.

II

I see the Deep's untrampled floor   10
    With green and purple seaweeds strown;
I see the waves upon the shore,
    Like light dissolved in star-showers, thrown:
    I sit upon the sands alone,—
The lightning of the noontide ocean
    Is flashing round me, and a tone
Arises from its measured motion,
How sweet! did any heart now share in my emotion.

III

Alas! I have nor hope nor health,
    Nor peace within nor calm around,   20
Nor that content surpassing wealth
    The sage in meditation found,
    And walked with inward glory crowned—
Nor fame, nor power, nor love, nor leisure.
    Others I see whom these surround—
Smiling they live, and call life pleasure;—
To me that cup has been dealt in another measure.

IV

Yet now despair itself is mild,
    Even as the winds and waters are;
I could lie down like a tired child,   30
    And weep away the life of care
    Which I have borne and yet must bear,
Till death like sleep might steal on me,
    And I might feel in the warm air
My cheek grow cold, and hear the sea
Breathe o'er my dying brain its last monotony.

V

Some might lament that I were cold,
　As I, when this sweet day is gone,
Which my lost heart, too soon grown old,
　Insults with this untimely moan;　　40
　They might lament—for I am one
Whom men love not,—and yet regret,
　Unlike this day, which, when the sun
Shall on its stainless glory set,
Will linger, though enjoyed, like joy in
　memory yet.

1818

SONNET

Lift not.the painted veil which those who live
Call Life: though unreal shapes be pictured
　there,
And it but mimic all we would believe
With colours idly spread,—behind, lurk Fear
And Hope, twin Destinies; who ever weave
Their shadows, o'er the chasm, sightless and
　drear.
I knew one who had lifted it—he sought,
For his lost heart was tender, things to love,
But found them not, alas! nor was there aught
The world contains, the which he could ap-
　prove.　　　　　　　　　　　　　　10
Through the unheeding many he did move,
A splendour among shadows, a bright blot
Upon this gloomy scene, a Spirit that strove
For truth, and like the Preacher found it not.

1818

SONG TO THE MEN OF ENGLAND

I

Men of England, wherefore plough
For the lords who lay ye low?
Wherefore weave with toil and care
The rich robes your tyrants wear?

II

Wherefore feed, and clothe, and save,
From the cradle to the grave,
Those ungrateful drones who would
Drain your sweat—nay, drink your blood?

III

Wherefore, Bees of England, forge
Many a weapon, chain, and scourge,　　10
That these stingless drones may spoil
The forced produce of your toil?

IV

Have ye leisure, comfort, calm,
Shelter, food, love's gentle balm?
Or what is it ye buy so dear
With your pain and with your fear?

V

The seed ye sow, another reaps;
The wealth ye find, another keeps;
The robes ye weave, another wears;
The arms ye forge, another bears.　　20

VI

Sow seed,—but let no tyrant reap;
Find wealth,—let no impostor heap;
Weave robes,—let not the idle wear;
Forge arms,—in your defence to bear.

VII

Shrink to your cellars, holes, and cells;
In halls ye deck another dwells.
Why shake the chains ye wrought? Ye see
The steel ye tempered glance on ye.

VIII

With plough and spade, and hoe and loom,
Trace your grave, and build your tomb,　30
And weave your winding-sheet, till fair
England be your sepulchre.

1819

ODE TO THE WEST WIND

I

O wild West Wind, thou breath of Autumn's
　being,
Thou, from whose unseen presence the leaves
　dead
Are driven, like ghosts from an enchanter
　fleeing,

Yellow, and black, and pale, and hectic red,
Pestilence-stricken multitudes: O thou,
Who chariotest to their dark wintry bed

The wingèd seeds, where they lie cold and low,
Each like a corpse within its grave, until
Thine azure sister of the Spring shall blow

Her clarion o'er the dreaming earth, and fill 10
(Driving sweet buds like flocks to feed in air)
With living hues and odours plain and hill:

Wild Spirit, which art moving everywhere;
Destroyer and preserver; hear, oh, hear!

II

Thou on whose stream, mid the steep sky's
    commotion,
Loose clouds like earth's decaying leaves are
    shed,
Shook from the tangled boughs of Heaven
    and Ocean,

Angels of rain and lightning: there are spread
On the blue surface of thine aëry surge,
Like the bright hair uplifted from the head 20

Of some fierce Maenad, even from the dim
    verge
Of the horizon to the zenith's height,
The locks of the approaching storm. Thou
    dirge

Of the dying year, to which this closing night
Will be the dome of a vast sepulchre,
Vaulted with all thy congregated might

Of vapours, from whose solid atmosphere
Black rain, and fire, and hail will burst: oh,
    hear!

III

Thou who didst waken from his summer
    dreams
The blue Mediterranean, where he lay,   30
Lulled by the coil of his crystàlline streams,

Beside a pumice isle in Baiae's bay,
And saw in sleep old palaces and towers
Quivering within the wave's intenser day,

All overgrown with azure moss and flowers
So sweet, the sense faints picturing them! Thou
For whose path the Atlantic's level powers

Cleave themselves into chasms, while far
    below
The sea-blooms and the oozy woods which
    wear
The sapless foliage of the ocean, know   40

Thy voice, and suddenly grow gray with fear,
And tremble and despoil themselves: oh, hear!

IV

If I were a dead leaf thou mightest bear;
If I were a swift cloud to fly with thee;
A wave to pant beneath thy power, and share

The impulse of thy strength, only less free
Than thou, O uncontrollable! If even
I were as in my boyhood, and could be

The comrade of thy wanderings over Heaven,
As then, when to outstrip thy skiey speed 50
Scarce seemed a vision; I would ne'er have
    striven

As thus with thee in prayer in my sore
    need.
Oh, lift me as a wave, a leaf, a cloud!
I fall upon the thorns of life! I bleed!

A heavy weight of hours has chained and
    bowed
One too like thee: tameless, and swift, and
    proud.

V

Make me thy lyre, even as the forest is:
What if my leaves are falling like its
    own!
The tumult of thy mighty harmonies

Will take from both a deep, autumnal tone, 60
Sweet though in sadness. Be thou, Spirit
    fierce,
My spirit! Be thou me, impetuous one!

Drive my dead thoughts over the universe
Like withered leaves to quicken a new birth!
And, by the incantation of this verse,

Scatter, as from an unextinguished hearth
Ashes and sparks, my words among man-
    kind!
Be through my lips to unawakened earth

The trumpet of a prophecy! O, Wind,   69
If Winter comes, can Spring be far behind?
1819

THE INDIAN SERENADE

I

I ARISE from dreams of thee
In the first sweet sleep of night,
When the winds are breathing low,
And the stars are shining bright:
I arise from dreams of thee,
And a spirit in my feet
Hath led me—who knows how?
To thy chamber window, Sweet!

II

The wandering airs they faint
On the dark, the silent stream—   10
The Champak odours fail
Like sweet thoughts in a dream;
The nightingale's complaint,
It dies upon her heart;—
As I must on thine,
Oh, belovèd as thou art!

III

Oh lift me from the grass!
I die! I faint! I fail!
Let thy love in kisses rain
On my lips and eyelids pale.   20
My cheek is cold and white, alas!
My heart beats loud and fast;—
Oh! press it to thine own again,
Where it will break at last.

1819

LOVE'S PHILOSOPHY

I

The fountains mingle with the river
    And the rivers with the Ocean,
The winds of Heaven mix for ever
    With a sweet emotion;
Nothing in the world is single;
    All things by a law divine
In one spirit meet and mingle.
    Why not I with thine?—

II

See the mountains kiss high Heaven
    And the waves clasp one another;   10
No sister-flower would be forgiven
    If it disdained its brother;
And the sunlight clasps the earth
    And the moonbeams kiss the sea:
What is all this sweet work worth
    If thou kiss not me?

1819

THE SENSITIVE PLANT

Part First

A Sensitive Plant in a garden grew,
And the young winds fed it with silver dew,
And it opened its fan-like leaves to the light,
And closed them beneath the kisses of Night.

And the Spring arose on the garden fair,
Like the Spirit of Love felt everywhere;
And each flower and herb on Earth's dark
    breast
Rose from the dreams of its wintry rest.

But none ever trembled and panted with bliss
In the garden, the field, or the wilderness,   10
Like a doe in the noontide with love's sweet
    want,
As the companionless Sensitive Plant.

The snowdrop, and then the violet,
Arose from the ground with warm rain wet,
And their breath was mixed with fresh odour,
    sent
From the turf, like the voice and the instru-
    ment.

Then the pied wind-flowers and the tulip tall,
And narcissi, the fairest among them all,
Who gaze on their eyes in the stream's recess,
Till they die of their own dear loveliness;   20

And the Naiad-like lily of the vale,
Whom youth makes so fair and passion so pale,
That the light of its tremulous bells is seen
Through their pavilions of tender green;

And the hyacinth purple, and white, and blue,
Which flung from its bells a sweet peal anew
Of music so delicate, soft, and intense,
It was felt like an odour within the sense;

And the rose like a nymph to the bath ad-
    dressed,
Which unveiled the depth of her glowing
    breast,   30
Till, fold after fold, to the fainting air
The soul of her beauty and love lay bare:

And the wand-like lily, which lifted up,
As a Maenad its moonlight-coloured cup,
Till the fiery star, which is its eye,
Gazed through clear dew on the tender sky;

And the jessamine faint, and the sweet tube-
    rose,
The sweetest flower for scent that blows;
And all rare blossoms from every clime
Grew in that garden in perfect prime.   40

And on the stream whose inconstant bosom
Was pranked, under boughs of embowering
    blossom,
With golden and green light, slanting through
Their heaven of many a tangled hue,

Broad water-lilies lay tremulously,
And starry river-buds glimmered by,
And around them the soft stream did glide
    and dance
With a motion of sweet sound and radiance.

And the sinuous paths of lawn and of moss,
Which led through the garden along and
    across,   50
Some open at once to the sun and the breeze,
Some lost among bowers of blossoming trees,

Were all paved with daisies and delicate bells
As fair as the fabulous asphodels,
And flow'rets which, drooping as day drooped
    too,
Fell into pavilions, white, purple, and blue,
To roof the glow-worm from the evening dew.

And from this undefilèd Paradise
The flowers (as an infant's awakening eyes
Smile on its mother, whose singing sweet 60
Can first lull, and at last must awaken it),

When Heaven's blithe winds had unfolded
    them,
As mine-lamps enkindle a hidden gem,
Shone smiling to Heaven, and every one
Shared joy in the light of the gentle sun;

For each one was interpenetrated
With the light and the odour its neighbour
    shed,
Like young lovers whom youth and love make
    dear
Wrapped and filled by their mutual atmos-
    phere.

But the Sensitive Plant which could give small
    fruit   70
Of the love which it felt from the leaf to the
    root,
Received more than all, it loved more than
    ever,
Where none wanted but it, could belong to
    the giver,—

For the Sensitive Plant has no bright flower;
Radiance and odour are not its dower;
It loves, even like Love, its deep heart is full,
It desires what it has not, the Beautiful!

The light winds which from unsustaining
    wings
Shed the music of many murmurings;
The beams which dart from many a star   80
Of the flowers whose hues they bear afar;

The plumèd insects swift and free,
Like golden boats on a sunny sea,
Laden with light and odour, which pass
Over the gleam of the living grass;

The unseen clouds of the dew, which lie
Like fire in the flowers till the sun rides high,
Then wander like spirits among the spheres,
Each cloud faint with the fragrance it bears;

The quivering vapours of dim noontide, 90
Which like a sea o'er the warm earth glide,
In which every sound, and odour, and beam,
Move, as reeds in a single stream;

Each and all like ministering angels were
For the Sensitive Plant sweet joy to bear,
Whilst the lagging hours of the day went by
Like windless clouds o'er a tender sky.

And when evening descended from Heaven
    above,
And the Earth was all rest, and the air was all
    love,
And delight, though less bright, was far more
    deep,   100
And the day's veil fell from the world of sleep,

And the beasts, and the birds, and the insects
    were drowned
In an ocean of dreams without a sound;
Whose waves never mark, though they ever
    impress
The light sand which paves it, consciousness;

(Only overhead the sweet nightingale
Ever sang more sweet as the day might fail,
And snatches of its Elysian chant
Were mixed with the dreams of the Sensitive
    Plant);—

The Sensitive Plant was the earliest   110
Upgathered into the bosom of rest;
A sweet child weary of its delight,
The feeblest and yet the favourite,
Cradled within the embrace of Night.

PART SECOND

There was a Power in this sweet place,
An Eve in this Eden; a ruling Grace
Which to the flowers, did they waken or
     dream,
Was as God is to the starry scheme.

A Lady, the wonder of her kind,
Whose form was upborne by a lovely mind
Which, dilating, had moulded her mien and
     motion
Like a sea-flower unfolded beneath the ocean,

Tended the garden from morn to even:
And the meteors of that sublunar Heaven, 10
Like the lamps of the air when Night walks
     forth,
Laughed round her footsteps up from the
     Earth!

She had no companion of mortal race,
But her tremulous breath and her flushing face
Told, whilst the morn kissed the sleep from
     her eyes,
That her dreams were less slumber than Para-
     dise:

As if some bright Spirit for her sweet sake
Had deserted Heaven while the stars were
     awake,
As if yet around her he lingering were,
Though the veil of daylight concealed him
     from her.   20

Her step seemed to pity the grass it pressed;
You might hear by the heaving of her breast,
That the coming and going of the wind
Brought pleasure there and left passion be-
     hind.

And wherever her aëry footstep trod,
Her trailing hair from the grassy sod
Erased its light vestige, with shadowy sweep,
Like a sunny storm o'er the dark green deep.

I doubt not the flowers of that garden sweet
Rejoiced in the sound of her gentle feet;   30
I doubt not they felt that spirit that came
From her glowing fingers through all their
     frame.

She sprinkled bright water from the stream
On those that were faint with the sunny beam;
And out of the cups of the heavy flowers
She emptied the rain of the thunder-showers.

She lifted their heads with her tender hands,
And sustained them with rods and osier-
     bands;
If the flowers had been her own infants, she
Could never have nursed them more
     tenderly.   40

And all killing insects and gnawing worms,
And things of obscene and unlovely forms,
She bore, in a basket of Indian woof,
Into the rough woods far aloof,—

In a basket, of grasses and wild-flowers full,
The freshest her gentle hands could pull
For the poor banished insects, whose intent,
Although they did ill, was innocent.

But the bee and the beamlike ephemeris
Whose path is the lightning's, and soft moths
     that kiss   50
The sweet lips of the flowers, and harm not,
     did she
Make her attendant angels be.

And many an antenatal tomb,
Where butterflies dream of the life to come,
She left clinging round the smooth and dark
Edge of the odorous cedar bark.

This fairest creature from earliest Spring
Thus moved through the garden ministering
All the sweet season of Summertide,
And ere the first leaf looked brown—she
     died!   60

PART THIRD

Three days the flowers of the garden fair,
Like stars when the moon is awakened, were,
Or the waves of Baiae, ere luminous
She floats up through the smoke of Vesuvius.

And on the fourth, the Sensitive Plant
Felt the sound of the funeral chant,
And the steps of the bearers, heavy and slow,
And the sobs of the mourners, deep and low;

The weary sound and the heavy breath,
And the silent motions of passing death,   10
And the smell, cold, oppressive, and dank,
Sent through the pores of the coffin-plank;

The dark grass, and the flowers among the
    grass,
Were bright with tears as the crowd did pass;
From their sighs the wind caught a mournful
    tone,
And sate in the pines, and gave groan for
    groan.

The garden, once fair, became cold and foul,
Like the corpse of her who had been its soul,
Which at first was lovely as if in sleep,
Then slowly changed, till it grew a heap   20
To make men tremble who never weep.

Swift Summer into the Autumn flowed,
And frost in the midst of the morning rode,
Though the noonday sun looked clear and
    bright,
Mocking the spoil of the secret night.

The rose-leaves, like flakes of crimson snow,
Paved the turf and the moss below.
The lilies were drooping, and white, and wan,
Like the head and the skin of a dying man.

And Indian plants, of scent and hue   30
The sweetest that ever were fed on dew,
Leaf by leaf, day after day,
Were massed into the common clay.

And the leaves, brown, yellow, and gray, and
    red,
And white with the whiteness of what is dead,
Like troops of ghosts on the dry wind passed;
Their whistling noise made the birds aghast.

And the gusty winds waked the wingèd seeds,
Out of their birthplace of ugly weeds,
Till they clung round many a sweet flower's
    stem,   40
Which rotted into the earth with them.

The water-blooms under the rivulet
Fell from the stalks on which they were set;
And the eddies drove them here and there,
As the winds did those of the upper air.

Then the rain came down, and the broken
    stalks
Were bent and tangled across the walks;
And the leafless network of parasite bowers
Massed into ruin; and all sweet flowers.

Between the time of the wind and the snow   50
All loathliest weeds began to grow,
Whose coarse leaves were splashed with many
    a speck,
Like the water-snake's belly and the toad's
    back.

And thistles, and nettles, and darnels rank,
And the dock, and henbane, and hemlock
    dank,
Stretched out its long and hollow shank,
And stifled the air till the dead wind stank.

And plants, at whose names the verse feels
    loath,
Filled the place with a monstrous undergrowth,
Prickly, and pulpous, and blistering, and
    blue,   60
Livid, and starred with a lurid dew.

And agarics, and fungi, with mildew and mould
Started like mist from the wet ground cold;
Pale, fleshy, as if the decaying dead
With a spirit of growth had been animated!

Spawn, weeds, and filth, a leprous scum,
Made the running rivulet thick and dumb,
And at its outlet flags huge as stakes
Dammed it up with roots knotted like water-
    snakes.

And hour by hour, when the air was still,   70
The vapours arose which have strength to kill,
At morn they were seen, at noon they were
    felt,
At night they were darkness no star could
    melt.

And unctuous meteors from spray to spray
Crept and flitted in broad noonday
Unseen; every branch on which they alit
By a venomous blight was burned and bit.

The Sensitive Plant, like one forbid,
Wept, and the tears within each lid
Of its folded leaves, which together grew, 80
Were changed to a blight of frozen glue.

For the leaves soon fell, and the branches soon
By the heavy axe of the blast were hewn;
The sap shrank to the root through every pore
As blood to a heart that will beat no more.

For Winter came: the wind was his whip:
One choppy finger was on his lip:
He had torn the cataracts from the hills
And they clanked at his girdle like manacles;

His breath was a chain which without a sound
The earth, and the air, and the water bound; 91
He came, fiercely driven, in his chariot-throne
By the tenfold blasts of the Arctic zone.

Then the weeds which were forms of living
        death
Fled from the frost to the earth beneath.
Their decay and sudden flight from frost
Was but like the vanishing of a ghost!

And under the roots of the Sensitive Plant
The moles and the dormice died for want:
The birds dropped stiff from the frozen air 100
And were caught in the branches naked and
        bare.

First there came down a thawing rain
And its dull drops froze on the boughs again;
Then there steamed up a freezing dew
Which to the drops of the thaw-rain grew;

And a northern whirlwind, wandering about
Like a wolf that had smelt a dead child out,
Shook the boughs thus laden, and heavy, and
        stiff,
And snapped them off with his rigid griff.

When Winter had gone and Spring came back
The Sensitive Plant was a leafless wreck; 111
But the mandrakes, and toadstools, and docks,
        and darnels,
Rose like the dead from their ruined charnels.

CONCLUSION

Whether the Sensitive Plant, or that
Which within its boughs like a Spirit sat,
Ere its outward form had known decay,
Now felt this change, I cannot say.

Whether that Lady's gentle mind,
No longer with the form combined
Which scattered love, as stars do light,   120
Found sadness, where it left delight,

I dare not guess; but in this life
Of error, ignorance, and strife,
Where nothing is, but all things seem,
And we the shadows of the dream,

It is a modest creed, and yet
Pleasant if one considers it,
To own that death itself must be,
Like all the rest, a mockery.

That garden sweet, that lady fair,   130
And all sweet shapes and odours there,
In truth have never passed away:
'Tis we, 'tis ours, are changed; not they.

For love, and beauty, and delight,
There is no death nor change: their might
Exceeds our organs, which endure
No light, being themselves obscure.

1820

THE CLOUD

I BRING fresh showers for the thirsting flowers,
    From the seas and the streams;
I bear light shade for the leaves when laid
    In their noonday dreams.
From my wings are shaken the dews that
        waken
    The sweet buds every one,
When rocked to rest on their mother's breast,
    As she dances about the sun.
I wield the flail of the lashing hail,
    And whiten the green plains under,   10
And then again I dissolve it in rain,
    And laugh as I pass in thunder.

I sift the snow on the mountains below,
    And their great pines groan aghast;
And all the night 'tis my pillow white,
    While I sleep in the arms of the blast.
Sublime on the towers of my skiey bowers,
    Lightning my pilot sits;
In a cavern under is fettered the thunder,
    It struggles and howls at fits;   20
Over earth and ocean, with gentle motion,
    This pilot is guiding me,

Lured by the love of the genii that move
  In the depths of the purple sea;
Over the rills, and the crags, and the hills,
  Over the lakes and the plains,
Wherever he dream, under mountain or stream,
  The Spirit he loves remains;
And I all the while bask in Heaven's blue
  smile,
  Whilst he is dissolving in rains.   30

The sanguine Sunrise, with his meteor eyes,
  And his burning plumes outspread,
Leaps on the back of my sailing rack,
  When the morning star shines dead;
As on the jag of a mountain crag,
  Which an earthquake rocks and swings,
An eagle alit one moment may sit
  In the light of its golden wings.
And when Sunset may breathe, from the lit
  sea beneath,
  Its ardours of rest and of love,   40
And the crimson pall of eve may fall
  From the depth of Heaven above,
With wings folded I rest, on mine aëry nest,
  As still as a brooding dove.

That orbèd maiden with white fire laden,
  Whom mortals call the Moon,
Glides glimmering o'er my fleece-like floor,
  By the midnight breezes strewn;
And wherever the beat of her unseen feet,
  Which only the angels hear,   50
May have broken the woof of my tent's thin
  roof,
  The stars peep behind her and peer;
And I laugh to see them whirl and flee,
  Like a swarm of golden bees,
When I widen the rent in my wind-built tent,
  Till the calm rivers, lakes, and seas,
Like strips of the sky fallen through me on
  high,
  Are each paved with the moon and these.

I bind the Sun's throne with a burning zone,
  And the Moon's with a girdle of pearl;   60
The volcanoes are dim, and the stars reel and
  swim,
  When the whirlwinds my banner unfurl.
From cape to cape, with a bridge-like shape,
  Over a torrent sea,
Sunbeam-proof, I hang like a roof,—
  The mountains its columns be.

The triumphal arch through which I march
  With hurricane, fire, and snow,
When the Powers of the air are chained to my
  chair,
  Is the million-coloured bow;   70
The sphere-fire above its soft colours wove,
  While the moist Earth was laughing below.

I am the daughter of Earth and Water,
  And the nursling of the Sky;
I pass through the pores of the ocean and
  shores;
  I change, but I cannot die.
For after the rain when with never a stain
  The pavilion of Heaven is bare,
And the winds and sunbeams with their con-
  vex gleams
  Build up the blue dome of air,   80
I silently laugh at my own cenotaph,— *monument*
  And out of the caverns of rain,
Like a child from the womb, like a ghost from
  the tomb,
  I arise and unbuild it again.
1820

TO A SKYLARK

Hail to thee, blithe Spirit!
  Bird thou never wert,
That from Heaven, or near it,
  Pourest thy full heart
In profuse strains of unpremeditated art.

Higher still and higher
  From the earth thou springest
Like a cloud of fire;
  The blue deep thou wingest,
And singing still dost soar, and soaring ever
  singest.   10

In the golden lightning
  Of the sunken sun,
O'er which clouds are bright'ning,
  Thou dost float and run;
Like an unbodied joy whose race is just begun.

The pale purple even
  Melts around thy flight;
Like a star of Heaven,
  In the broad daylight
Thou art unseen, but yet I hear thy shrill
  delight,   20

Keen as are the arrows
  Of that silver sphere,
Whose intense lamp narrows
  In the white dawn clear
Until we hardly see—we feel that it is there.

All the earth and air
  With thy voice is loud,
As, when night is bare,
  From one lonely cloud
The moon rains out her beams, and Heaven is
  overflowed.   30

What thou art we know not;
  What is most like thee?
From rainbow clouds there flow not
  Drops so bright to see
As from thy presence showers a rain of mel-
  ody.

Like a Poet hidden
  In the light of thought,
Singing hymns unbidden,
  Till the world is wrought
To sympathy with hopes and fears it heeded
  not: 40

Like a high-born maiden
  In a palace-tower,
Soothing her love-laden
  Soul in secret hour
With music sweet as love, which overflows her
  bower:

Like a glow-worm golden
  In a dell of dew,
Scattering unbeholden
  Its aëreal hue
Among the flowers and grass, which screen it
  from the view!   50

Like a rose embowered
  In its own green leaves,
By warm winds deflowered,
  Till the scent it gives
Makes faint with too much sweet those heavy-
  wingèd thieves:

Sound of vernal showers
  On the twinkling grass,
Rain-awakened flowers,

All that ever was
Joyous, and clear, and fresh, thy music doth
  surpass: 60

Teach us, Sprite or Bird,
  What sweet thoughts are thine:
I have never heard
  Praise of love or wine
That panted forth a flood of rapture so divine.

Chorus Hymeneal,
  Or triumphal chant,
Matched with thine would be all
  But an empty vaunt,
A thing wherein we feel there is some hidden
  want.   70

What objects are the fountains
  Of thy happy strain?
What fields, or waves, or mountains?
  What shapes of sky or plain?
What love of thine own kind? what ignorance
  of pain?

With thy clear keen joyance
  Languor cannot be:
Shadow of annoyance
  Never came near thee:
Thou lovest—but ne'er knew love's sad sa-
  tiety.   80

Waking or asleep,
  Thou of death must deem
Things more true and deep
  Than we mortals dream,
Or how could thy notes flow in such a crystal
  stream?

We look before and after,
  And pine for what is not:
Our sincerest laughter
  With some pain is fraught;
Our sweetest songs are those that tell of sad-
  dest thought.   90

Yet if we could scorn
  Hate, and pride, and fear;
If we were things born
  Not to shed a tear,
I know not how thy joy we ever should come
  near.

Better than all measures
　　Of delightful sound,
Better than all treasures
　　That in books are found,
Thy skill to poet were, thou scorner of the
　　ground!   100

Teach me half the gladness
　　That thy brain must know,
Such harmonious madness
　　From my lips would flow
The world should listen then—as I am listen-
　　ing now.
1820

TO —

I

I FEAR thy kisses, gentle maiden,
　　Thou needest not fear mine;
My spirit is too deeply laden
　　Ever to burthen thine.

II

I fear thy mien, thy tones, thy motion,
　　Thou needest not fear mine;
Innocent is the heart's devotion
　　With which I worship thine.
1820

HYMN OF PAN

I

FROM the forests and highlands
　　We come, we come;
From the river-girt islands,
　　Where loud waves are dumb
　　　　Listening to my sweet pipings.
The wind in the reeds and the rushes,
　　The bees on the bells of thyme,
The birds on the myrtle bushes,
　　The cicale above in the lime,
And the lizards below in the grass,   10
　　　　Were as silent as ever old Tmolus was,
　　　　Listening to my sweet pipings.

II

Liquid Peneus was flowing,
　　And all dark Tempe lay
In Pelion's shadow, outgrowing
　　The light of the dying day,
　　　　Speeded by my sweet pipings.
The Sileni, and Sylvans, and Fauns,

And the Nymphs of the woods and the
　　waves,
To the edge of the moist river-lawns,   20
　　And the brink of the dewy caves,
And all that did then attend and follow,
Were silent with love, as you now, Apollo,
　　　　With envy of my sweet pipings.

III

I sang of the dancing stars,
　　I sang of the daedal Earth,
And of Heaven—and the giant wars,
　　And Love, and Death, and Birth,—
And then I changed my pipings,—
Singing how down the vale of Maenalus   30
　　I pursued a maiden and clasped a reed.
Gods and men, we are all deluded thus!
　　It breaks in our bosom and then we bleed:
All wept, as I think both ye now would,
If envy or age had not frozen your blood,
　　　　At the sorrow of my sweet pipings.
1820

THE TWO SPIRITS: AN ALLEGORY

First Spirit

O THOU, who plumed with strong desire
　　Wouldst float above the earth, beware!
A Shadow tracks thy flight of fire—
　　　　Night is coming!
Bright are the regions of the air,
And among the winds and beams
　　It were delight to wander there—
　　　　Night is coming!

Second Spirit

The deathless stars are bright above;
　　If I would cross the shade of night,   10
Within my heart is the lamp of love,
　　　　And that is day!
And the moon will smile with gentle light
On my golden plumes where'er they move;
　　The meteors will linger round my flight,
　　　　And make night day.

First Spirit

But if the whirlwinds of darkness waken
　　Hail, and lightning, and stormy rain;
See, the bounds of the air are shaken—
　　　　Night is coming!   20

The red swift clouds of the hurricane
Yon declining sun have overtaken,
   The clash of the hail sweeps over the
      plain—
        Night is coming!

Second Spirit

I see the light, and I hear the sound;
   I'll sail on the flood of the tempest dark,
With the calm within and the light around
      Which makes night day:
   And thou, when the gloom is deep and
      stark,
Look from thy dull earth, slumber-bound, 30
   My moon-like flight thou then mayst mark
      On high, far away.

Some say there is a precipice
   Where one vast pine is frozen to ruin
O'er piles of snow and chasms of ice
      Mid Alpine mountains;
   And that the languid storm pursuing
That wingèd shape, for ever flies
   Round those hoar branches, aye renewing
      Its aëry fountains.   40

Some say when nights are dry and clear,
   And the death-dews sleep on the morass,
Sweet whispers are heard by the traveller,
      Which make night day:
And a silver shape like his early love doth
      pass
Upborne by her wild and glittering hair,
   And when he awakes on the fragrant grass,
      He finds night day.
1820

THE WORLD'S WANDERERS

I

TELL me, thou Star, whose wings of light
Speed thee in thy fiery flight,
In what cavern of the night
    Will thy pinions close now?

II

Tell me, Moon, thou pale and gray
Pilgrim of Heaven's homeless way,
In what depth of night or day
    Seekest thou repose now?

III

Weary Wind, who wanderest
Like the world's rejected guest,   10
Hast thou still some secret nest
    On the tree or billow?

1820

TIME LONG PAST

I

LIKE the ghost of a dear friend dead
    Is Time long past.
A tone which is now forever fled,
A hope which is now forever past,
A love so sweet it could not last,
    Was time long past.

II

There were sweet dreams in the night
    Of Time long past:
And, was it sadness or delight,
Each day a shadow onward cast   10
Which made us wish it yet might last—
    That Time long past.

III

There is regret, almost remorse,
    For Time long past.
'Tis like a child's belovèd corse
A father watches, till at last
Beauty is like remembrance, cast
    From Time long past.

1820

TO NIGHT

I

SWIFTLY walk o'er the western wave,
    Spirit of Night!
Out of the misty eastern cave,
Where, all the long and lone daylight,
Thou wovest dreams of joy and fear,
Which make thee terrible and dear,—
    Swift be thy flight!

II

Wrap thy form in a mantle gray,
    Star-inwrought!
Blind with thine hair the eyes of Day;   10
Kiss her until she be wearied out,
Then wander o'er city, and sea, and land,
Touching all with thine opiate wand—
    Come, long-sought!

VIII.   QUEEN MAB.   99

Second Part

VIII.

THE present and the past thou hast beheld:
It was a desolate sight. Now, Spirit, learn
The secrets of the future.—Time!
Unfold the brooding pinion of thy gloom,
Render thou up thy half-devoured babes; —
And from the cradles of eternity,
Where millions lie lulled to their portioned sleep
By the deep murmuring stream of passing things,
Tear thou that gloomy shroud.—Spirit, behold
    Thy glorious destiny!
    Joy to the Spirit came.
Through the wide rent in Time's eternal veil,
Hope was seen beaming through the mists of fear:
    Earth was no longer hell;
    Love, freedom, health, had given
Their ripeness to the manhood of its prime,

A Page of *Queen Mab* with Shelley's Corrections.
(See Appendix I.)

III

When I arose and saw the dawn,
          I sighed for thee;
When light rode high, and the dew was gone,
And noon lay heavy on flower and tree,
And the weary Day turned to his rest,
Lingering like an unloved guest,   20
          I sighed for thee.

IV

Thy brother Death came, and cried,
          Wouldst thou me?
Thy sweet child Sleep, the filmy-eyed,
Murmured like a noontide bee,
Shall I nestle near thy side?
Wouldst thou me?—And I replied,
          No, not thee!

V

Death will come when thou art dead,
          Soon, too soon—   30
Sleep will come when thou art fled;
Of neither would I ask the boon
I ask of thee, belovèd Night—
Swift be thine approaching flight,
          Come soon, soon!

1821

TO ——

Music, when soft voices die,
Vibrates in the memory—
Odours, when sweet violets sicken,
Live within the sense they quicken.

Rose leaves, when the rose is dead,
Are heaped for the belovèd's bed;
And so thy thoughts, when thou art gone,
Love itself shall slumber on.

1821

SONG

I

RARELY, rarely, comest thou,
    Spirit of Delight!
Wherefore hast thou left me now
    Many a day and night?
Many a weary night and day
'Tis since thou art fled away.

II

How shall ever one like me
    Win thee back again?

With the joyous and the free
    Thou wilt scoff at pain.   10
Spirit false! thou hast forgot
All but those who need thee not.

III

As a lizard with the shade
    Of a trembling leaf,
Thou with sorrow art dismayed;
    Even the sighs of grief
Reproach thee, that thou art not near,
And reproach thou wilt not hear.

IV

Let me set my mournful ditty
    To a merry measure;   20
Thou wilt never come for pity,
    Thou wilt come for pleasure;
Pity then will cut away
Those cruel wings, and thou wilt stay.

V

I love all that thou lovest,
    Spirit of Delight!
The fresh Earth in new leaves dressed,
    And the starry night;
Autumn evening, and the morn
When the golden mists are born.   30

VI

I love snow, and all the forms
    Of the radiant frost;
I love waves, and winds, and storms,
    Everything almost
Which is Nature's, and may be
Untainted by man's misery.

VII

I love tranquil solitude,
    And such society
As is quiet, wise, and good;
    Between thee and me   40
What difference? but thou dost possess
The things I seek, not love them less.

VIII

I love Love—though he has wings,
    And like light can flee,
But above all other things,
    Spirit, I love thee—
Thou art love and life! Oh, come,
Make once more my heart thy home.

1821

MUTABILITY

I

THE flower that smiles to-day
    To-morrow dies;
All that we wish to stay
    Tempts and then flies.
What is this world's delight?
Lightning that mocks the night,
    Brief even as bright.

II

Virtue, how frail it is!
    Friendship how rare!
Love, how it sells poor bliss   10
    For proud despair!
But we, though soon they fall,
Survive their joy, and all
    Which ours we call.

III

Whilst skies are blue and bright,
    Whilst flowers are gay,
Whilst eyes that change ere night
    Make glad the day;
Whilst yet the calm hours creep,
Dream thou—and from thy sleep   20
    Then wake to weep.

1821

A LAMENT

I

O WORLD! O life! O time!
On whose last steps I climb,
    Trembling at that where I had stood before;
When will return the glory of your prime?
    No more—Oh, never more!

II

Out of the day and night
A joy has taken flight;
    Fresh spring, and summer, and winter hoar,
Move my faint heart with grief, but with de-
    light
    No more—Oh, never more!   10

1821

TO ——

I

ONE word is too often profaned
    For me to profane it,
One feeling too falsely disdained
    For thee to disdain it;

One hope is too like despair
    For prudence to smother,
And pity from thee more dear
    Than that from another.

II

I can give not what men call love,
    But wilt thou accept not   10
The worship the heart lifts above
    And the Heavens reject not,—
The desire of the moth for the star,
    Of the night for the morrow,
The devotion to something afar
    From the sphere of our sorrow?

1821

TO ——

I

WHEN passion's trance is overpast,
If tenderness and truth could last,
Or live, whilst all wild feelings keep
Some mortal slumber, dark and deep,
I should not weep, I should not weep!

II

It were enough to feel, to see,
Thy soft eyes gazing tenderly,
And dream the rest—and burn and be
The secret food of fires unseen,
Couldst thou but be as thou hast been.   10

III

After the slumber of the year
The woodland violets reappear;
All things revive in field or grove,
And sky and sea, but two, which move
And form all others, life and love.

1821

MUSIC

I

I PANT for the music which is divine,
    My heart in its thirst is a dying flower;
Pour forth the sound like enchanted wine,
    Loosen the notes in a silver shower;
Like a herbless plain, for the gentle rain,
I gasp, I faint, till they wake again.

II

Let me drink of the spirit of that sweet sound,
    More, oh more,—I am thirsting yet;

It loosens the serpent which care has bound
  Upon my heart to stifle it;   10
The dissolving strain, through every vein,
  Passes into my heart and brain.

III

As the scent of a violet withered up,
  Which grew by the brink of a silver lake,
When the hot noon has drained its dewy cup,
  And mist there was none its thirst to slake—
And the violet lay dead while the odour flew
On the wings of the wind o'er the waters
    blue—

IV

As one who drinks from a charmèd cup
  Of foaming, and sparkling, and murmuring
    wine,   20
Whom, a mighty Enchantress filling up,
  Invites to love with her kiss divine . . .

1821

FRAGMENT: "WHEN SOFT WINDS AND SUNNY SKIES"

When soft winds and sunny skies
  With the green earth harmonize,
And the young and dewy dawn,
  Bold as an unhunted fawn,
Up to the windless heaven is gone,—
Laugh—for ambushed in the day,—
Clouds and whirlwinds watch their prey.

1821

From HELLAS

Chorus

The world's great age begins anew,
  The golden years return,
The earth doth like a snake renew
  Her winter weeds outworn:
Heaven smiles, and faiths and empires gleam,
Like wrecks of a dissolving dream.

A brighter Hellas rears its mountains
  From waves serener far;
A new Peneus rolls his fountains
  Against the morning star.   10
Where fairer Tempes bloom, there sleep
Young Cyclads on a sunnier deep.

A loftier Argo cleaves the main,
  Fraught with a later prize;
Another Orpheus sings again,
  And loves, and weeps, and dies.

A new Ulysses leaves once more
Calypso for his native shore.

Oh, write no more the tale of Troy,
  If earth Death's scroll must be!   20
Nor mix with Laian rage the joy
  Which dawns upon the free:
Although a subtler Sphinx renew
Riddles of death Thebes never knew.

Another Athens shall arise,
  And to remoter time
Bequeath, like sunset to the skies,
  The splendour of its prime;
And leave, if nought so bright may live,
All earth can take or Heaven can give.   30

Saturn and Love their long repose
  Shall burst, more bright and good
Than all who fell, than One who rose,
  Than many unsubdued:
Not gold, not blood, their altar dowers,
But votive tears and symbol flowers.

Oh, cease! must hate and death return?
  Cease! must men kill and die?
Cease! drain not to its dregs the urn
  Of bitter prophecy.   40
The world is weary of the past,
Oh, might it die or rest at last!

1821

LINES: "WHEN THE LAMP IS SHATTERED"

I

When the lamp is shattered
The light in the dust lies dead—
  When the cloud is scattered
The rainbow's glory is shed.
  When the lute is broken,
Sweet tones are remembered not;
  When the lips have spoken,
Loved accents are soon forgot.

II

  As music and splendour
Survive not the lamp and the lute,   10
  The heart's echoes render
No song when the spirit is mute:—
  No song but sad dirges,
Like the wind through a ruined cell,
  Or the mournful surges
That rings the dead seaman's knell.

III

When hearts have once mingled
Love first leaves the well-built nest;
  The weak one is singled
To endure what it once possessed.   20
  O Love! who bewailest
The frailty of all things here,
  Why choose you the frailest
For your cradle, your home, and your bier?

IV

  Its passions will rock thee
As the storms rock the ravens on high;
  Bright reason will mock thee,
Like the sun from a wintry sky.
  From thy nest every rafter
Will rot, and thine eagle home   30
  Leave thee naked to laughter,
When leaves fall and cold winds come.

1822

TO JANE: THE INVITATION

BEST and brightest, come away!
Fairer far than this fair Day,
Which, like thee to those in sorrow,
Comes to bid a sweet good-morrow
To the rough Year just awake
In its cradle on the brake.
The brightest hour of unborn Spring,
Through the winter wandering,
Found, it seems, the halcyon Morn
To hoar February born.   10
Bending from Heaven, in azure mirth,
It kissed the forehead of the Earth,
And smiled upon the silent sea,
And bade the frozen streams be free,
And waked to music all their fountains,
And breathed upon the frozen mountains,
And like a prophetess of May
Strewed flowers upon the barren way,
Making the wintry world appear
Like one on whom thou smilest, dear.   20

Away, away, from men and towns,
To the wild wood and the downs—
To the silent wilderness
Where the soul need not repress
Its music lest it should not find
An echo in another's mind,
While the touch of Nature's art

Harmonizes heart to heart.
I leave this notice on my door
For each accustomed visitor:—   30
'I am gone into the fields
To take what this sweet hour yields,—
Reflection, you may come to-morrow,
Sit by the fireside with Sorrow.—
You with the unpaid bill, Despair,—
You, tiresome verse-reciter, Care,—
I will pay you in the grave,—
Death will listen to your stave.
Expectation too, be off!   40
To-day is for itself enough;
Hope, in pity mock not Woe
With smiles, nor follow where I go;
Long having lived on thy sweet food,
At length I find one moment's good
After long pain—with all your love,
This you never told me of.'

Radiant Sister of the Day,
Awake! arise! and come away!
To the wild woods and the plains,   50
And the pools where winter rains
Image all their roof of leaves,
Where the pine its garland weaves
Of sapless green and ivy dun
Round stems that never kiss the sun;
Where the lawns and pastures be,
And the sand hills of the sea;—
Where the melting hoar-frost wets
The daisy-star that never sets,
And wind-flowers, and violets,   60
Which yet join not scent to hue,
Crown the pale year weak and new;
When the night is left behind,
In the deep east, dun and blind,
And the blue noon is over us,
And the multitudinous
Billows murmur at our feet,
Where the earth and ocean meet,
And all things seem only one
In the universal sun.   70

1822

WITH A GUITAR, TO JANE

  ARIEL to Miranda:—Take
This slave of Music, for the sake
Of him who is the slave of thee,

And teach it all the harmony
In which thou canst, and only thou,
Make the delighted spirit glow,
Till joy denies itself again,
And, too intense, is turned to pain;
For by permission and command
Of thine own Prince Ferdinand,   10
Poor Ariel sends this silent token
Of more than ever can be spoken;
Your guardian spirit, Ariel, who,
From life to life, must still pursue
Your happiness;—for thus alone
Can Ariel ever find his own.
From Prospero's enchanted cell,
As the mighty verses tell,
To the throne of Naples, he
Lit you o'er the trackless sea,   20
Flitting on, your prow before,
Like a living meteor.
When you die, the silent Moon,
In her interlunar swoon,
Is not sadder in her cell
Than deserted Ariel.
When you live again on earth,
Like an unseen star of birth,
Ariel guides you o'er the sea
Of life from your nativity.   30
Many changes have been run
Since Ferdinand and you begun
Your course of love, and Ariel still
Has tracked your steps, and served your
    will;
Now, in humbler, happier lot,
This is all remembered not;
And now, alas! the poor sprite is
Imprisoned, for some fault of his,
In a body like a grave;—
From you he only dares to crave,   40
For his service and his sorrow,
A smile to-day, a song to-morrow.

The artist who this idol wrought,
To echo all harmonious thought,
Felled a tree, while on the steep
The woods were in their winter sleep,
Rocked in that repose divine
On the wind-swept Apennine;
And dreaming, some of Autumn past,
And some of Spring approaching fast,   50
And some of April buds and showers,
And some of songs in July bowers,

And all of love; and so this tree,—
O that such our death may be!—
Died in sleep, and felt no pain,
To live in happier form again:
From which, beneath Heaven's fairest star,
The artist wrought this loved Guitar,
And taught it justly to reply,
To all who question skilfully,   60
In language gentle as thine own;
Whispering in enamoured tone
Sweet oracles of woods and dells,
And summer winds in sylvan cells;
For it had learned all harmonies
Of the plains and of the skies,
Of the forests and the mountains,
And the many-voicèd fountains;
The clearest echoes of the hills,
The softest notes of falling rills,   70
The melodies of birds and bees,
The murmuring of summer seas,
And pattering rain, and breathing dew,
And airs of evening; and it knew
That seldom-heard mysterious sound,
Which, driven on its diurnal round,
As it floats through boundless day,
Our world enkindles on its way.—
All this it knows, but will not tell
To those who cannot question well   80
The Spirit that inhabits it;
It talks according to the wit
Of its companions; and no more
Is heard than has been felt before,
By those who tempt it to betray
These secrets of an elder day:
But, sweetly as its answers will
Flatter hands of perfect skill,
It keeps its highest, holiest tone
For our belovèd Jane alone.   90
1822

A DIRGE

Rough wind, that moanest loud
    Grief too sad for song;
Wild wind, when sullen cloud
    Knells all the night long;
Sad storm, whose tears are vain,
Bare woods, whose branches strain,
Deep caves and dreary main,—
    Wail, for the world's wrong!

1822

Sadak the Wanderer. a fragment

* * * * *
* * * * * *

He thro' Norway Iceland has gone
To see the Mountains topmost stone
He has climbed, to tear the food
From the Eagle's screaming brood;
By the turbid Jungle tide
For his meal the Wolf has died;
He has braved the Tyger's lair
In his bleeding prey to share
Mark the wounded Panther's yell
Flying from the torn Gazelle.
By the food wild, weary, wan,
Stands a thing that once was man.

I look upon that withered brow.
See the glance that burns below,
See the lank, & scattered hair,
See the limb, smart, withered, bare,
See the feet that leave their mark
On the soil in bloodstains dark,
Who thus o'er the world doth roam
With the desert for his home?

Hath he wandered with the brand
of the robber in his hand.
Hath his soul been steeped in crime
That hath smote him in his prime?
Stainless as the newborn child,
Strays this Wanderer thro the wild.

An Unpublished Fragment by Shelley (See Appendix I.)

[handwritten margin notes at top: "vague auto bio account of a yng. poets unsuccessful attempt to recapture his envisioned ideal mate"]

ALASTOR
[handwritten: "evil genius"]

OR

THE SPIRIT OF SOLITUDE

PREFACE

THE poem entitled Alastor may be considered as allegorical of one of the most interesting situations of the human mind. It represents a youth of uncorrupted feelings and adventurous genius led forth by an imagination inflamed and purified through familiarity with all that is excellent and majestic, to the contemplation of the universe. He drinks deep of the fountains of knowledge, and is still insatiate. The magnificence and beauty of the external world sinks profoundly into the frame of his conceptions, and affords to their modifications a variety not to be exhausted. So long as it is possible for his desires to point towards objects thus infinite and unmeasured, he is joyous, and tranquil, and self-possessed. But the period arrives when these objects cease to suffice. His mind is at length suddenly awakened and thirsts for intercourse with an intelligence similar to itself. He images to himself the Being whom he loves. Conversant with speculations of the sublimest and most perfect natures, the vision in which he embodies his own imaginations unites all of wonderful, or wise, or beautiful, which the poet, the philosopher, or the lover could depicture. The intellectual faculties, the imagination, the functions of sense, have their respective requisitions on the sympathy of corresponding powers in other human beings. The Poet is represented as uniting these requisitions, and attaching them to a single image. He seeks in vain for a prototype of his conception. Blasted by his disappointment, he descends to an untimely grave. 40

The picture is not barren of instruction to actual men. The Poet's self-centred seclusion was avenged by the furies of an irresistible passion pursuing him to speedy ruin. But that 5 Power which strikes the luminaries of the world with sudden darkness and extinction, by awakening them to too exquisite a perception of its influences, dooms to a slow and poisonous decay those meaner spirits that dare 10 to abjure its dominion. Their destiny is more abject and inglorious as their delinquency is more contemptible and pernicious. They who, deluded by no generous error, instigated by no sacred thirst of doubtful knowledge, duped 15 by no illustrious superstition, loving nothing on this earth, and cherishing no hopes beyond, yet keep aloof from sympathies with their kind, rejoicing neither in human joy nor mourning with human grief; these, and such 20 as they, have their apportioned curse. They languish, because none feel with them their common nature. They are morally dead. They are neither friends, nor lovers, nor fathers, nor citizens of the world, nor benefactors of their 25 country. Among those who attempt to exist without human sympathy, the pure and tenderhearted perish through the intensity and passion of their search after its communities, when the vacancy of their spirit suddenly 30 makes itself felt. All else, selfish, blind, and torpid, are those unforeseeing multitudes who constitute, together with their own, the lasting misery and loneliness of the world. Those who love not their fellow-beings live unfruit- 35 ful lives, and prepare for their old age a miserable grave.

"The good die first,
And those whose hearts are dry as summer dust
Burn to the socket!"

December 14, 1815

[handwritten: "Mary — Ruined Cottage"]

EARTH, ocean, air, belovèd brotherhood!
If our great Mother has imbued my soul
With aught of natural piety to feel
Your love, and recompense the boon with
    mine;
If dewy morn, and odorous noon, and even,
With sunset and its gorgeous ministers,
And solemn midnight's tingling silentness;
If autumn's hollow sighs in the sere wood,

And winter robing with pure snow and crowns
Of starry ice the grey grass and bare boughs;
If spring's voluptuous pantings when she
    breathes 11
Her first sweet kisses, have been dear to me;
If no bright bird, insect, or gentle beast
I consciously have injured, but still loved
And cherished these my kindred; then for-
    give

[handwritten left margin, vertical: "3. typical youth 4. dreaming on an ideal young of this fortune frustrated 1. wandering on an ideal young 2. nevery wild the youth pursues"]

This boast, belovèd brethren, and withdraw
No portion of your wonted favour now!

Mother of this unfathomable world!
Favour my solemn song, for I have loved
Thee ever, and thee only; I have watched   20
Thy shadow, and the darkness of thy steps,
And my heart ever gazes on the depth
Of thy deep mysteries. I have made my bed
In charnels and on coffins, where black death
Keeps record of the trophies won from thee,
Hoping to still these obstinate questionings
Of thee and thine, by forcing some lone ghost
Thy messenger, to render up the tale
Of what we are. In lone and silent hours,
When night makes a weird sound of its own
        stillness,   30
Like an inspired and desperate alchymist
Staking his very life on some dark hope,
Have I mixed awful talk and asking looks
With my most innocent love, until strange
        tears
Uniting with those breathless kisses, made
Such magic as compels the charmèd night
To render up thy charge: . . . and, though
        ne'er yet
Thou hast unveiled thy inmost sanctuary,
Enough from incommunicable dream,
And twilight phantasms, and deep noon-day
        thought,   40
Has shone within me, that serenely now
And moveless, as a long-forgotten lyre
Suspended in the solitary dome
Of some mysterious and deserted fane,
I wait thy breath, Great Parent, that my
        strain
May modulate with murmurs of the air,
And motions of the forests and the sea,
And voice of living beings, and woven hymns
Of night and day, and the deep heart of man.

There was a Poet whose untimely tomb   50
No human hands with pious reverence reared,
But the charmed eddies of autumnal winds
Built o'er his mouldering bones a pyramid
Of mouldering leaves in the waste wilder-
        ness:—
A lovely youth,—no mourning maiden decked
With weeping flowers, or votive cypress
        wreath,
The lone couch of his everlasting sleep:—

Gentle, and brave, and generous,—no lorn
        bard *Lycidas*
Breathed o'er his dark fate one melodious sigh:
He lived, he died, he sung, in solitude.   60
Strangers have wept to hear his passionate
        notes,
And virgins, as unknown he passed, have
        pined
And wasted for fond love of his wild eyes.
The fire of those soft orbs has ceased to burn,
And Silence, too enamoured of that voice,
Locks its mute music in her rugged cell.

By solemn vision, and bright silver dream,
His infancy was nurtured. Every sight
And sound from the vast earth and ambient air,
Sent to his heart its choicest impulses.   70
The fountains of divine philosophy
Fled not his thirsting lips, and all of great,
Or good, or lovely, which the sacred past
In truth or fable consecrates, he felt
And knew. When early youth had passed, he
        left
His cold fireside and alienated home *autobiog*
To seek strange truths in undiscovered lands.
Many a wide waste and tangled wilderness
Has lured his fearless steps; and he has bought
With his sweet voice and eyes, from savage
        men,   80
His rest and food. Nature's most secret steps
He like her shadow has pursued, where'er
The red volcano overcanopies
Its fields of snow and pinnacles of ice
With burning smoke, or where bitumen lakes
On black bare pointed islets ever beat
With sluggish surge, or where the secret caves
Rugged and dark, winding among the springs
Of fire and poison, inaccessible
To avarice or pride, their starry domes   90
Of diamond and of gold expand above
Numberless and immeasurable halls,
Frequent with crystal column, and clear shrines
Of pearl, and thrones radiant with chrysolite.
Nor had that scene of ampler majesty
Than gems or gold, the varying roof of heaven
And the green earth lost in his heart its claims
To love and wonder; he would linger long
In lonesome vales, making the wild his home,
Until the doves and squirrels would partake 100
From his innocuous hand his bloodless food,
Lured by the gentle meaning of his looks,

And the wild antelope, that starts whene'er
The dry leaf rustles in the brake, suspend
Her timid steps to gaze upon a form
More graceful than her own.   His wandering step
Obedient to high thoughts, has visited
The awful ruins of the days of old:
Athens, and Tyre, and Balbec, and the waste
Where stood Jerusalem, the fallen towers 110
Of Babylon, the eternal pyramids,
Memphis and Thebes, and whatsoe'er of
    strange
Sculptured on alabaster obelisk
Or jasper tomb, or mutilated sphynx,
Dark Æthiopia in her desert hills
Conceals. Among the ruined temples there,
Stupendous columns, and wild images
Of more than man, where marble daemons
    watch
The Zodiac's brazen mystery, and dead men
Hang their mute thoughts on the mute walls
    around,   120
He lingered, poring on memorials
Of the world's youth, through the long burn-
    ing day
Gazed on those speechless shapes, nor, when
    the moon
Filled the mysterious halls with floating shades
Suspended he that task, but ever gazed
And gazed, till meaning on his vacant mind
Flashed like strong inspiration, and he saw
The thrilling secrets of the birth of time.

    Meanwhile an Arab maiden brought his food,
Her daily portion, from her father's tent,   130
And spread her matting for his couch, and
    stole
From duties and repose to tend his steps:—
Enamoured, yet not daring for deep awe
To speak her love:—and watched his nightly
    sleep,
Sleepless herself, to gaze upon his lips
Parted in slumber, whence the regular breath
Of innocent dreams arose: then, when red
    morn
Made paler the pale moon, to her cold home
Wildered, and wan, and panting, she returned.

    The Poet wandering on, through Arabie 140
And Persia, and the wild Carmanian waste,
And o'er the aërial mountains which pour
    down

Indus and Oxus from their icy caves,
In joy and exultation held his way;
Till in the vale of Cashmire, far within
Its loneliest dell, where odorous plants en-
    twine
Beneath the hollow rocks a natural bower,
Beside a sparkling rivulet he stretched
His languid limbs. A vision on his sleep
There came, a dream of hopes that never yet
Had flushed his cheek. He dreamed a veilèd
    maid   151
Sate near him, talking in low solemn tones.
Her voice was like the voice of his own soul,
Heard in the calm of thought; its music long,
Like woven sounds of streams and breezes,
    held
His inmost sense suspended in its web
Of many-coloured woof and shifting hues.
Knowledge and truth and virtue were her
    theme,
And lofty hopes of divine liberty,
Thoughts the most dear to him, and poesy, 160
Herself a poet. Soon the solemn mood
Of her pure mind kindled through all her
    frame
A permeating fire: wild numbers then
She raised, with voice stifled in tremulous sobs
Subdued by its own pathos: her fair hands
Were bare alone, sweeping from some strange
    harp
Strange symphony, and in their branching
    veins
The eloquent blood told an ineffable tale.
The beating of her heart was heard to fill
The pauses of her music, and her breath   170
Tumultuously accorded with those fits
Of intermitted song. Sudden she rose,
As if her heart impatiently endured
Its bursting burthen: at the sound he turned,
And saw by the warm light of their own life
Her glowing limbs beneath the sinuous veil
Of woven wind, her outspread arms now bare,
Her dark locks floating in the breath of night,
Her beamy bending eyes, her parted lips
Outstretched, and pale, and quivering eagerly.
His strong heart sunk and sickened with ex-
    cess   181
Of love. He reared his shuddering limbs and
    quelled
His gasping breath, and spread his arms to
    meet

Her panting bosom: ... she drew back a while,
Then, yielding to the irresistible joy,
With frantic gesture and short breathless cry
Folded his frame in her dissolving arms.
Now blackness veiled his dizzy eyes, and night
Involved and swallowed up the vision; sleep,
Like a dark flood suspended in its course, 190
Rolled back its impulse on his vacant brain.

Roused by the shock he started from his trance—
The cold white light of morning, the blue moon
Low in the west, the clear and garish hills,
The distinct valley and the vacant woods,
Spread round him where he stood. Whither have fled
The hues of heaven that canopied his bower
Of yesternight? The sounds that soothed his sleep,
The mystery and the majesty of Earth,
The joy, the exultation? His wan eyes   200
Gaze on the empty scene as vacantly
As ocean's moon looks on the moon in heaven.
The spirit of sweet human love has sent
A vision to the sleep of him who spurned
Her choicest gifts. He eagerly pursues
Beyond the realms of dream that fleeting shade;
He overleaps the bounds. Alas! Alas!
Were limbs, and breath, and being intertwined
Thus treacherously? Lost, lost, for ever lost,
In the wide pathless desert of dim sleep,   210
That beautiful shape! Does the dark gate of death
Conduct to thy mysterious paradise,
O Sleep? Does the bright arch of rainbow clouds,
And pendent mountains seen in the calm lake,
Lead only to a black and watery depth,
While death's blue vault, with loathliest vapours hung,
Where every shade which the foul grave exhales
Hides its dead eye from the detested day,
Conducts, O Sleep, to thy delightful realms?
This doubt with sudden tide flowed on his heart,   220
The insatiate hope which it awakened, stung

His brain even like despair.
                    While daylight held
The sky, the Poet kept mute conference
With his still soul. At night the passion came,
Like the fierce fiend of a distempered dream,
And shook him from his rest, and led him forth
Into the darkness.—As an eagle grasped
In folds of the green serpent, feels her breast
Burn with the poison, and precipitates
Through night and day, tempest, and calm, and cloud,   230
Frantic with dizzying anguish, her blind flight
O'er the wide aëry wilderness: thus driven
By the bright shadow of that lovely dream,
Beneath the cold glare of the desolate night,
Through tangled swamps and deep precipitous dells,
Startling with careless step the moonlight snake,
He fled. Red morning dawned upon his flight,
Shedding the mockery of its vital hues
Upon his cheek of death. He wandered on
Till vast Aornos seen from Petra's steep   240
Hung o'er the low horizon like a cloud;
Through Balk, and where the desolated tombs
Of Parthian kings scatter to every wind
Their wasting dust, wildly he wandered on,
Day after day a weary waste of hours,
Bearing within his life the brooding care
That ever fed on its decaying flame.
And now his limbs were lean; his scattered hair
Sered by the autumn of strange suffering
Sung dirges in the wind; his listless hand   250
Hung like dead bone within its withered skin;
Life, and the lustre that consumed it, shone
As in a furnace burning secretly
From his dark eyes alone. The cottagers,
Who ministered with human charity
His human wants, beheld with wondering awe
Their fleeting visitant. The mountaineer,
Encountering on some dizzy precipice
That spectral form, deemed that the Spirit of wind
With lightning eyes, and eager breath, and feet   260
Disturbing not the drifted snow, had paused
In its career: the infant would conceal
His troubled visage in his mother's robe
In terror at the glare of those wild eyes,

To remember their strange light in many a
   dream
Of after-times; but youthful maidens, taught
By nature, would interpret half the woe
That wasted him, would call him with false
   names
Brother, and friend, would press his pallid
   hand
At parting, and watch, dim through tears, the
   path   270
Of his departure from their father's door.

   At length upon the lone Chorasmian shore
He paused, a wide and melancholy waste
Of putrid marshes. A strong impulse urged
His steps to the sea-shore. A swan was there,
Beside a sluggish stream among the reeds.
It rose as he approached, but with strong
   wings
Scaling the upward sky, bent its bright course
High over the immeasurable main.
His eyes pursued its flight.—'Thou hast a
   home,   280
Beautiful bird; thou voyagest to thine home,
Where thy sweet mate will twine her downy
   neck
With thine, and welcome thy return with
   eyes
Bright in the lustre of their own fond joy.
And what am I that I should linger here,
With voice far sweeter than thy dying notes,
Spirit more vast than thine, frame more at-
   tuned
To beauty, wasting these surpassing powers
In the deaf air, to the blind earth, and heaven
That echoes not my thoughts?' A gloomy
   smile   290
Of desperate hope wrinkled his quivering lips.
For sleep, he knew, kept most relentlessly
Its precious charge, and silent death exposed,
Faithless perhaps as sleep, a shadowy lure,
With doubtful smile mocking its own strange
   charms.

   Startled by his own thoughts he looked
   around.
There was no fair fiend near him, not a sight
Or sound of awe but in his own deep mind.
A little shallop floating near the shore
Caught the impatient wandering of his gaze.
It had been long abandoned, for its sides   301

Gaped wide with many a rift, and its frail
   joints
Swayed with the undulations of the tide.
A restless impulse urged him to embark
And meet lone Death on the drear ocean's
   waste;
For well he knew that mighty Shadow loves
The slimy caverns of the populous deep.

   The day was fair and sunny, sea and sky
Drank its inspiring radiance, and the wind
Swept strongly from the shore, blackening the
   waves.   310
Following his eager soul, the wanderer
Leaped in the boat, he spread his cloak aloft
On the bare mast, and took his lonely seat,
And felt the boat speed o'er the tranquil sea
Like a torn cloud before the hurricane.

   As one that in a silver vision floats
Obedient to the sweep of odorous winds
Upon resplendent clouds, so rapidly
Along the dark and ruffled waters fled   319
The straining boat.—A whirlwind swept it on,
With fierce gusts and precipitating force,
Through the white ridges of the chafèd sea.
The waves arose. Higher and higher still
Their fierce necks writhed beneath the tem-
   pest's scourge
Like serpents struggling in a vulture's grasp.
Calm and rejoicing in the fearful war
Of wave ruining on wave, and blast on blast
Descending, and black flood on whirlpool
   driven
With dark obliterating course, he sate:
As if their genii were the ministers   330
Appointed to conduct him to the light
Of those belovèd eyes the Poet sate
Holding the steady helm. Evening came on,
The beams of sunset hung their rainbow hues
High 'mid the shifting domes of sheeted spray
That canopied his path o'er the waste deep;
Twilight, ascending slowly from the east,
Entwined in duskier wreaths her braided locks
O'er the fair front and radiant eyes of day;
Night followed, clad with stars. On every
   side   340
More horribly the multitudinous streams
Of ocean's mountainous waste to mutual war
Rushed in dark tumult thundering, as to mock
The calm and spangled sky. The little boat

Still fled before the storm; still fled, like foam
Down the steep cataract of a wintry river;
Now pausing on the edge of the riven wave;
Now leaving far behind the bursting mass
That fell, convulsing ocean: safely fled—
As if that frail and wasted human form,   350
Had been an elemental god.
                    At midnight
The moon arose: and lo! the ethereal cliffs
Of Caucasus, whose icy summits shone
Among the stars like sunlight, and around
Whose caverned base the whirlpools and the
    waves
Bursting and eddying irresistibly
Rage and resound for ever.—Who shall
    save?—
The boat fled on,—the boiling torrent
    drove,—
The crags closed round with black and jagged
    arms,
                      359
The shattered mountain overhung the sea,
And faster still, beyond all human speed,
Suspended on the sweep of the smooth wave,
The little boat was driven. A cavern there
Yawned, and amid its slant and winding depths
Ingulfed the rushing sea. The boat fled on
With unrelaxing speed.—'Vision and Love!'
The Poet cried aloud, 'I have beheld
The path of thy departure. Sleep and death
Shall not divide us long!'

                  The boat pursued
The windings of the cavern. Daylight shone
At length upon that gloomy river's flow;   371
Now, where the fiercest war among the waves
Is calm, on the unfathomable stream
The boat moved slowly. Where the mountain,
    riven,
Exposed those black depths to the azure sky,
Ere yet the flood's enormous volume fèll
Even to the base of Caucasus, with sound
That shook the everlasting rocks, the mass
Filled with one whirlpool all that ample
    chasm;
Stair above stair the eddying waters rose,   380
Circling immeasurably fast, and laved
With alternating dash the gnarled roots
Of mighty trees, that stretched their giant
    arms
In darkness over it. I' the midst was left,
Reflecting, yet distorting every cloud,

A pool of treacherous and tremendous calm.
Seized by the sway of the ascending stream,
With dizzy swiftness, round, and round, and
    round,
Ridge after ridge the straining boat arose,
Till on the verge of the extremest curve,   390
Where, through an opening of the rocky bank,
The waters overflow, and a smooth spot
Of glassy quiet mid those battling tides
Is left, the boat paused shuddering.—Shall it
    sink
Down the abyss? Shall the reverting stress
Of that resistless gulf embosom it?
Now shall it fall?—A wandering stream of
    wind,
Breathed from the west, has caught the ex-
    panded sail,
And, lo! with gentle motion, between banks
Of mossy slope, and on a placid stream,   400
Beneath a woven grove it sails, and, hark!
The ghastly torrent mingles its far roar,
With the breeze murmuring in the musical
    woods.
Where the embowering trees recede, and leave
A little space of green expanse, the cove
Is closed by meeting banks, whose yellow
    flowers
For ever gaze on their own drooping eyes,
Reflected in the crystal calm. The wave
Of the boat's motion marred their pensive task,
Which nought but vagrant bird, or wanton
    wind,   410
Or falling spear-grass, or their own decay
Had e'er disturbed before. The Poet longed
To deck with their bright hues his withered
    hair,
But on his heart its solitude returned,
And he forbore. Not the strong impulse hid
In those flushed cheeks, bent eyes, and
    shadowy frame
Had yet performed its ministry: it hung
Upon his life, as lightning in a cloud
Gleams, hovering ere it vanish, ere the floods
Of night close over it.
                  The noonday sun   420
Now shone upon the forest, one vast mass
Of mingling shade, whose brown magnificence
A narrow vale embosoms. There, huge caves,
Scooped in the dark base of their aëry rocks
Mocking its moans, respond and roar for ever.

The meeting boughs and implicated leaves
Wove twilight o'er the Poet's path, as led
By love, or dream, or god, or mightier Death,
He sought in Nature's dearest haunt, some bank,
Her cradle, and his sepulchre. More dark 430
And dark the shades accumulate. The oak,
Expanding its immense and knotty arms,
Embraces the light beech. The pyramids
Of the tall cedar overarching, frame
Most solemn domes within, and far below,
Like clouds suspended in an emerald sky,
The ash and the acacia floating hang
Tremulous and pale. Like restless serpents, clothed
In rainbow and in fire, the parasites,
Starred with ten thousand blossoms, flow around 440
The grey trunks, and, as gamesome infants' eyes,
With gentle meanings, and most innocent wiles,
Fold their beams round the hearts of those that love,
These twine their tendrils with the wedded boughs
Uniting their close union; the woven leaves
Make net-work of the dark blue light of day,
And the night's noontide clearness, mutable
As shapes in the weird clouds. Soft mossy lawns
Beneath these canopies extend their swells,
Fragrant with perfumed herbs, and eyed with blooms 450
Minute yet beautiful. One darkest glen
Sends from its woods of musk-rose, twined with jasmine,
A soul-dissolving odour, to invite
To some more lovely mystery. Through the dell,
Silence and Twilight here, twin-sisters, keep
Their noonday watch, and sail among the shades,
Like vaporous shapes half seen; beyond, a well,
Dark, gleaming, and of most translucent wave,
Images all the woven boughs above, 459
And each depending leaf, and every speck
Of azure sky, darting between their chasms;
Nor aught else in the liquid mirror laves
Its portraiture, but some inconstant star
Between one foliaged lattice twinkling fair,

Or, painted bird, sleeping beneath the moon,
Or gorgeous insect floating motionless,
Unconscious of the day, ere yet his wings
Have spread their glories to the gaze of noon.

Hither the Poet came. His eyes beheld
Their own wan light through the reflected lines 470
Of his thin hair, distinct in the dark depth
Of that still fountain; as the human heart,
Gazing in dreams over the gloomy grave,
Sees its own treacherous likeness there. He heard
The motion of the leaves, the grass that sprung
Startled and glanced and trembled even to feel
An unaccustomed presence, and the sound
Of the sweet brook that from the secret springs
Of that dark fountain rose. A Spirit seemed
To stand beside him—clothed in no bright robes 480
Of shadowy silver or enshrining light,
Borrowed from aught the visible world affords
Of grace, or majesty, or mystery;—
But, undulating woods, and silent well,
And leaping rivulet, and evening gloom
Now deepening the dark shades, for speech assuming,
Held commune with him, as if he and it
Were all that was,—only . . . when his regard
Was raised by intense pensiveness, . . . two eyes,
Two starry eyes, hung in the gloom of thought, 490
And seemed with their serene and azure smiles
To beckon him.

              Obedient to the light
That shone within his soul, he went, pursuing
The windings of the dell.—The rivulet
Wanton and wild, through many a green ravine
Beneath the forest flowed. Sometimes it fell
Among the moss with hollow harmony
Dark and profound. Now on the polished stones
It danced; like childhood laughing as it went:
Then, through the plain in tranquil wanderings crept, 500
Reflecting every herb and drooping bud
That overhung its quietness.—'O stream!
Whose source is inaccessibly profound,

Whither do thy mysterious waters tend?
Thou imagest my life. Thy darksome stillness,
Thy dazzling waves, thy loud and hollow
    gulfs,
Thy searchless fountain, and invisible course
Have each their type in me; and the wide sky,
And measureless ocean may declare as soon
What oozy cavern or what wandering cloud
Contains thy waters, as the universe   511
Tell where these living thoughts reside, when
    stretched
Upon thy flowers my bloodless limbs shall
    waste
I' the passing wind!'

                    Beside the grassy shore
Of the small stream he went; he did impress
On the green moss his tremulous step, that
    caught
Strong shuddering from his burning limbs. As
    one
Roused by some joyous madness from the
    couch
Of fever, he did move; yet, not like him,
Forgetful of the grave, where, when the
    flame   520
Of his frail exultation shall be spent,
He must descend. With rapid steps he went
Beneath the shade of trees, beside the flow
Of the wild babbling rivulet; and now
The forest's solemn canopies were changed
For the uniform and lightsome evening sky.
Grey rocks did peep from the spare moss, and
    stemmed
The struggling brook: tall spires of windle-
    strae
Threw their thin shadows down the rugged
    slope,
And nought but gnarled roots of ancient
    pines   530
Branchless and blasted, clenched with grasp-
    ing roots
The unwilling soil. A gradual change was here,
Yet ghastly. For, as fast years flow away,
The smooth brow gathers, and the hair grows
    thin
And white, and where irradiate dewy eyes
Had shone, gleam stony orbs:—so from his
    steps
Bright flowers departed, and the beautiful
    shade

Of the green groves, with all their odorous
    winds
And musical motions. Calm, he still pursued
The stream, that with a larger volume now
Rolled through the labyrinthine dell; and
    there   541
Fretted a path through its descending curves
With its wintry speed. On every side now rose
Rocks, which, in unimaginable forms,
Lifted their black and barren pinnacles
In the light of evening, and, its precipice
Obscuring the ravine, disclosed above,
Mid toppling stones, black gulfs and yawning
    caves,
Whose windings gave ten thousand various
    tongues
To the loud stream. Lo! where the pass ex-
    pands   550
Its stony jaws, the abrupt mountain breaks,
And seems, with its accumulated crags,
To overhang the world: for wide expand
Beneath the wan stars and descending moon
Islanded seas, blue mountains, mighty streams,
Dim tracts and vast, robed in the lustrous
    gloom
Of leaden-coloured even, and fiery hills
Mingling their flames with twilight, on the
    verge
Of the remote horizon. The near scene,
In naked and severe simplicity,   560
Made contrast with the universe. A pine,
Rock-rooted, stretched athwart the vacancy
Its swinging boughs, to each inconstant blast
Yielding one only response, at each pause
In most familiar cadence, with the howl
The thunder and the hiss of homeless streams
Mingling its solemn song, whilst the broad
    river,
Foaming and hurrying o'er its rugged path,
Fell into that immeasurable void   569
Scattering its waters to the passing winds.

    Yet the grey precipice and solemn pine
And torrent, were not all;—one silent nook
Was there. Even on the edge of that vast
    mountain,
Upheld by knotty roots and fallen rocks,
It overlooked in its serenity
The dark earth, and the bending vault of
    stars.
It was a tranquil spot, that seemed to smile

Even in the lap of horror. Ivy clasped
The fissured stones with its entwining arms,
And did embower with leaves for ever
    green,   580
And berries dark, the smooth and even space
Of its inviolated floor, and here
The children of the autumnal whirlwind bore,
In wanton sport, those bright leaves, whose
    decay,
Red, yellow, or ethereally pale,
Rivals the pride of summer. 'Tis the haunt
Of every gentle wind, whose breath can teach
The wilds to love tranquillity. One step,
One human step alone, has ever broken
The stillness of its solitude:—one voice   590
Alone inspired its echoes;—even that voice
Which hither came, floating among the winds,
And led the loveliest among human forms
To make their wild haunts the depository
Of all the grace and beauty that endued
Its motions, render up its majesty,
Scatter its music on the unfeeling storm,
And to the damp leaves and blue cavern mould,
Nurses of rainbow flowers and branching moss,
Commit the colours of that varying cheek, 600
That snowy breast, those dark and drooping
    eyes.

   The dim and hornèd moon hung low, and
    poured
A sea of lustre on the horizon's verge
That overflowed its mountains. Yellow mist
Filled the unbounded atmosphere, and drank
Wan moonlight even to fulness: not a star
Shone, not a sound was heard; the very winds,
Danger's grim playmates, on that precipice
Slept, clasped in his embrace.—O, storm of
    death!
Whose sightless speed divides this sullen
    night: 610
And thou, colossal Skeleton, that, still
Guiding its irresistible career
In thy devastating omnipotence,
Art king of this frail world, from the red field
Of slaughter, from the reeking hospital,
The patriot's sacred couch, the snowy bed
Of innocence, the scaffold and the throne,
A mighty voice invokes thee. Ruin calls
His brother Death. A rare and regal prey
He hath prepared, prowling around the
    world;   620

Glutted with which thou mayst repose, and
    men
Go to their graves like flowers or creeping
    worms,
Nor ever more offer at thy dark shrine
The unheeded tribute of a broken heart.

   When on the threshold of the green recess
The wanderer's footsteps fell, he knew that
    death
Was on him. Yet a little, ere it fled,
Did he resign his high and holy soul
To images of the majestic past,
That paused within his passive being now, 630
Like winds that bear sweet music, when they
    breathe
Through some dim latticed chamber. He did
    place
His pale lean hand upon the rugged trunk
Of the old pine. Upon an ivied stone
Reclined his languid head, his limbs did rest,
Diffused and motionless, on the smooth
    brink
Of that obscurest chasm;—and thus he lay,
Surrendering to their final impulses
The hovering powers of life. Hope and de-
    spair,   639
The torturers, slept; no mortal pain or fear
Marred his repose, the influxes of sense,
And his own being unalloyed by pain,
Yet feebler and more feeble, calmly fed
The stream of thought, till he lay breathing
    there
At peace, and faintly smiling:—his last sight
Was the great moon, which o'er the western
    line
Of the wide world her mighty horn suspended,
With whose dun beams inwoven darkness
    seemed
To mingle. Now upon the jagged hills
It rests, and still as the divided frame   650
Of the vast meteor sunk, the Poet's blood,
That ever beat in mystic sympathy
With nature's ebb and flow, grew feebler still:
And when two lessening points of light alone
Gleamed through the darkness, the alternate
    gasp
Of his faint respiration scarce did stir
The stagnate night:—till the minutest ray
Was quenched, the pulse yet lingered in his
    heart.

It paused—it fluttered. But when heaven remained
Utterly black, the murky shades involved 660
An image, silent, cold, and motionless,
As their own voiceless earth and vacant air.
Even as a vapour fed with golden beams
That ministered on sunlight, ere the west
Eclipses it, was now that wondrous frame—
No sense, no motion, no divinity—
A fragile lute, on whose harmonious strings
The breath of heaven did wander—a bright
stream
Once fed with many-voicèd waves—a dream
Of youth, which night and time have quenched
for ever, 670
Still, dark, and dry, and unremembered now.

O, for Medea's wondrous alchemy,
Which wheresoe'er it fell made the earth
gleam
With bright flowers, and the wintry boughs
exhale
From vernal blooms fresh fragrance! O, that
God,
Profuse of poisons, would concede the chalice
Which but one living man has drained, who
now,
Vessel of deathless wrath, a slave that feels
No proud exemption in the blighting curse
He bears, over the world wanders for ever, 680
Lone as incarnate death! O, that the dream
Of dark magician in his visioned cave,
Raking the cinders of a crucible
For life and power, even when his feeble hand
Shakes in its last decay, were the true law
Of this so lovely world! But thou art fled
Like some frail exhalation; which the dawn
Robes in its golden beams,—ah! thou hast
fled!
The brave, the gentle, and the beautiful,
The child of grace and genius. Heartless
things 690
Are done and said i' the world, and many
worms
And beasts and men live on, and mighty Earth
From sea and mountain, city and wilderness,
In vesper low or joyous orison,
Lifts still its solemn voice:—but thou art fled—
Thou canst no longer know or love the shapes
Of this phantasmal scene, who have to thee
Been purest ministers, who are, alas!

Now thou art not. Upon those pallid lips
So sweet even in their silence, on those eyes
That image sleep in death, upon that form 701
Yet safe from the worm's outrage, let no tear
Be shed—not even in thought. Nor, when
those hues
Are gone, and those divinest lineaments,
Worn by the senseless wind, shall live alone
In the frail pauses of this simple strain,
Let not high verse, mourning the memory
Of that which is no more, or painting's woe
Or sculpture, speak in feeble imagery 709
Their own cold powers. Art and eloquence,
And all the shows o' the world are frail and vain
To weep a loss that turns their lights to shade.
It is a woe too 'deep for tears,' when all
Is reft at once, when some surpassing Spirit,
Whose light adorned the world around it,
leaves
Those who remain behind, not sobs or groans,
The passionate tumult of a clinging hope;
But pale despair and cold tranquillity,
Nature's vast frame, the web of human things,
Birth and the grave, that are not as they
were. 720

1815 Pub. 1816

PROMETHEUS UNBOUND

A LYRICAL DRAMA IN FOUR ACTS

AUDISNE HAEC AMPHIARAE, SUB TERRAM
ABDITE?

DRAMATIS PERSONÆ

PROMETHEUS	MERCURY
DEMOGORGON	HERCULES
JUPITER	ASIA
THE EARTH	PANTHEA } Oceanides
OCEAN	IONE
APOLLO	

THE PHANTASM OF JUPITER
THE SPIRIT OF THE EARTH
THE SPIRIT OF THE MOON
SPIRITS OF THE HOURS
SPIRITS. ECHOES. FAUNS. FURIES

ACT I

SCENE.—*A Ravine of Icy Rocks in the Indian
Caucasus.* PROMETHEUS *is discovered bound
to the Precipice.* PANTHEA *and* IONE *are
seated at his feet. Time, night. During
the Scene, morning slowly breaks.*

Prometheus. Monarch of Gods and Dæmons, and all Spirits
But One, who throng those bright and rolling worlds
Which Thou and I alone of living things
Behold with sleepless eyes! regard this Earth
Made multitudinous with thy slaves, whom thou
Requitest for knee-worship, prayer, and praise,
And toil, and hecatombs of broken hearts,
With fear and self-contempt and barren hope.
Whilst me, who am thy foe, eyeless in hate,
Hast thou made reign and triumph, to thy scorn,   10
O'er mine own misery and thy vain revenge.
Three thousand years of sleep-unsheltered hours,
And moments aye divided by keen pangs
Till they seemed years, torture and solitude,
Scorn and despair,—these are mine empire:—
More glorious far than that which thou surveyest
From thine unenvied throne, O Mighty God!
Almighty, had I deigned to share the shame
Of thine ill tyranny, and hung not here   19
Nailed to this wall of eagle-baffling mountain,
Black, wintry, dead, unmeasured; without herb,
Insect, or beast, or shape or sound of life.
Ah me! alas, pain, pain ever, for ever!

No change, no pause, no hope! Yet I endure.
I ask the Earth, have not the mountains felt?
I ask yon Heaven, the all-beholding Sun,
Hast it not seen? The Sea, in storm or calm,
Heaven's ever-changing Shadow, spread below,
Have its deaf waves not heard my agony?
Ah me! alas, pain, pain ever, for ever!   30

The crawling glaciers pierce me with the spears
Of their moon-freezing crystals, the bright chains
Eat with their burning cold into my bones.
Heaven's wingèd hound, polluting from thy lips
His beak in poison not his own, tears up
My heart; and shapeless sights come wandering by,

The ghastly people of the realm of dream,
Mocking me: and the Earthquake-fiends are charged
To wrench the rivets from my quivering wounds   39
When the rocks split and close again behind:
While from their loud abysses howling throng
The genii of the storm, urging the rage
Of whirlwind, and afflict me with keen hail.
And yet to me welcome is day and night,
Whether one breaks the hoar frost of the morn,
Or starry, dim, and slow, the other climbs
The leaden-coloured east; for then they lead
The wingless, crawling hours, one among whom
—As some dark Priest hales the reluctant victim—   49
Shall drag thee, cruel King, to kiss the blood
From these pale feet, which then might trample thee
If they disdained not such a prostrate slave.
Disdain! Ah no! I pity thee. What ruin
Will hunt thee undefended through wide Heaven!
How will thy soul, cloven to its depth with terror,
Gape like a hell within! I speak in grief,
Not exultation, for I hate no more,
As then ere misery made me wise. The curse
Once breathed on thee I would recall. Ye Mountains,   59
Whose many-voicèd Echoes, through the mist
Of cataracts, flung the thunder of that spell!
Ye icy Springs, stagnant with wrinkling frost,
Which vibrated to hear me, and then crept
Shuddering through India! Thou serenest Air,
Through which the Sun walks burning without beams!
And ye swift Whirlwinds, who on poisèd wings
Hung mute and moveless o'er yon hushed abyss,
As thunder, louder than your own, made rock
The orbèd world! If then my words had power,
Though I am changed so that aught evil wish
Is dead within; although no memory be   71
Of what is hate, let them not lose it now!
What was that curse? for ye all heard me speak.

affect yourself on

First Voice (*from the Mountains*)

Thrice three hundred thousand years
　O'er the Earthquake's couch we stood:
Oft, as men convulsed with fears,
　We trembled in our multitude.

Second Voice (*from the Springs*)

Thunderbolts had parched our water,
　We had been stained with bitter blood,
And had run mute, 'mid shrieks of slaughter,
　Thro' a city and a solitude.　　　　　81

Third Voice (*from the Air*)

I had clothed, since Earth uprose,
　Its wastes in colours not their own,
And oft had my serene repose
　Been cloven by many a rending groan.

Fourth Voice (*from the Whirlwinds*)

We had soared beneath these mountains
　Unresting ages; nor had thunder,
Nor yon volcano's flaming fountains,
　Nor any power above or under
　Ever made us mute with wonder.　　　90

First Voice

But never bowed our snowy crest
As at the voice of thine unrest.

Second Voice

Never such a sound before
To the Indian waves we bore.
A pilot asleep on the howling sea
Leaped up from the deck in agony,
And heard, and cried, 'Ah, woe is me!'
And died as mad as the wild waves be.

Third Voice

By such dread words from Earth to Heaven
My still realm was never riven:　　　100
When its wound was closed, there stood
Darkness o'er the day like blood.

Fourth Voice

And we shrank back: for dreams of ruin
To frozen caves our flight pursuing
Made us keep silence—thus—and thus—
Though silence is as hell to us.

The Earth. The tongueless Caverns of the
　craggy hills
Cried, 'Misery!' then; the hollow Heaven re-
　plied,
'Misery!' And the Ocean's purple waves,
Climbing the land, howled to the lashing
　winds,　　　　　　　　　　　　110
And the pale nations heard it, 'Misery!'
　Prometheus. I heard a sound of voices: not
　　the voice
Which I gave forth. Mother, thy sons and 　*Earth*
　thou
Scorn him, without whose all-enduring will
Beneath the fierce omnipotence of Jove,
Both they and thou had vanished, like thin
　mist
Unrolled on the morning wind. Know ye not
　me,
The Titan? He who made his agony
The barrier to your else all-conquering foe?
Oh, rock-embosomed lawns, and snow-fed
　streams,　　　　　　　　　　　120
Now seen athwart frore vapours, deep below,
Through whose o'ershadowing woods I wan-
　dered once
With Asia, drinking life from her loved eyes;
Why scorns the spirit which informs ye, now
To commune with me? me alone, who checked,
As one who checks a fiend-drawn charioteer,
The falsehood and the force of him who reigns
Supreme, and with the groans of pining slaves
Fills your dim glens and liquid wildernesses:
Why answer ye not, still? Brethren!
　The Earth.　　　　　　　They dare not.
　Prometheus. Who dares? for I would hear
　　that curse again.　　　　　　　131
Ha, what an awful whisper rises up!
'Tis scarce like sound: it tingles through the
　frame
As lightning tingles, hovering ere it strike.
Speak, Spirit! from thine inorganic voice
I only know that thou art moving near
And love. How cursed I him?
　The Earth.　　　How canst thou hear
Who knowest not the language of the dead?
　Prometheus. Thou art a living spirit; speak
　　as they.
　The Earth. I dare not speak like life, lest
　　Heaven's fell King　　　　　　140
Should hear, and link me to some wheel of
　pain

More torturing than the one whereon I roll.
Subtle thou art and good, and though the
  Gods
Hear not this voice, yet thou art more than
  God, *Jupiter*
Being wise and kind: earnestly hearken now.
  Prometheus. Obscurely through my brain,
  like shadows dim,
Sweep awful thoughts, rapid and thick. I feel
Faint, like one mingled in entwining love;
Yet 'tis not pleasure.
  The Earth.   No, thou canst not hear:
Thou art immortal, and this tongue is known
Only to those who die.
  Prometheus.   And what art thou, 151
O, melancholy Voice?
  The Earth.   I am the Earth,
Thy mother; she within whose stony veins,
To the last fibre of the loftiest tree
Whose thin leaves trembled in the frozen air,
Joy ran, as blood within a living frame,
When thou didst from her bosom, like a cloud
Of glory, arise, a spirit of keen joy!   158
And at thy voice her pining sons uplifted
Their prostrate brows from the polluting dust,
And our almighty Tyrant with fierce dread
Grew pale, until his thunder chained thee here.
Then, see those million worlds which burn
  and roll
Around us: their inhabitants beheld
My spherèd light wane in wide Heaven; the
  sea
Was lifted by strange tempest, and new fire
From earthquake-rifted mountains of bright
  snow
Shook its portentous hair beneath Heaven's
  frown;
Lightning and Inundation vexed the plains;
Blue thistles bloomed in cities; foodless toads
Within voluptuous chambers panting crawled:
When Plague had fallen on man, and beast,
  and worm,   172
And Famine; and black blight on herb and
  tree;
And in the corn, and vines, and meadow-
  grass,
Teemed ineradicable poisonous weeds
Draining their growth, for my wan breast
  was dry
With grief; and the thin air, my breath, was
  stained

With the contagion of a mother's hate
Breathed on her child's destroyer; ay, I heard
Thy curse, the which, if thou rememberest
  not,   180
Yet my innumerable seas and streams,
Mountains, and caves, and winds, and yon
  wide air,
And the inarticulate people of the dead,
Preserve, a treasured spell. We meditate
In secret joy and hope those dreadful words,
But dare not speak them.
  Prometheus.   Venerable mother!
All else who live and suffer take from thee
Some comfort; flowers, and fruits, and happy
  sounds,
And love, though fleeting; these may not be
  mine.
But mine own words, I pray, deny me not. 190
  The Earth. They shall be told. Ere Babylon
  was dust,
The Magus Zoroaster, my dead child,
Met his own image walking in the garden.
That apparition, sole of men, he saw.
For know there are two worlds of life and
  death:
One that which thou beholdest; but the other
Is underneath the grave, where do inhabit
The shadows of all forms that think and live
Till death unite them and they part no more;
Dreams and the light imaginings of men, 200
And all that faith creates or love desires,
Terrible, strange, sublime and beauteous
  shapes.
There thou art, and dost hang, a writhing
  shade,
'Mid whirlwind-peopled mountains; all the
  gods
Are there, and all the powers of nameless
  worlds,
Vast, sceptred phantoms; heroes, men, and
  beasts;
And Demogorgon, a tremendous gloom;
And he, the supreme Tyrant, on his throne
Of burning gold. Son, one of these shall utter
The curse which all remember. Call at will 210
Thine own ghost, or the ghost of Jupiter,
Hades or Typhon, or what mightier Gods
From all-prolific Evil, since thy ruin
Have sprung, and trampled on my prostrate
  sons.
Ask, and they must reply: so the revenge

Of the Supreme may sweep through vacant
    shades,
As rainy wind through the abandoned gate
Of a fallen palace.
    Prometheus. Mother, let not aught
Of that which may be evil, pass again
My lips, or those of aught resembling me. 220
Phantasm of Jupiter, arise, appear!

Ione

My wings are folded o'er mine ears:
    My wings are crossèd o'er mine eyes:
Yet through their silver shade appears,
    And through their lulling plumes arise,
A Shape, a throng of sounds;
    May it be no ill to thee
    O thou of many wounds!
Near whom, for our sweet sister's sake,
Ever thus we watch and wake.   230

Panthea

The sound is of whirlwind underground,
    Earthquake, and fire, and mountains
        cloven;
The shape is awful like the sound,
    Clothed in dark purple, star-inwoven.
A sceptre of pale gold
    To stay steps proud, o'er the slow cloud
His veinèd hand doth hold.
Cruel he looks, but calm and strong,
Like one who does, not suffers wrong.

Phantasm of Jupiter. Why have the secret
    powers of this strange world   240
Driven me, a frail and empty phantom, hither
On direst storms? What unaccustomed sounds
Are hovering on my lips, unlike the voice
With which our pallid race hold ghastly talk
In darkness? And, proud sufferer, who art
    thou?
    Prometheus. Tremendous Image, as thou art
    must be
He whom thou shadowest forth. I am his foe,
The Titan. Speak the words which I would
    hear,
Although no thought inform thine empty
    voice.
    The Earth. Listen! And though your echoes
    must be mute,   250
Gray mountains, and old woods, and haunted
    springs,

Prophetic caves, and isle-surrounding streams,
Rejoice to hear what yet ye cannot speak.
    Phantasm. A spirit seizes me and speaks
    within:
It tears me as fire tears a thunder-cloud.
    Panthea. See, how he lifts his mighty looks,
    the Heaven
Darkens above.
    Ione.   He speaks! O shelter me!
    Prometheus. I see the curse on gestures
    proud and cold,   258
And looks of firm defiance, and calm hate,
And such despair as mocks itself with smiles,
Written as on a scroll: yet speak: Oh, speak!

    Phantasm.
Fiend, I defy thee! with a calm, fixed mind,
    All that thou canst inflict I bid thee do;
Foul Tyrant both of Gods and Human-kind,
    One only being shalt thou not subdue.
Rain then thy plagues upon me here,
Ghastly disease, and frenzying fear;
And let alternate frost and fire
Eat into me, and be thine ire
Lightning, and cutting hail, and legioned
    forms   270
Of furies, driving by upon the wounding
    storms.

Ay, do thy worst. Thou art omnipotent.
    O'er all things but thyself I gave thee
    power,
And my own will. Be thy swift mischiefs
    sent
    To blast mankind, from yon ethereal
    tower.
Let thy malignant spirit move
In darkness over those I love:
On me and mine I imprecate
The utmost torture of thy hate;
And thus devote to sleepless agony,   280
This undeclining head while thou must reign
    on high.

But thou, who art the God and Lord: O,
    thou,
    Who fillest with thy soul this world of
    woe,
To whom all things of Earth and Heaven do
    bow
    In fear and worship: all-prevailing foe!

I curse thee! let a sufferer's curse
Clasp thee, his torturer, like remorse;
Till thine Infinity shall be
A robe of envenomed agony;
And thine Omnipotence a crown of pain, 290
To cling like burning gold round thy dissolv-
    ing brain.

Heap on thy soul, by virtue of this Curse,
    Ill deeds, then be thou damned, beholding
        good;
Both infinite as is the universe,
    And thou, and thy self-torturing solitude.
An awful image of calm power
Though now thou sittest, let the hour
Come, when thou must appear to be
That which thou art internally;
And after many a false and fruitless crime
Scorn track thy lagging fall through bound-
    less space and time.   301

Prometheus. Were these my words, O Par-
    ent?
The Earth.   They were thine.
Prometheus. It doth repent me: words are
    quick and vain;
Grief for a while is blind, and so was mine.
I wish not living thing to suffer pain.

The Earth

Misery, Oh misery to me,
That Jove at length should vanquish thee.
Wail, howl aloud, Land and Sea,
The Earth's rent heart shall answer ye.
Howl, Spirits of the living and the dead, 310
Your refuge, your defence lies fallen and
    vanquishèd.

First Echo

Lies fallen and vanquishèd!

Second Echo

                Fallen and vanquishèd!

Ione

Fear not: 'tis but some passing spasm,
    The Titan is unvanquished still.
But see, where through the azure chasm
    Of yon forked and snowy hill
Trampling the slant winds on high
    With golden-sandalled feet, that glow

Under plumes of purple dye,   320
Like rose-ensanguined ivory,
    A Shape comes now,
    Stretching on high from his right hand
A serpent-cinctured wand.

Panthea. 'Tis Jove's world-wandering her-
    ald, Mercury.

Ione

And who are those with hydra tresses
    And iron wings that climb the wind,
Whom the frowning God represses
    Like vapours steaming up behind,
Clanging loud, and endless crowd— 330

Panthea

These are Jove's tempest-walking hounds
Whom he gluts with groans and blood,
When charioted on sulphurous cloud
    He bursts Heaven's bounds.

Ione

Are they now led, from the thin dead
On new pangs to be fed?

Panthea

The Titan looks as ever, firm, not proud.

First Fury. Hå! I scent life!
Second Fury. Let me but look into his eyes!
Third Fury. The hope of torturing him
    smells like a heap
Of corpses to a death-bird after battle.   340
    First Fury. Darest thou delay, O Herald!
    take cheer, Hounds
Of Hell: what if the Son of Maia soon
Should make us food and sport—who can
    please long
The Omnipotent?
Mercury. Back to your towers of iron,
And gnash, beside the streams of fire and wail,
Your foodless teeth. Geryon, arise! and
    Gorgon,
Chimæra, and thou Sphinx, subtlest of fiends
Who ministered to Thebes Heaven's poisoned
    wine,
Unnatural love, and more unnatural hate:
These shall perform your task.

First Fury.   Oh, mercy! mercy! 350
We die with our desire: drive us not back!
Mercury. Crouch then in silence.
                              Awful Sufferer!
To thee unwilling, most unwillingly
I come, by the great Father's will driven
     down,   *Jove*
To execute a doom of new revenge.
Alas! I pity thee, and hate myself
That I can do no more: aye from thy sight
Returning, for a season, Heaven seems Hell,
So thy worn form pursues me night and day,
Smiling reproach. Wise art thou, firm and
     good,   360
But vainly wouldst stand forth alone in strife
Against the Omnipotent; as yon clear lamps
That measure and divide the weary years
From which there is no refuge, long have
     taught
And long must teach. Even now thy Tor-
     turer arms
With the strange might of unimagined pains
The powers who scheme slow agonies in Hell,
And my commission is to lead them here,
Or what more subtle, foul, or savage fiends
People the abyss, and leave them to their
     task.   370
Be it not so! there is a secret known
To thee, and to none else of living things,
Which may transfer the sceptre of wide
     Heaven,
The fear of which perplexes the Supreme:
Clothe it in words, and bid it clasp his throne
In intercession; bend thy soul in prayer,
And like a suppliant in some gorgeous fane,
Let the will kneel within thy haughty heart:
For benefits and meek submission tame
The fiercest and the mightiest.
     Prometheus.   Evil minds 380
Change good to their own nature. I gave all
He has; and in return he chains me here
Years, ages, night and day: whether the Sun
Split my parched skin, or in the moony night
The crystal-wingèd snow cling round my
     hair:
Whilst my belovèd race is trampled down
By his thought-executing ministers.
Such is the tyrant's recompense: 'tis just:
He who is evil can receive no good;
And for a world bestowed, or a friend lost, 390
He can feel hate, fear, shame; not gratitude:

He but requites me for his own misdeed.
Kindness to such is keen reproach, which
     breaks
With bitter stings the light sleep of Revenge.
Submission, thou dost know I cannot try:
For what submission but that fatal word,
The death-seal of mankind's captivity,
Like the Sicilian's hair-suspended sword,
Which trembles o'er his crown, would he
     accept,   399
Or could I yield? Which yet I will not yield.
Let others flatter Crime, where it sits throned
In brief Omnipotence: secure are they:
For Justice, when triumphant, will weep down
Pity, not punishment, on her own wrongs,
Too much avenged by those who err. I wait,
Enduring thus, the retributive hour
Which since we spake is even nearer now.
But hark, the hell-hounds clamour: fear delay:
Behold! Heaven lowers under thy Father's
     frown.
     Mercury. Oh, that we might be spared: I
     to inflict   410
And thou to suffer! Once more answer me:
Thou knowest not the period of Jove's power?
     Prometheus. I know but this, that it must
     come.
     Mercury.   Alas!
Thou canst not count thy years to come of pain?
     Prometheus. They last while Jove must
     reign: nor more, nor less
Do I desire or fear.
     Mercury.   Yet pause, and plunge
Into Eternity, where recorded time,
Even all that we imagine, age on age,
Seems but a point, and the reluctant mind
Flags wearily in its unending flight,   420
Till it sink, dizzy, blind, lost, shelterless;
Perchance it has not numbered the slow years
Which thou must spend in torture, unre-
     prieved?
     Prometheus. Perchance no thought can
     count them, yet they pass.
     Mercury. If thou might'st dwell among the
     Gods the while
Lapped in voluptuous joy?
     Prometheus.   I would not quit
This bleak ravine, these unrepentant pains.
     Mercury. Alas! I wonder at, yet pity thee.
     Prometheus. Pity the self-despising slaves
     of Heaven,   429

Not me, within whose mind sits peace serene,
As light in the sun, throned: how vain is talk!
Call up the fiends.

   Ione.   O, sister, look! White fire
Has cloven to the roots yon huge snow-
   loaded cedar;
How fearfully God's thunder howls behind!

   Mercury. I must obey his words and thine:
   alas!
Most heavily remorse hangs at my heart!

   Panthea. See where the child of Heaven,
   with wingèd feet,
Runs down the slanted sunlight of the dawn.

   Ione. Dear sister, close thy plumes over
   thine eyes
Lest thou behold and die: they come: they
   come   440
Blackening the birth of day with countless
   wings,
And hollow underneath, like death.

   First Fury.   Prometheus!

   Second Fury. Immortal Titan!

   Third Fury.   Champion of
   Heaven's slaves!

   Prometheus. He whom some dreadful voice
   invokes is here,
Prometheus, the chained Titan. Horrible
   forms,
What and who are ye? Never yet there came
Phantasms so foul through monster-teeming
   Hell
From the all-miscreative brain of Jove;
Whilst I behold such execrable shapes,
Methinks I grow like what I contemplate, 450
And laugh and stare in loathsome sympathy.

   First Fury. We are the ministers of pain,
   and fear,
And disappointment, and mistrust, and hate,
And clinging crime; and as lean dogs pursue
Through wood and lake some struck and
   sobbing fawn,
We track all things that weep, and bleed, and
   live,
When the great King betrays them to our will.

   Prometheus. Oh! many fearful natures in
   one name,
I know ye; and these lakes and echoes know
The darkness and the clangour of your wings.
But why more hideous than your loathèd
   selves   461
Gather ye up in legions from the deep?

   Second Fury. We knew not that: Sisters,
   rejoice, rejoice!

   Prometheus. Can aught exult in its deformity?

   Second Fury. The beauty of delight makes
   lovers glad,
Gazing on one another: so are we.
As from the rose which the pale priestess kneels
To gather for her festal crown of flowers
The aëreal crimson falls, flushing her cheek,
So from our victim's destined agony   470
The shade which is our form invests us round,
Else we are shapeless as our mother Night.

   Prometheus. I laugh your power, and his
   who sent you here,
To lowest scorn. Pour forth the cup of pain.

   First Fury. Thou thinkest we will rend thee
   bone from bone,
And nerve from nerve, working like fire within?

   Prometheus. Pain is my element, as hate is
   thine;
Ye rend me now: I care not.

   Second Fury.   Dost imagine
We will but laugh into thy lidless eyes?

   Prometheus. I weigh not what ye do, but
   what ye suffer,   480
Being evil. Cruel was the power which called
You, or aught else so wretched, into light.

   Third Fury. Thou think'st we will live
   through thee, one by one,
Like animal life, and though we can obscure
   not
The soul which burns within, that we will
   dwell
Beside it, like a vain loud multitude
Vexing the self-content of wisest men:
That we will be dread thought beneath thy
   brain,
And foul desire round thine astonished heart,
And blood within thy labyrinthine veins 490
Crawling like agony?

   Prometheus.   Why, ye are thus now;
Yet am I king over myself, and rule *Dante*
The torturing and conflicting throngs within,
As Joy rules you when Hell grows mutinous.

Chorus of Furies

From the ends of the earth, from the ends of
   the earth,
Where the night has its grave and the morning
   its birth,

Come, come come!
Oh, ye who shake hills with the scream of
    your mirth,
When cities sink howling in ruin; and ye   499
Who with wingless footsteps trample the sea,
And close upon Shipwreck and Famine's track,
Sit chattering with joy on the foodless wreck;
        Come, come, come!
    Leave the bed, low, cold, and red,
    Strewed beneath a nation dead;
    Leave the hatred, as in ashes
        Fire is left for future burning:
    It will burst in bloodier flashes
        When ye stir it, soon returning:
    Leave the self-contempt implanted   510
    In young spirits, sense-enchanted,
        Misery's yet unkindled fuel:
    Leave Hell's secrets half unchanted,
        To the maniac dreamer; cruel
    More than ye can be with hate
        Is he with fear.
        Come, come, come!
We are steaming up from Hell's wide gate
And we burthen the blast of the atmosphere,
But vainly we toil till ye come here.   520

Ione. Sister, I hear the thunder of new
    wings.
Panthea. These solid mountains quiver with
    the sound
Even as the tremulous air: their shadows make
The space within my plumes more black than
    night.

First Fury
Your call was as a wingèd car
Driven on whirlwinds fast and far;
It rapped us from red gulfs of war.

Second Fury
From wide cities, famine-wasted;

Third Fury
Groans half heard, and blood untasted;

Fourth Fury
Kingly conclaves stern and cold,   530
Where blood with gold is bought and sold;

Fifth Fury
From the furnace, white and hot,
In which—

A Fury
    Speak not: whisper not:
I know all that ye would tell,
But to speak might break the spell
Which must bend the Invincible,
    The stern of thought;
He yet defies the deepest power of Hell.

A Fury
Tear the veil!

Another Fury
    It is torn.

Chorus
        The pale stars of the morn
Shine on a misery, dire to be borne.   540
Dost thou faint, mighty Titan? We laugh thee
    to scorn.
Dost thou boast the clear knowledge thou
    waken'dst for man?
Then was kindled within him a thirst which
    outran
Those perishing waters; a thirst of fierce fever,
Hope, love, doubt, desire, which consume him
    for ever.
    One came forth of gentle worth
    Smiling on the sanguine earth;
    His words outlived him, like swift poison
        Withering up truth, peace, and pity.
    Look! where round the wide horizon 550
        Many a million-peopled city
    Vomits smoke in the bright air.
    Hark that outcry of despair!
    'Tis his mild and gentle ghost
        Wailing for the faith he kindled:
    Look again, the flames almost
        To a glow-worm's lamp have dwindled:
The survivors round the embers
    Gather in dread.
        Joy, joy, joy!   560
Past ages crowd on thee, but each one remem-
    bers,
And the future is dark, and the present is
    spread
Like a pillow of thorns for thy slumberless
    head.

Semichorus I
Drops of bloody agony flow
From his white and quivering brow.
Grant a little respite now:

See a disenchanted nation
Springs like day from desolation;
To Truth its state is dedicate,
And Freedom leads it forth, her mate; 570
A legioned band of linkèd brothers
Whom Love calls children—

Semichorus II

                    'Tis another's:
See how kindred murder kin:
'Tis the vintage-time for death and sin:
Blood, like new wine, bubbles within:
    Till Despair smothers
The struggling world, which slaves and ty-
    rants win.
        [*All the* FURIES *vanish, except one.*
Ione. Hark, sister! what a low yet dreadful
    groan
Quite unsuppressed is tearing up the heart
Of the good Titan, as storms tear the deep, 580
And beasts hear the sea moan in inland caves.
Darest thou observe how the fiends torture
    him?
Panthea. Alas! I looked forth twice, but will
    no more.
Ione. What didst thou see?
Panthea.   A woful sight: a youth
With patient looks nailed to a crucifix.
Ione. What next?
Panthea.   The heaven around, the earth
    below
Was peopled with thick shapes of human
    death,
All horrible, and wrought by human hands,
And some appeared the work of human hearts.
For men were slowly killed by frowns and
    smiles: 590
And other sights too foul to speak and live
Were wandering by. Let us not tempt worse
    fear
By looking forth: those groans are grief
    enough.
Fury. Behold an emblem: those who do
    endure
Deep wrongs for man, and scorn, and chains,
    but heap
Thousandfold torment on themselves and him.
    Prometheus. Remit the anguish of that
    lighted stare;
Close those wan lips; let that thorn-wounded
    brow

Stream not with blood; it mingles with thy
    tears!
Fix, fix those tortured orbs in peace and
    death, 600
So thy sick throes shake not that crucifix,
So those pale fingers play not with thy gore.
O, horrible! Thy name I will not speak,
It hath become a curse. I see, I see
The wise, the mild, the lofty, and the just,
Whom thy slaves hate for being like to thee,
Some hunted by foul lies from their heart's
    home,
An early-chosen, late-lamented home;
As hooded ounces cling to the driven hind;
Some linked to corpses in unwholesome cells:
Some—hear I not the multitude laugh
    loud?—   ,   611
Impaled in lingering fire: and mighty realms
Float by my feet, like sea-uprooted isles,
Whose sons are kneaded down in common
    blood
By the red light of their own burning homes.
    Fury. Blood thou canst see, and fire; and
    canst hear groans;
Worse things, unheard, unseen, remain be-
    hind.
    Prometheus. Worse?
    Fury.   In each human heart terror
    survives
The ravin it has gorged: the loftiest fear
All that they would disdain to think were
    true: 620
Hypocrisy and custom make their minds
The fanes of many a worship, now outworn.
They dare not devise good for man's estate,
And yet they know not that they do not dare.
The good want power, but to weep barren
    tears.
The powerful goodness want: worse need for
    them.
The wise want love; and those who love want
    wisdom;
And all best things are thus confused to ill.
Many are strong and rich, and would be just,
But live among their suffering fellow-men
As if none felt: they know not what they do.
    Prometheus. Thy words are like a cloud of
    wingèd snakes; 632
And yet I pity those they torture not.
    Fury. Thou pitiest them? I speak no more!
                        [*Vanishes.*

Prometheus.   Ah woe!
Ah woe! Alas! pain, pain ever, for ever!
I close my tearless eyes, but see more clear
Thy works within my woe-illumèd mind,
Thou subtle tyrant! Peace is in the grave.
The grave hides all things beautiful and good:
I am a God and cannot find it there,   640
Nor would I seek it: for, though dread re-
    venge,
This is defeat, fierce king, not victory.
The sights with which thou torturest gird my
    soul
With new endurance, till the hour arrives
When they shall be no types of things which
    are.
Panthea. Alas! what sawest thou more?
Prometheus.   There are two woes:
To speak, and to behold; thou spare me one.
Names are there, Nature's sacred watchwords,
    they
Were borne aloft in bright emblazonry;
The nations thronged around, and cried aloud,
As with one voice, Truth, liberty, and love! 651
Suddenly fierce confusion fell from heaven
Among them: there was strife, deceit, and
    fear:
Tyrants rushed in, and did divide the spoil.
This was the shadow of the truth I saw.
    The Earth. I felt thy torture, son; with
        such mixed joy
As pain and virtue give. To cheer thy state
I bid ascend those subtle and fair spirits,
Whose homes are the dim caves of human
    thought,
And who inhabit, as birds wing the wind, 660
Its world-surrounding æther: they behold
Beyond that twilight realm, as in a glass,
The future: may they speak comfort to thee!
    Panthea. Look, sister, where a troop of
        spirits gather,
Like flocks of clouds in spring's delightful
    weather,
Thronging in the blue air!
    Ione.   And see! more come,
Like fountain-vapours when the winds are
    dumb,
That climb up the ravine in scattered lines.
And, hark! is it the music of the pines?
Is it the lake? Is it the waterfall?   670
    Panthea. 'Tis something sadder, sweeter far
        than all.

Chorus of Spirits

From unremembered ages we
Gentle guides and guardians be
Of heaven-oppressed mortality;
And we breathe, and sicken not,
The atmosphere of human thought:
Be it dim, and dank, and gray,
Like a storm-extinguished day,
Travelled o'er by dying gleams;
    Be it bright as all between   680
Cloudless skies and windless streams,
    Silent, liquid, and serene;
As the birds within the wind,
    As the fish within the wave,
As the thoughts of man's own mind
    Float through all above the grave;
We make there our liquid lair,
Voyaging cloudlike and unpent
Through the boundless element:
Thence we bear the prophecy   690
Which begins and ends in thee!

Ione. More yet come, one by one: the air
    around them
Looks radiant as the air around a star.

First Spirit

On a battle-trumpet's blast
I fled hither, fast, fast, fast,
'Mid the darkness upward cast.
From the dust of creeds outworn,
From the tyrant's banner torn,
Gathering 'round me, onward borne,
There was mingled many a cry—   700
Freedom! Hope! Death! Victory!
Till they faded through the sky;
And one sound, above, around,
One sound beneath, around, above,
Was moving; 'twas the soul of Love;
'Twas the hope, the prophecy,
Which begins and ends in thee.

Second Spirit

A rainbow's arch stood on the sea,
Which rocked beneath, immovably;
And the triumphant storm did flee,   710
Like a conqueror, swift and proud,
Between, with many a captive cloud,
A shapeless, dark and rapid crowd,
Each by lightning riven in half:
I heard the thunder hoarsely laugh:

Mighty fleets were strewn like chaff
And spread beneath a hell of death
O'er the white waters. I alit
On a great ship lightning-split,
And speeded hither on the sigh   720
Of one who gave an enemy,
His plank, then plunged aside to die.

Third Spirit

I sate beside a sage's bed,
And the lamp was burning red
Near the book where he had fed,
When a Dream with plumes of flame,
To his pillow hovering came,
And I knew it was the same   *wisdom*
Which had kindled long ago
Pity, eloquence, and woe;   730
And the world awhile below
Wore the shade, its lustre made.
It has borne me here as fleet
As Desire's lightning feet:
I must ride it back ere morrow,
Or the sage will wake in sorrow.

Fourth Spirit

On a poet's lips I slept   *poetry*
Dreaming like a love-adept
In the sound his breathing kept;
Nor seeks nor finds he mortal blisses,   740
But feeds on the aëreal kisses
Of shapes that haunt thought's wildernesses.
He will watch from dawn to gloom
The lake-reflected sun illume
The yellow bees in the ivy-bloom,
Nor heed nor see, what things they be;
But from these create he can
Forms more real than living man,
Nurslings of immortality!
One of these awakened me,   750
And I sped to succour thee.

Ione

Behold'st thou not two shapes from the east
      and west
Come, as two doves to one belovèd nest,
Twin nurslings of the all-sustaining air
On swift still wings glide down the atmos-
      phere?
And, hark! their sweet, sad voices! 'tis despair
Mingled with love and then dissolved in sound.

Panthea. Canst thou speak, sister? all my
      words are drowned.
Ione. Their beauty gives me voice. See how
      they float
On their sustaining wings of skiey grain, 760
Orange and azure deepening into gold:
Their soft smiles light the air like a star's fire.

Chorus of Spirits

Hast thou beheld the form of Love?

Fifth Spirit

                  As over wide dominions
I sped, like some swift cloud that wings the
      wide air's wildernesses,
That planet-crested shape swept by on
      lightning-braided pinions,
Scattering the liquid joy of life from his
      ambrosial tresses:
His footsteps paved the world with light; but
      as I passed 'twas fading,
And hollow Ruin yawned behind: great
      sages bound in madness,
And headless patriots, and pale youths who
      perished, unupbraiding,   *not complaining*
Gleamed in the night. I wandered o'er, till
      thou, O King of sadness,   770
Turned by thy smile the worst I saw to
      recollected gladness.

Sixth Spirit

Ah, sister! Desolation is a delicate thing:
      It walks not on the earth, it floats not on
      the air,
But treads with lulling footsteps, and fans with
      silent wing
      The tender hopes which in their hearts the
      best and gentlest bear;
Who, soothed to false repose by the fanning
      plumes above
      And the music-stirring motion of its soft
      and busy feet,
Dream visions of aëreal joy, and call the mon-
      ster, Love,
      And wake, and find the shadow Pain, as he
      whom now we greet.

Chorus

Though Ruin now Love's shadow be,   780
Following him, destroyingly,
      On Death's white and wingèd steed,

Which the fleetest cannot flee,
  Trampling down both flower and weed,
Man and beast, and foul and fair,
Like a tempest through the air;
Thou shalt quell this horseman grim,
Woundless though in heart or limb.

  Prometheus. Spirits! how know ye this shall
  be?

Chorus

In the atmosphere we breathe,   790
As buds grow red when the snow-storms flee,
  From Spring gathering up beneath,
Whose mild winds shake the elder brake,
And the wandering herdsmen know
That the white-thorn soon will blow:
  Wisdom, Justice, Love, and Peace,
  When they struggle to increase,
    Are to us as soft winds be
    To shepherd boys, the prophecy
  Which begins and ends in thee.   800

Ione. Where are the Spirits fled?
Panthea.   Only a sense
Remains of them, like the omnipotence
Of music, when the inspired voice and lute
Languish, ere yet the responses are mute,
Which through the deep and labyrinthine soul,
Like echoes through long caverns, wind and
  roll.
  Prometheus. How fair these airborn shapes!
  and yet I feel
Most vain all hope but love; and thou art far,
Asia! who, when my being overflowed,
Wert like a golden chalice to bright wine 810
Which else had sunk into the thirsty dust.
All things are still: alas! how heavily
This quiet morning weighs upon my heart;
Though I should dream I could even sleep
  with grief
If slumber were denied not. I would fain
Be what it is my destiny to be,
The saviour and the strength of suffering man,
Or sink into the original gulf of things: .
There is no agony, and no solace left;
Earth can console, Heaven can torment no
  more.   820
  Panthea. Hast thou forgotten one who
  watches thee
The cold dark night, and never sleeps but when
The shadow of thy spirit falls on her?

  Prometheus. I said all hope was vain but
  love: thou lovest.
  Panthea. Deeply in truth; but the eastern
  star looks white,
And Asia waits in that far Indian vale,
The scene of her sad exile; rugged once
And desolate and frozen, like this ravine;
But now invested with fair flowers and herbs,
And haunted by sweet airs and sounds, which
  flow   830
Among the woods and waters, from the æther
Of her transforming presence, which would
  fade
If it were mingled not with thine. Farewell!
  END OF THE FIRST ACT

Act II

Scene I.—*Morning. A lovely Vale in the Indian Caucasus.* Asia *alone.*

  Asia. From all the blasts of heaven thou
  hast descended:
Yes, like a spirit, like a thought, which makes
Unwonted tears throng to the horny eyes,
And beatings haunt the desolated heart,
Which should have learnt repose: thou hast
  descended
Cradled in tempests; thou dost wake, O Spring!
O child of many winds! As suddenly
Thou comest as the memory of a dream,
Which now is sad because it hath been sweet;
Like genius, or like joy which riseth up   10
As from the earth, clothing with golden clouds
The desert of our life.
This is the season, this the day, the hour;
At sunrise thou shouldst come, sweet sister
  mine,
Too long desired, too long delaying, come!
How like death-worms the wingless moments
  crawl!
The point of one white star is quivering still
Deep in the orange light of widening morn
Beyond the purple mountains: through a
  chasm
Of wind-divided mist the darker lake   20
Reflects it: now it wanes: it gleams again
As the waves fade, and as the burning threads
Of woven cloud unravel in pale air:
'Tis lost! and through yon peaks of cloud-like
  snow

The roseate sunlight quivers: hear I not
The Æolian music of her sea-green plumes
Winnowing the crimson dawn?

                  [PANTHEA *enters.*

            I feel, I see
Those eyes which burn through smiles that
    fade in tears,
Like stars half quenched in mists of silver
    dew.
Belovèd and most beautiful, who wearest   30
The shadow of that soul by which I live,
How late thou art! the spherèd sun had
    climbed
The sea; my heart was sick with hope, before
The printless air felt thy belated plumes.
   Panthea. Pardon, great Sister! but my wings
    were faint
With the delight of a remembered dream,
As are the noontide plumes of summer winds
Satiate with sweet flowers. I was wont to
    sleep
Peacefully, and awake refreshed and calm
Before the sacred Titan's fall, and thy   40
Unhappy love, had made, through use and
    pity,
Both love and woe familiar to my heart
As they had grown to thine: erewhile I slept
Under the glaucous caverns of old Ocean
Within dim bowers of green and purple moss,
Our young Ione's soft and milky arms
Locked then, as now, behind my dark, moist
    hair,
While my shut eyes and cheek were pressed
    within
The folded depth of her life-breathing bosom:
But not as now, since I am made the wind 50
Which fails beneath the music that I bear
Of thy most wordless converse; since dis-
    solved
Into the sense with which love talks, my rest
Was troubled and yet sweet; my waking hours
Too full of care and pain.
   Asia.   Lift up thine eyes,
And let me read thy dream.
   Panthea.   As I have said
With our sea-sister at his feet I slept.
The mountain mists, condensing at our voice
Under the moon, had spread their snowy
    flakes,   59
From the keen ice shielding our linkèd sleep.
Then two dreams came. One, I remember not.

But in the other his pale wound-worn limbs
Fell from Prometheus, and the azure night
Grew radiant with the glory of that form
Which lives unchanged within, and his voice
    fell
Like music which makes giddy the dim brain,
Faint with intoxication of keen joy:
'Sister of her whose footsteps pave the world
With loveliness—more fair than aught but
    her,
Whose shadow thou art—lift thine eyes on
    me.'   70
I lifted them: the overpowering light
Of that immortal shape was shadowed o'er
By love; which, from his soft and flowing
    limbs,
And passion-parted lips, and keen, faint eyes,
Steamed forth like vaporous fire; an atmos-
    phere
Which wrapped me in its all-dissolving power,
As the warm æther of the morning sun
Wraps ere it drinks some cloud of wandering
    dew.
I saw not, heard not, moved not, only felt
His presence flow and mingle through my
    blood   80
Till it became his life, and his grew mine,
And I was thus absorbed, until it passed,
And like the vapours when the sun sinks
    down,
Gathering again in drops upon the pines,
And tremulous as they, in the deep night
My being was condensed; and as the rays
Of thought were slowly gathered, I could hear
His voice, whose accents lingered ere they
    died
Like footsteps of weak melody: thy name
Among the many sounds alone I heard   90
Of what might be articulate; though still
I listened through the night when sound was
    none.
Ione wakened then, and said to me:
'Canst thou divine what troubles me to-night?
I always knew what I desired before,
Nor ever found delight to wish in vain.
But now I cannot tell thee what I seek;
I know not; something sweet, since it is sweet
Even to desire; it is thy sport, false sister; 99
Thou hast discovered some enchantment old,
Whose spells have stolen my spirit as I slept
And mingled it with thine: for when just now

We kissed, I felt within thy parted lips
The sweet air that sustained me, and the
    warmth
Of the life-blood, for loss of which I faint,
Quivered between our intertwining arms.'
I answered not, for the Eastern star grew pale,
But fled to thee.
    Asia.   Thou speakest, but thy words
Are as the air: I feel them not: Oh, lift
Thine eyes, that I may read his written soul!
    Panthea. I lift them though they droop be-
    neath the load   111
Of that they would express: what canst thou see
But thine own fairest shadow imaged there?
    Asia. Thine eyes are like the deep, blue,
    boundless heaven
Contracted to two circles underneath
Their long, fine lashes; dark, far, measureless,
Orb within orb, and line through line in-
    woven.
    Panthea. Why lookest thou as if a spirit
    passed?
    Asia. There is a change: beyond their in-
    most depth
I see a shade, a shape: 'tis He, arrayed   120
In the soft light of his own smiles, which
    spread
Like radiance from the cloud-surrounded
    moon.
Prometheus, it is thine! depart not yet!
Say not those smiles that we shall meet again
Within that bright pavilion which their beams
Shall build o'er the waste world? The dream is
    told.
What shape is that between us? Its rude hair
Roughens the wind that lifts it, its regard
Is wild and quick, yet 'tis a thing of air,
For through its gray robe gleams the golden
    dew   130
Whose stars the noon has quenched not.
    Dream.   Follow! Follow!
    Panthea. It is mine other dream.
    Asia.   It disappears.
    Panthea. It passes now into my mind. Me-
    thought
As we sate here, the flower-infolding buds
Burst on yon lightning-blasted almond-tree,
When swift from the white Scythian wilder-
    ness
A wind swept forth wrinkling the Earth with
    frost:

I looked, and all the blossoms were blown
    down;
But on each leaf was stamped, as the blue bells
Of Hyacinth tell Apollo's written grief,   140
O, FOLLOW, FOLLOW!
    Asia.   As you speak, your words
Fill, pause by pause, my own forgotten sleep
With shapes. Methought among these lawns
    together
We wandered, underneath the young gray
    dawn,
And multitudes of dense white fleecy clouds
Were wandering in thick flocks along the
    mountains
Shepherded by the slow, unwilling wind;
And the white dew on the new-bladed grass,
Just piercing the dark earth, hung silently;
And there was more which I remember not:
But on the shadows of the morning clouds, 151
Athwart the purple mountain slope, was writ-
    ten
FOLLOW, O, FOLLOW! as they vanished by;
And on each herb, from which Heaven's dew
    had fallen,
The like was stamped, as with a withering fire;
A wind arose among the pines; it shook
The clinging music from their boughs, and
    then
Low, sweet, faint sounds, like the farewell of
    ghosts,
Were heard: O, FOLLOW, FOLLOW, FOLLOW ME!
And then I said: 'Panthea, look on me.'   160
But in the depth of those belovèd eyes
Still I saw, FOLLOW, FOLLOW!
    Echo.   Follow, follow!
    Panthea. The crags, this clear spring morn-
    ing, mock our voices
As they were spirit-tongued.
    Asia.   It is some being
Around the crags. What fine clear sounds! O,
    list!

        Echoes (unseen)

    Echoes we: listen!
        We cannot stay:
    As dew-stars glisten
        Then fade away—
            Child of Ocean!   170

    Asia. Hark! Spirits speak. The liquid re-
    sponses
Of their aëreal tongues yet sound.

Panthea.   I hear.

Echoes

O, follow, follow,
  As our voice recedeth
Through the caverns hollow,
  Where the forest spreadeth;

(More distant.)

O, follow, follow!
Through the caverns hollow,
As the song floats thou pursue,
Where the wild bee never flew,   180
Through the noontide darkness deep,
By the odour-breathing sleep
Of faint night flowers, and the waves
At the fountain-lighted caves
While our music, wild and sweet,
Mocks thy gently falling feet,
         Child of Ocean!

Asia. Shall we pursue the sound? It grows more faint
And distant.
Panthea. List! the strain floats nearer now.

Echoes

In the world unknown   190
  Sleeps a voice unspoken;
By thy step alone
  Can its rest be broken;
         Child of Ocean!

Asia. How the notes sink upon the ebbing wind!

Echoes

O, follow, follow!
Through the caverns hollow,
As the song floats thou pursue,
By the woodland noontide dew;
By the forest, lakes, and fountains,   200
Through the many-folded mountains;
To the rents, and gulfs, and chasms,
Where the Earth reposed from spasms,
On the day when He and thou
Parted, to commingle now:
         Child of Ocean!

Asia. Come, sweet Panthea, link thy hand in mine,
And follow, ere the voices fade away.

SCENE II.—*A Forest, intermingled with Rocks and Caverns.* ASIA *and* PANTHEA *pass into it. Two young Fauns are sitting on a Rock listening.*

Semichorus I of Spirits

The path through which that lovely twain
  Have passed, by cedar, pine, and yew,
  And each dark tree that ever grew,
  Is curtained out from Heaven's wide blue;
Nor sun, nor moon, nor wind, nor rain,
  Can pierce its interwoven bowers,
  Nor aught, save where some cloud of dew,
Drifted along the earth-creeping breeze,
Between the trunks of the hoar trees,
  Hangs each a pearl in the pale flowers   10
  Of the green laurel, blown anew;
And bends, and then fades silently,
One frail and fair anemone:
Or when some star of many a one
That climbs and wanders through steep night,
Has found the cleft through which alone
Beams fall from high those depths upon
Ere it is borne away, away,
By the swift Heavens that cannot stay,
It scatters drops of golden light,   20
Like lines of rain that ne'er unite:
And the gloom divine is all around,
And underneath is the mossy ground.

Semichorus II

There the voluptuous nightingales,
  Are awake through all the broad noon-day.
When one with bliss or sadness fails,
  And through the windless ivy-boughs,
  Sick with sweet love, droops dying away
On its mate's music-panting bosom;
Another from the swinging blossom,   30
  Watching to catch the languid close
  Of the last strain, then lifts on high
  The wings of the weak melody,
'Till some new strain of feeling bear
  The song, and all the woods are mute;
When there is heard through the dim air
  The rush of wings, and rising there
  Like many a lake-surrounded flute,
Sounds overflow the listener's brain
So sweet, that joy is almost pain.   40

Semichorus I

There those enchanted eddies play
 Of echoes, music-tongued, which draw,
 By Demogorgon's mighty law,
 With melting rapture, or sweet awe,
All spirits on that secret way;
 As inland boats are driven to Ocean
Down streams made strong with mountain-
 thaw:
 And first there comes a gentle sound
 To those in talk or slumber bound,
 And wakes the destined soft emotion,— 50
Attracts, impels them; those who saw
 Say from the breathing earth behind
There steams a plume-uplifting wind
Which drives them on their path, while they
 Believe their own swift wings and feet
The sweet desires within obey:
And so they float upon their way,
Until, still sweet, but loud and strong,
The storm of sound is driven along,
 Sucked up and hurrying: as they fleet 60
 Behind, its gathering billows meet
And to the fatal mountain bear
Like clouds amid the yielding air.

First Faun. Canst thou imagine where those
 spirits live
Which make such delicate music in the woods?
We haunt within the least frequented caves
And closest coverts, and we know these wilds,
Yet never meet them, though we hear them
 oft:
Where may they hide themselves?
Second Faun.   'Tis hard to tell:
I have heard those more skilled in spirits say,
The bubbles, which the enchantment of the
 sun   71
Sucks from the pale faint water-flowers that
 pave
The oozy bottom of clear lakes and pools,
Are the pavilions where such dwell and float
Under the green and golden atmosphere
Which noontide kindles through the woven
 leaves;
And when these burst, and the thin fiery air,
The which they breathed within those lucent
 domes,
Ascends to flow like meteors through the night,
They ride on them, and rein their headlong
 speed,   80

And bow their burning crests, and glide in fire
Under the waters of the earth again.
 First Faun. If such live thus, have others
 other lives,
Under pink blossoms or within the bells
Of meadow flowers, or folded violets deep,
Or on their dying odours, when they die,
Or in the sunlight of the spherèd dew?
 Second Faun. Ay, many more which we may
 well divine.
But, should we stay to speak, noontide would
 come,
And thwart Silenus find his goats undrawn, 90
And grudge to sing those wise and lovely
 songs
Of Fate, and Chance, and God, and Chaos old,
And Love, and the chained Titan's woful
 doom,
And how he shall be loosed, and make the
 earth
One brotherhood: delightful strains which
 cheer
Our solitary twilights, and which charm
To silence the unenvying nightingales.

SCENE III.—*A Pinnacle of Rock among
 Mountains.* ASIA *and* PANTHEA

Panthea. Hither the sound has borne us—
 to the realm
Of Demogorgon, and the mighty portal,
Like a volcano's meteor-breathing chasm,
Whence the oracular vapour is hurled up
Which lonely men drink wandering in their
 youth,
And call truth, virtue, love, genius, or joy,
That maddening wine of life, whose dregs
 they drain
To deep intoxication; and uplift,
Like Mænads who cry loud, Evoe! Evoe!
The voice which is contagion to the world. 10
 Asia. Fit throne for such a Power! Magnifi-
 cent!
How glorious art thou, Earth! And if thou be
The shadow of some spirit lovelier still,
Though evil stain its work, and it should be
Like its creation, weak yet beautiful,
I could fall down and worship that and thee.
Even now my heart adoreth: Wonderful!
Look, sister, ere the vapour dim thy brain:
Beneath is a wide plain of billowy mist,

As a lake, paving in the morning sky,   20
With azure waves which burst in silver light,
Some Indian vale. Behold it, rolling on
Under the curdling winds, and islanding
The peak whereon we stand, midway, around,
Encinctured by the dark and blooming forests,
Dim twilight-lawns, and stream-illumèd caves,
And wind-enchanted shapes of wandering
   mist;
And far on high the keen sky-cleaving moun-
   tains
From icy spires of sun-like radiance fling
The dawn, as lifted Ocean's dazzling spray,   30
From some Atlantic islet scattered up,
Spangles the wind with lamp-like water-drops.
The vale is girdled with their walls, a howl
Of cataracts from their thaw-cloven ravines,
Satiates the listening wind, continuous, vast,
Awful as silence. Hark! the rushing snow!
The sun-awakened avalanche! whose mass,
Thrice sifted by the storm, had gathered there
Flake after flake, in heaven-defying minds
As thought by thought is piled, till some great
   truth   40
Is loosened, and the nations echo round,
Shaken to their roots, as do the mountains
   now.
   Panthea. Look how the gusty sea of mist is
   breaking
In crimson foam, even at our feet! it rises
As Ocean at the enchantment of the moon
Round foodless men wrecked on some oozy
   isle.
   Asia. The fragments of the cloud are scat-
   tered up;
The wind that lifts them disentwines my hair;
Its billows now sweep o'er mine eyes; my
   brain
Grows dizzy; see'st thou shapes within the
   mist?   50
   Panthea. A countenance with beckoning
   smiles: there burns
An azure fire within its golden locks!
Another and another: hark! they speak!

Song of Spirits

To the deep, to the deep,
        Down, down!
Through the shade of sleep,
Through the cloudy strife
Of Death and of Life;

Through the veil and the bar
Of things which seem and are   60
Even to the steps of the remotest throne,
        Down, down!

While the sound whirls around,
        Down, down!
As the fawn draws the hound,
As the lightning the vapour,
As a weak moth the taper;
Death, despair; love, sorrow;
Time both; to-day, to-morrow;
As steel obeys the spirit of the stone,   70
        Down, down!

Through the gray, void abysm,
        Down, down!
Where the air is no prism,
And the moon and stars are not,
And the cavern-crags wear not
The radiance of Heaven,
Nor the gloom to Earth given,
Where there is One pervading, One alone,
        Down, down!   80

In the depth of the deep,
        Down, down!
Like veiled lightning asleep,
Like the spark nursed in embers,
The last look Love remembers,
Like a diamond, which shines
On the dark wealth of mines,
A spell is treasured but for thee alone.
        Down, down!

We have bound thee, we guide thee;   90
        Down, down!
With the bright form beside thee;
Resist not the weakness,
Such strength is in meekness
That the Eternal, the Immortal,
Must unloose through life's portal,
The snake-like Doom coiled underneath his
   throne
        By that alone.

SCENE IV.—*The Cave of* DEMOGORGON.
ASIA *and* PANTHEA

   Panthea. What veilèd form sits on that ebon
   throne?
   Asia. The veil has fallen.

Panthea.   I see a mighty darkness
Filling the seat of power, and rays of gloom
Dart round, as light from the meridian sun.
—Ungazed upon and shapeless; neither limb,
Nor form, nor outline; yet we feel it is
A living Spirit.
 Demogorgon. Ask what thou wouldst know.
 Asia. What canst thou tell?
 Demogorgon. All things thou dar'st demand.
 Asia. Who made the living world?
 Demogorgon.   God.
 Asia.   Who made all
That it contains? thought, passion, reason,
 will,   10
Imagination?
 Demogorgon. God: Almighty God.
 Asia. Who made that sense which, when the
 winds of Spring
In rarest visitation, or the voice
Of one belovèd heard in youth alone,
Fills the faint eyes with falling tears which
 dim
The radiant looks of unbewailing flowers,
And leaves this peopled earth a solitude
When it returns no more?
 Demogorgon.   Merciful God.
 Asia. And who made terror, madness, crime,
 remorse,
Which from the links of the great chain of
 things,   20
To every thought within the mind of man
Sway and drag heavily, and each one reels
Under the load towards the pit of death:
Abandoned hope, and love that turns to hate;
And self-contempt, bitterer to drink than
 blood;
Pain, whose unheeded and familiar speech
Is howling, and keen shrieks, day after day;
And Hell, or the sharp fear of Hell?
 Demogorgon.   He reigns.
 Asia. Utter his name: a world pining in pain
Asks but his name: curses shall drag him
 down.   30
 Demogorgon. He reigns.
 Asia.   I feel, I know it: who?
 Demogorgon.   He reigns.
 Asia. Who reigns? There was the Heaven
 and Earth at first,
And Light and Love; then Saturn, from whose
 throne
Time fell, an envious shadow: such the state

Of the earth's primal spirits beneath his sway,
As the calm joy of flowers and living leaves
Before the wind or sun has withered them
And semivital worms! but he refused
The birthright of their being, knowledge,
 power,
The skill which wields the elements, the
 thought   40
Which pierces this dim universe like light,
Self-empire, and the majesty of love;
For thirst of which they fainted. Then Prome-
 theus
Gave wisdom, which is strength, to Jupiter,
And with this law alone, 'Let man be free,'
Clothed him with the dominion of wide
 Heaven.
To know nor faith, nor love, nor law; to be
Omnipotent but friendless is to reign;
And Jove now reigned; for on the race of man
First famine, and then toil, and then disease, 50
Strife, wounds, and ghastly death unseen be-
 fore,
Fell; and the unseasonable seasons drove
With alternating shafts of frost and fire,
Their shelterless, pale tribes to mountain caves:
And in their desert hearts fierce wants he sent,
And mad disquietudes, and shadows idle
Of unreal good, which levied mutual war,
So ruining the lair wherein they raged.
Prometheus saw, and waked the legioned hopes
Which sleep within folded Elysian flowers, 60
Nepenthe, Moly, Amaranth, fadeless blooms,
That they might hide with thin and rainbow
 wings
The shape of Death; and Love he sent to bind
The disunited tendrils of that vine
Which bears the wine of life, the human heart;
And he tamed fire which, like some beast of
 prey,
Most terrible, but lovely, played beneath
The frown of man; and tortured to his will
Iron and gold, the slaves and signs of power,
And gems and poisons, and all subtlest forms
Hidden beneath the mountains and the waves.
He gave man speech, and speech created
 thought,   72
Which is the measure of the universe;
And Science struck the thrones of earth and
 heaven,
Which shook, but fell not; and the harmonious
 mind

Poured itself forth in all-prophetic song;
And music lifted up the listening spirit
Until it walked, exempt from mortal care,
Godlike, o'er the clear billows of sweet sound;
And human hands first mimicked and then
    mocked,   80
With moulded limbs more lovely than its own,
The human form, till marble grew divine;
And mothers, gazing, drank the love men see
Reflected in their race, behold, and perish.
He told the hidden power of herbs and springs,
And Disease drank and slept. Death grew like
    sleep.
He taught the implicated orbits woven
Of the wide-wandering stars; and how the sun
Changes his lair, and by what secret spell
The pale moon is transformed, when her broad
    eye   90
Gazes not on the interlunar sea:
He taught to rule, as life directs the limbs,
The tempest-wingèd chariots of the Ocean,
And the Celt knew the Indian. Cities then
Were built, and through their snow-like col-
    umns flowed
The warm winds, and the azure æther shone,
And the blue sea and shadowy hills were seen.
Such, the alleviations of his state,
Prometheus gave to man, for which he hangs
Withering in destined pain: but who rains
    down   100
Evil, the immedicable plague, which, while
Man looks on his creation like a God
And sees that it is glorious, drives him on,
The wreck of his own will, the scorn of earth,
The outcast, the abandoned, the alone?
Not Jove: while yet his frown shook Heaven,
    ay, when
His adversary from adamantine chains
Cursed him, he trembled like a slave. Declare
Who is his master? Is he too a slave?
    Demogorgon. All spirits are enslaved which
    serve things evil: 110
Thou knowest if Jupiter be such or no.
    Asia. Whom call'st thou God?
    Demogorgon.   I spoke but as ye speak,
For Jove is the supreme of living things.
    Asia. Who is the master of the slave?
    Demogorgon.   If the abysm
Could vomit forth its secrets. . . . But a voice
Is wanting, the deep truth is imageless;
For what would it avail to bid thee gaze

On the revolving world? What to bid speak
Fate, Time, Occasion, Chance, and Change?
    To these
All things are subject but eternal Love.   120
    Asia. So much I asked before, and my heart
    gave
The response thou hast given; and of such truths
Each to itself must be the oracle.
One more demand; and do thou answer me
As mine own soul would answer, did it know
That which I ask. Prometheus shall arise
Henceforth the sun of this rejoicing world:
When shall the destined hour arrive?
    Demogorgon.   Behold!
    Asia. The rocks are cloven, and through the
    purple night
I see cars drawn by rainbow-wingèd steeds 130
Which trample the dim winds: in each there
    stands
A wild-eyed charioteer urging their flight.
Some look behind, as fiends pursued them
    there,
And yet I see no shapes but the keen stars:
Others, with burning eyes, lean forth, and
    drink
With eager lips the wind of their own speed,
As if the thing they loved fled on before,
And now, even now, they clasped it. Their
    bright locks
Stream like a comet's flashing hair: they all 139
Sweep onward.
    Demogorgon. These are the immortal Hours,
Of whom thou didst demand. One waits for
    thee.
    Asia. A spirit with a dreadful countenance
Checks its dark chariot by the craggy gulf.
Unlike thy brethren, ghastly charioteer,
Who art thou? Whither wouldst thou bear
    me? Speak!
    Spirit. I am the shadow of a destiny
More dread than is my aspect: ere yon planet
Has set, the darkness which ascends with me
Shall wrap in lasting night heaven's kingless
    throne.   149
    Asia. What meanest thou?
    Panthea.   That terrible shadow floats
Up from its throne, as may the lurid smoke
Of earthquake-ruined cities o'er the sea.
Lo! it ascends the car; the coursers fly
Terrified: watch its path among the stars
Blackening the night!

Asia.   Thus I am answered: strange!
Panthea. See, near the verge, another chariot
   stays;
An ivory shell inlaid with crimson fire,
Which comes and goes within its sculptured
   rim   158
Of delicate strange tracery; the young spirit
That guides it has the dove-like eyes of hope;
How its soft smiles attract the soul! as light
Lures wingèd insects through the lampless air.

Spirit

My coursers are fed with the lightning,
   They drink of the whirlwind's stream,
And when the red morning is bright'ning
   They bathe in the fresh sunbeam;
   They have strength for their swiftness I
     deem,
Then ascend with me, daughter of Ocean.

I desire: and their speed makes night kindle;
   I fear: they outstrip the Typhoon;   170
Ere the cloud piled on Atlas can dwindle
   We encircle the earth and the moon:
   We shall rest from long labours at noon:
Then ascend with me, daughter of Ocean.

SCENE V.—*The Car pauses within a Cloud on
the top of a snowy Mountain.* ASIA, PAN-
THEA, *and the* SPIRIT OF THE HOUR.

Spirit

On the brink of the night and the morning
   My coursers are wont to respire;
But the Earth has just whispered a warning
   That their flight must be swifter than fire:
   They shall drink the hot speed of desire!

Asia. Thou breathest on their nostrils, but
   my breath
Would give them swifter speed.
Spirit.   Alas! it could not.
Panthea. Oh Spirit! pause, and tell whence
   is the light
Which fills this cloud? the sun is yet unrisen.
Spirit. The sun will rise not until noon.
   Apollo   10
Is held in heaven by wonder; and the light
Which fills this vapour, as the aëreal hue
Of fountain-gazing roses fills the water,
Flows from thy mighty sister.

Panthea.   Yes, I feel—
Asia. What is it with thee, sister? Thou art
   pale.
Panthea. How thou art changed! I dare not
   look on thee;
I feel but see thee not. I scarce endure
The radiance of thy beauty. Some good change
Is working in the elements, which suffer
Thy presence thus unveiled. The Nereids tell
That on the day when the clear hyaline   21
Was cloven at thine uprise, and thou didst stand
Within a veinèd shell, which floated on
Over the calm floor of the crystal sea,
Among the Ægean isles, and by the shores
Which bear thy name; love, like the atmos-
   phere
Of the sun's fire filling the living world,
Burst from thee, and illumined earth and
   heaven
And the deep ocean and the sunless caves
And all that dwells within them; till grief cast
Eclipse upon the soul from which it came: 31
Such art thou now; nor is it I alone,
Thy sister, thy companion, thine own chosen
   one,
But the whole world which seeks thy sympathy.
Hearest thou not sounds i' the air which speak
   the love
Of all articulate beings? Feelest thou not
The inanimate winds enamoured of thee? List!
                           [*Music.*
Asia. Thy words are sweeter than aught else
   but his
Whose echoes they are: yet all love is sweet,
Given or returned. Common as light is love,
And its familiar voice wearies not ever.   41
Like the wide heaven, the all-sustaining air,
It makes the reptile equal to the God:
They who inspire it most are fortunate,
As I am now; but those who feel it most
Are happier still, after long sufferings,
As I shall soon become.
Panthea.   List! Spirits speak.

Voice in the Air, *singing*

Life of Life! thy lips enkindle
   With their love the breath between them;
And thy smiles before they dwindle   50
   Make the cold air fire; then screen them
In those looks, where whoso gazes
Faints, entangled in their mazes.

Child of Light! thy limbs are burning
  Through the vest which seems to hide them;
As the radiant lines of morning
  Through the clouds ere they divide them;
And this atmosphere divinest
Shrouds thee wheresoe'er thou shinest.

Fair are others; none beholds thee,   60
  But thy voice sounds low and tender
Like the fairest, for it folds thee
  From the sight, that liquid splendour,
And all feel, yet see thee never,
As I feel now, lost for ever!

Lamp of Earth! where'er thou movest
  Its dim shapes are clad with brightness,
And the souls of whom thou lovest
  Walk upon the winds with lightness,
Till they fail, as I am failing,   70
Dizzy, lost, yet unbewailing!

Asia

My soul is an enchanted boat,
  Which, like a sleeping swan, doth float
Upon the silver waves of thy sweet singing;
  And thine doth like an angel sit
  Beside a helm conducting it,
Whilst all the winds with melody are ringing.
  It seems to float ever, for ever,
  Upon that many-winding river,
  Between mountains, woods, abysses,   80
  A paradise of wildernesses!
Till, like one in slumber bound,
Borne to the ocean, I float down, around,
Into a sea profound, of ever-spreading sound:

  Meanwhile thy spirit lifts its pinions
  In music's most serene dominions;
Catching the winds that fan that happy heaven.
  And we sail on, away, afar,
  Without a course, without a star,
But, by the instinct of sweet music driven; 90
  Till through Elysian garden islets
  By thee, most beautiful of pilots,
  Where never mortal pinnace glided,
  The boat of my desire is guided:
Realms where the air we breathe is love,
Which in the winds and on the waves doth
    move,
Harmonizing this earth with what we feel
    above.

We have passed Age's icy caves,
  And Manhood's dark and tossing waves,
And Youth's smooth ocean, smiling to betray:
  Beyond the glassy gulfs we flee   101
  Of shadow-peopled Infancy,
Through Death and Birth, to a diviner day;
  A paradise of vaulted bowers,
  Lit by downward-gazing flowers,
  And watery paths that wind between
  Wildernesses calm and green,
Peopled by shapes too bright to see,
And rest, having beheld; somewhat like thee;
Which walk upon the sea, and chant melodi-
    ously!   110

END OF THE SECOND ACT

ACT III

SCENE I.—*Heaven.* JUPITER *on his Throne;*
  THETIS *and the other Deities assembled*

Jupiter. Ye congregated powers of heaven,
    who share
The glory and the strength of him ye serve,
Rejoice! henceforth I am omnipotent,
All else had been subdued to me; alone
The soul of man, like unextinguished fire,
Yet burns towards heaven with fierce reproach,
    and doubt,
And lamentation, and reluctant prayer,
Hurling up insurrection, which might make
Our antique empire insecure, though built
On eldest faith, and hell's coeval, fear;   10
And though my curses through the pendulous
    air,
Like snow on herbless peaks, fall flake by
    flake,
And cling to it; though under my wrath's
    night
It climbs the crags of life, step after step,
Which wound it, as ice wounds unsandalled
    feet,
It yet remains supreme o'er misery,
Aspiring, unrepressed, yet soon to fall:
Even now have I begotten a strange wonder,
That fatal child, the terror of the earth,
Who waits but till the destined hour arrive, 20
Bearing from Demogorgon's vacant throne
The dreadful might of ever-living limbs
Which clothed that awful spirit unbeheld,
To redescend, and trample out the spark.

Pour forth heaven's wine, Idæan Ganymede,
And let it fill the Dædal cups like fire,
And from the flower-inwoven soil divine
Ye all-triumphant harmonies arise,
As dew from earth under the twilight stars:
Drink! be the nectar circling through your
    veins   30
The soul of joy, ye ever-living Gods,
Till exultation burst in one wide voice
Like music from Elysian winds.
                                 And thou
Ascend beside me, veilèd in the light
Of the desire which makes thee one with me,
Thetis, bright image of eternity!
When thou didst cry, 'Insufferable might!
God! Spare me! I sustain not the quick flames,
The penetrating presence; all my being,
Like him whom the Numidian seps did thaw
Into a dew with poison, is dissolved,   41
Sinking through its foundations': even then
Two mighty spirits, mingling, made a third
Mightier than either, which, unbodied now,
Between us floats, felt, although unbeheld,
Waiting the incarnation, which ascends,
(Hear ye the thunder of the fiery wheels
Griding the winds?) from Demogorgon's
    throne.
Victory! victory! Feel'st thou not, O world,
The earthquake of his chariot thundering up 50
Olympus?
    [*The Car of the* HOUR *arrives.* DEMO-
    GORGON *descends, and moves to-*
    wards the Throne of JUPITER.
    Awful shape, what art thou? Speak!
Demogorgon. Eternity. Demand no direr
    name.
Descend, and follow me down the abyss.
I am thy child, as thou wert Saturn's child;
Mightier than thee: and we must dwell to-
    gether
Henceforth in darkness. Lift thy lightnings
    not.
The tyranny of heaven none may retain,
Or reassume, or hold, succeeding thee:
Yet if thou wilt, as 'tis the destiny
Of trodden worms to writhe till they are
    dead,
Put forth thy might.
    Jupiter.   Detested prodigy!   61
Even thus beneath the deep Titanian prisons
I trample thee! thou lingerest?

                                  Mercy! mercy!
No pity, no release, no respite! Oh,
That thou wouldst make mine enemy my
    judge,
Even where he hangs, seared by my long re-
    venge,
On Caucasus! he would not doom me thus.
Gentle, and just, and dreadless, is he not
The monarch of the world? What then art
    thou?
No refuge! no appeal!
                      Sink with me then, 70
We two will sink on the wide waves of ruin,
Even as a vulture and a snake outspent
Drop, twisted in inextricable fight,
Into a shoreless sea. Let hell unlock
Its mounded oceans of tempestuous fire,
And whelm on them into the bottomless void
This desolated world, and thee, and me,
The conqueror and the conquered, and the
    wreck
Of that for which they combated.
                            Ai! Ai!
The elements obey me not. I sink   80
Dizzily down, ever, for ever, down.
And, like a cloud, mine enemy above
Darkens my fall with victory! Ai, Ai!

SCENE II.—*The Mouth of a great River in the*
    Island Atlantis. OCEAN *is discovered re-*
    clining near the Shore; APOLLO *stands be-*
    side him.

    Ocean. He fell, thou sayest, beneath his
    conqueror's frown?
    Apollo. Ay, when the strife was ended which
    made dim
The orb I rule, and shook the solid stars,
The terrors of his eye illumined heaven
With sanguine light, through the thick ragged
    skirts
Of the victorious darkness, as he fell:
Like the last glare of day's red agony,
Which, from a rent among the fiery clouds,
Burns far along the tempest-wrinkled deep.
    Ocean. He sunk to the abyss? To the dark
    void?   10
    Apollo. An eagle so caught in some bursting
    cloud
On Caucasus, his thunder-baffled wings
Entangled in the whirlwind, and his eyes

Which gazed on the undazzling sun, now
    blinded
By the white lightning, while the ponderous
    hail
Beats on his struggling form, which sinks at
    length
Prone, and the aëreal ice clings over it.
    Ocean. Henceforth the fields of heaven-
    reflecting sea
Which are my realm, will heave, unstained
    with blood,
Beneath the uplifting winds, like plains of
    corn   20
Swayed by the summer air; my streams will
    flow
Round many-peopled continents, and round
Fortunate isles; and from their glassy thrones
Blue Proteus and his humid nymphs shall
    mark
The shadow of fair ships, as mortals see
The floating bark of the light-laden moon
With that white star, its sightless pilot's crest,
Borne down the rapid sunset's ebbing sea;
Tracking their path no more by blood and
    groans,
And desolation, and the mingled voice   30
Of slavery and command; but by the light
Of wave-reflected flowers, and floating odours,
And music soft, and mild, free, gentle voices,
And sweetest music, such as spirits love.
    Apollo. And I shall gaze not on the deeds
    which make
My mind obscure with sorrow, as eclipse
Darkens the sphere I guide; but list, I hear
The small, clear, silver lute of the young Spirit
That sits i' the morning star.
    Ocean.   Thou must away;
Thy steeds will pause at even, till when fare-
    well: 40
The loud deep calls me home even now to feed
    it
With azure calm out of the emerald urns
Which stand for ever full beside my throne.
Behold the Nereids under the green sea,
Their wavering limbs borne on the wind-like
    stream,
Their white arms lifted o'er their streaming hair
With garlands pied and starry sea-flower
    crowns,
Hastening to grace their mighty sister's joy.
                  [*A sound of waves is heard.*

It is the unpastured sea hungering for calm.
Peace, monster; I come now. Farewell.
    Apollo.   Farewell. 50

SCENE III.—*Caucasus.* PROMETHEUS, HER-
    CULES, IONE, *the* EARTH, SPIRITS, ASIA,
    and PANTHEA, *borne in the Car with the*
    SPIRIT OF THE HOUR. HERCULES *unbinds*
    PROMETHEUS, *who descends.*

    Hercules. Most glorious among Spirits, thus
    doth strength
To wisdom, courage, and long-suffering love,
And thee, who art the form they animate,
Minister like a slave.
    Prometheus.   Thy gentle words
Are sweeter even than freedom long desired
And long delayed.
                    Asia, thou light of life,
Shadow of beauty unbeheld: and ye,
Fair sister nymphs, who made long years of
    pain
Sweet to remember, through your love and
    care:
Henceforth we will not part. There is a cave, 10
All overgrown with trailing odorous plants,
Which curtain out the day with leaves and
    flowers,
And paved with veinèd emerald, and a fountain
Leaps in the midst with an awakening sound.
From its curved roof the mountain's frozen
    tears
Like snow, or silver, or long diamond spires,
Hang downward, raining forth a doubtful
    light:
And there is heard the ever-moving air,
Whispering without from tree to tree, and
    birds,
And bees; and all around are mossy seats, 20
And the rough walls are clothed with long
    soft grass;
A simple dwelling, which shall be our own;
Where we will sit and talk of time and change,
As the world ebbs and flows, ourselves un-
    changed.
What can hide man from mutability?
And if ye sigh, then I will smile; and thou,
Ione, shalt chant fragments of sea-music,
Until I weep, when ye shall smile away
The tears she brought, which yet were sweet
    to shed.   29

We will entangle buds and flowers and beams
Which twinkle on the fountain's brim, and make
Strange combinations out of common things,
Like human babes in their brief innocence;
And we will search, with looks and words of love,
For hidden thoughts, each lovelier than the last,
Our unexhausted spirits; and like lutes
Touched by the skill of the enamoured wind,
Weave harmonies divine, yet ever new,
From difference sweet where discord cannot be;
And hither come, sped on the charmèd winds,
Which meet from all the points of heaven, as bees   41
From every flower aëreal Enna feeds,
At their known island-homes in Himera,
The echoes of the human world, which tell
Of the low voice of love, almost unheard,
And dove-eyed pity's murmured pain, and music,
Itself the echo of the heart, and all
That tempers or improves man's life, now free;
And lovely apparitions,—dim at first,
Then radiant, as the mind, arising bright   50
From the embrace of beauty (whence the forms
Of which these are the phantoms) casts on them
The gathered rays which are reality—
Shall visit us, the progeny immortal
Of Painting, Sculpture, and rapt Poesy,
And arts, though unimagined, yet to be.
The wandering voices and the shadows these
Of all that man becomes, the mediators
Of that best worship, love, by him and us
Given and returned; swift shapes and sounds, which grow   60
More fair and soft as man grows wise and kind,
And, veil by veil, evil and error fall:
Such virtue has the cave and place around.
          [*Turning to the* SPIRIT OF THE HOUR.
For thee, fair Spirit, one toil remains. Ione,
Give her that curvèd shell, which Proteus old
Made Asia's nuptial boon, breathing within it
A voice to be accomplished, and which thou
Didst hide in grass under the hollow rock.

Ione. Thou most desired Hour, more loved and lovely
Than all thy sisters, this is the mystic shell; 70
See the pale azure fading into silver
Lining it with a soft yet glowing light:
Looks it not like lulled music sleeping there?
          Spirit. It seems in truth the fairest shell of Ocean:
Its sounds must be at once both sweet and strange.
          Prometheus. Go, borne over the cities of mankind
On whirlwind-footed coursers: once again
Outspeed the sun around the orbèd world;
And as thy chariot cleaves the kindling air,
Thou breathe into the many-folded shell,   80
Loosening its mighty music; it shall be
As thunder mingled with clear echoes: then
Return; and thou shalt dwell beside our cave.
And thou, O, Mother Earth!—
          The Earth.   I hear, I feel;
Thy lips are on me, and their touch runs down
Even to the adamantine central gloom
Along these marble nerves; 'tis life, 'tis joy,
And through my withered, old, and icy frame
The warmth of an immortal youth shoots down
Circling. Henceforth the many children fair
Folded in my sustaining arms; all plants,   91
And creeping forms, and insects rainbow-winged,
And birds, and beasts, and fish, and human shapes,
Which drew disease and pain from my wan bosom,
Draining the poison of despair, shall take
And interchange sweet nutriment; to me
Shall they become like sister-antelopes
By one fair dam, snow-white and swift as wind,
Nursed among lilies near a brimming stream.
The dew-mists of my sunless sleep shall float
Under the stars like balm: night-folded flowers   101
Shall suck unwithering hues in their repose:
And men and beasts in happy dreams shall gather
Strength for the coming day, and all its joy:
And death shall be the last embrace of her
Who takes the life she gavè, even as a mother
Folding her child, says, 'Leave me not again.'

Asia. Oh, mother! wherefore speak the name
    of death?
Cease they to love, and move, and breathe,
    and speak,
Who die?
   The Earth. It would avail not to reply; 110
Thou art immortal, and this tongue is known
But to the uncommunicating dead.
Death is the veil which those who live call
    life:
They sleep, and it is lifted: and meanwhile
In mild variety the seasons mild
With rainbow-skirted showers, and odorous
    winds,
And long blue meteors cleansing the dull night,
And the life-kindling shafts of the keen sun's
All-piercing bow, and the dew-mingled rain
Of the calm moonbeams, a soft influence
    mild,   120
Shall clothe the forests and the fields, ay, even
The crag-built deserts of the barren deep,
With ever-living leaves, and fruits, and flow-
    ers.
And thou! There is a cavern where my spirit
Was panted forth in anguish whilst thy pain
Made my heart mad, and those who did inhale
    it
Became mad too, and built a temple there,
And spoke, and were oracular, and lured
The erring nations round to mutual war.
And faithless faith, such as Jove kept with
    thee;   130
Which breath now rises, as amongst tall weeds
A violet's exhalation, and it fills
With a serener light and crimson air
Intense, yet soft, the rocks and woods around;
It feeds the quick growth of the serpent vine,
And the dark linkèd ivy tangling wild,
And budding, blown, or odour-faded blooms
Which star the winds with points of coloured
    light,
As they rain through them, and bright golden
    globes
Of fruit, suspended in their own green heaven,
And through their veinèd leaves and amber
    stems   141
The flowers whose purple and translucid bowls
Stand ever mantling with aëreal dew,
The drink of spirits: and it circles round,
Like the soft waving wings of noonday dreams,
Inspiring calm and happy thoughts, like mine,

And thou art thus restored. This cave is thine.
Arise! Appear!
             [A SPIRIT *rises in the likeness*
                  of a winged child.
          This is my torch-bearer;
Who let his lamp out in old time gazing
On eyes from which he kindled it anew   150
With love, which is as fire, sweet daughter
    mine,
For such is that within thine own. Run, way-
    ward,
And guide this company beyond the peak
Of Bacchic Nysia, Mænad-haunted mountain,
And beyond Indus and its tribute rivers,
Trampling the torrent streams and glassy lakes
With feet unwet, unwearied, undelaying,
And up the green ravine, across the vale,
Beside the windless and crystalline pool,
Where ever lies, on unerasing waves,   160
The image of a temple, built above,
Distinct with column, arch, and architrave,
And palm-like capital, and over-wrought,
And populous with most living imagery,
Praxitelean shapes, whose marble smiles
Fill the hushed air with everlasting love.
It is deserted now, but once it bore
Thy name, Prometheus; there the emulous
    youths
Bore to thy honour through the divine gloom
The lamp which was thine emblem; even as
    those   170
Who bear the untransmitted torch of hope
Into the grave, across the night of life,
As thou hast borne it most triumphantly
To this far goal of Time. Depart, farewell.
Beside that temple is the destined cave.

SCENE IV.—*A Forest. In the Backbround a
    Cave.* PROMETHEUS, ASIA, PANTHEA,
    IONE, *and the* SPIRIT OF THE EARTH.

  Ione. Sister, it is not earthly: how it glides
Under the leaves! how on its head there burns
A light, like a green star, whose emerald beams
Are twined with its fair hair! how, as it moves,
The splendour drops in flakes upon the grass!
Knowest thou it?
   Panthea.   It is the delicate spirit
That guides the earth through heaven. From
    afar
The populous constellations call that light

The loveliest of the planets; and sometimes
It floats along the spray of the salt sea,   10
Or makes its chariot of a foggy cloud,
Or walks through fields or cities while men
  sleep,
Or o'er the mountain tops, or down the rivers,
Or through the green waste wilderness, as
  now,
Wondering at all it sees. Before Jove reigned
It loved our sister Asia, and it came
Each leisure hour to drink the liquid light
Out of her eyes, for which it said it thirsted
As one bit by a dipsas, and with her
It made its childish confidence, and told her 20
All it had known or seen, for it saw much,
Yet idly reasoned what it saw; and called her—
For whence it sprung it knew not, nor do I—
Mother, dear mother.

    The Spirit of the Earth (*running to Asia*).
                 Mother, dearest mother;
May I then talk with thee as I was wont?
May I then hide my eyes in thy soft arms,
After thy looks have made them tired of joy?
May I then play beside thee the long noons,
When work is none in the bright silent air?
    Asia. I love thee, gentlest being, and hence-
forth   30
Can cherish thee unenvied: speak, I pray:
Thy simple talk once solaced, now delights.
    Spirit of the Earth. Mother, I am grown
    wiser, though a child
Cannot be wise like thee, within this day;
And happier too; happier and wiser both.
Thou knowest that toads, and snakes, and
  loathly worms,
And venomous and malicious beasts, and
  boughs
That bore ill berries in the woods, were ever
An hindrance to my walks o'er the green
  world:
And that, among the haunts of humankind, 40
Hard-featured men, or with proud, angry
  looks,
Or cold, staid gait, or false and hollow smiles,
Or the dull sneer of self-loved ignorance,
Or other such foul masks, with which ill
  thoughts
Hide that fair being whom we spirits call man;
And women too, ugliest of all things evil,
(Though fair, even in a world where thou art
  fair,

When good and kind, free and sincere like
  thee),
When false or frowning made me sick at heart
To pass them, though they slept, and I un-
  seen.   50
Well, my path lately lay through a great city
Into the woody hills surrounding it:
A sentinel was sleeping at the gate:
When there was heard a sound, so loud, it
  shook
The towers amid the moonlight, yet more
  sweet
Than any voice but thine, sweetest of all;
A long, long sound, as it would never end:
And all the inhabitants leaped suddenly
Out of their rest, and gathered in the streets,
Looking in wonder up to Heaven, while yet
The music pealed along. I hid myself   61
Within a fountain in the public square,
Where I lay like the reflex of the moon
Seen in a wave under green leaves; and soon
Those ugly human shapes and visages
Of which I spoke as having wrought me pain,
Passed floating through the air, and fading still
Into the winds that scattered them; and those
From whom they passed seemed mild and
  lovely forms
After some foul disguise had fallen, and all 70
Were somewhat changed, and after brief sur-
  prise
And greetings of delighted wonder, all
Went to their sleep again: and when the dawn
Came, wouldst thou think that toads, and
  snakes, and efts,
Could e'er be beautiful? yet so they were,
And that with little change of shape or hue:
All things had put their evil nature off:
I cannot tell my joy, when o'er a lake
Upon a drooping bough with nightshade
  twined,
I saw two azure halcyons clinging downward
And thinning one bright bunch of amber ber-
  ries,   81
With quick long beaks, and in the deep there
  lay
Those lovely forms imaged as in a sky;
So, with my thoughts full of these happy
  changes,
We meet again, the happiest change of all.
    Asia. And never will we part, till thy chaste
    sister

Who guides the frozen and inconstant moon
Will look on thy more warm and equal light
Till her heart thaw like flakes of April snow
And love thee.
   Spirit of the Earth. What; as Asia loves
     Prometheus?   90
   Asia. Peace, wanton, thou art yet not old
     enough.
Think ye by gazing on each other's eyes
To multiply your lovely selves, and fill
With spherèd fires the interlunar air?
   Spirit of the Earth. Nay, mother, while my
     sister trims her lamp
'Tis hard I should go darkling.
   Asia.   Listen; look!
     [*The* SPIRIT OF THE HOUR *enters.*
   Prometheus. We feel what thou hast heard
     and seen: yet speak.
   Spirit of the Hour. Soon as the sound had
     ceased whose thunder filled
The abysses of the sky and the wide earth,
There was a change: the impalpable thin air
And the all-circling sunlight were transformed,
As if the sense of love dissolved in them   102
Had folded itself round the spherèd world.
My vision then grew clear, and I could see
Into the mysteries of the universe:
Dizzy as with delight I floated down,
Winnowing the lightsome air with languid
   plumes,
My coursers sought their birthplace in the sun,
Where they henceforth will live exempt from
   toil,
Pasturing flowers of vegetable fire;   110
And where my moonlike car will stand within
A temple, gazed upon by Phidian forms
Of thee, and Asia, and the Earth, and me,
And you fair nymphs looking the love we
   feel,—
In memory of the tidings it has borne,—
Beneath a dome fretted with graven flowers,
Poised on twelve columns of resplendent stone,
And open to the bright and liquid sky.
Yoked to it by an amphisbaenic snake   119
The likeness of those wingèd steeds will mock
The flight from which they find repose. Alas,
Whither has wandered now my partial tongue
When all remains untold which ye would hear?
As I have said, I floated to the earth:
It was, as it is still, the pain of bliss
To move, to breathe, to be; I wandering went

Among the haunts and dwellings of mankind,
And first was disappointed not to see
Such mighty change as I had felt within
Expressed in outward things; but soon I
   looked,   130
And behold, thrones were kingless, and men
   walked
One with the other even as spirits do,
None fawned, none trampled; hate, disdain, or
   fear,
Self-love or self-contempt, on human brows
No more inscribed, as o'er the gate of hell,
'All hope abandon ye who enter here';
None frowned, none trembled, none with
   eager fear
Gazed on another's eye of cold command,
Until the subject of a tyrant's will
Became, worse fate, the abject of his own, 140
Which spurred him, like an outspent horse,
   to death.
None wrought his lips in truth-entangling
   lines
Which smiled the lie his tongue disdained to
   speak;
None, with firm sneer, trod out in his own
   heart
The sparks of love and hope till these re-
   mained
Those bitter ashes, a soul self-consumed,
And the wretch crept a vampire among men,
Infecting all with his own hideous ill;
None talked that common, false, cold, hollow
   talk
Which makes the heart deny the *yes* it breathes,
Yet question that unmeant hypocrisy   151
With such a self-mistrust as has no name.
And women, too, frank, beautiful, and kind
As the free heaven which rains fresh light and
   dew
On the wide earth, past; gentle radiant forms,
From custom's evil taint exempt and pure;
Speaking the wisdom once they could not
   think,
Looking emotions once they feared to feel,
And changed to all which once they dared
   not be,
Yet being now, made earth like heaven; nor
   pride,   160
Nor jealousy, nor envy, nor ill shame,
The bitterest of those drops of treasured gall,
Spoilt the sweet taste of the nepenthe, love.

Thrones, altars, judgment-seats, and prisons; wherein,
And beside which, by wretched men were borne
Sceptres, tiaras, swords, and chains, and tomes
Of reasoned wrong, glozed on by ignorance,
Were like those monstrous and barbaric shapes,
The ghosts of a no-more-remembered fame,
Which, from their unworn obelisks, look forth   170
In triumph o'er the palaces and tombs
Of those who were their conquerors: mouldering round,
These imaged to the pride of kings and priests
A dark yet mighty faith, a power as wide
As is the world it wasted, and are now
But an astonishment; even so the tools
And emblems of its last captivity,
Amid the dwellings of the peopled earth,
Stand, not o'erthrown, but unregarded now.
And those foul shapes, abhorred by god and man,—   180
Which, under many a name and many a form
Strange, savage, ghastly, dark and execrable,
Were Jupiter, the tyrant of the world;
And which the nations, panic-stricken, served
With blood, and hearts broken by long hope, and love
Dragged to his altars soiled and garlandless,
And slain amid men's unreclaiming tears,
Flattering the thing they feared, which fear was hate,—
Frown, mouldering fast, o'er their abandoned shrines:
The painted veil, by those who were, called life,   190
Which mimicked, as with colours idly spread,
All men believed or hoped, is torn aside;
The loathsome mask has fallen, the man remains
Sceptreless, free, uncircumscribed, but man
Equal, unclassed, tribeless, and nationless,
Exempt from awe, worship, degree, the king
Over himself; just, gentle, wise: but man
Passionless?——no, yet free from guilt or pain,
Which were, for his will made or suffered them,
Nor yet exempt, though ruling them like slaves,   200

From chance, and death, and mutability,
The clogs of that which else might oversoar
The loftiest star of unascended heaven,
Pinnacled dim in the intense inane.

END OF THE THIRD ACT

ACT IV

SCENE.—*A Part of the Forest near the Cave of* PROMETHEUS. PANTHEA *and* IONE *are sleeping: they awaken gradually during the first song.*

Voice of unseen Spirits

The pale stars are gone!
For the sun, their swift shepherd,
To their folds them compelling,
In the depths of the dawn,
Hastes, in meteor-eclipsing array, and they flee
Beyond his blue dwelling,
As fawns flee the leopard.
But where are ye?

A Train of dark Forms and Shadows passes by confusedly, singing.

Here, oh, here:
We bear the bier   10
Of the Father of many a cancelled year!
Spectres we
Of the dead Hours be,
We bear Time to his tomb in eternity.

Strew, oh, strew
Hair, not yew!
Wet the dusty pall with tears, not dew!
Be the faded flowers
Of Death's bare bowers
Spread on the corpse of the King of Hours!   20

Haste, oh, haste!
As shades are chased,
Trembling, by day, from heaven's blue waste.
We melt away,
Like dissolving spray,
From the children of a diviner day,
With the lullaby
Of winds that die
On the bosom of their own harmony!

Ione

What dark forms were they?   30

Panthea

The past Hours weak and gray,
  With the spoil which their toil
    Raked together
From the conquest but One could foil.

Ione

Have they passed?

Panthea

        They have passed;
  They outspeeded the blast,
  While 'tis said, they are fled:

Ione

Whither, oh, whither?

Panthea

To the dark, to the past, to the dead.

Voice of unseen Spirits

Bright clouds float in heaven,   40
Dew-stars gleam on earth,
Waves assemble on ocean,
  They are gathered and driven
By the storm of delight, by the panic of glee!
  They shake with emotion,
  They dance in their mirth.
    But where are ye?

The pine boughs are singing
Old songs with new gladness,
The billows and fountains   50
  Fresh music are flinging,
Likes the notes of a spirit from land and from
    sea;
  The storms mock the mountains
  With the thunder of gladness.
    But where are ye?

Ione. What charioteers are these?
Panthea.   Where are their chariots?

Semichorus of Hours

The voice of the Spirits of Air and of Earth
  Have drawn back the figured curtain of sleep
Which covered our being and darkened our
    birth
  In the deep.

A Voice

In the deep?

Semichorus II

  Oh, below the deep.   60

Semichorus I

An hundred ages we had been kept
  Cradled in visions of hate and care,
And each one who waked as his brother slept,
  Found the truth—

Semichorus II

  Worse than his visions were!

Semichorus I

We have heard the lute of Hope in sleep;
  We have known the voice of Love in
    dreams;
We have felt the wand of Power, and leap—

Semichorus II

  As the billows leap in the morning beams!

Chorus

Weave the dance on the floor of the breeze,
  Pierce with song heaven's silent light,   70
Enchant the day that too swiftly flees,
  To check its flight ere the cave of Night.

Once the hungry Hours were hounds
  Which chased the day like a bleeding deer,
And it limped and stumbled with many
    wounds
  Through the nightly dells of the desert year.

But now, oh weave the mystic measure
  Of music, and dance, and shapes of light,
Let the Hours, and the spirits of might and
    pleasure,
  Like the clouds and sunbeams, unite.

A Voice

        Unite!   80
Panthea. See, where the Spirits of the human mind
Wrapped in sweet sounds, as in bright veils,
  approach.

Chorus of Spirits

We join the throng
  Of the dance and the song,
By the whirlwind of gladness borne along,
  As the flying-fish leap
  From the Indian deep,
And mix with the sea-birds, half asleep.

Chorus of Hours

Whence come ye, so wild and so fleet,
For sandals of lightning are on your feet,   90
And your wings are soft and swift as thought,
And your eyes are as love which is veilèd not?

Chorus of Spirits

We come from the mind
  Of human kind
Which was late so dusk, and obscene, and
    blind,
    Now 'tis an ocean
    Of clear emotion,
A heaven of serene and mighty motion.

From that deep abyss
  Of wonder and bliss,   100
Whose caverns are crystal palaces;
  From those skiey towers
  Where Thought's crowned powers
Sit watching your dance, ye happy Hours!
  From the dim recesses
  Of woven caresses,
Where lovers catch ye by your loose tresses;
  From the azure isles,
  Where sweet Wisdom smiles,
Delaying your ships with her siren wiles. 110

From the temples high
  Of Man's ear and eye,
Roofed over Sculpture and Poesy;
  From the murmurings
  Of the unsealed springs
Where Science bedews her Dædal wings.

Years after years,
  Through blood, and tears,
And a thick hell of hatreds, and hopes, and
    fears;
  We waded and flew,   120
  And the islets were few
Where the bud-blighted flowers of happiness
    grew.

Our feet now, every palm,
  Are sandalled with calm,
And the dew of our wings is a rain of balm;
  And, beyond our eyes,
  The human love lies
Which makes all it gazes on Paradise.

Chorus of Spirits and Hours

Then weave the web of the mystic meas-
  ure;
From the depths of the sky and the ends of
  the earth,   130
Come, swift Spirits of might and of pleas-
  ure,
Fill the dance and the music of mirth,
  As the waves of a thousand streams rush by
To an ocean of splendour and harmony!

Chorus of Spirits

Our spoil is won,
  Our task is done,
We are free to dive, or soar, or run;
  Beyond and around,
  Or within the bound
Which clips the world with darkness round.

We'll pass the eyes   141
  Of the starry skies
Into the hoar deep to colonize:
  Death, Chaos, and Night,
  From the sound of our flight,
Shall flee, like mist from a tempest's might.

And Earth, Air, and Light,
  And the Spirit of Might,
Which drives round the stars in their fiery
    flight;
  And love, Thought, and Breath,   150
  The powers that quell Death,
Wherever we soar shall assemble beneath.

And our singing shall build
  In the void's loose field
A world for the Spirit of Wisdom to wield;
  We will take our plan
  From the new world of man,
And our work shall be called the Promethean.

Chorus of Hours

Break the dance, and scatter the song;
  Let some depart, and some remain.   160

Semichorus I

We, beyond heaven, are driven along:

Semichorus II

Us the enchantments of earth retain:

Semichorus I

Ceaseless, and rapid, and fierce, and free,
With the Spirits which build a new earth and
    sea,
And a heaven where yet heaven could never
    be;

Semichorus II

Solemn, and slow, and serene, and bright,
Leading the Day and outspeeding the Night,
With the powers of a world of perfect light;

Semichorus I

We whirl, singing loud, round the gathering
    sphere,
Till the trees, and the beasts, and the clouds
    appear   170
From its chaos made calm by love, not fear.

Semichorus II

We encircle the ocean and mountains of earth,
And the happy forms of its death and birth
Change to the music of our sweet mirth.

Chorus of Hours and Spirits

Break the dance, and scatter the song,
  Let some depart, and some remain,
Wherever we fly we lead along
In leashes, like starbeams, soft yet strong,
  The clouds that are heavy with love's sweet
    rain.

Panthea. Ha! they are gone!
Ione.   Yet feel you no delight 180
From the past sweetness?
Panthea.   As the bare green hill
When some soft cloud vanishes into rain,
Laughs with a thousand drops of sunny water
To the unpavilioned sky!
Ione.   Even whilst we speak
New notes arise. What is that awful sound?
Panthea. 'Tis the deep music of the rolling
    world
Kindling within the strings of the waved air
Æolian modulations.
Ione.   Listen too,
How every pause is filled with under-notes,
Clear, silver, icy, keen, awakening tones, 190
Which pierce the sense, and live within the
    soul,
As the sharp stars pierce winter's crystal air
And gaze upon themselves within the sea.

Panthea. But see where through two open-
    ings in the forest
Which hanging branches overcanopy,
And where two runnels of a rivulet,
Between the close moss violet-inwoven,
Have made their path of melody, like sisters
Who part with sighs that they may meet in
    smiles,
Turning their dear disunion to an isle   200
Of lovely grief, a wood of sweet sad thoughts;
Two visions of strange radiance float upon
The ocean-like enchantment of strong sound,
Which flows intenser, keener, deeper yet
Under the ground and through the windless
    air.
Ione. I see a chariot like that thinnest boat,
In which the Mother of the Months is borne
By ebbing light into her western cave,
When she upsprings from interlunar dreams;
O'er which is curved an orblike canopy   210
Of gentle darkness, and the hills and woods,
Distinctly seen through that dusk aery veil,
Regard like shapes in an enchanter's glass;
Its wheels are solid clouds, azure and gold,
Such as the genii of the thunderstorm
Pile on the floor of the illumined sea
When the sun rushes under it; they roll
And move and grow as with an inward wind;
Within it sits a wingèd infant, white
Its countenance, like the whiteness of bright
    snow,   220
Its plumes are as feathers of sunny frost,
Its limbs gleam white, through the wind-
    flowing folds
Of its white robe, woof of ethereal pearl.
Its hair is white, the brightness of white light
Scattered in strings; yet its two eyes are
    heavens
Of liquid darkness, which the Deity
Within seems pouring, as a storm is poured
From jaggèd clouds, out of their arrowy
    lashes,
Tempering the cold and radiant air around,
With fire that is not brightness; in its hand
It sways a quivering moonbeam, from whose
    point   231
A guiding power directs the chariot's prow
Over its wheelèd clouds, which as they roll
Over the grass, and flowers, and waves, wake
    sounds,
Sweet as a singing rain of silver dew.

Panthea. And from the other opening in the wood
Rushes, with loud and whirlwind harmony,
A sphere, which is as many thousand spheres,
Solid as crystal, yet through all its mass
Flow, as through empty space, music and
light: 240
Ten thousand orbs involving and involved,
Purple and azure, white, and green, and golden,
Sphere within sphere; and every space between
Peopled with unimaginable shapes,
Such as ghosts dream dwell in the lampless deep,
Yet each inter-transpicuous, and they whirl
Over each other with a thousand motions,
Upon a thousand sightless axles spinning,
And with the force of self-destroying swiftness,
Intensely, slowly, solemnly roll on, 250
Kindling with mingled sounds, and many tones,
Intelligible words and music wild.
With mighty whirl the multitudinous orb
Grinds the bright brook into an azure mist
Of elemental subtlety, like light;
And the wild odour of the forest flowers,
The music of the living grass and air,
The emerald light of leaf-entangled beams
Round its intense yet self-conflicting speed,
Seem kneaded into one aëreal mass 260
Which drowns the sense. Within the orb itself,
Pillowed upon its alabaster arms,
Like to a child o'erwearied with sweet toil,
On its own folded wings, and wavy hair,
The Spirit of the Earth is laid asleep,
And you can see its little lips are moving,
Amid the changing light of their own smiles,
Like one who talks of what he loves in dream.
Ione. 'Tis only mocking the orb's harmony.
Panthea. And from a star upon its forehead, shoot, 270
Like swords of azure fire, or golden spears
With tyrant-quelling myrtle overtwined,
Embleming heaven and earth united now,
Vast beams like spokes of some invisible wheel
Which whirl as the orb whirls, swifter than thought,
Filling the abyss with sun-like lightenings,
And perpendicular now, and now transverse,
Pierce the dark soil, and as they pierce and pass,

Make bare the secrets of the earth's deep heart;
Infinite mines of adamant and gold, 280
Valueless stones, and unimagined gems,
And caverns on crystalline columns poised
With vegetable silver overspread;
Wells of unfathomed fire, and water springs
Whence the great sea, even as a child is fed,
Whose vapours clothe earth's monarch mountain-tops
With kingly, ermine snow. The beams flash on
And make appear the melancholy ruins
Of cancelled cycles; anchors, beaks of ships;
Planks turned to marble; quivers, helms, and spears, 290
And gorgon-headed targes, and the wheels
Of scythèd chariots, and the emblazonry
Of trophies, standards, and armorial beasts,
Round which death laughed, sepulchred emblems
Of dead destruction, ruin within ruin!
The wrecks beside of many a city vast,
Whose population which the earth grew over
Was mortal, but not human; see, they lie,
Their monstrous works, and uncouth skeletons,
Their statues, homes and fanes; prodigious shapes 300
Huddled in gray annihilation, split,
Jammed in the hard, black deep; and over these,
The anatomies of unknown wingèd things,
And fishes which were isles of living scale,
And serpents, bony chains, twisted around
The iron crags, or within heaps of dust
To which the tortuous strength of their last pangs
Had crushed the iron crags; and over these
The jagged alligator, and the might 309
Of earth-convulsing behemoth, which once
Were monarch beasts, and on the slimy shores,
And weed-overgrown continents of earth,
Increased and multiplied like summer worms
On an abandoned corpse, till the blue globe
Wrapped deluge round it like a cloak, and they
Yelled, gasped, and were abolished; or some God
Whose throne was in a comet, passed, and cried,
'Be not!' And like my words they were no more.

The Earth

The joy, the triumph, the delight, the mad-
    ness!
The boundless, overflowing, bursting glad-
    ness,   320
The vaporous exultation not to be confined!
    Ha! ha! the animation of delight
    Which wraps me, like an atmosphere of light,
And bears me as a cloud is borne by its own
    wind.

The Moon

Brother mine, calm wanderer,
Happy globe of land and air,
Some Spirit is darted like a beam from thee,
    Which penetrates my frozen frame,
    And passes with the warmth of flame,
With love, and odour, and deep melody   330
    Through me, through me!

The Earth

Ha! ha! the caverns of my hollow mountains,
    My cloven fire-crags, sound-exulting foun-
       tains
Laugh with a vast and inextinguishable
    laughter.
    The oceans, and the deserts, and the abysses,
    And the deep air's unmeasured wildernesses,
Answer from all their clouds and billows,
    echoing after.

    They cry aloud as I do. Sceptred curse,
    Who all our green and azure universe
Threatenedst to muffle round with black de-
    struction, sending   340
    A solid cloud to rain hot thunderstones,
    And splinter and knead down my children's
       bones,
All I bring forth, to one void mass battering
    and blending,—

    Until each crag-like tower, and storied
    column,
    Palace, and obelisk, and temple solemn,
My imperial mountains crowned with cloud,
    and snow, and fire;
    My sea-like forests, every blade and
    blossom
    Which finds a grave or cradle in my bosom,
Were stamped by thy strong hate into a life-
    less mire:

How art thou sunk, withdrawn, covered,
    drunk up   350
    By thirsty nothing, as the brackish cup
Drained by a desert-troop, a little drop for
    all;
    And from beneath, around, within, above,
    Filling thy void annihilation, love
Burst in like light on caves cloven by the
    thunder-ball.

The Moon

The snow upon my lifeless mountains
Is loosened into living fountains,
My solid oceans flow, and sing, and shine:
    A spirit from my heart bursts forth,
    It clothes with unexpected birth   360
My cold bare bosom: Oh! it must be thine
    On mine, on mine!

    Gazing on thee I feel, I know
    Green stalks burst forth, and bright flowers
    grow,
And living shapes upon my bosom move:
    Music is in the sea and air,
    Wingèd clouds soar here and there,
Dark with the rain new buds are dreaming of:
    'Tis love, all love!

The Earth

    It interpenetrates my granite mass,   370
    Through tangled roots and trodden clay
    doth pass
Into the utmost leaves and delicatest flowers;
    Upon the winds, among the clouds 'tis
    spread,
    It wakes a life in the forgotten dead,
They breathe a spirit up from their obscurest
    bowers.

    And like a storm bursting its cloudy
    prison
    With thunder, and with whirlwind, has
    arisen
Out of the lampless caves of unimagined be-
    ing:
    With earthquake shock and swiftness mak-
    ing shiver
    Thought's stagnant chaos, unremoved for
    ever,   380
Till hate, and fear, and pain, light-vanquished
    shadows, fleeing,

Leave Man, who was a many-sided mirror,
Which could distort to many a shape of
  error,
This true fair world of things, a sea reflecting
  love;
Which over all his kind, as the sun's heaven
Gliding o'er ocean, smooth, serene, and
  even,
Darting from starry depths radiance and life,
  doth move:

Leave Man, even as a leprous child is
  left,
Who follows a sick beast to some warm
  cleft
Of rocks, through which the might of healing
  springs is poured;   390
Then when it wanders home with rosy
  smile,
Unconscious, and its mother fears awhile
It is a spirit, then, weeps on her child restored.

Man, oh, not men! a chain of linkèd
  thought,
Of love and might to be divided not,
Compelling the elements with adamantine
  stress;
As the sun rules, even with a tyrant's gaze,
The unquiet republic of the maze
Of planets, struggling fierce towards heaven's
  free wilderness.

Man, one harmonious soul of many a soul,
Whose nature is its own divine control,
Where all things flow to all, as rivers to the
  sea;   402
Familiar acts are beautiful through love;
Labour, and pain, and grief, in life's green
  grove
Sport like tame beasts, none knew how gentle
  they could be!

His will, with all mean passions, bad de-
  lights,
And selfish cares, its trembling satellites,
A spirit ill to guide, but mighty to obey,
Is as a tempest-wingèd ship, whose helm
Love rules, through waves which dare not
  overwhelm,   410
Forcing life's wildest shores to own its
  sovereign sway.

All things confess his strength. Through the
  cold mass
Of marble and of colour his dreams pass;
Bright threads whence mothers weave the
  robes their children wear;
Language is a perpetual Orphic song,
Which rules with Dædal harmony a throng
Of thoughts and forms, which else senseless
  and shapeless were.

The lightning is his slave; heaven's utmost
  deep
Gives up her stars, and like a flock of sheep
They pass before his eye, are numbered, and
  roll on!   420
The tempest is his steed, he strides the
  air;
And the abyss shouts from her depth laid
  bare,
Heaven, hast thou secrets? Man unveils me;
  I have none.

The Moon

The shadow of white death has passed
From my path in heaven at last,
A clinging shroud of solid frost and sleep;
And through my newly-woven bowers,
Wander happy paramours,
Less mighty, but as mild as those who keep
  Thy vales more deep.   430

The Earth

As the dissolving warmth of dawn may
  fold
A half unfrozen dew-globe, green, and gold,
And crystalline, till it becomes a wingèd mist,
And wanders up the vault of the blue day,
Outlives the noon, and on the sun's last
  ray
Hangs o'er the sea, a fleece of fire and
  amethyst.

The Moon

Thou art folded, thou art lying
In the light which is undying
Of thine own joy, and heaven's smile divine;
All suns and constellations shower   440
On thee a light, a life, a power
Which doth array thy sphere; thou pourest
  thine
  On mine, on mine!

The Earth

I spin beneath my pyramid of night,
Which points into the heavens dreaming de-
    light,
Murmuring victorious joy in my enchanted
    sleep;
As a youth lulled in love-dreams faintly
    sighing,
Under the shadow of his beauty lying,
Which round his rest a watch of light and
    warmth doth keep.

The Moon

As in the soft and sweet eclipse,   450
    When soul meets soul on lovers' lips,
High hearts are calm, and brightest eyes are
    dull;
    So when thy shadow falls on me,
    Then am I mute and still, by thee
Covered; of thy love, Orb most beautiful,
        Full, oh, too full!

Thou art speeding round the sun
Brightest world of many a one;
Green and azure sphere which shinest
With a light which is divinest   460
Among all the lamps of Heaven
To whom life and light is given;
I, thy crystal paramour
Borne beside thee by a power
Like the polar Paradise,
Magnet-like of lovers' eyes;
I, a most enamoured maiden
Whose weak brain is overladen
With the pleasure of her love,
Maniac-like around thee move   470
Gazing, an insatiate bride,
On thy form from every side
Like a Mænad, round the cup
Which Agave lifted up
In the weird Cadmæan forest.
Brother, wheresoe'er thou soarest
I must hurry, whirl and follow
Through the heavens wide and hollow,
Sheltered by the warm embrace
Of thy soul from hungry space,   480
Drinking from thy sense and sight
Beauty, majesty, and might,
As a lover or a chameleon
Grows like what it looks upon,

As a violet's gentle eye
Gazes on the azure sky
Until its hue grows like what it beholds,
    As a gray and watery mist
    Glows like solid amethyst
Athwart the western mountain it enfolds, 490
    When the sunset sleeps
        Upon its snow—

The Earth

    And the weak day weeps
        That it should be so.
Oh, gentle Moon, the voice of thy delight
Falls on me like thy clear and tender light
Soothing the seaman, borne the summer night,
    Through isles for ever calm;
Oh, gentle Moon, thy crystal accents pierce
The caverns of my pride's deep universe, 500
Charming the tiger joy, whose tramplings
    fierce
Made wounds which need thy balm.

Panthea. I rise as from a bath of sparkling
    water,
A bath of azure light, among dark rocks,
Out of the stream of sound.
Ione.   Ah me! sweet sister,
The stream of sound has ebbed away from us,
And you pretend to rise out of its wave,
Because your words fall like the clear, soft
    dew
Shaken from a bathing wood-nymph's limbs
    and hair.
Panthea. Peace! peace! A mighty Power,
    which is as darkness,   510
Is rising out of Earth, and from the sky
Is showered like night, and from within the
    air
Bursts, like eclipse which had been gathered
    up
Into the pores of sunlight: the bright visions,
Wherein the singing spirits rode and shone,
Gleam like pale meteors through a watery
    night.
Ione. There is a sense of words upon mine
    ear.
Panthea. An universal sound like words:
Oh, list!

Demogorgon

Thou, Earth, calm empire of a happy soul,
    Sphere of divinest shapes and harmonies,

Beautiful orb! gathering as thou dost roll 521
  The love which paves thy path along the
    skies:

The Earth

I hear: I am as a drop of dew that dies.

Demogorgon

Thou, Moon, which gazest on the nightly
    Earth
  With wonder, as it gazes upon thee;
Whilst each to men, and beasts, and the swift
    birth
  Of birds, is beauty, love, calm, harmony:

The Moon

I hear: I am a leaf shaken by thee!

Demogorgon

Ye Kings of suns and stars, Dæmons and
    Gods,
  Æthereal Dominations, who possess   530
Elysian, windless, fortunate abodes
  Beyond Heaven's constellated wilderness:

A Voice from above

Our great Republic hears, we are blest, and
    bless.

Demogorgon

Ye happy Dead, whom beams of brightest
    verse
  Are clouds to hide, not colours to portray,
Whether your nature is that universe
  Which once ye saw and suffered—

A Voice from beneath

                    Or as they
Whom we have left, we change and pass away.

Demogorgon

Ye elemental Genii, who have homes
  From man's high mind even to the central
    stone   540
Of sullen lead; from heaven's star-fretted
    domes
To the dull weed some sea-worm battens
    on:

A confused Voice

We hear: thy words waken Oblivion.

Demogorgon

Spirits, whose homes are flesh: ye beasts and
    birds,
  Ye worms, and fish; ye living leaves and
    buds;
Lightning and wind; and ye untameable herds,
  Meteors and mists, which throng air's soli-
    tudes:—

A Voice

Thy voice to us is wind among still woods.

Demogorgon

Man, who wert once a despot and a slave;
  A dupe and a deceiver; a decay;   550
A traveller from the cradle to the grave   .
  Through the dim night of this immortal
    day:

All

Speak: thy strong words may never pass
    away.

Demogorgon

This is the day, which down the void abysm
At the Earth-born's spell yawns for Heaven's
    despotism,
  And Conquest is dragged captive through
    the deep:
Love, from its awful throne of patient power
In the wise heart, from the last giddy hour
  Of dread endurance, from the slippery,
    steep,
And narrow verge of crag-like agony, springs
And folds over the world its healing wings. 561

Gentleness, Virtue, Wisdom, and Endurance,
These are the seals of that most firm assurance
  Which bars the pit over Destruction's
    strength;
And if, with infirm hand, Eternity,
Mother of many acts and hours, should free
  The serpent that would clasp her with its
    length;
These are the spells by which to reassume
An empire o'er the disentangled doom.   569

To suffer woes which Hope thinks infinite;
To forgive wrongs darker than death or night;
  To defy Power, which seems omnipotent;
To love, and bear; to hope till Hope creates
From its own wreck the thing it contemplates;

Neither to change, nor falter, nor repent;
This, like thy glory, Titan, is to be
Good, great and joyous, beautiful and free;
This is alone Life, Joy, Empire, and Victory.
1819

EPIPSYCHIDION

VERSES ADDRESSED TO THE NOBLE AND
UNFORTUNATE LADY, EMILIA V——,
NOW IMPRISONED IN THE
CONVENT OF——

SWEET Spirit! Sister of that orphan one,
Whose empire is the name thou weepest on,
In my heart's temple I suspend to thee
These votive wreaths of withered memory.

Poor captive bird! who, from thy narrow
  cage,
Pourest such music, that it might assuage
The ruggèd hearts of those who prisoned thee,
Were they not deaf to all sweet melody;
This song shall be thy rose: its petals pale
Are dead, indeed, my adored Nightingale! 10
But soft and fragrant is the faded blossom,
And it has no thorn left to wound thy bosom.

High, spirit-wingèd Heart! who dost for
  ever
Beat thine unfeeling bars with vain endeavour,
Till those bright plumes of thought, in which
  arrayed
It over-soared this low and worldly shade,
Lie shattered; and thy panting, wounded breast
Stains with dear blood its unmaternal nest!
I weep vain tears: blood would less bitter be,
Yet poured forth gladlier, could it profit thee.

Seraph of Heaven! too gentle to be human,
Veiling beneath that radiant form of Woman
All that is insupportable in thee   23
Of light, and love, and immortality!
Sweet Benediction in the eternal Curse!
Veilèd Glory of this lampless Universe!
Thou Moon beyond the clouds! Thou living
  Form
Among the Dead! Thou Star above the Storm!
Thou Wonder, and thou Beauty, and thou
  Terror!
Thou Harmony of Nature's art! Thou Mirror
In whom, as in the splendour of the Sun,   31

All shapes look glorious which thou gazest on!
Ay, even the dim words which obscure thee
  now
Flash, lightning-like, with unaccustomed glow;
I pray thee that thou blot from this sad song
All of its much mortality and wrong,
With those clear drops, which start like sacred
  dew
From the twin lights thy sweet soul darkens
  through,
Weeping, till sorrow becomes ecstasy:
Then smile on it, so that it may not die.   40

I never thought before my death to see
Youth's vision thus made perfect. Emily,
I love thee; though the world by no thin name
Will hide that love from its unvalued shame.
Would we two had been twins of the same
  mother!
Or, that the name my heart lent to another
Could be a sister's bond for her and thee,
Blending two beams of one eternity!
Yet were one lawful and the other true,
These names, though dear, could paint not,
  as is due,   50
How beyond refuge I am thine. Ah me!
I am not thine: I am a part of thee.

Sweet Lamp! my moth-like Muse has burned
  its wings
Or, like a dying swan who soars and sings,
Young Love should teach Time, in his own
  gray style,
All that thou art. Art thou not void of guile,
A lovely soul formed to be blessed and bless?
A well of sealed and secret happiness,   58
Whose waters like blithe light and music are,
Vanquishing dissonance and gloom? A Star
Which moves not in the moving heavens, alone?
A Smile amid dark frowns? a gentle tone
Amid rude voices? a belovèd light?
A Solitude, a Refuge, a Delight?
A Lute, which those whom Love has taught to
  play
Make music on, to soothe the roughest day
And lull fond Grief asleep? a buried treasure?
A cradle of young thoughts of wingless
  pleasure?
A violet-shrouded grave of Woe?—I measure
The world of fancies, seeking one like thee,
And find—alas! mine own infirmity.   71

She met me, Stranger, upon life's rough way,
And lured me towards sweet Death; as Night by Day,
Winter by Spring, or Sorrow by swift Hope,
Led into light, life, peace. An antelope,
In the suspended impulse of its lightness,
Were less ethereally light: the brightness
Of her divinest presence trembles through
Her limbs, as underneath a cloud of dew
Embodied in the windless heaven of June 80
Amid the splendour-wingèd stars, the Moon
Burns, inextinguishably beautiful:
And from her lips, as from a hyacinth full
Of honey-dew, a liquid murmur drops,
Killing the sense with passion; sweet as stops
Of planetary music heard in trance.
In her mild lights the starry spirits dance,
The sunbeams of those wells which ever leap
Under the lightnings of the soul—too deep
For the brief fathom-line of thought or sense.
The glory of her being, issuing thence,   91
Stains the dead, blank, cold air with a warm shade
Of unentangled intermixture, made
By Love, of light and motion: one intense
Diffusion, one serene Omnipresence,
Whose flowing outlines mingle in their flowing,
Around her cheeks and utmost fingers glowing
With the unintermitted blood, which there
Quivers, (as in a fleece of snow-like air   99
The crimson pulse of living morning quiver,)
Continuously prolonged, and ending never,
Till they are lost, and in that Beauty furled
Which penetrates and clasps and fills the world;
Scarce visible from extreme loveliness.
Warm fragrance seems to fall from her light dress
And her loose hair; and where some heavy tress
The air of her own speed has disentwined,
The sweetness seems to satiate the faint wind;
And in the soul a wild odour is felt,
Beyond the sense, like fiery dews that melt
Into the bosom of a frozen bud.—   111
See where she stands! a mortal shape indued
With love and life and light and deity,
And motion which may change but cannot die;
An image of some bright Eternity;

A shadow of some golden dream; a Splendour
Leaving the third sphere pilotless; a tender
Reflection of the eternal Moon of Love
Under whose motions life's dull billows move;
A Metaphor of Spring and Youth and Morning;   120
A Vision like incarnate April, warning,
With smiles and tears, Frost the Anatomy
Into his summer grave.

          Ah, woe is me!
What have I dared? where am I lifted? how *mortal woman*
Shall I descend, and perish not? I know
That Love makes all things equal: I have heard
By mine own heart this joyous truth averred:
The spirit of the worm beneath the sod
In love and worship, blends itself with God.

Spouse! Sister! Angel! Pilot of the Fate 130
Whose course has been so starless! O too late
Belovèd! O too soon adored, by me!
For in the fields of Immortality
My spirit should at first have worshipped thine,
A divine presence in a place divine;
Or should have moved beside it on this earth,
A shadow of that substance, from its birth;
But not as now:—I love thee; yes, I feel
That on the fountain of my heart a seal
Is set, to keep its waters pure and bright 140
For thee, since in those *tears* thou hast delight.
We—are we not formed, as notes of music are,
For one another, though dissimilar;
Such difference without discord, as can make
Those sweetest sounds, in which all spirits shake
As trembling leaves in a continuous air?

Thy wisdom speaks in me, and bids me dare
Beacon the rocks on which high hearts are wrecked.
I never was attached to that great sect,   149
Whose doctrine is, that each one should select
Out of the crowd a mistress or a friend,
And all the rest, though fair and wise, commend
To cold oblivion, though it is in the code
Of modern morals, and the beaten road
Which those poor slaves with weary footsteps tread,
Who travel to their home among the dead
By the broad highway of the world, and so

With one chained friend, perhaps a jealous foe,
The dreariest and the longest journey go.

True Love in this differs from gold and clay,
That to divide is not to take away.   161
Love is like understanding, that grows bright,
Gazing on many truths; 'tis like thy light,
Imagination! which from earth and sky,
And from the depths of human fantasy,
As from a thousand prisms and mirrors, fills
The Universe with glorious beams, and kills
Error, the worm, with many a sun-like arrow
Of its reverberated lightning. Narrow
The heart that loves, the brain that contem-
     plates,   170
The life that wears, the spirit that creates
One object, and one form, and builds thereby
A sepulchre for its eternity.

Mind from its object differs most in this:
Evil from good; misery from happiness;
The baser from the nobler; the impure
And frail, from what is clear and must endure.
If you divide suffering and dross, you may
Diminish till it is consumed away;   179
If you divide pleasure and love and thought,
Each part exceeds the whole; and we know not
How much, while any yet remains unshared,
Of pleasure may be gained, of sorrow spared:
This truth is that deep well, whence sages draw
The unenvied light of hope; the eternal law
By which those live, to whom this world of
     life
Is as a garden ravaged, and whose strife
Tills for the promise of a later birth
The wilderness of this Elysian earth.

There was a Being whom my spirit oft 190
Met on its visioned wanderings, far aloft,
In the clear golden prime of my youth's dawn,
Upon the fairy isles of sunny lawn,
Amid the enchanted mountains, and the caves
Of divine sleep, and on the air-like waves
Of wonder-level dream, whose tremulous floor
Paved her light steps;—on an imagined shore,
Under the gray beak of some promontory
She met me, robed in such exceeding glory,
That I beheld her not. In solitudes   200
Her voice came to me through the whispering
     woods,
And from the fountains, and the odours deep

Of flowers, which, like lips murmuring in their
     sleep
Of the sweet kisses which had lulled them
     there,
Breathed but of *her* to the enamoured air;
And from the breezes whether low or loud,
And from the rain of every passing cloud,
And from the singing of the summer-birds,
And from all sounds, all silence. In the words
Of antique verse and high romance,—in form,
Sound, colour—in whatever checks that Storm
Which with the shattered present chokes the
     past;   212
And in that best philosophy, whose taste
Makes this cold common hell, our life, a doom
As glorious as a fiery martyrdom;
Her Spirit was the harmony of truth.—

Then, from the caverns of my dreamy youth
I sprang, as one sandalled with plumes of fire,
And towards the lodestar of my one desire,
I flitted, like a dizzy moth, whose flight 220
Is as a dead leaf's in the owlet light,
When it would seek in Hesper's setting sphere
A radiant death, a fiery sepulchre,
As if it were a lamp of earthly flame.—
But She, whom prayers or tears then could
     not tame,
Passed, like a God throned on a wingèd planet,
Whose burning plumes to tenfold swiftness
     fan it,
Into the dreary cone of our life's shade;
And as a man with mighty loss dismayed,
I would have followed, though the grave be-
     tween   230
Yawned like a gulf whose spectres are unseen:
When a voice said:—'O thou of hearts the
     weakest,
The phantom is beside thee whom thou
     seekest.'
Then I—'Where?'—the world's echo an-
     swered 'where?'
And in that silence, and in my despair,
I questioned every tongueless wind that flew
Over my tower of mourning, if it knew
Whither 'twas fled, this soul out of my soul;
And murmured names and spells which have
     control
Over the sightless tyrants of our fate;   240
But neither prayer nor verse could dissipate
The night which closed on her; nor uncreate

That world within this Chaos, mine and me,
Of which she was the veiled Divinity,
The world I say of thoughts that worshipped
    her:
And therefore I went forth, with hope and fear
And every gentle passion sick to death,
Feeding my course with expectation's breath,
Into the wintry forest of our life;
And struggling through its error with vain
    strife,   250
And stumbling in my weakness and my haste,
And half bewildered by new forms, I passed,
Seeking among those untaught foresters
If I could find one form resembling hers,
In which she might have masked herself from
    me.
There,—One, whose voice was venomed
    melody
Sate by a well, under blue nightshade bowers;
The breath of her false mouth was like faint
    flowers,
Her touch was as electric poison,—flame
Out of her looks into my vitals came,   260
And from her living cheeks and bosom flew
A killing air, which pierced like honey-dew
Into the core of my green heart, and lay
Upon its leaves; until, as hair grown gray
O'er a young brow, they hid its unblown
    prime
With ruins of unseasonable time.

In many mortal forms I rashly sought
The shadow of that idol of my thought.
And some were fair—but beauty dies away:
Others were wise—but honeyed words betray:
And One was true—oh! why not true to me?
Then, as hunted deer that could not flee,   272
I turned upon my thoughts, and stood at bay,
Wounded and weak and panting; the cold day
Trembled, for pity of my strife and pain.
When, like a noonday dawn, there shone again
Deliverance. One stood on my path who
    seemed
As like the glorious shape which I had dreamed
As is the Moon, whose changes ever run
Into themselves, to the eternal Sun;   280
The cold chaste Moon, the Queen of Heaven's
    bright isles,
Who makes all beautiful on which she smiles,
That wandering shrine of soft yet icy flame
Which ever is transformed, yet still the same,

And warms not but illumines. Young and fair
As the descended Spirit of that sphere,
She hid me, as the Moon may hide the night
From its own darkness, until all was bright
Between the Heaven and Earth of my calm
    mind,
And, as a cloud charioted by the wind,   290
She led me to a cave in that wild place,
And sate beside me, with her downward face
Illumining my slumbers, like the Moon
Waxing and waning o'er Endymion.
And I was laid asleep, spirit and limb,
And all my being became bright or dim
As the Moon's image in a summer sea,
According as she smiled or frowned on me;
And there I lay, within a chaste cold bed:
Alas, I then was nor alive nor dead:—   300
For at her silver voice came Death and Life,
Unmindful each of their accustomed strife,
Masked like twin babes, a sister and a brother,
The wandering hopes of one abandoned
    mother,
And through the cavern without wings they
    flew,
And cried 'Away, he is not of our crew.'
I wept, and though it be a dream, I weep.

    What storms then shook the ocean of my
    sleep,
Blotting that Moon, whose pale and waning lips
Then shrank as in the sickness of eclipse;—
And how my soul was as a lampless sea,   311
And who was then its Tempest; and when She,
The Planet of that hour, was quenched, what
    frost
Crept o'er those waters, till from coast to coast
The moving billows of my being fell
Into a death of ice, immovable;—
And then—what earthquakes made it gape
    and split,
The white Moon smiling all the while on it,
These words conceal:—If not, each word
    would be
The key of staunchless tears. Weep not for me!

    At length, into the obscure Forest came
The Vision I had sought through grief and
    shame.   322
Athwart that wintry wilderness of thorns
Flashed from her motion splendour like the
    Morn's,

And from her presence life was radiated
Through the gray earth and branches bare and
　　dead;
So that her way was paved, and roofed above
With flowers as soft as thoughts of budding
　　love;
And music from her respiration spread　329
Like light,—all other sounds were penetrated
By the small, still, sweet spirit of that sound,
So that the savage winds hung mute around;
And odours warm and fresh fell from her hair
Dissolving the dull cold in the frore air:
Soft as an Incarnation of the Sun,
When light is changed to love, this glorious
　　One
Floated into the cavern where I lay,
And called my Spirit, and the dreaming clay
Was lifted by the thing that dreamed below
As smoke by fire, and in her beauty's glow
I stood, and felt the dawn of my long night
Was penetrating me with living light:　342
I knew it was the Vision veiled from me
So many years—that it was Emily.

　　　Twin Spheres of light who rule this passive
　　　　　Earth,
This world of love, this *me;* and into birth
Awaken all its fruits and flowers, and dart
Magnetic might into its central heart;
And lift its billows and its mists, and guide
By everlasting laws, each wind and tide　350
To its fit cloud, and its appointed cave;
And lull its storms, each in the craggy grave
Which was its cradle, luring to faint bowers
The armies of the rainbow-wingèd showers;
And, as those married lights, which from the
　　towers
Of Heaven look forth and fold the wandering
　　globe
In liquid sleep and splendour, as a robe;
And all their many-mingled influence blend,
If equal, yet unlike, to one sweet end;—　359
So ye, bright regents, with alternate sway
Govern my sphere of being, night and day!
Thou, not disdaining even a borrowed might;
Thou, not eclipsing a remoter light;
And, through the shadow of the seasons three,
From Spring to Autumn's sere maturity,
Light it into the Winter of the tomb,
Where it may ripen to a brighter bloom.
Thou too, O Comet beautiful and fierce,

Who drew the heart of this frail Universe
Towards thine own; till, wrecked in that con-
　　vulsion,　370
Alternating attraction and repulsion,
Thine went astray and that was rent in twain;
Oh, float into our azure heaven again!
Be there Love's folding-star at thy return;
The living Sun will feed thee from its urn
Of golden fire; the Moon will veil her horn
In thy last smiles; adoring Even and Morn
Will worship thee with incense of calm breath
And lights and shadows; as the star of Death
And Birth is worshipped by those sisters wild
Called Hope and Fear—upon the heart are
　　piled　381
Their offerings,—of this sacrifice divine
A World shall be the altar.

　　　　　　　　　Lady mine,
Scorn not these flowers of thought, the fading
　　birth
Which from its heart of hearts that plant puts
　　forth
Whose fruit, made perfect by thy sunny eyes,
Will be as of the trees of Paradise.

　　　The day is come, and thou wilt fly with me.
To whatsoe'er of dull mortality
Is mine, remain a vestal sister still;　390
To the intense, the deep, the imperishable,
Not mine but me, henceforth be thou united
Even as a bride, delighting and delighted.
The hour is come:—the destined Star has risen
Which shall descend upon a vacant prison.
The walls are high, the gates are strong, thick
　　set
The sentinels—but true Love never yet
Was thus constrained: it overleaps all fence:
Like lightning, with invisible violence
Piercing its continents; like Heaven's free
　　breath,　400
Which he who grasps can hold not; liker
　　Death,
Who rides upon a thought, and makes his
　　way
Through temple, tower, and palace, and the
　　array
Of arms: more strength has Love than he or
　　they;
For it can burst his charnel, and make free
The limbs in chains, the heart in agony,
The soul in dust and chaos.

Emily,
A ship is floating in the harbour now,
A wind is hovering o'er the mountain's brow;
There is a path on the sea's azure floor, 410
No keel has ever ploughed that path before;
The halcyons brood around the foamless
    isles;
The treacherous Ocean has forsworn its wiles;
The merry mariners are bold and free:
Say, my heart's sister, wilt thou sail with me?
Our bark is as an albatross, whose nest
Is a far Eden of the purple East;
And we between her wings will sit, while
    Night,
And Day, and Storm, and Calm, pursue their
    flight,
Our ministers, along the boundless Sea, 420
Treading each other's heels, unheededly.
It is an isle under Ionian skies,
Beautiful as a wreck of Paradise,
And, for the harbours are not safe and good,
This land would have remained a solitude
But for some pastoral people native there,
Who from the Elysian, clear, and golden air
Draw the last spirit of the age of gold,
Simple and spirited; innocent and bold.
The blue Aegean girds this chosen home, 430
With ever-changing sound and light and foam,
Kissing the sifted sands, and caverns hoar;
And all the winds wandering along the shore
Undulate with the undulating tide:
There are thick woods where sylvan forms
    abide;
And many a fountain, rivulet, and pond,
As clear as elemental diamond,
Or serene morning air; and far beyond,
The mossy tracks made by the goats and deer
(Which the rough shepherd treads but once a
    year) 440
Pierce into glades, caverns, and bowers, and
    halls
Built round with ivy, which the waterfalls
Illumining, with sound that never fails
Accompany the noonday nightingales;
And all the place is peopled with sweet airs;
The light clear element which the isle wears
Is heavy with the scent of lemon-flowers,
Which floats like mist laden with unseen
    showers,
And falls upon the eyelids like faint sleep;
And from the moss violets and jonquils peep,

And dart their arrowy odour through the
    brain 451
Till you might faint with that delicious pain.
And every motion, odour, beam, and tone,
With that deep music is in unison:
Which is a soul within the soul—they seem
Like echoes of an antenatal dream.—
It is an isle 'twixt Heaven, Air, Earth, and Sea,
Cradled, and hung in clear tranquillity;
Bright as that wandering Eden Lucifer,
Washed by the soft blue Oceans of young air.
It is a favoured place. Famine or Blight, 461
Pestilence, War and Earthquake, never light
Upon its mountain-peaks; blind vultures, they
Sail onward far upon their fatal way:
The wingèd storms, chanting their thunder-
    psalm
To other lands, leave azure chasms of calm
Over this isle, or weep themselves in dew,
From which its fields and woods ever renew
Their green and golden immortality.
And from the sea there rise, and from the sky
There fall, clear exhalations, soft and bright,
Veil after veil, each hiding some delight, 472
Which Sun or Moon or zephyr draw aside,
Till the isle's beauty, like a naked bride
Glowing at once with love and loveliness,
Blushes and trembles at its own excess:
Yet, like a buried lamp, a Soul no less
Burns in the heart of this delicious isle,
An atom of th' Eternal, whose own smile
Unfolds itself, and may be felt, not seen 480
O'er the gray rocks, blue waves, and forests
    green,
Filling their bare and void interstices.—
But the chief marvel of the wilderness
Is a lone dwelling, built by whom or how
None of the rustic island-people know:
'Tis not a tower of strength, though with its
    height
It overtops the woods; but, for delight,
Some wise and tender Ocean-King, ere crime
Had been invented, in the world's young
    prime,
Reared it, a wonder of that simple time, 490
An envy of the isles, a pleasure-house
Made sacred to his sister and his spouse.
It scarce seems now a wreck of human art,
But, as it were Titanic; in the heart
Of Earth having assumed its form, then grown
Out of the mountains, from the living stone,

Lifting itself in caverns light and high:
For all the antique and learnèd imagery
Has been erased, and in the place of it
The ivy and the wild-vine interknit   500
The volumes of their many-twining stems;
Parasite flowers illume with dewy gems
The lampless halls, and when they fade, the
    sky
Peeps through their winter-woof of tracery
With moonlight patches, or star atoms keen,
Or fragments of the day's intense serene;—
Working mosaic on their Parian floors.
And, day and night, aloof, from the high
    towers
And terraces, the Earth and Ocean seem
To sleep in one another's arms, and dream 510
Of waves, flowers, clouds, woods, rocks, and
    all that we
Read in their smiles, and call reality.

    This isle and house are mine, and I have
    vowed
Thee to be lady of the solitude.—
And I have fitted up some chambers there
Looking towards the golden Eastern air,
And level with the living winds, which flow
Like waves above the living waves below.—
I have sent books and music there, and all
Those instruments with which high Spirits call
The future from its cradle, and the past   521
Out of its grave, and make the present last
In thoughts and joys which sleep, but cannot
    die,
Folded within their own eternity.
Our simple life wants little, and true taste
Hires not the pale drudge Luxury, to waste
The scene it would adorn, and therefore still,
Nature with all her children haunts the hill.
The ring-dove, in the embowering ivy, yet
Keeps up her love-lament, and the owls flit
Round the evening tower, and the young stars
    glance   531
Between the quick bats in their twilight dance;
The spotted deer bask in the fresh moonlight
Before our gate, and the slow, silent night
Is measured by the pants of their calm sleep.
Be this our home in Life, and when years heap
Their withered hours, like leaves, on our de-
    cay,
Let us become the overhanging day,
The living soul of this Elysian isle,

Conscious, inseparable, one. Meanwhile   540
We two will rise, and sit, and walk together,
Under the roof of blue Ionian weather,
And wander in the meadows, or ascend
The mossy mountains, where the blue heavens
    bend
With lightest winds, to touch their para-
    mour;
Or linger, where the pebble-paven shore,
Under the quick, faint kisses of the sea
Trembles and sparkles as with ecstasy,—
Possessing and possessed by all that is
Within that calm circumference of bliss,   550
And by each other, till to love and live
Be one:—or, at the noontide hour, arrive
Where some old cavern hoar seems yet to
    keep
The moonlight of the expired night asleep,
Through which the awakened day can never
    peep;
A veil for our seclusion, close as night's,
Where secure sleep may kill thine innocent
    lights;
Sleep, the fresh dew of languid love, the rain
Whose drops quench kisses till they burn
    again.
And we will talk, until thought's melody 560
Become too sweet for utterance, and it die
In words, to live again in looks, which dart
With thrilling tone into the voiceless heart,
Harmonizing silence without a sound.
Our breath shall intermix, our bosoms bound,
And our veins beat together; and our lips
With other eloquence than words, eclipse
The soul that burns between them, and the
    wells
Which boil under our being's inmost cells,
The fountains of our deepest life, shall be
Confused in Passion's golden purity,   571
As mountain-springs under the morning sun.
We shall become the same, we shall be one
Spirit within two frames, oh! wherefore two?
One passion in twin-hearts, which grows and
    grew,
Till like two meteors of expanding flame,
Those spheres instinct with it become the
    same,
Touch, mingle, are transfigured; ever still
Burning, yet ever inconsumable:
In one another's substance finding food,   580
Like flames too pure and light and unimbued

To nourish their bright lives with baser prey,
Which point to Heaven and cannot pass away:
One hope within two wills, one will beneath
Two overshadowing minds, one life, one death,
One Heaven, one Hell, one immortality,
And one annihilation. Woe is me!
The wingèd words on which my soul would
     pierce
Into the height of Love's rare Universe,
Are chains of lead around its flight of fire—
I pant, I sink, I tremble, I expire!   591

Weak Verses, go, kneel at your Sovereign's
     feet,
And say:—'We are the masters of thy slave;
What wouldest thou with us and ours and
     thine?'
Then call your sisters from Oblivion's cave,
All singing loud: 'Love's very pain is sweet,
But its reward is in the world divine
Which, if not here, it builds beyond the grave.'
So shall ye live when I am there. Then haste
Over the hearts of men, until ye meet   600
Marina, Vanna, Primus, and the rest,
And bid them love each other and be blessed:
And leave the troop which errs, and which re-
     proves,
And come and be my guest,—for I am Love's.

1821

ADONAIS

I

I WEEP for Adonais—he is dead!
O, weep for Adonais! though our tears
Thaw not the frost which binds so dear a
     head!
And thou, sad Hour, selected from all years
To mourn our loss, rouse thy obscure
     compeers,
And teach them thine own sorrow, say: 'With me
Died Adonais; till the Future dares
Forget the Past, his fate and fame shall be
An echo and a light unto eternity!'

II

Where wert thou, mighty Mother, when he
     lay,   10
When thy Son lay, pierced by the shaft
     which flies

In darkness? where was lorn Urania
When Adonais died? With veilèd eyes,
'Mid listening Echoes, in her Paradise
She sate, while one, with soft enamoured
     breath,
Rekindled all the fading melodies,
With which, like flowers that mock the
     corse beneath,
He had adorned and hid the coming bulk of
     Death.

III

Oh, weep for Adonais—he is dead!
Wake, melancholy Mother, wake and weep!
Yet wherefore? Quench within their burn-
     ing bed   21
Thy fiery tears, and let thy loud heart keep
Like his, a mute and uncomplaining sleep;
For he is gone, where all things wise and
     fair
Descend;—oh, dream not that the amorous
     Deep
Will yet restore him to the vital air;
Death feeds on his mute voice, and laughs at
     our despair.

IV

Most musical of mourners, weep again!
Lament anew, Urania!—He died,
Who was the Sire of an immortal strain, 30
Blind, old, and lonely, when his country's
     pride,
The priest, the slave, and the liberticide,
Trampled and mocked with many a loathèd
     rite
Of lust and blood; he went, unterrified,
Into the gulf of death; but his clear Sprite
Yet reigns o'er earth; the third among the sons
     of light.

V

Most musical of mourners, weep anew!
Not all to that bright station dared to
     climb;
And happier they their happiness who knew,
Whose tapers yet burn through that night
     of time   40
In which suns perished; others more sublime,
Struck by the envious wrath of man or god,
Have sunk, extinct in their refulgent prime;
And some yet live, treading the thorny road,
Which leads, through toil and hate, to Fame's
     serene abode.

Presentation Copy of *Adonais* from Shelley to Hogg.
(See Appendix I.)

VI

But now, thy youngest, dearest one, has
    perished—
The nursling of thy widowhood, who grew,
Like a pale flower by some sad maiden
    cherished,   *echo of Isabella by Keats!*
And fed with true-love tears, instead of dew;
Most musical of mourners, weep anew! 50
Thy extreme hope, the loveliest and the last,
The bloom, whose petals nipped before they
    blew
Died on the promise of the fruit, is waste;
The broken lily lies—the storm is overpast.

VII

To that high Capital, where kingly Death
Keeps his pale court in beauty and decay,
He came; and bought, with price of purest
    breath,
A grave among the eternal.—Come away!
Haste, while the vault of blue Italian day
Is yet his fitting charnel-roof! while still 60
He lies, as if in dewy sleep he lay;
Awake him not! surely he takes his fill
Of deep and liquid rest, forgetful of all ill.
    S.S. mode of death

VIII

He will awake no more, oh, never more!—
Within the twilight chamber spreads apace
The shadow of white Death, and at the door
Invisible Corruption waits to trace
His extreme way to her dim dwelling-place;
The eternal Hunger sits, but pity and awe
Soothe her pale rage, nor dares she to deface
So fair a prey, till darkness, and the law
Of change, shall o'er his sleep the mortal cur-
    tain draw.   *Keats* 72
    unfinished love poems

IX

Oh, weep for Adonais!—The quick Dreams,
The passion-wingèd Ministers of thought,
Who were his flocks, whom near the living
    streams
Of his young spirit he fed, and whom he
    taught
The love which was its music, wander
    not,—
Wander no more, from kindling brain to
    brain,
But droop there, whence they sprung; and
    mourn their lot

Round the cold heart, where, after their
    sweet pain, 80
They ne'er will gather strength, or find a home
    again.

X

And one with trembling hands clasps his
    cold head,
And fans him with her moonlight wings,
    and cries;
'Our love, our hope, our sorrow, is not
    dead;
See, on the silken fringe of his faint eyes,
Like dew upon a sleeping flower, there
    lies
A tear some Dream has loosened from his
    brain.'
Lost Angel of a ruined Paradise!
She knew not 'twas her own; as with no
    stain
She faded, like a cloud which had outwept its
    rain. 90
    prep for burial   *mourning of muses*

XI

One from a lucid urn of starry dew
Washed his light limbs as if embalming
    them;
Another clipped her profuse locks, and
    threw
The wreath upon him, like an anadem, *crown*
Which frozen tears instead of pearls begem;
Another in her wilful grief would break
Her bow and wingèd reeds, as if to stem
A greater loss with one which was more
    weak;
And dull the barbèd fire against his frozen
    cheek.
    nymph thought

XII

Another Splendour on his mouth alit, 100
That mouth, whence it was wont to draw
    the breath
Which gave it strength to pierce the guarded
    wit,
And pass into the panting heart beneath
With lightning and with music: the damp
    death
Quenched its caress upon his icy lips;
And, as a dying meteor stains a wreath
Of moonlight vapour, which the cold night
    clips,
It flushed through his pale limbs, and passed
    to its eclipse.
    reanimation of corpse

XIII

And others came ... Desires and Ado-
rations,
Wingèd Persuasions and veiled Destinies,
Splendours, and Glooms, and glimmering
Incarnations   111
Of hopes and fears, and twilight Phantasies;
And Sorrow, with her family of Sighs,
And Pleasure, blind with tears, led by the
gleam
Of her own dying smile instead of eyes,
Came in slow pomp;—the moving pomp
might seem
Like pageantry of mist on an autumnal stream.

XIV

All he had loved, and moulded into thought,
From shape, and hue, and odour, and sweet
sound,
Lamented Adonais. Morning sought   120
Her eastern watch-tower, and her hair un-
bound,
Wet with the tears which should adorn the
ground,
Dimmed the aëreal eyes that kindle day;
Afar the melancholy thunder moaned,
Pale Ocean in unquiet slumber lay,
And the wild Winds flew round, sobbing in
their dismay.

XV

Lost Echo sits amid the voiceless mountains,
And feeds her grief with his remembered lay,
And will no more reply to winds or fountains,
Or amorous birds perched on the young
green spray,   130
Or herdsman's horn, or bell at closing day;
Since she can mimic not his lips, more dear
Than those for whose disdain she pined
away
Into a shadow of all sounds:—a drear
Murmur, between their songs, is all the wood-
men hear.

XVI

Grief made the young Spring wild, and she
threw down
Her kindling buds, as if she Autumn were,
Or they dead leaves; since her delight is
flown,
For whom should she have waked the sullen
year?

To Phoebus was not Hyacinth so dear 140
Nor to himself Narcissus, as to both
Thou, Adonais: wan they stand and sere
Amid the faint companions of their youth,
With dew all turned to tears; odour, to sigh-
ing ruth.

XVII

Thy spirit's sister, the lorn nightingale
Mourns not her mate with such melodious
pain;
Not so the eagle, who like thee could scale
Heaven, and could nourish in the sun's
domain
Her mighty youth with morning, doth
complain,
Soaring and screaming round her empty
nest,   150
As Albion wails for thee: the curse of Cain
Light on his head who pierced thy innocent
breast,
And scared the angel soul that was its earthly
guest!

XVIII

Ah, woe is me! Winter is come and gone,
But grief returns with the revolving year;
The airs and streams renew their joyous
tone;
The ants, the bees, the swallows reappear;
Fresh leaves and flowers deck the dead
Seasons' bier;
The amorous birds now pair in every brake,
And build their mossy homes in field and
brere;   160
And the green lizard, and the golden snake,
Like unimprisoned flames, out of their trance
awake.

XIX

Through wood and stream and field and hill
and Ocean
A quickening life from the Earth's heart has
burst
As it has ever done, with change and motion,
From the great morning of the world when
first
God dawned on Chaos; in its stream immersed,
The lamps of Heaven flash with a softer
light;
All baser things pant with life's sacred
thirst;

Diffuse themselves; and spend in love's delight, 170
The beauty and the joy of their renewèd might.

XX *Immortality*

The leprous corpse, touched by this spirit
tender,
Exhales itself in flowers of gentle breath;
Like incarnations of the stars, when splen-
dour
Is changed to fragrance, they illumine death
And mock the merry worm that wakes
beneath;
Nought we know, dies. Shall that alone
which knows
Be as a sword consumed before the sheath
By sightless lightning?—the intense atom
glows
A moment, then is quenched in a most cold
repose. *Imm
the negative* 180

XXI

Alas! that all we loved of him should be,
But for our grief, as if it had not been,
And grief itself be mortal! Woe is me!
Whence are we, and why are we? of what
scene
The actors or spectators? Great and mean
Meet massed in death, who lends what life
must borrow.
As long as skies are blue, and fields are green,
Evening must usher night, night urge the
morrow,
Month follow month with woe, and year wake
year to sorrow.

XXII

He will awake no more, oh, never more!
'Wake thou,' cried Misery, 'childless Mother,
rise 191
Out of thy sleep, and slake, in thy heart's
core,
A wound more fierce than his, with tears
and sighs.'
And all the Dreams that watched Urania's
eyes,
And all the Echoes whom their sister's song
Had held in holy silence, cried: 'Arise!'
Swift as a Thought by the snake Memory
stung,
From her ambrosial rest the fading Splendour
sprung.

XXIII

She rose like an autumnal Night, that
springs
Out of the East, and follows wild and drear
The golden Day, which, on eternal wings,
Even as a ghost abandoning a bier, 202
Had left the Earth a corpse. Sorrow and fear
So struck, so roused, so rapped Urania;
So saddened round her like an atmosphere
Of stormy mist; so swept her on her way
Even to the mournful place where Adonais lay.

XXIV *Journey of Urania*

Out of her secret Paradise she sped,
Through camps and cities rough with stone, *suffers thru*
and steel,
And human hearts, which to her aery tread *hard hearts*
Yielding not, wounded the invisible 211
Palms of her tender feet where'er they fell:
And barbèd tongues, and thoughts more
sharp than they,
Rent the soft Form they never could re-
pel,
Whose sacred blood, like the young tears
of May,
Paved with eternal flowers that undeserving
way.

XXV *animation*
Carpe agas?

In the death-chamber for a moment Death,
Shamed by the presence of that living
Might,
Blushed to annihilation, and the breath
Revisited those lips, and Life's pale light
Flashed through those limbs, so late her
dear delight. 221
'Leave me not wild and drear and comfort-
less,
As silent lightning leaves the starless night!
Leave me not!' cried Urania: her distress
Roused Death: Death rose and smiled, and *(sounds like torrent of Venus*
met her vain caress. *for adonais)*

muse of poetry

XXVI

'Stay yet awhile! speak to me once again;
Kiss me, so long but as a kiss may live;
And in my heartless breast and burning
brain
That word, that kiss, shall all thoughts else
survive,
With food of saddest memory kept alive,

Now thou art dead, as if it were a part   231
Of thee, my Adonais! I would give
All that I am to be as thou now art!
But I am chained to Time, and cannot thence
   depart!

XXVII

'O gentle child, beautiful as thou wert,
Why didst thou leave the trodden paths of
   men
Too soon, and with weak hands though
   mighty heart
Dare the unpastured dragon in his den?
Defenceless as thou wert, oh, where was
   then
Wisdom the mirrored shield, or scorn the
   spear?   240
Or hadst thou waited the full cycle, when
Thy spirit should have filled its crescent
   sphere,
The monsters of life's waste had fled from thee
   like deer.

XXVIII

'The herded wolves, bold only to pursue;
The obscene ravens, clamorous o'er the
   dead;
The vultures to the conqueror's banner
   true
Who feed where Desolation first has fed,
And whose wings rain contagion;—how
   they fled,
When, like Apollo, from his golden bow
The Pythian of the age one arrow sped
And smiled!—The spoilers tempt no second
   blow,   251
They fawn on the proud feet that spurn them
   lying low.

XXIX

'The sun comes forth, and many reptiles
   spawn;
He sets, and each ephemeral insect then
Is gathered into death without a dawn,
And the immortal stars awake again;
So is it in the world of living men:
A godlike mind soars forth, in its delight
Making earth bare and veiling heaven, and
   when
It sinks, the swarms that dimmed or shared
   its light   260
Leave to its kindred lamps the spirit's awful
   night.'

XXX

Thus ceased she: and the mountain shep-
   herds came,
Their garlands sere, their magic mantles
   rent;
The Pilgrim of Eternity, whose fame
Over his living head like Heaven is bent,
An early but enduring monument,
Came, veiling all the lightnings of his song
In sorrow; from her wilds Ierne sent
The sweetest lyrist of her saddest wrong,
And Love taught Grief to fall like music from
   his tongue.   270

XXXI

Midst others of less note, came one frail
   Form,
A phantom among men; companionless
As the last cloud of an expiring storm
Whose thunder is its knell; he, as I guess,
Had gazed on Nature's naked loveliness,
Actaeon-like, and now he fled astray
With feeble steps o'er the world's wilder-
   ness,
And his own thoughts, along that rugged
   way,
Pursued, like raging hounds, their father and
   their prey.

XXXII

A pardlike Spirit beautiful and swift—   280
A Love in desolation masked;—a Power
Girt round with weakness;—it can scarce
   uplift
The weight of the superincumbent hour;
It is a dying lamp, a falling shower,
A breaking billow;—even whilst we speak
Is it not broken? On the withering flower
The killing sun smiles brightly: on a cheek
The life can burn in blood, even while the
   heart may break.

XXXIII

His head was bound with pansies overblown,
And faded violets, white, and pied, and
   blue;   290
And a light spear topped with a cypress
   cone,
Round whose rude shaft dark ivy-tresses
   grew
Yet dripping with the forest's noonday dew,
Vibrated, as the ever-beating heart

action

Shook the weak hand that grasped it; of that
crew
He came the last, neglected and apart;
A herd-abandoned deer struck by the hunter's
dart. *read & as you like it*

XXXIV

All stood aloof, and at his partial moan
Smiled through their tears; well knew that
gentle band
Who in another's fate now wept his own,
As in the accents of an unknown land   301
He sung new sorrow; sad Urania scanned
The Stranger's mien, and murmured: 'Who
art thou?'
He answered not, but with a sudden hand
Made bare his branded and ensanguined
brow,
Which was like Cain's or Christ's—oh! that
it should be so! *Leigh Hunt's*

XXXV

What softer voice is hushed over the dead?
Athwart what brow is that dark mantle
thrown?
What form leans sadly o'er the white death-
bed,
In mockery of monumental stone,   310
The heavy heart heaving without a moan?
If it be He, who, gentlest of the wise,
Taught, soothed, loved, honoured the de-
parted one,
Let me not vex, with inharmonious sighs,
The silence of that heart's accepted sacrifice.

XXXVI

Our Adonais has drunk poison—oh!
What deaf and viperous murderer could
crown *to poetry*
Life's early cup with such a draught of
woe? *author of reviews*
The nameless worm would now itself dis-
own:
It felt, yet could escape, the magic tone
Whose prelude held all envy, hate, and
wrong,   321
But what was howling in one breast
alone,
Silent with expectation of the song,
Whose master's hand is cold, whose silver lyre
unstrung.

XXXVII

Live thou, whose infamy is not thy fame!
Live! fear no heavier chastisement from me,
Thou noteless blot on a remembered name!
But be thyself, and know thyself to be! *critic*
And ever at thy season be thou free
To spill the venom when thy fangs o'er-
flow; *image avis satan*   330
Remorse and Self-contempt shall cling to
thee;
Hot Shame shall burn upon thy secret
brow,
And like a beaten hound tremble thou shalt—
as now. *(Byron uses the same*

XXXVIII

Nor let us weep that our delight is fled
Far from these carrion kites that scream be-
low;
He wakes or sleeps with the enduring dead;
Thou canst not soar where he is sitting
now—
Dust to the dust! but the pure spirit shall
flow
Back to the burning fountain whence it
came,
A portion of the Eternal, which must glow
Through time and change, unquenchably
the same,   341
Whilst thy cold embers choke the sordid hearth
of shame.

XXXIX

Peace, peace! he is not dead, he doth not
sleep—
He hath awakened from the dream of life—
'Tis we, who lost in stormy visions, keep
With phantoms an unprofitable strife,
And in mad trance, strike with our spirit's
knife
Invulnerable nothings.—*We* decay
Like corpses in a charnel; fear and grief
Convulse us and consume us day by day,
And cold hopes swarm like worms within
our living clay.   351

consolation

XL

He has outsoared the shadow of our night;
Envy and calumny and hate and pain,
And that unrest which men miscall delight,
Can touch him not and torture not again;

From the contagion of the world's slow stain
He is secure, and now can never mourn
A heart grown cold, a head grown gray in
  vain;
Nor, when the spirit's self has ceased to burn,
With sparkless ashes load an unlamented urn.

XLI

He lives, he wakes—'tis Death is dead, not
  he;   361
Mourn not for Adonais.—Thou young
  Dawn,
Turn all thy dew to splendour, for from thee
The spirit thou lamentest is not gone;
Ye caverns and ye forests, cease to moan!
Cease, ye faint flowers and fountains, and
  thou Air,
Which like a mourning veil thy scarf hadst
  thrown
O'er the abandoned Earth, now leave it bare
Even to the joyous stars which smile on its
  despair!

XLII

He is made one with Nature: there is heard
His voice in all her music, from the moan
Of thunder, to the song of night's sweet bird;
He is a presence to be felt and known   373
In darkness and in light, from herb and
  stone,
Spreading itself where'er that Power may
  move
Which has withdrawn his being to its own;
Which wields the world with never-wearied
  love,
Sustains it from beneath, and kindles it above.

XLIII

He is a portion of the loveliness
Which once he made more lovely: he doth
  bear   380
His part, while the one Spirit's plastic stress
Sweeps through the dull dense world, com-
  pelling there,
All new successions to the forms they wear;
Torturing th' unwilling dross that checks
  its flight
To its own likeness, as each mass may bear;
And bursting in its beauty and its might
From trees and beasts and men into the Heav-
  en's light.

XLIV

The splendours of the firmament of time
May be eclipsed, but are extinguished not;
Like stars to their appointed height they
  climb,   390
And death is a low mist which cannot blot
The brightness it may veil. When lofty
  thought
Lifts a young heart above its mortal lair,
And love and life contend in it, for what
Shall be its earthly doom, the dead live there
And move like winds of light on dark and
  stormy air.

XLV

The inheritors of unfulfilled renown
Rose from their thrones, built beyond mor-
  tal thought,
Far in the Unapparent. Chatterton
Rose pale,—his solemn agony had not   400
Yet faded from him; Sidney, as he fought
And as he fell and as he lived and loved
Sublimely mild, a Spirit without spot,
Arose; and Lucan, by his death approved:
Oblivion as they rose shrank like a thing re-
  proved.

XLVI

And many more, whose names on Earth are
  dark,
But whose transmitted effluence cannot die
So long as fire outlives the parent spark,
Rose, robed in dazzling immortality.   409
'Thou art become as one of us,' they cry,
'It was for thee yon kingless sphere has long
Swung blind in unascended majesty,
Silent alone amid an Heaven of Song.
Assume thy wingèd throne, thou Vesper of
  our throng!'

XLVII

Who mourns for Adonais? Oh, come forth,
Fond wretch! and know thyself and him
  aright.
Clasp with thy panting soul the pendulous
  Earth;
As from a centre, dart thy spirit's light
Beyond all worlds, until its spacious might
Satiate the void circumference: then shrink
Even to a point within our day and night;
And keep thy heart light lest it make thee sink
When hope has kindled hope, and lured thee
  to the brink.   423

XLVIII

Or go to Rome, which is the sepulchre,
Oh, not of him, but of our joy: 'tis nought
That ages, empires, and religions there
Lie buried in the ravage they have wrought;
For such as he can lend,—they borrow not
Glory from those who made the world their
    prey;
And he is gathered to the kings of thought
Who waged contention with their time's
    decay,   431
And of the past are all that cannot pass away.

XLIX

Go thou to Rome,—at once the Paradise,
The grave, the city, and the wilderness;
And where its wrecks like shattered moun-
    tains rise,
And flowering weeds, and fragrant copses
    dress
The bones of Desolation's nakedness
Pass, till the spirit of the spot shall lead
Thy footsteps to a slope of green access
Where, like an infant's smile, over the dead
A light of laughing flowers along the grass is
    spread;   441

L

And gray walls moulder round, on which
    dull Time
Feeds, like slow fire upon a hoary brand;
And one keen pyramid with wedge sublime,
Pavilioning the dust of him who planned
This refuge for his memory, doth stand
Like flame, transformed to marble; and be-
    neath,
A field is spread, on which a newer band
Have pitched in Heaven's smile their camp
    of death,
Welcoming him we lose with scarce extin-
    guished breath.   450

LI

Here pause: these graves are all too young
    as yet
To have outgrown the sorrow which con-
    signed
Its charge to each; and if the seal is set,
Here, on one fountain of a mourning mind,
Break it not thou! too surely shalt thou find
Thine own well full, if thou returnest home,
Of tears and gall. From the world's bitter
    wind
Seek shelter in the shadow of the tomb.
What Adonais is, why fear we to become?

LII

The One remains, the many change and
    pass;   460
Heaven's light forever shines, Earth's shad-
    ows fly;
Life, like a dome of many-coloured glass,
Stains the white radiance of Eternity,
Until Death tramples it to fragments.—Die,
If thou wouldst be with that which thou
    dost seek!
Follow where all is fled!—Rome's azure sky,
Flowers, ruins, statues, music, words, are
    weak
The glory they transfuse with fitting truth to
    speak.

LIII

Why linger, why turn back, why shrink, my
    Heart?
Thy hopes are gone before: from all things
    here   470
They have departed; thou shouldst now de-
    part!
A light is passed from the revolving year,
And man, and woman; and what still is
    dear
Attracts to crush, repels to make thee wither.
The soft sky smiles,—the low wind whis-
    pers near:
'Tis Adonais calls! oh, hasten thither,
No more let Life divide what Death can join
    together.

LIV

That Light whose smile kindles the Universe,
That Beauty in which all things work and
    move,   479
That Benediction which the eclipsing Curse
Of birth can quench not, that sustaining
    Love
Which through the web of being blindly
    wove
By man and beast and earth and air and sea,
Burns bright or dim, as each are mirrors of
The fire for which all thirst; now beams on
    me,
Consuming the last clouds of cold mortality.

LV

The breath whose might I have invoked in
    song
Descends on me; my spirit's bark is driven,
Far from the shore, far from the trembling
    throng
Whose sails were never to the tempest given;
The massy earth and spherèd skies are
    riven!   491
I am borne darkly, fearfully, afar;
Whilst, burning through the inmost veil of
    Heaven,
The soul of Adonais, like a star,
Beacons from the abode where the Eternal are.
1821

THE TRIUMPH OF LIFE

SWIFT as a spirit hastening to his task
Of glory and of good, the Sun sprang forth
Rejoicing in his splendour, and the mask

Of darkness fell from the awakened Earth—
The smokeless altars of the mountain snows
Flamed above crimson clouds, and at the birth

Of light, the Ocean's orison arose,
To which the birds tempered their matin lay.
All flowers in field or forest which unclose

Their trembling eyelids to the kiss of day, 10
Swinging their censers in the element,
With orient incense lit by the new ray

Burned slow and inconsumably, and sent
Their odorous sighs up to the smiling air;
And, in succession due, did continent,

Isle, ocean, and all things that in them wear
The form and character of mortal mould,
Rise as the Sun their father rose, to bear

Their portion of the toil, which he of old
Took as his own, and then imposed on them:
But I, whom thoughts which must remain un-
    told   21

Had kept as wakeful as the stars that gem
The cone of night, now they were laid asleep
Stretched my faint limbs beneath the hoary
    stem

Which an old chestnut flung athwart the steep
Of a green Apennine: before me fled
The night; behind me rose the day; the deep

Was at my feet, and Heaven above my head,—
When a strange trance over my fancy grew
Which was not slumber, for the shade it
    spread   30

Was so transparent, that the scene came through
As clear as when a veil of light is drawn
O'er evening hills they glimmer; and I knew

That I had felt the freshness of that dawn
Bathe in the same cold dew my brow and hair,
And sate as thus upon that slope of lawn

Under the self-same bough, and heard as there
The birds, the fountains and the ocean hold
Sweet talk in music through the enamoured
    air,
And then a vision on my brain was rolled. 40
                    —————

As in that trance of wondrous thought I lay,
This was the tenour of my waking dream:—
Methought I sate beside a public way

Thick strewn with summer dust, and a great
    stream
Of people there was hurrying to and fro,
Numerous as gnats upon the evening gleam,

All hastening onward, yet none seemed to
    know
Whither he went, or whence he came, or why
He made one of the multitude, and so

Was borne amid the crowd, as through the
    sky   50
One of the million leaves of summer's bier;
Old age and youth, manhood and infancy,

Mixed in one mighty torrent did appear,
Some flying from the thing they feared, and
    some
Seeking the object of another's fear;

And others, as with steps towards the tomb,
Pored on the trodden worms that crawled be-
    neath,
And others mournfully within the gloom

Of their own shadow walked, and called it
      death;
And some fled from it as it were a ghost,   60
Half fainting in the affliction of vain breath:

But more, with motions which each other
      crossed,
Pursued or shunned the shadows the clouds
      threw,
Or birds within the noonday aether lost,

Upon that path where flowers never grew,—
And, weary with vain toil and faint for thirst,
Heard not the fountains, whose melodious dew

Out of their mossy cells forever burst;
Nor felt the breeze which from the forest told
Of grassy paths and wood-lawns interspersed

With overarching elms and caverns cold,   71
And violet banks where sweet dreams brood,
      but they
Pursued their serious folly as of old.

And as I gazed, methought that in the way
The throng grew wilder, as the woods of June
When the south wind shakes the extinguished
      day,

And a cold glare, intenser than the noon,
But icy cold, obscured with blinding light
The sun, as he the stars. Like the young
      moon—

When on the sunlit limits of the night   80
Her white shell trembles amid crimson air,
And whilst the sleeping tempest gathers
      might—

Doth, as the herald of its coming, bear
The ghost of its dead mother, whose dim form
Bends in dark aether from her infant's chair,—

So came a chariot on the silent storm
Of its own rushing splendour, and a Shape
So sate within, as one whom years deform,

Beneath a dusky hood and double cape,
Crouching within the shadow of a tomb;   90
And o'er what seemed the head a cloud-like
      crape

Was bent, a dun and faint aethereal gloom
Tempering the light. Upon the chariot-beam
A Janus-visaged Shadow did assume

The guidance of that wonder-wingèd team;
The shapes which drew it in thick lightenings
Were lost:—I heard alone on the air's soft
      stream

The music of their ever-moving wings.
All the four faces of that Charioteer
Had their eyes banded; little profit brings 100

Speed in the van and blindness in the rear,
Nor then avail the beams that quench the
      sun,—
Or that with banded eyes could pierce the
      sphere

Of all that is, has been or will be done;
So ill was the car guided—but it passed
With solemn speed majestically on.

The crowd gave way, and I arose aghast,
Or seemed to rise, so mighty was the trance,
And saw, like clouds upon the thunder-blast,

The million with fierce song and maniac
      dance   110
Raging around—such seemed the jubilee
As when to greet some conqueror's advance

Imperial Rome poured forth her living sea
From senate-house, and forum, and theatre,
When   upon the free

Had bound a yoke, which soon they stooped
      to bear.
Nor wanted here the just similitude
Of a triumphal pageant, for where'er

The chariot rolled, a captive multitude
Was driven;—all those who had grown old in
      power   120
Or misery,—all who had their age subdued

By action or by suffering, and whose hour
Was drained to its last sand in weal or
      woe,
So that the trunk survived both fruit and
      flower;—

All those whose fame or infamy must grow
Till the great winter lay the form and name
Of this green earth with them for ever low;—

All but the sacred few who could not tame
Their spirits to the conquerors—but as soon
As they had touched the world with living
    flame,   130

Fled back like eagles to their native noon,
Or those who put aside the diadem
Of earthly thrones or gems . . .

Were there, of Athens or Jerusalem,
Were neither mid the mighty captives seen,
Nor mid the ribald crowd that followed them,

Nor those who went before fierce and obscene.
The wild dance maddens in the van, and those
Who lead it—fleet as shadows on the green,

Outspeed the chariot, and without repose 140
Mix with each other in tempestuous measure
To savage music, wilder as it grows,

They, tortured by their agonizing pleasure,
Convulsed and on the rapid whirlwinds spun
Of that fierce Spirit, whose unholy leisure

Was soothed by mischief since the world be-
    gun,
Throw back their heads and loose their stream-
    ing hair;
And in their dance round her who dims the sun,

Maidens and youths fling their wild arms in air
As their feet twinkle; they recede, and now 150
Bending within each other's atmosphere,

Kindle invisibly—and as they glow,
Like moths by light attracted and repelled,
Oft to their bright destruction come and go,

Till like two clouds into one vale impelled,
That shake the mountains when their light-
    nings mingle
And die in rain—the fiery band which held

Their natures, snaps—while the shock still
    may tingle;
One falls and then another in the path
Senseless—nor is the desolation single,   160

Yet ere I can say *where*—the chariot hath
Passed over them—nor other trace I find
But as of foam after the ocean's wrath

Is spent upon the desert shore;—behind,
Old men and women foully disarrayed,
Shake their gray hairs in the insulting wind,

And follow in the dance, with limbs decayed,
Seeking to reach the light which leaves them
    still
Farther behind and deeper in the shade.

But not the less with impotence of will   170
They wheel, though ghastly shadows inter-
    pose
Round them and round each other, and fulfil

Their work, and in the dust from whence they
    rose
Sink, and corruption veils them as they lie,
And past in these performs what   in those.

Struck to the heart by this sad pageantry,
Half to myself I said—"And what is this?
Whose shape is that within the car? And
    why—"

I would have added—"is all here amiss?—"
But a voice answered—"Life!"—I turned, and
    knew   180
(O Heaven, have mercy on such wretchedness!)

That what I thought was an old root which
    grew
To strange distortion out of the hill side,
Was indeed one of those deluded crew,

And that the grass, which methought hung so
    wide
And white, was but his thin discoloured hair,
And that the holes he vainly sought to hide,

Were or had been eyes:—"If thou canst, for-
    bear
To join the dance, which I had well forborne!"
Said the grim Feature (of my thought aware),

"I will unfold that which to this deep scorn 191
Led me and my companions, and relate
The progress of the pageant since the morn;

"If thirst of knowledge shall not then abate,
Follow it thou even to the night, but I
Am weary."—Then like one who with the
    weight

Of his own words is staggered, wearily
He paused; and ere he could resume, I cried:
"First, who art thou?"—"Before thy memory,

"I feared, loved, hated, suffered, did and died,
And if the spark with which Heaven lit my
    spirit   201
Had been with purer nutriment supplied,

"Corruption would not now thus much inherit
Of what was once Rousseau,—nor this dis-
    guise
Stain that which ought to have disdained to
    wear it;

"If I have been extinguished, yet there rise
A thousand beacons from the spark I bore"—
"And who are those chained to the car?"—
    "The wise,

"The great, the unforgotten,—they who wore
Mitres and helms and crowns, or wreaths of
    light,   210
Signs of thought's empire over thought—their
    lore

"Taught them not this, to know themselves;
    their might
Could not repress the mystery within,
And for the morn of truth they feigned, deep
    night

"Caught them ere evening."—"Who is he
    with chin
Upon his breast, and hands crossed on his
    chain?"—
"The child of a fierce hour; he sought to win

"The world, and lost all that it did contain
Of greatness, in its hope destroyed; and more
Of fame and peace than virtue's self can
    gain   220

"Without the opportunity which bore
Him on its eagle pinions to the peak
From which a thousand climbers have before

"Fallen, as Napoleon fell."—I felt my cheek
Alter, to see the shadow pass away,
Whose grasp had left the giant world so weak

That every pigmy kicked it as it lay;
That much I grieved to think how power and
    will
In opposition rule our mortal day,

And why God made irreconcilable   230
Good and the means of good; and for despair
I half disdained mine eyes' desire to fill

With the spent vision of the times that were
And scarce have ceased to be.—"Dost thou
    behold,"
Said my guide, "those spoilers spoiled, Voltaire,

"Frederick, and Paul, Catherine, and Leopold,
And hoary anarchs, demagogues, and sage—
    names which the world thinks always old,

"For in the battle Life and they did wage,
She remained conqueror. I was overcome 240
By my own heart alone, which neither age,

"Nor tears, nor infamy, nor now the tomb
Could temper to its object."—"Let them pass,"
I cried, "the world and its mysterious doom

"Is not so much more glorious than it was,
That I desire to worship those who drew
New figures on its false and fragile glass

"As the old faded."—"Figures ever new
Rise on the bubble, paint them as you may;
We have but thrown, as those before us threw,

"Our shadows on it as it passed away.   251
But mark how chained to the triumphal chair
The mighty phantoms of an elder day;

"All that is mortal of great Plato there
Expiates the joy and woe his master knew not;
The star that ruled his doom was far too fair.

"And life, where long that flower of Heaven
    grew not,
Conquered that heart by love, which gold, or
    pain,
Or age, or sloth, or slavery could subdue not.

"And near him walk the twain, 260
The tutor and his pupil, whom Dominion
Followed as tame as vulture in a chain.

"The world was darkened beneath either pinion
Of him whom from the flock of conquerors
Fame singled out for her thunder-bearing
minion;

"The other long outlived both woes and wars,
Throned in the thoughts of men, and still had
kept
The jealous key of Truth's eternal doors,

"If Bacon's eagle spirit had not leapt
Like lightning out of darkness—he com-
pelled 270
The Proteus shape of Nature, as it slept

"To wake, and lead him to the caves that held
The treasure of the secrets of its reign.
See the great bards of elder time, who quelled

"The passions which they sung, as by their
strain
May well be known: their living melody
Tempers its own contagion to the vein

"Of those who are infected with it—I
Have suffered what I wrote, or viler pain!
And so my words have seeds of misery— 280

"Even as the deeds of others, not as theirs."
And then he pointed to a company,

'Midst whom I quickly recognized the heirs
Of Caesar's crime, from him to Constantine;
The anarch chiefs, whose force and murderous
snares

Had founded many a sceptre-bearing line,
And spread the plague of gold and blood
abroad:
And Gregory and John, and men divine,

Who rose like shadows between man and God;
Till that eclipse, still hanging over heaven, 290
Was worshipped by the world o'er which they
strode,

For the true sun it quenched—"Their power
was given
But to destroy," replied the leader:—"I
Am one of those who have created, even

"If it be but a world of agony."—
"Whence camest thou? and whither goest thou?
How did thy course begin?" I said, "and why?

"Mine eyes are sick of this perpetual flow
Of people, and my heart sick of one sad
thought—
Speak!"—"Whence I am, I partly seem to
know, 300

"And how and by what paths I have been
brought
To this dread pass, methinks even thou mayst
guess;—
Why this should be, my mind can compass
not;

"Whither the conqueror hurries me, still less;—
But follow thou, and from spectator turn
Actor or victim in this wretchedness,

"And what thou wouldst be taught I then may
learn
From thee. Now listen:—In the April prime,
When all the forest-tips began to burn

"With kindling green, touched by the azure
clime 310
Of the young season, I was laid asleep
Under a mountain, which from unknown time

"Had yawned into a cavern, high and deep;
And from it came a gentle rivulet,
Whose water, like clear air, in its calm sweep

"Bent the soft grass, and kept for ever wet
The stems of the sweet flowers, and filled the
grove
With sounds, which whoso hears must needs
forget

"All pleasure and all pain, all hate and love,
Which they had known before that hour of
rest; 320
A sleeping mother then would dream not of

"Her only child who died upon the breast
At eventide—a king would mourn no more
The crown of which his brows were dispos-
    sessed

"When the sun lingered o'er his ocean floor
To gild his rival's new prosperity.
Thou wouldst forget thus vainly to deplore

"Ills, which if ills can find no cure from
    thee,
The thought of which no other sleep will quell,
Nor other music blot from memory,   330

"So sweet and deep is the oblivious spell;
And whether life had been before that sleep
The Heaven which I imagine, or a Hell

"Like this harsh world in which I wake to weep,
I know not. I arose, and for a space
The scene of woods and waters seemed to
    keep,

"Though it was now broad day, a gentle
    trace
Of light diviner than the common sun
Sheds on the common earth, and all the place

"Was filled with magic sounds woven into
    one   340
Oblivious melody, confusing sense
Amid the gliding waves and shadows dun;

"And, as I looked, the bright omnipresence
Of morning through the orient cavern flowed,
And the sun's image radiantly intense

"Burned on the waters of the well that glowed
Like gold, and threaded all the forest's maze
With winding paths of emerald fire; there
    stood

"Amid the sun, as he amid the blaze
Of his own glory, on the vibrating   350
Floor of the fountain, paved with flashing
    rays,

"A Shape all light, which with one hand did
    fling
Dew on the earth, as if she were the dawn,
And the invisible rain did ever sing

"A silver music on the mossy lawn;
And still before me on the dusky grass,
Iris her many-coloured scarf had drawn:

"In her right hand she bore a crystal glass,
Mantling with bright Nepenthe; the fierce
    splendour
Fell from her as she moved under the mass

"Of the deep cavern, and with palms so
    tender,   361
Their tread broke not the mirror of its billow,
Glided along the river, and did bend her

"Head under the dark boughs, till like a wil-
    low
Her fair hair swept the bosom of the stream
That whispered with delight to be its pillow.

"As one enamoured is upborne in dream
O'er lily-paven lakes, mid silver mist,
To wondrous music, so this shape might seem

"Partly to tread the waves with feet which
    kissed   370
The dancing foam; partly to glide along
The air which roughened the moist amethyst,

"Or the faint morning beams that fell among
The trees or the soft shadows of the trees;
And her feet, ever to the ceaseless song

"Of leaves, and winds, and waves, and birds,
    and bees,
And falling drops, moved in a measure new
Yet sweet, as on the summer evening breeze,

"Up from the lake a shape of golden dew
Between two rocks, athwart the rising moon,
Dances i' the wind, where never eagle flew; 381

"And still her feet, no less than the sweet tune
To which they moved, seemed as they moved
    to blot
The thoughts of him who gazed on them; and
    soon

"All that was, seemed as if it had been not;
And all the gazer's mind was strewn beneath
Her feet like embers; and she, thought by
    thought,

"Trampled its sparks into the dust of death;
As day upon the threshold of the east
Treads out the lamps of night, until the breath

"Of darkness re-illumine even the least   391
Of heaven's living eyes—like day she came,
Making the night a dream; and ere she ceased

"To move, as one between desire and shame
Suspended, I said—If, as it doth seem,
Thou comest from the realm without a name

"Into this valley of perpetual dream,
Show whence I came, and where I am, and
        why—
Pass not away upon the passing stream.

"Arise and quench thy thirst, was her reply. 400
And as a shut lily stricken by the wand
Of dewy morning's vital alchemy,

"I rose; and, bending at her sweet command,
Touched with faint lips the cup she raised,
And suddenly my brain became as sand

"Where the first wave had more than half erased
The track of deer on desert Labrador;
Whilst the wolf, from which they fled amazed,

"Leaves his stamp visibly upon the shore,
Until the second bursts;—so on my sight 410
Burst a new vision, never seen before,

"And the fair shape waned in the coming light,
As veil by veil the silent splendour drops
From Lucifer, amid the chrysolite

"Of sunrise, ere it tinge the mountain-tops;
And as the presence of that fairest planet,
Although unseen, is felt by one who hopes

"That his day's path may end as he began it,
In that star's smile, whose light is like the scent
Of a jonquil when evening breezes fan it, 420

"Or the soft note in which his dear lament
The Brescian [1] shepherd breathes, or the caress
That turned his weary slumber to content;

[1] The favourite song, *Stanco di pascolar le peco-relle*, is a Brescian national air.—[MRS. SHELLEY'S NOTE.]

"So knew I in that light's severe excess
The presence of that Shape which on the
        stream
Moved, as I moved along the wilderness,

"More dimly than a day-appearing dream,
The ghost of a forgotten form of sleep;
A light of heaven, whose half-extinguished
        beam

"Through the sick day in which we wake to
        weep   430
Glimmers, for ever sought, for ever lost;
So did that shape its obscure tenour keep

"Beside my path, as silent as a ghost;
But the new Vision, and the cold bright car,
With solemn speed and stunning music, crossed

"The forest, and as if from some dread war
Triumphantly returning, the loud million
Fiercely extolled the fortune of her star.

"A moving arch of victory, the vermillion
And green and azure plumes of Iris had   440
Built high over her wind-wingèd pavilion,

"And underneath aethereal glory clad
The wilderness, and far before her flew
The tempest of the splendour, which forbade

"Shadow to fall from leaf and stone; the crew
Seemed in that light, like atomies to dance
Within a sunbeam;—some upon the new

"Embroidery of flowers, that did enhance
The grassy vesture of the desert, played,
Forgetful of the chariot's swift advance; 450

"Others stood gazing, till within the shade
Of the great mountains its light left them
        dim;
Others outspeeded it; and others made

"Circles around it, like the clouds that swim
Round the high moon in a bright sea of air;
And more did follow, with exulting hymn,

"The chariot and the captives fettered there:—
But all the bubbles on an eddying flood
Fell into the same track at last, and were

"Borne onward.—I among the multitude 460
Was swept—me, sweetest flowers delayed not
    long;
Me, not the shadow nor the solitude;

"Me, not that falling stream's Lethean song;
Me, not the phantom of that early Form
Which moved upon its motion—but among

"The thickest billows of that living storm
I plunged, and bared my bosom to the clime
Of that cold light, whose airs too soon de-
    form.

"Before the chariot had begun to climb
The opposing steep of that mysterious dell, 470
Behold a wonder worthy of the rhyme

"Of him who from the lowest depths of
    hell,
Through every paradise and through all glory,
Love led serene, and who returned to tell

"The words of hate and awe; the wondrous
    story
How all things are transfigured except Love;
For deaf as is a sea, which wrath makes hoary,

"The world can hear not the sweet notes that
    move
The sphere whose light is melody to lovers—
A wonder worthy of his rhyme.—The grove

"Grew dense with shadows to its inmost cov-
    ers,   481
The earth was gray with phantoms, and the air
Was peopled with dim forms, as when there
    hovers

"A flock of vampire-bats before the glare
Of the tropic sun, bringing, ere evening,
Strange night upon some Indian isle;—thus
    were

"Phantoms diffused around; and some did fling
Shadows of shadows, yet unlike themselves,
Behind them; some like eaglets on the wing

"Were lost in the white day; others like elves
Danced in a thousand unimagined shapes 491
Upon the sunny streams and grassy shelves;

"And others sate chattering like restless apes
On vulgar hands, . . .
Some made a cradle of the ermined capes

"Of kingly mantles; some across the tiar
Of pontiffs sate like vultures; others played
Under the crown which girt with empire

"A baby's or an idiot's brow, and made
Their nests in it. The old anatomies   500
Sate hatching their bare broods under the
    shade

"Of daemon wings, and laughed from their
    dead eyes
To reassume the delegated power,
Arrayed in which those worms did monarch-
    ize,

"Who made this earth their charnel. Others
    more
Humble, like falcons, sate upon the fist
Of common men, and round their heads did
    soar;

"Or like small gnats and flies, as thick as
    mist
On evening marshes, thronged about the
    brow
Of lawyers, statesmen, priest and theorist;—

"And others, like discoloured flakes of snow
On fairest bosoms and the sunniest hair,   512
Fell, and were melted by the youthful glow

"Which they extinguished; and, like tears, they
    were
A veil to those from whose faint lids they
    rained
In drops of sorrow. I became aware

"Of whence those forms proceeded which thus
    stained
The track in which we moved. After brief
    space,
From every form the beauty slowly waned;

"From every firmest limb and fairest face
The strength and freshness fell like dust, and
    left   521
The action and the shape without the grace

"Of life. The marble brow of youth was cleft
With care; and in those eyes where once hope
    shone,
Desire, like a lioness bereft

"Of her last cub, glared ere it died; each one
Of that great crowd sent forth incessantly
These shadows, numerous as the dead leaves
    blown

"In autumn evening from a poplar tree.
Each like himself and like each other were 530
At first; but some distorted seemed to be

"Obscure clouds, moulded by the casual air;
And of this stuff the car's creative ray
Wrought all the busy phantoms that were there,

"As the sun shapes the clouds; thus on the way
Mask after mask fell from the countenance
And form of all; and long before the day

"Was old, the joy which waked like heaven's
    glance
The sleepers in the oblivious valley, died;
And some grew weary of the ghastly dance, 540

"And fell, as I have fallen, by the wayside;—
Those soonest from whose forms most shad-
    ows passed,
And least of strength and beauty did abide.

"Then, what is life? I cried."—
1822

STANZAS—APRIL, 1814

AWAY! the moor is dark beneath the moon.
  Rapid clouds have drank the last pale beam
    of even:
Away the gathering winds will call the dark-
    ness soon.
  And profoundest midnight shroud the se-
    rene lights of heaven.

Pause not! the time is past! Every voice cries,
  Away!
  Tempt not with one last tear thy friend's un-
    gentle mood:
Thy lover's eye, so glazed and cold, dares not
  entreat thy stay:
  Duty and dereliction guide thee back to
    solitude.

Away, away! to thy sad and silent home;
  Pour bitter tears on its desolated hearth; 10
Watch the dim shades as like ghosts they go
  and come,
  And complicate strange webs of melancholy
    mirth.

The leaves of wasted autumn woods shall
  float around thine head:
  The blooms of dewy spring shall gleam be-
    neath thy feet:
But thy soul or this world must fade in the
  frost that binds the dead,
  Ere midnight's frown and morning's smile,
    ere thou and peace may meet.

The cloud shadows of midnight possess their
  own repose,
  For the weary winds are silent, or the moon
    is in the deep:
Some respite to its turbulence unresting ocean
  knows,
  Whatever moves, or toils, or grieves, hath
    its appointed sleep.   20

Thou in the grave shalt rest—yet till the phantoms flee
  Which that house and heath and garden
    made dear to thee erewhile,
Thy remembrance, and repentance, and deep
  musings are not free
  From the music of two voices and the light
    of one sweet smile.
1814

A DEFENCE OF POETRY

1821

PART I [1]

ACCORDING to one mode of regarding those two classes of mental action, which are called reason and imagination, the former may be considered as mind contemplating the relations borne by one thought to another, however produced; and the latter, as mind acting upon those thoughts so as to colour them with its own light, and composing from them, as from elements, other thoughts, each containing within itself the principle of its own integrity. The one is the τὸ ποιεῖν, or the principle of synthesis, and has for its objects those forms which are common to universal nature and existence itself; the other is the τὸ λογίζειν, or principle of analysis, and its action regards the relations of things, simply as relations; considering thoughts, not in their integral unity, but as the algebraical representations which conduct to certain general results. Reason is the enumeration of quantities already known; imagination is the perception of the value of those quantities, both separately and as a whole. Reason respects the differences, and imagination the similitudes of things. Reason is to the imagination as the instrument to the agent, as the body to the spirit, as the shadow to the substance.

Poetry, in a general sense, may be defined to be "the expression of the imagination": and poetry is connate with the origin of man. Man is an instrument over which a series of external and internal impressions are driven, like the alternations of an ever-changing wind over an Aeolian lyre, which move it by their motion to ever-changing melody. But there is a principle within the human being, and perhaps within all sentient beings, which acts otherwise than in the lyre, and produces not melody alone, but harmony, by an internal adjustment of the sounds or motions thus excited to the impressions which excite them. It is as if the lyre could accommodate its chords to the motions of that which strikes them, in a determined proportion of sound; even as the

musician can accommodate his voice to the sound of the lyre. A child at play by itself will express its delight by its voice and motions; and every inflexion of tone and every gesture will bear exact relation to a corresponding antitype in the pleasurable impressions which awakened it; it will be the reflected image of that impression; and as the lyre trembles and sounds after the wind has died away, so the child seeks, by prolonging in its voice and motions the duration of the effect, to prolong also a consciousness of the cause. In relation to the objects which delight a child, these expressions are, what poetry is to higher objects. The savage (for the savage is to ages what the child is to years) expresses the emotions produced in him by surrounding objects in a similar manner; and language and gesture, together with plastic or pictorial imitation, become the image of the combined effect of those objects, and of his apprehension of them. Man in society, with all his passions and his pleasures, next becomes the object of the passions and pleasures of man; an additional class of emotions produces an augmented treasure of expressions; and language, gesture, and the imitative arts, become at once the representation and the medium, the pencil and the picture, the chisel and the statue, the chord and the harmony. The social sympathies, or those laws from which, as from its elements, society results, begin to develop themselves from the moment that two human beings co-exist; the future is contained within the present, as the plant within the seed; and equality, diversity, unity, contrast, mutual dependence, become the principles alone capable of affording the motives according to which the will of a social being is determined to action, inasmuch as he is social; and constitute pleasure in sensation, virtue in sentiment, beauty in art, truth in reasoning, and love in the intercourse of kind. Hence men, even in the infancy of society, observe a certain order in their words and actions, distinct from that of the objects and the impressions represented by them, all expression being subject to the laws of that from which it proceeds. But let us dismiss those more general considerations which might involve an inquiry into the principles of society itself, and restrict our view

[1] The projected second and third parts were never written.

to the manner in which the imagination is expressed upon its forms.

In the youth of the world, men dance and sing and imitate natural objects, observing in these actions, as in all others, a certain rhythm or order. And, although all men observe a similar, they observe not the same order, in the motions of the dance, in the melody of the song, in the combinations of language, in the series of their imitations of natural objects. For there is a certain order or rhythm belonging to each of these classes of mimetic representation, from which the hearer and the spectator receive an intenser and purer pleasure than from any other: the sense of an approximation to this order has been called taste by modern writers. Every man in the infancy of art observes an order which approximates more or less closely to that from which this highest delight results: but the diversity is not sufficiently marked, as that its gradations should be sensible, except in those instances where the predominance of this faculty of approximation to the beautiful (for so we may be permitted to name the relation between this highest pleasure and its cause) is very great. Those in whom it exists in excess are poets, in the most universal sense of the word; and the pleasure resulting from the manner in which they express the influence of society or nature upon their own minds, communicates itself to others, and gathers a sort of reduplication from that community. Their language is vitally metaphorical; that is, it marks the before unapprehended relations of things and perpetuates their apprehension, until the words which represent them become, through time, signs for portions or classes of thoughts instead of pictures of integral thoughts; and then if no new poets should arise to create afresh the associations which have been thus disorganized, language will be dead to all the nobler purposes of human intercourse. These similitudes or relations are finely said by Lord Bacon to be "the same footsteps of nature impressed upon the various subjects of the world"; and he considers the faculty which perceives them as the storehouse of axioms common to all knowledge. In the infancy of society every author is necessarily a poet, because language itself is poetry; and to be a poet is to apprehend the true and the beautiful, in a word, the good which exists in the relation, subsisting, first between existence and perception, and secondly between perception and expression. Every original language near to its source is in itself the chaos of a cyclic poem: the copiousness of lexicography and the distinctions of grammar are the works of a later age, and are merely the catalogue and the form of the creations of poetry.

But poets, or those who imagine and express this indestructible order, are not only the authors of language and of music, of the dance, and architecture, and statuary, and painting; they are the institutors of laws, and the founders of civil society, and the inventors of the arts of life, and the teachers, who draw into a certain propinquity with the beautiful and the true, that partial apprehension of the agencies of the invisible world which is called religion. Hence all original religions are allegorical, or susceptible of allegory, and, like Janus, have a double face of false and true. Poets, according to the circumstances of the age and nation in which they appeared, were called, in the earlier epochs of the world, legislators, or prophets: a poet essentially comprises and unites both these characters. For he not only beholds intensely the present as it is, and discovers those laws according to which present things ought to be ordered, but he beholds the future in the present, and his thoughts are the germs of the flower and the fruit of latest time. Not that I assert poets to be prophets in the gross sense of the word, or that they can foretell the form as surely as they foreknow the spirit of events: such is the pretence of superstition, which would make poetry an attribute of prophecy, rather than prophecy an attribute of poetry. A poet participates in the eternal, the infinite, and the one; as far as relates to his conceptions, time and place and number are not. The grammatical forms which express the moods of time, and the difference of persons, and the distinction of place, are convertible with respect to the highest poetry without injuring it as poetry; and the choruses of Aeschylus, and the book of *Job*, and Dante's *Paradise*, would afford, more than any other writings, examples of this fact, if the limits of this essay did not forbid citation. The creations of sculpture, painting, and music, are illustrations still more decisive.

Language, colour, form, and religious and civil habits of action, are all the instruments and materials of poetry; they may be called poetry by that figure of speech which considers the effect as a synonym of the cause. But poetry in a more restricted sense expresses those arrangements of language, and especially 10 metrical language, which are created by that imperial faculty, whose throne is curtained within the invisible nature of man. And this springs from the nature itself of language, which is a more direct representation of the 15 actions and passions of our internal being, and is susceptible of more various and delicate combinations, than colour, form, or motion, and is more plastic and obedient to the control of that faculty of which it is the creation. For 20 language is arbitrarily produced by the imagination, and has relation to thoughts alone; but all other materials, instruments, and conditions of art, have relations among each other, which limit and interpose between conception 25 and expression. The former is as a mirror which reflects, the latter as a cloud which enfeebles, the light of which both are mediums of communication. Hence the fame of sculptors, painters, and musicians, although the in- 30 trinsic powers of the great masters of these arts may yield in no degree to that of those who have employed language as the hieroglyphic of their thoughts, has never equalled that of poets in the restricted sense of the 35 term; as two performers of equal skill will produce unequal effects from a guitar and a harp. The fame of legislators and founders of religions, so long as their institutions last, alone seems to exceed that of poets in the 40 restricted sense; but it can scarcely be a question, whether, if we deduct the celebrity which their flattery of the gross opinions of the vulgar usually conciliates, together with that which belonged to them in their higher char- 45 acter of poets, any excess will remain.

We have thus circumscribed the word poetry within the limits of that art which is the most familiar and the most perfect expression of the faculty itself. It is necessary, however, to 50 make the circle still narrower, and to determine the distinction between measured and unmeasured language; for the popular division into prose and verse is inadmissible in accurate philosophy.

Sounds as well as thoughts have relation both between each other and towards that which they represent, and a perception of the order of those relations has always been found connected with a perception of the order of the relations of thoughts. Hence the language of poets has ever affected a certain uniform and harmonious recurrence of sound, without which it were not poetry, and which is scarcely less indispensable to the communication of its influence, than the words themselves, without reference to that peculiar order. Hence the vanity of translation; it were as wise to cast a violet into a crucible that you might discover the formal principle of its colour and odour, as seek to transfuse from one language into another the creations of a poet. The plant must spring again from its seed, or it will bear no flower—and this is the burthen of the curse of Babel.

An observation of the regular mode of the recurrence of harmony in the language of poetical minds, together with its relation to music, produced metre, or a certain system of traditional forms of harmony and language. Yet it is by no means essential that a poet should accommodate his language to this traditional form, so that the harmony, which is its spirit, be observed. The practice is indeed convenient and popular, and to be preferred, especially in such composition as includes much action: but every great poet must inevitably innovate upon the example of his predecessors in the exact structure of his peculiar versification. The distinction between poets and prose writers is a vulgar error. The distinction between philosophers and poets has been anticipated. Plato was essentially a poet —the truth and splendour of his imagery, and the melody of his language, are the most intense that it is possible to conceive. He rejected the measure of the epic, dramatic, and lyrical forms, because he sought to kindle a harmony in thoughts divested of shape and action, and he forbore to invent any regular plan of rhythm which would include, under determinate forms, the varied pauses of his style.

Cicero sought to imitate the cadence of his periods, but with little success. Lord Bacon was a poet. His language has a sweet and majestic rhythm, which satisfies the sense, no less than the almost superhuman wisdom of his philosophy satisfies the intellect; it is a strain which distends, and then bursts the circumference of the reader's mind, and pours itself forth together with it into the universal element with which it has perpetual sympathy. All the authors of revolutions in opinion are not only necessarily poets as they are inventors, nor even as their words unveil the permanent analogy of things by images which participate in the life of truth; but as their periods are harmonious and rhythmical, and contain in themselves the elements of verse; being the echo of the eternal music. Nor are those supreme poets, who have employed traditional forms of rhythm on account of the form and action of their subjects, less capable of perceiving and teaching the truth of things, than those who have omitted that form. Shakespeare, Dante, and Milton (to confine ourselves to modern writers) are philosophers of the very loftiest power.

A poem is the very image of life expressed in its eternal truth. There is this difference between a story and a poem, that a story is a catalogue of detached facts, which have no other connexion than time, place, circumstance, cause and effect; the other is the creation of actions according to the unchangeable forms of human nature, as existing in the mind of the Creator, which is itself the image of all other minds. The one is partial, and applies only to a definite period of time, and a certain combination of events which can never again recur; the other is universal, and contains within itself the germ of a relation to whatever motives or actions have place in the possible varieties of human nature. Time, which destroys the beauty and the use of the story of particular facts, stripped of the poetry which should invest them, augments that of poetry, and for ever develops new and wonderful applications of the eternal truth which it contains. Hence epitomes have been called the moths of just history; they eat out the poetry of it. A story of particular facts is as a mirror which obscures and distorts that which should be beautiful: poetry is a mirror which makes beautiful that which is distorted.

The parts of a composition may be poetical, without the composition as a whole being a poem. A single sentence may be considered as a whole, though it may be found in the midst of a series of unassimilated portions: a single word even may be a spark of inextinguishable thought. And thus all the great historians, Herodotus, Plutarch, Livy, were poets; and although the plan of these writers, especially that of Livy, restrained them from developing this faculty in its highest degree, they made copious and ample amends for their subjection, by filling all the interstices of their subjects with living images.

Having determined what is poetry, and who are poets, let us proceed to estimate its effects upon society.

Poetry is ever accompanied with pleasure: all spirits on which it falls open themselves to receive the wisdom which is mingled with its delight. In the infancy of the world, neither poets themselves nor their auditors are fully aware of the excellence of poetry: for it acts in a divine and unapprehended manner, beyond and above consciousness; and it is reserved for future generations to contemplate and measure the mighty cause and effect in all the strength and splendour of their union. Even in modern times, no living poet ever arrived at the fullness of his fame; the jury which sits in judgement upon a poet, belonging as he does to all time, must be composed of his peers: it must be impanelled by Time from the selectest of the wise of many generations. A poet is a nightingale, who sits in darkness and sings to cheer its own solitude with sweet sounds; his auditors are as men entranced by the melody of an unseen musician, who feel that they are moved and softened, yet know not whence or why. The poems of Homer and his contemporaries were the delight of infant Greece; they were the elements of that social system which is the column upon which all succeeding civilization has reposed. Homer embodied the ideal perfection of his age in human character; nor can we doubt that those who read his verses were awakened to an ambition of becoming like to Achilles, Hector, and Ulysses: the truth and beauty of friendship, patriotism, and persevering devotion to an object, were unveiled to the depths in these immortal creations: the sentiments of the auditors must have been refined and enlarged by a sympathy with such great and lovely impersonations, until from admiring they imitated, and from imitation they identified themselves with the objects of their admiration. Nor let it be objected, that these characters are remote from moral perfection, and that they can by no means be considered as edifying patterns for general imitation. Every epoch, under names more or less specious, has deified its peculiar errors; Revenge is the naked idol of the worship of a semibarbarous age; and Self-deceit is the veiled image of unknown evil, before which luxury and satiety lie prostrate. But a poet considers the vices of his contemporaries as a temporary dress in which his creations must be arrayed, and which cover without concealing the eternal proportions of their beauty. An epic or dramatic personage is understood to wear them around his soul, as he may the ancient armour or the modern uniform around his body; whilst it is easy to conceive a dress more graceful than either. The beauty of the internal nature cannot be so far concealed by its accidental vesture, but that the spirit of its form shall communicate itself to the very disguise, and indicate the shape it hides from the manner in which it is worn. A majestic form and graceful motions will express themselves through the most barbarous and tasteless costume. Few poets of the highest class have chosen to exhibit the beauty of their conceptions in its naked truth and splendour; and it is doubtful whether the alloy of costume, habit, &c., be not necessary to temper this planetary music for mortal ears.

The whole objection, however, of the immorality of poetry rests upon a misconception of the manner in which poetry acts to produce the moral improvement of man. Ethical science arranges the elements which poetry has created, and propounds schemes and proposes examples of civil and domestic life: nor is it for want of admirable doctrines that men hate, and despise, and censure, and deceive, and subjugate one another. But poetry acts in another and diviner manner. It awakens and enlarges the mind itself by rendering it the receptacle of a thousand unapprehended combinations of thought. Poetry lifts the veil from the hidden beauty of the world, and makes familiar objects be as if they were not familiar; it reproduces all that it represents, and the impersonations clothed in its Elysian light stand thenceforward in the minds of those who have once contemplated them, as memorials of that gentle and exalted content which extends itself over all thoughts and actions with which its coexists. The great secret of morals is love; or a going out of our own nature, and an identification of ourselves with the beautiful which exists in thought, action, or person, not our own. A man, to be greatly good, must imagine intensely and comprehensively; he must put himself in the place of another and of many others; the pains and pleasures of his species must become his own. The great instrument of moral good is the imagination; and poetry administers to the effect by acting upon the cause. Poetry enlarges the circumference of the imagination by replenishing it with thoughts of ever new delight, which have the power of attracting and assimilating to their own nature all other thoughts, and which form new intervals and interstices whose void for ever craves fresh food. Poetry strengthens the faculty which is the organ of the moral nature of man, in the same manner as exercise strengthens a limb. A poet therefore would do ill to embody his own conceptions of right and wrong, which are usually those of his place and time, in his poetical creations, which participate in neither. By this assumption of the inferior office of interpreting the effect, in which perhaps after all he might acquit himself but imperfectly, he would resign a glory in a participation in the cause. There was little danger that Homer, or any of the eternal poets, should have so far misunderstood themselves as to have abdicated this throne of their widest dominion. Those in whom the poetical faculty, though great, is less intense, as Euripides, Lucan, Tasso, Spenser, have frequently affected a moral aim, and the effect of their poetry is diminished in exact proportion to the degree in which they compel us to advert to this purpose.

Homer and the cyclic poets were followed

at a certain interval by the dramatic and lyrical poets of Athens, who flourished contemporaneously with all that is most perfect in the kindred expressions of the poetical faculty; architecture, painting, music, the dance, sculpture, philosophy, and, we may add, the forms of civil life. For although the scheme of Athenian society was deformed by many imperfections which the poetry existing in chivalry and Christianity has erased from the habits and institutions of modern Europe; yet never at any other period has so much energy, beauty, and virtue, been developed; never was blind strength and stubborn form so disciplined and rendered subject to the will of man, or that will less repugnant to the dictates of the beautiful and the true, as during the century which preceded the death of Socrates. Of no other epoch in the history of our species have we records and fragments stamped so visibly with the image of the divinity in man. But it is poetry alone, in form, in action, or in language, which has rendered this epoch memorable above all others, and the storehouse of examples to everlasting time. For written poetry existed at that epoch simultaneously with the other arts, and it is an idle inquiry to demand which gave and which received the light, which all, as from a common focus, have scattered over the darkest periods of succeeding time. We know no more of cause and effect than a constant conjunction of events: poetry is ever found to co-exist with whatever other arts contribute to the happiness and perfection of man. I appeal to what has already been established to distinguish between the cause and the effect.

It was at the period here adverted to, that the drama had its birth; and however a succeeding writer may have equalled or surpassed those few great specimens of the Athenian drama which have been preserved to us, it is indisputable that the art itself never was understood or practised according to the true philosophy of it, as at Athens. For the Athenians employed language, action, music, painting, the dance, and religious institutions, to produce a common effect in the representation of the highest idealisms of passion and of power; each division in the art was made perfect in its kind by artists of the most consummate skill, and was disciplined into a beautiful proportion and unity one towards the other. On the modern stage a few only of the elements capable of expressing the image of the poet's conception are employed at once. We have tragedy without music and dancing; and music and dancing without the highest impersonations of which they are the fit accompaniment, and both without religion and solemnity. Religious institution has indeed been usually banished from the stage. Our system of divesting the actor's face of a mask, on which the many expressions appropriated to his dramatic character might be moulded into one permanent and unchanging expression, is favourable only to a partial and inharmonious effect; it is fit for nothing but a monologue, where all the attention may be directed to some great master of ideal mimicry. The modern practice of blending comedy with tragedy, though liable to great abuse in point of practice, is undoubtedly an extension of the dramatic circle; but the comedy should be as in *King Lear*, universal, ideal, and sublime. It is perhaps the intervention of this principle which determines the balance in favour of *King Lear* against the *Oedipus Tyrannus* or the *Agamemnon*, or, if you will, the trilogies with which they are connected; unless the intense power of the choral poetry, especially that of the latter, should be considered as restoring the equilibrium. *King Lear*, if it can sustain this comparison, may be judged to be the most perfect specimen of the dramatic art existing in the world; in spite of the narrow conditions to which the poet was subjected by the ignorance of the philosophy of the drama which has prevailed in modern Europe. Calderon, in his religious *Autos*, has attempted to fulfil some of the high conditions of dramatic representation neglected by Shakespeare; such as the establishing a relation between the drama and religion, and the accommodating them to music and dancing; but he omits the observation of conditions still more important, and more is lost than gained by the substitution of the rigidly-defined and ever-repeated idealisms of a distorted superstition for the living impersonations of the truth of human passions.

But I digress.—The connexion of scenic exhibitions with the improvement or corruption of the manners of men, has been universally recognized: in other words, the presence or absence of poetry in its most perfect and universal form, has been found to be connected with good and evil in conduct or habit. The corruption which has been imputed to the drama as an effect, begins, when the poetry employed in its constitution ends: I appeal to the history of manners whether the periods of the growth of the one and the decline of the other have not corresponded with an exactness equal to any example of moral cause and effect.

The drama at Athens, or wheresoever else it may have approached to its perfection, ever co-existed with the moral and intellectual greatness of the age. The tragedies of the Athenian poets are as mirrors in which the spectator beholds himself, under a thin disguise of circumstance, stript of all but that ideal perfection and energy which every one feels to be the internal type of all that he loves, admires, and would become. The imagination is enlarged by a sympathy with pains and passions so mighty, that they distend in their conception the capacity of that by which they are conceived; the good affectations are strengthened by pity, indignation, terror, and sorrow; and an exalted calm is prolonged from the satiety of this high exercise of them into the tumult of familiar life: even crime is disarmed of half its horror and all its contagion by being represented as the fatal consequence of the unfathomable agencies of nature; error is thus divested of its wilfulness; men can no longer cherish it as the creation of their choice. In a drama of the highest order there is little food for censure or hatred; it teaches rather self-knowledge and self-respect. Neither the eye nor the mind can see itself, unless reflected upon that which it resembles. The drama, so long as it continues to express poetry, is as a prismatic and many-sided mirror, which collects the brightest rays of human nature and divides and reproduces them from the simplicity of these elementary forms, and touches them with majesty and beauty, and multiplies all that it reflects, and endows it with the power of propagating its like wherever it may fall.

But in periods of the decay of social life, the drama sympathizes with that decay. Tragedy becomes a cold imitation of the form of the great masterpieces of antiquity, divested of all harmonious accompaniment of the kindred arts; and often the very form misunderstood, or a weak attempt to teach certain doctrines, which the writer considers as moral truths; and which are usually no more than specious flatteries of some gross vice or weakness, with which the author, in common with his auditors, are infected. Hence what has been called the classical and domestic drama. Addison's *Cato* is a specimen of the one; and would it were not superfluous to cite examples of the other! To such purposes poetry cannot be made subservient. Poetry is a sword of lightning, ever unsheathed, which consumes the scabbard that would contain it. And thus we observe that all dramatic writings of this nature are unimaginative in a singular degree; they affect sentiment and passion, which, divested of imagination, are other names for caprice and appetite. The period in our own history of the grossest degradation of the drama is the reign of Charles II, when all forms in which poetry had been accustomed to be expressed became hymns to the triumph of kingly power over liberty and virtue. Milton stood alone illuminating an age unworthy of him. At such periods the calculating principle pervades all the forms of dramatic exhibition, and poetry ceases to be expressed upon them. Comedy loses its ideal universality: wit succeeds to humour; we laugh from self-complacency and triumph, instead of pleasure; malignity, sarcasm, and contempt, succeed to sympathetic merriment; we hardly laugh, but we smile. Obscenity, which is ever blasphemy against the divine beauty in life, becomes, from the very veil which it assumes, more active if less disgusting: it is a monster for which the corruption of society for ever brings forth new food, which it devours in secret.

The drama being that form under which a greater number of modes of expression of poetry are susceptible of being combined than any other, the connexion of poetry and social good is more observable in the drama than in whatever other form. And it is indisputable that the highest perfection of human society has ever corresponded with the highest dramatic excellence; and that the corruption or the extinction of the drama in a nation where it has once flourished, is a mark of a corruption of manners, and an extinction of the energies which sustain the soul of social life. But, as Machiavelli says of political institutions, that life may be preserved and renewed, if men should arise capable of bringing back the drama to its principles. And this is true with respect to poetry in its most extended sense: all language, institution and form, require not only to be produced but to be sustained: the office and character of a poet participates in the divine nature as regards providence, no less than as regards creation.

Civil war, the spoils of Asia, and the fatal predominance first of the Macedonian, and then of the Roman arms, were so many symbols of the extinction or suspension of the creative faculty in Greece. The bucolic writers, who found patronage under the lettered tyrants of Sicily and Egypt, were the latest representatives of its most glorious reign. Their poetry is intensely melodious; like the odour of the tuberose, it overcomes and sickens the spirit with excess of sweetness; whilst the poetry of the preceding age was as a meadow-gale of June, which mingles the fragrance of all the flowers of the field, and adds a quickening and harmonizing spirit of its own, which endows the sense with a power of sustaining its extreme delight. The bucolic and erotic delicacy in written poetry is correlative with that softness in statuary, music, and the kindred arts, and even in manners and institutions, which distinguished the epoch to which I now refer. Nor is it the poetical faculty itself, or any misapplication of it, to which this want of harmony is to be imputed. An equal sensibility to the influence of the senses and the affections is to be found in the writings of Homer and Sophocles: the former, especially, has clothed sensual and pathetic images with irresistible attractions. Their superiority over these succeeding writers consists in the presence of those thoughts which belong to the inner faculties of our nature, not in the absence of those which are connected with the external: their incomparable perfection consists in a harmony of the union of all. It is not what the erotic poets have, but what they have not, in which their imperfection consists. It is not inasmuch as they were poets, but inasmuch as they were not poets, that they can be considered with any plausibility as connected with the corruption of their age. Had that corruption availed so as to extinguish in them the sensibility to pleasure, passion, and natural scenery, which is imputed to them as an imperfection, the last triumph of evil would have been achieved. For the end of social corruption is to destroy all sensibility to pleasure; and, therefore, it is corruption. It begins at the imagination and the intellect as at the core, and distributes itself thence as a paralysing venom, through the affections into the very appetites, until all become a torpid mass in which hardly sense survives. At the approach of such a period, poetry ever addresses itself to those faculties which are the last to be destroyed, and its voice is heard, like the footsteps of Astraea, departing from the world. Poetry ever communicates all the pleasure which men are capable of receiving: it is ever still the light of life; the source of whatever of beautiful or generous or true can have place in an evil time. It will readily be confessed that those among the luxurious citizens of Syracuse and Alexandria, who were delighted with the poems of Theocritus, were less cold, cruel, and sensual than the remnant of their tribe. But corruption must utterly have destroyed the fabric of human society before poetry can ever cease. The sacred links of that chain have never been entirely disjoined, which descending through the minds of many men is attached to those great minds, whence as from a magnet the invisible effluence is sent forth, which at once connects, animates, and sustains the life of all. It is the faculty which contains within itself the seeds at once of its own and of social renovation. And let us not circumscribe the effects of the bucolic and erotic poetry within the limits of the sensibility of those to whom it was addressed. They may have perceived the beauty of those immortal compositions, simply as fragments and isolated portions: those who are more finely organized, or born in a happier age, may recognize them as episodes to that great poem, which all poets, like the co-operating thoughts of one great mind, have built up since the beginning of the world.

The same revolutions within a narrower sphere had place in ancient Rome; but the actions and forms of its social life never seem to have been perfectly saturated with the poetical element. The Romans appear to have considered the Greeks as the selectest treasuries of the selectest forms of manners and of nature, and to have abstained from creating in measured language, sculpture, music, or architecture, anything which might bear a particular relation to their own condition, whilst it should bear a general one to the universal constitution of the world. But we judge from partial evidence, and we judge perhaps partially. Ennius, Varro, Pacuvius, and Accius, all great poets, have been lost. Lucretius is in the highest, and Virgil in a very high sense, a creator. The chosen delicacy of expressions of the latter, are as a mist of light which conceal from us the intense and exceeding truth of his conceptions of nature. Livy is instinct with poetry. Yet Horace, Catullus, Ovid, and generally the other great writers of the Virgilian age, saw man and nature in the mirror of Greece. The institutions also, and the religion of Rome were less poetical than those of Greece, as the shadow is less vivid than the substance. Hence poetry in Rome, seemed to follow, rather than accompany, the perfection of political and domestic society. The true poetry of Rome lived in its institutions; for whatever of beautiful, true, and majestic, they contained, could have sprung only from the faculty which creates the order in which they consist. The life of Camillus, the death of Regulus; the expectation of the senators, in their godlike state, of the victorious Gauls: the refusal of the republic to make peace with Hannibal, after the battle of Cannae, were not the consequences of a refined calculation of the probable personal advantage to result from such a rhythm and order in the shows of life, to those who were at once the poets and the actors of these immortal dramas. The imagination beholding the beauty of this order, created it out of itself according to its own idea; the consequence was empire, and the reward everliving fame. These things are not the less

poetry *quia carent vate sacro*.[1] They are the episodes of that cyclic poem written by Time upon the memories of men. The Past, like an inspired rhapsodist, fills the theatre of everlasting generations with their harmony.

At length the ancient system of religion and manners had fulfilled the circle of its revolutions. And the world would have fallen into utter anarchy and darkness, but that there were found poets among the authors of the Christian and chivalric systems of manners and religion, who created forms of opinion and action never before conceived; which, copied into the imaginations of men, become as generals to the bewildered armies of their thoughts. It is foreign to the present purpose to touch upon the evil produced by these systems: except that we protest, on the ground of the principles already established, that no portion of it can be attributed to the poetry they contain.

It is probable that the poetry of Moses, Job, David, Solomon, and Isaiah, had produced a great effect upon the mind of Jesus and his disciples. The scattered fragments preserved to us by the biographers of this extraordinary person, are all instinct with the most vivid poetry. But his doctrines seem to have been quickly distorted. At a certain period after the prevalence of a system of opinions founded upon those promulgated by him, the three forms into which Plato had distributed the faculties of mind underwent a sort of apotheosis, and became the object of the worship of the civilized world. Here it is to be confessed that "Light seems to thicken," and

The crow makes wing to the rooky wood,
Good things of day begin to droop and drowse,
And night's black agents to their preys do rouze.

But mark how beautiful an order has sprung from the dust and blood of this fierce chaos! how the world, as from a resurrection, balancing itself on the golden wings of knowledge and of hope, has reassumed its yet unwearied flight into the heaven of time. Listen to the music, unheard by outward ears, which is as a ceaseless and invisible wind, nourishing its everlasting course with strength and swiftness. The poetry in the doctrines of Jesus Christ,

[1] "Because they lack a divinely inspired poet."

and the mythology and institutions of the Celtic conquerors of the Roman empire, outlived the darkness and the convulsions connected with their growth and victory, and blended themselves in a new fabric of manners and opinion. It is an error to impute the ignorance of the dark ages to the Christian doctrines or the predominance of the Celtic nations. Whatever of evil their agencies may have contained sprang from the extinction of the poetical principle, connected with the progress of despotism and superstition. Men, from causes too intricate to be here discussed, had become insensible and selfish: their own will had become feeble, and yet they were its slaves, and thence the slaves of the will of others: lust, fear, avarice, cruelty, and fraud, characterized a race amongst whom no one was to be found capable of *creating* in form, language, or institution. The moral anomalies of such a state of society are not justly to be charged upon any class of events immediately connected with them, and those events are most entitled to our approbation which could dissolve it most expeditiously. It is unfortunate for those who cannot distinguish words from thoughts, that many of these anomalies have been incorporated into our popular religion.

It was not until the eleventh century that the effects of the poetry of the Christian and chivalric systems began to manifest themselves. The principle of equality had been discovered and applied by Plato in his *Republic*, as the theoretical rule of the mode in which the materials of pleasure and of power, produced by the common skill and labour of human beings, ought to be distributed among them. The limitations of this rule were asserted by him to be determined only by the sensibility of each, or the utility to result to all. Plato, following the doctrines of Timaeus and Pythagoras, taught also a moral and intellectual system of doctrine, comprehending at once the past, present, and the future condition of man. Jesus Christ divulged the sacred and eternal truths contained in these views to mankind, and Christianity, in its abstract purity, became the exoteric expression of the esoteric doctrines of the poetry and wisdom of antiquity. The incorporation of the

Celtic nations with the exhausted population of the south, impressed upon it the figure of the poetry existing in their mythology and institutions. The result was a sum of the action and reaction of all the causes included in it; for it may be assumed as a maxim that no nation or religion can supersede any other without incorporating into itself a portion of that which it supersedes. The abolition of personal and domestic slavery, and the emancipation of women from a great part of the degrading restraints of antiquity, were among the consequences of these events.

The abolition of personal slavery is the basis of the highest political hope that it can enter into the mind of man to conceive. The freedom of women produced the poetry of sexual love. Love became a religion, the idols of whose worship were ever present. It was as if the statues of Apollo and the Muses had been endowed with life and motion, and had walked forth among their worshippers; so that earth became peopled by the inhabitants of a diviner world. The familiar appearance and proceedings of life became wonderful and heavenly, and a paradise was created as out of the wrecks of Eden. And as this creation itself is poetry, so its creators were poets; and language was the instrument of their art: "Galeotto fù il libro, e chi lo scrisse." The Provençal Trouveurs, or inventors, preceded Petrarch, whose verses are as spells, which unseal the inmost enchanted fountains of the delight which is in the grief of love. It is impossible to feel them without becoming a portion of that beauty which we contemplate: it were superfluous to explain how the gentleness and the elevation of mind connected with these sacred emotions can render men more amiable, more generous and wise, and lift them out of the dull vapours of the little world of self. Dante understood the secret things of love even more than Petrarch. His *Vita Nuova* is an inexhaustible fountain of purity of sentiment and language: it is the idealized history of that period, and those intervals of his life which were dedicated to love. His apotheosis of Beatrice in Paradise, and the gradations of his own love and her loveliness, by which as by steps he feigns himself to have ascended to the throne of the Supreme Cause, is the most glorious imagination of modern poetry. The acutest critics have justly reversed the judgement of the vulgar, and the order of the great acts of the "Divine Drama," in the measure of the admiration which they accord to the Hell, Purgatory, and Paradise. The latter is a perpetual hymn of everlasting love. Love, which found a worthy poet in Plato alone of all the ancients, has been celebrated by a chorus of the greatest writers of the renovated world; and the music has penetrated the caverns of society, and its echoes still drown the dissonance of arms and superstition. At successive intervals, Ariosto, Tasso, Shakespeare, Spenser, Calderon, Rousseau, and the great writers of our own age, have celebrated the dominion of love, planting as it were trophies in the human mind of that sublimest victory over sensuality and force. The true relation borne to each other by the sexes into which human kind is distributed, has become less misunderstood; and if the error which confounded diversity with inequality of the powers of the two sexes has been partially recognized in the opinions and institutions of modern Europe, we owe this great benefit to the worship of which chivalry was the law, and poets the prophets.

The poetry of Dante may be considered as the bridge thrown over the stream of time, which unites the modern and ancient world. The distorted notions of invisible things which Dante and his rival Milton have idealized, are merely the mask and the mantle in which these great poets walk through eternity enveloped and disguised. It is a difficult question to determine how far they were conscious of the distinction which must have subsisted in their minds between their own creeds and that of the people. Dante at least appears to wish to mark the full extent of it by placing Riphaeus, whom Virgil calls *justissimus unus*, in Paradise, and observing a most heretical caprice in his distribution of rewards and punishments. And Milton's poem contains within itself a philosophical refutation of that system, of which, by a strange and natural antithesis, it has been a chief popular support. Nothing can exceed the energy and magnificence of the character of Satan as expressed in *Paradise Lost*. It is a mistake to suppose that he could ever have been intended for the popular personification of evil. Implacable hate, patient cunning, and a sleepless refinement of device to inflict the extremest anguish on an enemy, these things are evil; and, although venial in a slave, are not to be forgiven in a tyrant; although redeemed by much that ennobles his defeat in one subdued, are marked by all that dishonours his conquest in the victor. Milton's Devil as a moral being is as far superior to his God, as one who perseveres in some purpose which he has conceived to be excellent in spite of adversity and torture, is to one who in the cold security of undoubted triumph inflicts the most horrible revenge upon his enemy, not from any mistaken notion of inducing him to repent of a perseverance in enmity, but with the alleged design of exasperating him to deserve new torments. Milton has so far violated the popular creed (if this shall be judged to be a violation) as to have alleged no superiority of moral virtue to his God over his Devil. And this bold neglect of a direct moral purpose is the most decisive proof of the supremacy of Milton's genius. He mingled as it were the elements of human nature as colours upon a single pallet, and arranged them in the composition of his great picture according to the laws of epic truth; that is, according to the laws of that principle by which a series of actions of the external universe and of intelligent and ethical beings is calculated to excite the sympathy of succeeding generations of mankind. The *Divina Commedia* and *Paradise Lost* have conferred upon modern mythology a systematic form; and when change and time shall have added one more superstition to the mass of those which have arisen and decayed upon the earth, commentators will be learnedly employed in elucidating the religion of ancestral Europe, not only utterly forgotten because it will have been stamped with the eternity of genius.

Homer was the first and Dante the second epic poet: that is, the second poet, the series of whose creations bore a defined and intelligible relation to the knowledge and sentiment and religion of the age in which he lived, and of the ages which followed it: developing itself in correspondence with their development.

For Lucretius had limed the wings of his swift spirit in the dregs of the sensible world; and Virgil, with a modesty that ill became his genius, had affected the fame of an imitator, even whilst he created anew all that he copied; and none among the flock of mock-birds, though their notes were sweet, Apollonius Rhodius, Quintus Calaber, Nonnus, Lucan, Statius, or Claudian, have sought even to fulfil a single condition of epic truth. Milton was the third epic poet. For if the title of epic in its highest sense be refused to the *Aeneid*, still less can it be conceded to the *Orlando Furioso*, the *Gerusalemme Liberata*, the *Lusiad*, or the *Fairy Queen*.

Dante and Milton were both deeply penetrated with the ancient religion of the civilized world; and its spirit exists in their poetry probably in the same proportion as its forms survived in the unreformed worship of modern Europe. The one preceded and the other followed the Reformation at almost equal intervals. Dante was the first religious reformer, and Luther surpassed him rather in the rudeness and acrimony, than in the boldness of his censures of papal usurpation. Dante was the first awakener of entranced Europe; he created a language, in itself music and persuasion, out of a chaos of inharmonious barbarisms. He was the congregator of those great spirits who presided over the resurrection of learning; the Lucifer of that starry flock which in the thirteenth century shone forth from republican Italy, as from a heaven, into the darkness of the benighted world. His very words are instinct with spirit; each is as a spark, a burning atom of inextinguishable thought; and many yet lie covered in the ashes of their birth, and pregnant with a lightning which has yet found no conductor. All high poetry is infinite; it is as the first acorn, which contained all oaks potentially. Veil after veil may be undrawn, and the inmost naked beauty of the meaning never exposed. A great poem is a fountain for ever overflowing with the waters of wisdom and delight; and after one person and one age has exhausted all its divine effluence which their peculiar relations enable them to share, another and yet another succeeds, and new relations are ever developed, the source of an unforeseen and an unconceived delight.

The age immediately succeeding to that of Dante, Petrarch, and Boccaccio, was characterized by a revival of painting, sculpture, and architecture. Chaucer caught the sacred inspiration, and the superstructure of English literature is based upon the materials of Italian invention.

But let us not be betrayed from a defence into a critical history of poetry and its influence on society. Be it enough to have pointed out the effects of poets, in the large and true sense of the word, upon their own and all succeeding times.

But poets have been challenged to resign the civic crown to reasoners and mechanists, on another plea. It is admitted that the exercise of the imagination is most delightful, but it is alleged that that of reason is more useful. Let us examine as the grounds of this distinction, what is here meant by utility. Pleasure or good, in a general sense, is that which the consciousness of a sensitive and intelligent being seeks, and in which, when found, it acquiesces. There are two kinds of pleasure, one durable, universal and permanent; the other transitory and particular. Utility may either express the means of producing the former or the latter. In the former sense, whatever strengthens and purifies the affections, enlarges the imagination, and adds spirit to sense, is useful. But a narrower meaning may be assigned to the word utility, confining it to express that which banishes the importunity of the wants of our animal nature, the surrounding men with security of life, the dispersing the grosser delusions of superstition, and the conciliating such a degree of mutual forbearance among men as may consist with the motives of personal advantage.

Undoubtedly the promoters of utility, in this limited sense, have their appointed office in society. They follow the footsteps of poets, and copy the sketches of their creations into the book of common life. They make space, and give time. Their exertions are of the highest value, so long as they confine their administration of the concerns of the inferior powers of our nature within the limits due to the superior ones. But whilst the sceptic destroys gross superstitions, let him spare to deface, as some of the French writers have defaced, the eternal truths charactered upon the imaginations of men. Whilst the mechanist abridges, and the political economist combines labour, let them beware that their speculations, for want of correspondence with those first principles which belong to the imagination, do not tend, as they have in modern England, to exasperate at once the extremes of luxury and want. They have exemplified the saying, "To him that hath, more shall be given; and from him that hath not, the little that he hath shall be taken away." The rich have become richer, and the poor have become poorer; and the vessel of the state is driven between the Scylla and Charybdis of anarchy and despotism. Such are the effects which must ever flow from an unmitigated exercise of the calculating faculty.

It is difficult to define pleasure in its highest sense; the definition involving a number of apparent paradoxes. For, from an inexplicable defect of harmony in the constitution of human nature, the pain of the inferior is frequently connected with the pleasures of the superior portions of our being. Sorrow, terror, anguish, despair itself, are often the chosen expressions of an approximation to the highest good. Our sympathy in tragic fiction depends on this principle; tragedy delights by affording a shadow of the pleasure which exists in pain. This is the source also of the melancholy which is inseparable from the sweetest melody. The pleasure that is in sorrow is sweeter than the pleasure of pleasure itself. And hence the saying, "It is better to go to the house of mourning, than to the house of mirth." Not that this highest species of pleasure is necessarily linked with pain. The delight of love and friendship, the ecstasy of the admiration of nature, the joy of the perception and still more of the creation of poetry, is often wholly unalloyed.

The production and assurance of pleasure in this highest sense is true utility. Those who produce and preserve this pleasure are poets or poetical philosophers.

The exertions of Locke, Hume, Gibbon, Voltaire, Rousseau,[1] and their disciples, in favour of oppressed and deluded humanity, are entitled to the gratitude of mankind. Yet it is easy to calculate the degree of moral and intellectual improvement which the world would have exhibited, had they never lived. A little more nonsense would have been talked for a century or two; and perhaps a few more men, women, and children, burnt as heretics. We might not at this moment have been congratulating each other on the abolition of the Inquisition in Spain. But it exceeds all imagination to conceive what would have been the moral condition of the world if neither Dante, Petrarch Boccaccio, Chaucer, Shakespeare, Calderon, Lord Bacon, nor Milton, had ever existed; if Raphael and Michael Angelo had never been born; if the Hebrew poetry had never been translated; if a revival of the study of Greek literature had never taken place; if no monuments of ancient sculpture had been handed down to us; and if the poetry of the religion of the ancient world had been extinguished together with its belief. The human mind could never, except by the intervention of these excitements, have been awakened to the invention of the grosser sciences, and that application of analytical reasoning to the aberrations of society, which it is now attempted to exalt over the direct expression of the inventive and creative faculty itself.

We have more moral, political and historical wisdom, than we know how to reduce into practice; we have more scientific and economical knowledge than can be accommodated to the just distribution of the produce which it multiplies. The poetry in these systems of thought, is concealed by the accumulation of facts and calculating processes. There is no want of knowledge respecting what is wisest and best in morals, government, and political economy, or at least, what is wiser and better than what men now practise and endure. But we let "*I dare not* wait upon *I would*, like the poor cat in the adage." We want the creative faculty to imagine that which we know; we want the generous impulse to act that which we imagine; we want the poetry of life: our calculations have outrun conception; we have eaten more than we can digest. The cultivation of those sciences which have enlarged the limits of the empire of man over the external world, has, for want of the poetical fac-

[1] Although Rousseau has been thus classed, he was essentially a poet. The others, even Voltaire, were mere reasoners.

ulty, proportionally circumscribed those of the internal world; and man, having enslaved the elements, remains himself a slave. To what but a cultivation of the mechanical arts in a degree disproportioned to the presence of the creative faculty, which is the basis of all knowledge, is to be attributed the abuse of all invention for abridging and combining labour, to the exasperation of the inequality of mankind? From what other cause has it arisen that the discoveries which should have lightened, have added a weight to the curse imposed on Adam? Poetry, and the principle of Self, of which money is the visible incarnation, are the God and Mammon of the world.

The functions of the poetical faculty are two-fold; by one it creates new materials of knowledge and power and pleasure; by the other it engenders in the mind a desire to reproduce and arrange them according to a certain rhythm and order which may be called the beautiful and the good. The cultivation of poetry is never more to be desired than at periods when, from an excess of the selfish and calculating principle, the accumulation of the materials of external life exceed the quantity of the power of assimilating them to the internal laws of human nature. The body has then become too unwieldy for that which animates it.

Poetry is indeed something divine. It is at once the centre and circumference of knowledge; it is that which comprehends all science, and that to which all science must be referred. It is at the same time the root and blossom of all other systems of thought; it is that from which all spring, and that which adorns all; and that which, if blighted, denies the fruit and the seed, and withholds from the barren world the nourishment and the succession of the scions of the tree of life. It is the perfect and consummate surface and bloom of all things; it is as the odour and the colour of the rose to the texture of the elements which compose it, as the form and splendour of unfaded beauty to the secrets of anatomy and corruption. What were virtue, love, patriotism, friendship—what were the scenery of this beautiful universe which we inhabit; what were our consolations on this side of the grave— and what were our aspirations beyond it, if

poetry did not ascend to bring light and fire from those eternal regions where the owl-winged faculty of calculation dare not ever soar? Poetry is not like reasoning, a power to 5 be exerted according to the determination of the will. A man cannot say, "I will compose poetry." The greatest poet even cannot say it; for the mind in creation is as a fading coal, which some invisible influence, like an incon- 10 stant wind, awakens to transitory brightness; this power arises from within, like the colour of a flower which fades and changes as it is developed, and the conscious portions of our natures are unprophetic either of its approach 15 or its departure. Could this influence be durable in its original purity and force, it is impossible to predict the greatness of the results; but when composition begins, inspiration is already on the decline, and the most glorious 20 poetry that has ever been communicated to the world is probably a feeble shadow of the original conceptions of the poet. I appeal to the greatest poets of the present day, whether it is not an error to assert that the finest passages 25 of poetry are produced by labour and study. The toil and the delay recommended by critics, can be justly interpreted to mean no more than a careful observation of the inspired moments, and an artificial connexion of the spaces be- 30 tween their suggestions by the inter-texture of conventional expressions; a necessity only imposed by the limitedness of the poetical faculty itself; for Milton conceived the *Paradise Lost* as a whole before he executed it in portions. 35 We have his own authority also for the muse having "dictated" to him the "unpremeditated song." And let this be an answer to those who would allege the fifty-six various readings of the first line of the *Orlando Furioso*. Compo- 40 sitions so produced are to poetry what mosaic is to painting. This instinct and intuition of the poetical faculty is still more observable in the plastic and pictorial arts; a great statue or picture grows under the power of the artist as 45 a child in the mother's womb; and the very mind which directs the hands in formation is incapable of accounting to itself for the origin, the gradations, or the media of the process.

Poetry is the record of the best and happiest 50 moments of the happiest and best minds. We are aware of evanescent visitations of thought and feeling sometimes associated with place or person, sometimes regarding our own mind alone, and always arising unforeseen and departing unbidden, but elevating and delightful beyond all expression: so that even in the desire and regret they leave, there cannot but be pleasure, participating as it does in the nature of its object. It is as it were the interpenetration of a diviner nature through our own; but its footsteps are like those of a wind over the sea, which the coming calm erases, and whose traces remain only, as on the wrinkled sand which paves it. These and corresponding conditions of being are experienced principally by those of the most delicate sensibility and the most enlarged imagination; and the state of mind produced by them is at war with every base desire. The enthusiasm of virtue, love, patriotism, and friendship, is essentially linked with such emotions; and whilst they last, self appears as what it is, an atom to a universe. Poets are not only subject to these experiences as spirits of the most refined organization, but they can colour all that they combine with the evanescent hues of this ethereal world; a word, a trait in the representation of a scene or a passion, will touch the enchanted chord, and reanimate, in those who have ever experienced these emotions, the sleeping, the cold, the buried image of the past. Poetry thus makes immortal all that is best and most beautiful in the world; it arrests the vanishing apparitions which haunt the interlunations of life, and veiling them, or in language or in form, sends them forth among mankind, bearing sweet news of kindred joy to those with whom their sisters abide—abide, because there is no portal of expression from the caverns of the spirit which they inhabit into the universe of things. Poetry redeems from decay the visitations of the divinity in man.

Poetry turns all things to loveliness; it exalts the beauty of that which is most beautiful, and it adds beauty to that which is most deformed; it marries exultation and horror, grief and pleasure, eternity and change; it subdues to union under its light yoke, all irreconcilable things. It transmutes all that it touches, and every form moving within the radiance of its presence is changed by wondrous sympathy to an incarnation of the spirit which it breathes: its secret alchemy turns to potable gold the poisonous waters which flow from death through life; it strips the veil of familiarity from the world, and lays bare the naked and sleeping beauty, which is the spirit of its forms.

All things exist as they are perceived; at least in relation to the percipient. "The mind is its own place, and of itself can make a heaven of hell, a hell of heaven." But poetry defeats the curse which binds us to be subjected to the accident of surrounding impressions. And whether it spreads its own figured curtain, or withdraws life's dark veil from before the scene of things, it equally creates for us a being within our being. It makes us the inhabitants of a world to which the familiar world is a chaos. It reproduces the common universe of which we are portions and percipients, and it purges from our inward sight the film of familiarity which obscures from us the wonder of our being. It compels us to feel that which we perceive, and to imagine that which we know. It creates anew the universe, after it has been annihilated in our minds by the recurrence of impressions blunted by reiteration. It justifies the bold and true words of Tasso: *Non merita nome di creatore, se non Iddio ed il Poeta.*[1]

A poet, as he is the author to others of the highest wisdom, pleasure, virtue and glory, so he ought personally to be the happiest, the best, the wisest, and the most illustrious of men. As to his glory, let time be challenged to declare whether the fame of any other institutor of human life be comparable to that of a poet. That he is the wisest, the happiest, and the best, inasmuch as he is a poet, is equally incontrovertible: the greatest poets have been men of the most spotless virtue, of the most consummate prudence, and, if we would look into the interior of their lives, the most fortunate of men: and the exceptions, as they regard those who possessed the poetic faculty in a high yet inferior degree, will be found on consideration to confine rather than destroy the rule. Let us for a moment stoop to the arbitration of popular breath, and usurping

[1] "No one deserves the name of creator except God and the poet."

and uniting in our own persons the incompatible characters of accuser, witness, judge, and executioner, let us decide without trial, testimony, or form, that certain motives of those who are "there sitting where we dare not soar," are reprehensible. Let us assume that Homer was a drunkard, that Virgil was a flatterer, that Horace was a coward, that Tasso was a madman, that Lord Bacon was a peculator, that Raphael was a libertine, that Spenser was a poet laureate. It is inconsistent with this division of our subject to cite living poets, but posterity has done ample justice to the great names now referred to. Their errors have been weighed and found to have been dust in the balance; if their sins "were as scarlet, they are now white as snow": they have been washed in the blood of the mediator and redeemer, Time. Observe in what a ludicrous chaos the imputations of real or fictitious crime have been confused in the contemporary calumnies against poetry and poets; consider how little is, as it appears—or appears, as it is; look to your own motives, and judge not, lest ye be judged.

Poetry, as has been said, differs in this respect from logic, that it is not subject to the control of the active powers of the mind, and that its birth and recurrence have no necessary connexion with the consciousness or will. It is presumptuous to determine that these are the necessary conditions of all mental causation, when mental effects are experienced unsusceptible of being referred to them. The frequent recurrence of the poetical power, it is obvious to suppose, may produce in the mind a habit of order and harmony correlative with its own nature and with its effects upon other minds. But in the intervals of inspiration, and they may be frequent without being durable, a poet becomes a man, and is abandoned to the sudden reflux of the influences under which others habitually live. But as he is more delicately organized than other men, and sensible to pain and pleasure, both his own and that of others, in a degree unknown to them, he will avoid the one and pursue the other with an ardour proportioned to this difference. And he renders himself obnoxious to calumny, when he neglects to observe the circumstances under which these objects of universal pursuit and flight

have disguised themselves in one another's garments.

But there is nothing necessarily evil in this error, and thus cruelty, envy, revenge, avarice, 5 and the passions purely evil, have never formed any portion of the popular imputations on the lives of poets.

I have thought it most favourable to the cause of truth to set down these remarks according to the order in which they were sug- 10 gested to my mind, by a consideration of the subject itself, instead of observing the formality of a polemical reply; but if the view which they contain be just, they will be found to involve a refutation of the arguers against 15 poetry, so far at least as regards the first division of the subject. I can readily conjecture what should have moved the gall of some learned and intelligent writers who quarrel with certain versifiers; I confess myself, like 20 them, unwilling to be stunned by the Theseids of the hoarse Codri of the day. Bavius and Maevius undoubtedly are, as they ever were, insufferable persons. But it belongs to a philosophical critic to distinguish rather than con- 25 found.

The first part of these remarks has related to poetry in its elements and principles; and it has been shown, as well as the narrow limits assigned them would permit, that what is called 30 poetry, in a restricted sense, has a common source with all other forms of order and of beauty, according to which the materials of human life are susceptible of being arranged, and which is poetry in a universal sense. 35

The second part will have for its object an application of these principles to the present state of the cultivation of poetry, and a defence of the attempt to idealize the modern forms of manners and opinions, and compel 40 them into a subordination to the imaginative and creative faculty. For the literature of England, an energetic development of which has ever preceded or accompanied a great and free development of the national will, has 45 arisen as it were from a new birth. In spite of the low-thoughted envy which would undervalue contemporary merit, our own will be a memorable age in intellectual achievements, and we live among such philosophers and 50 poets as surpass beyond comparison any who have appeared since the last national struggle for civil and religious liberty. The most unfailing herald, companion, and follower of the awakening of a great people to work a beneficial change in opinion or institution, is poetry. At such periods there is an accumulation of the power of communicating and receiving intense and impassioned conceptions respecting man and nature. The persons in whom this power resides may often, as far as regards many portions of their nature, have little apparent correspondence with that spirit of good of which they are the ministers. But even whilst they deny and abjure, they are yet compelled to serve, the power which is seated on the throne of their own soul. It is impossible to read the compositions of the most celebrated writers of the present day without being startled with the electric life which burns within their words. They measure the circumference and sound the depths of human nature with a comprehensive and all-penetrating spirit, and they are themselves perhaps the most sincerely astonished at its manifestations; for it is less their spirit than the spirit of the age. Poets are the hierophants of an unapprehended inspiration; the mirrors of the gigantic shadows which futurity casts upon the present; the words which express what they understand not; the trumpets which sing to battle, and feel not what they inspire; the influence which is moved not, but moves. Poets are the unacknowledged legislators of the world.

SELECTIONS FROM THE LETTERS OF SHELLEY

I To Thomas Jefferson Hogg

Field Place, January 3, 1811

My dear Friend,

Before we deny or believe the existence of anything, it is necessary that we should have a tolerably clear idea of what it is. The word "God," a vague word, has been, and will continue to be, the source of numberless errors, until it is erased from the nomenclature of philosophy. Does it not imply "the soul of the universe, the intelligent and *necessarily* beneficent, actuating principle." This it is impossible not to believe in; I may not be able to adduce proofs, but I think that the leaf of a tree, the meanest insect on which we trample, are, in themselves, arguments more conclusive than any which can be advanced, that some vast intellect animates infinity. If we disbelieve *this*, the strongest argument in support of the existence of a future state instantly becomes annihilated. I confess that I think Pope's

All are but parts of one stupendous whole,

something more than poetry. It has ever been my favourite theory, for the immoral soul, "never to be able to die, never to escape from some shrine as chilling as the clayformed dungeon, which now it inhabits"; it is the future punishment which I can most easily believe in.

Love, love *infinite in extent*, eternal in duration, yet (allowing your theory in that point) perfectible, should be the reward; but can we suppose that this reward will arise, spontaneously, as a necessary appendage to our nature, or that our nature itself could be without cause—a first cause—a God? When do we see effects arise without causes? What causes are there without corresponding effects? Yet here, I swear—and as I break my oaths, may Infinity, Eternity blast me—here I swear that never will I forgive intolerance! It is the only point on which I allow myself to encourage revenge; every moment shall be devoted to my object, which I can spare; and let me hope that it will not be a blow which spends itself, and leaves the wretch at rest,—but lasting, long revenge! I am convinced too, that it is of great disservice to society—that it encourages prejudices which strike at the root of the dearest, the tenderest of its ties. Oh! how I wish I were the avenger—that it were mine to crush the demon; to hurl him to his native hell, never to rise again, and thus to establish for ever perfect and universal toleration, I expect to gratify some of this insatiable feeling in poetry. You shall see—you shall hear—how it has injured me. She is no longer mine! she[1] abhors me as a sceptic, as what she was before! Oh, bigotry! When I pardon this last, this severest

[1] His second cousin, Harriet Grove, with whom he was in love. Her family objected to Shelley's sceptical opinions—to which he had tried to convert the girl.

of thy persecutions, may Heaven (if there be wrath in Heaven) blast me! Has vengeance, in its armoury of wrath, a punishment more dreadful? Yet, desire to know *why* I consider myself as the victim of severer anguish [? I do not think] that I could have entered into this brief recital.

I am afraid there is selfishness in the passion of love, for I cannot avoid feeling every instant as if my soul was bursting; but I will feel no more! It is selfish. I would feel for others, but for myself—oh! how much rather would I expire in the struggle! Yes, there was a relief! Is suicide wrong? I slept with a loaded pistol and some poison, last night, but did not die. I could not come on Monday, my sister would not part with me; but I must—I will see you soon. My sister is now comparatively happy; she has felt deeply for me. Had it not been for her—had it not been for a sense of what I owed to her, to you, I should have bidden you a final farewell some time ago. But can the dead feel; dawns any day-beam on the night of dissolution?

Pray publish your tale; demand one hundred pounds for it from any publisher;—he will give it in the event. It is delightful, it is divine —not that I like your heroine—but the poor Mary is a character worthy of Heaven. I adore her!

Adieu, my dear friend. Your sincere,

P.B.S.

W——[1] has written. I have read his letter. It is too long to answer. I continue to dissipate Elizabeth's melancholy by keeping her as much as possible employed in poetry. You shall see some to-morrow. I cannot tell you when I can come to town. I wish it very much.

II To Thomas Jefferson Hogg

Field Place, May 21, 1811

My dearest Friend,

She[2] is quite *well;* she is perfect in health!

[1] W—— is presumably one of those unfortunate individuals Shelley entrapped into correspondence on religious matters.

[2] This and the following letter apparently refer to Elizabeth Shelley who, after recovering from scarlet fever, showed herself much less enthusiastic about her brother's visionary schemes than before, to his great distress.

Now, that is enough; we have no fever to sympathize in: but who can minister to a *mind* diseased? She is very gay, very lively. I did not show her your last letter; it was too grave; and I think it is barbarous to diminish what the possessor considers a pleasure, although I have always considered that volatility of character evinces no capabilities for great affections. It is a kind of self-satisfaction in trivial things that is constantly exerting itself; it is a species of continually awakened pride; but it is not constitutional; it used not, however, to be the character of my sister—serious contemplative, affectionate; enthusiastically alive to the wildest schemes; despising the world.

Now, apathetic to all things, except the trivial amusements and despicable intercourse of restrained conversation; bowing before that hellish idol, the *world;* appealing to its unjust decisions, in cases which demand a trial at the higher tribunal of conscience. Yet I do not despair; what she *once was* she has a power to be again; but will that power ever be exerted? I do not hesitate to say, that I think she is not worthy of us; *once* she was; once the fondest, warmest wish which ever I cherished was to witness the *eternal* perfectibility of a being, who appeared to me made for perfection. But she is now *not* what she was; she is not the singular, angelic being, whom I loved, whom I adored: I mourn her as no more. I consider the sister, whose happiness is mine, as dead.

Yet have I not hopes of a resuscitation? Certainly, or I would not tear my heart with the narration. But it is necessary that you should be informed of the real state of the case.

I will think no more of her, for she has murdered thought. Yes; I will think, and devote myself with ardour! On me,—yes, on me, descends the whole weight of my affliction! What right had I, day after day, to expatiate upon to another, to magnify to myself the excellence of a being who might change, who *has* changed? What right had I to seek to introduce you to the destroyer?

I leave Field-place to-night; but return on Friday.

Your eternally affectionate,

P. B. Shelley.

III To Thomas Jefferson Hogg

Cuckfield, June 2, 1811

My dear Friend,

I have nothing to tell you which you will like to hear. The affected contempt of narrowed intellects for the exertion of mental powers, which they either will not, or cannot comprehend, is always a tale of disgust. What must it be, when involving a keen disappointment, I have hesitated for three days on what I should say. I am your friend, you acknowledge it. You have chosen me, and we are inseparable; not the little tyranny of idiots can affect it; not the misrepresentations of the interested. You are then my friend. I am sensible, and you must be sensible, that it is in conformity to the most rigid duty that I would advise you how I have combated with myself.

What is *Passion?* The very word implies an incapacity for action, otherwise than in unison with its dictates. What is reason? It is a thing independent, inflexible; it adapts thoughts and actions to the varying circumstances, which for ever change—adapts them so as to produce the greatest overbalance of happiness. And to whom do you now give happiness? Not to others, for you associate with but few; those few regard you with the highest feelings of admiration and friendship; but perhaps there is but one;—and here is self again—not to yourself; for the truth of this I choose *yourself*, as a testimony against you. I think; reason; listen; cast off prejudice; hear the dictates of plain common sense—surely is it not evident? I [1] loved a being, an idea in my own mind, which had no real existence. I concreted this abstract of perfection, I annexed this fictitious quality to the idea presented by a *name;* the being, whom that name signified, was by no means worthy of this. This is the truth: Unless I am determinedly blind—unless I am resolved causelessly and selfishly to seek destruc-

[1] This is the text as Hogg printed it, but he probably tampered with it. Lady Shelley, working from autograph letters, corrected the reading to "You loved a being" and altered the pronoun "I" to "you" throughout the remainder of this passage wherever it was necessary in order to make Hogg himself, not Shelley, the man whose illusions had been betrayed by Elizabeth's alteration in character.

tion, I must see it. Plain! is it not plain? I loved a being; the being, whom I loved, is not what she was; consequently, as love appertains to mind, and not body, she exists no longer. I regret when I find that she never existed, but in my mind; yet does it not border on wilful deception, deliberate, intentional self-deceit, to continue to love the body, when the soul is no more? As well might I court the worms which the soulless body of a beloved being generates—be lost to myself, and to those who love me for what is really amiable in me— in the damp, unintelligent vaults of a charnel-house. Surely, when it is carried to the dung-heap as a mass of putrefaction, the loveliness of the flower ceases to charm. Surely it would be irrational to annex to this inertness the properties which the flower in its state of beauty possessed, which now cease to exist, and then *did* merely exist, because adjoined to it. Yet you will call this *cold reasoning?* No; you will not! this would be the exclamation of the uniformed Werter, not of my noble friend. But, indeed, it is not *cold* reasoning, if you saw me at this moment. I wish I could reason coldly, I should then stand more chance of success. But let me reconsider it myself—exert my own reasoning powers; let me entreat myself to awake. This—I do not know what I say. I go to Field-place; to-morrow you shall hear again. I go to Field-place *now;* this moment, I have rung the bell for the horse.

Your eternal Friend.

I wrote to her to entreat that she would receive my letter kindly; I wrote very long. This is the answer. Are you deaf, are you dead? I am cold and icy, but I cannot refrain. Stay, I will come soon.—Adieu!

IV To Elizabeth Hitchener

Cuckfield, [about 12 October, 1811]

I do not know that I shall have time to see you my dear friend whilst in Sussex, on Monday or Tuesday I *must* return. The intervening periods will be employed in the hateful task of combating prejudice and mistake. Yet our souls can meet, for these become embodied on paper; all else is even emptier than the breath of fame.

I omitted mentioning something in my last: 'tis of your visiting us. You say that at some *remote period*, etc. What is this remote period? when will it arrive? The term is indefinite and friendship cannot be satisfied with this. I do not mean to-day, to-morrow, or this week, but the time approaches when you need not attend the business of the school, *then* you have your own choice to make of the place of your intermediate residence. If that choice were in favour of me!

I shall come to live in this county. My friend Hogg, Harriet, my new sister, . . . could but be added to these the sister of my soul! *That* I cannot hope: but still she may visit us.

I have been convinced of the eventual omnipotence of mind over matter: adequacy of motive is sufficient to anything, and *my* golden age is when the present potence will become omnipotence: this will be the millennium of Christians, when "the lions shall lie down with the lamb," tho' neither will it be accomplished to complete a prophecy, or by the intervention of a *miracle*. This has been the favourite idea of all religions, the thesis on which the impassioned and benevolent have delighted to dwell. Will it not be the task of human reason, human powers,—whose progression in improvement has been so great since the remotest tradition, tracing general history to the point where now we stand? The series is infinite—can never end!

Now you will laugh at what I am about to tell you. When think [you] this reasoning has arisen? Just [conceive] its possible origin! Never [could] you have [conceived] that three days on the outside of a coach caused it. [Yet] so it is. I am now at Cuckfield; I arrived this morning; and, tho' three nights without sleep, I feel now neither sleepy nor fatigued. *This* is adequacy of motive. During my journey I had the proposed end in view of *accumulating money to myself* for the motives which I stated in my last letter.

I know I have something more to tell you— I forget what. The Captain is talking.

I must settle my plan of attack for to-morrow.

Adieu, my dear friend.

Your   Percy S.

I am happy to hear what I have just heard. You are to come to dine here, and bring Emma on Monday 21st, in the coach.

V To Elizabeth Hitchener

Keswick, Cumberland,
Sunday, Nov. 24, 1811

I answer your letter my dearest Friend not by return of Post, because the Keswick post comes in at seven and goes out at nine, and we are some distance.

Your letters revive me, they resuscitate my slumbering hopes. The languid flame of life, which before burns feebly, glows at communication with that vivid spark of friendship. "Love" I do not think is so adequate a sign of the idea: its usual signification involves selfish monopoly, the sottish idiotism of frenzy-nourished fools, as once I was. But let that era be blotted from the memory of my shame, when purity, truth, reason, virtue all sanctify a friendship which shall endure when the "love" of common souls shall sleep where the shroud moulders around their soulless bodies.—What a rhapsody! But with you I feel half inspired; and *then* feel half ashamed lest my inspiration like that of others, result from a little vanity.

I am discouraged. His [1] letters of late appear to me to betray *cunning*, deep cunning. But I may be deceived: oh! that I were in all that these five weeks had brought forth! His letters are long, but they never express any conviction or unison, they appear merely calculated to bring about what he calls "intimacy on the same happy terms as formerly." This I have positively forbade the very thought of; I tell him that I am open to reason,—I wish, ardently wish, that he would reason sincerely; but that, were I even convinced that his conduct resulted from *disinterested* love of Virtue, he could not live with us, as I should thereby barter Harriet's happiness for his short-lived pleasure,—since my friend if it is true that *such* passions are unconquerable (which I do not believe), how much greater ascendency

[1] Hogg's letters; Hogg had attempted a flirtation with Harriet and there had been an estrangement.

will they gain when under the immediate influence of their original excitement.

Love of what? Not love of my wife, for love seeks the happiness of its object, *even* when combined with the common-place infatuation of novels and gay life (oh no! I don't know that). Love of self: aye, as genuine and complete as the most bigoted believer in original sin could desire to defile mankind,—these *fine susceptibilities*, to which casual deformity and advanced age are such wonderful cures and preventatives. But these have nothing to do with real love, with friendship. Suppose *your* frame were wasted by sickness, your brow covered with wrinkles, suppose age had bowed your form till it reached the ground, would you not be as lovely as now? Yet one of *these* beings would pass that intellect, that soul, that sensibility, with as much indifference as I would show to the nightstar of a ball-room, the magnet of the apes, asses, geese, its inhabitants. So much for real [? false] and so much for true love. The one perishes with the body whence on earth it never dares to soar, the other lives with soul which was the exclusive object of its homage. Oh if this last be but true.

You talk of a future state: "Is not this imagination," you ask, "a proof of it?" To me it appears so: to me everything proves it. But what we earnestly desire we are very much prejudiced in favour of. It seems to me that everything lives again.—What is the Soul? Look at yonder flower. The blast of the North sweeps it from the earth; it withers beneath the breath of the destroyer. Yet that flower hath a soul: for what is soul but that which makes an organized being to be what it is,— without which it would not be so? On this hypothesis, must not that (the soul) without which a flower cannot be a flower exist, when the earthly flower hath perished? Yet where does it exist, in what state of being? have not flowers also some end which Nature destines their being to answer? Doubtless, it ill becomes us to deny this because we cannot certainly discover it; since so many analogies seem to favour the probability of this hypothesis. I will say, then, that all Nature is animated, that microscopic vision, as it hath discovered to us millions of animated beings whose pursuits and passions are as eagerly followed as our own; so might it, if extended, find that Nature itself was but a mass of organized animation. Perhaps the animative intellect of all this is in a constant rotation of change; perhaps a future state is no other than a different mode of terrestrial existence to which we have fitted ourselves in *this* mode.

Is there any probability in this supposition? On this plan, *congenial* souls must meet; because, having fitted themselves for nearly the same mode of being, they cannot fail to be *near* each other. Free-will must give energy to this infinite mass of being, and thereby constitute Virtue. If *our* change be in this mortal life, do not fear that we shall be among the grovelling souls of heroes, aristocrats, and commercialists.—Adieu to this.

I have scribbled a great deal: all my feeling, all my ideas as they arise, are thus yours. My dear friend believe that thou art the cheering beam which gilds this wintry day of life, perhaps ere long to be the exhaustless sun which shall gild my millenniums of immortality. Adieu, my dearest friend.

Ever, ever yours,
Percy S.

VI To William Godwin

Keswick, Cumberland, January 3, 1812

You will be surprised at hearing from a stranger. No introduction has, nor in all probability ever will authorize that which common thinkers would call a liberty; it is, however, a liberty which, although not sanctioned by custom, is so far from being reprobated by reason, that the dearest interests of mankind imperiously demand that a certain etiquette of fashion should no longer keep "man at a distance from man," or impose its flimsy fancies between the free communication of intellect.

The name of Godwin has been used to excite in me feelings of reverence and admiration. I have been accustomed to consider him a luminary too dazzling for the darkness which surrounds him. From the earliest period of my knowledge of his principles, I have ardently desired to share, on the footing of intimacy, that intellect which I have delighted to contemplate in its emanations.

Considering, then, these feelings, you will not be surprised at the inconceivable emotions with which I learned your existence and your dwelling. I had enrolled your name in the list of the honourable dead. I had felt regret that the glory of your being had passed from this earth of ours. It is not so; you still live, and, I firmly believe, are still planning the welfare of human kind.

I have but just entered on the scene of human operations; yet my feelings and my reasonings correspond with what yours were. My course has been short, but eventful. I have seen much of human prejudice, suffered much from human persecution, yet I see no reason hence inferrible which should alter my wishes for their renovation. The ill treatment I have met with has more than ever impressed the truth of my principles on my judgment. I am young, I am ardent in the cause of philanthropy and truth; do not suppose that this is vanity; I am not conscious that it influences this portraiture. I imagine myself dispassionately describing the state of my mind. I am young; you have gone before me, I doubt not are a veteran to me in the years of persecution. Is it strange that, defying prejudice as I have done, I should outstep the limits of custom's prescription, and endeavour to make my desire useful by a friendship with William Godwin?

I pray you to answer this letter. Imperfect as may be my capacity, my desire is ardent and unintermitted. Half an hour would be at least humanely employed in the experiment. I may mistake your residence; certain feelings, of which I may be an inadequate arbiter, may induce you to desire concealment; I may not, in fine, have an answer to this letter. If I do not, when I come to London, I shall seek for you. I am convinced I could represent myself to you in such terms as not to be thought wholly unworthy of your friendship; at least, if desire for universal happiness has any claim upon your preference, that desire I can exhibit. Adieu! I shall earnestly await your answer.

Percy B. Shelley.

VII To William Godwin

Sackville Street, Dublin,
March 8, 1812

5 My dear Sir,

Your letter affords me much food for thought; guide thou and direct me. In all the weakness of my inconsistencies, bear with me; the genuine respect which I bear for your 10 character, the love with which your virtues have inspired me, is undiminished by any suspicion of externally constituted authority; when you reprove me, reason speaks; I acquiesce in her decisions. I know that I am vain, 15 that I assume a character which is perhaps unadapted to the limitedness of my experience, that I am without the modesty which is so generally considered an indispensable ornament to the ingenuousness of youth. I attempt 20 not to conceal from others, or myself, these deficiencies, if such they are. That I have erred in pursuance of this line of conduct I am well aware: in the opposite case, I think that my errors would have been more momentous and 25 overwhelming. "A preponderance of resulting good is imagined in every action." I certainly believe that the line of conduct which I am now pursuing will produce a preponderance of good; when I get rid of this conviction, my 30 conduct shall be changed.

Inquiry is doubtless necessary, nay, essential. I am eagerly open to every new information. I attempt to read a book which attacks my most cherished sentiments as calmly as 35 one which corroborates them. I have not read your writings slightly; they have made a deep impression on my mind; their arguments are fresh in my memory; I have daily occasion to recur to them, as allies in the cause which I 40 am here engaged in vindicating. To them, to you, I owe the inestimable boon of granted power, of arising from the state of intellectual sickliness and lethargy into which I was plunged two years ago, and of which "St. 45 Irvyne" and "Zastrozzi" were the distempered, although unoriginal visions.

I am not forgetful or unheeding of what you said of associations. But "Political Justice" was first published in 1793; nearly twenty 50 years have elapsed since the general diffusion of its doctrines. What has followed? Have men ceased to fight? Have vice and misery vanished from the earth? Have the fireside communications which it recommends taken place? Out of the many who have read that inestimable book, how many have been blinded by prejudice; how many, in short, have taken it up to gratify an ephemeral vanity, and when the hour of its novelty had passed, threw it aside, and yielded with fashion to the arguments of Mr. Malthus?

I have at length proposed a Philanthropic Association, which I conceive not to be contradictory, but strictly compatible with the principles of "Political Justice." The "Address" was principally designed to operate on the Irish *mob*. Can they be in a worse state than at present? Intemperance and hard labour have reduced them to machines. The oyster that is washed and driven at the mercy of the tides, appears to me an animal of almost equal elevation in the scale of intellectual being. Is it impossible to awaken a moral sense in the breasts of those who appear so unfitted for the high destination of their nature? Might not an unadorned display of moral truth, suited to their comprehensions, produce the best effects? The state of society appears to me to be retrogressive. If there be any truth in the hopes which I so fondly cherish, then this cannot be. Yet, even if it be stationary, the eager activity of philanthropists is demanded. I think of the last twenty years with impatient scepticism, as to the progress which the human mind has made during this period. I will own that I am eager that something should be done. But my association. In some Suggestions respecting it, I have the following—"That any number of persons who meet together for philanthropic purposes, should ascertain by friendly discussion those points of opinion wherein they differ and those wherein they coincide, and should, by subjecting them to rational analysis, produce an unanimity founded on reason, and not the superficial agreement too often exhibited at associations for mere party purposes; that the minority, whose belief could not subscribe to the opinion of the majority on a division in any question of moment and interest, should recede."

"Some associations might, by refinement of secessions, contain not more than three or four members." I do not think a society such as this is incompatible with your chapter on associations; it purposes no violent or immediate measures; its intentions are a facilitation of inquiry, and actually to carry into effect those confidential and private communications which you recommend. I send you with this the proposals, which will be followed by the "suggestions."

I had no conception of the depth of human misery until now. The poor of Dublin are assuredly the meanest and most miserable of all. In their narrow streets thousands seem huddled together,—one mass of animated filth. With what eagerness do such scenes as these inspire me! How self confident, too, do I feel in my assumption to teach the lessons of virtue to those who grind their fellow beings into worse than annihilation. These were the persons to whom, in my fancy, I had addressed myself; how quickly were my views on this subject changed; yet how deeply has this very change rooted the conviction on which I came hither.

I do not think that my book can in the slightest degree tend to violence. The pains which I have taken, even to tautology, to insist on pacific measures; the necessity which every warrior and rebel must lie under to deny almost every passage of my book before he can become so, must at least exculpate *me* from tending to make him so. I shudder to think, that for the very roof that covers me, for the bed whereon I lie, I am indebted to the selfishness of man. A remedy must somewhere have a beginning. Have I explained myself clearly? Are we now at issue? [1]

I have not seen Mr. Curran. I have called repeatedly, left my address and my pamphlet. I *will* see him before I leave Dublin. I send a newspaper and the "proposals." I had no conception that the packet I sent you would be sent by the post; I thought it would have reached you per coach.

Harriet joins in respects to you. Is your denial respecting Wales irrevocable? Would not your children gain health and spirits from the jaunt?

With sincerest respect, yours
P. B. Shelley.

[1] Godwin at once answered Shelley disapproving the Irish campaign, and concluding, "I wish to my heart you would come immediately to London."

You will see the account of ME in the newspapers. I am vain, but not so foolish as not to be rather piqued than gratified at the eulogia of a journal. I have repeated my injunctions concerning "St. I[rvyne]" and "Z[astrozzi.]"

Expenditure is used in my address in a moral sense.

VIII To Thomas Jefferson Hogg

Tanyrallt, Dec. 3, 1812

My dear Friend,

. . . The Brown Demon,[1] as we call our late tormentor and school-mistress, must receive her stipend. I pay it with a heavy heart and an unwilling hand; but it must be so. She was deprived by our misjudging haste of a situation, where she was going on smoothly: and now she says, that her reputation is gone, her health ruined, her peace of mind destroyed by my barbarity; a complete victim to all the woes mental and bodily, that heroine ever suffered! This is not all fact; but certainly she is embarrassed and poor, and we being in some degree the cause, we ought to obviate it. She is an artful, superficial, ugly, hermaphroditical beast of a woman, and my astonishment at my fatuity, inconsistency, and bad taste was never so great, as after living four months with her as an inmate. What would Hell be, were such a woman in Heaven?

The society in Wales is very stupid. They are all aristocrats and saints: but that, I tell you, I do not mind in the least; the unpleasant part of the business is, that they hunt people to death, who are not so likewise. . . .

IX To Leigh Hunt [2]

Marlow, December 8, 1816

I have received both your letters yesterday and to-day, and I accuse myself that my precipitancy should have given you the vexation you express. Your letters, however, give me unmingled pleasure, and that of a very exalted kind. I have not in all my intercourse with

mankind experienced sympathy and kindness with which I have been so affected or which my whole being has so sprung forward to meet and to return. My communications with you shall be such as to attempt to deserve this fortunate distinction. Meanwhile, let me lay aside preliminaries and their reserve; let me talk with you as with an old friend.

First I will answer your questions. By some fatality I have seen every *Examiner*,[3] but that of last week. Since I received your letter yesterday, I have made every exertion to get a sight of it, unsuccessfully. All the people who take it in here have forwarded it to their friends at a distance. I hear there is one at a village five miles off; as it is very uncertain whether I shall be able to procure it, I will accept your kind offer of sending it to me. I take in the *Examiner* generally, and therefore will not trouble you to send your own copy.

Next, will I own the "Hymn to Intellectual Beauty"? [4] I do not care—as you like. And yet the poem was composed under the influence of feelings which agitated me even to tears, so that I think it deserves a better fate than the being linked with so stigmatised and unpopular a name (so far as it is known) as mine. You will say that it is not thus, that I am morbidly sensitive to what I esteem the injustice of neglect—but I do not say that I am unjustly neglected, the oblivion which overtook my little attempt of "Alastor" I am ready to acknowledge was sufficiently merited in *itself;* but then it was not accorded in the correct proportion considering the success of the most contemptible drivellings. I am undeceived in the belief that I have powers deeply to interest, or substantially to improve, mankind. How far my conduct and my opinions have rendered the zeal and ardour with which I have engaged in the attempt ineffectual, I know not. Self-love prompts me to assign much weight to a cause which perhaps has none. But thus much I do

---

[1] Elizabeth Hitchener, the former "sister of his soul."

[2] Reprinted from *Literary Anecdotes of the Nineteenth Century*, edited by W. R. Nicoll and T. J. Wise, by permission of Dodd, Mead & Co., to whom thanks are due.

[3] The issue for December 1, 1816, which included Hunt's article on "Young Poets"—who were Shelley, Reynolds, and Keats.

[4] Shelley had sent Hunt his "Hymn to Intellectual Beauty" for insertion in the *Examiner*, where it appeared in the issue for January 19, 1817, with the signature, "Percy B. Shelley." Hunt states that the poem was originally signed Elfin Knight, Mary's familiar name for Shelley.

not seek to conceal from myself, that I am an outcast from human society; my name is execrated by all who understand its entire import —by those very beings whose happiness I ardently desire. I am an object of compassion to a few more benevolent than the rest, all else abhor and avoid me. With you, and perhaps some others (though in a less degree I fear) my gentleness and sincerity find favour, because they are themselves gentle and sincere: they believe in self-devotion and generosity, because they are themselves generous and self-devoted. Perhaps I should have shrunk from persisting in the task which I had undertaken in early life, of opposing myself in these evil times and among these evil tongues, to what I esteem misery and vice. If I must have lived in the solitude of the heart, fortunately my domestic circle incloses that within it which compensates for the loss. But these are subjects for conversation, and I find that in using the privilege which you have permitted me of friendship, I have indulged in that garrulity of self-love which only friendship can excuse and endure.

When will you send me your poems? I never knew that you had published any other than "Rimini," with which I was exceedingly delighted. The *story* of the poem has an interest of very uncommon and irresistible character,— though it appeared to me that you have subjected yourself to some rules in the composition which fetter your genius, and diminish the effect of the conceptions. Though in one sense I am no poet, I am not so insensible to poetry as to read "Rimini" unmoved.—When will you send me your other poems?

Peacock is the author of "Headlong Hall," —he expresses himself much pleased by your approbation—indeed, it is approbation which many would be happy to acquire! He is now writing "Melincourt" in the same style, but, as I judge, far superior to "Headlong Hall." He is an amiable man of great learning, considerable taste, an enemy to every shape of tyranny and superstitious imposture. I am now on the point of taking the lease of a house among these woody hills, these sweet green fields, and this delightful river—where, if I should ever have the happiness of seeing you, I will introduce you to Peacock. I have noth-

ing to do in London, but I am most strongly tempted to come, only to spend one evening with you; and if I can I will, though I am anxious as soon as my employments here are finished to return to Bath.

Last of all—you are in distress for a few hundred Pounds;—I saw Lord Byron at Geneva, who expressed to me the high esteem which he felt for your character and worth. I cannot doubt that he would hesitate in contributing at least £100 towards extricating one whom he regards so highly from a state of embarrassment. I have heard from him lately, dated from Milan; and as he has entrusted me with one or two commissions, I do not doubt but my letter would reach him by the direction he gave me. If you feel any delicacy on the subject, may I write to him about it? My letter shall express that zeal for your interests which I truly feel, and which would not confine itself to those barren protestations if I had the smallest superfluity.

My friend accepts your *interest* and is contented to be a Hebrew for your sake. But a request is made in return which in courtesy cannot be refused. There is some little literary luxury, some enjoyment of taste or fancy you have refused yourself, because you have not felt, through the difficulty of your situation, that you were entitled to indulge yourself in it. You are entreated,—and a refusal would give more pain than you are willing to inflict— to employ the enclosed in making yourself a present of this luxury, that may remind you of this not unfriendly contest, which has conferred a value on £5 which I believe it never had before.

Adieu,
Most affectionately yours,
P. B. Shelley

I will send you an "Alastor."

X To Charles and James Ollier

Leghorn, September 6, 1819
Dear Sir,

I received your packet with Hunt's picture about a fortnight ago; and your letter with Nos. 1, 2, and 3 yesterday, but not No. 4, which is probably lost or mislaid, through the extreme irregularity of the Italian post.

When will you send me your poems? I never knew that you had published any other than "Rimini," with which I was exceedingly delighted.—The story of the poem has an interest of a very uncommon & irresistible character,—but it appears to me that you have emspirited [superadded] many to some rules in the composition which rather your genius, & diminish the effect, that [of] the conception. You in me, issue. I am no poet, I am not so insensible to poetry. as I used Rimini unmoved.—When will you send me your other poems?"

The ill account you give of the success of my poetical attempts, sufficiently accounts for your silence; but I believe that the truth is, I write less for the public than for myself. Considering that perhaps the parcel will be another year on its voyage, I rather wish, if this letter arrives in time, that you would send the *Quarterly's* article by the post, and the rest of the *Review* in the parcel. Of course it gives me a certain degree of pleasure to know that anyone likes my writings; but it is objection and enmity alone that rouses my *curiosity*. My "Prometheus," which has been long finished, is now being transcribed, and will soon be forwarded to you for publication. It is, in my judgment, of a higher character than anything I have yet attempted, and is perhaps less an imitation of anything that has gone before it. I shall also send you another work, calculated to produce a very popular effect, and totally in a different style from anything I have yet composed. This will be sent already printed.[1] The "Prometheus" you will be so good as to print as usual. . . .

In the "Rosalind and Helen," I see there are some few errors, which are so much the worse because they are errors in the sense. If there should be any danger of a second edition, I will correct them.

I have read your "Altham," and Keats's poem,[2] and Lamb's works. For the second in this list, much praise is due to me for having read it, the author's intention appearing to be that no person should possibly get to the end of it. Yet it is full of some of the highest and the finest gleams of poetry; indeed, everything seems to be viewed by the mind of a poet which is described in it. I think if he had printed about fifty pages of fragments from it, I should have been led to admire Keats as a poet more than I ought, of which there is now no danger. In "Altham" you have surprised and delighted me. It is a natural story, most unaffectedly told, and what is more, told in a strain of very pure and powerful English, which is a very rare merit. You seem to have studied our language to some purpose; but I suppose I ought to have waited for "Inesilla."

The same day that your letter came, came the news of the Manchester work,[3] and the torrent of my indignation has not yet done boiling in my veins. I wait anxiously to hear how the country will express its sense of this bloody, murderous opposition of its destroyers. "Something must be done. What, yet I know not."

In your parcel (which I pray you to send in some safe manner, forwarding to me the bill of lading, etc., in a regular mechanical way, so that my parcel may come in six weeks, not twelve months) send me Jones's Greek Grammar and some sealing-wax.

Whenever I publish, send copies of my books to the following people from me:— Mr. Hunt, Mr. Godwin, Mr. Hogg, Mr. Peacock, Mr. Keats, Mr. Thomas Moore, Mr. Horace Smith, Lord Byron (at Murray's).

Yours, obliged and faithful,
Percy B. Shelley

XI To Leigh Hunt

Livorno, Monday, September 27, 1819

My dear Friend,

We are now on the point of leaving this place for Florence, where we have taken pleasant apartments for six months, which brings us to the 1st of April, the season at which new flowers and new thoughts spring forth upon the earth and in the mind. What is then our destination is yet undecided. I have not seen Florence, except as one sees the outside of the streets; but its *physiognomy* indicates it to be a city which, though the ghost of a republic, yet possesses most amiable qualities. I wish you could meet us there in the spring, and we would try to muster up a "lieta brigata," which, leaving behind them the pestilence of remembered misfortunes, might act over again the pleasures of the Interlocutors in Boccaccio. I have been lately reading this most divine writer. He is, in a high sense of the word, a poet, and his language has the rhythm and

---

[1] The work alluded to here, as being printed in Italy, was "The Cenci." In 1821 a second edition was printed in London and published by Ollier.

[2] "Endymion."

[3] It was this indignation aroused by the news of the Manchester massacre which caused Shelley to write "The Mask of Anarchy."

harmony of verse. I think him not equal certainly to Dante or Petrarch, but far superior to Tasso and Ariosto, the children of a later and of a colder day. I consider the three first as the productions of the vigour of the infancy of a new nation—as rivulets from the same spring as that which fed the greatness of the republics of Florence and Pisa, and which checked the influence of the German emperors; and from which, through obscurer channels, Raffael and Michael Angelo drew the light and the harmony of their inspiration. When the second-rate poets of Italy wrote, the corrupting blight of tyranny was already hanging on every bud of genius. Energy, and simplicity, and unity of idea, were no more. In vain do we seek in the finest passages of Ariosto and Tasso, any expression which at all approaches in this respect to those of Petrarch and Dante. How much do I admire Boccaccio! What descriptions of nature are those in his little introductions to every new day! It is the morning of life stripped of that mist of familiarity which makes it obscure to us. Boccaccio seems to me to have possessed a deep sense of the fair ideal of human life, considered in its social relations. His more serious theories of love agree especially with mine. He often expresses things lightly too, which have serious meanings of a very beautiful kind. He is a moral casuist, the opposite of the Christian, stoical, readymade, and worldly system of morals. Do you remember one little remark, or rather maxim of his, the application of which might do some good to the common narrowminded conceptions of love,—"Bocca bacciata non perde ventura; anzi rinnuova, come fa la luna?" . . .

It would give me much pleasure to know Mr. Lloyd. Do you know, when I was in Cumberland, I got Southey to borrow a copy of Berkeley from him, and I remember observing some pencil notes in it, probably written by Lloyd, which I thought particularly acute. One, especially, struck me as being the assertion of a doctrine, of which even then I had long been persuaded, and on which I had founded much of my persuasions, regarding the imagined cause of the Universe—"Mind cannot create, it can only perceive." Ask him if he remembers having written it.

Of Lamb you know my opinion, and you can bear witness to the regret which I felt, when I learned that the calumny of an enemy had deprived me of his society whilst in England. —Ollier tells me that the Quarterly are going to review me; I suppose it will be a pretty morsel, and as I am acquiring a taste for humour and drollery, I confess I am curious to see it. I have sent my "Prometheus Unbound" to Peacock—if you ask him for it he will show it you—I think it will please you. . . .

Most affectionately your friend, P. B. S.

XII To Charles and James Ollier

Pisa, March 6, 1820

Dear Sir,

I do not hear that you have received "Prometheus" and "The Cenci"; I therefore think it safest to tell you how and when to get them if you have not yet done so.

Give the bill of lading Mr. Gisborne sent you to a broker in the city, whom you employ to get the packages, and to pay the duty on the unbound books. The ship sailed in the middle of December, and will assuredly have arrived long before now.

"Prometheus Unbound," I must tell you, is my favourite poem; I charge you, therefore, specially to pet him and feed him with fine ink and good paper. "Cenci" is written for the multitude, and ought to sell well. I think, if I may judge by its merits, the "Prometheus" cannot sell beyond twenty copies. I hear nothing either from Hunt, or you, or any one. If you condescend to write to me, mention something about Keats.

Allow me particularly to request you to send copies of whatever I publish to Horace Smith. Maybe you will see me in the summer; but in that case I shall certainly return to this "Paradise of Exiles" by the ensuing winter.

If any of the Reviews abuse me, cut them out and send them. If they praise, you need not trouble yourself. I feel ashamed, if I could believe that I should deserve the latter; the former, I flatter myself, is no more than a just tribute. If Hunt praises me, send it, because that is of another character of things.

Dear Sir, yours very truly,

Percy B. Shelley

XIII To John Keats

Pisa, 27 July, 1820

My dear Keats,

I hear with great pain the dangerous acci- 5
dent that you have undergone, and Mr. Gisborne who gives me the account of it, adds
that you continue to wear a consumptive appearance. This consumption is a disease particularly fond of people who write such good 10
verses as you have done, and with the assistance
of an English winter it can often indulge its
selection;—I do not think that young and
amiable poets are at all bound to gratify its
taste; they have entered into no bond with the 15
Muses to that effect. But seriously (for I am
joking on what I am very anxious about) I
think you would do well to pass the winter
after so tremendous an accident, in Italy, and
if you think it as necessary as I do so long as 20
you could [find] Pisa or its neighbourhood
agreeable to you, Mrs. Shelley unites with myself in urging the request, that you would take
up your residence with us. You might come
by sea to Leghorn (France is not worth seeing, 25
and the sea is particularly good for weak
lungs), which is within a few miles of us. You
ought at all events, to see Italy, and your
health, which I suggest as a motive, might be
an excuse to you. I spare declamation about 30
the statues, and the paintings, and the ruins—
and what is a greater piece of forbearance—
about the mountain streams and the fields, the
colours of the sky, and the sky itself.

I have lately read your "Endymion" again 35
and ever with a new sense of the treasures of
poetry it contains, though treasures poured
forth with indistinct profusion. This, people
in general will not endure, and that is the
cause of the comparatively few copies which 40
have been sold. I feel persuaded that you are
capable of the greatest things, so you but will.

I always tell Ollier to send you copies of my
books.—"Prometheus Unbound" I imagine
you will receive nearly at the same time with 45
this letter. "The Cenci" I hope you have already received—it was studiously composed in
a different style

"*Below the good how far? but far above the* 50
great."

In poetry I have sought to avoid system and
mannerism; I wish those who excel me in
genius would pursue the same plan.

Whether you remain in England, or journey
to Italy,—believe that you carry with you my 5
anxious wishes for your health, happiness and
success wherever you are, or whatever you
undertake, and that I am, yours sincerely.

P. B. Shelley

XIV To the Editor of the "Quarterly Review"

(Pisa, 1820?)

Sir,

Should you cast your eye on the signature
of this letter before you read the contents, you
might imagine that they related to a slanderous
paper which appeared in your Review some
time since. I never notice anonymous attacks. The wretch who wrote it has doubtless
the additional reward of a consciousness of
his motives, besides the thirty guineas a sheet,
or whatever it is that you pay him. Of course
you cannot be answerable for all the writings
which you edit, and I certainly bear you no ill-
will for having edited the abuse to which I
allude—indeed, I was too much amused by
being compared to Pharaoh, not readily to forgive editor, printer, publisher, stitcher, or anyone, except the despicable writer, connected
with something so exquisitely entertaining.
Seriously speaking, I am not in the habit of
permitting myself to be disturbed by what is
said or written of me, though, I dare say, I may
be condemned sometimes justly enough. But
I feel, in respect to the writer in question, that
"I am there sitting, where he durst not soar."

The case is different with the unfortunate
subject of this letter, the author of "Endymion," to whose feelings and situation I entreat you to allow me to call your attention. I
write considerably in the dark; but if it is
Mr. Gifford that I am addressing, I am persuaded that in an appeal to his humanity and
justice, he will acknowledge the *fas ab hoste
doceri*.[1] I am aware that the first duty of a Reviewer is towards the public, and I am willing
to confess that the "Endymion" is a poem
considerably defective, and that, perhaps, it

[1] "Right to be taught by an enemy."

deserved as much censure as the pages of your Review record against it; but, not to mention that there is certain contemptuousness of phraseology from which it is difficult for a critic to abstain, in the review of "Endymion," I do not think that the writer has given it its due praise. Surely the poem, with all its faults, is a very remarkable production for a man of Keats's age, and the promise of ultimate excellence is such as has rarely been afforded even by such as has afterwards attained high literary eminence. Look at book ii, line 833 etc., and book iii, line 113 to 120— read down that page, and then again from line 193. I could cite many other passages, to convince you that it deserved milder usage. Why it should have been reviewed at all, excepting for the purpose of bringing its excellences into notice, I cannot conceive, for it was very little read, and there was no danger that it should become a model to the age of that false taste, with which I confess that it is replenished.

Poor Keats was thrown into a dreadful state of mind by this review, which, I am persuaded, was not written with any intention of producing the effect, to which it has, at least, greatly contributed, of embittering his existence, and inducing a disease from which there are now but faint hopes of his recovery.[1] The first effects are described to me to have resembled insanity, and it was by assiduous watching that he was restrained from effecting purposes of suicide. The agony of his sufferings at length produced the rupture of a blood-vessel in the lungs, and the usual process of consumption appears to have begun. He is coming to pay me a visit in Italy; but I fear that unless his mind can be kept tranquil, little is to be hoped from the mere influence of climate.

But let me not extort anything from your pity. I have just seen a second volume, published by him evidently in careless despair. I have desired my bookseller to send you a copy, and allow me to solicit your special attention to the fragment of a poem entitled

[1] That Keats died of a broken heart over a book review is now an entirely exploded opinion, although it was widely believed at the time of his death and led to many indignant expressions of sympathy. Keats died of natural causes.

"Hyperion," the composition of which was checked by the Review in question. The great proportion of this piece is surely in the very highest style of poetry. I speak impartially, for the canons of taste to which Keats has conformed in his other compositions are the very reverse of my own. I leave you to judge for yourself: it would be an insult to you to suppose that from motives, however honourable, you would lend yourself to a deception of the public.

* * *

(This letter was never sent.)

XV To Charles Ollier

Pisa, February 16, 1821

Dear Sir,

I send you three poems—"Ode to Naples," a sonnet, and a longer piece, entitled "Epipsychidion." The two former are my own; and you will be so obliging as to take the first opportunity of publishing according to your own discretion.

The longer poem, I desire, should not be considered as my own; indeed, in a certain sense, it is a production of a portion of me already dead; and in this sense the advertisement is no fiction. It is to be published simply for the esoteric few; and I make its author a secret, to avoid the malignity of those who turn sweet food into poison; transforming all they touch into the corruption of their own natures. My wish with respect to it is, that it should be printed immediately in the simplest form, and merely one hundred copies: those who are capable of judging and feeling rightly with respect to a composition of so abstruse a nature, certainly do not arrive at that number —among those, at least, who would ever be excited to read an obscure and anonymous production; and it would give me no pleasure that the vulgar should read it. If you have any bookselling reason against publishing so small a number as a hundred, merely, distribute copies among those to whom you think the poetry would afford any pleasure, and send me, as soon as you can, a copy by the post. I have written it so as to give very little trouble, I hope, to the printer, or the person who revises. I would be much obliged to you if you would take this office on yourself.

Is there any expectation of a second edition of the "Revolt of Islam"? I have many corrections to make in it, and one part will be wholly remodelled. I am employed in high and new designs in verse; but they are the labours of years, perhaps.

We expect here every day the news of a battle between the armies of Austria and Naples. The latter have advanced upon Rome; and the first affair will probably take place in the Ecclesiastical States. You may imagine the expectation of all here.

Pray send me news of my intellectual children. For "Prometheus" I expect and desire no great sale. "The Cenci" ought to have been popular.

I remain, dear Sir,
Your very obedient servant,
Percy B. Shelley.

XVI To the Editor of "The Examiner"

Pisa, June 22, 1821

Sir,

Having heard that a poem, entitled "Queen Mab," has been surreptitiously published in London, and that legal proceedings have been instituted against the publisher, I request the favour of your insertion of the following explanation of the affair as it relates to me.

A poem, entitled "Queen Mab," was written by me at the age of eighteen, I dare say in a sufficiently intemperate spirit—but even then was not intended for publication, and a few copies were struck off, to be distributed among my personal friends. I have not seen this production for several years; I doubt not but that it is perfectly worthless in point of literary composition; and that in all that concerns moral and political speculation, as well as in the subtler discriminations of metaphysical and religious doctrine, it is still more crude and immature. I am a devoted enemy to religious, political, and domestic oppression; and I regret this publication, not so much from literary vanity, as because I fear it is better fitted to injure than to serve the cause of freedom. I have directed my solicitor to apply to

Chancery for an injunction to restrain the sale; but after the precedent of Mr. Southey's "Wat Tyler" (a poem, written, I believe, at the same age, and with the same unreflecting enthusiasm), with little hopes of success.

Whilst I exonerate myself from all share in having divulged opinions hostile to existing sanctions, under the form, whatever it may be, which they assume in this poem, it is scarcely necessary for me to protest against the system of inculcating the truth of Christianity and the excellence of Monarchy, however true or however excellent they may be, by such equivocal arguments as confiscation, and imprisonment, and invective, and slander, and the insolent violation of the most sacred ties of nature and society.

Sir, I am,
Your obliged and obedient servant,
Percy B. Shelley

XVII To Thomas Love Peacock

Ravenna, August (probably 10th), 1821

My dear Peacock,

I received your last letter just as I was setting off from the Bagni on a visit to Lord Byron at this place. Many thanks for all your kind attention to my accursed affairs. . . .

I have sent you by the Gisbornes a copy of the *Elegy on Keats*. The subject, I know, will not please you; but the composition of the poetry, and the taste in which it is written, I do not think bad. You and the enlightened public will judge. Lord Byron is in excellent cue both of health and spirits. He has got rid of all those melancholy and degrading habits which he indulged [in] at Venice. He lives with one woman, a lady of rank here, to whom he is attached, and who is attached to him, and is in every respect an altered man. He has written three more cantos of "Don Juan." I have yet only heard the fifth, and I think that every word of it is pregnant with immortality. I have not seen his late plays, except "Marino Faliero," which is very well, but not so transcendently fine as the "Don Juan." Lord Byron gets up at *two*. I get up, quite contrary to my usual custom, but one must sleep or die, like Southey's sea-snake in "Kehama," at 12. After breakfast we sit talking till six. From six till eight we gallop through the pine forests which divide Ravenna from the sea; we then come home and dine, and sit up gossiping till six in the morning. I don't suppose this will kill me in a week or fortnight, but I shall not try it longer. Lord B.'s establishment consists, besides servants, of ten horses, eight enormous dogs, three monkeys, five cats, an eagle, a crow, and a falcon; and all these, except the horses, walk about the house, which every now and then resounds with their unarbitrated quarrels, as if they were the masters of it. Lord B. thinks you wrote a pamphlet signed "John Bull"; he says he knew it by the style resembling "Melincourt," of which he is a great admirer. I read it, and assured him that it could not possibly be yours. I write nothing, and probably shall write no more. It offends me to see my name classed among those who have no name. If I cannot be something better, I had rather be nothing, and the accursed cause to the downfall of which I dedicated what powers I may have had—flourishes like a cedar and covers England with its boughs. My motive was never the infirm desire of fame; and if I should continue an author, I feel that I should desire it. This cup is justly given to one only of an age; indeed, participation would make it worthless: and unfortunate they who seek it and find it not.

I congratulate you—I hope I ought to do so—on your expected stranger. He is introduced into a rough world. My regards to Hogg, Co[u]lson if you see him.

Ever most faithfully yours,
P. B. S.

After I have sealed my letter, I find that my enumeration of the animals in this Circean Palace was defective, and that in a material point. I have just met on the grand stair case five peacocks, two guinea hens, and an Egyptian crane. I wonder who all these animals were before they were changed into these shapes.

XVIII To John Gisborne

Pisa, October 22, 1821

My dear Gisborne,

At length the post brings a welcome letter from you and I am pleased to be assured of your health and safe arrival. I expect with interest and anxiety the intelligence of your progress in England, and how far the advantages there compensate the loss of Italy. I hear from Hunt that he is determined on emigration, and if I thought the letter would arrive in time, I should beg you to suggest some advice to him. But you ought to be incapable of forgiving me in the fact of depriving England of what it must lose when Hunt departs.

Did I tell you that Lord Byron comes to settle at Pisa, and that he has a plan of writing a periodical work in connection with Hunt? His house, Madame Felichi's, is already taken and fitted up for him, and he has been expected every day these six weeks. La Guiccioli, who awaits him impatiently, is a very pretty, sentimental, innocent Italian, who has sacrificed an immense fortune for the sake of Lord Byron, and who, if I know anything of my friend, of her and of human nature, will hereafter have plenty of leisure and opportunity to repent her rashness. Lord Byron is, however, quite cured of his gross habits, as far as habits; the perverse ideas on which they were formed are not yet eradicated.

We have furnished a house at Pisa, and mean to make it our head-quarters. I shall get all my books out, and entrench myself like a spider in a web. If you can assist P[eacock] in sending them to Leghorn, you would do me an especial favour; but do not buy me Calderon, Faust, or Kant, as H[orace] S[mith] promises to send them me from Paris, where I suppose you had not time to procure them. Any other books you or Henry think would accord with my design, Ollier will furnish you with.

I should like very much to hear what is said of my "Adonais," and you would oblige me by cutting out, or making Ollier cut out, any respectable criticism on it and sending it me; you know I do not mind a crown or two in postage. The Epipsychidion is a mystery; as to real flesh and blood, you know that I do not deal in those articles; you might as well go to a gin-ship for a leg of mutton, as expect anything human or earthly from me. I desire Ollier not to circulate this piece except to the συνετοί, and even they, it seems, are inclined to approximate me to the circle of a servant girl and her sweetheart, but I intend to write a Symposium of my own to set all this right.

I am just finishing a dramatic poem, called "Hellas," upon the contest now raging in Greece—a sort of imitation of the "Persae" of Aeschylus, full of lyrical poetry. I try to be what I might have been, but am not successful. I find that (I dare say I shall quote wrong)

"Den herrlichsten, den sich der Geist emprangt
Drangt immer fremd und fremder Stoff sich an." 10

The Edinburgh Review lies. Godwin's answer to Malthus is victorious and decisive; and that it should not be generally acknowledged as such, is full of evidence of the influence of 15 successful evil and tyranny. What Godwin is, compared to Plato and Lord Bacon, we well know; but compared with these miserable sciolists, he is a vulture to a worm.

I read the Greek dramatists and Plato for 20 ever. You are right about Antigone; how sublime a picture of a woman! and what think you of the choruses, and especially the lyrical complaints of the godlike victim? and the menaces of Tiresias, and their rapid fulfilment? Some 25 of us have, in a prior existence, been in love with an Antigone, and that makes us find no full content in any mortal tie. As to books, I advise you to live near the British Museum, and read there. I have read, since I saw you, 30 the "Jungfrau von Orleans" of Schiller,—a fine play, if the fifth act did not fall off. Some Greeks, escaped from the defeat in Wallachia, have passed through Pisa to re-embark at Leghorn for the Morea; and the Tuscan Govern- 35 ment allowed them, during their stay and passage, three lire each per day and their lodging; that is good. Remember me and Mary most kindly to Mrs. Gisborne and Henry, and believe me,

                    40
                    Yours most affectionately,
                         P. B. S.

XIX To Horace Smith

Pisa, April 11, 1822

My dear Smith,

I have, as yet, received neither the "Nympholept" nor his metaphysical companions— *Time, my Lord, has a wallet on his back*, and I 50 suppose he has bagged them by the way. As he

has had a good deal of *alms* for *oblivion* out of me, I think he might as well have favoured me this once; I have, indeed, just dropped another mite into his treasury, called "Hellas," which 5 I know not how to send to you; but I dare say, some fury of the Hades of authors will bring one to Paris. It is a poem written on the Greek cause last summer—a sort of lyrical, dramatic nondescript piece of business.

You will have heard of a *row* we have had here, which, I dare say, will grow to a serious size before it arrives at Paris. It was, in fact, a trifling piece of business enough, arising from an insult of a drunken dragoon, offered to one 15 of our party, and only serious, because one of Lord B.'s servants wounded the fellow dangerously with a pitchfork. He is now, however, recovering, and the echo of the affair will be heard long after the original report has ceased.

Lord Byron has read me one or two letters of Moore to him, in which Moore speaks with great kindness of me; and of course I cannot but feel flattered by the approbation of a man, my inferiority to whom I am proud to ac- 25 knowledge.—Amongst other things, however, Moore, after giving Lord B. much good advice about public opinion, etc., seems to deprecate MY influence on his mind, on the subject of religion, and to attribute the tone assumed in 30 "Cain" to my suggestions. Moore cautions him against my influence on this particular, with the most friendly zeal; and it is plain that his motive springs from a desire of benefiting Lord B., without degrading me. I think you 35 know Moore. Pray assure him that I have not the smallest influence over Lord Byron, in this particular, and if I had, I certainly should employ it to eradicate from his great mind the delusions of Christianity, which, in spite of 40 his reason, seem perpetually to recur, and to lay in ambush for the hours of sickness and distress. "Cain" was *conceived* many years ago, and begun before I saw him last year at Ravenna. How happy should I not be to at- 45 tribute to myself, however indirectly, any participation in that immortal work!—I differ with Moore in thinking Christianity useful to the world; no man of sense can think it true; and the alliance of the monstrous superstitions 50 of the popular worship with the pure doctrines of the Theism of such a man as Moore, turns to the profit of the former, and makes the latter the fountain of its own pollution. I agree with him, that the doctrines of the French, and Material Philosophy, are as false as they are pernicious; but still they are better than Christianity, inasmuch as anarchy is better than despotism; for this reason, that the former is for a season, and the latter is eternal. My admiration of the character, no less than of the genius of Moore, makes me rather wish that he should not have an ill opinion of me.

Where are you this summer?—Forever in Paris? Forever in France? . . . May not I hope to see you, even for a trip in Italy? I hope your . . . little ones are well. Mine grows a fine boy, and is quite well.

I have contrived to get my musical coals at Newcastle itself. My dear Smith, believe me,

Faithfully yours,

P. B. S.

XX To John Gisborne

Lerici, June 18, 1822

. . . I have written to Ollier to send his account to you. The "Adonais" I wished to have had a fair chance, both because it is a favourite with me and on account of the memory of Keats, who was a poet of great genius, let the classic party say what it will. "Hellas" too I liked on account of the subject —one always finds some reason or other for liking one's own composition. The "Epipsychidion" I cannot look at, the person whom it celebrates was a cloud instead of a Juno; and poor Ixion starts from the centaur that was the offspring of his own embrace. If you are curious, however, to hear what I am and have been, it will tell you something thereof. It is an idealized history of my life and feelings. I think one is always in love with something or other; the error, and I confess it is not easy for spirits cased in flesh and blood to avoid it, consists in seeking in a mortal image the likeness of what is perhaps eternal.

Hunt is not yet arrived, but I expect him every day. I shall see little of Lord Byron, nor shall I permit Hunt to form the intermediate link between him and me. I detest all society— almost all, at least—and Lord Byron is the nucleus of all that is hateful and tiresome in it.

He will be half mad to hear of these memoirs. As to me, you know my supreme indifference to such affairs, except that I must confess that I am sometimes amused by the ridiculous mistakes of these writers. Tell me a little of what they say of me besides my being an atheist. One thing I regret in it, I dread lest it should injure Hunt's prospects in the establishment of the journal, for Lord Byron is so mentally capricious that the least impulse drives him from his anchorage. The Williams's are now on a visit to us, and they are people who are very pleasing to me. But words are not the instruments of our intercourse. I like Jane more and more, and I find Williams the most amiable of companions. She has a taste for music, and an elegance of form and motions that compensate in some degree for the lack of literary refinement. You know my gross ideas of music, and will forgive me when I say that I listen the whole evening on our terrace to the simple melodies with excessive delight. I have a boat here. It costs me £80, and reduced me to some difficulty in point of money. However, it is swift and beautiful, and appears quite a vessel. Williams is captain, and, we drive along this delightful bay in the evening wind under the summer moon until earth appears another world. Jane brings her guitar, and if the past and future could be obliterated, the present would content me so well that I could say with Faust to the passing moment "Remain thou, thou art so beautiful." Clare is with us, and the death of her child seems to have restored her to tranquillity. Her character is somewhat altered. She is vivacious and talkative; and though she teases me sometimes, I like her. . . . Lord Byron, who is at Leghorn, has fitted up a splendid vessel, a small schooner on the American model, and Trelawny is to be captain. How long the fiery spirit of our pirate will accommodate itself to the caprice of the poet remains to be seen.

I write little now. It is impossible to compose except under the strong excitement of an assurance of finding sympathy in what you write. Imagine Demosthenes reciting a Philippic to the waves of the Atlantic. Lord Byron is in this respect fortunate. He touched a chord to which a million hearts responded, and the coarse music which he produced to please them, disciplined him to the perfection to which he now approaches. I do not go on with "Charles the First." I feel too little certainty of the future, and too little satisfaction with regard to the past to undertake any subject seriously and deeply. I stand, as it were, upon a precipice, which I have ascended with great, and cannot descend without greater peril, and I am content if the heaven above me is calm for the passing moment.

You don't tell me what you think of "Cain." You send me the opinion of the populace, which you know I do not esteem. I have read several more of the plays of Calderon. "Los Dos Amantes del Cielo," is the finest, if I except one scene in the "Devocion de la Cruz." I read Greek and think about writing.

I do not think much of Emma's not admiring Metastasio; the *nil admirari,* however justly applied, seems to me a bad sign in a young person. I had rather a pupil of mine had conceived a frantic passion for Marini himself, than that she had found out the critical defects of the most deficient author. When she becomes of her own accord full of genuine admiration for the finest scene in the "Purgatorio," or the opening of the "Paradiso," or some other neglected piece of excellence, hope great things.

Adieu, I must not exceed the limits of my paper however little scrupulous I seem about those of your patience. P. B. S.

I waited three days to get this pen mended, and at last was obliged to write.

JOHN KEATS

[October 29, 1795–February 23, 1821]

JOHN KEATS was born over his father's livery stable. His parents were well-to-do and ambitious for their children and, while John was still a child, moved to a more pretentious home. Keats, however, in later life never spoke of the stable, probably as Hunt conjectures, because of "a personal soreness which the world had exasperated."

When he was seven, Keats, along with his younger brother George, was sent away to Enfield School. Tom, the youngest brother, came later. At Enfield, John led a normal schoolboy life, except that he was remarkable for his pugnacity. Although he was small, "he would fight any one—morning, noon, and night,—his brother among the rest. It was meat and drink to him." It was not that he was quarrelsome (though the distinction is hard to make) but rather that he would always stand up for what he thought a good cause, regardless of odds, and the impression he made on the other boys in the end was one of generosity and unselfish courage. Years later on a London street he came on an apprentice tormenting a kitten. As Keats was only five feet tall and slightly built, and the apprentice stood six foot, there seemed not much hope for the kitten, but in the fight which followed Keats carried off the victory, and a black eye. To get any understanding of Keats's character it is necessary always to bear in mind his sturdiness and his thorough ability to take care of himself mentally and, if need be, physically. He was an acutely sensitive man but he was no frail flower.

At Enfield Keats showed no unschoolboyish enthusiasm for books until his last year. He had formed a friendship with one of the younger ushers, Charles Cowden Clarke, which meant much to him. And there was nothing half-hearted about Keats when he did begin reading, for he exhausted the small school library and turned to Clarke's private library for more.

Keats's parents died while he was at school, and in 1811 his guardian, Richard Abbey, took him out of school and apprenticed him for five years to a surgeon at Edmonton. Abbey at the same time took George into his office. From a worldly point of view the action was wise as it seemed to prepare a career for both boys, and John does not seem to have objected. Neither does he seem to have been a very enthusiastic apprentice in the years which followed, though he was capable. Edmonton, however, was near Enfield, and Keats tramped over to talk with Clarke. On one of these visits Clarke showed him a copy of Spenser. Keats was ecstatic. He borrowed the volume and went through it "as a young horse would through a spring meadow—ramping." This was the beginning of poetry for Keats. His first known poem is an *Imitation of Spenser* (1812 or 1813) and in the time which followed he tried his hand at other verses.

He grew tired of Edmonton and, with the plausibility of youth, persuaded both his guardian and the surgeon to whom he was apprenticed that he should be allowed to break his indentures and go to the London hospitals to finish his medical training. Go to London he did in the autumn of 1815. Through the winter he worked earnestly at his studies, but more and more frequently he wrote at poetry. And in the spring occurred a great event in Keats's life. Clarke had shown some of the poems to Leigh Hunt and in the issue of May 5, 1816, Hunt printed the *Sonnet to Solitude* in *The Examiner*. Soon after, Keats met Hunt.

Keats's association with Hunt was to work a great change in his life. The period of intimacy did not, however, begin until the autumn, for in the immediate spring months ahead Keats had work to do. He was studying for his examinations, which he passed on July 25, 1816, and was licensed to practice as an apothecary. There was nothing unstable about Keats, and he did not leave incomplete at the last moment five years of professional training. But poetry had been growing in him like a passion and, some time during this year, he had taken the definite decision to devote himself to literature. In the autumn he returned and registered for more study, but his interest was elsewhere, and medicine fades out of the story of his life.

With Hunt and the Hunt circle he became intimate, and his position was that of Hunt's favorite disciple. Keats later outgrew Hunt and dismissed him with the cruel phrase, "Hunt does one harm by making fine things petty"; but at the start Hunt did Keats great good. He was the editor of the Liberal *Examiner* who had had the courage to call the Prince Regent a "fat Adonis of fifty" and had been sent to jail for it; he was the author of *The Story of Rimini* which had delighted Keats; he was, above all, an appreciator of good literature wherever he found it. Praise from such a man was stimulating in the highest degree. And Keats began to move among the literary groups, recognized as a coming poet. He met at this time or soon after Shelley and Hazlitt and Charles Lamb. (Wordsworth he met later.) He became intimate with the young poet Reynolds and the painter Haydon.

It is necessary to think of this year 1816 as a time of elation, and enthusiasm, and success. The tragic close of Keats's life has obscured the fact that his career begins when he is a young man vitally alive and enthusiastically happy. In the spring of 1816 his first poem to be published appeared. And promptly he began *I Stood Tip-toe upon a Little Hill,* a poem which is effervescent with delight in the springtime. Then he buckled to his examinations. Having passed them and put an uncongenial work behind him, he returned to London after a vacation. A few days later, in October, occurred that celebrated episode when Clarke introduced him to Chapman's *Homer* and he wrote *On First Looking into Chapman's Homer*. The Hunt circle acclaimed it, and also the *I Stood Tip-toe*, and he rapidly became the "pet lamb" of the group. Haydon introduced him to the Elgin marbles and he stood, at once abashed and stirred, before Greek art. Truly the world was opening out before Keats and he entered it with a consciousness of his powers. And the Hunt circle through the winter were talking of his coming book. It appeared, called simply *Poems*, on March 3, 1817.

Unfortunately the world was not so enthusiastic as the Hunt circle. The book had no sale and the great reviews ignored it. Unquestionably hurt by the failure, Keats did no whimpering, but set to work in April on *Endymion,* which he finished in November. The proofs and revisions occupied him until the following April (1818), almost precisely a year from the time he had started. Long before he was through with it, he was weary of it, and he saw its short-comings perhaps more clearly than his critics. It was to him, however, a test of his power of invention, of his power of sustained flight; and he met the test. The poem is diffuse, but rich in one of the qualities of the essential Keats—his acute sensitiveness to the beauties of the world around him and his gift for translating those beauties into language. The story of the poem is not important and the allegory rather thin.

By the time *Endymion* was finished, Keats was outgrowing Hunt's influence, and the story of his life is really the story of his remarkable growth as an artist from *I Stood Tip-toe,* begun in the spring of 1816, to the great Odes of the spring of 1819. As early as November or December, 1816, when he was writing *Sleep and Poetry*, Keats had shown he was aware of one of the weaknesses of his poetry. Mere sensuous appreciation was not enough. The poet, as he said in *Sleep and Poetry*, must have a wise understanding of humanity, a deeper quality than mere delight in the springtime and pretty nymphs eating strawberries. *Endymion* showed little or no advance toward that deeper quality. Immediately after *Endymion* appeared we find Keats writing to his publisher, "I know nothing—I have read nothing—and I mean to follow Solomon's directions, 'get learning—get understanding.'" And a few days later he was writing (May 3, 1818) to Reynolds his famous letter upon life as a mansion of many chambers, from the "Chamber of Maiden-Thought" of which he was just emerging into the dark mysterious passages.

Besides depth, Keats's poetry still lacked form, precision of effect in a sheer technical sense. Keats had, however, been reading the great English poets ceaselessly, enthusiastically. And he possessed, himself, the artist's sure instinct. Recognizing his own faults in *Endymion*, within a year he had corrected them, and written a series of odes which are incomparable in the English language. But this is advancing the story.

Endymion was published in the spring of 1818. The financial affairs of the Keats brothers were by this time hopelessly entangled. There had been sufficient to spend upon their education, but John had spent and *not* gone into his profession, George had quarrelled with his employer, and what remained was tied up in trusteeships and in lawsuits. George resolved to take what he could get and set out with his young wife for America and a fortune (which he did not make). The intimacy between the two brothers had been great, and John was now left alone to face a series of crises which might have broken any man.

John saw his brother off from Liverpool and then went for a walking trip with Brown in Scotland. He had a rollicking time, but came back with a sore throat. It was the first open symptom of tuberculosis, although it was not recognized as such, and from this time on Keats was fighting disaster without and disease within.

Least of his troubles were the fierce attacks on *Endymion* in the reviews—*Blackwood's* and *The Quarterly*—which broke upon him about the time of his return, and were thought to have broken his heart. He must have foreseen them. There had been a series of attacks on Hunt and the "Cockney School of Poetry," and that Keats would have his turn had been hinted. Literary criticism was dictated by politics, and in association with the political liberal Hunt, Keats had automatically made enemies of the great Tory journals. The reviews were stupid and brutal but that did not keep them from hurting.

More serious to John Keats was the condition of his brother Tom. Tom had been ill for a long time, and John and George had cared for him. When John came back from his summer's tramping trip, he saw at once that it was not a case of Tom's invalidism—it was death now. Attacked by the Reviews, ill himself, separated from George and worrying about George, separated from his beloved little sister Fanny by the suspicions of his guardian, John Keats, the most susceptible of men, sat down by the bedside of Tom to watch his brother die slowly of tuberculosis, from August till December. So passed the black autumn of 1818.

During the course of the autumn he met Fanny Brawne. His letters to his brother George say little of her except to suggest that she at first irritated him. She unsettled him so completely that he dared not speak of her, even to George. Later he told Fanny Brawne herself that within the first week he wrote himself her slave. Genuine and intense as always in his responses, Keats was swept off his feet into what proved to him a tragic and disastrous love affair. It tore him finally to pieces. The fault was not that of the bewildered girl, who returned his love. Circumstances and Keats's own nature were to blame. The first obstacle between them was financial, and it was an obstacle which was greater than one of mere money because Keats's proud independence was involved. He would not, poor, marry a well-to-do girl. Then tuberculosis declared itself in Keats and made impossible the one thing he most desired in the world. He physically broke himself to pieces against obstacles he could not control.

But in the spring of 1819, exultant in the first knowledge that his love was returned, Keats had a great flare of poetic production. Whether it was love, or mere springtime, or the release of his matured power after Tom's dying which was responsible, no one can ever say. Between January and May (1819) Keats wrote *The Eve of St. Agnes, The Eve of St. Mark, Bright Star Would I Were as Steadfast as Thou Art, La Belle Dame sans Merci,* and the great odes— *To Psyche, On a Grecian Urn, On Melancholy, To a Nightingale, On Indolence.* And until April Keats was still at work intermittently on *Hyperion,* which had been begun the previous year. In five months Keats had placed himself among the great English poets.

The remainder of the story is brief. Keats left London for the summer to escape the torment that the nearness of Fanny Brawne was to him. Before returning he wrote *Lamia, To Autumn,* and, in collaboration with Brown, a tragedy called *Otho the Great.* But his strength was burning out before a disease he did not yet recognize as any thing more serious than a sore throat.

The great hope of the autumn (1819) was that *Otho the Great* would make the fortune of all concerned. Nothing came of it. Meanwhile Keats, for all his courage, was becoming less resilient, less quick. On the night of February 3, 1820, he came in looking wild and feverish and, as Brown put him to bed, he coughed a single drop of blood on the pillow. "Bring me the candle, Brown," he commanded, "and let me see this blood." He recognized it as arterial blood and said, "That drop of blood is my death-warrant;—I must die."

He fought death for a year, fought it at first living with Brown in half of a duplex house of which Fanny Brawne and her mother occupied the other half, fought it staring through the glass of windows at Fanny walking in the garden while he lived his "posthumous life" within. In July 1820 his greatest work appeared in the *Lamia, Isabella, The Eve of St. Agnes, and Other Poems* volume, and the *Edinburgh Review,* which should have supported him earlier against the Tory journals, soon broke silence in his favor. Keats was too ill, physically and emotionally, to care. In September he sailed for Italy "as a soldier marches up to a battery," but it was the only hope for his health. Brown, who had been Keats's steadiest friend since the departure of George, had been in the north and delayed mails had prevented his learning of the Italian trip. When he heard, he came by the fastest route to see Keats, but his ship, inward bound, passed in the Thames Keats's ship outward bound. The young painter Severn who accompanied Keats tended him carefully, and at first the trip seemed to do Keats good. But he was too ill for recovery. He died in Rome, February 23, 1821, and was buried in the Protestant Cemetery there.

BIBLIOGRAPHICAL LIST OF KEATS'S VOLUMES

NOTE: In the present Anthology, Keats's poems are given in the order of composition, except that *Hyperion* has been placed last and that, to make grouping possible, a few of the sonnets are slightly out of place. The following list gives the contents, in order, of the three volumes published by Keats during his lifetime. The list is given for the convenience of those who may wish to study Keats's selection and arrangement of his own work.

I. POEMS, | BY | JOHN KEATS. | 'WHAT MORE FELICITY CAN FALL TO CREATURE, | THAN TO ENJOY DELIGHT WITH LIBERTY' | *Fate of the Butterfly.*—SPENSER. | LONDON: | PRINTED FOR C. & J. OLLIER, 3 WELBECK STREET, | CAVENDISH SQUARE. | 1817.

Dedication. To Leigh Hunt, Esq.

'I stood tip-toe upon a little hill.'

Specimen of an Induction to a Poem.

Calidore. A Fragment.

To Some Ladies.

On receiving a curious shell, and a Copy of Verses from the same Ladies.

To ——. ['Hadst thou liv'd in days of old.']

To Hope.

Imitation of Spenser.

'Woman! when I behold thee flippant, vain.'

Epistles:

 To George Felton Mathew.

 To my Brother George.

 To Charles Cowden Clarke.

Sonnets:

 I. To my Brother George.

 II. To ——. ['Had I a man's fair form, then might my sighs.']

 III. Written on the day that Mr. Leigh Hunt left prison.

 IV. 'How many bards gild the lapses of time.'

 V. To a Friend who sent me some roses.

 VI. To G. A. W.

 VII. 'O Solitude, if I must with thee dwell.'

 VIII. To my Brothers.

 IX. 'Keen, fitful gusts are whisp'ring here and there.'

 X. 'To one who has been long in city pent.'

 XI. On first Looking into Chapman's Homer.

 XII. On leaving some friends at an early hour.

 XIII. Addressed to Haydon.

 XIV. Addressed to the same.

 XV. On the Grasshopper and Cricket.

 XVI. To Kosciusko.

 XVII. 'Happy is England.'

Sleep and Poetry.

II. ENDYMION: | A POETIC ROMANCE. | BY JOHN KEATS. | 'THE STRETCHED METRE OF AN ANTIQUE SONG.' | LONDON: | PRINTED FOR TAYLOR AND HESSEY, | 93, FLEET STREET, | 1818.

III. LAMIA, | ISABELLA, | THE EVE OF ST. AGNES, | AND OTHER POEMS. | BY JOHN KEATS, | AUTHOR OF ENDYMION. | LONDON: | PRINTED FOR TAYLOR AND HESSEY, | FLEET STREET | 1820.

Lamia.

Isabella; or the Pot of Basil.

The Eve of St. Agnes.

Ode to a Nightingale.

Ode on a Grecian Urn.

Ode to Psyche.

Fancy.

Ode ['Bards of Passion and of Mirth'].

Lines on the Mermaid Tavern.

Robin Hood. To a Friend.

To Autumn.

Ode on Melancholy.

Hyperion: a Fragment.

The First Published Volume of Keats's *Poems*. (See Appendix I.)

IMITATION OF SPENSER

* * *

Now Morning from her orient chamber
    came,
And her first footsteps touch'd a verdant hill;
Crowning its lawny crest with amber flame,
Silv'ring the untainted gushes of its rill;
Which, pure from mossy beds, did down
    distil,
And after parting beds of simple flowers,
By many streams a little lake did fill,
Which round its marge reflected woven
    bowers,
And, in its middle space, a sky that never
    lowers.

There the kingfisher saw his plumage bright,
Vying with fish of brilliant dye below; 11
Whose silken fins, and golden scales' light
Cast upward, through the waves, a ruby
    glow:
There saw the swan his neck of arched
    snow,
And oar'd himself along with majesty;
Sparkled his jetty eyes; his feet did show
Beneath the waves like Afric's ebony,
And on his back a fay reclined voluptuously.

Ah! could I tell the wonders of an isle
That in that fairest lake had placed been, 20
I could e'en Dido of her grief beguile;
Or rob from aged Lear his bitter teen:
For sure so fair a place was never seen,
Of all that ever charm'd romantic eye:
It seem'd an emerald in the silver sheen
Of the bright waters; or as when on high,
Through clouds of fleecy white, laughs the
    cœrulean sky.

And all around it dipp'd luxuriously
Slopings of verdure through the glossy tide,
Which, as it were in gentle amity, 30
Rippled delighted up the flowery side;
As if to glean the ruddy tears, it tried,
Which fell profusely from the rose-tree
    stem!
Haply it was the workings of its pride,
In strife to throw upon the shore a gem
Outvying all the buds in Flora's diadem.

* * *

1812–13

SONNETS

(1816–17)

I

O SOLITUDE! IF I MUST WITH THEE DWELL

O Solitude! if I must with thee dwell,
  Let it not be among the jumbled heap
  Of murky buildings; climb with me the
    steep,—
Nature's observatory—whence the dell,
Its flowery slopes, its river's crystal swell,
May seem a span; let me thy vigils keep
  'Mongst boughs pavillion'd, where the deer's
    swift leap
Startles the wild bee from the fox-glove bell.
But though I'll gladly trace these scenes with
    thee, 9
  Yet the sweet converse of an innocent mind,
  Whose words are images of thoughts refin'd,
Is my soul's pleasure; and it sure must be
  Almost the highest bliss of human-kind,
When to thy haunts two kindred spirits flee.

1815–16

II

HOW MANY BARDS GILD THE LAPSES OF TIME!

How many bards gild the lapses of time!
  A few of them have ever been the food
  Of my delighted fancy,—I could brood
Over their beauties, earthly, or sublime:
And often, when I sit me down to rhyme,
  These will in throngs before my mind in-
    trude:
  But no confusion, no disturbance rude
Do they occasion; 'tis a pleasing chime.
So the unnumber'd sounds that evening store;
  The songs of birds—the whisp'ring of the
    leaves— 10
  The voice of waters—the great bell that
    heaves
With solemn sound,—and thousand others
    more,
  That distance of recognizance bereaves,
Make pleasing music, and not wild uproar.

1816

III

TO ONE WHO HAS BEEN LONG IN CITY PENT

To one who has been long in city pent,
  'Tis very sweet to look into the fair

And open face of heaven,—to breathe a
  prayer
Full in the smile of the blue firmament.
Who is more happy, when, with heart's content,
  Fatigued he sinks into some pleasant lair
  Of wavy grass, and reads a debonair
And gentle tale of love and languishment?
Returning home at evening, with an ear
  Catching the notes of Philomel,—an eye 10
Watching the sailing cloudlet's bright career,
  He mourns that day so soon has glided by:
E'en like the passage of an angel's tear
  That falls through the clear ether silently.

1816

IV

ON FIRST LOOKING INTO CHAPMAN'S HOMER

MUCH have I travell'd in the realms of gold,
  And many goodly states and kingdoms seen;
  Round many western islands have I been
Which bards in fealty to Apollo hold.
Oft of one wide expanse had I been told
  That deep-brow'd Homer ruled as his de-
    mesne:
  Yet did I never breathe its pure serene
Till I heard Chapman speak out loud and bold:
Then felt I like some watcher of the skies
  When a new planet swims into his ken; 10
Or like stout Cortez when with eagle eyes
  He star'd at the Pacific—and all his men
Look'd at each other with a wild surmise—
  Silent, upon a peak in Darien.

1816

V

ADDRESSED TO HAYDON

GREAT spirits now on earth are sojourning;
  He of the cloud, the cataract, the lake,
  Who of Helvellyn's summit, wide awake,
Catches his freshness from Archangel's wing:
He of the rose, the violet, the spring,
  The social smile, the chain for Freedom's sake:
  And lo!—whose steadfastness would never
    take
A meaner sound than Raphael's whispering.
And other spirits there are standing apart
  Upon the forehead of the age to come; 10
These, these will give the world another heart
  And other pulses. Hear ye not the hum
Of mighty workings?—
  Listen awhile ye nations, and be dumb.

1816

VI

KEEN, FITFUL GUSTS ARE WHISP'RING HERE
AND THERE

KEEN, fitful gusts are whisp'ring here and there
  Among the bushes half leafless, and dry;
  The stars look very cold about the sky,
And I have many miles on foot to fare.
Yet feel I little of the cool bleak air,
  Or of the dead leaves rustling drearily,
  Or of those silver lamps that burn on high,
Or of the distance from home's pleasant lair:
For I am brimfull of the friendliness
  That in a little cottage I have found; 10
Of fair-hair'd Milton's eloquent distress,
  And all his love for gentle Lycid drown'd;
Of lovely Laura in her light green dress,
  And faithful Petrarch gloriously crown'd.

1816

VII

HAPPY IS ENGLAND! I COULD BE CONTENT

HAPPY is England! I could be content
  To see no other verdure than its own;
  To feel no other breezes than are blown
Through its tall woods with high romances
    blent:
Yet do I sometimes feel a languishment
  For skies Italian, and an inward groan
  To sit upon an Alp as on a throne,
And half forget what world or worldling
    meant.
Happy is England, sweet her artless daughters;
  Enough their simple loveliness for me, 10
    Enough their whitest arms in silence
    clinging:
Yet do I often warmly burn to see
  Beauties of deeper glance, and hear their
    singing,
And float with them about the summer waters.

1816

VIII

TO G. A. W.

NYMPH of the downward smile and sidelong
    glance,
  In what diviner moments of the day
  Art thou most lovely? When gone far astray
Into the labyrinths of sweet utterance?
Or when serenely wand'ring in a trance
  Of sober thought? Or when starting away,
  With careless robe, to meet the morning ray,

Thou spar'st the flowers in thy mazy dance?
Haply 'tis when thy ruby lips part sweetly,
   And so remain, because thou listenest: 10
But thou to please wert nurtured so completely
   That I can never tell what mood is best.
I shall as soon pronounce which Grace more
    neatly
   Trips it before Apollo than the rest.

1816

IX

ON THE GRASSHOPPER AND CRICKET

THE poetry of earth is never dead:
   When all the birds are faint with the hot sun,
   And hide in cooling trees, a voice will run
From hedge to hedge about the new-mown
    mead;
That is the Grasshopper's—he takes the lead
   In summer luxury,—he has never done
   With his delights; for when tired out with
    fun
He rests at ease beneath some pleasant weed.
The poetry of earth is ceasing never:
   On a lone winter evening, when the frost 10
   Has wrought a silence, from the stove
    there shrills
The Cricket's song, in warmth increasing ever,
   And seems to one in drowsiness half lost,
   The Grasshopper's among some grassy
    hills.

December 30, 1816

X

AFTER DARK VAPOURS HAVE OPPRESS'D OUR
PLAINS

AFTER dark vapours have oppress'd our plains
   For a long dreary season, comes a day
   Born of the gentle South, and clears away
From the sick heavens all unseemly stains.
The anxious month, relieved of its pains,
   Takes as a long-lost right the feel of May;
   The eyelids with the passing coolness play
Like rose leaves with the drip of Summer
    rains.
The calmest thoughts come round us; as of
    leaves
   Budding—fruit ripening in stillness—Au-
    tumn suns   10
Smiling at eve upon the quiet sheaves—
Sweet Sappho's cheek—a smiling infant's
    breath—

The gradual sand that through an hour-glass
    runs—
A woodland rivulet—a Poet's death.

1817

XI

TO LEIGH HUNT, ESQ.

(Dedication sonnet to *Poems*, 1817)

GLORY and loveliness have pass'd away;
   For if we wander out in early morn,
   No wreathed incense do we see upborne
Into the east, to meet the smiling day:
No crowd of nymphs soft voic'd and young,
    and gay,
   In woven baskets bringing ears of corn,
   Roses, and pinks, and violets, to adorn
The shrine of Flora in her early May.
But there are left delights as high as these,
   And I shall ever bless my destiny,   10
That in a time, when under pleasant trees
   Pan is no longer sought, I feel a free,
A leafy luxury, seeing I could please
   With these poor offerings, a man like thee.

1817

XII

ON SEEING THE ELGIN MARBLES

MY spirit is too weak—mortality
   Weighs heavily on me like unwilling sleep,
   And each imagin'd pinnacle and steep
Of godlike hardship, tells me I must die
Like a sick Eagle looking at the sky.
   Yet 'tis a gentle luxury to weep
   That I have not the cloudy winds to keep,
Fresh for the opening of the morning's eye.
Such dim-conceived glories of the brain
   Bring round the heart an undescribable
    feud;   10
So do these wonders a most dizzy pain,
   That mingles Grecian grandeur with the
    rude
Wasting of old Time—with a billowy main—
   A sun—a shadow of a magnitude.

1817

XIII

ON THE SEA

IT keeps eternal whisperings around
   Desolate shores, and with its mighty swell
   Gluts twice ten thousand Caverns, till the
    spell

Of Hecate leaves them their old shadowy
    sound.
Often 'tis in such gentle temper found,
  That scarcely will the very smallest shell
  Be mov'd for days from where it sometime
    fell,
When last the winds of Heaven were unbound.
Oh ye! who have your eye-balls vex'd and
    tir'd,
  Feast them upon the wideness of the Sea; 10
  Oh ye! whose ears are dinn'd with uproar
    rude,
  Or fed too much with cloying melody—
  Sit ye near some old Cavern's Mouth, and
    brood
Until ye start, as if the sea-nymphs quir'd!
1817

XIV

ON A PICTURE OF LEANDER

Come hither, all sweet maidens soberly,
  Down-looking aye, and with a chasten'd
    light
  Hid in the fringes of your eyelids white,
And meekly let your fair hands joined be,
As if so gentle that ye could not see,
  Untouch'd, a victim of your beauty bright,
  Sinking away to his young spirit's night,
Sinking bewilder'd 'mid the dreary sea:
'Tis young Leander toiling to his death;
  Nigh swooning, he doth purse his weary
    lips   10
  For Hero's cheek, and smiles against her
    smile.
  O horrid dream! see how his body dips
  Dead-heavy; arms and shoulders gleam
    awhile;
He's gone; up bubbles all his amorous breath!
?1817

SPECIMEN OF AN INDUCTION
TO A POEM

Lo! I must tell a tale of chivalry;
For large white plumes are dancing in mine eye.
Not like the formal crest of latter days:
But bending in a thousand graceful ways;
So graceful, that it seems no mortal hand,
Or e'en the touch of Archimago's wand,
Could charm them into such an attitude.
We must think rather, that in playful mood,

Some mountain breeze had turned its chief
    delight,
To show this wonder of its gentle might. 10
Lo! I must tell a tale of chivalry;
For while I muse, the lance points slantingly
Athwart the morning air; some lady sweet,
Who cannot feel for cold her tender feet,
From the worn top of some old battlement
Hails it with tears, her stout defender sent:
And from her own pure self no joy dissem-
    bling,
Wraps round her ample robe with happy
    trembling.
Sometimes, when the good Knight his rest
    would take,
It is reflected, clearly, in a lake,   20
With the young ashen boughs, 'gainst which
    it rests,
And th' half-seen mossiness of linnets' nests.
Ah! shall I ever tell its cruelty,
When the fire flashes from a warrior's eye,
And his tremendous hand is grasping it,
And his dark brow for very wrath is knit?
Or when his spirit, with more calm intent,
Leaps to the honours of a tournament,
And makes the gazers round about the ring
Stare at the grandeur of the balancing? 30
No, no! this is far off:—then how shall I
Revive the dying tones of minstrelsy,
Which linger yet about long gothic arches,
In dark green ivy, and among wild larches?
How sing the splendour of the revelries,
When butts of wine are drunk off to the lees?
And that bright lance, against the fretted wall,
Beneath the shade of stately banneral,
Is slung with shining cuirass, sword, and
    shield?
Where ye may see a spur in bloody field. 40
Light-footed damsels move with gentle paces
Round the wide hall, and show their happy
    faces;
Or stand in courtly talk by fives and sevens:
Like those fair stars that twinkle in the heavens.
Yet must I tell a tale of chivalry:
Or wherefore comes that knight so proudly by?
Wherefore more proudly does the gentle
    knight,
Rein in the swelling of his ample might?

Spenser! thy brows are archèd, open, kind,
And come like a clear sunrise to my mind; 50

And always does my heart with pleasure dance,
When I think on thy noble countenance:
Where never yet was aught more earthly seen
Than the pure freshness of thy laurels green.
Therefore, great bard, I not so fearfully
Call on thy gentle spirit to hover nigh
My daring steps: or if thy tender care,
Thus startled unaware,
Be jealous that the foot of other wight
Should madly follow that bright path of light
Trac'd by thy lov'd Libertas; he will speak, 61
And tell thee that my prayer is very meek;
That I will follow with due reverence,
And start with awe at mine own strange pretence.
Him thou wilt hear; so I will rest in hope
To see wide plains, fair trees and lawny slope:
The morn, the eve, the light, the shade, the flowers;
Clear streams, smooth lakes, and overlooking towers.

1816

I STOOD TIP–TOE UPON A LITTLE HILL

"Places of nestling green for Poets made."
Story of Rimini

I STOOD tip-toe upon a little hill,
The air was cooling, and so very still,
That the sweet buds which with a modest pride
Pull droopingly, in slanting curve aside,
Their scantly leav'd, and finely tapering stems,
Had not yet lost those starry diadems
Caught from the early sobbing of the morn.
The clouds were pure and white as flocks new shorn,
And fresh from the clear brook; sweetly they slept
On the blue fields of heaven, and then there crept 10
A little noiseless noise among the leaves,
Born of the very sigh that silence heaves:
For not the faintest motion could be seen
Of all the shades that slanted o'er the green.
There was wide wand'ring for the greediest eye,
To peer about upon variety;
Far round the horizon's crystal air to skim,
And trace the dwindled edgings of its brim;

To picture out the quaint, and curious bending
Of a fresh woodland alley, never ending; 20
Or by the bowery clefts, and leafy shelves,
Guess where the jaunty streams refresh themselves.
I gazed awhile, and felt as light, and free
As though the fanning wings of Mercury
Had play'd upon my heels: I was light-hearted,
And many pleasures to my vision started;
So I straightway began to pluck a posey
Of luxuries bright, milky, soft and rosy.

A bush of May flowers with the bees about them;
Ah, sure no tasteful nook would be without them; 30
And let a lush laburnum oversweep them,
And let long grass grow round the roots to keep them
Moist, cool and green; and shade the violets,
That they may bind the moss in leafy nets.

A filbert hedge with wild briar overtwined,
And clumps of woodbine taking the soft wind
Upon their summer thrones; there too should be
The frequent chequer of a youngling tree,
That with a score of light green brethren shoots
From the quaint mossiness of aged roots: 40
Round which is heard a spring-head of clear waters
Babbling so wildly of its lovely daughters
The spreading blue-bells: it may haply mourn
That such fair clusters should be rudely torn
From their fresh beds, and scattered thoughtlessly
By infant hands, left on the path to die.

Open afresh your round of starry folds,
Ye ardent marigolds!
Dry up the moisture from your golden lids,
For great Apollo bids 50
That in these days your praises should be sung
On many harps, which he has lately strung;
And when again your dewiness he kisses,
Tell him, I have you in my world of blisses:
So haply when I rove in some far vale,
His mighty voice may come upon the gale.

Here are sweet peas, on tip-toe for a flight:
With wings of gentle flush o'er delicate white,

And taper fingers catching at all things,
To bind them all about with tiny rings.   60

Linger awhile upon some bending planks
That lean against a streamlet's rushy banks,
And watch intently Nature's gentle doings:
They will be found softer than ring-dove's
    cooings.
How silent comes the water round that bend;
Not the minutest whisper does it send
To the o'erhanging sallows: blades of grass
Slowly across the chequer'd shadows pass.
Why, you might read two sonnets, ere they
    reach   69
To where the hurrying freshnesses aye preach
A natural sermon o'er their pebbly beds;
Where swarms of minnows show their little
    heads,
Staying their wavy bodies 'gainst the streams,
To taste the luxury of sunny beams
Temper'd with coolness. How they ever
    wrestle
With their own sweet delight, and ever nestle
Their silver bellies on the pebbly sand.
If you but scantily hold out the hand,
That very instant not one will remain;   79
But turn your eye, and they are there again.
The ripples seem right glad to reach those
    cresses,
And cool themselves among the em'rald tresses;
The while they cool themselves, they freshness
    give,
And moisture, that the bowery green may
    live:
So keeping up an interchange of favours,
Like good men in the truth of their behaviours.
Sometimes goldfinches one by one will drop
From low hung branches; little space they
    stop;
But sip, and twitter, and their feathers sleek;
Then off at once, as in a wanton freak: 90
Or perhaps, to show their black, and golden
    wings,
Pausing upon their yellow flutterings.
Were I in such a place, I sure should pray
That naught less sweet, might call my thoughts
    away,
Than the soft rustle of a maiden's gown
Fanning away the dandelion's down;
Than the light music of her nimble toes
Patting against the sorrel as she goes.

How she would start, and blush, thus to be
    caught
Playing in all her innocence of thought.   100
O let me lead her gently o'er the brook,
Watch her half-smiling lips, and downward
    look;
O let me for one moment touch her wrist;
Let me one moment to her breathing list;
And as she leaves me may she often turn
Her fair eyes looking through her locks au-
    burne.
What next? A tuft of evening primroses,
O'er which the mind may hover till it dozes;
O'er which it well might take a pleasant sleep,
But that 'tis ever startled by the leap   110
Of buds into ripe flowers; or by the flitting
Of diverse moths, that aye their rest are quit-
    ting;
Or by the moon lifting her silver rim
Above a cloud, and with a gradual swim
Coming into the blue with all her light.
O Maker of sweet poets, dear delight
Of this fair world, and all its gentle livers;
Spangler of clouds, halo of crystal rivers,
Mingler with leaves, and dew and tumbling
    streams,
Closer of lovely eyes to lovely dreams,   120
Lover of loneliness, and wandering,
Of upcast eye, and tender pondering!
Thee must I praise above all other glories
That smile us on to tell delightful stories.
For what has made the sage or poet write
But the fair paradise of Nature's light?
In the calm grandeur of a sober line,
We see the waving of the mountain pine;
And when a tale is beautifully staid,
We feel the safety of a hawthorn glade: 130
When it is moving on luxurious wings,
The soul is lost in pleasant smotherings:
Fair dewy roses brush against our faces,
And flowering laurels spring from diamond
    vases;
O'er head we see the jasmine and sweet briar,
And bloomy grapes laughing from green attire;
While at our feet, the voice of crystal bubbles
Charms us at once away from all our troubles:
So that we feel uplifted from the world,
Walking upon the white clouds wreath'd and
    curl'd.   140
So felt he, who first told, how Psyche went
On the smooth wind to realms of wonderment;

What Psyche felt, and Love, when their full
    lips
First touch'd; what amorous, and fondling
    nips
They gave each other's cheeks; with all their
    sighs,
And how they kist each other's tremulous
    eyes:
The silver lamp,—the ravishment,—the won-
    der—
The darkness,—loneliness,—the fearful thun-
    der;
Their woes gone by, and both to heaven up-
    flown,
To bow for gratitude before Jove's throne. 150
So did he feel, who pull'd the boughs aside,
That we might look into a forest wide,
To catch a glimpse of Fauns, and Dryades
Coming with softest rustle through the trees;
And garlands woven of flowers wild, and
    sweet,
Upheld on ivory wrists, or sporting feet:
Telling us how fair, trembling Syrinx fled
Arcadian Pan, with such a fearful dread.
Poor nymph,—poor Pan,—how he did weep
    to find,
Naught but a lovely sighing of the wind   160
Along the reedy stream; a half-heard strain,
Full of sweet desolation—balmy pain.

What first inspired a bard of old to sing
Narcissus pining o'er the untainted spring?
In some delicious ramble, he had found
A little space, with boughs all woven round;
And in the midst of all, a clearer pool
Than e'er reflected in its pleasant cool,
The blue sky here, and there, serenely peeping
Through tendril wreaths fantastically creep-
    ing.   170
And on the bank a lonely flower he spied,
A meek and forlorn flower, with naught of
    pride,
Drooping its beauty o'er the watery clearness,
To woo its own sad image into nearness:
Deaf to light Zephyrus it would not move;
But still would seem to droop, to pine, to
    love.
So while the poet stood in this sweet spot,
Some fainter gleamings o'er his fancy shot;
Nor was it long ere he had told the tale ·
Of young Narcissus, and sad Echo's bale. 180

Where had he been, from whose warm head
    out-flew
That sweetest of all songs, that ever new,
That aye refreshing, pure deliciousness,
Coming ever to bless
The wanderer by moonlight? to him bringing
Shapes from the invisible world, unearthly
    singing
From out the middle air, from flowery nests,
And from the pillowy silkiness that rests
Full in the speculation of the stars.
Ah! surely he had burst our mortal bars; 190
Into some wond'rous region he had gone,
To search for thee, divine Endymion!

He was a Poet, sure a lover too,
Who stood on Latmus' top, what time there
    blew
Soft breezes from the myrtle vale below;
And brought in faintness solemn, sweet, and
    slow
A hymn from Dian's temple; while upswelling,
The incense went to her own starry dwelling.
But though her face was clear as infant's eyes,
Though she stood smiling o'er the sacrifice,
The Poet wept at her so piteous fate,   201
Wept that such beauty should be desolate:
So in fine wrath some golden sounds he won,
And gave meek Cynthia her Endymion.

Queen of the wide air; thou most lovely queen
Of all the brightness that mine eyes have seen!
As thou exceedest all things in thy shine,
So every tale, does this sweet tale of thine.
O for three words of honey, that I might
Tell but one wonder of thy bridal night! 210

Where distant ships do seem to show their
    keels,
Phoebus awhile delay'd his mighty wheels,
And turn'd to smile upon thy bashful eyes,
Ere he his unseen pomp would solemnize.
The evening weather was so bright, and clear,
That men of health were of unusual cheer;
Stepping like Homer at the trumpet's call,
Or young Apollo on the pedestal:
And lovely women were as fair and warm,
As Venus looking sideways in alarm.   220
The breezes were ethereal, and pure,
And crept through half-closed lattices to cure
The languid sick; it cool'd their fever'd sleep,
And soothed them into slumbers full and deep.

Soon they awoke clear eyed: nor burnt with
    thirsting,
Nor with hot fingers, nor with temples burst-
    ing:
And springing up, they met the wond'ring
    sight
Of their dear friends, nigh foolish with de-
    light;
Who feel their arms, and breasts, and kiss and
    stare,
And on their placid foreheads part the hair. 230
Young men, and maidens at each other gaz'd
With hands held back, and motionless, amaz'd
To see the brightness in each other's eyes;
And so they stood, fill'd with a sweet surprise,
Until their tongues were loos'd in poesy.
Therefore no lover did of anguish die:
But the soft numbers, in that moment spoken,
Made silken ties, that never may be broken.
Cynthia! I cannot tell the greater blisses,
That follow'd thine, and thy dear shepherd's
    kisses: 240
Was there a poet born?—but now no more,
My wand'ring spirit must no further soar.—

1816

From SLEEP AND POETRY

(LINES 53–154; 181–247)

O Poesy! for thee I grasp my pen
That am not yet a glorious denizen
Of thy wide heaven; yet, to my ardent prayer,
Yield from thy sanctuary some clear air,
Smooth'd for intoxication by the breath
Of flowering bays, that I may die a death
Of luxury, and my young spirit follow
The morning sun-beams to the great Apollo
Like a fresh sacrifice; or, if I can bear   61
The o'erwhelming sweets, 'twill bring to me
    the fair
Visions of all places: a bowery nook
Will be elysium—an eternal book
Whence I may copy many a lovely saying
About the leaves, and flowers—about the play-
    ing
Of nymphs in woods, and fountains; and the
    shade
Keeping a silence round a sleeping maid;
And many a verse from so strange influence
That we must ever wonder how, and whence

It came. Also imaginings will hover   71
Round my fire-side, and haply there discover
Vistas of solemn beauty, where I'd wander
In happy silence, like the clear Meander
Through its lone vales; and where I found a
    spot
Of awfuller shade, or an enchanted grot,
Or a green hill o'erspread with chequer'd dress
Of flowers, and fearful from its loveliness,
Write on my tablets all that was permitted,
All that was for our human senses fitted.   80
Then the events of this wide world I'd seize
Like a strong giant, and my spirit teaze
Till at its shoulders it should proudly see
Wings to find out an immortality.

Stop and consider! life is but a day;
A fragile dew-drop on its perilous way
From a tree's summit; a poor Indian's sleep
While his boat hastens to the monstrous
    steep
Of Montmorenci. Why so sad a moan?
Life is the rose's hope while yet unblown;   90
The reading of an ever-changing tale;
The light uplifting of a maiden's veil;
A pigeon tumbling in clear summer air;
A laughing school-boy, without grief or care,
Riding the springy branches of an elm.
O for ten years, that I may overwhelm
Myself in poesy; so I may do the deed
That my own soul has to itself decreed.
Then will I pass the countries that I see
In long perspective, and continually   100
Taste their pure fountains. First the realm I'll
    pass
Of Flora, and old Pan: sleep in the grass,
Feed upon apples red, and strawberries,
And choose each pleasure that my fancy sees;
Catch the white-handed nymphs in shady
    places,
To woo sweet kisses from averted faces,—
Play with their fingers, touch their shoulders
    white
Into a pretty shrinking with a bite
As hard as lips can make it: till agreed,
A lovely tale of human life we'll read.   110
And one will teach a tame dove how it best
May fan the cool air gently o'er my rest;
Another, bending o'er her nimble tread,
Will set a green robe floating round her head,

And still will dance with ever varied ease,
Smiling upon the flowers and the trees:
Another will entice me on, and on
Through almond blossoms and rich cinnamon;
Till in the bosom of a leafy world
We rest in silence, like two gems upcurl'd 120
In the recesses of a pearly shell.

noble account· strife of human hearts

And can I ever bid these joys farewell?
Yes, I must pass them for a nobler life,
Where I may find the agonies, the strife
Of human hearts: for lo! I see afar,
O'ersailing the blue cragginess, a car
And steeds with streamy manes—the chariot-
eer
Looks out upon the winds with glorious
fear:
And now the numerous tramplings quiver
lightly
Along a huge cloud's ridge; and now with
sprightly 130
Wheel downward come they into fresher
skies,
Tipt round with silver from the sun's bright
eyes.
Still downward with capacious whirl they
glide;
And now I see them on the green-hill's side
In breezy rest among the nodding stalks.
The charioteer with wond'rous gesture talks
To the trees and mountains; and there soon
appear
Shapes of delight, of mystery, and fear,
Passing along before a dusky space
Made by some mighty oaks: as they would
chace 140
Some ever-fleeting music on they sweep.
Lo! how they murmur, laugh, and smile, and
weep:
Some with upholden hand and mouth severe;
Some with their faces muffled to the ear
Between their arms; some, clear in youthful
bloom,
Go glad and smilingly athwart the gloom;
Some looking back, and some with upward
gaze;
Yes, thousands in a thousand different ways
Flit onward—now a lovely wreath of girls
Dancing their sleek hair into tangled curls; 150
And now broad wings. Most awfully intent
The driver of those steeds is forward bent,

And seems to listen: O that I might know
All that he writes with such a hurrying glow.

* * *

Could all this be forgotten? Yes, a schism
Nurtured by foppery and barbarism,
Made great Apollo blush for this his land.
Men were thought wise who could not under-
stand
His glories: with a puling infant's force
They sway'd about upon a rocking horse,
And thought it Pegasus. Ah dismal soul'd!
The winds of heaven blew, the ocean roll'd
Its gathering waves—ye felt it not. The blue
Bared its eternal bosom, and the dew 190
Of summer nights collected still to make
The morning precious: beauty was awake!
Why were ye not awake? But ye were dead
To things ye knew not of,—were closely wed
To musty laws lined out with wretched rule
And compass vile: so that ye taught a school
Of dolts to smooth, inlay, and clip, and fit,
Till, like the certain wands of Jacob's wit,
Their verses tallied. Easy was the task:
A thousand handicraftsmen wore the mask
Of Poesy. Ill-fated, impious race! 201
That blasphemed the bright Lyrist to his face,
And did not know it,—no, they went about,
Holding a poor, decrepid standard out
Mark'd with most flimsy mottos, and in large
The name of one Boileau!

expresses allegiance to freedom

decadence even of the neo-class school of criticism O ye whose charge *1669 1674*

It is to hover round our pleasant hills!
Whose congregated majesty so fills
My boundly reverence, that I cannot trace
Your hallowed names, in this unholy place,
So near those common folk; did not their
shames 211
Affright you? Did our old lamenting Thames
Delight you? Did ye never cluster round
Delicious Avon, with a mournful sound,
And weep? Or did ye wholly bid adieu
To regions where no more the laurel grew?
Or did ye stay to give a welcoming
To some lone spirits who could proudly sing
Their youth away, and die? 'Twas even so:
But let me think away those times of woe: 220
Now 'tis a fairer season; ye have breathed
Rich benedictions o'er us; ye have wreathed
Fresh garlands: for sweet music has been heard
In many places;—some has been upstirr'd

new clause for poetry ing

From out its crystal dwelling in a lake,
By a swan's ebon bill; from a thick brake,
Nested and quiet in a valley mild,
Bubbles a pipe; fine sounds are floating wild
About the earth: happy are ye and glad.

These things are doubtless: yet in truth we've
　　had　　　　　　　　　　　　　　　　230
Strange thunders from the potency of song;
Mingled indeed with what is sweet and strong,
From majesty: but in clear truth the themes
Are ugly clubs, the Poets' Polyphemes
Disturbing the grand sea. A drainless shower
Of light is poesy; 'tis the supreme of power;
'Tis might half slumb'ring on its own right
　　arm.
The very archings of her eye-lids charm
A thousand willing agents to obey,
And still she governs with the mildest sway:
But strength alone though of the Muses born
Is like a fallen angel: trees uptorn,　　　242
Darkness, and worms, and shrouds, and sepul-
　　chres
Delight it; for it feeds upon the burrs,
And thorns of life; forgetting the great end
Of poesy, that it should be a friend
To soothe the cares, and lift the thoughts of
　　man.

1816

ENDYMION

From BOOK I

CREDO (LINES 1–62)

A THING of beauty is a joy for ever:
Its loveliness increases; it will never
Pass into nothingness; but still will keep
A bower quiet for us, and a sleep
Full of sweet dreams, and health, and quiet
　　breathing.
Therefore, on every morrow, are we wreathing
A flowery band to bind us to the earth,
Spite of despondence, of the inhuman dearth
Of noble natures, of the gloomy days,
Of all the unhealthy and o'er-darkened ways 10
Made for our searching: yes, in spite of all,
Some shape of beauty moves away the pall
From our dark spirits. Such the sun, the moon,
Trees old, and young, sprouting a shady boon
For simple sheep; and such are daffodils

With the green world they live in; and clear
　　rills
That for themselves a cooling covert make
'Gainst the hot season; the mid forest brake,
Rich with a sprinkling of fair musk-rose
　　blooms:
And such too is the grandeur of the dooms 20
We have imagined for the mighty dead;
All lovely tales that we have heard or read:
An endless fountain of immortal drink,
Pouring unto us from the heaven's brink.

Nor do we merely feel these essences
For one short hour; no, even as the trees
That whisper round a temple become soon
Dear as the temple's self, so does the moon,
The passion poesy, glories infinite,
Haunt us till they become a cheering light 30
Unto our souls, and bound to us so fast,
That, whether there be shine, or gloom o'er-
　　cast,
They always must be with us, or we die.

Therefore, 'tis with full happiness that I
Will trace the story of Endymion.
The very music of the name has gone
Into my being, and each pleasant scene
Is growing fresh before me as the green
Of our own vallies: so I will begin
Now while I cannot hear the city's din;　　40
Now while the early budders are just new,
And run in mazes of the youngest hue
About old forests; while the willow trails
Its delicate amber; and the dairy pails
Bring home increase of milk. And, as the
　　year
Grows lush in juicy stalks, I'll smoothly steer
My little boat, for many quiet hours,
With streams that deepen freshly into bowers.
Many and many a verse I hope to write,
Before the daisies, vermeil rimm'd and white,
Hide in deep herbage; and ere yet the bees 51
Hum about globes of clover and sweet
　　peas,
I must be near the middle of my story.
O may no wintry season, bare and hoary,
See it half finish'd: but let Autumn bold,
With universal tinge of sober gold,
Be all about me when I make an end.
And now at once, adventuresome, I send
My herald thought into a wilderness:

There let its trumpet blow, and quickly dress
My uncertain path with green, that I may
 speed   61
Easily onward, thorough flowers and weed.

[Following this passage the poem describes a
festival of Pan. A throng enters including the
handsome and popular Endymion in his chariot.
After a great hymn in honor of Pan the crowd devotes itself to games, dancing, and the telling of
rich old stories of mythology. Endymion, however,
has throughout been moody and depressed, and
after the festival his sister, Peona, leads him to a
bowery island, where he falls asleep. When he
wakens she coaxes him into telling what is troubling his spirit? Endymion speaks:]

ENDYMION'S VISION (LINES 538–712)

      . . . "I will ease my breast
Of secret grief, here in this bowery nest.

"This river does not see the naked sky, 540
Till it begins to progress silverly
Around the western border of the wood,
Whence, from a certain spot, its winding
 flood
Seems at the distance like a crescent moon:
And in that nook, the very pride of June,
Had I been used to pass my weary eves;
The rather for the sun unwilling leaves
So dear a picture of his sovereign power,
And I could witness his most kingly hour,
When he doth tighten up the golden reins, 550
And paces leisurely down amber plains
His snorting four. Now when his chariot last
Its beams against the zodiac-lion cast,
There blossom'd suddenly a magic bed
Of sacred ditamy, and poppies red:
At which I wondered greatly, knowing well
That but one night had wrought this flowery
 spell;
And, sitting down close by, began to muse
What it might mean. Perhaps, thought I,
 Morpheus,
In passing here, his owlet pinions shook; 560
Or, it may be, ere matron Night uptook
Her ebon urn, young Mercury, by stealth,
Had dipt his rod in it: such garland wealth
Came not by common growth. Thus on I
 thought,
Until my head was dizzy and distraught.
Moreover, through the dancing poppies stole
A breeze, most softly lulling to my soul;

And shaping visions all about my sight
Of colours, wings, and bursts of spangly
 light;
The which became more strange, and strange,
 and dim,   570
And then were gulf'd in a tumultuous swim:
And then I fell asleep. Ah, can I tell
The enchantment that afterwards befell?
Yet it was but a dream: yet such a dream
That never tongue, although it overteem
With mellow utterance, like a cavern spring,
Could figure out and to conception bring
All I beheld and felt. Methought I lay _dream_
Watching the zenith, where the milky way
Among the stars in virgin splendour pours; 580
And travelling my eye, until the doors
Of heaven appear'd to open for my flight,
I became loth and fearful to alight
From such high soaring by a downward
 glance:
So kept me steadfast in that airy trance,
Spreading imaginary pinions wide.
When, presently, the stars began to glide,
And faint away, before my eager view:
At which I sigh'd that I could not pursue,
And dropt my vision to the horizon's verge;
And lo! from opening clouds, I saw emerge 591 _could not go_
The loveliest moon, that ever silver'd o'er
A shell for Neptune's goblet; she did soar _Cynthia_
So passionately bright, my dazzled soul
Commingling with her argent spheres did roll
Through clear and cloudy, even when she
 went
At last into a dark and vapoury tent—
Whereat, methought, the lidless-eyed train
Of planets all were in the blue again.
To commune with those orbs, once more I
 raised   600
My sight right upward: but it was quite dazed
By a bright something, sailing down apace,
Making me quickly veil my eyes and face:
Again I look'd, and, O ye deities,
Who from Olympus watch our destinies!
Whence that completed form of all complete-
 ness?
Whence came that high perfection of all
 sweetness?
Speak, stubborn earth, and tell me where, O
 where
Hast thou a symbol of her golden hair? 609
Not oat-sheaves drooping in the western sun;

Not—thy soft hand, fair sister! let me shun
Such follying before thee—yet she had,
Indeed, locks bright enough to make me mad;
And they were simply gordian'd up and
    braided,
Leaving, in naked comeliness, unshaded,
Her pearl round ears, white neck, and orbed
    brow;
The which were blended in, I know not how,
With such a paradise of lips and eyes,
Blush-tinted cheeks, half smiles, and faintest
    sighs,
That, when I think thereon, my spirit clings
And plays about its fancy, till the stings 621
Of human neighbourhood envenom all.
Unto what awful power shall I call?
To what high fane?—Ah! see her hovering
    feet,
More bluely vein'd, more soft, more whitely
    sweet
Than those of sea-born Venus, when she rose
From out her cradle shell. The wind outblows
Her scarf into a fluttering pavilion;
'Tis blue, and over-spangled with a million
Of little eyes, as though thou wert to shed, 630
Over the darkest, lushest bluebell bed,
Handfuls of daisies."—"Endymion, how
    strange!
Dream within dream!"—"She took an airy
    range,
And then, towards me, like a very maid,
Came blushing, waning, willing, and afraid,
And press'd me by the hand: Ah! 'twas too
    much;
Methought I fainted at the charmed touch,
Yet held my recollection, even as one
Who dives three fathoms where the waters run
Gurgling in beds of coral: for anon,   640
I felt upmounted in that region
Where falling stars dart their artillery forth,
And eagles struggle with the buffeting north
That balances the heavy meteor-stone;—
Felt too, I was not fearful, nor alone,
But lapp'd and lull'd along the dangerous sky.
Soon, as it seem'd, we left our journeying high,
And straightway into frightful eddies swoop'd;
Such as aye muster where gray time has
    scoop'd
Huge dens and caverns in a mountain's side:
There hollow sounds aroused me, and I
    sigh'd   651

To faint once more by looking on my bliss—
I was distracted; madly did I kiss
The wooing arms which held me, and did give
My eyes at once to death: but 'twas to live,
To take in draughts of life from the gold fount
Of kind and passionate looks; to count, and
    count
The moments, by some greedy help that
    seem'd
A second self, that each might be redeem'd
And plunder'd of its load of blessedness. 660
Ah, desperate mortal! I ev'n dared to press
Her very cheek against my crowned lip,
And, at that moment, felt my body dip
Into a warmer air: a moment more,
Our feet were soft in flowers. There was store
Of newest joys upon that alp. Sometimes
A scent of violets, and blossoming limes,
Loiter'd around us; then of honey cells,
Made delicate from all white-flower bells;
And once, above the edges of our nest,   670
An arch face peep'd,—an Oread as I guess'd.

"Why did I dream that sleep o'erpower'd
    me
In midst of all this heaven? Why not see,
Far off, the shadows of his pinions dark,
And stare them from me? But no, like a spark
That needs must die, although its little beam
Reflects upon a diamond, my sweet dream
Fell into nothing—into stupid sleep.
And so it was, until a gentle creep,
A careful moving caught my waking ears, 680
And up I started: Ah! my sighs, my tears,
My clenched hands;—for lo! the poppies hung
Dew-dabbled on their stalks, the ouzel sung
A heavy ditty, and the sullen day
Had chidden herald Hesperus away,
With leaden looks: the solitary breeze
Bluster'd, and slept, and its wild self did teaze
With wayward melancholy; and I thought,
Mark me, Peona! that sometimes it brought
Faint   fare-thee-wells,   and   sigh-shrilled
    adieus!—   690
Away I wander'd—all the pleasant hues
Of heaven and earth had faded: deepest shades
Were deepest dungeons: heaths and sunny
    glades
Were full of pestilent light; our taintless rills
Seem'd sooty, and o'er-spread with upturn'd
    gills

Of dying fish; the vermeil rose had blown
In frightful scarlet, and its thorns out-grown
Like spiked aloe. If an innocent bird
Before my heedless footsteps stirr'd, and stirr'd
In little journeys, I beheld in it   700
A disguis'd demon, missioned to knit
My soul with under darkness; to entice
My stumblings down some monstrous preci-
      pice:
Therefore I eager followed, and did curse
The disappointment. Time, that aged nurse,
Rock'd me to patience. Now, thank gentle
      heaven!
These things, with all their comfortings, are
      given
To my down-sunken hours, and with thee,
Sweet sister, help to stem the ebbing sea
Of weary life."
                    Thus ended he, and both 710
Sat silent: for the maid was very loth
To answer.

WHEREIN LIES HAPPINESS (LINES 769–857)

[Peona thinks this is nothing but a dream, and
very sensibly, but with a gentle timidity, she urges
him to put it aside and take his proper place in the
world again. Endymion replies:]

"Peona! ever have I long'd to slake
My thirst for the world's praises: nothing
      base,   770
No merely slumberous phantasm, could un-
      lace
The stubborn canvas for my voyage pre-
      pared—
Though now 'tis tatter'd; leaving my bark
      bared
And sullenly drifting: yet my higher hope
Is of too wide, too rainbow-large a scope,
To fret at myriads of earthly wrecks.
Wherein lies happiness? In that which becks
Our ready minds to fellowship divine,
A fellowship with essence; till we shine,
Full alchemized, and free of space. Behold 780
The clear religion of heaven! Fold
A rose leaf round thy finger's taperness,
And soothe thy lips: hist, when the airy stress
Of music's kiss impregnates the free winds,
And with a sympathetic touch unbinds
Æolian magic from their lucid wombs:
Then old songs waken from enclouded tombs;

Old ditties sigh above their father's grave;
Ghosts of melodious prophesyings rave
Round every spot where trod Apollo's foot;
Bronze clarions awake, and faintly bruit, 791
Where long ago a giant battle was;
And, from the turf, a lullaby doth pass
In every place where infant Orpheus slept.
Feel we these things?—that moment have we
      stept
Into a sort of oneness, and our state
Is like a floating spirit's. But there are
Richer entanglements, enthralments far
More self-destroying, leading, by degrees,
To the chief intensity: the crown of these 800
Is made of love and friendship, and sits high
Upon the forehead of humanity.
All its more ponderous and bulky worth
Is friendship, whence there ever issues forth
A steady splendour; but at the tip-top,
There hangs by unseen film, an orbed drop
Of light, and that is love: its influence
Thrown in our eyes genders a novel sense,
At which we start and fret: till in the end,
Melting into its radiance, we blend,   810
Mingle, and so become a part of it,—
Nor with aught else can our souls interknit
So wingedly: when we combine therewith,
Life's self is nourish'd by its proper pith,
And we are nurtured like a pelican brood.
Aye, so delicious is the unsating food,
That men, who might have tower'd in the
      van
Of all the congregated world, to fan
And winnow from the coming step of time
All chaff of custom, wipe away all slime 820
Left by men-slugs and human serpentry,
Have been content to let occasion die,
Whilst they did sleep in love's Elysium.
And, truly, I would rather be struck dumb,
Than speak against this ardent listlessness:
For I have ever thought that it might bless
The world with benefits unknowingly;
As does the nightingale, up-perched high,
And cloister'd among cool and bunched
      leaves—   829
She sings but to her love, nor e'er conceives
How tiptoe Night holds back her dark-gray
      hood.
Just so may love, although 'tis understood
The mere commingling of passionate breath,
Produce more than our searching witnesseth:

What I know not: but who, of men, can tell
That flowers would bloom, or that green
     fruit would swell
To melting pulp, that fish would have bright
     mail,
The earth its dower of river, wood, and vale,
The meadows runnels, runnels pebblestones,
The seed its harvest, or the lute its tones, 840
Tones ravishment, or ravishment its sweet,
If human souls did never kiss and greet?

    "Now, if this earthly love has power to
       make
Men's being mortal, immortal; to shake
Ambition from their memories, and brim
Their measure of content; what merest whim,
Seems all this poor endeavour after fame,
To one, who keeps within his steadfast aim
A love immortal, an immortal too.
Look not so wilder'd; for these things are true
And never can be born of atomies   851
That buzz about our slumbers, like brain-flies,
Leaving us fancy-sick. No, no, I'm sure,
My restless spirit never could endure
To brood so long upon one luxury,
Unless it did, though fearfully, espy
A hope beyond the shadow of a dream."

[Endymion goes on to express doubt that he was
dreaming, and in the remainder of Book I, he tells
of two further meetings he has had with the goddess. In the first she was but the glimmer of a face
reflected smiling from well-water, in the next he
had once more met her in the flesh.]

From BOOK II

INDUCTION (LINES 1–43)

O SOVEREIGN power of love! O grief! O balm!
All records, saving thine, come cool, and calm,
And shadowy, through the mist of passed
     years:
For other, good or bad, hatred and tears
Have become indolent; but touching thine,
One sigh doth echo, one poor sob doth pine,
One kiss brings honey-dew from buried days.
The woes of Troy, towers smothering o'er
     their blaze,
Stiff-holden shields, far-piercing spears, keen
     blades,
Struggling, and blood, and shrieks—all dimly
     fades   10

Into some backward corner of the brain;
Yet, in our very souls, we feel amain
The close of Troilus and Cressid sweet.
Hence, pageant history! hence, gilded cheat!
Swart planet in the universe of deeds!
Wide sea, that one continuous murmur breeds
Along the pebbled shore of memory!
Many old rotten-timber'd boats there be
Upon thy vaporous bosom, magnified
To goodly vessels; many a sail of pride,   20
And golden keel'd, is left unlaunch'd and dry.
But wherefore this? What care, though owl
     did fly
About the great Athenian admiral's mast?
What care, though striding Alexander past
The Indus with his Macedonian numbers?
Though old Ulysses tortured from his slum-
     bers
The glutted Cyclops, what care?—Juliet lean-
     ing
Amid her window-flowers,—sighing,—wean-
     ing
Tenderly her fancy from its maiden snow,
Doth more avail than these: the silver flow 30
Of Hero's tears, the swoon of Imogen,
Fair Pastorella in the bandit's den,
Are things to brood on with more ardency
Than the death-day of empires. Fearfully
Must such conviction come upon his head,
Who, thus far, discontent, has dared to tread,
Without one muse's smile, or kind behest,
The path of love and poesy. But rest,
In chaffing restlessness, is yet more drear
Than to be crush'd, in striving to uprear   40
Love's standard on the battlements of song.
So once more days and nights aid me along,
Like legion'd soldiers.

[Endymion follows a butterfly to a beautiful
fountain where it vanishes in the surface of the
water. A nymph rises and tells Endymion he must
wander far. He cries out for wings with which to
soar up to Cynthia. Instead he is bidden descend
into a cavern. Mysterious and aweful, Endymion
finds it, and, anxious for the open air again, he
appeals to Diana to guide him out. Flowers grow
up before him and, encouraged, he continues on.
He comes on a sleeping youth, Adonis.]

ADONIS IN SLUMBER (LINES 387–427)

    After a thousand mazes overgone,
At last, with sudden step, he came upon
A chamber, myrtle-wall'd, embower'd high,

Full of light, incense, tender minstrelsy, 390
And more of beautiful and strange beside:
For on a silken couch of rosy pride,
In midst of all, there lay a sleeping youth
Of fondest beauty; fonder, in fair sooth,
Than sighs could fathom, or contentment reach:
And coverlids gold-tinted like the peach,
Or ripe October's faded marigolds,
Fell sleek about him in a thousand folds—
Not hiding up an Apollonian curve
Of neck and shoulder, nor the tenting
    swerve 400
Of knee from knee, nor ankles pointing light;
But rather, giving them to the fill'd sight
Officiously. Sideway his face reposed
On one white arm, and tenderly unclosed,
By tenderest pressure, a faint damask mouth
To slumbery pout; just as the morning south
Disparts a dew-lipp'd rose. Above his head,
Four lily stalks did their white honours wed
To make a coronal; and round him grew
All tendrils green, of every bloom and hue, 410
Together intertwined and trammell'd fresh:
The vine of glossy sprout; the ivy mesh,
Shading its Ethiop berries; and woodbine,
Of velvet-leaves and bugle-blooms divine;
Convolvulus in streaked vases flush;
The creeper, mellowing for an autumn blush;
And virgin's bower, trailing airily;
With others of the sisterhood. Hard by,
Stood serene Cupids watching silently. 419
One, kneeling to a lyre, touch'd the strings,
Muffling to death the pathos with his wings;
And, ever and anon, uprose to look
At the youth's slumber; while another took
A willow bough, distilling odorous dew,
And shook it on his hair; another flew
In through the woven roof, and fluttering-wise
Rain'd violets upon his sleeping eyes.

[A cupid welcomes Endymion and tells him the story of Venus and Adonis. Endymion witnesses the arrival of Venus and the awakening of Adonis. Venus pities Endymion on his long and apparently hopeless quest and tells him all will end well. Endymion, left alone again, comes to the end of the path, and an eagle carries him swiftly down through darkness and unknown things to a jasmine bower. He lies down to sleep and suddenly finds Cynthia in his arms again. She leaves him once more while he sleeps and, continuing his pursuit, Endymion steps into "a cooler light" and suddenly "He saw the giant sea above his head." He is on the floor of the sea.]

From BOOK III

[Endymion continues his way across the sea floor past wrecks and skeletons of man, of beast, and of leviathan. He addresses the moon, unaware that the goddess he is pursuing is the moon goddess.]

ADDRESS TO THE MOON (LINES 142–187)

"What is there in thee, Moon! that thou
    shouldst move
My heart so potently? When yet a child
I oft have dried my tears when thou hast
    smiled.
Thou seem'dst my sister: hand in hand we
    went
From eve to morn across the firmament.
No apples would I gather from the tree,
Till thou hadst cool'd their cheeks deliciously:
No tumbling water ever spake romance,
But when my eyes with thine thereon could
    dance: 150
No woods were green enough, no bower
    divine,
Until thou liftedst up thine eyelids fine:
In sowing-time ne'er would I dibble take,
Or drop a seed, till thou wast wide awake;
And, in the summer tide of blossoming,
No one but thee hath heard me blithely sing
And mesh my dewy flowers all the night.
No melody was like a passing spright
If it went not to solemnize thy reign.
Yes, in my boyhood, every joy and pain 160
By thee were fashion'd to the self-same end;
And as I grew in years, still didst thou blend
With all my ardours; thou wast the deep glen;
Thou wast the mountain-top—the sage's
    pen—
The poet's harp—the voice of friends—the
    sun;
Thou wast the river—thou wast glory won;
Thou wast my clarion's blast—thou wast my
    steed—
My goblet full of wine—my topmost deed:—
Thou wast the charm of women, lovely
    Moon!
O what a wild and harmonized tune 170
My spirit struck from all the beautiful!
On some bright essence could I lean, and lull
Myself to immortality: I prest
Nature's soft pillow in a wakeful rest.
But gentle Orb! there came a nearer bliss—

My strange love came—Felicity's abyss!
She came, and thou didst fade, and fade away—
Yet not entirely; no, thy starry sway
Has been an under-passion to this hour.
Now I begin to feel thine orby power   180
Is coming fresh upon me: O be kind,
Keep back thine influence, and do not blind
My sovereign vision.—Dearest love, forgive
That I can think away from thee and live!—
Pardon me, airy planet, that I prize
One thought beyond thine argent luxuries!
How far beyond!"

[Endymion encounters an old man, Glaucus,
who has been condemned by Circe to one thousand
years of old age and then a nameless grave beneath
the sea. Glaucus can be made young again, and all
drowned lovers beneath the sea can be revived
and reunited if, at the right time, "A youth by
heavenly power loved and led" shall appear. It is
Endymion. He performs the necessary magical
acts. The drowned lovers waken and there is great
feasting and rejoicing at the Palace of Neptune.
Endymion, however, in his love-grief, faints away.
When he wakens he is on earth again in a grassy
place.]

From BOOK IV

[Endymion, pursuing the golden-haired and
blue-eyed Cynthia, stumbles upon a dark-haired
Indian maid and instantly is smitten with an overwhelming love for her. He is aghast at his own
apparent faithlessness to the goddess whom he
feels he still loves as intensely as ever.]

THE INDIAN MAID (LINES 98–181)

And so he groan'd, as one by beauty slain.
The lady's heart beat quick, and he could see
Her gentle bosom heave tumultuously.   100
He sprang from his green covert: there she lay,
Sweet as a musk-rose upon new-made hay;
With all her limbs on tremble, and her eyes
Shut softly up alive. To speak he tries:
"Fair damsel, pity me! forgive that I
Thus violate thy bower's sanctity!
O pardon me, for I am full of grief—
Grief born of thee, young angel! fairest thief!
Who stolen hast away the wings wherewith
I was to top the heavens. Dear maid, sith
Thou art my executioner, and I feel   111
Loving and hatred, misery and weal,
Will in a few short hours be nothing to me,
And all my story that much passion slew me;
Do smile upon the evening of my days;

And, for my tortured brain begins to craze,
Be thou my nurse; and let me understand
How dying I shall kiss that lily hand.—
Dost weep for me? Then should I be content.
Scowl on, ye fates! until the firmament   120
Outblackens Erebus, and the full-cavern'd
     earth
Crumbles into itself. By the cloud-girth
Of Jove, those tears have given me a thirst
To meet oblivion."—As her heart would
     burst
The maiden sobb'd awhile, and then replied:
"Why must such desolation betide
As that thou speakest of? Are not these green
     nooks
Empty of all misfortune? Do the brooks
Utter a gorgon voice? Does yonder thrush,
Schooling its half-fledged little one to brush
About the dewy forest, whisper tales?—   131
Speak not of grief, young stranger, or cold
     snails
Will slime the rose to-night. Though if thou
     wilt,
Methinks 'twould be a guilt—a very guilt—
Not to companion thee, and sigh away
The light—the dusk—the dark—till break
     of day!"
"Dear lady," said Endymion, "'tis past:
I love thee! and my days can never last.
That I may pass in patience still speak:
Let me have music dying, and I seek   140
No more delight—I bid adieu to all.
Didst thou not after other climates call,
And murmur about Indian streams?"— Then
     she,
Sitting beneath the midmost forest tree,
For pity sang this roundelay——

     "O Sorrow,
     Why dost borrow
The natural hue of health, from vermeil lips?—
     To give maiden blushes
     To the white rose bushes?   150
Or is 't thy dewy hand the daisy tips?

     "O Sorrow,
     Why dost borrow
The lustrous passion from a falcon-eye?—
     To give the glow-worm light?
     Or, on a moonless night,
To tinge, on siren shores, the salt sea-spry?

"O Sorrow,
Why dost borrow   159
The mellow ditties from a mourning tongue?
    To give at evening pale
    Unto the nightingale,
That thou mayst listen the cold dews among?

"O Sorrow,
Why dost borrow
Heart's lightness from the merriment of
    May?—
    A lover would not tread
    A cowslip on the head,
Though he should dance from eve till peep
    of day—
    Nor any drooping flower   170
    Held sacred for thy bower,
Wherever he may sport himself and play.

"To Sorrow,
    I bade good morrow,
And thought to leave her far away behind;
    But cheerly, cheerly,
    She loves me dearly;
She is so constant to me, and so kind:
    I would deceive her,
    And so leave her,   180
But ah! she is so constant and so kind."

[She explains her presence here and her loneliness, and Endymion comforts her while voices in
the air echo dismally "Woe! woe to that Endymion." Two winged steeds appear out of the earth
and Endymion and the Indian maid mount them.
In their flight they come into a dim benumbing
atmosphere. It is the God of Sleep on his way
to Endymion's own marriage with Cynthia in
heaven.]

ENCOUNTER WITH SLEEP (LINES 362–408)

There is a sleepy dusk, an odorous shade
From some approaching wonder, and behold
Those winged steeds, with snorting nostrils
    bold
Snuff at its faint extreme, and seem to tire,
Dying to embers from their native fire!

There curl'd a purple mist around them;
    soon,
It seem'd as when around the pale new moon
Sad Zephyr droops the clouds like weeping
    willow:

'Twas Sleep slow journeying with head on
    pillow.   370
For the first time, since he came nigh dead-
    born
From the old womb of night, his cave forlorn
Had he left more forlorn; for the first time,
He felt aloof the day and morning's prime—
Because into his depth Cimmerian
There came a dream, showing how a young
    man,
Ere a lean bat could plump its wintery skin,
Would at high Jove's empyreal footstool win
An immortality, and how espouse
Jove's daughter, and be reckon'd of his
    house.   380
Now was he slumbering towards heaven's
    gate,
That he might at the threshold one hour wait
To hear the marriage melodies, and then
Sink downward to his dusky cave again.
His litter of smooth semilucent mist,
Diversely tinged with rose and amethyst,
Puzzled those eyes that for the centre sought;
And scarcely for one moment could be caught
His sluggish form reposing motionless.
Those two on winged steeds, with all the
    stress   390
Of vision search'd for him, as one would look
Athwart the sallows of a river nook
To catch a glance at silver-throated eels,—
Or from old Skiddaw's top, when fog conceals
His rugged forehead in a mantle pale,
With an eye-guess towards some pleasant vale
Descry a favourite hamlet faint and far.

These raven horses, though they foster'd are
Of earth's splenetic fire, dully drop
Their full-vein'd ears, nostrils blood wide,
    and stop;   400
Upon the spiritless mist have they outspread
Their ample feathers, are in slumber dead,—
And on those pinions, level in mid air,
Endymion sleepeth and the lady fair.
Slowly they sail, slowly as icy isle
Upon a calm sea drifting: and meanwhile
The mournful wanderer dreams. Behold! he
    walks
On heaven's pavement.

[Fact and dream become confused. Endymion
dreams that he walks with the Gods come as guests
to his own wedding. He awakes to find the Indian

maid beside him, but strangely, and now awake, he perceives about him still the figures of his dream. He is distracted between the golden Cynthia and the dark Indian. The shadow of Cynthia weeps and melts away as Endymion kisses the mortal maiden. The two drive their winged horses from this terrifying place.]

LOSS OF THE MORTAL MAIDEN
(LINES 496–512)

Full facing their swift flight, from ebon
  streak,
The moon put forth a little diamond peak,
No bigger than an unobserved star,
Or tiny point of fairy scimetar;
Bright signal that she only stoop'd to tie 500
Her silver sandals, ere deliciously
She bow'd into the heavens her timid head.
Slowly she rose, as though she would have
  fled,
While to his lady meek the Carian turn'd,
To mark if her dark eyes had yet discern'd
This beauty in its birth—Despair! despair!
He saw her body fading gaunt and spare
In the cold moonshine. Straight he seized her
  wrist;
It melted from his grasp; her hand he kiss'd,
And, horror! kiss'd his own—he was alone.
Her steed a little higher soar'd, and then 511
Dropt hawk-wise to the earth.

[Endymion is left in a stupor by this so that he fails to hear or see various deities who pass him in the air, still journeying joyously toward his wedding. The steed brings Endymion to earth. He finds his mortal love sleeping.]

ENDYMION CHOOSES MORTAL LOVE
(LINES 615–721)

"Alas!" said he, "were I but always borne
Through dangerous winds, had but my foot-
  steps worn
A path in hell, for ever would I bless
Horrors which nourish an uneasiness
For my own sullen conquering: to him
Who lives beyond earth's boundary, grief is
  dim,   620
Sorrow is but a shadow: now I see
The grass; I feel the solid ground—Ah, me!
It is thy voice—divinest! Where?—who? who
Left thee so quiet on this bed of dew?
Behold upon this happy earth we are;
Let us aye love each other; let us fare

On forest-fruits, and never, never go
Among the abodes of mortals here below,
Or be by phantoms duped. O destiny!
Into a labyrinth now my soul would fly, 630
But with thy beauty will I deaden it.
Where didst thou melt to? By thee will I sit
For ever: let our fate stop here—a kid
I on this spot will offer: Pan will bid
Us live in peace, in love and peace among
His forest wildernesses. I have clung
To nothing, lov'd a nothing, nothing seen
Or felt but a great dream! O I have been,
Presumptuous against love, against the sky,
Against all elements, against the tie 640
Of mortals each to each, against the blooms
Of flowers, rush of rivers, and the tombs
Of heroes gone! Against his proper glory
Has my own soul conspired: so my story
Will I to children utter, and repent.
There never liv'd a mortal man, who bent
His appetite beyond his natural sphere,
But starv'd and died. My sweetest Indian, here,
Here will I kneel, for thou redeemed hast
My life from too thin breathing: gone and
  past   650
Are cloudy phantasms. Caverns lone, farewell!
And air of visions, and the monstrous swell
Of visionary seas! No, never more
Shall airy voices cheat me to the shore
Of tangled wonder, breathless and aghast.
Adieu, my daintiest Dream! although so vast
My love is still for thee. The hour may come
When we shall meet in pure elysium.
On earth I may not love thee; and therefore
Doves will I offer up, and sweetest store 660
All through the teeming year: so thou wilt
  shine
On me, and on this damsel fair of mine,
And bless our simple lives. My Indian bliss!
My river-lily bud! one human kiss!
One sigh of real breath—one gentle squeeze,
Warm as a dove's nest among summer trees,
And warm with dew at ooze from living blood!
Whither didst melt? Ah, what of that?—all good
We'll talk about—no more of dreaming.—
  Now,
Where shall our dwelling be? Under the
  brow   670
Of some steep mossy hill, where ivy dun
Would hide us up, although spring leaves
  were none;

And where dark yew trees, as we rustle
 through
Will drop their scarlet berry cups of dew?
O thou wouldst joy to live in such a place;
Dusk for our loves, yet light enough to grace
Those gentle limbs on mossy bed reclined:
For by one step the blue sky shouldst thou
 find,
And by another, in deep dell below,
See, through the trees, a little river go   680
All in its mid-day gold and glimmering.
Honey from out the gnarled hive I'll bring,
And apples, wan with sweetness, gather thee,—
Cresses that grow where no man may them see,
And sorrel untorn by the dew-claw'd stag:
Pipes will I fashion of the syrinx flag,
That thou mayst always know whither I roam,
When it shall please thee in our quiet home
To listen and think of love. Still let me speak;
Still let me dive into the joy I seek,—   690
For yet the past doth prison me. The rill,
Thou haply mayst delight in, will I fill
With fairy fishes from the mountain tarn,
And thou shalt feed them from the squirrel's
 barn.
Its bottom will I strew with amber shells,
And pebbles blue from deep enchanted wells.
Its sides I'll plant with dew-sweet eglantine,
And honeysuckles full of clear bee-wine.
I will entice this crystal rill to trace
Love's silver name upon the meadow's face.
I'll kneel to Vesta, for a flame of fire;   701
And to god Phœbus, for a golden lyre;
To Empress Dian, for a hunting-spear;
To Vesper, for a taper silver-clear,
That I may see thy beauty through the night;
To Flora, and a nightingale shall light
Tame on thy finger; to the River-gods,
And they shall bring thee taper fishing-rods
Of gold, and lines of Naiads' long bright tress.
Heaven shield thee for thine utter loveliness!
Thy mossy footstool shall the altar be   711
'Fore which I'll bend, bending, dear love, to
 thee:
Those lips shall be my Delphos, and shall
 speak
Laws to my footsteps, colour to my cheek,
Trembling or steadfastness to this same voice,
And of three sweetest pleasurings the choice:
And that affectionate light, those diamond
 things,

Those eyes, those passions, those supreme
 pearl springs,
Shall be my grief, or twinkle me to pleasure.
Say, is not bliss within our perfect seizure? 720
O that I could not doubt!"

CONCLUSION: THE DECISION OF THE GODS
(LINES 969–1003)

[The Indian Maiden feels that she is "forbidden," that strange powers are about them, and that she must bid him adieu. Nevertheless she wanders with him, hand in hand, and they come back to the scenes of Endymion's childhood. She seems to have a secret, and to be not displeased at his grief. They separate, he to become a hermit, she a priestess of Diana (Cynthia), but one last meeting is arranged for at twilight back of the temple. He is too engrossed, when the meeting time comes, to notice her approach, accompanied by Peona.]

He saw not the two maidens, nor their smiles,
Wan as primroses gather'd at midnight   970
By chilly-finger'd spring. "Unhappy wight!
Endymion!" said Peona, "we are here!
What wouldst thou ere we all are laid on
 bier?"
Then he embraced her, and his lady's hand
Press'd, saying: "Sister, I would have command,
If it were heaven's will, on our sad fate."
At which that dark-eyed stranger stood elate
And said, in a new voice, but sweet as love,
To Endymion's amaze: "By Cupid's dove,
And so thou shalt! and by the lily truth   980
Of my own breast thou shalt, beloved youth!"
And as she spake, into her face there came
Light, as reflected from a silver flame:
Her long black hair swell'd ampler, in display
Full golden; in her eyes a brighter day
Dawn'd blue, and full of love. Aye, he beheld
Phœbe, his passion! joyous she upheld
Her lucid bow, continuing thus: "Drear, drear
Has our delaying been; but foolish fear
Withheld me first; and then decrees of fate; 990
And then 'twas fit that from this mortal state
Thou shouldst, my love, by some unlook'd-for
 change
Be spiritualized. Peona, we shall range
These forests, and to thee they safe shall be
As was thy cradle; hither shalt thou flee
To meet us many a time." Next Cynthia bright
Peona kiss'd, and bless'd with fair good night:

Her brother kiss'd her too, and knelt adown
Before his goddess, in a blissful swoon.   999
She gave her fair hand to him, and behold,
Before three swiftest kisses he had told,
They vanish'd far away!—Peona went
Home through the gloomy wood in wonder-
      ment.

April–November, 1817

STANZAS

I

In a drear-nighted December,
      Too happy, happy tree,
Thy branches ne'er remember
      Their green felicity:
The north cannot undo them,
With a sleety whistle through them;
Nor frozen thawings glue them
      From budding at the prime.

II

In a drear-nighted December,
      Too happy, happy brook,   10
Thy bubblings ne'er remember
      Apollo's summer look;
But with a sweet forgetting,
They stay their crystal fretting,
Never, never petting
      About the frozen time.

III

Ah! would 'twere so with many
      A gentle girl and boy!
But were there ever any
      Writh'd not at passed joy?   20
To know the change and feel it,
When there is none to heal it,
Nor numbed sense to steel it,
      Was never said in rhyme.

1817

ISABELLA;
OR
THE POT OF BASIL

A Story from Boccaccio

I

FAIR Isabel, poor simple Isabel!
   Lorenzo, a young palmer in Love's eye!
They could not in the self-same mansion dwell
   Without some stir of heart, some malady;

They could not sit at meals but feel how well
   It soothed each to be the other by;
They could not, sure, beneath the same roof
      sleep
But to each other dream, and nightly weep.

II

With every morn their love grew tenderer,
   With every eve deeper and tenderer still; 10
He might not in house, field, or garden stir,
   But her full shape would all his seeing fill;
And his continual voice was pleasanter
   To her, than noise of trees or hidden rill;
Her lute-string gave an echo of his name,
She spoilt her half-done broidery with the same.

III

He knew whose gentle hand was at the latch
   Before the door had given her to his eyes;
And from her chamber-window he would
      catch
   Her beauty farther than the falcon spies; 20
And constant as her vespers would he watch,
   Because her face was turn'd to the same
      skies;
And with sick longing all the night outwear,
To hear her morning-step upon the stair.

IV

A whole long month of May in this sad plight
   Made their cheeks paler by the break of
      June:
"To-morrow will I bow to my delight,
   "To-morrow will I ask my lady's boon."—
"O may I never see another night,
   "Lorenzo, if thy lips breathe not love's
      tune."—   30
So spake they to their pillows; but, alas,
Honeyless days and days did he let pass;

V

Until sweet Isabella's untouch'd cheek
   Fell sick within the rose's just domain,
Fell thin as a young mother's, who doth
      seek
   By every lull to cool her infant's pain:
"How ill she is," said he, "I may not speak,
   "And yet I will, and tell my love all plain:
"If looks speak love-laws, I will drink her
      tears,   39
"And at the least 'twill startle off her cares."

VI

So said he one fair morning, and all day
  His heart beat awfully against his side;
And to his heart he inwardly did pray
  For power to speak; but still the ruddy tide
Stifled his voice, and puls'd resolve away—
  Fever'd his high conceit of such a bride,
Yet brought him to the meekness of a child:
Alas! when passion is both meek and wild!

VII

So once more he had wak'd and anguished
  A dreary night of love and misery,   50
If Isabel's quick eye had not been wed
  To every symbol on his forehead nigh;
She saw it waxing very pale and dead,
  And straight all flush'd; so, lisped tenderly,
"Lorenzo!"—here she ceas'd her timid quest,
But in her tone and look he read the rest.

VIII

"O Isabella, I can half perceive
  "That I may speak my grief into thine ear;
"If thou didst ever anything believe,   59
  "Believe how I love thee, believe how near
"My soul is to its doom: I would not grieve
  "Thy hand by unwelcome pressing, would
     not fear
"Thine eyes by gazing; but I cannot live
"Another night, and not my passion shrive.

IX

"Love! thou art leading me from wintry cold,
  "Lady! thou leadest me to summer clime,
"And I must taste the blossoms that unfold
  "In its ripe warmth this gracious morning
     time."
So said, his erewhile timid lips grew bold,
  And poesied with hers in dewy rhyme: 70
Great bliss was with them, and great happiness
Grew, like a lusty flower in June's caress.

X

Parting they seem'd to tread upon the air,
  Twin roses by the zephyr blown apart
Only to meet again more close, and share
  The inward fragrance of each other's heart.
She, to her chamber gone, a ditty fair
  Sang, of delicious love and honey'd dart;
He with light steps went up a western hill, 79
And bade the sun farewell, and joy'd his fill.

XI

All close they met again, before the dusk
  Had taken from the stars its pleasant veil,
All close they met, all eves, before the dusk
  Had taken from the stars its pleasant veil,
Close in a bower of hyacinth and musk,
  Unknown of any, free from whispering tale.
Ah! better had it been for ever so,
Than idle ears should pleasure in their woe.

XII

Were they unhappy then?—It cannot be—
  Too many tears for lovers have been shed,
Too many sighs give we to them in fee,   91
  Too much of pity after they are dead,
Too many doleful stories do we see,
  Whose matter in bright gold were best be
     read;
Except in such a page where Theseus' spouse
Over the pathless waves towards him bows.

XIII

But, for the general award of love,
  The little sweet doth kill much bitterness;
Though Dido silent is in under-grove,
  And Isabella's was a great distress,   100
Though Young Lorenzo in warm Indian clove
  Was not embalm'd, this truth is not the
     less—
Even bees, the little almsmen of spring-bowers,
Know there is richest juice in poison-flowers.

XIV

With her two brothers this fair lady dwelt,
  Enriched from ancestral merchandize,
And for them many a weary hand did swelt
  In torched mines and noisy factories
And many once proud-quiver'd loins did melt
  In blood from stinging whip;—with hollow
     eyes   110
Many all day in dazzling river stood,
To take the rich-ored driftings of the flood.

XV

For them the Ceylon diver held his breath,
  And went all naked to the hungry shark;
For them his ears gush'd blood; for them in
     death
  The seal on the cold ice with piteous bark
Lay full of darts; for them alone did seethe
  A thousand men in troubles wide and dark:

Half-ignorant, they turn'd an easy wheel,
That set sharp racks at work, to pinch and
   peel.   120

XVI

Why were they proud? Because their marble
   founts
   Gush'd with more pride than do a wretch's
      tears?—
Why were they proud? Because fair orange
   mounts
   Were of more soft ascent than lazar stairs?—
Why were they proud? Because red-lin'd ac-
   counts
   Were richer than the songs of Grecian
      years?—
Why were they proud? again we ask aloud,
Why in the name of Glory were they proud?

XVII

Yet were these Florentines as self-retired   129
   In hungry pride and gainful cowardice,
As two close Hebrews in that land inspired,
   Paled in and vineyarded from beggar-spies;
The hawks of ship-mast forests—the untired
   And pannier'd mules for ducats and old
      lies—
Quick cat's-paws on the generous stray-
   away,—
Great wits in Spanish, Tuscan, and Malay.

XVIII

How was it these same ledger-men could spy
   Fair Isabella in her downy nest?
How could they find out in Lorenzo's eye
   A straying from his toil? Hot Egypt's pest
Into their vision covetous and sly!   141
   How could these money-bags see east and
      west?—
Yet so they did—and every dealer fair
Must see behind, as doth the hunted hare.

XIX

O eloquent and famed Boccaccio!
   Of thee we now should ask forgiving boon,
And of thy spicy myrtles as they blow,
   And of thy roses amorous of the moon,
And of thy lillies, that do paler grow
   Now they can no more hear thy ghittern's
      tune,   150
For venturing syllables that ill beseem
The quiet glooms of such a piteous theme.

XX

Grant thou a pardon here, and then the tale
   Shall move on soberly, as it is meet;
There is no other crime, no mad assail
   To make old prose in modern rhyme more
      sweet:
But it is done—succeed the verse or fail—
   To honour thee, and thy gone spirit greet;
To stead thee as a verse in English tongue,
An echo of thee in the north-wind sung.   160

XXI

These brethren having found by many signs
   What love Lorenzo for their sister had,
And how she lov'd him too, each unconfines
   His bitter thoughts to other, well nigh
      mad
That he, the servant of their trade designs,
   Should in their sister's love be blithe and
      glad,
When 'twas their plan to coax her by degrees
To some high noble and his olive-trees.

XXII

And many a jealous conference had they,
   And many times they bit their lips alone,
Before they fix'd upon a surest way   171
   To make the youngster for his crime atone;
And at the last, these men of cruel clay
   Cut Mercy with a sharp knife to the bone;
For they resolved in some forest dim
To kill Lorenzo, and there bury him.

XXIII

So on a pleasant morning, as he leant
   Into the sun-rise, o'er the balustrade
Of the garden-terrace, towards him they bent
   Their footing through the dews; and to him
      said,   180
"You seem there in the quiet of content,
   "Lorenzo, and we are most loth to invade
"Calm speculation; but if you are wise,
"Bestride your steed while cold is in the skies.

XXIV

"To-day we purpose, aye, this hour we mount
   "To spur three leagues towards the Apen-
      nine;
"Come down, we pray thee, ere the hot sun
   count
   "His dewy rosary on the eglantine."

Lorenzo, courteously as he was wont,
  Bow'd a fair greeting to these serpents'
    whine;   190
And went in haste, to get in readiness,
With belt, and spur, and bracing huntsman's
  dress.

XXV

And as he to the court-yard pass'd along,
  Each third step did he pause, and listen'd oft
If he could hear his lady's matin-song,
  Or the light whisper of her footstep soft;
And as he thus over his passion hung,
  He heard a laugh full musical aloft;   198
When, looking up, he saw her features bright
Smile through an in-door lattice, all delight.

XXVI

"Love, Isabel!" said he, "I was in pain
  "Lest I should miss to bid thee a good mor-
    row:
"Ah! what if I should lose thee, when so fain
  "I am to stifle all the heavy sorrow
"Of a poor three hours' absence? but we'll gain
  "Out of the amorous dark what day doth
    borrow.
"Good bye! I'll soon be back."—"Good bye!"
  said she:—
And as he went she chanted merrily.

XXVII

So the two brothers and their murder'd man
  Rode past fair Florence, to where Arno's
    stream   210
Gurgles through straiten'd banks, and still
  doth fan
Itself with dancing bulrush, and the bream
Keeps head against the freshets. Sick and wan
  The brothers' faces in the ford did seem,
Lorenzo's flush with love.—They pass'd the
  water
Into a forest quiet for the slaughter.

XXVIII

There was Lorenzo slain and buried in,
  There in that forest did his great love cease;
Ah! when a soul doth thus its freedom win,
  It aches in loneliness—is ill at peace   220
As the break-covert blood-hounds of such sin:
  They dipp'd their swords in the water, and
    did tease
Their horses homeward, with convulsed spur,
Each richer by his being a murderer.

XXIX

They told their sister how, with sudden speed,
  Lorenzo had ta'en ship for foreign lands,
Because of some great urgency and need
  In their affairs, requiring trusty hands.
Poor Girl! put on thy stifling widow's weed,
  And 'scape at once from Hope's accursed
    bands;   230
To-day thou wilt not see him, nor to-morrow,
And the next day will be a day of sorrow.

XXX

She weeps alone for pleasures not to be;
  Sorely she wept until the night came on,
And then, instead of love, O misery!
  She brooded o'er the luxury alone:
His image in the dusk she seem'd to see,
  And to the silence made a gentle moan,
Spreading her perfect arms upon the air,
And on her couch low murmuring "Where?
  O where?"   240

XXXI

But Selfishness, Love's cousin, held not long
  Its fiery vigil in her single breast;
She fretted for the golden hour, and hung
  Upon the time with feverish unrest—
Not long—for soon into her heart a throng
  Of higher occupants, a richer zest,
Came tragic; passion not to be subdued,
And sorrow for her love in travels rude.

XXXII

In the mid days of autumn, on their eves
  The breath of Winter comes from far away,
And the sick west continually bereaves   251
  Of some gold tinge, and plays a roundelay
Of death among the bushes and the leaves,
  To make all bare before he dares to stray
From his north cavern. So sweet Isabel
By gradual decay from beauty fell,

XXXIII

Because Lorenzo came not. Oftentimes
  She ask'd her brothers, with an eye all pale,
Striving to be itself, what dungeon climes 259
  Could keep him off so long? They spake a tale
Time after time, to quiet her. Their crimes
  Came on them, like a smoke from Hin-
    nom's vale;
And every night in dreams they groan'd aloud,
To see their sister in her snowy shroud.

XXXIV

And she had died in drowsy ignorance,
  But for a thing more deadly dark than all;
It came like a fierce potion, drunk by chance,
  Which saves a sick man from the feather'd
    pall
For some few gasping moments; like a lance,
  Waking an Indian from his cloudy hall 270
With cruel pierce, and bringing him again
Sense of the gnawing fire at heart and brain.

XXXV

It was a vision.—In the drowsy gloom,
  The dull of midnight, at her couch's foot
Lorenzo stood, and wept: the forest tomb
  Had marr'd his glossy hair which once could
    shoot
Lustre into the sun, and put cold doom
  Upon his lips, and taken the soft lute
From his lorn voice, and past his loamed ears
Had made a miry channel for his tears. 280

XXXVI

Strange sound it was, when the pale shadow
    spake;
  For there was striving, in its piteous tongue,
To speak as when on earth it was awake,
  And Isabella on its music hung:
Languor there was in it, and tremulous shake,
  As in a palsied Druid's harp unstrung;
And through it moan'd a ghostly under-song,
Like hoarse night-gusts sepulchral briars
    among.

XXXVII

Its eyes, though wild, were still all dewy
    bright 289
  With love, and kept all phantom fear aloof
From the poor girl by magic of their light,
  The while it did unthread the horrid woof
Of the late darken'd time,—the murderous
    spite
  Of pride and avarice,—the dark pine roof
In the forest,—and the sodden turfed dell,
Where, without any word, from stabs he fell.

XXXVIII

Saying moreover, "Isabel, my sweet!
  "Red whortle-berries droop above my head,
"And a large flint-stone weighs upon my feet;
  "Around me beeches and high chestnuts
    shed 300

"Their leaves and prickly nuts; a sheep-fold
    bleat
  "Comes from beyond the river to my bed:
"Go, shed one tear upon my heather-bloom,
  "And it shall comfort me within the tomb.

XXXIX

"I am a shadow now, alas! alas!
  "Upon the skirts of human-nature dwelling
"Alone: I chant alone the holy mass,
  "While little sounds of life are round me
    knelling,
"And glossy bees at noon do fieldward pass,
  "And many a chapel bell the hour is telling,
"Paining me through: those sounds grow
    strange to me, 311
"And thou art distant in Humanity.

XL

"I know what was, I feel full well what is,
  "And I should rage, if spirits could go mad;
"Though I forget the taste of earthly bliss,
  "That paleness warms my grave, as though
    I had
"A Seraph chosen from the bright abyss
  "To be my spouse: thy paleness makes me
    glad;
"Thy beauty grows upon me, and I feel 319
"A greater love through all my essence steal."

XLI

The Spirit mourn'd "Adieu!"—dissolv'd and
    left
  The atom darkness in a slow turmoil;
As when of healthful midnight sleep bereft,
  Thinking on rugged hours and fruitless toil,
We put our eyes into a pillowy cleft,
  And see the spangly gloom froth up and boil:
It made sad Isabella's eyelids ache,
And in the dawn she started up awake;

XLII

"Ha! ha!" said she, "I knew not this hard life,
  "I thought the worst was simple misery;
"I thought some Fate with pleasure or with
    strife 331
  "Portion'd us—happy days, or else to die;
"But there is crime—a brother's bloody knife!
  "Sweet Spirit, thou hast school'd my in-
    fancy:
"I'll visit thee for this, and kiss thine eyes,
  "And greet thee morn and even in the skies."

XLIII

When the full morning came, she had devised
  How she might secret to the forest hie;
How she might find the clay, so dearly prized,
  And sing to it one latest lullaby;   340
How her short absence might be unsurmised,
  While she the inmost of the dream would
    try.
Resolv'd, she took with her an aged nurse,
And went into that dismal forest-hearse.

XLIV

See, as they creep along the river side,
  How she doth whisper to that aged Dame,
And, after looking round the champaign wide,
  Shows her a knife.—"What feverous hectic
    flame
"Burns in thee, child?—What good can thee
    betide,
  "That thou should'st smile again?"—The
    evening came,   350
And they had found Lorenzo's earthly bed;
The flint was there, the berries at his head.

XLV

Who hath not loiter'd in a green church-yard,
  And let his spirit, like a demon-mole,
Work through the clayey soil and gravel hard,
  To see scull, coffin'd bones, and funeral
    stole;
Pitying each form that hungry Death hath
    marr'd,
  And filling it once more with human soul?
Ah! this is holiday to what was felt
When Isabella by Lorenzo knelt.   360

XLVI

She gaz'd into the fresh-thrown mould, as
  though
  One glance did fully all its secrets tell;
Clearly she saw, as other eyes would know
  Pale limbs at bottom of a crystal well;
Upon the murderous spot she seem'd to grow,
  Like to a native lilly of the dell:
Then with her knife, all sudden, she began
To dig more fervently than misers can.

XLVII

Soon she turn'd up a soiled glove, whereon
  Her silk had play'd in purple phantasies,
She kiss'd it with a lip more chill than stone,
  And put it in her bosom, where it dries

And freezes utterly unto the bone   373
  Those dainties made to still an infant's cries:
Then 'gan she work again; nor stay'd her care,
But to throw back at times her veiling hair.

XLVIII

That old nurse stood beside her wondering,
  Until her heart felt pity to the core
At sight of such a dismal labouring,   379
  And so she kneeled, with her locks all hoar,
And put her lean hands to the horrid thing:
  Three hours they labour'd at this travail
    sore;
At last they felt the kernel of the grave,
And Isabella did not stamp and rave.

XLIX

Ah! wherefore all this wormy circumstance?
  Why linger at the yawning tomb so long?
O for the gentleness of old Romance,
  The simple plaining of a minstrel's song!
Fair reader, at the old tale take a glance,   389
  For here, in truth, it doth not well belong
To speak:—O turn thee to the very tale,
And taste the music of that vision pale.

L

With duller steel than the Perséan sword
  They cut away no formless monster's head,
But one, whose gentleness did well accord
  With death, as life. The ancient harps have
    said,
Love never dies, but lives, immortal Lord:
  If Love impersonate was ever dead,
Pale Isabella kiss'd it, and low moan'd.
'Twas love; cold,—dead indeed, but not de-
    thron'd.   400

LI

In anxious secrecy they took it home,
  And then the prize was all for Isabel:
She calm'd its wild hair with a golden comb,
  And all around each eye's sepulchral cell
Pointed each fringed lash; the smeared loam
  With tears, as chilly as a dripping well,
She drench'd away:—and still she comb'd, and
    kept
Sighing all day—and still she kiss'd, and wept.

LII

Then in a silken scarf,—sweet with the dews
  Of precious flowers pluck'd in Araby,   410

And divine liquids come with odorous ooze
  Through the cold serpent-pipe refresh-
    fully,—
She wrapp'd it up; and for its tomb did choose
  A garden-pot, wherein she laid it by,
And cover'd it with mould, and o'er it set
Sweet Basil, which her tears kept ever wet.

LIII

And she forgot the stars, the moon, and sun,
  And she forgot the blue above the trees,
And she forgot the dells where waters run,
  And she forgot the chilly autumn breeze;
She had no knowledge when the day was
    done,   421
  And the new morn she saw not: but in peace
Hung over her sweet Basil evermore,
And moisten'd it with tears unto the core.

LIV

And so she ever fed it with thin tears,
  Whence thick, and green, and beautiful it
    grew,
So that it smelt more balmy than its peers
  Of Basil-tufts in Florence; for it drew
Nurture besides, and life, from human fears,
  From the fast mouldering head there shut
    from view: 430
So that the jewel, safely casketed,
Came forth, and in perfumed leafits spread.

LV

O Melancholy, linger here awhile!
  O Music, Music, breathe despondingly!
O Echo, Echo, from some sombre isle,
  Unknown, Lethean, sigh to us—O sigh!
Spirits in grief, lift up your heads, and
    smile;
  Lift up your heads, sweet Spirits, heavily,
And make a pale light in your cypress glooms,
Tinting with silver wan your marble tombs.

LVI

Moan hither, all ye syllables of woe,   441
  From the deep throat of sad Melpomene!
Through bronzed lyre in tragic order go,
  And touch the strings into a mystery;
Sound mournfully upon the winds and low;
  For simple Isabel is soon to be
Among the dead: She withers, like a palm
Cut by an Indian for its juicy balm.

LVII

O leave the palm to wither by itself;
  Let not quick Winter chill its dying hour!—
It may not be—those Baälites of pelf,   451
  Her brethren, noted the continual shower
From her dead eyes; and many a curious elf,
  Among her kindred, wonder'd that such
    dower
Of youth and beauty should be thrown aside
By one mark'd out to be a Noble's bride.

LVIII

And, furthermore, her brethren wonder'd
    much
  Why she sat drooping by the Basil green,
And why it flourish'd, as by magic touch;
  Greatly they wonder'd what the thing might
    mean: 460
They could not surely give belief, that such
  A very nothing would have power to wean
Her from her own fair youth, and pleasures
    gay,
And even remembrance of her love's delay.

LIX

Therefore they watch'd a time when they
    might sift
  This hidden whim; and long they watch'd
    in vain;
For seldom did she go to chapel-shrift,
  And seldom felt she any hunger-pain;
And when she left, she hurried back, as swift
  As bird on wing to breast its eggs again; 470
And, patient as a hen-bird, sat her there
Beside her Basil, weeping through her hair.

LX

Yet they contriv'd to steal the Basil-pot,
  And to examine it in secret place;
The thing was vile with green and livid spot,
  And yet they knew it was Lorenzo's face:
The guerdon of their murder they had got,
  And so left Florence in a moment's space,
Never to turn again.—Away they went,   479
With blood upon their heads, to banishment.

LXI

O Melancholy, turn thine eyes away!
  O Music, Music, breathe despondingly!
O Echo, Echo, on some other day,
  From isles Lethean, sigh to us—O sigh!

Spirits of grief, sing not your "Well-a-way!"
   For Isabel, sweet Isabel, will die;
Will die a death too lone and incomplete,
Now they have ta'en away her Basil sweet.

LXII

Piteous she look'd on dead and senseless
      things,
   Asking for her lost Basil amorously;   490
And with melodious chuckle in the strings
   Of her lorn voice, she oftentimes would cry
After the Pilgrim in his wanderings,
   To ask him where her Basil was; and why
'Twas hid from her: "For cruel 'tis," said
      she,
"To steal my Basil-pot away from me."

LXIII

And so she pin'd, and so she died forlorn,
   Imploring for her Basil to the last.
No heart was there in Florence but did mourn
   In pity of her love, so overcast.   500
And a sad ditty of this story born
   From mouth to mouth through all the
      country pass'd:
Still is the burthen sung—"O cruelty,
"To steal my Basil-pot away from me!"

February–April 1818

LINES ON THE MERMAID TAVERN

   Souls of Poets dead and gone,
   What Elysium have ye known,
   Happy field or mossy cavern,
   Choicer than the Mermaid Tavern?
   Have ye tippled drink more fine
   Than mine host's Canary wine?
   Or are fruits of Paradise
   Sweeter than those dainty pies
   Of venison? O generous food!
   Drest as though bold Robin Hood   10
   Would, with his maid Marian,
   Sup and bowse from horn and can.

   I have heard that on a day
   Mine host's sign-board flew away,
   Nobody knew whither, till
   An astrologer's old quill
   To a sheepskin gave the story,
   Said he saw you in your glory,

Underneath a new old sign
Sipping beverage divine,   20
And pledging with contented smack
The Mermaid in the Zodiac.

   Souls of Poets dead and gone,
   What Elysium have ye known,
   Happy field or mossy cavern,
   Choicer than the Mermaid Tavern?

1818

MEG MERRILIES

I

Old Meg she was a Gipsy,
   And liv'd upon the Moors:
Her bed it was the brown heath turf,
   And her house was out of doors.

II

Her apples were swart blackberries,
   Her currants pods o' broom;
Her wine was dew of the wild white rose,
   Her book a churchyard tomb.

III

Her Brothers were the craggy hills,
   Her Sisters larchen trees—   10
Alone with her great family
   She liv'd as she did please.

IV

No breakfast had she many a morn,
   No dinner many a noon,
And 'stead of supper she would stare
   Full hard against the Moon.

V

But every morn of woodbine fresh
   She made her garlanding,
And every night the dark glen Yew
   She wove, and she would sing.   20

VI

And with her fingers old and brown
   She plaited Mats o' Rushes,
And gave them to the Cottagers
   She met among the Bushes.

VII

Old Meg was brave as Margaret Queen
   And tall as Amazon:

An old red blanket cloak she wore;
  A chip hat had she on.
God rest her aged bones somewhere—
  She died full long agone!   30
1818

ODE

[Written on the blank page before Beaumont and
Fletcher's tragi-comedy, *The Fair Maid of the Inn.*]

BARDS of Passion and of Mirth,
Ye have left your souls on earth!
Have ye souls in heaven too,
Double-liv'd in regions new?
Yes, and those of heaven commune
With the spheres of sun and moon;
With the noise of fountains wond'rous
And the parle of voices thund'rous;
With the whisper of heaven's trees
And one another, in soft ease   10
Seated on Elysian lawns
Browsed by none but Dian's fawns;
Underneath large blue-bells tented,
Where the daisies are rose-scented,
And the rose herself has got
Perfume which on earth is not;
Where the nightingale doth sing
Not a senseless, tranced thing,
But divine melodious truth;
Philosophic numbers smooth;   20
Tales and golden histories
Of heaven and its mysteries.

  Thus ye live on high, and then
On the earth ye live again;
And the souls ye left behind you
Teach us, here, the way to find you,
Where your other souls are joying,
Never slumber'd, never cloying.
Here, your earth-born souls still speak
To mortals, of their little week;   30
Of their sorrows and delights;
Of their passions and their spites;
Of their glory and their shame;
What doth strengthen and what maim.
Thus ye teach us, every day,
Wisdom, though fled far away.

  Bards of Passion and of Mirth,
Ye have left your souls on earth!
Ye have souls in heaven too,
Double-liv'd in regions new!   40
1818

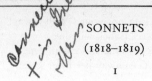

SONNETS
(1818–1819)

I

WHEN I HAVE FEARS THAT I MAY CEASE TO BE

WHEN I have fears that I may cease to be
  Before my pen has glean'd my teeming
    brain,
Before high-piled books, in charactery,
  Hold like rich garners the full ripen'd
    grain;
When I behold, upon the night's starr'd face,
  Huge cloudy symbols of a high romance,
And think that I may never live to trace
  Their shadows, with the magic hand of
    chance;
And when I feel, fair creature of an hour,
  That I shall never look upon thee more, 10
Never have relish in the faery power
  Of unreflecting love;—then on the shore
Of the wide world I stand alone, and think
Till love and fame to nothingness do sink.
1818

II

BRIGHT STAR, WOULD I WERE STEDFAST AS
THOU ART—

[Written on a blank page in Shakespeare's Poems,
facing *A Lover's Complaint.*]

BRIGHT star, would I were stedfast as thou
    art—
  Not in lone splendour hung aloft the
    night
And watching, with eternal lids apart,
  Like nature's patient, sleepless Eremite,
The moving waters at their priestlike task
  Of pure ablution round earth's human
    shores,
Or gazing on the new soft-fallen mask
  Of snow upon the mountains and the
    moors—
No—yet still stedfast, still unchangeable,
  Pillow'd upon my fair love's ripening
    breast,   10
To feel for ever its soft fall and swell,
  Awake for ever in a sweet unrest,
Still, still to hear her tender-taken breath,
And so live ever—or else swoon to death.
1819

III

WHY DID I LAUGH TO-NIGHT? NO VOICE WILL TELL

WHY did I laugh to-night? No voice will tell:
　No God, no Demon of severe response,
Deigns to reply from Heaven or from Hell.
　Then to my human heart I turn at once.
Heart! Thou and I are here sad and alone;
　I say, why did I laugh! O mortal pain!
O Darkness! Darkness! ever must I moan,
　To question Heaven and Hell and Heart in
　　vain.
Why did I laugh? I know this Being's lease,
　My fancy to its utmost blisses spreads; 10
Yet would I on this very midnight cease,
　And the world's gaudy ensigns see in shreds;
Verse, Fame, and Beauty are intense indeed,
But Death intenser—Death is Life's high
　meed.
1819

IV

ON FAME

FAME, like a wayward Girl, will still be coy
　To those who woo her with too slavish
　　knees,
But makes surrender to some thoughtless Boy,
　And dotes the more upon a heart at ease;
She is a Gipsey, will not speak to those
　Who have not learnt to be content without
　　her;
A Jilt, whose ear was never whisper'd close,
　Who thinks they scandal her who talk
　　about her;
A very Gipsey is she, Nilus-born,
　Sister-in-law to jealous Potiphar; 10
Ye love-sick Bards, repay her scorn for
　scorn,
　Ye Artists lovelorn, madmen that ye are!
Make your best bow to her and bid adieu,
Then, if she likes it, she will follow you.
1819

V

ON FAME

"You cannot eat your cake and have it too."
　　　　　　　　　　　　—*Proverb*

How fever'd is the man, who cannot look
　Upon his mortal days with temperate blood,
Who vexes all the leaves of his life's book,
　And robs his fair name of its maidenhood;

It is as if the rose should pluck herself,
　Or the ripe plum finger its misty bloom,
As if a Naiad, like a meddling elf,
　Should darken her pure grot with muddy
　　gloom,
But the rose leaves herself upon the briar, 9
　For winds to kiss and grateful bees to feed,
And the ripe plum still wears its dim attire,
　The undisturbed lake has crystal space,
　Why then should man, teasing the world
　　for grace,
Spoil his salvation for a fierce miscreed?
1819

VI

ON THE SONNET

IF by dull rhymes our English must be
　chain'd,
And, like Andromeda, the Sonnet sweet
Fetter'd, in spite of pained loveliness,
Let us find, if we must be constrain'd,
Sandals more interwoven and complete
To fit the naked foot of Poesy:
Let us inspect the Lyre, and weigh the stress
Of every chord, and see what may be gain'd
By ear industrious, and attention meet;
Misers of sound and syllable, no less 10
Than Midas of his coinage, let us be
Jealous of dead leaves in the bay wreath crown;
So, if we may not let the Muse be free,
She will be bound with garlands of her own.
1819

VII

TO FANNY

I CRY your mercy—pity—love!—aye, love!
　Merciful love that tantalizes not,
One-thoughted, never-wandering, guileless
　love,
　Unmask'd, and being seen—without a blot!
O! let me have thee whole,—all—all—be mine!
　That shape, that fairness, that sweet minor
　　zest
Of love, your kiss,—those hands, those eyes
　divine,
　That warm, white, lucent, million-pleasured
　　breast,—
Yourself—your soul—in pity give me all,
　Withhold no atom's atom or I die, 10
Or living on perhaps, your wretched thrall,
　Forget, in the mist of idle misery,

Life's purposes,—the palate of my mind
Losing its gust, and my ambition blind!

1819

THE EVE OF ST. AGNES

I

St. Agnes' Eve—Ah, bitter chill it was!
The owl, for all his feathers, was a-cold;
The hare limp'd trembling through the frozen grass,
And silent was the flock in woolly fold:
Numb were the Beadsman's fingers, while he told
His rosary, and while his frosted breath,
Like pious incense from a censer old,
Seem'd taking flight for heaven, without a death,
Past the sweet Virgin's picture, while his prayer he saith.

II

His prayer he saith, this patient, holy man; 10
Then takes his lamp, and riseth from his knees,
And back returneth, meagre, barefoot, wan,
Along the chapel aisle by slow degrees:
The sculptured dead, on each side, seem to freeze,
Emprison'd in black, purgatorial rails:
Knights, ladies, praying in dumb orat'ries,
He passeth by; and his weak spirit fails
To think how they may ache in icy hoods and mails.

III

Northward he turneth through a little door,
And scarce three steps, ere Music's golden tongue 20
Flatter'd to tears this aged man and poor;
But no—already had his death-bell rung;
The joys of all his life were said and sung:
His was harsh penance on St. Agnes' Eve:
Another way he went, and soon among
Rough ashes sat he for his soul's reprieve,
And all night kept awake, for sinners' sake to grieve.

IV

That ancient Beadsman heard the prelude soft;
And so it chanced, for many a door was wide,
From hurry to and fro. Soon, up aloft, 30

The silver, snarling trumpets 'gan to chide:
The level chambers, ready with their pride,
Were glowing to receive a thousand guests:
The carved angels, ever eager-eyed,
Stared, where upon their heads the cornice rests,
With hair blown back, and wings put crosswise on their breasts.

V

At length burst in the argent revelry,
With plume, tiara, and all rich array,
Numerous as shadows haunting fairily
The brain, new-stuff'd, in youth, with triumphs gay 40
Of old romance. These let us wish away,
And turn, sole-thoughted, to one Lady there,
Whose heart had brooded, all that wintry day,
On love, and wing'd St. Agnes' saintly care,
As she had heard old dames full many times declare.

VI

They told her how, upon St. Agnes' Eve,
Young virgins might have visions of delight,
And soft adorings from their loves receive
Upon the honey'd middle of the night,
If ceremonies due they did aright; 50
As, supperless to bed they must retire,
And couch supine their beauties, lily white;
Nor look behind, nor sideways, but require
Of Heaven with upward eyes for all that they desire.

VII

Full of this whim was thoughtful Madeline:
The music, yearning like a God in pain,
She scarcely heard: her maiden eyes divine,
Fix'd on the floor, saw many a sweeping train
Pass by—she heeded not at all: in vain
Came many a tiptoe, amorous cavalier, 60
And back retired; not cool'd by high disdain,
But she saw not: her heart was otherwhere;
She sigh'd for Agnes' dreams, the sweetest of the year.

VIII

She danced along with vague, regardless
  eyes,
Anxious her lips, her breathing quick and
  short:
The hallow'd hour was near at hand: she
  sighs
Amid the timbrels, and the throng'd resort
Of whisperers in anger, or in sport;
'Mid looks of love, defiance, hate, and scorn,
Hoodwink'd with faery fancy; all amort, 70
Save to St. Agnes and her lambs unshorn,
And all the bliss to be before to-morrow
  morn.

IX

So, purposing each moment to retire,
She linger'd still. Meantime, across the
  moors,
Had come young Porphyro, with heart on
  fire
For Madeline. Beside the portal doors,
Buttress'd from moonlight, stands he, and
  implores
All saints to give him sight of Madeline,
But for one moment in the tedious hours,
That he might gaze and worship all unseen;
Perchance speak, kneel, touch, kiss—in sooth
  such things have been. 81

X

He ventures in: let no buzz'd whisper tell:
All eyes be muffled, or a hundred swords
Will storm his heart, Love's fev'rous cita-
  del:
For him, those chambers held barbarian
  hordes,
Hyena foemen, and hot-blooded lords,
Whose very dogs would execrations howl
Against his lineage: not one breast affords
Him any mercy, in that mansion foul,
Save one old beldame, weak in body and in
  soul. 90

XI

Ah, happy chance! the aged creature came,
Shuffling along with ivory-headed wand,
To where he stood, hid from the torch's
  flame,
Behind a broad hall-pillar, far beyond
The sound of merriment and chorus bland:
He startled her; but soon she knew his face,
And grasp'd his fingers in her palsied hand,
Saying, 'Mercy, Porphyro! hie thee from
  this place;
They are all here to-night, the whole blood-
  thirsty race!

XII

'Get hence! get hence! there's dwarfish
  Hildebrand; 100
He had a fever late, and in the fit
He cursed thee and thine, both house and
  land:
Then there's that old Lord Maurice, not a
  whit
More tame for his gray hairs—Alas me! flit!
Flit like a ghost away.'—'Ah, Gossip dear,
We're safe enough; here in this armchair sit,
And tell me how'—'Good Saints! not here,
  not here;
Follow me, child, or else these stones will be
  thy bier.' 108

XIII

He follow'd through a lowly arched way,
Brushing the cobwebs with his lofty plume;
And as she mutter'd 'Well-a—well-a-day!'
He found him in a little moonlight room,
Pale, latticed, chill, and silent as a tomb.
'Now tell me where is Madeline,' said he,
'O tell me, Angela, by the holy loom
Which none but secret sisterhood may see,
When they St. Agnes' wool are weaving
  piously.'

XIV

'St. Agnes! Ah! it is St. Agnes' Eve—
Yet men will murder upon holy days: 119
Thou must hold water in a witch's sieve,
And be liege-lord of all the Elves and Fays,
To venture so: it fills me with amaze
To see thee, Porphyro!—St. Agnes' Eve!
God's help! my lady fair the conjuror plays
This very night: good angels her deceive!
But let me laugh awhile, I've mickle time to
  grieve.'

XV

Feebly she laugheth in the languid moon,
While Porphyro upon her face doth look,
Like puzzled urchin on an aged crone
Who keepeth closed a wond'rous riddle-
  book, 130
As spectacled she sits in chimney nook.

But soon his eyes grew brilliant, when she
    told
His lady's purpose; and he scarce could
    brook
Tears, at the thought of those enchant-
    ments cold,
And Madeline asleep in lap of legends old.

XVI

Sudden a thought came like a full-blown
    rose,
Flushing his brow, and in his pained heart
Made purple riot: then doth he propose
A stratagem, that makes the beldame start:
'A cruel man and impious thou art: 140
Sweet lady, let her pray, and sleep, and
    dream
Alone with her good angels, far apart
From wicked men like thee. Go, go! I deem
Thou canst not surely be the same that thou
    didst seem.'

XVII

'I will not harm her, by all saints I swear,'
Quoth Porphyro: 'O may I ne'er find grace
When my weak voice shall whisper its last
    prayer,
If one of her soft ringlets I displace,
Or look with ruffian passion in her face.
Good Angela, believe me by these tears;
Or I will, even in a moment's space,   151
Awake, with horrid shout, my foemen's
    ears,
And beard them, though they be more fang'd
    than wolves and bears.'

XVIII

'Ah! why wilt thou affright a feeble soul?
A poor, weak, palsy-stricken, church-yard
    thing,
Whose passing-bell may ere the midnight
    toll;
Whose prayers for thee, each morn and
    evening,
Were never miss'd.' Thus plaining, doth she
    bring
A gentler speech from burning Porphyro;
So woful, and of such deep sorrowing,
That Angela gives promise she will do   161
Whatever he shall wish, betide her weal or
    woe.

XIX

Which was, to lead him, in close secrecy,
Even to Madeline's chamber, and there hide
Him in a closet, of such privacy
That he might see her beauty unespied,
And win perhaps that night a peerless bride,
While legion'd fairies paced the coverlet,
And pale enchantment held her sleepy-eyed.
Never on such a night have lovers met,
Since Merlin paid his Demon all the monstrous
    debt.   171

XX

'It shall be as thou wishest,' said the Dame:
'All cates and dainties shall be stored there
Quickly on this feast-night: by the tambour
    frame *Tambourine*
Her own lute thou wilt see: no time to spare,
For I am slow and feeble, and scarce dare
On such a catering trust my dizzy head.
Wait here, my child, with patience; kneel
    in prayer
The while: Ah! thou must needs the lady
    wed,
Or may I never leave my grave among the
    dead.'   180

XXI

So saying she hobbled off with busy fear.
The lover's endless minutes slowly pass'd;
The Dame return'd, and whisper'd in his
    ear
To follow her; with aged eyes aghast
From fright of dim espial. Safe at last,
Through many a dusky gallery, they gain
The maiden's chamber, silken, hush'd and
    chaste;
Where Porphyro took covert, pleased a-
    main.
His poor guide hurried back with agues in her
    brain.

XXII

Her falt'ring hand upon the balustrade,   190
Old Angela was feeling for the stair,
When Madeline, St. Agnes' charmed maid,
Rose, like a mission'd spirit, unaware:
With silver taper's light, and pious care,
She turn'd, and down the aged gossip led
To a safe level matting. Now prepare,
Young Porphyro, for gazing on that bed;
She comes, she comes again, like ring-dove
    fray'd and fled.

XXIII

Out went the taper as she hurried in;   199
Its little smoke, in pallid moonshine, died:
She closed the door, she panted, all akin
To spirits of the air, and visions wide:
No uttered syllable, or, woe betide!
But to her heart, her heart was voluble,
Paining with eloquence her balmy side;
As though a tongueless nightingale should swell
Her throat in vain, and die, heart-stifled in her dell.

XXIV

A casement high and triple arch'd there was,
All garlanded with carven imag'ries
Of fruits, and flowers, and bunches of knot-grass,   210
And diamonded with panes of quaint device,
Innumerable of stains and splendid dyes,
As are the tiger-moth's deep-damask'd wings;
And in the midst, 'mong thousand herald-ries,
And twilight saints, and dim emblazonings,
A shielded scutcheon blush'd with blood of queens and kings.

XXV

Full on this casement shone the wintry moon,
And threw warm gules on Madeline's fair breast,
As down she knelt for heaven's grace and boon;
Rose-bloom fell on her hands, together prest,   220
And on her silver cross soft amethyst,
And on her hair a glory, like a saint:
She seem'd a splendid angel, newly drest,
Save wings, for heaven:—Porphyro grew faint;
She knelt, so pure a thing, so free from mortal taint.

XXVI

Anon his heart revives: her vespers done,
Of all its wreathed pearls her hair she frees;
Unclasps her warmed jewels one by one;
Loosens her fragrant bodice; by degrees   229
Her rich attire creeps rustling to her knees:
Half-hidden, like a mermaid in sea-weed,

Pensive awhile she dreams awake, and sees,
In fancy, fair St. Agnes in her bed,
But dares not look behind, or all the charm is fled.

XXVII

Soon, trembling in her soft and chilly nest,
In sort of wakeful swoon, perplex'd she lay,
Until the poppied warmth of sleep oppress'd
Her soothed limbs, and soul fatigued away;
Flown, like a thought, until the morrow-day;   239
Blissfully haven'd both from joy and pain;
Clasp'd like a missal where swart Paynims pray;
Blinded alike from sunshine and from rain,
As though a rose should shut, and be a bud again.

XXVIII

Stol'n to this paradise, and so entranced,
Porphyro gazed upon her empty dress,
And listen'd to her breathing, if it chanced
To wake into a slumberous tenderness;
Which when he heard, that minute did he bless,
And breathed himself: then from the closet crept,
Noiseless as fear in a wide wilderness,   250
And over the hush'd carpet, silent, stept,
And 'tween the curtains peep'd, where, lo!
—how fast she slept.

XXIX

Then by the bed-side, where the faded moon
Made a dim, silver twilight, soft he set
A table, and, half anguish'd, threw thereon
A cloth of woven crimson, gold, and jet:—
O for some drowsy Morphean amulet!
The boisterous, midnight, festive clarion,
The kettle-drum, and far-heard clarionet,
Affray his ears, though but in dying tone:—
The hall-door shuts again, and all the noise is gone.   261

XXX

And still she slept an azure-lidded sleep,
In blanched linen, smooth, and lavender'd,
While he from forth the closet brought a heap
Of candied apple, quince, and plum, and gourd;
With jellies soother than the creamy curd,

And lucent syrops, tinct with cinnamon;
Manna and dates, in argosy transferr'd 268
From Fez; and spiced dainties, every one,
From silken Samarcand to cedar'd Lebanon.

XXXI

These delicates he heap'd with glowing hand
On golden dishes and in baskets bright
Of wreathed silver: sumptuous they stand
In the retired quiet of the night,
Filling the chilly room with perfume light.—
'And now, my love, my seraph fair, awake!
Thou art my heaven, and I thine eremite:
Open thine eyes, for meek St. Agnes' sake,
Or I shall drowse beside thee, so my soul doth
    ache.' 279

XXXII

Thus whispering, his warm, unnerved arm
Sank in her pillow. Shaded was her dream
By the dusk curtains:—'twas a midnight
    charm
Impossible to melt as iced stream:
The lustrous salvers in the moonlight gleam;
Broad golden fringe upon the carpet lies:
It seem'd he never, never could redeem
From such a steadfast spell his lady's eyes;
So mused awhile, entoil'd in woofed phan-
    tasies. 288

XXXIII

Awakening up, he took her hollow lute,—
Tumultuous,—and, in chords that tender-
    est be,
He play'd an ancient ditty, long since mute,
In Provence call'd 'La belle dame sans
    mercy:'
Close to her ear touching the melody;—
Wherewith disturb'd, she utter'd a soft
    moan:
He ceased—she panted quick—and suddenly
Her blue affrayed eyes wide open shone:
Upon his knees he sank, pale as smooth-
    sculptured stone.

XXXIV

Her eyes were open, but she still beheld,
Now wide awake, the vision of her sleep:
There was a painful change, that nigh ex-
    pell'd 300
The blisses of her dream so pure and deep
At which fair Madeline began to weep,

And moan forth witless words with many a
    sigh;
While still her gaze on Porphyro would keep;
Who knelt, with joined hands and piteous
    eye,
Fearing to move or speak, she look'd so
    dreamingly.

XXXV

'Ah, Porphyro!' said she, 'but even now
Thy voice was at sweet tremble in mine ear,
Made tuneable with every sweetest vow;
And those sad eyes were spiritual and clear:
How changed thou art! how pallid, chill, and
    drear! 311
Give me that voice again, my Porphyro,
Those looks immortal, those complainings
    dear!
Oh leave me not in this eternal woe,
For if thou diest, my Love, I know not where
    to go.'

XXXVI

Beyond a mortal man impassion'd far
At these voluptuous accents, he arose,
Ethereal, flush'd, and like a throbbing star
Seen mid the sapphire heaven's deep repose;
Into her dream he melted, as the rose 320
Blendeth its odour with the violet,—
Solution sweet: meantime the frost-wind
    blows
Like Love's alarum pattering the sharp sleet
Against the window-panes; St. Agnes' moon
    hath set.

XXXVII

'Tis dark: quick pattereth the flaw-blown
    sleet:
'This is no dream, my bride, my Madeline!'
'Tis dark: the iced gusts still rave and beat:
'No dream, alas! alas! and woe is mine!
Porphyro will leave me here to fade and
    pine.— 329
Cruel! what traitor could thee hither bring?
I curse not, for my heart is lost in thine,
Though thou forsakest a deceived thing;—
A dove forlorn and lost with sick unpruned
    wing.'

XXXVIII

'My Madeline! sweet dreamer! lovely bride!
Say, may I be for aye thy vassal blest?
Thy beauty's shield, heart-shaped and ver-
    meil dyed?

Ah, silver shrine, here will I take my rest
After so many hours of toil and quest,
A famish'd pilgrim,—saved by miracle.
Though I have found, I will not rob thy
   nest   340
Saving of thy sweet self; if thou think'st well
To trust, fair Madeline, to no rude infidel.

XXXIX

'Hark! 'tis an elfin storm from faery land,
Of haggard seeming, but a boon indeed:
Arise—arise! the morning is at hand:—
The bloated wassailers will never heed:—
Let us away, my love, with happy speed;
There are no ears to hear, or eyes to see,—
Drown'd all in Rhenish and the sleepy
   mead:
Awake! arise! my love, and fearless be, 350
For o'er the southern moors I have a home
   for thee.'

XL

She hurried at his words, beset with fears,
For there were sleeping dragons all around,
At glaring watch, perhaps, with ready
   spears—
Down the wide stairs a darkling way they
   found.—
In all the house was heard no human sound.
A chain-droop'd lamp was flickering by each
   door;
The arras, rich with horseman, hawk, and
   hound,   358
Flutter'd in the besieging wind's uproar;
And the long carpets rose along the gusty
   floor.

XLI

They glide, like phantoms, into the wide
   hall;
Like phantoms to the iron porch they
   glide,
Where lay the Porter, in an uneasy sprawl,
With a huge empty flagon by his side:
The wakeful bloodhound rose, and shook
   his hide,
But his sagacious eye an inmate owns:
By one, and one, the bolts full easy slide:—
The chains lie silent on the footworn
   stones;—
The key turns, and the door upon its hinges
   groans.   369

XLII

And they are gone: aye, ages long ago
These lovers fled away into the storm.
That night the Baron dreamt of many a woe,
And all his warrior-guests, with shade and
   form
Of witch, and demon, and large coffin-worm,
Were long be-nightmared. Angela the old
Died palsy-twitch'd, with meagre face de-
   form;
The Beadsman, after thousand aves told,
For aye unsought-for slept among his ashes
   cold.

1819

THE EVE OF ST. MARK

A FRAGMENT

Upon a Sabbath-day it fell;
Twice holy was the Sabbath-bell,
That call'd the folk to evening prayer;
The city streets were clean and fair
From wholesome drench of April rains;
And, on the western window panes,
The chilly sunset faintly told
Of unmatured green valleys cold,
Of the green thorny bloomless hedge,
Of rivers new with spring-tide sedge,   10
Of primroses by shelter'd rills,
And daisies on the aguish hills.
Twice holy was the Sabbath-bell:
The silent streets were crowded well
With staid and pious companies,
Warm from their fireside orat'ries;
And moving, with demurest air,
To even-song, and vesper prayer.
Each arched porch, and entry low,
Was fill'd with patient folk and slow,   20
With whispers hush, and shuffling feet,
While play'd the organ loud and sweet.

The bells had ceas'd, the prayers begun,
And Bertha had not yet half done
A curious volume, patch'd and torn,
That all day long, from earliest morn,
Had taken captive her two eyes,
Among its golden broideries;
Perplex'd her with a thousand things,—
The stars of Heaven, and angels' wings,   30
Martyrs in a fiery blaze,
Azure saints and silver rays,

Moses' breastplate, and the seven
Candlesticks John saw in Heaven,
The winged Lion of Saint Mark,
And the Covenantal Ark,
With its many mysteries,
Cherubim and golden mice.

Bertha was a maiden fair,
Dwelling in th' old Minster-square;   40
From her fireside she could see,
Sidelong, its rich antiquity,
Far as the Bishop's garden-wall;
Where sycamores and elm-trees tall,
Full-leav'd, the forest had outstript,
By no sharp north-wind ever nipt,
So shelter'd by the mighty pile.
Bertha arose, and read awhile,
With forehead 'gainst the window-pane.
Again she tried, and then again,   50
Until the dusk eve left her dark
Upon the legend of St. Mark.
From plaited lawn-frill, fine and thin,
She lifted up her soft warm chin,
With aching neck and swimming eyes,
And daz'd with saintly imag'ries.

All was gloom, and silent all,
Save now and then the still foot-fall
Of one returning homewards late,
Past the echoing minster-gate.   60
The clamorous daws, that all the day
Above tree-tops and towers play,
Pair by pair had gone to rest,
Each in its ancient belfry-nest,
Where asleep they fall betimes,
To music and the drowsy chimes.

All was silent, all was gloom,
Abroad and in the homely room:
Down she sat, poor cheated soul!
And struck a lamp from the dismal coal;   70
Lean'd forward, with bright drooping hair
And slant book, full against the glare.
Her shadow, in uneasy guise,
Hover'd about, a giant size,
On ceiling-beam and old oak chair,
The parrot's cage, and panel-square;
And the warm angled winter-screen,
On which were many monsters seen,
Call'd doves of Siam, Lima mice,
And legless birds of Paradise,   80

Macaw, and tender Avadavat,
And silken-furr'd Angora cat.
Untired she read, her shadow still
Glower'd about, as it would fill
The room with wildest forms and shades,
As though some ghostly queen of spades
Had come to mock behind her back,
And dance, and ruffle her garments black.
Untired she read the legend page,
Of holy Mark, from youth to age,   90
On land, on sea, in pagan chains,
Rejoicing for his many pains.
Sometimes the learned eremite,
With golden star, or dagger bright,
Referr'd to pious poesies
Written in smallest crow-quill size
Beneath the text; and thus the rhyme
Was parcell'd out from time to time:
——'Als writith he of swevenis,
Men han beforne they wake in bliss,   100
Whanne that hir friendes thinke him bound
In crimped shroude farre under grounde;
And how a litling child mote be
A saint er its nativitie,
Gif that the modre (God her blesse!)
Kepen in solitarinesse,
And kissen devoute the holy croce,
Of Goddes love, and Sathan's force,—
He writith; and thinges many mo
Of swiche thinges I may not show.   110
Bot I must tellen verilie
Somdel of Saintè Cicilie,
And chieflie what he auctorethe
Of Saintè Markis life and dethe:'

At length her constant eyelids come
Upon the fervent martyrdom;
Then lastly to his holy shrine,
Exalt amid the tapers' shine
At Venice,—

1819

LA BELLE DAME SANS MERCI

O what can ail thee, knight at arms,
    Alone and palely loitering?
The sedge has withered from the lake,
    And no birds sing!

O what can ail thee, knight at arms,
    So haggard and so woe-begone?

The squirrel's granary is full,
And the harvest's done.

I see a lily on thy brow,
With anguish moist and fever dew;   10
And on thy cheeks a fading rose
Fast withereth too.—

I met a lady in the meads,
Full beautiful, a faery's child;
Her hair was long, her foot was light,
And her eyes were wild.

I made a garland for her head,
And bracelets, too, and fragrant zone;
She looked at me as she did love,
And made sweet moan.   20

I set her on my pacing steed,
And nothing else saw, all day long;
For sidelong would she bend, and sing
A faery's song.

She found me roots of relish sweet,
And honey wild, and manna dew;
And sure in language strange she said,
"I love thee true."

She took me to her elfin grot,   29
And there she wept and sighed full sore;
And there I shut her wild, wild eyes
With kisses four.

And there she lullèd me asleep,
And there I dreamed, ah woe betide!
The latest dream I ever dreamt,
On the cold hillside.

I saw pale kings, and princes too,
Pale warriors, death-pale were they all,
Who cried, "La belle dame sans merci
Thee hath in thrall!"   40

I saw their starved lips in the gloam
With horrid warning gapèd wide—
And I awoke, and found me here,
On the cold hill's side.

And this is why I sojourn here,
Alone and palely loitering;
Though the sedge is withered from the lake,
And no birds sing.

1819

ODE TO PSYCHE

I

O GODDESS! hear these tuneless numbers, wrung
    By sweet enforcement and remembrance dear,
And pardon that thy secrets should be sung
    Even into thine own soft-conchèd ear:
Surely I dreamt to-day, or did I see
    The wingèd Psyche with awaken'd eyes?
I wander'd in a forest thoughtlessly,
    And, on the sudden, fainting with surprise,
Saw two fair creatures, couchèd side by side
    In deepest grass, beneath the whisp'ring roof   10
Of leaves and trembled blossoms, where there ran
        A brooklet, scarce espied:

II

'Mid hush'd, cool-rooted flowers fragrant-eyed,
    Blue, silver-white, and budded Tyrian,
They lay calm-breathing on the bedded grass;
    Their arms embraced, and their pinions too;
    Their lips touch'd not, but had not bade adieu,
As if disjoined by soft-handed slumber,
And ready still past kisses to outnumber
    At tender eye-dawn of aurorean love: 20
        The wingèd boy I knew;
    But who wast thou, O happy, happy dove?
        His Psyche true!

III

O latest-born and loveliest vision far
    Of all Olympus' faded hierarchy!
Fairer than Phœbe's sapphire-region'd star,
    Or Vesper, amorous glow-worm of the sky;
Fairer than these, though temple thou hast none,
        Nor altar heap'd with flowers;
Nor virgin-choir to make delicious moan   30
        Upon the midnight hours;
No voice, no lute, no pipe, no incense sweet
    From chain-swung censer teeming;
No shrine, no grove, no oracle, no heat
    Of pale-mouth'd prophet dreaming.

IV

O brightest! though too late for antique vows,
  Too, too late for the fond believing lyre,
When holy were the haunted forest boughs,
  Holy the air, the water, and the fire;
Yet even in these days so far retired   40
  From happy pieties, thy lucent fans,
  Fluttering among the faint Olympians,
I see, and sing, by my own eyes inspired.
So let me be thy choir, and make a moan
      Upon the midnight hours;
Thy voice, thy lute, thy pipe, thy incense
    sweet
  From swinged censer teeming;
Thy shrine, thy grove, thy oracle, thy heat
  Of pale-mouth'd prophet dreaming.

V

Yes, I will be thy priest, and build a fane   50
  In some untrodden region of my mind,
Where branched thoughts, new-grown with
    pleasant pain,
  Instead of pines shall murmur in the wind:
Far, far around shall those dark-cluster'd trees
  Fledge the wild-ridged mountains steep by
    steep;
And there by zephyrs, streams, and birds, and
    bees,
  The moss-lain Dryads shall be lulled to
    sleep;
And in the midst of this wide quietness
A rosy sanctuary will I dress   59
With the wreath'd trellis of a working brain,
  With buds, and bells, and stars without a
    name,
With all the gardener Fancy e'er could feign,
  Who breeding flowers, will never breed the
    same:
And there shall be for thee all soft delight
  That shadowy thought can win,
A bright torch, and a casement ope at night,
  To let the warm Love in!

1819

ODE ON A GRECIAN URN

I

Thou still unravish'd bride of quietness,
  Thou foster-child of silence and slow time,
Sylvan historian, who canst thus express
  A flowery tale more sweetly than our rhyme:
What leaf-fring'd legend haunts about thy
    shape
  Of deities or mortals, or of both,
    In Tempe or the dales of Arcady?
  What men or gods are these? What maidens
    loth?
What mad pursuit? What struggle to escape?
    What pipes and timbrels? What wild
    ecstasy?   10

II

Heard melodies are sweet, but those unheard
  Are sweeter; therefore, ye soft pipes, play
    on;
Not to the sensual ear, but, more endear'd,
  Pipe to the spirit ditties of no tone:
Fair youth, beneath the trees, thou canst not
    leave
  Thy song, nor ever can those trees be bare;
    Bold Lover, never, never canst thou kiss,
Though winning near the goal—yet, do not
    grieve;
  She cannot fade, though thou hast not thy
    bliss,   19
    For ever wilt thou love, and she be fair!

III

Ah, happy, happy boughs! that cannot shed
  Your leaves, nor ever bid the Spring adieu;
And, happy melodist, unwearied,
  For ever piping songs for ever new;
More happy love! more happy, happy love!
  For ever warm and still to be enjoy'd,
    For ever panting, and for ever young;
All breathing human passion far above,
  That leaves a heart high-sorrowful and
    cloy'd,
    A burning forehead, and a parching
    tongue.   30

IV

Who are these coming to the sacrifice?
  To what green altar, O mysterious priest,
Lead'st thou that heifer lowing at the skies,
  And all her silken flanks with garlands drest?
What little town by river or sea shore,
  Or mountain-built with peaceful citadel,
    Is emptied of this folk, this pious morn?
And, little town, thy streets for evermore
  Will silent be; and not a soul to tell   39
    Why thou art desolate, can e'er return.

V

O Attic shape! Fair attitude! with brede
. Of marble men and maidens overwrought,
With forest branches and the trodden weed;
    Thou, silent form, dost tease us out of
        thought
As doth eternity: Cold Pastoral!
    When old age shall this generation waste,
        Thou shalt remain, in midst of other woe
Than ours, a friend to man, to whom thou
    say'st,
    "Beauty is truth, truth beauty,"—that is all
    Ye know on earth, and all ye need to
        know.   50
1819

ODE ON MELANCHOLY

I

No, no, go not to Lethe, neither twist
    Wolf's-bane, tight-rooted, for its poisonous
        wine;
Nor suffer thy pale forehead to be kiss'd
    By nightshade, ruby grape of Proserpine;
Make not your rosary of yew-berries,
    Nor let the beetle, nor the death-moth be
        Your mournful Psyche, nor the downy
            owl
A partner in your sorrow's mysteries:
    For shade to shade will come too drowsily,
        And drown the wakeful anguish of the
            soul.   10

II

But when the melancholy fit shall fall
    Sudden from heaven like a weeping cloud,
That fosters the droop-headed flowers all,
    And hides the green hill in an April shroud;
Then glut thy sorrow on a morning rose,
    Or on the rainbow of the salt sand-wave,
        Or on the wealth of globed peonies;
Or if thy mistress some rich anger shows,
    Emprison her soft hand, and let her rave,
        And feed deep, deep upon her peerless
            eyes.   20

III

She dwells with Beauty—Beauty that must die;
    And joy, whose hand is ever at his lips
Bidding adieu; and aching Pleasure nigh,
    Turning to poison while the bee-mouth sips:
Ay, in the very temple of Delight
    Veil'd Melancholy has her sovran shrine,

Though seen of none save him whose
    strenuous tongue   27
Can burst Joy's grape against his palate fine;
His soul shall taste the sadness of her might,
    And be among her cloudy trophies hung.
1819

ODE TO A NIGHTINGALE

I

My heart aches, and a drowsy numbness pains
    My sense, as though of hemlock I had drunk,
Or emptied some dull opiate to the drains
    One minute past, and Lethe-wards had sunk:
'Tis not through envy of thy happy lot,
    But being too happy in thine happiness,—
        That thou, light winged Dryad of the trees,
            In some melodious plot   8
Of beechen green, and shadows numberless,
    Singest of summer in full-throated ease.

II

O, for a draught of vintage! that hath been
    Cool'd a long age in the deep-delved earth,
Tasting of Flora and the country green,
    Dance, and Provençal song, and sunburnt
        mirth!
O for a beaker full of the warm South,
    Full of the true, the blushful Hippocrene,
        With beaded bubbles winking at the brim,
            And purple-stained mouth;
That I might drink, and leave the world un-
        seen,
    And with thee fade away into the forest
        dim: 20

III

Fade far away, dissolve, and quite forget
    What thou among the leaves hast never
        known,
The weariness, the fever, and the fret
    Here, where men sit and hear each other
        groan;
Where palsy shakes a few, sad, last grey hairs,
    Where youth grows pale, and spectre-thin,
        and dies;
    Where but to think is to be full of sorrow
        And leaden-ey'd despairs,
    Where Beauty cannot keep her lustrous
        eyes,
        Or new Love pine at them beyond to-
            morrow.   30

She lives in Beauty - Beauty that must die
And Joy whose hand is ever at his lips
Bidding Adieu; and aching Pleasure nigh
Turning to Poison while the Bee-mouth sips
Aye, in the very temple of delight
  Veil'd Melancholy has her sovran shrine
    Though seen of none but him whose strenuous
Can burst Joy's grape against his palate fine
  His soul shall the anguish of her might
And be among her cloudy trophies hung

The Concluding Stanza of *Ode to Melancholy* in Keats's Handwriting.
(See Appendix I.)

IV

Away! away! for I will fly to thee,
  Not charioted by Bacchus and his pards,
But on the viewless wings of Poesy,
  Though the dull brain perplexes and re-
    tards:
Already with thee! tender is the night,
  And haply the Queen-Moon is on her
    throne,
    Cluster'd around by all her starry Fays;
    But here there is no light,
  Save what from heaven is with the breezes
    blown
  Through verdurous glooms and winding
    mossy ways. 40

V

I cannot see what flowers are at my feet,
  Nor what soft incense hangs upon the
    boughs,
But, in embalmed darkness, guess each sweet
  Wherewith the seasonable month endows
The grass, the thicket, and the fruit-tree
    wild;
  White hawthorn, and the pastoral eglantine;
  Fast fading violets cover'd up in leaves;
    And mid-May's eldest child,
  The coming musk-rose, full of dewy wine,
  The murmurous haunt of flies on summer
    eves. 50

VI

Darkling I listen; and, for many a time
  I have been half in love with easeful Death,
Call'd him soft names in many a mused rhyme,
  To take into the air my quiet breath;
    Now more than ever seems it rich to
    die,
  To cease upon the midnight with no pain,
    While thou art pouring forth thy soul
    abroad
    In such an ecstasy!
  Still wouldst thou sing, and I have ears in
    vain—
  To thy high requiem become a sod. 60

VII

Thou wast not born for death, immortal Bird!
  No hungry generations tread thee down;
The voice I hear this passing night was heard
  In ancient days by emperor and clown:

Perhaps the self-same song that found a path
  Through the sad heart of Ruth, when, sick
    for home,
    She stood in tears amid the alien corn;
    The same that oft-times hath
  Charm'd magic casements, opening on the
    foam
  Of perilous seas, in faery lands forlorn. 70

VIII

Forlorn! the very word is like a bell
  To toll me back from thee to my sole self!
Adieu! the fancy cannot cheat so well
  As she is famed to do, deceiving elf.
Adieu! adieu! thy plaintive anthem fades
  Past the near meadows, over the still stream,
    Up the hill-side; and now 'tis buried deep
    In the next valley-glades:
  Was it a vision, or a waking dream? 79
  Fled is that music:—Do I wake or sleep?

1819

TO AUTUMN

I

Season of mists and mellow fruitfulness,
  Close bosom-friend of the maturing sun;
Conspiring with him how to load and bless
  With fruit the vines that round the thatch-
    eves run;
To bend with apples the moss'd cottage-trees,
  And fill all fruit with ripeness to the core;
    To swell the gourd, and plump the hazel
    shells
  With a sweet kernel; to set budding more,
And still more, later flowers for the bees, 9
Until they think warm days will never cease,
    For Summer has o'er-brimm'd their
    clammy cells.

II

Who hath not seen thee oft amid thy store?
  Sometimes whoever seeks abroad may find
Thee sitting careless on a granary floor,
  Thy hair soft-lifted by the winnowing wind;
Or on a half-reap'd furrow sound asleep,
  Drows'd with the fume of poppies, while
    thy hook
    Spares the next swath and all its twined
    flowers:
And sometimes like a gleaner thou dost keep
  Steady thy laden head across a brook; 20

Or by a cyder-press, with patient look,
  Thou watchest the last oozings hours by
      hours.

                III

Where are the songs of Spring? Ay, where are
      they?
  Think not of them, thou hast thy music
      too,—
While barred clouds bloom the soft-dying day,
  And touch the stubble-plains with rosy hue;
Then in a wailful choir the small gnats mourn
  Among the river sallows, borne aloft
    Or sinking as the light wind lives or
        dies;
And full-grown lambs loud bleat from hilly
      bourn;   30
  Hedge-crickets sing; and now with treble
      soft
  The red-breast whistles from a garden-
      croft;
    And gathering swallows twitter in the
        skies.

1819

LAMIA

PART I

Upon a time, before the faery broods
Drove Nymph and Satyr from the prosperous
      woods,
Before king Oberon's bright diadem,
Sceptre, and mantle, clasp'd with dewy gem,
Frighted away the Dryads and the Fauns
From rushes green, and brakes, and cowslip'd
      lawns,
The ever-smitten Hermes empty left
His golden throne, bent warm on amorous
      theft:
From high Olympus had he stolen light,
On this side of Jove's clouds, to escape the
      sight
Of his great summoner, and made retreat
Into a forest on the shores of Crete.
For somewhere in that sacred island dwelt
A nymph, to whom all hoofed Satyrs knelt;
At whose white feet the languid Tritons poured
Pearls, while on land they wither'd and adored.
Fast by the springs where she to bathe was
      wont,
And in those meads where sometime she might
      haunt,

Were strewn rich gifts, unknown to any Muse,
Though Fancy's casket were unlock'd to
      choose.   20
Ah, what a world of love was at her feet!
So Hermes thought, and a celestial heat
Burnt from his winged heels to either ear,
That from a whiteness, as the lilly clear,
Blush'd into roses 'mid his golden hair,
Fallen in jealous curls about his shoulders
      bare.

  From vale to vale, from wood to wood, he
      flew,
Breathing upon the flowers his passion new,
And wound with many a river to its head,
To find where this sweet nymph prepar'd her
      secret bed: 30
In vain; the sweet nymph might nowhere be
      found,
And so he rested, on the lonely ground,
Pensive, and full of painful jealousies
Of the Wood-Gods, and even the very trees.
There as he stood, he heard a mournful voice,
Such as once heard, in gentle heart, destroys
All pain but pity: thus the lone voice spake:
"When from this wreathed tomb shall I awake!
"When move in a sweet body fit for life,   39
"And love, and pleasure, and the ruddy strife
"Of hearts and lips! Ah, miserable me!"
The God, dove-footed, glided silently
Round bush and tree, soft-brushing, in his
      speed,
The taller grasses and full-flowering weed,
Until he found a palpitating snake,
Bright, and cirque-couchant in a dusky brake.

  She was a gordian shape of dazzling hue,
Vermilion-spotted, golden, green, and blue;
Striped like a zebra, freckled like a pard,
Eyed like a peacock, and all crimson barr'd; 50
And full of silver moons, that, as she breathed,
Dissolv'd, or brighter shone, or interwreathed
Their lustres with the gloomier tapestries—
So rainbow-sided, touch'd with miseries,
She seem'd, at once, some penanced lady elf,
Some demon's mistress, or the demon's self.
Upon her crest she wore a wannish fire
Sprinkled with stars, like Ariadne's tiar:
Her head was serpent, but ah, bitter-sweet!
She had a woman's mouth with all its pearls
      complete: 60

And for her eyes: what could such eyes do
there
But weep, and weep, that they were born so
fair? *goddess of agriculture*
As Proserpine still weeps for her Sicilian air.
Her throat was serpent, but the words she
spake
Came, as through bubbling honey, for Love's
sake,
And thus; while Hermes on his pinions lay,
Like a stoop'd falcon ere he takes his prey.

"Fair Hermes, crown'd with feathers, flut-
tering light,
"I had a splendid dream of thee last night:
"I saw thee sitting, on a throne of gold,   70
"Among the Gods, upon Olympus old,
"The only sad one; for thou didst not hear
"The soft, lute-finger'd Muses chaunting clear,
"Nor even Apollo when he sang alone,
"Deaf to his throbbing throat's long, long
melodious moan.
"I dreamt I saw thee, robed in purple flakes,
"Break amorous through the clouds, as morn-
ing breaks,
"And, swiftly as a bright Phœbean dart,
"Strike for the Cretan isle; and here thou art!
"Too gentle Hermes, hast thou found the
maid?"   80
Whereat the star of Lethe not delay'd
His rosy eloquence, and thus inquired:
"Thou smooth-lipp'd serpent, surely high in-
spired!
"Thou beauteous wreath, with melancholy
eyes,
"Possess whatever bliss thou canst devise,
"Telling me only where my nymph is fled,—
"Where she doth breathe!" "Bright planet, *Mercury*
thou hast said,"
Return'd the snake, "but seal with oaths, fair
God!"
"I swear," said Hermes, "by my serpent rod,
"And by thine eyes, and by thy starry crown!"
Light flew his earnest words, among the blos-
soms blown.   *Mercury again who*   91
Then thus again the brilliance feminine:
"Too frail of heart! for this lost nymph of
thine,
"Free as the air, invisibly, she strays
"About these thornless wilds; her pleasant days
"She tastes unseen; unseen her nimble feet

"Leave traces in the grass and flowers sweet;
"From weary tendrils, and bow'd branches
green,
"She plucks the fruit unseen, she bathes un-
seen:
"And by my power is her beauty veil'd   100 *invisible*
"To keep it unaffronted, unassail'd
"By the love-glances of unlovely eyes,
"Of Satyrs, Fauns, and blear'd Silenus' sighs.
"Pale grew her immortality, for woe
"Of all these lovers, and she grieved so
"I took compassion on her, bade her steep
"Her hair in weïrd syrops, that would keep
"Her loveliness invisible, yet free
"To wander as she loves, in liberty.
"Thou shalt behold her, Hermes, thou alone,
"If thou wilt, as thou swearest, grant my
boon!"   III
Then, once again, the charmed God began
An oath, and through the serpent's ears it ran
Warm, tremulous, devout, psalterian.
Ravish'd, she lifted her Circean head,
Blush'd a live damask, and swift-lisping said,
"I was a woman, let me have once more
"A woman's shape, and charming as before.
"I love a youth of Corinth—O the bliss!
"Give me my woman's form, and place me   *X*
where he is.   120   *touches*
"Stoop, Hermes, let me breathe upon thy   *her*
brow,   *with*
"And thou shalt see thy sweet nymph even   *rod*
now."
The God on half-shut feathers sank serene,
She breath'd upon his eyes, and swift was seen
Of both the guarded nymph near-smiling on
the green.
It was no dream; or say a dream it was,
Real are the dreams of Gods, and smoothly
pass
Their pleasures in a long immortal dream.
One warm, flush'd moment, hovering, it might
seem
Dash'd by the wood-nymph's beauty, so he
burn'd;   130
Then, lighting on the printless verdure, turn'd
To the swoon'd serpent, and with languid
arm,
Delicate, put to proof the lythe Caducean
charm.
So done, upon the nymph his eyes he bent
Full of adoring tears and blandishment,

And towards her stept: she, like a moon in
    wane,
Faded before him, cower'd, nor could restrain
Her fearful sobs, self-folding like a flower
That faints into itself at evening hour:
But the God fostering her chilled hand,   140
She felt the warmth, her eyelids open'd bland,
And, like new flowers at morning song of bees,
Bloom'd, and gave up her honey to the lees.
Into the green-recessed woods they flew;
Nor grew they pale, as mortal lovers do.

Left to herself, the serpent now began
To change; her elfin blood in madness ran,
Her mouth foam'd and the grass, therewith
    besprent,
Wither'd at dew so sweet and virulent;
Her eyes in torture fix'd, and anguish drear, 150
Hot, glaz'd, and wide, with lid-lashes all sear,
Flash'd phosphor and sharp sparks, without
    one cooling tear.
The colours all inflam'd throughout her train,
She writh'd about, convulsed with scarlet pain:
A deep volcanian yellow took the place
Of all her milder-mooned body's grace;
And, as the lava ravishes the mead,
Spoilt all her silver mail, and golden brede;
Made gloom of all her frecklings, streaks and
    bars,
Eclips'd her crescents, and lick'd up her stars:
So that, in moments few, she was undrest 161
Of all her sapphires, greens, and amethyst,
And rubious-argent: of all these bereft,
Nothing but pain and ugliness were left.
Still shone her crown; that vanish'd, also she
Melted and disappear'd as suddenly;
And in the air, her new voice luting soft,
Cried, "Lycius! gentle Lycius!"—Borne aloft
With the bright mists about the mountains
    hoar
These words dissolv'd: Crete's forests heard
    no more.   170

Whither fled Lamia, now a lady bright,
A full-born beauty new and exquisite?
She fled into that valley they pass o'er
Who go to Corinth from Cenchreas' shore;
And rested at the foot of those wild hills,
The rugged founts of the Peræan rills,
And of that other ridge whose barren back
Stretches, with all its mist and cloudy rack,

South-westward to Cleone. There she stood
About a young bird's flutter from a wood, 180
Fair, on a sloping green of mossy tread,
By a clear pool, wherein she passioned
To see herself escap'd from so sore ills,
While her robes flaunted with the daffodils.

Ah, happy Lycius!—for she was a maid
More beautiful than ever twisted braid,
Or sigh'd, or blush'd, or on spring-flowered
    lea
Spread a green kirtle to the minstrelsy:
A virgin purest lipp'd, yet in the lore
Of love deep learned to the red heart's core: 190
Not one hour old, yet of sciential brain
To unperplex bliss from its neighbour pain;
Define their pettish limits, and estrange
Their points of contact, and swift counter-
    change;
Intrigue with the specious chaos, and dispart
Its most ambiguous atoms with sure art;
As though in Cupid's college she had spent
Sweet days a lovely graduate, still unshent,
And kept his rosy terms in idle languishment.

Why this fair creature chose so faerily   200
By the wayside to linger, we shall see;
But first 'tis fit to tell how she could muse
And dream, when in the serpent prison-house,
Of all she list, strange or magnificent:
How, ever, where she will'd, her spirit went;
Whether to faint Elysium, or where
Down through tress-lifting waves the Nereids
    fair
Wind into Thetis' bower by many a pearly
    stair;
Or where God Bacchus drains his cups divine,
Stretch'd out, at ease, beneath a glutinous
    pine;   210
Or where in Pluto's gardens palatine
Mulciber's columns gleam in far piazzian line.
And sometimes into cities she would send
Her dream, with feast and rioting to blend;
And once, while among mortals dreaming thus,
She saw the young Corinthian Lycius
Charioting foremost in the envious race,
Like a young Jove with calm uneager face,
And fell into a swooning love of him.
Now on the moth-time of that evening dim 220
He would return that way, as well she knew,
To Corinth from the shore; for freshly blew

The eastern soft wind, and his galley now
Grated the quaystones with her brazen prow
In port Cenchreas, from Egina isle
Fresh anchor'd; whither he had been awhile
To sacrifice to Jove, whose temple there
Waits with high marble doors for blood and
    incense rare.   228
Jove heard his vows, and better'd his desire;
For by some freakful chance he made retire
From his companions, and set forth to walk,
Perhaps grown wearied of their Corinth talk:
Over the solitary hills he fared,
Thoughtless at first, but ere eve's star appeared
His phantasy was lost, where reason fades,
In the calm'd twilight of Platonic shades.
Lamia beheld him coming, near, more near—
Close to her passing, in indifference drear,
His silent sandals swept the mossy green;
So neighbour'd to him, and yet so unseen 240
She stood: he pass'd, shut up in mysteries,
His mind wrapp'd like his mantle, while her eyes
Follow'd his steps, and her neck regal white
Turn'd—syllabling thus, "Ah, Lycius bright,
"And will you leave me on the hills alone?
"Lycius, look back! and be some pity shown."
He did; not with cold wonder fearingly,
But Orpheus-like at an Eurydice;
For so delicious were the words she sung,
It seem'd he had lov'd them a whole summer
    long: 250
And soon his eyes had drunk her beauty up,
Leaving no drop in the bewildering cup,
And still the cup was full,—while he, afraid
Lest she should vanish ere his lip had paid
Due adoration, thus began to adore;
Her soft look growing coy, she saw his chain
    so sure:
"Leave thee alone! Look back! Ah, Goddess,
    see
"Whether my eyes can ever turn from thee!
"For pity do not this sad heart belie—
"Even as thou vanishest so shall I die.   260
"Stay! though a Naiad of the rivers, stay!
"To thy far wishes will thy streams obey:
"Stay! though the greenest woods be thy
    domain,
"Alone they can drink up the morning rain:
"Though a descended Pleiad, will not one
"Of thine harmonious sisters keep in tune
"Thy spheres, and as thy silver proxy shine?
"So sweetly to these ravish'd ears of mine

"Came thy sweet greeting, that if thou shouldst
    fade
"Thy memory will waste me to a shade:— 270
"For pity do not melt!"—"If I should stay,"
Said Lamia, "here, upon this floor of clay,
"And pain my steps upon these flowers too
    rough,
"What canst thou say or do of charm enough
"To dull the nice remembrance of my home?
"Thou canst not ask me with thee here to
    roam
"Over these hills and vales, where no joy is,—
"Empty of immortality and bliss!
"Thou art a scholar, Lycius, and must know
"That finer spirits cannot breathe below   280
"In human climes, and live: Alas! poor youth,
"What taste of purer air hast thou to soothe
"My essence? What serener palaces,
"Where I may all my many senses please,
"And by mysterious sleights a hundred thirsts
    appease?
"It cannot be—Adieu!" So said, she rose
Tiptoe with white arms spread. He, sick to lose
The amorous promise of her lone complain,
Swoon'd, murmuring of love, and pale with
    pain.
The cruel lady, without any show   290
Of sorrow for her tender favourite's woe,
But rather, if her eyes could brighter be,
With brighter eyes and slow amenity,
Put her new lips to his, and gave afresh
The life she had so tangled in her mesh:
And as he from one trance was wakening
Into another, she began to sing,
Happy in beauty, life, and love, and every thing,
A song of love, too sweet for earthly lyres,
While, like held breath, the stars drew in their
    panting fires.   300
And then she whisper'd in such trembling tone,
As those who, safe together met alone
For the first time through many anguish'd
    days,
Use other speech than looks; bidding him raise
His drooping head, and clear his soul of doubt,
For that she was a woman, and without
Any more subtle fluid in her veins
Than throbbing blood, and that the self-same
    pains
Inhabited her frail-strung heart as his.
And next she wonder'd how his eyes could
    miss   310

Her face so long in Corinth, where, she said,
She dwelt but half retir'd, and there had led
Days happy as the gold coin could invent
Without the aid of love; yet in content
Till she saw him, as once she pass'd him by,
Where 'gainst a column he leant thoughtfully
At Venus' temple porch, 'mid baskets heap'd
Of amorous herbs and flowers, newly reap'd
Late on that eve, as 'twas the night before
The Adonian feast; whereof she saw no more,
But wept alone those days, for why should she
      adore?   321
Lycius from death awoke into amaze,
To see her still, and singing so sweet lays;
Then from amaze into delight he fell
To hear her whisper woman's lore so well;
And every word she spake entic'd him on
To unperplex'd delight and pleasure known.
Let the mad poets say whate'er they please
Of the sweets of Faeries, Peris, Goddesses,
There is not such a treat among them all, 330
Haunters of cavern, lake, and waterfall,
As a real woman, lineal indeed
From Pyrrha's pebbles or old Adam's seed.
Thus gentle Lamia judg'd, and judg'd aright,
That Lycius could not love in half a fright,
So threw the goddess off, and won his heart
More pleasantly by playing woman's part,
With no more awe than what her beauty gave,
That, while it smote, still guaranteed to save.
Lycius to all made eloquent reply,   340
Marrying to every word a twinborn sigh;
And last, pointing to Corinth, ask'd her sweet,
If 'twas too far that night for her soft feet.
The way was short, for Lamia's eagerness
Made, by a spell, the triple league decrease
To a few paces; not at all surmised
By blinded Lycius, so in her comprized.
They pass'd the city gates, he knew not how,
So noiseless, and he never thought to know.

As men talk in a dream, so Corinth all, 350
Throughout her palaces imperial,
And all her populous streets and temples lewd,
Mutter'd, like tempest in the distance brew'd,
To the wide-spreaded night above her towers.
Men, women, rich and poor, in the cool hours,
Shuffled their sandals o'er the pavement white,
Companion'd or alone; while many a light
Flared, here and there, from wealthy festivals,
And threw their moving shadows on the walls,

Or found them cluster'd in the corniced
      shade   360
Of some arch'd temple door, or dusky colon-
      nade.

Muffling his face, of greeting friends in
      fear,
Her fingers he press'd hard, as one came near
With curl'd gray beard, sharp eyes, and smooth
      bald crown,
Slow-stepp'd, and robed in philosophic gown:
Lycius shrank closer, as they met and past,
Into his mantle, adding wings to haste,
While hurried Lamia trembled: "Ah," said he,
"Why do you shudder, love, so ruefully?
"Why does your tender palm dissolve in
      dew?"—   370
"I'm wearied," said fair Lamia: "tell me who
"Is that old man? I cannot bring to mind
"His features:—Lycius! wherefore did you
      blind
"Yourself from his quick eyes?" Lycius replied,
"'Tis Apollonius sage, my trusty guide
"And good instructor; but to-night he seems
"The ghost of folly haunting my sweet
      dreams."

While yet he spake they had arriv'd before
A pillar'd porch, with lofty portal door.
Where hung a silver lamp, whose phosphor
      glow   380
Reflected in the slabbed steps below,
Mild as a star in water; for so new,
And so unsullied was the marble's hue,
So through the crystal polish, liquid fine,
Ran the dark veins, that none but feet divine
Could e'er have touch'd there. Sounds Æolian
Breath'd from the hinges, as the ample span
Of the wide doors disclos'd a place unknown
Some time to any, but these two alone,
And a few Persian mutes, who that same year
Were seen about the markets: none knew
      where   391
They could inhabit; the most curious
Were foil'd, who watch'd to trace them to their
      house:
And but the flitter-winged verse must tell,
For truth's sake, what woes afterwards befel,
'Twould humour many a heart to leave them
      thus,
Shut from the busy world of more incredulous.

PART II

Love in a hut, with water and a crust,
Is—Love, forgive us!—cinders, ashes, dust;
Love in a palace is perhaps at last
More grievous torment than a hermit's fast:—
That is a doubtful tale from faery land,
Hard for the non-elect to understand.
Had Lycius liv'd to hand his story down,
He might have given the moral a fresh frown,
Or clench'd it quite: but too short was their bliss
To breed distrust and hate, that make the soft voice hiss.   10
Beside, there, nightly, with terrific glare,
Love, jealous grown of so complete a pair,
Hover'd and buzz'd his wings, with fearful roar,
Above the lintel of their chamber door,
And down the passage cast a glow upon the floor.

For all this came a ruin: side by side
They were enthroned, in the even tide,
Upon a couch, near to a curtaining
Whose airy texture, from a golden string,
Floated into the room, and let appear   20
Unveil'd the summer heaven, blue and clear,
Betwixt two marble shafts:—there they reposed,
Where use had made it sweet, with eyelids closed,
Saving a tythe which love still open kept,
That they might see each other while they almost slept;
When from the slope side of a suburb hill,
Deafening the swallow's twitter, came a thrill
Of trumpets—Lycius started—the sounds fled,
But left a thought, a buzzing in his head.
For the first time, since first he harbour'd in   30
That purple-lined palace of sweet sin,
His spirit pass'd beyond its golden bourn
Into the noisy world almost forsworn.
The lady, ever watchful, penetrant,
Saw this with pain, so arguing a want
Of something more, more than her empery
Of joys; and she began to moan and sigh
Because he mused beyond her, knowing well
That but a moment's thought is passion's passing bell.

"Why do you sigh, fair creature?" whisper'd he: 40
"Why do you think?" return'd she tenderly:
"You have deserted me;—where am I now?
"Not in your heart while care weighs on your brow:
"No, no, you have dismiss'd me; and I go
"From your breast houseless: aye, it must be so."
He answer'd, bending to her open eyes,
Where he was mirror'd small in paradise,
"My silver planet, both of eve and morn!
"Why will you plead yourself so sad forlorn,
"While I am striving how to fill my heart   50
"With deeper crimson, and a double smart?
"How to entangle, trammel up and snare
"Your soul in mine, and labyrinth you there
"Like the hid scent in an unbudded rose?
"Aye, a sweet kiss—you see your mighty woes.
"My thoughts! shall I unveil them? Listen then!
"What mortal hath a prize, that other men
"May be confounded and abash'd withal,
"But lets it sometimes pace abroad majestical,
"And triumph, as in thee I should rejoice   60
"Amid the hoarse alarm of Corinth's voice.
"Let my foes choke, and my friends shout afar,
"While through the thronged streets your bridal car
"Wheels round its dazzling spokes."—The lady's cheek
Trembled; she nothing said, but, pale and meek,
Arose and knelt before him, wept a rain
Of sorrows at his words; at last with pain
Beseeching him, the while his hand she wrung,
To change his purpose. He thereat was stung,
Perverse, with stronger fancy to reclaim   70
Her wild and timid nature to his aim:
Besides, for all his love, in self despite,
Against his better self, he took delight
Luxurious in her sorrows, soft and new.
His passion, cruel grown, took on a hue
Fierce and sanguineous as 'twas possible
In one whose brow had no dark veins to swell.
Fine was the mitigated fury, like
Apollo's presence when in act to strike
The serpent—Ha, the serpent! certes, she   80
Was none. She burnt, she lov'd the tyranny,
And, all subdued, consented to the hour
When to the bridal he should lead his paramour.

Whispering in midnight silence, said the youth,
"Sure some sweet name thou hast, though, by
  my truth,
"I have not ask'd it, ever thinking thee
"Not mortal, but of heavenly progeny,
"As still I do. Hast any mortal name,
"Fit appellation for this dazzling frame?
"Or friends or kinsfolk on the citied earth, 90
"To share our marriage feast and nuptial
  mirth?"
"I have no friends," said Lamia, "no, not one;
"My presence in wide Corinth hardly known:
"My parents' bones are in their dusty urns
"Sepulchred, where no kindled incense burns,
"Seeing all their luckless race are dead, save me,
"And I neglect the holy rite for thee.
"Even as you list invite your many guests;
"But if, as now it seems, your vision rests
"With any pleasure on me, do not bid   100
"Old Apollonius—from him keep me hid."
Lycius, perplex'd at words so blind and blank,
Made close inquiry; from whose touch she
  shrank,
Feigning a sleep; and he to the dull shade
Of deep sleep in a moment was betray'd.

      It was the custom then to bring away
The bride from home at blushing shut of day,
Veil'd, in a chariot, heralded along
By strewn flowers, torches, and a marriage
  song,
With other pageants: but this fair unknown 110
Had not a friend. So being left alone,
(Lycius was gone to summon all his kin)
And knowing surely she could never win
His foolish heart from its mad pompousness,
She set herself, high-thoughted, how to dress
The misery in fit magnificence.
She did so, but 'tis doubtful how and whence
Came, and who were her subtle servitors.
About the halls, and to and from the doors,
There was a noise of wings, till in short space
The glowing banquet-room shone with wide-
  arched grace.   121
A haunting music, sole perhaps and lone
Supportress of the faery-roof, made moan
Throughout, as fearful the whole charm might
  fade.
Fresh carved cedar, mimicking a glade
Of palm and plantain, met from either side,
High in the midst, in honour of the bride:

Two palms and then two plantains, and so on,
From either side their stems branch'd one to
  one
All down the aisled place; and beneath all 130
There ran a stream of lamps straight on from
  wall to wall.
So canopied, lay an untasted feast
Teeming with odours. Lamia, regal drest,
Silently paced about, and as she went,
In pale contented sort of discontent,
Mission'd her viewless servants to enrich
The fretted splendour of each nook and
  niche.
Between the tree-stems, marbled plain at first,
Came jasper pannels; then, anon, there burst
Forth creeping imagery of slighter trees, 140
And with the larger wove in small intricacies.
Approving all, she faded at self-will,
And shut the chamber up, close, hush'd and
  still,
Complete and ready for the revels rude,
When dreadful guests would come to spoil
  her solitude.

      The day appear'd, and all the gossip rout.
O senseless Lycius! Madman! wherefore flout
The silent-blessing fate, warm cloister'd hours,
And show to common eyes these secret bow-
  ers?
The herd approach'd; each guest, with busy
  brain,   150
Arriving at the portal, gaz'd amain,
And enter'd marveling: for they knew the
  street,
Remember'd it from childhood all complete
Without a gap, yet ne'er before had seen
That royal porch, that high-built fair de-
  mesne;
So in they hurried all, maz'd, curious and keen:
Save one, who look'd thereon with eye severe,
And with calm-planted steps walk'd in austere;
'Twas Apollonius: something too he laugh'd,
As though some knotty problem, that had
  daft   160
His patient thought, had now begun to thaw,
And solve and melt:—'twas just as he foresaw.

      He met within the murmurous vestibule
His young disciple. "'Tis no common rule,
Lycius," said he, "for uninvited guest
"To force himself upon you, and infest

"With an unbidden presence the bright throng
"Of younger friends; yet must I do this wrong,
"And you forgive me." Lycius blush'd, and led
The old man through the inner doors broad-
 spread;   •   170
With reconciling words and courteous mien
Turning into sweet milk the sophist's spleen.

 Of wealthy lustre was the banquet-room,
Fill'd with pervading brilliance and perfume:
Before each lucid pannel fuming stood
A censer fed with myrrh and spiced wood,
Each by a sacred tripod held aloft,   .
Whose slender feet wide-swerv'd upon the
 soft
Wool-woofed carpets: fifty wreaths of smoke
From fifty censers their light voyage took 180
To the high roof, still mimick'd as they rose
Along the mirror'd walls by twin-clouds odor-
 ous.
Twelve sphered tables, by silk seats insphered,
High as the level of a man's breast rear'd
On libbard's paws, upheld the heavy gold
Of cups and goblets, and the store thrice told
Of Ceres' horn, and, in huge vessels, wine
Come from the gloomy tun with merry shine.
Thus loaded with a feast the tables stood,
Each shrining in the midst the image of a
 God.   190

 When in an antichamber every guest
Had felt the cold full sponge to pleasure
 press'd,
By minist'ring slaves, upon his hands and feet,
And fragrant oils with ceremony meet
Pour'd on his hair, they all mov'd to the
 feast
In white robes, and themselves in order placed
Around the silken couches, wondering
Whence all this mighty cost and blaze of
 wealth could spring.

 Soft went the music the soft air along,
While fluent Greek a vowel'd undersong 200
Kept up among the guests, discoursing low
At first, for scarcely was the wine at flow;
But when the happy vintage touch'd their
 brains,
Louder they talk, and louder come the strains
Of powerful instruments:—the gorgeous dyes,
The space, the splendour of the draperies,

The roof of awful richness, nectarous cheer,
Beautiful slaves, and Lamia's self, appear,
Now, when the wine has done its rosy deed,
And every soul from human trammels freed,
No more so strange; for merry wine, sweet
 wine,   211
Will make Elysian shades not too fair, too
 divine.
Soon was God Bacchus at meridian height;
Flush'd were their cheeks, and bright eyes
 double bright:
Garlands of every green, and every scent
From vales deflower'd, or forest-trees branch-
 rent,
In baskets of bright osier'd gold were brought
High as the handles heap'd, to suit the thought
Of every guest; that each, as he did please,
Might fancy-fit his brows, silk-pillow'd at his
 ease.   220

 What wreath for Lamia? What for Lycius?
What for the sage, old Apollonius?
Upon her aching forehead be there hung
The leaves of willow and of adder's tongue;
And for the youth, quick, let us strip for
 him
The thyrsus, that his watching eyes may swim
Into forgetfulness; and, for the sage,
Let spear-grass and the spiteful thistle wage
War on his temples. Do not all charms fly
At the mere touch of cold philosophy? 230
There was an awful rainbow once in heaven:
We know her woof, her texture; she is given
In the dull catalogue of common things.
Philosophy will clip an Angel's wings,
Conquer all mysteries by rule and line,
Empty the haunted air, and gnomed mine—
Unweave a rainbow, as it erewhile made
The tender-person'd Lamia melt into a shade.

 By her glad Lycius sitting, in chief place,
Scarce saw in all the room another face,   240
Till, checking his love trance, a cup he took
Full brimm'd, and opposite sent forth a look
'Cross the broad table to beseech a glance
From his old teacher's wrinkled countenance,
And pledge him. The bald-head philosopher
Had fix'd his eye, without a twinkle or stir
Full on the alarmed beauty of the bride,
Brow-beating her fair form, and troubling her
 sweet pride.

Lycius then press'd her hand, with devout
  touch,
As pale it lay upon the rosy couch: 250
'Twas icy, and the cold ran through his veins;
Then sudden it grew hot, and all the pains
Of an unnatural heat shot to his heart.
"Lamia, what means this? Wherefore dost
  thou start?
"Know'st thou that man?" Poor Lamia an-
  swer'd not.
He gaz'd into her eyes, and not a jot
Own'd they the lovelorn piteous appeal:
More, more he gaz'd: his human senses reel:
Some hungry spell that loveliness absorbs;
There was no recognition in those orbs.   260
"Lamia!" he cried—and no soft-toned reply.
The many heard, and the loud revelry
Grew hush; the stately music no more breathes;
The myrtle sicken'd in a thousand wreaths.
By faint degrees, voice, lute, and pleasure
  ceased;
A deadly silence step by step increased,
Until it seem'd a horrid presence there,
And not a man but felt the terror in his hair.
"Lamia!" he shriek'd; and nothing but the
  shriek
With its sad echo did the silence break.   270
"Begone, foul dream!" he cried, gazing again
In the bride's face, where now no azure vein
Wander'd on fair-spaced temples; no soft
  ·bloom
Misted the cheek; no passion to illume
The deep-recessed vision:—all was blight;
Lamia, no longer fair, there sat a deadly white.
"Shut, shut those juggling eyes, thou ruthless
  man!
"Turn them aside, wretch! or the righteous
  ban
"Of all the Gods, whose dreadful images
"Here represent their shadowy presences, 280
"May pierce them on the sudden with the
  thorn
"Of painful blindness; leaving thee forlorn,
"In trembling dotage to the feeblest fright
"Of conscience, for their long offended might,
"For all thine impious proud-heart sophistries,
"Unlawful magic, and enticing lies.
"Corinthians! look upon that grey-beard
  wretch!
"Mark how, possess'd, his lashless eyelids
  stretch

"Around his demon eyes! Corinthians, see!
"My sweet bride withers at their potency." 290
"Fool!" said the sophist, in an under-tone
Gruff with contempt; which a death-nighing
  moan   •
From Lycius answer'd, as heart-struck and
  lost,
He sank supine beside the aching ghost.
"Fool! Fool!" repeated he, while his eyes still
Relented not, nor mov'd; "from every ill
"Of life have I preserv'd thee to this day,
"And shall I see thee made a serpent's prey?"
Then Lamia breath'd death breath; the soph-
  ist's eye,   299
Like a sharp spear, went through her utterly,
Keen, cruel, perceant, stinging: she, as well
As her weak hand could any meaning tell,
Motion'd him to be silent; vainly so,
He look'd and look'd again a level—No!
"A serpent!" echoed he; no sooner said,
Than with a frightful scream she vanished:
And Lycius' arms were empty of delight,
As were his limbs of life, from that same night.
On the high couch he lay!—his friends came
  round—
Supported him—no pulse, or breath they
  found,   310
And, in its marriage robe, the heavy body
  wound.

1819

HYPERION

A FRAGMENT

BOOK I

DEEP in the shady sadness of a vale
Far sunken from the healthy breath of morn,
Far from the fiery noon, and eve's one star,
Sat gray-hair'd Saturn, quiet as a stone,
Still as the silence round about his lair;
Forest on forest hung about his head
Like cloud on cloud. No stir of air was there,
Not so much life as on a summer's day
Robs not one light seed from the feather'd
  grass,
But where the dead leaf fell, there did it rest. 10
A stream went voiceless by, still deadened
  more
By reason of his fallen divinity
Spreading a shade: the Naiad 'mid her reeds
Press'd her cold finger closer to her lips.

Along the margin-sand large foot-marks
   went,
No further than to where his feet had stray'd,
And slept there since. Upon the sodden ground
His old right hand lay nerveless, listless, dead,
Unsceptred; and his realmless eyes were closed;
While his bow'd head seem'd list'ning to the
   Earth,   20
His ancient mother, for some comfort yet.

It seem'd no force could wake him from his
   place;
But there came one, who with a kindred hand
Touch'd his wide shoulders, after bending low
With reverence, though to one who knew it
   not.
She was a Goddess of the infant world;
By her in stature the tall Amazon
Had stood a pigmy's height: she would have
   ta'en
Achilles by the hair and bent his neck;
Or with a finger stay'd Ixion's wheel.   30
Her face was large as that of Memphian sphinx,
Pedestal'd haply in a palace court,
When sages look'd to Egypt for their lore.
But oh! how unlike marble was that face:
How beautiful, if sorrow had not made
Sorrow more beautiful than Beauty's self.
There was a listening fear in her regard,
As if calamity had but begun;
As if the vanward clouds of evil days
Had spent their malice, and the sullen rear   40
Was with its stored thunder labouring up.
One hand she press'd upon that aching spot
Where beats the human heart, as if just there,
Though an immortal, she felt cruel pain:
The other upon Saturn's bended neck
She laid, and to the level of his ear
Leaning with parted lips, some words she spake
In solemn tenour and deep organ tone:
Some mourning words, which in our feeble
   tongue
Would come in these like accents; O how
   frail   50
To that large utterance of the early Gods!
"Saturn, look up!—though wherefore, poor
   old King?
"I have no comfort for thee, no not one:
"I cannot say, 'O wherefore sleepest thou?'
"For heaven is parted from thee, and the earth
"Knows thee not, thus afflicted, for a God;

"And ocean too, with all its solemn noise,
"Has from thy sceptre pass'd; and all the air
"Is emptied of thine hoary majesty.
"Thy thunder, conscious of the new com-
   mand,   60
"Rumbles reluctant o'er our fallen house;
"And thy sharp lightning in unpractis'd hands
"Scorches and burns our once serene domain.
"O aching time! O moments big as years!
"All as ye pass swell out the monstrous truth,
"And press it so upon our weary griefs
"That unbelief has not a space to breathe.
"Saturn, sleep on:—O thoughtless, why did I
"Thus violate thy slumbrous solitude?
"Why should I ope thy melancholy eyes? 70
"Saturn, sleep on! while at thy feet I weep."

As when, upon a tranced summer-night,
Those green-rob'd senators of mighty woods,
Tall oaks, branch-charmed by the earnest stars,
Dream, and so dream all night without a stir,
Save from one gradual solitary gust
Which comes upon the silence, and dies off,
As if the ebbing air had but one wave;
So came these words and went; the while in
   tears
She touch'd her fair large forehead to the
   ground,   80
Just where her falling hair might be outspread
A soft and silken mat for Saturn's feet.
One moon, with alteration slow, had shed
Her silver seasons four upon the night,
And still these two were postured motionless,
Like natural sculpture in cathedral cavern;
The frozen God still couchant on the earth,
And the sad Goddess weeping at his feet:
Until at length old Saturn lifted up
His faded eyes, and saw his kingdom gone, 90
And all the gloom and sorrow of the place,
And that fair kneeling Goddess; and then spake,
As with a palsied tongue, and while his beard
Shook horrid with such aspen-malady:
"O tender spouse of gold Hyperion,
"Thea, I feel thee ere I see thy face;
"Look up, and let me see our doom in it;
"Look up, and tell me if this feeble shape
"Is Saturn's; tell me, if thou hear'st the voice
"Of Saturn; tell me, if this wrinkling brow, 100
"Naked and bare of its great diadem,
"Peers like the front of Saturn. Who had
   power

"To make me desolate? whence came the strength?

"How was it nurtur'd to such bursting forth,

"While Fate seem'd strangled in my nervous grasp?

"But it is so; and I am smother'd up,

"And buried from all godlike exercise

"Of influence benign on planets pale,

"Of admonitions to the winds and seas,

"Of peaceful sway above man's harvesting, 110

"And all those acts which Deity supreme

"Doth ease its heart of love in.—I am gone

"Away from my own bosom: I have left

"My strong identity, my real self,

"Somewhere between the throne, and where I sit

"Here on this spot of earth. Search, Thea, search!

"Open thine eyes eterne, and sphere them round

"Upon all space: space starr'd, and lorn of light;

"Space region'd with life-air; and barren void;

"Spaces of fire, and all the yawn of hell.— 120

"Search, Thea, search! and tell me, if thou seest

"A certain shape or shadow, making way

"With wings or chariot fierce to repossess

"A heaven he lost erewhile: it must—it must

"Be of ripe progress—Saturn must be King.

"Yes, there must be a golden victory;

"There must be Gods thrown down, and trumpets blown

"Of triumph calm, and hymns of festival

"Upon the gold clouds metropolitan,

"Voices of soft proclaim, and silver stir   130

"Of strings in hollow shells; and there shall be

"Beautiful things made new, for the surprise

"Of the sky-children; I will give command:

"Thea! Thea! Thea! where is Saturn?"

This passion lifted him upon his feet,
And made his hands to struggle in the air,
His Druid locks to shake and ooze with sweat,
His eyes to fever out, his voice to cease.
He stood, and heard not Thea's sobbing deep;
A little time, and then again he snatch'd   140
Utterance thus.—"But cannot I create?

"Cannot I form? Cannot I fashion forth

"Another world, another universe,

"To overbear and crumble this to naught?

"Where is another chaos? Where?"—That word
Found way unto Olympus, and made quake
The rebel three.—Thea was startled up,
And in her bearing was a sort of hope,
As thus she quick-voic'd spake, yet full of awe.

"This cheers our fallen house: come to our friends,   150

"O Saturn! come away, and give them heart;

"I know the covert, for thence came I hither."

Thus brief; then with beseeching eyes she went
With backward footing through the shade a space:
He follow'd, and she turn'd to lead the way
Through aged boughs, that yielded like the mist
Which eagles cleave upmounting from their nest.

Meanwhile in other realms big tears were shed,
More sorrow like to this, and such like woe,
Too huge for mortal tongue or pen of scribe:
The Titans fierce, self-hid, or prison-bound,
Groan'd for the old allegiance once more, 162
And listen'd in sharp pain for Saturn's voice.
But one of the whole mammoth-brood still kept
His sov'reignty, and rule, and majesty;—
Blazing Hyperion on his orbed fire
Still sat, still snuff'd the incense, teeming up
From man to the sun's God; yet unsecure:
For as among us mortals omens drear
Fright and perplex, so also shuddered he— 170
Not at dog's howl, or gloom-bird's hated screech,
Or the familiar visiting of one
Upon the first toll of his passing-bell,
Or prophesyings of the midnight lamp;
But horrors, portion'd to a giant nerve,
Oft made Hyperion ache. His palace bright
Bastion'd with pyramids of glowing gold,
And touch'd with shade of bronzed obelisks,
Glar'd a blood-red through all its thousand courts,
Arches, and domes, and fiery galleries;   180
And all its curtains of Aurorian clouds
Flush'd angerly: while sometimes eagles' wings,
Unseen before by Gods or wondering men,

Darken'd the place; and neighing steeds were
    heard,
Not heard before by Gods or wondering men.
Also, when he would taste the spicy wreaths
Of incense, breath'd aloft from sacred hills,
Instead of sweets, his ample palate took
Savour of poisonous brass and metal sick:
And so, when harbour'd in the sleepy west, 190
After the full completion of fair day,—
For rest divine upon exalted couch
And slumber in the arms of melody
He pac'd away the pleasant hours of ease
With stride colossal, on from hall to hall;
While far within each aisle and deep recess,
His winged minions in close clusters stood,
Amaz'd and full of fear; like anxious men
Who on wide plains gather in panting troops,
When earthquakes jar their battlements and
    towers.   200
Even now, while Saturn, rous'd from icy
    trance,
Went step for step with Thea through the
    woods,
Hyperion, leaving twilight in the rear,
Came slope upon the threshold of the west;
Then, as was wont, his palace-door flew ope
In smoothest silence, save what solemn tubes,
Blown by the serious Zephyrs, gave of sweet
And wandering sounds, slow-breathed melo-
    dies;
And like a rose in vermeil tint and shape,
In fragrance soft, and coolness to the eye, 210
That inlet to severe magnificence
Stood full blown, for the God to enter in.

    He enter'd, but he enter'd full of wrath;
His flaming robes stream'd out beyond his
    heels,
And gave a roar, as if of earthly fire,
That scar'd away the meek ethereal Hours
And made their dove-wings tremble. On he
    flared,
From stately nave to nave, from vault to vault,
Through bowers of fragrant and enwreathed
    light,
And diamond-paved lustrous long arcades, 220
Until he reach'd the great main cupola;
There standing fierce beneath, he stamped his
    foot,
And from the basements deep to the high
    towers

Jarr'd his own golden region; and before
The quavering thunder thereupon had ceas'd,
His voice leapt out, despite of godlike curb,
To this result: "O dreams of day and night!
"O monstrous forms! O effigies of pain!
"O spectres busy in a cold, cold gloom!
"O lank-ear'd Phantoms of black-weeded
    pools!   230
"Why do I know ye? why have I seen ye? why
"Is my eternal essence thus distraught
"To see and to behold these horrors new?
"Saturn is fallen, am I too to fall?
"Am I to leave this haven of my rest,
"This cradle of my glory, this soft clime,
"This calm luxuriance of blissful light,
"These crystalline pavilions, and pure fanes,
"Of all my lucent empire? It is left
"Deserted, void, nor any haunt of mine. 240
"The blaze, the splendour, and the symmetry,
"I cannot see—but darkness, death and dark-
    ness.
"Even here, into my centre of repose,
"The shady visions come to domineer,
"Insult, and blind, and stifle up my pomp.—
"Fall!—No, by Tellus and her briny robes!
"Over the fiery frontier of my realms
"I will advance a terrible right arm
"Shall scare the infant thunderer, rebel Jove,
"And bid old Saturn take his throne again."—
He spake, and ceas'd, the while a heavier
    threat   251
Held struggle with his throat but came not
    forth;
For as in theatres of crowded men
Hubbub increases more they call out "Hush!"
So at Hyperion's words the Phantoms pale
Bestirr'd themselves, thrice horrible and cold;
And from the mirror'd level where he stood
A mist arose, as from a scummy marsh.
At this, through all his bulk an agony
Crept gradual, from the feet unto the crown,
Like a lithe serpent vast and muscular 261
Making slow way, with head and neck con-
    vuls'd
From over-strained might. Releas'd, he fled
To the eastern gates, and full six dewy hours
Before the dawn in season due should blush,
He breath'd fierce breath against the sleepy
    portals,
Clear'd them of heavy vapours, burst them
    wide

Suddenly on the ocean's chilly streams.
The planet orb of fire, whereon he rode
Each day from east to west the heavens
    through,   270
Spun round in sable curtaining of clouds;
Not therefore veiled quite, blindfold, and hid,
But ever and anon the glancing spheres,
Circles, and arcs, and broad-belting colure,
Glow'd through, and wrought upon the muf-
    fling dark
Sweet-shaped lightnings from the nadir deep
Up to the zenith,—hieroglyphics old
Which sages and keen-eyed astrologers
Then living on the earth, with labouring
    thought
Won from the gaze of many centuries: 280
Now lost, save what we find on remnants huge
Of stone, or marble swart; their import gone,
Their wisdom long since fled.—Two wings
    this orb
Possess'd for glory, two fair argent wings,
Ever exalted at the God's approach:
And now, from forth the gloom their plumes
    immense
Rose, one by one, till all outspreaded were;
While still the dazzling globe maintain'd
    eclipse,
Awaiting for Hyperion's command.
Fain would he have commanded, fain took
    throne   290
And bid the day begin, if but for change.
He might not:—No, though a primeval God:
The sacred seasons might not be disturb'd.
Therefore the operations of the dawn
Stay'd in their birth, even as here 'tis told.
Those silver wings expanded sisterly,
Eager to sail their orb; the porches wide
Open'd upon the dusk demesnes of night;
And the bright Titan, phrenzied with new woes,
Unus'd to bend, by hard compulsion bent 300
His spirit to the sorrow of the time;
And all along a dismal rack of clouds,
Upon the boundaries of day and night,
He stretch'd himself in grief and radiance faint.
There as he lay, the Heaven with its stars
Look'd down on him with pity, and the voice
Of Cœlus, from the universal space,
Thus whisper'd low and solemn in his ear.
"O brightest of my children dear, earth-born
"And sky-engendered, Son of Mysteries 310
"All unrevealed even to the powers

"Which met at thy creating; at whose joys
"And palpitations sweet, and pleasures soft,
"I, Cœlus, wonder, how they came and
    whence;
"And at the fruits thereof what shapes they be,
"Distinct, and visible; symbols divine,
"Manifestations of that beauteous life
"Diffus'd unseen throughout eternal space:
"Of these new-form'd art thou, oh brightest
    child!   319
"Of these, thy brethren and the Goddesses!
"There is sad feud among ye, and rebellion
"Of son against his sire. I saw him fall,
"I saw my first-born tumbled from his throne!
"To me his arms were spread, to me his voice
"Found way from forth the thunders round
    his head!
"Pale wox I, and in vapours hid my face.
"Art thou, too, near such doom? vague fear
    there is:
"For I have seen my sons most unlike Gods.
"Divine ye were created, and divine
"In sad demeanour, solemn, undisturb'd, 330
"Unruffled, like high Gods, ye liv'd and ruled:
"Now I behold in you fear, hope, and wrath;
"Actions of rage and passion; even as
"I see them, on the mortal world beneath,
"In men who die.—This is the grief, O Son!
"Sad sign of ruin, sudden dismay, and fall!
"Yet do thou strive; as thou art capable,
"As thou canst move about, an evident God;
"And canst oppose to each malignant hour
"Ethereal presence:—I am but a voice; 340
"My life is but the life of winds and tides,
"No more than winds and tides can I avail:—
"But thou canst.—Be thou therefore in the van
"Of circumstance; yea, seize the arrow's barb
"Before the tense string murmur.—To the
    earth!
"For there thou wilt find Saturn, and his woes.
"Meantime I will keep watch on thy bright sun,
"And of thy seasons be a careful nurse."—
Ere half this region-whisper had come down,
Hyperion arose, and on the stars 350
Lifted his curved lids, and kept them wide
Until it ceased; and still he kept them wide:
And still they were the same bright, patient stars.
Then with a slow incline of his broad breast,
Like to a diver in the pearly seas,
Forward he stoop'd over the airy shore,
And plung'd all noiseless into the deep night.

BOOK II

Just at the self-same beat of Time's wide
 wings
Hyperion slid into the rustled air,
And Saturn gain'd with Thea that sad place
Where Cybele and the bruised Titans mourn'd.
It was a den where no insulting light
Could glimmer on their tears; where their own
 groans
They felt, but heard not, for the solid roar
Of thunderous waterfalls and torrents hoarse,
Pouring a constant bulk, uncertain where.
Crag jutting forth to crag, and rocks that
 seem'd   10
Ever as if just rising from a sleep,
Forehead to forehead held their monstrous
 horns;
And thus in thousand hugest phantasies
Made a fit roofing to this nest of woe.
Instead of thrones, hard flint they sat upon,
Couches of rugged stone, and slaty ridge
Stubborn'd with iron. All were not assembled:
Some chain'd in torture, and some wandering.
Cœus, and Gyges, and Briareüs,
Typhon, and Dolor, and Porphyrion, 20
With many more, the brawniest in assault,
Were pent in regions of laborious breath;
Dungeon'd in opaque element, to keep
Their clenched teeth still clench'd, and all their
 limbs
Lock'd up like veins of metal, crampt and
 screw'd;
Without a motion, save of their big hearts
Heaving in pain, and horribly convuls'd
With sanguine feverous boiling gurge of pulse,
Mnemosyne was straying in the world;
Far from her moon had Phœbe wandered; 30
And many else were free to roam abroad,
But for the main, here found they covert
 drear.
Scarce images of life, one here, one there,
Lay vast and edgeways; like a dismal cirque
Of Druid stones, upon a forlorn moor,
When the chill rain begins at shut of eve,
In dull November, and their chancel vault,
The Heaven itself, is blinded throughout
 night.
Each one kept shroud, nor to his neighbour
 gave
Or word, or look, or action of despair. 40

Creüs was one; his ponderous iron mace
Lay by him, and a shatter'd rib of rock
Told of his rage, ere he thus sank and pined.
Iäpetus another; in his grasp,
A serpent's plashy neck; its barbed tongue
Squeez'd from the gorge, and all its uncurl'd
 length
Dead; and because the creature could not spit
Its poison in the eyes of conquering Jove.
Next Cottus: prone he lay, chin uppermost,
As though in pain; for still upon the flint 50
He ground severe his skull, with open mouth
And eyes at horrid working. Nearest him
Asia, born of most enormous Caf,
Who cost her mother Tellus keener pangs,
Though feminine, than any of her sons:
More thought than woe was in her dusky face,
For she was prophesying of her glory;
And in her wide imagination stood
Palm-shaded temples, and high rival fanes,
By Oxus or in Ganges' sacred isles. 60
Even as Hope upon her anchor leans,
So leant she, not so fair, upon a tusk
Shed from the broadest of her elephants.
Above her, on a crag's uneasy shelve,
Upon his elbow rais'd, all prostrate else,
Shadow'd Enceladus; once tame and mild
As grazing on unworried in the meads;
Now tiger-passion'd, lion-thoughted, wroth,
He meditated, plotted, and even now
Was hurling mountains in that second war, 70
Not long delay'd, that scar'd the younger Gods
To hide themselves in forms of beast and bird.
Not far hence Atlas; and beside him prone
Phorcus, the sire of Gorgons. Neighbour'd
 close
Oceanus, and Tethys, in whose lap
Sobb'd Clymene among her tangled hair.
In midst of all lay Themis, at the feet
Of Ops the queen all clouded round from sight;
No shape distinguishable, more than when
Thick night confounds the pine-tops with the
 clouds: 80
And many else whose names may not be told.
For when the Muse's wings are air-ward
 spread,
Who shall delay her flight? And she must
 chaunt
Of Saturn, and his guide, who now had
 climb'd
With damp and slippery footing from a depth

More horrid still. Above a sombre cliff
Their heads appear'd, and up their stature
　　grew
Till on the level height their steps found ease:
Then Thea spread abroad her trembling arms
Upon the precincts of this nest of pain,　　90
And sidelong fix'd her eye on Saturn's face:
There saw she direst strife; the supreme God
At war with all the frailty of grief,
Of rage, of fear, anxiety, revenge,
Remorse, spleen, hope, but most of all
　　despair.
Against these plagues he strove in vain; for
　　Fate
Had pour'd a mortal oil upon his head,
A disanointing poison: so that Thea,
Affrighted, kept her still, and let him pass
First onwards in, among the fallen tribe.　100

　　As with us mortal men, the laden heart
Is persecuted more, and fever'd more,
When it is nighing to the mournful house
Where other hearts are sick of the same
　　bruise;
So Saturn, as he walk'd into the midst,
Felt faint, and would have sunk among the
　　rest,
But that he met Enceladus's eye,
Whose mightiness, and awe of him, at once
Came like an inspiration; and he shouted,
"Titans, behold your God!" at which some
　　groan'd;　　　　　　　　　　110
Some started on their feet; some also shouted;
Some wept, some wail'd, all bow'd with rever-
　　ence:
And Ops, uplifting her black folded veil,
Show'd her pale cheeks, and all her forehead
　　wan,
Her eye-brows thin and jet, and hollow eyes.
There is a roaring in the bleak-grown pines
When Winter lifts his voice; there is a noise
Among immortals when a God gives sign,
With hushing finger, how he means to load
His tongue with the full weight of utterless
　　thought,　　　　　　　　　　120
With thunder, and with music, and with pomp:
Such noise is like the roar of bleak-grown
　　pinés:
Which, when it ceases in this mountain'd
　　world,
No other sound succeeds; but ceasing here,

Among these fallen, Saturn's voice therefrom
Grew up like organ, that begins anew
Its strain, when other harmonies, stopt short,
Leave the dinn'd air vibrating silverly.
Thus grew it up—"Not in my own sad breast,
"Which is its own great judge and searcher
　　out,　　　　　　　　　　　　130
"Can I find reason why ye should be thus:
"Not in the legends of the first of days,
"Studied from that old spirit-leaved book
"Which starry Uranus with finger bright
"Sav'd from the shores of darkness, when the
　　waves
"Low-ebb'd still hid it up in shallow gloom;—
"And the which book ye know I ever kept
"For my firm-based footstool:—Ah, infirm!
"Not there, nor in sign, symbol, or portent
"Of element, earth, water, air, and fire,—140
"At war, at peace, or inter-quarreling
"One against one, or two, or three, or all
"Each several one against the other three,
"As fire with air loud warring when rain-floods
"Drown both, and press them both against
　　earth's face,
"Where, finding sulphur, a quadruple wrath
"Unhinges the poor world;—not in that strife,
"Wherefrom I take strange lore, and read it
　　deep,
"Can I find reason why ye should be thus:
"No, no-where can unriddle, though I search,
"And pore on Nature's universal scroll　　151
"Even to swooning, why ye, Divinities,
"The first-born of all shap'd and palpable
　　Gods,
"Should cower beneath what, in comparison,
"Is untremendous might. Yet ye are here,
"O'erwhelm'd, and spurn'd, and batter'd, ye
　　are here!
"O Titans, shall I say, 'Arise!'—Ye groan:
"Shall I say 'Crouch!'—Ye groan. What can I
　　then?
"O Heaven wide! O unseen parent dear!
"What can I? Tell me, all ye brethren Gods,160
"How we can war, how engine our great
　　wrath!
"O speak your counsel now, for Saturn's ear
"Is all a-hunger'd. Thou, Oceanus,
"Ponderest high and deep; and in thy face
"I see, astonied, that severe content
"Which comes of thought and musing: give
　　us help!"

So ended Saturn; and the God of the Sea,
Sophist and sage, from no Athenian grove,
But cogitation in his watery shades,
Arose, with locks not oozy, and began,   170
In murmurs, which his first-endeavouring
        tongue
Caught infant-like from the far-foamed sands.
"O ye, whom wrath consumes! who, passion-
        strung,
"Writhe at defeat, and nurse your agonies!
"Shut up your senses, stifle up your ears,
"My voice is not a bellows unto ire.
"Yet listen, ye who will, whilst I bring proof
"How ye, perforce, must be content to stoop:
"And in the proof much comfort will I give,
"If ye will take that comfort in its truth.   180
"We fall by course of Nature's law, not force
"Of thunder, or of Jove. Great Saturn, thou
"Hast sifted well the atom-universe;
"But for this reason, that thou art the King,
"And only blind from sheer supremacy,
"One avenue was shaded from thine eyes,
"Through which I wandered to eternal truth.
"And first, as thou wast not the first of powers,
"So art thou not the last; it cannot be:
"Thou art not the beginning nor the end. 190
"From chaos and parental darkness came
"Light, the first fruits of that intestine broil,
"That sullen ferment, which for wondrous
        ends
"Was ripening in itself. The ripe hour came,
"And with it light, and light, engendering
"Upon its own producer, forthwith touch'd
"The whole enormous matter into life.
"Upon that very hour, our parentage,
"The Heavens and the Earth, were manifest:
"Then thou first born, and we the giant race,
"Found ourselves ruling new and beauteous
        realms.   201
"Now comes the pain of truth, to whom 'tis
        pain;
"O folly! for to bear all naked truths,
"And to envisage circumstance, all calm,
"That is the top of sovereignty. Mark well!
"As Heaven and Earth are fairer, fairer far
"Than Chaos and blank Darkness, though
        once chiefs;
"And as we show beyond that Heaven and
        Earth
"In form and shape compact and beautiful,
"In will, in action free, companionship,   210

"And thousand other signs of purer life;
"So on our heels a fresh perfection treads,
"A power more strong in beauty, born of us
"And fated to excel us, as we pass
"In glory that old Darkness: nor are we
"Thereby more conquer'd, than by us the rule
"Of shapeless Chaos. Say, doth the dull soil
"Quarrel with the proud forests it hath fed,
"And feedeth still, more comely than itself?
"Can it deny the chiefdom of green groves? 220
"Or shall the tree be envious of the dove
"Because it cooeth, and hath snowy wings
"To wander wherewithal and find its joys?
"We are such forest-trees, and our fair boughs
"Have bred forth, not pale solitary doves,
"But eagles golden-feather'd, who do tower
"Above us in their beauty, and must reign
"In right thereof; for 'tis the eternal law
"That first in beauty should be first in might:
"Yea, by that law, another race may drive 230
"Our conquerors to mourn as we do now.
"Have ye beheld the young God of the Seas,
"My dispossessor? Have ye seen his face?
"Have ye beheld his chariot, foam'd along
"By noble winged creatures he hath made?
"I saw him on the calmed waters scud,
"With such a glow of beauty in his eyes,
"That it enforc'd me to bid sad farewell
"To all my empire: farewell sad I took,   239
"And hither came, to see how dolorous fate
"Had wrought upon ye; and how I might best
"Give consolation in this woe extreme.
"Receive the truth, and let it be your balm."

    Whether through poz'd conviction, or dis-
        dain,
They guarded silence, when Oceanus
Left murmuring, what deepest thought can tell?
But so it was, none answer'd for a space,
Save one whom none regarded, Clymene;
And yet she answer'd not, only complain'd,
With hectic lips, and eyes up-looking mild, 250
Thus wording timidly among the fierce:
"O Father, I am here the simplest voice,
"And all my knowledge is that joy is gone,
"And this thing woe crept in among our hearts,
"There to remain for ever, as I fear:
"I would not bode of evil, if I thought
"So weak a creature could turn off the help
"Which by just right should come of mighty
        Gods;

"Yet let me tell my sorrow, let me tell
"Of what I heard, and how it made me
   weep, 260
"And know that we had parted from all hope.
"I stood upon a shore, a pleasant shore,
"Where a sweet clime was breathed from a
   land
"Of fragrance, quietness, and trees, and
   flowers.
"Full of calm joy it was, as I of grief;
"Too full of joy and soft delicious warmth;
"So that I felt a movement in my heart
"To chide, and to reproach that solitude
"With songs of misery, music of our woes;
"And sat me down, and took a mouthed
   shell 270
"And murmur'd into it, and made melody—
"O melody no more! for while I sang,
"And with poor skill let pass into the breeze
"The dull shell's echo, from a bowery strand
"Just opposite, an island of the sea,
"There came enchantment with the shifting
   wind,
"That did both drown and keep alive my
   ears.
"I threw my shell away upon the sand,
"And a wave fill'd it, as my sense was fill'd
"With that new blissful golden melody. 280
"A living death was in each gush of sounds,
"Each family of rapturous hurried notes,
"That fell, one after one, yet all at once,
"Like pearl beads dropping sudden from their
   string:
"And then another, then another strain,
"Each like a dove leaving its olive perch,
"With music wing'd instead of silent plumes,
"To hover round my head, and make me sick
"Of joy and grief at once. Grief overcame,
"And I was stopping up my frantic ears, 290
"When, past all hindrance of my trembling
   hands,
"A voice came sweeter, sweeter than all tune,
"And still it cried, 'Apollo! young Apollo!
"'The morning-bright Apollo! young Apollo!'
"I fled, it follow'd me, and cried 'Apollo!'
"O Father, and O Brethren, had ye felt
"Those pains of mine; O Saturn, hadst thou
   felt,
"Ye would not call this too indulged tongue
"Presumptuous, in thus venturing to be
   heard."

So far her voice flow'd on, like timorous
   brook 300
That, lingering along a pebbled coast,
Doth fear to meet the sea: but sea it met,
And shudder'd; for the overwhelming voice
Of huge Enceladus swallow'd it in wrath:
The ponderous syllables, like sullen waves
In the half-glutted hollows of reef-rocks,
Came booming thus, while still upon his arm
He lean'd; not rising, from supreme contempt.
"Or shall we listen to the over-wise,
"Or to the over-foolish, Giant-Gods? 310
"Not thunderbolt on thunderbolt, till all
"That rebel Jove's whole armoury were spent,
"Not world on world upon these shoulders
   piled,
"Could agonize me more than baby-words
"In midst of this dethronement horrible.
"Speak! roar! shout! yell! ye sleepy Titans all.
"Do ye forget the blows, the buffets vile?
"Are ye not smitten by a youngling arm?
"Dost thou forget, sham Monarch of the
   Waves,
"Thy scalding in the seas? What, have I
   rous'd 320
"Your spleens with so few simple words as
   these?
"O joy! for now I see ye are not lost:
"O joy! for now I see a thousand eyes
"Wide-glaring for revenge!"—As this he said,
He lifted up his stature vast, and stood,
Still without intermission speaking thus:
"Now ye are flames, I'll tell you how to burn,
"And purge the ether of our enemies;
"How to feed fierce the crooked stings of
   fire,
"And singe away the swollen clouds of
   Jove, 330
"Stifling that puny essence in its tent.
"O let him feel the evil he hath done;
"For though I scorn Oceanus's lore,
"Much pain have I for more than loss of
   realms:
"The days of peace and slumberous calm are
   fled;
"Those days, all innocent of scathing war,
"When all the fair Existences of heaven
"Came open-eyed to guess what we would
   speak:—
"That was before our brows were taught to
   frown,

"Before our lips knew else but solemn
    sounds;   340
"That was before we knew the winged thing,
"Victory, might be lost, or might be won.
"And be ye mindful that Hyperion,
"Our brightest brother, still is undisgraced—
"Hyperion, lo! his radiance is here!"

All eyes were on Enceladus's face,
And they beheld, while still Hyperion's name
Flew from his lips up to the vaulted rocks,
A pallid gleam across his features stern:
Not savage, for he saw full many a God   350
Wroth as himself. He look'd upon them all,
And in each face he saw a gleam of light,
But splendider in Saturn's, whose hoar locks
Shone like the bubbling foam about a keel
When the prow sweeps into a midnight cove.
In pale and silver silence they remain'd,
Till suddenly a splendour, like the morn,
Pervaded all the beetling gloomy steeps,
All the sad spaces of oblivion,
And every gulf, and every chasm old,   360
And every height, and every sullen depth,
Voiceless, or hoarse with loud tormented
    streams:
And all the everlasting cataracts,
And all the headlong torrents far and near,
Mantled before in darkness and huge shade,
Now saw the light and made it terrible.
It was Hyperion:—a granite peak
His bright feet touch'd, and there he stay'd to
    view
The misery his brilliance had betray'd
To the most hateful seeing of itself.   370
Golden his hair of short Numidian curl,
Regal his shape majestic, a vast shade
In midst of his own brightness, like the bulk
Of Memnon's image at the set of sun
To one who travels from the dusking East:
Sighs, too, as mournful as that Memnon's harp
He utter'd, while his hands contemplative
He press'd together, and in silence stood.
Despondence seiz'd again the fallen Gods
At sight of the dejected King of Day,   380
And many hid their faces from the light:
But fierce Enceladus sent forth his eyes
Among the brotherhood; and, at their glare,
Uprose Iäpetus, and Creüs, too,
And Phorcus, sea-born, and together strode
To where he towered on his eminence.

There those four shouted forth old Saturn's
    name;
Hyperion from the peak loud answered,
    "Saturn!"
Saturn sat near the Mother of the Gods,
In whose face was no joy, though all the
    Gods   390
Gave from their hollow throats the name of
    "Saturn!"

BOOK III

THUS in alternate uproar and sad peace,
Amazed were those Titans utterly.
O leave them, Muse! O leave them to their
    woes;
For thou art weak to sing such tumults dire:
A solitary sorrow best befits
Thy lips, and antheming a lonely grief.
Leave them, O Muse! for thou anon wilt find
Many a fallen old Divinity
Wandering in vain about bewildered shores.
Meantime touch piously the Delphic harp, 10
And not a wind of heaven but will breathe
In aid soft warble from the Dorian flute;
For lo! 'tis for the Father of all verse.
Flush every thing that hath a vermeil hue,
Let the rose glow intense and warm the air,
And let the clouds of even and of morn
Float in voluptuous fleeces o'er the hills;
Let the red wine within the goblet boil,   18
Cold as a bubbling well; let faint-lipp'd shells,
On sands, or in great deeps, vermilion turn
Through all their labyrinths; and let the maid
Blush keenly, as with some warm kiss sur-
    pris'd.
Chief isle of the embowered Cyclades,
Rejoice, O Delos, with thine olives green,
And poplars, and lawn-shading palms, and
    beech,
In which the Zephyr breathes the loudest
    song,
And hazels thick, dark-stemm'd beneath the
    shade:
Apollo is once more the golden theme!
Where was he, when the Giant of the Sun
Stood bright, amid the sorrow of his peers? 30
Together had he left his mother fair
And his twin-sister sleeping in their bower,
And in the morning twilight wandered forth
Beside the osiers of a rivulet,
Full ankle-deep in lilies of the vale.

The nightingale had ceas'd, and a few stars
Were lingering in the heavens, while the
   thrush
Began calm-throated. Throughout all the isle
There was no covert, no retired cave   39
Unhaunted by the murmurous noise of waves,
Though scarcely heard in many a green recess.
He listen'd, and he wept, and his bright tears
Went trickling down the golden bow he held.
Thus with half-shut suffused eyes he stood,
While from beneath some cumbrous boughs
   hard by
With solemn step an awful Goddess came,
And there was purport in her looks for him,
Which he with eager guess began to read
Perplex'd, the while melodiously he said:
"How cam'st thou over the unfooted sea? 50
"Or hath that antique mien and robed form
"Mov'd in these vales invisible till now?
"Sure I have heard those vestments sweeping
   o'er
"The fallen leaves, when I have sat alone
"In cool mid-forest. Surely I have traced
"The rustle of those ample skirts about
"These grassy solitudes, and seen the flowers
"Lift up their heads, as still the whisper pass'd.
"Goddess! I have beheld those eyes before,
"And their eternal calm, and all that face, 60
"Or I have dream'd."—"Yes," said the su-
   preme shape,
"Thou hast dream'd of me; and awaking up
"Didst find a lyre all golden by thy side,
"Whose strings touch'd by thy fingers, all the
   vast
"Unwearied ear of the whole universe
"Listen'd in pain and pleasure at the birth
"Of such new tuneful wonder. Is't not strange
"That thou shouldst weep, so gifted? Tell me,
   youth,
"What sorrow thou canst feel; for I am sad
"When thou dost shed a tear: explain thy
   griefs   70
"To one who in this lonely isle hath been
"The watcher of thy sleep and hours of life,
"From the young day when first thy infant
   hand
"Pluck'd witless the weak flowers, till thine
   arm
"Could bend that bow heroic to all times.
"Show thy heart's secret to an ancient Power
"Who hath forsaken old and sacred thrones

"For prophecies of thee, and for the sake
"Of loveliness new born."—Apollo then,
With sudden scrutiny and gloomless eyes, 80
Thus answer'd, while his white melodious
   throat
Throbb'd with the syllables.—"Mnemosyne!
"Thy name is on my tongue, I know not how;
"Why should I tell thee what thou so well
   seest?
"Why should I strive to show what from thy
   lips
"Would come no mystery? For me, dark,
   dark,
"And painful vile oblivion seals my eyes:
"I strive to search wherefore I am so sad,
"Until a melancholy numbs my limbs;
"And then upon the grass I sit, and moan, 90
"Like one who once had wings.—O why
   should I
"Feel curs'd and thwarted, when the liegeless
   air
"Yields to my step aspirant? why should I
"Spurn the green turf as hateful to my feet?
"Goddess benign, point forth some unknown
   thing:
"Are there not other regions than this isle?
"What are the stars? There is the sun, the sun!
"And the most patient brilliance of the moon!
"And stars by thousands! Point me out the
   way
"To any one particular beauteous star,   100
"And I will flit into it with my lyre,
"And make its silvery splendour pant with
   bliss.
"I have heard the cloudy thunder: Where is
   power?
"Whose hand, whose essence, what divinity
"Makes this alarum in the elements,
"While I here idle listen on the shores
"In fearless yet in aching ignorance?
"O tell me, lonely Goddess, by thy harp,
"That waileth every morn and eventide,
"Tell me why thus I rave, about these
   groves!   110
"Mute thou remainest—mute! yet I can read
"A wondrous lesson in thy silent face:
"Knowledge enormous makes a God of me.
"Names, deeds, grey legends, dire events, re-
   bellions,
"Majesties, sovran voices, agonies,
"Creations and destroyings, all at once

"Pour into the wide hollows of my brain,
"And deify me, as if some blithe wine
"Or bright elixir peerless I had drunk,
"And so become immortal."—Thus the
    God,   120
While his enkindled eyes, with level glance
Beneath his white soft temples, stedfast kept
Trembling with light upon Mnemosyne.
Soon wild commotions shook him, and made
    flush
All the immortal fairness of his limbs;
Most like the struggle at the gate of death;
Or liker still to one who should take leave

Of pale immortal death, and with a pang
As hot as death's is chill, with fierce con-
    vulse
Die into life: so young Apollo anguish'd: 130
His very hair, his golden tresses famed
Kept undulation round his eager neck.
During the pain Mnemosyne upheld
Her arms as one who prophesied.—At length
Apollo shriek'd;—and lo! from all his limbs
Celestial

         *   *   *

1818–1819

SELECTIONS FROM THE LETTERS OF JOHN KEATS

I To John Hamilton Reynolds

Carisbrooke, April 17th [1817]

... The wind is in a sulky fit, and I feel that it would be no bad thing to be the favourite of some Fairy, who would give one the power of seeing how our Friends got on at a Distance. I should like, of all Loves, a sketch of you and Tom and George in ink which Haydon will do if you tell him how I want them. From want of regular rest I have been rather *narvus*— and the passage in *Lear*—'Do you not hear the sea?'—has haunted me intensely.

[Here follows the sonnet 'On the Sea.']

April 18th

... Whenever you write say a word or two on some Passage in Shakespeare that may have come rather new to you, which must be continually happening, notwithstanding that we read the same Play forty times—for instance, the following from the Tempest never struck me so forcibly as at present,
                'Urchins
Shall, for the vast of night that they may work,
All exercise on thee—'
How can I help bringing to your mind the line—
   In the dark backward and abysm of time—
I find I cannot exist without Poetry—without eternal Poetry—half the day will not do—the whole of it—I began with a little, but habit has made me a Leviathan. I had become all in a Tremble from not having written anything of late—the Sonnet overleaf did me good. I slept the better last night for it—this Morning, however, I am nearly as bad again. ...

II To Leigh Hunt

Margate, May 10, 1817

My dear Hunt—The little gentleman that sometimes lurks in a gossip's bowl, ought to have come in the very likeness of a *roasted* crab, and choaked me outright for not answering your letter ere this: however, you must not suppose that I was in town to receive it: no, it followed me to the Isle of Wight, and I got it just as I was going to pack up for Margate, for reasons which you anon shall hear. ...

I went to the Isle of Wight, thought so much about poetry, so long together, that I could not get to sleep at night; and, moreover, I know not how it was, I could not get wholesome food. By this means, in a week or so, I became not over capable in my upper stories, and set off pell-mell for Margate, at least a hundred and fifty miles, because, forsooth, I fancied that I should like my old lodging here, and could contrive to do without trees. Another thing, I was too much in solitude, and consequently was obliged to be in continual burning of thought, as an only resource. However, Tom is with me at present, and we are very comfortable. We intend, though, to get among some trees. How have you got on among them? ...

I vow that I have been down in the mouth lately at this work. These last two days, however, I have felt more confident—I have asked myself so often why I should be a poet more than other men, seeing how great a thing it is, —how great things are to be gained by it, what a thing to be in the mouth of Fame,— that at last the idea has grown so monstrously beyond my seeming power of attainment, that the other day I nearly consented with myself to drop into a Phaethon. Yet 'tis a disgrace to fail, even in a huge attempt; and at this moment I drive the thought from me. I began my poem about a fortnight since, and have done some every day, except travelling ones. Perhaps I may have done a good deal for the time, but it appears such a pin's point to me, that I will not copy any out. When I consider that so many of these pin-points go to form a bodkin-point (God send I end not my life with a bare bodkin, in its modern sense!), and that it requires a thousand bodkins to make a spear bright enough to throw any light to posterity, I see nothing but continual uphill journeying. Now is there anything more unpleasant (it may come among the thousand and one) than to be so journeying and to miss the goal at last? But I intend to whistle all these cogitations into the sea, where I hope they will breed storms violent enough to block up all exit from Russia. Does Shelley go on telling strange stories of the deaths of kings? Tell him, there are strange stories of the deaths of poets. Some have died before they were conceived. 'How do you make that out, Master Vellum?' Does Mrs. S. cut bread and butter as neatly as ever? Tell her to procure some fatal scissors, and cut the thread of life of all to-be-disappointed poets. Does Mrs. Hunt tear linen as straight as ever? Tell her to tear from the book of life all blank leaves. Remember me to them all; to Miss Kent and the little ones all.

Your sincere Friend

JOHN KEATS *alias* JUNKETS.

You shall hear where we move.

III TO BENJAMIN BAILEY

Hampstead, Wednesday [October 8, 1817]

... You may see the whole of the case by the following Extract from a Letter I wrote

to George in the Spring—'As to what you say about my being a Poet, I can return no Answer but by saying that the high Idea I have of poetical fame makes me think I see it towering too high above me. At any rate, I have no right to talk until Endymion is finished—it will be a test, a trial of my Powers of Imagination, and chiefly of my invention, which is a rare thing indeed—by which I must make 4000 lines of one bare circumstance, and fill them with poetry: and when I consider that this is a great task, and that when done it will take me but a dozen paces towards the temple of fame—it makes me say—God forbid that I should be without such a task! I have heard Hunt say, and I may be asked—*why endeavour after a long Poem?* To which I should answer, Do not the Lovers of Poetry like to have a little Region to wander in, where they may pick and choose, and in which the images are so numerous that many are forgotten and found new in a second Reading: which may be food for a Week's stroll in the Summer? Do not they like this better than what they can read through before Mrs. Williams comes down stairs? a Morning work at most.

'Besides, a long poem is a test of invention, which I take to be the Polar star of Poetry, as Fancy is the Sails—and Imagination the rudder. Did our great Poets ever write short Pieces? I mean in the shape of Tales—this same invention seems indeed of late years to have been forgotten as a Poetical excellence— But enough of this, I put on no Laurels till I shall have finished Endymion, and I hope Apollo is not angered at my having made a Mockery at him at Hunt's—'

You see, Bailey, how independent my Writing has been. Hunt's dissuasion was of no avail—I refused to visit Shelley that I might have my own unfettered scope;—and after all, I shall have the Reputation of Hunt's élève. His corrections and amputations will by the knowing ones be traced in the Poem. This is, to be sure, the vexation of a day, nor would I say so many words about it to any but those whom I know to have my welfare and reputation at heart.

A Letter from Keats to Jane Reynolds. (See Appendix I.)

IV TO BENJAMIN BAILEY

*[Fragment from an outside sheet:
postmark* London, November 5, 1817]

. . . I will speak of something else, or my
spleen will get higher and higher—and I am a
bearer of the two-edged sword.—I hope you
will receive an answer from Haydon soon—
if not, Pride! Pride! Pride! I have received no
more subscription—but shall soon have a full
health, Liberty and leisure to give a good part
of my time to him. I will certainly be in time
for him. We have promised him one year: let
that have elapsed, then do as we think proper.
If I did not know how impossible it is, I should
say—'do not at this time of disappointments,
disturb yourself about others.'

There has been a flaming attack upon Hunt
in the Endinburgh Magazine. I never read anything so virulent—accusing him of the greatest
Crimes, depreciating his Wife, his Poetry, his
Habits, his Company, his Conversation. These
Philippics are to come out in numbers—called
'the Cockney School of Poetry.' There has
been but one number published—that on
Hunt—to which they have prefixed a motto
from one Cornelius Webb, Poetaster—who
unfortunately was of our party occasionally at
Hampstead and took it into his head to write
the following,—something about 'we'll talk
on Wordsworth, Byron, a theme we never
tire on;' and so forth till he comes to Hunt and
Keats. In the Motto they have put Hunt and
Keats in large letters—I have no doubt that
the second number was intended for me: but
have hopes of its non-appearance, from the
following Advertisement in last Sunday's
Examiner:—'To Z.—The writer of the Article
signed Z., in Blackwood's Edinburgh Magazine for October 1817 is invited to send his
address to the printer of the Examiner, in order
that Justice may be Executed on the proper
person.' I don't mind the thing much—but
if he should go to such lengths with me as
he has done with Hunt, I must infallibly call
him to an Account if he be a human being,
and appears in Squares and Theatres, where
we might possibly meet—I don't relish his
abuse. . . .

V TO BENJAMIN BAILEY

[Burford Bridge, November 22, 1817]

MY DEAR BAILEY—I will get over the first
part of this (*un*said) Letter as soon as possible,
for it relates to the affairs of poor Cripps.—To
a Man of your nature such a Letter as Haydon's
must have been extremely cutting—What
occasions the greater part of the World's
Quarrels?—simply this—two Minds meet,
and do not understand each other time enough
to prevent any shock or surprise at the conduct
of either party—As soon as I had known
Haydon three days, I had got enough of his
Character not to have been surprised at such
a Letter as he has hurt you with. Nor, when I
knew it, was it a principle with me to drop his
acquaintance; although with you it would have
been an imperious feeling. I wish you knew all
that I think about Genius and the Heart—and
yet I think that you are thoroughly acquainted
with my innermost breast in that respect, or
you could not have known me even thus long,
and still hold me worthy to be your dear
Friend. In passing, however, I must say one
thing that has pressed upon me lately, and increased my Humility and capability of submission—and that is this truth—Men of
Genius are great as certain ethereal Chemicals
operating on the Mass of neutral intellect—but
they have not any individuality, any determined Character—I would call the top and
head of those who have a proper self Men of
Power.

But I am running my head into a subject
which I am certain I could not do justice to
under five Years' study, and 3 vols. octavo—
and, moreover, I long to be talking about the
Imagination—so my dear Bailey, do not think
of this unpleasant affair, if possible do not—I
defy any harm to come of it—I defy. I shall
write to Cripps this week, and request him to
tell me all his goings-on from time to time by
Letter wherever I may be. It will go on well—
so don't because you have suddenly discovered
a Coldness in Haydon suffer yourself to be
teased—Do not my dear fellow—O! I wish I
was as certain of the end of all your troubles as
that of your momentary start about the authenticity of the Imagination. I am certain of
nothing but of the holiness of the Heart's

affections, and the truth of Imagination. What the Imagination seizes as Beauty must be truth—whether it existed before or not,—for I have the same idea of all our passions as of Love: they are all, in their sublime, creative of essential Beauty. In a Word, you may know my favourite speculation by my first Book, and the little Song I sent in my last, which is a representation from the fancy of the probable mode of operating in these Matters. The Imagination may be compared to Adam's dream,—he awoke and found it truth:—I am more zealous in this affair, because I have never yet been able to perceive how anything can be known for truth by consecutive reasoning—and yet it must be. Can it be that even the greatest Philosopher ever arrived at his Goal without putting aside numerous objections? However it may be, O for a life of Sensations rather than of Thoughts! It is 'a Vision in the form of Youth,' a shadow of reality to come—And this consideration has further convinced me,—for it has come as auxiliary to another favourite speculation of mine,—that we shall enjoy ourselves hereafter by having what we called happiness on Earth repeated in a finer tone. And yet such a fate can only befall those who delight in Sensation, rather than hunger as you do after Truth. Adam's dream will do here, and seems to be a Conviction that Imagination and its empyreal reflection, is the same as human life and its spiritual repetition. But, as I was saying, the Simple imaginative Mind may have its rewards in the repetition of its own silent Working coming continually on the Spirit with a fine Suddenness—to compare great things with small, have you never by being surprised with an old Melody, in a delicious place by a delicious voice, *felt* over again your very speculations and surmises at the time it first operated on your soul?—do you not remember forming to yourself the Singer's face—more beautiful than it was possible, and yet with the elevation of the Moment you did not think so? Even then you were mounted on the Wings of Imagination, so high that the prototype must be hereafter—that delicious face you will see. What a time! I am continually running away from the subject. Sure this cannot be exactly the Case with a complex mind—one that is imaginative, and

at the same time careful of its fruits,—who would exist partly on Sensation, partly on thought—to whom it is necessary that years should bring the philosophic Mind? Such a one I consider yours, and therefore it is necessary to your eternal happiness that you not only drink this old Wine of Heaven, which I shall call the redigestion of our most ethereal Musings upon Earth, but also increase in knowledge and know all things. I am glad to hear that you are in a fair way for Easter. You will soon get through your unpleasant reading, and then!—but the world is full of troubles, and I have not much reason to think myself pestered with many.

I think Jane or Marianne has a better opinion of me than I deserve: for, really and truly, I do not think my Brother's illness connected with mine—you know more of the real Cause than they do; nor have I any chance of being rack'd as you have been. You perhaps at one time thought there was such a thing as worldly happiness to be arrived at, at certain periods of time marked out,—you have of necessity from your disposition been thus led away—I scarcely remember counting upon any Happiness—I look not for it if it be not in the present hour,—nothing startles me beyond the moment. The Setting Sun will always set me to rights, or if a Sparrow come before my Window, I take part in its existence and pick about the gravel. The first thing that strikes me on hearing a Misfortune having befallen another is this—'Well, it cannot be helped: he will have the pleasure of trying the resources of his Spirit'—and I beg now, my dear Bailey, that hereafter should you observe anything cold in me not to put it to the account of heartlessness, but abstraction—for I assure you I sometimes feel not the influence of a passion or affection during a whole Week—and so long this sometimes continues, I begin to suspect myself, and the genuineness of my feelings at other times—thinking them a few barren Tragedy Tears.

My brother Tom is much improved—he is going to Devonshire—whither I shall follow him. At present, I am just arrived at Dorking—to change the Scene—change the Air, and give me a spur to wind up my Poem, of which there are wanting 500 lines. I should have been here a day sooner, but the Reynoldses persuaded me to stop in Town to meet your friend Christie. There were Rice and Martin—we talked about Ghosts. I will have some Talk with Taylor and let you know,—when please God I come down at Christmas. I will find that Examiner if possible. My best regards to Gleig, my Brothers' to you and Mrs. Bentley.

Your affectionate Friend

JOHN KEATS.

I want to say much more to you—a few hints will set me going. Direct Burford Bridge near Dorking.

VI TO GEORGE AND THOMAS KEATS

Hampstead, December 22, 1817

MY DEAR BROTHERS—I must crave your pardon for not having written ere this. . . . I saw Kean return to the public in Richard III., and finely he did it, and, at the request of Reynolds, I went to criticise his *Duke* in Rich^d. —the critique is in to-day's Champion, which I send you with the Examiner, in which you will find very proper lamentation on the obsoletion of Christmas Gambols and pastimes: but it was mixed up with so much egotism of that drivelling nature that pleasure is entirely lost. Hone the publisher's trial, you must find very amusing, and as Englishmen very encouraging: his *Not Guilty* is a thing, which not to have been, would have dulled still more Liberty's Emblazoning—Lord Ellenborough has been paid in his own coin—Wooler and Hone have done us an essential service. I have had two very pleasant evenings with Dilke yesterday and to-day, and am at this moment just come from him, and feel in the humour to go on with this, begun in the morning, and from which he came to fetch me. I spent Friday evening with Wells and went next morning to see *Death on the Pale horse*. It is a wonderful picture, when West's age is considered; but there is nothing to be intense upon, no women one feels mad to kiss, no face swelling into reality. The excellence of every art is its intensity, capable of making all disagreeables evaporate from their being in close relationship with Beauty and Truth—Examine King Lear, and you will find this exemplified throughout; but in this picture we have unpleasantness without any momentous depth of speculation excited, in which to bury its repulsiveness—The picture is larger than Christ rejected.

I dined with Haydon the Sunday after you left, and had a very pleasant day. I dined too (for I have been out too much lately) with Horace Smith and met his two Brothers with Hill and Kingston and one Du Bois, they only served to convince me how superior humour is to wit, in respect to enjoyment—These men say things which make one start, without making one feel; they are all alike; their manners are alike; they all know fashionables; they have all a mannerism in their very eating and drinking, in their mere handling a Decanter. They talked of Kean and his low company—would I were with that company instead of yours said I to myself! I know such like acquaintance will never do for me and yet I am going to Reynolds, on Wednesday. Brown and Dilke walked with me and back from the Christmas pantomime. I had not a dispute, but a disquisition, with Dilke upon various subjects; several things dove-tailed in my mind, and at once it struck me what quality went to form a Man of Achievement, especially in Literature, and which Shakespeare possessed so enormously—I mean *Negative Capability*, that is, when a man is capable of being in uncertainties, mysteries, doubts, without any irritable reaching after fact and reason. Coleridge, for instance, would let go by a fine isolated verisimilitude caught from the Penetralium of mystery, from being incapable of remaining content with half-knowledge. This pursued through volumes would perhaps take us no further than this, that with a great poet the sense of Beauty overcomes every other consideration, or rather obliterates all consideration.

Shelley's poem is out and there are words about its being objected to, as much as Queen Mab was. Poor Shelley I think he has his Quota of good qualities, in sooth la! Write soon to your most sincere friend and affectionate Brother

JOHN.

VII To George and Thomas Keats

Featherstone Buildings
Monday [January 5, 1818]

... Thursday I promised to dine with Wordsworth, and the weather is so bad that I am undecided, for he lives at Mortimer Street. I had an invitation to meet him at Kingston's, but not liking that place I sent my excuse. What I think of doing to-day is to dine in Mortimer Street (Words^th), and sup here in the Feath^s buildings, as Mr. Wells has invited me. On Saturday, I called on Wordsworth before he went to Kingston's, and was surprised to find him with a stiff collar. I saw his spouse, and I think his daughter. I forget whether I had written my last before my Sunday evening at Haydon's—no, I did not, or I should have told you, Tom, of a young man you met at Paris, at Scott's, ... Ritchie. I think he is going to Fezan, in Africa; then to proceed if possible like Mungo Park. He was very polite to me, and inquired very particularly after you. Then there was Wordsworth, Lamb, Monkhouse, Landseer, Kingston, and your humble servant. Lamb got tipsy and blew up Kingston—proceeding so far as to take the candle across the room, hold it to his face, and show us what a soft fellow he was. I astonished Kingston at supper with a pertinacity in favour of drinking, keeping my two glasses at work in a knowing way.

... I have seen Fanny twice lately—she inquired particularly after you and wants a co-partnership letter from you. She has been unwell, but is improving. I think she will be quick. Mrs. Abbey was saying that the Keatses were ever indolent, that they would ever be so, and that it is born in them. Well, whispered Fanny to me, if it is born with us, how can we help it? ...

VIII To George and Thomas Keats

[Hampstead,] Friday 23d January [1818]

My dear Brothers—I was thinking what hindered me from writing so long, for I have so many things to say to you, and know not where to begin. It shall be upon a thing most interesting to you, my Poem. Well! I have given the first Book to Taylor; he seemed more than satisfied with it, and to my surprise proposed publishing it in Quarto if Haydon would make a drawing of some event therein, for a Frontispiece. I called on Haydon, he said he would do anything I liked, but said he would rather paint a finished picture, from it, which he seems eager to do; this in a year or two will be a glorious thing for us; and it will be, for Haydon is struck with the 1st Book. I left Haydon and the next day received a letter from him, proposing to make, as he says, with all his might, a finished chalk sketch of my head, to be engraved in the first style and put at the head of my Poem, saying at the same time he had never done the thing for any human being, and that it must have considerable effect as he will put his name to it—I begin to-day to copy my 2nd Book—'thus far into the bowels of the land'—You shall hear whether it will be Quarto or non Quarto, picture or non picture. Leigh Hunt I showed my 1st Book to——he allows it not much merit as a whole; says it is unnatural and made ten objections to it in the mere skimming over. He says the conversation is unnatural and too high-flown for Brother and Sister—says it should be simple forgetting do ye mind that they are both overshadowed by a supernatural Power, and of force could not speak like Francesca in the Rimini. He must first prove that Caliban's poetry is unnatural—This with me completely overturns his objections—the fact is he and Shelley are hurt, and perhaps justly, at my not having showed them the affair officiously and from several hints I have had they appear much disposed to dissect and anatomise any trip or slip I may have made. —But who's afraid? Ay! Tom! Demme if I am. I went last Tuesday, an hour too late, to Hazlitt's Lecture on poetry, got there just as they were coming out, when all these pounced upon me. Hazlitt, John Hunt and Son, Wells, Bewick, all the Landseers, Bob Harris, aye and more—the Landseers enquired after you particularly—I know not whether Wordsworth has left town—But Sunday I dined with Hazlitt and Haydon, also that I took Haslam with me—I dined with Brown lately. Dilke having taken the Champion Theatricals was obliged to be in town—Fanny has returned to Walthamstow.—Mr. Abbey appeared very glum, the last time I went to see her, and said in an indirect way, that I had no business there —Rice has been ill, but has been mending much lately—

I think a little change has taken place in my intellect lately—I cannot bear to be uninterested or unemployed, I, who for so long a time have been addicted to passiveness. Nothing is finer for the purposes of great productions than a very gradual ripening of the intellectual powers. As an instance of this—observe—I sat down yesterday to read King Lear once again: the thing appeared to demand the prologue of a sonnet, I wrote it, and began to read—(I know you would like to see it.) 15

[Here follows the Sonnet, *On Sitting Down to Read 'King Lear' Once Again.*]

So you see I am getting at it, with a sort of determination and strength, though verily I do not feel it at this moment—this is my fourth letter this morning, and I feel rather tired, and my head rather swimming—so I will leave it open till tomorrow's post.— . . .

IX To John Taylor

[Hampstead, January 30, 1818]

MY DEAR TAYLOR—These lines as they now stand about 'happiness,' having rung in my ears like 'a chime a mending'—See here,

'Behold
Wherein lies happiness, Peona? fold, etc.'

It appears to me the very contrary of blessed. I hope this will appear to you more eligible.

'Wherein lies Happiness? In that which becks
Our ready minds to fellowship divine,
A fellowship with Essence till we shine
Full alchemised, and free of space—Behold
The clear religion of Heaven—fold, etc.'[1]

You must indulge me by putting this in, for setting aside the badness of the other, such a preface is necessary to the subject. The whole thing must, I think, have appeared to you, who are a consecutive man, as a thing almost of mere words, but I assure you that, when I wrote it, it was a regular stepping of the Imagination towards a truth. My having written that argument will perhaps be of the greatest

[1] See Endymion I, li. 769 et seq.

service to me of anything I ever did. It set before me the gradations of happiness, even like a kind of pleasure thermometer, and is my first step towards the chief attempt in the drama. The playing of different natures with joy and Sorrow—

Do me this favour, and believe me
Your sincere friend   J. KEATS.

I hope your next work will be of a more general Interest. I suppose you cogitate a little about it, now and then.

X To John Hamilton Reynolds

Hampstead, Tuesday [February 3, 1818]

MY DEAR REYNOLDS—I thank you for your dish of Filberts—would I could get a basket of them by way of dessert every day for the sum of twopence. Would we were a sort of ethereal Pigs, and turned loose to feed upon spiritual Mast and Acorns—which would be merely being a squirrel and feeding upon filberts, for what is a squirrel but an airy pig, or a filbert but a sort of archangelical acorn? About the nuts being worth cracking, all I can say is, that where there are a throng of delightful Images ready drawn, simplicity is the only thing. The first is the best on account of the first line, and the 'arrow, foil'd of its antler'd food,' and moreover (and this is the only word or two I find fault with, the more because I have had so much reason to shun it as a quicksand) the last has 'tender and true.' We must cut this, and not be rattlesnaked into any more of the like. It may be said that we ought to read our contemporaries, that Wordsworth, etc. should have their due from us. But, for the sake of a few fine imaginative or domestic passages, are we to be bullied into a certain Philosophy engendered in the whims of an Egotist? Every man has his speculations, but every man does not brood and peacock over them till he makes a false coinage and deceives himself. Many a man can travel to the very bourne of Heaven, and yet want confidence to put down his half-seeing. Sancho will invent a Journey heavenward as well as anybody. We hate poetry that has a palpable design upon us, and, if we do not agree, seems to put its hand into its breeches pocket. Poetry should be great and unobtrusive, a thing which enters into one's soul, and does not startle it or amaze it with itself—but with its subject. How beautiful are the retired flowers!—how would they lose their beauty were they to throng into the highway, crying out, 'Admire me, I am a violet! Dote upon me, I am a primrose!' Modern poets differ from the Elizabethans in this: each of the moderns like an Elector of Hanover governs his petty state and knows how many straws are swept daily from the Causeways in all his dominions, and has a continual itching that all the Housewives should have their coppers well scoured: The ancients were Emperors of vast Provinces, they had only heard of the remote ones and scarcely cared to visit them. I will cut all this— I will have no more of Wordsworth or Hunt in particular—Why should we be of the tribe of Manasseh, when we can wander with Esau? Why should we kick against the Pricks, when we can walk on Roses? Why should we be owls, when we can be eagles? Why be teased with 'nice-eyed wagtails,' when we have in sight 'the Cherub Contemplation'? Why with Wordsworth's 'Matthew with a bough of wilding in his hand,' when we can have Jacques 'under an oak,' etc.? The secret of the Bough of Wilding will run through your head faster than I can write it. Old Matthew spoke to him some years ago on some nothing, and because he happens in an Evening Walk to imagine the figure of the Old Man, he must stamp it down in black and white, and it is henceforth sacred. I don't mean to deny Wordsworth's grandeur and Hunt's merit, but I mean to say we need not be teased with grandeur and merit when we can have them uncontaminated and unobtrusive. Let us have the old Poets and Robin Hood. Your letter and its sonnets gave me more pleasure than will the Fourth Book of Childe Harold and the whole of anybody's life and opinions. In return for your Dish of Filberts, I have gatherd a few Catkins, I hope they'll look pretty.

[To J. H. R. in answer to his Robin Hood Sonnets.]

I hope you will like them—they are at least written in the Spirit of Outlawry. Here are the Mermaid lines, . . .

I will call on you at 4 tomorrow, and we will trudge together, for it is not the thing to be a stranger in the Land of Harpsicols. I hope also to bring you my 2nd Book. In the hope that these Scribblings will be some amusement for you this Evening, I remain, copying on the Hill,

Your sincere friend and Co-scribbler

JOHN KEATS.

XI To JOHN TAYLOR

Hampstead, February 27 [1818]

MY DEAR TAYLOR—Your alteration strikes me as being a great Improvement—And now I will attend to the punctuations you speak of— The comma should be at *soberly*, and in the other passage, the Comma should follow *quiet*. I am extremely indebted to you for this alteration, and also for your after admonitions. It is a sorry thing for me that any one should have to overcome prejudices in reading my verses—that affects me more than any hypercriticism on any particular passage—In Endymion, I have most likely but moved into the go-cart from the leading-strings—In poetry I have a few axioms, and you will see how far I am from their centre.

1st. I think poetry should surprise by a fine excess, and not by singularity; it should strike the reader as a wording of his own highest thoughts, and appear almost a remembrance.

2d. Its touches of beauty should never be half-way, thereby making the reader breathless, instead of content. The rise, the progress, the setting of Imagery should, like the sun, come natural to him, shine over him, and set soberly, although in magnificence, leaving him in the luxury of twilight. But it is easier to think what poetry should be, than to write it— And this leads me to

Another axiom—That if poetry comes not as naturally as the leaves to a tree, it had better not come at all.—However it may be with me, I cannot help looking into new countries with 'O for a Muse of Fire to ascend!' If Endymion serves me as a pioneer, perhaps I ought to be content—I have great reason to be content, for thank God I can read, and perhaps understand Shakespeare to his depths, and I have I am sure many friends, who, if I fail; will attribute any change in my life and temper to humbleness rather than pride—to a cowering under the wings of great poets, rather than to a bitterness that I am not appreciated. I am anxious to get Endymion printed that I may forget it and proceed. I have copied the 3rd Book and begun the 4th. On running my eye over the proofs, I saw one mistake—I will notice it presently, and also any others, if there be any. There should be no comma in 'the raft branch down sweeping from a tall ash-top.' I have besides made one or two alterations, and also altered the thirteenth line p. 32 to make sense of it, as you will see. I will take care the printer shall not trip up my heels. There should be no dash after Dryope, in the line 'Dryope's lone lulling of her child.'

Remember me to Percy Street.

Your sincere and obliged friend

JOHN KEATS.

P. S.—You shall have a short preface in good time.

his remembrances to you. I think of seeing the Dart and Plymouth—but I don't know. It has as yet been a Mystery to me how and where Wordsworth went. I can't help thinking he has returned to his Shell—with his beautiful Wife and his enchanting Sister. It is a great Pity that People should by associating themselves with the finest things, spoil them. Hunt has damned Hampstead and masks and sonnets and Italian tales. Wordsworth has damned the lakes—Milman has damned the old drama—West has damned——wholesale. Peacock has damned satire—Ollier has damn'd Music—Hazlitt has damned the bigoted and the blue-stockinged; how durst the Man? he is your only good damner, and if ever I am damn'd—damn me if I shouldn't like him tó damn me. It will not be long ere I see you, but I thought I would just give you a line out of Devon.

Yours affectionately   JOHN KEATS.

Remember me to all we know.

XII To BENJAMIN ROBERT HAYDON

Teignmouth, Saturday Morn [March 21, 1818]

... I know not if this rhyming fit has done anything—it will be safe with you if worthy to put among my Lyrics. Here's some doggrel for you—Perhaps you would like a bit of b——hrell—

Where be ye going, you Devon Maid?
  And what have ye there in the Basket?
Ye tight little fairy just fresh from the dairy,
  Will ye give me some cream if I ask it?

I love your Meads, and I love your flowers,
  And I love your junkets mainly,
But 'hind the door I love kissing more,
  O look not so disdainly.

I love your hills, and I love your dales,
  And I love your flocks a-bleating—
But O, on the heather to lie together,
  With both our hearts a-beating!

I'll put your Basket all safe in a nook,
  Your shawl I hang up on the willow,
And we will sigh in the daisy's eye
  And kiss on a grass green pillow.

How does the work go on? I should like to bring out my 'Dentatus' at the time your Epic makes its appearance. I expect to have my Mind soon clear for something new. Tom has been much worse: but is now getting better—

XIII To JOHN HAMILTON REYNOLDS

Thy. morng., [Teignmouth, April 9, 1818]

MY DEAR REYNOLDS—Since you all agree that the thing [the first preface to *Endymion*] is bad, it must be so—though I am not aware there is anything like Hunt in it (and if there is, it is my natural way, and I have something in common with Hunt). Look it over again, and examine into the motives, the seeds, from which any one sentence sprung—I have not the slightest feel of humility towards the public—or to anything in existence,—but the eternal Being, the Principle of Beauty, and the Memory of great Men. When I am writing for myself for the mere sake of the moment's enjoyment, perhaps nature has its course with me—but a Preface is written to the Public; a thing I cannot help looking upon as an Enemy, and which I cannot address without feelings of Hostility. If I write a Preface in a supple or subdued style, it will not be in character with me as a public speaker—I would be subdued before my friends, and thank them for sub-·duing me—but among Multitudes of Men—I have no feel of stooping, I hate the idea of humility to them.

I never wrote one single Line of Poetry with the least Shadow of public thought.

Forgive me for vexing you and making a Trojan horse of such a Trifle, both with respect to the matter in Question, and myself—but it eases me to tell you—I could not live without the love of my friends—I would jump down Ætna for any great Public good—but I hate a Mawkish Popularity. I cannot be subdued before them—My glory would be to daunt and dazzle the thousand jabberers about Pictures and Books—I see swarms of Porcupines with their Quills erect 'like lime-twigs set to catch my Wingèd Book,' and I would fright them away with a torch. You will say my Preface is not much of a Torch. It would have been too insulting 'to begin from Jove,' and I could not set a golden head upon a thing of clay. If there is any fault in the Preface it is not affectation, but an undersong of disrespect to the Public—if I write another Preface it must be done without a thought of those people—I will think about it. If it should not reach you in four or five days, tell Taylor to publish it without a Preface, and let the Dedication simply stand—'inscribed to the Memory of Thomas Chatterton.'

I had resolved last night to write to you this morning—I wish it had been about something else—something to greet you towards the close of your long illness. I have had one or two intimations of your going to Hampstead for a space; and I regret to see your confounded Rheumatism keeps you in Little Britain where I am sure the air is too confined. Devonshire continues rainy. As the drops beat against the window, they give me the same sensation as a quart of cold water offered to revive a half-drowned devil—no feel of the clouds dropping fatness; but as if the roots of the earth were rotten, cold, and drenched. I have not been able to go to Kent's cave at Babbicombe—however on one very beautiful day I had a fine Clamber over the rocks all along as far as that place. I shall be in Town in about Ten days—We go by way of Bath on purpose to call on Bailey. I hope soon to be writing to you about the things of the north, purposing to wayfare all over those parts. I have settled my accoutrements in my own mind, and will go to gorge wonders. However, we'll have some days together before I set out— I have many reasons for going wonder-ways:

to make my winter chair free from spleen—to enlarge my vision—to escape disquisitions on Poetry and Kingston Criticism; to promote digestion and economise shoe-leather. I'll have leather buttons and belt; and, if Brown holds his mind, over the Hills we go. If my Books will help me to it, then will I take all Europe in turn, and see the Kingdoms of the Earth and the glory of them. Tom is getting better, he hopes you may meet him at the top o' the hill. My Love to your nurses. I am ever

Your affectionate Friend JOHN KEATS.

XIV TO JOHN TAYLOR

Teignmouth, Friday [April 24, 1818]

MY DEAR TAYLOR—I think I did wrong to leave to you all the trouble of Endymion—But I could not help it then—another time I shall be more bent to all sorts of troubles and disagreeables. Young men for some time have an idea that such a thing as happiness is to be had, and therefore are extremely impatient under any unpleasant restraining. In time however, of such stuff is the world about them, they know better, and instead of striving from uneasiness, greet it as an habitual sensation, a pannier which is to weigh upon them through life—And in proportion to my disgust at the task is my sense of your kindness and anxiety. The book pleased me much. It is very free from faults: and, although there are one or two words I should wish replaced, I see in many places an improvement greatly to the purpose. . . .

. . . I was proposing to travel over the North this summer. There is but one thing to prevent me.—I know nothing—I have read nothing—and I mean to follow Solomon's directions, 'Get learning—get understanding.' I find earlier days are gone by—I find that I can have no enjoyment in the world but continual drinking of knowledge. I find there is no worthy pursuit but the idea of doing some good for the world—Some do it with their Society—some with their wit—some with their benevolence—some with a sort of power of conferring pleasure and good-humour on all they meet—and in a thousand ways, all dutiful to the command of great Nature—there is but one way for me. The road lies through application, study, and thought.—I will pursue it; and for that end, purpose retiring for some years. I have been hovering for some time between an exquisite sense of the luxurious, and a love for philosophy,—were I calculated for the former, I should be glad. But as I am not, I shall turn all my soul to the latter.— My brother Tom is getting better, and I hope I shall see both him and Reynolds better before I retire from the world. I shall see you soon, and have some talk about what Books I shall take with me.

Your very sincere friend JOHN KEATS.

Pray remember me to Hessey Woodhouse and Percy Street.

XV To JOHN HAMILTON REYNOLDS

Teignmouth, May 3d [1818]

. . . Every department of Knowledge we see excellent and calculated towards a great whole —I am so convinced of this that I am glad at not having given away my medical Books, which I shall again look over to keep alive the little I know thitherwards; and moreover intend through you and Rice to become a sort of pip-civilian. An extensive knowledge is needful to thinking people—it takes away the heat and fever; and helps, by widening speculation, to ease the Burden of the Mystery, a thing which I begin to understand a little, and which weighed upon you in the most gloomy and true sentence in your Letter. The difference of high Sensations with and without knowledge appears to me this: in the latter case we are falling continually ten thousand fathoms deep and being blown up again, without wings, and with all horror of a bare-shouldered Creature—in the former case, our shoulders are fledged, and we go through the same air and space without fear. This is running one's rigs on the score of abstracted benefit—when we come to human Life and the affections, it is impossible to know how a parallel of breast and head can be drawn (you will forgive me for thus privately treading out of my depth, and take it for treading as school-boys tread the water); it is impossible to know how far knowledge will console us for the death of a friend, and the ill 'that flesh is heir to.' With respect to the affections and Poetry

you must know by a sympathy my thoughts that way, and I daresay these few lines will be but a ratification: I wrote them on Mayday— and intend to finish the ode all in good time—

'Mother of Hermes! and still youthful Maia!'

. . . You may perhaps be anxious to know for fact to what sentence in your Letter I allude. You say, 'I fear there is little chance of anything else in this life'—you seem by that to have been going through with a more painful and acute zest the same labyrinth that I have—I have come to the same conclusion thus far. My Branchings out therefrom have been numerous: one of them is the consideration of Wordsworth's genius and as a help, in the manner of gold being the meridian Line of worldly wealth, how he differs from Milton. And here I have nothing but surmises, from an uncertainty whether Milton's apparently less anxiety for Humanity proceeds from his seeing further or not than Wordsworth: And whether Wordsworth has in truth epic passion, and martyrs himself to the human heart, the main region of his song. In regard to his genius alone—we find what he says true as far as we have experienced, and we can judge no further but by larger experience—for axioms in philosophy are not axioms until they are proved upon our pulses. We read fine things, but never feel them to the full until we have gone the same steps as the author.—I know this is not plain; you will know exactly my meaning when I say that now I shall relish Hamlet more than I ever have done—Or, better—you are sensible no man can set down Venery as a bestial or joyless thing until he is sick of it, and therefore all philosophising on it would be mere wording. Until we are sick, we understand not; in fine, as Byron says, 'Knowledge is sorrow'; and I go on to say that 'Sorrow is wisdom'—and further for aught we can know for certainty 'Wisdom is folly'—So you see how I have run away from Wordsworth and Milton, and shall still run away from what was in my head, to observe, that some kind of letters are good squares, others handsome ovals, and other some orbicular, others spheroid—and why should not there be another species with two rough edges like a Rat-trap? I hope you will find all my long letters of that species, and all will be well; for by merely touching the spring delicately and ethereally, the rough-edged will fly immediately into a proper compactness; and thus you may make a good wholesome loaf, with your own leaven in it, of my fragments—If you cannot find this said Rat-trap sufficiently tractable, alas for me, it being an impossibility in grain for my ink to stain otherwise: If I scribble long letters I must play my vagaries—I must be too heavy, or too light, for whole pages—I must be quaint and free of Tropes and figures—I must play my draughts as I please, and for my advantage and your erudition, crown a white with a black, or a black with a white, and move into black or white, far and near as I please—I must go from Hazlitt to Patmore, and make Wordsworth and Coleman play at leap-frog, or keep one of them down a whole half-holiday at fly-the-garter—'From Gray to Gay, from Little to Shakespeare.' Also as a long cause requires two or more sittings of the Court, so a long letter will require two or more sittings of the Breech, wherefore I shall resume after dinner—

Have you not seen a Gull, an orc, a Sea-Mew, or anything to bring this Line to a proper length, and also fill up this clear part; that like the Gull I may *dip*[1]—I hope, not out of sight—and also, like a Gull, I hope to be lucky in a good-sized fish—This crossing a letter is not without its association—for chequer-work leads us naturally to a Milkmaid, a Milkmaid to Hogarth, Hogarth to Shakespeare —Shakespeare to Hazlitt—Hazlitt to Shake-speare—and thus by merely pulling an apron-string we set a pretty peal of Chimes at work —Let them chime on while, with your patience, I will return to Wordsworth—whether or no he has an extended vision or a circum-scribed grandeur—whether he is an eagle in his nest or on the wing—And to be more explicit and to show you how tall I stand by the giant, I will put down a simile of human life as far as I now perceive it; that is, to the point to which I say we both have arrived at— Well—I compare human life to a large Mansion of Many apartments, two of which I can only describe, the doors of the rest being as yet shut upon me—The first we step into we call the infant or thoughtless Chamber, in which we remain as long as we do not think— We remain there a long while, and notwith-standing the doors of the second Chamber remain wide open, showing a bright appear-ance, we care not to hasten to it; but are at length imperceptibly impelled by the awaken-ing of the thinking principle within us—we no sooner get into the second Chamber, which I shall call the Chamber of Maiden-Thought, than we become intoxicated with the light and the atmosphere, we see nothing but pleasant wonders, and think of delaying there for ever in delight: However among the effects this breathing is father of is that tremendous one of sharpening one's vision into the heart and nature of Man—of convincing one's nerves that the world is full of Misery and Heart-break, Pain, Sickness, and oppression—whereby this Chamber of Maiden-Thought becomes grad-ually darkened, and at the same time, on all sides of it, many doors are set open—but all dark—all leading to dark passages—We see not the balance of good and evil—we are in a mist—*we* are now in that state—We feel the 'burden of the Mystery.' To this point was Wordsworth come, as far as I can conceive, when he wrote 'Tintern Abbey,' and it seems to me that his Genius is explorative of those dark Passages. Now if we live, and go on thinking, we too shall explore them . . .

XVI To Fanny Keats

Dumfries, July 2nd [1818]

My dear Fanny—I intended to have writ-ten to you from Kirkcudbright, the town I shall be in to-morrow—but I will write now because my Knapsack has worn my coat in the Seams, my coat has gone to the Tailor's and I have but one Coat to my back in these parts. I must tell you how I went to Liverpool with George and our new Sister and the Gentleman my fellow traveller through the Summer and autumn—We had a tolerable journey to Liver-pool—which I left the next morning before George was up for Lancaster—Then we set off from Lancaster on foot with our Knapsacks on, and have walked a Little zig-zag through the mountains and Lakes of Cumberland and

---

[1] The crossing of the letter, begun at the words 'Have you not,' here *dips* into the original writing.

Westmoreland—We came from Carlisle yesterday to this place—We are employed in going up Mountains, looking at strange towns, prying into old ruins and eating very hearty breakfasts. Here we are full in the Midst of 5 broad Scotch 'How is it a' wi' yoursel'—the Girls are walking about bare-footed and in the worst cottages the smoke finds its way out of the door. I shall come home full of news for you and for fear I should choak you 10 by too great a dose at once I must make you used to it by a letter or two. We have been taken for travelling Jewellers, Razor sellers and Spectacle vendors because friend Brown wears a pair. The first place we stopped at 15 with our Knapsacks contained one Richard Bradshaw, a notorious tippler. He stood in the shape of a 3 and balanced himself as well as he could saying with his nose right in Mr. Brown's face 'Do—yo—u sell spect—ta— 20 cles?' Mr. Abbey says we are Don Quixotes— tell him we are more generally taken for Pedlars. All I hope is that we may not be taken for excisemen in this whisky country. We are generally up about 5 walking before 25 breakfast and we complete our 20 miles before dinner.—Yesterday we visited Burns's Tomb and this morning the fine Ruins of Lincluden.

[Auchencairn, same day, July 2]

I had done thus far when my coat came back fortified at all points—so as we lose no time 30 we set forth again through Galloway—all very pleasant and pretty with no fatigue when one is used to it—We are in the midst of Meg Merrilies's country of whom I suppose you have heard.   35

[Here follow the lines, 'Meg Merrilies.']

If you like these sort of ballads I will now and then scribble one for you—if I send any to Tom I'll tell him to send them to you.

[Kirkcudbright, evening of same day, July 2]

I have so many interruptions that I cannot manage to fill a Letter in one day—since 40 I scribbled the song we have walked through a beautiful Country to Kirkcudbright—at which place I will write you a song about myself—

There was a naughty Boy,
  A naughty boy was he,
He would not stop at home,
  He could not quiet be—
    He took
    In his Knapsack
    A Book
    Full of vowels;
    And a shirt
    With some towels—
    A slight cap
    For night cap—
    A hair brush,
    Comb ditto,
    New Stockings,
    For old ones
    Would split O!
    This Knapsack,
    Tight at 's back,
    He rivetted close
And follow'd his Nose
    To the North,
    To the North,
And follow'd his nose
    To the North.

*   *   *

There was a naughty Boy,
  And a naughty Boy was he,
He ran away to Scotland
  The people for to see—
    Then he found
    That the ground
    Was as hard,
    That a yard
    Was as long,
    That a song
    Was as merry,
    That a cherry
    Was as red—
    That lead
    Was as weighty,
    That fourscore
    Was as eighty,
    That a door
    Was as wooden
    As in England—
So he stood in his shoes
    And he wonder'd,
    He wonder'd,
He stood in his shoes
    And he wonder'd.

[Newton Stewart, July 4]

My dear Fanny, I am ashamed of writing you such stuff, nor would I if it were not for being tired after my day's walking, and ready to tumble into bed so fatigued that when I am asleep you might sew my nose to my great toe and trundle me round the town, like a

Hoop, without waking me. Then I get so hungry a Ham goes but a very little way and fowls are like Larks to me—A Batch of Bread I make no more ado with than a sheet of parliament; and I can eat a Bull's head as easily as I used to do Bull's eyes. I take a whole string of Pork Sausages down as easily as a Pen'orth of Lady's fingers. Ah dear I must soon be contented with an acre or two of oaten cake a hogshead of Milk and a Clothes-basket of Eggs morning noon and night when I get among the Highlanders. Before we see them we shall pass into Ireland and have a chat with the Paddies, and look at the Giant's Causeway which you must have heard of—I have not time to tell you particularly for I have to send a Journal to Tom of whom you shall hear all particulars or from me when I return. Since I began this we have walked sixty miles to Newton Stewart at which place I put in this Letter—to-night we sleep at Glenluce—to-morrow at Portpatrick and the next day we shall cross in the passage boat to Ireland. I hope Miss Abbey has quite recovered. Present my Respects to her and to Mr. and Mrs. Abbey. God bless you.

Your affectionate Brother   JOHN.

Do write me a Letter directed to *Inverness*, Scotland.

XVII To JOHN HAMILTON REYNOLDS

[Kingswells, July 13, 1818]

. . . We were talking on different and indifferent things, when on a sudden we turned a corner upon the immediate Country of Ayr—the Sight was as rich as possible. I had no Conception that the native place of Burns was so beautiful—the idea I had was more desolate, his 'rigs of Barley' seemed always to me but a few strips of Green on a cold hill—O prejudice! it was as rich as Devon—I endeavoured to drink in the Prospect, that I might spin it out to you as the Silkworm makes silk from Mulberry leaves—I cannot recollect it—Besides all the Beauty, there were the Mountains of Arran Isle, black and huge over the Sea. We came down upon everything suddenly—there were in our way the 'bonny Doon,' with the Brig that Tam o' Shanter crossed, Kirk Alloway, Burns's Cottage, and

then the Brigs of Ayr. First we stood upon the Bridge across the Doon; surrounded by every Phantasy of green in Tree, Meadow, and Hill,—the stream of the Doon, as a Farmer told us, is covered with trees from head to foot—you know those beautiful heaths so fresh against the weather of a summer's evening—there was one stretching along behind the trees. I wish I knew always the humour my friends would be in at opening a letter of mine, to suit it to them as nearly as possible. I could always find an egg shell for Melancholy, and as for Merriment a Witty humour will turn anything to Account—My head is sometimes in such a whirl in considering the million likings and antipathies of our Moments—that I can get into no settled strain in my Letters. My Wig! Burns and sentimentality coming across you and Frank Fladgate in the office—O scenery that thou shouldst be crushed between two Puns—As for them I venture the rascalliest in the Scotch Region—I hope Brown does not put them punctually in his journal—If he does I must sit on the cutty-stool all next winter. We went to Kirk Allo-way—'a Prophet is no Prophet in his own Country'—We went to the Cottage and took some Whisky. I wrote a sonnet for the mere sake of writing some lines under the roof—they are so bad I cannot transcribe them—The Man at the Cottage was a great Bore with his Anecdotes—I hate the rascal—his Life consists in fuz, fuzzy, fuzziest—He drinks glasses five for the Quarter and twelve for the hour—he is a mahogany-faced old Jackass who knew Burns—He ought to have been kicked for having spoken to him. He calls himself 'a curious old Bitch'—but he is a flat old dog—I should like to employ Caliph Vathek to kick him. O the flummery of a birthplace! Cant! Cant! Cant! It is enough to give a spirit the guts-ache—Many a true word, they say, is spoken in jest—this may be because his gab hindered my sublimity: the flat dog made me write a flat sonnet. My dear Reynolds—I cannot write about scenery and visitings—Fancy is indeed less than a present palpable reality, but it is greater than remembrance—you would lift your eyes from Homer only to see close before you the real Isle of Tenedos—you would rather read Homer afterwards than remember yourself—One song of Burns's is of more worth to you than all I could think for a whole year in his native country. His Misery is a dead weight upon the nimbleness of one's quill—I tried to forget it—to drink Toddy without any Care—to write a merry sonnet— it won't do—he talked with Bitches—he drank with Blackguards, he was miserable—We can see horribly clear, in the works of such a Man his whole life, as if we were God's spies. 10

XVIII To James Augustus Hessey

[Hampstead, October 9, 1818]

My dear Hessey—You are very good in sending me the letters from the Chronicle— and I am very bad in not acknowledging such 15 a kindness sooner—pray forgive me. It has so chanced that I have had that paper every day—I have seen to-day's. I cannot but feel indebted to those Gentlemen who have taken my part—As for the rest, I begin to get a little 20 acquainted with my own strength and weakness.—Praise or blame has but a momentary effect on the man whose love of beauty in the abstract makes him a severe critic on his own Works. My own domestic criticism has given 25 me pain without comparison beyond what Blackwood or the Quarterly could possibly inflict—and also when I feel I am right, no external praise can give me such a glow as my own solitary reperception and ratification of 30 what is fine. J. S. is perfectly right in regard to the slip-shod Endymion. That it is so is no fault of mine. No!—though it may sound a little paradoxical. It is as good as I had power to make it—by myself—Had I been nervous 35 about its being a perfect piece, and with that view asked advice, and trembled over every page, it would not have been written; for it is not in my nature to fumble—I will write independently.—I have written independently 40 *without Judgment*. I may write independently, and *with Judgment* hereafter. The Genius of Poetry must work out its own salvation in a man: It cannot be matured by law and precept, but by sensation and watchfulness in 45 itself—That which is creative must create itself—In Endymion, I leaped headlong into the sea, and thereby have become better acquainted with the Soundings, the quicksands, and the rocks, than if I had stayed upon the green shore, and piped a silly pipe, and took tea and comfortable advice. I was never afraid of failure; for I would sooner fail than not be 5 among the greatest—But I am nigh getting into a rant. So, with remembrances to Taylor and Woodhouse etc. I am

Yours very sincerely　　John Keats.

XIX To George and Georgiana Keats

[October 14 or 15, 1818]

I came by ship from Inverness, and was nine days at Sea without being sick—a little Qualm now and then put me in mind of you— however as soon as you touch the shore all the horrors of Sickness are soon forgotten, as was the case with a Lady on board who could not hold her head up all the way. We had not been in the Thames an hour before her tongue began to some tune; paying off 20 as it was fit she should all old scores. I was the only Englishman on board. There was a downright Scotchman who hearing that there had been a bad crop of Potatoes in England had brought some triumphant specimens from 25 Scotland—these he exhibited with national pride to all the Lightermen and Watermen from the Nore to the Bridge. I fed upon beef all the way; not being able to eat the thick Porridge which the Ladies managed to man-30 age with large awkward horn spoons into the bargain. Severn has had a narrow escape of his Life from a Typhus fever: he is now gaining strength—Reynolds has returned from a six weeks' enjoyment in Devonshire—he is well, 35 and persuades me to publish my pot of Basil as an answer to the attacks made on me in Blackwood's Magazine and the Quarterly Review. There have been two Letters in my defence in the Chronicle and one in the Examiner, 40 copied from the Alfred Exeter Paper, and written by Reynolds. I do not know who wrote those in the Chronicle. This is a mere matter of the moment—I think I shall be among the English Poets after my death. Even 45 as a Matter of present interest the attempt to crush me in the Quarterly has only brought me more into notice, and it is a common expression among book men 'I wonder the Quarterly should cut its own throat.'

It does me not the least harm in Society to make me appear little and ridiculous: I know when a man is superior to me and give him all due respect—he will be the last to laugh at me and as for the rest I feel that I make an impression upon them which insures me personal respect while I am in sight whatever they may say when my back is turned. Poor Haydon's eyes will not suffer him to proceed with his picture—he has been in the Country—I have 10 seen him but once since my return. I hurry matters together here because I do not know when the Mail sails—I shall enquire tomorrow, and then shall know whether to be particular or general in my letter—You shall 15 have at least two sheets a day till it does sail whether it be three days or a fortnight—and then I will begin a fresh one for the next Month. The Miss Reynoldses are very kind to me, but they have lately displeased me 20 much, and in this way—Now I am coming the Richardson. On my return the first day I called they were in a sort of taking or bustle about a Cousin of theirs who having fallen out with her Grandpapa in a serious manner 25 was invited by Mrs. R. to take Asylum in her house. She is an east indian and ought to be her Grandfather's Heir. At the time I called Mrs. R. was in conference with her up stairs, and the young Ladies were warm in her 30 praises down stairs, calling her genteel, interesting and a thousand other pretty things to which I gave no heed, not being partial to 9 days' wonders—Now all is completely changed—they hate her, and from what I hear 35 she is not without faults—of a real kind: but she has others which are more apt to make women of inferior charms hate her. She is not a Cleopatra, but she is at least a Charmian. She has a rich Eastern look; she has fine eyes 40 and fine manners. When she comes into a room she makes an impression the same as the Beauty of a Leopardess. She is too fine and too conscious of herself to repulse any Man who may address her—from habit she 45 thinks that nothing *particular*. I always find myself more at ease with such a woman; the picture before me always gives me a life and animation which I cannot possible feel with anything inferior. I am at such times too much 50 occupied in admiring to be awkward or in a

tremble. I forget myself entirely because I live in her. You will by this time think I am in love with her; so before I go any further I will tell you I am not—she kept me awake one 5 Night as a tune of Mozart's might do. I speak of the thing as a pastime and an amusement, than which I can feel none deeper than a conversation with an imperial woman, the very 'yes' and 'no' of whose Lips is to me a Banquet. I don't cry to take the moon home with me in my Pocket nor do I fret to leave her behind me. I like her and her like because one has no *sensations*—what we both are is taken for granted. You will suppose I have 15 by this had much talk with her—no such thing —there are the Miss Reynoldses on the look out—They think I don't admire her because I did not stare at her.

They call her a flirt to me—What a want of knowledge! She walks across a room in such 20 a manner that a Man is drawn towards her with a magnetic Power. This they call flirting! they do not know things. They do not know what a Woman is. I believe though she has faults—the same as Charmian and Cleopatra 25 might have had. Yet she is a fine thing speaking in a worldly way: for there are two distinct tempers of mind in which we judge of things— the worldly, theatrical and pantomimical; and the unearthly, spiritual and ethereal—in the 30 former Buonaparte, Lord Byron and this Charmian hold the first place in our Minds; in the latter, John Howard, Bishop Hooker rocking his child's cradle and you my dear Sister are the conquering feelings. As a Man 35 in the world I love the rich talk of a Charmian; as an eternal Being I love the thought of you. I should like her to ruin me, and I should like you to save me. Do not think, my dear Brother, from this that my Passions 40 are headlong, or likely to be ever of any pain to you—

'I am free from Men of Pleasure's cares,
By dint of feelings far more deep than theirs.'

This is Lord Byron, and is one of the finest things he has said. I have no town talk for you, as I have not been much among people —as for Politics they are in my opinion only 50 sleepy because they will soon be too wide awake . . .

[Hampstead, about October 25, 1818]

... I shall in a short time write you as far as I know how I intend to pass my Life—I cannot think of those things now Tom is so unwell and weak. Notwithstanding your Happiness and your recommendation I hope I shall never marry. Though the most beautiful Creature were waiting for me at the end of a Journey or a Walk; though the Carpet were of Silk, the Curtains of the morning Clouds; the chairs and Sofa stuffed with Cygnet's down; the food Manna, the Wine beyond Claret, the Window opening on Winander mere, I should not feel—or rather my Happiness would not be so fine, as my Solitude is sublime. Then instead of what I have described, there is a sublimity to welcome me home—The roaring of the wind is my wife and the Stars through the window pane are my Children. The mighty abstract Idea I have of Beauty in all things stifles the more divided and minute domestic happiness—an amiable wife and sweet Children I contemplate as a part of that Beauty, but I must have a thousand of those beautiful particles to fill up my heart. I feel more and more every day, as my imagination strengthens, that I do not live in this world alone but in a thousand worlds—No sooner am I alone than shapes of epic greatness are stationed around me, and serve my Spirit the office which is equivalent to a King's bodyguard—then 'Tragedy with sceptred pall comes sweeping by.' According to my state of mind I am with Achilles shouting in the Trenches or with Theocritus in the Vales of Sicily. Or I throw my whole being into Troilus, and repeating those lines, 'I wander like a lost Soul upon the stygian Banks staying for waftage,' I melt into the air with a voluptuousness so delicate that I am content to be alone. These things, combined with the opinion I have of the generality of women—who appear to me as children to whom I would rather give a sugar Plum than my time, form a barrier against Matrimony which I rejoice in.

I have written this that you might see I have my share of the highest pleasures, and that though I may choose to pass my days alone I shall be no Solitary. You see there is nothing spleenical in all this. The only thing that can ever affect me personally for more than one short passing day, is any doubt about my powers for poetry—I seldom have any, and I look with hope to the nighing time when I shall have none. I am as happy as a Man can be—that is, in myself I should be happy if Tom was well, and I knew you were passing pleasant days. Then I should be most enviable —with the yearning Passion I have for the beautiful, connected and made one with the ambition of my intellect. Think of my Pleasure in Solitude in comparison of my commerce with the world—there I am a child—there they do not know me, not even my most intimate acquaintance—I give in to their feelings as though I were refraining from irritating a little child. Some think me middling, others silly, others foolish—every one thinks he sees my weak side against my will, when in truth it is with my will—I am content to be thought all this because I have in my own breast so great a resource. This is one great reason why they like me so: because they can all show to advantage in a room and eclipse from a certain tact one who is reckoned to be a good Poet. I hope I am not here playing tricks 'to make the angels weep': I think not: for I have not the least contempt for my species, and though it may sound paradoxical, my greatest elevations of soul leave me every time more humbled— Enough of this—though in your Love for me you will not think it enough. ...

XX To Richard Woodhouse

[Hampstead, October 27, 1818]

My dear Woodhouse—Your letter gave me great satisfaction, more on account of its friendliness than any relish of that matter in it which is accounted so acceptable to the 'genus irritabile.' The best answer I can give you is in a clerklike manner to make some observations on two principal points which seem to point like indices into the midst of the whole pro and con about genius, and views, and achievements, and ambition, et cætera.—1st. As to the poetical Character itself (I mean that sort, of which, if I am anything, I am a member; that sort distinguished from the Wordsworthian, or egotistical Sublime; which is a thing per se, and stands alone,) it is not itself—it has no self—It is everything and nothing—It has no character—it enjoys light and shade; it lives in gusto, be it foul or fair, high or low, rich or poor, mean or elevated—It has as much delight in conceiving an Iago as an Imogen. What shocks the virtuous philosopher delights the chameleon poet. It does no harm from its relish of the dark side of things, any more than from its taste for the bright one, because they both end in speculation. A poet is the most unpoetical of anything in existence, because he has no Identity—he is continually in for and filling some other body. The Sun,—the Moon,—the Sea, and men and women, who are creatures of impulse, are poetical, and have about them an unchangeable attribute; the poet has none, no identity—he is certainly the most unpoetical of all God's creatures.—If then he has no self, and if I am a poet, where is the wonder that I should say I would write no more? Might I not at that very instant have been cogitating on the Characters of Saturn and Ops? It is a wretched thing to confess; but it is a very fact, that not one word I ever utter can be taken for granted as an opinion growing out of my identical Nature—how can it, when I have no Nature? When I am in a room with people, if I ever am free from speculating on creations of my own brain, then, not myself goes home to myself, but the identity of every one in the room begins to press upon me, so that I am in a very little time annihilated—not only among men; it would be the same in a nursery of Children. I know not whether I make myself wholly understood: I hope enough so to let you see that no dependence is to be placed on what I said that day.

In the 2d place, I will speak of my views, and of the life I purpose to myself. I am ambitious of doing the world some good: if I should be spared, that may be the work of maturer years—in the interval I will assay to reach to as high a summit in poetry as the nerve bestowed upon me will suffer. The faint conceptions I have of poems to come bring the blood frequently into my forehead—All I hope is, that I may not lose all interest in human affairs—that the solitary Indifference l feel for applause, even from the finest spirits, will not blunt any acuteness of vision I may have. I

do not think it will. I feel assured I should write from the mere yearning and fondness I have for the beautiful, even if my night's labours should be burnt every Morning, and no eye ever shine upon them. But even now I am perhaps not speaking from myself, but from some Character in whose soul I now live.

I am sure however that this next sentence is from myself—I feel your anxiety, good opinion, and friendship, in the highest degree, and am

Yours most sincerely   JOHN KEATS.

XXI To George and Georgiana Keats
[Hampstead, about Dec.ʳ 18, 1818]

MY DEAR BROTHER AND SISTER—You will have been prepared before this reaches you for the worst news you could have, nay, if Haslam's letter arrives in proper time, I have a consolation in thinking that the first shock will be past before you receive this. The last days of poor Tom were of the most distressing nature; but his last moments were not so painful, and his very last was without a pang. I will not enter into any parsonic comments on death—yet the common observations of the commonest people on death are as true as their proverbs. I have scarce a doubt of immortality of some nature or other—neither had Tom. My friends have been exceedingly kind to me every one of them—Brown detained me at his House. I suppose no one could have had their time made smoother than mine has been. During poor Tom's illness I was not able to write and since his death the task of beginning has been a hindrance to me. Within this last Week I have been everywhere —and I will tell you as nearly as possible how all go on. With Dilke and Brown I am quite thick—with Brown indeed I am going to domesticate—that is, we shall keep house together. I shall have the front parlour and he the back one, by which I shall avoid the noise of Bentley's Children—and be the better able to go on with my Studies—which have been greatly interrupted lately, so that I have not the shadow of an idea of a book in my head, and my pen seems to have grown too gouty for sense. How are you going on now? The goings on of the world makes me dizzy

—There you are with Birkbeck—here I am with Brown—sometimes I fancy an immense separation, and sometimes as at present, a direct communication of Spirit with you. That will be one of the grandeurs of immortality—There will be no space, and consequently the only commerce between spirits will be by their intelligence of each other—when they will completely understand each other, while we in this world merely comprehend each other in different degrees—the higher the degree of good so higher is our Love and friendship. . . .

. . . Mrs. Brawne who took Brown's house for the Summer, still resides in Hampstead. She is a very nice woman, and her daughter senior is I think beautiful and elegant, graceful, silly, fashionable and strange. We have a little tiff now and then—and she behaves a little better, or I must have sheered off. I find by a sidelong report from your Mother that I am to be invited to Miss Millar's birthday dance. Shall I dance with Miss Waldegrave? Eh! I shall be obliged to shirk a good many there. I shall be the only Dandy there—and indeed I merely comply with the invitation that the party may not be entirely destitute of a specimen of that race. I shall appear in a complete dress of purple, Hat and all—with a list of the beauties I have conquered embroidered round my Calves.

Thursday [December 24]

This morning is so very fine, I should have walked over to Walthamstow if I had thought of it yesterday. What are you doing this morning? Have you a clear hard frost as we have? How do you come on with the gun? Have you shot a Buffalo? Have you met with any Pheasants? My Thoughts are very frequently in a foreign Country—I live more out of England than in it. The Mountains of Tartary are a favourite lounge, if I happen to miss the Alleghany ridge, or have no whim for Savoy. There must be great pleasure in pursuing game—pointing your gun—no, it won't do—now, no—rabbit it—now bang—smoke and feathers—where is it? Shall you be able to get a good pointer or so? Have you seen Mr. Trimmer? He is an acquaintance of

Peachey's. Now I am not addressing myself to G. Minor, and yet I am—for you are one. Have you some warm furs? By your next Letters I shall expect to hear exactly how you go on—smother nothing—let us have all; fair and foul, all plain. Will the little bairn have made his entrance before you have this? Kiss it for me, and when it can first know a cheese from a Caterpillar show it my picture twice a week. . . .

. . . Hunt has asked me to meet Tom Moore some day—so you shall hear of him. The Night we went to Novello's there was a complete set to of Mozart and punning. I was so completely tired of it that if I were to follow my own inclinations I should never meet any one of that set again, not even Hunt, who is certainly a pleasant fellow in the main when you are with him—but in reality he is vain, egotistical, and disgusting in matters of taste and in morals. He understands many a beautiful thing; but then, instead of giving other minds credit for the same degree of perception as he himself professes—he begins an explanation in such a curious manner that our taste and self-love is offended continually. Hunt does one harm by making fine things petty, and beautiful things hateful. Through him I am indifferent to Mozart, I care not for white Busts—and many a glorious thing when associated with him becomes a nothing. This distorts one's mind—makes one's thoughts bizarre—perplexes one in the standard of Beauty. . . .

Friday [December 25]

I think you knew before you left England that my next subject would be 'the fall of Hyperion.' I went on a little with it last night, but it will take some time to get into the vein again. I will not give you any extracts because I wish the whole to make an impression. I have however a few Poems which you will like, and I will copy out on the next sheet. . . .

Shall I give you Miss Brawne? She is about my height—with a fine style of countenance of the lengthened sort—she wants sentiment in every feature—she manages to make her hair look well—her nostrils are fine—though a little painful—her mouth is bad and good—her Profile is better than her full-face which indeed is not full but pale and thin without showing any bone. Her shape is very graceful and so are her movements—her Arms are good her hands baddish—her feet tolerable. She is not seventeen—but she is ignorant—monstrous in her behaviour, flying out in all directions—calling people such names that I was forced lately to make use of the term *Minx*—this is I think not from any innate vice, but from a penchant she has for acting stylishly—I am however tired of such style and shall decline any more of it. She had a friend to visit her lately—you have known plenty such—her face is raw as if she was standing out in a frost; her lips raw and seem always ready for a Pullet—she plays the Music without one sensation but the feel of the ivory at her fingers. She is a downright Miss without one set off—We hated her and smoked her and baited her and I think drove her away. Miss B. thinks her a Paragon of fashion, and says she is the only woman she would change persons with. What a stupe—She is superior as a Rose to a Dandelion. When we went to bed Brown observed as he put out the Taper what a very ugly old woman that Miss Robinson would make—at which I must have groaned aloud for I'm sure ten minutes. I have not seen the thing Kingston again—George will describe him to you—I shall insinuate some of these Creatures into a Comedy some day—and perhaps have Hunt among them— . . .

Thursday [December 31]

. . . My thoughts have turned lately this way—The more we know the more inadequacy we find in the world to satisfy us—this is an old observation; but I have made up my Mind never to take anything for granted—but even to examine the truth of the commonest proverbs—This however is true. Mrs. Tighe and Beattie once delighted me—now I see through them and can find nothing in them but weakness, and yet how many they still delight! Perhaps a superior being may look upon Shakespeare in the same light—is it possible? No—This same inadequacy is dis-

covered (forgive me, little George, you know I don't mean to put you in the mess) in Women with few exceptions—the Dress Maker, the blue Stocking, and the most charming sentimentalist differ but in a slight degree and are equally smokeable. But I will go no further—I may be speaking sacrilegiously—and on my word I have thought so little that I have not one opinion upon anything except in matters of taste—I never can feel certain of any truth but from a clear perception of its Beauty—and I find myself very young minded even in that perceptive power—which I hope will increase. A year ago I could not understand in the slightest degree Raphael's cartoons—now I begin to read them a little—And how did I learn to do so? By seeing something done in quite an opposite spirit—I mean a picture of Guido's in which all the Saints, instead of that heroic simplicity and unaffected grandeur which they inherit from Raphael, had each of them both in countenance and gesture all the canting, solemn, melodramatic mawkishness of Mackenzie's father Nicholas. When I was last at Haydon's I looked over a Book of Prints taken from the fresco of the Church at Milan, the name of which I forget—in it are comprised Specimens of the first and second age of art in Italy. I do not think I ever had a greater treat out of Shakespeare. Full of Romance and the most tender feeling—magnificence of draperies beyond any I ever saw, not excepting Raphael's. But Grotesque to a curious pitch—yet still making up a fine whole—even finer to me than more accomplish'd works—as there was left so much room for Imagination. I have not heard one of this last course of Hazlitt's lectures. They were upon 'Wit and Humour,' 'the English comic writers.'

Saturday, Jany. 2nd [1819]

Yesterday Mr. and Mrs. D. and myself dined at Mrs. Brawne's—nothing particular passed. I never intend hereafter to spend any time with Ladies unless they are handsome—you lose time to no purpose. For that reason I shall beg leave to decline going again to Redall's or Butler's or any Squad where a fine feature cannot be mustered among them all—and where all the evening's amusement consists in saying 'your good health, *your* good health, and YOUR good health—and (O I beg your pardon) yours, Miss ——,' and such thing not even dull enough to keep one awake—With respect to amiable speaking I can read—let my eyes be fed or I'll never go out to dinner anywhere. . . .

XXII To George and Georgiana Keats

Friday, Feby. 18, 1819

The day before yesterday I went to Romney Street—your Mother was not at home—but I have just written her that I shall see her on Wednesday. I call'd on Mr. Lewis this morning—he is very well—and tells me not to be uneasy about Letters, the chances being so arbitrary. He is going on as usual among his favourite democrat papers. We had a chat as usual about Cobbett and the Westminster electors. Dilke has lately been very much harrassed about the manner of educating his son—he at length decided for a public school—and then he did not know what school—he at last has decided for Westminster; and as Charley is to be a day boy, Dilke will remove to Westminster. We lead very quiet lives here—Dilke is at present in Greek histories and antiquities, and talks of nothing but the electors of Westminster and the retreat of the ten-thousand. I never drink now above three glasses of wine—and never any spirits and water. Though by the bye, the other day Woodhouse took me to his coffee house and ordered a Bottle of Claret—now I like Claret, whenever I can have Claret I must drink it,—'tis the only palate affair that I am at all sensual in. Would it not be a good spec. to send you some vine roots—could it be done? I'll enquire—If you could make some wine like Claret to drink on summer evenings in an arbour! For really 'tis so fine—it fills one's mouth with a gushing freshness—then goes down cool and feverless—then you do not feel it quarrelling with your liver—no, it is rather a Peacemaker, and lies as quiet as it did in the grape; then it is as fragrant as the Queen Bee, and the more ethereal Part of it mounts into the brain, not assaulting the cerebral apartments like a bully in a bad-house looking for his trull and hurry-ing from door to door bouncing against the wainscoat, but rather walks like Aladdin about his own enchanted palace so gently that you do not feel his step. Other wines of a heavy and spirituous nature transform a Man to a Silenus: this makes him a Hermes—and gives a Woman the soul and immortality of Ariadne, for whom Bacchus always kept a good cellar of claret—and even of that he could never persuade her to take above two cups. I said this same claret is the only palate-passion I have—I forgot game—I must plead guilty to the breast of a Partridge, the back of a hare, the backbone of a grouse, the wing and side of a Pheasant and a Woodcock *passim*. Talking of game (I wish I could make it), the Lady whom I met at Hastings and of whom I said something in my last I think has lately made me many presents of game, and enabled me to make as many. She made me take home a Pheasant the other day, which I gave to Mrs. Dilke; on which to-morrow Rice, Reynolds and the Wentworthians will dine next door. The next I intend for your Mother. These moderate sheets of paper are much more pleasant to write upon than those large thin sheets which I hope you by this time have received—though that can't be, now I think of it. I have not said in any Letter yet a word about my affairs—in a word I am in no despair about them—my poem has not at all succeeded; in the course of a year or so I think I shall try the public again—in a selfish point of view I should suffer my pride and my contempt of public opinion to hold me silent—but for yours and Fanny's sake I will pluck up a spirit and try again. I have no doubt of success in a course of years if I persevere—but it must be patience, for the Reviews have enervated and made indolent men's minds—few think for themselves. These Reviews too are getting more and more powerful, especially the Quarterly—they are like a superstition which the more it prostrates the Crowd and the longer it continues the more powerful it becomes just in proportion to their increasing weakness. I was in hopes that when people saw, as they must do now, all the trickery and iniquity of these Plagues they would scout them, but no, they are like the spectators at the Westminster cock-pit—they like the battle and do not care who wins or who loses. Brown is going on this morning with the story of his old woman and the Devil—He makes but slow progress— The fact is it is a Libel on the Devil, and as that person is Brown's Muse, look ye, if he libels his own Muse how can he expect to write? Either Brown or his Muse must turn tail. Yesterday was Charley Dilke's birthday. Brown and I were invited to tea. During the evening nothing passed worth notice but a little conversation between Mrs. Dilke and Mrs. Brawne. The subject was the Watchman. It was ten o'clock, and Mrs. Brawne, who lived during the summer in Brown's house and now lives in the Road, recognized her old Watchman's voice, and said that he came as far as her now. 'Indeed,' said Mrs. D., 'does he turn the Corner?' There have been some letters passed between me and Haslam but I have not seen him lately. The day before yesterday— which I made a day of Business—I called upon him—he was out as usual. Brown has been walking up and down the room a-breeding—now at this moment he is being delivered of a couplet, and I daresay will be as well as can be expected. Gracious—he has twins! . . .

XXIII To George and Georgiana Keats

Friday, 19th March [1819]

This morning I have been reading 'the False One.' Shameful to say, I was in bed at ten—I mean this morning. The Blackwood Reviewers have committed themselves in a scandalous heresy—they have been putting up Hogg, the Ettrick Shepherd, against Burns: the senseless villains! The Scotch cannot manage themselves at all, they want imagination, and that is why they are so fond of Hogg, who has a little of it. This morning I am in a sort of temper, indolent and supremely careless—I long after a Stanza or two of Thomson's Castle of Indolence—my passions are all asleep, from my having slumbered till nearly eleven, and weakened the animal fibre all over me, to a delightful sensation, about three degrees on this side of faintness. If I had teeth of pearl and the breath of lilies I should call it languor, but as I am set [1] I must call it laziness. In this state of effeminacy the fibres of the brain are relaxed in common with the rest of the body, and to such a happy degree that pleasure has no show of enticement and pain no unbearable power. Neither Poetry, nor Ambition, nor Love have any alertness of countenance as they pass by me; they seem rather like figures on a Greek vase—a Man and two women whom no one but myself could distinguish in their disguisement. This is the only happiness, and is a rare instance of the advantage of the body overpowering the Mind. I have this moment received a note from Haslam, in which he expects the death of his Father, who has been for some time in a state of insensibility; his mother bears up he says very well—I shall go to town to-morrow to see him. This is the world—thus we cannot expect to give way many hours to pleasure. Circumstances are like Clouds continually gathering and bursting— While we are laughing, the seed of some trouble is put into the wide arable land of events—while we are laughing it sprouts it grows and suddenly bears a poison fruit which we must pluck. Even so we have leisure to reason on the misfortunes of our friends; our own touch us too nearly for words. Very few men have ever arrived at a complete disinterestedness of Mind: very few have been influenced by a pure desire of the benefit of others,—in the greater part of the Benefactors to Humanity some meretricious motive has sullied their greatness—some melodramatic scenery has fascinated them. From the manner in which I feel Haslam's misfortune I perceive how far I am from any humble standard of disinterestedness. Yet this feeling ought to be carried to its highest pitch, as there is no fear of its ever injuring society—which it would do, I fear, pushed to an extremity. For in wild nature the Hawk would lose his Breakfast of Robins and the Robin his of Worms—The Lion must starve as well as the swallow. The greater part of Men make their way with the same instinctiveness, the same unwandering eye from their purposes, the same animal eagerness as the Hawk. The Hawk wants a Mate, so does the Man—look at them both, they set about it and procure one in the same manner. They want both a nest and they both set about one in the same manner—they get their food in the same manner. The noble animal

[1] Especially as I have a black eye.

Man for his amusement smokes his pipe— the Hawk balances about the Clouds—that is the only difference of their leisures. This it is that makes the Amusement of Life—to a speculative Mind—I go among the Fields and catch a glimpse of a Stoat or a fieldmouse peeping out of the withered grass—the creature hath a purpose, and its eyes are bright with it. I go amongst the buildings of a city and I see a Man hurrying along—to what? The Creature has a purpose and his eyes are bright with it. But then, as Wordsworth says, 'we have all one human heart——' There is an electric fire in human nature tending to purify—so that among these human creatures there is continually some birth of new heroism. The pity is that we must wonder at it, as we should at finding a pearl in rubbish. I have no doubt that thousands of people never heard of have had hearts completely disinterested: I can remember but two—Socrates and Jesus— Their histories evince it. What I heard a little time ago, Taylor observe with respect to Socrates, may be said of Jesus—That he was so great a man that though he transmitted no writing of his own to posterity, we have his Mind and his sayings and his greatness handed to us by others. It is to be lamented that the history of the latter was written and revised by Men interested in the pious frauds of Religion. Yet through all this I see his splendour. Even here, though I myself am pursuing the same instinctive course as the veriest human animal you can think of, I am, however young, writing at random, straining at particles of light in the midst of a great darkness, without knowing the bearing of any one assertion, of any one opinion. Yet may I not in this be free from sin? May there not be superior beings amused with any graceful, though instinctive, attitude my mind may fall into as I am entertained with the alertness of a Stoat or the anxiety of a Deer? Though a quarrel in the Streets is a thing to be hated, the energies displayed in it are fine; the commonest Man shows a grace in his quarrel. By a superior Being our reasonings may take the same tone —though erroneous they may be fine. This is the very thing in which consists Poetry, and if so it is not so fine a thing as philosophy— For the same reason that an eagle is not so fine a thing as a truth. Give me this credit— Do you not think I strive—to know myself? Give me this credit, and you will not think that on my own account I repeat Milton's lines—

> How charming is divine Philosophy,
> Not harsh and crabbed, as dull fools suppose,
> But musical as is Apollo's lute.

No—not for myself—feeling grateful as I do to have got into a state of mind to relish them properly. Nothing ever becomes real till it is experienced—Even a Proverb is no proverb to you till your Life has illustrated it. I am ever afraid that your anxiety for me will lead you to fear for the violence of my temperament continually smothered down: for that reason I did not intend to have sent you the following sonnet—but look over the two last pages and ask yourselves whether I have not that in me which will bear the buffets of the world. It will be the best comment on my sonnet; it will show you that it was written with no Agony but that of ignorance; with no thirst of anything but Knowledge when pushed to the point though the first steps to it were through my human passions—they went away and I wrote with my Mind—and perhaps I must confess a little bit of my heart—

[Here follows the sonnet, 'Why did I laugh tonight? No voice will tell.']

I went to bed and enjoyed an uninterrupted sleep. Sane I went to bed and sane I arose. . . .

XXIV   To George and Georgiana Keats

[April 15, 1819]

. . . Brown is gone to bed—and I am tired of rhyming—there is a north wind blowing playing young gooseberry with the trees—I don't care so it helps even with a side wind a Letter to me—for I cannot put faith in any reports I hear of the Settlement; some are good and some bad. Last Sunday I took a Walk towards Highgate and in the lane that winds by the side of Lord Mansfield's park I met Mr. Green our Demonstrator at Guy's in conversation with Coleridge—I joined them, after enquiring by a look whether it would be agreeable—I walked with him at his alderman-after-dinner pace for near two miles I suppose. In those two Miles he broached a thousand things—let me see if I can give you a list—Nightingales—Poetry—on Poetical Sensation—Metaphysics—Different genera and species of Dreams—Nightmare—a dream accompanied by a sense of touch—single and double touch—a dream related—First and second consciousness—the difference explained between will and volition—so say metaphysicians from a want of smoking the second consciousness—Monsters—the Kraken—Mermaids—Southey believes in them—Southey's belief too much diluted—a Ghost story—Good morning—I heard his voice as he came towards me—I heard it as he moved away—I had heard it all the interval—if it may be called so. He was civil enough to ask me to call on him at Highgate. Good-night! . . .

[Later, April 16 or 17]

It looks so much like rain I shall not go to town to-day: but put it off till to-morrow. Brown this morning is writing some Spenserian stanzas against Mrs., Miss Brawne and me; so I shall amuse myself with him a little: in the manner of Spenser—

He is to weet a melancholy Carle:
Thin in the waist, with bushy head of hair,
As hath the seeded thistle when in parle
It holds the Zephyr, ere it sendeth fair
Its light balloons into the summer air;
There to his beard had not begun to bloom,
No brush had touch'd his chin, or razor sheer;
No care had touched his cheek with mortal
    doom,
But new he was, and bright, as scarf from Persian
    loom.

Ne cared he for wine, or half-and-half;
Ne cared he for fish, or flesh, or fowl;
And sauces held he worthless as the chaff;
He's deigned the swineherd at the wassail bowl;
Ne with lewd ribalds sat he cheek by jowl;
Ne with sly Lemans in the scorner's chair;
But after water-brooks this Pilgrim's soul
Panted, and all his food was woodland air;
Though he would oft-times feast on gilliflowers
    rare.

The slang of cities in no wise he knew;
Tipping the wink to him was heathen Greek;
He sipp'd no 'olden Tom,' or 'ruin blue,'
Or Nantz, or cherry-brandy, drunk full meek
By many a Damsel hoarse, and rouge of cheek;

Nor did he know each aged Watchman's beat,
Nor in obscured purlieus would he seek
For curled Jewesses, with ankles neat,
Who, as they walk abroad, make tinkling with
    their feet.

This character would ensure him a situation in the establishment of patient Griselda. The servant has come for the little Browns this morning—they have been a toothache to me which I shall enjoy the riddance of—Their little voices are like wasps' stings—Sometimes am I all wound with Browns. We had a claret feast some little while ago. There were Dilke, Reynolds, Skinner, Mancur, John Brown, Martin, Brown and I. We all got a little tipsy—but pleasantly so—I enjoy Claret to a degree.

XXV To George and Georgiana Keats

April 28 [1819]

. . . The whole appears to resolve into this—that Man is originally a poor forked creature subject to the same mischances as the beasts of the forest, destined to hardships and disquietude of some kind or other. If he improves by degrees his bodily accommodations and comforts—at each stage, at each ascent there are waiting for him a fresh set of annoyances—he is mortal, and there is still a heaven with its Stars above his head. The most interesting question that can come before us is, How far by the persevering endeavours of a seldom appearing Socrates Mankind may be made happy—I can imagine such happiness carried to an extreme, but what must it end in?—Death—and who could in such a case bear with death? The whole troubles of life, which are now frittered away in a series of years, would then be accumulated for the last days of a being who instead of hailing its approach would leave this world as Eve left Paradise. But in truth I do not at all believe in this sort of perfectibility—the nature of the world will not admit of it—the inhabitants of the world will correspond to itself. Let the fish Philosophise the ice away from the Rivers in winter time, and they shall be at continual play in the tepid delight of summer. Look at the Poles and at the Sands of Africa, whirlpools and volcanoes—Let men exterminate them and I will say that they may arrive at earthly Happiness. The point at which Man may arrive is as far as the parallel state in inanimate nature, and no further. For instance suppose a rose to have sensation, it blooms on a beautiful morning, it enjoys itself, but then comes a cold wind, a hot sun—it cannot escape it, it cannot destroy its annoyances—they are as native to the world as itself: no more can man be happy in spite, the worldly elements will prey upon his nature. The common cognomen of this world among the misguided and superstitious is 'a vale of tears,' from which we are to be redeemed by a certain arbitrary interposition of God and taken to Heaven—What a little circumscribed straightened notion! Call the world if you please 'The vale of Soul-making.' Then you will find out the use of the world (I am speaking now in the highest terms for human nature admitting it to be immortal which I will here take for granted for the purpose of showing a thought which has struck me concerning it) I say '*Soul-making*'—Soul as distinguished from an Intelligence. There may be intelligences or sparks of the divinity in millions—but they are not Souls till they acquire identities, till each one is personally itself. Intelligences are atoms of perception—they know and they see and they are pure, in short they are God—how then are the Souls to be made? How then are these sparks which are God to have identity given them—so as ever to possess a bliss peculiar to each one's individual existence? How, but by the medium of a world like this? . . . Do you not see how necessary a World of Pains and troubles is to school an Intelligence and make it a soul? . . . Seriously I think it probable that this system of Soul-making may have been the Parent of all the more palpable and personal schemes of Redemption among the Zoroastrians the Christians and the Hindoos. For as one part of the human species must have their carved Jupiter; so another part must have the palpable and named Mediator and Saviour, their Christ, their Oromanes, and their Vishnu. If what I have said should not be plain enough, as I fear it may not be, I will put you in the place where I began in this series of thoughts—I mean I began by seeing how man was formed by circumstances—and what are circumstances but touchstones of his heart? and what are touchstones but provings of his heart, but fortifiers or alterers of his nature? and what is his altered nature but his Soul?—and what was his Soul before it came into the world and had these provings and alterations and perfectionings?—An intelligence without Identity—and how is this Identity to be made? Through the medium of the Heart? and how is the heart to become this Medium but in a world of Circumstances?

There now I think what with Poetry and Theology, you may thank your stars that my pen is not very long-winded. Yesterday I received two Letters from your Mother and Henry, which I shall send by young Birkbeck with this.

Friday, April 30

Brown has been here rummaging up some of my old sins—that is to say sonnets. I do not think you remember them, so I will copy them out, as well as two or three lately written. I have just written one on Fame—which Brown is transcribing and he has his book and mine. I must employ myself perhaps in a sonnet on the same subject.—

[Here are given the two sonnets on 'Fame,' and the one 'To Sleep.']

The following Poem—the last I have written—is the first and the only one with which I have taken even moderate pains. I have for the most part dash'd off my lines in a hurry. This I have done leisurely—I think it reads the more richly for it, and will I hope encourage me to write other things in even a more peaceable and healthy spirit. You must recollect that Psyche was not embodied as a goddess before the time of Apuleius the Platonist who lived after the Augustan age, and consequently the Goddess was never worshipped or sacrificed to with any of the ancient fervour—and perhaps never thought of in the old religion—I am more orthodox than to let a heathen Goddess be so neglected—

[The 'Ode to Psyche' here follows.]

Incipit altera Sonneta

I have been endeavouring to discover a better Sonnet Stanza than we have. The legitimate does not suit the language over well from the pouncing rhymes—the other kind appears too elegiac—and the couplet at the end of it has seldom a pleasing effect—I do not pretend to have succeeded—it will explain itself.

[Sonnet, 'If By Dull Rhymes.']

[May 3]

This is the third of May, and everything is in delightful forwardness; the violets are not withered before the peeping of the first rose. You must let me know everything—how parcels go and come, what papers you have, and what newspapers you want, and other things. God bless you, my dear brother and sister.

Your ever affectionate Brother

JOHN KEATS.

XXVI TO BENJAMIN ROBERT HAYDON

Wentworth Place,
[Postmark, March 8, 1819]

MY DEAR HAYDON,—You must be wondering where I am and what I am about! I am mostly at Hampstead, and about nothing; being in a sort of qui bono temper, not exactly on the road to an epic poem. Nor must you think I have forgotten you. No, I have about every three days been to Abbey's and to the Law[y]ers. Do let me know how you have been getting on, and in what spirits you are.

You got out gloriously in yesterday's Examiner. What a set of little people we live amongst! I went the other day into an ironmonger's shop—without any change in my sensations—men and tin kettles are much the same in these days—they do not study like children at five and thirty—but they talk like men of twenty. Conversation is not a search after knowledge, but an endeavour at effect.

In this respect two most opposite men, Wordsworth and Hunt, are the same. A friend of mine observed the other day that if Lord Bacon were to make any remark in a party of the present day, the conversation would stop on the sudden. I am convinced of this, and from this I have come to this resolution— never to write for the sake of writing or making a poem, but from running over with any little knowledge or experience which many years of reflection may perhaps give me; otherwise I will be dumb. What imagination I have I shall enjoy, and greatly, for I have experienced the satisfaction of having great conceptions without the trouble of sonnetteering. I will not spoil my love of gloom by writing an Ode to Darkness!

With respect to my livelihood, I will not write for it,—for I will not run with that most vulgar of all crowds, the literary. Such things I ratify by looking upon myself, and trying myself at lifting mental weights, as it were. I am three and twenty with little knowledge and middling intellect. It is true that in the height of enthusiasm I have been cheated into some fine passages; but that is not the thing.

I have not been to see you because all my going out has been to town, and that has been a great deal. Write soon.

Yours constantly,   JOHN KEATS.

XXVII TO BENJAMIN ROBERT HAYDON

Tuesday [April 13, 1819]

MY DEAR HAYDON—When I offered you assistance I thought I had it in my hand; I thought I had nothing to do but to do. The difficulties I met with arose from the alertness and suspicion of Abbey: and especially from the affairs being still in a Lawyer's hand— who has been draining our Property for the last six years of every charge he could make. I cannot do two things at once, and thus this affair has stopped my pursuits in every way— from the first prospect I had of difficulty. I assure you I have harrassed myself ten times more than if I alone had been concerned in so much gain or loss. I have also ever told you the exact particulars as well as and as literally as any hopes or fear could translate them: for it was only by parcels that I found all those petty obstacles which for my own sake should not exist a moment—and yet why not--for from my own imprudence and neglect all my accounts are entirely in my Guardian's Power. This has taught me a Lesson. Hereafter I will be more correct. I find myself possessed of much less than I thought for and now if I had all on the table all I could do would be to take from it a moderate two years' subsistence and lend you the rest; but I cannot say how soon I could become possessed of it. This would be on sacrifice nor any matter worth thinking of—much less than parting as I have more than once done with little sums which might have gradually formed a library to my taste. These sums amount together to nearly £200, which I have but a chance of ever being repaid or paid at a very distant period. I am humble enough to put this in writing from the sense I have of your struggling situation and the great desire that you should do me the justice to credit me the unostentatious and willing state of my nerves on all such occasions. It has not been my fault. I am doubly hurt at the slightly reproachful tone of your note and at the occasion of it,—for it must be some other disappointment; you seem'd so sure of some important help when I last saw you—now you have maimed me again; I was whole, I had began reading again—when your note came I was engaged in a Book. I dread as much as a Plague the idle fever of two months more without any fruit. I will walk over the first fine day: then see what aspect your affairs have taken, and if they should continue gloomy walk into the City to Abbey and get his consent for I am persuaded that to me alone he will not concede a jot.

XXVIII   To Fanny Keats

Wentworth Place [April 13, 1819]

My dear Fanny . . . I ordered some bulbous roots for you at the Gardener's, and they sent me some, but they were all in bud—and could not be sent—so I put them in our Garden. There are some beautiful heaths now in bloom in Pots—either heaths or some seasonable plants I will send you instead—perhaps some that are not yet in bloom that you may see them come out . . . I hope you have good store of double violets—I think they are the Princesses of flowers, and in a shower of rain, almost as fine as barley sugar drops are to a schoolboy's tongue. I suppose this fine weather the lambs' tails give a frisk or two extraordinary—when a boy would cry huzzah and a Girl O my! a little Lamb frisks its tail. I have not been lately through Leicester Square—the first time I do I will remember your Seals. I have thought it best to live in Town this Summer, chiefly for the sake of books, which cannot be had with any comfort in the Country—besides my Scotch journey gave me a dose of the Picturesque with which I ought to be contented for some time. Westminster is the place I have pitched upon—the City or any place very confined would soon turn me pale and thin—which is to be avoided. You must make up your mind to get stout this summer—indeed I have an idea we shall both be corpulent old folks with tripple chins and stumpy thumbs.

Your affectionate Brother   John.

XXIX   To Fanny Brawne

July 8, [1819]

My sweet Girl—Your Letter gave me more delight than any thing in the world but yourself could do; indeed I am almost astonished that any absent one should have that luxurious power over my senses which I feel. Even when I am not thinking of you I receive your influence and a tenderer nature stealing upon me. All my thoughts, my unhappiest days and nights, have I find not at all cured me of my love of Beauty, but made it so intense that I am miserable that you are not with me: or rather breathe in that dull sort of patience that cannot be called Life. I never knew before, what such a love as you have made me feel, was; I did not believe in it; my Fancy was afraid of it, lest it should burn me up. But if you will fully love me, though there may be some fire, 'twill not be more than we can bear when moistened and bedewed with Pleasures. You mention 'horrid people' and ask me whether it depend upon them whether I see you again. Do understand me, my love, in this. I have so much of you in my heart that I must turn Mentor when I see a chance of harm befalling you. I would never see any thing but Pleasure in your eyes, love on your lips, and Happiness in your steps. I would wish to see you among those amusements suitable to your inclinations and spirits; so that our loves might be a delight in the midst of Pleasures agreeable enough, rather than a resource from vexations and cares. But I doubt much, in case of the worst, whether I shall be philosopher enough to follow my own Lessons: if I saw my resolution give you a pain I could not. Why may I not speak of your Beauty, since without that I could never have lov'd you?—I cannot conceive any beginning of such love as I have for you but Beauty. There may be a sort of love for which, without the least sneer at it, I have the highest respect and can admire it in others: but it has not the richness, the bloom, the full form, the enchantment of love after my own heart. So let me speak of your Beauty, though to my own endangering; if you could be so cruel to me as to try elsewhere its Power. You say you are afraid I shall think you do not love me —in saying this you make me ache the more to be near you. I am at the diligent use of my faculties here, I do not pass a day without sprawling some blank verse or tagging some rhymes; and here I must confess, that (since I am on that subject) I love you the more in that I believe you have liked me for my own sake and for nothing else. I have met with women whom I really think would like to be married to a Poem and to be given away by a Novel. I have seen your Comet, and only wish it was a sign that poor Rice would get well whose illness makes him rather a melancholy companion: and the more so as to conquer his feelings and hide them from me, with a forc'd Pun. I kiss'd your writing over in the hope you had indulg'd me by leaving a trace of honey. What was your dream? Tell it me and I will tell you the interpretation thereof.

Ever yours, my love!
JOHN KEATS.

Do not accuse me of delay—we have not here an opportunity of sending letters every day. Write speedily.

XXX TO FANNY BRAWNE

Sunday Night. [Postmark, July 27, 1819]

MY SWEET GIRL—I hope you did not blame me much for not obeying your request of a Letter on Saturday: we have had four in our small room playing at cards night and morning leaving me no undisturb'd opportunity to write. Now Rice and Martin are gone I am at liberty. Brown to my sorrow confirms the account you give of your ill health. You cannot conceive how I ache to be with you: how I would die for one hour——for what is in the world? I say you cannot conceive; it is impossible you should look with such eyes upon me as I have upon you: it cannot be. Forgive me if I wander a little this evening, for I have been all day employ'd in a very abstract Poem and I am in deep love with you—two things which must excuse me. I have, believe me, not been an age in letting you take possession of me; the very first week I knew you I wrote myself your vassal; but burnt the Letter as the very next time I saw you I thought you manifested some dislike to me. If you should ever feel for Man at the first sight what I did for you, I am lost. Yet I should not quarrel with you, but hate myself if such a thing were to happen—only I should burst if the thing were not as fine as a Man as you are as a Woman. Perhaps I am too vehement, then fancy me on my knees, especially when I mention a part of your Letter which hurt me; you say speaking of Mr. Severn 'but you must be satisfied in knowing that I admire you much more than your friend.' My dear love, I cannot believe there ever was or ever could be any thing to admire in me especially as far as sight goes—I cannot be admired, I am not a thing to be admired. You are, I love you; all I can bring you is a swooning admiration of your Beauty. I hold that place among Men which snub-nos'd brunettes with meeting eyebrows do among women— they are trash to me—unless I should find one among them with a fire in her heart like the one that burns in mine. You absorb me in spite of myself—you alone: for I look not forward with any pleasure to what is call'd being settled in the world; I tremble at domestic cares—yet for you I would meet them, though if it would leave you the happier I would rather die than do so. I have two luxuries to brood over in my walks, your Loveliness and the hour of my death. O that I could have possession of them both in the same minute. I hate the world: it batters too much the wings of my self-will, and would I could take a sweet poison from your lips to send me out of it. From no others would I take it. I am indeed astonish'd to find myself so careless of all charms but yours—remembering as I do the time when even a bit of ribband was a matter of interest with me. What softer words can I find for you after this—what it is I will not read. Nor will I say more here, but in a Postscript answer any thing else you may have mentioned in your Letter in so many words— for I am distracted with a thousand thoughts. I will imagine you Venus tonight and pray, pray, pray to your star like a Heathen.

Your's ever, fair Star,   JOHN KEATS.

XXXI To CHARLES WENTWORTH DILKE

Shanklin, Saturday Evening [July 31, 1819]

MY DEAR DILKE—I will not make my diligence an excuse for not writing to you sooner —because I consider idleness a much better plea. A Man in the hurry of business of any sort is expected and ought to be expected to look to everything—his mind is in a whirl, and what matters it what whirl? But to require a Letter of a Man lost in idleness is the utmost cruelty; you cut the thread of his existence, you beat, you pummel him, you sell his goods and chattels, you put him in prison; you impale him; you crucify him. If I had not put pen to paper since I saw you this would be to me a vi et armis taking up before the Judge; but having got over my darling lounging habits a little, it is with scarcely any pain I come to this dating from Shanklin and Dear Dilke. The Isle of Wight is but so so, etc. Rice and I passed rather a dull time of it. I hope he will not repent coming with me. He was unwell, and I was not in very good health: and I am afraid we made each other worse by acting upon each other's spirits. We would grow as melancholy as need be. I confess I cannot bear a sick person in a House, especially alone—it weighs upon me day and night— and more so when perhaps the Case is irretrievable. Indeed I think Rice is in a dangerous state. I have had a Letter from him which speaks favourably of his health at present. Brown and I are pretty well harnessed again to our dog-cart. I mean the Tragedy, which goes on sinkingly. We are thinking of introducing an Elephant, but have not historical reference within reach to determine us as to Otho's Menagerie. When Brown first men-

tioned this I took it for a joke; however he brings such plausible reasons, and discourses so eloquently on the dramatic effect that I am giving it a serious consideration. The Art of Poetry is not sufficient for us, and if we get on in that as well as we do in painting, we shall by next winter crush the Reviews and the Royal Academy. Indeed, if Brown would take a little of my advice, he could not fail to be first palette of his day. But odd as it may appear, he says plainly that he cannot see any force in my plea of putting skies in the background, and leaving Indian ink out of an ash tree. The other day he was sketching Shanklin Church, and as I saw how the business was going on, I challenged him to a trial of skill—he lent me Pencil and Paper— we keep the Sketches to contend for the Prize at the Gallery. I will not say whose I think best—but really I do not think Brown's done to the top of the Art.

A word or two on the Isle of Wight. I have been no further than Steephill. If I may guess, I should say that there is no finer part in the Island than from this Place to Steephill. I do not hesitate to say it is fine. Bonchurch is the best. But I have been so many finer walks, with a background of lake and mountain instead of the sea, that I am not much touch'd with it, though I credit it for all the Surprise I should have felt if it had taken my cockney maidenhead. But I may call myself an old Stager in the picturesque, and unless it be something very large and overpowering, I cannot receive any extraordinary relish.

I am sorry to hear that Charles is so much oppress'd at Westminster, though I am sure it will be the finest touchstone for his Metal in the world. His troubles will grow day by day less, as his age and strength increase. The very first Battle he wins will lift him from the Tribe of Manasseh. I do not know how I should feel were I a Father—but I hope I should strive with all my Power not to let the present trouble me. When your Boy shall be twenty, ask him about his childish troubles and he will have no more memory of them than you have of yours. Brown tells me Mrs. Dilke sets off to-day for Chichester. I am glad—I was going to say she had a fine day—but there had been a great Thunder cloud muttering over Hampshire all day—I hope she is now at supper with a good appetite.

So Reynold's Piece succeeded—that is all well. Papers have with thanks been duly received. We leave this place on the 13th, and will let you know where we may be a few days after—Brown says he will write when the fit comes on him. If you will stand law expenses I'll beat him into one before his time. When I come to town I shall have a little talk with you about Brown and one Jenny Jacobs. Open daylight! he don't care. I am afraid there will be some more feet for little stockings—[*of Keats's making. (I mean the feet.*[1])] Brown here tried at a piece of Wit but it failed him, as you see, though long a brewing—[*this is a 2*[d] *lie.*[1]] Men should never despair—you see he·has tried again and succeeded to a miracle.—He wants to try again, but as I have a right to an inside place in my own Letter—I take possession.

Your sincere friend   JOHN KEATS.

XXXII To JOHN TAYLOR

Winchester, Monday morn
[August 23, 1819]

MY DEAR TAYLOR—. . . Brown and I have together been engaged (this I should wish to remain secret) on a Tragedy which I have just finished and from which we hope to share moderate profits. . . . I feel every confidence that, if I choose, I may be a popular writer. That I will never be; but for all that I will get a livelihood. I equally dislike the favour of the public with the love of a woman. They are both a cloying treacle to the wings of Independence. I shall ever consider them (People) as debtors to me for verses, not myself to them for admiration—which I can do without. I have of late been indulging my spleen by composing a preface AT them: after all resolving never to write a preface at all. 'There are so many verses,' would I have said to them, 'give so much means for me to buy pleasure with, as a relief to my hours of labour'—You will observe at the end of this if you put down the letter, 'How a solitary life engenders pride and egotism!' True—I know it does: but this pride and egotism will enable me to write

¹ The bracketed portions are by Brown.

finer things than anything else could—so I will indulge it. Just so much as I am humbled by the genius above my grasp am I exalted and look with hate and contempt upon the literary world.—A drummer-boy who holds out his hand familiarly to a field Marshal,—that drummer-boy with me is the good word and favour of the public. Who could wish to be among the common-place crowd of the little famous—who are each individually lost in a throng made up of themselves? Is this worth louting or playing the hypocrite for? To beg suffrages for a seat on the benches of a myriad-aristocracy in letters? This is not wise. —I am not a wise man—'Tis pride—I will give you a definition of a proud man—He is a man who has neither Vanity nor Wisdom— One filled with hatreds cannot be vain, neither can he be wise. Pardon me for hammering instead of writing. Remember me to Woodhouse Hessey and all in Percy Street.

Ever yours sincerely   JOHN KEATS.

XXXIII To BENJAMIN BAILEY

[*Fragment (outside sheet) of a letter addressed to Bailey at St. Andrews.*]

Winchester, August 15, 1819].

We removed to Winchester for the convenience of a library, and find it an exceeding pleasant town, enriched with a beautiful Cathedral and surrounded by a fresh-looking country. We are in tolerably good and cheap lodgings—Within these two months I have written 1500 lines, most of which, besides many more of prior composition, you will probably see by next winter. I have written 2 tales, one from Boccaccio, called the Pot of Basil, and another called St. Agnes's Eve, on a popular Superstition, and a 3rd called Lamia (half finished). I have also been writing parts of my 'Hyperion,' and completed 4 Acts of a tragedy. It was the opinion of most of my friends that I should never be able to write a scene. I will endeavour to wipe away the prejudice—I sincerely hope you will be pleased when my labours, since we last saw each other, shall reach you. One of my Ambitions is to make as great a revolution in modern dramatic writing as Kean has done in acting. Another to upset the drawling of the blue-stocking literary world—if in the Course of a few years I do these two things, I ought to die content, and my friends should drink a dozen of claret on my tomb. I am convinced more and more every day that (excepting the human friend philosopher), a fine writer is the most genuine being in the world. Shakespeare and the Paradise lost every day become greater wonders to me. I look upon fine phrases like a lover. I was glad to see by a passage of one of Brown's letters, some time ago, from the North that you were in such good spirits. Since that you have been married, and in congratulating you I wish you every continuance of them. Present my respects to Mrs. Bailey. This sounds oddly to me, and I daresay I do it awkwardly enough: but I suppose by this time it is nothing new to you. Brown's remembrances to you. As far as I know, we shall remain at Winchester for a goodish while.

Ever your sincere friend

JOHN KEATS.

XXXIV TO GEORGE AND GEORGIANA KEATS

Winchester, September [17, 1819], Friday
... I have passed my time in reading, writing, and fretting—the last I intend to give up, and stick to the other two. They are the only chances of benefit to us. Your wants will be a fresh spur to me. I assure you you shall more than share what I can get whilst I am still young. The time may come when age will make me more selfish. I have not been well treated by the world, and yet I have, capitally well. I do not know a person to whom so many purse-strings would fly open as to me, if I could possibly take advantage of them, which I cannot do, for none of the owners of these purses are rich. Your present situation I will not suffer myself to dwell upon. When misfortunes are so real, we are glad enough to escape them and the thought of them. I cannot help thinking Mr. Audubon a dishonest man. Why did he make you believe that he was a man of property? How is it that his circumstances have altered so suddenly? In truth, I do not believe you fit to deal with the world, or at least the American world. But, good God!

who can avoid these chances? You have done your best. Take matters as coolly as you can; and confidently expecting help from England, act as if no help were nigh. Mine, I am sure, is a tolerable tragedy; it would have been a bank to me, if just as I had finished it, I had not heard of Kean's resolution to go to America. That was the worst news I could have had. There is no actor can do the principal character besides Kean. At Covent Garden there is a great chance of its being damm'd. Were it to succeed even there it would lift me out of the mire; I mean the mire of a bad reputation which is continually rising against me. My name with the literary fashionables is vulgar. I am a weaver-boy to them. A tragedy would lift me out of this mess, and mess it is as far as regards our pockets. But be not cast down any more than I am; I feel that I can bear real ills better than imaginary ones. Whenever I find myself growing vapourish, I rouse myself, wash, and put on a clean shirt, brush my hair and clothes, tie my shoestrings neatly, and in fact adonise as I were going out. Then, all clean and comfortable, I sit down to write. This I find the greatest relief. Besides I am becoming accustomed to the privations of the pleasures of sense. In the midst of the world I live like a hermit. I have forgot how to lay plans for the enjoyment of any pleasure. I feel I can bear anything,—any misery, even imprisonment, so long as I have neither wife nor child. Perhaps you will say yours are your only comfort; they must be. I returned to Winchester the day before yesterday, and am now here alone, for Brown, some days before I left, went to Bedhampton, and there he will be for the next fortnight ...

I saw Haslam. He is very much occupied with love and business, being one of Mr. Saunders' executors and lover to a young woman. He showed me her picture by Severn. I think she is, though not very cunning, too cunning for him. Nothing strikes me so forcibly with a sense of the ridiculous as love. A man in love I do think cuts the sorriest figure in the world; queer, when I know a poor fool to be really in pain about it, I could burst out laughing in his face. His pathetic visage becomes irresistible. Not that I take Haslam as a pattern for lovers; he is a very worthy man and a good friend. His love is very amusing. Somewhere in the Spectator is related an account of a man inviting a party of stutterers and squinters to his table. It would please me more to scrape together a party of lovers—not to dinner, but to tea. There would be no fighting as among knights of old.

Pensive they sit, and roll their languid eyes,
Nibble their toast, and cool their tea with sighs,
Or else forget the purpose of the night,
Forget their tea—forget their appetite.
See with cross'd arms they sit—ah! happy crew,
The fire is going out and no one rings
For coals, and therefore no coals Betty brings.
A fly is in the milk-pot—must he die
    By a humane society?
No, no; there Mr. Werter takes his spoon,
Inserts it, dips the handle, and lo! soon
The little straggler, sav'd from perils dark,
Across the teaboard draws a long wet mark. . . .

You see, I cannot get on without writing, as boys do at school, a few nonsense verses. I begin them and before I have written six the whim has passed—if there is anything deserving so respectable a name in them. I shall put in a bit of information anywhere, just as it strikes me. Mr. Abbey is to write to me as soon as he can bring matters to bear, and then I am to go to town and tell him the means of forwarding to you through Capper and Hazlewood. I wonder I did not put this before. I shall go on to-morrow; it is so fine now I must take a bit of a walk.

Saturday [September 18]

With my inconstant disposition it is no wonder that this morning, amid all our bad times and misfortunes, I should feel so alert and well-spirited. At this moment you are perhaps in a very different state of mind. It is because my hopes are ever paramount to my despair. I have been reading over a part of a short poem I have composed lately, called Lamia, and I am certain there is that sort of fire in it that must take hold of people some way. Give them either pleasant or unpleasant sensation—what they want is a sensation of some sort. I wish I could pitch the key of your spirits as high as mine is; but your organ-loft is beyond the reach of my voice.

. . . You speak of Lord Byron and me.

There is this great difference between us: he describes what he sees—I describe what I imagine. Mine is the hardest task; now see the immense difference. The Edinburgh Reviewers are afraid to touch upon my poem. They do not know what to make of it; they do not like to condemn it, and they will not praise it for fear. They are as shy of it as I should be of wearing a Quaker's hat. The fact is, they have no real taste. They dare not compromise their judgments on so puzzling a question. If on my next publication they should praise me, and so lug in Endymion, I will address them in a manner they will not at all relish. The cowardliness of the Edinburgh is more than the abuse of the Quarterly. . . .

Monday [September 20]

. . . I hope you will like this for all its carelessness. I must take an opportunity here to observe that though I am writing to you, I am all the while writing at your wife. This explanation will account for my speaking sometimes hoity-toity-ishly, whereas if you were alone, I should sport a little more sober sadness. I am like a squinty gentleman, who, saying soft things to one lady ogles another, or what is as bad, in arguing with a person on his left hand, appeals with his eyes to one on the right. His vision is elastic; he bends it to a certain object, but having a patent spring it flies off. Writing has this disadvantage of speaking —one cannot write a wink, or a nod, or a grin, or a purse of the lips, or a smile—O law! One cannot put one's finger to one's nose, or yerk ye in the ribs, or lay hold of your button in writing; but in all the most lively and titterly parts of my letter you must not fail to imagine me, as the epic poets say, now here, now there; now with one foot pointed at the ceiling, now with another; now with my pen on my ear, now with my elbow in my mouth. O, my friends, you lose the action, and attitude is everything, as Fuseli said when he took up his leg like a musket to shoot a swallow just darting behind his shoulder. And yet does not the word 'mum' go for one's finger beside the nose? I hope it does. I have to make use of the word 'mum' before I tell you that Severn has got a little baby—all his own, let us hope. He told Brown he had given up painting, and had turned modeller. I hope sincerely 'tis not a party concern—that no Mr.——or——is the real Pinxit and Severn the poor Sculpsit to this work of art. You know he has long studied in the life Academy. 'Haydon—yes,' your wife will say, 'Here is a sum total account of Haydon again. I wonder your brother don't put a monthly bulletin in the Philadelphia papers about him. I won't hear—no. Skip down to the bottom, and there are some more of his verses—skip (lullaby-by) them too.'—'No, let's go regularly through.'—'I won't hear a word about Haydon—bless the child, how rioty she is—there, go on there.'

Now, pray go on here, for I have a few words to say about Haydon. Before this chancery threat had cut off every legitimate supply of cash from me, I had a little at my disposal. Haydon being very much in want, I lent him £30 of it. Now in this see-saw game of life, I got nearest to the ground, and this chancery business riveted me there, so that I was sitting in that uneasy position where the seat slants so abominably. I applied to him for payment. He could not. That was no wonder; but Goodman Delver, where was the wonder then? Why marry in this: he did not seem to care much about it, and let me go without my money with almost nonchalance, when he ought to have sold his drawings to supply me. I shall perhaps still be acquainted with him, but for friendship, that is at an end. Brown has been my friend in this. He got him to sign a bond, payable at three months. Haslam has assisted me with the return of part of the money you lent him. . . .

Tuesday [September 21]

You see I keep adding a sheet daily till I send the packet off, which I shall not do for a few days, as I am inclined to write a good deal; for there can be nothing so remembrancing and enchaining as a good long letter, be it composed of what it may. From the time you left me our friends say I have altered completely—am not the same person. Perhaps in this letter I am, for in a letter one takes up one's existence from the time we last met. I daresay you have altered also—every man does—our bodies every seven years are completely material'd. Seven years ago it was not this hand that clinched itself against Hammond. We are like the relict garments of a saint—the same and not the same, for the careful monks patch it and patch it till there's not a thread of the original garment left, and still they show it for St. Anthony's shirt. This is the reason why men who have been bosom friends, on being separated for any number of years meet coldly, neither of them knowing why. The fact is they are both altered.

Men who live together have a silent moulding and influencing power over each other. They interassimilate. 'Tis an uneasy thought, that in seven years the same hands cannot greet each other again. All this may be obviated by a wilful and dramatic exercise of our minds towards each other. Some think I have lost that poetic ardour and fire 'tis said I once had—the fact is, perhaps I have; but, instead of that, I hope I shall substitute a more thoughtful and quiet power. I am more frequently now contented to read and think, but now and then haunted with ambitious thoughts. Quieter in my pulse, improved in my digestion, exerting myself against vexing speculations, scarcely content to write the best verses for the fever they leave behind. I want to compose without this fever. I hope I one day shall. . . .

XXXV To Charles Armitage Brown

Winchester, September 23, 1819

* * *

Do not suffer me to disturb you unpleasantly: I do not mean that you should not suffer me to occupy your thoughts, but to occupy them pleasantly; for I assure you I am as far from being unhappy as possible. Imaginary grievances have always been more my torment than real ones—You know this well—Real ones will never have any other effect upon me than to stimulate me to get out of or avoid them. This is easily accounted for—Our imaginary woes are conjured up by our passions, and are fostered by passionate feeling: our real ones come of themselves, and are opposed by an abstract exertion of mind. Real grievances are displacers of passion. The imaginary nail a man down for a sufferer, as on a cross; the real spur him up into an agent. I wish, at one view, you would see my heart towards you. 'Tis only from a high tone of feeling that I can put that word upon paper— out of poetry. I ought to have waited for your answer to my last before I wrote this. I felt however compelled to make a joinder to yours. I had written to Dilke on the subject of my last, I scarcely know whether I shall send my letter now. I think he would approve of my plan; it is so evident. Nay, I am convinced, out and out, that by prosing for a while in periodical works I may maintain myself decently.

* * *

XXXVI To GEORGIANA AUGUSTA KEATS

Thursday, January 13, 1820

MY DEAR SIS.: By the time you receive this your trouble will be over. I wish you knew they were half over. I mean that George is safe in England [1] and in good health. . . .

We smoke George about his little girl. He runs the common-beaten road of every father, as I dare say you do of every mother: there is no child like his child, so original,—original forsooth! However, I take you at your words. I have a lively faith that yours is the very gem of all children. Ain't I its uncle? . . .

. . . My pen is no more garrulous than my tongue. Any third person would think I was addressing myself to a lover of scandal. But we know we do not love scandal, but fun; and if scandal happens to be fun, that is no fault of ours. There were very good pickings for me in George's letters about the prairie settle-ment, if I had any taste to turn them to account in England.

. . . I was surprised to hear of the state of society at Louisville; it seems to me you are just as ridiculous there as we are here—three-penny parties, halfpenny dances. The best thing I have heard of is your shooting; for it seems you follow the gun. Give my compli-ments to Mrs. Audubon, and tell her I cannot think her either good-looking or honest. Tell Mr. Audubon he's a fool, and Briggs that 'tis well I was not Mr. A. . . .

[1] George Keats returned to England for a few weeks in January 1820, on business.

Saturday, January 15

. . . Were you now in England I dare say you would be able (setting aside the pleasure you would have in seeing your mother) to suck out more amusement for society than I am able to do. To me it is all as dull here as Louisville could be. I am tired of the theatres. Almost all the parties I may chance to fall into I know by heart. I know the different styles of talk in different places,—what subjects will be started, how it will proceed like an acted play, from the first to the last act. If I go to Hunt's I run my head into many tunes heard before, old puns, and old music; to Haydon's worn-out discourses of poetry and painting. The Miss —— I am afraid to speak to, for fear of some sickly reiteration of phrase or sentiment. When they were at the dance the other night I tried manfully to sit near and talk to them, but to no purpose; and if I had it would have been to no purpose still. My ques-tion or observation must have been an old one, and the rejoinder very antique indeed. At Dilke's I fall foul of politics. 'Tis best to re-main aloof from people and like their good parts without being eternally troubled with the dull process of their every-day lives. When once a person has smoked the vapidness of the routine of society he must either have self-interest or the love of some sort of distinction to keep him in good humour with it. All I can say is that, standing at Charing Cross and looking east, west, north, and south, I can see nothing but dulness. I hope while I am young to live retired in the country. When I grow in years and have a right to be idle, I shall enjoy cities more. If the American ladies are worse than the English they must be very bad. You say you should like your Emily brought up here. You had better bring her up yourself. You know a good number of English ladies; what encomium could you give of half a dozen of them? The greater part seems to me down-right American. I have known more than one Mrs. Audubon. Her affectation of fashion and politeness cannot transcend ours. Look at our Cheapside tradesmen's sons and daughters— only fit to be taken off by a plague. I hope now soon to come to the time when I shall never be forced to walk through the city and hate as I walk.

Monday, January 17

George had a quick rejoinder to his letter of excuse to Haslam, so we had not his company yesterday, which I was sorry for as there was our old set. I know three witty people all distinct in their excellence—Rice, Reynolds, and Richards. Rice is the wisest, Reynolds the playfulest, Richards the out-o'-the-wayest. The first makes you laugh and think, the second makes you laugh and not think, the third puzzles your head. I admire the first, I enjoy the second, I stare at the third. The first is claret, the second ginger-beer, the third crême de Byrapymdrag. The first is inspired by Minerva, the second by Mercury, the third by Harlequin Epigram, Esq. The first is neat in his dress, the second slovenly, the third uncomfortable. The first speaks adagio, the second allegretto, the third both together. The first is Swiftean, the second Tom-Crib-ean, the third Shandean. And yet these three eans are not three eans but one ean. . . .

I know three people of no wit at all, each distinct in his excellence—A, B, and C. A is the foolishest, B the sulkiest, C is a negative. A makes you yawn, B makes you hate, as for C you never see him at all though he were six feet high—I bear the first, I forbear the second, I am not certain that the third is. The first is gruel, the second ditch-water, the third is spilt—he ought to be wip'd up. A is inspired by Jack-o'-the-clock, B has been drilled by a Russian serjeant, C, they say, is not his mother's true child, but she bought him of the man who cries, Young lambs to sell.

XXXVII To James Rice

Wentworth Place, February 16, 1820

My dear Rice—I have not been well enough to make any tolerable rejoinder to your kind letter. I will, as you advise, be very chary of my health and spirits. I am sorry to hear of your relapse and hypochondriac symptoms attending it. Let us hope for the best, as you say. I shall follow your example in looking to the future good rather than brooding upon the present ill. I have not been so worn with lengthened illnesses as you have, therefore cannot answer you on your own ground with

respect to those haunting and deformed thoughts and feelings you speak of. When I have been, or supposed myself in health, I have had my share of them, especially within the last year. I may say, that for six months before I was taken ill I had not passed a tranquil day. Either that gloom overspread me, or I was suffering under some passionate feeling, or if I turned to versify, that acerbated the poison of either sensation. The beauties of nature had lost their power over me. How astonishingly (here I must premise that illness, as far as I can judge in so short a time, has relieved my mind of a load of deceptive thoughts and images, and makes me perceive things in a truer light),—how astonishingly does the chance of leaving the world impress a sense of its natural beauties upon us! Like poor Falstaff, though I do not 'babble,' I think of green fields; I muse with the greatest affection on every flower I have known from my infancy—their shapes and colours are as new to me as if I had just created them with a superhuman fancy. It is because they are connected with the most thoughtless and the happiest moments of our lives. I have seen foreign flowers in hothouses, of the most beautiful nature, but I do not care a straw for them. The simple flowers of our Spring are what I want to see again.

Brown has left the inventive and taken to the imitative art. He is doing his forte, which is copying Hogarth's heads. He has just made a purchase of the Methodist Meeting picture, which gave me a horrid dream a few nights ago. I hope I shall sit under the trees with you again in some such place as the Isle of Wight. I do not mind a game of cards in a saw-pit or waggon, but if ever you catch me on a stage-coach in the winter full against the wind, bring me down with a brace of bullets, and I promise not to 'peach. Remember me to Reynolds, and say how much I should like to hear from him; that Brown returned immediately after he went on Sunday, and that I was vexed at forgetting to ask him to lunch; for as he went towards the gate, I saw he was fatigued and hungry.

I am, my dear Rice, ever most sincerely yours

John Keats.

I have broken this open to let you know I was surprised at seeing it on the table this morning, thinking it had gone long ago.

XXXVIII To Fanny Brawne

MY DEAR FANNY,—Do not let your mother suppose that you hurt me by writing at night. For some reason or other your last night's note was not so treasureable as former ones. I would fain that you call me *Love* still. To see you happy and in high spirits is a great consolation to me—still let me believe that you are not half so happy as my restoration would make you. I am nervous, I own, and may think myself worse than I really am; if so you must indulge me, and pamper with that sort of tenderness you have manifested towards me in different Letters. My sweet creature when I look back upon the pains and torments I have suffer'd for you from the day I left you to go to the Isle of Wight; the ecstasies in which I have pass'd some days and the miseries in their turn, I wonder the more at the Beauty which has kept up the spell so fervently. When I send this round I shall be in the front parlour watching to see you show yourself for a minute in the garden. How illness stands as a barrier betwixt me and you! Even if I was well—I must make myself as good a Philosopher as possible. Now I have had opportunities of passing nights anxious and awake I have found other thoughts intrude upon me. 'If I should die,' said I to myself, 'I have left no immortal work behind me—nothing to make my friends proud of my memory—but I have lov'd the principle of beauty in all things, and if I had had time I would have made myself remember'd.' Thoughts like these came very feebly whilst I was in health and every pulse beat for you—now you divide with this (may *I* say it?) 'Last infirmity of noble minds' all my reflection.

God bless you, Love. J. KEATS.

XXXIX To Fanny Brawne

MY DEAREST GIRL—Indeed I will not deceive you with respect to my Health. This is the fact as far as I know. I have been confined three weeks and am not yet well—this proves that there is something wrong about me which my constitution will either conquer or give way to. Let us hope for the best. Do you hear the Thrush singing over the field? I think it is a sign of mild weather—so much the better for me. Like all Sinners now I am ill I philosophize, aye out of my attachment to every thing, Trees, flowers, Thrushes, Spring, Summer, Claret, &c. &c.—aye every thing but you.—My sister would be glad of my company a little longer. That Thrush is a fine fellow. I hope he was fortunate in his choice this year. Do not send any more of my Books home. I have a great pleasure in the thought of you looking on them.

Ever yours my sweet Fanny   J. K.

XL To Fanny Brawne

MY DEAR FANNY—I think you had better not make any long stay with me when Mr. Brown is at home. Whenever he goes out you may bring your work. You will have a pleasant walk today. I shall see you pass. I shall follow you with my eyes over the Heath. Will you come towards evening instead of before dinner? When you are gone, 'tis past—if you do not come till the evening I have something to look forward to all day. Come round to my window for a moment when you have read this. Thank your Mother, for the preserves, for me. The raspberry will be too sweet not having any acid; therefore as you are so good a girl I shall make you a present of it. Good bye My sweet Love!   J. KEATS.

XLI To Fanny Brawne

MY DEAREST GIRL—I endeavour to make myself as patient as possible. Hunt amuses me very kindly—besides I have your ring on my finger and your flowers on the table. I shall not expect to see you yet because it would be so much pain to part with you again. When the Books you want come you shall have them. I am very well this afternoon. My dearest. . . .

[Signature cut off.]

XLII To Fanny Brawne

Tuesday Afternoon

MY DEAREST FANNY—For this Week past I have been employed in marking the most beautiful passages in Spenser, intending it for you, and comforting myself in being somehow occupied to give you however small a pleasure. It has lightened my time very much. I am much better. God bless you.

Your affectionate

J. KEATS.

XLIII To Fanny Brawne

Tuesday Morn

MY DEAREST GIRL—I wrote a letter for you yesterday expecting to have seen your mother. I shall be selfish enough to send it though I know it may give you a little pain, because I wish you to see how unhappy I am for love of you, and endeavour as much as I can to entice you to give up your whole heart to me whose whole existence hangs upon you. You could not step or move an eyelid but it would shoot to my heart—I am greedy of you. Do not think of anything but me. Do not live as if I was not existing. Do not forget me—But have I any right to say you forget me? Perhaps you think of me all day. Have I any right to wish you to be unhappy for me? You would forgive me for wishing it if you knew the extreme passion I have that you should love me—and for you to love me as I do you, you must think of no one but me, much less write that sentence. Yesterday and this morning I have been haunted with a sweet vision—I have seen you the whole time in your shepherdess dress. How my senses have ached at it! How my heart has been devoted to it! How my eyes have been full of tears at it! I[n]deed I think a real love is enough to occupy the widest heart. Your going to town alone when I heard of it was a shock to me—yet I expected it—*promise me you will not for some time till I get better.* Promise me this and fill the paper full of the most endearing names. If you cannot do so with good will, do my love tell me—say what you think—confess if your heart is too much fasten'd on the world. Perhaps then I may see you at a greater distance, I may not be able to appropriate you so closely to myself. Were you to loose a favourite bird from the cage, how would your eyes ache after it as long as it was in sight; when out of sight you would recover a little. Perhaps if you would, if so it

is, confess to me how many things are necessary to you besides me, I might be happier; by being less tantaliz'd. Well may you exclaim, how selfish, how cruel not to let me enjoy my youth! to wish me to be unhappy! You must be so if you love me. Upon my soul I can be contented with nothing else. If you would really what is call'd enjoy yourself at a Party—if you can smile in people's faces, and wish them to admire you *now*—you never have nor ever will love me. I see *life* in nothing but the certainty of your Love—convince me of it my sweetest. If I am not somehow convinced I shall die of agony. If we love we must not live as other men and women do—I cannot brook the wolfsbane of fashion and foppery and tattle—you must be mine to die upon the rack if I want you. I do not pretend to say that I have more feeling than my fellows, but I wish you seriously to look over my letters kind and unkind and consider whether the person who wrote them can be able to endure much longer the agonies and uncertainties which you are so peculiarly made to create. My recovery of bodily health will be of no benefit to me if you are not mine when I am well. For God's sake save me—or tell me my passion is of too awful a nature for you. Again God bless you.

J. K.

No—my sweet Fanny—I am wrong—I do not wish you to be unhappy—and yet I do, I must while there is so sweet a Beauty—my loveliest, my darling! good bye! I kiss you—O the torments!

XLIV To Benjamin Robert Haydon

[Mortimer Terrace, July, 1820]

MY DEAR HAYDON—I am sorry to be obliged to try your patience a few more days when you will have the Book [Chapman's *Homer*] sent from Town. I am glad to hear you are in progress with another Picture. Go on. I am afraid I shall pop off just when my mind is able to run alone.

Your sincere friend

JOHN KEATS.

XLV To Fanny Brawne

*I do not write this till the last,
that no eye may catch it.*

My dearest Girl—I wish you could invent some means to make me at all happy without you. Every hour I am more and more concentrated in you; every thing else tastes like chaff in my Mouth. I feel it almost impossible to go to Italy—the fact is I cannot leave you, and shall never taste one minute's content until it pleases chance to let me live with you for good. But I will not go on at this rate. A person in health as you are can have no conception of the horrors that nerves and a temper like mine go through. What Island do your friends propose retiring to? I should be happy to go with you there alone, but in company I should object to it; the back-bitings and jealousies of new colonists who have nothing else to amuse themselves, is unbearable. Mr. Dilke came to see me yesterday, and gave me a very great deal more pain than pleasure. I shall never be able any more to endure the society of any of those who used to meet at Elm Cottage and Wentworth Place. The last two years taste like brass upon my Palate. If I cannot live with you I will live alone. I do not think my health will improve much while I am separated from you. For all this I am averse to seeing you—I cannot bear flashes of light and return into my gloom again. I am not so unhappy now as I should be if I had seen you yesterday. To be happy with you seems such an impossibility! it requires a luckier Star than mine! it will never be. I enclose a passage from one of your letters which I want you to alter a little—I want (if you will have it so) the matter express'd less coldly to me. If my health would bear it, I could write a Poem which I have in my head, which would be a consolation for people in such a situation as mine. I would show some one in Love as I am, with a person living in such Liberty as you do. Shakespeare always sums up matters in the most sovereign manner. Hamlet's heart was full of such Misery as mine is when he said to Ophelia 'Go to a Nunnery, go, go!' Indeed I should like to give up the matter at once—I should like to die. I am sickened at the brute world which you are smiling with.

I hate men, and women more. I see nothing but thorns for the future—wherever I may be next winter, in Italy or nowhere, Brown will be living near you with his indecencies. I see no prospect of any rest. Suppose me in Rome—well, I should there see you as in a magic glass going to and from town at all hours,——I wish you could infuse a little confidence of human nature into my heart. I cannot muster any—the world is too brutal for me—I am glad there is such a thing as the grave—I am sure I shall never have any rest till I get there. At any rate I will indulge myself by never seeing any more Dilke or Brown or any of their Friends. I wish I was either in your arms full of faith or that a Thunder bolt would strike me.

God bless you.   J. K.

XLVI To Percy Bysshe Shelley

[Wentworth Place, Hampstead, August, 1820]

My dear Shelley—I am very much gratified that you, in a foreign country, and with a mind almost over-occupied, should write to me in the strain of the letter beside me. If I do not take advantage of your invitation, it will be prevented by a circumstance I have very much at heart to prophesy. There is no doubt that an English winter would put an end to me, and do so in a lingering hateful manner. Therefore, I must either voyage or journey to Italy, as a soldier marches up to a battery. My nerves at present are the worst part of me, yet they feel soothed that, come what extreme may, I shall not be destined to remain in one spot long enough to take a hatred of any four particular bedposts. I am glad you take any pleasure in my poor poem, which I would willingly take the trouble to unwrite, if possible, did I care so much as I have done about reputation. I received a copy of the Cenci, as from yourself, from Hunt. There is only one part of it I am judge of—the poetry and dramatic effect, which by many spirits nowadays is considered the Mammon. A modern work, it is said, must have a purpose, which may be the God. An artist must serve Mammon; he must have 'self-concentration'—selfishness, perhaps. You, I am sure, will forgive me for sincerely remarking that you might curb your magnanimity, and be more of an artist, and load every rift of your subject with ore. The thought of such discipline must fall like cold chains upon you, who perhaps never sat with your wings furled for six months together. And is this not extraordinary talk for the writer of Endymion, whose mind was like a pack of scattered cards? I am picked up and sorted to a pip. My imagination is a monastery, and I am its monk. I am in expectation of Prometheus every day. Could I have my own wish effected, you would have it still in manuscript, or be but now putting an end to the second act. I remember you advising me not to publish my first blights, on Hampstead Heath. I am returning advice upon your hands. Most of the poems in the volume I send you have been written above two years, and would never have been published but for hope of gain; so you see I am inclined enough to take your advice now. I must express once more my deep sense of your kindness, adding my sincere thanks and respects for Mrs. Shelley.

In the hope of soon seeing you, I remain most sincerely yours JOHN KEATS.

XLVII To Charles Armitage Brown

Rome, November 30, 1820

MY DEAR BROWN—'Tis the most difficult thing in the world to me to write a letter. My stomach continues so bad, that I feel it worse on opening any book,—yet I am much better than I was in quarantine. Then I am afraid to encounter the pro-ing and con-ing of anything interesting to me in England. I have an habitual feeling of my real life having passed, and that I am leading a posthumous existence. God knows how it would have been—but it appears to me—however, I will not speak of that subject. I must have been at Bedhampton nearly at the time you were writing to me from Chichester—how unfortunate—and to pass

on the river too! There was my star predominant! I cannot answer anything in your letter, which followed me from Naples to Rome, because I am afraid to look it over again. I am so weak (in mind) that I cannot bear the sight of any handwriting of a friend I love so much as I do you. Yet I ride the little horse, and at my worst even in quarantine, summoned up more puns, in a sort of desperation, in one week than in any year of my life. There is one thought enough to kill me; I have been well, healthy, alert, etc., walking with her, and now —the knowledge of contrast, feeling for light and shade, all that information (primitive sense) necessary for a poem, are great enemies to the recovery of the stomach. There, you rogue, I put you to the torture; but you must bring your philosophy to bear, as I do mine, really, or how should I be able to live? Dr. Clark is very attentive to me; he says there is very little the matter with my lungs, but my stomach, he says, is very bad. I am well disappointed in hearing good news from George, for it runs in my head we shall all die young. I have not written to Reynolds yet, which he must think very neglectful; being anxious to send him a good account of my health, I have delayed it from week to week. If I recover, I will do all in my power to correct the mistakes made during sickness; and if I should not, all my faults will be forgiven. Severn is very well, though he leads so dull a life with me. Remember me to all friends, and tell Haslam I should not have left London without taking leave of him, but from being so low in body and mind. Write to George as soon as you receive this, and tell him how I am, as far as you can guess; and also a note to my sister— who walks about my imagination like a ghost —she is so like Tom. I can scarcely bid you good-bye, even in a letter. I always made an awkward bow.

God bless you! JOHN KEATS.

THOMAS LOVELL BEDDOES
[July 20, 1803–January 26, 1849]

THOMAS LOVELL BEDDOES was educated at Charterhouse and Pembroke College, Oxford, at both of which places he showed himself to be of a picturesque and rebellious temperament. While still an undergraduate he published a poetic play called *The Brides' Tragedy* (1822) which was highly praised, though not widely bought. With the exception of a juvenile volume this was all that Beddoes published during his lifetime. He became interested in medicine and in 1825 went to Germany to study anatomy. Save for brief visits to England, he remained abroad the remainder of his life, and little is known of his doings there. In 1846 he reappeared at the house of relatives in England, bearded and grave and riding solemnly upon a donkey. His eccentric behavior during this visit led to doubt of his sanity, one of his acts having been an attempt to set fire to Drury Lane Theatre with a £5 note, because of his disapproval of the condition of the English stage. He was, however, sane enough in his grim way. He returned to the continent and died at Basle in 1849, but he did *not* die of a strange poison as is stated in some editions of his works.

After his death a friend published his *Death's Jest-Book* (1850), a poetic play which Beddoes had begun in 1825, finished in 1829, and revised until his death in 1849. The year after *Death's Jest-Book* appeared, the same friend published Beddoes's fragmentary dramas and lyrics. Two small volumes contain the whole of Beddoes's work which has survived.

Of all the secondary figures of the Romantic Period Beddoes has the most original and striking talent. The blank verse of his quite unactable *Death's Jest-Book* has a fierce imaginative splendor which challenges comparison with the great Elizabethans. The play has no structure, but it has great scenes in it. The lyrics are simpler, but they reflect, as do the plays, Beddoes's absorption in the theme of death. *The Phantom-Wooer* is perhaps his most characteristic lyric, and no one who has ever heard his "little snakes of silver throat—ever singing 'die, oh! die' " can quite forget them. It is the peculiarity of Beddoes that he alone of the poets of death can become the spokesman for death as something sensuous, subtle, and delicious. A reading of the poem or of the scene from *Death's Jest-Book* given below will illustrate the point. Or if Beddoes does not choose to be the spokesman for death, he can hob-nob with it. There is an element of grim jocularity in such a poem as *Old Adam, the Carrion Crow*. In the passage of nervous prose which gives *Death's Jest-Book* its title, the court fool surrenders his office with the speech, "I will yield Death the crown of folly. He hath no hair, and in this weather might catch cold and die . . . and when the world is old and dead, the thin wit [Death] shall find the angel's record of man's works and deeds, and write with a lipless grin on the innocent first page for a title, 'Here begins Death's Jest-Book.' "

Work of this type is admittedly strange and off the beaten track. It is for the few who like such things. To the few Beddoes has always appealed, but with a steadily increasing reputation while greater names than his have been going into eclipse.

HOW MANY TIMES DO I LOVE THEE, DEAR?

From TORRISMOND (ACT I, SCENE III)

A garden by moonlight
VERONICA, ELVIRA, *and other female attendants*

Veron. Come then, a song; a winding, gentle
    song,
To lead me into sleep. Let it be low
As zephyr, telling secrets to his rose,
For I would hear the murmuring of my
    thoughts;
And more of voice than of that other music
That grows around the strings of quivering
    lutes;
But most of thought; for with my mind I listen,
And when the leaves of sound are shed upon it,
If there's no seed remembrance grows not
    there.
So life, so death; a song, and then a dream! 10
Begin before another dewdrop fall
From the soft hold of these disturbed flowers,
For sleep is filling up my senses fast,
And from these words I sink.

Song

How many times do I love thee, dear?
    Tell me how many thoughts there be
        In the atmosphere
        Of a new-fall'n year,
Whose white and sable hours appear
    The latest flake of Eternity: 20
So many times do I love thee, dear.

How many times do I love again?
    Tell me how many beads there are
        In a silver chain
        Of evening rain,
Unravelled from the tumbling main,
    And threading the eye of a yellow star:
So many times do I love again.

Elvira. She sees no longer: leave her then
    alone,   29
Encompassed by this round and moony night.
A rose-leaf for thy lips, and then good-night:
So life, so death; a song, and then a dream!
            [*Exeunt* ELVIRA *and attendants,*
            leaving VERONICA *asleep.*
                    *   *   *

1823–1824

STREW NOT EARTH WITH EMPTY STARS

From THE SECOND BROTHER

Strew not earth with empty stars,
    Strew it not with roses,
Nor feathers from the crest of Mars,
    Nor summer's idle posies.
'Tis not the primrose-sandalled moon,
    Nor cold and silent morn,
Nor he that climbs the dusty noon,
Nor mower war with scythe that drops,
Stuck with helmed and turbaned tops
    Of enemies new shorn.   10

Ye cups, ye lyres, ye trumpets know,
Pour your music, let it flow,
'Tis Bacchus' son who walks below.

1824–1825

SONGS FROM DEATH'S JEST-BOOK

THE SWALLOW LEAVES HER NEST

(ACT I, SCENE IV)

The swallow leaves her nest,
The soul my weary breast;
But therefore let the rain
    On my grave
Fall pure; for why complain?
Since both will come again
    O'er the wave.

The wind dead leaves and snow
Doth hurry to and fro;
And, once, a day shall break   10
    O'er the wave,
When a storm of ghosts shall shake
The dead, until they wake
    In the grave.

1844

II IF THOU WILT EASE THINE HEART

(ACT II, SCENE I)

If thou wilt ease thine heart
Of love and all its smart,
    Then sleep, dear, sleep;
And not a sorrow
    Hang any tear on your eyelashes;
    Lie still and deep,

Sad soul, until the sea-wave washes
The rim o' the sun to-morrow.
    In eastern sky.

But wilt thou cure thine heart   10
Of love and all its smart,
    Then die, dear, die;
'Tis deeper, sweeter,
    Than on a rose bank to lie dreaming
        With folded eye;
And then alone, amid the beaming
Of love's stars, thou'lt meet her
    In eastern sky.

1829

III   OLD ADAM, THE CARRION CROW

(ACT V, SCENE IV)

Old Adam, the carrion crow,
    The old crow of Cairo;
He sat in the shower, and let it flow
Under his tail and over his crest;
    And through every feather
    Leaked the wet weather;
And the bough swung under his nest;
For his beak it was heavy with marrow.
    Is that the wind dying? O no;
    It's only two devils, that blow   10
    Through a murderer's bones, to and fro,
        In the ghosts' moonshine.

Ho! Eve, my grey carrion wife,
    When we have supped on kings' marrow,
Where shall we drink and make merry our life?
    Our nest it is queen Cleopatra's skull,
        'Tis cloven and cracked,
        And battered and hacked,
    But with tears of blue eyes it is full:
Let us drink them, my raven of Cairo.   20
    Is that the wind dying? O no;
    It's only two devils, that blow
    Through a murderer's bones, to and fro,
        In the ghosts' moonshine.

1824

IV   WE DO LIE BENEATH THE GRASS

(ACT V, SCENE IV)

We do lie beneath the grass
    In the moonlight, in the shade
Of the yew-tree. They that pass
    Hear us not. We are afraid

They would envy our delight,
    In our graves by glow-worm night.
Come follow us, and smile as we;
    We sail to the rock in the ancient waves,
Where the snow falls by thousands into the
        sea,
    And the drowned and the shipwrecked
        have happy graves.   10

? 1829

SCENE FROM DEATH'S JEST-BOOK

(ACT IV, SCENE II)

A garden: SIBYLLA

* * *

Sibyl. Then no one hears me. O! the world's
        too loud,
With trade and battle, for my feeble cry
To rouse the living. The invisible
Hears best what is unspoken; and my thoughts
Have long been calling comfort from the grave.

WOLFRAM [1] *suddenly appears, in the garment
        of a monk.*

Wolfr. Lady, you called me.
Sibyl.   I?
Wolfr.   The word was *Comfort:*
A name by which the master, whose I am,   30
Is named by many wise and many wretched.
Will you with me to the place where sighs are
        not;
A shore of blessing, which disease doth beat
Sea-like, and dashes those whom he would
        wreck
Into the arms of Peace? But ah! what say I?
You're young and must be merry in the world;
Have friends to envy, lovers to betray you;
And feed young children with the blood of
        your heart,
Till they have sucked up strength enough to
        break it.
Poor woman! Art thou nothing but the
        straw   40
Bearing a heavy poison, and, that shed,
Cut down to be stamped on? But thou'rt i'
        th' blade;

[1] The Wolfram of this scene is really a spectre
returned to seek revenge on the man who had
murdered him. This explains his appearance at
first in disguise to Sibylla, the girl who had loved
him.

The green and milky sun-deceived grass:
So stand till the scythe comes, take shine and
    shower,
And the wind fell you gently.
  Sibyl.   Do not go.
Speak as at first you did; there was in the
    words
A mystery and music, which did thaw
The hard old rocky world into a flood,
Whereon a swan-drawn boat seemed at my
    feet
Rocking on its blue billows; and I heard   50
Harmonies, and breathed odours from an isle,
Whose flowers cast tremulous shadows in the
    day
Of an immortal sun, and crowd the banks
Whereon immortal human kind doth couch.
This I have dreamt before: your speech re-
    called it.
So speak to soothe me once again.
  Wolfr.   (*Aside*) Snake Death,
Sweet as the cowslip's honey is thy whisper:
O let this dove escape thee! I'll not plead,
I will not be thy suitor to this innocent:
Open thy craggy jaws; speak, coffin-tongued,
Persuasions through the dancing of the yew-
    bough   61
And the crow's nest upon it. (*Aloud*) Lady
    fair,
Listen not to me, look not on me more.
I have a fascination in my words,
A magnet in my look, which drags you down-
    wards,
From hope and life. You set your eyes upon
    me,
And think I stand upon this earth beside you:
Alas! I am upon a jutting stone,
Which crumbles down the steeps of an abyss;
And you, above me far, grow wild and giddy:
Leave me, or you must fall into the deep. 71
  Sibyl. I leave thee never, nor thou me. O no!
You know not what a heart you spurn away;
How good it might be, if love cherished it;
And how deserted 'tis; ah, so deserted,
That I have often wished a ghost would come,
Whose love might haunt it. Turn not thou,
    the last.
Thou see'st I'm young: how happy might I be!
And yet I only wish these tears I shed
Were raining on my grave. If thou'lt not love
    me,   80

Then do me the next office; show me only
The shortest path to solitary death.
  Wolfr. You're moved to wildness, maiden.
    Beg not of me.
I can grant nothing good: quiet thyself,
And seek heaven's help. Farewell.
  Sibyl.   Wilt thou leave me?
Unpitying, aye unmoved in cheek and heart,
Stern, selfish mortal? Hast thou heard my
    prayer;
Hast see me weep; hast seen my limbs to quiver,
Like a storm-shaken tree over its roots?   89
Art thou alive, and canst thou see this wretch,
Without a care?
  Wolfr.   Thou see'st I am unmoved:
Infer the truth.
  Sibyl.   Thy soul indeed is dead.
  Wolfr. My soul, my soul! O that it wore not
    now
The semblance of a garb it hath cast off;
O that it was disrobed of these mock limbs,
Shed by a rocky birth unnaturally,
Long after their decease and burial!
O woe that I must speak! for she, who hears,
Is marked for no more breathing. There are
    histories
Of women, nature's bounties, who dis-
    dained   100
The mortal love of the embodied man,
And sought the solitude which spirits cast
Around their darksome presence. These have
    loved,
Wooed, wedded, and brought home their
    moonstruck brides
Unto the world-sanded eternity.
Hast faith in such reports?
  Sibyl.   So lonely am I,
That I dare wish to prove them true.
  Wolfr.   Dar'st die?
A grave-deep question. Answer it religiously,
  Sibyl. With him I loved, I dared.
  Wolfr.   With me and for me.
I am a ghost. Tremble not; fear not me. 110
The dead are ever good and innocent,
And love the living. They are cheerful creatures,
And quiet as the sunbeams, and most like,
In grace and patient love and spotless beauty,
The new-born of mankind. 'Tis better too
To die, as thou art, young, in the first grace
And full of beauty, and so be remembered
As one chosen from the earth to be an angel;

Not left to droop and wither, and be borne
Down by the breath of time. Come then,
   Sibylla,   120
For I am Wolfram!
   Sibyl.   Thou art come to fetch me!
It is indeed a proof of boundless love,
That thou hadst need of me even in thy bliss.
I go with thee. O Death! I am thy friend,
I struggle not with thee, I love thy state:
Thou canst be sweet and gentle, be so now;
And let me pass praying away into thee,
As twilight still does into starry night.
                 [*The scene closes.*

Voices in the air

  As sudden thunder
    Pierces night;   130
  As magic wonder,
    Wild affright,
  Rives asunder
    Men's delight:
  Our ghost, our corpse; and we
    Rise to be.

  As flies the lizard
    Serpent fell;
  As goblin vizard,
    At the spell   140
  Of the wizard,
    Sinks to hell:
  Our life, our laugh, our lay
    Pass away.

  As wake the morning
    Trumpets bright;
  As snowdrop, scorning
    Winter's might,
  Rises warning
    Like a spright: 150
  We buried, dead, and slain
    Rise again.

Pub. 1850

FRAGMENTS INTENDED FOR THE DRAMAS

I SUBTERRANEAN CITY

CAN it then be, that the earth loved some city,
Another planet's child, so long, so truly,
That here we find its image next her heart,
Like an abandoned, melancholy thought
Yet legible?

II DREAM OF DYING

SHIVERING in fever, weak and parched to sand,
My ears, those entrances of word-dressed
   thoughts,
My pictured eyes, and my assuring touch,
Fell from me, and my body turned me forth
From its beloved abode: then I was dead;
And in my grave beside my corpse I sat,
In vain attempting to return: meantime
There came the untimely spectres of two
   babes,
And played in my abandoned body's ruins; 9
They went away; and, one by one, by snakes
My limbs were swallowed; and, at last, I sat
With only one, blue-eyed, curled round my
   ribs,
Eating the last remainder of my heart,
And hissing to himself. O sleep, thou fiend!
Thou blackness of the night! how sad and
   frightful
Are these thy dreams!

III INSIGNIFICANCE OF THE WORLD

WHY what's the world and time? a fleeting
   thought
In the great meditating universe,
A brief parenthesis in chaos.

IV A BEAUTIFUL NIGHT

How lovely is the heaven of this night,
How deadly still its earth! the forest brute
Has crept into his cave, and laid himself
Where sleep has made him harmless like the
   lamb.
The horrid snake, his venom now forgot,
Is still and innocent as the honied flower
Under his head: and man, in whom are met
Leopard and snake, and all the gentleness
And beauty of the young lamb and the bud,
Has let his ghost out, put his thoughts aside
And lent his senses unto death himself.   11

V A LOFTY MIND

HIS thoughts are so much higher than his
   state,
That, like a mountain hanging o'er a hut,
They chill and darken it.
? 1823–1825

SILENUS IN PROTEUS

OH those were happy days, heaped up with
  wine-skins,
And ivy-wreathed and thyrsus-swinging days,
Swimming like streamy-tressed wanton Bac-
  chantes,
When I was with thee, and sat kingly on thee,
My ass of asses. Then quite full of wine—
Morning, eve—and leaning on a fawn,
Still pretty steady, and on t'other side
Some vinous-lipped nymph of Ariadne,
Her bosom a soft cushion for my right: 9
Half dreaming and half waking, both in bliss,
I sat upon my ass and laughed at Jove.
But thou are dead, my dapple, and I too
Shall ride thee soon about the Elysian meadow,
Almost a skeleton as well as thou.
And why, oh dearest, couldst not keep thy legs
That sacred hair, sacred to sacred me?
Was this thy gratitude for pats and fondlings,
To die like any other mortal ass?
Was it for this, oh son of Semele,
I taught thee then, a little tumbling one,   20
To suck the goatskin oftener than the goat?

c. 1825

DREAM–PEDLARY

I

IF there were dreams to sell,
  What would you buy?
Some cost a passing bell;
  Some a light sigh,
That shakes from Life's fresh crown
Only a rose-leaf down.
If there were dreams to sell,
Merry and sad to tell,
And the crier rung the bell,
  What would you buy?   10

II

A cottage lone and still,
  With bowers nigh,
Shadowy, my woes to still,
  Until I die.
Such pearl from Life's fresh crown
Fain would I shake me down.
Were dreams to have at will,
This would best heal my ill,
  This would I buy.

III

But there were dreams to sell   20
  Ill didst thou buy;
Life is a dream, they tell,
  Waking, to die.
Dreaming a dream to prize,
Is wishing ghosts to rise;
  And, if I had the spell
  To call the buried well,
    Which one would I?

IV

If there are ghosts to raise,
  What shall I call,   30
Out of hell's murky haze,
  Heaven's blue pall?
Raise my loved long-lost boy
To lead me to his joy.
  There are no ghosts to raise;
  Out of death lead no ways;
    Vain is the call.

V

Know'st thou not ghosts to sue?
  No love thou hast.
Else lie, as I will do,   40
  And breathe thy last.
So out of Life's fresh crown
Fall like a rose-leaf down.
  Thus are the ghosts to woo;
  Thus are all dreams made true,
    Ever to last!

1829–1830

SONG

TRANSLATED FROM THE GERMAN OF WAL-
THER VON DER VOGELWEIDE

I

UNDER the lime-tree, on the daisied ground,
  Two that I know of made their bed;
There you may see, heaped and scattered
  round,
  Grass and blossoms, broken and shed,
All in a thicket down in the dale;
    Tandaradei—
Sweetly sang the nightingale.

II

Ere I set foot in the meadow, already
  Some one was waiting for somebody;

There was a meeting—O gracious Lady!   10
  There is no pleasure again for me.
Thousands of kisses there he took—
      Tandaradei—
See my lips, how red they look!

III

Leaf and blossom he had pulled and piled
  For a couch, a green one, soft and high;
And many a one hath gazed and smiled,
  Passing the bower and pressed grass by;
And the roses crushed hath seen—
      Tandaradei—   20
Where I laid my head between.

IV

In this love passage, if any one had been there,
  How sad and shamed should I be!
But what were we a-doing alone among the
    green there,
  No soul shall ever know except my love and
    me,
And the little nightingale.—
      Tandaradei—
She, I think, will tell no tale.
1829

THE PHANTOM–WOOER

I

A GHOST, that loved a lady fair,
Ever in the starry air
  Of midnight at her pillow stood;
And, with a sweetness skies above
The luring words of human love,
  Her soul the phantom wooed.
Sweet and sweet is their poisoned note,
The little snakes of silver throat,
In mossy skulls that nest and lie,
Ever singing 'die, oh! die.'   10

II

Young soul put off your flesh, and come
With me into the quiet tomb,
  Our bed is lovely, dark, and sweet;
The earth will swing us, as she goes,
Beneath our coverlid of snows,
  And the warm leaden sheet.
Dear and dear is their poisoned note,
The little snakes of silver throat,

In mossy skulls that nest and lie,
Ever singing 'die, oh! die.'   20
Pub. 1851

DIRGE FOR A YOUNG MAIDEN

HUSHED be sighing, near the string,
O'er whose tremors deep we sing
The youngest Death, who hath no fears,
Blood, nor pang, nor any tears.
  Hushed be sighing!
Fair and young as Venus' child,
Only paler, and most mild;
End of all that's dear and young,
  Thee we mean, soft Drop of roses;
Hush of birds that sweetest sung,   10
  That beginn'st when music closes;
    The maiden's Dying!
Pub. 1851

DIRGE

To her couch of evening rest
'Neath the sun's divinest west,
Bear we, in the silent car,
This consumed incense star,
This dear maid whose life is shed,
And whose sweets are sweetly dead.

SONG ON THE WATER

I

As mad sexton's bell, tolling
  For earth's loveliest daughter
Night's dumbness breaks rolling
    Ghostily:
So our boat breaks the water
    Witchingly.

II

As her look the dream troubles
  Of her tearful-eyed lover,
So our sails in the bubbles
    Ghostily   10
  Are mirrored, and hover
    Moonily.
Pub. 1851

SONG OF THE STYGIAN NAIADES

I

PROSERPINE may pull her flowers,
  Wet with dew or wet with tears,

Red with anger, pale with fears,
Is it any fault of ours,
If Pluto be an amorous king,
  And comes home nightly, laden,
Underneath his broad bat-wing,
  With a gentle, mortal maiden?
Is it so, Wind, is it so?
All that you and I do know   10
Is, that we saw fly and fix
'Mongst the reeds and flowers of Styx,
        Yesterday,
Where the Furies made their hay
For a bed of tiger cubs,
A great fly of Beelzebub's,
The bee of hearts, which mortals name
Cupid, Love, and Fie for shame.

II

Proserpine may weep in rage,
  But, ere I and you have done   20
  Kissing, bathing in the sun,
What I have in yonder cage,
Bird or serpent, wild or tame,
  She shall guess and ask in vain;
  But, if Pluto does't again,
It shall sing out loud his shame.
  What hast caught then? What hast caught?
  Nothing but a poet's thought,
  Which so light did fall and fix
'Mongst the reeds and flowers of Styx,   30
        Yesterday,
Where the Furies made their hay
For a bed of tiger cubs,
A great fly of Beelzebub's.
The bee of hearts, which mortals name
Cupid, Love, and Fie for shame.

Pub. 1851

LYRICAL FRAGMENTS

I LINES

WRITTEN AT GENEVA; JULY, 1824

THE hour is starry, and the airs that stray,
Sad wanderers from their golden home of day
On night's black mountain, melt and fade away
In sorrow that is music. Some there be
Make them blue pillows on Geneva's sea,
And sleep upon their best-loved planet's
    shade:
And every herb is sleeping in the glade;

They have drunk sunshine and the linnet's
    song,
Till every leaf's soft sleep is dark and strong.
Or was there ever sound, or can what was 10
Now be so dead? Although no flowers or grass
Grow from the corpse of a deceased sound,
Somewhat, methinks, should mark the air
    around
Its dying place and tomb,
A gentle music, or a pale perfume:
For hath it not a body and a spirit,
A noise and meaning? and, when one doth
    hear it
Twice born, twice dying, doubly found and
    lost,
That second self, that echo, is its ghost.
But even the dead are all asleep this time, 20
And not a grave shakes with the dreams of
    crime:
The earth is full of chambers for the dead,
And every soul is quiet in his bed;
Some who have seen their bodies moulder
    away,
Antediluvian minds, most happy they,
Who have no body but the beauteous air,
No body but their minds. Some wretches are
Now lying with the last and only bone
Of their old selves, and that one worm alone
That ate their heart: some, buried just, behold
The weary flesh, like an used mansion, sold
Unto a stranger, and see enter it   32
The earthquake winds and waters of the pit,
Or children's spirits in its holes to play.

* * *

1824

II STANZAS FROM THE IVORY GATE

THE mighty thought of an old world
Fans, like a dragon's wing unfurled,
  The surface of my yearnings deep;
And solemn shadows then awake,
Like the fish-lizard in the lake,
  Troubling a planet's morning sleep.

My waking is a Titan's dream,
Where a strange sun, long set, doth beam
  Through Montezuma's cypress bough:
Through the fern wilderness forlorn 10
Glisten the giant harts' great horn,
  And serpents vast with helmed brow.

The measureless from caverns rise
With steps of earthquake, thunderous cries,
  And graze upon the lofty wood;
The palmy grove, through which doth gleam
Such antediluvian ocean's stream,
  Haunts shadowy my domestic mood.

    *   *   *

c.1837

III THRENODY

No sunny ray, no silver night,
  Here cruelly alight!
    Glare of noontide, star of e'en,
      Otherwhere descend!
  No violet-eyed green,

      ' With its daisies' yellow end,
The dewy debt receive of any eye!
It is a grave: and *she* doth lie
    'Neath roses' root,
      And the fawn's mossy foot,   10
    Under the skylark's grassy floor,
Whose graceful life held every day—
As lilies, dew—as dews, the starry ray—
More music, grace, delight than they.
When stars are few let light be here,
  Of the softest, through the boughs
    Berry-laden, sad and few;
And the wings of one small bird,
His form unseen, his voice unheard—

    *   *   *

Pub. 1851

THOMAS CAMPBELL
[July 22, 1777–June 15, 1844]

THOMAS CAMPBELL was the eleventh and youngest child of a Glasgow merchant. His father had been wealthy but, just before the poet's birth, had lost most of his fortune, and the boy grew up in straitened circumstances. At the university (he studied at the University of Glasgow) he was obliged to supplement his income by doing tutoring work. There was a bleak prospect before him when he went to Edinburgh in 1797, resolved to study law. At first he drudged as a copying clerk, but he soon received some hack literary work to do. It was during this dreary period that he consoled himself by writing *The Pleasures of Hope* (1799). The poem was an instantaneous success and confirmed the reputation as a poet which he had won at the university. On the proceeds he visited the continent, remaining abroad nearly a year. One of his experiences was the witnessing of a battle in which the French defeated the Austrians, and his vivid impressions later found expression in *Hohenlinden*. From this continental trip Campbell also brought back *Ye Mariners of England*. In recognition of his talent he was given a crown pension of £200 annually, beginning in 1805, and in 1826 was elected Lord Rector of Glasgow University, an honorary office of distinction. From 1820 to 1830 he was editor of the *New Monthly Magazine* but gave up the editorship because of the "interminable scrapes." In the main his life was the cloistered one of a man of letters, but he was sympathetic to the cause of the Greek and Polish revolutionaries, and at his burial in Westminster Abbey one of the Polish patriots sprinkled a handful of earth from the grave of Kosciusko into the earth which covered Campbell.

As a poet, Campbell was an exasperation to his contemporaries—so much was expected of him and he did so little. After *The Pleasures of Hope* he wrote several long poems, such as *Gertrude of Wyoming* (1809) and *Theodoric* (1824), which are not very good, and his total production is perhaps not more than 7000 lines. On a handful of short lyrics including the three fine war pieces—*Ye Mariners of England*, *The Battle of the Baltic*, and *Hohenlinden*—his reputation rests. He was perhaps too cautious, too self-conscious in the face of the standards he deliberately set up for himself. What he did do has a clarity and force which marks Campbell's poetic talent as one of the finest of the period, despite his limited accomplishment.

THE HARPER

ON the green banks of Shannon, when Sheelah
was nigh,
No blithe Irish lad was so happy as I;
No harp like my own could so cheerily play,
And wherever I went was my poor dog Tray.

When at last I was forced from my Sheelah
to part,
She said, (while the sorrow was big at her
heart,)
Oh! remember your Sheelah when far, far away:
And be kind, my dear Pat, to our poor dog
Tray.

Poor dog! he was faithful and kind, to be
sure,
And he constantly loved me, although I was
poor;   10
When the sour-looking folks sent me heartless away,
I had always a friend in my poor dog Tray.

When the road was so dark, and the night
was so cold,
And Pat and his dog were grown weary and
old,
How snugly we slept in my old coat of gray,
And he licked me for kindness—my poor dog
Tray.

Though my wallet was scant, I remembered
his case,
Nor refused my last crust to his pitiful face;
But he died at my feet on a cold winter day,
And I played a sad lament for my poor dog
Tray.   20

Where now shall I go, poor, forsaken, and
blind?
Can I find one to guide me, so faithful, and
kind?
To my sweet native village, so far, far away,
I can never more return with my poor dog Tray.
Pub. 1799

YE MARINERS OF ENGLAND

A NAVAL ODE

YE mariners of England,
  That guard our native seas;

Whose flag has braved, a thousand years,
  The battle and the breeze!
Your glorious standard launch again
To match another foe,
And sweep through the deep,
  While the stormy winds do blow;
While the battle rages loud and long,
  And the stormy winds do blow.   10

The spirits of your fathers
  Shall start from every wave!
For the deck it was their field of fame,
  And Ocean was their grave.
Where Blake and mighty Nelson fell,
  Your manly hearts shall glow,
As ye sweep through the deep,
  While the stormy winds do blow;
While the battle rages loud and long,
  And the stormy winds do blow.   20

Britannia needs no bulwarks,
  No towers along the steep;
Her march is o'er the mountain-waves,
  Her home is on the deep.
With thunders from her native oak,
  She quells the floods below,
As they roar on the shore,
  When the stormy winds do blow;
When the battle rages loud and long,
  And the stormy winds do blow.   30

The meteor flag of England
  Shall yet terrific burn,
Till danger's troubled night depart,
  And the star of peace return.
Then, then, ye ocean-warriors!
  Our song and feast shall flow
To the fame of your name,
  When the storm has ceased to blow;
When the fiery fight is heard no more,
  And the storm has ceased to blow.   40
1800

HOHENLINDEN

ON Linden, when the sun was low,
All bloodless lay the untrodden snow,
And dark as winter was the flow
  Of Iser, rolling rapidly.

But Linden saw another sight,
When the drum beat, at dead of night,
Commanding fires of death to light
  The darkness of her scenery.

3

He prays to Heaven. for England's King he says
And dares he to the God of Mercy kneel
Besmear'd with massacres from head to heel
No—Moloch is his God—to him he prays
And if his lizard-like prayers had power to bring
An influence their power would be to curse—
His hate is baleful but his love is worse—
A serpent's slaver deadlier than its sting
Oh feeble statesmen—ignominious times ✳
That lick the tyrant's feet & smile upon his crimes
—————————— T. Campbell.

✳ Note There is not upon record a more disgusting scene of
Russian hypocrisy & (woe that must be written) of
British humiliation than that which pass'd on board the
Talavera—When British sailors accepted money from the
Emperor Nicholas & gave him cheers——It will require
the Talavera to fight well with the first Russian Ship that
she may have to encounter to make us forget that day—

Page of MS of a Poem by Thomas Campbell. (See Appendix I.)

By torch and trumpet fast arrayed,
Each horseman drew his battle-blade,   10
And furious every charger neighed,
   To join the dreadful revelry.

Then shook the hills with thunder riven,
Then rushed the steed to battle driven,
And louder than the bolts of heaven,
   Far flashed the red artillery.

But redder yet that light shall glow
On Linden's hills of stainèd snow,
And bloodier yet the torrent flow
   Of Iser, rolling rapidly.   20

'Tis morn, but scarce yon level sun
Can pierce the war-clouds, rolling dun,
Where furious Frank, and fiery Hun,
   Shout in their sulphurous canopy.

The combat deepens. On, ye brave,
Who rush to glory, or the grave!
Wave, Munich! all thy banners wave,
   And charge with all thy chivalry!

Few, few, shall part where many meet!
The snow shall be their winding-sheet,   30
And every turf beneath their feet
   Shall be a soldier's sepulchre.

1802

LOCHIEL'S WARNING

WIZARD

LOCHIEL! Lochiel! beware of the day
When the lowlands shall meet thee in battle
   array!
For a field of the dead rushes red on my sight,
And the clans of Culloden are scattered in
   fight.
They rally, they bleed, for their kingdom and
   crown;
Woe, woe to the riders that trample them
   down!
Proud Cumberland prances, insulting the
   slain,
And their hoof-beaten bosoms are trod to the
   plain.
But hark! through the fast-flashing lightning
   of war,
What steed to the desert flies frantic and far?   10
'Tis thine, oh Glenullin! whose bride shall
   await,

Like a love-lighted watch-fire, all night at the
   gate.
A steed comes at morning: no rider is there;
But its bridle is red with the sign of despair.
Weep, Albin! to death and captivity led!
Oh weep, but thy tears cannot number the
   dead:
For a merciless sword on Culloden shall wave,
Culloden! that reeks with the blood of the
   brave.

LOCHIEL

Go, preach to the coward, thou death-telling
   seer;
Or, if gory Culloden so dreadful appear,   20
Draw, dotard, around thy old wavering
   sight
This mantle, to cover the phantoms of fright.

WIZARD

Ha! laugh'st thou, Lochiel, my vision to
   scorn?
Proud bird of the mountain, thy plume shall
   be torn:
Say, rushed the bold eagle exultingly forth,
From his home, in the dark rolling clouds of
   the north?
Lo! the death-shot of foemen outspeeding, he
   rode
Companionless, bearing destruction abroad;
But down let him stoop from his havoc on
   high!
Ah! home let him speed,—for the spoiler is
   nigh.   30
Why flames the far summit? Why shoot to
   the blast
Those embers, like stars from the firmament
   cast?
'Tis the fire-shower of ruin, all dreadfully
   driven
From his eyrie, that beacons the darkness of
   heaven.
Oh, crested Lochiel! the peerless in might,
Whose banners arise on the battlements'
   height,
Heaven's fire is around thee, to blast and to
   burn;
Return to thy dwelling! all lonely return!
For the blackness of ashes shall mark where
   it stood,
And a wild mother scream o'er her famishing
   brood.   40

LOCHIEL

False Wizard, avaunt! I have marshalled my
clan,
Their swords are a thousand, their bosoms
are one!
They are true to the last of their blood and
their breath,
And like reapers descend to the harvest of
death.
Then welcome be Cumberland's steed to the
shock!
Let him dash his proud foam like a wave on
the rock!
But woe to his kindred, and woe to his cause,
When Albin her claymore indignantly draws;
When her bonneted chieftains to victory
crowd,
Clanronald the dauntless, and Moray the
proud, 50
All plaided and plumed in their tartan
array——

WIZARD

——Lochiel, Lochiel! beware of the day;
For, dark and despairing, my sight I may seal,
But man cannot cover what God would re-
veal;
'Tis the sunset of life gives me mystical lore,
And coming events cast their shadows before.
I tell thee, Culloden's dread echoes shall ring
With the bloodhounds that bark for thy fugi-
tive king.
Lo! anointed by Heaven with the vials of
wrath,
Behold where he flies on his desolate path! 60
Now in darkness and billows, he sweeps from
my sight:
Rise, rise! ye wild tempests, and cover his
flight!
'Tis finished. Their thunders are hushed on
the moors:
Culloden is lost, and my country deplores.
But where is the iron-bound prisoner? Where
For the red eye of battle is shut in despair.
Say, mounts he the ocean-wave, banished,
forlorn,
Like a limb from his country cast bleeding
and torn?
Ah, no! for a darker departure is near;
The war-drum is muffled, and black is the
bier; 70

His death-bell is tolling: oh! mercy, dispel
Yon sight, that it freezes my spirit to tell!
Life flutters convulsed in his quivering limbs,
And his blood-streaming nostril in agony
swims.
Accursed be the fagots, that blaze at his feet,
Where his heart shall be thrown, ere it ceases
to beat,
With the smoke of its ashes to poison the
gale——

LOCHIEL

——Down, soothless insulter! I trust not the
tale:
For never shall Albin a destiny meet, 79
So black with dishonor, so foul with retreat.
Tho' my perishing ranks should be strewed
in their gore,
Like ocean-weeds heaped on the surf-beaten
shore.
Lochiel, untainted by flight or by chains,
While the kindling of life in his bosom re-
mains,
Shall victor exult, or in death be laid low,
With his back to the field, and his feet to the
foe!
And leaving in battle no blot on his name,
Look proudly to Heaven from the death-bed
of fame.
1802

BATTLE OF THE BALTIC

I

Of Nelson and the North,
Sing the glorious day's renown,
When to battle fierce came forth
All the might of Denmark's crown,
And her arms along the deep proudly shone;
By each gun the lighted brand,
In a bold determined hand,
And the Prince of all the land
Led them on.——

II

Like leviathans afloat, 10
Lay their bulwarks on the brine;
While the sign of battle flew
On the lofty British line;
It was ten of April morn by the chime
As they drifted on their path,
There was silence deep as death;
And the boldest held his breath,
For a time.——

III

But the might of England flushed
To anticipate the scene;   20
And her van the fleeter rushed
O'er the deadly space between.
"Hearts of oak!" our captain cried; when each
      gun
From its adamantine lips
Spread a death-shade round the ships,
Like the hurricane eclipse
Of the sun.

IV

Again! again! again!
And the havoc did not slack,
Till a feeble cheer the Dane   30
To our cheering sent us back;—
Their shots along the deep slowly boom:—
Then ceased—and all is wail,
As they strike the shattered sail:
Or, in conflagration pale,
Light the gloom.—

V

Out spoke the victor then,
As he hailed them o'er the wave;
"Ye are brothers! ye are men!
And we conquer but to save:—   40
So peace instead of death let us bring;
But yield, proud foe, thy fleet,
With the crews, at England's feet,
And make submission meet
To our King."—

VI

Then Denmark blessed our chief,
That he gave her wounds repose;
And the sounds of joy and grief
From her people wildly rose,
As death withdrew his shades from the day. 50
While the sun looked smiling bright
O'er a wide and woful sight,
Where the fires of funeral light
Died away.

VII

Now joy, Old England, raise!
For the tidings of thy might,
By the festal cities' blaze,
Whilst the wine-cup shines in light;
And yet amidst that joy and uproar,
Let us think of them that sleep,   60
Full many a fathom deep,
By thy wild and stormy steep,
Elsinore!

VIII

Brave hearts! to Britain's pride
Once so faithful and so true,
On the deck of fame that died;—
With the gallant good Riou;
Soft sigh the winds of Heaven o'er their
      grave,
While the billow mournful rolls,
And the mermaid's song condoles,   70
Singing glory to the souls
Of the brave!

1805

LORD ULLIN'S DAUGHTER

A CHIEFTAIN, to the Highlands bound,
  Cries, "Boatman, do not tarry!
And I'll give thee a silver pound,
  To row us o'er the ferry."—

"Now who be ye, would cross Lochgyle
  This dark and stormy water?"
"O, I'm the chief of Ulva's isle,
  And this Lord Ullin's daughter.—

And fast before her father's men
  Three days we've fled together,   10
For should he find us in the glen,
  My blood would stain the heather.

His horsemen hard behind us ride;
  Should they our steps discover,
Then who will cheer my bonny bride
  When they have slain her lover?"—

Out spoke the hardy Highland wight,
  "I'll go, my chief—I'm ready:—
It is not for your silver bright;
  But for your winsome lady: 20

And by my word! the bonny bird
  In danger shall not tarry:
So though the waves are raging white,
  I'll row you o'er the ferry."—

By this the storm grew loud apace,
  The water-wraith was shrieking;
And in the scowl of heaven each face
  Grew dark as they were speaking.

But still as wilder blew the wind,
  And as the night grew drearer,   30
Adown the glen rode armed men,
  Their trampling sounded nearer.

"Oh haste thee, haste!" the lady cries,
    "Though tempests round us gather;
I'll meet the raging of the skies,
    But not an angry father."—

The boat has left a stormy land,
    A stormy sea before her,—
When, oh! too strong for human hand,
    The tempest gathered o'er her.—   40

And still they rowed amidst the roar
    Of waters fast prevailing:
Lord Ullin reached that fatal shore,
    His wrath was changed to wailing.—

For sore dismayed, through storm and shade,
    His child he did discover:—
One lovely hand she stretched for aid,
    And one was round her lover.

"Come back! come back!" he cried in grief,
    "Across this stormy water: 50
And I'll forgive your Highland chief,
    My daughter!—oh, my daughter!"—

'Twas vain: the loud waves lashed the shore,
    Return or aid preventing:—
The waters wild went o'er his child,
    And he was left lamenting.

1804–1805

TO THE RAINBOW

TRIUMPHAL arch, that fill'st the sky
    When storms prepare to part,
I ask not proud Philosophy
    To teach me what thou art—

Still seem, as to my childhood's sight,
    A midway station given
For happy spirits to alight
    Betwixt the earth and heaven.

Can all that Optics teach, unfold
    Thy form to please me so,   10
As when I dreamt of gems and gold
    Hid in thy radiant bow?

When Science from Creation's face
    Enchantment's veil withdraws,
What lovely visions yield their place
    To cold material laws!

And yet, fair bow, no fabling dreams,
    But words of the Most High,
Have told why first thy robe of beams
    Was woven in the sky.   20

When o'er the green undeluged earth
    Heaven's covenant thou didst shine,
How came the world's gray fathers forth
    To watch thy sacred sign!

And when its yellow lustre smiled
    O'er mountains yet untrod,
Each mother held aloft her child
    To bless the bow of God.

Methinks, thy jubilee to keep,
    The first-made anthem rang   30
On earth delivered from the deep,
    And the first poet sang.

Nor ever shall the Muse's eye
    Unraptured greet thy beam;
Theme of primeval prophecy,
    Be still the prophet's theme!

The earth to thee her incense yields,
    The lark thy welcome sings,
When glittering in the freshened fields
    The snowy mushroom springs.   40

How glorious is thy girdle, cast
    O'er mountain, tower, and town,
Or mirrored in the ocean vast,
    A thousand fathoms down!

As fresh in yon horizon dark,
    As young thy beauties seem,
As when the eagle from the ark
    First sported in thy beam:

For, faithful to its sacred page,
    Heaven still rebuilds thy span,   50
Nor lets the type grow pale with age
    That first spoke peace to man.

1819

SONG

TO THE EVENING STAR

STAR that bringest home the bee,
And sett'st the weary laborer free!
If any star shed peace, 'tis thou,
    That send'st it from above,

Appearing when Heaven's breath and brow
  Are sweet as hers we love.

Come to the luxuriant skies,
Whilst the landscape's odors rise,
Whilst far-off lowing herds are heard,
  And songs when toil is done,   10
From cottages whose smoke unstirred
  Curls yellow in the sun.

Star of love's soft interviews,
Parted lovers on the muse;
Their remembrancer in Heaven
  Of thrilling vows thou art
Too delicious to be riven
  By absence from the heart.

Pub. 1822

TO MARY SINCLAIR, WITH A VOLUME OF HIS POEMS

Go, simple Book of Ballads, go
From Eaton-street, in Pimlico;
It is a gift, my love to show—
                    To Mary!

And, more its value to increase,
I swear, by all the gods of Greece,
It cost a seven-shilling piece—
                    My Mary!

But what is gold, so bright that looks,
Or all the coins of miser's nooks,   10
Compared to be in thy *good books*—
                    My Mary!

Now witness earth, and skies, and main!
The book to thee shall appertain;
I'll never ask it back again—
                    My Mary!

But what, you say, shall you bestow?
For, as the world now goes, you know,
There always is a *quid pro quo*—   19
                    My Mary!

I ask not twenty hundred kisses,
Nor smile, the lover's heart that blesses,
As poets ask from other Misses—
                    My Mary!

I ask that, till the day you die,
You'll never pull my wig awry,
Nor ever quiz my poetrye—
                    My Mary!

THE DEAD EAGLE
WRITTEN AT ORAN

FALLEN as he is, this king of birds still seems
Like royalty in ruins. Though his eyes
Are shut, that look undazzled on the sun,
He was the sultan of the sky, and earth
Paid tribute to his eyry. It was perched
Higher than human conqueror ever built
His bannered fort. Where Atlas' top looks o'er
Zahara's desert to the equator's line:
From thence the winged despot marked his
    prey,
Above th' encampments of the Bedouins, ere
Their watchfires were extinct, or camels
    knelt   11
To take their loads, or horsemen scoured the
    plain,
And there he dried his feathers in the dawn,
Whilst yet th' unwakened world was dark
    below.

There's such a charm in natural strength and
    power,
That human fancy has for ever paid
Poetic homage to the bird of Jove
Hence, 'neath his image, Rome arrayed her
    turms
And cohorts for the conquest of the world.
And figuring his flight, the mind is filled   20
With thoughts that mock the pride of wing-
    less man.
True, the carred aeronaut can mount as high;
But what's the triumph of his volant art?
A rash intrusion on the realms of air.
His helmless vehicle, a silken toy,
A bubble bursting in the thunder-cloud;
His course has no volition, and he drifts
The passive plaything of the winds. Not such
Was this proud bird: he clove the adverse
    storm,
And cuffed it with his wings. He stopped his
    flight   30
As easily as the Arab reigns his steed,
And stood at pleasure 'neath Heaven's zenith,
    like
A lamp suspended from its azure dome,
Whilst underneath him the world's moun-
    tains lay
Like mole hills, and her streams like lucid
    threads,

Then downward, faster than a falling star,
He neared the earth, until his shape distinct
Was blackly shadowed on the sunny ground;
And deeper terror hushed the wilderness,
To hear his nearer whoop. Then, up again   40
He soared and wheeled. There was an air of scorn
In all his movements, whether he threw round
His crested head to look behind him; or
Lay vertical and sportively displayed
The inside whiteness of his wing declined,
In gyres and undulations full of grace,
An object beautifying Heaven itself.
He—reckless who was victor, and above
The hearing of their guns—saw fleets engaged
In flaming combat. It was nought to him   50
What carnage, Moor or Christian, strewed their decks.
But if his intellect had matched his wings,
Methinks he would have scorned man's vaunted power
To plough the deep; his pinions bore him down
To Algiers the warlike, or the coral groves,
That blush beneath the green of Bona's waves;
And traversed in an hour a wider space
Than yonder gallant ship, with all her sails
Wooing the winds, can cross from morn till eve.
His bright eyes were his compass, earth his chart,   60
His talons anchored on the stormiest cliff,
And on the very light-house rock he perched,
When winds churned white the waves.
                        The earthquake's self
Disturbed not him that memorable day,
When, o'er yon table-land, where Spain had built,
Cathedrals, cannoned forts, and palaces,
A palsy stroke of Nature shook Oran,
Turning her city to a sepulchre,
And strewing into rubbish all her homes;

Amidst whose traceable foundations now,   70
Of streets and squares, the hyæna hides himself.
That hour beheld him fly as careless o'er
The stifled shrieks of thousands buried quick,
As lately when he pounced the speckled snake,
Coiled in yon mallows and wide nettled fields
That mantle o'er the dead old Spanish town.

Strange is the imagination's dread delight
In objects linked with danger, death and pain!
Fresh from the luxuries of polished life,
The echo of these wilds enchanted me;   80
And my heart beat with joy when first I hear
A lion's roar come down the Lybian wind,
Across yon long, wide, lonely inland lake,
Where boat ne'er sails from homeless shore to shore
And yet Numidia's landscape has its spots
Of pastoral pleasantness—though far between,
The village planted near the Maraboot's
Round roof has aye its feathery palm trees
Paired, for in solitude they bear no fruits.
Here nature's hues all harmonize—fields white   90
With alasum, or blue with bugloss—banks
Of glossy fennel, blent with tulips wild,
And sunflowers, like a garment prankt with gold;
Acres and miles of opal asphodel,
Where sports and couches the black-eyed gazelle.
Here, too, the air's harmonious—deep-toned doves
Coo to the fife-like carol of the lark;
And when they cease, the holy nightingale
Winds up his long, long shakes of ecstasy,
With notes that seem but the protracted sounds   100
Of glassy runnels bubbling over rocks.
c. 1835

JOHN CLARE

[July 13, 1793–May 20, 1864]

CLARE's life, which began in a hovel and ended in a madhouse, was unhappy in the extreme. The son of a pauper farm-laborer, at seven he was set to work tending sheep and at thirteen, although physically frail, he was working in the fields. Such schooling as he got was in night classes. An old woman who tended cows had filled his head with songs and a reading of Thomson's *The Seasons* convinced him he was himself a poet. In intervals of heavy labor he began to scribble on scraps of paper—scribblings which his mother used to light the fire. At the time of his marriage (1820) Clare had come almost to literal beggary. Taylor, however, in 1820 published his *Poems Descriptive of Rural Life and Scenery* and the book was a success. Clare spent some time in London, where he was lionized, and dined with lords. A subscription was taken, enough to buy him an annuity of £45 a year. But, back in the country, Clare found £45 not enough to support his father, mother, wife, and many children. Two later books published in his lifetime failed to aid him and, crushed by ill-health, poverty, and drink, he sank into madness, spending the last twenty-two years of his life in an asylum. There, in his lucid intervals, he continued to write poems which were published after his death.

The distinguishing mark of his poetry is its extraordinary closeness to the facts of field and country. In his extreme sensibility, which resulted finally in madness, Clare was not a peasant, but he had a peasant's instinct for the earth. When he is "literary," he is not good, and some of his early editors and publishers unfortunately tried to polish him a bit. When he is natural there is the vigor and sharpness of reality about him. One might cite as an illustration of Clare's fidelity to his world his half line about a mouse in a barn "quirking round" for kernels. What else does a mouse do but "quirk," and who but Clare ever said so? The example is but one of a type of writing which is common in Clare.

APPROACH OF SPRING

Sweet are the omens of approaching Spring
    When gay the elder sprouts her winged
    leaves;
When tooting robins carol-welcomes sing,
    And sparrows chelp glad tidings from the
    eaves.
What lovely prospects wait each wakening
    hour,
    When each new day some novelty dis-
    plays;
How sweet the sun-beam melts the crocus
    flower,
    Whose borrow'd pride shines dizen'd in
    his rays:
Sweet, new-laid hedges flush their tender
    greens;
Sweet peep the arum-leaves their shelter
    screens;   10
    Ah! sweet is all which I'm denied to
    share:
Want's painful hindrance sticks me to her
    stall;—
    But still Hope's smiles unpoint the thorns
    of Care,
Since Heaven's eternal Spring is free for all.

Pub. 1820

NOON

All how silent and how still;
Nothing heard but yonder mill:
While the dazzled eye surveys
All around a liquid blaze;
And amid the scorching gleams,
If we earnest look, it seems
As if crooked bits of glass
Seem'd repeatedly to pass.
Oh, for a puffing breeze to blow!
But breezes are all strangers now;   10
Not a twig is seen to shake,
Nor the smallest bent to quake;
From the river's muddy side
Not a curve is seen to glide;
And no longer on the stream
Watching lies the silver bream,
Forcing, from repeated springs,
'Verges in successive rings.'
Bees are faint, and cease to hum;
Birds are overpower'd and dumb.   20
Rural voices all are mute,
Tuneless lie the pipe and flute:
Shepherds, with their panting sheep,
In the swaliest corner creep;
And from the tormenting heat
All are wishing to retreat.

Huddled up in grass and flowers,
Mowers wait for cooler hours;
And the cow-boy seeks the sedge,
Ramping in the woodland hedge,   30
While his cattle o'er the vales
Scamper, with uplifted tails;
Others not so wild and mad,
That can better bear the gad,
Underneath the hedge-row lunge,
Or, if nigh, in waters plunge.
Oh! to see how flowers are took,
How it grieves me when I look:
Ragged-robins, once so pink,
Now are turn'd as black as ink,   40
And the leaves, being scorch'd so much,
Even crumble at the touch;
Drowking lies the meadow-sweet,
Flopping down beneath one's feet:
While to all the flowers that blow,
If in open air they grow,
Th' injurious deed alike is done
By the hot relentless sun.
E'en the dew is parched up
From the teasel's jointed cup: 50
O poor birds! where must ye fly,
Now your water-pots are dry?
If ye stay upon the heath,
Ye'll be choak'd and clamm'd to death.
Therefore leave the shadeless goss,
Seek the spring-head lin'd with moss;
There your little feet may stand,
Safely printing on the sand;
While, in full possession, where
Purling eddies ripple clear,   60
You with ease and plenty blest,
Sip the coolest and the best.
Then away! and wet your throats;
Cheer me with your warbling notes;
'Twill hot noon the more revive;
While I wander to contrive
For myself a place as good,
In the middle of a wood:
There aside some mossy bank,
Where the grass in bunches rank   70
Lifts its down on spindles high,
Shall be where I'll choose to lie;
Fearless of the things that creep,
There I'll think, and there I'll sleep;
Caring not to stir at all,
Till the dew begins to fall.

Pub. 1820

RECOLLECTIONS AFTER AN EVENING WALK

JUST as the even-bell rang, we set out
To wander the fields and the meadows about;
And the first thing we mark'd that was lovely
    to view,
Was the sun hung on nothing, just bidding
    adieu:
He seem'd like a ball of pure gold in the west,
In a cloud like a mountain blue, dropping to
    rest;
The skies all around him were ting'd with
    his rays,
And the trees at a distance seem'd all on a
    blaze,
Till, lower and lower, he sank from our
    sight,
And the blue mist came creeping with silence
    and night.   10
The woodman then ceas'd with his hatchet
    to hack,
And bent away home with his kid on his back;
The mower too lapt up his scythe from our
    sight,
And put on his jacket, and bid us good-night;
The thresher once lumping, we heard him no
    more,
He left his barn-dust, and had shut up his
    door;
The shepherd had told all his sheep in his pen,
And humming his song, sought his cottage
    agen:
But the sweetest of all seeming music to me,
Were the songs of the clumsy brown-beetle
    and bee;   20
The one was seen hast'ning away to his hive,
The other was just from his sleeping alive,—
'Gainst our hats he kept knocking as if he'd
    no eyes,
And when batter'd down he was puzzled to
    rise.
The little gay moth too was lovely to view,
A-dancing with lily-white wings in the dew;
He whisk'd o'er the water-pudge flirting and
    airy,
And perch'd on the down-headed grass like
    a fairy.
And there came the snail from his shell peep-
    ing out,
As fearful and cautious as thieves on the rout;

The sly jumping frog too had ventur'd to
    tramp,   31
And the glow-worm had just 'gun to light up
    his lamp;
To sip of the dew the worm peep'd from his
    den,
But dreading our footsteps soon vanish'd agen:
And numbers of creatures appear'd in our
    sight,
That live in the silence and sweetness of night,
Climbing up the tall grasses or scaling the
    bough,
But these were all nameless, unnotic'd till now.
And then we wound round 'neath the brook's
    willow row,
And look'd at the clouds that kept passing
    below;   40
The moon's image too, in the brook we
    could see't,
As if 'twas the other world under our feet;
And we listen'd well pleas'd at the guggles
    and groans
The water made passing the pebbles and
    stones.
And then we turn'd up by the rut-rifted lane,
And sought for our cot and the village again;
For night gather'd round, and shut all from
    the eye,
And a black sultry cloud crept all over the sky;
The dew on the bush, soon as touch'd it
    would drop,
And the grass 'neath our feet was as wet as a
    mop: 50
And, as to the town we approach'd very fast,
The bat even popp'd in our face as he past;
And the crickets sang loud as we went by the
    house,
And by the barn-side we saw many a mouse
Quirking round for the kernels that, litter'd
    about,
Were shook from the straw which the thresher
    hurl'd out.
And then we came up to our cottage once
    more,
And shut out the night-dew, and lock'd up
    the door;
The dog bark'd a welcome, well-pleas'd at
    our sight,
And the owl o'er our cot flew, and whoop'd
    a "good-night."   60

Pub. 1821

THE WOOD–CUTTER'S NIGHT SONG

Welcome, red and roundy sun,
    Dropping lowly in the west;
Now my hard day's work is done,
    I'm as happy as the best.

Joyful are the thoughts of home,
    Now I'm ready for my chair,
So, till morrow-morning's come,
    Bill and mittens, lie ye there!

Though to leave your pretty song,
    Little birds, it gives me pain,   10
Yet to-morrow is not long,
    Then I'm with you all again.

If I stop, and stand about,
    Well I know how things will be,
Judy will be looking out
    Every now-and-then for me.

So fare ye well! and hold your tongues,
    Sing no more until I come;
They're not worthy of your songs
    That never care to drop a crumb.   20

All day long I love the oaks,
    But, at nights, yon little cot,
Where I see the chimney smokes,
    Is by far the prettiest spot.

Wife and children all are there,
    To revive with pleasant looks,
Table ready set, and chair,
    Supper hanging on the hooks.

Soon as ever I get in,
    When my faggot down I fling,   30
Little prattlers they begin
    Teasing me to talk and sing.

Welcome, red and roundy sun,
    Dropping lowly in the west;
Now my hard day's work is done,
    I'm as happy as the best.

Joyful are the thoughts of home,
    Now I'm ready for my chair,
So, till morrow-morning's come,
    Bill and mittens, lie ye there!   40

Pub. 1821

SOLITUDE

Now as even's warning bell
Rings the day's departing knell,
Leaving me from labour free,
Solitude, I'll walk with thee:
Whether 'side the woods we rove,
Or sweep beneath the willow grove;
Whether sauntering we proceed
Cross the green, or down the mead;
Whether, sitting down, we look
On the bubbles of the brook;　　　10
Whether, curious, waste an hour,
Pausing o'er each tasty flower;
Or, expounding nature's spells,
From the sand pick out the shells;
Or, while lingering by the streams,
Where more sweet the music seems,
Listen to the soft'ning swells
Of some distant chiming bells
Mellowing sweetly on the breeze,
Rising, falling by degrees,　　　20
Dying now, then wak'd again
In full many a 'witching strain,
Sounding, as the gale flits by,
Flats and sharps of melody.

Sweet it is to wind the rill,
Sweet with thee to climb the hill,
On whose lap the bullock free
Chews his cud most placidly;
Or o'er fallows bare and brown
Beaten sheep-tracks wander down,　　　30
Where the mole unwearied still
Roots up many a crumbling hill,
And the little chumbling mouse
Gnarls the dead weed for her house,
While the plough's unfeeling share
Lays full many a dwelling bare;—
Where the lark with russet breast
'Hind the big clod hides her nest,
And the black snail's founder'd pace
Finds from noon a hiding-place,　　　40
Breaking off the scorching sun
Where the matted twitches run.

Solitude! I love thee well,
Brushing through the wilder'd dell,
Picking from the ramping grass
Nameless blossoms as I pass,
Which the dews of eve bedeck,
Fair as pearls on woman's neck;

Marking shepherds rous'd from sleep
Blundering off to fold their sheep;　　　50
And the swain, with toils distrest,
Hide his tools to seek his rest:
While the cows, with hobbling strides,
Twitching slow their fly-bit hides,
Rub the pasture's creaking gate,
Milking maids and boys to wait.
Or as sunshine leaves the sky,
As the daylight shuts her eye,
Sweet it is to meet the breeze
'Neath the shade of hawthorn trees,　　　60
By the pasture's wilder'd round,
Where the pismire hills abound,
Where the blushing fin-weed's flower
Closes up at even's hour:
Leaving then the green behind,
Narrow hoof-plod lanes to wind,
Oak and ash embower'd beneath,
Leading to the lonely heath,
Where the unmolested furze
And the burdock's clinging burs,　　　70
And the briars, by freedom sown,
Claim the wilder'd spots their own.

There while we the scene survey
Deck'd in nature's wild array,
Swell'd with ling-clad hillocks green
Suiting the disorder'd scene,
Haply we may rest us then
In the banish'd herdsman's den;
Where the wattled hulk is fixt,
Propt some double oak betwixt,　　　80
Where the swain the branches lops,
And o'erhead with rushes tops;
Where, with woodbine's sweet perfume,
And the rose's blushing bloom,
Loveliest ceiling of the bower,
Arching in, peeps many a flower;
While a hill of thyme so sweet,
Or a moss'd stone, forms a seat.
There, as 'tween-light hangs the eve,
I will watch thy bosom heave;　　　90
Marking then the darksome flows
Night's gloom o'er thy mantle throws;
Fondly gazing on thine eye
As it rolls its extasy,
When thy solemn musings caught
Tell thy soul's absorb'd in thought;
When thy finely folded arm
O'er thy bosom beating warm

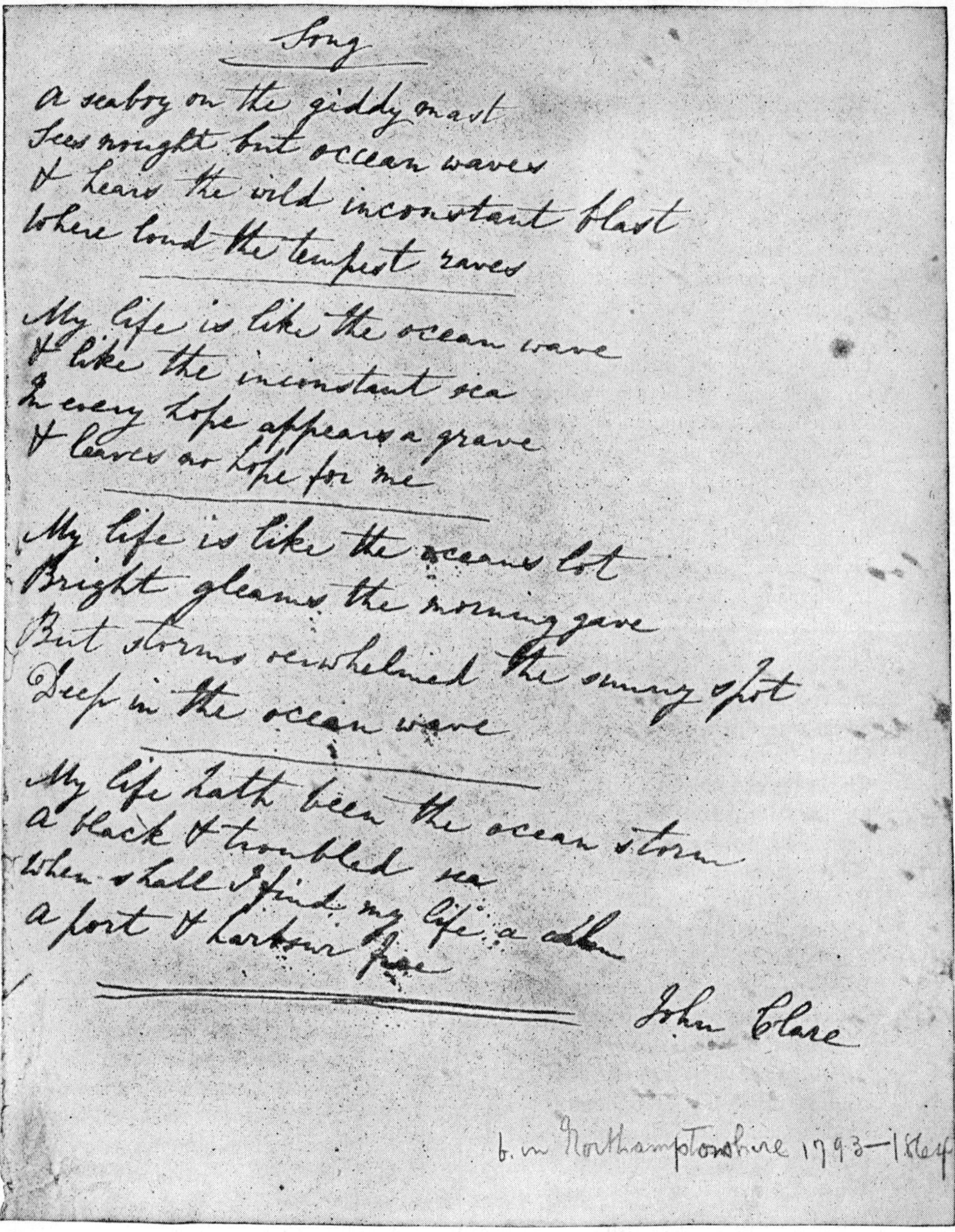
Song

a seaboy on the giddy mast
Sees nought but ocean waves
& hears the wild inconstant blast
Where loud the tempest raves

My life is like the ocean wave
& like the inconstant sea
In every hope appears a grave
& leaves no hope for me

My life is like the oceans lot
Bright gleams the morning gave
But storms oerwhelmed the sunny spot
Deep in the ocean wave

My life hath been the ocean storm
a black & troubled sea
When shall I find my life a calm
a port & harbour free

John Clare

b. in Northamptonshire 1793—1864

A Poem by John Clare. (See Appendix I.)

Wraps thee melancholy round;
And thy ringlets wild unbound 100
On thy lily shoulders lie,
Like dark streaks in morning's sky.
Peace and silence sit with thee,
And peace alone is heaven to me:
While the moonlight's infant hour
Faint 'gins creep to gild the bower,
And the wattled hedge gleams round
Its diamond shadows on the ground.
—O thou soothing Solitude,
From the vain and from the rude, 110
When this silent hour is come,
And I meet thy welcome home,
What balm is thine to troubles deep,
As on thy breast I sink to sleep;
What bliss on even's silence flows,
When thy wish'd opiate brings repose.

And I have found thee wondrous sweet,
Sheltering from the noon-day heat,
As 'neath hazels I have stood
In the gloomy hanging wood, 120
Where the sunbeams, filtering small,
Freckling through the branches fall;
And the flapping leaf the ground
Shadows, flitting round and round:
Where the glimmering streamlets wreathe
Many a crooked root beneath,
Unseen gliding day by day
O'er their solitary way,
Smooth or rough, as onward led
Where the wild-weed dips its head, 130
Murmuring,—dribbling drop by drop
When dead leaves their progress stop,—
Or winding sweet their restless way
While the frothy bubbles play.
And I love thy presence drear
In such wildernesses, where
Ne'er an axe was heard to sound,
Or a tree's fall gulsh'd the ground,
Where (as if that spot could be)
First foot-mark'd the ground by me, 140
All is still, and wild, and gay,
Left as at creation's day.
Pleasant too it is to look
For thy steps in shady nook,
Where, by hedge-side coolly led,
Brooks curl o'er their sandy bed;
On whose tide the clouds reflect,
In whose margin flags are freckt;

Where the waters, winding blue,
Single-arch'd brig flutter through, 150
While the willow-branches grey
Damp the sultry eye of day,
And in whispers mildly sooth
Chafe the mossy keystone smooth;
Where the banks, beneath them spread,
Level in an easy bed;
While the wild-thyme's pinky bells
Circulate reviving smells;
And the breeze, with feather-feet,
Crimping o'er the waters sweet, 160
Trembling fans the sun-tann'd cheek,
And gives the comfort one would seek.
Stretching there in soft repose,
Far from peace and freedom's foes,
In a spot, so wild, so rude,
Dear to me is solitude!
Soothing then to watch the ground,—
Every insect flitting round,
Such as painted summer brings;—
Lady-fly with freckled wings, 170
Watch her up the tall bent climb;
And from knotted flowers of thyme,
Where the woodland banks are deckt,
See the bee his load collect;
Mark him turn the petals by,
Gold dust gathering on his thigh,
As full many a hum he heaves,
While he pats th' intruding leaves,
Lost in many a heedless spring,
Then wearing home on heavy wing. 180

But when sorrows more oppress,
When the world brings more distress,
Wishing to despise as then
Brunts of fate, and scorn of men;
When fate's demons thus intrude,
Then I seek thee, Solitude,
Where the abbey's height appears
Hoary 'neath a weight of years;
Where the mouldering walls are seen
Hung with pellitory green; 190
Where the steeple's taper stretch
Tires the eye its length to reach,
Dizzy, nauntling high and proud,
Top-stone losing in a cloud;
Where the cross, to time resign'd,
Creaking harshly in the wind,
Crowning high the rifted dome,
Points the pilgrim's wish'd-for home;

While the look fear turns away,
Shuddering at its dread decay.   200
There let me my peace pursue
'Neath the shades of gloomy yew,
Doleful hung with mourning green,
Suiting well the solemn scene;
There, that I may learn to scan
Mites illustrious, called man,
Turn with thee the nettles by
Where the grave-stone meets the eye,
Soon, full soon to read and see
That all below is vanity;   210
And man, to me a galling thing,
Own'd creation's lord and king,
A minute's length, a zephyr's breath,
Sport of fate, and prey of death;
Tyrant to-day, to-morrow gone;
Distinguish'd only by a stone,
That fain would have the eye to know
Pride's better dust is lodg'd below,—
While worms like me are mouldering laid,
With nothing set to say "they're dead;"— 220
All the difference, trifling thing,
That notes at last the slave and king.
As wither'd leaves, life's bloom when stopt,
That drop in autumn, so they dropt:
As snails, which in their painted shell
So snugly once were known to dwell,
When in the school-boy's care we view
The pleasing toys of varied hue.—
By age or accident are flown,
The shell left empty,—tenant gone;—   230
So pass we from the world's affairs,
And careless vanish from its cares;
So leave, with silent, long farewell,
Vain life—as left the snail his shell.

    All this when there my eyes behold
On every stone and heap of mould,
Solitude, though thou art sweet,
Solemn art thou then to meet;
When with list'ning pause I look
Round the pillar's ruin'd nook,   240
Glooms revealing, dim descried,
Ghosts, companion'd by thy side;
Where in old deformity
Ancient arches sweep on high;
And the aisles, to light unknown,
Create a darkness all their own:
Save the moon, as on we pass,
Splinters through the broken glass,

Or the torn roof, patch'd with cloud,
Or the crack'd wall, bulg'd and bow'd,— 250
Glimmering faint along the ground,
Shooting solemn and profound,
Lighting up the silent gloom
Just to read an ancient tomb:
'Neath where, as it gilding creeps,
We may see some abbot sleeps;
And as on we mete the aisle,
Daring scarce to breathe the while,
Soft as creeping feet can fall,
While the damp green-stained wall   260
Swift the startled ghost flits by,
Mocking murmurs faintly sigh;
Reminding our intruding fear
Such visits are unwelcome here.
Seemly then, from hollow urn,
Gentle steps our steps return:
E'er so soft and e'er so still,
Check our breath or how we will,
List'ning spirits still reply
Step for step, and sigh for sigh.   270
Murmuring o'er one's weary woe,
Such as once 'twas theirs to know,
They whisper to such slaves as me,
A buried tale of misery:—
"We once had life, ere life's decline,
Flesh, blood, and bones, the same as thine;
We knew its pains, and shar'd its grief,
Till death, long wish'd-for, brought relief;
We had our hopes, and like to thee,
Hop'd morrow's better day to see,   280
But like to thine, our hope the same,
To-morrow's kindness never came:
We had our tyrants, e'en as thou;
Our wants met many a scornful brow;
But death laid low their wealthy powers,
Their harmless ashes mix with ours:
And this vain world, its pride, its form,
That treads on thee as on a worm,
Its mighty heirs—the time shall be
When they as quiet sleep by thee!"   290

    O here's thy comfort, Solitude,
When overpowering woes intrude!
Then thy sad, thy solemn dress
Owns the balm my soul to bless:
Here I judge the world aright;
Here see vain man in his true light;
Learn patience, in this trying hour,
To gild life's brambles with a flower;

Take pattern from the hints thou'st given,
And follow in thy steps to heaven.   300
Pub. 1821

From SUMMER IMAGES

I love at early morn, from new mown swath,
  To see the startled frog his route pursue;
To mark while, leaping o'er the dripping path,
  His bright sides scatter dew,   102
The early lark that, from its bustle flies,
  To hail his matin new;
    And watch him to the skies.

To note on hedgerow baulks, in moisture
    sprent,
  The jetty snail creep from the mossy thorn,
With earnest heed, and tremulous intent,
  Frail brother of the morn,
That from the tiny bent's dew-misted leaves
  Withdraws his timid horn,   111
    And fearful vision weaves.

Or swallow heed on smoke-tanned chimney
    top,
  Wont to be first unsealing Morning's eye,
Ere yet the bee hath gleaned one wayward
    drop
  Of honey on his thigh;
To see him seek morn's airy couch to sing,
  Until the golden sky
    Bepaint his russet wing.

Or sauntering boy by tanning corn to spy, 120
  With clapping noise to startle birds away,
And hear him bawl to every passer by
  To know the hour of day;
While the uncradled breezes, fresh and
    strong,
  With waking blossoms play,
    And breathe Æolian song.

I love the south-west wind, or low or loud,
  And not the less when sudden drops of
    rain
Moisten my glowing cheek from ebon cloud,
  Threatening soft showers again,   130
That over lands new ploughed and meadow
    grounds,
  Summer's sweet breath unchain,
    And wake harmonious sounds.

Rich music breathes in Summer's every sound;
  And in her harmony of varied greens,
Woods, meadows, hedge-rows, corn-fields,
    all around
  Much beauty intervenes,
Filling with harmony the ear and eye;
  While o'er the mingling scenes
    Far spreads the laughing sky.   140

See, how the wind-enamoured aspen leaves
  Turn up their silver lining to the sun!
And hark! the rustling noise, that oft deceives,
  And makes the sheep-boy run:
The sound so mimics fast-approaching
    showers,
  He thinks the rain's begun,
    And hastes to sheltering bowers.

But now the evening curdles dank and grey,
  Changing her watchet hue for sombre
    weed;
And moping owls, to close the lids of day, 150
  On drowsy wing proceed;
While chickering crickets, tremulous and long,
  Light's farewell inly heed,
    And give it parting song.

The pranking bat its flighty circlet makes;
  The glow-worm burnishes its lamp anew;
O'er meadows dew-besprent, the beetle
    wakes
  Inquiries ever new,
Teazing each passing ear with murmurs vain,
  As wanting to pursue   160
    His homeward path again.

Hark! 'tis the melody of distant bells
  That on the wind with pleasing hum re-
    bounds
By fitful starts, then musically swells
  O'er the dim stilly grounds;
While on the meadow-bridge the pausing boy
  Listens the mellow sounds,
    And hums in vacant joy.
Pub. 1835

THE SWALLOW

Swift goes the sooty swallow o'er the heath,
Swifter than skims the cloud-rack of the skies;
As swiftly flies its shadow underneath,
And on his wing the twittering sunbeam lies,

As bright as water glitters in the eyes
Of those it passes; 'tis a pretty thing,
The ornament of meadows and clear skies:
With dingy breast and narrow pointed
wing,
Its daily twittering is a song to Spring.

Pub. 1873

YOUNG JENNY

THE cockchafer hums down the rut-rifted lane
Where the wild roses hang and the woodbines
entwine,
And the shrill squeaking bat makes his circles
again
Round the side of the tavern close by the sign.
The sun is gone down like a wearisome queen,
In curtains the richest that ever were seen.

The dew falls on flowers in a mist of small
rain,
And, beating the hedges, low fly the barn owls;
The moon with her horns is just peeping
again,
And deep in the forest the dog-badger howls;
In best bib and tucker then wanders my Jane
By the side of the woodbines which grow in
the lane.   12

On a sweet eventide I walk by her side;
In green hoods the daisies have shut up their
eyes.
Young Jenny is handsome without any pride;
Her eyes (O how bright!) have the hue of the
skies.
O 'tis pleasant to walk by the side of my Jane
At the close of the day, down the mossy
green lane.

We stand by the brook, by the gate, and the
stile,
While the even star hangs out his lamp in the
sky;   20
And on her calm face dwells a sweet sunny
smile,

While her soul fondly speaks through the
light of her eye.
Sweet are the moments while waiting for Jane;
'Tis her footsteps I hear coming down the
green lane.

Pub. 1873

THE DYING CHILD

HE could not die when trees were green,
  For he loved the time too well.
His little hands, when flowers were seen,
  Were held for the bluebell,
    As he was carried o'er the green.

His eye glanced at the white-nosed bee;
  He knew those children of the Spring:
When he was well and on the lea
  He held one in his hands to sing,
    Which filled his heart with glee.   10

Infants, the children of the Spring!
  How can an infant die
When butterflies are on the wing,
  Green grass, and such a sky?
    How can they die at Spring?

He held his hands for daisies white,
  And then for violets blue,
And took them all to bed at night
  That in the green fields grew,
    As childhood's sweet delight.   20

And then he shut his little eyes,
  And flowers would notice not;
Birds' nests and eggs caused no surprise,
  He now no blossoms got:
    They met with plaintive sighs.

When Winter came and blasts did sigh,
  And bare were plain and tree,
As he for ease in bed did lie
  His soul seemed with the free,
    He died so quietly.   30

Pub. 1873

HARTLEY COLERIDGE
[September 19, 1796–January 6, 1849]

HARTLEY COLERIDGE was the child of whom his greater father thought when he wrote *Frost at Midnight*, and the child actually had the upbringing his father dreamed for him. He did not, however, become a great poet. He was a sensitive man with a friendliness toward small gay things such as crickets and children, and frittered away a talent which was fine, but not great, in a life which was rather aimless. Of sustained poetic effort he was incapable. In the sonnet he did his best work, and it has been said by friends who knew him that his sonnets were written at an impulse, rarely costing him more than ten minutes time to complete, once the impulse struck him.

SONG: SHE IS NOT FAIR

SHE is not fair to outward view
    As many maidens be,
Her loveliness I never knew
    Until she smil'd on me;
Oh! then I saw her eye was bright,
A well of love, a spring of light.

But now her looks are coy and cold,
    To mine they ne'er reply,
And yet I cease not to behold
    The love-light in her eye: 10
Her very frowns are fairer far
Than smiles of other maidens are.

Pub. 1833

"MULTUM DILEXIT" [1]

SHE sat and wept beside His feet; the weight
Of sin oppress'd her heart; for all the blame,
And the poor malice of the worldly shame,
To her was past, extinct, and out of date:
Only the sin remain'd,—the leprous state;
She would be melted by the heart of love,
By fires far fiercer than are blown to prove
And purge the silver ore adulterate.

    [1] "She loved greatly."

She sat and wept, and with her untress'd hair
Still wip'd the feet she was so bless'd to touch;
And He wip'd off the soiling of despair   11
From her sweet soul, because she lov'd so
    much.
I am a sinner, full of doubts and fears:
Make me a humble thing of love and tears.

Pub. 1851

SONNET: LONG TIME A CHILD

LONG time a child, and still a child, when
    years
Had painted manhood on my cheek, was I,—
For yet I lived like one not born to die;
A thriftless prodigal of smiles and tears,
No hope I needed, and I knew no fears.
But sleep, though sweet, is only sleep, and
    waking,
I waked to sleep no more, at once o'ertaking
The vanguard of my age, with all arrears
Of duty on my back. Nor child, nor man,
Nor youth, nor sage, I find my head is grey, 10
For I have lost the race I never ran:
A rathe December blights my lagging May;
And still I am a child, though I be old,
Time is my debtor for my years untold.

Pub. 1851

ALLAN CUNNINGHAM
[December 7, 1784–October 30, 1842]

"HONEST ALLAN CUNNINGHAM" was apprenticed to a stonemason at the age of eleven. In his youth he was welcome at local merry-makings but he found time for poetry and spent twenty-four of his scarce shillings on a volume by Scott. Later he tramped over to Edinburgh merely to catch a glimpse of the great man in the streets. A London publisher printed his *Remains of Nithsdale and Galloway Song* in 1810, ostensibly a collection of old songs, but with the exception of two pieces, really by Cunningham. His pay for this volume was a bound copy of it. The same year he went up to London where he became, and remained until 1841, secretary to the sculptor Chantrey, supplementing his income by hack literary work. Although Cunningham was a landsman, the poem printed below is one of the most swinging sea poems in English.

A WET SHEET AND A FLOWING SEA

A WET sheet and a flowing sea,
  A wind that follows fast,
And fills the white and rustling sail
  And bends the gallant mast;
And bends the gallant mast, my boys,
  While, like the eagle free,
Away the good ship flies, and leaves
  Old England on the lee.

"O for a soft and gentle wind!"
  I heard a fair one cry;   10
But give to me the snoring breeze
  And white waves heaving high;

And white waves heaving high, my lads,
  The good ship tight and free,—
The world of waters is our home,
  And merry men are we.

There's tempest in yon hornéd moon,
  And lightning in yon cloud;
But hark the music, mariners!
  The wind is piping loud;   20
The wind is piping loud, my boys,
  The lightning flashes free,—
While the hollow oak our palace is,
  Our heritage the sea.

Pub. 1825

ROBERT STEPHEN HAWKER
[December 3, 1803–August 15, 1875]

ROBERT STEPHEN HAWKER was educated at Oxford where he won the Newdigate Prize in 1827 with a poem about Pompeii. His life was spent at Morwenstow in Cornwall where he was vicar. There he labored stoutly for the upbuilding of his parish. His interest in the stormy and picturesque district, once infamous for its wreckers of ships who used to light false beacons on the coast, led him into antiquarian researches and is reflected in his poetry. As a cleric he was sympathetic to the views of the Tractarian movement. A few hours before his death he was formally accepted into the Catholic Church. Of his poetry the best is found in his *Records of the Western Shore*, published in 1832 and revised in later editions, and in his *The Quest of the San Graal* (1864).

THE SONG OF THE WESTERN MEN

A GOOD sword and a trusty hand!
  A merry heart and true!
King James's men shall understand
  What Cornish lads can do.

And have they fix'd the where and when?
  And shall Trelawny die?
Here's twenty thousand Cornish men
  Will know the reason why!

Out spake their captain brave and bold,
  A merry wight was he: 10
"If London Tower were Michael's hold,
  We'll set Trelawny free!

"We'll cross the Tamar, land to land,
  The Severn is no stay,
With 'one and all,' and hand in hand,
  And who shall bid us nay?

"And when we come to London Wall,
  A pleasant sight to view,
Come forth! come forth, ye cowards all,
  Here's men as good as you!   20

"Trelawny he's in keep and hold,
  Trelawny he may die;
But here's twenty thousand Cornish bold
  Will know the reason why!"

1825

FELICIA DOROTHEA HEMANS
[September 25, 1793–May 16, 1835]

ASIDE from her marriage and separation, Mrs. Hemans's life may be described as uneventful. In 1812 she married an Irish army officer, and in 1818 they separated for reasons unexplained, and never met again, although they corresponded concerning their five sons.

Mrs. Hemans had begun writing young. As early as 1808 her parents published a volume of her poems, and, from that time, she wrote and published with regularity, and her life after her separation continued to be that of the writer, studious and prolific of poetry.

The bulk of her work is considerable. It suffers from its easiness. Mrs. Hemans's pen was quickly responsive to the surface emotions and wrote fluently. Nevertheless, some of her short pieces have merit. And her *Casabianca* probably has the distinction of having been recited aloud by unwilling American schoolboys more often than any other poem of the last century.

THE LANDING OF THE PILGRIM FATHERS IN NEW ENGLAND

"Look now abroad! Another race has filled
  Those populous borders—wide the wood re-
    cedes,
And towns shoot up, and fertile realms are
    tilled;
  The land is full of harvests and green meads."
                                    BRYANT

THE breaking waves dashed high
  On a stern and rock-bound coast,
And the woods against a stormy sky
  Their giant branches tossed;

And the heavy night hung dark
  The hills and waters o'er,
When a band of exiles moored their bark
  On the wild New England shore.

Not as the conqueror comes,
  They, the true-hearted, came;   10
Not with the roll of the stirring drums,
  And the trumpet that sings of fame;

Not as the flying come,
  In silence and in fear;—
They shook the depths of the desert gloom
  With their hymns of lofty cheer.

Amidst the storm they sang,
  And the stars heard and the sea;
And the sounding aisles of the dim woods rang
  To the anthem of the free!   20

The ocean eagle soared
  From his nest by the white wave's foam;
And the rocking pines of the forest roared—
  This was their welcome home!

There were men with hoary hair
  Amidst that pilgrim band;—
Why had *they* come to wither there,
  Away from their childhood's land?

There was woman's fearless eye,
  Lit by her deep love's truth;   30
There was manhood's brow, serenely high
  And the fiery heart of youth.

What sought they thus afar?—
  Bright jewels of the mine?
The wealth of seas, the spoils of war?—
  They sought a faith's pure shrine!

Ay, call it holy ground,
  The soil where first they trod;
They have left unstained what there they
    found—
  Freedom to worship God.   40

Pub. 1826

THE PALM TREE

It waved not through an Eastern sky,
Beside a fount of Araby;
It was not fanned by Southern breeze
In some green isle of Indian seas;
Nor did its graceful shadow sleep
O'er stream of Afric, lone and deep.

But fair the exiled palm tree grew
'Midst foliage of no kindred hue;
Through the laburnum's dropping gold
Rose the light shaft of Orient mould,   10
And Europe's violets, faintly sweet,
Purpled the moss beds at its feet.

Strange looked it there! The willow streamed
Where silvery waters near it gleamed;
The lime bough lured the honey bee
To murmur by the desert's tree,
And showers of snowy roses made
A lustre in its fan-like shade.

There came an eve of festal hours—
Rich music filled that garden's bowers;   20
Lamps, that from flowering branches hung,
On sparks of dew soft color flung;
And bright forms glanced—a fairy show—
Under the blossoms to and fro.

But one, a lone one, 'midst the throng,
Seemed reckless all of dance or song:
He was a youth of dusky mien,
Whereon the Indian sun had been,
Of crested brow and long black hair—
A stranger, like the palm tree, there.   30

And slowly, sadly, moved his plumes,
Glittering athwart the leafy glooms.
He passed the pale-green olives by,
Nor won the chestnut flowers his eye;
But when to that sole palm he came,
Then shot a rapture through his frame!

To him, to him its rustling spoke—
The silence of his soul it broke!
It whispered of his own bright isle,
That lit the ocean with a smile;   40
Ay, to his ear that native tone
Had something of the sea-wave's moan!

His mother's cabin home, that lay
Where feathery cocoas fringed the bay;
The dashing of his brethren's oar—
The conch note heard along the shore;
All through his wakening bosom swept—
He clasped his country's tree, and wept!

O, scorn him not! The strength whereby
The patriot girds himself to die,   50
Th' unconquerable power which fills
The freeman battling on his hills,
These have one fountain deep and clear—
The same whence gushed that childlike tear!

Pub. 1826

COME TO ME, GENTLE SLEEP!

Come to me, gentle Sleep!
  I pine, I pine for thee;
Come with thy spells, the soft, the deep,
  And set my spirit free!
Each lonely, burning thought
  In twilight languor steep—
Come to the full heart, long o'erwrought,
  O gentle, gentle Sleep!

Come with thine urn of dew,
  Sleep, gentle Sleep! yet bring   10
No voice, love's yearning to renew,
  No vision on thy wing!

Come, as to folding flowers,
  To birds in forests deep—
Long, dark, and dreamless be thine hours,
  O gentle, gentle Sleep!

Pub. 1834

EVENING SONG OF THE WEARY

FATHER of heaven and earth!
  I bless thee for the night,
  The soft, still night!
The holy pause of care and mirth,
  Of sound and light!

Now, far in glade and dell,
Flower cup, and bud, and bell

Have shut around the sleeping woodlark's nest;
  The bee's long-murmuring toils are done,
  And I, the o'erwearied one,   10
  O'erwearied and o'erwrought,
Bless thee, O God! O Father of the op-
    pressed!
With my last waking thought,
    In the still night!
Yes! e'er I sink to rest,
By the fire's dying light,
Thou Lord of earth and heaven!
  I bless thee, who hast given,
Unto life's fainting travellers, the night—
  The soft, still, holy night.   20

Pub. 1834

THOMAS HOOD
[May 23, 1799–May 3, 1845]

ALTHOUGH in his youth he had been trained as an engraver, Thomas Hood in 1821 became sub-editor of the *London Magazine*. At the monthly dinners to contributors the young man became acquainted among others with Lamb, Clare, Cunningham, De Quincey, and Reynolds. Better still, the publishers allowed him to publish his own verse, serious and light. Taylor and Hessey, publishers of the *London*, were Keats's publishers, and had just brought out Keats's last (1820) volume. Hood fell greatly under the influence of Keats's verse. He also became intimate with Keats's friend, John Hamilton Reynolds, and in 1825 married his sister, the Jane Reynolds whom Keats had admired. In 1825 Hood and Reynolds published anonymously *Odes and Addresses to Great People*, and Hood followed up the success in the next two years with two volumes of *Whims and Oddities in Prose and Verse*. In 1827 he published the only volume of serious verse to appear in his lifetime, but the volume was passed over by the same generation which was ignoring Keats and Shelley. Compelled to earn a living (he had left the *London Magazine* in 1823 for free-lancing), Hood at Christmas 1830 published the first issue of his *Comic Annual* which was his chief support for the next dozen years. In ill health, and harassed by debts due to the expenses of ill health, Hood lived abroad from 1835 to 1840 in an effort to economize. On his return he held various literary jobs and in 1843 launched his *Hood's Magazine and Comic Miscellany*, a magazine which could not have continued, because of Hood's ill health, except for the assistance of friends, Browning and Dickens being among those who contributed.

Hood's contributions became fewer and fewer, but the May 1844 issue contained his *Bridge of Sighs* and the November issue his *Lay of the Labourer*. The latter poem was really a plea for pardon for a farm boy of eighteen who had asked for work and, because he threatened to burn the farmers' ricks if he did not receive it, had been sentenced to transportation for life. In the previous year (1843) the great comic weekly *Punch* had startled England by publishing in the Christmas Number, Hood's *Song of the Shirt*, giving it a whole page to itself. The poem, inspired by disclosures of the shameful underpayment of sempstresses by commercial employers, provoked a sensation in direct proportion to the unexpectedness of its appearance in the *Punch*

Christmas Number. Thus, at the close of his life (Hood died in 1845) the poet who had lived for fifteen years by his comic writing was returning to serious themes, inspired by a deep humanitarian sympathy.

It is not exact to say that Hood had abandoned serious themes in the interval. Some of his comics are merely that and nothing more, and some are merely pot-boilers. But there is a middle ground in Hood's work when his wit and verbal dexterity blend with his poetic sentiment. His *I Remember, I Remember* and poems of its type have a grace and wit of handling which smack of light verse, and yet are so purely poetic in sentiment as to make difficult any merely arbitrary division of Hood's work into "humorous" and "serious." It *is* exact to say of Hood that, because of the public's demand for work of his lighter touch, he never found strength to explore and exhaust the capacities of a talent which could write such grim poems as *The Last Man* or *The Dream of Eugene Aram*, could write with such a Keatsian richness of phrase as he showed in early poems such as *Ode: Autumn*, and such a passionate social consciousness as he showed in *The Lay of the Labourer* and kindred poems. It may be that all these were flashes accidental to a minor talent, but it seems hard to believe.

THE LAST MAN

'Twas in the year two thousand and one,
A pleasant morning of May,
I sat on the gallows-tree all alone,
A chaunting a merry lay,—
To think how the pest had spared my life,
To sing with the larks that day!

When up the heath came a jolly knave,
Like a scarecrow, all in rags:
It made me crow to see his old duds
All abroad in the wind, like flags:—   10
So up he came to the timbers' foot
And pitch'd down his greasy bags.—

Good Lord! how blythe the old beggar was!
At pulling out his scraps,—
The very sight of his broken orts
Made a work in his wrinkled chaps:
"Come down," says he, "you Newgate bird,
And have a taste of my snaps!"—

Then down the rope, like a tar from the mast,
I slided, and by him stood;   20
But I wished myself on the gallows again
When I smelt that beggar's food,
A foul beef-bone and a mouldy crust;
"Oh!" quoth he, "the heavens are good!"

Then after this grace he cast him down:
Says I, "You'll get sweeter air
A pace or two off, on the windward side,"
For the felons' bones lay there.

But he only laugh'd at the empty skulls,
And offered them part of his fare.   30

"I never harm'd *them*, and they won't harm
     me:
Let the proud and the rich be cravens!"
I did not like that strange beggar man,
He look'd so up at the heavens.
Anon he shook out his empty old poke;
"There's the crumbs," saith he, "for the
     ravens!"

It made me angry to see his face,
It had such a jesting look;
But while I made up my mind to speak,
A small case-bottle he took: 40
Quoth he, "Though I gather the green water-
     cress,
My drink is not of the brook!"

Full manners-like he tender'd the dram;
Oh, it came of a dainty cask!
But, whenever it came to his turn to pull,
"Your leave, good sir, I must ask;
But I always wipe the brim with my sleeve,
When a hangman sups at my flask!"

And then he laugh'd so loudly and long,
The churl was quite out of breath;   50
I thought the very Old One was come
To mock me before my death,
And wish'd I had buried the dead men's bones
That were lying about the heath!

But the beggar gave me a jolly clap—
"Come, let us pledge each other,
For all the wide world is dead beside,
And we are brother and brother—
I've a yearning for thee in my heart,
As if we had come of one mother.   60

"I've a yearning for thee in my heart
That almost makes me weep,
For as I pass'd from town to town
The folks were all stone-asleep,—
But when I saw thee sitting aloft,
It made me both laugh and leap!"

Now a curse (I thought) be on his love,
And a curse upon his mirth,—
An' if it were not for that beggar man
I'd be the King of the earth,—   70
But I promis'd myself an hour should come
To make him rue his birth—

So down we sat and bous'd again
Till the sun was in mid-sky,
When, just when the gentle west-wind came,
We hearken'd a dismal cry;
"Up, up, on the tree," quoth the beggar man,
"Till these horrible dogs go by!"

And, lo! from the forest's far-off skirts,
They came all yelling for gore,   80
A hundred hounds pursuing at once,
And a panting hart before,
Till he sunk down at the gallows' foot,
And there his haunches they tore!

His haunches they tore, without a horn
To tell when the chase was done;
And there was not a single scarlet coat
To flaunt it in the sun!—
I turn'd, and look'd at the beggar man,
And his tears dropt one by one!   90

And with curses sore he chid at the hounds,
Till the last dropt out of sight,
Anon, saith he, "Let's down again,
And ramble for our delight,
For the world's all free, and we may choose
A right cozie barn for to-night!"

With that, he set up his staff on end,
And it fell with the point due West;
So we far'd that way to a city great,

Where the folks had died of the pest—   100
It was fine to enter in house and hall
Wherever it liked me best;

For the porters all were stiff and cold,
And could not lift their heads;
And when we came where their masters lay,
The rats leapt out of the beds;
The grandest palaces in the land
Were as free as workhouse sheds.

But the beggar man made a mumping face,
And knocked at every gate: 110
It made me curse to hear how he whined,
So our fellowship turned to hate,
And I bade him walk the world by himself,
For I scorn'd so humble a mate!

So *he* turn'd right, and *I* turn'd left,
As if we had never met;
And I chose a fair stone house for myself,
For the city was all to let;
And for three brave holidays drank my fill
Of the choicest that I could get.   120

And because my jerkin was coarse and worn,
I got me a properer vest;
It was purple velvet, stitch'd o'er with
    gold,
And a shining star at the breast!—
'Twas enough to fetch old Joan from her
    grave
To see me so purely drest!

But Joan was dead and under the mould,
And every buxom lass;
In vain I watch'd, at the window pane
For a Christian soul to pass!   130
But sheep and kine wander'd up the street,
And browz'd on the new-come grass.—

When lo! I spied the old beggar man,
And lustily he did sing!—
His rags were lapp'd in a scarlet cloak,
And a crown he had like a King;
So he stept right up before my gate
And danc'd me a saucy fling!

Heaven mend us all!—but, within my mind,
I had killed him then and there;   140
To see him lording so braggart-like

That was born to his beggar's fare,
And how he had stolen the royal crown
His betters were meant to wear.

But God forbid that a thief should die
Without his share of the laws!
So I nimbly whipt my tackle out,
And soon tied up his claws,—
I was judge myself, and jury, and all,
And solemnly tried the cause.   150

But the beggar man would not plead, but cried
Like a babe without its corals,
For he knew how hard it is apt to go
When the law and a thief have quarrels,—
There was not a Christian soul alive
To speak a word for his morals.

Oh, how gaily I doff'd my costly gear,
And put on my work-day clothes;
I was tired of such a long Sunday life,—
And never was one of the sloths;   160
But the beggar man grumbled a weary deal,
And made many crooked mouths.

So I haul'd him off to the gallows' foot,
And blinded him in his bags;
'Twas a weary job to heave him up,
For a doom'd man always lags;
But by ten of the clock he was off his legs
In the wind, and airing his rags!

So there he hung, and there I stood,
The LAST MAN left alive,   170
To have my own will of all the earth:
Quoth I, now I shall thrive!
But when was ever honey made
With one bee in a hive?

My conscience began to gnaw my heart,
Before the day was done,
For other men's lives had all gone out,
Like candles in the sun!—
But it seem'd as if I had broke, at last,
A thousand necks in one!   180

So I went and cut his body down
To bury it decentlie;—
God send there were any good soul alive
To do the like by me!
But the wild dogs came with terrible speed,
And bade me up the tree!

My sight was like a drunkard's sight,
And my head began to swim,
To see their jaws all white with foam,
Like the ravenous ocean brim;—   190
But when the wild dogs trotted away
Their jaws were bloody and grim!

Their jaws were bloody and grim, good Lord!
But the beggar man, where was he?—
There was naught of him but some ribbons
    of rags
Below the gallows' tree!—
I know the Devil, when I am dead,
Will send his hounds for me!—

I've buried my babies one by one,
And dug the deep hole for Joan,   200
And covered the faces of kith and kin,
And felt the old churchyard stone
Go cold to my heart, full many a time,
But I never felt so lone!

For the lion and Adam were company,
And the tiger him beguiled:
But the simple kine are foes to my life,
And the household brutes are wild.
If the veriest cur would lick my hand,
I could love it like a child!   210

And the beggar man's ghost besets my dream,
At night to make me madder,—
And my wretched conscience within my
    breast,
Is like a stinging adder;—
I sigh when I pass the gallows' foot,
And look at the rope and ladder!—

For hanging looks sweet,—but, alas! in vain
My desperate fancy begs,—
I must turn my cup of sorrows quite up,
And drink it to the dregs,—   220
For there is not another man alive,
In the world, to pull my legs!

Pub. 1826

FAITHLESS SALLY BROWN

AN OLD BALLAD

YOUNG BEN he was a nice young man,
  A carpenter by trade;
And he fell in love with Sally Brown,
  That was a lady's maid.

But as they fetch'd a walk one day,
  They met a press-gang crew;
And Sally she did faint away,
  Whilst Ben he was brought to.

The Boatswain swore with wicked words,
  Enough to shock a saint,   10
That though she did seem in a fit,
  'Twas nothing but a feint.

"Come, girl," said he, "hold up your head,
  He'll be as good as me;
For when your swain is in our boat,
  A boatswain he will be."

So when they'd made their game of her,
  And taken off her elf,
She roused, and found she only was
  A coming to herself.   20

"And is he gone, and is he gone?"
  She cried, and wept outright:
"Then I will to the water side,
  And see him out of sight."

A waterman came up to her,—
  "Now, young woman," said he,
"If you weep on so, you will make
  Eye-water in the sea."

"Alas! they've taken my beau Ben
  To sail with old Benbow;"   30
And her woe began to run afresh,
  As if she'd said Gee woe!

Says he, "They've only taken him
  To the Tender ship, you see;"
"The Tender-ship," cried Sally Brown,
  "What a hard-ship that must be!

"O! would I were a mermaid now,
  For then I'd follow him;
But Oh!—I'm not a fish-woman,
  And so I cannot swim.   40

"Alas! I was not born beneath
  The virgin and the scales,
So I must curse my cruel stars,
  And walk about in Wales."

Now Ben had sail'd to many a place
  That's underneath the world;
But in two years the ship came home,
  And all her sails were furl'd.

But when he call'd on Sally Brown,
  To see how she went on,   50
He found she'd got another Ben,
  Whose Christian-name was John.

"O Sally Brown, O Sally Brown,
  How could you serve me so?
I've met with many a breeze before,
  But never such a blow:"

Then reading on his 'bacco box
  He heaved a bitter sigh,
And then began to eye his pipe,
  And then to pipe his eye.   60

And then he tried to sing "All's Well,"
  But could not though he tried;
His head was turn'd, and so he chew'd
  His pigtail till he died.

His death, which happen'd in his berth,
  At forty-odd befell:
They went and told the sexton, and
  The sexton toll'd the bell.

Pub. 1826

THE MERMAID OF MARGATE

  "Alas! what perils do environ
    That man who meddles with a siren!"
                          HUDIBRAS

ON Margate beach, where the sick one roams,
  And the sentimental reads;
Where the maiden flirts, and the widow
    comes—
  Like the ocean—to cast her weeds,—

Where urchins wander to pick up shells,
  And the Cit to spy at the ships,—
Like the water gala at Sadler's Wells,—
  And the Chandler for watery dips;—

There's a maiden sits by the ocean brim,
  As lovely and fair as sin!   10
But woe, deep water and woe to him,
  That she snareth like Peter Fin!

Her head is crown'd with pretty seawares,
  And her locks are golden and loose:
And seek to her feet, like other folks' heirs,
  To stand, of course, in her shoes!

And, all day long, she combeth them well,
  With a sea-shark's prickly jaw;
And her mouth is just like a rose-lipp'd shell,
  The fairest that man e'er saw!   20

And the Fishmonger, humble as love may be,
  Hath planted his seat by her side;
"Good even, fair maid! Is thy lover at sea,
  To make thee so watch the tide?"

She turn'd about with her pearly brows,
  And clasp'd him by the hand:—
"Come, love, with me; I've a bonny house
  On the golden Goodwin Sand."

And then she gave him a siren kiss,
  No honeycomb e'er was sweeter;   30
Poor wretch! how little he dreamt for this
  That Peter should be salt-Peter:

And away with her prize to the wave she
    leapt,
  Not walking, as damsels do,
With toe and heel, as she ought to have stept,
  But she hopt like a Kangaroo;

One plunge, and then the victim was blind,
  Whilst they galloped across the tide;
At last, on the bank he waked in his mind,
  And the Beauty was by his side.   40

One half on the sand, and half in the sea,
  But his hair began to stiffen;
For when he look'd where her feet should be,
  She had no more feet than Miss Biffen!

But a scaly tail, of a dolphin's growth,
  In the dabbling brine did soak:
At last she open'd her pearly mouth,
  Like an oyster, and thus she spoke:—

"You crimpt my father, who was a skate;—
  And my sister you sold—a maid;   50
So here remain for a fish'ry fate,
  For lost you are, and betray'd!"

And away she went, with a seagull's scream,
  And a splash of her saucy tail;
In a moment he lost the silvery gleam
  That shone on her splendid mail!

The sun went down with a blood-red flame,
  And the sky grew cloudy and black,
And the tumbling billows like leapfrog came,
  Each over the other's back!   60

Ah, me! it had been a beautiful scene,
  With a safe terra-firma round;
But the green water-hillocks all seem'd to him
  Like those in a church-yard ground;

And Christians love in the turf to lie,
  Not in watery graves to be;
Nay, the very fishes will sooner die
  On the land than in the sea.

And whilst he stood, the watery strife
  Encroached on every hand,   70
And the ground decreas'd—his moments of life
  Seem'd measur'd, like Time's, by sand;

And still the waters foam'd in, like ale,
  In front, and on either flank,
He knew that Goodwin and Co. must fail,
  There was such a run on the bank.

A little more, and a little more,
  The surges came tumbling in;
He sang the evening hymn twice o'er,
  And thought of every sin!   80

Each flounder and plaice lay cold at his heart,
  As cold as his marble slab;
And he thought he felt, in every part,
  The pincers of scalded crab!

The squealing lobsters that he had boil'd,
  And the little potted shrimps,
All the horny prawns he had ever spoil'd,
  Gnawed into his soul, like imps!

And the billows were wandering to and fro,
  And the glorious sun was sunk,   90
And Day, getting black in the face, as though
  Of the night-shade she had drunk!

Had there been but a smuggler's cargo adrift,
  One tub, or keg, to be seen,
It might have given his spirits a lift
  Or an *anker* where *Hope* might lean!

But there was not a box or a beam afloat,
  To raft him from that sad place;
Not a skiff, not a yawl, or a mackarel boat,
  Nor a smack upon Neptune's face.   100

At last, his lingering hopes to buoy,
  He saw a sail and a mast,
And called "Ahoy!"—but it was not a hoy,
  And so the vessel went past.

WHIMS AND ODDITIES,

In Prose and Verse:

WITH FORTY ORIGINAL DESIGNS,

BY

THOMAS HOOD,

ONE OF THE AUTHORS OF ODES AND ADDRESSES TO GREAT PEOPLE
AND THE DESIGNER OF THE PROGRESS OF CANT.

"O Cicero! Cicero! if to pun be a crime, 'tis a crime I have learned
of thee: O Bias! Bias! if to pun be a crime, by thy example I was biassed!"

SCRIBLERUS.

LONDON:

LUPTON RELFE, 13, CORNHILL.

—

1826.

Presentation Copy from Thomas Hood to S. T. Coleridge. (See Appendix I.)

And with saucy wing that flapp'd in his face,
   The wild bird about him flew,
With a shrilly scream, that twitted his case,
   "Why, thou art a sea-gull too!"

And lo! the tide was over his feet;
   Oh! his heart began to freeze,   110
And slowly to pulse:—in another beat
   The wave was up to his knees!

He was deafen'd amidst the mountain-tops,
   And the salt spray blinded his eyes,
And wash'd away the other salt-drops
   That grief had caused to arise:—

But just as his body was all afloat,
   And the surges above him broke,
He was saved from the hungry deep by a boat,
   Of Deal—(but builded of oak.)   120

The skipper gave him a dram, as he lay,
   And chafed his shivering skin;
And the Angel return'd that was flying away
   With the spirit of Peter Fin!

Pub. 1826

FAITHLESS NELLY GRAY

A PATHETIC BALLAD

BEN BATTLE was a soldier bold,
   And used to war's alarms:
But a cannon-ball took off his legs,
   So he laid down his arms!

Now as they bore him off the field,
   Said he, "Let others shoot,
For here I leave my second leg,
   And the Forty-second Foot!"

The army-surgeons made him limbs:
   Said he,—"They're only pegs: 10
But there's as wooden members quite
   As represent my legs!"

Now Ben he loved a pretty maid,
   Her name was Nelly Gray;
So he went to pay her his devours
   When he'd devoured his pay!

But when he called on Nelly Gray,
   She made him quite a scoff;
And when she saw his wooden legs,
   Began to take them off!   20

"O Nelly Gray! O Nelly Gray!
   Is this your love so warm?
The love that loves a scarlet coat
   Should be more uniform!"

Said she, "I loved a soldier once,
   For he was blythe and brave;
But I will never have a man
   With both legs in the grave!

"Before you had those timber toes,
   Your love I did allow,   30
But then, you know, you stand upon
   Another footing now!"

"O Nelly Gray! O Nelly Gray!
   For all your jeering speeches,
At duty's call, I left my legs
   In Badajos's *breaches!*"

"Why, then," said she, "you've lost the feet
   Of legs in war's alarms,
And now you cannot wear your shoes
   Upon your feats of arms!"   40

"Oh false and fickle Nelly Gray;
   I know why you refuse:—
Though I've no feet—some other man
   Is standing in my shoes!

"I wish I ne'er had seen your face;
   But, now, a long farewell!
For you will be my death;—alas!
   You will not be my *Nell!*"

Now when he went from Nelly Gray,
   His heart so heavy got—   50
And life was such a burthen grown,
   It made him take a knot!

So round his melancholy neck,
   A rope he did entwine,
And, for his second time in life,
   Enlisted in the Line!

One end he tied around a beam,
   And then removed his pegs,
And, as his legs were off,—of course,
   He soon was off his legs!   60

And there he hung, till he was dead
   As any nail in town,—
For though distress had cut him up,
   It could not cut him down!

A dozen men sat on his corpse,
  To find out why he died—
And they buried Ben in four crossroads,
  With a *stake* in his inside!

Pub. 1826

From HERO AND LEANDER

"O POPPY death!—sweet poisoner of sleep;
Where shall I seek for thee, oblivious drug,
That I may steep thee in my drink, and creep
Out of life's coil? Look, Idol! how I hug
Thy dainty image in this strict embrace,
And kiss this clay-cold model of thy face!

"Put out, put out these sun-consuming lamps!
I do but read my sorrows by their shine;
O, come and quench them with thy oozy
    damps,
And let my darkness intermix with thine; 10
Since love is blinded, wherefore should I see?
Now love is death,—death will be love to me!

"Away, away, this vain complaining breath,
It does but stir the troubles that I weep;
Let it be hushed and quieted, sweet Death;
The wind must settle ere the wave can sleep,—
Since love is silent I would fain be mute;
O, Death, be gracious to my dying suit!"

Pub. 1827

FAIR INES

I

O SAW ye not fair Ines?
  She's gone into the West,
To dazzle when the sun is down,
  And rob the world of rest:
She took our daylight with her,
  The smiles that we love best,
With morning blushes on her cheek,
  And pearls upon her breast.

II

O turn again, fair Ines,
  Before the fall of night, 10
For fear the Moon should shine alone,
  And stars unrivall'd bright;
And blessed will the lover be
  That walks beneath their light,
And breathes the love against thy cheek
  I dare not even write!

III

Would I had been, fair Ines,
  That gallant cavalier,
Who rode so gaily by thy side,
  And whisper'd thee so near!— 20
Were there no bonny dames at home
  Or no true lovers here,
That he should cross the seas to win
  The dearest of the dear?

IV

I saw thee, lovely Ines,
  Descend along the shore,
With bands of noble gentlemen,
  And banners wav'd before;
And gentle youth and maidens gay,
  And snowy plumes they wore;— 30
It would have been a beauteous dream,—
  If it had been no more!

V

Alas, alas, fair Ines,
  She went away with song,
With Music waiting on her steps,
  And shoutings of the throng;
But some were sad, and felt no mirth,
  But only Music's wrong,
In sounds that sang Farewell, Farewell,
  To her you've loved so long. 40

VI

Farewell, farewell, fair Ines,
  That vessel never bore
So fair a lady on its deck,
  Nor danc'd so light before,—
Alas for pleasure on the sea,
  And sorrow on the shore!
The smile that blest one lover's heart
  Has broken many more!

Pub. 1827

ODE

AUTUMN

I

I SAW old Autumn in the misty morn
Stand shadowless like Silence, listening
To silence, for no lonely bird would sing
Into his hollow ear from woods forlorn,
Nor lowly hedge nor solitary thorn;—

Shaking his languid locks, all dewy bright
With tangled gossamer that fell by night,
  Pearling his coronet of golden corn.

II

Where are the songs of summer?—With the
    sun,
Oping the dusky eyelids of the south,   10
Till shade and silence waken up as one,
And Morning sings with a warm odorous
    mouth.
Where are the merry birds?—Away, away,
On panting wings through the inclement skies,
  Lest owls should prey
  Undazzled at noon-day,
And tear with horny beak their lustrous eyes.

III

Where are the blooms of Summer?—In the
    west,
Blushing their last to the last sunny hours,
When the mild Eve by sudden Night is prest
Like tearful Proserpine, snatch'd from her
    flow'rs   21
  To a most gloomy breast.
Where is the pride of Summer,—the green
    prime,—
The many, many leaves all twinkling?—Three
  On the moss'd elm; three on the naked lime
Trembling,—and one upon the old oak tree!
  Where is the Dryads' immortality?—
Gone into mournful cypress and dark yew,
Or wearing the long gloomy Winter through
  In the smooth holly's green eternity.   30

IV

The squirrel gloats on his accomplish'd hoard,
The ants have brimm'd their garners with ripe
    grain,
  And honey bees have stor'd
The sweets of Summer in their luscious cells;
The swallows all have wing'd across the main;
But here the Autumn melancholy dwells,
  And sighs her tearful spells
Amongst the sunless shadows of the plain.
  Alone, alone,
  Upon a mossy stone,   40
She sits and reckons up the dead and gone
With the last leaves for a love-rosary,
Whilst all the wither'd world looks drearily,

Like a dim picture of the drowned past
In the hush'd mind's mysterious far away,
Doubtful what ghostly thing will steal the last
Into that distance, grey upon the grey.

V

O go and sit with her, and be o'ershaded
Under the languid downfall of her hair:
She wears a coronal of flowers faded   50
Upon her forehead, and a face of care;—
There is enough of wither'd every where
To make her bower,—and enough of gloom;
There is enough of sadness to invite,
If only for the rose that died,—whose doom
Is Beauty's,—she that with the living bloom
Of conscious cheeks most beautifies the
    light;—
There is enough of sorrowing, and quite
Enough of bitter fruits the earth doth bear,—
Enough of chilly droppings for her bowl;   60
Enough of fear and shadowy despair,
To frame her cloudy prison for the soul!
Pub. 1827

BALLAD

Spring it is cheery,
  Winter is dreary,
Green leaves hang, but the brown must fly;
  When he's forsaken,
  Wither'd and shaken
What can an old man do but die?

  Love will not clip him,
  Maids will not lip him,
Maud and Marian pass him by;
  Youth it is sunny,   10
  Age has no honey,—
What can an old man do but die?

  June it was jolly,
  O for its folly!
A dancing leg and a laughing eye;
  Youth may be silly,
  Wisdom is chilly,—
What can an old man do but die?

  Friends, they are scanty,
  Beggars are plenty,   20
If he has followers, I know why;
  Gold's in his clutches,
  (Buying him crutches!)—
What can an old man do but die?
Pub. 1827

RUTH

She stood breast-high amid the corn,
Clasp'd by the golden light of morn,
Like the sweetheart of the sun,
Who many a glowing kiss had won.

On her cheek an autumn flush,
Deeply ripen'd;—such a blush
In the midst of brown was born,
Like red poppies grown with corn.

Round her eyes her tresses fell;
Which were blackest none could tell,   10
But long lashes veil'd a light
That had else been all too bright.

And her hat, with shady brim,
Made her tressy forehead dim;—
Thus she stood amid the stooks,
Praising God with sweetest looks:—

Sure, I said, Heaven did not mean
Where I reap thou shouldst but glean;
Lay thy sheaf adown, and come,
Share my harvest and my home.   20

Pub. 1827

I REMEMBER, I REMEMBER

I

I remember, I remember,
The house where I was born,
The little window where the sun
Came peeping in at morn;
He never came a wink too soon,
Nor brought too long a day,
But now, I often wish the night
Had borne my breath away!

II

I remember, I remember,
The roses, red and white,   10
The vi'lets, and the lily-cups,
Those flowers made of light!
The lilacs where the robin built,
And where my brother set
The laburnum on his birthday,—
The tree is living yet!

III

I remember, I remember,
Where I was used to swing,
And thought the air must rush as fresh
To swallows on the wing;   20
My spirit flew in feathers then,
That is so heavy now,
And summer pools could hardly cool
The fever on my brow!

IV

I remember, I remember,
The fir trees dark and high;
I used to think their slender tops
Were close against the sky:
It was a childish ignorance,
But now 'tis little joy   30
To know I'm farther off from heav'n
Than when I was a boy.

Pub. 1827

SONG

I

The stars are with the voyager
    Wherever he may sail;
The moon is constant to her time;
    The sun will never fail;
But follow, follow round the world,
    The green earth and the sea;
So love is with the lover's heart,
    Wherever he may be.

II

Wherever he may be, the stars
    Must daily lose their light;   10
The moon will veil her in the shade;
    The sun will set at night.
The sun may set, but constant love
    Will shine when he's away;
So that dull night is never night,
    And day is brighter day.

Pub. 1827

SILENCE

There is a silence where hath been no sound,
    There is a silence where no sound may be,
    In the cold grave—under the deep deep sea,
Or in wide desert where no life is found,
Which hath been mute, and still must sleep
    profound;

No voice is hush'd—no life treads silently,
　　But clouds and cloudy shadows wander free,
That never spoke, over the idle ground:
But in green ruins, in the desolate walls
　　Of antique palaces, where Man hath been, 10
Though the dun fox, or wild hyena, calls,
　　And owls, that flit continually between,
Shriek to the echo, and the low winds moan,
There the true Silence is, self-conscious and
　　alone.

Pub. 1827

THE DREAM OF EUGENE ARAM, THE MURDERER

'TWAS in the prime of summer time,
　　An evening calm and cool,
And four-and-twenty happy boys
　　Came bounding out of school:
There were some that ran and some that
　　leap'd,
　　Like troutlets in a pool.

Away they sped with gamesome minds,
　　And souls untouch'd by sin;
To a level mead they came, and there
　　They drave the wickets in: 10
Pleasantly shone the setting sun
　　Over the town of Lynn.

Like sportive deer they cours'd about,
　　And shouted as they ran,—
Turning to mirth all things of earth,
　　As only boyhood can;
But the Usher sat remote from all,
　　A melancholy man!

His hat was off, his vest apart,
　　To catch heaven's blessed breeze; 20
For a burning thought was in his brow,
　　And his bosom ill at ease:
So he lean'd his head on his hands, and read
　　The book between his knees!

Leaf after leaf, he turn'd it o'er,
　　Nor ever glanc'd aside,
For the peace of his soul he read that book.
　　In the golden eventide:
Much study had made him very lean,
　　And pale, and leaden-ey'd. 30

At last he shut the ponderous tome,
　　With a fast and fervent grasp
He strain'd the dusky covers close,
　　And fix'd the brazen hasp:
"Oh, God! could I so close my mind,
　　And clasp it with a clasp!"

Then leaping on his feet upright,
　　Some moody turns he took,—
Now up the mead, then down the mead,
　　And past a shady nook,— 40
And, lo! he saw a little boy
　　That pored upon a book!

"My gentle lad, what is't you read—
　　Romance or fairy fable?
Or is it some historic page,
　　Of kings and crowns unstable?"
The young boy gave an upward glance,—
　　"It is 'The Death of Abel.'"

The Usher took six hasty strides,
　　As smit with sudden pain,— 50
Six hasty strides beyond the place,
　　Then slowly back again;
And down he sat beside the lad,
　　And talk'd with him of Cain;

And, long since then, of bloody men,
　　Whose deeds tradition saves;
Of lonely folk cut off unseen,
　　And hid in sudden graves;
Of horrid stabs, in groves forlorn,
　　And murders done in caves; 60

And how the sprites of injur'd men
　　Shriek upward from the sod,—
Aye, how the ghostly hand will point
　　To show the burial clod;
And unknown facts of guilty acts
　　Are seen in dreams from God!

He told how murderers walk the earth
　　Beneath the curse of Cain,—
With crimson clouds before their eyes,
　　And flames about their brain: 70
For blood has left upon their souls
　　Its everlasting stain!

"And well," quoth he, "I know, for truth,
　　Their pangs must be extreme,—
Woe, woe, unutterable woe,—

Who spill life's sacred stream!
For why? Methought, last night, I wrought
  A murder, in a dream!

"One that had never done me wrong—
  A feeble man, and old;   80
I led him to a lonely field,—
  The moon shone clear and cold:
Now here, said I, this man shall die,
  And I will have his gold!

"Two sudden blows with a ragged stick,
  And one with a heavy stone,
One hurried gash with a hasty knife,—
  And then the deed was done:
There was nothing lying at my foot
  But lifeless flesh and bone!   90

"Nothing but lifeless flesh and bone,
  That could not do me ill;
And yet I fear'd him all the more,
  For lying there so still:
There was a manhood in his look,
  That murder could not kill!

"And, lo! the universal air
  Seem'd lit with ghastly flame;—
Ten thousand thousand dreadful eyes
  Were looking down in blame: 100
I took the dead man by his hand,
  And call'd upon his name!

"Oh, God! it made me quake to see
  Such sense within the slain!
But when I touch'd the lifeless clay,
  The blood gush'd out amain!
For every clot, a burning spot,
  Was scorching in my brain!

"My head was like an ardent coal,
  My heart as solid ice;   110
My wretched, wretched soul, I knew,
  Was at the Devil's price:
A dozen times I groan'd; the dead
  Had never groan'd but twice!

"And now, from forth the frowning sky,
  From the Heaven's topmost height,
I heard a voice—the awful voice
  Of the blood-avenging Sprite:—
'Thou guilty man! take up thy dead,
  And hide it from my sight!'   120

"I took the dreary body up,
  And cast it in a stream,—
A sluggish water, black as ink,
  The depth was so extreme:—
My gentle Boy, remember this
  Is nothing but a dream!

"Down went the corse with a hollow plunge,
  And vanish'd in the pool;
Anon I cleans'd my bloody hands,
  And wash'd my forehead cool,   130
And sat among the urchins young
  That evening in the school.

"Oh, Heaven! to think of their white souls,
  And mine so black and grim!
I could not share in childish prayer,
  Nor join in Evening Hymn:
Like a Devil of the Pit, I seem'd,
  'Mid holy Cherubim!

"And Peace went with them, one and all,
  And each calm pillow spread;   140
But Guilt was my grim Chamberlain
  That lighted me to bed;
And drew my midnight curtains round
  With fingers bloody red!

"All night I lay in agony,
  In anguish dark and deep;
My fever'd eyes I dared not close,
  But stared aghast at Sleep:
For Sin had render'd unto her
  The keys of Hell to keep!   150

"All night I lay in agony,
  From weary chime to chime,
With one besetting horrid hint,
  That rack'd me all the time,—
A mighty yearning, like the first
  Fierce impulse unto crime;

"One stern tyrannic thought, that made
  All other thoughts its slave;
Stronger and stronger every pulse
  Did that temptation crave,—   160
Still urging me to go and see
  The Dead Man in his grave!

"Heavily I rose up, as soon
  As light was in the sky,

And sought the black accursed pool
With a wild misgiving eye;
And I saw the Dead in the river bed,
For the faithless stream was dry!

"Merrily rose the lark, and shook
The dew-drop from its wing;   170
But I never mark'd its morning flight,
I never heard it sing:
For I was stooping once again
Under the horrid thing.

"With breathless speed, like a soul in chase,
I took him up and ran;—
There was no time to dig a grave
Before the day began:
In a lonesome wood, with heaps of leaves,
I hid the murder'd man!   180

"And all that day I read in school,
But my thought was other where;
As soon as the mid-day task was done,
In secret I was there:
And a mighty wind had swept the leaves,
And still the corse was bare!

"Then down I cast me on my face,
And first began to weep,
For I knew my secret then was one
That earth refus'd to keep: 190
Or land, or sea, though he should be
Ten thousand fathoms deep.

"So wills the fierce avenging Sprite,
Till blood for blood atones!
Ay, though he's buried in a cave,
And trodden down with stones,
And years have rotted off his flesh,—
The world shall see his bones.

"Oh, God! that horrid, horrid dream
Besets me now awake!   200
Again—again, with a dizzy brain,
The human life I take;
And my red right hand grows raging hot,
Like Cranmer's at the stake.

"And still no peace for the restless clay,
Will wave or mould allow;
The horrid thing pursues my soul,—
It stands before me now!"
The fearful Boy look'd up, and saw
Huge drops upon his brow.   210

That very night, while gentle sleep
The urchin eyelids kiss'd,
Two stern-faced men set out from Lynn,
Through the cold and heavy mist;
And Eugene Aram walk'd between,
With gyves upon his wrist.[1]

1829

DOMESTIC ASIDES; OR, TRUTH IN PARENTHESES

"I REALLY take it very kind,
This visit, Mrs. Skinner!
I have not seen you such an age—
(The wretch has come to dinner!)

"Your daughters, too, what loves of girls—
What heads for painters' easels!
Come here and kiss the infant, dears,—
(And give it p'rhaps the measles!)

"Your charming boys I see are home
From Reverend Mr. Russel's;   10
'Twas very kind to bring them both,—
(What boots for my new Brussels!)

"What! little Clara left at home?
Well now I call that shabby:
I should have lov'd to kiss her so,—
(A flabby, dabby, babby!)

"And Mr. S., I hope he's well,
Ah! though he lives so handy,
He never now drops in to sup,—
(The better for our brandy!)   20

"Come, take a seat—I long to hear
About Matilda's marriage;
You're come, of course, to spend the day!—
(Thank Heav'n, I hear the carriage!)

"What! must you go? next time I hope
You'll give me longer measure;
Nay—I shall see you down the stairs—
(With most uncommon pleasure!)

[1] The late Admiral Burney went to school at an establishment where the unhappy Eugene Aram was Usher, subsequent to his crime. The Admiral stated that Aram was generally liked by the boys; and that he used to discourse to them about *murder*, in somewhat of the spirit which is attributed to him in the Poem.

"Good-bye! good-bye! remember all
Next time you'll take your dinners!   30
(Now, David, mind I'm not at home
In future to the Skinners!)"

Pub. 1839

SALLY SIMPKIN'S LAMENT

OR, JOHN JONES'S KIT-CAT-ASTROPHE

"He left his body to the sea,
  And made a shark his legatee."
                    BRYAN *and* PERENNE

"OH! what is that comes gliding in,
  And quite in middling haste?
It is the picture of my Jones,
  And painted to the waist.

"It is not painted to the life,
  For where's the trowsers blue?
Oh Jones, my dear!—Oh dear! my Jones,
  What is become of you?"

"Oh! Sally dear, it is too true,—
  The half that you remark   10
Is come to say my other half
  Is bit off by a shark!

"Oh! Sally, sharks do things by halves,
  Yet most completely do!
A bite in one place seems enough,
  But I've been bit in two.

"You know I once was all your own,
  But now a shark must share!
But let that pass—for now to you
  I'm neither here nor there.   20

"Alas! death has a strange divorce
  Effected in the sea,
It has divided me from you,
  And even me from me!

"Don't fear my ghost will walk o' nights
  To haunt, as people say;
My ghost *can't* walk, for, oh! my legs
  Are many leagues away!

"Lord! think when I am swimming round,
  And looking where the boat is,   30
A shark just snaps away a *half*,
  Without 'a *quarter's* notice.'

"One half is here, the other half
  Is near Columbia placed;
Oh! Sally, I have got the whole
  Atlantic for my waist.

"But now, adieu—a long adieu!
  I've solved death's awful riddle,
And would say more, but I am doomed
  To break off in the middle."   40

Pub. 1839

EPICUREAN REMINISCENCES OF A SENTIMENTALIST

"My *Tables! Meat* it is, *I set it* down!"
                    HAMLET

I THINK it was Spring—but not certain I am—
  When my passion began first to work;
But I know we were certainly looking for lamb,
  And the season was over for pork.

'Twas at Christmas, I think, when I met with .
  Miss Chase,
  Yes,—for Morris had asked me to dine,—
And I thought I had never beheld such a face,
  Or so noble a turkey and chine.

Placed close by her side, it made others quite
  wild,
  With sheer envy to witness my luck;   10
How she blushed as I gave her some turtle,
  and smil'd
  As I afterwards offered some duck.

I looked and I languished, alas, to my cost,
  Through three courses of dishes and meats;
Getting deeper in love—but my heart was
  quite lost,
  When it came to the trifle and sweets!

With a rent-roll that told of my houses and
  land,
  To her parents I told my designs—
And then to herself I presented my hand,
  With a very fine pottle of pines!   20

I asked her to have me for weal or for woe,
  And she did not object in the least;—
I can't tell the date—but we married, I know,
  Just in time to have game at the feast.

We went to——it certainly was the seaside;
  For the next, the most blessed of morns,
I remember how fondly I gazed at my bride,
  Sitting down to a plateful of prawns.

O never may mem'ry lose sight of that year,
  But still hallow the time as it ought,   30
That season the "grass" was remarkably dear,
  And the peas at a guinea a quart.

So happy, like hours, all our days seem'd to
    haste,
  A fond pair, such as poets have drawn,
So united in heart—so congenial in taste,
  We were both of us partial to brawn!

A long life I looked for of bliss with my bride,
  But then Death—I ne'er dreamt about that!
Oh there's nothing is certain in life, as I cried,
  When my turbot eloped with the cat!   40

My dearest took ill at the turn of the year,
  But the cause no physician could nab;
But something it seemed like consumption, I
    fear,
  It was just after supping on crab.

In vain she was doctor'd, in vain she was dosed,
  Still her strength and her appetite pined;
She lost relish for what she had relish'd the
    most,
  Even salmon she deeply declin'd.

For months still I linger'd in hope and in
    doubt,
  While her form it grew wasted and thin; 50
But the last dying spark of existence went out,
  As the oysters were just coming in!

She died, and she left me the saddest of men
  To indulge in a widower's moan,
Oh, I felt all the power of solitude then,
  As I ate my first natives alone!

But when I beheld Virtue's friends in their
    cloaks,
  And with sorrowful crape on their hats,
O my grief poured a flood! and the out-of-
    doors folks
  Were all crying—I think it was sprats! 60
Pub. 1839

FRENCH AND ENGLISH

  Good heaven! Why even the little children in
France speak French!"—ADDISON

I

NEVER go to France
Unless you know the lingo,
If you do, like me,
You will repent, by jingo.
Staring like a fool,
And silent as a mummy,
There I stood alone,
A nation with a dummy:

II

Chaises stand for chairs,
They christen letters *Billies*,   10
They call their mother *mares*,
And all their daughters *fillies;*
Strange it was to hear,
I'll tell you what's a good 'un,
They call their leather *queer*,
And half their shoes are wooden.

III

Signs I had to make
For every little notion,
Limbs all going like
A telegraph in motion,   20
For wine I reel'd about,
To show my meaning fully,
And made a pair of horns,
To ask for "beef and bully."

IV

Moo! I cried for milk;
I got my sweet things snugger,
When I kissed Jeanette,
'Twas understood for sugar.
If I wanted bread,
My jaws I set a-going,   30
And asked for new-laid eggs,
By clapping hands and crowing!

V

If I wish'd a ride,
I'll tell you how I got it;
On my stick astride
I made believe to trot it;
Then their cash was strange,
It bored me every minute,
Now here's a *hog* to change,
How many *sows* are in it!   40

VI

Never go to France,
Unless you know the lingo;
If you do, like me,
You will repent, by jingo;
Staring like a fool,
And silent as a mummy,
There I stood alone,
A nation with a dummy!

Pub. 1839

PAIR'D, *NOT* MATCH'D

Of wedded bliss
Bards sing amiss,
I cannot make a song of it;
For I am small,
My wife is tall,
And that's the short and long of it;

When we debate
It is my fate
To always have the wrong of it;
For I am small   10
And she is tall,
And that's the short and long of it!

And when I speak
My voice is weak,
But hers—she makes a gong of it;
For I am small,
And she is tall,
And that's the short and long of it;

She has, in brief,
Command in Chief,   20
And I'm but Aide-de-camp of it;
For I am small,
And she is tall,
And that's the short and long of it!

She gives to me
The weakest tea,
And takes the whole Souchong of it;
For I am small,
And she is tall,
And that's the short and long of it;   30

She'll sometimes grip
My buggy whip,
And make me feel the thong of it;

For I am small,
And she is tall,
And that's the short and long of it!

Against my life
She'll take a knife,
Or fork, and dart the prong of it;
For I am small,   40
And she is tall,
And that's the short and long of it!

I sometimes think
I'll take a drink,
And hector when I'm strong of it;
For I am small,
And she is tall,
And that's the short and long of it!

O, if the bell
Would ring her knell,   50
I'd make a gay ding dong of it;
For I am small,
And she is tall,
And that's the short and long of it!

Pub. 1839

THE SONG OF THE SHIRT

With fingers weary and worn,
With eyelids heavy and red,
A Woman sat, in unwomanly rags,
Plying her needle and thread—
Stitch! stitch! stitch!
In poverty, hunger, and dirt,
And still with a voice of dolorous pitch
She sang the "Song of the Shirt!"

"Work! work! work!
While the cock is crowing aloof!   10
And work—work—work,
Till the stars shine through the roof!
It 's O! to be a slave
Along with the barbarous Turk,
Where woman has never a soul to save.
If this is Christian work!

"Work—work—work
Till the brain begins to swim;
Work—work—work
Till the eyes are heavy and dim!   20

Seam, and gusset, and band,
  Band, and gusset, and seam,
Till over the buttons I fall asleep,
  And sew them on in a dream!

"O! Men with Sisters dear!
  O! Men! with Mothers and Wives!
It is not linen you're wearing out,
  But human creatures' lives!
    Stitch—stitch—stitch,
  In poverty, hunger, and dirt,   30
Sewing at once, with a double thread,
  A Shroud as well as a Shirt.

"But why do I talk of Death?
  That Phantom of grisly bone,
I hardly fear his terrible shape,
  It seems so like my own—
It seems so like my own,
  Because of the fasts I keep,
Oh! God! that bread should be so dear,
  And flesh and blood so cheap!   40

"Work—work—work!
  My labour never flags;
And what are its wages? A bed of straw,
  A crust of bread—and rags.
That shatter'd roof,—and this naked floor—
  A table—a broken chair—
And a wall so blank, my shadow I thank
  For sometimes falling there!

"Work—work—work!
  From weary chime to chime,   50
Work—work—work,
  As prisoners work for crime!
Band, and gusset, and seam,
  Seam, and gusset, and band,
Till the heart is sick, and the brain benumb'd,
  As well as the weary hand.

"Work—work—work,
  In the dull December light,
And work—work—work,
  When the weather is warm and bright—   60
While underneath the eaves
  The brooding swallows cling
As if to show me their sunny backs
  And twit me with the spring.

"Oh! but to breathe the breath
  Of the cowslip and primrose sweet—

With the sky above my head,
  And the grass beneath my feet,
For only one short hour
  To feel as I used to feel,   70
Before I knew the woes of want
  And the walk that costs a meal!

"Oh but for one short hour!
  A respite however brief!
No blessed leisure for Love or Hope,
  But only time for Grief!
A little weeping would ease my heart,
  But in their briny bed
My tears must stop, for every drop
  Hinders needle and thread!"   80

[Seam, and gusset, and band,
  Band, and gusset, and seam,
Work, work, work,
  Like the Engine that works by Steam!
A mere machine of iron and wood
  That toils for Mammon's sake—
Without a brain to ponder and craze
  Or a heart to feel—and break!][1]

With fingers weary and worn,
  With eyelids heavy and red,   90
A Woman sat, in unwomanly rags,
  Plying her needle and thread—
    Stitch! stitch! stitch!
  In poverty, hunger, and dirt,
And still with a voice of dolorous pitch,
Would that its tone could reach the Rich!—
  She sang this "Song of the Shirt!"
1843

THE BRIDGE OF SIGHS

    "Drown'd! drown'd!"—HAMLET

ONE more Unfortunate,
  Weary of breath,
Rashly importunate,
  Gone to her death!

Take her up tenderly,
  Lift her with care;
Fashion'd so slenderly,
  Young, and so fair!

Look at her garments
  Clinging like cerements;   10
Whilst the wave constantly

---

[1] The stanza in brackets was omitted when the "Song" was originally published.

Drips from her clothing;
Take her up instantly,
Loving, not loathing.—

Touch her not scornfully;
Think of her mournfully,
Gently and humanly;
Not of the stains of her,
All that remains of her
Now is pure womanly.   20

Make no deep scrutiny
Into her mutiny
Rash and undutiful:
Past all dishonour
Death has left on her
Only the beautiful.

Still, for all slips of hers,
One of Eve's family—
Wipe those poor lips of hers
Oozing so clammily.   30

Loop up her tresses
Escaped from the comb,
Her fair auburn tresses;
Whilst wonderment guesses
Where was her home?

Who was her father?
Who was her mother?
Had she a sister?
Had she a brother?
Or was there a dearer one   40
Still, and a nearer one
Yet, than all other?

Alas! for the rarity
Of Christian charity
Under the sun!
Oh! it was pitiful!
Near a whole city full,
Home she had none!

Sisterly, brotherly,
Fatherly, motherly,   50
Feelings had changed:
Love, by harsh evidence,
Thrown from its eminence;
Even God's providence
Seeming estranged.

Where the lamps quiver
So far in the river,
With many a light
From window and casement,
From garret to basement,   60
She stood, with amazement,
Houseless by night.

The bleak wind of March
Made her tremble and shiver;
But not the dark arch,
Or the black flowing river:
Mad from life's history,
Glad to death's mystery,
Swift to be hurl'd—
Anywhere, anywhere,   70
Out of the world!

In she plunged boldly,
No matter how coldly
The rough river ran,—
Over the brink of it,
Picture it—think of it,
Dissolute man!
Lave in it, drink of it,
Then, if you can!

Take her up tenderly,   80
Lift her with care;
Fashion'd so slenderly,
Young, and so fair!

Ere her limbs frigidly
Stiffen too rigidly,
Decently,—kindly,—
Smoothe and compose them:
And her eyes, close them,
Staring so blindly!

Dreadfully staring   90
Thro' muddy impurity,
As when with the daring
Last look of despairing,
Fix'd on futurity.

Perishing gloomily,
Spurr'd by contumely,
Cold inhumanity,
Burning insanity,
Into her rest.—
Cross her hands humbly,   100
As if praying dumbly,
Over her breast!

Owning her weakness,
Her evil behaviour,
And leaving, with meekness,
Her sins to her Saviour!

1844

THE LAY OF THE LABOURER

A SPADE! a rake! a hoe!
  A pickaxe, or a bill!
A hook to reap, or a scythe to mow,
  A flail, or what ye will—
And here's a ready hand
  To ply the needful tool,
And skill'd enough, by lessons rough,
  In Labour's rugged school.

To hedge, or dig the ditch,
  To lop or fell the tree,   10
To lay the swarth on the sultry field,
  Or plough the stubborn lea;
The harvest stack to bind,
  The wheaten rick to thatch,
And never fear in my pouch to find
  The tinder or the match.

To a flaming barn or farm
  My fancies never roam;
The fire I yearn to kindle and burn
  Is on the hearth of Home;   20
Where children huddle and crouch
  Through dark long winter days,
Where starving children huddle and crouch,
  To see the cheerful rays,
A-glowing on the haggard cheek,
  And not in the haggard's blaze!

To Him who sends a drought
  To parch the fields forlorn,
The rain to flood the meadows with mud,
  The lights to blast the corn,   30
To Him I leave to guide
  The bolt in its crooked path.
To strike the miser's rick, and show
  The skies blood-red with wrath.

A spade! a rake! a hoe!
  A pickaxe, or a bill!
A hook to reap, or a scythe to mow,
  A flail, or what ye will—
The corn to thrash, or the hedge to plash,
  The market-team to drive,   40

Or mend the fence by the cover side,
  And leave the game alive.

Ay, only give me work,
  And then you need not fear
That I shall snare his worship's hare,
  Or kill his grace's deer;
Break into his lordship's house,
  To steal the plate so rich;
Or leave the yeoman that had a purse
  To welter in a ditch.   50

Wherever Nature needs
  Wherever Labour calls,
No job I'll shirk of the hardest work,
  To shun the workhouse walls;
Where savage laws begrudge
  The pauper babe its breath,
And doom a wife to a widow's life,
  Before her partner's death.

My only claim is this,
  With labour stiff and stark,   60
By lawful turn, my living to earn,
  Between the light and dark;
My daily bread, and nightly bed,
  My bacon, and drop of beer—
But all from the hand that holds the land,
  And none from the overseer!

No parish money, or loaf,
  No pauper badges for me,
A son of the soil, by right of toil
  Entitled to my fee.   70
No alms I ask, give me my task:
  Here are the arm, the leg,
The strength, the sinews of a Man,
  To work, and not to beg.

Still one of Adam's heirs,
  Though doom'd by chance of birth
To dress so mean, and to eat the lean
  Instead of the fat of the earth;
To make such humble meals
  As honest labour can,   80
A bone and a crust, with a grace to God,
  And little thanks to man!

A spade! a rake! a hoe!
  A pickaxe, or a bill!
A hook to reap, or a scythe to mow,
  A flail, or what ye will—

Whatever the tool to ply,
  Here is a willing drudge,
With muscle and limb, and woe to him
  Who does their pay begrudge!   90

Who every weekly score
  Docks labour's little mite,
Bestows on the poor at the temple door,
  But robb'd them over night.
The very shilling he hoped to save,
  As health and morals fail,
Shall visit me in the New Bastille,
The Spital, or the Gaol!

1844

STANZAS

FAREWELL, Life! My senses swim;
And the world is growing dim;

Thronging shadows cloud the light,
Like the advent of the night,—
Colder, colder, colder still
Upward steals a vapour chill—
Strong the earthy odour grows—
I smell the Mould above the Rose!

Welcome, Life! the Spirit strives!
Strength returns, and hope revives;   10
Cloudy fears and shapes forlorn
Fly like shadows at the morn,—
O'er the earth there comes a bloom—
Sunny light for sullen gloom,
Warm perfume for vapour cold—
I smell the Rose above the Mould!

Pub. 1845

LEIGH HUNT
[October 19, 1784–August 28, 1859]

LEIGH HUNT's life touches that of greater men at so many points that he is a figure of more importance in literary history than his own powers could command. His life was that of a bookman. His father published a volume of his poems when he was sixteen, and by the time he was twenty he was contributing to journals. He continued as an industrious essayist, poet, editor, and critic until his death, the bulk of his work being truly considerable. Essentially a bookish life, it was disturbed occasionally by more dramatic events, including a two-year term in jail.

In 1808 in conjunction with his brother he started *The Examiner*, a weekly, which he continued for fourteen years. The magazine had no party connections but was strongly liberal in its sympathies. The authorities watched it with disfavor and prosecuted the Hunts several times, finally securing a conviction over an article in which Hunt called the Prince Regent "a fat Adonis of fifty." The incarceration was scarcely cruel: Hunt was allowed to redecorate his walls with a trellis of roses and paint the ceiling with sky and clouds. His family was with him, he was allowed the use of a garden, and visitors were freely admitted—Byron, indeed, once gave a dinner party in his honor at the jail. Nevertheless, the imprisonment made Hunt a martyr to the liberal cause, and when he was released in February 1815 he was a marked man. It was unfortunate, because Hunt was not really politically-minded. The result was that the liberal groups naturally tended to laud Hunt, and the Tories, equally naturally, were hostile to him and all his circle. The attacks on Hunt in which Keats became involved are to be understood against this political background.

In 1822 Hunt gave up *The Examiner* and went to Italy to collaborate on a quarterly, *The Liberal*, with Shelley and Byron. The idea was probably Shelley's—an effort to help Hunt financially—and Shelley's death left Hunt to deal with the temperamental Byron alone. The magazine suspended after four issues, both Hunt and Byron feeling personally aggrieved, the removal of Shelley, the intermediary, having led to a series of misunderstandings. Hunt expressed his feelings in 1828 when he published his *Lord Byron and His Contemporaries*. This volume and Hunt's *Autobiography* (1850; completed version, 1860) are now perhaps Hunt's most widely-read works—read, not for interest in Hunt, but for what he has to report of greater men.

The bulk of Hunt's writing is very great. His *The Story of Rimini* (1816) is important because of its influence on the early Keats. The poem is tawdry, and one need only compare the passage printed in this anthology with the corresponding passage at the close of Dante's fifth canto (*Inferno*) to understand what the mature Keats meant when he said that Hunt made fine things petty. Nevertheless the book had influence, especially from a technical point of view, in the impetus it gave to the relaxation of the couplet from the more rigid technique employed by the Augustans. The other extracts printed here show Hunt as a finer poet, and show also something of the quality of appreciation which he had for literature and art. He had a flair for discovering fine things, even if he could not often write them, and this appears most clearly in his essays, where his most important work was done.

THE STORY OF RIMINI

(*From* CANTO III)

ONE day,—'twas on a gentle, autumn noon,
When the cicale cease to mar the tune   371
Of birds and brooks—and morning work is
  done,
And shades have heavy outlines in the sun,—
The Princess came to her accustomed bower
To get her, if she could, a soothing hour;
Trying, as she was used, to leave her cares
Without, and slumberously enjoy the airs,
And the low-talking leaves, and that cool
  light
The vines let in, and all that hushing sight
Of closing wood seen through the opening
  door,   380
And distant plash of waters tumbling o'er,
And smell of citron blooms, and fifty luxuries
  more.

She tried as usual for the trial's sake,
For even that diminish'd her heart-ache;
And never yet, how ill soe'er at ease,
Came she for nothing 'midst the flowers and
  trees.
Yet how it was she knew not, but that day
She seem'd to feel too lightly borne away,—
Too much reliev'd,—too much inclin'd to
  draw
A careless joy from everything she saw,   390
And looking round her with a new-born eye,
As if some tree of knowledge had been nigh,
To taste of nature primitive and free,
And bask at ease in her heart's liberty.

Painfully clear those rising thoughts ap-
  pear'd,
With something dark at bottom that she fear'd:
And turning from the trees her thoughtful look,
She reach'd o'erhead, and took her down a
  book,
And fell to reading with as fix'd an air,
As though she had been wrapt since morning
  there.   400

'Twas "Launcelot of the Lake," a bright ro-
  mance,
That like a trumpet made young pulses dance,
Yet had a softer note that shook still more:—
She had begun it but the day before,
And read with a full heart, half sweet, half sad,
How old King Ban was spoil'd of all he had
But one fair castle: how one summer's day
With his fair queen and child he went away
In hopes King Arthur might resent his wrong;
How reaching by himself a hill ere long,   410
He turn'd to give his castle a last look,
And saw its calm white face; and how a smoke,
As he was looking, burst in volumes forth,
And good King Ban saw all that he was worth,
And his fair castle burning to the ground,
So that his wearied pulse felt overwound,
And he lay down, and said a prayer apart
For those he lov'd, and broke his poor old
  heart.
Then read she of the queen with her young
  child,
How she came up, and nearly had gone wild,
And how in journeying on in her despair,   421
She reach'd a lake, and met a lady there,

To Hampstead.

Winter has reached thee once again at last;
   And now the rambler, whom thy groves yet please,
   Feels on his house-warm lips the thin air freeze;
While in his shrugging neck the resolute blast
Comes edging; & the leaves, in heaps down cast,
   He shuffles with his hastening foot, & sees
   The cold sky whitening through the wiry trees,
And sighs to think his loitering noons have passed.

And do I love thee less to paint thee so?
   No: this the season is of beauty still
      Doubled at heart,— of smoke with whirling glee
Uptumbling ever from the blaze below. —
   And home remembered most,— & oh, loved hill,
      The second, & the last, away from thee!

                                          L. H. Hunt

Surry Jail nov: 1814

Copy of a Poem by Leigh Hunt, written while the Author was
in Surrey Jail. (See Appendix I.)

Who pitied her, and took the baby sweet
Into her arms, when lo! with closing feet
She sprang up all at once, like bird from brake,
And vanish'd with him underneath the lake.
Like stone thereat the mother stood, alas!—
The fairy of the place the lady was,
And Launcelot (so the boy was called) became
Her pupil, till in search of knightly fame   430
He went to Arthur's court, and play'd his part
So rarely, and display'd so frank a heart,
That what with all his charms of look and limb,
The Queen Geneura fell in love with him:—
And here, such interest in the tale she took,
Francesca's eyes went deeper in the book.

Ready she sat with one hand to turn o'er
The leaf, to which her thoughts ran on before,
The other on the table, half enwreath'd
In the thick tresses over which she breath'd.
So sat she fix'd, and so observ'd was she   441
Of one, who at the door stood tenderly,—
Paulo,—who from a window seeing her
Go straight across the lawn, and guessing
    where,
Had thought she was in tears, and found, that
    day,
His usual efforts vain to keep away.
Twice had he seen her since the Prince was
    gone,
On some small matter needing unison;
Twice linger'd, and convers'd, and grown long
    friends;
But not till now where no one else attends.—
"May I come in?" said he:—it made her
    start,—   451
That smiling voice;—she colour'd, press'd her
    heart
A moment, as for breath, and then with free
And usual tone said,—"O yes,——certainly."
There's wont to be, at conscious times like
    these,
An affectation of a bright-eyed ease,
An air of something quite serene and sure,
As if to seem so, were to be, secure.
With this the lovers met, with this they spoke,
With this sat down to read the self-same
    book,   460
And Paulo, by degrees, gently embrac'd
With one permitted arm her lovely waist;
And both their cheeks, like peaches on a tree,
Came with a touch together thrillingly,

And o'er the book they hung, and nothing
    said,
And every lingering page grew longer as they
    read.

As thus they sat, and felt with leaps of heart
Their colour change, they came upon the part
Where fond Geneura, with her flame long
    nurst,
Smil'd upon Launcelot, when he kiss'd her
    first:—   470
That touch, at last, through every fibre slid;
And Paulo turn'd, scarce knowing what he did,
Only he felt he could no more dissemble,
And kiss'd her, mouth to mouth, all in a
    tremble.—
Oh then she wept,—the poor Francesca wept;
And pardon oft he pray'd; and then she swept
The tears away, and look'd him in the face,
And, well as words might save the truth dis-
    grace,
She told him all, up to that very hour,
The father's guile, th' undwelt-in bridal
    bower,—   480
And wish'd for wings on which they two
    might soar
Far, far away, as doves to their own shore,
With claim from none.—That day they read
    no more.
Pub. 1816

THE POETS

WERE I to name, out of the times gone by,
    The poets dearest to me, I should say,
    Pulci for spirits, and a fine, free way;
Chaucer for manners, and close, silent eye;
Milton for classic taste, and harp strung high;
    Spenser for luxury, and sweet, sylvan play;
    Horace for chatting with, from day to day;
Shakespeare for all, but most, society.

But which take with me, could I take but one?
    Shakespeare,—as long as I was unoppressed
        With the world's weight, making sad
            thoughts intenser;   11
But did I wish, out of the common sun,
    To lay a wounded heart in leafy rest,
        And dream of things far off and healing,
            —Spenser.
Pub. 1815

Sonnets.

X.

The Poets.

Were I to name, out of the times gone by,
  The poets dearest to me, I should say,
Pulci for spirits of a ~~merry free~~ *airy free* way;
Chaucer for nature, & close, silent eye:
Milton for classic taste, & harp strung high;
  Spenser for luxury, & sweet sylvan play;
  Horace for chatting with, from day to day;
Shakespeare for all, but most, society.

But which take with me, could I take but one?
  Shakespeare,—as long as I was unoppress'd
    With the world's weight, & thought it made intenser;
But if I wish'd, out of the common sun,
  To lay a wounded heart in leafy rest,
    And dream of things far off & healing,—Spenser.

8. Nov. 1815.

A Sonnet by Leigh Hunt. (See Appendix I.)

WRITTEN UNDER THE ENGRAVING OF A PORTRAIT OF RAFAEL, PAINTED BY HIMSELF WHEN HE WAS YOUNG

RAFAEL! It must be he; we only miss
　　Something which manhood gave him, and
　　　the fair;
　　A look still sweeter and more thoughtful air;
But for the rest, 'tis every feature his,
The oval cheek, clear eye, mouth made to kiss,
　　Terse lightsome chin, and flush of gentle
　　　hair
　　Clipped ere it loitered into ringlets there,—
The beauty, the benignity, the bliss.

How sweetly sure he looks! how unforlorn!
　　There is but one such visage at a time;　10
'Tis like the budding of an age new born,
　　Remembered youth, the cuckoo in the
　　　prime,
The maid's first kiss, or any other thing
Most lovely, and alone, and promising.

Pub. 1816

TO THE GRASSHOPPER AND THE CRICKET

GREEN little vaulter in the sunny grass,
　　Catching your heart up at the feel of June,
　　Sole voice that's heard amidst the lazy noon,
When ev'n the bees lag at the summoning
　　brass;—
And you, warm little housekeeper, who class
　　With those who think the candles come too
　　　soon,
　　Loving the fire, and with your tricksome
　　　tune
Nick the glad silent moments as they pass;—

Oh, sweet and tiny cousins, that belong,
　　One to the fields, the other to the hearth, 10
Both have your sunshine; both, though small,
　　are strong
　　At your clear hearts; and both were sent
　　　on earth
To sing in thoughtful ears this natural song—
　　In doors and out,—summer and winter,—
　　　Mirth.

Pub. 1817

THE PRAYER IN THE BOWER

TURNING down, goatherd, by the oaks, you'll
　　see
A fig-tree statue, put up recently,
Three-footed, with the bark on, without ears;
Yet plain enough Priapus it appears.
A sacred hedge runs round it; and a brook,
Flowing from out a little gravelly nook,
Keeps green the laurel and the myrtle trees,
And odorous cypresses:
And there's a vine there, heaping all about
Its tendrilled clusters out;　　　　　　　10
And vernal blackbirds through the sprays
Shake their shrill notes a thousand ways;
And yellow nightingales reply,
Murmuring a honied song deliciously.
Sit you down there; and the kind god implore,
That I may yearn for Psamathe no more;
Myself with a fine kid will follow you,
And sacrifice; and should the deity nod,
A heifer and a goat shall thank him too,
And a house-lamb. Hear then, kind-hearted
　　god.　　　　　　　　　　　　　　20

Pub. 1818

ABOU BEN ADHEM

ABOU BEN ADHEM (may his tribe increase!)
Awoke one night from a deep dream of peace,
And saw, within the moonlight in his room,
Making it rich, and like a lily in bloom,
An angel writing in a book of gold:—
Exceeding peace had made Ben Adhem bold,
And to the presence in the room he said,
"What writest thou?"—The vision rais'd its
　　head,
And with a look made of all sweet accord,
Answer'd, "The names of those who love the
　　Lord."　　　　　　　　　　　　　10
"And is mine one?" said Abou. "Nay, not so,"
Replied the angel. Abou spoke more low,
But cheerly still; and said, "I pray thee then,
Write me as one that loves his fellow-men."

　　The angel wrote, and vanished. The next
　　　night
It came again with a great wakening light,
And show'd the names whom love of God had
　　bless'd,
And lo! Ben Adhem's name led all the rest.

Pub. 1838

John Keats
from his affectionate friend the Author.

FOLIAGE;

OR

POEMS ORIGINAL AND TRANSLATED,

BY

LEIGH HUNT.

Still climbing trees in the Hesperides.—SHAKSPEARE.

LONDON:

PRINTED FOR C. AND J. OLLIER, WELBECK STREET.

1818.

Presentation Copy to Keats from Leigh Hunt.
(See Appendix I.)

RONDEAU

JENNY kissed me when we met,
　Jumping from the chair she sat in;
Time, you thief, who love to get
　Sweets into your list, put that in:
Say I'm weary, say I'm sad,
　Say that health and wealth have missed me,
Say I'm growing old, but add,
　Jenny kissed me.

Pub. 1838

DIRGE FOR AN INFANT

HE is dead and gone—a flower
Born and withered in an hour.
Coldly lies the death-frost now
On his little rounded brow;
And the seal of darkness lies
Ever on his shrouded eyes.
He will never feel again
Touch of human joy or pain,
Never will his once bright eyes
Open with a glad surprise;　　　　　　　10
Nor the death-frost leave his brow—
All is over with him now.

Vacant now his cradle-bed,
As a nest from whence hath fled
Some dear little bird, whose wings
Rest from timid flutterings.
Thrown aside the childish rattle;
Hushed for aye the infant prattle—

Little broken words that could
By none else be understood,　　　　　　20
Save the childless one who weeps
O'er the grave where now he sleeps.
Closed his eyes, and cold his brow—
All is over with him now!

Pub. 1849

ON THE DEATH OF HIS SON VINCENT

WAKING at morn, with the accustomed sigh
For what no morn could ever bring me
　　more,
And again sighing, while collecting strength
To meet the pangs that waited me, like one
Whose sleep the rack hath watched: I tried to
　　feel
How good for me had been strange griefs of
　　old,
That for long days, months, years, inured my
　　wits
To bear the dreadful burden of one thought.
One thought with woful need turned many
　　ways,
Which, shunned at first, and scaring me, as
　　wounds　　　　　　　　　　　　　　　10
Thrusting in wound, became, oh! almost
　　clasped
And blest, as saviours from the one dire pang
That mocked the will to move it.

Pub. 1862

CHARLES LAMB
[February 10, 1775–December 27, 1834]

SEVEN years before he died Charles Lamb wrote a short autobiography which remained unpublished for almost a hundred years. So well does it characterize him and so typical is it of his delightful humor that we reproduce it here:

"Charles Lamb, born in the Inner Temple, 10 Feb. 1775, educated in Christ's Hospital, afterwards a clerk in the Accountant's Office, East India House, pensioned off from the service 1825 after 33 years service, is now a gentleman at large, can remember few specialities in his life worth noting, except that he once caught a swallow flying (*teste sua manu* [witness his hand]); below the middle stature; cast of face slightly Jewish, with no Judaic tinge in his complexional religion; stammers abominably, and is therefore more apt to discharge his occasional conversation in a quaint aphorism, or a poor quibble, than in set and edifying speeches; has consequently been libelled as a person always aiming at wit, which as he told a dull fellow that charges him

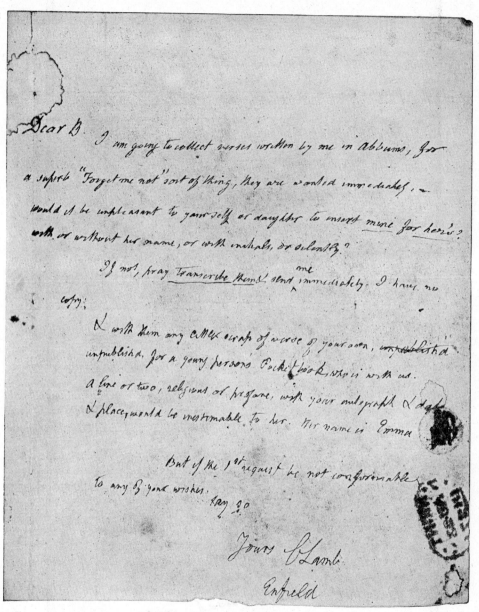

Letter from Charles Lamb to Bernard Barton. (See Appendix I.)

Dear Gilman, Pray do you, or
S. T. C., immediately write to say
you have received back the golden works
of the dear fine old Angel,
which I part from bleeding —
and to say how the winter has used
you all. It is our intention soon,
weather permitting, to come over
for a day at Highgate for a
quiet gossip and a cup of
tea. Be sure to tell us if we
may come casually, for in this change
of climate, there is no naming a
day for walking. With best loves
to Mrs Gilman & Eolese —
            Yours, mopish but in
      health, Lamb
I shall be uneasy till I hear of
Fuller's safe arrival —

Letter from Charles Lamb to James Gilman. (See Appendix I.)

with it, is at least as good as aiming at dullness; a small eater but not drinker, confesses a partiality for the product of the Juniper Berry; was a fiercer smoker of Tobacco, but may be resembled to a volcano burnt out, emitting only now and then a casual puff. Has been guilty of obtruding upon the Public a Tale in Prose called Rosamund Gray, a Dramatic Sketch named John Woodvil, a Farewell Ode to Tobacco, with sundry other poems and light prose matter, collected in two slight crown octavos and pompously christen'd his works, tho' in fact they were his Recreations, and his true works may be found on the shelves of Leaden Hall Street, filling some hundred Folios. He is also the true Elia, whose essays are extant in a little volume, published a year or two since; and rather better known from that name without a meaning, than for anything he has done, or can hope to do, in his own. He also was the first to draw the Public Attention to the Old English Dramatists in a work called Specimens of English Dramatic Writers who lived about the time of Shakespeare, published about fifteen years since. In short all his merits and demerits to set forth would take to the end of Mr. Upcott's book, and then not be told truly. He died   18   much lamented. To Anybody: Please fill up these blanks. Witness his Hand, Charles Lamb, 10th Apr. 1827."

Lamb's first published work was four sonnets which Coleridge, his old Christ's Hospital schoolmate, included in his volume of poems in 1796. The second edition of Coleridge's poems in 1797 also contained poems by Lamb, and in 1798 Lamb and Charles Lloyd brought out a small book of poems. In all these Lamb showed only moderate ability. From 1798 to 1820 he published newspaper jokes and epigrams, tales, dramas, and criticism. In 1820 he began writing for the *London Magazine* the *Elia* essays, published in book form in 1823, and in 1833 he published *The Last Essays of Elia*. In the writing of the familiar essay he reached heights unequaled by any other essayist in English.

The year with which "Anybody" is to "fill up the blanks" near the end of his autobiography is 1834.

THE OLD FAMILIAR FACES

WHERE are they gone, the old familiar faces?[1]

I have had playmates, I have had companions,
In my days of childhood, in my joyful schooldays—
All, all are gone, the old familiar faces.

I have been laughing, I have been carousing,
Drinking late, sitting late, with my bosom cronies—
All, all are gone, the old familiar faces.

I loved a love once, fairest among women.
Closed are her doors on me, I must not see her—
All, all are gone, the old familiar faces.   10

I have a friend, a kinder friend has no man.
Like an ingrate, I left my friend abruptly;
Left him, to muse on the old familiar faces.

Ghost-like, I paced round the haunts of my childhood.
Earth seemed a desert I was bound to traverse,
Seeking to find the old familiar faces.

Friend of my bosom, thou more than a brother!
Why wert not thou born in my father's dwelling?
So might we talk of the old familiar faces.

For some they have died, and some they have left me,   20
And some are taken from me; all are departed;
All, all are gone, the old familiar faces.

1798

[1] The first edition of the poem opened with this line and three following lines referring to the killing of Lamb's mother by Mary Lamb in a fit of insanity. Subsequent editions omitted the first four lines. In the present version the opening line is restored as integral to the poem. The other omitted lines are not restored as contrary to its spirit and wisely omitted.

HESTER

WHEN maidens such as Hester die,
Their place ye may not well supply,
Though ye among a thousand try,
      With vain endeavour.

A month or more hath she been dead,
Yet cannot I by force be led
To think upon the wormy bed,
      And her together.

A springy motion in her gait,
A rising step, did indicate   10
Of pride and joy no common rate,
      That flushed her spirit.

I know not by what name beside
I shall it call:—if 'twas not pride,
It was a joy to that allied,
      She did inherit.

Her parents held the Quaker rule,
Which doth the human feeling cool,
But she was train'd in Nature's school,
      Nature had blest her.   20

A waking eye, a prying mind,
A heart that stirs, is hard to bind,
A hawk's keen sight ye cannot blind,
      Ye could not Hester.

My sprightly neighbour, gone before
To that unknown and silent shore,
Shall we not meet, as heretofore,
      Some summer morning,

When from thy cheerful eyes a ray
Hath struck a bliss upon the day,   30
A bliss that would not go away,
      A sweet fore-warning?

1803

WALTER SAVAGE LANDOR
[January 30, 1775–September 17, 1864]

IT was as an old man with only a few pennies in his pocket that Landor took refuge with the Brownings in Italy, and Elizabeth Barrett Browning found herself with two poets in her house—an alarming situation for any woman. Wrote she in a letter, "Dear, darling Robert amuses me by talking of his [Landor's] gentleness and sweetness. A most courteous and refined gentleman he is, of course, and very affectionate to Robert (as he ought to be), but of self-restraint he has not a grain, and of suspicion many grains. What do you really say to dashing down a plate on the floor when you don't like what's on it? Robert succeeded in soothing him, and the poor old lion is very quiet on the whole, roaring softly to beguile the time in Latin alcaics against his wife and Louis Napoleon."

"Darling Robert" also succeeded in soothing the wife and family to whom Landor had made over his fortune, so that an allowance was arranged for, and Landor was no longer penniless, but Elizabeth Barrett Browning had been given the opportunity for her pen sketch of Landor. Violent Landor was, as Elizabeth suggested. The legend of his life contains stories of his thrashing a schoolmaster, shooting at a college professor he disliked (the worthy man took cover in time to avoid serious hurt), and assaulting a lawyer who cross-examined him. But tender he could be, as Robert declared. And at times the diverse qualities combined in odd ways as in one famous episode in which Landor flung an offending servant out of the window—a window beneath which there were flower beds. The full enormity of his act struck him in a flash. "My God!" he exclaimed, "I forgot the violets!"

The dates of Landor's life should be considered. He was almost of an age with Coleridge and Wordsworth and he published his *Gebir*, a long blank-verse poem in seven books, in 1798—the year of the *Lyrical Ballads*. He published his *Simonidea* (which contained his most popular lyric, *Rose Aylmer*) in 1806 when Shelley was in his teens and had not yet gone to Oxford. He was supervising the publication of his *Works* in 1846 when Tennyson and Browning were in their full power. *Works* was no true title, for he promptly set to work on his *Hellenics* which occupied him intermittently until 1859. He published in 1853 his *Last Fruit from an Old Tree*. Titles were becoming difficult. There was yet to come, in 1858, *Dry Sticks* containing his *God Scatters Beauty* which, though brief, is as fresh and fine as his *Rose Aylmer* of half a century before. Tennyson, by this time, had passed the peak of his accomplishment, Arnold and Rossetti had been in the field for nearly a decade. Landor died in 1864, just a year before Swinburne, who might be described as of the third poetical generation, published *Atalanta in Calydon*. In this sweep of poetical time Landor had seen, politically, the whole of the French Revolution, the rise and fall of the first Napoleon, the post-Napoleonic era of the Holy Alliance, the Reform Bill of 1832 in England, the revolutions of 1848, the rise of Napoleon the Third. He had undergone the disappointments which alienated Coleridge and Wordsworth from the democratic idea of the Revolution and, preserving his faith in the idea, he had lived long enough to see it coming to accomplishment.

The imagination is a little staggered by such a life, and through it Landor moved with a personal violence, indicated above, suggestive of an itinerant volcano, and yet with an essential nobility about him which made his violences seem unessential to the real truth of his character. He could write and publish his *I Strove with None*, which was absolutely at variance with the known facts of his life, without appearing absurd. It was truer of him than were the facts.

As a writer Landor seems to have missed the first rank by some curious accident in public and critical reaction. He was as distinguished in his prose as in his poetry, his *Imaginary Conversations* bulking large in his work, and his *Pericles and Aspasia* (1836) deserving much more popularity than it has ever had. It is a fresh and human book. Prose, however, is naturally perishable and, in the accident which has befallen Landor's name, his prose has merely diffused the attention given him. Half of critical attention only is then left to Landor's poetry, and this half is disturbed by the fact that in his longer efforts in the *Hellenics* and in *Gebir*, in spite of purple passages and in spite of such occasional fine poems as *Iphigeneia and Agamemnon*, Landor is dull. The praise justly due to Landor's brief pieces is thus always preceded by critical reservations justly due to his longer efforts. The short pieces are done with such a classical precision and simplicity of workmanship that it is hard to over-praise them.

ROSE AYLMER

Ah what avails the sceptred race,
  Ah what the form divine!
What every virtue, every grace!
  Rose Aylmer, all were thine.
Rose Aylmer, whom these wakeful eyes
  May weep, but never see,
A night of memories and of sighs
  I consecrate to thee.

1806[1]

REGENERATION

We are what suns and winds and waters make us;
The mountains are our sponsors, and the rills

[1] Dates given in connection with Landor's poems are of first appearance in book form.

Fashion and win their nursling with their smiles.
But where the land is dim from tyranny,
There tiny pleasures occupy the place
Of glories and of duties; as the feet
Of fabled fairies when the sun goes down
Trip o'er the grass where wrestlers strove by day.
Then Justice, call'd the Eternal One above,
Is more inconstant than the buoyant form   10
That burst into existence from the froth
Of ever-varying ocean: what is best
Then becomes worst; what loveliest, most deformed.
The heart is hardest in the softest climes,
The passions flourish, the affections die.
O thou vast tablet of these awful truths,

[17]

Threw a pale luſtre on his native ſhore;
When ſuddenly the ſound "*Conſpirator*,"   ~~135~~
(How harſh from thoſe we ſerve and thoſe we love!)
Burſt with inſulting blow the enchanting ſtrain,
And the fair viſion vaniſh into air.
The pleaſant ſolitude of ſunny beach,
The yellow bank ſcoopt out with idle hands,   ~~140~~
And near, white birds, and further, naked boys,
Who o'er the level of the luſtrous ſand,
Like kindred broods, ſeem ready to unite,
The tempeſt whirls away, and where they ſtood
Up ſtarts a monſter, that with hiſs and howl,   ~~145~~
Seizes the wretch who runs to looſe it's chain.

When Arganthonius ſaw him, he exclaim'd
"Hymneus! and thou too here! thy glowing words
Could once, arouſing in the warrior's breaſt
Enthuſiaſtic rage, ſublime the ſoul   ~~150~~
So far above the rocks where Danger broods,
That ſhe and all her monſtrous progeny
Groveling, and breathing fire, and ſhadow-winged,
Become inviſible. O thou of power
With magic tones Affliction to diſarm!   ~~155~~
Thou canſt conjure up fury, call down hope,
Or whiſper comfort, or inſpire revenge.
Riſe! trace the wanderings of thy comrades, ſhew
What men, relying on the Gods, can bear."
He ended here, and Hymneus thus began,   ~~160~~
Hymneus, who knew the times and deeds of old
And tales and songs recording them, ohad claspt
The lyre, but never ſhuddered at the sword.

That fillest all the space between the seas,
Spreading from Venice's deserted courts
To the Tarentine and Hydruntine mole,
What lifts thee up? what shakes thee? 'tis the
    breath   20
Of God. Awake, ye nations! spring to life!
Let the last work of his right hand appear
Fresh with his image, Man. Thou recreant
    slave
That sittest afar off and helpest not,
O thou degenerate Albion! with what shame
Do I survey thee, pushing forth the sponge
At thy spear's length, in mockery at the thirst
Of holy Freedom in his agony,
And prompt and keen to pierce the wounded
    side!
Must Italy then wholly rot away   30
Amid her slime, before she germinate
Into fresh vigor, into form again?
What thunder bursts upon mine ear! some isle
Hath surely risen from the gulfs profound,
Eager to suck the sunshine from the breast
Of beauteous Nature, and to catch the gale
From golden Hermus and Melena's brow.
A greater thing than isle, than continent,
Than earth itself, than ocean circling earth,
Hath risen there; regenerate Man hath risen. 40
Generous old bard of Chios! not that Jove
Deprived thee in thy latter days of sight
Would I complain, but that no higher theme
Than a disdainful youth, a lawless king,
A pestilence, a pyre, awoke thy song,
When on the Chian coast, one javelin's throw
From where thy tombstone, where thy cradle,
    stood,
Twice twenty self-devoted Greeks assail'd
The naval host of Asia, at one blow
Scattered it into air . . . and Greece was
    free . . .   50
And ere these glories beam'd, thy day had
    closed.
Let all that Elis ever saw, give way,
All that Olympian Jove e'er smiled upon:
The Marathonian columns never told
A tale more glorious, never Salamis,
Nor, faithful in the centre of the false,
Platea, nor Anthela, from whose mount
Benignant Ceres wards the blessed Laws,
And sees the Amphictyon dip his weary foot
In the warm streamlet of the strait below. 60
Goddess! altho' thy brow was never rear'd

Among the powers that guarded or assail'd
Perfidious Ilion, parricidal Thebes,
Or other walls whose war-belt e'er inclosed
Man's congregated crimes and vengeful pain,
Yet hast thou touched the extremes of grief
    and joy;
Grief upon Enna's mead and Hell's ascent,
A solitary mother; joy beyond,
Far beyond, that thy woe, in this thy fane:
The tears were human, but the bliss divine. 70
I, in the land of strangers, and depressed
With sad and certain presage for my own,
Exult at hope's fresh dayspring, tho' afar,
There where my youth was not unexercised
By chiefs in willing war and faithful song:
Shades as they were, they were not empty
    shades,
Whose bodies haunt our world and blear our
    sun,
Obstruction worse than swamp and shapeless
    sands.
Peace, praise, eternal gladness, to the souls
That, rising from the seas into the heavens, 80
Have ransom'd first their country with their
    blood!
O thou immortal Spartan! at whose name
The marble table sounds beneath my palms,
Leonidas! even thou wilt not disdain
To mingle names august as these with thine;
Nor thou, twin-star of glory, thou whose rays
Stream'd over Corinth on the double sea,
Achaian and Saronic; whom the sons
Of Syracuse, when Death removed thy light,
Wept more than slavery ever made them weep,
But shed (if gratitude is sweet) sweet tears. 91
The hand that then pour'd ashes o'er their
    heads
Was loosen'd from its desperate chain by thee.
What now can press mankind into one mass,
For Tyranny to tread the more secure?
From gold alone is drawn the guilty wire
That Adulation trills: she mocks the tone
Of Duty, Courage, Virtue, Piety,
And under her sits Hope. O how unlike
That graceful form in azure vest array'd, 100
With brow serene, and eyes on heaven alone
In patience fixed, in fondness unobscured!
What monsters coil beneath the spreading tree
Of Despotism! what wastes extend around!
What poison floats upon the distant breeze!
But who are those that cull and deal its fruit?

Creatures that shun the light and fear the shade,
Bloated and fierce, Sleep's mien and Famine's cry.
Rise up again, rise in thy dignity,
Dejected Man! and scare this brood away. 110

1824

FIESOLAN IDYL

HERE, where precipitate Spring, with one light bound
Into hot Summer's lusty arms, expires,
And where go forth at morn, at eve, at night,
Soft airs that want the lute to play with 'em,
And softer sighs that know not what they want,
Aside a wall, beneath an orange-tree
Whose tallest flowers could tell the lowlier ones
Of sights in Fiesolè right up above,
While I was gazing a few paces off
At what they seem'd to show me with their nods, 10
Their frequent whispers and their pointing shoots,
A gentle maid came down the garden-steps
And gathered the pure treasure in her lap.
I heard the branches rustle, and stept forth
To drive the ox away, or mule, or goat,
Such I believed it must be. How could I
Let beast o'erpower them? When hath wind or rain
Borne hard upon weak plant that wanted me,
And I (however they might bluster round)
Walkt off? 'Twere most ungrateful: for sweet scents 20
Are the swift vehicles of still sweeter thoughts,
And nurse and pillow the dull memory
That would let drop without them her best stores.
They bring me tales of youth and tones of love,
And 'tis and ever was my wish and way
To let all flowers live freely, and all die,
(Whene'er their Genius bids their souls depart)
Among their kindred in their native place.
I never pluck the rose; the violet's head
Hath shaken with my breath upon its bank
And not reproacht me; the ever-sacred cup

Of the pure lily hath between my hands 32
Felt safe, unsoil'd, nor lost one grain of gold.
I saw the light that made the glossy leaves
More glossy; the fair arm, the fairer cheek
Warmed by the eye intent on its pursuit;
I saw the foot, that altho' half-erect
From its grey slipper, could not lift her up
To what she wanted: I held down a branch
And gather'd her some blossoms; since their hour 40
Was come, and bees had wounded them, and flies
Of harder wing were working their way thro'
And scattering them in fragments under-foot.
So crisp were some, they rattled unevolved,
Others, ere broken off, fell into shells,
For such appear the petals when detacht,
Unbending, brittle, lucid, white like snow,
And like snow not seen thro', by eye or sun:
Yet every one her gown received from me
Was fairer than the first. I thought not so, 50
But so she praised them to reward my care,
I said: "You find the largest."
                                    "This indeed,"
Cried she, "is large and sweet." She held one forth,
Whether for me to look at or to take
She knew not, nor did I; but taking it
Would best have solved (and this she felt) her doubt.
I dared not touch it; for it seemed a part
Of her own self; fresh, full, the most mature
Of blossoms, yet a blossom; with a touch
To fall, and yet unfallen. She drew back 60
The boon she tender'd, and then, finding not
The ribbon at her waist to fix it in,
Dropt it, as loth to drop it, on the rest.

1831

TO CORINTH

QUEEN of the double sea, beloved of him
Who shakes the world's foundations, thou hast seen
Glory in all her beauty, all her forms;
Seen her walk back with Theseus when he left
The bones of Sciron bleaching to the wind,
Above the ocean's roar and cormorant's flight,
So high that vastest billows from above
Shew but like herbage waving in the mead;
Seen generations throng thy Isthmian games.

And pass away; the beautiful, the brave, 10
And them who sang their praises. But, O Queen,
Audible still, and far beyond thy cliffs,
As when they first were utter'd, are those words
Divine which praised the valiant and the just;
And tears have often stopt, upon that ridge
So perilous, him who brought before his eye
The Colchian babes. "Stay! spare him! save the last!
Medea! Is that blood? again! it drops
From my imploring hand upon my feet!
I will invoke the Eumenides no more, 20
I will forgive thee, bless thee, bend to thee
In all thy wishes, do but thou, Medea,
Tell me, one lives." "And shall I too deceive?"
Cries from the fiery car an angry voice;
And swifter than two falling stars descend
Two breathless bodies; warm, soft, motionless,
As flowers in stillest noon before the sun,
They lie three paces from him: such they lie
As when he left them sleeping side by side, 29
A mother's arm round each, a mother's cheeks
Between them, flusht with happiness and love.
He was more changed than they were, doomed to show
Thee and the stranger, how defaced and scarr'd
Grief hunts us down the precipice of years,
And whom the faithless prey upon the last.

To give the inertest masses of our earth
Her loveliest forms was thine, to fix the Gods
Within thy walls, and hang their tripods round
With fruits and foliage knowing not decay.
A nobler work remains: thy citadel 40
Invites all Greece: o'er lands and floods remote
Many are the hearts that still beat high for thee:
Confide then in thy strength, and unappall'd
Look down upon the plain, while yokemate kings
Run bellowing, where their herdsmen goad them on.
Instinct is sharp in them and terror true,
They smell the floor whereon their necks must lie.

1831

THE DEATH OF ARTEMIDORA

[From Pericles and Aspasia.]

"Artemidora! Gods invisible,
While thou art lying faint along the couch,
Have tied the sandal to thy slender feet

And stand beside thee, ready to convey
Thy weary steps where other rivers flow.
Refreshing shades will waft thy weariness
Away, and voices like thy own come near
And nearer, and solicit an embrace."
Artemidora sigh'd, and would have pressed
The hand now pressing hers, but was too weak. 10
Iris stood over her dark hair unseen
While thus Elpenor spake. He looked into
Eyes that had given light and life erewhile
To those above them, but now dim with tears
And wakefulness. Again he spake of joy
Eternal. At that word, that sad word, *joy*,
Faithful and fond her bosom heav'd once more:
Her head fell back; and now a loud deep sob
Swell'd thro' the darken'd chamber; 'twas not hers.

1836

From the HELLENICS

I

ON THE HELLENICS

Come back, ye wandering Muses, come back home,
Ye seem to have forgotten where it lies:
Come, let us walk upon the silent sands
Of Simois, where deep footmarks show long strides;
Thence we may mount, perhaps, to higher ground,
Where Aphroditè from Athenè won
The golden apple, and from Herè too,
And happy Ares shouted far below.
Or would ye rather choose the grassy vale
Where flows Anapos thro' anemones, 10
Hyacinths, and narcissuses, that bend
To show their rival beauty in the stream?
Bring with you each her lyre, and each in turn
Temper a graver with a lighter song.

1847

II

IPHIGENEIA AND AGAMEMNON

Iphigeneia, when she heard her doom
At Aulis, and when all beside the King
Had gone away, took his right hand, and said,
"O father! I am young and very happy.

I do not think the pious Calchas heard
Distinctly what the Goddess spake. Old-age
Obscures the senses. If my nurse, who knew
My voice so well, sometimes misunderstood
While I was resting on her knee both arms
And hitting it to make her mind my words, 10
And looking in her face, and she in mine,
Might he not also hear one word amiss,
Spoken from so far off, even from Olympus?"
The father placed his cheek upon her head,
And tears dropt down it, but the king of men
Replied not. Then the maiden spake once
    more.
"O father! sayst thou nothing? Hear'st thou
    not
Me, whom thou ever hast, until this hour,
Listened to fondly, and awakened me
To hear my voice amid the voice of birds, 20
When it was inarticulate as theirs,
And the down deadened it within the nest?"
He moved her gently from him, silent still,
And this, and this alone, brought tears from
    her,
Although she saw fate nearer: then with sighs,
"I thought to have laid down my hair before
Benignant Artemis, and not have dimmed
Her polisht altar with my virgin blood;
I thought to have selected the white flowers
To please the Nymphs, and to have asked of
    each   30
By name, and with no sorrowful regret,
Whether, since both my parents willed the
    change,
I might at Hymen's feet bend my clipt brow;
And (after those who mind us girls the most)
Adore our own Athena, that she would
Regard me mildly with her azure eyes.
But, father! to see you no more, and see
Your love, O father! go ere I am gone." ...
Gently he moved her off, and drew her back,
Bending his lofty head far over hers,   40
And the dark depths of nature heaved and
    burst.
He turned away; not far, but silent still.
She now first shuddered; for in him, so nigh,
So long a silence seemed the approach of death,
And like it. Once again she raised her voice.
"O father! if the ships are now detained,
And all your vows move not the Gods above,
When the knife strikes me there will be one
    prayer

The less to them: and purer can there be
Any, or more fervent than the daughter's
    prayer   50
For her dear father's safety and success?"
A groan that shook him shook not his resolve.
An aged man now entered, and without
One word, stept slowly on, and took the wrist
Of the pale maiden. She looked up, and saw
The fillet of the priest and calm cold eyes.
Then turned she where her parent stood, and
    cried
"O father! grieve no more: the ships can sail."
1846

III

THE HAMADRYAD

RHAICOS was born amid the hills wherefrom
Gnidos, the light of Caria, is discerned.
And small are the white-crested that play near,
And smaller onward are the purple waves.
Thence festal choirs were visible, all crowned
With rose and myrtle if they were inborn;
If from Pandion sprang they, on the coast
Where stern Athene raised her citadel,
Then olive was entwined with violets
Clustered in bosses, regular and large.   10
For various men wore various coronals,
But one was their devotion; 'twas to her
Whose laws all follow, her whose smile with-
    draws
The sword from Ares, thunderbolt from Zeus,
And whom in his chill caves the mutable
Of mind, Poseidon, the sea-king, reveres,
And whom his brother, stubborn Dis, hath
    prayed
To turn in pity the averted cheek
Of her he bore away, with promises,   19
Nay, with loud oath before dread Styx itself,
To give her daily more and sweeter flowers
Than he made drop from her on Enna's dell.
    Rhaicos was looking from his father's door
At the long trains that hastened to the town
From all the valleys, like bright rivulets
Gurgling with gladness, wave outrunning
    wave,
And thought it hard he might not also go
And offer up one prayer, and press one hand,
He knew not whose. The father called him in
And said, "Son Rhaicos! those are idle games;
Long enough I have lived to find them so." 31

And ere he ended, sighed; as old men do
Always, to think how idle such games are.
"I have not yet," thought Rhaicos in his heart,
And wanted proof. "Suppose thou go and help
Echeion at the hill, to bark yon oak
And lop its branches off, before we delve
About the trunk and ply the root with axe;
This we may do in winter."

                    Rhaicos went;
For thence he could see farther, and see more
Of those who hurried to the city-gate.   41
Echeion he found there, with naked arm
Swart-haired, strong-sinewed, and his eyes
    intent
Upon the place where first the axe should fall:
He held it upright. "There are bees about,
Or wasps, or hornets," said the cautious eld,
"Look sharp, O son of Thallinos!" The youth
Inclined his ear, afar, and warily,
And caverned in his hand. He heard a buzz
At first, and then the sound grew soft and
    clear,   50
And then divided into what seemed tune,
And there were words upon it, plaintive words.
He turned, and said, "Echeion! do not strike
That tree; it must be hollow, for some god
Speaks from within. Come thyself near." Again
Both turned toward it; and behold! there sat
Upon the moss below, with her two palms
Pressing it, on each side, a maid in form.
Downcast were her long eyelashes, and pale
Her cheek, but never mountain-ash displayed
Berries of colour like her lips so pure,   61
Nor were the anemones about her hair
Soft, smooth, and wavering like the face be-
    neath.

    "What dost thou here?" Echeion, half-
    afraid,
Half-angry, cried. She lifted up her eyes,
But nothing spake she. Rhaicos drew one step
Backward, for fear came likewise over him,
But not such fear: he panted, gaspt, drew in
His breath, and would have turned it into
    words,
But could not into one.

                  "O send away   70
That sad old man!" said she. The old man
    went
Without a warning from his master's son,
Glad to escape, for sorely he now feared;
And the axe shone behind him in their eyes.

    Hamad. And wouldst thou too shed the
    most innocent
Of blood? No vow demands it; no god wills
The oak to bleed.
    Rhaicos. Who art thou? whence? why here?
And whither wouldst thou go? Among the
    robed
In white or saffron, or the hue that most
Resembles dawn or the clear sky, is none   80
Arrayed as thou art. What so beautiful
As that gray robe which clings about thee
    close,
Like moss to stones adhering, leaves to trees,
Yet lets thy bosom rise and fall in turn,
As, toucht by zephyrs, fall and rise the boughs
Of graceful platane by the river-side?
    Hamad. Lovest thou well thy father's
    house?
    Rhaicos. Indeed
I love it, well I love it, yet would leave   88
For thine, where'er it be, my father's house,
With all the marks upon the door, that show
My growth at every birthday since the third,
And all the charms, o'erpowering evil eyes,
My mother nailed for me against my bed,
And the Cydonian bow (which thou shalt see)
Won in my race last spring from Eutychos.
    Hamad. Bethink thee what it is to leave a
    home
Thou never yet has left, one night, one day.
    Rhaicos. No, 'tis not hard to leave it; 'tis not
    hard   98
To leave, O maiden, that paternal home,
If there be one on earth whom we may love
First, last, forever, one who says that she
Will love forever too. To say which word,
Only to say it, surely is enough—
It shows such kindness—if 'twere possible
We at the moment think she would indeed.
    Hamad. Who taught thee all this folly at
    thy age?
    Rhaicos. I have seen lovers and have learnt
    to love.
    Hamad. But wilt thou spare the tree?
    Rhaicos.   My father wants
The bark; the tree may hold its place awhile.
    Hamad. Awhile! thy father numbers then
    my days?   110
    Rhaicos. Are there no others where the moss
    beneath
Is quite as tufty? Who would send thee forth,

Or ask thee why thou tarriest? Is thy flock
Anywhere near?
   Hamad.   I have no flock: I kill
Nothing that breathes, that stirs, that feels
   the air,
The sun, the dew. Why should the beautiful
(And thou art beautiful) disturb the source
Whence springs all beauty? Hast thou never
   heard
Of hamadryads?
   Rhaicos.   Heard of them I have;
Tell me some tale about them. May I sit   120
Beside thy feet? Art thou not tired? The herbs
Are very soft; I will not come too nigh;
Do but sit there, nor tremble so, nor doubt.
Stay, stay an instant: let me first explore
If any acorn of last year be left
Within it; thy thin robe too ill protects
Thy dainty limbs against the harm one small
Acorn may do. Here's none. Another day
Trust me; till then let me sit opposite.
   Hamad. I seat me; be thou seated, and con-
   tent.   130
   Rhaicos. O sight for gods! ye men **below**,
   adore
The Aphrodite! *Is* she there below?
Or sits she here before me? as she sate
Before the shepherd on those highths that
   shade
The Hellespont, and brought his kindred woe.
   Hamad. Reverence the higher Powers; nor
   deem amiss
Of her who pleads to thee, and would repay—
Ask not how much—but very much. Rise
   not—
No, Rhaicos, no! Without the nuptial vow
Love is unholy. Swear to me that none   140
Of mortal maids shall ever taste thy kiss,
Then take thou mine; then take it, not before.
   Rhaicos. Hearken, all gods above! O Aphro-
   dite
O Herè! Let my vow be ratified!
But wilt thou come into my father's house?
   Hamad. Nay; and of mine I cannot give thee
   part.
   Rhaicos. Where is it?
   Hamad.   In this oak.
   Rhaicos.   Ay, now **begins**
The tale of hamadryad; tell it through.
   Hamad. Pray of thy father never to cut
   down   149

My tree; and promise him, as well thou mayst,
That every year he shall receive from me
More honey than will buy him nine fat sheep,
More wax than he will burn to all the gods.
Why fallest thou upon thy face? Some thorn
May scratch it, rash young man! Rise up; for
   shame!
   Rhaicos. For shame I cannot rise. O pity
   me!
I dare not sue for love—but do not hate!
Let me once more behold thee—not once
   more,
But many days; let me love on—unloved!
I aimed too high: on my own head the bolt
Falls back, and pierces to the very brain.   161
   Hamad. Go—rather go than make me say I
   love.
   Rhaicos. If happiness is immortality
(And whence enjoy it else the gods above?)
I am immortal too: my vow is heard—
Hark! on the left.—Nay, turn not from me
   now,
I claim my kiss.
   Hamad.   Do men take first, then claim?
Do thus the seasons run their course with
   them?

Her lips were sealed; her head sank on his
   breast.
'Tis said that laughs were heard within the
   wood;   170
But who should hear them? and whose laughs?
   and why?

Savoury was the smell, and long past noon,
Thallinos, in thy house; for marjoram,
Basil and mint, and thyme and rosemary,
Were sprinkled on the kid's well-roasted
   length,
Awaiting Rhaicos. Home he came at last,
Not hungry, but pretending hunger keen,
With head and eyes just o'er the maple plate.
"Thou seest but badly, coming from the sun,
Boy Rhaicos!" said the father. "That oak's
   bark   180
Must have been tough, with little sap between;
It ought to run; but it and I are old."
Rhaicos, although each morsel of the bread
Increased by chewing, and the meat grew cold
And tasteless to his palate, took a draught
Of gold-bright wine, which, thirsty as he was,

He thought not of, until his father filled
The cup, averring water was amiss,
But wine had been at all times poured on kid—
It was religion.
    He, thus fortified,   190
Said, not quite boldly and not quite abasht,
"Father, that oak is Zeus's own; that oak
Year after year will bring thee wealth from wax
And honey. There is one who fears the gods
And the gods love;—that one" (he blushed, nor said
What one) "hast promist this, and may do more.
Thou hast not many moons to wait until
The bees have done their best; if then there come
Nor wax nor honey, let the tree be hewn."
 "Zeus hath bestowed on thee a prudent mind,"   200
Said the glad sire; "but look thou often there,
And gather all the honey thou canst find
In every crevice, over and above
What has been promist; would they reckon that?"
 Rhaicos went daily; but the nymph as oft,
Invisible. To play at love, she knew,
Stopping its breathings when it breathes most soft,
Is sweeter than to play on any pipe.
She played on his: she fed upon his sighs;
They pleased her when they gently waved her hair,   210
Cooling the pulses of her purple veins;
And when her absence brought them out, they pleased.
Even among the fondest of them all,
What mortal or immortal maid is more
Content with giving happiness than pain?
One day he was returning from the wood
Despondently. She pitied him, and said,
"Come back!" and twined her fingers in the hem
Above his shoulder. Then she led his steps
To a cool rill that ran o'er level sand   220
Through lentisk and through oleander; there
Bathed she his feet, lifting them on her lap
When bathed, and drying them in both her hands.
He dared complain; for those who most are loved

Most dare it; but not harsh was his complaint.
"O thou inconstant!" said he, "if stern law
Bind thee, or will, stronger than sternest law,
O, let me know henceforward when to hope
The fruit of love that grows for me but here."
He spake; and pluckt it from its pliant stem.
"Impatient Rhaicos! Why thus intercept
The answer I would give? There is a bee
Whom I have fed, a bee who knows my thoughts   233
And executes my wishes: I will send
That messenger. If ever thou art false,
Drawn by another, own it not, but drive
My bee away; then shall I know my fate,
And—for thou must be wretched—weep at thine.
But often as my heart persuades to lay
Its cares on thine and throb itself to rest,   240
Expect her with thee, whether it be morn
Or eve, at any time when woods are safe."
 Day after day the Hours beheld them blest,
And season after season: years had past,
Blest were they still. He who asserts that Love
Ever is sated of sweet things, the same
Sweet things he fretted for in earlier days,
Never, by Zeus! loved he a hamadryad.
 The nights had now grown longer, and perhaps
The hamadryads find them lone and dull
Among their woods; one did, alas! She called
Her faithful bee; 'twas when all bees should sleep,   252
And all did sleep but hers. She was sent forth
To bring that light which never wintry blast
Blows out, nor rain nor snow extinguishes,
The light that shines from loving eyes upon
Eyes that love back, till they can see no more.
 Rhaicos was sitting at his father's hearth:
Between them stood the table, not o'erspread
With fruits which autumn now profusely bore,   260
Nor anise cakes, nor odorous wine, but there
The draft-board was expanded; at which game
Triumphant sat old Thallinos; the son
Was puzzled, vext, discomforted, distraught.
A buzz was at his ear; up went his hand,
And it was heard no longer. The poor bee
Returned (but not until the morn shone bright),
And found the hamadryad with her head
Upon her aching wrist, and showed one wing

Half broken off, the other's meshes marred,
And there were bruises which no eye could see
Saving a hamadryad's. At this sight   272
Down fell the languid brow, both hands fell
    down;
A shriek was carried to the ancient hall
Of Thallinos: he heard it not; his son
Heard it, and ran forthwith into the wood.
No bark was on the tree, no leaf was green,
The trunk was riven through. From that day
    forth
Nor word nor whisper soothed his ear, nor
    sound
Even of insect wing; but loud laments   280
The woodmen and the shepherds one long year
Heard day and night, for Rhaicos would not
    quit
The solitary place, but moaned and died.
    Hence milk and honey wonder not, O guest,
To find set duly on the hollow stone.
1846

LYRICS AND EPIGRAMS

I

MILD is the parting year, and sweet
    The odor of the falling spray;
Life passes on more rudely fleet,
    And balmless is its closing day.

I wait its close, I court its gloom,
    But mourn that never must there fall
Or on my breast or on my tomb
    The tear that would have soothed it all.
1831

II

IN Clementina's artless mien
    Lucilla asks me what I see,
And are the roses of sixteen
            Enough for me?

Lucilla asks, if that be all,
    Have I not cull'd as sweet before:
Ah yes, Lucilla! and their fall
            I still deplore.

I now behold another scene,
    Where Pleasure beams with heaven's own
        light,   10
More pure, more constant, more serene,
            And not less bright:

Faith, on whose breast the Loves repose,
    Whose chain of flowers no force can sever,
And Modesty who, when she goes,
            Is gone for ever.
1831

III

PURSUITS! alas, I now have none,
    But idling where were once pursuits,
Often, all morning quite alone,
    I sit upon those twisted roots
Which rise above the grass, and shield
    Our harebell, when the churlish year
Catches her coming first afield,
    And she looks pale tho' spring is near;
I chase the violets, that would hide
    Their little prudish heads away,   10
And argue with the rills, that chide
    When we discover them at play.
1846

IV

PROUD word you never spoke, but you will
    speak
Four not exempt from pride some future
    day.
Resting on one white hand a warm wet cheek
    Over my open volume you will say,
"This man loved *me!*" then rise and trip
    away.
1846

V

LITTLE you think, my lovely friend,
While o'er these easy lines you bend
    That they can give you many days,
You little think, to whom belong
The purer streams of sacred song,
    He from the tomb the prey of Death can
        raise:
He can, and will; for this is due
From him above the rest to you,
    Tho' with the rest he shares your smile:
Ah! most he wants it, as you know . . .   10
One, only one, would soothe his woe . . .
    Beguile not him . . . and all but him beguile!

VI

DULL is my verse: not even thou
    Who movest many cares away
From this lone breast and weary brow,
    Canst make, as once, its fountain play;

"What is really my belief?"

My faith is this. I do believe
That ladies never would deceive,
And that the little fault of Eve
Is very easy to retrieve.

She lost us immortality,
But in good earnest what care I.
If you receive my latest sigh
And give me one — before I die

W S L

A Poem by Walter Savage Landor. (See Appendix I.)

No, nor those gentle words that now
   Support my heart to hear thee say:
"The bird upon its lonely bough
   Sings sweetest at the close of day."

1846

VII

THE day returns, my natal day,
   Borne on the storm and pale with snow,
And seems to ask me why I stay,
   Stricken by Time and bowed by Woe.

Many were once the friends who came
   To wish me joy; and there are some
Who wish it now; but not the same:
   They are whence friend can never come.

Nor are they you my love watched o'er
   Cradled in innocence and sleep;   10
You smile into my eyes no more,
   Nor see the bitter tears they weep.

1846

VIII

TWENTY years hence my eyes may grow
If not quite dim, yet rather so,
Still yours from others they shall know
    Twenty years hence.

Twenty years hence tho' it may hap
That I be call'd to take a nap
In a cool cell where thunder-clap
    Was never heard,

There breathe but o'er my arch of grass
A not too sadly sigh'd *Alas*,   10
And I shall catch, ere you can pass,
    That wingèd word.

1846

IX

I CANNOT tell, not I, why she
   Awhile so gracious, now should be
So grave: I cannot tell you why
   The violet hangs its head awry.
It shall be cull'd, it shall be worn,
   In spite of every sign of scorn,
Dark look, and overhanging thorn.

1846

X

THE maid I love ne'er thought of me
   Amid the scenes of gaiety;
But when her heart or mine sank low,
   Ah then it was no longer so,

From the slant palm she rais'd her head,
And kiss'd the cheek whence youth had fled.
Angels! some future day for this,
Give her as sweet and pure a kiss.

1846

XI

MOTHER, I cannot mind my wheel;
   My fingers ache, my lips are dry:
Oh! if you felt the pain I feel!
   But oh, who ever felt as I?
No longer could I doubt him true—
   All other men may use deceit;
He always said my eyes were blue,
   And often swore my lips were sweet.

1846

XII

ONE year ago my path was green,
My footstep light, my brow serene;
Alas! and could it have been so
    One year ago?
There is a love that is to last
When the hot days of youth are past:
Such love did a sweet maid bestow
    One year ago.
I took a leaflet from her braid
And gave it to another maid.   10
Love! broken should have been thy bow
    One year ago.

1846

XIII

YES: I write verses now and then,
But blunt and flaccid is my pen,
No longer talked of by young men
    As rather clever:
In the last quarter are my eyes,
You see it by their form and size,
Is it not time then to be wise?
    Or now or never.

Fairest that ever sprang from Eve!
While Time allows the short reprieve,   10
Just look at me! would you believe
    'Twas once a lover?
I cannot clear the five-bar gate,
But, trying first its timbers' state,
Climb stiffly up, take breath, and wait
    To trundle over.

Thro' gallopade I cannot swing
The entangling blooms of Beauty's spring:
I cannot say the tender thing,
    Be't true or false,   20

And am beginning to opine
Those girls are only half-divine
Whose waists yon wicked boys entwine
    In giddy waltz.

I fear that arm above that shoulder,
I wish them wiser, graver, older,
Sedater, and no harm if colder
    And panting less.
Ah! people were not half so wild
In former days, when, starchly mild,   30
Upon her high-heel'd Essex smiled
    The brave Queen Bess.

1846

XIV

Why, why repine, my pensive friend,
    At pleasure slipped away?
Some the stern Fates will never lend,
    And all refuse to stay.

I see the rainbow in the sky,
    The dew upon the grass,
I see them, and I ask not why
    They glimmer or they pass.

With folded arms I linger not
    To call them back; 'twere vain;   10
In this, or in some other spot,
    I know they'll shine again.

1846

XV

I know not whether I am proud,
But this I know, I hate the crowd:
Therefore pray let me disengage
My verses from the motley page,
Where others far more sure to please
Pour out their choral song with ease.
And yet perhaps, if some should tire
With too much froth or too much fire,
There is an ear that may incline
Even to words so dull as mine.   10

1846

XVI

Ye little household gods, that make
    My heart leap lighter with your play,
And never let it sink or ache,
    Unless you are too far away;

Eight years have flown, and never yet
    One day has risen up between
The kisses of my earlier pet,
    And few the hours he was not seen.

How can I call to you from Rome?
    Will mamma teach what babbo said?   10
Have ye not heard him talk at home
    About the city of the dead?

Marvellous tales will babbo tell,
    If you don't clasp his throat too tight,
Tales which you, Arnold, will love well,
    Tho' Julia's cheek turns pale with fright.

How, swimming o'er the Tiber, Clelia
    Headed the rescued virgin train;
And, loftier virtue! how Cornelia   19
    Lived when her two brave sons were slain.

This is my birthday: may ye waltz
    Till mamma cracks her best guitar!
Yours are true pleasures; those are false
    We wise ones follow from afar.

What shall I bring you? would you like
    Urn, image, glass, red, yellow, blue,
Stricken by Time, who soon must strike
    As deep the heart that beats for you.

1846

XVII

Alas, how soon the hours are over
Counted us out to play the lover!
And how much narrower is the stage
Allotted us to play the sage!
But when we play the fool, how wide,
The theatre expands! beside,
How long the audience sits before us!
How many prompters! what a chorus!

1846

XVIII

TO ROBERT BROWNING

There is delight in singing, tho' none hear
Beside the singer; and there is delight
In praising, tho' the praiser sit alone
And see the prais'd far off him, far above.
Shakespeare is not our poet, but the world's,
Therefore on him no speech! and brief for thee,
Browning! Since Chaucer was alive and hale,
No man hath walked along our roads with step
So active, so inquiring eye, or tongue
So varied in discourse. But warmer climes
Give brighter plumage, strong wing: the breeze
Of Alpine heights thou playest with, borne on

Beyond Sorrento and Amalfi, where   13
The Siren waits thee, singing song for song.
1846

XIX

I STROVE with none, for none was worth my
      strife,
   Nature I loved, and next to Nature, Art;
I warmed both hands before the fire of life,
   It sinks, and I am ready to depart.
1853

XX

A PROVIDENT and wakeful fear
   Impels me, while I read, to say,
When Poesy invites, forbear
   Sometimes to walk her tempting way:
Readier is she to swell the tear
   Than its sharp tinglings to allay.

"But there are stories fit for song,
   And fit for maiden lips to sing."
Yes; and to you they all belong,
   About your knee they fondly cling;   10
They love the accents of your tongue,
   They seek the shadow of your wing.

Ah! let the Hours be light and gay,
   With Hope for ever at their side,
And let the Muses chaunt a lay
   Of pleasures that await the bride,
Of sunny Life's untroubled sea,
   Smooth sands, and gently swelling tide.

A time will come when steps are slow,
   And prone on ancient scenes to rest,   20
When life shall lose its former glow,
   And, leaf by leaf, the shrinking breast
Shall drop the blossom yet to blow
   For the most blessed of the blest.

Then, nor till then, in spring go forth
   "The graves of waiting friends to see."
It would be pleasant to my earth
   To know your step, if that might be.
A verse is more than I am worth,
   A thought is not undue to me.   30
1853

XXI

GOD scatters beauty as he scatters flowers
O'er the wide earth, and tells us all are ours.
A hundred lights in every temple burn,
And at each shrine I bend my knee in turn.
1853

XXII

DEATH stands above me, whispering low
   I know not what into my ear:
Of this strange language all I know
   Is, there is not a word of fear.
1853

XXIII

So then, I feel not deeply! if I did,
I should have seized the pen and pierced there-
      with
The passive world!
                  And thus thou reasonest?
Well hast thou known the lover's, not so well
The poet's heart: while that heart bleeds, the
      hand
Presses it close. Grief must run on and pass
Into near Memory's more quiet shade
Before it can compose itself in song.
He who is agonized and turns to show
His agony to those who sit around,   10
Seizes the pen in vain: thought, fancy, power,
Rush back into his bosom; all the strength
Of genius can not draw them into light
From under mastering Grief; but Memory,
The Muse's mother, nurses, rears them up,
Informs, and keeps them with her all her days.
1853

XXIV

TO YOUTH

WHERE art thou gone, light-ankled Youth?
   With wing at either shoulder,
And smile that never left thy mouth
   Until the Hours grew colder:

Then somewhat seem'd to whisper near
   That thou and I must part;
I doubted it: I felt no fear,
   No weight upon the heart:

If aught befell it, Love was by
   And roll'd it off again;   10
So, if there ever was a sigh,
   'Twas not a sigh of pain.

I may not call thee back; but thou
   Returnest when the hand
Of gentle Sleep waves o'er my brow
   His poppy-crested wand;

Then smiling eyes bend over mine,
   Then lips once pressed invite;

Dear Browning,

It is now several weeks since I totally lost my voice and hearing. My last effort of writing is being made now, to thank you for your innumerable proofs of kindness, and to say that I have ever been most justly and affectionately

your obliged

Walter Landor

Need I tell you how grateful I am to Mrs Twisleton?

June 26. '64.

A Letter to Robert Browning, written by Walter Savage Landor in the last year of his life.
(See Appendix I.)

But sleep hath given a silent sign,
  And both, alas! take flight.   20

1853

XXV

TO AGE

WELCOME, old friend! These many years
  Have we lived door by door:
The Fates have laid aside their shears
  Perhaps for some few more.

I was indocile at an age
  When better boys were taught,
But thou at length hast made me sage,
  If I am sage in aught.

Little I know from other men,
  Too little they from me,   10
But thou hast pointed well the pen
  That writes these lines to thee.

Thanks for expelling Fear and Hope,
  One vile, the other vain;
One's scourge, the other's telescope,
  I shall not see again:

Rather what lies before my feet
  My notice shall engage—
He who hath braved Youth's dizzy heat
  Dreads not the frost of Age.   20

1853

XXVI

To my ninth decade I have totter'd on,
  And no soft arm bends now my steps to
    steady;
She, who once led me where she would, is
    gone,
  So when he calls me, Death shall find me
  ready.

1863

JAMES (CLARENCE) MANGAN
[May 1, 1803–June 20, 1849]

JAMES MANGAN, perhaps the greatest poet Ireland produced in the first half of the century, was born in Dublin, and there his life was wholly lived. Forced to go to work early, he drudged for seven years in a scrivener's office and for another three with an attorney. Friends secured him a position in the Ordinance Survey Office and later in the library of Trinity College, but the increasing irregularity of his habits, due to drink and narcotics, made it impossible for him to hold any position, and made him entirely dependent upon his pen. As early as 1822 he had published verse in Dublin almanacs. In 1831 he was elected to the Comet Club, a group of Dublin wits, and his contributions to the club journal appeared over the signature "Clarence," a name he later appropriated for himself. All of his work appeared in Dublin magazines, his most important contributions being to the *Dublin University Magazine* beginning in 1834 and to the *Nation* beginning in 1842. The only collection to appear during his lifetime was the *Anthologia Germanica*, which was published in 1845. In 1849 Mangan died in the Meath Hospital —of cholera, say some accounts; of starvation and exhaustion, say others.

Mangan published many adaptations from modern tongues, chiefly the German, and others which he pretended were from Turkish, Persian, or Arabic sources. But it is generally agreed that the greatest of his poems are those adapted from the Gaelic. A dreamer, with the wreck of his own broken life about him, he found in Ireland's tragic history themes and old songs sympathetic to him. It was not merely a matter of patriotism but something deeper and more obscure, a matter of those subtle sympathies which govern creative impulse. The fierce and anguished *O'Hussey's Ode to the Maguire* is an Irish poem; it is also a poem of the broken and unhappy Mangan. *Kathaleen Ny-Houlahan* is not only a song to Ireland; it is also a poem by the distressed lover of beautiful things who sees them soiled. It is in this sense that the poet Mangan, feeling within himself "the asp, the worm that will not sleep and cannot die" found in the history of his country the tragic symbol of his own frustration.

DARK ROSALEEN [1]

OH! my dark Rosaleen,
  Do not sigh, do not weep!
The priests are on the ocean green,
  They march along the deep.
There's wine from the royal Pope
  Upon the ocean green,
And Spanish ale shall give you hope,
  My dark Rosaleen!
  My own Rosaleen!
Shall glad your heart, shall give you hope, 10
Shall give you health, and help, and hope,
  My dark Rosaleen!

Over hills and through dales
  Have I roamed for your sake;
All yesterday I sailed with sails
  On river and on lake.
The Erne, at its highest flood,
  I dashed across unseen,
For there was lightning in my blood,
  My dark Rosaleen!   20
  My own Rosaleen!
Oh! there was lightning in my blood,
Red lightning lightened through my blood,
  My dark Rosaleen!

All day long, in unrest,
  To and fro do I move.
The very soul within my breast
  Is wasted for you, love!
The heart in my bosom faints
  To think of you, my Queen,   30
My life of life, my saint of saints,
  My dark Rosaleen!
  My own Rosaleen!
To hear your sweet and sad complaints,
My life, my love, my saint of saints,
  My dark Rosaleen!

Woe and pain, pain and woe,
  Are my lot, night and noon,
To see your bright face clouded so,
  Like to the mournful moon.   40
But yet will I rear your throne
  Again in golden sheen;
'Tis you shall reign, shall reign alone,
  My dark Rosaleen!
  My own Rosaleen!
'Tis you shall have the golden throne,
'Tis you shall reign, and reign alone,
  My dark Rosaleen!

Over dews, over sands,
  Will I fly for your weal: 50
Your holy delicate white hands
  Shall girdle me with steel.
At home in your emerald bowers,
  From morning's dawn till e'en,
You'll pray for me, my flower of flowers,
  My dark Rosaleen!
  My own Rosaleen!
You'll think of me through daylight's hours,
My virgin flower, my flower of flowers,
  My dark Rosaleen!   60

I could scale the blue air,
  I could plough the high hills,
Oh! I could kneel all night in prayer,
  To heal your many ills!
And one beamy smile from you
  Would float like light between
My toils and me, my own, my true,
  My dark Rosaleen!
  My own Rosaleen!
Would give me life and soul anew,   70
A second life, a soul anew,
  My dark Rosaleen!

Oh! the Erne shall run red
  With redundance of blood,
The earth shall rock beneath our tread,
  And flames wrap hill and wood,
And gun-peal and slogan-cry
  Wake many a glen serene,
Ere you shall fade, ere you shall die,
  My dark Rosaleen!   80
  My own Rosaleen!
The Judgment Hour must first be nigh,
Ere you can fade, ere you can die,
  My dark Rosaleen!

[1] "Dark Rosaleen" (Roisin Dubh, "Dark-haired little Rose," or Rois Gheal Dubh, "Dark-haired, fair-skinned Rose) is Ireland, after the custom of the Celtic bards of personifying their country as a distressed maiden. The Gaelic originals which inspired Mangan's free rendering refer to the time of the struggle of the northern clans against Queen Elizabeth. The Irish at this time were encouraged by promises of aid from the Pope and the King of Spain, which accounts for the references to Spain and the Pope in the first stanza.

Friday, at noon —

My dear Tighe,

      I send you inclosed what you request —
I also send you the "chisselld" original. — The latter take
care not to let Elliott see, because, as I think or am half
inclined to believe you do not delight in cruelty. His feelings
shall not be put upon the rack — Do you smile — oh! you
know he is a gentleman and therefore must possess sensations
which the Canaille know nothing about — But what am I
saying — "where was I" as they say, aye I was speaking of
the inclosure — Be good enough to give it to Elliott, telling him
at the same time, that you have made such few alterations
as you thought necessary, and that he has an excellent taste
for Poetry — The rest you know yourself —

           I am your's sincerely
           James Mangan.

P.S. I have a droll peculiarity
which is, that I never wish to hear
any thing further of a Letter after
it escapes from my hands. this may
that is, must, arise from the consciousness
I entertain of the wretched stile in
which I pen it — You will therefore
be so kind as never to speak a word
concerning this to me —

A Letter by James (Clarence) Mangan. (See Appendix I.)

O'HUSSEY'S ODE TO THE MAGUIRE

From the Irish

WHERE is my Chief, my Master, this bleak
    night, mavrone!
  Oh, cold, cold, miserably cold, is this bleak
    night for Hugh;
  Its showery, arrowy, speary sleet pierceth
    one through and through—
Pierceth one to the very bone!

Rolls real thunder? Or was that red livid light
  Only a meteor? I scarce know; but through
    the midnight dim
  The pitiless ice-wind streams. Except the
    hate that persecutes him,
Nothing hath crueller venomy might.

An awful, a tremendous night is this, meseems!
  The flood-gates of the rivers of heaven, I
    think, have been burst wide—   10
  Down from the overcharged clouds, like
    unto headlong ocean's tide,
Descends grey rain in roaring streams.

Though he were even a wolf raging the round
    green woods,
  Though he were even a pleasant salmon in
    the unchainable sea,
  Though he were a wild mountain eagle, he
    could scarce bear, he,
This sharp, sore sleet, these howling floods.

Oh! mournful is my soul this night for Hugh
    Maguire!
  Darkly, as in a dream he strays! Before him
    and behind
  Triumphs the tyrannous anger of the
    wounding wind,
The wounding wind that burns as fire!   20

It is my bitter grief—it cuts me to the heart—
  That in the country of Clan Darry this
    should be his fate!
  Oh, woe is me, where is he? Wandering,
    houseless, desolate,
Alone, without or guide or chart!

Medreams I see just now his face, the straw-
    berry-bright,
  Uplifted to the blackened heavens, while
    the tempestuous winds

Blow fiercely over and round him, and the
    smiting sleet-shower blinds
The hero of Galang to-night!

Large, large affliction unto me and mine
    it is,
  That one of his majestic bearing, his fair,
    stately form,   30
  Should thus be tortured and o'erborne—
    that this unsparing storm
Should wreak its wrath on head like his!

That his great hand, so oft the avenger of the
    oppressed,
  Should this chill, churlish night, perchance,
    be paralysed by frost—
  While through some icicle-hung thicket—
    as one lorn and lost—
He walks and wanders without rest.

The tempest-driven torrent deluges the mead;
  It overflows the low banks of the rivulets
    and ponds—
  The lawns and pasture-grounds lie locked
    in icy bonds,
So that the cattle cannot feed.   40

The pale bright margins of the streams are seen
    by none;
  Rushes and sweeps along the untamable
    flood on every side—
  It penetrates and fills the cottagers' dwell-
    ings far and wide—
Water and land are blent in one.

Through some dark wood, 'mid bones of
    monsters, Hugh now strays,
  As he confronts the storm with anguished
    heart, but manly brow—
  Oh! what a sword-wound to that tender
    heart of his were now
A backward glance at peaceful days!

But other thoughts are his—thoughts that can
    still inspire
  With joy and an onward-bounding hope
    the bosom of MacNee—   50
  Thoughts of his warriors charging like
    bright billows of the sea,
Borne on the wind's wings, flashing fire!

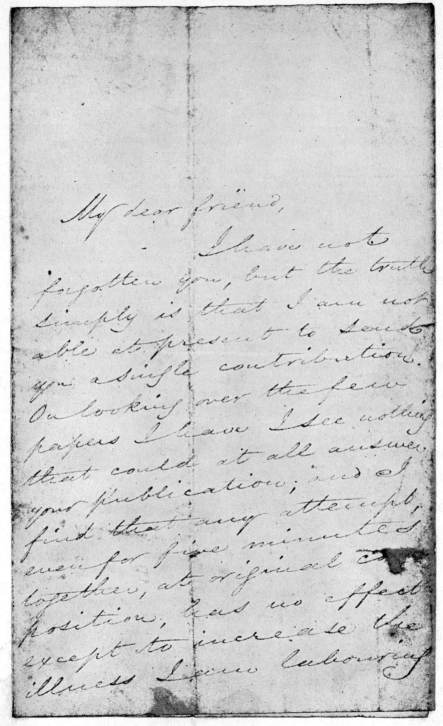

First Page of a Letter by Mangan. (See Appendix I.)

Second and Third Pages of the Letter by Mangan, beginning on opposite page. Much Reduced.
(See Appendix I.)

And though frost glaze to-night the clear dew
    of his eyes,
    And white gauntlets glove his noble fine
        fair fingers o'er,
    A warm dress is to him that lightning-garb
        he ever wore,
The lightning of the soul, not skies.

AVRAN

Hugh marched forth to the fight—I grieved to
    see him so depart;
    And lo! to-night he wanders frozen, rain-
        drenched, sad, betrayed—
    But the memory of the lime-white mansions
        his right hand hath laid
In ashes warms the hero's heart.   60

KATHALEEN NY-HOULAHAN [1]

A Jacobite Relic—from the Irish

Long they pine in weary woe—the nobles of
    our land—
Long they wander to and fro, proscribed, alas!
    and banned;
Feastless, houseless, altarless, they bear the
    exile's brand,
    But their hope is in the coming-to of Katha-
    leen Ny-Houlahan.

Think not her a ghastly hag, too hideous to
    be seen;
Call her not unseemly names, our matchless
    Kathaleen;
Young she is, and fair she is, and would be
    crowned a queen,
    Were the king's son at home here with
    Kathaleen Ny-Houlahan.

Sweet and mild would look her face—Oh!
    none so sweet and mild—
Could she crush the foes by whom her beauty
    is reviled;   10
Woollen plaids would grace herself and robes
    of silk her child,
    If the king's son were living here with
    Kathaleen Ny-Houlahan.

Sore disgrace it is to see the Arbitress of
    thrones
Vassal to a Saxoneen of cold and sapless bones!

[1] Kathaleen Ny-Houlahan is Ireland, again
personified as a distressed maiden.

Bitter anguish wrings our souls—with heavy
    sighs and groans
    We wait the Young Deliverer of Kathaleen
    Ny-Houlahan.

Let us pray to Him who holds life's issues in
    His hands,
Him who formed the mighty globe, with all its
    thousand lands:
Girding them with sea and mountains, rivers
    deep, and strands,
    To cast a look of pity upon Kathaleen Ny-
    Houlahan.   20

He who over sands and waves led Israel
    along—
He who fed, with heavenly bread, that chosen
    tribe and throng;
He who stood by Moses when his foes were
    fierce and strong,
    May He show forth His might in saving
    Kathaleen Ny-Houlahan!

SIBERIA

In Siberia's wastes
    The ice-wind's breath
Woundeth like the toothed steel.
Lost Siberia doth reveal
    Only blight and death.

Blight and death alone.
    No Summer shines.
Night is interblent with Day.
In Siberia's wastes alway
    The blood blackens, the heart pines.   10

In Siberia's wastes
    No tears are shed,
For they freeze within the brain.
Nought is felt but dullest pain,
    Pain acute, yet dead;

Pain as in a dream,
    When years go by
Funeral-paced, yet fugitive—
When man lives and doth not live
    Doth not live—nor die.   20

In Siberia's wastes
    Are sands and rocks.

Nothing blooms of green or soft,
But the snowpeaks rise aloft
  And the gaunt ice-blocks.

And the exile there
  Is one with those;
They are part, and he is part,
For the sands are in his heart,
  And the killing snows.   30

Therefore in those wastes
  None curse the Czar;
Each man's tongue is cloven by
The North Blast, who heweth nigh
  With sharp scimitar.

And such doom each drees,
  Till, hunger-gnawn
And cold slain, he at length sinks there,
Yet scarce more a corpse than ere
  His last breath was drawn.   40

SHAPES AND SIGNS

I SEE black dragons mount the sky,
  I see earth yawn beneath my feet—
  I feel within the asp, the worm
That will not sleep and cannot die,
  Fair though may show the winding-sheet!
  I hear all night as through a storm
  Hoarse voices calling, calling
    My name upon the wind—
  All omens monstrous and appalling
    Affright my guilty mind.   10

I exult alone in one wild hour—
  That hour in which the red cup drowns
    The memories it anon renews
In ghastlier guise, in fiercer power—
  Then Fancy brings me golden crowns,
  And visions of all brilliant hues
  Lap my lost soul in gladness,
    Until I wake again,
  And the dark lava-fires of madness
    Once more sweep through my brain. 20

THOMAS MOORE
[May 28, 1779–February 25, 1852]

IT has been said that "Tommy loved a lord" rather as a reproach and with the implication that he was a time-server and toady to the great. Time-server Thomas Moore was not, and the truer statement might be, "Great people loved Tommy." His own talent opened the great world to him without subservience on his part, and his own charm made him everywhere beloved. A brilliant society was open to him and he moved freely in it, but he never forgot his wife, Bessy, and his children at home, and his perfectly frank devotion to them is one of the pleasantest touches in the literary history of his day.

As a poet, Moore pressed Byron and Scott hard for popular acclaim. His friends forced Longmans to offer him for the copyright of *Lalla Rookh* (1817) as much as "had ever been paid a poet before." The publishers met the challenge and paid him £3000, the equal of what Scott received for *Rokeby*, for a manuscript they had never seen. *Lalla Rookh*, a long narrative poem in an oriental setting, now seems the product of industry rather than inspiration, and Moore's reputation does not rest upon it, in spite of its importance in its own day. Moore also did satirical work, such as the *Twopenny Post Bag* (1813). The *Irish Melodies* (published in groups from 1807 to 1834 with accompanying music) were immensely popular, and from Moore's works it is lyrical work of this type which has retained real vitality.

Moore's reputation must ultimately rest upon his singing quality. Poetry is a wedding of emotionalized idea with sound. These two qualities remain fundamental in the art, although the balance is never perfect between them and the pendulum swings. The greater poets have been intense of idea, with their musical richness obvious and taken for granted. Moore is not intense of idea. He is simple and rather sentimental. But although he is sentimental in a fashion that smart intellectuals can easily make sport of, there is a certain compelling genuineness to his sentimentality. It is an expression of the honest feeling of the man who left London society to go home to "Bessy" and the children.

In ideology, then, Moore does not possess the flaming venturesomeness of, say, a Shelley, and his literary reputation has suffered from the lack. He has never been given quite the credit which is due him for the essential trueness of the sentiment which he does express, and praise for the one quality which he possesses in superlative degree has been given to him in rather niggardly critical fashion. In the marrying of words to music, Moore stands with the very greatest in the language. As one looks back through the whole history of English literature for songs which stay alive on men's lips as do those of Thomas Moore, one has difficulty in finding Moore's equal. And Moore himself was the first to regret the separation of his lyrics from music. "It is," he wrote, when his words were published without their music, "with a feeling which I can hardly expect my unlyrical readers to understand, that I see such a swarm of songs as crowd these pages all separated from the beautiful airs which have formed hitherto their chief ornament and strength."

The time has come for the reëstimation of Thomas Moore on the basis of the powers he possessed. The lyrics upon which Moore's fame rests were meant to be sung: a certain simplification of sentiment and idea is essential to meet this condition. It may be that Moore was emotionally and intellectually incapable of meeting other standards, and evidence rather indicates as much. The fact remains that he has met those standards of song to which his talent was adjusted.

From IRISH MELODIES

(Published 1807–1834)

OH, BREATHE NOT HIS NAME

OH, breathe not his name, let it sleep in the
    shade,
Where cold and unhonor'd his relics are laid:
Sad, silent, and dark, be the tears that we shed,
As the night dew that falls on the grass o'er his
    head.

But the night dew that falls, though in silence
    it weeps,
Shall brighten with verdure the grave where he
    sleeps;
And the tear that we shed, though in secret it
    rolls,
Shall long keep his memory green in our souls.

THE HARP THAT ONCE THROUGH TARA'S HALLS

THE harp that once through Tara's halls
    The soul of music shed,
Now hangs as mute on Tara's walls,
    As if that soul were fled.—

So sleeps the pride of former days,
    So glory's thrill is o'er,
And hearts, that once beat high for praise,
    Now feel that pulse no more.

No more to chiefs and ladies bright
    The harp of Tara swells; ·   10
The chord alone, that breaks at night,
    Its tale of ruin tells.
Thus Freedom now so seldom wakes,
    The only throb she gives,
Is when some heart indignant breaks,
    To show that still she lives.

RICH AND RARE WERE THE GEMS SHE WORE

RICH and rare were the gems she wore,
And a bright gold ring on her wand she bore;
But O, her beauty was far beyond
Her sparkling gems, or snow-white wand.

"Lady! dost thou not fear to stray,
So lone and lovely through this bleak way?
Are Erin's sons so good or so cold,
As not to be tempted by woman or gold?"

"Sir Knight! I feel not the least alarm,
No son of Erin will offer me harm:— 10
For though they love woman and golden
    store,
Sir Knight! they love honor and virtue more!"

On she went, and her maiden smile
In safety lighted her round the green isle;
And blest forever is she who relied
Upon Erin's honor and Erin's pride.

THE MEETING OF THE WATERS

THERE is not in the wide world a valley so
    sweet
As that vale in whose bosom the bright waters
    meet;
O, the last rays of feeling and life must depart,
Ere the bloom of that valley shall fade from
    my heart.

Yet it *was* not that nature had shed o'er the
    scene
Her purest of crystal and brightest of green;
'Twas *not* her soft magic of streamlet or hill,
O, no, it was something more exquisite still.

'Twas that friends, the belov'd of my bosom,
    were near,
Who made every dear scene of enchantment
    more dear, 10
And who felt how the best charms of nature
    improve,
When we see them reflected from looks that
    we love.

Sweet vale of Avoca! how calm could I rest
In thy bosom of shade, with the friends I love
    best,
Where the storms that we feel in this cold
    world should cease,
And our hearts, like thy waters, be mingled in
    peace.

HOW DEAR TO ME THE HOUR

How dear to me the hour when daylight dies,
    And sunbeams melt along the silent sea;
For then sweet dreams of other days arise,
    And memory breathes her vesper sigh to
    thee.

And, as I watch the line of light, that plays
    Along the smooth wave toward the burning
    west,
I long to tread that golden path of rays,
    And think 'twould lead to some bright isle
    of rest.

LET ERIN REMEMBER THE DAYS
OF OLD

LET Erin remember the days of old,
    Ere her faithless sons betray'd her;
When Malachi wore the collar of gold,
    Which he won from her proud invader,
When her kings, with standard of green un-
    furl'd,
    Led the Red-Branch Knights to danger;—
Ere the emerald gem of the western world
    Was set in the crown of a stranger.

On Lough Neagh's bank as the fisherman
    strays,
    When the clear cold eve's declining, 10
He sees the round towers of other days
    In the wave beneath him shining;
Thus shall memory often, in dreams sublime,
    Catch a glimpse of the days that are over;
Thus, sighing, look through the waves of time
    For the long-faded glories they cover.

THE SONG OF FIONNUALA

SILENT, O Moyle, be the roar of thy water,
    Break not, ye breezes, your chain of repose,
While, murmuring mournfully, Lir's lonely
    daughter
    Tells to the night star her tale of woes.
When shall the swan, her death note singing,
    Sleep, with wings in darkness furl'd?
When will heaven, its sweet bell ringing,
    Call my spirit from this stormy world?

Sadly, O Moyle, to thy winter wave weeping,
    Fate bids me languish long ages away; 10
Yet still in her darkness doth Erin lie sleeping,
    Still doth the pure light its dawning delay.
When will that daystar, mildly springing,
    Warm our isle with peace and love?
When will heaven, its sweet bell ringing,
    Call my spirit to the fields above?

BELIEVE ME, IF ALL THOSE EN-
DEARING YOUNG CHARMS

BELIEVE me, if all those endearing young
    charms,
  Which I gaze on so fondly to-day,
Were to change by to-morrow, and fleet in
    my arms,
  Like fairy gifts fading away,
Thou wouldst still be ador'd, as this moment
    thou art,
  Let thy loveliness fade as it will,
And around the dear ruin each wish of my
    heart
  Would intwine itself verdantly still.

It is not while beauty and youth are thine
    own,
  And thy cheeks unprofan'd by a tear,   10
That the fervor and faith of a soul can be
    known,
  To which time will but make thee more
    dear;
No, the heart that has truly lov'd never for-
    gets,
  But as truly loves on to the close,
As the sunflower turns on her god, when he
    sets,
  The same look which she turn'd when he
    rose.

AFTER THE BATTLE

NIGHT clos'd around the conqueror's way,
  And lightnings show'd the distant hill,
Where those who lost that dreadful day,
  Stood few and faint, but fearless still.
The soldier's hope, the patriot's zeal,
  Forever dimm'd, forever cross'd—
O, who shall say what heroes feel,
  When all but life and honor's lost?

The last sad hour of freedom's dream,
  And valor's task, moved slowly by,   10
While mute they watch'd, till morning's
    beam
  Should rise and give them light to die.
There's yet a world, where souls are free,
  Where tyrants taint not nature's bliss;—
If death that world's bright opening be,
  O, who would live a slave in this?

SHE IS FAR FROM THE LAND

SHE is far from the land where her young hero
    sleeps,
  And lovers are round her, sighing:
But coldly she turns from their gaze, and
    weeps,
  For her heart in his grave is lying.

She sings the wild song of her dear native
    plains,
  Every note which he lov'd awaking;—
Ah! little they think who delight in her
    strains
  How the heart of the Minstrel is breaking.

He had liv'd for his love, for his country he
    died,
  They were all that to life had intwin'd
    him;   10
Nor soon shall the tears of his country be
    dried,
  Nor long will his love stay behind him.

O, make her a grave where the sunbeams
    rest,
  When they promise a glorious morrow;
They'll shine o'er her sleep, like a smile from
    the West,
  From her own lov'd island of sorrow.

'TIS THE LAST ROSE OF SUMMER

'TIS the last rose of summer
  Left blooming alone;
All her lovely companions
  Are faded and gone;
No flower of her kindred,
  No rosebud is nigh,
To reflect back her blushes,
  Or give sigh for sigh.

I'll not leave thee, thou lone one!
  To pine on the stem;   10
Since the lovely are sleeping,
  Go, sleep thou with them.
Thus kindly I scatter
  Thy leaves o'er the bed,
Where thy mates of the garden
  Lie scentless and dead.

So soon may *I* follow,
 When friendships decay,
 And from Love's shining circle
  The gems drop away. 20
When true hearts lie wither'd,
 And fond ones are flown,
 O, who would inhabit
  This bleak world alone?

THE MINSTREL BOY

THE Minstrel Boy to the war is gone,
 In the ranks of death you'll find him;
His father's sword he has girded on,
 And his wild harp slung behind him.—
"Land of song!" said the warrior bard,
 "Though all the world betrays thee,
One sword, at least, thy rights shall guard,
 One faithful harp shall praise thee!"

The Minstrel fell!—but the foeman's chain
 Could not bring his proud soul under; 10
The harp he lov'd ne'er spoke again,
 For he tore its chords asunder;
And said, "No chains shall sully thee,
 Thou soul of love and bravery!
Thy songs were made for the pure and free,
 They shall never sound in slavery."

THE TIME I'VE LOST IN WOOING

 THE time I've lost in wooing,
 In watching and pursuing
  The light, that lies
  In woman's eyes,
 Has been my heart's undoing.
 Though Wisdom oft has sought me,
 I scorn'd the lore she brought me.
  My only books
  Were woman's looks,
 And folly's all they've taught me. 10

 Her smile when Beauty granted,
 I hung with gaze enchanted,
 Like him the Sprite,
  Whom maids by night
 Oft meet in glen that's haunted.
 Like him, too, Beauty won me,
 But while her eyes were on me,
  If once their ray
  Was turn'd away,
 O, winds could not outrun me. 20

And are those follies going?
And is my proud heart growing
  Too cold or wise
  For brilliant eyes
Again to set it glowing?
No, vain, alas! th' endeavor
From bonds so sweet to sever;—
  Poor Wisdom's chance
  Against a glance
Is now as weak as ever. 30

COME, REST IN THIS BOSOM

COME, rest in this bosom, my own stricken deer,
Though the herd have fled from thee, thy
 home is still here;
Here still is the smile, that no cloud can o'er-
 cast,
And a heart and a hand all thy own to the last.

O, what was love made for, if 'tis not the same
Through joy and through torment, through
 glory and shame?
I know not, I ask not, if guilt's in that heart,
I but know that I love thee, whatever thou art.

Thou hast call'd me thy Angel in moments of
 bliss,
And thy Angel I'll be, 'mid the horrors of
 this,— 10
Through the furnace, unshrinking, thy steps
 to pursue,
And shield thee, and save thee,—or perish
 there too!

DEAR HARP OF MY COUNTRY

DEAR Harp of my Country! in darkness I
 found thee,
 The cold chain of silence had hung o'er thee
  long,
When proudly, my own Island Harp, I unbound thee,
 And gave all thy chords to light, freedom,
  and song!
The warm lay of love and the light note of
 gladness
 Have waken'd thy fondest, thy liveliest thrill;
But, so oft hast thou echoed the deep sigh of
 sadness,
 That ev'n in thy mirth it will steal from thee
  still.

Dear Harp of my Country! farewell to thy
    numbers,
  This sweet wreath of song is the last we
    shall twine!   10
Go, sleep with sunshine of Fame on thy
    slumbers,
  Till touch'd by some hand less unworthy
    than mine;
If the pulse of the patriot, soldier, or lover,
  Have throbb'd at our lay, 'tis thy glory alone;
I was *but* as the wind, passing heedlessly over,
  And all the wild sweetness I wak'd was thy
    own.

I WISH I WAS BY THAT DIM LAKE

I wish I was by that dim Lake,
Where sinful souls their farewell take
Of this vain world, and half way lie
In death's cold shadow, ere they die.
There, there, far from thee,
Deceitful world, my home should be;
Where, come what might of gloom and pain,
False hope should ne'er deceive again.

The lifeless sky, the mournful sound
Of unseen waters falling round;   10
The dry leaves, quiv'ring o'er my head,
Like man, unquiet ev'n when dead!
These, ay, these shall wean
My soul from life's deluding scene,
And turn each thought, o'ercharged with
    gloom,
Like willows, downwards towards the tomb.

As they, who to their couch at night
Would win repose, first quench the light,
So must the hopes, that keep this breast
Awake, be quench'd, ere it can rest.   20
Cold, cold, this heart must grow,
Unmoved by either joy or woe,
Like freezing founts, where all that's thrown
Within their current turns to stone.

From NATIONAL AIRS

(Published 1815)

OFT, IN THE STILLY NIGHT

(Scotch Air)

Oft, in the stilly night,
  Ere Slumber's chain has bound me,

Fond Memory brings the light
  Of other days around me;
    The smiles, the tears,
    Of boyhood's years,
The words of love then spoken;
    The eyes that shone,
    Now dimm'd and gone,
The cheerful hearts now broken!   10
Thus, in the stilly night,
  Ere Slumber's chain has bound me,
Sad Memory brings the light
  Of other days around me.

When I remember all
  The friends, so link'd together,
I've seen around me fall,
  Like leaves in wintry weather;
    I feel like one,
    Who treads alone   20
Some banquet hall deserted,
    Whose lights are fled,
    Whose garlands dead,
And all but he departed!
Thus, in the stilly night,
  Ere Slumber's chain has bound me,
Sad Memory brings the light
  Of other days around me.

HARK! THE VESPER HYMN IS STEALING

(Russian Air)

Hark! the vesper hymn is stealing
  O'er the waters soft and clear;
Nearer yet and nearer pealing,
  And now bursts upon the ear:
    Jubilate, Amen.
Farther now, now farther stealing,
  Soft it fades upon the ear:
    Jubilate, Amen.

Now, like moonlight waves retreating
  To the shore, it dies along;   10
Now, like angry surges meeting,
  Breaks the mingled tide of song:
    Jubilate, Amen.
Hush! again, like waves, retreating
  To the shore, it dies along:
    Jubilate, Amen.

From BALLADS, SONGS,
MISCELLANEOUS POEMS, ETC.

CHILD'S SONG. FROM A MASK

I HAVE a garden of my own,
  Shining with flowers of every hue;
I loved it dearly while alone,
  But I shall love it more with you:
And there the golden bees shall come,
  In summer time at break of morn,
And wake us with their busy hum
  Around the Siha's fragrant thorn.

I have a fawn from Aden's land,
  On leafy buds and berries nurs'd,   10
And you shall feed him from your hand,
  Though he may start with fear at first.
And I will lead you where he lies
  For shelter in the noontide heat;
And you may touch his sleeping eyes,
  And feel his little silv'ry feet.

WILLIAM MOTHERWELL
[October 13, 1797–November 1, 1835]

WILLIAM MOTHERWELL was the son of a Glasgow ironmonger. He worked in the office of the Sheriff Clerk at Paisley for ten years (1819–29) during the latter part of which he also edited a Tory newspaper. From Paisley he went to Glasgow to edit *The Glasgow Courier* and died at Glasgow of apoplexy at the age of thirty-seven. His energies were almost exclusively devoted to editorial work and to fiercely partisan political debate. The only product of his very real poetic ability was a small volume, *Poems, Narrative and Lyrical*, published in 1832.

BONNIE GEORGE CAMPBELL

HIE upon Hielands
  And low upon Tay,
Bonny George Campbell
  Rade out on a day.
Saddled and bridled
  And gallant rade he;
Hame cam his gude horse,
  But never cam he!

Out cam his auld mither
  Greeting fu' sair,   10
And out cam his bonnie bride
  Rivin' her hair.

Saddled and bridled
  And booted rade he;
Toom hame cam the saddle,
  But never cam he!

"My meadow lies green,
  And my corn is unshorn;
My barn is to big,
  And my babie's unborn."   20
Saddled and bridled
  And booted rade he;
Toom hame cam the saddle,
  But never cam he!

Pub. 1832

THOMAS LOVE PEACOCK
[October 18, 1785–January 23, 1866]

THOMAS LOVE PEACOCK lived long enough to be the intimate friend of Shelley and the friendly father-in-law of Meredith, two of the more interesting poets of the century. From 1819 till 1856 he was a clerk in the East India Company, and his life in this respect is similar to that of Charles Lamb. He is chiefly known as a satirical novelist of caustic wit with a clean-cut English style and a brain which objected to the vulgarities of "progress." Peacock's reputation as a novelist has obscured his talent as a poet, but scattered through the novels are songs which unquestionably show him to be a poet. His longer poems, *The Genius of the Thames* (1810) and *Rhododaphne* (1818), are not so successful. Other poetical publications were *Palmyra* (1806) and *Paper Money Lyrics* (1837). His novel *Nightmare Abbey* is a vivacious satire on some of the poets of the period, the caricatures of Coleridge and Shelley being especially amusing. It was Peacock's *The Four Ages of Poetry* which provoked Shelley's *A Defence of Poetry*.

THE GRAVE OF LOVE

I DUG, beneath the cypress shade,
   What well might seem an elfin's grave;
And every pledge in earth I laid,
   That erst thy false affection gave.

I pressed them down the sod beneath;
   I placed one mossy stone above;
And twined the rose's fading wreath
   Around the sepulchre of love.

Frail as thy love, the flowers were dead,
   Ere yet the evening sun was set: 10
But years shall see the cypress spread,
   Immutable as my regret.

1806

FOR THE SLENDER BEECH AND THE SAPLING OAK

[From *Maid Marian*]

FOR the slender beech and the sapling oak
   That grow by the shadowy rill,
You may cut down both at a single stroke,
   You may cut down which you will.

But this you must know, that as long as they
   grow,
   Whatever change may be,
You never can teach either oak or beech
   To be aught but a greenwood tree.

1822

THOUGH I BE NOW A GRAY, GRAY FRIAR

[From *Maid Marian*]

THOUGH I be now a gray, gray friar,
   Yet I was once a hale young knight:
The cry of my dogs was the only choir
   In which my spirit did take delight.
Little I recked of matin bell,
   But drowned its toll with my clanging horn

And the only beads I loved to tell
   Were the beads of dew on the spangled thorn.

Little I reck of matin bell,
   But drown its toll with my clanging horn: 10
And the only beads I love to tell
   Are the beads of dew on the spangled
    thorn.

An archer keen I was withal,
   As ever did lean on greenwood tree;
And could make the fleetest roebuck fall,
   A good three hundred yards from me.
Though changeful time, with hand severe,
   Has made me now these joys forego,
Yet my heart bounds whene'er I hear
   Yoicks! hark away! and tally ho!   20

Though changeful time, with hand severe,
   Has made me now these joys forego,
Yet my heart bounds whene'er I hear
   Yoicks! hark away! and tally ho!

1822

THE WAR-SONG OF DINAS VAWR

[From *The Misfortunes of Elphin*]

THE mountain sheep are sweeter,
But the valley sheep are fatter;
We therefore deemed it meeter
To carry off the latter.
We made an expedition;
We met an host and quelled it;
We forced a strong position,
And killed the men who held it.

On Dyfed's richest valley,
Where herds of kine were browsing,   10
We made a mighty sally,
To furnish our carousing.
Fierce warriors rushed to meet us;
We met them, and o'erthrew them:
They struggled hard to beat us;
But we conquered them, and slew them.

printed respecting you. but he has not even alluded to it. Medwin thought himself justified in repeating what Moore had said in his Life of Byron, as if any thing said or done by that little dirty, paltry, pitiful rascal, could justify any one in doing the same.

Hogg has published two thick volumes of a Life of Shelley, which is to be in four. It comes down to the point, preceding his separation from Harriet. More than half of the whole is about himself, or about matters which have not the remotest relation to Shelley.

I am writing an article on these works for Fraser. but I shall stop for the present where Hogg stops

Page of a Letter from Thomas Love Peacock to Jane Clairmont. (See Appendix I.)

As we drove our prize at leisure,
The king marched forth to catch us:
His rage surpassed all measure,
But his people could not match us.   20
He fled to his hall-pillars;
And, ere our force we led off,
Some sacked his house and cellars,
While others cut his head off.

We there, in strife bewildering,
Spilt blood enough to swim in:
We orphaned many children,
And widowed many women.
The eagles and the ravens

We glutted with our foemen: 30
The heroes and the cravens,
The spearmen and the bowmen.

We brought away from battle,
And much their land bemoaned them,
Two thousand head of cattle,
And the head of him who owned them:
Ednyfed, King of Dyfed,
His head was borne before us;
His wine and beasts supplied our feasts,
And his overthrow, our chorus.   40

1829

WINTHROP MACKWORTH PRAED
[July 26, 1802–July 15, 1839]

PRAED was educated at Eton and Trinity College, Cambridge. At Eton his social charm and his gift for verse had already distinguished him. There, in 1820, he circulated a manuscript journal, the *Apis Matina*, and later was a moving spirit in *The Etonian*, a schoolboy magazine of exceptional merit. His reputation preceded him to Cambridge where he at once took his place as one of the most brilliant men of his college generation. Scholarship to him, however, was a thing of grace rather than passion, but he won several medals for Greek odes and epigrams and twice he won the Chancellor's medal for English verse. After graduation he was a tutor at Eton for a brief period, then studied law and entered politics. In college debates he had taken the radical side but he entered parliament in 1830 as a conservative, explaining, "I am not going to stem a torrent, but I confess I should like to confine its fury within some bounds. I am in no small degree an alarmist, and I would readily give a cart load of abstract ideas for a certainty of fifty years' peace and quietness." Political and legal affairs occupied the remainder of his short life.

While at college he had contributed to various periodicals including *Knight's Quarterly Magazine* and *The Brazen Head*. During his later years he contributed frequently to the *Morning Post*, which, partly because of Praed's contributions, became the leading conservative paper. The first collections of Praed's poems were published in America, three American editions having appeared before the authorized edition was published in 1864.

The gaiety and charm of the man, which captivated all who associated with him, are plainly apparent in his lighter verses which are written with the clarity and point of true wit. A sensitiveness to human values, often lacking in the mere wit, is equally apparent in Praed. *The Vicar*, for example, is written in a spirit of real tenderness. Now and again Praed abandons his bantering vein entirely and writes a personal lyric. But in the main he wore his wit like armor, bright and shining, and kept his heart to himself.

TO ——

I

WE met but in one giddy dance,
   Good-night joined hands with greeting;
And twenty thousand things may chance
   Before our second meeting:
For oh! I have been often told
   That all the world grows older,
And hearts and hopes, to-day so cold,
   To-morrow must be colder.

II

If I have never touched the string
   Beneath your chamber, dear one,   10
And never said one civil thing
   When you were by to hear one,—
If I have made no rhymes about
   Those looks which conquer Stoics,
And heard those angel tones, without
   One fit of fair heroics,—

III

Yet do not, though the world's cold school
   Some bitter truths has taught me,
O do not deem me quite the fool
   Which wiser friends have thought me!   20
There is one charm I still could feel,
   If no one laughed at feeling;
One dream my lute could still reveal,—
   If it were worth revealing.

IV

But Folly little cares what name
   Of friend or foe she handles,
When merriment directs the game,
   And midnight dims the candles;
I know that Folly's breath is weak
   And would not stir a feather;   30
But yet I would not have her speak
   Your name and mine together.

V

Oh no! this life is dark and bright,
   Half rapture and half sorrow;
My heart is very full to-night,
   My cup shall be to-morrow:
But they shall never know from me,
   On any one condition,
Whose health made bright my Burgundy,
   Whose beauty was my vision!   40

? 1822–1825

PEACE BE THINE

WHEN Sorrow moves with silent tread
   Around some mortal's buried dust,
And muses on the mouldering dead
   Who sleep beneath their crumbling bust,
Though all unheard and all unknown
   The name on that sepulchral stone,
   She looks on its recording line,
   And whispers kindly, "Peace be thine!"

O Lady! me thou knowest not,
   And what I am, or am to be;   10
The pain and pleasure of my lot
   Are naught, and must be naught, to thee;
Thou seest not my hopes and fears;
Yet thou perhaps, in other years,
   Wilt look on this recording line,
   And whisper kindly, "Peace be thine!"

? 1822–1825

LOVE AT A ROUT

WHEN some mad bard sits down to muse
About the lilies and the dews,
The grassy vales and sloping lawns,
Fairies and Satyrs, Nymphs and Fauns,
He's apt to think, he's apt to swear,
That Cupid reigns not anywhere
Except in some sequestered village
Where peasants live on truth and tillage;
That none are fair enough for witches
But maids who frisk through dells and
   ditches;   10
That dreams are twice as sweet as dances,
That cities never breed romances;
That Beauty always keeps a cottage,
And Purity grows pale on pottage.
Yes! those dear dreams are all divine;
And those dear dreams have all been mine.
I like the stream, the rock, the bay,
I like the smell of new-mown hay,
I like the babbling of the brooks,
I like the creaking of the crooks,   20
I like the peaches and the posies,—
But chiefly, when the season closes,
And often, in the month of fun,
When every poacher cleans his gun,
And cockneys tell enormous lies,
And stocks are pretty sure to rise,
And e'en the Chancellor, they say,
Goes to a point the nearest way—

I hurry from my drowsy desk
To revel in the picturesque; 30
To hear beneath those ancient trees
The far-off murmur of the bees,
Or trace yon river's mazy channels
With Petrarch, and a brace of spaniels,
Combining foolish rhymes together,
And killing sorrow, and shoe-leather.

Then, as I see some rural maid
Come dancing up the sunny glade,
Coquetting with her fond adorer
Just as her mother did before her, 40
"Give me," I cry, "the quiet bliss
Of souls like these, of scenes like this;
Where ladies eat and sleep in peace,
Where gallants never heard of Greece,
Where day is day, and night is night,
Where frocks—and morals—both are white;
Blue eyes below—blue skies above—
These are the homes, the hearts, for Love!"

But this is idle; I have been
A sojourner in many a scene, 50
And picked up wisdom in my way,
And cared not what I had to pay;
Smiling and weeping all the while,
As other people weep and smile;
And I have learned that Love is not
Confined to any hour or spot;
He lights the smile and fires the frown
Alike in country and in town.
I own fair faces not more fair
In Ettrick, than in Portman Square, 60
And silly danglers just as silly
In Sherwood, as in Piccadilly.
Soft tones are not the worse, no doubt,
For having harps to help them out;
And smiles are not a ray more bright
By moonbeams, than by candle-light;
I know much magic oft reposes
On wreaths of artificial roses,
And snowy necks,—I never found them
Quite spoilt by having cameos round them. 70
In short, I'm very sure that all
Who seek or sigh for Beauty's thrall
May breathe their vows, and feed their passion,
Though whist and waltzing keep in fashion,
And make the most delicious sonnets,
In spite of diamonds, and French bonnets!

1824

REMEMBER ME

In Seville, when the feast was long,
  And lips and lutes grew free,
At Inez' feet, amid the throng,
  A masquer bent his knee;
And still the burden of his song
  Was, "Sweet, remember me!

"Remember me in shine and shower,
  In sorrow and in glee;
When summer breathes upon the flower,
  When winter blasts the tree; 10
When there are dances in the bower,
  Or sails upon the sea.

"Remember me beneath far skies,
  On foreign lawn or lea;
When others worship those wild eyes
  Which I no more may see;
When others wake the melodies
  Of which I mar the key.

"Remember me! my heart will claim
  No love, no trust from thee; 20
Remember me, though doubt and blame
  Linked with the record be;
Remember me,—with scorn or shame,—
  But yet, remember me!"

1827

HOW AM I LIKE HER?

"You are very like her."—*Miss H— E—*

"Resemblances begin to strike
  In things exceedingly unlike."—*MS. Poem*

How am I like her?—for no trace
  Of pain, of passion, or of aught
That stings or stains, is on her face:
  Mild eyes, clear forehead,—ne'er was
    wrought
A fitter, fairer dwelling-place
  For tranquil joy and holy thought.

How am I like her?—for the fawn
  Not lighter bounds o'er rock and rill
Than she, beneath the intruding dawn
  Threading, all mirth, our gay quadrille; 10
Or tripping o'er our level lawn
  To those she loves upon the hill.

How am I like her?—for the ear
  Thrills with her voice. Its breezy tone
Goes forth, as eloquently clear
  As are the lutes at Heaven's high throne;
And makes the hearts of those who hear
  As pure and peaceful as her own.

How am I like her?—for her ways
  Are full of bliss. She never knew   20
Stern Avarice, nor the thirst of praise
  Insatiable;—Love never threw
Upon her calm and sunny days
  The venom of his deadly dew.

How am I like her?—for her arts
  Are blessing. Sorrow owns her thrall;
She dries the tear-drop as it starts,
  And checks the murmurs as they fall;
She is the day-star of our hearts,
  Consoling, guiding, gladdening all.   30

How am I like her?—for she steals
  All sympathies. Glad Childhood's play
Is left for her; and wild Youth kneels
  Obedient to her gentle sway;
And age beholds her smile, and feels
  December brightening into May.

How am I like her?—The rude fir
  Is little like the sweet rose-tree:—
Unless, perchance, fair flatterer,
  In this your fabled likeness be,—   40
That all who are most dear to her
  Are apt to be most dear to me.
October 10, 1829

THE VICAR

SOME years ago, ere time and taste
  Had turned our parish topsy-turvy,
When Darnel Park was Darnel Waste,
  And roads as little known as scurvy,
The man who lost his way, between
  St. Mary's Hill and Sandy Thicket,
Was always shown across the green,
  And guided to the Parson's wicket.

Back flew the bolt of lissom lath;
  Fair Margaret, in her tidy kirtle,   10
Led the lorn traveller up the path,
  Through clean-clipt rows of box and
    myrtle;

And Don and Sancho, Tramp and Tray,
  Upon the parlour steps collected,
Wagged all their tails, and seemed to say—
  "Our master knows you—you're expected."

Uprose the Reverend Dr. Brown,
  Uprose the Doctor's winsome marrow;
The lady laid her knitting down,
  Her husband clasped his ponderous Bar-
    row;   20
Whate'er the stranger's caste or creed,
  Pundit or Papist, saint or sinner,
He found a stable for his steed,
  And welcome for himself, and dinner.

If, when he reached his journey's end,
  And warmed himself in Court or College,
He had not gained an honest friend
  And twenty curious scraps of knowledge,—
If he departed as he came,
  With no new light on love or liquor,—   30
Good sooth, the traveller was to blame,
  And not the Vicarage, nor the Vicar.

His talk was like a stream, which runs
  With rapid change from rocks to roses:
It slipped from politics to puns,
  It passed from Mahomet to Moses;
Beginning with the laws which keep
  The planets in their radiant courses,
And ending with some precept deep
  For dressing eels, or shoeing horses.   40

He was a shrewd and sound Divine,
  Of loud Dissent the mortal terror;
And when, by dint of page and line,
  He 'stablished Truth, or startled Error,
The Baptist found him far too deep;
  The Deist sighed with saving sorrow;
And the lean Levite went to sleep,
  And dreamed of tasting pork to-morrow.

His sermon never said or showed
  That Earth is foul, that Heaven is gracious,
Without refreshment on the road   51
  From Jerome, or from Athanasius:
And sure a righteous zeal inspired
  The hand and head that penned and planned
    them,
For all who understood admired,
  And some who did not understand them.

He wrote, too, in a quiet way,
   Small treatises, and smaller verses,
And sage remarks on chalk and clay,
   And hints to noble Lords—and nurses;   60
True histories of last year's ghost,
   Lines to a ringlet, or a turban,
And trifles for the Morning Post,
   And nothings for Sylvanus Urban.

He did not think all mischief fair,
   Although he had a knack of joking;
He did not make himself a bear,
   Although he had a taste for smoking;
And when religious sects ran mad,
   He held, in spite of all his learning,   70
That if a man's belief is bad,
   It will not be improved by burning.

And he was kind, and loved to sit
   In the low hut or garnished cottage,
And praise the farmer's homely wit,
   And share the widow's homelier pottage!
At his approach complaint grew mild;
   And when his hand unbarred the shutter,
The clammy lips of fever smiled
   The welcome which they could not utter. 80

He always had a tale for me
   Of Julius Caesar, or of Venus;
From him I learnt the rule of three,
   Cat's cradle, leap-frog, and *Quae genus:*
I used to singe his powdered wig,
   To steal the staff he put such trust in,
And make the puppy dance a jig,
   When he began to quote Augustine.

Alack the change! in vain I look
   For haunts in which my boyhood trifled,—
The level lawn, the trickling brook,   91
   The trees I climbed, the beds I rifled:
The church is larger than before;
   You reach it by a carriage entry;
It holds three hundred people more,
   And pews are fitted up for gentry.

Sit in the Vicar's seat: you'll hear
   The doctrine of a gentle Johnian,
Whose hand is white, whose tone is clear,
   Whose phrase is very Ciceronian.   100
Where is the old man laid?—look down,
   And construe on the slab before you,

"Hic jacet GVLIELMVS BROWN,
   Vir nullâ non donandus lauru."

1829

THE BELLE OF THE BALL-ROOM

Il faut juger des femmes depuis la chaussure jusqu' à la coiffure exclusivement, à peu près comme on mesure le poisson entre queue et tête.—LA BRUYÈRE.

YEARS—years ago,—ere yet my dreams
   Had been of being wise or witty,—
Ere I had done with writing themes,
   Or yawned o'er this infernal Chitty;—
Years—years ago,—while all my joy
   Was in my fowling-piece and filly,—
In short, while I was yet a boy,
   I fell in love with Laura Lily.

I saw her at the County Ball:
   There, when the sounds of flute and fiddle
Gave signal sweet in that old hall   11
   Of hands across and down the middle,
Hers was the subtlest spell by far
   Of all that set young hearts romancing;
She was our queen, our rose, our star;
   And then she danced—O Heaven, her dancing!

Dark was her hair, her hand was white;
   Her voice was exquisitely tender;
Her eyes were full of liquid light;
   I never saw a waist so slender!   20
Her every look, her every smile,
   Shot right and left a score of arrows;
I thought 'twas Venus from her isle,
   And wondered where she'd left her sparrows.

She talked,—of politics or prayers,—
   Of Southey's prose or Wordsworth's sonnets,—
Of danglers—or of dancing bears,
   Of battles—or the last new bonnets,
By candlelight, at twelve o'clock,
   To me it mattered not a tittle;   30
If those bright lips had quoted Locke,
   I might have thought they murmured Little.

Through sunny May, through sultry June,
   I loved her with a love eternal;
I spoke her praises to the moon,
   I wrote them to *The Sunday Journal:*

My mother laughed; I soon found out
 That ancient ladies have no feeling;
My father frowned; but how should gout
 See any happiness in kneeling?   40

She was the daughter of a Dean,
 Rich, fat, and rather apoplectic;
She had one brother, just thirteen,
 Whose color was extremely hectic;
Her grandmother for many a year
 Had fed the parish with her bounty;
Her second cousin was a peer,
 And Lord Lieutenant of the County.

But titles, and the three per cents,
 And mortgages, and great relations,   50
And India bonds, and tithes and rents,
 Oh, what are they to love's sensations?
Black eyes, fair forehead, clustering locks—
 Such wealth, such honors, Cupid chooses;
He cares as little for the Stocks,
 As Baron Rothschild for the Muses.

She sketched; the vale, the wood, the beach,
 Grew lovelier from her pencil's shading:
She botanized; I envied each
 Young blossom in her boudoir fading: 60
She warbled Handel; it was grand;
 She made the Catalani jealous:
She touched the organ; I could stand
 For hours and hours to blow the bellows.

She kept an album, too, at home,
 Well filled with all an album's glories;
Paintings of butterflies, and Rome,
 Patterns for trimmings, Persian stories;
Soft songs to Julia's cockatoo,
 Fierce odes to Famine and to Slaughter; 70
And autographs of Prince Leboo,
 And recipes for elder-water.

And she was flattered, worshipped, bored;
 Her steps were watched, her dress was
  noted,
Her poodle dog was quite adored,
 Her sayings were extremely quoted;
She laughed, and every heart was glad,
 As if the taxes were abolished;
She frowned, and every look was sad,
 As if the Opera were demolished.   80

She smiled on many, just for fun,—
 I knew that there was nothing in it;
I was the first—the only one
 Her heart had thought of for a minute.—
I knew it, for she told me so,
 In phrase which was divinely moulded;
She wrote a charming hand,—and oh!
 How sweetly all her notes were folded!

Our love was like most other loves;—
 A little glow, a little shiver,   90
A rose-bud, and a pair of gloves,
 And "Fly not yet"—upon the river;
Some jealousy of some one's heir,
 Some hopes of dying broken-hearted;
A miniature, a lock of hair,
 The usual vows,—and then we parted.

We parted; months and years rolled by;
 We met again four summers after:
Our parting was all sob and sigh;
 Our meeting was all mirth and laughter: 100
For in my heart's most secret cell
 There had been many other lodgers;
And she was not the ball-room's belle,
 But only—Mrs. Something Rogers!
1830

THE TALENTED MAN

A Letter from a Lady in London to a Lady at Lausanne.

DEAR Alice! you'll laugh when you know
  it,—
 Last week, at the Duchess's ball,
I danced with the clever new poet,—
 You've heard of him,—Tully St. Paul.
Miss Jonquil was perfectly frantic;
 I wish you had seen Lady Anne!
It really was very romantic,
 He is such a talented man!

He came up from Brazen Nose College,
 Just caught, as they call it, this spring;   10
And his head, love, is stuffed full of knowl-
  edge
 Of every conceivable thing.
Of science and logic he chatters,
 As fine and as fast as he can;
Though I am no judge of such matters,
 I'm sure he's a talented man.

His stories and jests are delightful;—
    Not stories or jests, dear, for you;
The jests are exceedingly spiteful,
    The stories not always quite true.   20
Perhaps to be kind and veracious
    May do pretty well at Lausanne;
But it never would answer,—good gracious!
    Chez nous—in a talented man.

He sneers,—how my Alice would scold
    him!—
    At the bliss of a sigh or a tear;
He laughed—only think!—when I told him
    How we cried o'er Trevelyan last year;
I vow I was quite in a passion;
    I broke all the sticks of my fan;   30
But sentiment's quite out of fashion,
    It seems, in a talented man.

Lady Bab, who is terribly moral,
    Has told me that Tully is vain,
And apt—which is silly—to quarrel,
    And fond—which is sad—of champagne.
I listened, and doubted, dear Alice,
    For I saw, when my Lady began,
It was only the Dowager's malice;—
    She does hate a talented man!   40

He's hideous, I own it. But fame, love,
    Is all that these eyes can adore;
He's lame,—but Lord Byron was lame, love,
    And dumpy,—but so is Tom Moore.
Then his voice,—such a voice! my sweet
    creature,
    It's like your Aunt Lucy's toucan:
But lo! what's a tone or a feature,
    When once one's a talented man?

My mother, you know, all the season,
    Has talked of Sir Geoffrey's estate;   50
And truly, to do the fool reason,
    He has been less horrid of late.
But to-day, when we drive in the carriage,
    I'll tell her to lay down her plan;—
If ever I venture on marriage,
    It must be a talented man!

P.S.—I have found, on reflection,
    One fault in my friend,—entre nous;
Without it, he'd just be perfection;—
    Poor fellow, he has not a soul!   60
And so, when he comes in September
    To shoot with my uncle, Sir Dan,

I've promised mamma to remember
    He's only a talented man!

1831

LATIN HYMN TO THE VIRGIN

I

Virgin Mother, thou hast known
Joy and sorrow like my own;
In thy arms the bright Babe lay,
As my own in mine to-day;
    So he wept and so he smiled;
    Ave Mary! guard my child!

II

From the pains and perils spread
Round about our path and bed,
Fierce desires, ambitious schemes,
Moody doubts, fantastic dreams,   10
    Pleasures idle, passions wild,
    Ave Mary! guard my child!

III

Make him whatsoe'er may be
Dearest to the saints and thee;
Tell him, from the throne above,
What to loathe and what to love;
    To be true and just and mild,
    Ave Mary! teach my child!

IV

By the wondrous mercy won
For the world by thy blest Son,   20
By the rest his labours wrought,
By the bliss his tortures bought,
    By the Heaven he reconciled,
    Ave Mary! bless my child!

V

If about his after fate
Sin and sorrow darkly wait,
Take him rather to thine arms
From the world and the world's harms;
    Thus unscathed, thus undefiled,
    Ave Mary! take my child!   30

? 1834–1835

THE NEWLY-WEDDED

I

Now the rite is duly done;
    Now the word is spoken;
And the spell has made us one
    Which may ne'er be broken:

Rest we, dearest, in our home,—
  Roam we o'er the heather,—
We shall rest, and we shall roam,
  Shall we not? together.

II

From this hour the summer rose
  Sweeter breathes to charm us;   10
From this hour the winter snows
  Lighter fall to harm us:
Fair or foul—on land or sea—
  Come the wind or weather,

Best and worst, whate'er they be,
  We shall share together.

III

Death, who friend from friend can part,
  Brother rend from brother,
Shall but link us, heart and heart,
  Closer to each other: 20
We will call his anger play,
  Deem his dart a feather,
When we meet him on our way
  Hand in hand together.

1835

SAMUEL ROGERS
[July 30, 1763–December 18, 1855]

SAMUEL ROGERS in his own day was a person of importance, though little of his work now has vitality. As a young man he scored a poetic success with his *The Pleasures of Memory* (1792) and, soon after, he inherited his father's substantial banking interests, two events which established him as a man of letters and a man of the world.

His means he employed in gathering about him in his bachelor establishment an art collection of excellent taste and rarity. To his art objects he added an excellent cook, his own gift for playing host, and his wit, so that an invitation to one of Rogers's famous breakfasts or dinners was desired by all and a compliment to any man, no matter how great he was. It was Rogers who brought Byron and Moore together at dinner to reconcile a quarrel and begin a fast friendship. And as host and wit he now chiefly lives.

Rogers's sharp wit has been often spoken of because it *was* sharp. Washington Irving once wrote that he had dined with Rogers who "served up his friends as he served up his fish, with a squeeze of lemon over each. It was very piquant, but it rather set my teeth on edge." But Rogers's sharp wit in public was balanced by his generosity in private for, without saying anything about it, he was almost as ready to help a poor poet quietly as to make a stinging comment where every one could hear it.

His poem *The Pleasures of Memory* offended no conventional critic of his day, but belonged to a dying school of poetry. It deserved its success in its own time and it deserved its fate, which was oblivion in later days. Nor was *Italy* (of which the first part was published in 1822 and of which revisions and extensions were made later until the first complete edition came out in 1834) deserving of more success, save in rare parts. These two poems are Rogers's challenges to immortality, and they have failed. He was a gentleman of conventional taste and talent, but in him was a consciousness of the new wind, and no less a person than Byron was pleased to find a long poem of his own published in the same volume with Rogers's *Jacqueline*.

POEMS

BY

SAMUEL ROGERS.

LONDON:

PRINTED FOR T. CADELL, STRAND; AND E. MOXON,
DOVER-STREET.

1834.

To Mrs Shelley

from her very sincere Friend

The Author.

Presentation Copy from Samuel Rogers to Mrs. Shelley. (See Appendix I.)

A WISH

MINE be a cot beside the hill,
A bee-hive's hum shall soothe my ear;
A willowy brook, that turns a mill,
With many a fall shall linger near.

The swallow, oft, beneath my thatch,
Shall twitter from her clay-built nest;
Oft shall the pilgrim lift the latch,
And share my meal, a welcome guest.

Around my ivy'd porch shall spring
Each fragrant flower that drinks the dew;   10
And Lucy, at her wheel, shall sing
In russet gown and apron blue.

The village-church, among the trees,
Where first our marriage-vows were given,
With many peals shall swell the breeze,
And point with taper spire to heaven.

1786

SIR WALTER SCOTT
[August 15, 1771–September 21, 1832]

SIR WALTER SCOTT was born at Edinburgh in 1771 of parents who were gentlefolk. As he was a sickly infant, he was sent to his grandfather's farmhouse at Sandyknowe, where his earlier childhood was spent near the crags of a ruined baronial tower in a district famous in border history. He was returned to Edinburgh and after attending the High School there (1778–1783) he studied at the University of Edinburgh for a time, entering in 1783. His success as a scholar was not conspicuous at either place, and, after he had written an essay maintaining Ariosto was a greater poet than Homer, an exasperated University teacher was moved to exclaim that "dunce he was and dunce he would remain." Scott, however, from his childhood on had filled his dunce's head with a great deal of miscellaneous reading in the histories, voyages, travels, romances, and fairy tales which delighted him.

His health being fully recovered, and his father wishing him to study law, Scott began his studies, first as his father's apprentice and later at the University, and was called to the bar in 1792. Soon after, he made the first of his series of "raids" into the secluded districts where he began picking up the materials which later went into his *Minstrelsy of the Scottish Border* (1802–3). To all appearances he was one among many promising young lawyers, although in 1796 he had published his translations of Bürger and in 1799 he had written several ballads which he himself called his "first serious attempts at verse." The appearance of the *Minstrelsy* won him immediate recognition in literary circles. He followed it up with an edition of the old poem of *Sir Tristrem* (1804) and in 1805 published *The Lay of the Last Minstrel* which he had been working on for several years. Its popular success was immense.

It behooved the young lawyer to reconsider his career. Scott himself in a preface to a later (1830) edition of *The Lay* summed up his attitude toward law by quoting Slender's speech on Mistress Anne Page: "There was no great love between us at the beginning, and it pleased Heaven to decrease it on further acquaintance." Scott at the same time took two resolutions. The first was that he would not be dependent upon literature for his ordinary expenses and, accordingly, he applied for, and obtained in 1806, a principal clerkship in the Scottish Court of Session. He had in 1799 been appointed Sheriff-depute of Selkirkshire. These two offices, exacting very little work, assured him a respectable income. Scott's second resolution was to mingle in general society, not literary society alone, and thereby avoid the bickerings and jealousies of the lower slopes of Parnassus.

The Lay of the Last Minstrel was but the beginning. There followed *Marmion* (1808),

The Lady of the Lake (1810), *Rokeby* (1813), and *The Lord of the Isles* (1815), to mention only his chief productions. The copyright of *Rokeby* brought the highest price ever paid for an English poem up to that time. But, although Scott's rise had been brilliant, a decline in popular favor began to be apparent in 1813–14.

Years before Scott had begun a novel and cast it aside. He now picked it up and, finishing it with surprising rapidity, published it anonymously in the summer of 1814. The novel was *Waverley*, and its success was as instantaneous and dramatic as had been that of *The Lay of the Last Minstrel*. Only Scott in the history of English letters has won the glory of immediate success in two fields of literature. The reason for the anonymous publication of *Waverley* has never been fully explained. It was "his humour," Scott said afterwards. And probably there was a wish that his prose should find its own place, not be bracketed with his poetry. It was not until 1827 that Scott publicly acknowledged his novels, although the secret had become an open one before this.

Meanwhile, however, novels "by the author of *Waverley*" continued to pour from the presses. Years before, on the appearance of the *Minstrelsy*, an inspired critic had declared that the book contained "the elements of an hundred historical romances," and upon this great storehouse, and upon other stores of knowledge, Scott began to draw. His output was prodigious. If one will consider a Scott novel and imagine the mere physical effort, quite aside from the creative, necessary to put the required number of words on paper with a quill pen, and then consider that Scott's output was nearly two novels a year over a considerable period, one may judge of the scale, at least of his effort, if not of its quality. The novels, however, belong to the history of prose.

In 1811 Scott had bought a small farm of a hundred acres which he named Abbotsford. The original plans called for a modest manor house with two spare bedrooms but, as Scott's means expanded, his dreams expanded, and in the end Abbotsford was a baronial castle set in a large estate. It was a folly, but it was a folly in keeping with the fascination feudal days exercised over Scott's imagination, and with the scale of that imagination.

And at Abbotsford we see Scott at his greatest. His refusal, long before, to confine himself to merely literary society or to become involved in its bickerings bore its final fruit, and at Abbotsford he lived as genial host and a great gentleman, without enemies and without pettiness. So fine a man does he appear, that his greatness as a writer seems almost incidental to his greatness as a man.

To maintain the estate, however, required a great income, and Scott had become involved as a silent partner in the printing and publishing houses of the Ballantynes in Edinburgh. The Ballantynes failed early in 1826 and Scott, through no fault of his own, found himself not only ruined but, as a partner, heaped with debt. He refused the ordinary procedure of the bankruptcy court and, assuming his share of the debt, he set to work, haggard and driven, to pay it with his pen. It is said that in two years (1826–28) he realized £40,000 for the creditors. In the end the work killed him. Early in 1830 he suffered a paralytic shock, but he continued working for another year, when renewed attacks made further labor impossible. He died in 1832, and his executors paid the last of the debt a few years after his death.

The geniality and courage of Scott the gentleman have made posterity reluctant to pass final judgement on his longer and more pretentious poems. It seems such a pity they should be what time has inexorably shown them to be—rather second-rate. They are healthy and honest in spirit; anything the good Sir Walter did would be so. Because they deal with glamorous times and places there is a pseudo-glamor about them. There is a swing to the verse, and there is undeniably in them the instinct of Scott the great story-teller. But of that final magic which constitutes poetic significance they are lacking, just as the particular group of Byron poems which eclipsed them (*The Bride of Abydos, The Corsair*, etc.) were lacking. Byron's narratives of that period have gone to oblivion. Scott's narratives have made a harder struggle for life because Scott was the better story-teller. Byron could write to Scott in 1822, "of whom could you be jealous?—of none of the living certainly, and (taking all in all into consideration) of which of the dead?" Posterity has reversed the verdict, and now, so far as the longer poems are concerned, there is no living poet so poor as to be jealous of Scott, save possibly of fragments of *The Lady of the Lake*.

Scattered through the longer narratives, however, scattered through the novels, and scatteringly published elsewhere are shorter pieces, usually akin to the ballad in spirit, which are totally different in their poetic vitality. Homely and simple and vigorous, they have in them the vitality of that folklore which so delighted Scott, and Scott's own vigor and swing of expression. Upon such songs and ballads Scott's reputation as a poet must rest in the end, it seems.

From THE LAY OF THE LAST MINSTREL

(1802–1804. Pub. 1805)

SWEET TEVIOT

(Canto IV, i, ii)

SWEET Teviot! on thy silver tide
  The glaring bale-fires blaze no more;
No longer steel-clad warriors ride
  Along thy wild and willow'd shore;
Where'er thou wind'st, by dale or hill,
All, all is peaceful, all is still,
  As if thy waves, since Time was born,
Since first they roll'd upon the Tweed,
Had only heard the shepherd's reed,
  Nor started at the bugle-horn.   10

Unlike the tide of human time,
  Which, though it change in ceaseless flow,
Retains each grief, retains each crime,
  Its earliest course was doom'd to know;
And, darker as it downward bears,
Is stain'd with past and present tears.
  Low as that tide has ebb'd with me,
It still reflects to Memory's eye
The hour my brave, my only boy,
  Fell by the side of great Dundee.   20
Why, when the volleying musket play'd
Against the bloody Highland blade,
Why was not I beside him laid!—
Enough—he died the death of fame;
Enough—he died with conquering Græme.

BREATHES THERE THE MAN

(Canto VI)

I

BREATHES there the man, with soul so dead,
Who never to himself hath said,
  This is my own, my native land!
Whose heart hath ne'er within him burn'd,
As home his footsteps he hath turn'd,
  From wandering on a foreign strand!
If such there breathe, go, mark him well;
For him no Minstrel raptures swell;
High though his titles, proud his name,
Boundless his wealth as wish can claim;   10
Despite those titles, power, and pelf,
The wretch, concentred all in self,
Living, shall forfeit fair renown,
And, doubly dying, shall go down
To the vile dust, from whence he sprung,
Unwept, unhonour'd, and unsung.

II

O Caledonia! stern and wild,
Meet nurse for a poetic child!
Land of brown heath and shaggy wood,
Land of the mountain and the flood,   20
Land of my sires! what mortal hand
Can e'er untie the filial band,
That knits me to thy rugged strand!
Still, as I view each well-known scene,
Think what is now, and what hath been,
Seems as, to me, of all bereft,
Sole friends thy woods and streams were
  left

And thus I love them better still,
Even in extremity of ill.
By Yarrow's streams still let me stray,   30
Though none should guide my feeble way;
Still feel the breeze down Ettrick break,
Although it chill my wither'd cheek;
Still lay my head by Teviot Stone,
Though there, forgotten and alone,
The Bard may draw his parting groan.

SONG OF ALBERT GRÆME

(Canto VI, xi, xii)

It was an English ladye bright,
  (The sun shines fair on Carlisle wall,)
And she would marry a Scottish knight,
  For Love will still be lord of all.

Blithely they saw the rising sun,
  When he shone fair on Carlisle wall;
But they were sad ere day was done,
  Though Love was still the lord of all.

Her sire gave brooch and jewel fine,
  Where the sun shines fair on Carlisle wall;
Her brother gave but a flask of wine,   11
  For ire that Love was lord of all.

For she had lands, both meadow and lea,
  Where the sun shines fair on Carlisle wall,
And he swore her death, ere he would see
  A Scottish knight the lord of all!

That wine she had not tasted well,
  (The sun shines fair on Carlisle wall,)
When dead, in her true love's arms, she fell,
  For Love was still the lord of all!   20

He pierced her brother to the heart,
  Where the sun shines fair on Carlisle wall:—
So perish all would true love part,
  That Love may still be lord of all!

And then he took the cross divine,
  (Where the sun shines fair on Carlisle wall,)
And died for her sake in Palestine,
  So Love was still the lord of all.

Now all ye lovers, that faithful prove,
  (The sun shines fair on Carlisle wall,)   30
Pray for their souls who died for love,
  For Love shall still be lord of all!

HAROLD'S SONG

(Canto VI, xxiii)

O listen, listen, ladies gay!
  No haughty feat of arms I tell;
Soft is the note, and sad the lay,
  That mourns the lovely Rosabelle.

—"Moor, moor the barge, ye gallant crew!
  And, gentle ladye, deign to stay!
Rest thee in Castle Ravensheuch,
  Nor tempt the stormy firth to-day.

"The blackening wave is edg'd with white:
  To inch and rock the sea-mews fly;   10
The fishers have heard the Water-Sprite,
  Whose screams forebode that wreck is nigh.

"Last night the gifted Seer did view
  A wet shroud swathed round ladye gay;
Then stay thee, Fair, in Ravensheuch:
  Why cross the gloomy firth to-day?"

"'Tis not because Lord Lindesay's heir
  To-night at Roslin leads the ball,
But that my ladye-mother there
  Sits lonely in her castle-hall.   20

"'Tis not because the ring they ride,
  And Lindesay at the ring rides well,
But that my sire the wine will chide,
  If 'tis not fill'd by Rosabelle."

O'er Roslin all that dreary night
  A wondrous blaze was seen to gleam;
'Twas broader than the watch-fire's light,
  And redder than the bright moon-beam.

It glar'd on Roslin's castled rock,
  It ruddied all the copse-wood glen;   30
'Twas seen from Dryden's groves of oak,
  And seen from cavern'd Hawthornden.

Seem'd all on fire that chapel proud,
  Where Roslin's chiefs uncoffin'd lie,
Each Baron, for a sable shroud,
  Sheath'd in his iron panoply.

Seem'd all on fire within, around,
  Deep sacristy and altar's pale;
Shone every pillar foliage-bound,
  And glimmer'd all the dead men's mail.   40

Blaz'd battlement and pinnet high,
  Blaz'd every rose-carved buttress fair—
So still they blaze when fate is nigh
  The lordly line of high St. Clair.

There are twenty of Roslin's barons bold
  Lie buried within that proud chapelle;
Each one the holy vault doth hold—
  But the sea holds lovely Rosabelle!

And each St. Clair was buried there,
  With candle, with book, and with knell; 50
But the sea-caves rung, and the wild winds
    sung,
  The dirge of lovely Rosabelle.

From MARMION

(1806–1807. Pub. 1808)

THE SHEPHERD

(Introduction to Canto IV)

When red hath set the beamless sun,
Through heavy vapours dark and dun;
When the tired ploughman, dry and warm,
Hears, half asleep, the rising storm
Hurling the hail, and sleeted rain,
Against the casement's tinkling pane;
The sounds that drive wild deer, and fox, 60
To shelter in the brake and rocks,
Are warnings which the shepherd ask
To dismal and to dangerous task.
Oft he looks forth, and hopes, in vain,
The blast may sink in mellowing rain;
Till, dark above, and white below,
Decided drives the flaky snow,
And forth the hardy swain must go.
Long, with dejected look and whine,
To leave the hearth his dogs repine; 70
Whistling and cheering them to aid,
Around his back he wreathes the plaid:
His flock he gathers, and he guides,
To open downs, and mountain sides,
Where fiercest though the tempest blow,
Least deeply lies the drift below.
The blast, that whistles o'er the fells,
Stiffens his locks to icicles;
Oft he looks back, while streaming far,
His cottage window seems a star,— 80
Loses its feeble gleam,—and then
Turns patient to the blast again,

And, facing to the tempest's sweep,
Drives through the gloom his lagging sheep.
If fails his heart, if his limbs fail,
Benumbing death is in the gale:
His paths, his landmarks, all unknown,
Close to the hut, no more his own,
Close to the aid he sought in vain,
The morn may find the stiffened swain: 90
The widow sees, at dawning pale,
His orphans raise their feeble wail;
And, close beside him, in the snow,
Poor Yarrow, partner of their wo,
Crouches upon his master's breast,
And licks his cheek, to break his rest.

  Who envies now the shepherd's lot,
His healthy fare, his rural cot,
His summer couch by greenwood tree,
His rustic kirn's loud revelry, 100
His native hill-notes, tuned on high,
To Marion of the blithesome eye;
His crook, his scrip, his oaten reed,
And all Arcadia's golden creed?

LOCHINVAR

(Canto V, xii)

O, YOUNG Lochinvar is come out of the west,
Through all the wide border his steed was the
    best;
And save his good broadsword, he weapons
    had none,
He rode all unarmed, and he rode all alone.
So faithful in love, and so dauntless in war,
There never was knight like the young Loch-
    invar.

He staid not for brake, and he stopped not
    for stone,
He swam the Eske river where ford there was
    none;
But, ere he alighted at Netherby gate,
The bride had consented, the gallant came
    late: 10
For a laggard in love, and a dastard in war,
Was to wed the fair Ellen of brave Lochinvar.

So boldly he entered the Netherby hall,
Among bride's-men, and kinsmen, and broth-
    ers, and all:
Then spoke the bride's father, his hand on his
    sword,

(For the poor craven bridegroom said never a word,)
"O come ye in peace here, or come ye in war,
Or to dance at our bridal, young Lord Lochinvar?"

"I long woo'd your daughter, my suit you denied;
Love swells like the Solway, but ebbs like its tide;   20
And now am I come, with this lost love of mine,
To lead but one measure, drink one cup of wine.
There are maidens in Scotland, more lovely by far,
That would gladly be bride to the young Lochinvar."

The bride kissed the goblet; the knight took it up,
He quaffed off the wine, and he threw down the cup.
She looked down to blush, and she looked up to sigh,
With a smile on her lips, and a tear in her eye.
He took her soft hand, ere her mother could bar,—
"Now tread we a measure!" said young Lochinvar.   30

So stately his form, and so lovely her face,
That never a hall such a galliard did grace:
While her mother did fret, and her father did fume,
And the bridegroom stood dangling his bonnet and plume;
And the bride-maidens whispered, "'Twere better by far
To have matched our fair cousin with young Lochinvar."

One touch to her hand, and one word in her ear,
When they reached the hall-door, and the charger stood near;
So light to the croupe the fair lady he swung,
So light to the saddle before her he sprung!   40
"She is won! we are gone, over bank, bush, and scaur;
They'll have fleet steeds that follow," quoth young Lochinvar.

There was mounting 'mong Græmes of the Netherby clan;
Forsters, Fenwicks, and Musgraves, they rode and they ran:
There was racing and chasing, on Cannobie Lee,
But the lost bride of Netherby ne'er did they see.
So daring in love, and so dauntless in war,
Have ye e'er heard of gallant like young Lochinvar?

CHRISTMAS

(Introduction to Canto VI)

And well our Christian sires of old
Loved when the year its course had rolled,
And brought blithe Christmas back again,
With all his hospitable train.
Domestic and religious rite
Gave honour to the holy night;
On Christmas eve the bells were rung;   30
On Christmas eve the mass was sung:
That only night, in all the year,
Saw the stoled priest the chalice rear.
The damsel donned her kirtle sheen;
The hall was dressed with holy green;
Forth to the wood did merry-men go,
To gather in the mistletoe.
Then opened wide the baron's hall
To vassal, tenant, serf, and all;
Power laid his rod of rule aside,   40
And ceremony doffed his pride.
The heir, with roses in his shoes,
That night might village partner choose;
The lord, underogating, share
The vulgar game of "post and pair."
All hailed, with uncontrolled delight,
And general voice, the happy night,
That to the cottage, as the crown,
Brought tidings of salvation down.

The fire, with well-dried logs supplied,   50
Went roaring up the chimney wide;
The huge hall-table's oaken face,
Scrubbed till it shone, the day to grace,
Bore then upon its massive board
No mark to part the squire and lord.
Then was brought in the lusty brawn,
By old blue-coated serving-man;
Then the grim boar's-head frowned on high,
Crested with bays and rosemary.

Well can the green-garbed ranger tell, 60
How, when, and where, the monster fell;
What dogs before his death he tore,
And all the baiting of the boar.
The wassel round, in good brown bowls,
Garnished with ribbons, blithely trowls.
There the huge sirloin reeked; hard by
Plum-porridge stood, and Christmas pie;
Nor failed old Scotland to produce,
At such high-tide, her savoury goose.
Then came the merry maskers in, 70
And carols roared with blithesome din;
If unmelodious was the song,
It was a hearty note, and strong.
Who lists may in their mumming see
Traces of ancient mystery;
White shirts supplied the masquerade,
And smutted cheeks the visors made;
But, O! what maskers, richly dight,
Can boast of bosoms half so light!
England was merry England, when 80
Old Christmas brought his sports again.
'Twas Christmas broached the mightiest ale;
'Twas Christmas told the merriest tale;
A Christmas gambol oft could cheer
The poor man's heart through half the year.

Still linger, in our northern clime,
Some remnants of the good old time;
And still, within our valleys here,
We hold the kindred title dear,
Even when, perchance, its far-fetched claim 90
To southern ear sounds empty name;
For course of blood, our proverbs deem,
Is warmer than the mountain-stream.
And thus, my Christmas still I hold,
Where my great-grandsire came of old,
With amber beard, and flaxen hair,
And reverend, apostolic air—
The feast and holy-tide to share,
And mix sobriety with wine,
And honest mirth with thoughts divine. 100

THE BATTLE[1]

(Canto VI)

XXI

Ere yet the bands met Marmion's eye,
Fitz-Eustace shouted loud and high,—

[1] Marmion, a brave warrior but evil in his deeds and a treacherous friend, is riding with his troop to

"Hark! hark! my lord, an English drum!
And see, ascending squadrons come
    Between Tweed's river and the hill,
Foot, horse, and cannon:—hap what hap,
My basnet to a 'prentice cap,
    Lord Surrey's o'er the Till!—
Yet more! yet more! how far arrayed
They file from out the hawthorn shade, 630
    And sweep so gallant by!
With all their banners bravely spread,
    And all their armour flashing high,
Saint George might waken from the dead,
    To see fair England's standards fly."—
"Stint in thy prate," quoth Blount, "thou'dst best,
And listen to our lord's behest."—
With kindling brow Lord Marmion said—
"This instant be our band arrayed;
The river must be quickly crossed, 640
That we may join Lord Surrey's host.
If fight King James,—as well I trust,
That fight he will, and fight he must,—
The Lady Clare behind our lines
Shall tarry, while the battle joins."

XXII

Himself he swift on horseback threw,
Scarce to the Abbot bade adieu;
Far less would listen to his prayer,
To leave behind the helpless Clare,
Down to the Tweed his band he drew, 650
And muttered, as the flood they view,
"The pheasant in the falcon's claw,
He scarce will yield to please a daw:
Lord Angus may the Abbot awe,
    So Clare shall bide with me."
Then on that dangerous ford, and deep,
Where to the Tweed Leat's eddies creep
    He ventured desperately:
And not a moment will he bide,
Till squire, or groom, before him ride; 660
Headmost of all he stems the tide,
    And stems it gallantly.
Eustace held Clare upon her horse,
    Old Hubert led her rein,
Stoutly they braved the current's course,
And, though far downward driven per force,
    The southern bank they gain;

join the English army before the battle of Flodden Field. Clare, whom circumstances have put in his company, loves another man and fears Marmion.

Behind them, straggling, came to shore,
　　As best they might, the train:
Each o'er his head his yew-bow bore,　　670
　　A caution not in vain;
Deep need that day that every string,
By wet unharmed should sharply ring.
A moment then Lord Marmion staid,
And breathed his steed, his men arrayed,
　　Then forward moved his band,
Until, Lord Surrey's rear-guard won,
He halted by a cross of stone,
That, on a hillock standing lone,
　　Did all the field command.　　680

XXIII

Hence might they see the full array
Of either host, for deadly fray;
Their marshalled lines stretched east and west,
　　And fronted north and south,
And distant salutation pass'd
　　From the loud cannon mouth;
Not in the close successive rattle,
That breathes the voice of modern battle,
　　But slow and far between.—
The hillock gained, Lord Marmion staid:　　690
"Here, by this cross," he gently said,
　　"You well may view the scene.
Here shalt thou tarry, lovely Clare:
O! think of Marmion in thy prayer!—
Thou wilt not?—well,—no less my care
Shall, watchful, for thy weal prepare.—
You, Blount and Eustace, are her guard,
　　With ten picked archers of my train;
With England if the day go hard,
　　To Berwick speed amain.—　　700
But, if we conquer, cruel maid,
My spoils shall at your feet be laid,
　　When here we meet again."
He waited not for answer there,
And would not mark the maid's despair,
　　Nor heed the discontented look
From either squire; but spurred amain,
And, dashing through the battle plain,
　　His way to Surrey took.

XXIV

"The good Lord Marmion, by my life!
　　Welcome to danger's hour!—　　711
Short greeting serves in time of strife:—
　　Thus have I ranged my power:

Myself will rule this central host,
　　Stout Stanley fronts their right,
My sons command the vaward post,
　　With Brian Tunstall, stainless knight;
Lord Dacre, with his horsemen light,
Shall be in rearward of the fight,
And succour those that need it most.　　720
　　Now, gallant Marmion, well I know,
Would gladly to the vanguard go;
Edmund, the admiral, Tunstall there,
With thee their charge will blithely share;
There fight thine own retainers too,
Beneath De Burgh, thy steward true."—
"Thanks, noble Surrey!" Marmion said,
Nor farther greeting there he paid;
But, parting like a thunderbolt,
First in the vanguard made a halt,　　730
　　Where such a shout there rose
Of "Marmion! Marmion!" that the cry,
Up Flodden mountain shrilling high,
　　Startled the Scottish foes.

XXV

Blount and Fitz-Eustace rested still
With lady Clare upon the hill;
On which (for far the day was spent)
The western sunbeams now were bent;
The cry they heard, its meaning knew,
Could plain their distant comrades view;　　740
Sadly to Blount did Eustace say,
"Unworthy office here to stay!
No hope of gilded spurs to-day.—
But see! look up—on Flodden bent,
The Scottish foe has fired his tent."
　　And sudden, as he spoke,
From the sharp ridges of the hill,
All downward to the banks of Till,
　　Was wreathed in sable smoke.
Volumed and fast, and rolling far,　　750
The cloud enveloped Scotland's war,
　　As down the hill they broke;
Nor martial shout, nor minstrel tone,
Announced their march; their tread alone,
At times one warning trumpet blown,
　　At times a stifled hum
Told England, from his mountain throne,
　　King James did rushing come.—
Scarce could they hear, or see their foes,
Until at weapon-point they close.—　　760
They close, in clouds of smoke and dust,
With sword-sway, and with lance's thrust;

And such a yell was there,
Of sudden and portentous birth,
As if men fought upon the earth,
　And fiends in upper air;
O life and death were in the shout,
Recoil and rally, charge and rout,
　And triumph and despair.
Long looked the anxious squires; their eye 770
Could in the darkness naught descry.

XXVI

At length the freshening western blast
Aside the shroud of battle cast;
And, first, the ridge of mingled spears
Above the brightening cloud appears;
And in the smoke the pennons flew,
As in the storm the white sea-mew.
Then marked they, dashing broad and far
The broken billows of the war,
And plumed crest of chieftains brave, 780
Floating like foam upon the wave;
　But naught distinct they see:
Wide raged the battle on the plain;
Spears shook, and falchions flashed amain;
Fell England's arrow-flight like rain;
Crests rose, and stooped, and rose again,
　Wild and disorderly.
Amid the scene of tumult, high
They saw Lord Marmion's falcon fly:
And stainless Tunstall's banner white, 790
And Edmund Howard's lion bright,
Still bear them bravely in the fight;
　Although against them come,
Of gallant Gordons many a one,
And many a stubborn Badenoch-man,
And many a rugged border clan,
　With Huntley, and with Home.

XXVII

Far on the left, unseen the while,
Stanley broke Lennox and Argyle;
Though there the western mountaineer 800
Rushed with bare bosom on the spear,
And flung the feeble targe aside,
And with both hands the broadsword plied.
'Twas vain:—But fortune, on the right,
With fickle smile, cheered Scotland's fight.
Then fell that spotless banner white,
　The Howard's lion fell;
Yet still Lord Marmion's falcon flew
With wavering flight, while fiercer grew

Around the battle yell. 810
The border slogan rent the sky!
A Home! a Gordon! was the cry;
　Loud were the clanging blows;
Advanced,—forced back,—now low, now high
　The pennon sunk and rose;
As bends the bark's mast in the gale,
When rent are rigging, shrouds, and sail,
　It wavered 'mid the foes.
No longer Blount the view could bear:
"By heaven, and all its saints! I swear, 820
　I will not see it lost!
Fitz-Eustace, you with lady Clare
May bid your beads, and patter prayer,—
　I gallop to the host."
And to the fray he rode amain,
Followed by all the archer train.
The fiery youth, with desperate charge,
Made, for a space, an opening large,—
　The rescued banner rose,—
But darkly closed the war around, 830
Like pine-tree, rooted from the ground,
　It sunk among the foes.
Then Eustace mounted too:—yet staid,
As loath to leave the helpless maid,
　When, fast as shaft can fly,
Blood-shot his eyes, his nostrils spread,
The loose rein dangling from his head,
Housing and saddle bloody red,
　Lord Marmion's steed rushed by;
And Eustace, maddening at the sight, 840
　A look and sign to Clara cast,
　To mark he would return in haste,
Then plunged into the fight.

XXVIII

Ask me not what the maiden feels,
　Left in that dreadful hour alone:
Perchance her reason stoops, or reels;
　Perchance a courage, not her own,
　Braces her mind to desperate tone.—
The scattered van of England wheels;—
　She only said, as loud in air 850
　The tumult roared, "Is Wilton there?"—
They fly, or, maddened by despair,
　Fight but to die,—"Is Wilton there?"
With that, straight up the hill there rode,
　Two horsemen drenched with gore,
And in their arms, a helpless load,
　A wounded knight they bore.

His hand still strained the broken brand;
His arms were smeared with blood and sand:
Dragged from among the horses' feet,   860
With dinted shield, and helmet beat,
The falcon crest and plumage gone,
Can that be haughty Marmion! . . .
Young Blount his armour did unlace,
And, gazing on his ghastly face,
    Said—"By Saint George, he's gone!
That spear-wound has our master sped,
And see the deep cut on his head!
    Good night to Marmion."—
"Unnurtured Blount! thy brawling cease: 870
He opes his eyes," said Eustace; "peace!"

XXIX

When, doffed his casque, he felt free air,
Around 'gan Marmion wildly stare:—
"Where's Harry Blount? Fitz-Eustace where?
Linger ye here, ye hearts of hare!
Redeem my pennon,—charge again!
Cry—'Marmion to the rescue!'—Vain!
Last of my race, on battle-plain
That shout shall ne'er be heard again!—
    Yet my last thought is England's—fly, 880
To Dacre bear my signet-ring—
Tell him his squadrons up to bring.
    Fitz-Eustace, to Lord Surrey hie;
Tunstall lies dead upon the field,
His life-blood stains the spotless shield:
Edmund is down:—my life is reft;—
The Admiral alone is left.
Let Stanley charge with spur of fire,—
With Chester charge, and Lancashire,
Full upon Scotland's central host,   890
Or victory and England's lost.—
Must I bid twice?—hence, varlets, fly!
Leave Marmion here alone—to die."
They parted, and alone he lay;
Clare drew her from the sight away,
Till pain wrung forth a lowly moan,
And half he murmured,—"Is there none,
    Of all my halls have nurst,
Page, squire, or groom, one cup to bring
Of blessed water from the spring;   900
    To slake my dying thirst!"

XXX

O, woman! in our hours of ease,
Uncertain, coy, and hard to please,
And variable as the shade
By the light quivering aspen made;
When pain and anguish wring the brow,
A ministering angel thou!—
Scarce were the piteous accents said,
When, with the Baron's casque, the maid
    To the nigh streamlet ran: 910
Forgot were hatred, wrongs, and fears;
The plaintive voice alone she hears,
    Sees but the dying man.
She stooped her by the runnel's side,
    But in abhorrence backward drew;
For, oozing from the mountain's side,
Where raged the war, a dark-red tide
    Was curdling in the streamlet blue.
Where shall she turn!—behold her mark
    A little fountain cell,   920
Where water, clear as diamond-spark,
    In a stone basin fell.
Above, some half-worn letters say,
Drink, weary pilgrim, drink and pray
For the kind soul of Sybil Grey,
    Who built this cross and well.
She filled the helm, and back she hied,
And with surprise and joy espied
    A Monk supporting Marmion's head;
A pious man, whom duty brought   930
To dubious verge of battle fought,
    To shrive the dying, bless the dead.

XXXI

Deep drank Lord Marmion of the wave,
And, as she stooped his brow to lave—
"Is it the hand of Clare," he said,
"Or injured Constance, bathes my head?"
    Then, as remembrance rose,—
"Speak not to me of shrift or prayer!
    I must redress her woes.
Short space, few words are mine to spare; 940
Forgive and listen, gentle Clare!"—
    "Alas!" she said, "the while,—
O, think of your immortal weal!
In vain for Constance is your zeal;
    She——died at Holy Isle."
Lord Marmion started from the ground,
As light as if he felt no wound;
Though in the action burst the tide,
In torrents, from his wounded side.
"Then it was truth,"—he said—"I knew 950
That the dark presage must be true.—
    I would the fiend, to whom belongs

The vengeance due to all her wrongs,
　　Would spare me but a day!
For wasting fire, and dying groan,
And priest slain on the altar stone,
　　Might bribe him for delay.
It may not be!—this dizzy trance—
Curse on yon base marauder's lance,
And doubly cursed my failing brand！　　960
A sinful heart makes feeble hand."
Then, fainting, down on earth he sunk,
Supported by the trembling Monk.

XXXII

With fruitless labour, Clara bound,
And strove to stanch the gushing wound:
The Monk, with unavailing cares,
Exhausted all the church's prayers.
Ever, he said, that, close and near,
A lady's voice was in his ear,
And that the priest he could not hear；　　970
　　For that she ever sung,
"In the lost battle, borne down by the flying,
Where mingles war's rattle with groans of the
　　dying!"
　　So the notes rung;—
"Avoid thee, fiend!—with cruel hand,
Shake not the dying sinner's sand!
O, look, my son, upon yon sign
Of the Redeemer's grace divine;
　　O, think on faith and bliss!—
By many a death-bed I have been,　　980
And many a sinner's parting seen,
　　But never aught like this."—
The war, that for a space did fail,
Now trebly thundering swelled the gale.
　　And—Stanley! was the cry;—
A light on Marmion's visage spread,
　　And fired his glazing eye:
With dying hand, above his head,
He shook the fragment of his blade,
　　And shouted "Victory!—　　990
Charge, Chester, charge! On, Stanley, on!"
Were the last words of Marmion.

XXXIII

By this, though deep the evening fell,
Still rose the battle's deadly swell,
For still the Scots, around their king,
Unbroken, fought in desperate ring.
Where's now their victor vaward wing,

Where Huntly, and where Home?—
O, for a blast of that dread horn,
On Fontarabian echoes borne,　　1000
　　That to king Charles did come,
When Rowland brave, and Olivier,
And every paladin and peer,
　　On Roncesvalles died!
Such blast might warn them, not in vain,
To quit the plunder of the slain,
And turn the doubtful day again,
　　While yet on Flodden side,
Afar, the royal standard flies,
And round it toils, and bleeds, and dies,　1010
　　Our Caledonian pride!
In vain the wish—for, far away,
While spoil and havoc mark their way,
Near Sybil's cross the plunderers stray.—
"O, Lady," cried the Monk, "away!"
　　And placed her on her steed,
And led her to the chapel fair,
　　Of Tilmouth upon Tweed.
There all the night they spent in prayer,
And at the dawn of morning, there　　1020
She met her kinsman, Lord Fitz-Clare.

* * *

XXXVII

Less easy task it were, to show
Lord Marmion's nameless grave, and low. 1120
　　They dug his grave e'en where he lay,
　　　　But every mark is gone;
　　Time's wasting hand has done away
　　The simple cross of Sybil Grey,
　　　　And broke her font of stone:
But yet from out the little hill
Oozes the slender springlet still.
　　Oft halts the stranger there,
For thence may best his curious eye
The memorable field descry;　　1130
　　And shepherd boys repair
To seek the water-flag and rush,
And rest them by the hazel bush,
　　And plait their garlands fair;
Nor dream they sit upon the grave,
That holds the bones of Marmion brave.—
When thou shalt find the little hill,
With thy heart commune, and be still.
If ever, in temptation strong,
Thou left'st the right path for the wrong；1140
If every devious step thus trod,
Still led thee farther from the road;

Dread thou to speak presumptuous doom
On noble Marmion's lowly tomb;
But say, "He died a gallant knight,
With sword in hand, for England's right."

From THE LADY OF THE LAKE

(1809–1810. Pub. 1810)

HARP OF THE NORTH

(Introduction, Canto I)

HARP of the North! that mouldering long hast
    hung
  On the witch-elm that shades Saint Fillan's
    spring,
And down the fitful breeze thy numbers flung,
  Till envious ivy did around thee cling,
Muffling with verdant ringlet every string,—
  O minstrel harp, still must thine accents
    sleep?
Mid rustling leaves and fountains murmuring,
  Still must thy sweeter sounds their silence
    keep,
Nor bid a warrior smile, nor teach a maid to
    weep?

Not thus, in ancient days of Caledon,   10
  Was thy voice mute amid the festal crowd,
When lay of hopeless love, or glory won,
  Aroused the fearful, or subdued the proud.
At each according pause, was heard aloud
  Thine ardent symphony sublime and high!
Fair dames and crested chiefs attention bowed;
  For still the burden of thy minstrelsy
Was knighthood's dauntless deed and beauty's
    matchless eye.

O wake once more! how rude soe'er the hand
  That ventures o'er thy magic maze to
    stray;   20
O wake once more! tho' scarce my skill com-
    mand,
  Some feeble echoing of thine earlier lay:
Though harsh and faint, and soon to die away,
  And all unworthy of thy nobler strain,
Yet, if one heart throb higher at its sway,
  The wizard note has not been touched in
    vain.
Then silent be no more! Enchantress, wake
    again!

SOLDIER, REST

(Canto I, xxxi)

SOLDIER, rest! thy warfare o'er,
  Sleep the sleep that knows not breaking;
Dream of battled fields no more,
  Days of danger, nights of waking.
In our isle's enchanted hall,
  Hands unseen thy couch are strewing,
Fairy strains of music fall,
  Every sense in slumber dewing.
Soldier, rest! thy warfare o'er,
Dream of fighting fields no more;   10
Sleep the sleep that knows not breaking,
Morn of toil, nor night of waking.

No rude sound shall reach thine ear,
  Armour's clan, or war-steed champing,
Trump nor pibroch summon here
  Mustering clan, or squadron tramping.
Yet the lark's shrill fife may come,
  At the day-break from the fallow,
And the bittern sound his drum,
  Booming from the sedgy shallow.   20
Ruder sounds shall none be near,
Guards nor warders challenge here,
Here's no war-steed's neigh and champing
Shouting clans or squadrons stamping.

THE FIERY CROSS

(Canto III)

VIII

'Twas all prepared;—and from the rock,
A goat, the patriarch of the flock,   190
Before the kindling pile was laid,
And pierced by Roderick's ready blade.
Patient the sickening victim eyed
The life-blood ebb in crimson tide,
Down his clogg'd beard and shaggy limb,
Till darkness glazed his eyeballs dim.
The grisly priest, with murmuring prayer,
A slender crosslet form'd with care,
A cubit's length in measure due;
The shaft and limbs were rods of yew,   200
Whose parents in Inch-Cailliach wave
Their shadows o'er Clan-Alpine's grave,
And, answering Lomond's breezes deep,
Soothe many a chieftain's endless sleep.

The Cross, thus form'd, he held on high,
With wasted hand, and haggard eye,
And strange and mingled feelings woke,
While his anathema he spoke:

IX

"Wo to the clansman, who shall view
This symbol of sepulchral yew, 210
Forgetful that its branches grew
Where weep the heavens their holiest dew
  On Alpine's dwelling low!
Deserter of his Chieftain's trust,
He ne'er shall mingle with their dust,
But, from his sires and kindred thrust,
Each clansman's execration just
  Shall doom him wrath and wo."
He paused;—the word the vassals took,
With forward step and fiery look, 220
On high their naked brands they shook,
Their clattering targets wildly strook;
  And first in murmur low,
Then, like the billow in his course,
That far to seaward finds his source,
And flings to shore his muster'd force,
Burst, with loud roar, their answer hoarse,
  "Wo to the traitor, wo!"
Ben-an's gray scalp the accents knew,
The joyous wolf from covert drew, 230
The exulting eagle scream'd afar,—
They knew the voice of Alpine's war.

X

The shout was hush'd on lake and fell,
The monk resumed his mutter'd spell:
Dismal and low its accents came,
The while he scathed the cross with flame;
And the few words that reach'd the air,
Although the holiest name was there,
Had more of blasphemy than prayer.
But when he shook above the crowd 240
Its kindled points, he spoke aloud:—
"Wo to the wretch, who fails to rear
At this dread sign the ready spear!
For, as the flames this symbol sear,
His home, the refuge of his fear,
  A kindred fate shall know;
Far o'er its roof the volumed flame
Clan-Alpine's vengeance shall proclaim,
While maids and matrons on his name
Shall call down wretchedness and shame, 250
  And infamy and wo."

Then rose the cry of females shrill,
As goss-hawk's whistle on the hill,
Denouncing misery and ill,
Mingled with childhood's babbling trill
  Of curses stammer'd slow;
Answering with imprecation dread,
"Sunk be his home in embers red!
And cursed be the meanest shed
That e'er shall hide the houseless head, 260
  We doom to want and wo!"
A sharp and shrieking echo gave,
Coir-Uriskin, thy goblin cave!
And the gray pass where birches wave,
  On Beala-nam-bo.

XI

Then deeper paused the priest anew,
And hard his labouring breath he drew,
While, with set teeth and clenched hand,
And eyes that glowed like fiery brand,
He meditated curse more dread, 270
And deadlier, on the clansman's head,
Who, summon'd to his Chieftain's aid,
The signal saw and disobey'd.
The crosslet's points of sparkling wood,
He quench'd among the bubbling blood,
And, as again the sign he rear'd,
Hollow and hoarse his voice was heard:
"When flits this Cross from man to man,
Vich-Alpine's summons to his clan,
Burst be the ear that fails to heed! 280
Palsied the foot that shuns to speed!
May ravens tear the careless eyes,
Wolves make the coward heart their prize!
As sinks that blood-stream in the earth,
So may his heart's-blood drench his hearth!
As dies in hissing gore the spark,
Quench thou his light, Destruction dark!
And be the grace to him denied,
Bought by this sign to all beside!"
He ceased; no echo gave agen 290
The murmur of the deep Amen.

XII

Then Roderick, with impatient look,
From Brian's hand the symbol took:
"Speed, Malise, speed!" he said, and gave
The crosslet to his henchman brave.
"The muster-place be Lanrick mead—
Instant the time—speed, Malise, speed!"
Like heath-bird, when the hawks pursue,
A barge across Loch Katrine flew;

High stood the henchman on the prow, 300
So rapidly the barge-men row,
The bubbles, where they launch'd the boat,
Were all unbroken and afloat,
Dancing in foam and ripple still,
When it had neared the mainland hill;
And from the silver beach's side
Still was the prow three fathom wide,
When lightly bounded to the land
The messenger of blood and brand.

XIII

Speed, Malise, speed! the dun deer's hide 310
On fleeter foot was never tied.
Speed, Malise, speed! such cause of haste
Thine active sinews never braced.
Bend 'gainst the steepy hill thy breast,
Burst down like torrent from its crest;
With short and springing footstep pass
The trembling bog and false morass;
Across the brook like roebuck bound,
And thread the brake like questing hound,
The crag is high, the scaur is deep, 320
Yet shrink not from the desperate leap:
Parch'd are thy burning lips and brow,
Yet by the fountain pause not now;
Herald of battle, fate, and fear,
Stretch onward in thy fleet career!
The wounded hind thou track'st not now,
Pursuest not maid through greenwood bough,
Nor pliest thou now thy flying pace;
With rivals in the mountain race;
But danger, death, and warrior deed, 330
Are in thy course—speed, Malise, speed!

XIV

Fast as the fatal symbol flies,
In arms the huts and hamlets rise:
From winding glen, from upland brown,
They pour'd each hardy tenant down.
Nor slack'd the messenger his pace;
He show'd the sign, he named the place.
And, pressing forward like the wind,
Left clamour and surprise behind.
The fisherman forsook the strand, 340
The swarthy smith took dirk and brand;
With changed cheer, the mower blithe
Left in the half-cut swathe the scythe;
The herds without a keeper stray'd,
The plough was in mid-furrow staid,
The falc'ner toss'd his hawk away,

The hunter left the stag at bay;
Prompt at the signal of alarms,
Each son of Alpine rush'd to arms;
So swept the tumult and affray 350
Along the margin of Achray.
Alas, thou lovely lake! that e'er
Thy banks should echo sounds of fear!
The rocks, the bosky thickets, sleep
So stilly on thy bosom deep,
The lark's blithe carol, from the cloud,
Seems for the scene too gayly loud.

XV

Speed, Malise, speed! the lake is past,
Duncraggan's huts appear at last,
And peep, like moss-grown rocks, half seen,
Half hidden in the copse so green; 361
There mayst thou rest, thy labour done,
Their lord shall speed the signal on.—
As stoops the hawk upon his prey,
The henchman shot him down the way.
—What woful accents load the gale?
The funeral yell, the female wail!
A gallant hunter's sport is o'er,
A valiant warrior fights no more.
Who, in the battle or the chase, 370
At Roderick's side shall fill his place!—
Within the hall, where torches' ray
Supplies the excluded beams of day,
Lies Duncan on his lowly bier,
And o'er him streams his widow's tear.
His stripling son stands mournful by,
His youngest weeps, but knows not why;
The village maids and matrons round
The dismal coronach resound.

CORONACH

(Canto III, xvi)

He is gone to the mountain,
  He is lost to the forest,
Like a summer-dried fountain,
  When our need was the sorest.
The font, reappearing,
  From the rain-drops shall borrow,
But to us comes no cheering,
  To Duncan no morrow!

The hand of the reaper
  Takes the ears that are hoary, 10
But the voice of the weeper
  Wails manhood in glory.

The autumn winds rushing
  Waft the leaves that are searest,
But our flower was in flushing,
  When blighting was nearest.

Fleetfoot on the correi,
  Sage counsel in cumber,
Red hand in the foray,
  How sound is thy slumber!   20
Like the dew on the mountain,
  Like the foam on the river,
Like the bubble on the fountain,
  Thou art gone, and for ever!

THE HEATH THIS NIGHT MUST BE MY BED

(Canto III, xxiii)

THE heath this night must be my bed,
The bracken curtain for my head,
My lullaby the warder's tread,
  Far, far from love and thee, Mary;
To-morrow eve more stilly laid,
My couch may be my bloody plaid,
My vesper song, thy wail, sweet maid!
  It will not waken me, Mary!

I may not, dare not, fancy now
The grief that clouds thy lovely brow,   10
I dare not think upon thy vow,
  And all it promised me, Mary.
No fond regret must Norman know;
When bursts Clan-Alpine on the foe,
His heart must be like bended bow,
  His foot like arrow free, Mary.

A time will come with feeling fraught,
For if I fall in battle fought,
Thy hapless lover's dying thought
  Shall be a thought on thee, Mary.   20
And if returned from conquer'd foes,
How blithely will the evening close,
How sweet the linnet sing repose,
  To my young bride and me, Mary!

THE TOILS ARE PITCHED

(Canto IV, xxv)

THE toils are pitch'd, and the stakes are set,
  Ever sing merrily, merrily;
The bows they bend, and the knives they whet,
  Hunters live so cheerily.

It was a stag, a stag of ten,
  Bearing his branches sturdily;
He came stately down the glen,
  Ever sing hardily, hardily.

It was there he met with a wounded doe,
  She was bleeding deathfully;   10
She warn'd him of the toils below,
  O, so faithfully, faithfully!

He had an eye, and he could heed,
  Ever sing warily, warily;
He had a foot, and he could speed—
  Hunters watch so narrowly.

From ROKEBY

(1812. Pub. 1813)

BRIGNALL BANKS

(Canto III, xvi–xviii)

O, BRIGNALL banks are wild and fair,
  And Greta woods are green,
And you may gather garlands there
  Would grace a summer queen.
And as I rode by Dalton-hall,
  Beneath the turrets high,
A maiden on the castle wall
  Was singing merrily:—
"O Brignall banks are fresh and fair,
  And Greta woods are green;   10
I'd rather rove with Edmund there,
  Than reign our English queen."

"If, maiden, thou wouldst wend with me,
  To leave both tower and town,
Thou first must guess what life lead we,
  That dwell by dale and down.
And if thou canst that riddle read,
  As read full well you may,
Then to the greenwood shalt thou speed,
  As blithe as Queen of May."   20
Yet sung she, "Brignall banks are fair,
  And Greta woods are green;
I'd rather rove with Edmund there,
  Than reign our English queen.

"I read you, by your bugle-horn,
  And by your palfrey good,
I read you for a ranger sworn,
  To keep the king's greenwood."

J. W. Croker

from the Author's

THE

VISION

OF

DON RODERICK;

A POEM.

BY

WALTER SCOTT, Esq.

Quid dignum memorare tuis, Hispania, terris,
Vox humana valet.————————CLAUDIAN.

(*Author's Copy.*)

EDINBURGH :

Printed by James Ballantyne and Company,
AT
The Border Press.

1811.

Presentation Copy from Sir Walter Scott to J. W. Croker. (See Appendix I.)

"A ranger, lady, winds his horn,
  And 'tis at peep of light; 30
His blast is heard at merry morn,
  And mine at dead of night."
Yet sung she, "Brignall banks are fair,
  And Greta woods are gay;
I would I were with Edmund there,
  To reign his Queen of May!

"With burnish'd brand and musketoon,
  So gallantly you come,
I read you for a bold dragoon,
  That lists the tuck of drum." 40
"I list no more the tuck of drum,
  No more the trumpet hear;
But when the beetle sounds his hum,
  My comrades take the spear.
And O! though Brignall banks be fair,
  And Greta woods be gay,
Yet mickle must the maiden dare,
  Would reign my Queen of May!

"Maiden! a nameless life I lead,
  A nameless death I'll die; 50
The fiend, whose lantern lights the mead,
  Were better mate than I!
And when I'm with my comrades met
  Beneath the greenwood bough,
What once we were we all forget,
  Nor think what we are now.
Yet Brignall banks are fresh and fair,
  And Greta woods are green,
And you may gather garlands there
  Would grace a summer queen." 60

ALLEN–A–DALE

(Canto III, xxx)

ALLEN-A-DALE has no fagot for burning,
Allen-a-Dale has no furrow for turning,
Allen-a-Dale has no fleece for the spinning,
Yet Allen-a-Dale has red gold for the winning.
Come, read me my riddle! come, hearken my tale!
And tell me the craft of bold Allen-a-Dale.

The Baron of Ravensworth prances in pride,
And he views his domains upon Arkindale side.
The mere for his net, and the land for his game,
The chase for the wild, and the park for the tame:
Yet the fish of the lake, and the deer of the vale,
Are less free to Lord Dacre than Allen-a-Dale!

Allen-a-Dale was ne'er belted a knight, 13
Though his spur be as sharp, and his blade be as bright;
Allen-a-Dale is no baron or lord,
Yet twenty tall yeomen will draw at his word;
And the best of our nobles his bonnet will vail,
Who at Rere-cross on Stanmore meets Allen-a Dale.

Allen-a-Dale to his wooing is come;
The mother, she ask'd of his household and home; 20
"Though the castle of Richmond stand fair on the hill,
My hall," quoth bold Allen, "shows gallanter still;
'Tis the blue vault of heaven, with its crescent so pale,
And with all its bright spangles!" said Allen-a-Dale.

The father was steel, and the mother was stone;
They lifted the latch, and they bade him be gone:
But loud, on the morrow, their wail and their cry:
He had laugh'd on the lass with his bonny black eye,
And she fled to the forest to hear a love-tale,
And the youth it was told by was Allen-a-Dale! 30

THE CYPRESS WREATH

(Canto V, xiii)

O, LADY, twine no wreath for me,
Or twine it of the cypress-tree!
Too lively glow the lilies light,
The varnish'd holly's all too bright,
The May-flower and the eglantine
May shade a brow less sad than mine,
But, Lady, weave no wreath for me,
Or weave it of the cypress-tree!

Let dimpled Mirth his temples twine
With tendrils of the laughing vine; 10
The manly oak, the pensive yew,
To patriot and to sage be due;
The myrtle bow bids lovers live,
But that Matilda will not give;
Then, Lady, twine no wreath for me,
Or twine it of the cypress-tree!

Let merry England proudly rear
Her blended roses, bought so dear;
Let Albin bind her bonnet blue
With heath and harebell dipp'd in dew; 20
On favour'd Erin's crest be seen
The flower she loves of emerald green—
But, Lady, twine no wreath for me,
Or twine it of the cypress-tree.

Strike the wild harp, while maids prepare
The ivy meet for minstrel's hair:
And, while his crown of laurel-leaves,
With bloody hand the victor weaves,
Let the loud trump his triumph tell;
But when you hear the passing bell, 30
Then, Lady, twine a wreath for me,
And twine it of the cypress-tree.

Yes! twine for me the cypress bough:
But, O Matilda, twine not now!
Stay till a few brief months are past,
And I have look'd and loved my last!
When villagers my shroud bestrew
With panzies, rosemary, and rue,—
Then, Lady, weave a wreath for me,
And weave it of the cypress-tree. 40

BALLAD

(Canto V, xxvii)

"AND whither would you lead me then?"
  Quoth the Friar of orders gray;
And the Ruffians twain replied again,
  "By a dying woman to pray."—

"I see," he said, "a lovely sight,
  A sight bodes little harm,
A lady as a lily bright,
  With an infant on her arm."—

"Then do thine office, Friar gray,
  And see thou shrive her free! 10
Else shall the sprite, that parts to-night
  Fling all its guilt on thee.

"Let mass be said, and trentals read,
  When thou'rt to convent gone,
And bid the bell of St. Benedict
  Toll out its deepest tone."

The shrift is done, the Friar is gone,
  Blindfolded as he came—
Next morning, all in Littlecot Hall
  Were weeping for their dame. 20

Wild Darrell is an alter'd man,
  The village crones can tell;
He looks pale as clay, and strives to pray
  If he hears the convent bell.

If prince or peer cross Darrell's way,
  He'll beard him in his pride—
If he meet a Friar of orders gray,
  He droops and turns aside.

SONGS AND BALLADS

WILLIAM AND HELEN [1]

FROM heavy dreams fair Helen rose,
  And eyed the dawning red:
"Alas, my love, thou tarriest long!
  O art thou false or dead?"

With gallant Fred'rick's princely power
  He sought the bold Crusade;
But not a word from Judah's wars
  Told Helen how he sped.

With Paynim and with Saracen
  At length a truce was made, 10
And every knight return'd to dry
  The tears his love had shed.

Our gallant host was homeward bound
  With many a song of joy;
Green waved the laurel in each plume,
  The badge of victory.

And old and young, and sire and son,
  To meet them crowd the way,
With shouts, and mirth, and melody,
  The debt of love to pay. 20

Full many a maid her true-love met,
  And sobb'd in his embrace,
And flutt'ring joy in tears and smiles
  Array'd full many a face.

Nor joy nor smile for Helen sad;
  She sought the host in vain;
For none could tell her William's fate,
  If faithless, or if slain.

The martial band is past and gone;
  She rends her raven hair, 30
And in distraction's bitter mood
  She weeps with wild despair.

  [1] Imitated from the *Lenore* of Bürger.

"O rise, my child," her mother said,
 "Nor sorrow thus in vain;
A perjured lover's fleeting heart
 No tears recall again."

"O mother, what is gone, is gone,
 What's lost for ever lorn:
Death, death alone can comfort me;
 O had I ne'er been born!   40

"O break, my heart—O break at once!
 Drink my life-blood, Despair!
No joy remains on earth for me,
 For me in heaven no share."

"O enter not in judgment, Lord!"
 The pious mother prays;
"Impute not guilt to thy frail child!
 She knows not what she says.

"O say thy pater noster, child!
 O turn to God and grace!   50
His will, that turn'd thy bliss to bale,
 Can change thy bale to bliss."

"O mother, mother, what is bliss?
 O mother, what is bale?
My William's love was heaven on earth,
 Without it earth is hell.

"Why should I pray to ruthless Heaven,
 Since my loved William's slain?
I only pray'd for William's sake,
 And all my prayers were vain."   60

"O take the sacrament, my child,
 And check these tears that flow;
By resignation's humble prayer,
 O hallow'd be thy woe!"

"No sacrament can quench this fire,
 Or slake this scorching pain;
No sacrament can bid the dead
 Arise and live again.

"O break, my heart—O break at once!
 Be thou my god, Despair!   70
Heaven's heaviest blow has fallen on me,
 And vain each fruitless prayer."

"O enter not in judgment, Lord,
 With thy frail child of clay!
She knows not what her tongue has spoke;
 Impute it not, I pray!

"Forbear, my child, this desperate woe,
 And turn to God and grace;
Well can devotion's heavenly glow
 Convert thy bale to bliss."   80

"O mother, mother, what is bliss?
 O mother, what is bale?
Without my William what were heaven,
 Or with him what were hell?"

Wild she arraigns the eternal doom,
 Upbraids each sacred power,
Till, spent, she sought her silent room,
 All in the lonely tower.

She beat her breast, she wrung her hands,
 Till sun and day were o'er,   90
And through the glimmering lattice shone
 The twinkling of the star.

Then, crash! the heavy drawbridge fell
 That o'er the moat was hung;
And, clatter! clatter! on its boards
 The hoof of courser rung.

The clank of echoing steel was heard
 As off the rider bounded;
And slowly on the winding stair
 A heavy footstep sounded.   100

And hark! and hark! a knock—tap! tap!
 A rustling stifled noise;
Door-latch and tinkling staples ring;
 At length a whispering voice:

"Awake, awake, arise, my love!
 How, Helen, dost thou fare?
Wak'st thou, or sleep'st? laugh'st thou, or
  weep'st?
 Hast thought on me, my fair?"

"My love! my love!—so late by night!
 I waked, I wept for thee: 110
Much have I borne since dawn of morn;
 Where, William, couldst thou be?"

"We saddle late—from Hungary
 I rode since darkness fell;
And to its bourne we both return
 Before the matin-bell."

"O rest this night within my arms,
 And warm thee in their fold!
Chill howls through hawthorn bush the wind:
 My love is deadly cold."   120

"Let the wind howl through hawthorn bush!
  This night we must away;
The steed is wight, the spur is bright;
  I cannot stay till day."

"Busk, busk, and boune! thou mount'st behind
  Upon my black barb steed:
O'er stock and stile, a hundred miles,
  We haste to bridal bed."

"To-night—to-night, a hundred miles?
  O dearest William, stay!   130
The bell strikes twelve—dark, dismal hour!
  O wait, my love, till day!"

"Look here, look here—the moon shines
      clear—
  Full fast I ween we ride;
Mount and away! for ere the day
  We reach our bridal bed.

"The black barb snorts, the bridle rings;
  Haste, busk, and boune, and seat thee!
The feast is made, the chamber spread,
  The bridal guests await thee."   140

Strong love prevail'd. She busks, she bounes,
  She mounts the barb behind,
And round her darling William's waist
  Her lily arms she twined.

And, hurry! hurry! off they rode,
  As fast as fast might be;
Spurn'd from the courser's thundering heels
  The flashing pebbles flee.

And on the right, and on the left,
  Ere they could snatch a view,   150
Fast, fast each mountain, mead, and plain,
  And cot, and castle flew.

"Sit fast—dost fear? The moon shines clear;
  Fleet goes my barb—keep hold!
Fear'st thou?" "O no!" she faintly said;
  "But why so stern and cold?

"What yonder rings? what yonder sings?
  Why shrieks the owlet grey?"
"'Tis death-bell's clang, 'tis funeral song,
  The body to the clay.   160

"With song and clang, at morrow's dawn,
  Ye may inter the dead:
To-night I ride, with my young bride,
  To deck our bridal bed.

"Come with thy choir, thou coffin'd guest,
  To swell our nuptial song!
Come, priest, to bless our marriage feast!
  Come all, come all along!"

Ceased clang and song; down sunk the bier;
  The shrouded corpse arose: 170
And, hurry! hurry! all the train
  The thundering steed pursues.

And, forward! forward! on they go;
  High snorts the straining steed;
Thick pants the rider's labouring breath,
  As headlong on they speed.

"O William, why this savage haste?
  And where thy bridal bed?"
"'Tis distant far, low, damp, and chill,
  And narrow, trustless maid."   180

"No room for me?" "Enough for both;
  Speed, speed, my barb, thy course!"
O'er thundering bridge, through boiling surge
  He drove the furious horse.

Tramp! tramp! along the land they rode,
  Splash! splash! along the sea;
The scourge is wight, the spur is bright,
  The flashing pebbles flee.

Fled past on right and left how fast
  Each forest, grove, and bower!   190
On right and left fled past how fast
  Each city, town, and tower!

"Dost fear? dost fear? The moon shines clear,
  Dost fear to ride with me?
Hurrah! hurrah! the dead can ride!"
  "O William, let them be!

"See there, see there! What yonder swings,
  And creaks 'mid whistling rain?"
"Gibbet and steel, th' accursed wheel;
  A murderer in his chain.   200

"Hollo! thou felon, follow here:
  To bridal bed we ride;
And thou shalt prance a fetter dance
  Before me and my bride."

And, hurry! hurry! clash! clash! clash!
  The wasted form descends;
And fleet as wind through hazel bush
  The wild career attends.

Tramp tramp! along the land they rode,
  Splash! splash! along the sea;   210
The scourge is red, the spur drops blood,
  The flashing pebbles flee.

How fled what moonshine faintly show'd!
  How fled what darkness hid!
How fled the earth beneath their feet,
  The heaven above their head!

"Dost fear? dost fear? The moon shines clear,
  And well the dead can ride;
Does faithful Helen fear for them?"
  "O leave in peace the dead!"   220

"Barb! barb! methinks I hear the cock;
  The sand will soon be run:
Barb! barb! I smell the morning air;
  The race is wellnigh done."

Tramp! tramp! along the land they rode,
  Splash! splash! along the sea;
The scourge is red, the spur drops blood,
  The flashing pebbles flee.

"Hurrah! hurrah! well ride the dead;
  The bride, the bride is come;   230
And soon we reach the bridal bed,
  For, Helen, here's my home."

Reluctant on its rusty hinge
  Revolved an iron door,
And by the pale moon's setting beam
  Were seen a church and tower.

With many a shriek and cry, whiz round
  The birds of midnight, scared;
And rustling like autumnal leaves
  Unhallow'd ghosts were heard.   240

O'er many a tomb and tombstone pale
  He spurr'd the fiery horse,
Till sudden at an open grave
  He check'd the wondrous course.

The falling gauntlet quits the rein,
  Down drops the casque of steel,
The cuirass leaves his shrinking side,
  The spur his gory heel.

The eyes desert the naked skull,
  The mould'ring flesh the bone,   250
Till Helen's lily arms entwine
  A ghastly skeleton.

The furious barb snorts fire and foam,
  And, with a fearful bound,
Dissolves at once in empty air,
  And leaves her on the ground.

Half seen by fits, by fits half heard,
  Pale spectres flit along,
Wheel round the maid in dismal dance,
  And howl the funeral song;   260

"E'en when the heart's with anguish cleft,
  Revere the doom of Heaven!
Her soul is from her body reft;
  Her spirit be forgiven!"
1795

THE MAID OF NEIDPATH

O LOVERS' eyes are sharp to see,
  And lovers' ears in hearing;
And love, in life's extremity,
  Can lend an hour of cheering.
Disease had been in Mary's bower,
  And slow decay from mourning,
Though now she sits on Neidpath's tower,
  To watch her love's returning.

All sunk and dim her eyes so bright,
  Her form decay'd by pining,   10
Till through her wasted hand, at night,
  You saw the taper shining;
By fits a sultry hectic hue
  Across her cheek was flying:
By fits, so ashy pale she grew,
  Her maidens thought her dying.

Yet keenest powers to see and hear,
  Seem'd in her frame residing;
Before the watch-dog prick'd his ear,
  She heard her lover's riding: 20
Ere scarce a distant form was ken'd,
  She knew, and waved to greet him;
And o'er the battlement did bend,
  As on the wing to meet him.

He came—he pass'd—a heedless gaze,
  As o'er some stranger glancing;
Her welcome spoke in faltering phrase,
  Lost in his courser's prancing—
The castle arch, whose hollow tone
  Returns each whisper spoken,   30
Could scarcely catch the feeble moan,
  Which told her heart was broken.

Pub. 1806

LULLABY OF AN INFANT CHIEF

AIR—"*Cadul gu lo.*" [1]

O HUSH thee, my babie, thy sire was a knight,
Thy mother a lady, both lovely and bright;
The woods and the glens, from the towers
    which we see,
They all are belonging, dear babie, to thee
        O ho ro, i ri ri, cadul gu lo,
        O ho ro, i ri ri, &c.

O, fear not the bugle, though loudly it
    blows,
It calls but the warders that guard thy repose;
Their bows would be bended, their blades
    would be red,
Ere the step of a foeman draws near to thy
    bed.   10
        O ho ro, i ri ri, &c.

O, hush thee, my babie, the time soon will
    come,
When thy sleep shall be broken by trumpet
    and drum;
Then hush thee, my darling, take rest while
    you may,
For strife comes with manhood, and waking
    with day.
        O ho ro, i ri, ri, &c.

c. 1816

JOCK OF HAZELDEAN

"WHY weep ye by the tide, ladie?
    Why weep ye by the tide?
I'll wed ye to my youngest son,
    And ye sall be his bride;
And ye sall be his bride, ladie,
    Sae comely to be seen"—
But aye she loot the tears down fa'
    For Jock of Hazeldean.

"Now let this wilfu' grief be done,
    And dry that cheek so pale;   10
Young Frank is chief of Errington,
    And Lord of Langley-dale;
His step is first in peaceful ha',
    His sword in battle keen"—
But aye she loot the tears down fa'
    For Jock of Hazeldean.

[1] "Sleep on till day."

"A chain of gold ye sall not lack,
    Nor braid to bind your hair;
Nor mettled hound, nor managed hawk,
    Nor palfrey fresh and fair;   20
And you, the foremost o' them a',
    Shall ride our forest queen"—
But aye she loot the tears down fa'
    For Jock of Hazeldean.

The kirk was deck'd at morning-tide,
    The tapers glimmer'd fair;
The priest and bridegroom wait the bride,
    And dame and knight are there.
They sought her baith by bower and ha';
    The ladie was not seen!   30
She's o'er the Border, and awa'
    Wi' Jock of Hazeldean.

Pub. 1816

SOUND THE CLARION

(From *Old Mortality*)

SOUND, sound the clarion, fill the fife!
    To all the sensual world proclaim,
One crowded hour of glorious life
    Is worth an age without a name.

Pub. 1816

PROUD MAISIE

(From *The Heart of Midlothian*)

PROUD Maisie is in the wood,
    Walking so early.
Sweet robin sits on the bush,
    Singing so rarely.

"Tell me, thou bonny bird,
    When shall I marry me?"
"When six braw gentlemen
    Kirkward shall carry ye."

"Who makes the bridal bed,
    Birdie, say truly?"   10
"The grey-headed sexton,
    That delves the grave duly.

"The glowworm o'er grave and stone
    Shall light thee steady;
The owl from the steeple sing,
    'Welcome, proud lady.'"

Pub. 1818

BONNY DUNDEE

(From *The Doom of Devorgoil*)

To the Lords of Convention 'twas Claver'se
  who spoke,
"Ere the King's crown shall fall there are
  crowns to be broke;
So let each Cavalier who loves honor and me,
Come follow the bonnet of Bonny Dundee.

  "Come fill up my cup, come fill up my can,
  Come saddle your horses, and call up your
    men;
  Come open the West Port, and let me gang
    free,
  And it's room for the bonnets of Bonny
    Dundee!"

Dundee he is mounted, he rides up the street,
The bells are rung backward, the drums they
  are beat;   10
But the Provost, douce man, said, "Just e'en
  let him be,
The Gude Town is weel quit of that Deil of
  Dundee."
        Come fill up my cup, etc.

As he rode down the sanctified bends of the
  Bow,
Ilk carline was flyting and shaking her pow;
But the young plants of grace they look'd
  couthie and slee,
Thinking, "Luck to thy bonnet, thou Bonny
  Dundee!"
        Come fill up my cup, etc.

With sour-featured Whigs the Grass-market
  was cramm'd   19
As if half the West had set tryst to be hang'd;
There was spite in each look, there was fear
  in each e'e,
As they watch'd for the bonnets of Bonny
  Dundee.
        Come fill up my cup, etc.

These cowls of Kilmarnock had spits and had
  spears,
And lang-hafted gullies to kill Cavaliers;
But they shrunk to close-heads, and the cause-
  way was free,
At the toss of the bonnet of Bonny Dundee.
        Come fill up my cup, etc.

He spurr'd at the foot of the proud Castle
  rock,
And with the gay Gordon he gallantly
  spoke;   30
"Let Mons Meg and her marrows speak twa
  words or three,
For the love of the bonnet of Bonny Dundee."
        Come fill up my cup, etc.

The Gordon demands of him which way he
  goes—
"Where'er shall direct me the shade of Montrose!
Your Grace in short space shall hear tidings of
  me,
Or that low lies the bonnet of Bonny Dundee.
        Come fill up my cup, etc.

"There are hills beyond Pentland, and lands
  beyond Forth,
If there's lords in the Lowlands, there's chiefs
  in the North;   40
There are wild Duniewassals, three thousand
  times three,
Will cry *hoigh!* for the bonnet of Bonny
  Dundee.
        Come fill up my cup, etc.

"There's brass on the target of barken'd
  bull-hide;
There's steel in the scabbard that dangles
  beside;
The brass shall be burnish'd, the steel shall
  flash free,
At a toss of the bonnet of Bonny Dundee.
        Come fill up my cup, etc.

"Away to the hills, to the caves, to the rocks—
Ere I own an usurper, I'll couch with the
  fox;   50
And tremble, false Whigs, in the midst of your
  glee,
You have not seen the last of my bonnet and
  me!"
        Come fill up my cup, etc.

He waved his proud hand, and the trumpets
  were blown,
The kettle-drums clash'd, and the horsemen
  rode on,

Till on Ravelston's cliffs and on Clermiston's
    lee,
Died away the wild war-notes of Bonny
    Dundee.

  Come fill up my cup, come fill up my can,

Come saddle the horses, and call up the men,
Come open your gates, and let me gae free,
For it's up with the bonnets of Bonny
    Dundee!   61

Pub. 1830

ROBERT SOUTHEY
[August 12, 1774–March 21, 1843]

"To think how many mouths I must feed out of one inkstand" exclaimed Southey once, and told the story of his later life. An industrious and capable writer, he did his duty as he saw it, supporting his own family and, for a time, that of Coleridge also with his pen. His industry may be judged from his total output—some ten good sized volumes of poetry and forty of prose. Hack work was thrust upon him, and at times he brought it to the dignity of literature.

There were other ideas in his head when (1792) he went up from Westminster school to Oxford with "a heart full of poetry and feeling, a head full of Rousseau and Werther." He was one of the young liberals, sympathetic with France, and was soon at work on *Joan of Arc*, an epic which, in its praise of French patriotism, indirectly expressed Southey's approval of the French Revolution. Two years later (1794) he became associated with Coleridge in the Pantisocracy scheme—a scheme which, coupled with his marriage to Edith Fricker, led to his being turned out of the house, practically penniless, by the aunt who had brought him up from childhood. About the same time he was writing *Wat Tyler*, a revolutionary epic.

Southey's association with liberalism, and with greater men than himself, has brought him discredit he does not altogether deserve. His enthusiasm for the French cause ended with the fall of the Girondins and the execution of his idol Brissot, when the ink was scarcely yet dry on the first draft of *Joan of Arc*. Temperamentally, he had not the spread of wing to maintain flight with Coleridge. When he abandoned Pantisocracy and went to Portugal with an uncle (having been disowned by an aunt) he was behaving reasonably, if not gloriously. By 1803 he was settled with his wife and children at Greta Hall, Keswick. There he lived as an industrious and conservative man of letters until his death. He became Poet Laureate in 1813. He received a D.C.L. from Oxford in 1820. From 1808 until 1839 he was a valued and well paid contributor to the Tory *Quarterly Review*, for whose policies he was not to blame.

Southey held the views and led the life of a sturdy worthy Englishman. As the world goes, Southey deserved the honors which he won, and did not deserve his defeats. Unfortunately for him his unpublished *Wat Tyler* appeared in a pirated edition in 1817 to emphasize his change of political opinions. Unfortunately for him as Poet Laureate he wrote well (which was his best) while Byron and Shelley were flaming. Unfortunately for him he quarreled with Byron. And as a consequence he undeservedly looks the fool in literary history.

Southey's prose has worn better than his poetry. As a poet, besides many shorter pieces, he wrote a series of long poems, now unread, including *Madoc*, *Thalaba*, and *The Curse of Kehama*. As a Laureate his most famous piece is *The Vision of Judgement* (1821)—famous because Byron answered it. As a Laureate, however, Southey did do one thing, and one very great thing. The office, when he took it, was in actual disrepute. In his period the compulsory odes were abolished, and his personal dignity restored it sufficiently so that greater poets could accept it after him. Gray had flatly refused the office in the preceding century.

SONNET

Go, Valentine, and tell that lovely Maid
Whom fancy still will portray to my sight,
How here I linger in this sullen shade,
This dreary gloom of dull, monastic night;
Say, that from every joy of life remote
At evening's closing hour I quit the throng,
Listening in solitude the ring-dove's note,
Who pours like me her solitary song;
Say, that her absence calls the sorrowing sigh;
Say, that of all her charms I love to speak,   10
In fancy feel the magic of her eye,
In fancy view the smile illume her cheek,
Court the·lone hour when silence stills the
      grove,
And heave the sigh of memory and of love.

1794

THE BATTLE OF BLENHEIM

1

It was a summer evening;
   Old Kaspar's work was done,
And he before his cottage door
   Was sitting in the sun;
And by him sported on the green
His little grandchild Wilhelmine.

2

She saw her brother Peterkin
   Roll something large and round,
Which he beside the rivulet,
   In playing there, had found;   10
He came to ask what he had found,
That was so large, and smooth, and round.

3

Old Kaspar took it from the boy,
   Who stood expectant by;
And then the old man shook his head,
   And with a natural sigh,
"'Tis some poor fellow's skull," said he,
"Who fell in the great victory.

4

"I find them in the garden,
   For there's many here about;   20
And often, when I go to plough,
   The ploughshare turns them out;
For many thousand men," said he,
"Were slain in that great victory."

5

"Now tell us what 'twas all about,"
   Young Peterkin he cries;
And little Wilhelmine looks up
   With wonder-waiting eyes;
"Now tell us all about the war,
And what they fought each other for."   30

6

"It was the English," Kaspar cried,
   "Who put the French to rout;
But what they fought each other for,
   I could not well make out;
But every body said," quoth he,
"That 'twas a famous victory.

7

"My father lived at Blenheim then,
   Yon little stream hard by;
They burnt his dwelling to the ground,
   And he was forced to fly;   40
So with his wife and child he fled,
Nor had he where to rest his head.

8

"With fire and sword the country round
   Was wasted far and wide,
And many a childing mother then,
   And new-born baby died;
But things like that, you know, must be
At every famous victory.

9

"They say it was a shocking sight
   After the field was won;   50
For many thousand bodies here
   Lay rotting in the sun;
But things like that, you know, must be
After a famous victory.

10

"Great praise the Duke of Marlbro' won,
   And our good Prince Eugene."
"Why, 'twas a very wicked thing!"
   Said little Wilhelmine.
"Nay—nay—my little girl," quoth he,
"It was a famous victory.   60

11

"And every body praised the Duke,
   Who this great fight did win."
"But what good came of it at last?"
   Quoth little Peterkin.

267

Keswick. Cumberland - 2 May 1826

Sir
I have the honour to acknowledge your letter of the 28th last, this day received, informing me that the Royal Society of Literature has been pleased to elect me one of its Honorary Associates & accompanying a Diploma which certifies that election. - If I am not acting according to form, in transmitting herewith the prescribed form of Obligation, the error may be amended in the course of the present month, on my arrival in London.

With a due sense of the honour thus conferred on me

I remain
Sir
Your most obedient humble servant

Robert Southey.

Reverend Richard Cattermole.

Letter from Robert Southey on His Election to the Royal Society of Literature.
(See Appendix I.)

"Why, that I cannot tell," said he;
"But 'twas a famous victory."
Westbury, 1798

THE HOLLY–TREE

1

O READER! hast thou ever stood to see
  The Holly-Tree?
The eye that contemplates it well perceives
  Its glossy leaves
Order'd by an intelligence so wise,
As might confound the Atheist's sophistries.

2

Below, a circling fence, its leaves are seen
  Wrinkled and keen;
No grazing cattle through their prickly round
  Can reach to wound;   10
But as they grow where nothing is to fear,
Smooth and unarm'd the pointless leaves appear.

3

I love to view these things with curious eyes,
  And moralize;
And in this wisdom of the Holly-Tree
  Can emblem see
Wherewith perchance to make a pleasant rhyme,
One which may profit in the after time.

4

Thus, though abroad perchance I might appear
  Harsh and austere,   20
To those who on my leisure would intrude
  Reserved and rude,
Gentle at home amid my friends I'd be
Like the high leaves upon the Holly-Tree.

5

And should my youth, as youth is apt, I know,
  Some harshness show,
All vain asperities I day by day
  Would wear away,   28
Till the smooth temper of my age should be
Like the high leaves upon the Holly-Tree.

6

And as, when all the summer trees are seen
  So bright and green,
The Holly leaves a sober hue display
  Less bright than they;

But when the bare and wintry woods we see,
What then so cheerful as the Holly-Tree?

7

So serious should my youth appear among
  The thoughtless throng;
So would I seem amid the young and gay
  More grave than they,   40
That in my age as cheerful I might be
As the green winter of the Holly-Tree.
Westbury, 1798

WRITTEN IMMEDIATELY AFTER READING

THE SPEECH OF ROBERT EMMET

ON HIS TRIAL AND CONVICTION FOR HIGH
TREASON, SEPTEMBER, 1803

"LET no man write my epitaph; let my grave
Be uninscribed, and let my memory rest
Till other times are come, and other men,
Who then may do me justice."[1]
                              Emmet, no!
No withering curse hath dried my spirit up,
That I should now be silent,—that my soul
Should from the stirring inspiration shrink,
Now when it shakes her, and withhold her
  voice,
Of that divinest impulse never more
Worthy, if impious I withheld it now,   10
Hardening my heart. Here, here in this free Isle,
To which in thy young virtue's erring zeal
Thou wert so perilous an enemy,
Here in free England shall an English hand
Build thy imperishable monument;
Oh,—to thine own misfortune and to ours,
By thine own deadly error so beguiled,
Here in free England shall an English voice
Raise up thy mourning-song. For thou hast
  paid
The bitter penalty of that misdeed;   20

[1] These were the words in his speech: "Let there
be no inscription upon my tomb. Let no man write
my epitaph. No man can write my epitaph. I am
here ready to die. I am not allowed to vindicate
my character; and when I am prevented from
vindicating myself, let no man dare to calumniate
me. Let my character and my motives repose in
obscurity and peace, till other times and other men
can do them justice. Then shall my character be
vindicated; then may my epitaph be written.
I HAVE DONE."

Justice hath done her unrelenting part,
If she in truth be Justice who drives on,
Bloody and blind, the chariot wheels of death.

So young, so glowing for the general good,
Oh, what a lovely manhood had been thine,
When all the violent workings of thy youth
Had passed away, hadst thou been wisely
    spared,
Left to the slow and certain influences
Of silent feeling and maturing thought!
How had that heart,—that noble heart of
    thine,   .   30
Which even now had snapp'd one spell,
    which beat
With such brave indignation at the shame
And guilt of France, and of her miscreant
    Lord,—
How had it clung to England! With what
    love,
What pure and perfect love, return'd to her,
Now worthy of thy love, the champion now
For freedom,—yea, the only champion now,
And soon to be the Avenger. But the blow
Hath fallen, the indiscriminating blow,   39
That for its portion to the Grave consign'd
Youth, Genius, generous Virtue. Oh, grief,
    grief!
Oh, sorrow and reproach! Have ye to learn,
Deaf to the past, and to the future blind,
Ye who thus irremissibly exact
The forfeit life, how lightly life is staked,
When in distempered times the feverish mind
To strong delusion yields? Have ye to learn
With what a deep and spirit-stirring voice
Pity doth call Revenge? Have ye no hearts
To feel and understand how Mercy tames 50
The rebel nature, madden'd by old wrongs,
And binds it in the gentle bands of love,
When steel and adamant were weak to hold
That Samson-strength subdued!
                     Let no man write
Thy epitaph! Emmet, nay; thou shalt not go
Without thy funeral strain! Oh, young, and
    good,
And wise, though erring here, thou shalt not
    go
Unhonor'd nor unsung. And better thus
Beneath that indiscriminating stroke,
Better to fall, than to have lived to mourn, 60
As sure thou wouldst, in misery and remorse,

Thine own disastrous triumph; to have seen,
If the Almighty at that awful hour
Had turn'd away his face, wild Ignorance
Let loose, and frantic Vengeance, and dark
    Zeal,
And all bad passions tyrannous, and the
    fires
Of Persecution once again ablaze.
How had it sunk into thy soul to see,
Last curse of all, the ruffian slaves of
    France
In thy dear native country lording it!   70
How happier thus, in that heroic mood
That takes away the sting of death, to die,
By all the good and all the wise forgiven,
Yea, in all ages by the wise and good
To be remember'd, mourn'd, and honor'd still.
Keswick

MY DAYS AMONG THE DEAD ARE PAST

My days among the dead are past;
    Around me I behold,
Where'er these casual eyes are cast,
    The mighty minds of old;
My never-failing friends are they,
With whom I converse day by day.

With them I take delight in weal,
    And seek relief in woe;
And while I understand and feel
    How much to them I owe,   10
My cheeks have often been bedew'd
With tears of thoughtful gratitude.

My thoughts are with the dead, with them
    I live in long-past years,
Their virtues love, their faults condemn,
    Partake their hopes and fears,
And from their lessons seek and find
Instruction with an humble mind.

My hopes are with the dead, anon
    My place with them will be,   20
And I with them shall travel on
    Through all futurity;
Yet leaving here a name, I trust,
That will not perish in the dust.
1818

IMITATED FROM THE PERSIAN

Lord! who art merciful as well as just,
Incline thine ear to me, a child of dust!
Not what I would, O Lord! I offer thee,
    Alas! but what I can.
Father Almighty, who hast made me man,
And bade me look to Heaven, for Thou art
    there,
Accept my sacrifice and humble prayer.
Four things which are not in thy treasury,
I lay before thee, Lord, with this petition:—
    My nothingness, my wants,   10
    My sins, and my contrition.

Lowther Castle, 1828

PRELUDE

"Tell us a story, old Robin Gray!
  This merry Christmas time;
We are all in our glory; so tell us a story,
  Either in prose or in rhyme.

"Open your budget, old Robin Gray!
  We very well know it is full:
Come! out with a murder,—a Goblin,
    —a Ghost,
  Or a tale of a Cock and a Bull!"

"I have no tale of a Cock and a Bull,
  My good little women and men;   10
But 'twill do as well, perhaps, if I tell
  A tale of a Cock and a Hen."

Pub. 1829

From A VISION OF JUDGEMENT

(Part VI)

THE ABSOLVERS

Ho! he exclaim'd, King George of England
  standeth in judgment!
Hell hath been dumb in his presence. Ye who
  on earth arraign'd him,
Come ye before him now, and here accuse or
  absolve him!
For injustice hath here no place.

        From the Souls of the Blessed
Some were there then who advanced; and more
  from the skirts of the meeting—

Spirits who had not yet accomplish'd their
  purification,
Yet, being cleansed from pride, from faction
  and error deliver'd,
Purged of the film wherewith the eye of the
  mind is clouded,
They, in their better state, saw all things clear;
  and discerning
Now, in the light of truth, what tortuous views
  had deceived them,   10
They acknowledged their fault, and own'd the
  wrong they had offer'd;
Not without ingenuous shame, and a sense of
  compunction,
More or less, as each had more or less to atone
  for.
One alone remain'd, when the rest had retired
  to their station:
Silently he had stood, and still unmoved and
  in silence,
With a steady mien, regarded the face of the
  Monarch.
Thoughtful awhile he gazed; severe, but
  serene, was his aspect;
Calm, but stern; like one whom no compassion
  could weaken,
Neither could doubt deter, nor violent im-
  pulses alter;
Lord of his own resolves,—of his own heart
  absolute master.   20
Awful Spirit; his place was with ancient sages
  and heroes;
Fabius, Aristides, and Solon, and Epami-
  nondas.

  Here then at the Gate of Heaven we are
    met! said the Spirit;
King of England! albeit in life opposed to each
  other,
Here we meet at last. Not unprepared for the
  meeting
Ween I; for we had both outlived all enmity,
  rendering
Each to each that justice which each from each
  had withholden.
In the course of events, to thee I seem'd as a
  Rebel,
Thou a Tyrant to me;—so strongly doth cir-
  cumstance rule men
During evil days, when right and wrong are
  confounded.   30

or if you think it necessary that I don't tax brains which are bona
fide and better employed?

If you are of opinion that I may hold myself absolved, shall I
insert these lines in a copy of Roderick, for presentation. Understand
I pray you that I am far from wishing to be thought offensive
with such things, & only wish to do it, if it ought to be done
& could not without some impropriety be left undone.

    Prince, I approach thee not with annual strain
    On temporal theme, soon framed nor lasting long,
    Nor seek I now with gratulations vain
    To win thine ear. What need the Poet's song
    To join the general praise when all rejoice,
    And grateful nations with one heart & voice
    Thee & thy counsels bless? Let History pay,
    Then most extolling both when most sincere,
    The eternal meed to George & England due.
    Hither I come with this elaborate lay,
    The thoughtful work of many a studious year;
    So may I best becoming zeal display
    Of the high honour by thy hand conferred
    On no unworthy servant of the Muse.

Page of a Southey Letter. (See Appendix I.)

Left to our hearts we were just. For me, my
    actions have spoken,
That not for lawless desires, nor goaded by
    desperate fortunes,
Nor for ambition, I chose my part; but ob-
    servant of duty,
Self-approved. And here, this witness I will-
    ingly bear thee,—
Here, before Angels and Men, in the awful
    hour of judgment,—
Thou too didst act with upright heart, as be-
    fitted a Sovereign
True to his sacred trust, to his crown, his
    kingdom, and people.
Heaven in these things fulfill'd its wise, though
    inscrutable purpose,
While we work'd its will, doing each in his
    place as became him.

Washington! said the Monarch, well hast
    thou spoken and truly,   40

Just to thyself and to me. On them is the guilt
    of the contest,
Who for wicked ends, with foul arts of faction
    and falsehood,
Kindled and fed the flame; but verily they have
    their guerdon.
Thou and I are free from offence. And would
    that the nations,
Learning of us, would lay aside all wrongful
    resentment,
All injurious thought, and, honoring each in
    the other
Kindred courage and virtue, and cognate
    knowledge and freedom,
Live in brotherhood wisely conjoin'd. We set
    the example.
They who stir up strife, and would break that
    natural concord,
Evil they sow, and sorrow will they reap for
    their harvest.   50
1821

HENRY KIRKE WHITE
[March 21, 1785–October 19, 1806]

HENRY KIRKE WHITE was born the son of a butcher in Nottingham and, although he showed astonishing precocity in his studies, was put to work at a stocking-loom at the age of fourteen. Soon after, however, he left this work and was articled to a lawyer. He continued his studies, and the habits of work which ultimately killed him may be understood from the fact that at this time, while still in his early teens, he would, after a full day at the office, study until one, two, or three in the morning and then rise at five, for more study. *Clifton Grove* (1803), the only volume to appear during his lifetime, was published in the hope of obtaining funds to attend the University. It failed to sell, but a sizarship was obtained for him at St. John's College, Cambridge, which college he entered in October 1805. He died, literally of overwork, in his college rooms the following year.

In his preface to *Clifton Grove* White stated, "Men are not, I believe, frequently known to bestow much labour on their amusements; and these poems were, most of them, written merely to beguile a leisure hour, or to fill up the languid intervals of studies of a severer nature." The preface is unfortunate—there is a good deal of the false modesty of a boy of eighteen in it, but, nevertheless, Kirke White *did* begin his literary career by announcing that his poems were the product of "languid intervals." Southey was won by the ingenuousness of the statement and so angered by the treatment White received in certain reviews that he became White's champion. It was Southey who issued *The Remains of Henry Kirke White* in two volumes in 1807. It ran through ten editions in about fifteen years. Southey added a supplementary volume of *Remains* in 1822. Posterity, in spite of Southey's enthusiasm, has been inclined to accept White's own statement that the poems are products of "languid intervals."

DESCRIPTION OF A SUMMER'S EVE

Down the sultry arc of day,
The burning wheels have urged their way,
And Eve along the western skies
Sheds her intermingling dyes.
Down the deep, the miry lane,
Creeking comes the empty wain,
And Driver on the shaft-horse sits,
Whistling now and then by fits;
And oft, with his accustomed call,
Urging on the sluggish Ball.   10
The barn is still, the master's gone,
And Thresher puts his jacket on,
While Dick, upon the ladder tall,
Nails the dead kite to the wall.
Here comes shepherd Jack at last,
He has penned the sheep-cote fast,
For 'twas but two nights before,
A lamb was eaten on the moor:
His empty wallet *Rover* carries,
Nor for Jack, when near home, tarries.   20
With lolling tongue he runs to try,
If the horse-trough be not dry,
The milk is settled in the pans,
And supper messes in the cans;
In the hovel carts are wheeled,
And both the colts are drove a-field;
The horses are all bedded up,
And the ewe is with the tup.
The snare for Mister Fox is set,
The leaven laid, the thatching wet,   30
And Bess has slinked away to talk
With Roger in the holly-walk.

Now on the settle all, but Bess,
Are set to eat their supper mess;
And little Tom, and roguish Kate,
Are swinging on the meadow gate.
Now they chat of various things,
Of taxes, ministers, and kings,
Or else tell all the village news,
How madam did the squire refuse;   40
How parson on his tithes was bent,
And landlord oft distrained for rent.
Thus do they talk, till in the sky
The pale eyed moon is mounted high,
And from the alehouse drunken Ned
Had reeled—then hasten all to bed.
The mistress sees that lazy Kate
The happing coal on kitchen grate

Has laid—while master goes throughout,
Sees shutters fast, the mastiff out,   50
The candles safe, the hearths all clear,
And nought from thieves or fire to fear;
Then both to bed together creep,
And join the general troop of sleep.

1803–1806

VERSES

When pride and envy, and the scorn
    Of wealth, my heart with gall imbued,
I thought how pleasant were the morn
    Of silence in the solitude;
To hear the forest bee on wing;
Or by the stream, or woodland spring,
To lie and muse alone—alone,
While the tinkling waters moan,
Or such wild sounds arise, as say,
Man and noise are far away.   10

Now, surely, thought I, there's enow
    To fill life's dusty way;
And who will miss a poet's feet,
    Or wonder where he stray?
So to the woods and waste I'll go,
    And I will build an osier bower;
And sweetly there to me shall flow
    The meditative hour.

And when the Autumn's withering hand
Shall strew with leaves the sylvan land,   20
I'll to the forest caverns hie:
And in the dark and stormy nights
I'll listen to the shrieking sprites,
Who, in the wintry wolds and floods,
Keep jubilee, and shred the woods;
Or, as it drifted soft and slow,
Hurl in ten thousand shapes the snow.

1803–1806

A PASTORAL SONG

Come, Anna! come, the morning dawns,
    Faint streaks of radiance tinge the skies;
Come, let us seek the dewy lawns,
    And watch the early lark arise;
    While nature clad in vesture gay,
    Hails the loved return of day.

Our flocks that nip the scanty blade
    Upon the moor, shall seek the vale;

And then, secure beneath the shade,
 We'll listen to the throstle's tale; 10
 And watch the silver clouds above,
 As o'er the azure vault they rove.

Come, Anna! come, and bring thy lute,
 That with its tones, so softly sweet,
In cadence with my mellow flute,
 We may beguile the noon-tide heat;
 While near the mellow bee shall join,
 To raise a harmony divine.

And then at eve, when silence reigns,
 Except when heard the beetle's hum; 20
We'll leave the sober-tinted plains,
 To these sweet heights again we'll come;
 And thou to thy soft lute shalt play
 A solemn vesper to departing day.

1803–1806

FRAGMENT

O PALE art thou, my lamp, and faint
 Thy melancholy ray:

When the still night's unclouded saint
 Is walking on her way.
 Through my lattice leaf embowered,
 Fair she sheds her shadowy beam;
 And o'er my silent sacred room,
 Casts a chequered twilight gloom;
 I throw aside the learnèd sheet,
I cannot choose but gaze, she looks so mildly
 sweet. 10
 Sad vestal why art thou so fair,
 Or why am I so frail?

Methinks thou lookest kindly on me, Moon,
 And cheerest my lone hours with sweet re-
 gards!
Surely like me thou'rt sad, but dost not speak
 Thy sadness to the cold unheeding crowd;
So mournfully compos'd, o'er yonder cloud
Thou shinest, like a cresset, beaming far
From the rude watch-tower, o'er the Atlantic
 wave.

1803–1806

CHARLES WOLFE

[December 14, 1791–February 21, 1823]

CHARLES WOLFE, an Irish poet, had his earlier schooling in England but returned to Trinity College, Dublin, where he took his B.A. in 1814. He entered the church in 1817, but in 1821 was obliged to give up his work because of failing health. He died at Cork in 1823. *The Burial of Sir John Moore* is Wolfe's only poem of consequence. It was written in the rooms of a college friend in 1816 and circulated in manuscript until it was printed over the initials C. W. in the *Newry Telegraph*, an Ulster newspaper, in 1817. Reprinted in English papers, some confusion arose as to its authorship, and it was by some attributed to Byron, who praised the poem but disclaimed it.

THE BURIAL OF SIR JOHN MOORE
AT CORUNNA

NOT a drum was heard, not a funeral note,
 As his corse to the rampart we hurried;
Not a soldier discharged his farewell shot
 O'er the grave where our hero we buried.

We buried him darkly at dead of night,
 The sods with our bayonets turning;
By the struggling moonbeam's misty light,
 And the lantern dimly burning.

No useless coffin enclosed his breast,
 Not in sheet nor in shroud we wound
 him, 10
But he lay like a warrior taking his rest
 With his martial cloak around him.

Few and short were the prayers we said,
 And we spoke not a word of sorrow;
But we stedfastly gazed on the face that was
 dead,
 And we bitterly thought of the morrow.

We thought as we hollowed his narrow bed,
  And smoothed down his lonely pillow,
That the foe and the stranger would tread o'er
    his head,
  And we far away on the billow!   20

Lightly they'll talk of the spirit that's gone,
  And o'er his cold ashes upbraid him,—
But little he'll reck, if they let him sleep on
  In the grave where a Briton has laid
    him.

But half of our weary task was done
  When the clock struck the hour for retiring;
And we heard the distant and random gun
  That the foe was sullenly firing.

Slowly and sadly we laid him down,
  From the field of his fame fresh and gory; 30
We carved not a line, and we raised not a
    stone—
  But we left him alone with his glory.
1816

THE APPENDIX

I. THE ILLUSTRATIONS
II. BIBLIOGRAPHIES AND NOTES
III. INDEX OF AUTHORS, TITLES, AND
FIRST LINES OF POETRY

APPENDIX I

THE ILLUSTRATIONS

The facsimiles used in illustrating this volume are all made from originals in the collection of Mr. William T. H. Howe, who has placed them at the disposal of the Editors.

PAGE 6.—A Page from Wordsworth's MS of *The Excursion*.

> Wild is the music of the Autumn west wind
> Among the faded woods; but these blithe notes
> Strike the deserted to the heart; I speak
> Of what I know and what we feel within.
> Beside the Cottage in which Emma dwelt
> Stands a tall ashtree, to whose top most twig
> A Thrush resorts and annually chants
> At morn or evening, from that naked perch
> While all the undergrove is thick with leaves
> A time-beguiling ditty for delight
> Of his fond partner, silent in the nest.
> Ah why, said Emma, sighing to herself,
> Why do not words and kiss and solemn pledges
> And nature which is kind in woman's breast
> And reason that in man is wise and good
> And fear of him who is a righteous judge—
> Why do not these prevail for human life
> To keep two hearts together that began
> Their spring time with one love, and that have need
> Of mutual pity and forgiveness, sweet
> To grant, or to receive?— while that poor Bird—
> O come and hear him. Thou who hast to me
> Been faithless, hear him, though a lowly creature,
> One of God's simple children that as yet know not
> The universal Parent, how he sings
> As if he wished the firmament of heaven

These lines are from Book VI, lines 858–883. Note that this passage varies from the published version in the opening lines. Compare with the above the following:

> With spirit-saddening power
> Winds pipe through fading woods; but those blithe notes
> Strike the deserted to the heart;

Note also that the name *Emma* was later changed to *Ellen*.

PAGE 78.—Title-page of a Presentation Copy of *The Waggoner*.

Edith May Southey was the daughter of Robert Southey, the poet. *The Waggoner* appeared, with a few shorter poems, in 1819, with the following dedication to Lamb:

My dear friend—When I sent you, a few weeks ago, "The Tale of Peter Bell," you asked "Why *The Waggoner* was not added?" To say the truth, from the higher tone of imagination and the deeper touches of passion aimed at in the former, I apprehended this little piece could not accompany it without disadvantage. In the year 1806, if I am not mistaken, *The Waggoner* was read to you in manuscript, and as you have remembered it for so long a time, I am the more encouraged to hope that, since the localities on which the Poem partly depends did not prevent its being interesting to you, it may prove acceptable to others. Being, therefore, in some measure the cause of its present appearance, you must allow me the gratification of inscribing it to you; in acknowledgment of the pleasure I have derived from your writings, and of the high esteem with which

> I am very truly yours,
> William Wordsworth.

PAGE 97.—Presentation Copy of Wordsworth's *The Excursion.*

This is a facsimile of the cover of the 1814 edition of *The Excursion.* The identity of Mrs. Lees is not known.

PAGE 120.—Reduced Facsimile of a Statement about an Agreement with Moxon, the Publisher. In Wordsworth's Handwriting.

In consideration of the liberal terms of the agreement concluded this day between Mr Moxon and Mr Wordsworth, Mr Wordsworth hereby declares that he considers Mr Moxon as entitled to especial consideration in preference to other Publishers for any future edition which may be required of his works, and he hereby expresses wish that if he should die before the present Edition be disposed of that his Executor would act in conformity to this declaration.

> Wm Wordsworth

London June 25
      1836

Edward Moxon was one of the foremost publishers of his day. He married Emma Isola, the adopted daughter of Charles and Mary Lamb.

PAGE 146.—A Page of Coleridge's Corrected Copy for the 1797 edition of the *Poems.*

The passage is from *Ode to the Departing Year,* lines 144–158. The note at the bottom of the page is addressed to Joseph Cottle, an enterprising and ambitious young publisher of Bristol, and reads: I suspect, almost suspect, that the word "dark" was *intentionally* substituted for "lank"—if so, twas the most *tasteless* thing thou ever didst,

> Dear Joseph!—

PAGE 172.—Lines 76–90 of the 1790 version of *Monody on the Death of Chatterton.*

PAGE 180.—Reduced Facsimile of the First Page of the MS of Coleridge's *The Raven.*

> Beneath a goodly old Oak-tree
> There was of swine a large company
> They were making a rude repast
> Grunting as they crunch'd the mast
> Then they trotted away, for the wind grew high
> One acorn they left and no more mote you spy.
> But soon came a Raven, who lik'd not such folly
> He belong'd, I believe, to the Witch Melancholy!
> Blacker was he than the blackest jet—,
> Flew low in the rain, his feathers were wet
> He pick'd up the acorn and buried it strait
> By the side of a River both deep and great
> Where then did the Raven go?
> He went high and low:
> Over hill, over dale did the black Raven go.
> Many Autumns, many Springs
> Travell'd he on wandering wings:
> Many Summers, many Winters—
> I can't tell half his adventures!

This MS, which was first printed in the *Morning Post,* March 10, 1798, is probably the earliest version of the poem.

PAGE 192.—Lines 1–38 of *Youth and Age* in Coleridge's Handwriting.

These lines were, in all probability, composed in 1823. They were first published with the heading *Youth and Age* in the *Literary Souvenir*, 1828 and also in the *Bijou*, 1828. Eleven lines were added, later. The variations between this version and the text as reprinted in *Poetical Works* are as follows:

line 10   O'er *aery cliffs* and *glittering* sands
12   Like those trim *skiffs*, unknown of yore
21   Of *Friendship, Love*, and Liberty
25   O Youth! for years so *many* and sweet
34   This *drooping* gait, this altered size

PAGE 241.—Six Stanzas of Byron's MS of *Love and Gold*.

This poem when published was entitled *Love and Gold* and was in all probability addressed to the poet's future wife. An entry in the Diary for November 30, 1813, in which Annabella (Miss Milbanke) is described "as an heiress, a girl of twenty, a peeress that is to be," etc., and a letter from Byron to Miss Milbanke dated November 29, 1813, in which he alludes to her would-be suitors, "your thousand and one pretendants," etc., suggest that the lines were addressed to Miss Milbanke when he first made her acquaintance in 1812 or 1813.

The facsimile does not include stanzas 5, 6, and 7. The complete poem is as follows:

LOVE AND GOLD

I

I cannot talk of Love to thee,
    Though thou art young and free and fair!
There is a spell thou dost not see,
    That bids a genuine love despair.

2

And yet that spell invites each youth,
    For thee to sigh, or seem to sigh;
Makes falsehood wear the garb of truth,
    And Truth itself appear a lie.

3

If ever Doubt a place possest
    In woman's heart, 'twere wise in thine:
Admit not Love into thy breast,
    Doubt others' love, nor trust in mine.

4

Perchance 'tis feigned, perchance sincere,
    But false or true thou canst not tell;
So much hast thou from all to fear,
    In that unconquerable spell.

5

Of all the herd that throng around,
    Thy simpering or thy sighing train,
Come tell me who to thee is bound
    By Love's or Plutus' heavier chain.

6

In some 'tis Nature, some 'tis Art
    That bids them worship at thy shrine;
But thou deserv'st a better heart,
    Than they or I can give for thine.

7

For thee, and such as thee, behold,
    Is Fortune painted truly—blind!
Who doomed thee to be bought or sold,
    Has proved too bounteous to be kind.

8

Each day some tempter's crafty suit
　　Would woo thee to a loveless bed:
I see thee to the altar's foot
　　A decorated victim led.

9

Adieu, dear maid! I must not speak
　　Whate'er my secret thoughts may be;
Though thou art all that man can reck
　　I dare not talk of Love to thee.

PAGE 249.—A Page from Byron's *Childe Harold's Pilgrimage*.

Let such approach this consecrated land
　　And pass in peace along the magic waste
But spare its relics—let no wanton hand
　　Deface the scenes already how effaced!
Not for such portion were these altars placed—
　　Revere the remnant nations once revered
So may our country's name be undisgraced!
　　So mayst thou prosper where thy youth was reared
By every honest joy of love and life endeared!

For thee, who thus in too protracted song
　　Hast soothed thine idlesse with inglorious lays,
Soon shall thy voice be lost amid the throng
　　Of louder minstrels of these later days,
To these resign the strife for fading Bays.

These lines are from Canto II, Stanzas 93 and 94 (in part). Note that the published version has **busy** instead of *wanton* in line 3.

PAGE 293.—Stanza III of the *Dedication to Don Juan* in Byron's Handwriting.

You Bob—are rather insolent, you know—
　　As being disappointed in your wish
To supersede all warblers now below,
　　And be the only blackbird in the dish;
And then you overstrain yourself, or so
　　And tumble downward like the flying fish
Gasping on deck because you were too high, Bob
And fall for lack of moisture quite a dry Bob!

PAGES 394 AND 395.—Two Pages of a Letter from Byron to Leigh Hunt.

January 10ᵗʰ 1823

Dear H.

It appears to me that your brother might direct his counsel to cite from "Watt Tyler" and ask *why that* is not prosecuted? Also a little from *his* Vision. But it would be as well to send off your *Collectanea* quickly that they may have time to prepare them for the Court and Courtiers. I have sent to Mrs S[helley] for the benefit of being copied a poem of about seven hundred and fifty lines length —the Age of Bronze—or Carmen Seculare et Annus Mirabilis—with this epigraph "Impar *Congressus* Achilli" It is calculated for the reading part of the million—being all on politics, etc., etc., etc., and a review of the day in general—in my early English Bards style—but a little more stilted and somewhat too full of "epithets of war" and classical and historical allusions. If notes are necessary, they can be added. If it will do for "the Liberal," it and the Pulci will form (in size that is) a good half number. But of this you can judge. It is in the heroic couplet measure, which is an old friend with a new face.

I congratulate you on the weather.

Yours ever

N. B.

The brother referred to is John Hunt who, in 1821, had been once more prosecuted for his liberal political opinions and had been sentenced to two years' imprisonment. *Watt Tyler*, a social drama, was published by Southey in 1817. The reference to *"his* Vision" is to Southey's *A Vision of Judgment,* 1821. Byron's poem, *The Age of Bronze, Carmen Seculare et Annus haud Mirabilis 1822,* was published in London (but not in the *Liberal*) by John Hunt in June, 1823. The brazen age which Byron here satirizes was 1822, the year after Napoleon's death, which witnessed a revolution in Spain and the Congress of Allied Sovereigns in Vienna. The *Liberal* was a political collaboration in the form of a periodical which Byron attempted with Leigh Hunt and Shelley. It ran through part of 1822 and 1823, terminating with the death of Shelley.

PAGES 418 AND 419.—Two Pages of Shelley's MS of *The Revolt of Islam.*

Is God itself, the priests its downfall knew
As day by day their altars lonelier grew,
Till they were left alone within the fane;
The shafts of falsehood unpolluting flew,
And the cold sneers of calumny were vain,
The union of the free with discord's brand to stain.

19

The rest thou knowest—lo! we two are here
We have survived a ruin wide and deep
Strange thoughts are mine—I cannot grieve or fear,
Sitting with thee upon the lonely steep
I smile tho' human love should make me weep;
We have survived a joy that knows no sorrow,
And I do feel a mighty calmness creep
Over my heart, which can no longer borrow
Its hues from chance or change, dark children of tomorrow.

20

We know not what will come—yet Laon, dearest,
Cythna shall be the prophetess of Love,
Her lips shall rob thee of the grace thou wearest
To hide thy heart, and clothe the shapes which rove
Within the homeless Future's wintry grove,—
For I now, sitting thus beside thee, seem
Even with thy breath and blood to live and move,
And violence and wrong are as a dream
Which rolls from steadfast truth an unreturning stream.

This fragment is lines 3624–3648 of *The Revolt of Islam.* The poem was originally called *Laon and Cythna* after its principal characters, and a few copies were printed under this title in 1817. Attention is called to the variations between the first three lines of the MS and the reading of the published version. The note in the lower right-hand corner of the second sheet was made by William Bell Scott, a friend of G. H. Lewes whom he met through Leigh Hunt, and reads as follows: Leaf of the MS of the "Revolt of Islam" in Shelley's Handwriting. Given me by G. H. Lewes. W. B. S.

PAGE 437.—A Page of *Queen Mab* with Shelley's Corrections.

Queen Mab, principally written, as it would seem, in 1812 was privately printed under the title *Queen Mab: A Philosophical Poem,* London, 1813. Shelley later revised this juvenile effort and published it in 1816 as *The Dæmon of the World, A Fragment.* This page with Shelley's corrections belonged to Shelley's own copy of *Queen Mab* and constitutes lines 1–16 of Canto VIII. When reprinted, this passage became lines 316–330 of *The Dæmon of the World.* In the revised copy the first four lines which are struck out are replaced by lines which resemble the original but slightly, either in ideas or phrasing. The remaining lines were worked into the later poem as they stand corrected here. The variations may be accounted for on the supposition that Shelley worked a little on the proof sheets.

PAGE 443.—An Unpublished Fragment by Shelley.

SADAK THE WANDERER *A fragment*

. . . . . .

He thro' Storm and Wind has gone!
To the Mountains' topmost stone
He has climbed, to bear the food
From the Eagle's screaming brood;
By the turbid Jungle tide
For his meal the wolf has died;
He has braved the Tyger's lair
In his bleeding prey to share
Hark the wounded Panther's yell
Flying from the torn gazelle
By the food wild, weary, wan,
Stands a thing that once was man.

Look upon that withered brow
See the glance that burns below,
See the lank and scattered hair
See the limb, swart, withered, bare,
See the feet that leave their mark
On the rail in bloodstains dark
Who thus o'er the World doth roam
With the Desert for his home?

Hath he wandered with the brand
Of the robber in his hand.
Hath his soul been steeped in crime
That hath smote him in his prime?
Stainless as the newborn child,
Strays this Wanderer thro' the Wild.

PAGE 498.—Presentation Copy of *Adonais* from Shelley to Hogg.

Thomas Jefferson Hogg was a young man from Durham whom Shelley met at Oxford in the autumn of 1810. The two youths struck up a warm friendship at once. The results of their extended discussions was the pamphlet *The Necessity of Atheism* which occasioned their expulsion from the university. Their intimacy continued throughout life, and after Shelley's death Hogg became his official biographer. See note to page 749.

PAGE 540.—A Paragraph from Shelley's Letter to Leigh Hunt, December 8, 1816.

In the earlier part of this very interesting letter Shelley asks Hunt to send him a copy of the *Examiner* for December 1, 1816. This copy of the *Examiner* contained an article entitled "Young Poets" in which Leigh Hunt refers to the work of Shelley, John Hamilton Reynolds, and John Keats. His comments upon *Alastor* pronounce Shelley to be "a very striking and original thinker," and probably constitute the first public recognition of Shelley as a poet. Keats had not then published a volume, but Leigh Hunt had the good fortune of printing in this article for the first time the sonnet "On First Looking into Chapman's Homer."

The portion of the letter here reproduced is as follows:

When will you send me your poems? I never knew that you had published any other than "Rimini," with which I was exceedingly delighted. The *story* of the poem has an interest of a very uncommon and irresistible character,—though it appeared to me that you have subjected yourself to some rules in the composition which fetter your genius, and diminish the effect of the conceptions. Though in one sense, I am no poet, I am not so insensible to poetry as to read "Rimini" unmoved.—When will you send me your other poems?

Besides the boyish collection of *Juvenilia*, 1801, the following volumes of Leigh Hunt's poetry had been published: *The Feast of the Poets*, 1814 and 1815; *The Descent of Liberty*, a mask 1815; and *The Story of Rimini*, 1816.

PAGE 556.—The First Published Volume of Keats's Poems.

Keats's first volume of verse was dedicated to Leigh Hunt and published with his encouragement in March, 1817. Hunt had printed two of the sonnets contained in it the year before in the *Examiner*. It was a copy of this edition of Keats's poems that was found in Shelley's pocket when his dead body was washed ashore near Viareggio.

PAGE 596.—The Concluding Stanza of *Ode to Melancholy* in Keats's Handwriting.

She lives with Beauty—Beauty that must die;
And Joy, whose hand is ever at his lips
Bidding adieu; and aching Pleasure nigh,
Turning to poison while the bee-mouth sips:
Ay, in the very temple of Delight
Veiled Melancholy has her sovran shrine,
Though seen of none but him whose strenuous tongue
Can burst Joy's grape against his palate fine;
His soul shall taste the anguish of her might,
And be among her cloudy trophies hung.

Note the felicitous substitution of *dwells* for *lives* in the first line of the published version. Other changes are *save* for *but* in line 7 and *sadness* for *anguish* in the ninth line of the stanza.

PAGE 619.—An Unpublished Letter from John Keats to Jane Reynolds.

Jane and Marianne Reynolds were the sisters of Keats's good friend John Hamilton Reynolds, the poet. Marianne, the elder of these sisters, married a Mr. Green and was the mother of the two distinguished artists, Charles and Townley Green. Jane married Thomas Hood, the poet, on May 5, 1824.
This letter to Jane shows that Keats was on very pleasant terms with the sisters:

My dear Jane,
You must not expect that your Porcupine quill is to be shot at me with impunity without you mean to question the existence of the Pyramids or rout Sir Isaac Newton out of his coffin. If I did not think you had a kind of preference yourself for Juliet, I would not say a word more about it—but, as I know, people have to be reminded of those they most love. 'Tis with me a certain thing that you are merely fishing for a little proing and conning thereon—As for you[r] accusations, I perhaps may answer them like Haydon in a Postscript. If you go on at this rate I shall always have you in my imagination side by side with Bayley's Picture of Jeremy Taylor who always looks as if he were going to hit me a rap with a Book he hold[s] in a very threatening position. My head is always in imminent danger. However with the armour of words and the Sword of Syllables I hope to attack you in a very short time more at length

My love to Marianne   Yours sincerely
John Keats.

PAGE 667.—Page of MS of a Poem by Thomas Campbell.

He prays to Heaven for England's king, he says:
And dares he to the God of Mercy kneel,
Besmeared with massacres from head to heel?
No; Moloch is his god—to him he prays;
And if his weird-like prayers had power to bring
An influence, their power would be to curse.
His hate is baleful, but his love is worse—
A serpent's slaver deadlier than its sting!
Oh, feeble statesmen—ignominious times,*
That lick the tyrant's feet, and smile upon his crimes.

* NOTE. There is not upon record a more disgusting scene of Russian hypocrisy and (woe that must be written!) of British humiliation than that which passed on board the Talavera when British sailors accepted money from the Emperor Nicholas and gave him cheers—It will require the Talavera to fight well with the first Russian ship that she may have to encounter to make us forget that day—

This fragment represents the concluding lines of Thomas Campbell's poem entitled *To Sir Francis Burdett*, on his speech delivered in Parliament, August 7, 1832, respecting the foreign policy of Great Britain. The starred notation is Campbell's own comment upon the situation.

PAGE 678.—A Poem by John Clare.

John Clare was known as the "Northamptonshire Peasant Poet," and his most successful poems portray the Northampton country which he knew so well. This poem seems not to have been published.

PAGE 693.—Presentation Copy from Thomas Hood to Coleridge.

This is a copy of the first series of *Whims and Oddities* which was so successful that a second series followed in 1827. The quotation on the title page is intended as a defense of punning, a habit to which Hood was addicted. His excesses in this direction annoyed his more serious readers.

PAGE 709.—Copy of a Poem by Leigh Hunt Written while the Author was in Surrey Jail.

To Hampstead

[First published in the *Examiner*, December 18, 1814, as "Sonnet to Hampstead IV"; reprinted 1815, 1860.]

Winter has reached thee once at last;
  And now the rambler, whom thy groves yet please,
  Feels on his house-warm lips the thin air freeze;
While in his shrugging neck the resolute blast
Comes edging; and the leaves, in heaps down cast
  He shuffles with his hastening foot, and sees
  The cold sky whitening through the wiry trees,
And sighs to think his loitering noons have passed.

And do I love thee less to paint thee so?
  No: this the season is of beauty still
    Doubled at heart,—of smoke with whirling glee
Uptumbling ever from the blaze below,
  And home remembered most,—and oh, loved hill,
    The second, and the last, away from thee!

                           L. Hunt

Surrey Jail, November 1814

In 1808 Leigh Hunt formed a partnership with his brother John to issue the *Examiner*, a journal of liberal politics, which attained under his editorship a high reputation for literary merit. In December, 1812, the brothers were condemned to pay each a fine of five hundred pounds and to be imprisoned two years for a satirical article in which the prince regent was styled an "Adonis of fifty." All through his imprisonment Leigh Hunt continued to edit the *Examiner*. He left prison in February, 1815.

PAGE 711.—A Sonnet by Leigh Hunt.

The Poets

[First published in the *Examiner*, December 24, 1815; not reprinted.]

Were I to name, out of the times gone by,
  The poets dearest to me, I should say,
  Pulci for spirits, and a fine, free way;
Chaucer for manners, and close, silent eye;
Milton for classic taste, and harp strung high;
  Spenser for luxury, and sweet, sylvan play;
  Horace for chatting with, from day to day;
Shakspeare for all, but most, society

But which take with me, could I take but one?
  Shakspeare,—as long as I was unoppressed
    With the world's weight, making sad thoughts intenser;
But did I wish, out of the common sun,
  To lay a wounded heart in leafy rest,
    And dream of things far off and healing,—Spenser.

8 November 1815

PAGE 713.—Presentation Copy to Keats from Leigh Hunt.

Keats's first volume of verse was dedicated to Leigh Hunt and published with his encouragement in March, 1817. This presentation copy published in the following year is further evidence of the friendship between these two youthful writers.

PAGE 715.—Letter from Charles Lamb to Bernard Barton.

[August, 1827]

Dear B.

I am going to collect verses written by me in Albums for a superb "Forget me not" sort of thing; they are wanted immediately. Would it be unpleasant to yourself or daughter to insert *mine* for *hers?* with or without her name, or with initials, or silently?

If not, pray *transcribe them* and send me immediately. I have no copy:

And with them any little scrap of verse of your own, unpublished, for a young person's pocket-book, who is with us. A line or two, religious or profane, with your autograph and date and place, would be inestimable to her. Her name is Emma.

But if the first request be not conformable to any of your wishes,

Say so

Yours, C Lamb

Enfield

Bernard Barton was a Quaker and a poet with whom Lamb carried on an extensive correspondence for some years. The "young person" referred to in the letter is Emma Isola whom Charles and Mary Lamb had adopted. She married Edward Moxon, the publisher, in 1833.

This letter is not published by either Ainger or Lucas. That Barton complied, however, is seen by the following note from Lamb to Barton to be found in both collections under date of August 28, 1827.

Dear B. B.—I am thankful to you for your ready compliance with my wishes. Emma is delighted with your verses, to which I have appended this notice, "The sixth line refers to the child of a dear friend of the author's, named Emma," without which it must be obscure, and have sent it with four album poems of my own (your daughter's with your heading, requesting it a place next mine) to a Mr. Fraser, who is to be editor of a more superb pocket-book than has yet appeared by far!

Lamb's *Album Verses* were published in 1830.

PAGE 716.—Letter from Charles Lamb to James Gilman.

[?Early Spring, 1830.]

Dear Gilman,

Pray do you or S. T. C. immediately write to say you have received back the golden works of the dear fine old Angel which I part from bleeding—and to say how the winter has used you all. It is our intention soon, weather permitting, to come over for a day at Highgate for a quiet gossip and a cup of tea. Be sure to tell us if we may come casually for in this change of climate, there is no naming a day for walking. With best loves to Mrs Gilman, etc.

Yours, mopish but in health,

C Lamb

I shall be uneasy till I hear of Fuller's safe arrival

This letter to James Gilman was written during the period in which Samuel Taylor Coleridge was making his home with the Gilman family at Highgate. The "dear fine old Angel" was Thomas Fuller, a seventeenth century divine, author of *The Church History of Britain, The History of the Worthies of England, Collected Sermons*, etc. Lamb's enthusiasm for Fuller is further attested by his volume, *Specimens from the Writings of T. Fuller*, to be found in L. Hutchinson's edition of Lamb, vol. I pp. 142–150.

PAGE 720.—Page of the Rare First Edition of Landor's Poems of 1802, with the Author's Corrections.

This volume bears the title *Poetry*, by the author of *Gebir*. This passage is probably a part of the projected epic of *The Phocæans*. It was not reprinted in the editions of Landor's works published in 1846 and 1876.

PAGE 729.—A Poem by Walter Savage Landor.

This charming bit of *vers de société* was published as XCIV of the "Epigrams" in *Last Fruit Off an Old Tree* (1853). He collected the poems of this volume from his friends for whom they had been written as occasional verses, and published them in his seventy-ninth year. This poem when published was revised to read:

> What is my faith? I do believe
> That Ladies never would deceive
> And that the little fault of Eve
> Is very easy to retrieve.
>
> *She lost us immortality!*
> Well, so she might; and what care I?
> Eden and Paradise are nigh
> As ever: should we pass them by.

Note the more personal coloring of the two concluding lines of the manuscript version.

PAGE 733.—A Letter to Robert Browning Written in the Last Year of His Life.

Dear Browning

It is now several weeks since I totally lost my voice and hearing. My last effort of writing is being made now, to thank you for your innumerable proofs of kindness and to say that I have ever been most justly and affectionately

Your obliged
Walter Landor

Need I tell you how grateful I am to Mr. Twisleton
June 26 '64

This letter to Robert Browning was written by Landor in his eighty-ninth year. He died on September 17, 1864. In 1863 Landor had published *Heroic Idyls*, the manuscript of which had been taken from Landor's residence in Florence to London by Mr. Edward Twisleton. Mr. Twisleton had gone to Italy armed with an introduction to Landor from Browning. His visits to the old man during the summer of 1863 were among his last intellectual pleasures. The new book was dedicated to this new friend.

This letter with its expression of thanks shows how deeply grateful the aged poet was to Browning for his services in financial and domestic affairs. When well past 80, Landor had, after a long period of estrangement, rejoined his family at Fiesole. But the arrangement did not answer. He was ungoverned in speech and temper. Violent quarrels took place. Three times he flung himself out of the house and after each such occasion he was brought back to it. On the fourth occasion he refused absolutely to return. His family, to whom he had made over his property, would make no provision for him outside their own walls. He was now homeless. With eighteen pence in his pocket he appeared at Casa Guidi. Browning at once took charge of his affairs and got for him an invitation to stop with the Storys at Siena while he arranged for more permanent lodgings for him in Florence. Meanwhile he wrote to Forster, Landor's publisher in London, who, after corresponding with Landor's brothers, reported that £200 would be supplied annually for his maintenance. Browning was made trustee of this allowance. It is only fair to add that Landor responded to the tact and kindness shown by Browning and proved amiable to the last.

The date in the lower left-hand corner of the letter is in a handwriting other than Landor's.

PAGE 736.—A Letter by James (Clarence) Mangan.

Friday at noon

My dear Tighe,

I send you inclosed what you request. I also send you the "chisseled" original. The latter take care not to let Elliott see, because, as I think or am half inclined to believe, you do not delight in cruelty, *his* feelings shall not be put upon the rack—Do you smile—oh! you know *he* is a gentleman and *therefore* must profess sensations which the *canaille* know nothing about—But what am I saying?—"where was I" as they say, aye I was speaking of the inclosure—Be good enough to give it to Elliott, telling him at the same time, that you have made such few alterations as you thought necessary, and that he has an excellent taste for Poetry—The rest you know yourself.

I am yours sincerely
James Mangan.

P.S. I have a droll peculiarity which is, that I never wish to hear anything further of a Letter after it escapes from my hands. This may, that is, must, arise from the consciousness I entertain of the wretched stile in which I pen it. You will therefore be so kind as never to speak a word concerning this to me.

This letter is addressed to James Tighe (1795–1869), who was one of Mangan's fellow clerks in the scrivener's office which Mangan entered in 1818. Tighe was the author of some clever literary efforts, among which were some verses addressed to Mangan written about 1826. He was probably the person who first induced Mangan to write for the Dublin and Belfast almanacs, which were at that time the recognized receptacles in Ireland for the poetical output of rhymesters all over the country.

PAGES 738 AND 739.—A Letter from Mangan to the Editor of a Dublin Magazine.

My dear friend,

I have not forgotten you, but the truth simply is that I am not able at present to send you a single contribution. On looking over the few papers I have, I see nothing that could at all answer your publication; and I find that any attempt, even for five minutes together, at original composition, has no effect except to increase the illness I am labouring under, to a degree almost unendurable. I have been obliged even to discontinue writing for the Magazine; and in short I begin to see that for me literature in any shape is the most unfit of all occupations. If I ever recover my health I shall endeavour to dedicate the very limited powers I possess to Something of a more practical and profitable character. Meantime I know you too well, and I know that you know the world too well, to be displeased with me for what I really cannot avoid,—my inability to be of the slightest use to you in your undertaking. I can do no more than wish your exertions all the success they undoubtedly deserve.

Believe me
Ever yours faithfully
J. C. Mangan

5 Richmond St
10th October, 1838.

PAGE 749.—Page of a Letter from Thomas Love Peacock to Jane Clairmont.

printed respecting you but he has not even alluded to it. Medwin thought himself justified in repeating what Moore had said in his Life of Byron, as if anything said or done by that little dirty, paltry, pitiful rascal, could justify any one in doing the same.

Hogg has published two thick volumes of a Life of Shelley, which is to be in four. It comes down to the point preceding his separation from Harriet. More tnan half of the whole is about himself, or about matters which have not the remotest relation to Shelley.

I am writing an article on these works for Frazer, but I shall stop for the present where Hogg stops

This letter to Jane Clairmont, the stepsister of Mary Godwin Shelley, is interesting because of the comments upon Shelley's two earliest biographers, Thomas Medwin and Thomas Jefferson Hogg. Medwin had also published a *Journal of the Conversations of Lord Byron*, which excited great interest especially because of certain statements made therein in regard to Lady Byron.

PAGE 757.—Presentation Copy from Samuel Rogers to Mrs. Shelley.

In 1844 Mrs. Shelley returned the compliment of this presentation by dedicating her *Rambles in Germany and Italy* to Samuel Rogers.

PAGE 774.—Presentation Copy from Sir Walter Scott to J. W. Croker.

John Wilson Croker, author, critic, and politician, was born in Galway, Ireland, in 1780. He was elected to Parliament in 1807, and appointed secretary to the admiralty in 1809. In this year Scott, Croker, and others founded the *London Quarterly Review*. This presentation copy with its imprint "Authors Copy" indicates that it is one of an advance printing made for Scott by his publishers.

PAGE 784.—Letter from Robert Southey on his Election to the Royal Society of Literature.

The Royal Society of Literature which had been founded in 1821 under the patronage of the newly crowned George IV. The Rev. Richard Cattermole was an English author who published several volumes dealing with English history.

Keswick, Cumberland, 2 May 1826

Sir

I have the honour to acknowledge your letter of the 28th last, this day received, informing me that the Royal Society of Literature has been pleased to elect me one of its Honorary Associates and accompanying a Diploma which certifies that election. If I am not acting according to form, in transmitting herewith the prescribed form of obligation, the error may be amended in the course of the present month, on my arrival in London.

With a due sense of the honour thus conferred on me

I remain

Sir

Your most obedient humble servant

Robert Southey

Reverend Richard Cattermole

PAGE 788.—Page of a Southey Letter.

This is the second page of a letter from Robert Southey written in 1814, correspondent unknown: or if you think it necessary that I dont tax brains that are *bona fide* much better employed?

If you are of opinion that I may hold myself absolved shall I insert these lines in a copy of Roderick for presentation. Understand I pray you, that I am far from wishing to be thought obtrusive with such things, and only wish to do it if it ought to be done and could not without some impropriety be left undone.

> Prince, I approach thee not with annual strain
> On temporal theme, soon framed nor lasting long,
> Nor seek I not with gratulations vain
> To win thine ear. What need the Poets song
> To join the general praise when all rejoice,
> And grateful nations with one heart and voice
> Thee and thy counsels bless? Let History pay,
> Then most extolling both when most sincere,
> The eternal meed to George and England due.
> Fitlier I come with this elaborate lay
> The thoughtful work of many a studious year;
> So may I best becoming sense display
> Of the high honour by thy hand conferr'd
> On no unworthy servant of the Muse.

Southey was made poet laureate in 1813 by the Prince Regent (George Augustus Frederick, Prince of Wales, afterwards George IV, who during his father's dementia, 1810–1820, administered affairs under the guidance of Parliament). In 1814 Southey published his second poem, *Roderick, the Last of the Goths*, a copy of which with appropriate verses he wishes to present to his benefactor.

APPENDIX II

BIBLIOGRAPHIES AND NOTES

The editors of *English Romantic Poets* are greatly indebted to Tom B. Haber, Ph.D., of Ohio State University, for the preparation of all the bibliographies included in the following pages. While these bibliographies are frankly selective, an attempt has been made to indicate all the more important books and articles dealing with each poet—editions of works as well as biographical and critical discussions. The descriptive comments accompanying the entries give the student some clear notion of the nature and value of each.

Biographical accounts of the poets precede each group of selections throughout the text. Additional biographical facts are given in the following notes only when needed to help in the understanding of some particular poem.

Guides in heavy-faced type are inserted to indicate the pages on which poems begin. Unless otherwise indicated all page references are to *English Romantic Poets*.

WILLIAM WORDSWORTH

BIBLIOGRAPHY

I. WORKS

Poetical Works, ed. by Thomas Hutchinson. 5 vols. (Oxford University Press: 1895.) The standard edition of the poetry, equipped with an introduction and complete critical apparatus.

Poetical Works, ed. by Edward Dowden. Aldine Edition. 7 vols. (Macmillan: New York, 1892–3.) One of the most useful of the earlier complete collections: Vol. I contains a memoir; Vol. VII, a bibliography and chronological table of poems.

Poems, selected and ed. by G. M. Harper. (Scribner: New York, 1923.) A good one-volume collection by the poet's most recent authoritative biographer: furnished with a critical introduction.

Complete Poetical Works, ed. by John Morley. Globe Edition. (Macmillan: New York, 1905.) A very satisfactory one-volume edition, provided with a brief introduction.

The Poems of William Wordsworth, ed. by Thomas Hutchinson. (Oxford University Press: 1911.) A recommended edition, complete and inexpensive.

Complete Poetical Works, ed. by A. J. George. Cambridge Edition. (Houghton: Boston, 1904.) A good edition for student use.

Shorter Poems. (Dutton: New York, 1927.) A useful inexpensive edition, provided with a short introduction by Ernest Rhys.

Longer Poems. (Dutton: New York, 1928.) A good cheap edition, containing *The Prelude* and the *Excursion*, together with *The Borderers*.

The Prelude, ed. by Ernest de Sélincourt. (Oxford University Press: 1926.) This edition, of manifold usefulness, is admirably furnished with an introduction and textual and critical notes: it is collated from thirteen MSS of the poem. The right-hand pages give the authorized (1850) text; the left-hand pages, the text as it stood in 1805. (There is an abridgement in the Oxford Edition of Standard Authors, 1935.)

Lyrical Ballads, a reprint, ed. by H. Littledale. (Oxford University Press: 1911.) An excellent edition for student use: it offers a good historical introduction and useful notes calling attention to later changes in the text. The appendix gives Wordsworth's Prefaces of 1800 and 1802.

Sonnets, ed. by C. G. Moore Smith. Temple Classics. (Dent: London, 1902.) Includes the whole body of this important work, providing notes and the poet's preface to the 1838 edition.

Poems and Prose, selected and ed. by E. H. Moorhouse. (Browne: Chicago, 1913.) An appreciative critique forms an introduction: included are critical estimates by contemporary and later writers.

Prose Works, ed. by W. A. Knight. Eversley Edition. 2 vols. (Macmillan: New York, 1896.) The best student edition of the outstanding prose works.

Letters of the Wordsworth Family from 1787 to 1855, ed. by W. A. Knight. 3 vols. (Ginn: Boston, 1907.) This useful work will no doubt be superseded by the new edition which is being prepared by Ernest de Sélincourt.

Literary Criticism, ed. by N. C. Smith. (Frowde: London, 1906.) Many scattered writings are here collected; this edition also provides an introduction and notes.

Guide to the Lakes, ed. by Ernest de Sélincourt. (Oxford University Press: 1906.) The editor has added an introduction, appendices, and textual and illustrative notes: a map and eight engravings are included.

II. BIOGRAPHY AND CRITICISM

Babenroth, A. C. *English Childhood.* (Columbia University Press: 1922.) Places Wordsworth's poetry of childhood in perspective against the 18th-century tradition from Prior to Crabbe.

Batho, Edith C. *The Later Wordsworth.* (Cambridge University Press: 1933.) Attempts to round out Harper's rather cursory account of the poet's life from 1815 to 1850: traces a consistent development in his politics and religion; shows the damaging results of the failure of Wordsworth's eyesight from about 1815 on.

Beatty, Arthur. *William Wordsworth: His Doctrine and Art in Their Historical Relations.* (University of Wisconsin Press: 1927.) Shows the influence of the psychologist Hartley in the poet's prefaces, *The Prelude,* and some of the shorter poems; leans away from the mystical interpretation.

Boas, F. S. *Wordsworth's Patriotic Poems and Their Significance Today.* (English Association Pamphlet XXX, 1914.) A patriotic "dated" analysis of a portion of the poet's work, showing his influence upon British national thought.

Campbell, O. J., and Mueschke, P. *Wordsworth's Aesthetic Development, 1795–1802.* (University of Michigan Publications: 1935.) A comprehensive survey of the subject, based on the work of many researchers and offering fresh inferences and conclusions.

Coleridge, Samuel T. *Biographia Literaria* (1817), ed. by John Shawcross. 2 vols. (Oxford University Press: 1907.) Contains many scattered references to Wordsworth, the most abundant material being in chapters V, XIV, XVII–XXII. These eulogistic pronouncements did much to bring Wordsworth into favorable public notice.

Cooper, Lane. *A Concordance to the Poems of William Wordsworth.* (Dutton: New York, 1911.) Brings into alphabetical arrangement the complete vocabulary of the poet; the intention of the compiler is to make more apparent the relations between the longer and shorter poems.

Dicey, A. V. *The Statesmanship of Wordsworth.* (Oxford University Press: 1917.) A survey of the poet's theory of British insularity, expressed in his Liberty Sonnets and the Cintra Tract; points out the recrudescence of his nationalistic opinions during the World War.

Fausset, H. I'A. *The Lost Leader.* (Harcourt: New York, 1933.) A study of the poet's inner life, tracing the decline of his productive powers to "the natural man rising up against the spiritual man."

Garrod, H. W. *Wordsworth: Lectures and Essays.* (Oxford University Press: 1923.) A collection of Oxford lectures by a member of the school of Arnold, including valuable discussions on *The Borderers,* the "immortal Ode," the Prefaces to the *Lyrical Ballads,* and *The Prelude:* develops the theory of the inspirational influence of Coleridge.

Grey, Viscount. *Wordsworth's Prelude.* (Oxford University Press: 1923.) An inspiring discussion by one of the poet's most famous spiritual descendants: originally an address before the English Association, it was reprinted in the *Falloden Papers,* 1926.

Harper, G. M. *William Wordsworth: His Life, Works, and Influences.* 2 vols. (Scribner: New York, 1916.) Compendious and exact: the most recent authoritative biography; following the new emphasis proposed by Legouis, it is concerned chiefly with the early life of the poet. There is a later (1929) edition, but the first inclusive edition is preferable.

Harper, G. M. *Wordsworth's French Daughter.* (Princeton University Press: 1921.) The story of her birth, with the certificates of her baptism and marriage, authenticated by the discovery of some interesting letters written by Dorothy Wordsworth in 1814–15, together with documents from the French archives.

Herford, C. H. *Wordsworth.* (Dutton: New York, 1930.) Making acknowledgment to Harper's numerous studies and to De Sélincourt's edition of *The Prelude,* this book reviews the poet's life, observing about the same time-divisions as those suggested by Harper and Legouis. The concluding section of the final chapter points out the enduring qualities of Wordsworth's poetry.

Hudson, H. N. *Studies in Wordsworth.* (Little: Boston, 1884.) Emphasizes the ethical and spiritual qualities of the poet, his significance as a moral guide. The writer is a fervent Wordsworthian (against his ilk Arnold warned us to be on our guard).

Knight, W. A. *The Life of William Wordsworth.* 3 vols. (Macmillan: New York, 1896.) This compendious work, by the poet's editor, superseded Christopher Wordsworth's; it is now likewise overshadowed by Harper's: suffers from an inclination to preserve a rigid distinction between the tasks of the biographer and the literary critic.

Knight, W. A. *Coleridge and Wordsworth in the West Country: Their Friendship, Work, and Surroundings.* (Scribner: New York, 1914.) Letters and diaries, with many extracts from Dorothy's Alfoxden *Journals,* have contributed to this informal account of the most fruitful period of the association of the two poets, 1795–98.

Legouis, E. H. *The Early Life of William Wordsworth, 1770–98.* Trans. by J. W. Matthews. (Dent: London, 1921.) A fine survey of the schoolboy period and early manhood of the poet; of especial interest in connection with a study of *The Prelude:* an appendix acknowledges Harper's researches.

Legouis, E. H. *William Wordsworth and Annette Vallon.* (Dutton: New York, 1922.) Largely a collection of articles written for the *Revue des Deux Mondes,* 1922, this study presents the ascertainable facts in the poet's romantic story: the author states that he is not only completing a portrait of the poet, but also doing justice to the Vallon family.

Legouis, E. H. *Wordsworth in a New Light.* (Harvard University Press: 1923.) A brief candid presentation of the facts concerning the relations of the poet and Annette Vallon, which nevertheless confirms the traditional opinion of his character.

MacLean, Catherine M. *Dorothy and William Wordsworth.* (Cambridge University Press: 1927.) Not so much a record of the unique association of brother and sister as a re-interpretation of Wordsworth's poetry in the light of Dorothy's influence upon it as witnessed in her *Journals.*

Magnus, Laurie. *A Primer of Wordsworth.* (Methuen: London, 1897.) Considers the poet's life and work as the expression of a consistent philosophy of nature and man: offers a useful chronological bibliography.

Mead, Marian. *Four Studies in Wordsworth.* (Banta: Menasha, Wis., 1929.) Titles: "Wordsworth's Eye," "Light and Color in Wordsworth," "The Idiot Boy," "The Happiest-Looking Homes of Men." The appendix adds a study of Wordsworth's and of Keats's use of light and color words. The first two essays are especially noteworthy.

Morley, F. V. *Dora Wordsworth, Her Book.* (Houghton: Boston, 1925.) Based chiefly on the album of the poet's daughter, this study provides a fairly clear biography of her, with many references to her literary acquaintances.

Myers, F. W. H. *Wordsworth.* English Men of Letters series. (Harper: New York, 1894.) A good brief biography, the best in the field before the Life by Harper, though in places unnecessarily dull: presents Wordsworth as the poet of *Tintern Abbey* and the founder of a religion of nature.

Rader, M. M. *Presiding Ideas in Wordsworth's Poetry.* (University of Washington Press: 1931.) A description of the development of the poet's thought, the influence of Hartley, Kant, Plato, and (especially) of Coleridge.

Raleigh, W. A. *Wordsworth.* (Longmans: New York, 1921.) A thoroughly sound favorable criticism of the poet's work, with a minimum of biographical material: a book which has, however, been in part superseded by more recent research into the poet's heredity and biography.

Read, Herbert. *Wordsworth.* (Cape: London, 1930.) Traces the maturing of the poet's personality through emotional development and analyzes the poetry as illustrating certain processes of the creative mind; attempts to identify the "real" and the "legendary" Wordsworth.

Robertson, E. S. *Wordsworthshire.* (Appleton: New York, 1911.) Written determinedly apart from books, this "series of suggestions about a poet's mind in relation to the country in which he dwelt" illuminates many of his most significant poems.

Sneath, E. H. *Wordsworth: Poet of Nature and Poet of Man.* (Ginn: Boston, 1912.) An exhaustive scholarly work, considering the poet from a wholly objective standpoint as a product of his social and physical environments.

Sperry, W. L. *Wordsworth's Anti-Climax.* (Harvard University Press: 1935.) A scholarly study of the last forty years of the poet's life, finding the cause of the decline of his artistic power in some of the outward events of his life and in the hardening of his intellectual fiber.

Winchester, C. T. *William Wordsworth: How to Know Him.* (Bobbs: Indianapolis, 1916.) A kind of "Wordsworth primer" providing an easy introduction to his poetical tenets, philosophy, etc.

Woods, Mrs. Margaret L. *A Poet's Youth.* (Chapman: London, 1924.) Cast in the spirit of Maurois's *Ariel*, this book rewrites the poet's love story, finding in his *Vaudracour and Julia* a reflection of his romance with Annette Vallon.

Wordsworth, Christopher. *Memoirs of William Wordsworth.* 2 vols. (Moxon: London, 1851.) The earliest Life, by the poet's bishop-nephew, from memoranda dictated by Wordsworth in November, 1847. It is naturally partisan and over-cautious, but presents a graphic record of the poet's life in England.

Wordsworth, Dorothy. *Journals,* ed. by W. A. Knight. (Macmillan: New York, 1924.) Invaluable for intimate details of the poet's life: his methods of work, circumstances of the composition of certain poems, his friends, etc.

III. ARTICLES FROM BOOKS

Arnold, Matthew. "Wordsworth," in *Essays in Criticism,* Second Series. (Macmillan: London, 1889.) The poet's most distinguished disciple here gives a conservative and typically British summary of the value of Wordsworth's poetry: four-fifths of it is of little worth, but the golden remainder, unspoiled by his philosophy, is a "great and ample body of powerful work" that will rank him above all moderns, save Dante, Shakespeare, Molière, Milton, and Goethe.

De Sélincourt, Ernest. "Wordsworth's Preface to The Borderers," in *Oxford Lectures on Poetry.* (Oxford University Press: 1934.) Prints the complete text, hitherto unpublished: discusses the early influence of Godwin and his school.

Dowden, Edward. "The Text of Wordsworth's Poems," in *Transcripts and Studies.* (Paul: London, 1910.) Remarks that there is no great need for a definitive text for Wordsworth's poetry, each of the successive revisions having its intrinsic value, even though some of the later re-touchings were not happy.

Fairchild, H. N. Chapters V–XI in *The Romantic Quest.* (Columbia University Press: 1931.) Here are discussed prominently *The Prelude* and the great *Ode,* the poet's religion of nature, and his transcendental philosophy. Chapter XI explains the poet's conservatism as an outgrowth of political exigencies.

Garrod, H. W. "Wordsworth's Lucy," in *The Profession of Poetry.* (Oxford University Press: 1929.) Suggests that the Lucy poems may be addressed to Dorothy, death being seen as "no tragic antithesis at all" in the poet's concept of man and nature.

Gingerich, S. F. "Wordsworth," in *Essays in the Romantic Poets.* (Macmillan: New York, 1924.) Recommended for an easy introduction: it contains lucid summaries of most of the principal poems.

Gingerich, S. F. "Wordsworth," in *Wordsworth, Tennyson, and Browning.* (Wahr: Ann Arbor, 1911.) Points out the domination of the will in the poet's work, his dependence on memories of childhood; shows his mysticism to be the blending of these forces.

Huxley, Aldous. "Wordsworth in the Tropics," in *Do What You Will.* (Doubleday: New York, 1929.) A hostile *reductio ad absurdum* of the poet's theory of the benignity of nature; asks what becomes of the theory amidst the wanton luxuriance of tropical life.

Legouis, E. H. "William Wordsworth," in *Cambridge History of English Literature,* XI. (Putnam: New York, 1914.) A fine illustrative essay, showing the influence of Rousseau and the clash between the poet's philosophy and his poetical genius.

More, P. E. "Wordsworth," in *Shelburne Essays*, Seventh Series. (Houghton: Boston, 1910.) A review of Knight's edition of the letters of the Wordsworth family; finds in them new reasons to complain of the poet's admitted prosiness.

Noyes, Alfred. "Wordsworth," in *Some Aspects of Modern Poetry*. (Stokes: New York, 1924.) Sees the poet as the apostle of the abiding truths of nature, which he interprets as the "shadowing forth of the Infinite Being."

Pater, Walter. "Wordsworth," in *Appreciations*. (Macmillan: New York, 1922.) Discusses the significance of the poet's perception of the immanence of life in natural objects, with man considered as an elevated part of nature: a tribute to Wordsworth's influence as a moral teacher.

Payne, W. M. "William Wordsworth," in *Greater English Poets of the Nineteenth Century*. (Holt: New York, 1907.) Emphasizes the intellectual element of the poet's work, and its effect upon contemporary politics and religion.

Stephen, Leslie. "Wordsworth's Ethics," in *Hours in a Library*, III. (Putnam: New York, 1907.) This essay, first printed in 1874, is historically interesting in that it called forth Arnold's famous reply, which evaded rather than challenged this unsympathetic analysis of the poet's philosophy.

Strong, A. T. "An Essay on Nature in Wordsworth and Meredith," in *Three Studies in Shelley*. (Oxford University Press: 1921.) Points out a common intensity of observation in the two writers, with Wordsworth's belief in personal immortality contrasting with Meredith's faith in the theory of evolution.

Swinburne, A. C. "Wordsworth and Byron," in *Miscellanies*. (Scribner: New York, 1911.) An indirect thrust at Arnold, to whom "years have brought the unphilosophic mind": grudgingly admits Wordsworth's genius in "meditation and sympathy," especially in his patriotic verse.

Symons, Arthur. "William Wordsworth," in *The Romantic Movement in English Poetry*. (Dutton: New York, 1909.) Praises the sonnets, discounts the blank verse; insists upon the poet's sincerity, even in his lapses; places high among early influences his sense of animated nature.

IV. ARTICLES FROM PERIODICALS

Barnard, C. C. "Wordsworth and the *Ancient Mariner*," *Englische Studien*, LX, 262–71 (1926). Points out discrepancies in the accounts of Wordsworth and Coleridge, and comments on the former's disparaging references to the poem in 1800.

Beach, J. W. "Expostulation and Reply," *Publications of the Modern Language Association*, XL, 346–61 (June, 1925). A well-considered rebuttal to Cerf's article (see following note); presents the Wordsworthian gospel of nature as the majority of students see it: the interpretation of man as a part of nature.

Cerf, Barry. "Wordsworth's Gospel of Nature," *Publications of the Modern Language Association*, XXXVII, 615–38 (Dec., 1922). A provocative analysis of the poet's central theme: nature as the teacher of man; the poet's nerveless, effortless philosophy is attacked.

Clutton-Brock, A. "The Problem of Wordsworth," *London Mercury*, II, 700–10 (Oct., 1920). The "problem" is Wordsworth's dullness; the article suggests a way of bearing it.

Cooper, Lane. "A Glance at Wordsworth's Reading," *Modern Language Notes*, XXII, 83–9, 110–17 (Mar., Apr., 1907). Decries the idea that the poet was no reader; points to the sale-list of his Rydal library, where many works of travel were included: traces their effects throughout his poetry.

Darbishire, Helen. "Wordsworth's *Prelude*," *Nineteenth Century*, XCIX, 718–31 (May, 1926). Drawn from the original version published by De Sélincourt, this article comments on the evils wrought in the revisions of the poem by Wordsworth's Anglican doctrine.

Eagleston, A. J. "Wordsworth, Coleridge, and the Spy," *Nineteenth Century*, LXIV, 300–10 (Aug., 1908). Treats of their being watched as suspected Alfoxden revolutionaries during the exciting 1797 epoch.

Gray, C. H. "Wordsworth's First Visit to Tintern Abbey," *Publications of the Modern Language Association*, XLIX, 123–33 (Mar., 1934). Analyzes the poet's mood in the poem; compares it with the tone of passages in *The Prelude*, in which the "period of degradation" is also reflected.

Harper, G. M. "Did Wordsworth Defy the Guillotine?" *Quarterly Review*, CCXLVIII, 254–64 (Apr., 1927). Offers seemingly irrefutable proof that in 1793 Wordsworth attempted to rejoin Annette Vallon in France.

Hartman, Herbert. "Wordsworth's 'Lucy' Poems," *Publications of the Modern Language Association*, XLIX, 134–42 (Mar., 1934). A review of the five Lucy poems, with a restatement of the problems of identification, to which a new issue is added in a possible original Lucy in a song of Collins.

Herzberg, M. J. "Wordsworth and German Literature," *Publications of the Modern Language Association*, XL, 302–45 (June, 1925). Tends to diminish the theory that the poet's work shows significant traces of German influence.

Howard, Leon. "Wordsworth in America," *Modern Language Notes*, XLVIII, 359–65 (June, 1933). Discusses the comparatively successful effect of the *Lyrical Ballads* in Philadelphia and elsewhere in America.

Kirtlan, E. J. B. "Did Wordsworth Recant?" *Contemporary Review*, CXIV, 87–9 (July, 1918). Defends the poet's later conservatism as the natural influence of the age in which he lived.

Knaplaund, Paul. "The Grant of a Civil List Pension," *Modern Language Notes*, XLII, 385–90 (June, 1927). Offers evidence as to the poet's financial condition about 1842.

Knowlton, E. C. "The Novelty of Wordsworth's 'Michael' as a Pastoral," *Publications of the Modern Language Association*, XXXV, 432–46 (Dec., 1920). Commenting on the lack of immediate literary models, the author here traces influences from Theocritus, powerfully supplemented by the poet's knowledge of English rural life.

Merrill, L. R. "Vaughan's Influence upon Wordsworth's Poetry," *Modern Language Notes*, XXXVII, 91–6 (Feb., 1922). Makes the usual comparison between *The Retreat* and the *Ode* with references to other related poems: refers to Wordsworth's "much-thumbed copy" of Vaughan.

Moore, J. R. "Wordsworth's Unacknowledged Debt to Macpherson's *Ossian*," *Publications of the Modern Language Association*, XL, 362–78 (June, 1925). Treats of stylistic influences, particularly in descriptions of natural scenery.

Paul, H. W. "The Permanence of Wordsworth," *Nineteenth Century*, LXIII, 987–98 (June, 1908). A naïve uncritical account of some of the poet's outstanding themes.

Pennington, W. "The 'Lucy' Poems," *Modern Language Notes*, XLI, 314–16 (May, 1926). Suggests that the five poems have one central theme, an incident related by Dorothy.

Rader, Melvin. "The Transcendentalism of William Wordsworth," *Modern Philology*, XXVI, 169–90 (Nov., 1928). A valuable complement to Beatty's *William Wordsworth* (see note under *Biography and Criticism*); discounts Hartleian influence.

Rea, J. D. "Coleridge's Intimations of Immortality from Proclus," *Modern Philology*, XXVI, 201–13 (Nov., 1928). Shows that Wordsworth's *Ode* derives many significant elements from the reading of Coleridge.

Roberts, E. C. "The Ascendancy of Wordsworth," *Contemporary Review*, CIII, 703–11 (May, 1913). Compares the poet's vitality with the reputation of other romantic poets.

Shackford, Martha H. "Wordsworth's Italy," *Publications of the Modern Language Association*, XXXVIII, 236–52 (Mar., 1923). An attempt to dispel the opinion of the poet's insularity; attention is directed toward poems showing the influence of Italian writers and of those dealing with Italian subjects.

Stallknecht, N. P. "Wordsworth and Philosophy: Suggestions Concerning the Source of the Poet's Doctrines and the Nature of his Mystical Experience," *Publications of the Modern Language Association*, XLIV, 1116–43 (Dec., 1929). A useful supplement to Beatty's study of sources: a thorough review of the poet's reading, and his changing philosophical attitudes, from Godwin to Kant.

Stork, C. W. "The Influence of the Popular Ballad on Wordsworth and Coleridge," *Publications of the Modern Language Association*, XXIX, 299–326 (Sept., 1914). Shows the poet's interest in the simplicity of the ballad, his being led astray by poor 18th-century versions, his lessening interest after the publication of the *Lyrical Ballads*.

Thorpe, C. D. "Wordsworth and Keats," *Publications of the Modern Language Association*, XLII, 1010–26 (Dec., 1927). Discusses Wordsworth's disdain of Keats, the younger poet's adverse comment upon Wordsworth, with instances of more kindly reference, notably in Keats's letter to Reynolds, May 3, 1818.

Wordsworth, G. G. "The Boyhood of Wordsworth," *Cornhill Magazine*, XLVIII, 410–20 (Apr., 1920). Based on unpublished documents, the article discloses matters of fact in reference to the poet's household and his school days.

NOTES

Page 7. LINES

This poem was written in part when Wordsworth was at school at Hawkshead. The yew tree, which stood on the eastern side of the lake, a few minutes' walk from Hawkshead, was destroyed "owing to the popular belief that its leaves were poisonous and might injure the cattle grazing in the common." Wordsworth said of the spot that it was his favorite walk in the evenings during the latter part of his schooltime. Of the man in ll. 12–13,

"who owned no common soul,"

Wordsworth wrote that he was "a gentleman of the neighbourhood, a man of talent and learning, who had been educated at one of the Universities, and returned to pass his time in seclusion on his own estate."

Although the moral wisdom expressed in the poem is that which is usually associated with age and experience, Wordsworth was only twenty-five in the year in which the poem is dated.

MARGARET: OR THE RUINED COTTAGE

The argument with which Wordsworth introduces Book I of *The Excursion*, of which this poem is a part, is as follows: "A summer forenoon. The Author reaches a ruined Cottage upon a Common, and there meets with a revered Friend, the Wanderer, of whose education and course of life he gives an account. The Wanderer, while resting under the shade of the Trees that surround the cottage, relates the History of its last Inhabitant." Ll. 38–433 of Book I of *The Excursion*, which deal with the "education and course of life" of the Wanderer, are omitted here. The Wanderer was a pedlar, a native of "the hills of Athol," in Scotland. He was an educated man, however, sound in character, devout in temper, and philosophic in his outlook on life.

The justification for printing this fragment of Book I and entitling it *Margaret: or the Ruined Cottage*, is to be found in the fact that Wordsworth seems originally to have designed it for a separate poem. Indeed he proposed the title, *The Ruined Cottage*.

Page 14. LINES WRITTEN IN EARLY SPRING

"Actually composed while I was sitting by the side of the brook that runs down from the Comb, in which stands the village of Alford, through the grounds of Alfoxden. It was a chosen resort of mine. The brook fell down a sloping rock so as to make a waterfall considerable for that country, and across the pool below had fallen a tree, an ash, if I rightly remember, from which rose perpendicularly, boughs in search of the light intercepted by the deep shade above. The boughs bore leaves of green that for want of sunshine had faded into almost lily-white; and from the underside of this natural sylvan bridge depended long and beautiful tresses of ivy which waved gently in the breeze that might poetically speaking be called the breath of the waterfall. This motion varied of course in proportion to the power of water in the brook. When, with dear friends, I revisited this spot, after an interval of more than forty years, this interesting feature of the scene was gone. To the owner of the place I could not but regret that the beauty of this retired part of the grounds had not tempted him to make it more accessible by a path, not broad or obtrusive, but sufficient for persons who love such scenes to creep along without difficulty." (Wordsworth's note.)

A WHIRL-BLAST FROM BEHIND THE HILL

Wordsworth said that the incident described in this poem was "observed in the holly-grove at Alfoxden." He had the pleasure of "again seeing this grove in unimpaired beauty forty-one years after." In her journal of the Alfoxden days for March 18, 1798, Dorothy Wordsworth wrote: "A cold, windy morning. Walked with them [the Coleridges] half way [to their home]. On our return, sheltered under the hollies, during a hail-shower. The withered leaves danced with the hailstones. William wrote a description of the storm."
Professor H. J. Hall says that this poem, together with *Lines Written in Early Spring* (p. 14) and *To My Sister* (p. 15), holds "in condensed form the whole of Wordsworth's belief in the value of nature to man."

Page 15.   TO MY SISTER

On a seat between two large elms in front of Alfoxden House, the spacious home in the Quantock Hills which Wordsworth and his sister Dorothy lived in for a short time, the poet used to sit, reading and composing poetry. This poem and the poems *Expostulation and Reply* (p. 18) and *The Tables Turned* (p. 18) were composed there.
Mr. E. Paxton Hood wrote the following of Wordsworth and his sister: "Not Laura with Petrarch, nor Beatrice with Dante, nor the fair Geraldine with Surrey, are more really connected than is Wordsworth with his sister Dorothy."
"My little boy-messenger [the Edward of l. 13] on this occasion," Wordsworth said, "was the son of Basil Montagu [a friend of the Wordsworths]. The larch mentioned in the first stanza was standing when I revisited the place in May, 1841, more than forty years after."

SIMON LEE

Although the scene of this poem is in Wales, Simon Lee, Wordsworth writes, had been huntsman to the squires of Alfoxden. "I dearly love their voice" (see l. 24) was the old man's comment, word for word, on the baying of the hunting dogs. A good deal of ridicule has been aimed at the piece for its flat simplicity, its triviality, and its prosaic realism. Wordsworth's reply to the ridicule was that the poem should excite pity, not mirth. Whatever truth there may be in his reply, a comparison of *Simon Lee* with poems like *Michael* (p. 44) and *Resolution and Independence* (p. 55) will show that there is something about the manner of treatment of the two last-named poems that places them beyond any charge of ridicule, even though their details are just as realistic as those of *Simon Lee*.

Page 16.   WE ARE SEVEN

In 1793 while Wordsworth was on a walking tour he met near Goodrich Castle the little girl who five years later appeared as the heroine of this poem, composed while the poet was walking in the grove at Alfoxden. Wordsworth was not satisfied with the poem when he had finished it, and after reciting it to his sister Dorothy and to Coleridge he remarked that it should have an introductory stanza. Coleridge at once threw out

"A simple child, dear brother Jem,"

the name Jem referring to a friend of his and the Wordsworths, Mr. James Tobin, brother of John Tobin, the dramatist. Wordsworth disliked the phrase "dear brother Jem," but nevertheless the line formed the beginning of the poem until 1815, when it was revised for the present reading.
In the fourth line of the first stanza Coleridge (the entire stanza is his) stated the problem or idea of the poem—the inability of a child, whose sense of physical being is so keen, to conceive of death. The child does not distinguish between life and death, between the seen and the unseen. And according to Wordsworth she may be nearer the truth in her simplicity than is the mature person in his wisdom. The student should compare this poem with *Ode: Intimations of Immortality* (text p. 63).

Page 17.   THERE WAS A BOY

This poem, written in Germany in the "bitter winter" of 1798, Wordsworth in 1804 inserted as lines 364 to 397 of Book V of *The Prelude*. Coleridge, to whom Wordsworth sent a copy of the poem, wrote from Ratzeburg of the lines—

"uncertain heaven received
Into the bosom of the steady lake":

"I should have recognized [them] anywhere; and had I met these lines running wild in the deserts of Arabia, I should have instantly screamed out, 'Wordsworth!'" Wordsworth's schoolmate, William Raincock, of Rayrigg, has been mentioned as the Boy, but in reality the Boy's identity is not known.

2. *Winander.* Windermere or Winandermere in Westmoreland.

Page 18. EXPOSTULATION AND REPLY

See note *To My Sister,* above.

The scene of this poem is Esthwaite, near Hawkshead, where Wordsworth attended school from his eighth to his sixteenth year and where he developed a great affection for the headmaster, William Taylor. There is good reason to believe that the Matthew of this poem and of other of Wordsworth's poems is this "honored teacher of his youth," or a composite figure much of which goes back to Taylor. The poem, Wordsworth said, was a favorite with the Quakers, lines 21–24 harmonizing perfectly with their beliefs.

THE TABLES TURNED

See note on *To My Sister,* above.

Professor Dowden points out that some critics have found fault with the stanza beginning "One impulse from a vernal wood" on the ground of exaggeration; and then defends Wordsworth by explaining that his meaning simply is that "in communion with external nature a moment may come which will evoke from the heart more moral energy than can be taught by books."

A narrow interpretation may see a hatred of science in the last two stanzas, but certainly they make no attack on "a science which recognizes the truths of the imagination as well as those of experiment."

Compare this poem with *To My Sister,* (text p. 15).

THE IDIOT BOY

For Wordsworth's defense of this poem see the letter to John Wilson, text p. 112.

Wordsworth said that the lines in the last stanza—

"The cocks did crow to-whoo, to-whoo,
And the sun did shine so cold!"—

were the foundation of the whole. "The words were reported to me," he continued, "by my dear friend, Thomas Poole; but I have since heard the same repeated of other Idiots. . . . This long poem was composed in the groves of Alfoxden, almost extempore; not a word, I believe, being corrected, though one stanza was omitted. I mention this in gratitude to those

happy moments, for, in truth, I never wrote anything with so much glee."

In her journal for March 4, 1802, Dorothy Wordsworth wrote: "I worked and read the L. B. [*Lyrical Ballads*], enchanted with *The Idiot Boy.*"

Page 24. LINES, COMPOSED A FEW MILES ABOVE TINTERN ABBEY

In June, 1798, Wordsworth and his sister went to Bristol to see the *Lyrical Ballads* through the press. Within a week they tired of the noise and confusion of the city and went on a walking tour through the beautiful country which Wordsworth and his college friend, Robert Jones, had tramped five years before, after the poet's return from his stormy months in France. "We crossed the Severn ferry," he writes, "and walked ten miles further to Tintern Abbey, a very beautiful ruin on the Wye. The next morning we walked along the river through Monmouth to Goodrich Castle, there slept, and returned the next day to Tintern, thence to Chepstow, and from Chepstow back again in a boat to Tintern, where we slept, and thence back in a small vessel to Bristol." The vacation was four or five days long. Wordsworth began the poem upon leaving Tintern and finished it just as he was entering Bristol. No part of the poem was written down till he reached Bristol.

The poem is important as an expression of Wordsworth's philosophy of nature.

65–110. Here are described the three periods through which the poet's feeling for nature passed They are (1) that in which the animal enjoyment of nature was supreme; (2) that in which the love of man predominated over the love of nature; (3) that in which a spiritual presence becomes manifest through a deepened sympathy with man and nature.

Professor de Sélincourt says that lines 114 to the end were Wordsworth's greatest contribution to *Lyrical Ballads* and the fullest tribute to what Dorothy had been to him ever since she had joined him at Racedown.

Cf. *Ode: Intimations of Immortality* (text p. 63).

Page 25 THE OLD CUMBERLAND BEGGAR

"The class of Beggars, to which the Old Man here described belongs, will probably soon be extinct. It consisted of poor, and, mostly, old and infirm persons, who confined themselves to a stated round in their neighborhood, and had certain fixed days, on which, at different houses, they regularly received alms, sometimes in money, but mostly in provisions." (Wordsworth's note.)

Wordsworth called the war of the political economists upon mendicity in all its forms and upon alms-giving also, a heartless process. In "Postscript, 1835" he expresses his views of pauperism.

1–66. These lines picture with great clearness the old pauper who in the eyes of the "political economists" has completely passed his days of usefulness.

87–170. The poet points out that the beggar "confers real service on his fellows in receiving service," compelling the soul of the giver to love and so awakening in him the realization of his

> "kindred with a world
> Where want and sorrow were."

175. *chartered*. Privileged. In *King Henry V* Shakespeare speaks of the air "as a chartered libertine."

179. *House*. A poorhouse.

Page 28.
STRANGE FITS OF PASSION HAVE I KNOWN

This poem and the four immediately following it were written in Germany and are known as "the Lucy poems." Most students of the poems say that nothing is known of the identity of the beautiful Lucy, and point out that in his autobiographical notes Wordsworth is silent concerning these poems. Professor de Sélincourt, in his biography of Dorothy Wordsworth, says that we shall never know whether they were inspired by an early episode in Wordsworth's life of which we know nothing, or are the creation of the poet's imagination. He believes, however, that much of the feeling expressed for Lucy arose from the poet's passionate devotion for his sister, and quotes Coleridge as having said that he always felt that the sublime epitaph, *A Slumber Did My Spirit Seal*, had been prompted by the thought of Dorothy's death. De Sélincourt points out further that the same thought may have prompted the irrational fear of Lucy's death in *Strange Fits of Passion*, a poem of which Dorothy wrote, "it is a favourite of mine." The reader who sees Dorothy Wordsworth in the beautiful Lucy may not be far astray.

SHE DWELT AMONG THE UNTRODDEN WAYS

2. *Dove*. A river forming part of the boundary between Derby and Stafford.

Page 29.   NUTTING

This poem, which was written in Germany, Wordsworth intended as a part of a poem on his own life (*The Prelude*), but struck out as not being wanted there. "Like most of my school-fellows," he said, "I was an impassioned nutter. For this pleasure the vale of Esthwaite, abounding in coppice wood, furnished a very wide range. These verses arose out of the re-

membrance of feelings I had often had when a boy, and particularly in the extensive woods that still [1843] stretch from the side of Esthwaite Lake towards Graythwaite." For an impressive delineation of the poet's boyhood feelings see lines 301–339 of Book I of *The Prelude* (text p. 85)

The poem presents some of the incidents and experiences arising out of Wordsworth's animal enjoyment of nature in boyhood and records his recognition, even then, of the spiritual influences of nature. It is, says Professor Raleigh, "the reflections of one who has studied the mind of man as reverently and patiently as the scientific observer studies the works of nature."

9. *weeds*. Clothes.

11. During his schooldays at Hawkshead Wordsworth lived with Dame Anne Tyson.

54. *dearest Maiden*. Dorothy Wordsworth.

Page 30.   MATTHEW

In a note concerning this poem Wordsworth wrote: "In the school of Hawkshead is a tablet, on which are inscribed, in gilt letters, the names of the several persons who have been schoolmasters there since the foundation of the school, with the time at which they entered upon and quitted their office. Opposite to one of those names the author wrote the following lines [*Matthew*]."

Some of the characteristics of the Matthew of the poem are taken from the Rev. William Taylor, who was Wordsworth's loved teacher at Hawkshead and who died the year Wordsworth left the school. The portrait is a composite one, however, rather than the single portrait of Taylor. Wordsworth said that this and the other "Matthew poems (*The Two April Mornings*, *The Fountain*, and *Address to the Scholars of the Village School of ——*) would not gain by a literal detail of facts. . . . This schoolmaster was made up of several, both of his class and men of other occupations."

Page 31.   THE TWO APRIL MORNINGS

60. *wilding*. A branch of crabapple blossoms.

THE FOUNTAIN

4. *Matthew seventy-two*. Our understanding of the liberty with which Wordsworth drew upon the characteristics of the Rev. William Taylor for the several portraits of Matthew, and yet constructed an ideal figure of a schoolmaster in the "Matthew poems," becomes clear when we learn that the Hawkshead schoolmaster died at the age of thirty-two. Wordsworth said that he did not ask pardon for what there was of untruth in these verses, considered strictly as matters of fact. Truth and consistency in spirit, so that they might "move and teach in

a manner not unworthy of a poet's calling," was the great essential.

Page 32. RUTH

Wordsworth said that this poem, which was written in Germany, was suggested to him by an account he had of a wanderer in Somersetshire. De Quincey, in his *Autobiographic Sketches*, says that the story of the poem is based in fact. "Wordsworth himself told me, in general terms," he writes, "that the case which suggested the poem was that of an American lady, whose husband forsook her at the very place of embarkation from England, under circumstances and under expectations, upon her part, very much the same as those of Ruth."

Professor Dowden says that in this poem are exhibited the dangers to the heart and life arising from nature as impulse, apart from its restraining power. Usually in Wordsworth's poems the influence of nature upon man's spirit and life is a beneficent one.

Page 35. LUCY GRAY

Wordsworth wrote as follows of this poem: "Written at Goslar in Germany. It was founded on a circumstance told me by my sister, of a little girl who, not far from Halifax in Yorkshire, was bewildered in a snowstorm. Her footsteps were traced by her parents to the middle of the lock of a canal, and no other vestige of her, backward or forward, could be traced. The body, however, was found in the canal. The way in which the incident was treated and the spiritualizing of the character might furnish hints for contrasting the imaginative influences which I have endeavored to throw over common life with Crabbe's matter of fact style of treating subjects of the same kind."

THE SIMPLON PASS

In the summer vacation of 1790 Wordsworth and his Welsh friend, Robert Jones, went on a walking tour in France, Switzerland, and Italy. Crossing the Alps on this trip gave the poet the impressions recorded in *The Simplon Pass*. 18. *Characters of the great Apocalypse*, etc. Letters, tokens, evidences of the spirit which reveals itself to man through nature.

Page 36. TO M. H.

This and the three poems immediately following it Wordsworth placed in a section of his poems with the heading, "Poems on the Naming of Places." The poet introduced this section, comprising seven poems, with the following explanation: "By persons resident in the country, and attached to rural objects, many places will be found unnamed or of unknown names, where little Incidents must have occurred, or feelings been experienced, which will have given to such places a private and peculiar interest. From a wish to give some sort of record to such Incidents, and renew the gratification of such feelings, Names have been given to Places by the Author and some of his Friends, and the following Poems written in consequence."

Though many attempts have been made to find the exact location of the scene of the poem, it still remains unknown. The pool is in Rydal Upper Park, and the place must be near Rydal Mount or in the grounds of the Park.

23. *Mary.* Mary Hutchinson, who became Mrs. Wordsworth in 1802.

IT WAS AN APRIL MORNING

Wordsworth said that this poem, which was written at Grasmere, "was suggested on the banks of the brook that runs through Easedale, which is, in some parts of its course, as wild and beautiful as brook can be. I have composed thousands of verses by the side of it."

Easedale was a half-hour's walk from Dove Cottage. Wordsworth and Dorothy discovered the path "through this wild nook" three days after they had moved into the Cottage, and, as the poet said, it long remained their favorite haunt.

39. *My Emma.* Wordsworth frequently referred to his sister Dorothy as Emma or Emmeline.

Page 37. THERE IS AN EMINENCE

The "Eminence," which Wordsworth said could not actually be seen from the orchard seat, is Stone-Arthur. "It rises above the road by the side of Grasmere Lake, towards Keswick."

There is a special fitness in associating this "loneliest place among the clouds" with the contemplative lover of solitude, William Wordsworth.

14. *She who dwells with me*, etc. Dorothy Wordsworth.

WHEN, TO THE ATTRACTIONS OF THE BUSY WORLD

John Wordsworth, the poet's beloved brother who died in shipwreck in 1805, made his home in the little Grasmere cottage from late January, 1800, to the end of September. The brothers had seen little of each other since John "quitted Esthwaite's pleasant shore," where they had been together in the Hawkshead school. In the eight months of intimate association Wordsworth found that his brother was deeply appreciative of his poetry, and the two spent many hours in the Fir Grove talking over the *Lyrical Ballads*. The grove, which Wordsworth said was a "favorite haunt with us all while we lived at Town-end," is not far from the Wishing Gate on the road over White Moss Common.

Coleridge, the companion of John Wordsworth and William on a walking tour in the Lake Country in October, 1799, saw with a poet's intuition that John was a being of some moment, and wrote, "John is one of you, a man who hath solitary musings of his own intellect, with a subtle tact, a swift instinct of Truth and Beauty." Dorothy Wordsworth found almost at the beginning of her brother's visit that Coleridge's opinion was right, and she wrote to Mrs. John Marshall, March 16, 1805, that John (who, indeed, "had been set down as the dunce of the family") loved solitude and rejoiced in society; "he would wander alone among these hills with his fishing rod, or led on merely by the pleasure of walking—or he would walk with William or me or both of us, ... he had so fine an eye that no distinction was unnoticed by him, and so tender a feeling that he never noticed anything in vain."

See note on *The Happy Warrior*, below.

80. *A silent Poet.* One with all the feelings of a poet, endowed with

"The vision and the faculty divine;
Yet wanting the accomplishment of verse."
                        Excursion, Book I, 79–80

82. *inevitable ear.* One that heard all things.

Page 38.   THE BROTHERS

Of this poem Wordsworth wrote: "This poem was composed in a grove at the northeastern end of Grasmere Lake, which grove was in a great measure destroyed by turning the highroad along the side of the water. The few trees that are left were spared at my intercession. The poem arose out of the fact, mentioned to me at Ennerdale, that a shepherd had fallen asleep upon the top of the rock called the Pillar, and perished as here described. The abruptness with which the poem begins is accounted for by the fact that it was intended to be a concluding poem of a series of pastorals, the scene of which is laid among the mountains of Cumberland and Westmoreland."

Leslie Stephen points to this poem as exemplifying his idea that Wordsworth "loves his native hills, not in the Byronic fashion, as a savage wilderness, but as the appropriate framework in which a healthy social order can permanently maintain itself."

16. *Ennerdale.* A beautiful vale lying within high, steep mountains in the western part of the Lake Region.

139. *pike.* Peak, hill.

204-15. The meaning probably is that gen-

erations of Walter Ewbank's family had had the heart, i.e., the energy, ambition, to try to acquire more lands and property; that in so doing they had contracted more and more debt, which they passed on to each new generation of Ewbanks; and that finally, in his turn, Walter had to assume the burden. Although he had the family heart, he found the struggle to carry on, burdened "with bond, interest, and mortgages," a killing thing, and at last "went into his grave before his time."

310. *Great Gavel.* A mountain at the head of Ennerdale.

Leeza's banks. The Leeza is a stream that flows westerly into the vale of Ennerdale.

311. *the Enna.* A stream flowing out of Ennerdale Water into the Irish sea.

Egremont. A market town in Ennerdale near the sea.

Page 44.   MICHAEL

Wordsworth said of this poem: "[It was] written at Town-end, Grasmere, about the same time as *The Brothers*. The sheepfold, on which so much of the poem turns, remains, or rather the ruins of it. The character and circumstances of Luke were taken from a family to whom had belonged, many years before, the house we lived in at Town-end, along with some fields and woodlands on the eastern shore of Grasmere. The name of the Evening Star was not in fact given to this house, but to another on the same side of the valley, more to the north."

To Thomas Poole, his friend, he wrote of the poem: "I have attempted to give a picture of a man, of strong mind and lively sensibility, agitated by two of the most powerful affections of the human heart; the parental affection, and the love of property, *landed* property, including the feelings of inheritance, home, and personal and family independence. . . . In writing it I had your character often before my eyes."

To Charles J. Fox he wrote: "In the two poems, *The Brothers* and *Michael*, I have attempted to draw a picture of the domestic affections, as I know they exist among a class of men who are now almost confined to the north of England. . . . The poems . . . were written with a view to show that men who do not wear fine clothes can feel deeply. . . . The poems are faithful copies from Nature."

2. *Green-head Ghyll.* A valley near Dove Cottage. Ghyll, Wordsworth said, was the local name for a steep, narrow valley with a dashing stream running through it.

51. *subterraneous music.* Professor Dowden suggests that this may be "the sound of the wind under overhanging cliffs and in hollows of the hills."

134. *Easedale* is near Grasmere; *Dunmail-Raise* is a pass about three miles from Grasmere.

169. *Clipping Tree.* "Clipping is the word used in the north of England for shearing." (Wordsworth.)

Page 50. THE SPARROW'S NEST

"Written in the orchard, Town-end, Grasmere. At the end of the garden of my father's house at Cockermouth was a high terrace that commanded a fine view of the River Derwent and Cockermouth Castle. This was our favorite playground. The terrace-wall, a low one, was covered with closely-clipt privet and roses, which gave an almost impervious shelter to birds that built their nests there. The latter of these stanzas alludes to one of those nests." (Wordsworth's note.)

9. *Emmeline.* His sister Dorothy.

THE AFFLICTION OF MARGARET ——

The poet said of this poem: "Written at Town-end, Grasmere. This was taken from the case of a poor widow who lived in the town of Penrith. Her sorrow was well known to Mrs. Wordsworth, to my sister, and, I believe, to the whole town. She kept a shop, and when she saw a stranger passing by she was in the habit of going out into the street to enquire of him after her son."

Professor Gingerich points out that this "study in maternal sorrow" is an excellent example of Wordsworth's power to create characters who, although their feelings are profoundly stirred, nevertheless remain outwardly calm.

Page 51. MY HEART LEAPS UP

This poem, which is a condensed utterance of Wordsworth's belief in Nature's power to influence man, was written at Town-end, Grasmere. Professor George speaks of it as the keynote of Wordsworth's poetry, and says that it is all *The Prelude* rendered in a lyric. It should be noted that it expresses the germ thought of the great *Ode: Intimations of Immortality*, of which its last three lines are the motto.

7. *The Child is father of the Man.* Cf. Milton's

The childhood shows the man
As morning shows the day.

9. *natural piety.* Piety is used in the Latin sense of "filial reverence."

TO A BUTTERFLY

Dorothy Wordsworth gives us a vivid picture of her brother's absorption in writing this poem: ". . . While we were at breakfast . . . with his basin of broth beside him untouched, and a little plate of bread and butter, he wrote the Poem to a Butterfly. He ate not a morsel, nor put on his stockings, but sate with his shirt neck unbuttoned, and his waistcoat open while he did it. The thought first came upon him as we were talking about the pleasure we both always feel at the sight of a butterfly. I told him that I used to chase them a little, but that I was afraid of brushing the dust off their wings, and did not catch them."

Page 52. TO THE SMALL CELANDINE

In her Journal Dorothy Wordsworth wrote: "We came into the orchard directly after breakfast and sat there. . . . William began to write the poem of The Celandine. . . . I walked backwards and forwards with William. He repeated his poem to me."

Wordsworth thought it remarkable that, since so many bright and beautiful celandines came out very early in the spring, they had not been noticed earlier in English verse.

TO THE DAISY, TO THE SAME FLOWER (p. 53), TO THE DAISY (p. 54)

The three "Daisy" poems were composed at Town-end, Grasmere, in the earlier part of the poet's residence there.

The quotation prefixed to the poem on page 52 is from *The Shepherd's Hunting*, by George Wither, a minor English poet of the seventeenth century. By "Her" in the first line Wither meant his muse. "Titan," in the ninth line, is the sun.

17. *morrice.* A dance once common in England in pageants, processions, and May-day games. Commonly spelled "morris."

25. *mews.* Hiding places.

76. *leveret.* A young hare.

Speaking of the third "Daisy" poem (p. 54) Wordsworth said that his use of the words "thy function apostolical" (line 23) had been criticised as "little less than profane." "How could it be thought so?" he asked, and then continued: "The word is adopted with reference to its derivation, implying something sent on a mission; and assuredly this little flower . . . may be regarded . . . as administering both to moral and to spiritual purposes."

Page 54. TO THE CUCKOO

This poem, Wordsworth's favorite among his shorter poems, is another of the numerous pieces composed in the Town-end orchard. Of this poem and of *The Green Linnet* (p. 59), Mr. E. A. G. Lamborn says: "The contrast between Shelley's lark [p. 433] and Wordsworth's [p. 80] is happily repeated" in the comparison between two English birds. "The greenfinch is a real bird in the real world, a beautiful material thing; but the cuckoo is a voice" from the far off "world of youthful dreams, that for an enchanted moment retransfigures this one, investing it with 'the light that never was on sea or land' but only in the vision of the child and the poet."

Page 55.   RESOLUTION AND INDEPENDENCE

"This old man," Wordsworth wrote in Fenwick Notes, "I met a few hundred yards from my cottage; and the account of him is taken from his own mouth. I was in the state of feeling described in the beginning of the poem, while crossing over Barton Fell from Mr. Clarkson's, at the foot of Ullswater, towards Askham. The image of the hare I then observed on the ridge of the Fell."

To some friends he wrote: "I cannot conceive a figure more impressive than that of an old man like this, the survivor of a wife and ten children, travelling alone among the mountains and all lonely places, carrying with him his own fortitude, and the necessities which an unjust state of society has laid upon him."

Wordsworth's mood in this poem is not surprising. His work had been received with ridicule, his income brought him but a bare subsistence, and the little money that was to be his by inheritance had not been paid—conditions which seemed to thrust far into the future the fulfillment of his desire to marry. He had chosen to shape his life by a high idealism, and he had unshaken belief in the rightness of his theory of poetry and in the purity of his poetic inspiration. But others, alas—Burns, Chatterton—with aspirations just as understandable to them had struggled and gone down in spite of their high visions. Little wonder then that fears and fancies came thick upon him and that he saw gloomily that the glad youth of the poet may come in the end to despondency and madness. The old Leech-gatherer, met when the poet's spirit has touched the depths, gives him a "new insight into the mystery of man's inward power of being," and transforms him from a being of gloom and despondency to one easily adequate to his crisis.

43. *Chatterton, the marvellous Boy.* Thomas Chatterton, an English poet of considerable talent—some say genius—born in 1752. He died by suicide when he was eighteen years old.

45. *Him.* Robert Burns.

Page 57.   IT IS A BEAUTEOUS EVENING

Arising out of a month's stay in France which William and Dorothy made in August, 1802. Dorothy wrote two significant notes in her Journal. For the first see note to *Composed by the Sea-Side Near Calais*, below. For the second see text page 4.

The last six lines of the poem are not addressed to Dorothy Wordsworth, as has often been said, but to the poet's daughter Caroline, whose mother was the French girl, Annette Vallon. Caroline was ten years old at the time this poem was composed.

12. *in Abraham's bosom.* See Luke 16 : 23.

WITH HOW SAD STEPS

9. *Merlin.* In medieval romance, a famous prophet and magician of the fifth century.

13. *Cynthia.* An epithet for Artemis, an Olympian goddess associated with the moon. "Cynthia" as used here, therefore, means "moon."

COMPOSED UPON WESTMINSTER BRIDGE

This sonnet was composed upon the top of the coach in which Wordsworth and Dorothy were beginning their journey to France in July, 1802, by way of Dover. Wordsworth, who assigned the date, September 3, either was mistaken as to the exact time or, as Professor Dowden suggests, may have thought that the "fierce light" of July was less in harmony with the sonnet than the more subdued light of September.

The sonnet is a good example of Wordsworth's power to transfigure a real thing and give it a realness and a permanence beyond those which it possesses in its material existence. The London of the Thames may sometime be no more, but as long as there is a discerning human soul, the city of Wordsworth's sonnet will endure.

WRITTEN IN LONDON

This and the seven sonnets immediately following it are on political themes and express the poet's appreciation of his native country and his praise of the liberty-loving spirit in man. Wordsworth tells us that as a result of hearing his sister Dorothy read Milton's sonnets one morning in May, 1802, he took fire and produced three sonnets the same afternoon, the first he had ever written, except an irregular one at school. A comparison of the sonnets of the two poets will show that Wordsworth's have much of that quality which has been so often praised as "Miltonic grandeur."

Of this poem, which was written immediately after his return from his first trip to France, Wordsworth wrote: "I could not but be struck, as here described, with the vanity and parade of our own country, especially in great towns and cities, as contrasted with the quiet, and I may say the desolation, that the revolution had produced in France. This must be borne in mind, or else the reader will think that in this and succeeding sonnets I have exaggerated the mischief engendered and fostered among us by undisturbed wealth."

1. *Friend.* Coleridge.

Page 58. LONDON, 1802

This sonnet majestically and solemnly calls England's attention to one of her greatest sons, Milton, who, if he were living, would lift her from the corruption into which she has fallen.
4. *hall and bower.* The resort of knights and ladies respectively.

IT IS NOT TO BE THOUGHT OF

This expression of a "calm, clear, triumphant faith in freedom" was published in the *Morning Post*, April 16, 1803, at which time the English heart was stirred at the threat of an invasion by Napoleon.
4. *"with pomp of waters, unwithstood."* From Samuel Daniel's *Civil Wars between the Two Houses of Lancaster and York*, 1595, Book II, stanza 7.

ON THE EXTINCTION OF THE VENETIAN
REPUBLIC

Venice became an independent state in 997 and for centuries maintained a government republican in form but markedly oligarchical in reality. In 1797 Bonaparte occupied the city and by the treaty of Campo Formio dissolved the republic, Austria receiving most of the Venetian territory and holding it until 1866, when it was joined with Italy.
4. *The eldest Child of Liberty.* In 697 many citizens of the towns in the north of Italy fled to islands in the northern Adriatic to escape the Huns under Attila. They prospered and grew strong in this inaccessible situation, and began the groundwork of their republic.
8. *espouse the everlasting Sea.* In 998 the doge constituted Venice the protector of the North Adriatic. The custom arose of symbolizing this office by celebrating the wedding of Venice and the Adriatic on Ascension Day by dropping a gold ring into the water. The annual celebration became a ceremony of much magnificence in the late years of the twelfth century. Cf. *Childe Harold*, Canto IV, 1–36 (text p. 266).

TO TOUSSAINT L'OUVERTURE

Toussaint (surnamed L'Ouverture, the Opener, because he broke through the Spanish entrenchments) was born a negro slave in Haiti in 1743. He rose to military leadership in the negro army of his country, and in 1793, when Haiti declared for France, saw negro slavery abolished in that island. In 1796 the French made him chief of the army of San Domingo. In 1802, however, when Bonaparte proclaimed the return of slavery in San Domingo, Toussaint rebelled. Declared an outlaw, he was captured and thrown in prison in France, where he died in 1803.

COMPOSED IN THE VALLEY NEAR DOVER
ON THE DAY OF LANDING

August 30, 1802, Wordsworth and his sister returned home after a month in France.
9. *Europe is yet in bonds.* To Napoleon, through the Treaty of Amiens, March 25, 1802.

Page 59. SEPTEMBER, 1802. NEAR DOVER

In connection with this sonnet it is interesting to note that Dorothy Wordsworth wrote in her Journal: "On Sunday, the 29th of August, we left Calais at twelve o'clock in the morning and landed at Dover at one on Monday the 30th. . . . The next day was very hot. We . . . bathed, and sate upon the Dover Cliffs, and looked upon France with many a melancholy and tender thought. We could see the shores almost as plain as if it were but an English lake."
A year later Napoleon, who was threatening to invade England, was reported to have said, as he looked across the narrow Strait, "Make me master of that strip of water for twelve hours, and I am master of the world."
12. *themselves.* Winds and waters, mentioned in line 10.
13. *them.* Same as "themselves" in preceding line.

COMPOSED BY THE SEA-SIDE NEAR CALAIS,
AUGUST, 1802

Wordsworth and Dorothy reached Calais at four o'clock on the morning of July 31st. "We had delightful walks," Dorothy wrote, "after the heat of the day was past,—seeing far off in the west the coast of England like a cloud, crested with Dover Castle, which was but like the summit of a cloud—the evening star and the glory of the sky; the reflections in the water were more beautiful than the sky itself; purple waves brighter than precious stones forever melting far away upon the sands. . . . Nothing in romance was ever half so beautiful."
12. *with many a fear.* The poet was fearful that the situation between England and France might become critical.

THE GREEN LINNET

See note to *To the Cuckoo*, above.

Page 60. THE SOLITARY REAPER

In 1803 Wordsworth and his sister, accompanied by Coleridge, visited Scotland. Of that part of their trip along Loch Voil, Dorothy wrote: "It was harvest-time, and the fields were quietly—might I say pensively?—enlivened by small companies of reapers. It is not uncommon in the more lonely parts of the

Highlands to see a single person so employed. The following poem was suggested to William by a beautiful sentence in Thomas Wilkinson's *Tour in Scotland*."

The passage in Wilkinson to which Dorothy refers is this: "Passed a female who was reaping alone; she sung in Erse as she bended over her sickle;—the sweetest human voice I ever heard; her strains were tenderly melancholy, and felt delicious, long after they were heard no more."

Mr. Herbert Read says, "I would always send out *The Solitary Reaper* into the world of letters to represent the quintessence of English poetry."

19–20. In his paper, "Wordsworth and Byron," Swinburne wrote of these two lines: "In the whole expanse of poetry there can hardly be two verses of more perfect and profound and exalted beauty. But if anybody does not happen to see this, no critic . . . could succeed in making visible the certainty of this truth to the mind's eye of that person."

TO A HIGHLAND GIRL

This poem, like *The Solitary Reaper* (p. 60), *At the Grave of Burns* (p. 61), *Yarrow Unvisited* (p. 62), and *Stepping Westward* (p. 63), belongs to a group of seventeen poems which Wordsworth collected under the heading "Memorials of a Tour in Scotland, 1803."

Dorothy Wordsworth's Journal for August 28 had the following entry: "When beginning to descend the hill toward Loch Lomond we overtook two girls, who told us we could not cross the ferry till evening, for the boat was gone with a number of people to church. One of the girls was exceedingly beautiful: and the figures of both of them, in gray plaids falling to their feet, their faces only being uncovered, excited our attention before we spoke to them. . . . I think I never heard the English language sound more sweetly than from the mouth of the elder of these girls, while she stood at the gate answering our inquiries, her face flushed with the rain."

In a note to this poem Wordsworth wrote: "The sort of prophecy with which the verses conclude has, through God's goodness, been realized; and now approaching the close of my seventy-third year I have a most vivid remembrance of her and the beautiful objects with which she was surrounded."

This poem should be compared with *The Solitary Reaper*. Both poems have the same subject, but *The Solitary Reaper* has a beauty, a memorableness, that is missing from the *Highland Girl*. In the haunting music of the *Reaper* and in its magical phrasing the poet has given life everlasting to the Scotch girl and to the lonely mountain field in which she "cuts and binds the grain." Both poems are evidence of

Wordsworth's marked ability to recall and renew, in all their first impressiveness, scenes or experiences by whose beauty he had been deeply stirred.

Professor Herford says that "the Highland Maids," the subjects of these poems, "with their shy elusive beauty, their natural grace, overcame the reticence which the lover of Annette had hitherto almost completely observed in poetry."

Page 61.   YEW-TREES

Of the yew-trees that are the subject of this poem, Wordsworth wrote that they "are still standing, but the spread of that at Lorton is much diminished by mutilation." He was so impressed by the gigantic size of a yew trunk that lay on the Rosthwaite-Stonethwaite road that he believed it must have been as old as the Christian era. An old Keswick guide, he said, "used gravely to tell strangers that there could be no doubt of its having been in existence before the flood."

Coleridge pointed to this poem in support of this statement: "In imaginative power he [Wordsworth] stands nearest of all modern writers to Shakespeare and Milton; and yet in a kind perfectly unborrowed and his own." (See text p. 230.) Ruskin spoke of the poem as the "most vigorous and solemn bit of forest landscape ever painted."

Note the use of personification in the poem and see if you can justify it from what the poet says in his "Preface to the Lyrical Ballads," on text p. 103.

1. *Lorton Vale*. A little valley a few miles south of Cockermouth, the poet's birthplace.

4. *furnish weapons*. The wood of the yew is unsurpassed for making bows.

5. *Umfraville or Percy*. The Umfraville and Percy families were active against the Scots in the medieval border wars in which the English and Scots frequently engaged. The Percy of the poem is Henry Percy, known as Hotspur. He is the hero of the old ballad, *Chevy Chace*.

7. *Azincour*. This battle between the English and the French was fought in 1415.

8. *Crecy, or Poictiers*. These battles between the English and the French were fought, respectively, in 1346 and 1356.

14. *those fraternal Four of Borrowdale*. The "fraternal Four" were uprooted by a tornado in 1883. Borrowdale is a valley a short distance northwest of Grasmere.

33. *Glaramara*. A mountain about 2500 feet high at the head of Borrowdale.

AT THE GRAVE OF BURNS

See first paragraph of notes on *To a Highland Girl*, above.

For August 18, 1803, Dorothy Wordsworth

wrote as follows in her Journal: "Went to the churchyard where Burns is buried. . . . He lies at a corner of the churchyard, and his son Francis Wallace beside him. . . . We looked at the grave with melancholy and painful reflections, repeating to each other his own verses:—

'Is there a man whose judgment clear
Can others teach the course to steer,
Yet runs himself life's mad career
    Wild as the wave?—
Here let him pause and through a tear
    Survey this grave.'"

The lines which the poet and his sister repeated compose the third stanza of Burns's poem, *A Bard's Epitaph*. *At the Grave of Burns*, in which Wordsworth generously acknowledges his indebtedness to Burns, is written in the measure of *A Bard's Epitaph*, a measure so frequently employed by Burns that it is not inaccurate to speak of it as his favorite poetic melody.

6. *Where Burns is laid*. At Dumfries.
20. *"glinted" forth*. Suggested by a line in Burns's *To a Mountain Daisy*.
39. *Criffel's hoary top*. Criffel, or Crowfell, a mountain in the county of Kirkcudbright, near Dumfries.
40. *Skiddaw*. A mountain near Keswick in the Lake District not quite thirty miles from Criffel.
50. *"poor Inhabitant below."* The fourth stanza of *A Bard's Epitaph* contains the lines—

The poor inhabitant below
Was quick to learn and wise to know.

53. *gowans*. Daisies.

Page 62.   YARROW UNVISITED

See first paragraph of note on *To a Highland Girl*, above.
On their rambling trip through Scotland Wordsworth and his sister reached Clovenford, near "the bonny holms of Yarrow," September 18. They talked of "going thither" but concluded to reserve "the pleasure for some future time." As a result of this decision Wordsworth wrote *Yarrow Unvisited*. The Yarrow is a romantic river in the Scottish Lowlands which flows into the Ettrick.
6. *"winsome Marrow."* From a ballad, *Busk ye, busk ye, my bonnie, bonnie bride*, by William Hamilton (1704–1754). A marrow is a mate or companion, here referring, of course, to Dorothy Wordsworth.
17. *Galla Water, Leader Haughs*. Galla Water, a northern tributary of the Tweed. The Leader is a river emptying into the Tweed near Melrose. Haughs, or holms, are the lowlands or "bottom" near a stream.
19. *Dryborough*. A town on the Tweed.
20. *lintwhites*. A poetical form of the word linnet.

21. *Tiviot-dale*. The Teviot, or Tiviot, a tributary of the Tweed.
35. This line is from Hamilton's ballad.
37. *Strath*. A flat, wide river-valley.
43. *St. Mary's Lake*. The Yarrow flows from the lake. Mrs. Andrew Lang, in an essay on "Poets as Landscape Painters," said that Wordsworth was strictly accurate in the number of swans on the lake.
For Wordsworth's comment on this line see text p. 140.

Page 63.   STEPPING WESTWARD

See first paragraph of note on *To a Highland Girl*, above.
Dorothy Wordsworth wrote the following of the experience which this poem records: "I cannot describe how affecting this simple expression ['What! you are stepping westward?'] was in that remote place, with the western sky in front, yet glowing with the departed sun. William wrote the poem long after, in remembrance of his feelings and mine."

ODE: INTIMATIONS OF IMMORTALITY

In a note on this poem Wordsworth said: "Nothing was more difficult for me in childhood than to admit the notion of death as a state applicable to my own being. . . . It was not so much from feelings of animal vivacity that *my* difficulty came as from a sense of the indomitableness of the spirit within me. I used to brood over the stories of Enoch and Elijah, and almost to persuade myself that, whatever might become of others, I should be translated, in something of the same way, to heaven. With a feeling congenial to this, I was often unable to think of external things as having external existence, and I communed with all that I saw as something not apart from, but inherent in, my own immaterial nature. Many times while going to school have I grasped at a wall or tree to recall myself from this abyss of idealism to the reality. . . . In later periods of life I have deplored . . . a subjugation of an opposite character, and have rejoiced over the remembrances, as is expressed in the lines—

'obstinate questionings
Of sense and outward things,
Fallings from us, vanishings.'"

Concerning the doctrine of pre-existence contained in lines 58–65, a passage which, the poet said, "has given pain to some good and pious persons," he wrote that he did not mean to inculcate such a belief. "It is far too shadowy a notion," he believes, "to be recommended to faith, as more than an element in our instincts of immortality. But let us bear in mind that, though the idea is not advanced in revelation, there is nothing there to contradict it, and the fall of man presents an analogy in its favor. Accordingly, a pre-existent state has entered into the popular creeds of many nations; and . . . is . . . an ingredient in Platonic philosophy. . . . When I was impelled to write this poem on the Immortality of the Soul, I took hold of the notion of pre-existence as having sufficient foundation in humanity for authorizing me to make for my purpose the best use of it I could as a poet."

The *Ode*, Professor Herford points out, deals with the spiritual crisis which the poet had to face in the period 1802–6, just as *The Prelude* records the political and personal crisis of 1793–97. A comparison of the *Ode* with *Tintern Abbey* should result in one's seeing that the theme of each is the same—with what difference?

For Coleridge's comment on the *Ode*, see text pages 224, 225, 228, 230, and 231.

Mr. E. A. G. Lamborn, pointing to such lines as 12–13, 25, 28, and 158–9, says that this poem is kept alive in men's hearts not by its philosophy but by its beauty. Such lines, he concludes, "transfigure and make significant for us the world of sense, and certify us of the reality that lies behind it."

Motto. *The Child is father of the Man.* See note on *My Heart Leaps Up*, above.

28. *the fields of sleep.* Professor Dowden asks: "Are 'the fields of sleep' those deep and shadowy parts of our own souls which lie out of the view of consciousness?" Another commentator says: "I take the phrase to mean the fields where the winds had slept through the night."

103. "*humorous stage.*" Fulke Greville (1554–1628) has a sonnet containing the line—

"I do not here upon this humorous stage."

Wordsworth may have taken the phrase from this sonnet, or he may have had in mind Shakespeare's "All the world's a stage" (*As You Like It*, II, vii); however, the word "humorous," evidently meaning of different humors or moods, does not appear in this passage.

Page 66.　FRENCH REVOLUTION

Wordsworth prefixed a note to this poem in which he described it as "an extract from the long poem on my own poetical education. It was first published by Coleridge in his *Friend*, which is the reason of its having had a place in every edition of my poems since." The poem comprises lines 105–44 of Book XI of *The Prelude*, the long poem on the author's poetical education.

I WANDERED LONELY AS A CLOUD

Dorothy Wordsworth's Journal for Tuesday, April 15, 1802, reads: "When we were in the woods beyond Gowbarrow Park [at the south-western shore of Ullswater] we saw a few daffodils close to the water-side. We fancied that the sea had floated the seeds ashore, and that the little colony had so sprung up. But as we went along there were more, and yet more; and, at last, under the boughs of the trees, we saw there was a long belt of them along the shore, about the breadth of a country turnpike road. I never saw daffodils so beautiful. They grew among the mossy stones, about and above them; some rested their heads on these stones as on a pillow for weariness; and the rest tossed, and reeled, and danced, and seemed as if they verily laughed with the wind that blew upon them over the lake. They looked so gay, ever glancing, ever changing. The wind blew directly over the lake to them. There was here and there a little knot, and a few stragglers higher up; but they were so few as not to disturb the simplicity, unity, and life of that one busy highway."

Why does the experience related in the final stanza seem to be in keeping with the poet's theory of poetry set forth in lines 40 ff., text page 110?

Lines 21 and 22 were suggested or perhaps even composed by Mrs. Wordsworth. Their thought, however, is intensely Wordsworthian. For Coleridge's comment on the poem see text page 224, lines 10 ff.

Page 67.　SHE WAS A PHANTOM OF DELIGHT

The inspiration of this poem was Mrs. Wordsworth. The first four lines were originally composed as a part of the poem *To a Highland Girl*. 22. *machine.* The poet has been severely criticized for having spoken of a "lovely girl in a love poem as a piece of machinery." Shakespeare makes Hamlet use it of himself in *Hamlet*, II, ii, 124—but sneeringly. As Wordsworth uses it does it necessarily mean human body?

TO A YOUNG LADY

The young lady is doubtless Dorothy Wordsworth.

CHARACTER OF THE HAPPY WARRIOR

Many of the character elements approved of in this poem were to be found, Wordsworth believed, in the character of Admiral Nelson, "shaker of the Baltic and the Nile," who in October, 1805, gained a decisive victory over the combined French and Spanish fleets off Cape Trafalgar, but was himself fatally wounded. A few years before Trafalgar, Nelson had fallen in love with Lady Hamilton, the wife of Sir William Hamilton, and so great was his infatuation for her that he disobeyed orders to leave Naples and join a Mediterranean squadron. It was this "one great crime" that Wordsworth had in mind when he wrote that "though many . . . of these lines were suggested by what was . . . known as excellent in [Nelson's] conduct, I have not been able to connect his name with the poem as I could wish, or even to think of him with satisfaction in reference to the idea of what a warrior ought to be." He then stated that "many elements of the characters here portrayed were found" in his brother John, who was drowned off Weymouth in February, 1805, when his command, the East Indiaman *Earl of Abergavenny*, struck a rock and sank. Captain Beaupuy, his French friend, was probably in his mind also when he wrote the poem.

When Wordsworth was told by Harriet Martineau that this poem was the favorite of Channing, the American Unitarian divine, he replied, somewhat humorously: "Ay, that was not on account of the poetic conditions being best fulfilled in that poem, but because it is a chain of extremely *valooable* thoughts." The student will find it an excellent aid to his grasping the poem to make a list of the links composing this chain of valuable thoughts.

Mr. Spencer Spring-Rice had copies of *The Happy Warrior* circulated among the troops in the Crimea on the ground that it was much more likely to inspire them than pious tracts. See the note on *When, To the Attractions of the Busy World*, above.

Page 68. ODE TO DUTY

Wordsworth wrote of this sermon in verse: "This *Ode* is on the model of Gray's *Ode to Adversity*, which is copied from Horace's *Ode to Fortune*. Many and many a time have I been twitted by my wife and sister for having forgotten this dedication of myself to the stern lawgiver. Transgressor indeed I have been, from hour to hour, from day to day: I would fain hope, however, not more flagrantly or in a worse way than most of my tuneful brethren. But these last words are in a wrong strain. We should be rigorous to ourselves and forbearing, if not indulgent, to others, and, if we make comparisons at all, it ought to be with those who have morally excelled us."

Miss E. C. Batho points out the "clear kinship of thought between Dante's submission to the Love that moves the sun and the other stars, and the great declaration" of the four lines of the *Ode* beginning,

Flowers laugh before thee on their beds.

Professor Walter Raleigh wrote of this poem: "Flowers, and laughter, and fragrance—all that plays on the surface and fades in the air—are the offspring of the same unalterable law which disciplines the stars in their squadrons, and which, in human hearts, is the law of sanity and order, of faith and of peace."

The stanza in brackets appeared in the edition of 1807 only.

Page 69. ELEGIAC STANZAS

In a note Wordsworth said that his friend, Sir George H. Beaumont, the landscape painter, painted two pictures of Peele Castle, one of which he gave to Mrs. Wordsworth. Lady Beaumont "interfered," and after Sir George's death she gave the picture to Sir Uvedale Price. Wordsworth was the neighbor of the "rugged Pile" when he spent four weeks with his cousin, Mrs. Barker, in Rampside, a village of Low Furness, Lancashire, right opposite the Castle, which lies between Walney Isle and the mainland. The year of this visit has been set as 1788, but there is better reason for dating it in August, 1794, after Wordsworth and his sister, who had been "rambling about the country on foot," separated for more than a year. It was this roaming the countryside with a revolutionary brother—their first vacation together —that brought Dorothy a severe reproof from her Aunt Crackanthorpe, whom Dorothy had characterized as a "mixture of ignorance, pride, affectation, self-conceit, and affected notability."

This poem, which Professor Gingerich calls the finest fruit of the poet's bereavement (the death of his brother John), should be read with *Ode to Duty, Character of the Happy Warrior, When, to the Attractions of the Busy World*, and *Elegiac Verses in Memory of My Brother*. 54. *the Kind*. Human beings.

Page 70. NUNS FRET NOT

In the entire realm of English poetry the technical perfection, dignity of thought, and sheer poetical beauty of Milton's sonnets have never been surpassed, if indeed they have been equalled. With the passing of Milton, however, the sonnet went into an eclipse from which it did not emerge for almost a century and a half, Dryden and Pope, each the leader of a period after Milton, apparently not even attempting it, and Thomson, Gray, and Cowper composing only a very few poems in the sonnet form. In the pages of Main's *Treasury of English Sonnets*, which covers the field of English poetry from Sir Thomas Wyatt (1503-1542) to O. M. Brown (1855-1874), there are four hundred sixty-three sonnets, but to this number the long period of 130 years beginning with the death of Milton and ending with Wordsworth's appearance as a sonneteer contributed only twenty-one.

The publication in 1789 of William Lisle Bowles's little book, *Fourteen Sonnets*, stirred the youthful Coleridge and awakened an interest in the long neglected form in a number of other young poets of his time. There was not a single sonnet in *Lyrical Ballads*, that book which in 1798 marked a new dawn for poetry; but the fact that Coleridge was moved to write of "the genial influence of a style of poetry, so tender and yet so manly, so natural and real, and yet so dignified and harmonious, as the sonnets . . . of Mr. Bowles," and that by 1802 Wordsworth had begun composing "sonnets of Miltonic grandeur," is unmistakable evidence that the long neglect of the sonnet form was over. It is natural to believe that if Bowles's sonnets aroused the enthusiasm of Coleridge they must have made some impression on Wordsworth (see letter to Bowles, text p. 145); but it is to be remembered that, in Wordsworth's own words, he "took fire" over Milton's sonnets as a result of his sister Dorothy's reading them aloud one day in May, 1802, and that that very afternoon he composed three sonnets, the first he ever wrote. In the words (approximately) of Mr. Houston Peterson, "the sonnet's scanty plot of ground" had an early attraction for Wordsworth, and in spite of his revolutionary views concerning poetic form and diction, so long and so thorough was his cultivation of the "plot" that the result was more than four hundred sonnets, some of them, of course, of little merit. In near a score of them, however, he reached a depth and richness which led the late Professor W. Sharp to say, Wordsworth "at his best is the greatest" [sonnet-writer in English].

The fine accomplishment of Wordsworth in the Petrarchan sonnet did much to establish the supremacy of the sonnet of that form over the Shakespearean sonnet, from Wordsworth's day to the present.

The student who would have an adequate appreciation of the poet's greatness as a sonneteer must first have a thorough understanding of the structure of the sonnet.

For an interesting criticism by Wordsworth of a sonnet by Gray, see text p. 104.

6. *Furness-fells.* The downs or uplands of Furness, on the coast of Lancashire.

THE WORLD IS TOO MUCH WITH US

13. *Proteus.* A prophetic sea-god who had the power of changing his shape.

14. *Triton.* A sea-god, the son of Poseidon (Neptune).

PERSONAL TALK

7. *Forms with chalk.* Marks to guide dancers.

41. *Lady married to the Moor.* Desdemona.

42. *Una with her milk-white Lamb.* A lovely lady in Spenser's *Faerie Queene* (Book I) intended as a personification of Truth.

51-6. These lines, which point out that the poet's function is to give two things, "truth" and "pure delight," are inscribed on the pedestal of the statue of Wordsworth in Westminster Abbey.

Page 71.   YES, IT WAS THE MOUNTAIN ECHO

In a note to this poem, which is another of the Town-end, Grasmere, compositions, Wordsworth said: "The echo came from Nab-scar, when I was walking on the opposite side of Rydal Mere. I will here mention, for my dear sister's sake, that, while she was sitting alone one day high up on this part of Loughrigg Fell, she was so affected by the voice of the cuckoo heard from the crags at some distance that she could not suppress a wish to have a stone inscribed with her name among the rocks from which the sound proceeded. On my return from my walk I recited these verses to Mrs. Wordsworth."

SONG AT THE FEAST OF BROUGHAM CASTLE

In a note Wordsworth said that he composed this poem while "walking to and fro along the path which led from Sir George Beaumont's farm-house, where we resided, to the Hall, which was building at that time."

Mr. A. J. George speaks as follows of the historical background of the poem: "The history of Westmereland—the country of the Western lakes—is closely connected with that long and illustrious line which began in Roger de Clifford. The eighth in the line was John Lord Clifford, who espoused the cause of the Lancastrians. After the battle of Wakefield he slew the son of the Duke of York, in revenge for the death of his father at the hands of the Yorkists, and was himself slain at Ferrybridge the day before the battle of Towton (1461). The family were deprived of their estates, and Henry, the subject of the poem, was obliged to live in concealment for twenty-four years, during which time he lived the life of a shepherd. After the battle of Bosworth Field the Shepherd Lord was restored to his own by Henry VII. He spent his time in peaceful pursuits until 1513, when, at the age of sixty, he was appointed to a command over the army which fought at Flodden. He died at the age of seventy, and was buried at Bolton Priory."

Brougham Castle suffered the fate of most of the numerous castles erected by "brave and bonny Cumberland" during the Border Wars and the Wars of the Roses, the fate namely of falling into ruin. The ruins of Brougham are on a hill overlooking the rivers Esmont and Lowther, near Penrith.

7. *thirty years.* The Wars of the Roses ran from 1455–1485.

11–14. A reference to the marriage of Henry VII to Elizabeth of York.

27. "This line," Wordsworth wrote, "is from *The Battle of Bosworth Field*, by Sir John Beaumont."

36. *Skipton, Pendragon* (l. 40), and *Brough* (l. 44) are castles of the Cliffords.

46. *she that keepeth.* Appleby Castle, on the Eden river.

51. *one fair House.* Brougham Castle.

54. *Him, and his Lady-mother dear.* The "shepherd-lord," Henry Clifford, and Margaret his mother, daughter of Lord Vesci.

73. *Carrock's side.* Carrock-fell is three miles southwest from Castle Sowerby in Cumberland. A fell is a hill or mountain.

89. *Mosedale's groves.* The vale of Mosedale is north of Blencathara, or Saddleback.

92. Glenderamakin's source is in the high ground near Saddleback.

95–101. *Sir Lancelot Threlkeld.* Father-in-law of the "shepherd-lord" Henry Clifford, whom he concealed on his estate in Cumberland.

122–3. *the undying fish.* There was a legend of olden time, Wordsworth tells us, that "two immortal fish" lived in this tarn, "which lies in the mountains not far from Threlkeld."

157–72. These lines are much more Wordsworthian than are those in which the poet catches the martial spirit and romance of the medieval minstrel's song. In the main body of the composition he catches that spirit remarkably well; but the sure Wordsworthian quality is to be found in the idea that love of humanity is engendered "in huts where poor men lie." "This Clifford's heart" was endeared to all, not because he had

> In him the savage virtue of the Race,

but because

> His daily teachers had been woods and rills
> . . . the starry sky . . . the lonely hills.

Page 73. TWO VOICES ARE THERE

This poem, which was composed while the poet was "pacing to and fro between the Hall of Coleorton . . . and the principal farm-house of the estate," usually bears the long but significant title, *Thought of a Briton on the Subjugation of Switzerland.*

Napoleon gained control of Switzerland, the mountain voice of Liberty, in 1802, and in 1807, when this poem appeared, was preparing to invade England, the voice of Liberty from the sea.

Aubrey de Vere felt in the poem the "passion of a great thought taken up in stillness into a great imagination." Wordsworth himself called it his best sonnet.

Page 74.

COMPOSED BY THE SIDE OF GRASMERE LAKE

Wordsworth left Coleorton, where he had lived for almost ten months, in August, 1807, and went back to Grasmere, in Westmoreland County. This sonnet, though written in 1807, was not published until 1819.

FEELINGS OF THE TYROLESE

The Tyrolese inhabited the Alpine province of Tyrol. They were herdsmen, who fought valiantly but vainly against the French. Their leader, Andreas Hofer, was an innkeeper, but Wordsworth, who wrote several sonnets celebrating the devotion of the Tyrolese to the cause of liberty, has made him the subject of a sonnet in which he becomes a "godlike warrior." Hofer was defeated by the Bavarians in 1809 and executed the next year. This sonnet, which Wordsworth included in a group under the heading "Poems Dedicated to National Independence and Liberty," voices the passion for freedom that swayed the poet in his youth.

SURPRISED BY JOY

This poem came of the poet's reflections on the death of his three-year-old daughter Catherine, which occurred in June, 1812. The idea of the sonnet, he said, was suggested long after the child's death.

See introductory note to Wordsworth, *English Romantic Poets*, near top of page 5.

YARROW VISITED

"As mentioned in my verses on the death of the Ettrick Shepherd" [James Hogg], Wordsworth wrote, "my first visit to Yarrow was in his company. We had lodged the night before at Traquhair, where Hogg had joined us, and also Dr. Anderson, the Editor of the British Poets, who was on a visit to the Manse. Dr. A. walked with us till we came in view of the vale of Yarrow, and, being advanced in life, he then turned back." On this journey Mrs. Wordsworth and her sister Sara Hutchinson were the poet's companions. Wordsworth deeply regretted that his sister Dorothy "was not of the party, as she would have had so much delight in recalling the time when, travelling together in Scotland, we declined going in search of this celebrated stream, not altogether, I will frankly confess, for the reasons assigned in the poem on the occasion."

It was in the summer of 1803 that Wordsworth and his sister Dorothy came near Yarrow in their rambling journey through Scotland, a journey one result of which was the poem *Yarrow Unvisited.* The visit to the vale of Yarrow on which Hogg was a member of Wordsworth's party and out of which came the present poem, occurred eleven years later, in the autumn of 1814. Seventeen years after that date, in the autumn of 1831, Wordsworth, this time with his daughter, was again a visitor at Yarrow. Sir Walter Scott, whom the Wordsworths visited for several days at Abbotsford, and who was about to go to Italy in an effort to regain his health, was their companion on the Yarrow expedition this time. Wordsworth wrote his third Yarrow poem—*Yarrow Revisited*—as a result of this excursion.

13. *Saint Mary's Lake*. See notes on *Yarrow Unvisited*, above.

25–6. Professor Dowden in his "Poems of Wordsworth," Athenaeum Press Series, writes: "Principal Shairp in his *Aspects of Poetry* ('The Three Yarrows') says that here Wordsworth fell into an inaccuracy; for Mary Scott of Dryhope, the real 'Flower of Yarrow,' never did lie bleeding on Yarrow, but became the wife of Wat of Harden and the mother of a wide-branching race. Yet Wordsworth speaks of *his* bed, evidently confounding the lady 'Flower of Yarrow' with that 'slaughtered youth' for whom so many ballads have sung lament. But doubtless Wordsworth had Logan's *Braes of Yarrow* in his mind, where the lady laments her lover and names him 'the flower of Yarrow.' "

31. *The Water-wraith ascended thrice*. Lines twenty-three and twenty-four of J. Logan's *The Braes of Yarrow* are—

> Thrice did the water-wraith ascend,
> And gave a doleful groan thro' Yarrow.

55. *Newark's Towers*. Newark Castle is on the lower course of the Yarrow about five miles west of Selkirk. It is the scene of Scott's *Lay of the Last Minstel*.

Page 75. LAODAMIA

The passage in the sixth book of the *Aeneid* which speaks of trees withering in sympathy with the spirit of the dead was probably what prompted Wordsworth to write *Laodamia*. His interest in classical literature was never great, but it was enlivened at least temporarily in the years 1814–16 by the fact that he was engaged in tutoring his elder son, John, for entrance in the university. "The incident of the trees growing and withering," he said, "put the subject into my thoughts, and I wrote with the hope of giving it a loftier tone than, so far as I know, has been given to it by any of the ancients who have treated of it. It cost me more trouble than almost anything of equal length I have ever written."

11–12. *Her bosom heaves*, etc. An interesting comparison with Virgil's Sybil (*Aeneid*, VI, 46 ff.), whose

> . . . heart with frenzy heaves,
> And, larger grown, dilating to the eye, etc.,

is suggested by these lines.

18–19. *Mercury* (Greek Hermes). The conductor of souls to the lower world.

48. *Hector*. Eldest son of Priam and bravest of the Trojan warriors. He was slain by Achilles.

60. *Thessalian air*. Protesilaus was a prince of Thessaly.

65. *Parcæ*. The Fates.

66. *Stygian hue*. The hue of death. From Styx, the principal river of the lower world.

71. *Erebus*. A region of the lower world, a place of nether darkness, through which the soul passed to Hades.

81. *Alcestis*. The title and heroine of a tragedy by Euripides (see Browning's *Balaustion's Adventure*). King Admetus, of Thessaly, was mortally sick, but the Fates agreed to spare his life on condition that someone should die in his stead. Alcestis offered herself but was rescued by Hercules.

83–4. *Medea's . . . Æson*. According to Ovid, Medea restored the aged Æson to youth by letting his blood and pouring in a magic preparation.

120. *fleet at Aulis*. The Greek fleet, assembled at Aulis, a Bœotian port, for the attack on Troy, was "enchained" by calm because Agamemnon, the leader, had slain a stag of Artemis (Diana). To appease the wrath of the goddess, Agamemnon offered his daughter Iphigenia as a sacrifice, but the goddess, relenting, rescued her and made her a priestess, and brought the winds to release the fleet.

158–63. *Thus, all in vain . . . 'mid unfading bowers*. In 1815 and 1820 these lines stood as follows:

> "Ah, judge her gently who so deeply loved!
> Her, who, in reason's spite, yet without crime,
> Was in a trance of passion thus removed;
> Delivered from the galling yoke of time
> And these frail elements—to gather flowers
> Of blissful quiet mid unfading bowers."

In 1827 Wordsworth placed a sterner punishment on Laodamia, and these lines became:

> "By no weak pity might the Gods be moved;
> She who thus perished not without the crime
> Of Lovers that in Reason's spite have loved,
> Was doomed to wander in a grosser clime
> Apart from happy Ghosts—that gather flowers
> Of blissful quiet 'mid unfading bowers."

The present form of the poem, which provides for a slight mitigation of the punishment, i.e. the substitution of "a purgatory of limited duration for eternal damnation," became fixed in 1845.

Wordsworth has been severely criticized for changing the decree of mercy which he recommended in 1815 to the stern punishment of the later editions. Swinburne said, "the change was unquestionably and inexpressibly for the worse." Mr. Herbert Read says that the poet allowed "moral judgments to interfere with his poetic sensibility," and suggests that "into the hapless figure of Laodamia he was merely projecting the moral condemnation of his own youthful conduct." In defense of the change

Wordsworth wrote as follows to his nephew, John Wordsworth, in 1831: "As first written, the heroine was dismissed to happiness in Elysium. To what purpose then the mission of Protesilaus? He exhorts her to moderate her passion; the exhortation is fruitless, and no punishment follows. So it stood: at present she is placed among the unhappy ghosts for disregard of that exhortation. Virgil also places her there."

Page 79.

COMPOSED ON AN EVENING OF EXTRAOR-DINARY SPLENDOUR AND BEAUTY

In a note to the poem Wordsworth wrote: "Felt and in a great measure composed upon the little mount in front of our abode at Rydal. In concluding my notices of this class of poems it may be as well to observe that among the Miscellaneous Sonnets are a few alluding to morning impressions which might be read with mutual benefit in connection with these Evening Voluntaries. See, for example, that one on Westminster Bridge, that composed on a May morning, the one on the song of the thrush, and that beginning—'While beams of orient light shoot wide and high.'"

Mr. A. J. George said of this composition: "Surely the purity, the sublimity, the grace, and simplicity of the *Ode* are here reproduced with an element of 'peace supreme' which is the product of Christian Faith."

So deep is the feeling in this poem and in the two immediately following it, and so impassioned the language, that one is reminded of the inspired creations of the youthful Wordsworth; but even so these poems of the later years fall somewhat short of "that thrilling utterance [the phrase is Housman's] which pierces the heart" of man and "by touching something in him that is older than the present organization of his nature," dims his eyes with tears.

43–52. *Yon hazy ridges . . . practicable way.* In a note Wordsworth said: "The multiplication of mountain-ridges, described at the commencement of the third Stanza of this Ode as a kind of Jacob's Ladder, leading to Heaven, is produced either by watery vapors or sunny haze;—in the present instance by the latter cause. Allusions to the Ode entitled *Intimations of Immortality* pervade the last Stanza."

TO ——

See note on *Composed Upon An Evening*, above, for a reference to this poem, which was written at Rydal Mount, and addressed, so the poet said, to Mrs. Wordsworth.

8. *"sober certainties."* From Milton's *Comus*, ll. 263–5.

Page 80. TO A SKYLARK

Mr. E. A. G. Lamborn, comparing this poem with Shelley's *To a Skylark* (text p. 433), says, "Wordsworth's music is the grave voice of the thinker, Shelley's the ecstatic song of the lark itself, with its short bursts of melody rising to a long-sustained climax." Lamborn has nothing but praise for both these poems, whereas Mr. I. A. Richards remarks that "some of the greatest favorites of the anthologies figure there through their 'bad eminence,'" and says that Shelley's *Skylark* reaches that bad eminence, in "its best known parts at least."

As originally published the poem had a second stanza, which Wordsworth removed to his poem *A Morning Exercise* in 1846. The stanza was as follows:

"To the last point of vision, and beyond,
Mount, daring warbler!—that love-prompted strain,
('Twixt thee and thine a never-failing bond)
Thrills not the less the bosom of the plain:
Yet might'st thou seem, proud privilege! to sing
All independent of the leafy spring."

8. Compare lines 36–7 in Shelley's *To a Skylark:*

> "Like a Poet hidden
> In the light of thought."

SCORN NOT THE SONNET

Wordsworth said in a note that this sonnet was "composed almost extempore in a short walk on the western side of Rydal Lake."

1. *Scorn not*, etc. In the early part of the 18th century the sonnet was not held in high repute.

2–3. When Robert Browning quotes in his poem *House*,

> With this [same] key
> Shakespeare unlocked his heart,

and then remarks, "If so, the less Shakespeare he!" he allies himself either with those who do not believe that Shakespeare's sonnets were autobiographical or with those who regretfully accept the autobiographical interpretation because the evidence convinces them that no other interpretation is so valid. Sidney Lee, leading the first group, holds that the sonnets are exercises in imagination and did not grow out of a real situation in Shakespeare's life. There are, however, many readers of the sonnets who believe with Wordsworth that they record the profound personal experiences of the dramatist; that "with this key he did indeed unlock his heart."

4. *Petrarch's wound.* The grief of Petrarch, a famous Italian poet (1304–1374), at the death of Laura, the lady whose praises he sang in his

sonnets. Laura has been identified, traditionally, with Laura de Noves, an Avignonese lady who died of the plague in 1348, and who was already married to Hugues de Sade when, in 1327, Petrarch is said to have first seen her.

5. *Tasso*. An Italian poet (1544–1595).

6. *Camöens*. A Portuguese poet (1524–1580). He was exiled from Lisbon because of his love for Donna Caterina.

8. *Dante*. The great Italian poet (1265–1321), author of *Divina Commedia*.

10. *Spenser*. English poet (1552?–1599), author of *The Faerie Queene*.

WHY ART THOU SILENT

Concerning this poem Wordsworth wrote: "In the month of January, when Dora and I were walking from Town-end, Grasmere, across the vale, snow being on the ground, she espied, in the thick though leafless hedge, a bird's nest half filled with snow. Out of this comfortless appearance arose this Sonnet, which was, in fact, written without the least reference to any individual object, but merely to prove to myself that I could, if I thought fit, write in a strain that Poets have been fond of. On the 14th of February in the same year, my daughter, in a sportive mood, sent it as a Valentine, under a fictitious name, to her cousin C. W."

MOST SWEET IT IS WITH UNUPLIFTED EYES

This poem was suggested to Wordsworth by a tour he, his son John, and H. Crabb Robinson took in the summer of 1833 in Scotland and in the Isle of Man.

It is interesting to consider the differences of critics concerning the poem. One of them says that it has "neither the nature nor the true form of a sonnet," and Matthew Arnold writes of it: "This sonnet cannot be matched from Milton." Professor Herford believes that a "meditative walk has never been more subtly described" than in this composition, which he considers "one of the finest of the later sonnets." Yet he adds it is the work "of a mind for which nature has come to provide delightful interludes rather than transforming experience."

The reader who remembers that Wordsworth defined poetry as "emotion recollected in tranquility" will see in the Wordsworth of this "meditative walk" a being closely akin to the Wordsworth of "pensive mood" in *I Wandered Lonely as a Cloud*, and to him who "bears away his recompense" and "prizes his memory" in *To a Highland Girl*.

Page 81.

A POET!—HE HATH PUT HIS HEART TO SCHOOL

"I was impelled to write this [somewhat satirical] sonnet," Wordsworth said, "by the dis-

gusting frequency with which the word *artistical*, imported with other impertinences from the Germans, is employed by writers of the present day: for *artistical* let them substitute *artificial*, and the poetry written on this system, both at home and abroad, will be for the most part much better characterized."

THE PRELUDE

The Prelude, which is a poem in fourteen Books, having for its subject "The Growth of a Poet's Mind," was published July 20, 1850. Professor de Sélincourt characterizes it as "the essential living document for the interpretation of Wordsworth's life and poetry."

The following "Advertisement" was prefixed to the poem:

"The following Poem was commenced in the beginning of the year 1799, and completed in the summer of 1805.

"The design and occasion of the work are described by the Author in his Preface to the 'Excursion,' first published in 1814, where he thus speaks:—

"'Several years ago, when the Author retired to his native mountains with the hope of being enabled to construct a literary work that might live, it was a reasonable thing that he should take a review of his own mind, and examine how far Nature and Education had qualified him for such an employment.

"'As subsidiary to this preparation, he undertook to record, in verse, the origin and progress of his own powers, as far as he was acquainted with them.

"'That work, addressed to a dear friend, most distinguished for his knowledge and genius, and to whom the Author's intellect is deeply indebted, has been long finished; and the result of the investigation which gave rise to it, was a determination to compose a philosophical Poem, containing views of Man, Nature, and Society, and to be entitled the 'Recluse'; as having for its principal subject the sensations and opinions of a poet living in retirement.

"'The preparatory poem is biographical, and conducts the history of the Author's mind to the point when he was emboldened to hope that his faculties were sufficiently matured for entering upon the arduous labour which he had proposed to himself; and the two works have the same kind of relation to each other, if he may so express himself, as the Ante-chapel has to the body of a Gothic Church. Continuing this allusion, he may be permitted to add, that his minor pieces, which have been long before the public, when they shall be properly arranged, will be found by the attentive reader to have such connection with the main work as may give them claim to be likened to the little cells, oratories, and sepulchral recesses, ordinarily included in those edifices.'

"Such was the Author's language in the year 1814.

"It will thence be seen, that the present Poem was intended to be introductory to the 'Recluse,' and that the 'Recluse,' if completed, would have consisted of Three Parts. Of these, the Second Part alone, viz. the 'Excursion,' was finished, and given to the world by the Author.

"The First Book of the First Part of the 'Recluse' still [1850] remains in manuscript; but the Third Part was only planned. The materials, of which it would have been formed have however, been incorporated, for the most part, in the Author's other Publications, written subsequently to the 'Excursion.'

"The Friend, to whom the present Poem is addressed, was the late Samuel Taylor Coleridge, who was resident in Malta, for the restoration of his health, when the greater part of it was composed.

"Mr. Coleridge read a considerable portion of the Poem while he was abroad; and his feelings, on hearing it recited by the Author (after his return to his own country) are recorded in his Verses, addressed to Mr. Wordsworth, which will be found in the 'Sibylline Leaves,' p. 197, ed. 1817, or 'Poetical Works,' by S. T. Coleridge, vol. i, p. 206.''

The details set forth in this "Advertisement" are accurate in the main, but depart from strict fact in a few unimportant matters; as, for example, the poet conceived the idea of "reviewing his mind" and actually wrote part of the review in 1798, *before* he had "retired to his native mountains," not *after* his retirement. The selections from *The Prelude* appearing in *English Romantic Poets* are from the text of 1850. For the original version of the poem as it was completed in May, 1805, see Ernest de Sélincourt's edition of *The Prelude*, Oxford University Press.

Mr. Herbert Read, after cautioning the reader to remember that the subtitle of *The Prelude* is the "Growth of a Poet's Mind," says that Wordsworth always considered the poem "as the history of his mental development." "For his theoretical structure," he continues, the poet "went to Hartley," the philosopher who repudiated Shaftesbury's view that the moral sense is instinctively innate in man, and attributed it to the association of ideas. Hartley, reasoning from "Locke, Berkeley, and Hume, divided the development of the mind into three stages, corresponding to the processes of association. Just as, in knowledge, you have first impressions of sensations, then simple ideas derived from these impressions, and finally complex ideas formed by the association of simple ideas, so, in the evolution of the mind you have first the age of sensation, or child-

hood; then the age of simple ideas, or youth; and finally the age of complex ideas, or maturity. In the *Prelude*, and in fact everywhere in his poetry, Wordsworth adheres closely to this scheme, and indeed the *Prelude* is nothing but an interpretation of this scheme in terms of his own experience. . . . The theory," Mr. Read finds, "was already fully absorbed by 1798, for there are distinct traces of it in the *Tintern Abbey* poem, where the characteristics of each stage of development are given, the 'glad animal movements' of childhood, the 'passions' and 'appetites' of youth, and lastly 'that serene and blessed mood' when 'we are laid asleep in body, and becoming a living soul.'"

BOOK I. INTRODUCTION—CHILDHOOD AND
SCHOOL-TIME

1–45. These lines depict Wordsworth's feelings in September, 1795, when after eight months' residence in London, he was journeying to Racedown, where he was to live with his sister Dorothy.

8. *now free.* Free because he had been bequeathed a legacy of £900 by Raisley Calvert.

21–2. Cf. *Tintern Abbey*, ll. 37–41.

46–7. *not used to make A present joy the matter of a song.* Consider these lines in the light of the poet's remark in the Preface to *Lyrical Ballads* that poetry "takes its origin from emotion recollected in tranquility."

72. *Of a known Vale.* Racedown. The 1805 text reads "one sweet Vale," which is defensible on the ground that in 1795 Racedown was "known" to the poet only by hearsay.

96. *Æolian visitations.* Thoughts that come and go like the rise and fall of melodies on the Aeolian harp, or harp of the winds.

133–4. *for present gifts Of humbler industry.* Early in 1798 Wordsworth was working on *The Wanderer (Excursion,* I), *The Cumberland Beggar,* and, later, on some of the *Lyrical Ballads,* and *Peter Bell.*

169. *by Milton left unsung.* This expression of a youthful yearning to sing Miltonic themes is not without significance.

187. *vanquished Mithridates.* A king of Pontus, (132?–63 B.C.), who proclaimed himself Asia's deliverer from the yoke of the Romans, imperiled Roman rule for a number of years. In 66 B.C. he was defeated by Pompey and "northward passed" intending to invade Italy from that direction. The connection of Mithridates with Odin (189), who was the chief of a tribe of barbarians dwelling on the banks of Lake Maeotis, was suggested by Gibbon in chapter X of his *Decline and Fall of the Roman Empire.*

191. *Sertorius.* A Roman general (B.C.?–72) who during the Sullan proscriptions had es-

caped to Spain. The Spanish tribes were chafing under Roman rule, and Sertorius planned to deliver the land from Rome and set up an independent republic. Mithridates aided him with ships and men, and the revolutionists defeated Pompey, who had been sent against them, so decisively that they came near destroying his army. Finally fortune turned and Sertorius was conquered by Pompey, and in the end murdered by one of his own lieutenants.

192. *Fortunate Isles*. Ancient name of the Canary Isles.

212. *Gustavus*. Gustavus I (1496–1560), king of Sweden, freed his country from Denmark.

213. *Dalecarlia's mines*. In Dalecarlia, a division of Sweden in which there is much mining, Gustavus laid his plans for Swedish freedom.

214. *Wallace*. In her *Journal* for August 21, 1803, Dorothy Wordsworth speaks of passing two of Wallace's caves and says, "there is scarcely a noted glen in Scotland that has not a cave for Wallace, or some other hero."

275. *Derwent*. A river in Cumberland flowing into the Cocker.

283. *those towers*. Cockermouth Castle was in sight of Wordsworth's birthplace.

304. *belovèd Vale*. Esthwaite, at the northwest end of which is Hawkshead, the scene of the poet's schooldays.

357 ff. The scene of this boating experience has always been thought to be Esthwaite, but the 1805 text makes it "by the shores of Patterdale," which would fix the scene at Lake Ullswater.

371. *far above*. This should probably be "*for* above." Of the five extant MSS of *The Prelude* only one has *far*. It is from this one that the text of 1850 was copied. The 1805 text reads "for behind."

531. *Vulcan*. God of the fiery element. He was hurled from Heaven by Jupiter.

543. *Bothnic Main*. That part of the Baltic Sea bordering Bothnia.

551. *motions*. Emotions, impulses.

553–6. Cf. *Ode: Intimations of Immortality*.

615. *the breath of spring*. "Breath" is probably a printer's error for "birth." Not one of the five MSS reads "breath," but the word is "breath" in the 1850 text.

Page 89. BOOK II. SCHOOL-TIME

Book II begins with and carries on for some lines a description of the life—particularly its sports and outdoor experiences—lived by the young boy Wordsworth while he was at Hawkshead School.

419–51. "Recollecting in tranquility" his boyhood days among the mountains, lakes, and sounding cataracts, the poet attributes his purity of heart, his modest content, his freedom from enmity and low desire, to the sweet influence of Nature. Nov. 7, 1794, in a letter to William Mathews (see note to Letter XXI below) Wordsworth made this startling and, in contrast with the sentiment of these lines, most un-Wordsworthian statement: "I begin to wish much to be in town. Cataracts and mountains are good occasional society, but they will not do for constant companions." The sentiment here expressed, so unlike that of *The Prelude*, has led some students to "doubt the autobiographical validity of that idealistic structure." One should not forget, however, that this letter to Mathews was written in the dark days of 1794–95 when the poet was still brooding over the personal, political, and social problems arising out of his life in France. Book III, from which no lines are reprinted in the text, has for its subject "Residence at Cambridge." Wordsworth entered St. John's College, Cambridge, in October, 1787.

Page 90. BOOK IV. SUMMER VACATION

Book IV recounts the poet's experiences during the long summer vacation of 1788, most of which he spent at Hawkshead, revisiting his schoolboy haunts, meeting his old friends and companions, and entering into a genial comradeship with the village folk.

143. *Our cottage door*. The cottage of Anne Tyson, the "good creature" with whom he lived during his Hawkshead schooldays.

BOOK V. BOOKS

In Book V Wordsworth writes of the importance for youth of books. Christopher Wordsworth in his *Memoirs* quotes the poet as saying: "My earliest days at school . . . were very happy ones, chiefly because I was left at liberty, then and in the vacations, to read whatever books I liked . . . I read all Fielding's works, *Don Quixote*, *Gil Blas*, and any part of Swift that I liked; *Gulliver's Travels* and the *Tale of a Tub*, being both much to my taste." It is in the *Memoirs*, too, that we read that Wordsworth's "father set him very early to learn portions of the works of the best English poets by heart, so that at an early age he could repeat large portions of Shakespeare, Milton, and Spenser." Books, then, the poet believes, are of immense value for the right forming of the youth. The two great agencies of education are nature and books; books that are

> Powers
> Forever to be hallowed; only less,
> For what we are and what we may become,
> Than nature's self.

Page 91. BOOK VI

In this book Wordsworth writes of his life at Cambridge, particularly of his third year there, and of the walking tour in central Europe he and his Welsh friend, Robert Jones, took in the summer vacation of 1790. Cambridge, though an important formative influence, did not stir his mind as deeply as did his contact with nature.

592–608. Professor de Sélincourt points out that "Wordsworth made many efforts to give a satisfactory philosophic account of the imagination . . ." which "was to him 'the vision and the faculty divine.'"

BOOK VII

It may be that Wordsworth considered this, the least interesting book in the poem, of less importance than the other books, since he did not believe his London experiences of deep significance in the growth and shaping of his mind.

Page 92. BOOK VIII

Commenting on this book Professor George says: "In the rush and roar of London . . . Wordsworth seems to have been drifting aimlessly. But the poet's heart was beating . . . all the more rapidly because of the contrast of the city's din to the quiet of his cloister life at Cambridge; and at each pulse he felt himself drawn nearer to the life of man. Until this time, Nature was first, and Man second; here in the centre of the great metropolis the transition was made. . . . At the beginning of the eighth book, he looks back and gives us an inside view of the workings of his own soul while it was being played upon by the influence of Nature and Man."

BOOK IX

Books IX, X, and XI relate the trials and experiences, the deeply moving scenes on which the poet entered when, at twenty-one, he began his adventures in France. Whether he was drawn to France by a newly awakened interest in man and, hence, by a sympathy for the Revolutionists, or whether, as the text of 1805 indicates, he was

> Led thither chiefly by a personal wish
> To speak the language more familiarly,

is unimportant. The significant thing is that the French adventures came and that they left on the mind of the poet the deep mark he records in *The Prelude*.

It is usually said that one moving experience—the story of the youthful poet's love for Annette Vallon—is strangely missing from this study of his life in France. Professor de Sélincourt, however, sees in the story of "Vaudracour and Julia," which is in the ninth book of the 1805 text, an allusion, in veiled language, to the love of the poet and Annette. The incidents in "Vaudracour and Julia" are very uneven in merit, but certain of them have all the vividness and intensity of feeling that were charac-

teristic of Wordsworth when he was writing of actual personal experience. "Vaudracour and Julia" of 1820, which is the version usually found in complete editions of the poems, should be compared with the text of the story as it appears in the *Prelude* MS of 1805.

392. *Rotha's stream.* The Rotha is a river flowing by the Grasmere churchyard (the place of Wordsworth's burial) and emptying into Rydal Water.

393. *Greta, or Derwent.* Greta, a river in Keswick. Derwent, a river in Cumberland.

408. *Attic shades.* Athenian or Grecian.

409–16. *Dion.* The brother-in-law of Dionysius the elder, tyrant of Syracuse, was the disciple of Plato. After the accession of the weak and dissolute Dionysius the younger to the tyranny, Dion tried to reform the young man and induced Plato also to attempt his reformation. Both failed. Dion then made war against the tyrant and sailed with his soldiers in two vessels from Zacynthus, one of the Cyclades. Endemus and Timonides were philosophers who assisted Dion.

Page 93. BOOK XII

This book, beginning by pointing out the "loss of hope itself" occasioned by the spectacle of "human ignorance and guilt" detailed in Books IX, X, and XI, tells us that "when the spirit of evil reached its height," Wordsworth, "still glorying in Nature," found "a secret happiness" there. Realizing, though, that the "bodily eye" often held his mind "in absolute dominion" and hence forced his inner faculties to sleep, the poet, soothed and sustained by the presence of a maid—Mary Hutchinson—"a young enthusiast" whose "eye was not the mistress of her heart," shook off forever the tyranny of the bodily eye, and became, in nature's presence, "a sensitive being, a *creative* soul."

Page 95. BOOK XIII

This book continues in much the same vein the subject of Book XII, and discloses the poet's conviction of the worth of "men as they are men within themselves"; those whom he sees daily "in the familiar circuit of his home," whose "words are but under-agents in their souls." A comparison should be made of the ideas herein expressed concerning the lives and language of common men with the thought of those passages in the preface of 1800 (text pp. 101–12) in which the poet speaks of the value for poetry of "humble and rustic life."

BOOK XIV

This book begins by describing a marvelous "billowy ocean" of mist which the poet looked down upon from moonlit mountain heights when he was in Wales in the summer of 1793, and which, as he reflected upon it, seemed to him an emblem of "majestic intellect." As the history approaches "its appointed close" he pays tribute to his sister Dorothy, who "didst soften down" his "over-sternness," to Mary Hutchinson, who is "no more [merely] a phantom to adorn a moment," to Raisley Calvert, who, dying, made him a bequest that freed him from the "hazard to his finer sense," and finally to Coleridge, who, when he remembers the happiness of the old Quantock days—the time of the *Lyrical Ballads*—will have a perfect understanding of the "Growth of a Poet's Mind." The poem touches sadly upon "a private grief," the death by drowning of Wordsworth's brother John, and ends with the fine utterance that Wordsworth and his brother poet, "joint labourers in the work" of man's deliverance, "prophets of Nature," shall speak, even after their race is run, "a lasting inspiration" to an age "too weak to tread the ways of truth."

Page 96.   THE EXCURSION

This long poem of nine books consists of a series of moral stories which the poet strung together one after the other with little or no thought of dramatic structure. It is the middle section of a great philosophical poem "on man, on nature, and on human life," which Wordsworth planned to write in three parts. The three-part poem was to be called *The Recluse*, "as having for its principal subject the sensations and opinions of a poet living in retirement." *The Excursion* alone was completed.

The Wanderer of the poem is an old philosophic Scotch pedlar whom the author encounters on various occasions and into whose mouth he puts his favorite doctrines. The Wanderer has a despondent friend whose despondency arises out of his lack of faith in religion and his doubt of the goodness of man. Wordsworth through the pedlar reproves the despondent one in lengthy discourses. The fifth book introduces the Pastor, who "illustrates the harmonizing effect of virtue and religion" by telling of the lives of the good men who lie buried in his churchyard. The last two books point out the unhappiness and degradation of the humbler classes resulting from the great expansion of industry in the early nineteenth century, and call attention to the fact that proper education of children must provide the remedy for these evils.

Margaret: or the Ruined Cottage (text p. 7) is a part of Book I of this poem.

Jeffrey, of the *Edinburgh Review*, in his famous "This-will-never-do" attack on *The Excursion* asked this pointed question: "Did Mr. Wordsworth really imagine, that his favourite doctrines were likely to gain anything in point of effect or authority by being put into the mouth of a person accustomed to higgle about tape, or brass sleeve-buttons?"

Page 101.   PREFACE TO LYRICAL BALLADS

The first edition of *Lyrical Ballads* was published in September, 1798. The price of the copyright agreed upon by the authors and Cottle, the publisher, was thirty guineas. Wordsworth and Coleridge needed the money, they said, to pay the expenses of visiting Germany and living there for a time in order to study the German language and to furnish themselves "with a tolerable stock of information in natural science." The book, which was published anonymously, contained twenty-three poems, four of which were Coleridge's. The titles of the poems and the order in which they were arranged by the authors were as follows:

The Rime of the Ancient Mariner (Coleridge)
The Foster-Mother's Tale (Coleridge)
Lines Left upon a Seat in a Yew Tree
The Nightingale (Coleridge)
The Female Vagrant
Goody Blake and Harry Gill
Lines Written at a Small Distance from My House
Simon Lee
Anecdote for Fathers
We Are Seven
Lines Written in Early Spring
The Thorn
The Last of the Flock
The Dungeon (Coleridge)
The Mad Mother
The Idiot Boy
Lines Written near Richmond
Expostulation and Reply
The Tables Turned
Old Man Travelling
The Complaint of a Forsaken Indian Woman
The Convict
Lines, Composed a Few Miles above Tintern Abbey

The reviews of the volume were unfavorable, but the professional reviewers were not alone in finding things in the book to condemn. Southey and the descriptive poet Charles Lloyd as well as the reviewers were shocked by the *Ancient Mariner*. Even Wordsworth himself was said to have been "a little shocked" by this poem. On the other hand Charles Lamb said that it contained "fifty passages as miraculous as the miracles they celebrate." *Goody Blake*, *The Thorn*, and *The Idiot Boy* each came in for praise from a number of readers, but the *Lines Left upon a Seat in a Yew Tree* and the beautiful *Tintern Abbey* nobody noticed except Southey and Lamb, the latter writing, "that last poem is one of the finest written." The sales of the little book were very small, and the only report the authors got while they were in Germany was a letter from Mrs. Coleridge bringing them the cold comfort, "*Lyrical Ballads* are not liked at all by any."

Page 112. WORDSWORTH'S LETTERS

I. In 1802 John Wilson (1785–1854), then only seventeen, wrote Wordsworth a letter praising *Lyrical Ballads* but condemning "The Idiot Boy" as having for its subject a "feeling that does not please." (See Knight's *Life of Wordsworth*, I, 390–97.) In 1817 Wilson, using the pseudonym "Christopher North," became a reviewer for *Blackwood's Magazine*.

Page 116.

III. Sir George Beaumont (1753–1827), an art patron and landscape painter. See note on *Elegiac Stanzas*, above.

Page 117.

IV. Lady Beaumont, wife of Sir George Beaumont.

Page 118.

V. Henry Reed (1808–1854) was a native of Philadelphia. In 1831 he was made assistant professor of English literature in the University of Pennsylvania and soon after assistant professor of moral philosophy. In 1835 his title became professor of rhetoric and English literature. He was an industrious writer and editor in the fields of history and English literature, his principal work being *Lectures on English Literature* (1855). His intimate relations with Wordsworth began in 1837, when he directed the editing and publishing of an American edition of Wordsworth's poems.

Page 119.

VI. Bernard Barton (1784–1849), a poet of Quaker parentage. He was a close friend of Lamb and an acquaintance of Wordsworth, Southey, and other literary men.

VII. Edward Moxon (1801–1858), became a publisher in London in 1830. He published for Southey, Wordsworth, Landor, Tennyson, and Browning. In 1826 and again in 1837 he published volumes of his own sonnets. Wordsworth's letter is in the nature of a warning to Moxon upon the occasion of his 1826 volume.

VIII. Lieutenant-General Sir William M. Gomm (1784–1875) distinguished himself at the battle of Salamanca, in 1812, and was on the staff of the fifth division at Waterloo. He was commander in chief in India from 1850 to 1855, and within that period was promoted to a full generalship. His "modest and cultivated letters" to his aunt and sister, written

"from the stirring scenes of the Peninsula," were published in 1881.

Page 121.

IX. W. Rowan Hamilton (1805–1865), a mathematician who discovered the science of quaternions. At sixteen he detected an error of reasoning in Laplace's *Mécanique céleste*, and about 1830 he was made astronomer royal for Ireland. At Trinity College, Dublin, he twice won the vice-chancellor's prize for English verse. His taste in poetical compositions was excellent, and he wrote many sonnets and other poems. Wordsworth, Coleridge, and Southey were correspondents of his.

X. The Rev. Robert Montgomery (1807–1855) was the natural son of Robert Gomery, a clown at the Bath Theatre. Partly because the friends of Robert's father predicted that the boy would become a future Byron and partly because of vanity, he assumed the aristocratic prefix Mont. According to Macaulay he never became more than a "wretched poetaster," the author of a number of volumes of "detestable verse." In May, 1835, the same year of Wordsworth's letter, he was ordained and, beginning to serve a curacy, acquired the title Wordsworth gave him.

XI. Alexander Dyce (1798–1869) would have gone into the service of the East India Company if he had yielded to the wishes of his father, Lieutenant-General Alexander Dyce, of the Company. The younger Dyce did not care for such a career, however, and accepted the alternative of taking orders. In 1825 he published *Specimens of British Poetesses*, a book which induced Wordsworth to write concerning the Countess of Winchelsea. His *Specimens of English Sonnets*, published in 1833, led to Wordsworth's writing the letters that are numbered XV and XVI in the text (pp. 122–3).

Page 125.

XX. The Rev. Christopher Wordsworth (1774–1846) was Wordsworth's youngest brother. Charles Manners-Sutton, to whom Christopher Wordsworth had been tutor, became Archbishop of Canterbury in 1805 and made his old tutor his domestic chaplain. In 1817, when Manners-Sutton was elected speaker of the House of Commons, Wordsworth was appointed chaplain. In 1820 he was made Master of Trinity College, Cambridge, on the recommendation of the archbishop.

XXI. William Mathews was Wordsworth's college friend and correspondent, one of a group of advanced political thinkers with which the poet was in sympathy and with which he was probably associated in London from January to September, 1795. Other members of the group were Mary Wollstonecraft, Thomas Paine, Horne Tooke, and Joseph Fawcett, a dissenting preacher of eloquence and power. If Wordsworth was not in the heart of the group, he was at least an interested and brooding member on the outer edge.

Wordsworth's letters to Mathews are of especial interest because he expressed in them his political opinions with the utmost freedom. The poet has given us no more extreme declaration of his intense devotion to his ideal of republicanism than the following paragraph from a note to Mathews: "I solemnly affirm that in no writings of mine will I ever admit of any sentiment which can have the least tendency to induce my readers to suppose that the doctrines which are now enforced by banishment, imprisonment, etc., etc., are other than pregnant with every species of misery. You know perhaps already that I am of that odious class of men called democrats, and of that class I shall ever continue."

XXII. The original editor of this letter conceals the identity of L—— by saying that he was "an old and valued friend" of the poet.

Page 126.

XXIII. Early in 1793 Richard Watson, Bishop of Llandaff, published one of his sermons entitled "The Wisdom and Goodness of God in having made both Rich and Poor." Writing from the text, "The rich and poor meet together; the Lord is the maker of them all" (Proverbs 22:2), the Bishop found in these words much consolation—for the rich! Accompanying the printed sermon was an appendix in which, under date of January 25, the Bishop lauded the Constitution of England and expressed his disapproval of affairs in France, where, four days before, Louis XVI had been guillotined. The chief opinions of the Bishop as set forth in the appendix were the following: his extreme dislike of the republican form of government and his approval of monarchy; his horror at the execution of a king; his conviction that the British Constitution insures to every individual the greatest freedom possible in civil society; his belief in aristocratic institutions; and his dislike of the Press "when employed to infuse into the minds of the lowest orders of the community disparaging ideas concerning the constitution of their country." Incensed at these opinions the youthful Wordsworth, but lately returned from France with a fervent belief in the sincerity and the principles of the Revolutionists, wrote his long letter "To the Bishop of Llandaff" ("Apology for the French Revolution"), which, indeed, he may never have sent to the Bishop and which was not published for more than eighty years. Professor George M. Harper, commenting on the letter, says that it "deserves to rank with the writings of Burke, Paine, and Mackintosh, as one of the most

philosophical treatises occasioned in England by the Revolutionary movement."

20. *a sublime allegory.* "The Vision of Mirzah."

32. *continuing your way,* etc. Bishop Watson had been at one time a warm supporter of the Revolution.

Page 127.

13. *National Convention.* The elected assembly which governed France from Sept. 20, 1792, to Oct. 26, 1795. It abolished royalty and established a republic.

19–20. *"Tyran, voilà ton ouvrage."* "Tyrant, here's what you have done."

Page 128.

8. *Racine.* Jean Baptiste Racine (1639–1699), French (tragic) dramatic poet.

42. *Prince de Rohan.* A French cardinal (1734–1803), a notorious spendthrift. An adventuress and her companions led him to believe that he could gain the favor of Queen Marie Antoinette, a lady who lived for pleasure and loved jewelry, by buying her a famous diamond necklace worth more than a million and a half livres. The dupe Rohan bought the necklace and kept moonlight engagements with a woman who impersonated the queen. The fraud came out when the thieves disappeared with the necklace and it was discovered that the contract Rohan passed on for payment bore the forged signature of the queen. Marie refused to honor the contract, and Rohan, brought to trial by the outraged king, was acquitted.

Page 129.

41. *Mr. Burke.* Edmund Burke (1729–1797), English statesman and orator.

26–32. *"Tout homme né dans . . . aimaient leur abrutissement."* "Every man born into slavery is born for slavery; nothing is more true. Slaves lose everything in their bonds, even the desire to escape them: they love their servitude even as the companions of Ulysses loved their transformation into beasts."

Page 130.

12. *the philosophic Priestley.* Joseph Priestley (1733–1804), English chemist and physicist, the discoverer of oxygen. He studied for the ministry but was rejected because of certain doctrinal opinions. His liberal ideas made him unpopular in England, where feeling against the French Revolution was high, and in 1791 his home and laboratory in Birmingham were burned by a mob. To escape persecution he left England in 1794 and came to America, where he remained till his death.

Page 134.

15. *Tarpeian rock.* A steep rock forming part of the Capitoline Hill, Rome. Traitors to

Rome were hurled to their death from this rock.

Page 135.

11. *ministerial maxim of Sir Robert Walpole.* Walpole's maxim was, "Quieta non movere," a free translation of which is, "Let sleeping dogs lie."

Page 136.

4. *like the inveterate enemy of Philip.* Charles Rollin tells in his *Ancient History* this story of Philip of Macedon: "Aster of Amphipolis had offered his service to Philip, as so excellent a marksman that he could bring down birds in their most rapid flight. The monarch made answer: 'I will take you into my service when I make war upon starlings'; which answer stung the cross-bow-man to the quick.... After having thrown himself into the city [Methone], he shot an arrow on which was written, 'to Philip's right eye,' and . . . hit him in his right eye. Philip sent him back the same arrow, with this inscription, 'If Philip takes the city, he will hang up Aster'; and he was as good as his word." Rollin adds that ever after Philip became angry when anyone mentioned the word "Cyclops" or even the word "eye" in his presence.

Page 137.

26 ff. *Maury or a Cazalès . . . La Fayette or a Mirabeau.* Maury and Cazalès were leaders of the conservatives in the National assembly, 1789–91; La Fayette and Mirabeau were leaders of the reactionaries.

XXV. 23. *esprits forts.* Freethinkers.

27. *par nobile fratrum.* A notorious pair of brothers.

XXVI. The Right Hon. Earl De La Warr, Lord Chamberlain, was "the truly noble and honorable person who filled the office of Lord Chamberlain" at the time the death of Southey made vacant the laureateship.

SAMUEL TAYLOR COLERIDGE

BIBLIOGRAPHY

I. WORKS

Complete Works, ed. by William G. T. Shedd. 7 vols. (Harper: New York, 1884.) Divides with the Ashe 8-vol. collection the claim to being the nearest approach to a definitive edition; an introductory essay discusses Coleridge's philosophical and theological opinions.

Works, ed. by Thomas Ashe. 8 vols. Bohn Library. (Macmillan: New York, 1895.) A more accessible edition than the Shedd collection, which is only slightly less complete.

Complete Poetical Works, ed. by E. H. Coleridge. 2 vols. (Oxford University Press: 1912.) Textually, the best collection of the poetry, of which many variants are supplied: the text is based upon the last edition issued in the poet's lifetime (the editor is the poet's grandson).

Poetical Works, ed. by J. D. Campbell. Globe Edition. (Macmillan: London, 1909.) The preferred one-vol. edition, furnished with a biographical introduction and valuable notes.

Poetry, ed. by Richard Garnett. The Muses' Library. (Scribner: New York, 1898.) A recommended inexpensive edition.

The Best of Coleridge, ed. by E. L. Griggs. (Nelson: New York, 1932.) Contains all the standard selections: an excellent introduction to the poet.

The Golden Book of Coleridge. (Dutton: New York, 1932.) A desirable cheap edition, furnished with a brief preface by Stopford Brooke.

Coleridge: Poetry and Prose, ed. by H. W. Garrod. (Oxford University Press: 1925.) A recommended compact edition: valuable for its comprehensive, though brief, introduction; includes many prose comments by Hazlitt, De Quincey, Carlyle, and others.

Coleridge: Select Poetry and Prose, ed. by Stephen Potter. (Nonesuch Press: London, 1933.) Draws largely upon the *Anima Poetæ;* provides two versions of *The Ancient Mariner.*

Biographia Literaria, ed. by John Shawcross. 2 vols. (Oxford University Press: 1907.) The best edition: based upon the edition of 1817; the introduction gives an excellent résumé of Coleridge's literary theory, and considers the problem of German influence.

Biographia Literaria, ed. by J. C. Metcalf. (Macmillan: New York, 1926.) A recommended recent edition, but secondary to the Shawcross work for the use of the advanced student.

Shakesperean Criticism, ed. by T. M. Raysor. 2 vols. (Harvard University Press: 1930.) Provides an excellent introduction, taking up the troublesome question of German influence; discounts the Helmholtz theory; shows Coleridge's descent from the 18th-century English critics; points out his chief contribution—his analysis of character.

Prose and Table-Talk, ed. by W. H. Dircks. (Scott: London, 1886.) An inexpensive, convenient collection of important material.

Table-Talk and Omniana, ed. by Thomas Ashe. (Bell: London, 1923.) A valuable collection, including and superseding the 1883 edition by Morley.

Anima Poetæ, ed. by E. H. Coleridge. (Houghton: Boston, 1895.) The contents are fragments and longer sketches from the Notebooks, collected after 1803.

Letters, ed. by E. H. Coleridge. 2 vols. (Houghton: Boston, 1895.) A record of the correspondence from 1785 to 1834.

Unpublished Letters, ed. by E. L. Griggs. 2 vols. (Yale University Press: 1933.) Contains a treasury of new information for the specializing student; Coleridge is here revealed as a man possessing an acute sense of social responsibilities and at the same time possessed by his own self-sufficiency: thus is shown the paradox of his life.

II. BIOGRAPHY AND CRITICISM

Blunden, Edmund, and Griggs, E. L., eds. *Studies by Several Hands*. (Constable: London, 1934.) Especially valuable for the fragment of the Life by E. H. Coleridge; the final item is also interesting: a letter from Sara to Hartley, describing the poet's death.

Caine, Hall. *Life of Samuel Taylor Coleridge*. (Scott: London, 1887.) A brief and vigorous Life, giving the essential biographical data, with little critical discussion.

Campbell, J. D. *Samuel Taylor Coleridge*. (Macmillan: New York, 1894.) Still recognized as an indispensable authority for the facts of the poet's life.

Charpentier, John. *Coleridge, the Sublime Somnambulist*. Trans. by M. V. Nugent. (Dodd: New York, 1929.) A re-presentation of all the essential facts, with much anecdotal material: one of the most interesting recent Lives, offering sound literary criticism.

Cottle, Joseph. *Early Recollections, Chiefly Relating to the Late S. T. Coleridge*. 2 vols. (Longmans: London, 1837.) Intended to fill gaps in the *Biographia Literaria* relative to the poet's Bristol days: written from first-hand information, with a tendency to bespeak indulgence for the faults of the man.

Fausset, H. I'A. *Samuel Taylor Coleridge*. (Cape: London, 1926.) An impressionistic study of the inner life of the poet, whose unresolved spiritual conflict is shown to be the shaping influence of a major portion of his poetry, which is termed an "escape from reality."

Greever, Garland. *A Wiltshire Parson and His Friends*. (Houghton: Boston, 1926.) Gives Coleridge's four hitherto unidentified critiques on the romances of terror, together with the correspondence of the poet W. L. Bowles.

Howard, Claud. *Coleridge's Idealism: A Study of Its Relationship to Kant and the Cambridge Platonists*. (Badger: Boston, 1924.) Endeavors to show that German thinkers, especially Kant, have been greatly overestimated as the source of Coleridge's idealism; upholds the English Platonists of the 17th century as a prior influence.

Knight, W. A. *Coleridge and Wordsworth in the West Country: Their Friendship, Work, and Surroundings*. (Scribner: New York, 1914.) Letters and diaries, with many extracts from Dorothy Wordsworth's Alfoxden *Journal*, have contributed to this informal account of the most fruitful period of the two poets' association, 1795–98.

Lowes, J. L. *The Road to Xanadu*. (Houghton: Boston, 1927.) "A study in the ways of the imagination," it attempts to reveal how the poet's curious reading became sublimated into poetry, notably *The Ancient Mariner* and *Kubla Khan*: the most learned treatment of any phase of Coleridge's work.

Phelan, Mrs. Anna A. *The Indebtedness of S. T. Coleridge to August Wilhelm von Schlegel*. (University of Wisconsin Press: 1907.) Arranges a formidable series of parallel passages, but inclines to overrate their significance in suggesting deliberate plagiarism.

Potter, Stephen. *Coleridge and S. T. C.* (Cape: London, 1935.) A clear positing of the problem of Coleridge's dual nature, involving a study of his degeneration as an artist and of the struggle between his "true self" and the later character which finally possessed him.

Richards, I. A. *Coleridge on Imagination*. (Paul: London, 1934.) Comprehensive analysis of the poet's theory of creative imagination and poetic experience: unlike Lowes, Richards maintains a distinction between "fancy" and "imagination."

Sandford, Mrs. Henry. *Thomas Poole and His Friends*. 2 vols. (Macmillan: London, 1888.) A useful, but latterly somewhat rare, book: it deals with the relations between the poet and one of his benefactors, the merchant who came to his rescue after the failure of *The Watchman*.

Snyder, Alice D. *The Critical Principle of the Reconciliation of Opposites as Employed by Coleridge*. (Ann Arbor Press: 1918.) A well-documented study of the poet's critical principles, showing how his lively sense of dualism was a paramount influence in his literary criticism, especially of Shakespeare, whose works represented for him the perfect balance between nature and art, the ideal and the actual, the universal and the individual.

Traill, H. D. *Coleridge*. English Men of Letters series. (Harper: New York, 1884.) A concise, satisfactory Life, one of the earliest authoritative studies.

Watson, Lucy E. G. *Coleridge at Highgate*. (Longmans: New York, 1925.) A comprehensive review of the events of the poet's life from 1816 to the end, during the time of his residence with Dr. Gillman; the interpretation seems at times over-sympathetic, which may be attributed to the fact that the author is a granddaughter of Dr. Gillman.

Wordsworth, Dorothy. *Journals*, ed. by W. A. Knight. (Macmillan: New York, 1924.) The time covered is Jan. 20, 1798–July 10, 1828: the first four divisions of this edition contain many allusions to Coleridge.

III. ARTICLES FROM BOOKS

Dowden, Edward. "Coleridge as a Poet," in *New Studies in Literature*. (Paul: London, 1902.) Calls attention to the "fine humanity" of the poet, his social message, and his descriptions of the supernatural.

Drinkwater, John. "Coleridge, Milton, and Warton," and "Coleridge's *Zapolya*," in *A Book for Bookmen*. (Doran: New York, 1927.) The first essay reviews Coleridge's life at Highgate, when he was reading Warton's edition of Milton (pub. 1785, 1791); provides forty-two annotated passages. The second essay pleads for a reading-appreciation of the play; gives some notes on the author's revisions of it.

Fairchild, H. N. "The Pantisocratic Phase," "The Medievalism of Wordsworth and Coleridge," "Coleridge and Transcendentalism," in *The Romantic Quest*. (Columbia University Press: 1931.) The first essay discusses the poet of the days of the American project and of the period of the French Revolution. The second shows how from the 1796 volume the middle-age spirit permeates much of Coleridge's finest verse. The last points out his utilization of Kantian metaphysic in dealing with the problems of sense, understanding, and reason.

Feiling, Keith. "Coleridge," in *Sketches in Nineteenth Century Biography*. (Longmans: London, 1930.) Comments on the poet's attitude toward the political turmoil of his day.

Garrod, H. W. "Coleridge," in *The Profession of Poetry*. (Oxford University Press: 1929.) Reviews the association with Wordsworth, insists on reading Coleridge unanthologized, comments feelingly on his unfinished work.

Marks, Jeannette. "Coleridge," in *Genius and Disaster*. (Adelphi: New York, 1925.) A highly colored portrayal of the poet as an opium-addict: his "drug mentality" is psychoanalyzed, and its taint indicated in his life and work.

Murry, J. M. "Coleridge's Criticism," in *Aspects of Literature*. (Knopf: New York, 1920.) A searching examination of the *Biographia Literaria*, which is impugned for its verbosity: only the chapters on Wordsworth and his poetical creed justify its reputation.

Pater, Walter. "Coleridge," in *Appreciations*. (Macmillan: New York, 1922.) An enthusiastic appraisal of the poet's power of imagination; provides a fairly clear biographical outline.

Payne, W. M. "Samuel Taylor Coleridge," in *Greater English Poets of the Nineteenth Century*. (Holt: New York, 1907.) An interesting review of the work of the poet and his contributions to English criticism and philosophy.

Robertson, J. M. "Coleridge," in *New Essays toward a Critical Method*. (Lane: London, 1897.) A carefully planned attack on the theories of Coleridge's poetic imagination: shows his poetry to be the product of opium dreams, scorns his philosophy, and pitilessly exposes his moral weaknesses.

Shafer, Robert. "Coleridge," in *Christianity and Naturalism*. (Yale University Press: 1926.) A wholesome evaluation of the man's spiritual life; his acceptance of certain limitations of church dogma is interpreted as a marked limitation.

Stephen, Leslie. "Coleridge," in *Hours in a Library*, IV. (Putnam: New York, 1907.) Takes the materialistic point of view: emphasizes the effects of opium, admits the poet's great influence.

Swinburne, A. C. "Coleridge," in *Essays and Studies*. (Chatto: London, 1888.) Sees in the poetry little philosophic depth and values it for its aesthetic and dreamlike strain, the "height and perfection of imaginative quality."

Symons, Arthur. "Samuel Taylor Coleridge," in *The Romantic Movement in English Poetry*. (Dutton: New York, 1909.) Shows the poet's lifelong quest for the absolute, discusses the effect of dreams, his sensitiveness to color.

Vaughan, C. E. "Coleridge," in *The Cambridge History of English Literature*, XI. (Putnam: New York, 1914.) An excellent summary, with a good conclusion on the main points of the poet's philosophy and critical theory.

Woodberry, G. E. "Coleridge," in *Makers of Literature*. (Macmillan: New York, 1900.) Emphasizes the element of change in the poet's career, refuses to lament for the unfinished poems, sees his prose as the ashes of his creative fire.

IV. ARTICLES FROM PERIODICALS

Cooper, Lane. "The Abyssinian Paradise in Coleridge and Milton," *Modern Philology*, III, 327–32 (Jan., 1906). Identifies Mount Abora with the "Hill Amara" of Purchas's *Pilgrimage*.

Dunstan, A. C. "The German Influence on Coleridge," *Modern Language Review*, XVII, 272–81 (July, 1922), and XVIII, 183–201 (Apr., 1923). Two valuable papers, supplementing the study by Mrs. Phelan: Herder and Schiller are here proposed as influential sources—somewhat at the expense of the Schlegel theory.

Eagleston, A. J. "Wordsworth, Coleridge, and the Spy," *Nineteenth Century*, LXIV, 300–10 (Aug., 1908). Tells of their being under surveillance as suspected Alfoxden revolutionaries during the nervous epoch of 1797.

Gingerich, S. F. "From Necessity to Transcendentalism in Coleridge," *Publications of the Modern Language Association*, XXXV, 1–59 (Jan., 1920). With special allusion to the *Rime*, the article shows Coleridge's early preference for creating passive characters; the influence of Kantian philosophy is seen as the compelling force toward his later transcendental tendencies.

Graham, Walter. "An Important Coleridge Letter," *Journal of English and Germanic Philology*, XXI, 530–5 (1922). A discussion of Coleridge's opinions upon revolutionary France, as stated in his *Watchman* in 1796; the letter is to Benjamin Flower, editor of the *Cambridge Intelligencer*.

Griggs, E. L. "Coleridge and His Son," *Studies in Philology*, XXVII, 634–47 (Oct., 1930). An interesting review of the poet's relations with his children, especially with his favorite, Hartley.

Griggs, E. L. "Coleridge and Byron," *Publications of the Modern Language Association*, XLV, 1085–97 (Dec., 1930). Finds in five new letters of Coleridge evidence of his gratitude for Byron's interest in his dramas.

Harper, G. M. "Coleridge's Conversation Poems," *Quarterly Review*, CCXLIV, 284–98 (Apr., 1925). Comments delicately on eight poems: *The Eolian Harp, Reflections on Having Left a Place of Retirement, This Lime-Tree Bower My Prison, Frost at Midnight, Fears in Solitude, The Nightingale, Dejection, To William Wordsworth*.

Kaufman, Paul. "The Reading of Southey and Coleridge," *Modern Philology*, XXI, 317–20 (Feb., 1924). Gives the record of their borrowings from the Bristol library, 1793–98.

McElderry, B. R., Jr. "Coleridge's Revision of *The Ancient Mariner*," *Studies in Philology*, XXIX, 68–94 (Jan., 1932). Holds that the poet revised the original version in 1800 and 1817 upon a consideration of criticism, largely Southey's; the marginal gloss of 1817 is seen as the result of studied retouching of his masterpiece.

Morrill, Dorothy I. "Coleridge's Theory of Dramatic Illusion," *Modern Language Notes*, XLII, 436–44 (Nov., 1927). Traces three origins: the dream-figure (from Herder and Schlegel), his own early concept of the suspension of judgment, and the idea of the assistance of the will in this suspension (Schlegel).

Nitchie, Elizabeth. "The Moral of *The Ancient Mariner* Reconsidered," *Publications of the Modern Language Association*, XLVIII, 867–76

(Sept., 1933). Finds a simple explanation only within the poem itself: the natural result of a harrowing dream is a restatement of the humanitarian principle.

Potter, G. R. "Coleridge and the Idea of Evolution," *Publications of the Modern Language Association*, XL, 370–97 (June, 1925). Tends to rebuke the vulgar error that the poet understood evolution as a scientist and supported it as such.

Ratchford, Fannie E. "S. T. Coleridge and the London Philosophical Library," *Modern Language Review*, XX, 76–80 (Jan., 1925). Calls attention to a letter by Coleridge, now in the Wrenn Library of the University of Texas: indicates his political conservatism, 1810 and after.

Raysor, T. M. "Coleridge's Manuscript Lectures," *Modern Philology*, XXII, 17–25 (Aug., 1924). Gives evidence that the poet's lecture-notes were edited with the view of posthumous publication.

Raysor, T. M. "Some Marginalia on Shakespeare," *Publications of the Modern Language Association*, XLII, 762–5 (Sept., 1927). A brief interesting report of annotations made by Coleridge in two sets of Shakespeare, now in the British Museum.

Raysor, T. M. "The Study of Shakespeare's Characters in the Eighteenth Century," *Modern Language Notes*, XLII, 495–500 (Dec., 1927). Points to Coleridge's lack of novelty in his criticisms of Shakespearean figures; shows that many 18th-century English critics had anticipated his sympathetic point of view and his emphasis on Shakespeare's art.

Raysor, T. M. "Coleridge and 'Asra,'" *Studies in Philology*, XXVI, 305–24 (Apr., 1929). A highly valuable and suggestive presentation of the facts in the personal relations of Coleridge and Sara Hutchinson—based on documentary sources.

Rea, J. D. "Coleridge's Intimations of Immortality from Proclus," *Modern Philology*, XXVI, 201–13 (Nov., 1928). Shows that Wordsworth's *Ode* derived many of its important ideas from Coleridge's reading.

Rea, J. D. "Hartley Coleridge and Wordsworth's 'Lucy,'" *Studies in Philology*, XXVIII, 118–35 (Jan., 1931). Finds the source of the paternal tone of the Lucy poems in Coleridge's affection for his son Hartley.

Snyder, Alice D. "A Note on Coleridge's Shakespeare Criticism," *Modern Language Notes*, XXXVIII, 23–31 (Jan., 1923). Bases the poet's criticism on recognized psychological grounds, though admitting his eclecticism and lack of any consistent system.

Stallknecht, N. P. "The Moral of *The Ancient Mariner*," *Publications of the Modern Language Association*, XLVII, 559–69 (June, 1932). Finds the inspiration of the poem in a romanticized view of life, possibly derived from Spinoza.

Stork, C. W. "The Influence of the Popular Ballad on Wordsworth and Coleridge," *Publications of the Modern Language Association*, XXIX, 299–326 (Sept., 1914). Shows the attraction of Coleridge to the ballad's free remoteness from modern life; sees the ballad as a formative power in the *Rime* and the lack of it as the cause for the incompleteness of the two unfinished masterpieces.

Wright, Herbert. "The Tour of Coleridge and His Friend Hucks in Wales, in 1794," *Nineteenth Century*, XCIX, 732–44 (May, 1926). Gives some instances of their romantic tendency to over-idealize people and situations.

NOTES

Page 145.   TO THE REV. W. L. BOWLES

Coleridge in the first chapter of the *Biographia Literaria* expresses his obligation to Bowles as follows:

"I had just entered on my seventeenth year, when the sonnets of Mr. Bowles, twenty in number, and just then published in a quarto pamphlet, were first made known and presented to me, by a schoolfellow who had quitted us for the University, and who, during the whole time that he was in our first form (or in our school language a Grecian,) had been my patron and protector. I refer to Dr. Middleton, the truly learned, ånd every way excellent Bishop of Calcutta. . . .

"It was a double pleasure to me, and still remains a tender recollection, that I should have received from a friend so reverend the first knowledge of a poet, by whose works, year after year, I was so enthusiastically delighted and inspired. My earliest acquaintances will not have forgotten the undisciplined eagerness and impetuous zeal, with which I laboured to make proselytes, not only of my companions, but of all with whom I conversed, of whatever rank, and in whatever place. As my school finances did not permit me to purchase copies, I made, within less than a year and a half, more than forty transcriptions, as the best presents I could offer to those, who had in any way won my regard. And with almost equal delight did I receive the three or four following publications of the same author. . . . My obligations to Mr. Bowles were indeed important, and for radical good. At a very premature age, even before my fifteenth year, I had bewildered myself in metaphysics, and in theological controversy. Nothing else pleased me. History, and particular facts, lost all interest in my mind . . . —poetry itself, yea, novels and romances, became insipid to me. In my friendless wanderings on our *leave-days*, (for I was an orphan, and had scarcely any connections in London,) highly was I delighted, if any passenger, especially if he were dressed in black, would enter into conversation with me. For I soon found the means of directing it to my favourite subjects

'Of providence, fore-knowledge, will, and fate,
Fixed fate, free will, fore-knowledge absolute,
And found no end in wandering mazes lost.'

This preposterous pursuit was, beyond doubt, injurious both to my natural powers, and to the progress of my education. It would perhaps have been destructive, had it been continued; but from this I was auspiciously withdrawn, partly indeed by an accidental introduction to an amiable family, chiefly however, by the genial influence of a style of poetry, so tender and yet so manly, so natural and real, and yet so dignified and harmonious, as the sonnets and other early poems of Mr. Bowles. Well would it have been for me, perhaps, had I never relapsed into the same mental disease; if I had continued to pluck the flower and reap the harvest from the cultivated surface, instead of delving in the unwholesome quicksilver mines of metaphysic lore. And if in after time I have sought refuge from bodily pain and mismanaged sensibility in abstruse researches, which exercised the strength and subtility of the understanding without awakening the feelings of the heart; still there was a long and blessed interval, during which my natural faculties were allowed to expand, and my original tendencies to develop themselves; —my fancy, and the love of nature, and the sense of beauty in forms and sounds."

THE EOLIAN HARP

1. *pensive Sara*. Sara Fricker, whom Coleridge married about two months after the composition of this poem.
12. *that simplest Lute*. The eolian harp—an instrument of delicately tuned strings which was played upon by currents of air, for which reason it was often placed in the window.
49. *But thy more serious eye a mild reproof Darts*. "In Coleridge's early period (before 1798–1799) he was clearly influenced by Unitarian ideas, and tended towards the idea that God is pervasive through all things, that man is a part of nature and sharer in God's love along with the rest of creation. This point of view was closer to the evolutionary spirit than the orthodox Trinitarian doctrines of the time were. But Coleridge never became so profoundly influenced by this type of philosophy as to lose a certain substratum of orthodox belief. . . .
"The ending of his poem *The Eolian Harp* is significant of his frame of mind. The poet loses himself momentarily in a dream that all of animated nature may be as harps for 'one intellectual breeze, at once the Soul of each, and God of all,' but his Sara brings him back to orthodoxy again, and he rests content. . . ." (George R. Potter, "Coleridge and the Idea of Evolution," *Publications of the Modern Language Association*, XL, 388–9.)

Page 147. *From* RELIGIOUS MUSINGS

Coleridge's earlier admirers considered that the *Religious Musings* marked him out as a great

poet. It was published in 1797 and went into a second edition. There was more than a little eloquence in the poem, but later critics have not treated it too gently.
"To the second edition of these poems, which was published in the following year, Coleridge, at all times a candid critic (to the limited extent to which it is possible even for the finest judges to be so) of his own works, prefixed a preface, wherein he remarks that his poems have been 'rightly charged with a profusion of double epithets and a general turgidness,' and adds that he has 'pruned the double epithets with no sparing hand,' and used his best efforts to tame the swell and glitter both of thought and diction. 'The latter fault, however, had,' he continues, 'so insinuated itself into my *Religious Musings* with such intricacy of union that sometimes I have omitted to disentangle the weed from fear of snapping the flower.' This is plain-spoken criticism, but I do not think that any reader who is competent to pronounce judgment on the point will be inclined to deprecate its severity." (H. D. Traill, *Coleridge*, pp. 22–3.)

THIS LIME-TREE BOWER MY PRISON

The friends referred to in Coleridge's introductory note were William and Dorothy Wordsworth and Charles Lamb.
28. *gentle-hearted Charles*. When the poem was published in 1800 in the *Annual Anthology*, Lamb wrote Coleridge protesting against the epithet: ". . . For God's sake (I never was more serious), don't make me ridiculous any more by terming me gentle-hearted in print, or do it in better verses. It did well enough five years ago when I came to see you, and was moral coxcomb enough at the time you wrote the lines, to feed upon such epithets; but, besides that, the meaning of gentle is equivocal at best, and almost always means poor-spirited, the very quality of gentleness is abhorrent to such vile trumpetings. . . . In the next edition of the 'Anthology' (which Phoebus avert and those nine other wandering maids also!) please to blot out *gentle-hearted*, and substitute drunken-dog, ragged-head, seld-shaven, odd-eyed, stuttering, or any other epithet which truly and properly belongs to the gentleman in question. And for Charles read Tom, or Bob, or Richard *for more delicacy*." Coleridge did not alter it. On his death-bed in 1834 Coleridge wrote against this poem: "Ch. and Mary Lamb—dear to my heart, yea, as it were, my heart.—S. T. C. Aet. 63, 1834. 1797–1834 = 37 years!"

Page 149.

THE RIME OF THE ANCIENT MARINER

Coleridge's account of the origin of the *Lyrical Ballads* is given in *Biographia Literaria*, ch. XIV (see text p. 195, et seq.). Coleridge's statement in the first two paragraphs of his own part in the *Lyrical Ballads* is of primary value in establishing an approach to this poem. The version which appeared in 1798 in the *Lyrical Ballads* was revised for the 1800 edition. The marginal gloss first appeared in Coleridge's *Sibylline Leaves* (1817) in which the poem was reprinted. It was preceded by an extract from Burnet's Latin *Archaeologiae Philosophicae* which, translated, reads: "I readily believe that there are in the universe more invisible than visible Natures. But who shall declare to us the family, the ranks, the relationships, the differences, the respective functions of all these beings? What do they? Where do they dwell? Human nature has ever circled (ambivit) about this knowledge, but has never reached it. In the meantime I doubt not that it is profitable to contemplate at times with the inner eye, as in a picture, the prospect of this greater, better world, to the end that the mind, used to the petty details of daily life, be not too narrowed, and lapse entirely into mean thoughts. But at the same time we must be on the lookout for truth and observe restraint, in order that we may distinguish certain from the uncertain, day from darkness."

The Ancient Mariner now stands accepted without question as one of the perfect poems of the language—a thing in itself. It was not always so. Lamb was its first great champion. He preferred it to any thing else in the first *Lyrical Ballads* and in 1811 Crabb Robinson reports in his *Diary* a conversation with Lamb in which the word "surprise" may be noted: "We spoke of Wordsworth and Coleridge. To my surprise Lamb asserted the latter to be the greater man. He preferred the 'Ancient Mariner' to anything Wordsworth had written."

Wordsworth himself added a note to *The Ancient Mariner* in the 1800 edition. He apparently thought that *The Ancient Mariner* had been responsible for the poor public reception of the poems; sensing which, Coleridge may have been first hurt and desirous of withdrawing, then spurred on to revision. (See Lowes, *The Road to Xanadu*, p. 520, n. 17.) Wordsworth's note (1800) is as follows: "I cannot refuse myself the gratification of informing such Readers as may have been pleased with this Poem, or with any part of it, that they owe their pleasure in some sort to me; as the Author was himself very desirous that it should be suppressed. This wish had arisen from a consciousness of the defects of the Poem, and from a knowledge that many persons had been much displeased with it. The Poem of my Friend has indeed great defects; first, that the principal person has no

distinct character, either in his profession of Mariner, or as a human being who having been long under the controul of supernatural impressions might be supposed himself to partake of something supernatural: secondly, that he does not act, but is continually acted upon: thirdly, that the events having no necessary connection do not produce each other; and lastly, that the imagery is somewhat too laboriously accumulated. Yet the Poem contains many delicate touches of passion, and indeed the passion is everywhere true to nature; a great number of the stanzas present beautiful images, and are expressed with unusual felicity of language; and the versification, though the metre is itself unfit for long poems, is harmonious and artfully varied, exhibiting the utmost powers of that metre, and every variety of which it is capable. It therefore appeared to me that these several merits (the first of which, namely that of the passion, is of the highest kind,) gave to the Poem a value which is not often possessed by better Poems. On this account I requested of my Friend to permit me to republish it."

Wordsworth, in a statement dictated to Miss Fenwick about 1843, said of the origins of *The Ancient Mariner:* ". . . In the spring of the year 1798, he, my sister, and myself, started from Alfoxden, pretty late in the afternoon, with a view to visit Lenton and the valley of Stones near it: and as our united funds were very small, we agreed to defray the expense of the tour by writing a poem, to be sent to the *New Monthly Magazine. . . .* Accordingly we set off and proceeded along the Quantock Hills toward Watchet, and in the course of this walk was planned the poem of *The Ancient Mariner*, founded on a dream, as Mr. Coleridge said, of his friend, Mr. Cruikshank. Much the greatest part of the story was Mr. Coleridge's invention; but certain parts I myself suggested:—for example, some crime was to be committed which should bring upon the old navigator, as Coleridge afterwards delighted to call him, the spectral persecution, as a consequence of that crime, and his own wanderings. I had been reading in Shelvocke's *Voyages* a day or two before that, while doubling Cape Horn, they frequently saw albatrosses in that latitude, the largest sort of sea-fowl, some extending their wings twelve or fifteen feet. 'Suppose,' said I, 'you represent him as having killed one of these birds on entering the South Sea, and that the tutelary Spirits of those regions take upon them to avenge the crime.' The incident was thought fit for the purpose and adopted accordingly. I also suggested the navigation of the ship by the dead men, but do not recollect that I had anything more to do with the scheme of the poem. The Gloss with which it was subsequently accompanied was not thought of by either of us at the time; at least, not a hint of it was given to me, and I have no doubt it was a gratuitous afterthought. We began the composition together on that, to me, memorable evening. I furnished two or three lines at the beginning of the poem, in particular:—

'And listened like a three years' child;
The Mariner had his will.'

These trifling contributions, all but one (which Mr. C. has with unnecessary scrupulosity recorded) slipt out of his mind as they well might. As we endeavored to proceed conjointly (I speak of the same evening) our respective manners proved so widely different that it would have been quite presumptuous in me to do anything but separate from an undertaking upon which I could only have been a clog. . . . *The Ancient Mariner* grew and grew till it became too important for our first object, which was limited to our expectation of five pounds, and we began to talk of a volume. . . ."

Campbell in his edition of the *Works* of Coleridge has a note based on a statement reported by the Rev. Alexander Dyce from which the following is extracted: "I [Wordsworth] had very little share in the composition of it, for I soon found that the style of Coleridge and myself would not assimilate. Besides the lines (in the fourth part):

'And thou art long, and lank, and brown,
As is the ribbed sea-sand'—

I wrote the stanza (in the first part):

'He holds him with his glittering eye—
The Wedding-Guest stood still,
And listens like a three-years' child:
The Mariner hath his will'—

and four or five lines more in different parts of the poem, which I could not now point out. The idea of 'shooting an albatross' was mine; for I had been reading Shelvocke's *Voyages*, which probably Coleridge never saw. I also suggested the reanimation of the dead bodies, to work the ship."

Much has been made of the moral of this poem. ". . . Mrs. Barbauld once told me that she admired *The Ancient Mariner* very much, but that there were two faults in it,—it was improbable, and had no moral. As for the probability, I owned that that might admit some question; but as to the want of a moral, I told her that in my own judgment the poem had too much; and that the only, or chief fault, if I might say so, was the obtrusion of the moral sentiment so openly on the reader as a principle or cause of action in a work of

pure imagination. It ought to have had no more moral than the *Arabian Nights'* tale of the merchant's sitting down to eat dates by the side of a well and throwing the shells aside, and lo! a genie starts up and says he *must* kill the aforesaid merchant *because* one of the date shells had, it seems, put out the eye of the genie's son." (Coleridge, *Table Talk*, May 31, 1800.)

Professor Lowes gives brilliantly the answer to the Mrs. Barbaulds:
"The sequence, then, which follows from the Mariner's initial act accomplishes two ends: it unifies and (again to borrow Coleridge's coinage) it 'credibilizes' the poem. Has it still another end, to wit, edification? I am well aware of Coleridge's homiletical propensity. Nevertheless, to interpret the drift of *The Ancient Mariner* as didactic in its intention is to stultify both Coleridge and one's self. For such an interpretation shatters that world of illusion which is the very essence of the poem. . . . Coleridge is not intent on teaching (profoundly as he believed the truth) that what a man soweth, that shall he also reap; he is giving coherence and inner congruity to the dream-like fabric of an imagined world. *Given that world*—and were it not given, there would be no poem, and were it otherwise given, this poem would not be—given that world, its inviolate keeping with itself becomes the sole condition of our acceptance, 'for the moment,' of its validity. And that requirement Coleridge, with surpassing skill, has met.
". . . For that inner consistency which creates the illusion of reality is attained at the expense of the integrity of the elements which enter into it. . . . Even poetry cannot transform reality and have it, untransmuted, too. And through the very completeness of their incorporation with the texture of *The Ancient Mariner*, the truths of experience which run in sequence through it have lost, so far as any inculcation of a moral through the poem is concerned, all didactic value.
"For the 'moral' of the poem, *outside the poem*, will not hold water. It is valid only within that magic circle. The great loop of the voyage from Equator to Equator around the Cape runs true to the chart. But dæmons, and spectres, and angels, and *revenants* haunt its course, and the Mariner's voyage, magnificent metamorphosis of fact though it be, can scarcely be regarded as a profitable guide to the fauna of equatorial and arctic seas. The relentless line of cause and consequence runs likewise, unswerving as the voyage, through the poem. But consequence and cause, *in terms of the world of reality*, are ridiculously incommensurable. The shooting of a sea-bird carries in its train the vengeance of an aquatic dæmon,

acting in conjunction with a spectre-bark; and an impulse of love for other living creatures of the deep summons a troop of angels to navigate an unmanned ship. Moreover, because the Mariner has shot a bird, four times fifty sailors drop down dead, and the slayer himself is doomed to an endless life. The punishment, measured by the standards of a world of balanced penalties, palpably does not fit the crime. But the sphere of balanced penalties is not the given world in which the poem moves. Within *that* world, where birds have tutelary dæmons and ships are driven by spectral and angelic powers, consequence and antecedent are in keeping—if for the poet's moment we accept the poet's premises. And the function of the ethical background of *The Ancient Mariner*, as Coleridge employs it, is to give the illusion of inevitable sequence to that superb inconsequence. The imaginative use of familiar moral values, like the imaginative use of the familiar outline of a voyage, is leagues away from the promulgation of edifying doctrine through the vehicle of a fairy-tale. . . .

"For the very triviality of the act which precipitates its astounding train of consequences is the *sine qua non* of the impression which the poem was intended to convey. The discrepancy is essential to the design. . . . Springing from the fall of a feather, it becomes a dome in air, built with music, yet with the shadows of supporting arch and pillar floating midway in the wave. For its world is, in essence, the world of a dream. Its inconsequence is the dream's irrelevance, and by a miracle of art we are possessed, as we read, with that sense of an intimate logic, consecutive and irresistible and more real than reality, which is the dream's supreme illusion. 'The events having no necessary consequence do not produce each other,' Wordsworth complained in his deplorable strictures on the poem. The events in a dream do not produce each other, but they *seem* to. And that is the sole requirement of the action of the poem." (J. L. Lowes, *The Road to Xanadu*, pp. 299–303, extracts.)

Professor Lowes considers the progress of the moral idea only one of the three great structural elements of the poem which give it its coherence and vivid actuality. The other two are the structural line of the voyage and the balance of angelic and dæmonic forces. The moral idea that deeds have consequences is inescapable and that the spreading circle of results may be regretted, but cannot ever be stopped. This is the moral Coleridge has embedded in his poem, transforming it to fit his imaginary world. Professor Lowes (*op. cit.*, pp. 296–8) calls attention to lines which mark the progress of the idea:

81–2.	The deed.
141–2.	Consequences fall upon the doer of the deed.
216–20.	The consequences extend to others.
283–91.	The Mariner rejoins by sympathy the company of living things and the symbol of his alienation falls.
406–9.	The deed, however, cannot be cancelled and there is "penance more" to do.
511–12.	There is an absolution of guilt but, as the next part indicates, there can be no cancelling of consequence.
582–90.	At certain times the Mariner in a seizure must tell the story—this is the continuing consequence.

Page 164.   CHRISTABEL

This poem was begun in 1797 at Nether Stowey and continued in 1800 at Keswick after Coleridge's return from Germany. It was not published until 1816 when, at Byron's suggestion, Murray brought it out (along with *Kubla Khan* and *The Pains of Sleep*). Meanwhile it had circulated in quotation by those who had been privileged to hear it read and requoted. Scott heard it in 1801 and it influenced the music of his *Lay of the Last Minstrel*. Its curious music spread a contagion in the poetic air and Byron, working on *The Siege of Corinth* wrote some Coleridgean lines in section XIX, 521–32. Soon after he heard Scott recite *Christabel* and wrote to Coleridge offering to cancel in his own manuscript poem the lines most reminiscent of *Christabel*. Coleridge did not ask for the cancellation, but in his own preface (1816) gave the dates of composition in order to protect himself from the charge of plagiarism. He also in the preface explained the musical principle of *Christabel* as follows: "I have only to add that the metre of the *Christabel* is not, properly speaking, irregular, though it may seem so from its being founded on a new principle: namely, that of counting in each line the accents, not the syllables. Though the latter may vary from seven to twelve, yet in each line the accents will be found to be only four. Nevertheless, this occasional variation in number of syllables is not introduced wantonly, or for the mere ends of convenience, but in correspondence with some transition in the nature of the imagery or passion."

Byron's *Siege of Corinth* came out in 1816 two months earlier than did Coleridge's poems and to the lines in question Byron added the following note: ". . . I must here acknowledge a close though unintentional resemblance in these twelve lines to a passage in an unpublished poem of Mr. Coleridge, called *Christabel*. It was not till after these lines were written that

I heard that wild and singularly original and beautiful poem recited. . . . The original idea undoubtedly pertains to Mr. Coleridge, whose poem has been composed above fourteen years. Let me conclude by a hope that he will not longer delay the publication. . . ."

The passage of his own in which Byron felt the resemblance between the two poems most marked, reads as follows:

Was it the wind, through some hollow stone,
Sent that soft and tender moan?
He lifted his head, and he look'd on the sea,
But it was unrippled as glass may be;
He look'd on the long grass—it waved not a
    blade;
How was that gentle sound convey'd?
He look'd to the banners—each flag lay still,
So did the leaves on Cithaeron's hill,
And he felt not a breath come over his cheek;
What did that sudden sound bespeak?
He turn'd to the left—is he sure of sight?
There sate a lady, youthful and bright!

Christabel was never completed. As late as 1833, when it was apparent even to Coleridge's most devoted admirers that the poem would never be completed, Coleridge said, "I could write as good verses now as ever I did, if I were perfectly free from vexations, and were in the ad libitum hearing of fine music, which has a sensible effect in harmonizing my thoughts, and in animating and, as it were lubricating my inventive faculty. The reason of my not finishing *Christabel* is not, that I don't know how to do it—for I have, as I always had, the whole plan entire from beginning to end in my mind; but I fear I could not carry on with equal success the execution of the idea, an extremely subtle and difficult one. Besides, after this continuation of [Goethe's] *Faust* [part I, pub. 1806; part II, 1832] which they tell me is very poor, who can have courage to attempt a reversal of the judgment of all criticism against continuation?" (*Table Talk*, July 6, 1833.)

Wordsworth later said that he did not think Coleridge had ever conceived in his own mind any definite plan for the poem, but Dr. Gillman, who cared for Coleridge from 1816 until his death in 1834, states that Coleridge's plan for the completion of the poem was as follows: ". . . The following relation was to have occupied a third and fourth canto, and to have closed the tale. Over the mountains, the Bard, as directed by Sir Leoline, hastes with his disciple; but in consequence of one of those inundations supposed to be common to this country, the spot only where the castle once stood is discovered—the edifice itself being washed away. He determines to return. Geraldine. being acquainted with all that is passing, like the weird sisters in *Macbeth*, vanishes.

Reappearing, however, she awaits the return of the Bard, exciting in the meantime, by her wily arts, all the anger she could rouse in the Baron's breast, as well as that jealousy of which he is described to have been susceptible. The old Bard and the youth at length arrive, and therefore she can no longer personate the character of Geraldine, the daughter of Lord Roland de Vaux, but changes her appearance to that of the accepted though absent lover of Christabel. Now ensues a courtship most distressing to Christabel, who feels, she knows not why, great disgust for her once favored knight. This coldness is very painful to the Baron, who has no more conception than herself of the supernatural transformation. She at last yields to her father's entreaties, and consents to approach the altar with this hated suitor. The real lover, returning enters at this moment, and produces the ring which she had once given him in sign of her betrothment. Thus defeated, the supernatural being Geraldine disappears. As predicted, the castle bell tolls, the mother's voice is heard, and, to the exceeding great joy of the parties, the rightful marriage takes place, after which follows a reconciliation and explanation between the father and daughter." (Gillman's *The Life of Samuel Taylor Coleridge*.)

20. *The night is chill, the cloud is gray.* Professor Lowes in *The Road to Xanadu* (chap. XI, n. 65), although he is writing of *The Ancient Mariner*, summarizes the relationship of *Christabel* to Dorothy Wordsworth's *Journals*: ". . . Now at just this period the relations between the *Journals* and Coleridge's verse were singularly close. The very next night (March 25), for example, Dorothy writes: 'Walked to Coleridge's after tea. Arrived at home at one o'clock. *The night cloudy but not dark*' (I, 15). Line 15 of 'Christabel' reads 'The night is chilly, but not dark.' On March 7 she had written: 'One only leaf upon the top of a tree—the sole remaining leaf—danced round and round like a rag blown by the wind' (I, 12–13). And Coleridge wrote in 'Christabel': 'The one red leaf, the last of its clan, That dances as often as dance it can, Hanging so light, and hanging so high, On the topmost twig that looks up at the sky' (ll. 49–52). The words which immediately follow 'The stars dim' in our entry of March 24 are these: 'The spring continues to advance very slowly' (I, 14); line 22 of 'Christabel' reads: 'And the Spring comes slowly up this way.' Compare further 'Christabel,' l. 12 (the mastiff's howls) with the entry for Jan. 27 (I, 5); and 'Christabel,' ll. 16–17 (and the jotting in the Note Book; see p. 7, above) with the entry for Jan. 31 (I, 5–6). All these parallels, of course, are noted in E. H. Coleridge, *Christabel*, pp. 62–65, and in Sir Arthur Quiller-Couch's

Introduction to Sampson's edition of B. L., pp. xxiv–xxvi; but for my present purpose I must have some, at least, of the facts before our eyes. . . .

"Now we have just seen . . . how phrases heard from poems read by Coleridge clung to Dorothy Wordsworth's memory, and, revived by the sight of the objects portrayed, were set down in her *Journals*. That similar recollection accounts for some (though certainly not for all) of the parallels with 'Christabel,' I have little doubt. The phrases passed, in a word, from Coleridge to the *Journals*, and not the other way around. . . ."

129. *The lady sank, belike through pain.* The threshold had received Christian blessing; the witch had not power to cross it herself. Coleridge has given the clue to Geraldine's nature here and developed it in following lines.

Page 168.

PART II. "Certain Verses of Crashaw's 'Hymn to Saint Teresa,' said Coleridge once, 'were ever present to my mind whilst writing the second part of *Christabel;* if, indeed by some subtle process of the mind they did not suggest the first thought of the whole poem." The process of the mind must have indeed been subtle. The suggested inspiring lines, beautiful in themselves, are given in the old form:

Since 'tis not to be had at home
She'l travail to a Martyrdom.
No home for hers confesses she
But where she may a Martyr be.
   She'l to the Moores; And trade with them,
For this unvalued Diadem.
She'l offer them her dearest Breath,
With CHRIST'S Name in't, in change for
   death.
She'l bargain with them; & will give
Them GOD; teach them how to live
In him: or, if they this deny,
For him she'l teach them how to DY.
So shall she leave amongst them sown
Her LORD'S Blood; or at lest her own.
   FAREWELL then, all the world! Adieu.
TERESA is no more for you.
Farewell, all pleasures, sports, & joyes,
(Never till now esteemed toyes)
Farewell what ever deare may be,
MOTHER'S armes or FATHER'S knee,
Farewell house, & farewell home!
SHE'S for the Moores, & MARTYRDOM.

Page 171.

CONCLUSION TO PART II. Writing to Southey on May 6, 1801, Coleridge exclaimed of his child, "Dear Hartley! we are at times alarmed by the state of his health, but at present he is well. If I were to lose him, I am afraid it would

exceedingly deaden my affection for any other children I may have." Whereupon without comment Coleridge wrote out in the letter the lines finally printed as the conclusion of Part II of *Christabel*. The lines have little or no connection with the rest of the poem. They may have been preparing the way for some curious development in an unwritten Part III of which no apparent trace of the whole original idea survives. Young Hartley Coleridge, however, was clearly in Coleridge's mind in connection with the lines, or he would not have written Southey as he did.

Page 173.   FROST AT MIDNIGHT

7. *My cradled infant.* Hartley Coleridge. Another direct reference to Hartley occurs in *The Nightingale* (text p. 181, ll. 91–110). See also poems by Hartley Coleridge, text p. 683.
15. *that film, which fluttered on the grate.* A certain flicker of the flame in an open fire, according to old superstition, indicated the coming of a visitor, and the tradition has persisted even in America and well into the era of artificial heating systems.
24. *How oft, at school.* Coleridge, a country child, spent nine of his most impressionable years at Christ's Hospital in London—a city and a school built mostly of stone, as such are apt to be. Brooding by his child's cradle he resolves the infant shall have "lakes and sandy shores" as a growing environment.
26. *fluttering stranger.* See note on l. 15.

Page 174.   FRANCE: AN ODE

This Ode marks Coleridge's break with the French Revolution—it is in effect a recantation. Note that his recantation is based upon two grounds—religious and political. Line 43 et seq. refers to the celebrated Feast of Reason of Nov. 1793, when a comely opera singer was enthroned on the high altar of the Cathedral of Notre Dame in Paris as the Goddess of Reason amid ceremonies more enthusiastic than decorous. Line 66 refers to the aggressive policy of France toward Switzerland, the traditional "free country" of the continent.
Coleridge's recantation has not always been well accepted. Aynard says, and his remarks have specific reference to the fifth stanza: "But if liberty is thus the effect of an individual revelation, and does not exist in any political form, it necessarily follows that all revolution is immoral, and in particular the French Revolution because 'the sensual and the blind ['aveugles'—Aynard's French rendering of 'dark'] rebel in vain, slaves by their own compulsion.' When liberation is accomplished within souls all revolution is useless; it is made in advance because it cannot possibly come to accomplishment outside of souls.

"This very noble philosophy has, as a practical consequence, reaction against all revolution since the people which rises violently shows by such action that it is still slave of its passions. Coleridge rejoined by a winding way the majority of his compatriots: the French were incapable of liberty and unworthy of it. It remained only that he should persuade himself that England had all the liberty necessary, that she had the understanding and custom of possible liberty for him to reach the same point as Burke—an optimism which is the natural complement of a robust and aggressive patriotism." (Joseph Aynard, *La Vie d'un Poète: Coleridge*, p. 161.)

George Brandes, a Danish scholar, summarizes the political attitude of four of the chief poets of the English Romantic Movement with a generalization worthy of note:

". . . But the word liberty in their mouths meant something different from what it did in Moore's, or Shelley's, or Byron's. To understand this we must dissect the word by means of two simple questions: freedom, from what? —liberty, to do what?

"To these conservative poets freedom is a perfectly definite thing, a right which England has and the other countries of Europe have not—the right of a country to govern itself, untyrannised over by an autocratic ruler of foreign extraction. The country which has this privilege is free. By liberty, then, the men in question understood freedom from foreign political tyranny; there is no thought of liberty of action in their conception at all. Look through Wordsworth's *Sonnets Dedicated to Liberty*, and see what it is they celebrate. . . .

"He always comes back to England. His sonnets are one long declaration of love to the country for which he feels 'as a lover or a child,' the country of which he writes: 'Earth's best hopes are all with thee.' He follows her through her long war, celebrating, like Southey, each of her victories; and it is significant of his attitude that, appended to the *Sonnets Dedicated to Liberty*, we find the great, pompous thanksgiving ode for the battle of Waterloo. We of to-day ask what kind of liberty it was that Waterloo gained. . . . Wordsworth and his school considered the nation ideal as it was, whereas the others tried to compel it to turn its eyes towards the ideal, not only unattained, but as yet unrecognised; the former flattered it, and were rewarded with laurels; the latter educated and castigated it, and were spurned by it. Scott was offered the post of Poet Laureate, and Southey and Wordsworth in turn occupied it; but to this day the English nation has shown no public recognition of what it owes to Shelley and Byron. And the reason is, that these men's conception of liberty was utterly different from that of the Lake School. To them it was not realised in a nation or a constitution—for it was no accomplished, finished thing; neither was their idea of the struggle for liberty realised in a highly egoistic war against a revolutionary conqueror. They felt strongly what an absence of liberty, political as well as intellectual, religious as well as social, there might be under a so-called *free* constitution. They had no inclination to write poems in honour of the glorious attainments of the human race, and more especially of their own countrymen; for in the so-called land of freedom they felt a terrible, oppressive want of freedom—of liberty to think without consideration of recognised dogmas, to write without paying homage to public opinion, to act as it was natural to men of their character to act, without injury from the verdict of those who, because they had no particular character of their own, were the most clamorous and unmerciful condemners of the faults which accompanied independence, originality, and genius. They saw that in this 'free' country the ruling caste canted and lied, extorted and plundered, curbed and constrained quite as much as did the one great autocrat with his absolute power—and without his excuse, the authority of intellect and of genius.

". . . When Shelley sings to liberty:—

'But keener thy gaze than the lightning's glare,
    And swifter thy step than the earthquake's
        tramp;
Thou deafenest the rage of the ocean; thy stare
Makes blind the volcanoes; the sun's bright
        lamp
            To thine is a fen-fire damp;'

we feel that this liberty is not a thing which we can grasp with our hands, or confer as a gift in a constitution, or inscribe among the articles of a state-church. It is the eternal cry of the human spirit, its never-ending requirement of itself; it is the spark of heavenly fire which Prometheus placed in the human heart when he formed it, and which it has been the work of the greatest among men to fan into the flame that is the source of all light and all warmth in those who feel that life would be dark as the grave and cold as stone without it. This liberty makes its appearance in each new century with a new name. In the Middle Ages it was persecuted and stamped out under the name of heresy; in the sixteenth century it was championed and opposed under the name of the Reformation; in the seventeenth it was sentenced to the stake as witchcraft and atheism; in the eighteenth it became first a philosophical gospel, and then, through the Revolution, a political power; in the nineteenth it receives from the champions of the past the new nickname of Radicalism.

"What the poets of the Lake School extolled was a definite, actually existing *sum of liberties* —not liberty. What the revolutionary poets extolled was undoubtedly true liberty; but their conception was so extremely ideal, that in practical matters they too often shot beyond the mark. . . ." (George Brandes, *Main Currents in Nineteenth Century Literature*, IV, 85–9.)

Page 175.   LEWTI

". . . Now I do affirm that 'Lewti' is a very beautiful poem. I *was* in earnest when I praised it. It describes a silly species of one not the wisest of passions. *Therefore* it cannot deeply affect a disenthralled mind. But such imagery, such novelty, such delicacy, and such versification never got into an 'Anthology' before. I am only sorry that the cause of all the passionate complaint is not greater than the trifling circumstance of Lewti being out of temper one day. . . ." (Lamb to Coleridge, Aug. 14, 1800.)

". . . 'Lewti' for instance, an early sample of his admirable melody, of tender color and dim grace as of clouds, but effeminate in build, loose-hung, weak of eye and foot. Yet nothing of more precious and rare sweetness exists in verse than that stanza of the swans disturbed. His style indeed was a plant of strangely slow growth, but perfect and wonderful in its final flower." (A. C. Swinburne, *Works*, Bonchurch Edition, XV, 142.)

It was intended to include this poem in the *Lyrical Ballads* (1798) but at the last moment the sheet was cancelled and *The Nightingale* substituted. The poem first appeared in the *Morning Post*, April 13, 1798.

Page 176.   FEARS IN SOLITUDE

There was a rumor in England in 1798 of a projected invasion of England which may or may not have been spread by the French to "cover" Napoleon's expedition to Egypt. The poem provokes a discussion of the definition of true patriotism—Coleridge's willingness to condemn his own country while expressing love for her, his insistence upon the necessity of defense while deploring the brutality of war, his vigorous insistence on a spiritual housecleaning all raise questions which have a strangely modern ring.

Dykes Campbell in a note calls attention to an autographed copy, initialled " S. T. C.," which has the following note: "N.B.—The above is perhaps not Poetry,—but rather a sort of middle thing between Poetry and Oratory— *sermoni propriora.*—Some parts are, I am conscious, too tame even for animated prose."

Page 179.   THE NIGHTINGALE

13. "*Most musical, most melancholy.*"

"Sweet bird, that shunn'st the noise of folly,
Most musical, most melancholy!
Thee, Chauntress, oft the woods among
I woo, to hear thy even-song."

           Milton, *Lycidas*, ll. 61–5.

Compare Coleridge's statement in the lines which follow with *Dejection: An Ode*, stanza IV.
40. *My Friend, and thou, our Sister!* William and Dorothy Wordsworth.
91. *My dear babe.* Hartley Coleridge. See notes on *Frost at Midnight*, above.

Page 181.   BALLAD OF THE DARK LADIÉ

See note on *Love*, below.

Page 182.   KUBLA KHAN

The poem was originally published with two others—*Christabel* and *The Pains of Sleep*—by Murray in 1816. Lamb wrote to Wordsworth on April 26 of that year: ". . . Coleridge is printing Xtabel, by Ld Byron's recommendation to Murray, with what he calls a vision, Kubla Khan—which said vision he repeats so enchantingly that it irradiates and brings heaven and Elysian bowers into my parlor while he sings or says it, but there is an observation 'Never tell thy dreams,' and I am almost afraid that Kubla Khan is an owl that won't bear day light, I fear lest it should be discovered by the lantern of typography and clear reducting to letters, no better than nonsense or no sense. . . ."

In spite of his misgivings, Lamb, with his usual happy faculty, hit upon a happy critical word. The poem "irradiates" with the splendor and irrationality of a dream—which was what it was.

Swinburne's judgment of Coleridge's work may be fitly quoted in connection with this poem: ". . . Judged by the justice of other men, he is assailable and condemnable on several sides; his good work is the scantiest in quantity ever done by a man so famous in so long a life; and much of his work is bad. His genius is fluctuant and moonstruck as the sea is, and yet his mind is not, what he described Shakespeare's to be, 'an oceanic mind.' His plea against all accusers must be that of Shakespeare, a plea unanswerable:

'I am that I am; and they that level
At my abuses reckon up their own.'

". . . The *Christabel*, the *Kubla Khan*, with one or two more, are outside all law and jurisdiction of ours. When it has been said that such melodies were never heard, such dreams never dreamed, such speech never spoken, the chief thing remains unsaid, and unspeakable. There is a charm upon these poems which can only be felt in silent submission of wonder. Any separate line has its own heavenly beauty, but to cite separate lines is intolerable. They are to be received in a rapture of silence. . . .

"Nevertheless, were we compelled to the choice, I for one would rather preserve *Kubla Khan* and *Christabel* than any other of Coleridge's poems. It is more conceivable that another man should be born capable of writing *The Ancient Mariner* than one capable of writing these. The former is perhaps the most wonderful of all poems. In reading it we seem rapt into that paradise revealed to Swedenborg, where music and colour and perfume were one, where you could hear the hues and see the harmonies of heaven. For absolute melody and splendour it were hardly rash to call it the first poem in the language. . . .

". . . Other and stronger men, with fuller control and concentration of genius, may do more service, may bear more fruit; but such as his was they will not have in them to give. The highest lyric work is either passionate or imaginative; of passion Coleridge's has nothing; but for height and perfection of imaginative quality he is the greatest of lyric poets. This was his special power, and this is his special praise." (A. C. Swinburne, *Works*, Bonchurch Edition, XV, 141–54, extracts.)

Page 183.   LOVE

Published in the second edition of the *Lyrical Ballads* (1800). An earlier version had appeared in the *Morning Post*, December 21, 1799. In an introductory letter there, Coleridge described it as intended to be the introduction to a somewhat longer companion poem—*The Ballad of the Dark Ladié*. Both, of course, are poems of love in a medieval setting.

Page 184.   DEJECTION: AN ODE

This poem, in the first version addressed to Wordsworth, was published on Wordsworth's wedding-day, October 4, 1802—a sad enough gift for the occasion. In the spring, when the poem was composed, Coleridge was in the Lake District and on April 4, the day of the composition of the poem, Wordsworth and Dorothy visited him, and Wordsworth read some of his work. Wordsworth at this time was writing some of his best and his happiest poems (*My Heart Leaps Up, To a Butterfly, To the Cuckoo*—see text pp. 51–4). What was more, he was courting Mary Hutchinson—a courtship which ended in his happy marriage. Coleridge, on the other hand, was unhappy. He

was writing little, he was in poor health (partly because of his opium-taking), he was estranged from his wife and in love with Sara Hutchinson, sister of the girl Wordsworth was to marry. The contrast was too striking and bitter. Coleridge thereupon composed this Ode—a sad and beautiful thing. Later it was altered and addressed to the "Dear Lady" (line 138) of the present version who was Sara Hutchinson; —the hopelessness of Coleridge's love for Sara, since he was already bound, being a sufficient explanation of his dejection. Formerly it was believed the "Dear Lady" of the poem was Dorothy Wordsworth. It has been conjectured (Fred Manning Smith, *PMLA*, L, 233) that Wordsworth's *Resolution and Independence*, written a month later, when next the new moon had the old moon in her arms, was Wordsworth's reply to Coleridge's *Dejection*.

89. *by abstruse research*. See Coleridge's own comment on this tendency of his character given in the extract from *Biographia Literaria* quoted in the notes on *To the Rev. W. L. Bowles*, above.

121. *'Tis of a little child*. Wordsworth's *Lucy Gray*, although Otway was made to father it in the final public version of Coleridge's ode.

Page 186.   HYMN BEFORE SUN-RISE IN THE VALE OF CHAMOUNI

Coleridge had never been to Chamouni and he based his poem very largely on a German poem addressed by Friederika Brun to Klopstock. When it first appeared in the *Morning Post* it was preceded by a lengthy prose note describing the scene and designed to give the impression it was the report of an eyewitness. In later editions this note was shortened to the brief note which appears in the text.

Page 188.   THE PAINS OF SLEEP

Coleridge in his letters tells the story of the horror of his nights. Writing to Southey (September 10, 1803), he includes a copy of this poem and says, ". . . My spirits are dreadful, owing entirely to the horrors of every night —I truly dread to sleep. It is no shadow with me, but substantial misery foot-thick, that makes me sit by my bedside of a morning and cry.—I have abandoned all opiates, except ether be one. . . . And when you see me drink a glass of spirit-and-water, except by proscription of a physician, you shall despise me, —but still I cannot get quiet rest. . . .

"I do not know how I came to scribble down these verses to you—my heart was aching, my head all confused—but they are, doggerel as they may be, a true portrait of my nights. What to do, I am at a loss; for it is hard thus to be withered, having the faculties and attainments which I have. . . ." A month later (Oct. 3, 1803), writing to Poole, he adds: "God forbid that my worst enemy should ever have the nights and the sleeps that I have had night after night—surprised by sleep, while I struggled to remain awake, starting up to bless my own loud scream that had awakened me— yea, dear friend! till my repeated night-yells had made me a nuisance in my own house. As I live and am a man, this is an unexaggerated tale. My dreams became the substances of my life."

TO WILLIAM WORDSWORTH

Coleridge when he went to Malta carried with him a copy of the first five books of Wordsworth's *The Prelude*. When he returned, the poem was completed—and addressed to him. Wordsworth read it aloud, the reading taking several evenings, and Coleridge was deeply moved. This poem was his reply. In the original version there were the following lines, later omitted, following l. 60:

" Dear shall it be to every human heart,
To me how more than dearest! me, on whom
Comfort from thee, and utterance of thy love,
Came with such heights and depths of harmony.
Such sense of wings unlifting, that its might
Scatter'd and quell'd me, till my thoughts became
A bodily tumult; and thy faithful hopes,
Thy hopes of me, dear friend, by me unfelt!
Were troublous to me, almost as a voice,
Familiar once, and more than musical;
As a dear woman's voice to one cast forth,
A wanderer with a worn-out heart forlorn,
Mid strangers pining with untended wounds.
O friend, too well thou know'st of what sad years
The long suppression had benumb'd my soul."

The contrast between the condition of the two friends was becoming even more acute than it had been at the time of *Dejection: An Ode* (see note on that poem). Coleridge returned from Malta broken in health, completely in the grip of the opium habit, and with the darkest years of his life just ahead of him, to hear his friend read the great poem which he had completed in the very period when Coleridge was sinking lower and lower.

29. *Where France.* See *The Prelude*, Books IX, X, and XI.

74. *Strewed on my corse.* Corpse. The passage preceding refers to the ruin of Coleridge's career and his desperate situation at the time.

83-4. *that hour Of thy communion with my nobler mind.* The period of association at Nether Stowey in 1797, when Coleridge was writing his greatest poems.

Page 190.   GLYCINE'S SONG

Coleridge several times attempted the stage. *Osorio* was his first attempt. It was later revised and under the title *Remorse* finally got on the stage of Drury Lane on January 23, 1813, about fifteen years after its original composition. It had a very respectable run. Byron, who had sponsored *Remorse*, urged that Coleridge write another play and *Zapolya* was the result. The Theatre Committee asked for certain alterations to adapt it to the stage but Coleridge did not complete them and the play was never acted. It was printed in 1817 and had a successful sale—some 2000 copies in six weeks.

LIMBO

Limbo is the outer circle of hell. According to medieval theology those souls were confined in Limbo which had belonged to men who had done no evil, but had had no opportunity to accept the Christian religion and, dying unbaptised, could not therefore be accepted among the blessed. According to Dante (*Inferno*, IV) their only punishment was that they, without hope, should live in desire of being accepted among the blessed.

Page 191.   WORK WITHOUT HOPE

For the edition of 1828 Coleridge prefixed to this poem the date "Lines Composed 21st February 1827." Actually they seem to have been composed in 1825. The confusion of dates would indicate that the lines still expressed his feeling of the moment. In the interval (on March 18, 1826) he had written to Lady Beaumont, and the letter which stands between the composition and publication of the poem expresses a similar idea. Writes Coleridge: "Though I am at present sadly below even *my* par of health, or rather unhealth, and am the more depressed thereby from the consciousness that in this yearly resurrection of Nature from her winter sleep, amid young leaves and blossoms and twittering nest-building birds, and sun so gladsome, the breezes with such healing on their wings, all good and lovely things are beneath me, above me, and everywhere around me, and all from God, while my incapability of enjoying, or, at best, languor in receiving them, is directly or indirectly from myself, from past procrastination, and cowardly impatience of pain."
Work without Hope is more truly Coleridge's epitaph than that he wrote for himself (see text p. 193). If ever a man had known "the banks where amaranths blow," it was Coleridge. And those fadeless flowers of poetic legend bloomed for him no more.

Page 193. BIOGRAPHIA LITERARIA

Coleridge's career is filled with the ghosts of books planned and never written, and among these ghosts the *Biographia Literaria* is a startlingly solid object, for in this case he wrote very much more than he had planned. He was preparing a volume of poems for the press in 1815 and a prose preface was planned. The preface expanded into a literary autobiography and acquired a preface of its own which in turn grew formidably until finally it was embodied in the autobiography. The result overflowed one volume, and was too short for two, so additional material was added and the *Biographia Literaria*, which Coleridge has begun in 1815, appeared in two volumes in 1817. *Sibylline Leaves*, the collection of poems for which it had originally been intended as a preface, appeared in the same year—in one volume.

Arthur Symons declares, perhaps extremely, that the *Biographia Literaria* "is the greatest book of criticism in English, and one of the most annoying books in any language." Into it Coleridge's discursive mind poured a wealth of material personal, philosophic, and literary so oddly assorted that no general plan can be detected in the volume. Between chapter IV (text p. 193) in which the *Lyrical Ballads* first make a prominent appearance and chapter XIV (text p. 195) in which they next appear, occur the following chapters (Coleridge's chapter summaries are given):

V. On the law of Association—Its history traced from Aristotle to Hartley.

VI. That Hartley's system, as far as it differs from that of Aristotle, is neither tenable in theory, nor founded in facts.

VII. Of the necessary consequences of the Hartleian Theory—Of the original mistake or equivocation which procured its admission—*Memoria technica*.

VIII. The system of Dualism introduced by Des Cartes—Refined first by Spinoza and afterwards by Leibnitz into the doctrine of *Harmonia præstabilita*—Hylozoism—Materialism—None of these systems, or any possible theory of Association, supplies or supersedes a theory of Perception, or explains the formation of the Associable.

IX. Is Philosophy possible as a science, and what are its conditions?—Giordano Bruno—Literary Aristocracy, or the existence of a tacit compact among the learned as a privileged order—The Author's obligations to the Mystics—To Immanuel Kant—The difference between the letter and the spirit of Kant's writings, and a vindication of prudence in the teaching of Philosophy—Fichte's attempt to complete the Critical system—Its partial success and ultimate failure—Obligations to Schelling; and among English writers to Saumarez.

X. A Chapter of digression and anecdotes, as an interlude preceding that on the nature and genesis of the Imagination or Plastic Power—On Pedantry and pedantic expressions—Advice to young authors respecting publication—Various anecdotes of the Author's literary life, and the progress of his opinions in Religion and Politics.

XI. An affectionate exhortation to those who in early life feel themselves disposed to become authors.

XII. A Chapter of requests and premonitions concerning the perusal or omission of the chapter that follows.

XIII. On the Imagination, or Esemplastic power.

The discursive nature of the *Biographia Literaria* is obvious. Its richness is real but not so obvious. The fourteenth chapter, says I. A. Richards (*Principles of Literary Criticism*), "contains more hints towards a theory of poetry than all the rest ever written upon the subject." The book is full of lightning flashes. Among its more obvious qualities is the sustained analysis of Wordsworth, which remains one of the most acute criticisms of that poet ever written, and the chapter on Shakespeare's *Venus and Adonis* and *The Rape of Lucrece* as evidences of "the specific symptoms of poetic power."

Coleridge ranks among the great English critics, despite the fragmentary nature of his work, and the *Biographia Literaria* is the only volume of criticism which he himself saw through the press.

GEORGE GORDON, LORD BYRON

BIBLIOGRAPHY

I. WORKS

The Works of Lord Byron, poetry in 7 vols. ed. by E. H. Coleridge; letters and journals in 6 vols. ed. by R. E. Prothero. (Murray: London, 1898–1904.) The standard edition: although practically all of the poetry had already appeared, this edition included a great many hitherto unpublished letters in possession of John Murray, the grandson of Byron's original publisher.

Poetical Works, ed. by E. H. Coleridge. (Murray: London, 1905.) An excellent one-volume edition, with an introductory memoir.

Complete Poetical Works, ed. by P. E. More. Cambridge Edition. (Houghton: Boston, 1906.) A good one-volume text, with a biographical introduction.

Poems of Lord Byron, ed. by H. J. C. Grierson. (Chatto: London, 1922.) A selection of poems arranged in chronological order, including three cantos (II–IV) of *Don Juan:* the preface claims for Byron the merit of rendering life as it is understood by the average man.

The Best of Byron, ed. by R. A. Rice. (Nelson: New York, 1933.) A good selection, containing the standard anthology-pieces, together with some early poems included for their historical interest.

Poems and Plays. 2 vols. (Dutton: New York, 1927.) A recommended cheap edition, furnished with a brief introduction by W. P. Trent; *Don Juan* is in Vol. II.

Letters and Journals, ed. by Mathilde Blind. (Scott: London, 1886.) An excellent inexpensive collection; the introduction discounts the "theatricals" of the Greek expedition; remarks Carlyle's injustice in denouncing Byron as "a sham strong man."

Correspondence, ed. by John Murray. 2 vols. (Scribner: New York, 1922.) Includes letters to Lady Melbourne, Hobhouse, Douglas Kinnaird, and Shelley; a number of the letters to Lady Melbourne in Vol. I tend to support Lord Lovelace's accusation; Vol. II contains several letters from Shelley, here published for the first time.

Lord Byron in His Letters, ed. by V. H. Collins. (Murray: London, 1927.) An avowed selection from the Prothero edition, arranged to represent all phases of the poet's career revealed in his correspondence and journals; the prefaces and notes are valuable.

Byron and Greece, ed. by Harold Spender. (Murray: London, 1924.) An autobiographical record of Byron's two visits to Greece: the editor has arranged in chronological order passages from the letters and poems, showing that the poet's passionate love of Greece was a dominant influence in his life and gave it its one heroic touch.

II. BIOGRAPHY AND CRITICISM

Bellamy, R. L. *Byron the Man.* (Paul: London, 1924.) Concerned primarily with the poet in his public and personal life; makes no attempt at any critical evaluations.

Briscoe, W. A., ed. *Byron the Poet.* (Routledge: London, 1924.) A centenary collection of very uneven "tributes" and studies; outstanding are Quiller-Couch's reprinted "Byron: A Study" and Grierson's "Byron and English Society"— showing the poet's reaction against religious dogma.

Chew, S. C. *Byron in England: His Fame and After-Fame.* (Scribner: New York, 1924.) An exhaustive survey of the history of Byron's reputation in England, supported by many references to journals, reviews, and other documentary sources.

Clarke, Isabel C. *Shelley and Byron.* (Hutchinson: London, 1934.) A very adequate statement of familiar material concerning the Italian residence of the two poets; begins with 1812, carries to Trelawney's death in 1881.

Drinkwater, John. *The Pilgrim of Eternity: Byron —A Conflict.* (Doran: New York, 1926.) The best recent biography; interesting in its references to numerous foregoing Lives, especially *Astarte* by Lord Lovelace; puts the most favorable interpretation on Byron's faults, rebukes the modern disparagement of cantos III and IV of *Childe Harold.*

Du Bos, Charles. *Byron and the Need of Fatality*, trans. by Ethel C. Mayne. (Putnam: New York, 1932.) An intensive psychological study of the four years from the publication of *Childe Harold*, 1812, to the poet's departure from England, 1816; the *Journals* are held to be Byron's masterpiece; Miss Mayne has profited from the collaboration of the author himself, her Life of Lady Byron supplying him with much new data for the final chapter of the English edition.

Edgcumbe, Richard. *Byron: The Last Phase.* (Scribner: New York, 1909.) A doubtfully successful attempt to identify the addressee of the famous letter of May 17, 1819, as Mary Chaworth, who is alleged to be the mother of Medora Leigh. The account of Byron's Greek expedition is thoroughly reliable.

Fox, Sir John C. *The Byron Mystery.* (Richards: London, 1924.) A lawyer's sifting of the evidence of the charge of incest, tending to this conclusion: the offense, although admitted before Byron's marriage, cannot be proved thereafter; however, Byron did attempt it, giving Lady Byron cause for repudiating him.

Galt, John. *The Life of Lord Byron.* (Cassell: New York, 1911.) The original edition, 1830, was intended to supplement Moore's Life by dwelling particularly on the intellectual side; good for the personal recollections, 1809–11; underestimates Byron's motives for the Greek expedition.

Gordon, A. C. *Allegra: The Story of Byron and Miss Clairmont.* (Minton: New York, 1926.) A somewhat superficial biography, covering the whole extent of Byron's life, with emphasis upon the Claire Clairmont episode; contains many references to Shelley.

Gribble, F. H. *The Love-Affairs of Byron.* (Scribner: New York, 1910.) Pretends to show that Byron's love-affairs were the principal incidents in his life.

Jeaffreson, J. C. *The Real Lord Byron.* 2 vols. (Osgood: Boston, 1883.) A singularly dark study of the unpleasant passages in Byron's life, told with candor and with knowledge of some hitherto unpublished documents which ostensibly rid Byron of complicity with Mrs. Leigh.

Leonard, W. E. *Byron and Byronism in America.* (Columbia University Press: 1907.) An apparently exhaustive survey of Byron's reputation in America, but revealing less popularity than might be expected by students of romantic poetry.

Lovelace, R. G. N. K. *Astarte: A Fragment of Truth concerning George Gordon Byron.* (Christophers: London, 1921.) A now generally repudiated defense of the memory of the grandmother of the author at the expense of Byron and Mrs. Leigh; this reprinted edition, published for the first time thirty-four letters of Byron.

Maurois, André. *Byron.* Trans. by Hamish Miles. (Appleton: New York, 1930.) A highly romanticized account of Byron, in which his human errors are stated and accepted, with no effort at apology; gives little critical comment on his writing.

Mayne, Ethel C. *Byron*. (Scribner: New York, 1924.) A revised edition of the 1913 study, regarded by many as the authoritative biography; the author contrasts Byron's dealings in his friendships with men and women.

Moore, Thomas. *The Life of Lord Byron, with His Letters and Journals*. (Murray: London, 1830.) An indispensable Life (frequently reprinted), though not a great biography; noteworthy in that it first gave to the public the bulk of the letters and journals: a loyal, if somewhat shallow tribute.

Nichol, John. *Byron*. English Men of Letters series. (Harper: New York, 1887.) The best brief biography; prepared in consultation with Swinburne, it takes note of Byron's sincerity, eloquence, satire, and the impulse he imparted to the democratic movement.

Nicholson, H. G. *Byron: The Last Journey, April 1823–April 1824*. (Houghton: Boston, 1924.) A brilliantly written account of the last days in Italy, the Greek expedition, and the circumstances of Byron's death.

Noel, Roden. *The Life of Byron*. (Scott: London, 1890.) A recommended brief biography, sound on the critical side though presenting little of novelty.

Quennell, Peter. *Byron*. (Duckworth: London, 1934.) Accepts the *Astarte* story, deflates somewhat the Byron legend, showing Byron as its author and its victim; singles out as the best of the poetry *Childe Harold*, *Don Juan*, and *English Bards and Scotch Reviewers*.

Raymond, Mrs. Dora N. *The Political Career of Lord Byron*. (Holt: New York, 1924.) A compendious, if ill-written and uncritical, arrangement of the material on the subject.

Symon, J. D. *Byron in Perspective*. (Stokes: New York, 1924.) A detailed examination of the influence of Scottish ancestry, early associations in Aberdeen, and later connections; elucidating, but with a tendency to overstate— e.g., that Byron's use of *river* to rhyme with *ever* proves Aberdeen influence.

Trelawney, E. J. *Recollections of the Last Days of Shelley and Byron*, ed. by Edward Dowden. (Oxford University Press: 1906.) Originally published in 1858, this book covers the year 1822; presents a vivid first-hand portrayal of the poet; in places unsympathetic and unreliable, but fairer in the first edition than in the later *Records*, published in 1878.

III. ARTICLES FROM BOOKS

Arnold, Matthew. "Byron," in *Essays in Criticism*, Second Series. (Macmillan: New York, 1891.) Claims Byron as an ally in opposing the "Philistines"; suggests that the poet is best represented in selections, discovering in his poetry no useful social criticism; ranks him next to Wordsworth in the category of romantic poets.

Austin, Alfred. "Byron and Wordsworth," in *The Bridling of Pegasus*. (Macmillan: London, 1910.) Maintains that Arnold's selections are inade-quate to represent Byron; praises his poetic vigor and powers of invention.

Brandes, Georg. "Byron, the Passionate Personality," in *Main Currents in Nineteenth Century Literature*. (Boni: New York, 1923.) The essay in Vol. IV depicts the poet as the inspirer of liberalism, especially effective in continental Europe.

Collins, J. C. "The Collected Works of Byron," in *Studies in Poetry and Criticism*. (Macmillan: New York, 1906.) Regards the Coleridge-Prothero edition as definitely complete; ranks Byron after only Shakespeare in versatility.

Dowden, Edward. "Renewed Revolutionary Advance," in *The French Revolution and English Literature*. (Scribner: New York, 1897.) Suggests that interest in contemporary politics unified Byron's poetic forces; makes again the frequent assertion that the unmergeable contradictions in his character forbid piecemeal reading of his poetry.

Fairchild, H. N. "Byron and Transcendentalism," in *The Romantic Quest*. (Columbia University Press: 1931.) Traces a thin but continuous thread of transcendental thought in *Manfred*, *Cain*, and *Childe Harold*.

Garrod, H. W. "Byron 1824–1924," in *The Profession of Poetry*. (Oxford University Press: 1929.) Generally unfavorable; it briefly reviews the poet's life, contrasts his work with Shelley's; would persuade that, even in *Don Juan*, "Byron's deeper passions were not engaged."

Gingerich, S. F. "Byron," in *Essays in the Romantic Poets*. (Macmillan: New York, 1923.) Confidently states that "the great law of fatality" drove Byron away from Wordsworthian influences (evidenced in canto III of *Childe Harold*) to the satirical outlook of his later poetry.

Grierson, H. J. C. "Lord Byron: Arnold and Swinburne," in *The Background of English Literature*. (Chatto: London, 1925.) Presents the issues involved in the celebrated quarrel, concluding with a dispassionate judgment of them.

Henley, W. E. "Byron," in *Views and Reviews*. (Scribner: New York, 1890.) A reply to Arnold's essay (first published, 1881): deprecates his apologetic tone, attacks his "touchstone" method of judgment of poetry, considers his selections of Byron an inadequate representation.

Moorman, F. W. "Byron," in *The Cambridge History of English Literature*, XII. (Putnam: New York, 1916.) An adequate though unoriginal discussion, with some attention given in detail to the longer poems.

Morley, John. "Byron," in *Critical Miscellanies*, I. (Macmillan: New York, 1908.) One of the earliest rational summaries of Byron; discusses the poet as a European revolutionary, tending toward the modern spirit.

Quiller-Couch, Sir Arthur. "Byron," in *Studies in Literature*, Second Series. (Cambridge University Press: 1922.) The date April 25, 1816, is set up to divide the good from the bad in Byron's verse; *Don Juan* is reviewed in some detail: "it belongs with heart and soul to its age."

Swinburne, A. C. "Byron," in *Essays and Studies*. (Chatto: London, 1888.) Formerly a preface to the 1865 *Selections*, this essay dwells upon the poet's perception of nature, his sincerity, lack of dramatic power, and his sense of human interest; insists upon the need of understanding the whole of Byron's poetry.

Swinburne, A. C. "Wordsworth and Byron," in *Miscellanies.* (Scribner: New York, 1911.) A violent protest against Arnold's famous 1881 preface, in which Byron is ranked above Coleridge and Shelley; Swinburne, here at his worst, finds nothing but the worst in Byron.

Symons, Arthur. "Byron," in *The Romantic Movement in English Poetry.* (Dutton: New York, 1909.) A discriminating, open-minded discussion, in which Byron's weakness and strength are fairly weighed: his disjointed philosophy is seen as the reason for his unsuccesses as a poet and a man.

Trent, W. P. "The Byron Revival," in *The Authority of Criticism and Other Essays.* (Scribner: New York, 1899.) Reviews the vicissitudes of the poet's fame, foresees no favorable permanent reaction from the recent publication (by Murray) of the *Letters*, but contends for the recognition of Byron's poetic vigor, revealed especially in *Don Juan.*

Vincent, L. H. "Episodes in the Life of a Noble Poet," in *Dandies and Men of Letters.* (Houghton: Boston, 1913.) Commends Moore's *Life*, describes Byron's adventures in the London literary and social worlds.

Woodberry, G. E. "Byron's Centenary," in *Makers of Literature.* (Macmillan: New York, 1900.) Comments rationally on the Westminster Abbey refusal; rebukes Landor's attack; praises *Don Juan*, but faintheartedly.

IV. ARTICLES FROM PERIODICALS

Briscoe, W. A. "Byron as Politician," *Contemporary Review*, CXXV, 460–7 (Mar., 1924). Begins with his appearances in the House of Lords; points out in his poetry references to English politics and affairs of Italy and Greece; reviews the Greek expedition.

Chew, S. C. "Byron in America," *American Mercury*, I, 335–44 (Mar., 1924). Shows how the republican spirit in Byron found friends for him in America after a period of moralizing; traces permanent, but not always happy, influences of *Don Juan.*

Elliott, G. R. "Byron and the Comic Spirit," *Publications of the Modern Language Association*, XXXIX, 897–909 (Dec., 1924). A study of Byron's poetry showing a progression toward a sense of universal comedy, unlimited by prejudice or personal animadversion.

Griggs, E. L. "Coleridge and Byron," *Publications of the Modern Language Association*, XLV, 1085–97 (Dec., 1930). Finds in five new letters of Coleridge evidence of his gratitude for Byron's interest in his dramas.

Jones, F. L. "Byron's Last Poem," *Studies in Philology*, XXXI, 487–9 (July, 1934). Sees the poet's role in "On This Day I Complete My Thirty-sixth Year" as a combination of his "usual heroics" plus a dash of Macbeth's defiance.

Jones, H. M. "The Byron Centenary," *Yale Review*, XIII, 730–45 (July, 1924). Shows the poet's artistic lineage from the eighteenth century; compares him with Burns in his "fierce flippancy."

More, P. E. "The Wholesome Revival of Byron," *Atlantic Monthly*, LXXXII, 801–9 (Nov., 1898). Grounds Byron's strength on his classicism, which saves him from the effeminacy of Shelley and Wordsworth; praises his broad scope as a genius, while admitting artistic faults.

Murray, John. "The Popularity of Byron," *Cornhill Magazine*, LVI, 385–91 (Apr., 1924). Reviews the progress of British criticism of the poet, largely in reference to Chew's study; speaks from the publisher's point of view of Byron's popularity, concluding with a pleasant bit of personal reminiscence.

Prothero, R. E. "The Poetry of Byron," *Quarterly Review*, CCXLI, 229–53 (Apr., 1924). Discusses the poet's practical revolutionary ideas; winnowing out his affectation, reviews *Don Juan.*

Pyre, J. F. A. "Byron in Our Day," *Atlantic Monthly*, XCIX, 542–52 (Apr., 1907). Really involving a study of the decadence of Romanticism, this essay defends Byron's egotism and palliates his love-affairs.

Sichel, Walter. "The Humor of Lord Byron," *Nineteenth Century*, LXXXVIII, 1026–36 (Dec., 1920). Names the poet's humor "the humor of good sense," and compares him with Sheridan in this respect; shows Byron's humor arising out of his feeling for the drama.

Sichel, Walter. "Byron as a War Poet," *Fortnightly Review*, XCIX, 127–33 (Jan., 1916). Shows by abundant quotation the best of Byron's war poetry; praises him as the supreme English poet in this field.

Stauffer, Ruth M. "Byron and Shelley in Italy," *Poet Lore*, XXVIII, 554–66; 703–21 (Autumn, Winter, 1917). Traces the relationship of the two poets during the months of May, 1816–Oct., 1821; suggests mutual influences.

Strahan, J. A. "Byron in England," *Edinburgh Review*, CCXXXIV, 331–45 (Oct., 1921). A review of *Astarte*, this article discusses cautiously Byron's marriage and his relations with Augusta Leigh.

Street, G. S. "Byron Reconsidered," *Nineteenth Century*, XCI, 775–81 (May, 1922). Comments on Murray's publication of the *Letters* and upon *Astarte;* casts an oblique eye upon Byron's romances.

NOTES

Page 238.   WELL! THOU ART HAPPY

This was written to Mary Chaworth, two years older than Byron, and with whom as a schoolboy of fifteen he fell violently in love—so much so that after the summer vacation of 1803 he refused for some time to go back to school because of her. She married another. In 1808 Byron dined with her and her husband, and her two year old daughter was exhibited. Byron "started involuntarily" and had trouble in concealing his emotion.

Page 239.   MAID OF ATHENS, ERE WE PART

The Maid of Athens was Teresa Macri, daughter of the widow of the English vice-consul at

Athens in whose house Byron stopped for ten weeks on his first Near Eastern trip. He wrote to Drury: "I almost forgot to tell you that I am dying for love of three Greek girls at Athens, sisters. I lived in the same house. Teresa, Mariana, and Katinka are the names of these divinities—all of them under fifteen."

Page 240. LINES TO A LADY WEEPING

It had been reported that the Princess Charlotte had burst into tears at the time her father, the Prince Regent, quarrelled with his Whig ministers. Byron, politically sympathetic with the Whigs, promptly wrote the *Lines* and published them anonymously. They attracted no attention. He had them printed with *The Corsair* (1814), acknowledging authorship in spite of Murray's warning of the danger involved. "I care nothing for consequences on this point," he said. A furore promptly followed and Byron was violently attacked. The episode was significant as indicating how intense was the latent hostility to Byron. As Maurois says (p. 246): "Here was a poet who flourished in London's face the triple insolence of beauty, genius and free speech: against him was held in suspension so strong a rancour that the slightest shock would precipitate a most powerful solution of hate." The uproar over the *Lines* was the first open sign of Byron's approaching downfall.

SHE WALKS IN BEAUTY

Written to Lady Wilmot Horton who appeared at a ball in mourning but with numerous spangles on her dress—suggesting the imagery of the first two lines.

Page 242. THE DESTRUCTION OF SENNACHERIB

The biblical basis of this poem may be found in II Kings 18 : 13; 19 : 15–19, 35–36.

STANZAS FOR MUSIC

Mayne conjectures this poem to have been inspired by Claire Clairmont, who also inspired Shelley's *To Constantia Singing*. See p. 387 of text for a letter from Byron to Augusta Leigh referring to Claire.

FARE THEE WELL

The poem was written after Byron was aware that Lady Byron would not return to him. The student may form his own conclusions as to its sincerity. Byron said tears fell fast as he wrote it and Moore confirmed him, having seen a manuscript sheet all blotted with tears. The original manuscript, however, which was sold at Sotheby's in 1885, showed no such traces and it was probably over a "fair copy" that Byron wept. This poem, together with

A Sketch (a violent attack on Mrs. Clermont, Lady Byron's old nurse, whom he thought responsible for alienating her), Byron ordered printed for private distribution only, but copies leaked out and were printed on April 14 by the *Champion*, a Tory newspaper. The outcry of condemnation which followed was similar to that caused by the *Lines to a Lady Weeping*. Lady Byron at this time was also in great distress and confusion of mind. Although she made the resolution to separate, and adhered to it, a servant reported her "rolling on the floor in a paroxysm of grief at having promised to separate." The appearance of *Fare Thee Well*, which put her in the light of a faithless and hard-hearted wife, offended her deeply (if offense is the proper word in such a conflict of passions) and helped to steel her resolution. A skeptic, aware of Byron's temperament and the circumstances surrounding the case, might well distrust the sentiment of this poem—and might easily do an injustice. Byron had the faculty of creating a mood and of living in it with perfect sincerity for the moment. Such a faculty is merely "play-acting" when measured against the standard of human deeds; it is unhealthy and undesirable in a world where men should be measured by their deeds; but it is not insincere.

See letters XVI, XVIII, XIX, and XXI (pp. 383–7 of the text) for an expression of Byron's feelings just before and just after his marriage, and just after the breach. See also number XXII (p. 387) for his farewell to Lady Byron (the last sentence of paragraph two is noticeably bitter) and number XXIX (p. 393) for a bitter letter some years later. See also numbers XIII and XIV (pp. 380–1) and XVII (p. 383) for letters written to his wife before the marriage.

Page 244. STANZAS TO AUGUSTA

The fourth stanza, implying that Lady Byron was everything which Augusta was not, should be compared with the sentiment of *Fare Thee Well*. In justice to Byron it should be pointed out that both might be completely sincere. Variable of temper as he was, and under severe strain, he might quite easily pass through contradictory moods and express them both honestly.

Augusta Leigh, to whom the poem was written, was Byron's half-sister and her child, Medora, is said to have been Byron's. It was on Byron's relations with Augusta that Lady Byron's separation case was based. Whatever the guilt involved, Byron's affection for her, in a life rather filled with casual affairs, was certainly deep and enduring.

One of the wisest scholars of this century has this to say, in an informal mood, of the personalities involved, and his letter might close the discussion of this group of poems: ". . . I like Shelley better than Byron, as a book, but if they were alive and I knew them I know that I should take to Byron and have no patience with Shelley. I have no use for him except in a book, where he does very well. He was just a bright Being, not a man. You can't blame him, because, you see, he was merely a bright Being. I could live in a tent with Byron, who was never unreal or faddy about ordinary things and was as sincere as an angel when there was no public present. Juan and Haidee and even the stanzas to Augusta (which make me cry) were all for the public. He got a bad woman for his wife (by his own silly youthful lordliness and desire to show that nothing mattered) and, as it happened, this mattered a great deal to him. If she had been as good as Lady Hamilton we should have heard of him outside society verses. As it was she gibbered and lied, because he broke a watch with a poker, and said 'Damnably,' and asked if he was in hell, when he woke and saw red bedcurtains. A badhearted, narrow, prig, I fear. She should have stayed Miss Milbanke. Augusta was quite obviously a duck." (*The Letters of Sir Walter Raleigh*, edited by Lady Raleigh, II, 282.)

See letter XXII (p. 387) in which Byron leaves Augusta under the care of Lady Byron, who did as a matter of fact repeatedly assist Augusta in later years. See letters XXIII (p. 387) and XLIX (p. 407), written to Augusta.

EPISTLE TO AUGUSTA

See notes on *Stanzas to Augusta*, above.
73–5. *our own dear Lake . . . old Hall . . . Leman's.* The *old Hall* was Newstead Abbey, Byron's family seat, where Augusta had visited. *Leman* is Lake Geneva. Byron was in Switzerland at the time of writing.

Page 246.   SO, WE'LL GO NO MORE A-ROVING

On February 28, 1817, Byron wrote Moore that the Carnival and "sitting up late o' nights" had put him on an "invalid regimen." "Though I did not dissipate much upon the whole, yet I find 'the sword wearing out the scabbard,' though I have but just turned the corner of twenty-nine." The poem follows in the letter with no further comment.

Attention has frequently been called to the broken rhythm of the last line, "like a sob in the throat."

TO THOMAS MOORE

On July 10, 1817, Byron wrote to Moore, "Ah, Master Shallow, we have heard the chimes at midnight. But—" and followed with this poem, adding afterwards: "This should have been

written fifteen moons ago—the first stanza was. I am just come out from an hour's swim in the Adriatic; and I write to you with a black-eyed Venetian girl before me, reading Boccacio."

Page 247.   ON THIS DAY I COMPLETE MY THIRTY-SIXTH YEAR

Moore tells the circumstances under which this poem was first read: "On the morning of the 22d of January, his birthday,—the last my poor friend was ever fated to see,—he came from his bedroom into the apartment where Colonel Stanhope and some others were assembled, and said with a smile, 'You were complaining the other day that I never write any poetry now. This is my birthday, and I have just finished something which, I think, is better than what I usually write.' He then produced to them those beautiful stanzas which, though already known to most readers, are far too affectingly associated with this closing scene of his life to be omitted among its details. Taking into consideration, indeed, everything connected with these verses,—the last tender aspirations of a loving spirit which they breathe, the self-devotion to a noble cause which they so nobly express, and that consciousness of a near grave glimmering sadly through the whole,—there is perhaps no production within the range of mere human composition, round which the circumstances and feelings under which it was written cast so touching an interest." (Thomas Moore, *Letters and Journals of Lord Byron with Notices of his Life* [Murray, 1830], II, 718–9.)

It is interesting to compare this birthday with that of three years before. See entries in Byron's *Diary* for Jan. 21 and 22, 1821 (text p. 367).

CHILDE HAROLD'S PILGRIMAGE

The first two cantos of *Childe Harold* were published in March, 1812, and, perfectly catching the temper of the time, established Byron's reputation. In the *Preface* Byron expressly denies that the Childe represented any real person—meaning himself. In the third and fourth cantos he frankly makes the Childe his spokesman. The third canto was written in Switzerland, being completed in July, 1816; the fourth was done at Venice between June, 1817, and the following January. There are references to these cantos and the state of mind in which he wrote them in the text, p. 390, col. 1, l. 18 ff. and p. 391, col. 1, l. 48 ff. Any student who is puzzled by the contrast of the misanthropic Byron of these cantos and the zestful Byron of the letters might do well to read a passage in the letters (text p. 401, col. 1, l. 40 ff.)—and ponder this passage well. It was as a master of the "eloquence of despair" that Byron first impressed his own generation. In the reaction which occurred after his death his sentiments were attacked as sham and his workmanship as shoddy. Swinburne puts the case for the prosecution vigorously: ". . . But what shall be said of a poet whose work not only does not lose, but gains, by translation into foreign prose? and gains so greatly and indefinitely by that process as to assume a virtue which it has not? On taking up a fairly good version of *Childe Harold's Pilgrimage* in French or Italian prose, a reader whose eyes and ears are not hopelessly sealed against all distinction of good from bad in rhythm or in style will infallibly be struck by the vast improvement which the text has undergone in the course of translation. The blundering, floundering, lumbering and stumbling stanzas, transmuted into prose and transfigured into grammar, reveal the real and latent force of rhetorical energy that is in them: the gasping, ranting, wheezing, broken-winded verse has been transformed into really effective and fluent oratory. A ranter, of course, it is whose accents we hear in alternate moan and bellow from the trampled platform of theatrical misanthropy: but he rants no longer out of tune: and we are able to discern in the thick and troubled stream of his natural eloquence whatever of real value may be swept along in company with much drifting rubbish. It is impossible to express how much *Childe Harold* gains by being done out of wretchedly bad metre into decently good prose: the New Testament did not gain more by being translated out of canine Greek into divine English. Not that even under these improved conditions Byron's is comparable to the work of a firstrate orator or preacher; but one may perceive how men to whom English poetry was a strange tongue might mistake it for an impressive and effective example of English poetry." ("Wordsworth and Byron," in Swinburne's *Works*, Bonchurch Edition, XIV, 166–7.)

Critical opinion has veered again. Byron's real fame will probably rest upon his *Don Juan*, but few, if any, today would agree with so severe a criticism as Swinburne's of the *Childe Harold*. In any case, in the latter cantos of this poem and in *Manfred* are to be found the completest expression of Byron's "Byronism," a literary attitude which conquered a generation. And most critics will now concede real sweep and eloquence to the work. These two poems are directly expressive of Byron himself and of a mood of post-war disillusionment which followed the Napoleonic struggle. It was because he did so perfectly express that mood that Byron so completely conquered in his own day.

Professor Grierson has a revealing analysis of the poems as they related to Byron himself and to his period:

"To say that Byron was touched by the sweep of the Evangelical wave may seem strange but it is true. His early years had been spent, not in aristocratic, but in middle-class and pious circles. At Aberdeen he acquired the elements of that intimate knowledge of the Bible which he manifested throughout his life, and imbibed the Calvinist doctrine of predestination. For him to be religious meant to be Evangelical or Methodist. . . . "And when he was driven into exile, cast off by his country and the aristocracy to which he belonged, his first conflict was not with these—that came later—but in his own heart, with the sense of wrong-doing, and with the creed by which he had been taught to envisage and arraign his own wrong-doing. The central experience of *Childe Harold, Prometheus, Manfred, Cain, Sardanapalus*, is the sense of sin and the injustice of the decree which arraigns sin as guilt, as consciousness and conflict inexplicable to the 'invincible ignorance' or the purer and more enlightened eyes of Shelley. "*Childe Harold* is, of course, much besides a confession of Byron's sense of sin and conflict with the creed of his childhood. It is an almost classical—wanting indeed classical clarity of thought and perfection of form—an almost classical expression of the mind of Europe when the long period of high hopes and fierce conflicts which the French Revolution inaugurated had ended with Waterloo in shattering and complete disillusionment. Great men—Napoleon, Rousseau, Voltaire, Gibbon, Hannibal—great events, Waterloo, Cannae—great cities, Venice, Florence, above all, Rome—they all tell the same tale, *Vanitas Vanitatum*. Only Nature, only beauty endures,—the Alps, the Rhine, Thrasimene as it is now:

Her lake a sheet of silver, and her plain
Rent by no ravage save the gentle plow,

and the everlasting sea:

Dark-heaving, boundless, endless, and sublime,
The image of Eternity.

"Byron's was not the only mind that felt the Dionysiac mood which is the theme of his turbid, passionate, splendid rhapsody. But the deepest personal note in it all is that which I have indicated, the sense of sin, and a proud passionate conflict with the doctrine impressed on his mind in childhood—Evangelical, Calvinist, Augustinian, of predestined sin and predestined guilt; a passionate denial of the justice of the decree which makes man the victim of inherited passions and untoward circumstances and then condemns him as solely and entirely responsible. . . . "In *Childe Harold* this, though the central experience determining the mood of the whole poem, is subordinated to the elaboration of the more general theme of historical world disillusionment. In *Prometheus* and *Manfred* it becomes the principal topic. Each presents in a different form the same fixed, unyielding attitude of mind of one who acknowledges delinquency but rejects with defiance the doctrine which arraigns sin as guilt. In the great speech of Satan with which Milton opens the fourth book of *Paradise Lost* the poet drives home, with stroke after stroke, the responsibility of Satan for his own wrong-doing:

Had'st thou the same free will and power to
    stand?
Thou had'st. Whom hast thou then, or what,
    to accuse
But Heaven's free love dealt equally to all?
Be then his love accurst, since, love or hate,
To me alike it deals eternal woe.
Nay, curst be thou; since against his thy will
Chose freely what it now so justly rues.
Me miserable! which way shall I fly?
Infinite wrath and infinite despair.

"That is, I take it, the orthodox, essentially religious view. Man has no rights; but he has freedom and therefore complete responsibility. Paul, Augustine, Calvin, had doubts about the freedom, none about the responsibility. Byron and the sceptical mind find it difficult to accept either position. To call a conscious being into existence seems to him to involve moral obligations for a righteous creator. Man's free-will is not, experience and thought seem to indicate, thus absolute. If Satan rebelled it was in virtue of something in his nature, the nature which he did not himself make, but received. Free, a man's conscience tells him he is, within limits and relatively, relative to other created beings to whom he cannot transfer his individual responsibility. But neither conscience nor reason tells him that this complex being which is his responsible self, is of his own making, is free absolutely, i.e., in its relation to the absolute. So much Byron feels, but he is incapable of a philosophical solution of the enigma. The *Prometheus* is a defiant and unshakable arraignment of the conception of Providence taught him by Orthodox Evangelicalism. . . .
"In *Manfred* Byron endeavours to give the same theme dramatic form, the lyrical-dramatic form which Goethe's *Faust* had given vogue to, and in the same metaphysical strain. But Byron's genius was not dramatic nor had he the lyrical soul of Shelley. Shelley lacked solidity; Byron lacked wings. Yet *Manfred*, read aright, is an impressive and significant poem. Its closest parallel is Marlowe's *Dr. Faustus*, a poem which in its best passages has more of the essential music of poetry than Byron's, for a deficiency in essential music is Byron's greatest defect as a poet. But Byron's thought goes deeper than Marlowe's. Marlowe set two moods over against one another, on the one hand lust of knowledge and of the power which knowledge brings, on the other terror of the supernatural; but he failed to link them logically and dramatically. His sympathies, one feels, are with the soaring ambitions of Faustus, yet at the end he hands him over to the devils of superstition in a speech of splendid power. He failed to show, as Shakespeare did in *Macbeth*, that the forbidden fruit brought its *own* curse. Byron's poem is even less many-mooded than Marlowe's; but its logic, so far as it goes, is lucid and convincing. Manfred is the victim of sin and remorse but the defiant enemy of the orthodox conception of retribution. The punishment of sin is the consciousness of sin, the consciousness above all of wrong to another, to the one who is loved and has been the victim of passion. . . .
"And when the devils appear it is not to carry off Manfred as they had carried off Faustus. Retribution is not only useless, it is but to add crime to crime·

Must crimes be punished but by other crimes
And greater criminals? Back to thy hell!
Thou hast no power upon me, *that* I feel;
Thou never shalt possess me, *that* I know:
What I have done is done; I bear within
A torture which could nothing gain from thine.

A step more one feels might have led Byron to proclaim, with Blake and Tolstoi, that the fundamental principle of Christianity and true religion is the doctrine of the eternal forgiveness of sin." (H. J. C. Grierson: "Byron and English Society," amplified from a lecture given at University College, Nottingham, March 17, 1922, and first printed in *Byron the Poet, A Collection of Essays*, edited by W. A. Briscoe, pp. 67-75.)

Page 247.

CHILDE HAROLD: CANTO THE THIRD

19. *I did sing of One*. Reference to the first two cantos of Childe Harold published in 1812 (see l. 66). Byron tried to avoid identification of himself with the hero of cantos one and two (see letter, text p. 378, col. 1, ll. 1-9) but the disguise was always thin. In the last two cantos he speaks frankly through the lips of his hero.
145-53. *Stop!* et seq. Byron on his way to Switzerland and exile stopped on the field of Waterloo and, it has been said, wrote this stanza on the actual battlefield. Waterloo is "history" to the modern reader, but to Byron it was an event of the previous year.
158. "*pride of place*." A term of falconry which means the highest pitch of flight. The "eagle" is, of course, Napoleon.
180. *Harmodius*. Harmodius and Aristogiton delivered Athens from the tyranny of Hippias and Hipparchus. They have become symbolic figures in literature—the deliverers of a people.

181. *There was a sound of revelry.* A ball was given at Brussels by Lady de Ros, daughter of the Duchess of Richmond, on the night before Waterloo. Legend says that the dance was broken up by the sound of trumpets breaking in on the dance music and summoning the officers back to their regiments. Byron was the first to use the possibilities of dramatic contrast offered by the scene.

200. *Brunswick's fated chieftain.* The Duke of Brunswick, who was killed in the engagement at Quatre-Bras.

234. *Evan's, Donald's fame.* "Sir Evan Cameron, and his descendant Donald, the 'gentle Lochiel' of the 'forty-five.'" (Byron's note.)

235. *And Ardennes waves above them.* "The wood of Soignies is supposed to be a remnant of the forest of Ardennes, famous in Boiardo's *Orlando*, and immortal in Shakespeare's *As You Like It*. It is also celebrated in Tacitus, as being the spot of successful defence by the Germans against the Roman encroachments. I have ventured to adopt the name connected with nobler associations than those of mere slaughter." (Byron's note.)

270. *I turn'd from all she brought.* "My guide from Mont St. Jean over the field seemed intelligent and accurate. The place where Major Howard fell was not far from two tall and solitary trees (there was a third cut down, or shivered in the battle), which stand a few yards from each other at a pathway's side. Beneath these he died and was buried. The body has since been removed to England. A small hollow for the present marks where it lay, but will probably soon be effaced; the plough has been upon it, and the grain is. After pointing out the different spots where Picton and other gallant men had perished, the guide said, 'Here Major Howard lay: I was near him when wounded.' I told him my relationship, and he seemed then still more anxious to point out the particular spot and circumstances. The place is one of the most marked in the field, from the peculiarity of the two trees above mentioned. I went on horseback twice over the field, comparing it with my recollection of similar scenes. As a plain, Waterloo seems marked out for the scene of some great action, though this may be mere imagination: I have viewed with attention those of Platea, Troy, Mantinea, Leuctra, Chæronea, and Marathon: and the field around Mont St. Jean and Hougoumont appears to want little but a better cause, and that undefinable but impressive halo which the lapse of ages throws around a celebrated spot, to vie in interest with any or all of these, except, perhaps, the last mentioned." (Byron's note.)

303. *apples on the Dead Sea's shore.* "The (fabled) apples on the brink of the lake Asphaltites were said to be fair without, and, within,

ashes. Vide Tacitus, Histor. lib. v. 7." (Byron's note.)

335. *flying from the field.* Napoleon abandoned the *Grande Armée* towards the end of the retreat from Moscow. Early in his career he had abandoned an army in Egypt.

366. *Philip's son.* Alexander the Great, son of Philip of Macedon.

368. *Diogenes.* The ancient philosopher who searched, rather despairingly, for an honest man.

369. *For sceptred cynics.* "The great error of Napoleon, 'if we have writ our annals true,' was a continued obtrusion on mankind of his want of all community of feeling for or with them; perhaps more offensive to human vanity than the active cruelty of more trembling and suspicious tyranny. Such were his speeches to public assemblies as well as individuals; and the single expression which he is said to have used on returning to Paris after the Russian winter had destroyed his army, rubbing his hands over a fire, 'This is pleasanter than Moscow,' would probably alienate more favour from his cause than the destruction and reverses which led to the remark." (Byron's note.)

409. *majestic Rhine.* Harold's route parallels Byron's itinerary when he went into exile in 1816: Belgium and then up the Rhine to Switzerland.

413. *chiefless castles.* The natural scenery of the Rhine is picturesque and the romantic effect is increased by the existence of numerous castles, once the headquarters of robber barons, but now empty and ruinous.

496. *Drachenfels.* One of the more picturesque castles of the Rhine.

541. *Honour to Marceau!* "The monument of the young and lamented General Marceau (killed by a rifle-ball at Alterkirchen, on the last day of the fourth year of the French Republic) still remains as described. The inscriptions on his monument are rather too long, and not required: his name was enough; France adored, and her enemies admired; both wept over him. His funeral was attended by the generals and detachments from both armies." (Byron's note.)

554. *Ehrenbreitstein.* "Ehrenbreitstein, *i.e.* 'the broad stone of honour,' one of the strongest fortresses in Europe, was dismantled and blown up by the French at the truce of Leoben. It had been, and could only be, reduced by famine or treachery. It yielded to the former, aided by surprise." (Byron's note.)

601. *Morat! the proud, the patriot field!* At Morat in 1476 the Swiss defeated an invading army of Burgundians and retained their independence. The site of the battle was marked by a great heap of the bones of the slaughtered Burgundians and there still remained some of

these grisly relics when Byron visited the place, although in the interval, every Burgundian who had passed that way had carried off a few bones for burial in native soil.

608. *Cannæ's carnage.* Hannibal's greatest victory in the Second Punic War in which he annihilated the Roman army which had been sent to destroy him.

625. *Adventicum.* The former Roman capital of Helvetia, reduced to ruins.

634. *And held within their urn.* "Julia Alpinula, a young Aventian priestess, died soon after a vain endeavour to save her father, condemned to death as a traitor by Aulus Cæcina. Her epitaph was discovered many years ago;—it is thus:—'Julia Alpinula: Hic jaceo. Infelicis patris infelix proles. Deæ Aventiæ Sacerdos. Exorare patris necem non potui: Male mori in fatis ille erat. Vixi annos XXIII.' [Julia Alpinula, unhappy child of an unhappy father, priestess of the goddess Aventia. I was not able to save my father's life by pleading; he was fated to die miserably. I lived twenty three years.]—I know of no human composition so affecting as this, nor a history of deeper interest. These are the names and actions which ought not to perish, and to which we turn with a true and healthy tenderness, from the wretched and glittering detail of a confused mass of conquests and battles, with which the mind is roused for a time to a false and feverish sympathy, from whence it recurs at length with all the nausea consequent on such intoxication." (Byron's note.)
More, in the Cambridge Edition, points out that the inscription was a sixteenth century forgery.

644. *Lake Leman.* Lake Geneva.

743. *Julie.* The heroine of Rousseau's *La Nouvelle Héloïse.*

745. *the memorable kiss.* Byron in his note says this refers to Rousseau's account in his *Confessions* of his passion for the Comtesse d'Houdetot "and his long walk every morning, for the sake of the single kiss which was the common salutation of French acquaintance."

860. *The sky is changed.* "The thunder-storm to which these lines refer occurred on the 13th of June, 1816, at midnight. I have seen, among the Acroceraunian mountains of Chimari, several more terrible, but none more beautiful." (Byron's note.)

923. *Clarens.* On Lake Geneva; mentioned in Rousseau's *La Nouvelle Héloïse.* Byron in his note to l. 927 quotes from the novel a passage as authority for his color words "sunset into rose-hues" and then, in a long note on the locality, has this to say: "The feeling with which all around Clarens, and the opposite rocks of Meillerie, is invested, is of a still higher and more comprehensive order than the mere sympathy with individual passion; it is a sense

of the existence of love in its most extended and sublime capacity, and of our own participation of its good and of its glory: it is the great principle of the universe, which is there more condensed, but not less manifested; and of which, though knowing ourselves a part, we lose our individuality, and mingle in the beauty of the whole.—If Rousseau had never written, nor lived, the same associations would not less have belonged to such scenes. He has added to the interest of his works by their adoption; he has shown his sense of their beauty by the selection; but they have done that for him which no human being could do for them." (Byron's note.)

978. *Of names which unto you bequeath'd a name.* Gibbon lived at Lausanne and Voltaire at Ferney. Stanza CVI is devoted to Voltaire and CVII to Gibbon.

1024. *fierce Carthaginian.* Hannibal, whose invasion of Italy in the Second Punic War is one of the most spectacular campaigns in military history. See note on l. 608.

1064. *O'er others' griefs.* "It is said by Rochefoucault, that there is *always* something in the misfortunes of men's best friends not displeasing to them." (Byron's note.)

Page 266.

CHILDE HAROLD: CANTO THE FOURTH

Extracts from the Letter of Dedication to John Hobhouse:
"After an interval of eight years between the composition of the first and last cantos of *Childe Harold*, the conclusion of the poem is about to be submitted to the public. In parting with so old a friend, it is not extraordinary that I should recur to one still older and better, —to one who has beheld the birth and death of the other, and to whom I am far more indebted for the social advantages of an enlightened friendship, than—though not ungrateful—I can, or could be, to *Childe Harold*, for any public favour reflected through the poem on the poet,—to one, whom I have known long, and accompanied far, whom I have found wakeful over my sickness and kind in my sorrow, glad in my prosperity and firm in my adversity, true in counsel and trusty in peril,— to a friend often tried and never found wanting; —to yourself.
"In so doing, I recur from fiction to truth; and in dedicating to you, in its complete or at least concluded state, a poetical work which is the longest, the most thoughtful and comprehensive of my compositions, I wish to do honour to myself by the record of many years' intimacy with a man of learning, of talent, of steadiness, and of honour. It is not for minds like ours to give or receive flattery; yet the praises of sincerity have ever been permitted

to the voice of friendship; and it is not for you, nor even for others, but to relieve a heart which has not elsewhere, or lately, been so much accustomed to the encounter of good-will as to withstand the shock firmly, that I thus attempt to commemorate your good quali-ties, or rather the advantages which I have derived from their exertion. Even the recur-rence of the date of this letter, the anniversary of the most unfortunate day of my past exist-ence [his marriage], but which cannot poison my future while I retain the resource of your friendship, and of my own faculties, will hence-forth have a more agreeable recollection for both, inasmuch as it will remind us of this my attempt to thank you for an indefatigable regard, such as few men have experienced, and no one could experience without thinking better of his species and of himself. . . .

"With regard to the conduct of the last canto, there will be found less of the pilgrim than in any of the preceding, and that little slightly, if at all, separated from the author speaking in his own person. The fact is, that I had become weary of drawing a line which every one seemed determined not to perceive. Like the Chinese in Goldsmith's ' Citizen of the World,' whom nobody would believe to be a Chinese, it was in vain that I asserted, and imagined that I had drawn, a distinction between the author and the pilgrim; and the very anxiety to pre-serve this difference, and disappointment at finding it unavailing, so far crushed my efforts in the composition, that I determined to aban-don it altogether—and have done so. The opin-ions which have been, or may be, formed on that subject, are now a matter of indifference; the work is to depend on itself, and not on the writer; and the author, who has no resources in his own mind beyond the reputation, tran-sient or permanent, which is to arise from his literary efforts, deserves the fate of authors."

8. *winged Lion's marble piles.* The winged lion was the symbol of St. Mark, the patron saint of Venice. Several statues of the Lion stand in the city, placed on the top of tall, slender shafts of marble. The most conspicuous is near the Campanile in the Piazza San Marco.

10–11. *She looks a sea Cybele, fresh from ocean.* "Sabellicus, describing the appearance of Ven-ice, has made use of the above image, which would not be poetical were it not true.—'Quo fit ut qui superne urbem contempletur, turri-tam telluris imaginem medio Oceano figuratam se putet inspicere.' [By which it happens that he who gazes upon the city from above believes that he is looking upon an illusion of land crowned with towers in mid-ocean.]

19. *Tasso's echoes are no more.* "The well-known song of the gondoliers, of alternate stanzas from Tasso's *Jerusalem*, had died with

the independence of Venice. Editions of the poem, with the original on one column, and the Venetian variations on the other, as sung by the boatmen, were once common, and are still to be found." (More, Cambridge ed., p. 1008.)

31. *dogeless city.* The ruler of Venice was called the Doge until the extinction of the Venetian Republic. See note on Wordsworth's *On the Extinction of the Venetian Republic,* above.

34. *Pierre.* A character in Otway's *Venice Pre-served.* This play, written and first played in 1682, was revived at least as late as 1845. Roden Noel asserts that Byron was certainly indebted to this play in his *Marino Faliero.*

86. *Sparta hath many a worthier son.* "The answer of the mother of Brasidas, the Lace-dæmonian general, to the strangers who praised the memory of her son."

563. *Niobe.* Niobe had boasted that, with her seven sons and seven daughters, she was greater than Latona who had only two children, Apollo and Diana. The gods killed all her children and, stricken with grief, Niobe was turned to stone within and without, but her tears con-tinued to flow in never-ending grief.

567. *Scipios' tomb.* This tomb had been dis-covered and plundered in 1780.

591. *trebly hundred triumphs.* Byron cites his authorities for the statement that there were 320 triumphs celebrated at Rome.

600. *Sylla.* Sylla brought his eastern campaign to a conclusion before returning to Rome at the time (86 B.C.) his enemies were chosen consuls.

624. *day of double victory and death.* The third of September, on which day Cromwell won the victories of Dunbar (1650) and Worcester (1651), and on which day he died (1658).

644. *thunder-stricken nurse.* "The bronze statue of the wolf which nursed Romulus and Remus was, according to Cicero, struck by lightning. The present statue is of doubtful origin." (More, Cambridge Edition.)

1188. *Awake! thou shalt, and must.* Byron re-fers to this invocation of Nemesis in a letter to Lady Byron at the time of Sir Samuel Romilly's suicide. (See text p. 393, especially col. 2, ll. 13–15.)

1620. *there let him lay.* Byron on several oc-casions is careless in his use of the word "lay," and the fact that it is here used as a rhyme word emphasizes the error. See Swinburne's general comment in the introductory material to this poem, p. 855 above.

Page 274.   MANFRED

The first two acts were written in Switzerland in 1816, the third in Venice early the following year. Byron was obliged to rewrite practically the whole of the third act, and the poem finally was published in June, 1817.

See the introductory material to *Childe Harold,* especially the extract from Professor Grierson's article.

Much has been written about Byron's possible indebtedness to Marlowe and Goethe in this poem. Byron disclaimed any knowledge of Marlowe but said that once "Monk" Lewis had translated most of Goethe's *Faust* to him orally. Goethe, in a review of *Manfred* published in 1820, seemed to think Byron had taken much from him but had made it his own. Goethe said in part: "Byron's tragedy, *Manfred,* was to me a wonderful phenomenon, and one that closely touched me. This singularly intellectual poet has taken my *Faustus* to himself, and extracted from it the strangest nourishment for his hypochondriac humor. He has made use of the impelling principles in his own way, for his own purposes, so that no one of them remains the same; and it is particularly on this account that I cannot enough admire his genius. The whole is in this way so completely formed anew that it would be an interesting task for the critic to point out, not only the alterations he has made, but their degree of resemblance with, or dissimilarity to, the original; in the course of which I cannot deny that the gloomy heat of an unbounded and exuberant despair becomes at last oppressive to us. Yet is the dissatisfaction we feel always connected with esteem and admiration." Of the soliloquy beginning "We are the fools of time and terror" (II, II, 164), Goethe said, "Hamlet's soliloquy appears improved upon here"—which is praise indeed!

50. *First Spirit.* The spirits who speak represent: first, Air; second, Earth; third, Water; and fourth, Fire—the four elements; the fifth and the sixth are Storm and Darkness and the seventh is Manfred's guiding star, a wild comet.

Page 276.

192. *When the moon is on the wave,* et seq. These lines were written in Switzerland in 1816 and sent to England with the third canto of *Childe Harold.* Moore implies that they were written after the breakdown of negotiations for a reconciliation with Lady Byron and that she was in the poet's mind when he wrote.

Page 277.

250-1. *compel Thyself to be thy proper Hell!* This motivating idea runs through the whole drama and its significance should be noted.

Page 280.

8. *As told in the Apocalypse.* "And I looked, and behold a pale horse: and his name that sat on him was Death, and Hell followed with him. And power was given unto them over the fourth part of the earth, to kill with sword,

and with hunger, and with death, and with the beasts of the earth." (Revelation 6: 8.)

Page 281.

93. *Eros and Anteros, at Gadara.* Byron in his note gives as the source of this line an account in the life of Iamblicus, by Eunapius, in which the philosopher calls up the gods from the fountains named after them. Eros is, of course, the blind god of love; Anteros, his "reputed" brother, was sometimes represented as the avenger of slighted love.

Page 283.

181. *The buried Prophet.* "And Saul disguised himself, and put on other raiment, and he went, and two men with him, and they came to the woman by night: and he said, I pray thee, divine unto me by the familiar spirit, and bring me *him* up, whom I shall name unto thee. And the woman said unto him, Behold, thou knowest what Saul hath done, how he hath cut off those that have familiar spirits, and the wizards, out of the land: wherefore then layest thou a snare for my life, to cause me to die? And Saul sware to her by the LORD, saying, *As* the LORD liveth, there shall no punishment happen to thee for this thing. Then said the woman, Whom shall I bring up unto thee? And he said, Bring me up Samuel. And when the woman saw Samuel, she cried with a loud voice: and the woman spake to Saul, saying, Why hast thou deceived me? for thou *art* Saul. And the king said unto her, Be not afraid: for what sawest thou? And the woman said unto Saul, I saw gods ascending out of the earth. And he said unto her, What form *is* he of? And she said, An old man cometh up; and he *is* covered with a mantle. And Saul perceived that it *was* Samuel, and he stooped with *his* face to the ground, and bowed himself. And Samuel said to Saul, Why hast thou disquieted me, to bring me up? And Saul answered, I am sore distressed; for the Philistines make war against me, and God is departed from me, and answereth me no more, neither by prophets, nor by dreams: therefore I have called thee, that thou mayest make known unto me what I shall do." (I Samuel 28: 8–15).

182. *the Spartan Monarch,* et seq. See Plutarch's life of Cimon. Pausanias murdered Cleonice by mistake in the night. The deed haunted him until he invoked her spirit and was told that he would soon be delivered from all his troubles. Death delivered him soon after. See l. 191.

Page 287.

13. *Kalon.* The highest good of human existence.

19. *the abbot of St. Maurice.* See I, 1, 250-1.

Manfred feels that the spiritual struggle is entirely within himself, and that there can be no earthly intermediary, as the following lines show.

Page 289.

5–6. *Of undiseased mankind . . . angels.* "And it came to pass, when men began to multiply on the face of the earth, and daughters were born unto them, That the sons of God saw the daughters of men that they *were* fair; and they took them wives of all which they chose. And the LORD said, My spirit shall not always strive with man, for that he also *is* flesh: yet his days shall be an hundred and twenty years. There were giants in the earth in those days; and also after that, when the sons of God came in unto the daughters of men, and they bare *children* to them, the same *became* mighty men which *were* of old, men of renown. And God saw that the wickedness of man *was* great in the earth, and *that* every imagination of the thoughts of his hearts *was* only evil continually. And it repented the LORD that he had made man on the earth, and it grieved him at his heart." (Genesis 6 : 1–4.)

Page 292.   DON JUAN

Canto I was written in September, 1818; Canto II in December of that year and January of the following. They were published in July, 1819. Cantos III, IV, and V were published in August, 1821. Byron remained intermittently occupied on the poem thereafter and carried a few stanzas of a seventeenth canto with him when he went to Greece. At one time he gave up the poem altogether on the plea of the Countess Guiccioli. For an explanation of why she objected see Byron's letter (text p. 402, col. 1, l. 1 ff.). He returned to the poem, however. The student should consult certain references to *Don Juan* in the text (p. 393, col. 2, l. 32; p. 396, col. 1, l. 24; p. 398, col. 2, l. 14; p. 399, col. 2, l. 45). All of these are important. That Byron really had a coherent plan in mind when he began is doubtful. The poem seems to have grown under his hand. P. E. More says, "In one sense Don Juan is a satire, to many critics the greatest satire ever written; but it is something still more than that. It is the epic of modern life." With an astounding versatility and an astounding energy and all Europe for a stage, Byron launches his young hero on his way and the result is one of the great poems of the century.

Sir Arthur Quiller-Couch says of *Don Juan:* "And so—as it might seem by felicitous chance, out of an experiment in *Beppo*—but truly by destiny—all his fortunes with his insurgent wrath against them, his knowledge of men and cities, his fatal sensual half-knowledge of women, with that noble damning core of true intuition ever torturing our Lucifer wide-eyed for the best thing missed, for salvation lost— all his facility of wit, his perfectness in the note of conversation among well-bred men and women; his own very considerable grasp of politics; his sense of Europe; his sense of the hypocrisy underlying all received government, all received religion; his sense of seas and mountains and vast natural forces amid which man may be viewed at will as a controlling engineer or a derisory ape;—all these (I say) in the end miraculously met together, found the measure and stanza exactly suitable to them and to Byron's genius, and combined in *Don Juan.*

"I believe *Don Juan* will some day be recognized for one of the world's few greatest epics. I am sure that it is, after *Paradise Lost*, our second English Epic. *Don Juan* has this, at any rate, in common with the *Iliad* itself: it belongs with heart and soul to its age—a remarkable age, too, in human history—and it paints that age with such lively intensity, with such a sweep of power, that no generation to come will ever be able to dispute the picture. Still less will anyone dispute the play of life in the story, with its multitudinous variety of movement. It undulates like an ocean sweeping the reader along upon its waves, carrying him from shores familiar to shores romantic, from mart to mart of traffic, passion, intrigue, to shipwreck him but—as Odysseus was shipwrecked long ago—to leave him stretched, with the brine on his nakedness, on sands in the bland sunlight, caressed by soft winds, gazing up faint and half awake into the eyes of young love, innocent and startled. . . .

"Those who approach *Don Juan* with preconceived notions of what an Epic should be, may deny it the title if they will. *I* call it an Epic: but, Epic or not (as we consent or refuse to be slaves to definition), it is a tremendous poem. If I hesitate at all to commend it to the young, I should hesitate not in prudery—for youth, the natural time of temptation, is the time to meet it and be trained to overcome it. I should hesitate rather because the poem appeals less to the young than to intelligent and mature men and women who (as Nichol puts it) 'have grown weary of mere sentiment, and yet retain enough of sympathetic feeling to desire at times to recall it.' The poem, in short, addresses middle age, as Montaigne's Essays address middle age. If we are wise we shall come to them both at last.

"Anyhow (to quote Nichol again) 'in writing *Don Juan*, Byron attempted something that had never been done before, and his genius so chimed with his enterprise that it need never be done again.' Like many another epical undertaking—the *Faerie Queene* for example—it survives as a broken pillar on the author's grave. Byron himself, even in the act of writing it, scarcely suspected that this was his grand charge against the forts of hypocrisy and despotism. He dreamed of action: and the circumstances of his death have clouded in the biographies the glory of the greater performance. He had written:

And I will war, at least in words (and—should
    My chance so happen—deeds), with all who
        war
With Thought;—and of Thought's foes by far
    most rude
    Tyrants and sycophants have been and are,
I know not who may conquer; if I could
    Have such a prescience, it should be no bar
To this my plain, sworn downright detestation
Of every despotism in every nation.

The war against the forts of folly, the enemies of Thought, is—alas! must be—unending. But, for Byron's temporal victory, seek in *Don Juan*. *Don Juan* was his Heights of Abraham: and falling, he passes into a splendor of memory. "You know the end: how he died as a man should...." (*Studies in Literature*, Second Series, pp. 21–22, 26.)

The famous French critic, Taine, in his discussion of Byron's work, has the following to say of *Don Juan:*
"Is not this a singular apology? Does it not aggravate the fault? Let us wait; we know not yet the whole venom of the book: together with Juan there are Donna Julia, Haidee, Gulbeyaz, Dudu, and many more. It is here the diabolical poet digs in his sharpest claw, and he takes care to dig it into our weakest side. What will the clergymen and white-chokered reviewers say? For, to speak the truth, there is no preventing it: we must read on, in spite of ourselves. Twice or three times following we meet here with *happiness;* and when I say happiness, I mean profound and complete happiness—not mere voluptuousness, not obscene gaiety; we are far removed from the nicely-written ribaldry of Dorat, and the unbridled license of Rochester. Beauty is here, southern beauty, resplendent and harmonious, spread over everything, over the luminous sky, the calm scenery, corporal nudity, artlessness of heart. Is there a thing it does not deify? All sentiments are exalted under its hands. What was gross becomes noble; even in the nocturnal adventure in the seraglio, which seems worthy of Faublas, poetry embellishes licentiousness. The girls are lying in the large silent apartment, like precious flowers brought from all climates into a conservatory.... What will become now of Puritanic prudery? Can the proprieties prevent beauty from being beautiful? Will you condemn a picture of Titian for its nudity?

What gives value to human life, and nobility to human nature, if not the power of attaining delicious and sublime emotions? We have just had one—one worthy of a painter; is it not worth that of an alderman? Shall we refuse to acknowledge the divine because it appears in art and enjoyment, and not only in conscience and action? There is a world beside ours, and a civilisation beside ours; our rules are narrow, and our pedantry tyrannic; the human plant can be otherwise developed than in our compartments and under our snows, and the fruits it will then bear will not be less precious. We must confess it, since we relish them when they are offered to us. Who has read the love of Haidee, and has had any other thought than to envy and pity her? ...
"Besides British cant, there is universal hypocrisy; besides English pedantry, Byron wars against human roguery. Here is the general aim of the poem, and to this his character and genius tended. His great and gloomy dreams of juvenile imagination have vanished; experience has come; he knows man now; and what is man, once known? does the sublime abound in him? Do we think that the grand sentiments —those of Childe Harold, for instance,—are the ordinary course of life? The truth is, that man employs most of his time in sleeping, dining, yawning, working like a horse, amusing himself like an ape. According to Byron, he is an animal; except for a few minutes, his nerves, his blood, his instincts lead him. Routine works over it all, necessity whips him on, the animal advances. As the animal is proud, and moreover imaginative, it pretends to be marching for its own pleasure, that there is no whip, that at all events this whip rarely touches its flanks, that at least its stoic back can make-believe that it does not feel it. It thinks that it is decked with the most splendid trappings, and thus struts on with measured steps, fancying that it carries relics and treads on carpets and flowers, whilst in reality it tramples in the mud, and carries with it the stains and bad smells of every dunghill. What a pastime to touch its mangy back, to set before its eyes the sacks full of flour which it carries, and the goad which makes it go! What a pretty farce! It is the eternal farce; and not a sentiment thereof but provides him with an act.... You think yourself rational, humane; I admit it for to-day; you have dined, and you are comfortable in a pleasant room. Your human mechanism works without getting into disorder, because the wheels are oiled and well regulated; but place it in a shipwreck, a battle, let the failing or the plethora of blood for an instant derange the chief pieces, and we shall see you howling or drivelling like a madman or an idiot. Civilisation, education, reason, health, cloak us in their smooth and polished cases;

let us tear them away one by one, or all to-gether, and we laugh to see the brute, who is lying at the bottom. . . . These are the words of a sceptic, even of a cynic. Sceptic and cynic, it is in this he ends. Sceptic through misan-thropy, cynic through bravado, a sad and com-bative humour always impels him; southern voluptuousness has not conquered him; he is only an epicurean through contradiction and for a moment:

'Let us have wine and women, mirth and
    laughter,
Sermons and soda-water the day after.
Man, being reasonable must get drunk;
The best of life is but intoxication.'

We see clearly that he is always the same, going to extremes and unhappy, bent on de-stroying himself. His *Don Juan*, also, is a de-bauchery; in it he diverts himself outrageously at the expense of all respectable things, as a bull in a china shop. He is always violent, and often ferocious; a sombre imagination inter-sperses his love stories with horrors leisurely enjoyed, the despair and famine of shipwrecked men, and the emaciation of the raging skeletons feeding on each other. He laughs at it horribly, like Swift; he jests over it like Voltaire. . . . With his specimens in hand, Byron follows with a surgeon's exactness all the stages of death, gorging, rage, madness, howling, ex-haustion, stupor; he wishes to touch and ex-hibit the naked and ascertained truth, the last grotesque and hideous element of humanity. Let us read again the assault on Ismail,—the grape-shot and the bayonet, the street mas-sacres, the corpses used as fascines, and the thirty-eight thousand slaughtered Turks. There is blood enough to satiate a tiger, and this blood flows amidst an accompaniment of jests; it is in order to rail at war, and the butcheries dignified with the name of exploits. In this pitiless and universal demolition of all human vanities, what remains? What do we know ex-cept that life is 'a scene of all-confess'd in-anity,' and that men are,

'Dogs, or men!—for I flatter you in saying
That ye are dogs—your betters far—ye may
Read, or read not, what I am now essaying
To show ye what ye are in every way?'

Again, what remains? Himself, he alone, stand-ing amidst all this ruin. It is he who speaks here; his characters are but screens; half the time even he pushes them aside, to occupy the stage. He lavishes upon us his opinions, recollections, anger, tastes; his poem is a con-versation, a confidence, with the ups and downs, the rudeness and freedom of a conver-sation and a confidence, almost like the holo-graphic journal, in which, by night, at his writing-table, he opened his heart and dis-charged his feelings. Never was seen in such a clear glass the birth of lively thought, the tumult of great genius, the inner life of a genuine poet, always impassioned, inexhausti-bly fertile and creative, in whom suddenly, successively, finished and adorned, bloomed all human emotions and ideas,—sad, gay, lofty, low, hustling one another, mutually impeding one another, like swarms of insects who go humming and feeding on flowers and in the mud. He may say what he likes; willingly or unwillingly we listen to him; let him leap from sublime to burlesque, we leap with him. He has so much wit, so fresh a wit, so sudden, so biting, such a prodigality of knowledge, ideas, images picked up from the four corners of the horizon, in heaps and masses, that we are captivated, transported beyond all limits; we cannot dream of resisting. Too vigorous, and hence unbridled,—that is the word which ever recurs when we speak of Byron; too vigorous against others and himself, and so unbridled, that after spending his life in setting the world at defiance, and his poetry in depicting revolt, he can only find the fulfilment of his talent and the satisfaction of his heart, in a poem waging war on all human and poetic conventions. When a man lives in such a manner he must be great, but he becomes also morbid. There is a malady of heart and mind in the style of *Don Juan*, as in Swift. When a man jests amidst his tears, it is because he has a poisoned imagination. This kind of laughter is a spasm, and we see in one man a hardening of the heart, or madness; in another, excitement or disgust. Byron was exhausted, at least the poet was exhausted in him. The last cantos of *Don Juan* drag: the gaiety became forced, the escapades became digressions; the reader began to be bored. A new kind of poetry, which he had attempted, had given way in his hands: in the drama he only attained to powerful declamation, his characters had no life; when he forsook poetry, poetry forsook him; he went to Greece in search of action, and only found death." (H. A. Taine, *History of English Literature*, Bk. IV, Ch. II.)

Page 292.   DEDICATION

3–5. *Tory at Last . . . Epic Renegade.* See the introductory material to *The Vision of Judg-ment* for an account of Byron's relations with Southey (p. 866 below). See also the introduc-tory note on Southey (text p. 782).
6. *Lakers.* The "Lake Poets," so-called from their long connection with the Lake District in northern England. Wordsworth, Coleridge, and Southey were the most important figures of the group.
16. *I wish he would explain his Explanation.*

A reference to the *Biographia Literaria*. Others have shared Byron's feeling.

35. *Keswick*. In the Lake District. There Southey lived for many years.

46. *his place in the Excise*. "Wordsworth's place may be in the Customs—it is, I think, in that or the Excise—besides another at Lord Lonsdale's table, where this poetical charlatan and political parasite licks up the crumbs with a hardened alacrity; the converted Jacobin having long subsided into the clownish sycophant of the worst prejudices of the aristocracy." (Byron's note.)

55. *Scott, Rogers, Campbell, Moore, and Crabbe.* See also Byron's comment in his letters (text p. 391, col. 2, l. 37 et seq.; and p. 392, col. 1, l. 47 et seq.).

86. *And heartless daughters.* "'Pale, but not cadaverous:'—Milton's two elder daughters are said to have robbed him of his books, besides cheating and plaguing him in the economy of his house, etc. His feelings on such an outrage, both as a parent and a scholar, must have been singularly painful. Hayley compares him to Lear." (Byron's note.)

88. *The intellectual eunuch Castlereagh.*

'Would *he* subside into a hackney Laureate—
A scribbling, self-sold, soul-hired, scorn'd Iscariot?'

I doubt if 'Laureate' and 'Iscariot' be good rhymes, but must say, as Ben Jonson did to Sylvester, who challenged him to rhyme with—

I, John Sylvester
Lay with your sister.

Jonson answered,—'I, Ben Jonson, lay with your wife.' Sylvester answered,—'That is not rhyme.'—'No,' said Ben Jonson; 'but it is *true*.' (Byron's note.)

Castlereagh was the leader of the Tories, unalterably opposed to the revolutionary spirit, and as such Byron attacked him. In the preface to the sixth canto after Castlereagh's death, Byron has this to say: ". . . Had that person's oligarchy died with him, they [lines against him] would have been suppressed; as it is, I am aware of nothing in the manner of his death or of his life to prevent the free expression of the opinions of all whom his whole existence was consumed in endeavouring to enslave. That he was an amiable man in *private* life, may or may not be true; but with this the public have nothing to do; and as to lamenting his death, it will be time enough when Ireland has ceased to mourn for his birth. As a minister, I, for one of millions, looked upon him as the most despotic in intention, and the weakest in intellect, that ever tyrannised over a country."

102. *Ixion*. His punishment in hell was to be fixed to a ceaselessly revolving wheel.

117. *Eutropius*. A eunuch, minister at the court of Arcadius, referred to in Gibbon.

132. *"buff and blue."* The Whig colors.

136. *Ultra-Julian*. Byron's note makes it clear that he is referring to Julian the Apostate.

Page 295.   CANTO THE FIRST

41. *"in medias res."* In the middle of things. According to the rules of pseudo-classical poetic theory an epic was supposed to begin in the middle and tell its story backwards.

68. *Gothic gentlemen of Spain.* The Spanish aristocracy traced its descent from the Visigothic conquerors, much as the English aristocracy was inclined to trace back to the Norman Conquest.

73. *mother was a learned lady.* The portrait of Donna Inez is supposed to be a satire on Lady Byron.

85. *Feinagle's were an useless art.* Professor Feinagle in 1812 had delivered a course of lectures on Mnemonics.

116. *Sir Samuel Romilly.* See Byron's comments on Romilly's suicide in his letters (text p. 393, col. 1, l. 21 et seq.; and p. 398, col. 1, l. 8 et seq.).

122. *Miss Edgeworth's novels.* Some of Miss Edgeworth's shorter stories were collected in a volume with the repulsive title, *The Parent's Assistant*, which indicates the moral tone of the works to which Byron is referring.

136. *"incomparable oil," Macassar!* Macassar oil was used in hairdressing. It was advertised as having "des vertus incomparables."

209. *call'd some druggists and physicians.* Lady Byron, after she returned to her parents, had Byron watched to establish his sanity.

288. *death or Doctors' Commons.* Death or divorce.

333. *Longinus tells us.* Byron's note refers to Longinus, section 10.

351. *all in an appendix.* "Fact! There is, or was, such an edition, with all the obnoxious epigrams of Martial placed by themselves at the end." (Byron's note.)

376. *envy his transgressions.* "See his Confessions, l.i.c.ix. By the representation which Saint Augustine gives of himself in his youth, it is easy to see that he was what we should call a rake. He avoided the school as the plague; he loved nothing but gaming and public shows; he robbed his father of everything he could find; he invented a thousand lies to escape the rod, which they were obliged to make use of to punish his irregularities." (Byron's note.)

508. *St. Anthony to reason.* "For the particulars of St. Anthony's recipe for hot blood in cold weather, see Mr. Alban Butler's 'Lives of the Saints.'" (Byron's note.)

567. *Armida's fairy art.* A reference to the episode of Armida and Rinaldo in Tasso's *Gerusalemme Liberata.*

598. *have made a Tarquin quake.* Tarquinius Superbus was the last of the Tarquin kings of Rome who ruled before the establishment of the Republic. He is notable in legend for the "rape of Lucrece" in spite of her entreaties. See Shakespeare's poem.

701. *The bard I quote from.* Byron was quoting from memory from Campbell's *Gertrude of Wyoming*, a very dull poem much esteemed in its own day.

829. *Anacreon Moore.* Anacreon was one of the great lyric poets of ancient Greece; Thomas Moore had published his oriental poem, *Lalla Rookh*, in 1817.

1177. *Cortejo.* The Spanish equivalent of the Italian *Cavalier Servente.*

1183-4. *Count O'Reilly, Who took Algiers.* "Donna Julia here made a mistake. Count O'Reilly did not take Algiers—but Algiers very nearly took him: he and his army and fleet retreated with great loss, and not much credit, from before that city, in the year 1775." (Byron's note.)

1328. *Clarence in his Malmsey butt.* The Duke of Clarence was very fond of Malmsey wine. Given a choice of the method by which he was to die, he chose to be drowned in a butt of Malmsey. See Shakespeare's *Richard III*, 1, 4.

1772. *The world will find thee after many days.* Southey, *The Lay of the Laureate*, L'Envoy, ll. 1-4.

Page 321.   CANTO THE SECOND

56. *Venetian Fazzioli.* "*Fazzioli*—literally, the little handkerchiefs—the veils most availing of St. Mark." (Byron's note.)

194. *licentiate Pedrillo.* The licentiate in certain continental universities was a stage in academic advancement between the bachelor's degree and the doctorate.

202. *it blew a gale.* Byron had read much of ships and wrecks and had been in storms at sea. He always defended the accuracy of his account in this canto. "With regard to the charges about the Shipwreck, I think that I told you and Mr. Hobhouse, years ago, that there was not a circumstance of it not taken from fact; not, indeed, from any single shipwreck, but all from actual facts of different wrecks." (Byron, Letter to Murray, August 23, 1821.)

295. *Salamanca.* Site of one of the chief universities of Spain.

296. *Sancho Panca.* The plump and practical-minded squire of Don Quixote who was led by his master into many disasters.

391-2. *twelve days had Fear Been their familiar.* A familiar is an attendant spirit but the connotation of the word is evil. According to demonology witches had attendant spirits who took animal forms—a cat, a hedgehog, etc.

Page 331.

658-9. *Ugolino condescends To eat the head of his arch-enemy.* Dante in the thirty-third canto of the *Inferno* comes on Ugolino, gnawing the skull of Ruggieri. Ruggieri had betrayed Ugolino in life, imprisoned him with his sons and grandsons, and finally ordered the keys to the tower thrown into the river so that the prisoners starved to death. Ugolino concludes his narrative to Dante as follows: "After we had come to the fourth day, Gaddo threw himself stretched out at my feet, saying: 'My father, why dost thou not help me?' Here he died: and, even as thou seest me, I saw the three fall one by one between the fifth day and the sixth; then I betook me, already blind, to groping over each, and for two days I called them after they were dead: then fasting was more powerful than woe."

"When he had said this, with his eyes twisted, he seized again the wretched skull with his teeth, that were strong as a dog's upon the bone." (Norton's translation.)

840. *Leander, Mr. Ekenhead, and I did.* The story of Hero and Leander was one of the famous love stories of antiquity. Leander swam the Hellespont to be with his lady love in her tower on the opposite bank, slipping away before dawn. He was drowned on the return journey. (See Keats's *Sonnet on a Picture of Leander*, text p. 560; extract from Hood's *Hero and Leander*, text p. 695. There are numerous literary treatments of the story, the most notable being Christopher Marlowe's great but unfinished *Hero and Leander*.)

Byron with his flair for drama swam the Hellespont on his first Near Eastern trip.

Says Ethel Mayne, rather exasperated by the whole performance and the dispute which arose afterwards, "He did, and so did Mr. Ekenhead, the officer of the English frigate *Salsette;* and Byron was one hour and ten minutes in the water, and Ekenhead five minutes less; and it was more than four miles, and the current was very strong and cold, and they were not fatigued but a little chilled. It was the famous Swim across the Hellespont, and Byron (literally) never after that morning wrote a letter home without describing it." (Mayne, *Byron*, p. 115.) The dispute arose because the currents *are* strong in the Hellespont and the question was raised as to whether Byron hadn't swum it the easiest way.

1037. "*vous.*" Intellect; intelligence.

1096. *my grand-dad's "Narrative."* A *Narrative of the Honourable John Byron*, which was an account of his journey around the world.

1234. *old fable of the Minotaur.* Of Minos II, "it is related that when aiming at the crown of Crete, he boasted of his power to obtain by prayer whatever he desired, and as a test, he implored Neptune to send him a bull for sacrifice. The bull appeared; but Minos, astonished at its great beauty, declined to sacrifice the brute. Neptune, therefore incensed, drove the bull wild,—worse still, drove Pasiphaë, the wife of Minos, wild with love of it. The wonderful brute was finally caught and overcome by Hercules, who rode it through the waves to Greece. But its offspring, the Minotaur, a monster, bull-headed and man-bodied, remained, for many a day, a terror to Crete,—till finally a famous artificer, Dædalus, constructed for him a labyrinth, with passages and turnings winding in and about like the river Mæander, so that whoever was inclosed in it might by no means find his way out. The Minotaur, roaming therein, lived upon human victims." (Gayley, *Classic Myths*.)

1608. *play the devil, and then write a novel.* A reference to Lady Caroline Lamb and her novel *Glenarvon*, in which she gave her story of her affair with Byron. For Byron's comment on *Glenarvon* at the time of its appearance see text p. 389, col. 1, l. 43 et seq. Especially see Letter viii, text p. 378, a letter written at the time the affair was still "on."

Page 348.

FROM CANTO III: THE ISLES OF GREECE

1. *The isles of Greece.* See note immediately following. This poem is line-numbered as a complete unit in itself. It follows stanza lxxxvi of the narrative text.

Page 349.   FROM CANTO III: AVE MARIA

801. *T'our tale,—The feast was over.* Haidee had installed Juan in her father's place as master of the island, believing her father killed on his piratical expedition. There was music and feasting on the island and open hospitality. The song, *The Isles of Greece*, was sung at the feast. Through all this the young lovers have little attention for anything but one another. The *Ave Maria* stanzas conclude the feasting scene. Lambro, Haidee's father, is not dead and returns with his men. The consequences may be mildly described as—"regrettable." Juan is overpowered (and subsequently sold as a slave); Haidee dies of a broken heart.

Page 350.   THE VISION OF JUDGMENT

Character and conviction threw Southey and Byron into opposing political camps. Circumstance added a ferociously bitter personal animosity. The circumstance may be given as stated by Mayne:

". . . After Lewis came Hobhouse and Scrope Davies. Byron went with them and Polidori to Chamounix.

"The Shelley party had made the same tour in July, and it was then that Shelley made the famous 'atheist' entry in the hotel-album at Montanvert. Hobhouse said that Byron, showing him the words, observed: 'Do you not think I shall do Shelley a service by scratching this out?'—and forthwith defaced the entry; but evidently not with sufficient care, for in 1817 a second poet saw it at Montanvert. This was Robert Southey, Poet Laureate; and Southey thought it worth while to 'transcribe the names, the avowal, and the comment' (he says nothing of any defacement), and to speak of the circumstance on his return. Byron heard of this, and heard too that Southey had said that he (Byron) and Shelley were, during the Genevan sojourn, living in 'promiscuous intercourse with two sisters.'

"To anticipate a little, in the interest of coherence:—

"'He is a burning liar!' wrote Byron at once to Murray, and enclosed in a parcel of MS. the Dedication to Southey of the first canto of *Don Juan*. Shelley, who was then living in Italy, had heard Byron read this piece, and described it in a letter to Peacock as more like a mixture of wormwood and verdigrease [sic] than satire. It did not appear when *Don Juan* was published on July 15, 1819. 'As the Poem is to be published anonymously, *omit* the Dedication. I won't attack the dog in the dark.' Southey, who had had absolutely nothing to do with spreading the incest slander, heard of the Dedication and its character; and when King George III died in January, 1820, and he as Laureate sat down to his task of composing a funeral ode, he seized the occasion to compose a preface also, in which he 'repaid some of his obligations to Lord Byron by a few comments on *Don Juan*.' Southey's *Vision of Judgement* was published on April 11, 1821, with its preface." (Mayne, *Byron*, p. 279.)

The following extracts are from Southey's Preface:

". . . Would that this literary intolerance were under the influence of a saner judgment, and regarded the morals more than the manner of a composition; the spirit rather than the form! Would that it were directed against those monstrous combinations of horrors and mockery, lewdness and impiety, with which English poetry has, in our days, first been polluted! For more than half a century English literature had been distinguished by its moral purity, the effect, and, in its turn, the cause of an improvement in national manners. A father might, without apprehension of evil, have put into the hands of his children any book which issued from the press, if it did not bear, either in its title-page or frontispiece, manifest signs that it was intended as furniture for the brothel. There was no danger in any work which bore the name of a respectable publisher, or was to be procured at any respectable bookseller's. This was particularly the case with regard to our poetry. It is now no longer so; and woe to those by whom the offence cometh! The greater the talents of the offender, the greater is his guilt, and the more enduring will be his shame. . . . "The publication of a lascivious book is one of the worst offences that can be committed against the well-being of society. It is a sin, to the consequences of which no limits can be assigned, and those consequences no after-repentance in the writer can counteract. Whatever remorse of conscience he may feel when his hour comes (and come it must!) will be of no avail. The poignancy of a death-bed repentance cannot cancel one copy of the thousands which are sent abroad; and as long as it continues to be read, so long is he the pander of posterity, and so long is he heaping up guilt upon his soul in perpetual accumulation. "These remarks are not more severe than the offence deserves, even when applied to those immoral writers who have not been conscious of any evil intention in their writings, who would acknowledge a little levity, a little warmth of coloring, and so forth, in that sort of language with which men gloss over their favorite vices, and deceive themselves. What, then, should be said of those for whom the thoughtlessness and inebriety of wanton youth can no longer be pleaded, but who have written in sober manhood and with deliberate purpose? —Men of diseased hearts and depraved imaginations, who, forming a system of opinions to suit their own unhappy course of conduct, have rebelled against the holiest ordinances of human society, and hating that revealed religion which, with all their efforts and bravadoes, they are unable entirely to disbelieve, labor to make others as miserable as themselves, by infecting them with a moral virus that eats into the soul! The school which they have set up may properly be called the Satanic school; for though their productions breathe the spirit of Belial in their lascivious parts, and the spirit of Moloch in those loathsome images of atrocities and horrors which they delight to represent, they are more especially characterized by a Satanic spirit of pride and audacious impiety, which still betrays the wretched feeling of hopelessness wherewith it is allied. . . . "No apology is offered for these remarks. The subject led to them; and the occasion of introducing them was willingly taken, because it is the duty of every one, whose opinion may have any influence, to expose the drift and aim of those writers who are laboring to subvert the foundations of human virtue and of human happiness."

Byron replied to Southey by a note in the Appendix to *The Two Foscari*, published Dec. 11,

1821. To continue with Mayne's account: ". . . Southey answered in *The Courier* for January 6, 1822, giving 'a direct and positive denial' to the charge of slander; and in doing so expressed himself very caustically. He had 'made no inquiry concerning Byron when he was abroad, because he felt no curiosity. . . .' As regarded the entry in the hotel-album, 'the gentleman in question would not have thought himself slandered by having that recorded of him which he has so often recorded of himself.' He then pointed out that these were side-issues; and that *his* charges of impiety, lewdness, and so forth, in *Don Juan*, had not been answered, and were unanswerable. Lord Byron had called him a scribbler of all work. 'I will tell Lord Byron what I have *not* scribbled, what kind of work I have *not* done'—and it must be allowed that Southey scores heavily in this enumeration. He turned next to the work he *had* done, and in this sort pointed with exultation to the phrase Satanic School. 'I have sent a stone from my sling which has smitten their Goliath in the forehead. I have fastened his name upon the gibbet for reproach and ignominy as long as it shall endure. Take it down who can!'

"Medwin, in the Conversations, describes the effect of reading this on Byron. 'He looked perfectly awful; his colour changed almost prismatically; his lips were as pale as death. He said not a word. He threw down the paper, and asked me if I thought there was anything of a personal nature . . . that demanded satisfaction; as if there was, he would instantly set off for England, and call Southey to account. . . . I said that as to personality, his own expressions were much stronger than any in the letter before me. He paused a moment, and said, "Perhaps you are right; but I will consider of it. You have not seen MY *Vision of Judgment*. I wish I had a copy to show you; but the only one I have is in London. I had almost decided not to publish it, but it shall now go forth to the world." '" (Mayne, *Byron*, p. 280.)

The attention of the student is called to the note on the Concept of Liberty from Brandes quoted in connection with Coleridge's *France: An Ode*, to the second and third paragraphs of the introductory note on Southey (p. 782 of the text), and to the extract from Southey's *A Vision of Judgement* (p. 787 of the text). Students may also consult Byron's Preface to his poem (easily available in the Oxford edition, and most complete editions). A comparison of Byron's Preface with that of Southey quoted above, shows that Byron for once was having all the worst of it, in prose. Byron's Preface was signed "Quevedo Redivivus"— meaning roughly "Quevedo Alive Again!"

Quevedo was a Spanish satirist who was also a noted duellist. In the prose duel Byron as Quevedo Redivivus did not match Southey, but in poetry he had his revenge.

A recent scholar, writing of Byron as a satirist, says of this poem:

"Southey's name is mentioned only once before the 35th stanza of Byron's poem, but from that point until the conclusion the work deals entirely with him. These stanzas constitute what is probably Byron's happiest effort at personal satire. For once he did not act in haste, but carefully matured his project, studied its execution, and permitted his first impulsive anger to moderate into scorn. With due attention to craftsmanship, he surveyed and annihilated his enemy, laughing at him contemptuously and making every stroke tell. It should be observed too that he chose a method largely indirect and dramatic. He did not, as in *English Bards*, merely apply offensive epithets; rather he placed Southey in a ridiculous situation and made him the sport of other characters. The satire, is, therefore, exceedingly effective, since it allows the victim no chance for a reply. By turning the laugh on Southey, Byron closed the controversy by attaining what is probably the most desirable result of purely personal satire—the making an opponent seem not hateful but absurd.

"Byron's poem, however, was something more than a chapter in the satisfaction of a private quarrel. It is also a liberal polemic, assailing not only the whole system of constituted authority in England, but also tyranny and repression wherever they operate. The indictment of George III, which at times approaches sublimity, is in reality directed against the entire reactionary policy of contemporary European statesmen and rulers. The doctrines of the revolutionary Byron, already familiar to us in *Don Juan*, are to be found in the ironic stanzas upon the sumptuous funeral of the king, a passage admired by Goethe; respect for monarchy itself had died out in a nobleman who could say of George's entombment:

'It seem'd the mockery of hell to fold
The rottenness of eighty years in gold.'

With all its broad humor, the satire is aflame with indignation. In this respect the poem performed an important public service. In place of stupid content with things as they were, it offered critical comment on existing conditions, comment somewhat biassed, it is true, but nevertheless in refreshing contrast to the conventional submission of the great majority of the British public." (Claude M. Fuess, *Lord Byron as a Satirist in Verse*, pp. 194–5.)

Southey in his poem makes King George III face the bar of heaven before accusers and absolvers before that happy monarch is admitted to his harp. In full justice to Southey who, as Poet Laureate, was obliged to justify prompt admission, it may be stated that he had no easy task—George III having been insane for much of his reign and not too successful in his saner moments. In justice to Byron as a satirist, attention must be called to his complete success in stealing his enemy's entire machinery of war and turning it to his own purposes.

1. *Saint Peter*. Byron added a postscript to his Preface which may be quoted here.
"P.S.—It is possible that some readers may object, in these objectionable times, to the freedom with which saints, angels, and spiritual persons discourse in this 'Vision.' But, for precedents upon such points, I must refer him to Fielding's *Journey from this World to the next*, and to the Visions of myself, the said Quevedo, in Spanish or translated. The reader is also requested to observe, that no doctrinal tenets are insisted upon or discussed; that the person of the Deity is carefully withheld from sight, which is more than can be said for the Laureate, who hath thought proper to make him talk, not 'like a school divine,' but like the unscholarlike Mr. Southey. The whole action passes on the outside of heaven; and Chaucer's *Wife of Bath*, Pulci's *Morgante Maggiore*, Swift's *Tale of a Tub*, and the other works above referred to, are cases in point of the freedom with which saints, etc., may be permitted to converse in works not intended to be serious.—Q. R."

5. *Gallic era " eighty-eight."* 1788; a reference to the French Revolution.

55. *Like Saint John's foretold beast.* See Revelation 13.

57. *In the first year of freedom's second dawn.* George III died Jan. 29, 1820. The "stabilization" imposed by the conservative forces after the fall of Napoleon preserved an exterior but there were rumblings beneath the surface. See text (pp. 363–70) for references to revolutionary agitation in 1821, the year in which Byron published this poem.

58–9. *Although no tyrant, one Who shielded tyrants.* The Stuarts who ruled by the "Divine Right of Kings," had been dethroned in 1688 and defeated in the rebellions of 1715 and 1745 when they endeavored to recapture the throne and re-establish the "Divine Right." Byron, a very astute political warrior, keeps clear the constitutional issue settled in 1688 and does so even in the heat of a fierce poem. The King is *not* absolute; he had shielded ministers who tried to be so. See l. 345.

92. *unless he left a German will.* An allusion to the report which had been circulated about

George III, that he had destroyed his father's will. The Georges were German and Kings of Hanover as well as England.

157. *St. Bartholomew*. Historians differ on the manner of St. Bartholomew's martyrdom, Saint Theodore affirming that he was flayed alive. The *Legenda Aurea* states: "But, in fact, the contradiction is only apparent because nothing prevents one from assuming that the saint had first been crucified (head downwards); then, to add to his suffering, had been flayed alive, and had finally been decapitated."

216. *Captain Parry's crew*. Captain Edward Parry made an unsuccessful voyage in 1819–20 in an effort to discover the Northwest Passage.

224. *Johanna Southcote*. An earnest and enthusiastic virgin who developed symptoms of pregnancy. About her collected a group of the devout, awaiting the birth of the second Christ. It turned out that she merely had dropsy. Southey's feelings on finding himself bracketed with her may only be guessed at.

256. *champ clos*. Closed field for a tournament.

260. *"sons of God."* Job 1: 6–7: See the "Prologue in Heaven" of Goethe's *Faust* for a literary use of this idea which Byron expressly puts by.

330. *old, blind, mad, helpless, weak, poor worm*. George III ruled for 60 years (1760–1820) and was insane for a considerable portion of this time. The span of his reign covered both the American and French Revolutions.

345. *a tool from first to last*. See note above on ll. 58–9.

364. *Apicius' board*. Apicius was a noted epicure of the time of Augustus.

377. *Five millions of the primitive*. The primitive Catholic faith which antedated the church of England. Catholics were debarred from the franchise and the holding of certain offices under a settlement dating from the days of Elizabeth. Protestant dissenters from the church of England also suffered from certain restrictions. Pitt prepared a bill which would have raised both Catholic and dissenter to perfect equality of civil rights, but when George III heard of it he exclaimed, "I count any man my personal enemy who proposes any such measure," and Pitt (1801) was forced to resign.

393. *Cerberus*. The watchdog of hell; friendly to those who would enter, but not so friendly to those who wished to depart.

395. *Bedlam*. The hospital in London where lunatics were confined (Hospital of St. Mary of Bethlehem)—hence any lunatic asylum.

426. *gilt key*. Insignia of the lord chamberlain.

471–2. *Jonathan . . . I guess*. Jonathan is the typical American. It is a current superstition in America that no Englishman ever utters a sentence which does not include the words "jolly" and "bully"; similarly it is a superstition in England that no American ever arrives at a period in his speech without saying "I guess." It is interesting to see that the superstition was current as early as 1821 and crept into the works of one of the major English poets. The italics given to the word "our" are ironic. The American citizen felt he owned his president. The British nobleman felt free to insult his king but not to own him.

520. *Jack Wilkes as well as any*. Wilkes was a political leader whose name was anathema to the Tories. He had been expelled from the House of Commons in 1764 (after having been imprisoned as the author of what was before the courts as a "false, scandalous and seditious libel," having been freed on an habeas corpus writ, and after having fled to France) but in 1782 he succeeded in carrying a motion to expunge from the records of the House the resolution under which he had been expelled. A reference to this is made in l. 557. The beautiful insolence of having such a witness, called up by Lucifer himself, testify that he didn't care whether or not George III got into heaven, in fact that he was really "all for it," should be understood.

535–6. *candidate with unturn'd coat!* etc. Southey was a turncoat according to the liberal poets. Wilkes the demagogue tries to get St. Peter's vote for himself to get into Heaven because he himself (Wilkes) has *not* turned his coat.

552. *Have told them what I thought*. See note above on l. 520.

557. *beat him hollow*. See note above on l. 520.

585. *Junius*. A series of powerful and brilliantly written papers against the government came out over the signature "Junius." The author has never been satisfactorily identified.

601–2. *the less Could they distinguish*. The reference is still to the undisclosed identity of Junius.

650. *consult my title-page*. The motto of Junius on his title-page was *Stat Nominis Umbra* ("He stands the shadow of a dream").

710. *an ass . . . prates*. See Numbers 22: 25–31.

719. *hexameter*. Southey's poem was written in dactylic hexameter (see text p. 787). The hexameter is a six-foot measure and Byron states that Southey, with this plethora of "feet," couldn't get any of them moving.

728. *Non Di, non homines*. Neither gods nor men. The reference is to Horace's *Ars Poetica*. More in the Cambridge edition of Byron quotes from Martin's translation:

"But gods, and men, and booksellers refuse
To countenance a mediocre muse."

736. *Pye*. Henry James Pye, Southey's predecessor as Poet Laureate, had the distinction of being one of the worst poets of his century.

The distressed George III confuses Southey's accents with those of Pye and, at the risk of losing Heaven, exclaims, "No more of that!"

752. *"de se."* On himself; suicide.

768. *Wat Tyler,* etc. *Wat Tyler* was Southey's revolutionary poem written in his college days and published in a pirated edition in 1817. Byron in this line and in the next two stanzas points out with the insolence of contempt the weakness of Southey's intellectual position, making the most of Southey's reversal of policies. Attention of the student is called to the introductory note on Southey (text p. 782).

773. *pantisocracy.* See text pp. 141–2 (fifth paragraph of the introductory note to Coleridge).

807. *Like King Alfonso.* Alfonso, speaking of the Ptolomean system, said that "had he been consulted at the creation of the world, he would have spared the Maker some absurdities." (Byron's note.)

835. *For all corrupted things.* "A drowned body lies at the bottom till rotten; it then floats, as most people know." (Byron's note.) This was pleasant for Southey!

Page 363.
EXTRACTS FROM A DIARY OF LORD BYRON

First printed in Moore's *Letters and Journals of Lord Byron with Notices of his Life* (1830). Omissions are indicated by dots.

363a, l. 23. *Galignani's messengers.* Giovanni Galignani in 1800 opened an English Library in Paris and in 1814 began the publication of *Galignani's Messenger,* a newspaper in English.

364b, l. 10. *Count Pietro G.* Count Pietro Gamba, brother of the Countess Guiccioli. Byron became intimate with him. The two were associated in the Carbonari conspiracy and Gamba went with Byron to Greece.

365a, l. 29. *like Swift.* The great satirist was insane before his death.

365b, l. 27. *Carbonari.* Literally, charcoal-burners. At first the Italian patriots plotting to throw off the Austrian yoke met in the forests and made their way to the meeting-place disguised as carbonari. The name was applied to all members of the secret patriotic society.

366a, l. 4. *P. G.* Pietro Gamba.

366a, l. 39. *Pegasus.* The winged horse which had been tamed by Minerva and presented to the Muses.

367b, l. 38. *"highland hunting."* A reference to the favorite sport in the Scottish highlands. The phrase was proverbial and Byron gives its meaning in the lines immediately following in the text.

369a, l. 21. *my brethren C.* His Carbonari brothers. Secret revolutionary societies do not leave membership lists lying about, but Byron

is supposed to have been a member and his phraseology here is to be noted.

369b, l. 47. *Nam vita gaudet mortua floribus.* "For life delights though dead in flowers."

Page 370.   ON ARTIFICIALITY AND POPE

Although his own poetical practice was directly to the contrary, Byron always held a high critical admiration for Pope (see text p. 391, col. 2, l. 37 to the end of the letter; also p. 396, col. 1, ll. 45–51). In the *English Bards and Scotch Reviewers* (ll. 327–84) Byron printed some derisive lines in which he ridiculed some of Bowles's poems and then attacked him on the ground that Bowles in his edition of Pope (1806) had dug up some dead scandal, ending with the statement that if Bowles had lived in Pope's own day he would have found himself in *The Dunciad*—where he belonged. After Byron's exile Bowles became involved in a controversy over Pope provoked by Campbell's *Essay on English Poetry* (1819) and, because of his early lines, Byron's name was brought in. Byron entered the lists in defense of Pope with this "Letter." Bowles retorted with some "Observations" and Byron then made some "Observations on 'Observations,'" but by this time the controversy had degenerated to a squabble. The gist of Byron's critical position in defence of Pope is in the sections given in the text. (See R. E. Prothero [Lord Ernle], *Letters and Journals of Lord Byron,* V, 522–92, for details of the controversy.)

372b, l. 30. *as Plato would have done.* In the *Republic,* Plato urges the banishment of poets, his chief argument being that the Greek poets, in narrating the myths of the Greek gods, had given a fictitious and false picture of the gods who, if gods, must necessarily be just and always the same. The poets' works then were lies. Byron's point is that Pope's work, because of its ethical quality, stands on a higher plane.

Page 372.   LETTERS OF LORD BYRON

Francis Hodgson (1781–1852). Was appointed in 1807 to a resident tutorship at Cambridge where Byron met him. He left the University in 1816 after having been appointed to the living of Bakewell in Derbyshire.

373a, l. 2. *Hobhouse's forthcoming Book of Travels.* The name of John Hobhouse (1786–1869) appears repeatedly in Byron's correspondence. He was Byron's friend at Cambridge, was the "best man" at Byron's wedding, and accompanied Byron part of the way on the first Near Eastern trip. He visited Byron at the Villa Diodati in Switzerland near Geneva and traveled with him to Venice and Rome. It was Hobhouse who wrote the notes to Canto IV of *Childe Harold*, which was dedicated to him. He was a member of the "Greek Committee" in London during the confused days of Byron's campaign in Greece, and was one of Byron's executors.

373a, l. 36. *all the Ephesians.* Byron's convivial group at Cambridge called themselves the Ephesians.

374b, l. 48. *Fletcher.* Byron's faithful English valet who followed him through all his wanderings to the end at Missolonghi.

376b, l. 15. *Scrope Davies.* A contemporary of Byron's at Cambridge, but more intimate with him in the London days. Davies, a great wit and much beloved, ultimately ruined himself by gambling and had to flee to the Continent.

376b, l. 20. *My mother lies a corpse.* Byron on his return from the Near East was detained in London on business. He reached Newstead Abbey August 2. His mother had died the previous day.

376b, l. 20. *one of my best friends is drowned in a ditch.* Charles Skinner Mathews, whom Byron describes as the most brilliant of his Cambridge circle. Mathews was caught in the weeds in the Cam.

376b, l. 45. *Robert Charles Dallas* (1754–1824). Assisted Byron to find a publisher for *Childe Harold.* Byron gave to him the proceeds of the first two cantos and of *The Corsair*, being himself at that time too proud to accept money for his literary work.

378a, l. 26. *Lady Caroline Lamb* (1785–1828). (See Byron introduction, text p. 233, paragraph 4.) Lady Caroline, wife of William Lamb (later Lord Melbourne), was a picturesque and tempestuous beauty who from childhood had been noted for her ungovernable temper. Her spectacular affair with Byron was a London sensation. Byron finally broke it off in 1813 with a brutal letter which she reprinted in *Glenarvon*, her novel about the affair.

378b, l. 29. *the lines on Dermody.* Thomas Dermody (d. 1802) whose collected work had come out in 1807 as *The Harp of Erin.*

379a, l. 15. *Lord Holland.* Henry Richard Vassal Fox, third Lord Holland (1773–1840), was one of the Whig leaders in the House of Lords, where he was recognized as the exponent of the policies of Charles James Fox, his uncle. Byron had unfairly lampooned him in *English Bards*, but regretted it and admired Holland for his liberal statesmanship.

379a, l. 31. *poor B—'s adventure.* Beau Brummel who, after being favored by the Prince Regent, was "cut" by him.

379a, l. 33. *Mr. Pye.* Henry James Pye, who had been appointed Poet Laureate in 1790 and held the post until his death in 1813.

379b, l. 10. *Lady Melbourne.* The mother-in-law of Lady Caroline Lamb—which did not prevent her from being the friend and confidant of Byron. She was a woman of remarkable ability, and after her death Byron declared she was "the best, and kindest, and ablest female I have ever known, old or young."

380a, l. 19. *William Gifford* (1756–1826). Gifford, an orphan, had a difficult time in his childhood. In his maturity he has been reported as amiable in private life, kind to children, and fond of dogs. He became editor of the Tory *Quarterly Review* and although he may have been fond of dogs, his treatment of poets occasionally left something to be desired. Shelley incorrectly believed him the author of the *Quarterly* attack on Keats (see text p. 543). Byron always respected him. He was, among other things, the author of two satires, the *Baviad* and the *Maviad*, published together in 1797.

382a, l. 21. *Thomas Moore.* Moore and Byron at one time were close to a duel over a remark Byron made in *English Bards and Scotch Reviewers.* After Byron's return from the Near East, friends patched up the quarrel and the two became boon companions. See note on Moore, text p. 741.

384a, ll. 43–4. *one scene . . . C's style.* Lady Caroline Lamb's style.

385a, l. 17. *upper Beggar's Opera.* A reference to Gay's *Beggar's Opera*, comparing London society to the rogues of that merry operetta.

385a, l. 41. *Leigh Hunt.* See introductory note on Hunt, text p. 707.

386a, l. 34. *Rimini.* An extract from Hunt's *The Story of Rimini* is given in the text, p. 708.

387a, l. 40. *parted from Augusta.* Augusta Leigh, Byron's half-sister. See notes on *Fare Thee Well* and *Stanzas to Augusta.*

387b, l. 21. *only carried us to Halnaby, and London, and you to Kirkby.* To Halnaby they went on their honeymoon, to London to set up their home; to Kirkby Mallory she went with the baby to visit her parents—and never rejoined Byron. The bitterness of the lines is obvious.

388a, l. 22. *La Manche.* The English Channel.

389a, l. 44. *Glenarvon.* Lady Caroline Lamb's novel, in which she told her version of her affair with Byron.

389b, l. 28. *kept to Pythagoras.* Kept to a strict medical regimen.

391a, l. 36. *John Murray.* The second of the name, was Byron's publisher for many years, until he gave up the later cantos of *Don Juan.* ". . . The remarkable position which the second John Murray created for himself, has two aspects, one commercial, the other social. He was not only the publisher, but the friend, of the most distinguished men of the day; and he was both by reason, partly of his honorable character, partly of his personal attractiveness. Sir Walter Scott, writing, October 30, 1828, to Lockhart, speaks of Murray in words which sum up his character: 'By all means do what the Emperor says. He is what Emperor Nap was not, "much a gentleman."' Murray was the first to divorce the business of publishing from that of selling books; the first to see, as he wrote to Sir Walter Scott, October 13, 1825 (*A Publisher and His Friends*, II, 199), that 'the business of a publishing bookseller is not in his shop, or even his connection, but in his brains.' Quick-tempered and warm-hearted, he was endowed with a strong sense of humour, and a gift of felicitous expression, which made him at once an admirable talker and an excellent letter-writer, and enabled him to hold his own among the noted wits and brilliant men of letters whom he gathered under his roof. A man of ideas more than a man of business, of enterprise rather than of calculation, he was always on the watch for new writers and new openings. . . ." (R. E. Prothero, *Letters and Journals of Lord Byron*, I, 334.)

391b, l. 22. *Lalla Rookh.* Moore's oriental poem. See introductory material to Moore, text p. 741.

392a, l. 6. *Horace then, and Claudian now.* Horace was one of the greatest poets of the Augustan period; Claudian came in a later and less glorious literary era.

392a, l. 28. *my little legitimate.* Ada, daughter of Lady Byron. See *Childe Harold*, III, 2

392a, l. 29. *an illegitimate.* Allegra, daughter of Claire Clairmont, Mrs. Shelley's stepsister. See text p. 387, Letter xxiii.

392b, l. 3. *Lakers included.* The "Lake Poets," of whom Wordsworth, Coleridge, and Southey were the most prominent.

393a, l. 22. *Sir Samuel Romilly.* See also 398a, ll. 10–34. Romilly had a distinguished career as a lawyer and as a member of Parliament. He waged a long campaign for the reform of English criminal law and in 1808 secured the repeal of an Elizabethan statute which prescribed the death penalty for theft. Some of Byron's friends, notably Hobhouse, supported him in the campaign, but Byron hated him always with a deadly hatred. Romilly's wife died Oct. 29, 1818, and he committed suicide Nov. 2, aged 61.

393b, l. 33 et seq. *So you and Mr. Foscolo . . . want me to undertake.* This letter was sent in reply to one from Murray in which Murray had said: ". . . Here is Foscolo at my side, deploring that a man of your genius will not occupy some six or eight years in the composition of a work and subject worthy of you, and this you have promised to Gifford long ago, and to Hobhouse and Kinnaird since. Believe me, there is no character talked of in this country as yours is; it is the constant theme of all classes, and your portrait is engraved, and painted, and sold in every town through-

out the Kingdom. I wish you would suffer yourself to be fully aware of this high estimation of your countrymen, and not to run even a slight or doubtful chance of injuring what is to be the noblest inheritance of a descendant who promises to be so attractive. Let me have the second canto of *Don Juan*, and suffer Gifford, who never swerves in his admiration of your talents, to prepare what he thinks worthy of you. This I will instantly set up in proof, and send out for your final alteration and completion, and there will yet be time to bring it out in May." (Prothero, *Letters and Journals of Lord Byron*, IV, 283.)

396b, l. 2. *Douglas Kinnaird* (1788–1830) was in 1815 associated with Byron on a sub-committee of the Drury Lane Theatre. He was a graduate of Cambridge (M.A. 1811). Byron once described him as "my trusty and trustworthy trustee and banker, and crown and sheet anchor."

396b, l. 5. *the Vampire.* In the *New Monthly Magazine* had appeared a poem entitled *The Vampyre* which was ascribed to Byron. Actually it was by John William Polidori, the young doctor who had accompanied Byron into exile as his personal physician but had been dismissed because of incompatibility. Byron in Switzerland in 1818 had begun a poem of the same title but had dropped it in its initial stages.

398a, ll. 7–8. *Ada, the little Electra of my Mycenae.* Electra was the daughter of Agamemnon, King of Mycenae. In the Greek tragedies of Aeschylus and Euripides she spurred on her younger brother Orestes to avenge her father who had been murdered by her mother and her mother's lover.

398b, l. 25. *P—.* Francis Cohen, who embraced Christianity and changed his name to Palgrave.

399a, l. 25. *Prior and Paulo Purgante.* ". . . I asked whether Prior's poems were to be printed entire: Johnson said, they were. I mentioned Lord Hailes's censure of Prior, in his Preface to a collection of 'Sacred Poems,' by various hands, published by him at Edinburgh a great many years ago, where he mentions, 'Those impure tales which will be the eternal opprobrium of their ingenious author.' *Johnson:* 'Sir, Lord Hailes has forgot. There is nothing in Prior that will excite to lewdness. If Lord Hailes thinks there is, he must be more combustible than other people.' I instanced the tale of 'Paulo Purganti and his Wife.' *Johnson:* 'Sir, there is nothing there, but that his wife wanted to be kissed, when poor Paulo was out of pocket. No, Sir, Prior is a lady's book. No lady is ashamed to have it standing in her library.'" (Boswell, *Life of Johnson*, Globe Edition, p. 428.)

399a, l. 30. *I have read this book.* The book was

Mme de Staël's *Corinne*, in which an Italian poetess falls in love with an English nobleman. They travel together in Italy, but he ultimately deserts her and goes back into English life. She dies in despair.

399b, l. 49. *Anacharsis Cloots.* "Jean Baptiste Clootz (better known by the name of Anacharsis), a Prussian baron, born at Cleves in 1755, was the nephew of Cornelius de Pauw, author of *Recherches Philosophiques sur les Américains*, etc. In 1790, at the bar of the National Convention, he described himself a *l'orateur du genre humain*. Falling under the suspicion of Robespierre, he was, in March, 1794, condemned to death. On the scaffold, he begged the executioner to decapitate him the last, alleging that he wished to make some observations essential to the establishment of certain principles, while the heads of his companions were falling. The request was complied with." (Prothero's note.)

400a, l. 5. *Werther-faced man.* Werther was the hero of Goethe's short novel, *The Sorrows of Werther*. Thackeray's brief poem gives an insight into the nature of "Wertherism":

THE SORROWS OF WERTHER

Werther had a love for Charlotte
    Such as words could never utter;
Would you know how first he met her?
    She was cutting bread and butter.

Charlotte was a married lady,
    And a moral man was Werther,
And, for all the wealth of Indies,
    Would do nothing for to hurt her.

So he sighed and pined and ogled,
    And his passion boiled and bubbled,
Till he blew his silly brains out,
    And no more was by it troubled.

Charlotte, having seen his body
    Borne before her on a shutter,
Like a well-conducted person,
    Went on cutting bread and butter.

400b, l. 13. *The child.* Allegra, Claire Clairmont's daughter.

400b, l. 28. *the review of "Endymion."* See notes on that poem.

401a, ll. 10–11. *remarks . . . provoked by his attack upon Pope.* Keats's attack was in *Sleep and Poetry* (see text p. 565, ll. 181–206). Byron in his controversy with Bowles (see notes on *On Artificiality and Pope*) said, "A Mr. John Ketch has written some lines against him [Pope], of which it were better to be the subject than the author."

401a, l. 31. *I only regret that Bowles*, etc. Thomas Moore found himself in an awkward position in the Bowles-Byron controversy (see introductory note to *On Artificiality and*

Pope). He was an old acquaintance of Bowles and Bowles quoted, without naming the author, a remark which Moore had entirely forgotten. Byron, in replying, opened fire on this precise point and, to make matters worse, referred (also without naming the author) to a scandalous anecdote concerning Bowles's youth which Moore had told him one evening after an excellent dinner.

401a, l. 40. *your Mr. Irving.* Washington Irving, who was a boon companion of Moore's.

402a, l. 46. *With respect to "Religion."* Moore replied to this that he did not identify Byron with the "blasphemies" of *Cain*. "All I wish and implore is you, who are such a powerful manufacturer of these thunderbolts, would not choose subjects that make it necessary to launch them." Byron read this letter of Moore's to Shelley and the discussion provoked Shelley's comment in his letter of April 11, 1822, to Horace Smith. (See text p. 547b, l. 20 et seq.)

402b, l. 36. *in my time Watier's was the Dandy Club.* "I liked the Dandies; they were always very civil to *me*, though in general they disliked literary people, and persecuted and mystified M⁰ de Stael, Lewis, Horace Twiss, and the like, damnably. They persuaded M⁰ de Stael that Alvanley had a hundred thousand a year, etc., etc., till she praised him to his face for his *beauty!* and made a set at him for Albertine (*Libertine*, as Brummell baptized her, though the poor Girl was and is as correct as maid or wife can be, and very amiable withal), and a hundred fooleries besides.

"The truth is, that, though I gave up the business early, I had a tinge of Dandyism in my minority, and probably retained enough of it, to conciliate the great ones; at four and twenty I had gamed, and drank, and taken my degrees in most dissipations; and having no pedantry, and not being overbearing, we ran quietly together. I knew them all more or less, and they made me a Member of Watier's (a superb Club at that time), being, I take it, the only literary man (except *two others*, both men of the world, M. and S.) in it.

"Our Masquerade was a grand one; so was the Dandy Ball, too, at the Argyle, but *that* (the latter) was given by the four Chiefs, B., M., A. and P., if I err not.

"I was a Member of the Alfred too, being elected while in Greece. It was pleasant—a little too sober and literary, and bored with Sotheby and Sir Francis d'Ivernois! but one met Peel, and Ward, and Valentia, and many other pleasant or known people; and was upon the whole a decent resource on a rainy day, in a dearth of parties, or parliament, or an empty season.

"I belonged, or belong, to the following Clubs or Societies:—to the Alfred, to the Cocoa tree, to Watier's, to the Union, to Racker's (at Brighton), to the Pugilistic, to the Owls or 'Fly by Night,' to the *Cambridge* Whig Club, to the Harrow Club, Cambridge, and to one or two private Clubs, to the Hampden political Club, and to the Italian Carbonari, etc., etc., etc., 'though last *not least.*' I got into all these, and never stood for any other—at least to my own knowledge. I declined being proposed to several others; though pressed to stand Candidate." (Byron, *Detached Thoughts*, 1821.)

407a, l. 34. *Sir Charles James Napier* was, in 1819, appointed by the British as inspecting field officer in the Ionian Islands. Byron admired his ability highly and when he returned to England in 1824 sent a letter to the "Greek Committee" in London saying, he is "our man to lead a regular force or to organise a national one for the Greeks." Napier, however, did not come to agreement with the Committee and later carved out an illustrious career for himself in India.

407a, l. 19. *Glenarvoning.* A reference to Lady Caroline Lamb's novel *Glenarvon.*

408b, ll. 38–9. *like Garcilasso de la Vega*, etc. All these writers were wounded or killed in action.

PERCY BYSSHE SHELLEY
BIBLIOGRAPHY

I. WORKS

Complete Works, ed. by Roger Ingpen and Walter E. Peck. Julian Edition. 10 vols. (Scribner: New York, 1926–30.) An expensive limited edition but the best available; some alterations in the *Letters* (which appear in Vols. VIII–X, many hitherto unpublished) are re-corrected. The *Letters*, however, should be supplemented by the discoveries of Hotson; see below.

Complete Works, ed. by H. Buxton Forman. 8 vols. (Reeves: London, 1882.) The standard edition until the appearance of the work listed above.

Complete Poetical Works, ed. by Thomas Hutchinson. (Oxford University Press: 1933.) This newly reprinted edition is useful for its textual accuracy, the more important various readings being given in footnotes. It offers a biographical introduction by Benjamin P. Kurtz.

The Poems of Percy Bysshe Shelley, ed. by C. D. Locock. 2 vols. (Methuen: London, 1911.) Unusually full and readable notes are found in the appendices; there is a brief introduction by A. Clutton-Brock.

Complete Poetical Works, ed. by G. E. Woodberry. Cambridge Edition. (Houghton: Boston, 1901.) A good one-volume edition, with an introductory memoir.

Select Poems, ed. by W. J. Alexander. Athenaeum Press Edition. (Ginn: Boston, 1898.) Recommended for its annotations; the editor provides a biographical introduction.

The Narrative Poems of Percy Bysshe Shelley, ed. by C. H. Herford. 2 vols. (Chatto: London, 1927.) The arrangement is chronological; the introduction lays down the general principles of romantic narrative, discusses the important poems separately.

Poetical Works. 2 vols. (Dutton: New York, 1930.) A good inexpensive edition, provided with an introductory sketch by A. H. Koszul; the plays, translations, and longer poems are in Vol. II.

The Best of Shelley, ed. by Newman I. White. (Nelson: New York, 1932.) Includes the standard pieces, forming a very satisfactory introduction to the poet's work.

Essays and Letters, ed. by Ernest Rhys. (Scott: London, 1886.) A good inexpensive collection, equipped with an introduction by the editor.

A Defence of Poetry, ed. by H. F. B. Brett-Smith. Percy Reprints. (Blackwell: Oxford, 1923.) The essay (with Hunt's excisions given in the appendix) is reproduced in its complete original form, together with Peacock's *Four Ages of Poetry*, to which it was a rejoinder. Included also is Browning's celebrated *Essay on Shelley.*

Prose Works, ed. by R. H. Shepherd. 2 vols. (Chatto: London, 1912.) The most convenient collection of this important material.

Verse and Prose from MSS, ed. by Sir John C. E. Shelley-Rolls and Roger Ingpen. (Zaehnsdorf: London, 1934.) The Shelley Notebooks, now in possession of the first-named editor (the poet's great-nephew) supply the material; many variants and rejected passages are shown.

The Letters of Shelley, ed. by Roger Ingpen. 2 vols. (Macmillan: New York, 1915.) The collection contains about 480 letters, of which 38 were here published for the first time.

Literary and Philosophical Criticism, ed. by John Shawcross. (Frowde: London, 1909.) The most significant items are *A Defence of Poetry* and the *Essay on Christianity;* the introduction remarks Shelley's emancipation from Godwin, comments on the "breadth and tolerance" of his literary judgments.

Note Books, ed. by H. Buxton Forman. (Privately printed for W. K. Bixby: St. Louis, 1911.) The editor has provided a transcription and a full commentary.

II. BIOGRAPHY AND CRITICISM

Angeli, Helen Rossetti. *Shelley and His Friends in Italy.* (Brentano's: New York, 1911.) An entertaining account of the poet's last years, associating many of his poems with their original settings; relations with Byron and many other important figures are treated at length.

Brailsford, H. N. *Shelley, Godwin, and Their Circle.* (Holt: New York, 1913.) Valuable for its summary of the personal relations between Godwin and Shelley; compare the chapter "Skinner Street News," in A. E. Newton's *The Greatest Book in the World* (Little: Boston, 1925).

Campbell, Mrs. O. W. *Shelley and the Unromantics.* (Scribner: New York, 1924.) A stimulating, if over-enthusiastic, study of the man Shelley; somewhat at the expense of his fellow romantics, he is exalted above the scale of human judgment—a good book to balance against Jeaffreson's *The Real Shelley.*

Clarke, Isabel C. *Shelley and Byron.* (Hutchinson: London, 1934.) A summary of the abundant material on the subject of the two poets' relationship in Italy; begins with 1812, ends with Trelawney's death, 1881.

Clutton-Brock, Arthur. *Shelley the Man and the Poet.* (Dutton: New York, 1922.) Reveals Shelley as a developing personality, living between the worlds of reality and imagination; without apologizing, it claims tolerance for the poet's human weaknesses.

Dowden, Edward. *The Life of Percy Bysshe Shelley.* 2 vols. (Scribner: New York, 1896.) An indispensable source-book for matters of fact; still generally regarded as the standard Life, although occasionally lacking in frankness and sympathy.

Edmunds, E. W. *Shelley and His Poetry.* (Dodge: New York, 1918.) Takes the facts of the poet's life as a starting-point for the criticism of his poetry, showing that his powers of idealization were his peculiar creative agent.

Ellis, F. S. *A Lexical Concordance to the Poetical Works of Shelley.* (Quaritch: London, 1892.) Gives the reader access to passages illustrating Shelley's complete poetic diction.

Gordon, A. C. *Allegra, the Story of Byron and Miss Clairmont.* (Minton: New York, 1926.) Part II (pp. 93–198) contains many references to Shelley's part in the affairs of Byron and his mistress; gives a circumstantial account of the events connected with Shelley's death.

Gribble, F. H. *The Romantic Life of Shelley and the Sequel.* (Putnam: New York, 1911.) Brings the Harriet episode into rather over-due prominence; provides a fairly consecutive outline of biographical facts, with little literary comment. The Sequel is "Mary Shelley's Suitors."

Hoffmann, H. L. *An Odyssey of the Soul: Shelley's Alastor.* (Columbia University Press: 1933.) Reads the poem as Shelley's criticism of his past self; traces in it allusions to the poet's study and experience: a valuable book for the advanced student.

Hogg, T. J. *The Life of Percy Bysshe Shelley*, ed. by Edward Dowden. (Routledge: London, 1906.) A useful edition of an early life (1858) of the poet, vivid and amusing, but inaccurate and misleading in places; carries to 1813; should be read with Dowden's Life.

Hunt, Leigh. *Autobiography* (1850), ed. by Roger Ingpen. 2 vols. (Dutton: New York, 1903.) Important references to Shelley begin with the letters during the poet's Oxford residence; the passages recounting their Italian residence are necessarily few, but significant; prevailing tone is favorable to Shelley.

Ingpen, Roger. *Shelley in England.* (Paul: London, 1917.) An almost day-by-day record of the poet's life up to 1816, based on new facts from documents entrusted to the attorney of Sir Bysshe and Timothy Shelley. Appendix gives facsimiles of the *Notebooks*, with transcriptions.

Jeaffreson, J. C. *The Real Shelley: New Views of the Poet's Life.* 2 vols. (Hurst: London, 1885.) A relentless pursuit of Shelley's faults; no attempt at literary criticism, except to point out biographical stigma.

Johnson, R. B. *Shelley—Leigh Hunt: How Friendship Made History.* (Ingpen: London, 1928.) A valuable digest, based in part on unpublished material, of Hunt's editorial notices of Shelley in *The Examiner*, including many letters between Hunt and the Shelley family.

Kurtz, B. P. *The Pursuit of Death.* (Oxford University Press: 1933.) A brilliant "advanced" study of Shelley's attitude toward death, which is the symbol of the destruction of "the noble, the gentle, the beautiful"; the assumption is made that "in what a poet says about death the critics may discover much of his attitude toward life."

Liptzin, Solomon. *Shelley in Germany.* (Columbia University Press: 1924.) Traces the poet's reputation in Germany, which after 1830 hailed him as an apostle of liberty; points out important translations and adaptations of Shelley, the facts of his life being as significant in this latter respect as his literary productions.

Maurois, André. *Ariel: A Shelley Romance*, trans. by Ella d'Arcy. (Appleton: New York, 1924.) An extraordinary subjective study of the poet, giving the illusion of eyewitness reality; based on reliable sources.

Medwin, Thomas. *The Life of Percy Bysshe Shelley*, ed. by H. Buxton Forman. 2 vols. (Oxford University Press: 1913.) The information of the original edition (1847) is scanty and inaccurate, the general tone apologetic; an introduction and commentary by the editor attempt to provide a well-rounded portrayal.

Peacock, T. L. *Memoirs of Shelley with Shelley's Letters to Peacock*, ed. by H. F. B. Brett-Smith. (Oxford University Press: 1909.) A portrayal, by an anti-romantic, of the intimacy lasting to 1817–18; though not a full biography, it is the best of the early (1875) attempts; the editor's notes point out wanted information for the early winter and spring of 1814.

Peck, W. E. *Shelley, His Life and Work.* 2 vols. (Houghton: New York, 1927.) A compendious re-collection of the biographical material, with special attention to the life of Harriet Shelley; "interchapters" discuss the major poems; purpose is to explode the "ineffectual angel" view of Shelley.

Salt, H. S. *Shelley, Poet and Pioneer.* (Scribner: New York, 1896.) One of the earliest Lives to point out the development of the poet's personality; well-balanced and judicious.

Sharp, William. *Life of Shelley.* Great Writers series. (Scott: London, 1887.) A good brief biography; gives a favorable coloring to the main facts, comments little upon the poetry.

Solve, M. T. *Shelley: His Theory of Poetry.* (University of Chicago Press: 1927.) The best book on the subject, giving a succinct introduction to Shelley's views on poetry.

Stovall, Floyd. *Desire and Restraint in Shelley.* (Duke University Press: 1931.) Presenting Shelley as "the enthusiast, the combatant, and the sufferer," this study aims to give a consecutive record of the poet's development from revolt through conflict to final compromise.

Strong, A. T. *Three Studies in Shelley.* (Oxford University Press: 1922.) "The Faith of Shelley," "Shelley's Symbolism," and "The Sinister in Shelley" constitute a penetrating study of the poet's major works, revealing in them the outgrowth of Shelley's social philosophy.

Symonds, J. A. *Shelley.* English Men of Letters

series. (Harper: New York, 1925.) An excellent brief biography, improved by much revision; doing the poet full justice, it does not gloss over or conceal his faults.

Trelawney, E. J. *Recollections of the Last Days of Shelley and Byron*, ed. by Edward Dowden. (Oxford University Press: 1906.) Originally published in 1858, covers only the year 1822, vivid and picturesque; unreliable in its accounts of Mary Shelley.

Ullman, J. R. *Mad Shelley*. (Princeton University Press: 1931.) A high-pitched study of Shelley unbound by social restraints, surrendering only in his two marriages; he is seen as a part of the vital impulse of modern life.

Weaver, Bennett. *Toward the Understanding of Shelley*. (University of Michigan Press: 1932.) A thought-provoking essay to show the influence of the Bible upon Shelley, "ushering a great poet into a new light."

III. ARTICLES FROM BOOKS

Arnold, Matthew. "Shelley," in *Essays in Criticism*, Second Series. (Macmillan: New York, 1888.) A review of Dowden's *Life*, with a sober appraisal of the "ridiculous and odious" and the "beautiful and lovable"; points out the poet's lack of humor and his self-deception; source of the celebrated "beautiful and ineffectual angel" passage.

Bagehot, Walter. "Percy Bysshe Shelley," in *Literary Studies*. (Longmans: London, 1898.) Purports to find the poet's autobiography in his writings, where his revolutionary ideas are made clear; discusses his philosophy of religion, points out traces of Lucretius; compares Shelley with Keats.

Bradley, A. C. "Shelley's Views of Poetry," in *Oxford Lectures on Poetry*. (Macmillan: London, 1911.) The first important approach to the subject; shows the effect of Shelley's reading upon his poetry, reconstructs his theory of poetry from a close reading of his prose and verse.

Brooke, Stopford A. "The Lyrics of Shelley" and "*Epipsychidion*," in *Studies in Poetry*. (Duckworth: London, 1920.) The first essay remarks the poet's lack of self-consciousness, his humanitarian outlook; the second essay interprets the poem as a record of the poet's search for ideal Beauty, finding its culmination in "the living image of his own soul."

Fairchild, H. N. "Shelley and Transcendentalism," in *The Romantic Quest*. (Columbia University Press: 1931.) Points out traces of Spinoza in *Queen Mab* and *Alastor*, where also occur borrowings from Plato and Sir William Drummond; the decay of Shelley's faith is seen as the reason for the morbidity of his final poems.

Herford, C. H. "Shelley," in *Cambridge History of English Literature*, XII. (Putnam: New York, 1916.) An able brief essay, presenting both biographical and critical material.

More, P. E. "Shelley," in *Shelburne Essays*, Seventh Series. (Putnam: New York, 1910.) Marks the onset of the anti-romantic reaction; Shelley's unrestrained fancy is condemned.

Noyes, Alfred. "The Poet of Light," in *Some Aspects of Modern Poetry*. (Stokes: New York,

1924.) Presents an illuminating discussion of a number of famous passages; praises Browning's criticism, answers Arnold's.

Quiller-Couch, Sir Arthur. "Shelley," in *Studies in Literature*, Second Series. (Cambridge University Press: 1922.) Denies the theory that Shelley's boat was deliberately run down; puts his influence above Byron's and Wordsworth's; challenges some early and modern criticism.

Shairp, J. C. "Shelley as a Lyric Poet," in *Aspects of Poetry*. (Houghton: Boston, 1881.) Attempts to point out autobiographical traces in the poet's work; analyzes his philosophy of religion; comments upon some of the best-known lyrics.

Swinburne, A. C. "Notes on the Text of Shelley," in *Essays and Studies*. (Chatto: London, 1875.) Praises the poet's lyric gift with an unmeasured enthusiasm, frequently with the idea of exalting Shelley by debasing other romantics, Byron notably.

Symons, Arthur. "Percy Bysshe Shelley," in *The Romantic Movement in English Poetry*. (Dutton: New York, 1909.) Comments on the poet's fascination by the problem of evil; praises his lyrical cry, his sincerity, and the sureness of his intuition.

Thompson, Francis. "Shelley," in *Collected Works*, III. (Scribner: New York, 1913.) A brilliantly written essay, praising the lyrical powers of the poet, acclaiming him the "eternal child."

Trent, W. P. "Apropos of Shelley," in *The Authority of Criticism and Other Essays*. (Scribner: New York, 1899.) Ploughs through some of the critical contradictions, briefly reviews the life of the poet, attacks Arnold's critique, finds the poet at his best in his short lyrics.

Woodberry, G. E. "Remarks on Shelley," and "Shelley's Work," in *Makers of Literature*. (Macmillan: New York, 1900.) The final essay, "Shelley's Work," appraises the poet's social philosophy, shows its vitality in the modern age; the other essay discusses the poet's life from the point of view of its few years, mildly rebukes Arnold, enthusiastically comments on the Italian letters.

Yeats, W. B. "The Philosophy of Shelley," in *Ideas of Good and Evil*. (Macmillan: New York, 1903.) Maintains that, as the highest philosophy is essentially poetry, Shelley's works (especially *Prometheus Unbound*) embody the best political, social, and moral philosophy of his day.

IV. ARTICLES FROM PERIODICALS

Bald, Marjory A. "The Psychology of Shelley," *Contemporary Review*, CXXXI, 359–66 (Feb., 1927). A study of Shelley "between Christ and Cain"; comments on the poet's reaction to emotional stresses.

Burriss, E. E. "The Classical Culture of Percy Bysshe Shelley," *Classical Journal*, XXI, 344–54 (Feb., 1926). Traces references to Greek and Latin authors through Shelley's letters.

Croft, Margaret L. "A Strange Adventure of Shelley's," *Century Magazine*, LXX, 905–9 (Oct., 1905). A circumstantial account of the assault on Shelley at Tan-yr-allt in Wales: a tribute to his sense of truth.

Dunn, N. P. "Unknown Pictures of Shelley," *Century Magazine*, LXX, 909–17 (Oct., 1905).

An account of the discovery, in 1905, of two studies of Shelley by W. E. West; some good reproductions are in the article.

Gingerich, S. F. "Shelley's Doctrine of Necessity *versus* Christianity," *Publications of the Modern Language Association*, XXXIII, 444–73 (Sept., 1918). Shows Shelley's changing attitude toward the problem of evil; discusses his "thin idealism" which turned toward a passive outlook upon life.

Graham, Walter. "Shelley's Debt to Leigh Hunt and *The Examiner*," *Publications of the Modern Language Association*, XL, 185–92 (Mar., 1925). Shows Hunt's service as a reviewer in pointing out Shelley's social philosophy.

Havens, R. D. "Shelley's *Alastor*," *Publications of the Modern Language Association*, XLV, 1098–1115 (Dec., 1930). Attacks the idea of the avowed self-portrait in the poem; sees the hero as an idealized youth, lacking sympathy with his contemporaries.

Hotson, Leslie. "Shelley's Lost Letters to Harriet," *Atlantic Monthly*, CXLV, 122–33, 166–77 (Jun., Feb., 1930). Recounts the interesting circumstances of the discovery of the letters among the Master's Papers of the Chancery records, with a commentary on the letters, which date from 14 July, 1814, to 18 December, 1816.

Hotson, Leslie. "A Footnote to Shelley," *Atlantic Monthly*, CXLV, 350–8 (Mar., 1930). A review of the documentary evidence used in the case of Shelley's divorce.

Hughes, A. M. D. "Shelley and Nature," *North American Review*, CCVIII, 287–95 (Aug., 1918). Shows the process of softening and refinement in Shelley's descriptions of natural scenes.

Mitchell, Stewart. "A Century of Shelley," *Dial*, LXXII, 246–58 (Mar., 1922). A defense of the reliability of the biographies by Hogg and Trelawney.

Nicholson, A. P. "Shelley *Contra Mundum*," *Nineteenth Century*, LXIII, 794–810 (May, 1908). A review of various adverse critical points of view regarding the poet, from Arnold to Dowden.

Shanks, Edward. "Shelley," *London Mercury*, VI, 154–65 (June, 1922). A discussion of Shelley as a poet of youth: a distinction between him and Keats.

Slaughter, Gertrude. "Percy Bysshe Shelley," *North American Review*, CCXVI, 67–82 (July, 1922). Shows the poet's combination of "a mystic's faith with the humanitarian instincts of our time."

Slaughter, Gertrude. "A Poet's Heritage," *North American Review*, CCXVIII, 97–108 (July, 1923). A series of pen-pictures of Shelley's grandfather and father, presenting scenes of their affairs with the poet.

Stauffer, Ruth M. "Byron and Shelley in Italy," *Poet Lore*, XXVIII, 554–66, 703–21 (Autumn–Winter, 1917). Traces the relationship of the two poets during their Italian residence, May, 1816, to October, 1821, with suggestions of their mutual influence.

Stovall, Floyd. "Shelley's Doctrine of Love," *Publications of the Modern Language Association*, XLV, 283–303 (Mar., 1930). Points out love as a dominating theme in the poet's work; traces this concept through his poetry, showing its growing force as a factor in his social philosophy.

White, N. I. "Shelley's *Prometheus Unbound*, or Every Man His Own Allegorist," *Publications of the Modern Language Association*, XL, 172–84 (Mar., 1925). Asserts that the poem has the representative value of great art, but is subservient to no definite mode or system.

NOTES

Page 415.   TO WORDSWORTH

Wordsworth was felt by the more radical poets to have been in his later days a renegade to the cause of liberalism. Cf. Browning's *The Lost Leader*, and see Wordsworth's own defense of his opinions (Letter to L——, Dec. 4, 1821; text p. 125).

HYMN TO INTELLECTUAL BEAUTY

". . . He spent the summer on the shores of the Lake of Geneva. The *Hymn to Intellectual Beauty* was conceived during his voyage round the Lake with Lord Byron. He occupied himself during this voyage by reading the *Nouvelle Héloïse* for the first time. The reading it on the very spot where the scenes are laid, added to the interest; and he was at once surprised and charmed by the passionate eloquence and earnest enthralling interest that pervades this work. There was something in the character of Saint-Preux, in his abnegation of self, and in the worship he paid to Love, that coincided with Shelley's own disposition; and, though differing in many of the views, and shocked by others, yet the effect of the whole was fascinating and delightful." (Mrs. Shelley's note.)

In Plato's *Symposium* there is a climactic passage on the discipline of love, and its power to enable the lover to penetrate through the forms of beauty to the one eternal beauty, which deeply influenced Shelley's thinking. The passage follows in Shelley's translation: ". . . He ought, then, to consider that beauty in whatever form it resides is the brother of that beauty which subsists in another form; and if he ought to pursue that which is beautiful in form, it would be absurd to imagine that beauty is not one and the same thing in all forms, and would therefore remit much of his ardent preference towards one, through his perception of the multitude of claims upon his love. In addition, he would consider the beauty which is in souls more excellent than that which is in form. . . . Contemplating thus the universal beauty, no longer would he unworthily and meanly enslave himself to the attractions of one form in love, nor one subject of discipline or science, but would turn towards the wide ocean of intellectual beauty, and from the sight of the lovely and majestic forms which it contains, would abundantly bring forth his conceptions in philosophy; until, strengthened, and confirmed, he should at length steadily contemplate one science, which is the science of this universal beauty. . . . He who has been disciplined to this point in love, by contemplating beautiful objects gradually, and in their order, now arriving at the end of all that concerns love, on a sudden beholds a beauty wonderful in its nature. . . . It is eternal, unproduced, indestructible; neither subject to increase nor decay; not, like other things, partly beautiful and partly deformed; not at one time beautiful and at another time not; not beautiful in relation to one thing and deformed in relation to another; not here beautiful and there deformed; not beautiful in the estimation of one person and deformed in that of another; nor can this supreme beauty be figured to the imagination, like a beautiful face or beautiful hands or any portion of the body, nor like any discourse nor any science. Nor does it subsist in any other that lives or is, either in earth, or in heaven, or in any other place; but it is eternally uniform and consistent, and monoeidic with itself. All other things are beautiful through a participation of it, with this one condition, that, although they are subject to production and decay, it never becomes more or less, or endures any change. When any one, ascending from the correct system of love, begins to contemplate this supreme beauty, he already touches the consummation of his labor. For such as discipline themselves upon this system, or are conducted by another beginning to ascend through these transitory objects which are beautiful, toward that which is beauty itself, proceeding as on steps from the love of one form to that of two, and from that of two, to that of all forms which are beautiful; and from beautiful forms to beautiful habits and institutions, and from institutions to beautiful doctrines; until, from the meditation of many doctrines, they arrive at that which is nothing else than the doctrine of supreme beauty itself, in the knowledge and contemplation of which at length they repose. Such a life as this . . . spent in the contemplation of the beautiful, is the life for men to live; which if you chance ever to experience you will esteem far beyond gold and rich garments and even those lovely persons whom you and many others now gaze on with astonishment, and are prepared neither to eat nor drink so that you may behold and live forever with these objects of your love! What then shall we imagine to be the aspect of the supreme beauty itself, simple, pure, uncontaminated with the intermixture of human flesh and colors, and all other idle and unreal shapes attendant on mortality; the divine, the original, the supreme, the mono-eidic beautiful itself? What must be the life of him who dwells with and gazes on that which it becomes us all to seek? Think you not that to him alone is accorded the prerogative of bringing forth, not images and shadows of virtue, for he is in contact not with a shadow but with reality, with virtue itself, in the production and nourishment of which he becomes dear to the gods, and, if such a privilege is conceded to any human being, himself immortal." (Shelley's *Prose Works*, ed. Forman, Vol. III, 218–222.)

Page 416.　TO CONSTANTIA, SINGING

Constantia is Claire Clairmont, the notes of whose voice were once described as "like a string of pearls."

11. *Unseen.* The untidy first draft of the poem in the Bodleian has "Of dreams unseen" but the "Of dreams" for some reason was omitted from the *Posthumous Poems* published by Mrs. Shelley in 1824.

Page 417.

THE REVOLT OF ISLAM: DEDICATION

1. *Mary.* Mary Shelley.
3. *Knight of Faëry.* One of Mary's names for Shelley was "Elfin Knight."
25–36. *From the near schoolhouse,* etc. There is no reason to doubt that this incident of self-dedication was an actual occurrence of Shelley's boyhood.
58–9. *the mortal chain Of Custom.* A reference to Mary's elopement with Shelley.
60. *the clouds.* Of detraction which followed the elopement.
102. *One.* Mary Wollstonecraft, mother of Mary Shelley.

Page 421.　LINES WRITTEN AMONG THE
EUGANEAN HILLS

Shelley states in the Preface that this poem "was written after a day's excursion among those lovely mountains which surround what was once the retreat, and where is now the sepulchre, of Petrarch. If any one is inclined to condemn the insertion of the introductory lines, which image forth the sudden relief of a state of deep despondency by the radiant visions disclosed by the sudden burst of an Italian sunrise in autumn, on the highest peak of those delightful mountains, I can only offer as my excuse, that they were not erased at the request of a dear friend, with whom added years of intercourse only add to my apprehension of its value, and who would have had more right than any one to complain, that she has not been able to extinguish in me the very power of delineating sadness."

The Euganean Hills lie just to one side of the route from Venice to Padua. The poem was written at Este in October, 1818.

9, 11, 19. *above . . . behind . . . before.* Locock in his edition follows each of these adverbs of place with a comma to make them more emphatic and assist in giving the outline of the picture.

47. *lay.* Locock has "laid" for "lay" and conjectures the meaning to be: "As they (the tempests) once shook the wretch who lay down to sleep there."

97. *Amphitrite.* One of the Nereids, wife of Neptune, the God of the Sea.

115–6. *Sun-girt City . . . queen.* Venice. During the time when Venice was a great maritime power it was a custom annually to throw a ring into the sea with great ceremony to symbolize her wedding with the sea.

152. *Celtic Anarch.* Austria. Celtic is used to suggest Northern barbarians as opposed to the Latin-descended races of Italy. See l. 223, "the brutal Celt," and l. 248, "the mighty Austrian." See note on Ezzelin, l. 239.

174. *tempest-cleaving Swan.* Byron.

239. *Ezzelin.* Eccelino da Romano III, son of Eccelino II, who appears in Browning's *Sordello.* Eccelino III was the great but cruel captain who commanded the army of the Holy Roman Emperor Frederick II in an effort to subdue the free cities of Lombardy. He succeeded in forcing many of these republics to name him Captain of the People but the position on which he based his authority was only a legal fiction. ". . . He soon changed the authority which he derived from the people into a frightful tyranny: fixing his suspicions upon all who rose to any distinction, who in any way attracted the attention of their fellow-citizens, he did not wait for any expression of discontent, of symptom of resistance, in the nobles, merchants, priests, or lawyers, who by their eminence alone became suspected, to throw them into prison, and there, by the most excruciating torture, extract confessions of crimes that might justify his suspicions. The names which escaped their lips in the agony of torture were carefully registered, in order to supply fresh victims to the tyrant. In the single town of Padua there were eight prisons always full, notwithstanding the incessant toil of the executioner to empty them; two of these contained each 300 prisoners." Old associates disgusted by his crimes, finally betrayed him (in the year 1259) and, wounded and a prisoner, ". . . he refused to speak, rejected all the aid of medicine; tore off all the bandages from his wounds, and finally expired, on the eleventh day of his

captivity." (Sismondi's *History of the Italian Republics*, Ch. IV.)

An understanding of this story is necessary to a comprehension of Shelley's gamble between Death and Sin and the prophecy that at a destined time Sin should have its way with the Lombard plain. When Shelley wrote the poem Austria dominated Lombardy as Eccelino had failed to do for his master Frederick II.

256. *lamp of learning.* Padua was the seat of one of the great medieval universities.

315–9. *Be it love . . . universe.* "The passage admits of numerous interpretations, the precise meaning of 'all' (316) and the antecedent of 'Which' in the next line, being equally doubtful. On the whole the most satisfactory explanation seems to be—'Whether that which is now falling from Heaven be love, light, etc., or the Universal Mind which inspires this verse, and so peoples the universe with its subjective creations.'" (Locock.)

331. *this lone being.* Shelley.

Page 425. STANZAS, WRITTEN IN DEJECTION, NEAR NAPLES

"At the time, Shelley suffered greatly in health. He put himself under the care of a medical man, who promised great things, and made him endure severe bodily pain, without any good results. Constant and poignant physical suffering exhausted him; and though he preserved the appearance of cheerfulness, and often greatly enjoyed our wanderings in the environs of Naples, and our excursions on its sunny sea, yet many hours were passed when his thoughts, shadowed by illness, became gloomy,—and then he escaped to solitude, and in verses, which he hid from fear of wounding me, poured forth morbid but too natural bursts of discontent and sadness. One looks back with unspeakable regret and gnawing remorse to such periods; fancying that, had one been more alive to the nature of his feelings, and more attentive to soothe them, such would not have existed. And yet, enjoying as he appeared to do every sight or influence of earth or sky, it was difficult to imagine that any melancholy he showed was aught but the effect of the constant pain to which he was a martyr." (From Mrs. Shelley's note.)

The poem is a contrast between personal mood and beauty of setting. That Mary Shelley did not understand at the time the depth of Shelley's personal despondency she indicates in her note. A recent critic has itemized "the schedule" of Shelley's sorrows, referred to in the third stanza of the poem:

". . . *Nor hope:* at times it seemed to him that he was hunted by calamity. The suicides of Harriet and Fanny, the loss of his children by

Harriet, the turning of family and friends against him, his public reputation as a moral pariah, the death of his little daughter, Clara, in September of this year, a host of minor difficulties, financial and other, the constant worry about Claire and Allegra, some mysterious affair at Naples, concluding seemingly in the death of an English woman who was infatuated with him—all these events tortured his memory. It is little wonder that, as he wrote sometime later, it seemed to him as if the destruction that was consuming him was as an 'atmosphere which wrapt and infected' everything connected with him. *Nor health:* he had come to Italy for his health, he was continually subjected to intense physical pain and overwhelming lassitude, and at Naples he had suffered particularly through the egregious blundering of a physician. *Nor peace:* in the midst of all these wearing memories and ever-recurring problems, he had been cautioned to avoid even the comfort of composition, and not even the translating of the *Symposium* had restored the tranquillity of mind he had praised in the *Hymn*. *Nor fame:* his published works were neglected—for example, the public indifference to *Alastor;* or bigotedly rejected—for example, the *Quarterly Review* criticism of *The Revolt of Islam*, by John Taylor Coleridge, who vilified the author and pronounced the work a 'laboriously obscene' farrago of lawlessness, atheism, and immorality. *Nor power:* his hopes of bettering society had ended in failure, both his practical attempts, and his endeavours in his poetry to awaken men from 'the trance of ordinary life' and stimulate them to a noble rivalry in working for moral progress. On every side he saw the vast accumulation of stupid, selfish opinions and institutions, against which virtue itself seemed powerless. . . . *Nor love:* it was a time of loneliness for Mary and Shelley, for friends were few, especially at Naples. Then, too, there was his feeling that he ought to keep Mary in ignorance of his despondency, so far as possible. She curiously united, as Dowden has observed, to something of her father's desire for temperance of emotion a habit of looking 'over-intensely at the dark side of human things' (Leigh Hunt's words, in a letter addressed to her); so there was good reason for guarding her peace of mind. Much as she had always aided him to overcome his gloom, at this time, apparently, he suffered alone, preserving for her sake an appearance of cheerfulness. Later she came to realize a part, at least, of what he had kept from her: . . . Thus, dying daily, as it were, he suffered an accumulation of tortures that must have been like that 'cloud of winged snakes' with which the mind of Prometheus was tormented." (Benjamin P. Kurtz's *The Pursuit of Death*, pp. 151-3.)

Page 426.

SONNET: LIFT NOT THE PAINTED VEIL

6. *Their shadows*, etc. In the *Posthumous Poems* (1824) edited by Mary Shelley, this line reads: "The shadows, which the world calls substance, there."

Shelley's ideas of shadow and substance, illusion and reality, were derived from Plato, notably from the sixth and seventh books of *The Republic*. Book Seven opens with the famous figure of the den which perhaps Shelley had in mind when he wrote this sonnet: "And now, I said, let me show in a figure how far our nature is enlightened or unenlightened:—Behold! human beings living in an underground den, which has a mouth open towards the light and reaching all along the den; here they have been from their childhood, and have their legs and necks chained so that they cannot move, and can only see before them, being prevented by the chains from turning round their heads. Above and behind them a fire is blazing at a distance, and between the fire and the prisoners there is a raised way; and you will see, if you look, a low wall built along the way, like the screen which marionette players have in front of them, over which they show the puppets.—I see.—And do you see, I said, men passing along the wall carrying all sorts of vessels, and statues and figures of animals made of wood and stone and various materials, which appear over the wall? Some of them are talking, others silent. —You have shown me a strange image, and they are strange prisoners.—Like ourselves, I replied; and they see only their own shadows, or the shadows of one another, which the fire throws on the opposite wall of the cave?— True, he said; how could they see anything but the shadows if they were never allowed to move their heads?. . .—And if they were able to converse with one another, would they not suppose that they were naming what was actually before them?—Very true.—And suppose further that the prison had an echo which came from the other side, would they not be sure to fancy when one of the passers-by spoke that the voice which they heard came from the passing shadow?—No question, he replied.— To them, I said, the truth would be literally nothing but the shadows of the images.—That is certain.—And now look again, and see what will naturally follow if the prisoners are released and disabused of their error. At first, when any of them is liberated and compelled suddenly to stand up and turn his neck round and walk and look towards the light, he will suffer sharp pains; the glare will distress him, and he will be unable to see the realities of which in his former state he had seen the shadows; and then conceive some one saying to him, that what he saw before was an illusion, but that now, when he is approaching nearer to being and his eye is turned towards more real existence, he has a clearer vision,—what will be his reply? And you may further imagine that his instructor is pointing to the objects as they pass and requiring him to name them,—will he not be perplexed? Will he not fancy that the shadows which he formerly saw are truer than the objects which are now shown to him?—Far truer.—. . .—He will require to grow accustomed to the sight of the upper world. And first he will see the shadows best, next the reflections of men and other objects in the water, and then the objects themselves; then he will gaze upon the light of the moon and the stars and the spangled heaven; and he will see the sky and the stars by night better than the sun or the light of the sun by day?—Certainly.—Last of all he will be able to see the sun, and not mere reflections of him in the water, but he will see him in his own proper place, and not in another; and he will contemplate him as he is." (*The Republic*, Bk. VII, Jowett translation.)

SONG TO THE MEN OF ENGLAND

In 1819 Shelley composed a group of political poems written in a style simpler than was customary with him and which he hoped would have a direct popular appeal. They were not, however, published until after his death, when the first great battle for reform had been fought and won. The agitation in England was for parliamentary reform. On August 16, 1819, a great reform meeting had been held at St. Peter's Field, Manchester. The yeomanry interfered, arresting the speakers, and in the riot which followed several people were killed and many hurt. This "Manchester Massacre," resulting from interference with England's traditional right of assembly and free speech, deeply moved Shelley.

ODE TO THE WEST WIND

"This poem was conceived and chiefly written in a wood that skirts the Arno, near Florence, and on a day when that tempestuous wind, whose temperature is at once mild and animating, was collecting the vapors which pour down the autumnal rains. They began, as I foresaw, at sunset with a violent tempest of hail and rain, attended by that magnificent thunder and lightning peculiar to the Cisalpine regions." (Shelley's note.)

38. *Cleave themselves into chasms.* "The phenomenon alluded to at the conclusion of the third stanza is well known to naturalists. The vegetation at the bottom of the sea, of rivers, and of lakes, sympathizes with that of the land in the change of seasons, and is consequently influenced by the winds which announce it." (Shelley's note.)

Page 428.   THE SENSITIVE PLANT

The germinal idea for *The Sensitive Plant* may have been supplied to Shelley by an episode which occurred during his Oxford days. Hogg recounts it as follows:

"I followed him, but with less ardour, and passing through a narrow belt of wood and thicket, I presently found him standing motionless in one of his picturesque attitudes, riveted to the earth in speechless astonishment. He had thrown himself thus precipitately into a trim flower-garden, of a circular, or rather an oval form, of small dimensions, encompassed by a narrow, but close girdle of trees and underwood; it was apparently remote from all habitations, and it contrasted strongly with the bleak and bare country through which we had recently passed.

"Had the secluded scene been bright with the gay flowers of spring, with hyacinths and tulips; had it been powdered with mealy auriculas, or conspicuous for a gaudy show of all anemones and of every ranunculus; had it been profusely decorated by the innumerable roses of summer, it would be easy to understand why it was so cheerful. But we were now in the very heart of winter, and after much frost scarcely a single wretched brumal flower lingered and languished. There was no foliage, save the dark leaves of evergreens, and of them there were many, especially around and on the edges of the magic circle, on which account possibly, but chiefly perhaps through the symmetry of the numerous small parterres, the scrupulous neatness of the corresponding walks, the just ordonnance and disposition of certain benches, the integrity and freshness of the green trellices, and of the skeletons of some arbours, and through every leafless excellence which the dried anatomy of a flower-garden can exhibit, its past and its future wealth seemed to shine forth in its present poverty, and its potential glories adorn its actual disgrace.

"The sudden transition from the rugged fields to this garnished and decorated retreat was striking, and held my imagination captive a few moments; the impression, however, would probably have soon faded from my memory, had it not been fixed there by the recollection of the beings who gave animation and a permanent interest to the polished nook.

"We admired the trim and retired garden for some minutes in silence, and afterwards each answered in monosyllables the other's brief expressions of wonder. Neither of us had advanced a single step beyond the edge of the thicket through which we had entered; but I was about to precede, and to walk round the magic circle, in order fully to survey the place, when Shelley startled me by turning with astonishing rapidity, and dashing through the bushes and the gap in the fence with the mysterious and whimsical agility of a kangaroo. Had he caught a glimpse of a tiger crouching behind the laurels, and preparing to spring upon him, he could not have vanished more promptly, or more silently. I was habituated to his abrupt movements, nevertheless his alacrity surprised me, and I tried in vain to discover what object had scared him away.

. . . .

"Shelley had looked on the ornate inclosure with a poet's eye, and as we hastily pursued our course towards Oxford by the frozen and sounding way, whilst the day rapidly declined, he discoursed of it fancifully, and with a more glowing animation than ordinary, like one agitated by a divine fury, and by the impulse of inspiring Deity. He continued, indeed, so long to enlarge upon the marvels of the enchanted grove, that I hinted the enchantress might possibly be at hand, and since he was so eloquent concerning the nest, what would have been his astonishment had he been permitted to see the bird herself.

. . . .

". . . Shelley's lively fancy has painted a goodly portraiture of the mistress of the fair garden, nor were apt words wanting to convey to me a faithful copy of the bright original. It would be a cruel injustice to an orator, should a plain man attempt, after a silence of more than twenty years, to revive his glowing harangue from faded recollections; I will not seek, therefore, to portray the likeness of the ideal nymph of the flower-garden.

"'Since your fairy gardener,' I said, 'has so completely taken possession of your imagination'—and he was wonderfully excited by the unexpected scene and his own splendid decorations—'it is a pity we did not notice the situation, for I am quite sure I should not be able to return thither, to recover your Eden, and the Eve whom you created to till it; and I doubt whether you could guide me.'
"He acknowledged that he was as incapable of finding it again, as of leading me to that paradise to which I had compared it.

. . . .

"'No!' he exclaimed, pausing in the rapid career of words, and for a while he was somewhat troubled, 'the seclusion is too sweet, too holy, to be the theatre of ordinary love; the love of the sexes, however pure, still retains some taint of earthly grossness; we must not admit it within the sanctuary.'" (Hogg's *Life of Shelley*, ed. Dowden, pp. 76–80.)

The poem as finally composed is a parable lavishly overlaid with description. The seasonal changes are, obviously enough, symbols of life and growth and death. In the first part

the purely sensuous predominates, in the second we have the coming of soul, in the third the coming of death. There is a notable change, however, between Parts Second and Third. The flowers throughout Parts First and Second had been assumed to be "conscious" (see for example Part Second, 31–32); in Part Third, 14–16, they are still "conscious." But after that the garden, with the single exception of the Sensitive Plant, is treated purely as vegetable growth, and not very pleasant growth. When spring comes again even the Plant is dead. The Conclusion revolts from the rebirth of mandrakes and toadstools only and asserts that where all is the shadow of a dream, death also is illusion and beauty does not die. From a strictly logical point of view there are inconsistencies in the conclusion but it does not greatly abuse the permissibilities of poetic license and it makes its point.

The Sensitive Plant has been identified with Shelley himself, and Mr. Kurtz, one of the most brilliant of contemporary commentators on Shelley, accepts the identification as complete. Shelley is the most personal of the English romantic poets and almost all he wrote can be identified with him in one way or another. The poem in its responsiveness to beauty, revolt at its physical destruction, and Platonic assertion of the survival of the Ideal is Shelley; the Plant in its vegetable and helpless inactivity is no fair portrait. Shelley once remarked to Trelawney, "I go on until I am stopped. . . . And I never am stopped," and Trelawney, who had all the vigor of a bandit, did not challenge the statement. Before Shelley is too completely identified with the Sensitive Plant this aspect of his character should be considered.

72–3. *Received . . . giver.* This passage is not clearly expressed and has given rise to many interpretations. Rearranging the order and inserting the word "beauty" twice we arrive at this direct prose statement: "Where none wanted (i.e., lacked beauty) but it, it loved more beauty than ever could belong to the giver." And "loved" has the Platonic sense of "desired"—or "willed to have and be one with," if the word "desired" has too passionate a complexion in English. See extracts from the *Symposium* in the introductory material to the *Hymn to Intellectual Beauty*. So understood against the Platonic background the lines are plain enough and accord perfectly with ll. 76–77. Note in line 76 the capitalization of "It loves, even like Love"—the capitalizing of the second Love, taken in connection with the following line, indicating very clearly a reference to Socrates' reply to Agathon in the *Symposium*.

2. *An Eve in this Eden.* According to Medwin the original was Lady Mountcashell, a resident in Pisa. Shelley later described Jane Williams as "the exact antitype of the Lady—though this must have been a *pure anticipated cognition.*" Either or neither of these ladies may have been the model of the Lady, by anticipated cognition or otherwise, but, before both, there had been the purely imaginary garden nymph of Shelley's conversation with Hogg.
78. *one forbid.* One accurst.
131–2. *sweet shapes . . . have never passed away.* Logically, according to the preceding stanza, they should have done so. If one accepts the last four lines of the Conclusion as referring to Idea, not physical substance, the inconsistency is largely resolved.

Page 432.　THE CLOUD

Mrs. Shelley says, "There are others, such as the 'Ode to the Skylark,' and 'The Cloud,' which, in the opinion of many critics, bear a purer poetical stamp than any other of his productions. They were written as his mind prompted, listening to the carolling of the bird, aloft in the azure sky of Italy; or marking the cloud as it sped across the heavens, while he floated in his boat on the Thames."
A recent critic writes of *The Cloud:* ". . . The exhalation of the seas, the growth of the cloud, its processional thunder and lightning, its beautiful reflection of sunrise and moonlight, its precipitation in dew and rain, hail and snow, its dissipation, and the re-continuation of the whole process, are vivified in rapid succession. The shifting beauty of these changes produces no mood of pensive sadness in the poet, but intoxicates him with gladness. The vitality of the life-process takes hold of his imagination, as, really, it had informed Keats's when he spoke of life as "a pigeon tumbling in clear summer air." It energizes his susceptibility to impressions, and then exalts his intuition of the everlasting vitality of nature. Each loveliness passes, but only to yield place to its successor; and the anguish of each departure is absorbed into the glory of each advent. Death is swallowed up in the victory of a persistent and beautiful, beneficent process. This is that intuition of change, or of an *élan vital,* that comes to one contemplating the procession of nature: the realization that nature itself cannot use the word death with our egotistic, sorrow-bred meaning, for death is but the gate through which the procession passes on. . . . 'I change, but I cannot die': there, in a reference to death, is the culmination of this lyric of what I should like to call cosmic gladness, were not such a phrase long since spoiled by cheap usage on the part of superficial mystics." (Kurtz's *The Pursuit of Death,* pp. 223–5.)

Page 433.　TO A SKYLARK

"It was on a beautiful summer evening, while wandering among the lanes, whose myrtle hedges were the bowers of the butterflies, that we heard the carolling of the skylark, which inspired one of the most beautiful of his poems." (Mrs. Shelley's note.)
See notes on *The Cloud,* above. Shelley's *To a Skylark* shares with *The Cloud* the note of exultant acceptance.

Page 435.　HYMN OF PAN

This song is sung *by* Pan, not *to* him. It was composed by request for insertion in a short drama, *Midas,* probably by Mary Shelley, and is preceded by a similar "Hymn of Apollo." The two gods are in competition.
11. *Timolus.* The God of Mount Timolus who was the umpire between Apollo and Pan.
31. *pursued a maiden.* Syrinx in escaping from Pan was changed into a reed.

THE TWO SPIRITS: AN ALLEGORY

The opposition of the positive and negative spirits is clear enough, the positive carrying within his heart "the lamp of love" (l. 11) but the significance of the last two stanzas is not clear. The traveller (l. 43) is aware of both forces, the negative being symbolized by the unfriendly physical scene.

Page 438.

TO —— (MUSIC, WHEN SOFT VOICES DIE)

"What is important is that after plans for Emilia's marriage were first announced, in the spring of 1821, Shelley spoke of the *Epipsychidion* as "a portion of me already dead." The full significance of this when compared with his lines in the *Epipsychidion:*

> I am not thine: I am a part of *thee,*

and

> We shall become the same, we shall be one Spirit within two frames,

should be, but has not been apparent. Emilia, by marrying another, has slain half of the poet's own life; that portion of himself—for he considered her such—was dead. The consummation of that marriage, or its impending consummation, evoked from Shelley more deeply-moving poems on the death of someone deeply beloved by the poet, than were produced in any other similar period of his life. Witness the series, all belonging to the poems of 1821: *Lines,* 'Music, when soft voices die,' *Song, Mutability, A Lament, Remembrance,* 'When passion's trance is overpast,' and several fragments of this year, in the same melancholy tone." (Walter E. Peck's *Shelley: His Life and Work*, II, 207.)

Page 439.   MUTABILITY

See note on "To —— (Music, when Soft Voices Die)." Distress over the impending marriage of Emilia Viviani may have been the immediate provocation of this poem, but the theme was by no means new to Shelley. Like all acutely sensitive figures he was intensely aware of the transitoriness of beauty in the phenomenal world around him, and his distress at its evanescence was in exact proportion to his responsiveness to the beauty itself. In other words, by the law of compensation, every height implied a depth beyond.

A LAMENT (O WORLD! O LIFE! O TIME!)

"The most fashionable of Shelley's lyrics among latter-day critics. The sentiment and diction are to a great extent Wordsworthian." (Locock.)

TO —— (ONE WORD IS TOO OFTEN PROFANED)

This poem, unlike the three preceding, is generally agreed to have been inspired by Jane Williams. It takes its place as one of the most perfect of Shelley's lyrics. Had Shelley deliberately set out to write a motto for his life he could scarcely have done better than the last four lines of this poem.

TO —— (WHEN PASSION'S TRANCE IS OVERPAST)

See note on "To —— (Music, when Soft Voices Die)."
"Well may he have learned this lesson of cooling love from Harriet, or Mary, or Emilia. Who has not learned it? . . . The expression is at once general and intense enough to be true to human experience the world over; so piercingly eloquent that Everyman realizes himself in it, knowing himself, and mankind, more keenly than he had before; so musical that pain is purged of crude selfishness, beauty taking over the place of intemperate self-love." (Kurtz's *The Pursuit of Death*, pp. 242–3.)

Page 440.

From HELLAS: CHORUS (THE WORLD'S GREAT AGE BEGINS ANEW)

"The final chorus is indistinct and obscure, as the event of the living drama whose arrival it foretells. . . . Prophecies of wars, and rumours of wars, etc., may safely be made by poet or prophet in any age; but to anticipate, however darkly, a period of regeneration and happiness is a more hazardous exercise of the faculty which bards possess or feign. It will remind the reader, 'magno nec proximus intervallo' of Isaiah and Virgil, whose ardent spirits, overleaping the actual reign of evil which we endure and bewail, already saw the possible and perhaps approaching state of society in which the 'lion shall lie down with the lamb,' and 'omnis feret omnia tellus.' Let these great names be my authority and my excuse." (Shelley's note.)
Locock assumes that this chorus "describes the future Hellas in America."
21. *Laian rage.* Laius, father of Œdipus, was killed by his son, in accordance with the Delphic oracle. " 'Laian rage' might stand loosely for Œdipean rage; or it might allude to the command of Laius that his infant son should be put to death. Probably, as Rossetti suggests, it means simply 'rage of the Laian period,' the allusion being to the Sphinx, who was sent by Here to desolate Thebes." (Locock.)
31. *Saturn and Love.* "Saturn and Love were among the deities of a real or imaginary state of innocence and happiness. . . ." (From Shelley's note.)

Page 441.   WITH A GUITAR, TO JANE

The poem was sent to Jane Williams with a present of a guitar. The actual instrument is now preserved in the Bodleian Library.

". . . The suggestion for the poem is found by Dr. Garnett in the fact that 'the front portion of the guitar is made of Swiss pine.' He continues: 'It is now clear how the poem took shape in Shelley's mind. The actual thought of the imprisonment of the Spirit of Music in the material of the instrument suggested Ariel's penance in the cloven pine; the identification of himself with Ariel and of Jane Williams with Miranda was the easiest of feats to his brilliant imagination; and hence an allegory of unequalled grace and charm, which could never have existed if the instrument had not been partly made of pine wood." (G. E. Woodberry, Cambridge ed., Shelley's *Poetical Works.*)

Trelawney gives an account of the conditions under which the first draft of the poem was composed which gives an amusing picture of the Shelley group in the summer of 1822: ". . . When we got under the cool canopy of the pines, she (Mary Shelley) stopped and allowed me to hunt for her husband. I now strode along; the forest was on my right hand and extensive pastures on my left, with herds of oxen, camels, and horses grazing thereon. I came upon the open sea at a place called Gombo, from whence I could see Via Reggio, the Gulf of Spezzia, and the mountains beyond. After bathing, seeing nothing of the Poet, I penetrated the densest part of the forest, ever and anon making the woods ring with the name of Shelley, and scaring the herons and water-birds from the chain of stagnant pools which impeded my progress.

"With no landmarks to guide me, nor sky to be seen above, I was bewildered in this wilderness of pines and ponds; so I sat down, struck a light, and smoked a cigar. A red man would have known his course by the trees themselves, their growth, form, and colour; or if a footstep had passed that day, he would have hit upon its trail. As I mused upon his sagacity and my own stupidity, the braying of a brother jackass startled me. He was followed by an old man picking up pine cones. I asked him if he had seen a stranger?

"'O' Inglese malinclico haunts the wood maledetta. I will show you his nest.'

"As we advanced, the ground swelled into mounds and hollows. By-and-by the old fellow pointed with his stick to a hat, books, and loose papers lying about, and then to a deep pool of dark glimmering water, saying, 'Eccolo!' I thought he meant that Shelley was in or under the water. The careless, not to say impatient, way in which the Poet bore his burden of life, caused a vague dread amongst his family and friends that he might lose or cast it away at any moment.

"The strong light streamed through the opening of the trees. One of the pines, undermined by the water, had fallen into it. Under its lee, and nearly hidden, sat the Poet, gazing on the dark mirror beneath, so lost in his bardish reverie that he did not hear my approach. There the trees were stunted and bent, and their crowns were shorn like friars by the sea breezes, excepting a cluster of three, under which Shelley's traps were lying: these overtopped the rest. To avoid startling the Poet out of his dream, I squatted under the lofty trees, and opened his books. One was a volume of his favourite Greek dramatist, Sophocles,—the same that I found in his pocket after his death—and the other was a volume of Shakespeare. I then hailed him, and, turning his head, he answered faintly:

"'Hello, come in.'

"'Is this your study?' I asked.

"'Yes,' he answered, 'and these trees are my books—they tell no lies. You are sitting on the stool of inspiration,' he exclaimed. 'In those three pines the weird sisters are imprisoned, and this,' pointing to the water, 'is their caldron of black broth. The Pythian priestesses uttered their oracles from below—now they are muttered from above. Listen to the solemn music in the pine tops—don't you hear the mournful murmurings of the sea? Sometimes they rave and roar, shriek and howl, like a rabble of priests. In a tempest, when a ship

sinks, they catch the despairing groans of the drowning mariners. Their chorus is the eternal wailing of wretched men.'

"'They, like the world,' I observed, 'seem to take no note of wretched women. The sighs and wailing you talk about are not those of wretched men afar off, but are breathed by a woman near at hand—not from the pine tops, but by a forsaken lady.'

"'What do you mean?' he asked.

"'Why, that an hour or two ago I left your wife, Mary Shelley, at the entrance of this grove, in despair at not finding you.'

"He started up, snatched up his scattered books and papers, thrust them into his hat and jacket pockets, sighing 'Poor Mary! hers is a sad fate. Come along; she can't bear solitude, nor I society—the quick coupled with the dead.'

"He glided along with his usual swiftness, for nothing could make him pause for an instant when he had an object in view, until he had attained it. On hearing our voices, Mrs. Shelley joined us; her clear gray eyes and thoughtful brow expressing the love she could not speak. To stop Shelley's self-reproaches, or to hide her own emotions, she began in a bantering tone, chiding and coaxing him:

"'What a wild-goose you are, Percy; if my thoughts have strayed from my book, it was to the opera, and my new dress from Florence—and especially the ivy wreath so much admired for my hair, and not to you, you silly fellow! When I left home, my satin slippers had not arrived. These are serious matters to gentlewomen, enough to ruffle the serenest tempered. As to you and your ungallant companion, I had forgotten that such things are; but as it is the ridiculous custom to have men at balls and operas, I must take you with me, though, from your uncouth ways, you will be taken for Valentine and he for Orson.'

"Shelley, like other students, would, when the spell that bound his faculties was broken, shut his books, and indulge in the wildest flights of mirth and folly. As this is a sport all can join in, we talked and laughed, and shrieked, and shouted, as we emerged from under the shadows of the melancholy pines and their nodding plumes, into the now cool purple twilight and open country. The cheerful and graceful peasant girls, returning home from the vineyards and olive groves, stopped to look at us. The old man I had met in the morning gathering pine cones, passed hurriedly by with his donkey, giving Shelley a wide berth, and evidently thinking that the melancholy Englishman had now become a raving maniac. Sancho says, 'Blessings on the man who invented sleep'; the man who invented laughing deserves no less.

"The day I found Shelley in the pine forest he

was writing verses on a guitar. I picked up a
fragment, but could only make out the first
two lines:—

> Ariel, to Miranda take
> This slave of music.

It was a frightful scrawl; words smeared out
with his finger, and one upon the other, over
and over in tiers, and all run together in most
'admired disorder'; it might have been taken
for a sketch of a marsh overgrown with bul-
rushes, and the blots for wild ducks; such a
dashed off daub as self-conceited artists mistake for a manifestation of genius. On my
observing this to him, he answered,
"'When my brain gets heated with thought,
it soon boils, and throws off images and words
faster than I can skim them off. In the morning, when cooled down, out of the rude sketch
as you justly call it, I shall attempt a drawing.
If you ask me why I publish what few or none
will care to read, it is that the spirits I have
raised haunt me until they are sent to the
devil of a printer. All authors are anxious to
breech their bantings.'"

Page 444.   ALASTOR

The title and Preface presumably were added
after the completion of the poem. Of the title
Peacock says in his *Memoirs of Shelley:*
"He (Shelley) was at a loss for a title, and I
proposed that which he adopted: "Alastor;
or the Spirit of Solitude." The Greek word,
'Αλάστωρ, is an evil genius. . . . The poem
treated the spirit of solitude as a spirit of evil.
I mention the true meaning of the word because many have supposed "Alastor" to be
the name of the hero."

This distinction should be borne in mind. The
Preface as well as the title presents some difficulty. The ideas Shelley chose to emphasize
when he was writing in prose after the completion of the poem were not those he chose to
emphasize in the heat of poetic composition.
It is not that the poem and preface are at variance: but there is a marked difference of emphasis.

Shelley wrote to Godwin (February 24, 1812):
"Though I begin a subject in writing with no
definite view, it presently assumes a definite
form, in consequence of the method that grows
out of the induced train of thought." It is not
too much to assume that *Alastor* grew under
Shelley's hands in the course of composition.
In any case, the architectonics (never Shelley's
strong point) of the poem are uncertain. In
individual passages, however, and there are
many of them scattered through the poem, the
authentic voice of the great Shelley is heard

and *Alastor* rightfully takes its place as the
first (excluding *Queen Mab*, which was only a
succès de scandale) of his important poetic
productions. Mary Shelley in her note to the
poem says: "The poem ought rather to be considered didactic than narrative: it was the
outpouring of his own emotions, embodied in
the purest form he could conceive, painted in
the ideal hues which his brilliant imagination
inspired, and softened by the recent anticipation of death."

". . . The reader of *Alastor* is confused because
its author was confused. Instead of having, as
the preface implies, a single purpose in writing
it, he had in view at least four objects, although
they are so closely allied that one rises naturally
out of another and soon sinks back into it or
else passes imperceptibly into a third and then
to a fourth. The first thing he wished to do
was to narrate the wanderings (ending in death)
of an ideal youth; the second, to describe the
scenery through which the youth passes; the
third, to point out his neglect of human love
through his fondness for solitude; and the
fourth, to recount his dream of an ideal mate
and his attempted union with her through
death.
"To the first of these purposes, which domi-
nates some 400 lines of the poem, and to the
first part of the fourth, which controls 50 lines,
the preface gives approximately the same
space; to the second, which is responsible for
200 lines, it devotes a sentence; the second
part of the fourth purpose, which animates 80
lines, the preface does not mention; but upon
the third, which affects exactly two and a half
lines of the verse, it lays the chief stress. Some
descriptions of nature, to be sure, might be
expected in an account of a poet's wanderings
or a picture of a man unduly fond of solitude;
and yearning for an ideal mate could well be
introduced into the story of a wandering poet
or of a recluse. But in *Alastor* we have pictures
of nature for their own sake and adventurous
wandering for its own sake. For a time we have
also the yearnings for an ideal mate and the
attempted suicide of a solitary; but the remainder of the work would be unaffected if,
by the omission of a hundred or so lines, this
part were removed. The poem is not a unity,
it does not produce a single impression, it was
not the offspring of a single, dominating purpose. That such a purpose is ascribed to it in
the preface would seem to indicate that Shelley
had either forgotten or was imperfectly aware
of much that was in his mind when he wrote
the poem—that he unintentionally represented
the creative process, the ebb and flow of his
thoughts, as more simple, more logical, more
conscious than was the case." (Raymond D.
Havens, *P.M.L.A.*, XLV, 1108-9.)

Shelley's prose fragment "On Love" (1815) is somewhat similar in tone to the Preface of *Alastor* and may be compared with it: "Thou demandest what is love? It is that powerful attraction towards all that we conceive, or fear, or hope beyond ourselves, when we find within our own thoughts the chasm of an insufficient void, and seek to awaken in all things that are, a community with what we experience within ourselves. If we reason, we would be understood; if we imagine, we would that the airy children of our brain were born anew within another's; if we feel, we would that another's nerves should vibrate to our own, that the beams of their eyes should kindle at once and mix and melt into our own, that lips of motionless ice should not reply to lips quivering and burning with the heart's best blood. This is Love. This is the bond and the sanction which connects not only man with man, but with everything which exists. We are born into the world, and there is something within us which, from the instant that we live, more and more thirsts after its likeness. It is probably in correspondence with this law that the infant drains milk from the bosom of its mother; this propensity develops itself with the development of our nature. We dimly see within our intellectual nature a miniature as it were of our entire self, yet deprived of all that we condemn or despise, the ideal prototype of everything excellent or lovely that we are capable of conceiving as belonging to the nature of man. Not only the portrait of our external being, but an assemblage of the minutest particles of which our nature is composed; (These words are ineffectual and metaphorical. Most words are so—No help! [Shelley's note.]) a mirror whose surface reflects only the forms of purity and brightness; a soul within our soul that describes a circle around its proper paradise, which pain, and sorrow, and evil dare not overleap. To this we eagerly refer all sensations, thirsting that they should resemble or correspond with it. The discovery of its antitype; the meeting with an understanding capable of clearly estimating our own; an imagination which should enter into and seize upon the subtle and delicate peculiarities which we have delighted to cherish and unfold in secret; with a frame whose nerves, like the chords of two exquisite lyres, strung to the accompaniment of one delightful voice, vibrate with the vibrations of our own; and of a combination of all these in such proportion as the type within demands; this is the invisible and unattainable point to which Love tends; and to attain which, it urges forth the powers of man to arrest the faintest shadow of that, without the possession of which there is no rest nor respite to the heart over which it rules."

18. *Mother*. See note on l. 479.

23–4. *made my bed In charnels and on coffins*. Hogg (ch. II) reports that Shelley himself planned how he might get admission to the vault at Warnham Church that he "might sit there all night, harrowed by fear, yet trembling with expectation, to see one of the spiritualized owners of the bones piled around him."

85. *bitumen lakes*. A reference to the Dead Sea?

101. *bloodless food*. Shelley himself was for a time a practicing vegetarian. It did not help his health.

118. *dæmons*. Pronounced the same as *demons*, but not to be confused with the evil demons (devils) of Judaeo-Christian thought. A dæmon belongs to classical mythology and was a spirit above men but below the gods, and not necessarily evil or hostile unless offended.

119. *Zodiac's brazen mystery*. Shelley had been reading Volney's *Les Ruines*, which contains a passage referring to the Zodiac of the temple of Denderah in Upper Egypt—since removed to the Bibliothèque Nationale in Paris. On the ceiling of the portico of the temple mythological figures were arranged in the form of the Zodiac.

141. *wild Carmanian waste*. The desert of Kerman; the itinerary of Shelley's hero has a certain consistency and correspondence with the route of Alexander the Great on his invasion of India. Nevertheless there are difficulties which become acute when Shelley's hero becomes involved with whirlpools and tunnels under mountains. Havens suggests that the difficulties may be resolved by considering the journey a journey of the mind rather than an actual physical voyage.

151. *a veilèd maid*. "Woodberry identifies her as the spirit of the ideal, Forman as the ideal of female perfection. Cf. *Epipsychidion*, l. 190, etc., and the Preface to *Alastor*, ll. 17–26. In any case she is clearly the Alastor, or Spirit of Solitude, sent to avenge 'the Poet's self-centered seclusion.'" (Locock.) See note on ll. 203–5.

200–369. *His wan eyes*, etc. Havens declares this section of the poem most directly bears out the Preface and Peacock's interpretation of the title.

203–5. *The spirit of sweet human love has sent*. This is the origin of the dream of the veiled maid referred to in l. 151. "Yet if a loving spirit sent the dream, an evil one makes use of it, since the results are neither what might have been anticipated nor what the preface describes. For the young solitary, awakening to a world from which the beauty and joy have departed (192–202), wonders if he may not regain the ecstasy of companionship with his beloved through death. That is, he is tempted to suicide." (Havens, *P.M.L.A.*, XLV, 1099.)

211. *the dark gate of death*. Here is the temptation to suicide. See note on ll. 203–5.

291. *desperate hope*. That in death by suicide
he could meet again the Vision.

297. *fair fiend*. He has been tempted to suicide
(see note on l. 291), perhaps by the devil who
has the capacity to put on a fair form and hold
out sweet promises to lure a mortal to destruction. Cf. Hamlet's distrust of the ghost in
Act I.

304. *restless impulse*. Havens maintains that
by embarking in a frail shallop which, by all
the rules of common sense and physics, ought
to sink at once the hero becomes a "moral
suicide." That the actual physical event of
death did not befall him was not his doing.

479. *A Spirit*. Woodberry feels this to be
"apparently an embodiment of nature evoked
by and reflecting the death-melancholy in
the Poet" while Havens makes it equivalent
to the "Mother of this unfathomable world"
of l. 18 and presumably the "pervading Spirit
co-eternal with the universe." The Spirit's
grayness of garb makes it clear that this Spirit
is not the Vision.

490. *Two starry eyes*. This is the last reference
to the Vision.

611. *Skeleton*. Death; the skeleton and the
hourglass are traditional symbols of death.

677. *one living man*. The Wandering Jew.

Page 453. PROMETHEUS UNBOUND

Prometheus Unbound, admittedly one of the
most difficult of Shelley's poems, has been
subjected to more commentary and elucidation than any other work of his. Elaborate
allegorical systems have been read into it, and
the significance of the various figures has been
debated. Prometheus is now the "Mind of
Man" and now simply "Humanity." Asia is
now "Nature," now "Divine Beauty and
Love," and now "Beauty, Love, and Nature"
all at once. Elsewhere she is simplified to mere
"Emotion." Panthea is "Faith" and Ione
"Hope" and Demogorgon passes among other
things as "Eternity," "Divine Justice," and
"Necessity." It is obvious from the very
wealth of meaning read into these figures that
the poem has carried an intense significance
for many minds.
Professor Newman I. White, however, in a
striking article ("Shelley's *Prometheus Unbound*, or Every Man His Own Allegorist,"
P.M.L.A., XL, 172–84) calls attention to the
fact that Aeschylus, from whom Shelley took
over the outlines of the story, thought of his
Prometheus as "simply a noble character . . . a
person in revolt against divine authority, not
an abstraction"; and that Shelley himself nowhere even hinted at an allegorical purpose.
Professor White, however, concedes "the

general representative value of all great art"
and admits "the recognized and indisputable
fact that the poem as a whole does represent
the struggle of humanity against oppression."

Accepting this point of view, one has a fresh
and clear approach to a poem which has been
made needlessly difficult. Shelley took over
and modified a fable, and as a fable his poem
should first be seen, not as a systematic ex-
position of a set of philosophical ideas. But
the fable—the story of a noble nature suffering for humanity and defying authoritarian
oppression until the latter fell, crushed by its
own evil, and the perfect world evolved—was
intensely sympathetic to Shelley, and touched
upon subjects which had been those most
burning in his mind. The result is a lyrical
drama. Instead of the objective impersonality
of the normal drama where the dramatist presents his story and conceals himself, there was
the closer identification of poet and subject
of the lyric. Shelley presents his story and,
when that story touches on subjects close to
his heart, he pours out his heart. The poem
then *is* something more than a story, because
it expresses Shelley's love of love, and hate
of hate, and triumphant hope in the human
heart in many ways, but to press too heavily
on every detail and person of the drama for
significance is a mistake. For example in Act
II it is necessary to the story for two nymphs
to go a journey. Shelley has them follow
echoes and spirit voices through "A Forest
intermingled with Rocks and Caverns" and
past "A Pinnacle of Rock among Mountains,"
and we can safely let it go at that as the story-
telling of a lyrical poet, without pausing to
consider whether the forest represents the
jungle of the physical senses and the mountain
peak the heights of the intellect. But on the
other hand, arrived at their destination, the
nymphs ask questions on the nature and power
of God which make the passage significant.
The problem of when to read in deeper meanings into the story-telling is more apparent
than real. The significant passages have a way
of declaring themselves from the pages of the
text.

For those who prefer the more elaborate approach to *Prometheus Unbound* another authoritative contemporary critic who adheres
to this method is quoted. He begins with a
summary of some preceding interpretations:

"Of interpretations of *Prometheus Unbound*,
as of Browning's *Sordello*, there is, and in the
nature of things can be, no end. Those that
are best known and most available, perhaps
most authoritative, were made by Rossetti
and Todhunter nearly half a century ago; Miss
Scudder's interpretation in the introduction

to her edition of *Prometheus* takes account of others which preceded it and is also valuable for its own sake. Rossetti offers the following interpretation of the principal characters: Prometheus is the Mind of Man, Asia is Nature, Jupiter is the anthropomorphic God, a creation of the Mind of Man, Demogorgon is the personification of Eternity; he makes no explanation of Panthea and Ione. Todhunter gives a considerably different interpretation: Prometheus is the incarnation of the genius of mankind; Jupiter is the evil principle, apparent as orthodoxy, authority, custom, etc.; Demogorgon is the spirit of rebellion, begotten of Jupiter, but, in a broader sense, Divine Justice itself; Panthea is the spirit of divine wisdom, seeing into the truth of things; Ione is hope; and Asia is the spirit of divine love and beauty. Miss Scudder's interpretation is: Prometheus represents all humanity; Jupiter stands for all those institutions, civil and religious, through which the authority of law is expressed; Thetis, whom Jupiter marries, is false glory; Demogorgon, the offspring of this marriage, is Revolution, or intellectual force, acting through reason, that makes revolution possible; Asia is the Spirit of Divine Love; and Panthea is Faith.

"It makes little difference whether Prometheus be the mind of man, the genius of mankind, or humanity itself, except for the sake of consistency within the poem; for if the mind or genius of man is bound, man himself is also bound. Perhaps it would be more accurate to say that Prometheus is the personification of wisdom which enlightens the human mind, not the mind itself. Jupiter is undoubtedly intended to represent the institutions of society, religious, political, and social, which have enslaved mankind and fettered wisdom. Demogorgon is both an abstraction and a personality; the personality is derived from the marriage of Jupiter and Thetis, and may be defined as revolution; the abstraction, however, is the eternal law which as cause and effect governs the operation of fate, time, occasion, chance, and change. Asia is the Spirit of Beauty or Love, but she may with equal truth be described as the Spirit of Nature—not as Nature itself, as Rossetti believed. Panthea and Ione may be faith and hope, but it is impossible to ascribe to them any definite character. Their function was to comfort Prometheus in his suffering, to act as messengers between him and Asia, and to rejoice with him in his freedom.

"The general meaning of the poem, if minor inconsistencies be disregarded, is clear enough. The long speech of Asia in the fourth scene of the second act outlines the history of the earth up to the moment of the liberation of Prometheus. In the beginning were Heaven and Earth and Light and Love, the elements which we may assume to have existed always. Light here is probably not the natural phenomenon but the spiritual element later incorporated in Prometheus, as Love is the spiritual element later incorporated in Asia. Heaven and Earth, of course, represent the material part of the universe. Of living things Saturn was first, and during his reign men had neither knowledge nor power, but were on the plane of animals and plants. After Saturn came Jupiter, to whom Prometheus "gave wisdom, which is strength," on the condition that man should be free. The reign of Jupiter marks the beginning of law in the world, the organization of men into social groups, without which progress was impossible. The granting of power to Jupiter, therefore, was not inconsistent with the perfect wisdom of Prometheus. The source of evil in Jupiter resided in his endowment with supreme power, for

To know nor faith, nor love, nor law; to be
Omnipotent but friendless is to reign;
And Jove now reigned.

"Shelley does not mean that law or order is evil, except when it lies within the disposition of a single being. When Jupiter broke his contract with Prometheus, not making man free but enslaving him, then began the conflict between the two, which is analogous to the conflict between the Principle of Evil and the Principle of Good that has already been pointed out in *Laon and Cythna*. Prometheus sent Hope and Love to mankind to comfort them, and also gave men the secrets of fire and speech, which enabled them to improve their condition materially and intellectually. But men came to worship Jupiter rather than Prometheus, and the latter was finally separated from Asia, or Love, and bound to a rock. Such the state of things is, and has been for three thousand years, when the drama opens. The Spirit of Wisdom which enlightens the human mind is not destroyed, but has been temporarily curtailed of its power by the influence of evil in the person of Jupiter." (Floyd Stovall, *Desire and Restraint in Shelley*, pp. 241–3.)

Shelley's Preface

"The Greek tragic writers, in selecting as their subject any portion of their national history or mythology, employed in their treatment of it a certain arbitrary discretion. They by no means conceived themselves bound to adhere to the common interpretation or to imitate in story as in title their rivals and predecessors. Such a system would have amounted to a resignation of those claims to a preference over their competitors which incited the composition. The Agamemnonian story was exhibited on the Athenian theatre with as many variations as dramas.

"I have presumed to employ a similar license. The *Prometheus Unbound* of Æschylus supposed the reconciliation of Jupiter with his victim as the price of the disclosure of the danger threatened to his empire by the consummation of his marriage with Thetis. Thetis, according to this view of the subject, was given in marriage to Peleus, and Prometheus, by the permission of Jupiter, delivered from his captivity by Hercules. Had I framed my story on this model, I should have done no more than have attempted to restore the lost drama of Æschylus; an ambition which, if my preference to this mode of treating the subject had incited me to cherish, the recollection of the high comparison such an attempt would challenge might well abate. But, in truth, I was averse from a catastrophe so feeble as that of reconciling the champion with the oppressor of mankind. The moral interest of the fable, which is so powerfully sustained by the sufferings and endurance of Prometheus, would be annihilated if we could conceive of him as unsaying his high language and quailing before his successful and perfidious adversary. The only imaginary being resembling in any degree Prometheus, is Satan; and Prometheus is, in my judgment, a more poetical character than Satan, because, in addition to courage, and majesty, and firm and patient opposition to omnipotent force, he is susceptible of being described as exempt from the taints of ambition, envy, revenge, and a desire for personal aggrandizement, which, in the hero of *Paradise Lost*, interfere with the interest. The character of Satan engenders in the mind a pernicious casuistry which leads us to weigh his faults with his wrongs, and to excuse the former because the latter exceed all measure. In the minds of those who consider that magnificent fiction with a religious feeling it engenders something worse. But Prometheus is, as it were, the type of the highest perfection of moral and intellectual nature, impelled by the purest and the truest motives to the best and noblest ends.

"This poem was chiefly written upon the mountainous ruins of the Baths of Caracalla, among the flowery glades, and thickets of odoriferous blossoming trees, which are extended in ever winding labyrinths upon its immense platforms and dizzy arches suspended in the air. The bright blue sky of Rome, and the effect of the vigorous awakening spring in that divinest climate, and the new life with which it drenches the spirits even to intoxication, were the inspiration of this drama.

"The imagery which I have employed will be found, in many instances, to have been drawn from the operations of the human mind, or from those external actions by which they are expressed. This is unusual in modern poetry, although Dante and Shakespeare are full of instances of the same kind: Dante indeed more than any other poet, and with greater success. But the Greek poets, as writers to whom no resource of awakening the sympathy of their contemporaries was unknown, were in the habitual use of this power; and it is the study of their works (since a higher merit would probably be denied me) to which I am willing that my readers should impute this singularity.

"One word is due in candor to the degree in which the study of contemporary writings may have tinged my composition, for such has been a topic of censure with regard to poems far more popular, and indeed more deservedly popular, than mine. It is impossible that any one who inhabits the same age with such writers as those who stand in the foremost ranks of our own, can conscientiously assure himself that his language and tone of thought may not have been modified by the study of the productions of those extraordinary intellects. It is true that, not the spirit of their genius, but the forms in which it has manifested itself, are due less to the peculiarities of their own minds than to the peculiarity of the moral and intellectual condition of the minds among which they have been produced. Thus a number of writers possess the form, whilst they want the spirit of those whom, it is alleged, they imitate; because the former is the endowment of the age in which they live, and the latter must be the uncommunicated lightning of their own mind.

"The peculiar style of intense and comprehensive imagery which distinguishes the modern literature of England, has not been, as a general power, the product of the imitation of any particular writer. The mass of capabilities remains at every period materially the same; the circumstances which awaken it to action perpetually change. If England were divided into forty republics, each equal in population and extent to Athens, there is no reason to suppose but that, under institutions not more perfect than those of Athens, each would produce philosophers and poets equal to those who (if we except Shakespeare) have never been surpassed. We owe the great writers of the golden age of our literature to that fervid awakening of the public mind which shook to dust the oldest and most oppressive form of the Christian religion. We owe Milton to the progress and development of the same spirit: the sacred Milton was, let it ever be remembered, a republican, and a bold inquirer into morals and religion. The great writers of our own age are, we have reason to suppose, the companions and forerunners of some unimagined change in our social condition or the opinions which cement it. The cloud of mind is discharging its collected lightning, and the equilibrium between institutions and opinions is now restoring, or is about to be restored.

"As to imitation, poetry is a mimetic art. It creates, but it creates by combination and representation. Poetical abstractions are beautiful and new, not because the portions of which they are composed had no previous existence in the mind of man or in nature, but because the whole produced by their combination has some intelligible and beautiful analogy with those sources of emotion and thought, and with the contemporary condition of them: one great poet is a masterpiece of nature which another not only ought to study but must study. He might as wisely and as easily determine that his mind should no longer be the mirror of all that is lovely in the visible universe, as exclude from his contemplation the beautiful which exists in the writings of a great contemporary. The pretence of doing it would be a presumption in any but the greatest; the effect, even in him, would be strained, unnatural, and ineffectual. A poet is the combined product of such internal powers as modify the nature of others; and of such external influences as excite and sustain these powers; he is not one, but both. Every man's mind is, in this respect, modified by all the objects of nature and art; by every word and every suggestion which he ever admitted to act upon his consciousness; it is the mirror upon which all forms are reflected, and in which they compose one form. Poets, not otherwise than philosophers, painters, sculptors, and musicians, are, in one sense, the creators, and, in another, the creations, of their age. From this subjection the loftiest do not escape. There is a similarity between Homer and Hesiod, between Æschylus and Euripides, between Virgil and Horace, between Dante and Petrarch, between Shakespeare and Fletcher, between Dryden and Pope; each has a generic resemblance under which their specific distinctions are arranged. If this similarity be the result of imitation, I am willing to confess that I have imitated.

"Let this opportunity be conceded to me of acknowledging that I have, what a Scotch philosopher characteristically terms, 'a passion for reforming the world': what passion incited him to write and publish his book, he omits to explain. For my part I had rather be damned with Plato and Lord Bacon, than go to Heaven with Paley and Malthus. But it is a mistake to suppose that I dedicate my poetical compositions solely to the direct enforcement of reform, or that I consider them in any degree as containing a reasoned system on the theory of human life. Didactic poetry is my abhorrence; nothing can be equally well expressed in prose that is not tedious and supererogatory in verse. My purpose has hitherto been simply to familiarize the highly refined imagination of the more select classes of poetical readers with beautiful idealisms of moral excellence; aware that until the mind can love, and admire, and trust, and hope, and endure, reasoned principles of moral conduct are seeds cast upon the highway of life which the unconscious passenger tramples into dust, although they would bear the harvest of his happiness. Should I live to accomplish what I purpose, that is, produce a systematical history of what appear to me to be the genuine elements of human society, let not the advocates of injustice and superstition flatter themselves that I should take Æschylus rather than Plato as my model.

"The having spoken of myself with unaffected freedom will need little apology with the candid, and let the uncandid consider that they injure me less than their own hearts and minds by misrepresentation. Whatever talents a person may possess to amuse and instruct others, be they ever so inconsiderable, he is yet bound to exert them: if his attempt be ineffectual, let the punishment of an unaccomplished purpose have been sufficient; let none trouble themselves to heap the dust of oblivion upon his efforts; the pile they raise will betray his grave which might otherwise have been unknown."

A considerable portion of Mrs. Shelley's "Note on *Prometheus Unbound*" is now quoted:

". . . The first aspect of Italy enchanted Shelley; it seemed a garden of delight placed beneath a clearer and brighter heaven than any he had lived under before. He wrote long descriptive letters during the first year of his residence in Italy, which, as compositions, are the most beautiful in the world, and show how truly he appreciated and studied the wonders of nature and art in that divine land.

"The poetical spirit within him speedily revived with all the power and with more than all the beauty of his first attempts. He meditated three subjects as the groundwork for lyrical dramas. One was the story of Tasso; of this a slight fragment of a song of Tasso remains. The other was one founded on the *Book of Job*, which he never abandoned in idea, but of which no trace remains among his papers. The third was the *Prometheus Unbound*. The Greek tragedians were now his most familiar companions in his wanderings, and the sublime majesty of Æschylus filled him with wonder and delight. The father of Greek tragedy does not possess the pathos of Sophocles, nor the variety and tenderness of Euripides; the interest on which he founds his dramas is often elevated above human vicissitudes into the mighty passions and throes of gods and demi-gods: such fascinated the abstract imagination of Shelley.

. . . .

"At first he completed the drama in three acts. It was not till several months after, when at Florence, that he conceived that a fourth act, a sort of hymn of rejoicing in the fulfillment of the prophecies with regard to Prometheus, ought to be added to complete the composition.

"The prominent feature of Shelley's theory of the destiny of the human species was that evil is not inherent in the system of the creation, but an accident that might be expelled. This also forms a portion of Christianity: God made earth and man perfect, till he, by his fall,

'Brought death into the world and all our woe.'

Shelley believed that mankind had only to will that there should be no evil, and there would be none. It is not my part in these notes to notice the arguments that have been urged against this opinion, but to mention the fact that he entertained it, and was indeed attached to it with fervent enthusiasm. That man could be so perfectionized as to be able to expel evil from his own nature, and from the greater part of the creation, was the cardinal point of his system. And the subject he loved best to dwell on was the image of One warring with the Evil Principle, oppressed not only by it, but by all—even the good, who were deluded into considering evil a necessary portion of humanity; a victim full of fortitude and hope and the spirit of triumph emanating from a reliance in the ultimate omnipotence of Good. Such he had depicted in his last poem [*The Revolt of Islam*] when he made Laon the enemy and the victim of tyrants. He now took a more idealized image of the same subject. He followed certain classical authorities in figuring Saturn as the good principle, Jupiter the usurping evil one, and Prometheus as the regenerator, who, unable to bring mankind back to primitive innocence, used knowledge as a weapon to defeat evil, by leading mankind, beyond the state wherein they are sinless through ignorance, to that in which they are virtuous through wisdom. Jupiter punished the temerity of the Titan by chaining him to a rock of Caucasus, and causing a vulture to devour his still-renewed heart. There was a prophecy afloat in heaven portending the fall of Jove, the secret of averting which was known only to Prometheus; and the god offered freedom from torture on condition of its being communicated to him. According to the mythological story, this referred to the offspring of Thetis, who was destined to be greater than his father. Prometheus at last bought pardon for his crime of enriching mankind with his gifts, by revealing the prophecy. Hercules killed the vulture, and set him free; and Thetis was married to Peleus, the father of Achilles.

"Shelley adapted the catastrophe of this story to his peculiar views. The son greater than his father, born of the nuptials of Jupiter and Thetis, was to dethrone Evil, and bring back a happier reign than that of Saturn. Prometheus defies the power of his enemy, and endures centuries of torture; till the hour arrives when Jove, blind to the real event, but darkly guessing that some great good to himself will flow, espouses Thetis. At the moment, the Primal Power of the world drives him from his usurped throne, and Strength, in the person of Hercules, liberates Humanity, typified in Prometheus, from the tortures generated by evil done or suffered. Asia, one of the Oceanides, is the wife of Prometheus—she was, according to other mythological interpretations, the same as Venus and Nature. When the benefactor of mankind is liberated, Nature resumes the beauty of her prime, and is united to her husband, the emblem of the human race, in perfect and happy union. In the Fourth Act, the poet gives further scope to his imagination, and idealizes the forms of creation—such as we know them, instead of such as they appeared to the Greeks. Maternal Earth, the mighty parent, is superseded by the Spirit of the Earth, the guide of our planet through the realms of sky; while his fair and weaker companion and attendant, the Spirit of the Moon, receives bliss from the annihilation of Evil in the superior sphere.

"Shelley develops, more particularly in the lyrics of this drama, his abstruse and imaginative theories with regard to the Creation. It requires a mind as subtle and penetrating as his own to understand the mystic meanings scattered throughout the poem. They elude the ordinary reader by their abstraction and delicacy of distinction, but they are far from vague. It was his design to write prose metaphysical essays on the nature of man, which would have served to explain much of what is obscure in his poetry; a few scattered fragments of observations and remarks alone remain. He considered these philosophical views of mind and nature to be instinct with the intensest spirit of poetry.

"More popular poets clothe the ideal with familiar and sensible imagery. Shelley loved to idealize the real—to gift the mechanism of the material universe with a soul and a voice, and to bestow such also on the most delicate and abstract emotions and thoughts of the mind. . . .

"Through the whole poem there reigns a sort of calm and holy spirit of love; it soothes the tortured, and is hope to the expectant, till the prophecy is fulfilled, and love, untainted by any evil, becomes the law of the world. . . .

"The charm of the Roman climate helped to clothe his thoughts in greater beauty than they had ever worn before. And, as he wandered among the ruins made one with nature in their decay, or gazed on the Praxitelean shapes that throng the Vatican, the Capitol, and the palaces of Rome, his soul imbibed forms of loveliness which became a portion of itself. There are many passages in the *Prometheus* which show the intense delight he received from such studies, and give back the impression with a beauty of poetical description peculiarly his own. . . ."

Page 454. *Act I*

2. *One.* Prometheus.

53–59. *I pity thee*, etc. See ll. 144–5, where the Earth tells Prometheus he is "more than God, Being wise and kind." G. E. Woodberry has an illuminating note on the pitying wisdom which has come to Prometheus: "The pity of Prometheus for Jupiter and his wish to recall the curse formerly pronounced mark the moral transformation of the character from that conceived by Aeschylus. This is the point of departure from the ancient myth, which is here left behind. Shelley thus clothes Prometheus with the same ideal previously depicted in Laon,—the spiritual power of high-minded and forgiving endurance of wrong, the opposition of love to force, the victory of the higher nature of man in its own occult and inherent right. It appears to me that this perfecting of Prometheus through suffering, so that he lays aside his hate of Jupiter for pity, shown in his repentance for the curse and his withdrawal of it, is the initial point of the action of the drama and marks the appointed time for the overthrow of the tyrant. The fulfilment of the moral ideal in Prometheus is the true cause of the end of the reign of evil, though this is dramatically brought about by the instrumentality of Demogorgon."

262–301. *Fiend, I defy thee*, etc. The phantasm is now not speaking in its own character, but is repeating the words uttered by Prometheus to the real Jupiter some three thousand years before.

292–301. Evil must by its own force inevitably destroy itself.

324. *A serpent-cinctured wand.* The caduceus, the winged staff circled by serpents which Mercury carried.

346–7. *Geryon, Gorgon, Chimæra, Sphinx.* Monsters in Greek mythology.

381–2. *I gave all He has.* Note the conception that the original source of Jupiter's power was not in absolute godhead but that it was derived from Prometheus. If Prometheus be

considered as humanity, then Jupiter is one of the false gods of man's own making who has enslaved him, and represents tyranny, not deity. See also ll. 272–4 in this connection.

398. *hair-suspended sword.* The sword of Damocles.

483–91. *Thou think'st*, etc. An obscure passage. Note that it ends with a question mark and hence "Thou think'st" might be paraphrased: "Have you thought?" Then the Furies describe how evil forces might attempt to creep within a soul and assail it from within.

541–5. *We laugh thee to scorn*, etc. The climax of Prometheus's torture is mental. The Furies show to him two visions of how good has been corrupted to evil by the forces of tyranny.

546. *One came forth.* Christ. There follows a vision of the agony of the Crucifixion followed by a vision of some of the evils which have been done to man in the name of religion.

648–55. *Nature's sacred watchwords.* The reference is to the French Revolution. There is also a brief reference in ll. 567–77.

676. *Chorus of Spirits.* Woodberry identifies the first four spirits who are summoned by Earth from the "dim caves of human thought" to console Prometheus as Revolution, Self-Sacrifice, Wisdom, and Poetry. The last two who sing of love and pain are not specifically identified. Note the chorus, ll. 780–800, which is the answer of the Spirits to the chorus of Furies, ll. 541–5.

Page 465. *Act II, Scene 1*

140. *Apollo's written grief.* Apollo accidentally killed Hyacinthus and caused a flower to spring up from his blood. The Greeks thought they could see in its color markings the interjection *ai* (*woe*) which Apollo inscribed on the flower.

204. *He and thou.* Probably Prometheus and Asia, figuratively separated at the time of Prometheus's enchainment and now approaching perfect union.

Page 468. *Act II, Scene 2*

62. *fatal mountain.* The mountain which the two Oceanides reach in the next scene; fatal in the sense of fateful because of the presence of Demogorgon.

Page 469. *Act II, Scene 3*

4. *oracular vapour.* Priestesses at the shrine at Delphi inhaled vapors. Their semi-delirious words were taken as the words of the god.

9. *Mænads.* Women who followed Bacchus in his festivals.

Page 470. *Act II, Scene 4*

This and the following scene are of the utmost importance in understanding the central thought of the poem.

9. *Who made the living world*, etc. Note the

antithesis between the creative God and the ruling Jupiter indicated in the answer to this question, and the answer in line 28 to the question concerning the source of evil. Tyranny as a source of evil was central in Shelley's thinking. When Asia tries to push her questioning further in the direction of the Absolute she receives a more vague answer (ll. 110–120) although Demogorgon declares Love to be outside the dominion of Fate, Time, Occasion, Chance, and Change. For note on Demogorgon see note on Act III, Sc. 1, l. 51, below.

12. *sense which, when*, etc. There was an error of some sort here when Shelley's text was first printed which can now be corrected only by guesswork. Perhaps a line was omitted. Although the construction of the passage as it stands is uncertain, the general sense is clear.

Page 473.   *Act II, Scene 5*

48–71. *Life of Life*, etc. In this poem, which is sung to Asia, the *Prometheus Unbound* reaches its highest point of lyrical intensity. Asia (Act III, sc. 3, ll 6–7) is spoken of as "thou light of life, Shadow of beauty unbeheld," and the student may compare this with the "shadow of some unseen Power" of the *Hymn to Intellectual Beauty*. She has an outward form and a place in the story, but the form is but the shadow of an inner potentiality. Whether one consider her as simply a nymph in the fable or as representative of some abstraction such as Love, Beauty, or Nature, the fable cannot be completed until the utmost inner potentiality is made a reality in the new world that is to be. Herein lies the significance of the lyric with its dazzling breaking forth of the spirit through the screen of form as the time of Prometheus's liberation approaches.

Page 474.   *Act III, Scene 1*

40. *Numidian seps*. A species of poisonous serpent.
51–2. *Demogorgon*. This figure has been variously identified as "Eternity," "Divine Justice," "the incarnate opposite of Prometheus," "The Ancient Principle of Reason," and "Necessity." Note that in Shelley's treatment of the figure the emphasis is on vague but irresistible power and almost complete absence of form as human beings know form. As Demogorgon is Jupiter's child (l. 54) we may deduce that Shelley meant that evil had within itself the seeds of its own destruction; possibly— since Demogorgon is friendly to Prometheus— that every nature, Good or Evil, is compelled to work out its own proper fate by a central compulsion. The fable would require a figure to represent this compulsion, but it would not need to be more fully characterized than Shelley characterized Demogorgon.

Page 476.   *Act III, Scene 3*

65. *shell. . .Proteus*. Proteus was one of the sea-gods and a son of Neptune. The shell is to be blown on like a trumpet by the Spirit of the Hour to announce to the world the coming of Universal Freedom and Love.

Page 478.   *Act IV, Scene 4*

54. *A sound*. The sound of the shell blown by the Spirit of the Hour. The Spirit of the Earth reports in the following passage that at the sound "all things had put their evil nature off."
119. *Amphisbaenic*. Two-headed.
124–204. *I floated to the earth*. The Spirit of the Hour reports the complete transformation of the world after the blowing of the shell-trumpet. The action of the play is properly completed with this speech.

Page 481.   *Act IV*

This act was written as an afterthought some months after the completion of Act III and has no proper place in the action. It is simply a hymn of triumph to the new order. The drama requires struggle, and with the establishment of the perfect world there seemed little left to do but sing. There are, however, some excellent lyrics in the Act, and Demogorgon's final speech is one of the finest things in the drama.
9–29. *Here, oh, here*, etc. Hymn of the dead hours. All is eternal now and therefore time has no meaning.

Page 490.   EPIPSYCHIDION

Epipsychidion, one of the best beloved of Shelley's poems, was completed by February 16, 1821, on which date Shelley sent the poem to Ollier, his publisher. (See letter, text p. 544.) Shelley prefixed to it an "Advertisement" declaring it to have been written by a young man who had "died at Florence, as he was preparing for a voyage to one of the wildest of the Sporades, which he had bought, and where he had fitted up the ruins of an old building, and where it was his hope to have realised a scheme of life, suited perhaps to that happier and better world of which he is now an inhabitant, but hardly practicable in this." The reasons for this anonymity Shelley states in his letter to Ollier.

The inspiration of the poem was the young "Contessina" Teresa Emilia Viviani. Some two years before, Emilia's father had remarried and the stepmother, finding herself not so beautiful as her stepdaughters, had (in the best manner of fairy tales) prevailed on the father to shut them up, each in a separate convent, on the pretense of completing their education. Professor Pacchiani spoke of them to the Shelley circle and Shelley, moved by the story, visited Emilia at the ruinous convent of St. Anna. Mary Shelley and Claire Clairmont had visited her before. The entire circle were entranced by her beauty: "profuse black hair," brow fair as marble and features of "a rare faultlessness," and eyes with "the sleepy voluptuousness, if not the colour, of Beatrice Cenci's." And Emilia's intelligence was judged to be as remarkable as her beauty. Some time in December, 1820, Shelley first met her, and by the middle of February he had completed the *Epipsychidion*.

The title of the poem has been much discussed. It is a "coined" Greek word and would seem to mean "A little additional soul" or, as Shelley puts it (l. 238), "this soul out of my soul." The last is the generally accepted meaning. The idea is similar to that expressed in the Preface to *Alastor* (q.v.: text p. 444, col. 1, ll. 24–27).

Shelley's enthusiasm for Emilia ended almost as abruptly as it began. By June 18, 1822, he was ready to declare her "a cloud instead of a Juno" (see letter to Gisborne: text p. 548) and there is a touch of the pathetic in his confession that "spirits cased in flesh and blood" make an error when they seek "in a mortal image the likeness of what is perhaps eternal."

The remainder of Emilia's story is as highly colored as the beginning, though not quite so like a fairy tale. She married in 1822 and, according to Mary Shelley, led her husband "a devil of a life." A few years after, Medwin, Shelley's cousin, saw her. Exhausted by ill-health she lay on a couch and extended a thin hand. There was no trace left of her beauty. And shortly after, she died of a fever. So living and so dying she had served as the symbol of something rarely beautiful and inspired one of the great lyrics of her century.

Stopford A. Brooke in *Studies in Poetry* has a discriminating essay which places *Epipsychidion* in relation to other Shelley poems and praises adequately the great section of the poem. Extracts follow:

"I have said that there was a personal element in this poem, that Shelley had some feeling for Emilia herself. But there was another element of personality in it different from that which had to do with Emilia. He infused a personality into the ideal Beauty to which he aspired to unite himself. Plato did not impersonate his idea of Beauty, but Shelley did this thing. He was forced by his nature to realise the idea in some form, and to realise it as belonging especially to himself. Hence he created an *Epipsychidion*—'a soul out of his soul'—a heightened, externalised personality of himself, conceived as perfect; an ideal image of his own being; different in sex; his complement; originally part of him, now separated from him; after whom he pursued; whom he felt in all that was calm and sublime and lovely in knowledge, in nature, and in woman; and to absolute union with whom, such union as is described in the latter half of *Epipsychidion*, he passionately aspired. And this being, since she was the essence of all the loveliness which he could conceive or feel, represented also to him and for him—ideal Beauty. This creation was not Platonic—Plato spoke only of the Idea of Beauty. This was an invention of Shelley's, an addition, to satisfy his cry for personality, to the Platonic theory of love. He expresses it fully enough in his essay on Love; and it reaches its extreme of mingled ideality and personality in the poem of *Epipsychidion*.

"The history of the development of this conception is written in his poetry. In the *Hymn to Intellectual Beauty*, he conceives of the Archetypal Beauty, the beauty which is the model and source of all beautiful forms, much as Plato might have conceived of it. It is not personal at all. It is a pervading spirit, whose shadow, but never whose substance, is seen. But this conception was soon changed. He wanted personality. He embodied this archetype in a feminine being, existing in the super-phenomenal world, glimpses of whom he saw at times, and she was the other half of his own soul. 'Her voice,' he says in *Alastor*,

> 'was like the voice of his own soul
> Heard in the calm of Thought.'

And if he could have been content with that— if he could have kept himself wholly to the ideal personality—it had been well. But he had not strength enough. He was always driven, by a weakness in his nature, to try and find her image in real women. His ideal love continually glided back into a desire of realising itself on earth; and yet, when he attempted to realise it in any woman, she fell, or earthly love itself fell, so far below the ideal image, that he was driven back again from the woman on earth to the ideal in his own soul. Thus smitten to and fro, he had no peace. He was, as he calls himself in *Adonais*, 'a power girt round with weakness'—the creator of thoughts which afterwards pursued their creator as wolves pursue a deer.

"*Alastor* records the coming of this vision and the agony of not being able to realise it.

". . . It is with Shelley as with all artists who are worthy of the name—as emotion deepens clearness deepens.

> 'The day is come and thou wilt fly with me'

begins the close. Shelley is alone—Mary, Emilia, all passed away—with the living image of his own soul in perfect peace, with his being of absolute Beauty. A splendid passage about love, closely knit, the metaphors hand in hand, introduces the new theme of his flight to the island with her who is the soul out of his soul. And then we possess the creation of the island of imagination, of himself as Love, of Emily as absolute joy, of their imperishable union in passion. This is the vision to which all the rest has led. It is clear, simple, astonishingly bright in the sunlight of thought, in the sunlight of feeling. It is realised to the smallest detail. The landscape is luminous, set in pellucid air, and is wholly at unity with itself. Every touch increases the impression, and I think it is the most beautiful thing—for pure beauty—which exists in English poetry. It is not sublime, it is not on the highest range of poetry, it is not of that primal emotion which redeems the heart from the world, but it is of an exquisite and solitary loveliness. And it runs without a break in its beauty to a noble end, to a perfect climax—to that fine and spiritual reality of passion, which is, when it is pure of self, the last summit of human joy and peace to which we attain in life."

". . . How little essential truth there was in the part ascribed to Emily is well known. The other passages, which have been interpreted as personal, may be similarly touched with tenuity as matters of fact, though correctly representing in allegory the moods of Shelley's inner life as he remembered them. The memory of a poet, especially if it be touched with pain and remorse, when he allows his eloquence to work in images of sorrow and despair to express what would otherwise remain forever unutterable by his lips, is an entirely untrustworthy witness of fact. Shelley's self-description has the truth of his poetic consciousness at the time, and its moods are sadly sustained by many passages of his verse; but to seek precise fact and named individuals as meant by his words is, I believe, futile, and may be misleading. It is only as a poem of the inner life that *Epipsychidion* has its high imaginative interest." (G. E. Woodberry, Cambridge ed., *Shelley's Poetical Works*, p. 629.)

1–2. *orphan one . . . empire . . . name.* The two lines are obscure. The common interpretation is that the "orphan one" is Mary Shelley and the name is Shelley's own; by metonymy— Shelley himself.

5. *captive bird.* It was Professor Pacchiani who first spoke to the Shelleys of Emilia Viviani. "Poverina," he said, "she pines like a bird in a cage—ardently longs to escape from her prison-house—pines with *ennui*, and wanders

about the corridors like an unquiet spirit; she sees her young days glide on without aim or purpose. She was made for love."

38. *lights.* Eyes. As also in ll. 87 and 557.

42. *Youth's vision.* The vision of Alastor.

50. *names.* Sister and wife.

68. *wingless pleasure.* I.e., pleasure which cannot take wing and so prove fleeting.

69. *violet-shrouded.* It is now the "grave of Woe" but the covering with violets suggests Emilia.

72. *She.* Both is and is not Emilia. In the preceding lines Shelley has been trying to find something to which to compare Emilia, and has failed. All he can find to which he can compare her is that vision of eternal loveliness he had glimpsed in *Hymn to Intellectual Beauty* and *Alastor* and he launches into a hymn to that vision—properly the "she" of l. 72. But before he has ended he has been carried away from this earth and has also partially identified Emilia with the vision. This explains the drop in ll. 123–9 when he returns more directly to the mortal woman. See note on l. 322.

117. *third sphere.* According to Ptolemaic astronomy each of the planets was set in a separate sphere which revolved about the earth. The third sphere was that of Venus.

123–9. See note on l. 72.

184. *This truth.* "Each part exceeds the whole, etc."

190. *There was a Being.* The Vision of Alastor.

222. *Hesper.* The evening star.

238. *this soul out of my soul.* Equals Epipsychidion, the title of the poem. See introductory note.

256. *One.* Sensual love.

269–71. *some were fair . . . Others were wise . . . One was true.* Various guesses have been made as to whom Shelley had in mind. The use of the plurals (some, others) would indicate he was thinking of no one in particular in the first two cases. The one who was not true to him has often (but perhaps incorrectly) been identified with his first wife, Harriet. It may have been Harriet Grove. See note on l. 368.

277. *One stood.* Mary Shelley.

312–3. *Tempest . . . Planet.* Possibly a mysterious Englishwoman Shelley had met at Naples.

322. *The Vision.* Emilia. The identification of Emilia with the Vision which was suggested in lines 72–123 is here complete and frankly accepted.

345. *Twin Spheres.* Mary as the moon and Emilia as the sun.

368. *O Comet.* Harriet, Shelley's first wife.

369. *heart.* Shelley's heart.

388. *The day is come.* See, in the introductory material to this poem, the final paragraph in the quotation from Stopford A. Brooke.

412. *halcyons.* Kingfishers. Jove, in pity for the sad story of Halcyone and Ceÿx, transformed them into kingfishers and commanded that the winds should not blow while Halcyone brooded on her nest. The bird is thus associated with tranquil and sunny seas.

601. *Marina, Vanna, Primus.* Mary Shelley, Jane Williams, Edward Williams.

Page 497. ADONAIS

Shelley regarded *Adonais* as one of the finest of his poems. On June 5, 1821, he wrote to the Gisbornes: "I have been engaged these last days in composing a poem on the death of Keats, which will shortly be finished—It is a highly-wrought *piece of art*, and perhaps better, in point of composition, than anything I have written." Eleven days later he added, "I have dipped my pen in consuming fire for his destroyers; otherwise the style is clear and solemn." And the following November he wrote Ollier, "I confess I should be surprised if *that* poem were born to an immortality of oblivion."

Shelley and Keats had never been intimate. They had met at Leigh Hunt's in 1817 and, on hearing of Keats's illness, Shelley had invited him to Italy. (The famous letters of invitation and refusal appear in this text on pp. 543 and 655-6.) Hunt, who had introduced the two poets, and, with his usual acuteness, sensed there was little personally sympathetic between them, realized that a great poem was open to a grave challenge from a certain type of mind —that it was based upon no real feeling. Hunt met the challenge by frankly picking up a sneering phrase of Dr. Johnson's concerning Milton's *Lycidas* and replying vigorously. Milton also had written in terms of grief about a man he scarcely knew. "Where," said Johnson of Milton—"Where there is leisure for fiction, there is little grief." Setting aside Hunt's very adequate answer (in *The Examiner,* July 7, 1822), one may ask how the question of sincerity could have been fairly raised even at the time the poem was published.

Always fiercely aroused by stories of oppression or unfairness, Shelley had been deeply stirred by the report that Keats's death had been caused by the savagery of a critical attack by J. W. Croker on Keats in *The Quarterly Review* for April, 1818. (See pp. 543-4 of the text, especially p. 544, col. 1, l. 24 et seq.) *Adonais* was the result. The lament is then not so much a personal lament for a lost friend as a lament for oppressed genius, and the elegy faces the problem of death on the universal plane rather than the personal. In this it is akin to Milton's *Lycidas* rather than Tennyson's *In Memoriam,* the only other two elegies in the language which can fairly be compared to it. All three poems follow the same pattern of progression from grief through hope and consolation, and finally to triumphant affirmation. The conclusion of *Adonais* can meet Milton's poem on equal terms and *In Memoriam* must be conceded the weakest in fire of the great trio.

The title of the poem is derived from the myth of Adonis with whom Venus fell so in love that she abandoned "Paphos, and Cnidos, and Amathus, rich in metals. She absented herself even from Olympus, for Adonis was dearer to her than heaven. Him she followed, and bore him company. She who loved to recline in the shade, with no care but to cultivate her charms, now rambled through the woods and over the hills, girt like the huntress Diana. She chased game that is safe to hunt, but kept clear of the wolves and bears. She charged Adonis, too, to beware of dangerous animals. 'Be brave toward the timid,' she would say, 'courage against the courageous is not safe.' Having thus, on one occasion, warned him, she mounted her chariot drawn by swans, and drove away through the air. But Adonis was too noble to heed such counsels. The dogs had roused a wild boar from his lair; and the youth threw his spear, and wounded the animal with a sidelong stroke. The beast drew out the weapon with his jaws, and rushing after Adonis, buried his tusks in the lad's side, and stretched him dying upon the plain." (Gayley's *Classic Myths.*) The symbolism of the youth beloved of the goddess who was too noble to be timid and who was slain by the beast he had enraged is sufficiently obvious.

The poem was first printed in Pisa in 1821. The first English edition, by an irony of literary fate, was printed in Cambridge in 1829 at the instance of Lord Houghton and Arthur Hallam, one of whom was to become the first important biographer of Keats and the other the inspiration of *In Memoriam.* The English edition was edited from a copy of the Pisa edition brought back from Italy by Hallam.

To the Pisa edition Shelley prefixed the following Preface:

"It is my intention to subjoin to the London edition of this poem, a criticism upon the claims of its lamented object to be classed among the writers of the highest genius who have adorned our age. My known repugnance to the narrow principles of taste on which several of his earlier compositions were modelled, prove, at least that I am an impartial judge. I consider the fragment of *Hyperion,* as second to nothing that was ever produced by a writer of the same years.

"John Keats, died at Rome of a consumption, in his twenty-fourth year, on the —— of —— 1821; and was buried in the romantic and lonely cemetery of the protestants in that city, under the pyramid which is the tomb of Cestius, and the massy walls and towers, now mouldering and desolate, which formed the circuit of ancient Rome. The cemetery is an open space among the ruins covered in winter with violets and daisies. It might make one in love with death, to think that one should be buried in so sweet a place.

"The genius of the lamented person to whose memory I have dedicated these unworthy verses, was not less delicate and fragile than it was beautiful; and where cankerworms abound, what wonder, if its young flower was blighted in the bud? The savage criticism on his *Endymion*, which appeared in the *Quarterly Review*,[1] produced the most violent effect on his susceptible mind; the agitation thus originated ended in the rupture of a blood-vessel in the lungs; a rapid consumption ensued, and the succeeding acknowledgements from more candid critics, of the true greatness of his powers, were ineffectual to heal the wound thus wantonly inflicted.

"It may be well said, that these wretched men know not what they do. They scatter their insults and their slanders without heed as to whether the poisoned shaft lights on a heart made callous by many blows, or one, like Keats's, composed of more penetrable stuff. One of their associates is, to my knowledge, a most base and unprincipled calumniator. As to *Endymion;* was it a poem whatever might be its defects, to be treated contemptuously by those who had celebrated with various degrees of complacency and panegyric, *Paris*, and *Woman*, and a *Syrian Tale*, and Mrs. Lefanu, and Mr. Barrett, and Mr. Howard Payne, and a long list of the illustrious obscure? Are these the men, who in their venal good nature, presumed to draw a parallel between the Rev. Mr. Milman and Lord Byron? What gnat did they strain at here, after having swallowed all those camels? Against what woman taken in adultery, dares the foremost of these literary prostitutes to cast his opprobrious stone? Miserable man! you, one of the meanest, have wantonly defaced one of the noblest specimens of the workmanship of God. Nor shall it be your excuse, that, murderer as you are, you have spoken daggers, but used none.

"The circumstances of the closing scene of poor Keats's life were not made known to me until the *Elegy* was ready for the press. I am given to understand that the wound which his sensitive spirit had received from the criticism of *Endymion*, was exasperated by the bitter sense of unrequited benefits; the poor fellow seems to have been hooted from the stage of life, no less by those on whom he had wasted

[1] Shelley was unaware of the even more savage attack in *Blackwood's Magazine*, August, 1818.

the promise of his genius, than those on whom he had lavished his fortune and his care. He was accompanied to Rome, and attended in his last illness by Mr. Severn, a young artist of the highest promise, who, I have been informed 'almost risked his own life, and sacrificed every prospect to unwearied attendance upon his dying friend.' Had I known these circumstances before the completion of my poem, I should have been tempted to add my feeble tribute of applause to the more solid recompense which the virtuous man finds in the recollection of his own motives. Mr. Severn can dispense with a reward from 'such stuff as dreams are made of.' His conduct is a golden augury of the success of his future career—may the unextinguished Spirit of his illustrious friend animate the creations of his pencil, and plead against Oblivion for his name!"

10. *mighty Mother*. Urania. Shelley may have remembered Plato's statement in the Symposium that there were two Aphrodites: Aphrodite Urania and Aphrodite Pandemos. The "mighty Mother" then really was Aphrodite Urania, the goddess of the higher forms of love. The connection of Aphrodite (or Venus) with the Adonis story makes this consistent.

29. *He died*. Milton.

36. *the third*. If epic poets are meant the three would be Homer, Dante, and Milton. Otherwise it might be either Homer or Sophocles and Shakespeare and Milton.

55. *high Capital*. Rome.

69. *eternal Hunger*. Corruption, called eternal because all the beauty of the world can never satisfy her, and decay goes on forever.

73. *quick Dreams*. The first of the mourners are Keats's unwritten dreams—poems which never will be written now.

94. *anadem*. A garland for the head.

107. *clips*. Embraces.

133. *for whose disdain*. Narcissus. The Oread Echo repulsed by Narcissus faded away until there was nothing left of her but her voice. Narcissus in turn, the symbol of self-conceit, fell in love with his own image in the water. See l. 141.

177-9. *Shall that alone*, etc. Shall the conscious spirit only be destroyed while the body (the mere sheath of the sword) renews itself in other ways?

191. *Mother*. Urania.

250. *Pythian of the age*. Byron, whom Shelley deems to have silenced the critics with his *English Bards and Scotch Reviewers*. Apollo slew with arrows the python, a monster born out of the slime which covered the earth after the flood, and instituted the Pythian games in honor of the event.

264. *Pilgrim of Eternity*. Byron.

269. *The sweetest lyrist*. Thomas Moore.

271. *one frail Form.* Shelley himself.

289–92. *With pansies overblown*, etc. In the "language of flowers" the pansy symbolizes thought, the violet modesty, the cypress grief, and the ivy constancy.

306. *like Cain's or Christ's.* The world crowns two types with thorns—its enemies and its unrecognized benefactors. Therefore, says Shelley, from the mere fact that a brow is branded and bloody, you can judge nothing.

307. *What softer voice.* Leigh Hunt's.

319. *The nameless worm.* The author of the unsigned criticism of *Endymion* in the *Quarterly Review.*

414. *Vesper of our throng.* Vesper is the evening star and Keats is so hailed because he comes late in the poetic line. Milton had compared his subject to the day-star that sinks to rise again and "Flames in the forehead of the morning sky."

439. *a slope of green access.* The Protestant Cemetery at Rome where Keats was buried. The cemetery is bounded on one side by a portion of the medieval city wall and close to Keats's grave is the Roman pyramidal tomb of Caius Cestius—both of which are referred to in the following stanza.

Page 506. THE TRIUMPH OF LIFE

"This leads us to the questions, not to be longer postponed, what, after all, does Shelley mean in the poem by 'the world' and 'Life' and 'the struggle with Life'? To attempt an answer in detail we must recall the main outlines of the poem, so far as it was completed.

"The poet is resting at sunrise on a mountain-slope, and suddenly he falls into a trance through which the real scene can only be discerned faintly, while across it he sees, in what appears high noon, a dusty 'public way,' crowded with human beings of all ages, drifting in a torrent of fear or futile pursuit. While he gazes the crowd thickens, and then he sees an icy glare making the sun look dim, and in the glare a cold bright Car, drawn by strange winged creatures, and on the Car a sinister woman-shape, and on the chariot-beam of it a four-faced blindfolded charioteer. Round the Car now surges a wild dancing multitude, young figures in the van, and in the rear a 'ribald crowd,' old men and women, 'with limbs decayed,' and ghastly shadows winding in among them. Chained to the Car are mighty captives, all the great ones of the earth, except a chosen few, such as Christ and Socrates, and those,

> the sacred few who could not tame
> Their spirits to the conqueror's—but as soon
> As they had touched the world with living flame,
> Fled back like eagles to their native noon.

When the rearguard is fully in sight the poet asks sadly, and half to himself, what it all can mean. He is answered by the word 'Life!' a word uttered by one of the last-comers who has fallen by the wayside, a figure so distorted as to be more like an old root than a man. This 'grim Feature' shows him who the mighty captives are, and tells his own story, how he is 'what was once Rousseau,' and how, at dawn in the oblivious valley of his youth, he was met by a radiant vision that gave him a cup of Nepenthe to drink, and on that he saw the Car of Life sweeping past him, and flung himself into the thickest of the throng around it, and grew deformed under its influence, and how he had watched other creatures like himself, surging about the Car and sending out shadows from their own being, and perishing as the shadows issued.

"The Car of Life, it is clear from such a scheme, cannot mean the whole of Being, nor even, I think, the whole of human life on earth apart from man's conscious will. Rather, it would seem, Shelley uses the word 'life,' much as the New Testament speaks of 'the world,' simply to describe the evil side of human society in the earthly order, those elements, terrible and alluring, in the rush of circumstance and in the passions of men that combine to fetter, deform, and crush personality. So that 'Life' conquers when a man fails in right action, and still more when his character becomes the plaything of circumstance." (F. Melian Stawell, "Shelley's *Triumph of Life*," in *Essays and Studies by Members of the English Association*. Vol. V, pp. 112–4.)

The Triumph of Life was the poem upon which Shelley was engaged at the time of his death, and incompleteness in some of the lines of the text as printed is due to the incompleteness of his manuscript, not to censorship. The poem should be read as one of that great series of poems, including *Alastor* and *Epipsychidion*, in which Shelley deals with the pursuit of the ideal and presents his doctrine of love,—but as a startling and contradictory member of the series. In the earlier poems, sympathy with the seeker of the ideal was dominant. Here Shelley, without denying the beauty and realness of Love, considers it as a terrible and destructive force, capable not only of destroying the body but also of corrupting the soul. It is this last idea, that love can lead to spiritual corruption which, coming from Shelley, is so striking. The poem is unfinished and it ends as suddenly as Shelley's life.

As the poem is somewhat difficult to follow, an analysis of the development of the thought is given as an aid to the student. The following division of the poem into sections is an

arbitrary editorial device for the convenience
of the student. Shelley made no such division.

1–40. "Before me fled the night; behind me
rose the day"; and in a trance Shelley faces
the vision which makes the poem.
41–180. He "sees a torrent of people" and is
startled by the appearance of a chariot driven
furiously by a blindfolded shape. The four faces
of the charioteer (l. 99) probably represent the
Past, Present, Future, and Eternity. A "captive multitude" is driven on by or follows
the car and Shelley observes that "All but the
sacred few—were there." He exclaims "Whose
shape is that?" A voice answers "Life."
180–295. The voice is that of Rousseau. He
discusses "The mighty phantoms of an elder
day" who make up the multitude. Most are
called by name. "The child of a fierce hour"
(l. 217) is Napoleon. Plato is there (l. 254) and
the student of Shelley's thought should particularly note by what means Life conquered
him. In l. 261, "the tutor and his pupil" are
Aristotle and Alexander. The section closes
in more general terms: Poets, Emperors, and
Popes are of the multitude.
296–544. Shelley asks Rousseau concerning
his own case and this whole concluding section
is of great significance. To avoid confusion it
should be noted Rousseau's story develops in
clear stages: (a) His "April time"; (b) his
vision of a female image in a reflection of the
Sun and his surrender to her (note that the
evil is not in the cup itself which she offers
him, but in him who drinks it unworthily);
(c) the development of a second and sinister
image paralleling the first, and Rousseau's
surrender to life; (d) Rousseau's account of
how he saw grow out of the multitude a cloud
of shadows "like vampire bats." Members of
the multitude wane in beauty and fall, those
falling first from whom most shadows sprang.
The symbolism here represents the dissolution
of personality through surrender to caprice.
The figure who appears at l. 472 is Dante
and, in a poem dealing with destructive forces
and the collapse of personality, the lines are
significant in their indication that Love itself
is good.

Page 514.   STANZAS—APRIL, 1814

The rift had been growing between Shelley and
his first wife and at the time the poem was
composed Harriet was with her sister while
Shelley was with the Boinvilles at Bracknell.
"The beautiful 'Stanzas,' dated 'April, 1814,'
read like a fantasia of sorrow, the motives of
which are supplied by Shelley's anticipated
farewell to Bracknell, and his return, at the
call of duty, to a home which seemed to him
loveless." (Dowden, *Life of Shelley*, 1920 ed.,
p. 223.)

Page 515.   A DEFENCE OF POETRY

Thomas Love Peacock (see text p. 747), the
satirist, was a friend of Shelley's of some intimacy. His *The Four Ages of Poetry* appeared
in *Ollier's Literary Miscellany* in 1820. Shelley
knew the attack on poetry was coming and,
when he had read it, wrote back to Peacock
(Feb. 15, 1821) that "your anathemas against
poetry itself excited me to a sacred rage."
Shelley's essay then is a reply to a specific
attack, although Shelley lifts the discussion
to a general plane. Peacock's "four ages" were
those of primitive iron, Homeric gold, Augustan
silver, and the age of brass. His classical examples were well enough chosen and so were
his English parallels until he chose to develop
the full venom of his attack—which made his
own period the English age of brass. Having
reached this point, Peacock remarks:

"A poet in our times is a semi-barbarian in a
civilized community. He lives in the days that
are past. His ideas, thoughts, feelings, associations, are all with barbarous manners, obsolete
customs, and exploded superstitions. The march
of his intellect is like that of a crab, backward.
The brighter the light diffused around him by
the progress of reason, the thicker is the darkness of antiquated barbarism, in which he
buries himself like a mole, to throw up the
barren hillocks of his Cimmerian labours. The
philosophic mental tranquillity which looks
round with an equal eye on all external things,
collects a store of ideas, discriminates their
relative value, assigns to all their proper place,
and from the materials of useful knowledge
thus collected, appreciated, and arranged,
forms new combinations that impress the stamp
of their power and utility on the real business
of life, is diametrically the reverse of that
frame of mind which poetry inspires, or from
which poetry can emanate. . . ." He then takes
a side shot at "the promiscuous rubbish" of the
"unpoetical times" and adds: "But in whatever degree poetry is cultivated, it must necessarily be to the neglect of some branch of useful
study: and it is a lamentable spectacle to see
minds, capable of better things, running to
seed in the specious indolence of these empty
aimless mockeries of intellectual exertion.
Poetry was the mental rattle that awakened
the attention of intellect in the infancy of
civil society: but for the maturity of mind to
make a serious business of the playthings of its
childhood, is as absurd as for a full-grown man
to rub his gums with coral, and cry to be
charmed to sleep by the jingle of silver bells."

Peacock's writing was lively and the vivacity
of his satirical attack provoked Shelley into an
earnest reply.

Prior to Shelley there had been Sir Philip Sidney's famous *Apologie for Poetrie* (1595)— a defense of poetry provoked by Gosson's *The Schoole of Abuse* which attacked poetry on moral grounds. Shelley had Sidney's treatise in mind and there are some interesting parallelisms of thought. The following extracts from Sidney's *Apologie for Poetrie* have the points of most striking parallelism indicated by the references enclosed in brackets:

". . . And first, truly to al them that professing learning inveigh against Poetry, may justly be objected, that they goe very neer to ungratfulnes, to seek to deface that, which in the noblest nations and languages that are knowne, hath been the first light-giver to ignorance, and first Nurse, whose milk by little and little enabled them to feed afterwards of tougher knowledges: and will they now play the Hedghog, that being received into the den, drave out his host? or rather the Vipers, that with theyr birth kill their Parents? Let learned Greece in any of her manifold Sciences, be able to shew me one booke, before *Musæus, Homer*, and *Hesiodus*, all three nothing els but Poets. . . . This did so notably shewe it selfe, that the Phylosophers of Greece, durst not a long time appeare to the worlde but under the masks of Poets [p. 518b, l. 43].

". . . And truely, even *Plato*, whosoever well considereth, shall find, that in the body of his work, though the inside and strength were Philosophy, the skinne as it were and beautie, depended most of Poetrie [p. 517b, l. 43]: for all standeth upon Dialogues, wherein he *faineth* many honest Burgesses of Athens to speake of such matters, that if they had been sette on the racke, they would never have confessed them. Besides, his poetical describing the circumstances of their meetings, as the well ordering of a banquet, the delicacie of a walke, with enterlacing meere tales, as *Giges* Ring, and others, which who knoweth not to be flowers of Poetrie, did never walke into *Appolos* Garden. "Among the Romans a Poet was called *Vates* [p. 516b, l. 23], which is as much as a Diviner, Fore-seer, or Prophet, as by his conjoyned words *Vaticinium* and *Vaticinari*, is manifest: so heavenly a title did that excellent people bestow upon his hart-ravishing knowledge. And so farre were they carried into the admiration thereof, that they thought in the chaunceable hitting uppon any such verses great fore-tokens of their following fortunes were placed. . . .

"But now, let us see how the Greekes named it, and howe they deemed it. The Greeks called him a Poet, which name, hath as the most excellent, gone thorough other Languages. It commeth of this word *Poiein*, which is, to make: wherein I know not whether by lucke or wisedome, wee Englishmen have mette with the Greekes, in calling him a maker: which name, how high and incomparable a title it is [p. 515a, l. 16], I had rather were knowne by marking the scope of other Sciences, then by my partiall allegation.

". . . The naturall Philosopher thereon hath his name, and the Morrall Philosopher standeth upon the naturall vertues, vices, and passions of man; and followe Nature (saith hee) therein, and thou shalt not erre. The Lawyer sayth what men have determined. The Historian what men have done. The Grammarian speaketh onely of the rules of Speech, and the Rethorician, and Logitian, considering what in Nature will soonest prove and perswade, thereon give artificiall rules, which still are compassed within the circle of a question, according to the proposed matter. The Phisition waigheth the nature of a mans bodie, and the nature of things helpful, or hurtfull into it. And the Metaphisick, though it be in the seconde and abstract notions, and therefore be counted supernaturall: yet doth hee indeede builde upon the depth of Nature: onely the Poet, disdayning to be tied to any such subjection, lifted up with the vigor of his owne invention, dooth growe in effect, another nature, in making things either better than Nature bringeth forth, or quite a newe formes such as never were in Nature, as the *Heroes, Demigods, Cyclops, Chimeras, Furies*, and such like: so as hee goeth hand in hand with Nature, not inclosed within the narrow warrant of her guifts, but freely ranging onely within the Zodiack of his owne wit. . . .

". . . The greatest part of Poets have apparelled their poetical inventions in that numbrous kinde of writing which is called verse: indeed but apparelled, verse being but an ornament and no cause to Poetry: sith there have beene many most excellent Poets, that never versified, and now swarme many versifiers that neede never aunswere to the name of Poets. . . . It is not riming and versing that maketh a Poet, no more then a long gowne maketh an Advocate: who though he pleaded in armor should be an Advocate and no Souldier. But it is that fayning notable images of vertues, vices, or what els, with that delightful teaching which must be the right describing note to know a Poet by [p. 517b, l. 39].

". . . Therefore compare we the Poet with the Historian, and with the Morrall Phylosopher, and, if hee goe beyond them both, no other humaine skill can match him. . . .

"The Philosopher therfore and the Historian, are they which would win the gole: the one by precept, the other by example. But both not having both, doe both halte. For the Philosopher, setting downe with thorny argument the bare rule, is so hard of utterance, and so mistie to bee conceived, that one that hath no other guide but him, shall wade in him till hee be olde, before he shall finde sufficient cause to bee honest: for his knowledge standeth so upon the abstract and generall, that happie is that man who may understande him, and more happie, that can applye what hee dooth understand.

"On the other side, the Historian wanting the precept, is so tyed, not to what shoulde bee, but to what is, to the particuler truth of things, and not to the general reason of things, that hys example draweth no necessary consequence and therefore a lesse fruitfull doctrine. "Nowe dooth the peerelesse Poet performe both: for whatsoever the Philosopher sayth should be doone, hee giveth a perfect picture of it in some one, by whom hee presupposeth it was done. So as hee coupleth the generall notion with the particuler example. A perfect picture I say, for hee yeeldeth to the powers of the minde, an image of that whereof the Philosopher bestoweth but a woordish description: which dooth neyther strike, pierce, nor possesse the sight of the soule, so much as that other dooth [p. 518a, l. 27].

"Nowe therein of all Sciences, (I speak still of humane, and according to the humane conceits) is our Poet the Monarch [p. 518a, l. 27]. For he dooth not only show the way, but giveth so sweete a prospect into the way, as will intice any man to enter into it. Nay, he dooth as if your journey should lye through a fayre Vineyard, at the first give you a cluster of Grapes: that full of that taste, you may long to passe further. He beginneth not with obscure definitions, which must blur the margent with interpretations, and load the memory with doubtfulnesse: but hee commeth to you with words sent in delightfull proportion, either accompanied with, or prepared for the well inchaunting skill of Musicke; and with a tale forsooth he commeth unto you: with a tale which holdeth children from play, and old men from the chimney corner. And pretending no more, doth intende the winning of the mind from wickednesse to vertue: even as the childe is often brought to take most wholsom things, by hiding them in such other as have a pleasant tast: which, if one should beginne to tell them the nature of Aloes or Rubarb they shoulde receive, woulde sooner take their Phisicke at their eares, then at their mouth. So is it in men (most of which are childish in the best things, till they bee cradled in their graves,) glad they will be to heare the tales of Hercules, Achilles, Cyrus, and Æneas: and hearing them, must needs heare the right description of wisdom, valure, and justice; which, if they had been barely, that is to say, Philosophically set out, they would sweare they bee brought to schools againe [p. 518b, l. 47, and p. 519a, l. 41].

". . . Nowe then goe wee to the most important

imputations laid to the poore Poets, for ought I can yet learne, they are these, first, that there beeing many other more fruitefull knowledges, a man might better spend his tyme in them, then in this. Secondly, that it is the mother of lyes. Thirdly, that it is the Nurse of abuse, infecting us with many pestilent desires: with a Syrens sweetnes, drawing the mind to the Serpents tayle of sinfull fancy. And heerein especially, Comedies give the largest field to erre, as Chaucer sayth: howe both in other Nations and in ours, before Poets did soften us, we were full of courage, given to martiall exercises; the pillers of manlyke liberty, and not lulled a sleepe in shady idlenes with Poets pastimes. And lastly, and chiefely, they cry out with an open mouth, as if they out shot Robin Hood, that Plato banished them out of hys Common-wealth. Truely, this is much, if there be much truth in it. . . .

"They alledge heere-with, that before Poets beganne to be in price, our Nation, hath set their harts delight upon action, and not upon imagination: rather doing things worthy to bee written, then writing things fitte to be done. What that before tyme was, I thinke scarcely Sphinx can tell: Sith no memory is so auncient, that hath the precedence of Poetrie. And certaine it is, that in our plainest homelines, yet never was the Albion Nation without Poetrie. Mary, thys argument, though it bee leaveld against Poetrie, yet is it indeed, a chaine-shot against all learning, or bookishnes, as they commonly tearme it. Of such minde were certaine Goethes, of whom it is written, that having in the spoile of a famous Citie, taken a fayre librarie: one hangman (bee like fitte to execute the fruites of their wits) who had murthered a great number of bodies, would have set fire on it: no sayde another, very gravely, take heede what you doe, for whyle they are busie about these toyes, wee shall with more leysure conquer their Countries.

"This indeede is the ordinary doctrine of ignorance, and many wordes sometymes I have heard spent in it: but because this reason is generally against all learning, as well as Poetrie; or rather, all learning but Poetry: because it were too large a digression, to handle, or at least, to superfluous: (sith it is manifest, that all government of action, is to be gotten by knowledg, and knowledge best, by gathering many knowledges, which is, reading,) I onely with Horace, to him that is of that opinion,

Iubeo stultum esse libenter;

for as for Poetrie it selfe, it is the freest from thys objection. For Poetrie is the companion of the Campes.

"I dare undertake, Orlando Furioso, or honest King Arthur, will never displease a Souldier: but the quiddity of Ens, and Prima materia, will hardely agree with a Corslet: and therefore, as I said in the beginning, even Turks and Tartares are delighted with Poets. . . ."

515a, ll, 16–19. τὸ ποιεῖν . . . τὸ λογίζειν. "The creative principle . . . the rational principle."

518a, l. 27. *A poem is the very image*, etc. Cf. Aristotle's *Poetics* (IX): "It is, moreover, evident from what has been said, that it is not the function of the poet to relate what has happened, but what may happen—what is possible according to the law of probability or necessity. The poet and the historian differ not by writing in verse or in prose. The work of Herodotus might be put into verse, and it would still be a species of history, with metre no less than without it. The true difference is that one relates what has happened, the other what may happen. Poetry, therefore, is a more philosophical and a higher thing than history: for poetry tends to express the universal, history the particular."

522b, l. 35. *The sacred links of that chain*. The image of the chain derives from Plato's *Ion* where the original inspiration is conceived as coming direct from the Muses: ". . . The gift which you possess is not an art, but, as I was just saying, an inspiration; there is a divinity moving you, like that contained in the stone which Euripides calls a magnet, but which is commonly known as the stone of Heraclea. This stone not only attracts iron rings; and sometimes you may see a number of pieces of iron and rings suspended from one another so as to form quite a long chain: and all of them derive their power of suspension from the original stone. In like manner the Muse first of all inspires men herself; and from these inspired persons a chain of other persons is suspended, who take the inspiration. For all good poets, epic as well as lyric, compose their beautiful poems not by art, but because they are inspired and possessed. . . ."

524b, l. 30. *Galeotto fù il libro*, etc.: "Gallehaut was the book and he who wrote it" (Dante, *Inferno*, V, 137). This was the book Paolo and Francesca were reading together before their first kiss.

525a, ll. 7–8. *Love, which found a worthy poet in Plato*. The reference is to Agathon's speech in the *Symposium*.

528a, ll. 31–46. *Poetry . . . divine*, etc. Cf. Wordsworth's *Preface*, text p. 107b, ll. 3–23.

Page 531. THE LETTERS OF SHELLEY

Thomas Jefferson Hogg (1792–1862). Hogg was Shelley's closest friend at Oxford and was expelled with him. After the expulsion he went into law in which he had only a moderate success. After the elopement of Shelley and Harriet, Hogg joined them at York and his attempted flirtation with Harriet (see letter to

Elizabeth Hitchener, text p. 534 and footnote) caused a break in the friendship. The two were reconciled in 1813 and saw much of one another until Shelley left England in 1818. Hogg's *Life* gives a vivid picture of Shelley in the Oxford days. The family turned over to him the papers necessary for a biography but disapproved so completely of the first two volumes that the documents were withdrawn and the *Life* is complete only to 1814. See footnote, text p. 533.

Page 533.

Elizabeth Hitchener. Taught a school at Cuckfield near the home of Shelley's uncle, Captain Pilfold, and there Shelley met her in June, 1811. Despite the fact she was about ten years Shelley's senior, a platonically earnest correspondence developed in which Harriet also took part later. The Shelleys invited her to join them and, after much misgiving, she closed her school and joined them in the middle of 1812. She was rather a masculine individual but the first impression she made was favorable. The second was not so happy (see Shelley's letter to Hogg, text p. 538). Shelley pensioned her. She afterwards conducted a school and later married an officer in the Austrian army and went abroad.

Page 535.

William Godwin (1756–1836). Godwin's *An Enquiry concerning Political Justice* (1793) was an important book in its day and took its part in the controversy to which Burke and Thomas Paine contributed. And he stood up manfully with an article in the *Morning Chronicle* in defense of his friends Holcroft, Thelwall, and Tooke, when they were on trial for high treason (1794) in the days of war hysteria and suppression. This was the Godwin, the husband of the brilliant feminist Mary Wollstonecraft, whom Shelley admired and to whom he wrote. Unfortunately *when* he wrote (1812), Godwin was a publisher of juvenile text books, in very serious financial difficulties, and remarried, after the death of Mary Wollstonecraft, to an unpleasant widow—Mrs. Clairmont. Godwin was still a strong man, but there were possibilities of disillusion in the situation. It was while calling on the philosopher that Shelley met Mary Godwin, the daughter of Mary Wollstonecraft.

Page 537.

537a, l. 11. *a Philanthropic Association*. The pamphlet was entitled: "*Proposals for an AS-SOCIATION of those PHILANTHROPISTS, who, convinced of the inadequacy of the moral and political state of Ireland to produce benefits which are nevertheless attainable, are willing to unite to accomplish its regeneration."* Immediately preceding the text was a brief summary of the purpose of the project—brief but formidably comprehensive: "I propose an Association which shall have for its immediate objects Catholic Emancipation and the Repeal of the Act of Union between Great Britain and Ireland; and grounding on the removal of these grievances, an annihilation or palliation of whatever moral or political evil it may be within the compass of human power to assuage or eradicate."

537a, l. 14. *The "Address." An Address to the Irish People* carried the following "Advertisement": "The lowest possible price [five pence] is set on this publication, because it is the intention of the Author to awaken in the minds of the Irish poor, a knowledge of their real state, summarily pointing out the evils of that state, and suggesting rational means of remedy.— Catholic Emancipation, and a Repeal of the Union Act, (the latter, the most successful engine that England ever wielded over the misery of fallen Ireland,) being treated of in the following address, as grievances which unanimity and resolution may remove, and associations conducted with peaceable firmness, being earnestly recommended, as means for embodying that unanimity and firmness, which must finally be successful."

537a, l. 36. *some Suggestions.* Apparently never printed.

537b, l. 40. *the "proposals."* See note on 537a, l. 11 above.

537b, l. 42. *sent by the post.* Shelley's error in not seeing that the pamphlet *did* go by coach cost the unfortunate philosopher one pound one shilling and eight pence in postage charges.

Page 538.

5. *"St. Irvyne" and "Zastrozzi."* Two youthful novels published in 1811 and 1810 respectively.

Leigh Hunt (1784–1859). See Introduction to Hunt, text p. 707. Hunt was one of the many people whom Shelley helped financially.

Page 539.

Charles and James Ollier. Shelley's publishers. James attended to the commercial side of the business. Charles (1788–1859) was himself a writer. The firm at one time and another published Hunt, Keats, and Shelley.

Page 542.

40. *Mr. Lloyd.* Charles Lloyd, a young poet who lived for a time with Coleridge to profit by his instruction. Some gossip he repeated to Lamb about Coleridge led to a breach with the latter in 1798.

Page 543.

John Keats. See Keats's famous reply to this letter, text p. 655.

Page 545.

Thomas Love Peacock (1785–1866). See Introduction to Peacock, text p. 747. Peacock was seven years older than Shelley, an important number of years considering that Shelley was about 21 when they met in London (some time in 1813). Peacock was at once sane and sympathetic and the friendship was a healthy one for Shelley.

Page 546.

John Gisborne. Had rather an unsuccessful career as a merchant but he married the brilliant and charming widow of Willey Reveley. Shelley thought him a bore and made fun of his nose, but put up with him for his wife's sake. But Shelley also trusted Gisborne upon occasion, and Peacock thought him "agreeable and well-informed."

50. συνετοί. The intelligent.

Page 547.

9. *Den herrlichsten,* etc. "Strange and ever stranger materials force themselves upon the loftiest individual whom the spirit inspires." The lines, not correctly quoted, are from Goethe's *Faust*, Part I, 634–5.

Horace Smith (1779–1849). Received training for business and went on the stock exchange where he was highly successful. With his brother James as collaborator he published in 1812 a brilliant set of parodies—the *Rejected Addresses*. This was his only literary success in spite of more serious efforts.

48. *Nympholept.* Smith's *Amarynthus, the Nympholept* contained a poem "To Percy Bysshe Shelley, Esq., on his poems."

JOHN KEATS

BIBLIOGRAPHY

I. WORKS

Complete Works, ed. by H. Buxton Forman. 5 vols. (Gowans: Glasgow, 1901.) The standard edition, affording a memoir and full notes; Vols. IV and V, usually purchasable separately, contain the Letters.

Complete Poetical Works and Letters, ed. by H. E. Scudder. Cambridge Edition. (Houghton: Boston, 1899.) A good one-volume edition, with a biographical sketch.

Poems, ed. by Ernest de Sélincourt. (Dodd: New York, 1926.) A recommended edition, now reprinted for the fifth time; the annotations are valuable.

Poems, ed. by Sidney Colvin. 2 vols. (Chatto: London, 1915.) Arranges the poems in careful chronological order; offers an introductory memoir.

Poems, ed. by G. T. Drury. 2 vols. The Muses' Library. (Scribner: New York, 1896.) Valuable for its introductory critical essay by Robert Bridges, in which *Endymion* is read as a semi-allegory teaching the identity of sensuous and ideal passion.

Poetical Works, ed. by H. Buxton Forman. Oxford Edition. (Oxford University Press: 1926.) Furnished with an introduction and good textual notes.

Poems. (Dutton: New York, 1933.) A desirable inexpensive edition, giving the bare text of the poems.

Letters, ed. by M. B. Forman. 2 vols. (Oxford University Press: 1931.) A completion of the work begun by the editor's father who adds biographical notes on the correspondents.

Letters to Fanny Brawne, ed. by H. Buxton Forman. (Scribner: New York, 1890.) The first complete edition of the much-discussed correspondence (original edition, 1878); the introduction is a firm announcement of the editor's position.

Autobiography, compiled by E. V. Weller. (Stanford University Press: 1934.) The essays and letters are drawn upon to furnish a fairly clear record of the last four years of the poet's life; includes a post-lude by Cowden Clarke and Severn's description of Keats's death.

II. BIOGRAPHY AND CRITICISM

Baldwin, D. L., Broughton, L. N., and assistants. *A Concordance to the Poems of John Keats*. (Carnegie Institution of Washington: 1917.) Demonstrates Keats's entire poetic diction.

Colvin, Sidney. *John Keats: His Life and Poetry*. (Scribner: New York, 1925.) The revised edition of what will generally be regarded as the standard Life: treats *Endymion* as an allegory of self-purification, tending to the identity of earthly and spiritual beauty, etherealized by passion.

Colvin, Sidney. *Keats*. English Men of Letters series. (Harper: New York, 1894.) A thoroughly reliable brief biography, the nucleus of the work mentioned above.

Crawford, A. W. *The Genius of Keats*. (Stockwell: London, 1932.) A review of the poet's work in 1819, finding in it not merely the prophecy but the actual evidence of philosophic depth.

Evans, B. I. *Keats*. (Duckworth: London, 1934.) A good factual biography, but weak on the interpretative side.

Fausset, H. I'A. *Keats: A Study in Development*. (Secker: London, 1922). A stimulating psychological essay to follow the growth of the poet's mind in the development of his powers as a writer, advancing "from sensationalism to vision" and dying on "the very threshold of absolute truth."

Garrod, H. W. *Keats*. (Oxford University Press: 1926.) A study of Keats as thinker and poet; deprecates the over-emphasis of philosophy; of especial value for its analysis of the structure of the great Odes.

Hancock, A. E. *John Keats: A Literary Biography*. (Houghton: Boston, 1908.) Indicates but does not define the poet's theories on art and beauty: suggests that his "healthy humanism" anticipates Browning.

Hunt, Leigh. *Autobiography* (1850), ed. by Roger Ingpen. 2 vols. (Dutton: New York, 1903.) Many references to Keats, in the light of other known facts, reveal the extent of Hunt's influence on him.

Keats Memorial Volume, by the Keats House Committee. (Lane: London, 1921.) Contains about 100 miscellaneous unequal pieces: most interesting are Colvin's account of the autograph MSS of the Nightingale Ode, Abercrombie's discussion of the two *Hyperions*, and Bradley's study, "Keats and Philosophy."

Lowell, Amy. *John Keats*. 2 vols. (Houghton: Boston, 1925.) A "twentieth-century" estimate of the poet, written from a (perhaps too) sympathetic point of view; presents original analyses of some of the most important poems, besides other details unknown or unrecognized by previous biographers.

Milnes, R. M. (Lord Houghton). *Life, Letters, and Literary Remains of John Keats*. (Dutton: New York, 1927.) Valuable as the first complete Life (2 vols., 1848: revised 1857); includes many letters, drawing from them deductions which, ignored by Hunt and Rossetti, later biographies have generally ratified. Robert Lynd's introduction discusses Fanny Brawne's influence on Keats's poetry.

Murry, J. M. *Keats and Shakespere*. (Oxford University Press: 1925.) A penetrating criticism: it analyzes the poet's theories of art, drawing inferences sometimes of doubtful validity, but none which may be dismissed without careful consideration; furnishes a convincing expansion of Arnold's dictum that Keats is "with Shakespere."

Murry, J. M. *Studies in Keats*. (Oxford University Press: 1930.) Most valuable are "On First Looking into Chapman's Homer," showing how Keats's reading precipitated his matured feelings; and "The Meaning of *Endymion*," which undertakes a highly subjective interpretation of the poem.

Owen, Mrs. Frances M. *John Keats: A Study*. (Paul: London, 1880.) Latterly a rather rare book, but still an authority on certain phases of interpretation, notably in its references to *Endymion*, which is seen as an allegory in which the human race strives for spiritual uplift.

Ridley, M. R. *Keats' Craftsmanship*. (Oxford University Press: 1933.) A thoroughgoing discussion of the poet's methods of composition and his theories of the art of poetry; the studies of the writing of the Odes are especially valuable.

Rossetti, W. M. *Life of John Keats*. (Scott: London, 1887.) A judicious study, with a satisfactory balance between the biographical material and critical discussion of the poet's work.

Spurgeon, Caroline F. E. *Keats' Shakespeare: A Descriptive Study Based on New Material*. (Oxford University Press: 1928.) New light upon the poet's acquaintance with Shakespeare, based upon his 7-volume 1814 edition, now in the library of Mr. George Armour, Princeton, N. J.: gives Keats's underlinings, etc., for *The Tempest*,

Midsummer Night's Dream, Measure for Measure, Antony and Cleopatra.

Thorpe, C. D. *The Mind of John Keats.* (Oxford University Press: 1926.) Beginning with the conclusion of the *Ode on a Grecian Urn*, the author analyzes the development of the "poetic mind" of Keats as revealed in his entire work: sees it as a steady advance, culminating in the two *Hyperions.*

Weller, E. V. *Keats and Mary Tighe.* (Century: New York, 1928.) An elaborate display of parallel passages tending to show a very considerable influence of the minor Irish poet.

III. ARTICLES FROM BOOKS

Arnold, Matthew. "Keats," in *Essays in Criticism,* Second Series. (Macmillan: New York, 1891.) A famous Victorian pronouncement, self-complete and therefore unfair in part, although affirming that Keats is "with Shakespere"; the starting-point for numerous later critiques.

Bradley, A. C. "The Letters of Keats," in *Oxford Lectures on Poetry.* (Macmillan: London, 1909.) Shows how essential are the *Letters* in an interpretation of the poetry; finds in them strength of character and tenderness for a younger sister; traces in them the poet's philosophy of beauty.

Brooke, Stopford A. "Keats," in *Studies in Poetry.* (Duckworth: London, 1920.) Comments on the poet's lack of interest in contemporary events, his pursuit of beauty through the ancient and medieval traditions.

Clarke, C. C. and Mary. "Recollections of John Keats," in *Recollections of Writers.* (Scribner: New York, 1878.) Supplies many personal reminiscences of the poet.

De Sélincourt, Ernest. "John Keats," in *Proceedings of the British Academy,* X (1921–23). (Oxford University Press: 1921.) A Warton Lecture, delivered on the occasion of the centenary of the poet's death.

Fairchild, H. N. "The Medievalism of Keats" and "John Keats," in *The Romantic Quest.* (Columbia University Press: 1931.) The first essay shows how the poet progressed in his sources from the 18th-century medievalists to the great originals: Spenser, Shakespeare, Milton, Dante. The second essay analyzes the poet's idea of sensuous beauty, quoting liberally from his letters; remarks the frequency of the "aesthetic swoon."

Herford, C. H. "Keats," in *The Cambridge History of English Literature,* XII. (Putnam: New York, 1916.) A judicious short essay, concluding with suggestive comparisons.

Mackail, J. W. "The Composition of Keats' *Endymion*," in *Studies of English Poets.* (Longmans: New York, 1926.) Shows the effect upon the poem of places visited by the poet: Isle of Wight, Margate, Canterbury, Hampstead.

More, P. E. "John Keats," in *Shelburne Essays,* Fourth Series. (Putnam: New York, 1906.) Beginning with the idea that Keats was an artist preoccupied with the creation of beauty, the essay discusses his successes and failures—emphasizing the latter.

Suddard, S. J. Mary. "The Evolution of Keats's Mind," "Keats's Prelude," and "Keats's Style," in *Keats, Shelley, and Shakespeare Studies.* (Cambridge University Press: 1912.) These essays are definite contributions to the study of Keats as a developing personality: interprets *Sleep and Poetry* as implied autobiography.

Swinburne, A. C. "Keats," in *Miscellanies.* (Scribner: New York, 1911.) A loud deprecation of the poet's youthful unrestraint; glances obliquely at most of the long narratives, except *Hyperion;* rebukes other adverse critics.

Symons, Arthur. "John Keats," in *The Romantic Movement in English Poetry.* (Dutton: New York, 1909.) Over-stresses the morbid side of the poet; sees in his poetry the aspiration toward sensuous pleasure; points out metrical faults.

Woodberry, G. E. "On the Promise of Keats," in *Literary Essays.* (Harcourt: New York, 1920.) Quotes many of the poet's comments on his own mental growth and the "shadow of reality to come"; remarks the significance of his distaste for his pictorial skill as mind came to mean more to him.

IV. ARTICLES FROM PERIODICALS

Beach, J. W. "Keats's Realms of Gold," *Publications of the Modern Language Association,* XLIX, 246–57 (Mar., 1934). Notes the use made by the poet of Robertson's *History of America* in the Chapman sonnet.

Blunden, Edmund. "New Sidelights on Keats, Lamb, and Others from Letters to J. Clare," *London Mercury,* IV, 141–49 (June, 1921). Traces allusions to Keats in John Clare's letters, 1820–1837, many written by John Taylor, Keats's publisher.

Brown, Leonard. "The Genesis, Growth, and Meaning of *Endymion*," *Studies in Philology,* XXX, 618–53 (Oct., 1933). Finds the beginning of the poem in Drayton's *Man in the Moone,* Wordsworth being a shaping influence; *Alastor* is taken to be the clue to its allegorical significance.

Bush, Douglas. "The Date of Keats's *Fall of Hyperion*," *Modern Language Notes,* XLIX, 281–6 (May, 1934). Attacks Finney's view that the *Fall* was the first draft of the dual poems; cannot agree that Keats's loss of humanitarian faith accounts for his leaving the poem incomplete.

Chancellor, E. B. "Keats in Rome," *Nineteenth Century,* LXXXIX, 253–61 (Feb., 1921). Reviews in a somewhat exalted style the story of the poet's illness, departure for Italy, and his death.

Crawford, A. W. "*The Ode to a Nightingale*," *Modern Language Notes,* XXXVII, 476–81 (Dec., 1922). Discusses Brown's story of the composition of the Ode, analyzes its stanzas: points out the significance of the night-scenery—the symbol of the poet's grief.

Elliott, G. R. "The Real Tragedy of Keats," *Publications of the Modern Language Association,* XXXVI, 315–31 (Sept., 1921). A "post-centenary view," it ventures into the thorny field of speculating upon what a maturer Keats might have produced: it maintains that the poet's artistic powers lagged behind his intellectual development—this is the "real tragedy."

Finney, C. L. "Shakespeare and Keats's *Hyperion*," *Philological Quarterly,* III, 139–45 (Apr., 1924).

Advances the theory that Shakespeare was the greatest influence on Keats.

Finney, C. L. "*The Fall of Hyperion,*" *Journal of English and Germanic Philology,* XXVI, 304–24 (1927). From a reading of the poet's letters sees Milton and Wordsworth as the great influential factors in the poem; remarks Keats's disbelief in humanitarianism as the cause for leaving the poem unfinished.

Havens, R. D. "Concerning the *Ode on a Grecian Urn,*" *Modern Philology,* XXIV, 209–14 (Nov., 1926). Comments on Miss Lowell's analysis of the *Ode on a Grecian Urn* and the *Ode on Melancholy:* shows that there is no contradiction between them.

Landrum, Grace W. "More Concerning Chapman's Homer and Keats," *Publications of the Modern Language Association,* XLII, 986–1009 (Dec., 1927). Approaches the question of Keats's indebtedness to Chapman from the side of metre, careless rhyme, diction, epithets for classical deities, etc.: tends to narrow the range of real influence.

MacCracken, H. N. "The Source of Keats's *Eve of St. Agnes,*" *Modern Philology,* V, 145–50 (Oct., 1907). Calls attention to the scene in the tower in Boccaccio's *Filocolo,* describing the adventure in Alexandria.

Marsh, G. L., and White, N. I. "Keats and the Periodicals of His Time," *Modern Philology,* XXXII, 37–53 (Aug., 1934). An exhaustive list of notices of the poet, 1816–21, establishing the fact that the favorable comments outnumbered the unfavorable.

Moult, Thomas. "John Keats and the Poetry of Our Time," *Fortnightly Review,* CIX, 309–20 (Feb., 1921). Shows Keats's poetry as separate from the circumstances of his life; points out the fact that he has had few aesthetic followers.

Olney, Clarke. "John Keats and Robert Benjamin Haydon," *Publications of the Modern Language Association,* XLIX, 258–75 (Mar., 1934). Outlines their friendship; discusses the significance of the painter's influence upon the poet, which as a whole was beneficial.

Roberts, J. H. "Poetry of Sensation or of Thought," *Publications of the Modern Language Association,* XLV, 1129–39 (Dec., 1930). Sees Keats's crowning work as the result of the poet's surrender to sensuous beauty, which had hitherto conflicted with his empire of thought, *Endymion* and *Hyperion* being the products of his divided nature.

Roberts, J. H. "The Significance of 'Lamia,'" *Publications of the Modern Language Association,* L, 550–61 (June, 1935). Interprets *L mia* as Keats's reaffirmation of the sensuous ideal, which clashed with the theme of *Hyperion* and caused the abandonment of that poem, but found expression again in his *Ode to Autumn.*

Rusk, R. L. "Keats in the Wordsworth Country," *North American Review,* CCXIX, 392–7 (Mar., 1924). Prints a journal-letter from Keats to his brother George which was printed in an obscure Louisville, Kentucky, paper in 1836; suggests interesting changes in the dating of the "Bright star" sonnet.

Samuel, Herbert. "The Life and Poetry of John Keats," *Contemporary Review,* CXIX, 494–501 (Mar., 1921). A slightly condensed report of a centenary address; offers a brief biographical sketch, making many references to Colvin's Life.

Severn, Joseph. "On the Vicissitudes of Keats' Fame," *Atlantic Monthly,* XI, 401–7 (Apr., 1863). A retrospect of nearly fifty years by one of the poet's closest friends; speaks of meeting Keats's sister in Rome.

Shipman, Mary E. "Orthodoxy concerning Keats," *Publications of the Modern Language Association,* XLIV, 929–34 (Sept., 1929). A refutation of Mr. Snow's article (see below); puts Keats's inspiration above the surcharge of raw sensuousness.

Snow, R. H. "Heresy concerning Keats," *Publications of the Modern Language Association,* XLIII, 1142–9 (Dec., 1928). Suggests that the meaning of the *Ode on a Grecian Urn* may be discovered in the poem itself rather than in miscellaneous comments in the poet's letters; attempts an explanation of the last two lines and relates the Ode to the *Ode on Melancholy* and *Ode to a Nightingale.*

Thayer, Mary R. "Keats: *The Eve of St. Mark,*" *Modern Language Notes,* XXXIV, 149–55 (Mar., 1919). Discusses the legend in the "middle-English" passage; refers to earlier variants of the poem.

Thorpe, C. D. "Wordsworth and Keats," *Publications of the Modern Language Association,* XLII, 1010–26 (Dec., 1927). Speaks of Wordsworth's ignoring of Keats, the younger poet's adverse comments on Wordsworth, with instances of favorable allusion, notably in Keats's letter to Reynolds, May 3, 1818.

Warren, Herbert. "Keats as a Classical Scholar," *Nineteenth Century,* XCIII, 62–8 (Jan., 1923). Traces in Keats's poems and letters evidence of first-hand acquaintance with Vergil and Horace, and notes other classical gleanings derived from dictionaries, translations, etc.

NOTES

Page 557. IMITATION OF SPENSER

This poem is interesting as the earliest example of Keats's writing which has been preserved. It was written not later than the autumn of 1813, and may have been written as early as the beginning of 1812.

The following extract from Lord Houghton will indicate what Spenser meant to Keats in the early days when he was discovering that such a thing existed as poetry: "He was always borrowing books, which he devoured, rather than read. Yet so little expectation was formed of the direction his ability would take, that when, in the beginning of 1812, he asked for the loan of Spenser's *Faerie Queene,* Mr. Clarke remembers that it was supposed in the family that he merely desired, from a boyish ambition, to study an illustrious production of literature. The effect, however, produced on him by that great work of ideality was electrical: he was in the habit of walking over to Enfield at least once a week, to talk over his reading with his friend, and he would now speak of nothing but Spenser. A new world of delight seemed revealed to him: 'he ramped through the scenes of the romance,' writes Mr. Clarke, 'like a young horse turned into a spring meadow': he revelled in the gorgeousness of the imagery, as in the pleasures of a sense fresh-found: the force and felicity of an epithet (such, for example, as—'the sea-shouldering whale') would light up his countenance with ecstasy, and some fine touch of description would seem to strike on the secret chords of his soul and generate countless harmonies. This, in fact, was not only his open presentation at the Court of the Muses (for the lines in imitation of Spenser,

Now Morning from her orient chamber came, And her first footsteps touched a verdant hill, etc.

are the earliest known verses of his composition), but it was the great impulse of his poetic life, and the stream of his inspiration remained long coloured by the rich soil over which it first had flowed." (Houghton, *Life and Letters of John Keats*.)

The richness and surety of handling of the Spenserian stanza which Keats ultimately came to display may be discovered by a study of *The Eve of St. Agnes*. See note below on l. 6 of *Specimen of An Induction to a Poem*.

O SOLITUDE! IF I MUST WITH THEE DWELL

This was the first of Keats's poems to appear in print, appearing in Leigh Hunt's *The Examiner* for May 5, 1816.

HOW MANY BARDS GILD THE LAPSES OF TIME

". . . The main interest of the sonnet is its comparison of the working of Keats's miscellaneous poetic reading in his mind and memory with the effect of the confused but harmonious sounds of evening on the ear,—a frank and illuminating comment by himself on those stray echoes and reminiscences of the older poets which we catch now and again throughout his work. Such echoes and reminiscences are always permitted to genius, because genius cannot help turning whatever it takes into something new of its own: and Keats showed himself from the first one of those chartered borrowers who have the right to draw inspiration as they please. . . ." (Sidney Colvin, *John Keats*, pp. 88–9.)

TO ONE WHO HAS BEEN LONG IN CITY PENT

The uncertainty of Keats's early poetic accent may be studied by comparing ll. 1–4 with

ll. 5–8. The first four lines are refreshed and firm. The next four are mawkish and contain a confusion of debonairness and languishment, two qualities which do not agree with one another and have nothing to do with the theme as stated in the opening. The sestet returns to the tone of the opening quatrain.

Page 558.

ON FIRST LOOKING INTO CHAPMAN'S HOMER

Charles Cowden Clarke had borrowed a rich old folio edition of Chapman's Homer and he invited Keats over to read it with him. The two young men spent all one summer night dipping here and there into the volume. Keats's delight was intense. He left only at dawn, but when Clarke came down to breakfast, he found a copy of this sonnet which Keats had written and sent to him in the interval.

This, perhaps the first poem in which Keats showed the true measure of his power, has met with consistent critical praise. Mr. Middleton Murry gives an excellent analysis of its effect:

"What is the impression produced by the sonnet upon us? Impressions of this sort are hard to define: but here one seems to be predominant and recognizable.

"We receive an impression of excitement so intense that the declared and actual subject of the poem is as it were dissolved away by it. It is almost impossible not to forget that it is all about a book—Chapman's translation of *Homer*. There is a direct communication of emotion, which grows swifter and swifter, till in the final picture of Cortez, half visual, half abstract, it touches a consummation: the image is not merely stamped upon our minds by the emotional force of the poem, but the image gathers up, clinches, makes tangible, the emotional content of the poem. Cortez on the peak—it is the perfect culmination of the sonnet. All that the sonnet really means is crammed into that final image: it is the flower of the plant, the purpose and the essence of the created thing.

"Let us leave this for a moment and examine the sonnet more coldly, putting aside, if we can, the immediate and overwhelming impression. We observe that the imagery of exploration and discovery is maintained from the beginning. . . . From the first line the poet is a traveller, an explorer, voyaging among islands, discovering the realms of gold: he hears on his travels persistent rumours and reports of a great *El dorado*. The word of the conquistadors is helpful; for the phrase 'the realms of gold' is become so familiar, so much a part of current speech, that we forget that when Keats used it it was original. And it had come, I fancy, from the same reading whence came his picture of Cortez. '*El dorado*' means simply 'the realm, or the city, of gold.' Keats was, to his own mind, a conquistador, with Chapman's *Homer* for his new-found land.

"In the first two lines of the sestet . . . the imagery is slightly changed—he becomes the explorer not of earth but of heaven—an astronomer who has discovered a new planet; but the change, instead of weakening the poem, quite definitely strengthens and enriches it: it gives an infinite extension to its imaginative scope—to the yet unlimited earth the illimitable heavens are added, and by the exquisite use of the word 'swims' is created an impression of ethereal stillness, a background of quiet translunary spaces, against which the figure of Cortez on his peak emerges with tremendous and craggy definition.

"So that, on a colder examination, the immediate impression that the image of Cortez on the peak in Darien is the natural and, so to say, organic culmination of the poem, is fully substantiated. At the very outset Keats imagines himself as the explorer in search of *El dorado*, and when finally he likens himself to the mightiest of the conquistadors, at the supreme moment of discovery, he has carried the imagery with which he began to the pinnacle of its potentialities.

"It is one of the greatest sonnets in the English language: its immediate effect is startling, and perhaps this cold-blooded analysis has yielded some reason why this is so. The unity of the poem lies deep and is *organic:* in the first line the last is implicit, as a flower is implicit in a seed. . . ." (John Middleton Murry, *Studies in Keats*, pp. 17–18.)

11. *stout Cortez.* "History would here suggest Balboa," as Alfred Tennyson informed Francis Palgrave many years ago, and many commentators have noted since. The error is of no importance but has some slight interest in view of a remark in Leigh Hunt's *Recollections* that Keats had seen a striking portrait of Cortez by Titian and that the "eagle eyes" came direct from Titian. Keats then (if Hunt is correct), walking home wildly excited at about five in the morning, got his explorers mixed up, and Titian's genius influenced the poem to its present shape. The eyes, however, were "wond'ring eyes" in the version Keats first dashed off and sent to Clarke.

ADDRESSED TO HAYDON

2. *He of the cloud, the cataract, the lake.* Wordsworth. Haydon proposed sending the poem to Wordsworth, a suggestion which put Keats all "out of breath." Keats's attitude toward Wordsworth varied sharply from near reverence to irritation. See for example of the latter,

text p. 624, col. 2, l. 33 et seq. Professor Clarence D. Thorpe in *P.M.L.A.* for Dec., 1927 (XLII, 1010–26) has an article on Keats's varying feeling for Wordsworth. Professor Thorpe, quoting Bailey, among other things points out the frequency with which Keats referred to Wordsworth's *Tintern Abbey*, especially the passage beginning

"The blessed mood
In which the burthen of the mystery," etc.

KEEN, FITFUL GUSTS ARE WHISP'RING HERE AND THERE

By some esteemed one of the best of the sonnets in the 1817 volume, though, of course, not comparable to the *On First Looking into Chapman's Homer*.

TO G. A. W.

To Georgiana Wylie, who married Keats's brother George.

Page 559.

ON THE GRASSHOPPER AND CRICKET

At Hunt's, it was the custom occasionally to have rhyming competitions, the poets writing on set subjects. Cowden Clarke was present one evening when the talk got onto crickets— "the cheerful little grasshopper of the fireside." Hunt proposed they write on the title of this sonnet and the two poets set to work thereupon. "Such a prosperous opening!" was Hunt's exclamation when he read Keats's first line; and "Bravo, Keats!" at the tenth and eleventh lines.

Amy Lowell says of this sonnet: "Keats's sonnet, although not up to his best, is a delightful thing. The opening is an excellent picture, vivid and suggestive; one can see it, feel it, and smell it. The frost, as Hunt pointed out, is perfect; and the return of the grasshopper in the end, as being recollected through the sound of the cricket, well managed. This end is not only beautiful as regards the technical pattern, as I have said, it is so in regard to what I may call the mental pattern as well." (Amy Lowell, *John Keats*, I, 239.)

ON SEEING THE ELGIN MARBLES

Lord Elgin had secured in Greece the fragments of the Parthenon frieze, now one of the glories of the British Museum. In one of those attacks of singular obtuseness which occasionally overtake great nations on matters artistic there had been some hesitation in purchasing them for the nation. Haydon had been one of the leaders in the successful agitation to secure the marbles and, with his rather wild enthusiasms, was Keats's guide on his first visit to the marbles. Keats was both stunned and stirred and tried to express his feeling in this sonnet which he sent to Haydon along with another addressed to Haydon himself. Amy Lowell comments on the unevenness of this sonnet, calling attention to the strength of the opening lines and the concluding line.

ON THE SEA

This sonnet was included in letter to Reynolds, April 17–18, 1817, and Keats said he "slept the better" for it (see text p. 617). The line in *Lear* which Keats quotes in the letter is from IV, VI, 4—quoted from memory and not exactly. It is an unimportant line in itself but prepares the way for *Lear*, IV, VI, 11–25, which relate to Keats's sonnet.

Page 560.   ON A PICTURE OF LEANDER

So entitled in the earlier editions. It was really inspired by one of Tassie's colored paste reproductions of an engraved gem on the subject, which Keats had received as a gift. For a note on the Hero and Leander story see the note on *Don Juan*, II, 840.

SPECIMEN OF AN INDUCTION TO A POEM

6. *Archimago*. The magician in Spenser's *Faerie Queene*. Note this and the reference to Spenser in l. 49 as an indication of how great was Spenser's influence in Keats's formative period. Keats's first volume (see text p. 555) carried a motto from Spenser and a vignette of that poet on the title-page. In spite, however, of Keats's identification of Spenser with the chivalric, he is himself more independent as a poet than he was in the *Imitation of Spenser*. 61. *Libertas*. Leigh Hunt.

Page 561.

I STOOD TIP-TOE UPON A LITTLE HILL

This poem has often been called the "little Endymion" because "Endymion" was its first title, cancelled before the poem went to print in 1817. The longer poem may have been, and probably was, in Keats's mind to cause the cancellation of the title. Medwin (not a very reliable witness) tells a story of Keats and Shelley in 1816 each agreeing to write a long poem and says that Shelley's *Laon and Cythna* (published as *The Revolt of Islam*) and Keats's *Endymion* were the results. There is some dispute as to the date of composition of this poem. Leigh Hunt says it was inspired "by a delightful summer's day"; Amy Lowell agrees. Sir Sidney Colvin places the poem in the following December. It was, however, certainly being worked over in December, 1816. The poem then, to be arbitrary, was begun in the early summer and was being concluded in the late winter.

The poem breaks into two definite parts and both parts show clearly in different ways one of the true qualities of Keats's greatness—his immediate and powerful response to external stimuli. In this poem he responds to and puts into words with exquisite accuracy his feelings in two definitely divergent directions—an early summer day with its "luxuries" (see l. 28) and some stories from classical mythology which also have some luxury value. To each of these Keats responds with that powerful response which marks one side of his genius. This poem was a favorite with the Hunt circle.

In Appendix C of Amy Lowell's *John Keats* (II, 574–8) is an interesting bit of personalia connected with this poem. From the copy of the *Poems* (1817) which Keats gave to his brother George she has extracted the passages from this poem which George underscored. It is an interesting commentary of what the Keats brothers, in their intimate family circle, thought of the poem.

Page 564.   SLEEP AND POETRY

This poem belongs to the autumn and winter of 1816. It was planned and probably some of the lines actually composed one night when Keats, after an exciting evening of talk, was "put up" on an improvised bed on the sofa in Leigh Hunt's study. Unable to sleep and with Hunt's pictures and books about him Keats apparently thought a great deal about poetry and art. This poem is his *credo* to that date— his expression of what he believed and what he thought was yet before him to do. It was the concluding poem of the 1817 volume, as *I Stood Tip-toe* was the opening one. Keats himself settled the order of that volume and the student may draw such conclusions as he chooses from the position in which the poems were placed. The poem is 404 lines long and only extracts are presented in the text. 96. *O for ten years*. Keats had four and a fraction years actually, part of this brief period useless because of failing health. 122. *And can I ever bid these joys farewell?* Note that the preceding passage has been one of rather trivial luxuriousness—a matter of nymphs and strawberries. Now comes the decision for a nobler life which shall take into account "the agonies, the strife of human hearts." The passage is rather floundering poetry and ends surprisingly with a "wreath of girls" with "tangled curls," but the great charioteer of the deep imagination *has* come down and looked at other things than nymphs and strawberries. The passage is of the greatest significance to an understanding of Keats in spite of its inferiority as poetry. Consult Keats's letters (text p. 627, col. 2, l. 36 to the end of the letter; also p. 628, col. 2, ll. 32–43). Keats's distrust of his own particular bias has occupied much of modern scholarship and thrown a great deal of it into confusion over a supposed "dualism" in his nature, a conflict between the "sensuous," which he obviously had, and a desire for the "intellectual" which some have supposed him not to have possessed at this period. Keats himself stated the whole problem and the whole answer in his letters (text p. 629, col. 1, l. 38 to conclusion). A young man was growing up and adding to something he already had something more—maturity.

181. *Could all this be forgotten?* Keats launches his celebrated attack on the Augustans, having in the previous passage (not given in the text) referred to conceptions of poetry of which he more approved. Wordsworth with a sustained prose Preface (1800) had been before him. So had Leigh Hunt in the preface to *The Story of Rimini*. There is a certain rhetorical dash to Keats's lines which places them up in the front rank of the controversialists—so much so that Byron, who should have been one of Keats's first defenders, was enraged. Byron once called Keats "tadpole of Lakes." This was when Byron was defending Pope against himself and the whole Romantic Movement.

206. *Boileau.* In excellent French verse, between 1669 and 1674, Boileau summarized in his *L'Art Poétique* the decaying principles of the neo-classical school of criticism. He was respected by the chief English Augustans. He therefore became a "symbol" open to attack from the chief English Romantics.

Professor Thorpe has this to say of the passage in question:

"Here Keats expresses his allegiance to freedom-giving, truth-revealing intuitive imagination as the informing spirit of poetry, and his deep-rooted antagonism to the idea of verse coldly thought out, cut by feet and chiseled by rule, all unwarmed by the penetrative fires of feeling. . . . Yet, Keats and Boileau agreed on one essential: each knew that nothing is more dangerous than for a poet to write with the imagination only. Boileau believed this firmly, and Keats, at least after 1818, came to know that the highest poetry could not be written in this way. But Keats took the more balanced view. Where Boileau would make the imagination subordinate, Keats would have the imagination and the intellect work together, like twin sisters, as it were, except that the imaginative sister should have the stronger, clearer eyes and the deeper, more accurate seeing power, and so should always be the authority in case of dispute. In fact Keats refused to trust the intellectual sister's vision at all until he had appealed to the imaginative twin to corroborate her judgment—'I can never be sure of a truth except by a clear con-

ception of its beauty.' On the other hand he will even discredit or ignore the intellect if the imagination's penetrative vision has pierced some misty haze and caught gleams that her slower sister's eye cannot detect: 'What the Imagination seizes as beauty must be truth.' Boileau's mistake, as Brunetière points out in a statement with which Keats would agree, is that he failed to 'recognize that, in spite of all its excesses, the imagination, that is to say the faculty of transcending nature, of even seeing in it what is not there, provided only that he make us see it, that imagination remains the supreme faculty of the poet, his original aptitude, one whose place can be supplied by no other, without which one may indeed be artist, writer, orator, but never poet—for this it is we are bound to upbraid him. The reason is that he himself was not a poet.' . . . So it was not that Keats discarded knowledge; we have seen how earnestly he sought to know and understand: it was not that he despised conscious craftsmanship in verse building; we shall see how much thought he himself gave to fitting form for poetic substance: it was simply that he felt that without the operation of the imagination there could be no artistic perception nor revelation. In the education of the imagination, all knowledge and intellect have a place. . . ." (C. D. Thorpe, *The Mind of John Keats*, pp. 116–18.)

221. *Now 'tis a fairer season.* Young John Keats having recollected that poets have been abroad in the land in the past, and having disapproved of the Augustans in no uncertain terms, thinks there is still a chance for "poetry" in England. He was correct.

234. *the Poets' Polyphemes.* Supposed to refer to Byron "disturbing the grand sea."

235–6. *A drainless shower Of light is poesy.* That Keats should make this outright statement, after reference to disturbance in the previous lines, is worth considering.

Page 566. ENDYMION

Keats began the actual composition of this poem in April, 1817, the idea having been in his mind for some time, and completed it in November. It was published the following April (1818), almost exactly a year from the beginning of composition. His letters make frequent mention of the work and its progress (see especially text p. 618, col. 2, entire). The poem should be approached as what Keats in this letter describes it to be—"a little region to wander in," where the reader "may pick and choose." Thus understood the poem will be found to contain many isolated bits of great charm and beauty. Other references to *Endymion* occur in the text p. 621, col. 2; p. 623, col. 1; p. 624, col. 1; p. 625, col. 2; p. 626, cols.

1 and 2; p. 627, col. 2; p. 632, col. 1; and p. 649, col. 2, the last item being especially interesting as containing Keats's comparison of himself with Byron. See also Shelley's letter to the editor of the *Quarterly* (text p. 543).

Bridges has this to say of the poem: "To one who expects to be carried on by the interest of a story, this poem is more tedious and unreadable than can be imagined; and parts of it merit at least some of the condemnation which fell on the whole. Keats thought to 'surprise by a fine excess'; his excess rather confuses and blurs, and it is a severe task to keep the attention fixed. A want of definition in the actual narration,—so that important matters do not stand out,—a sameness in the variety, and the reiteration of languid epithets, are the chief cause of this; and in the second book, where Endymion is wandering in strange places, the uncertainty as to where he is, in the absence of explanatory statement as to what is intended, reduces the reader to despair. And yet it is nothing less than a marvel how even these faults can have obscured so completely the poetic excellences from a more general recognition. . . . In so far as the poem has an inner meaning, *Endymion* must be identified with the poet as Man. The Moon represents 'Poetry' or the Ideality of desired objects, *The principle of Beauty* in all things; it is the supersensuous quality which makes all desired objects ideal; and Cynthia, as moon goddess, crowns and personifies this, representing the ideal beauty or love of woman: and in so far as she is also actually the Moon as well as the Indian lady,—who clearly represents real or sensuous passion,—it follows that the love of woman is in its essence the same with all love of beauty; and this proposition and its converse will explain much that is otherwise strange and difficult." (Robert Bridges, Critical Introduction to *Poems*, in Muses' Library.)
The "inner meaning" referred to by Bridges can be followed in the extracts printed in the text but especial attention must be paid to the extracts from Book Four.

Colvin has this somewhat more amplified interpretation (note his sentences on the influence of two secondary moral ideas): "For such a clue to serve the reader, he must have it in his hand from the beginning. Let it be borne in mind, then, that besides the fundamental idea of treating the passion of Endymion for Cynthia as a type of the passion of the poetic soul for essential Beauty, Keats wrote under the influence of two secondary moral ideas or convictions, inchoate probably in his mind when he began but gaining definiteness as he went on. One was that the soul enamoured of and pursuing Beauty cannot achieve its quest in selfishness and isolation, but to succeed must first be taken out of itself and purified by active sympathy with the lives and sufferings of others: the other, that a passion for the manifold separate and dividual beauties of things and beings upon earth is in its nature identical with the passion for that transcendental and essential Beauty: hence the various human love-adventures which befall the hero in dreams or in reality, and seem to distract him from his divine quest, are shown in the end to be in truth no infidelities but only attractions exercised by his celestial mistress in disguise." (Sidney Colvin, *John Keats*, pp. 172–3.) In connection with either of these interpretations the student should consult Keats's letter of Nov. 22, 1817, to Bailey (text p. 620).

Keats cancelled his first preface (see his letter to Reynolds on the subject, text p. 626) and the poem finally appeared with the following Preface:

"Knowing within myself the manner in which this Poem has been produced, it is not without a feeling of regret that I make it public.
"What manner I mean, will be quite clear to the reader, who must soon perceive great inexperience, immaturity, and every error denoting a feverish attempt, rather than a deed accomplished. The two first books, and indeed the two last, I feel sensible are not of such completion as to warrant their passing the press; nor should they if I thought a year's castigation would do them any good;—it will not: the foundations are too sandy. It is just that this youngster should die away: a sad thought for me, if I had not some hope that while it is dwindling I may be plotting, and fitting myself for verses fit to live.
"This may be speaking too presumptuously, and may deserve a punishment: but no feeling man will be forward to inflict it: he will leave me alone, with the conviction that there is not a fiercer hell than the failure in a great object. This is not written with the least atom of purpose to forestall criticisms of course, but from the desire I have to conciliate men who are competent to look, and who do look with a zealous eye, to the honour of English literature.
"The imagination of a boy is healthy, and the mature imagination of a man is healthy; but there is a space of life between, in which the soul is in a ferment, the character undecided, the way of life uncertain, the ambition thick-sighted: thence proceeds mawkishness, and all the thousand bitters which those men I speak of must nesessarily taste in going over the following pages.
"I hope I have not in too late a day touched the beautiful mythology of Greece, and dulled its brightness: for I wish to try once more, before I bid it farewell."

It was *Endymion* which was attacked in the fierce reviews which were supposed, quite incorrectly, to have broken Keats's heart. Two extracts from these reviews follow:

"Of all the manias of this mad age, the most incurable, as well as the most common, seems to be no other than the *metromanie*. The just celebrity of Robert Burns and Miss Baillie has had the melancholy effect of turning the heads of we know not how many farm-servants and unmarried ladies; our very footmen compose tragedies, and there is scarcely a superannuated governess in the island that does not leave a roll of lyrics behind her in her bandbox. To witness the disease of any human understanding, however feeble, is distressing; but the spectacle of an able mind reduced to a state of insanity is of course ten times more afflicting. It is with such sorrow as this that we have contemplated the case of Mr. John Keats. This young man appears to have received from nature talents of an excellent, perhaps even of a superior order,—talents which, devoted to the purposes of any useful profession, must have rendered him a respectable if not an eminent citizen. His friends, we understand, destined him to the career of medicine, and he was bound apprentice some years ago to a worthy apothecary in town. But all has been undone by a sudden attack of the malady to which we have alluded. Whether Mr. John had been sent home with a diuretic or composing draught to some patient far gone in the poetical mania, we have not heard. This much is certain, that he has caught the infection, and that thoroughly. For some time we were in hopes that he might get off with a violent fit or two, but of late the symptoms are terrible. The frenzy of the *Poems* was bad enough in its way, but it did not alarm us half so seriously as the calm, settled, imperturbable driveling idiocy of the *Endymion*. We hope, however, that in so young a person, and with a constitution originally so good, even now the disease is not utterly incurable. Time, firm treatment, and rational restraint do much for many apparently hopeless invalids; and if Mr. Keats should happen, at some interval of reason, to cast his eye upon our pages, he may perhaps be convinced of the existence of his malady, which in such cases is often all that is necessary to put the patient in a fair way of being cured. . . . "Before giving any extracts, we must inform our readers that this romance is meant to be written in English heroic rhyme. To those who have read any of Hunt's poems, this hint might indeed be needless. Mr. Keats has adopted the loose, nerveless versification and Cockney rhymes of the poet of *Rimini*, but in fairness to that gentleman we must add that the defects of the system are tenfold more conspicuous in his disciple's work than his own. Mr. Hunt is a small poet, but he is a clever man. Mr. Keats is a still smaller poet, and he is only a boy of pretty abilities, which he has done everything in his power to spoil. . . . We venture to make one small prophecy, that his bookseller will not a second time venture fifty pounds upon anything he can write. It is a better and wiser thing to be a starved apothecary than a starved poet; so back to the shop, Mr. John, back to 'plasters, pills, and ointment boxes,' etc. But for heaven's sake, young Sangrado, be a little more sparing of extenuatives and soporifices in your practice than you have been in your poetry." (*Blackwood's Edinburgh Magazine*, August, 1818; signed "Z," probably written by John Gibson Lockhart.)

"Reviewers have been sometimes accused of not reading the works which they affected to criticize. On the present occasion we shall anticipate the author's complaint, and honestly confess that we have not read his work. Not that we have been wanting in our duty—far from it; indeed, we have made efforts almost as superhuman as the story itself appears to be, to get through it; but with the fullest stretch of our perseverance we are forced to confess that we have not been able to struggle beyond the first of the four books of which this Poetic Romance consists. We should extremely lament this want of energy, or whatever it may be, on our parts, were it not for one consolation,—namely, that we are no better acquainted with the meaning of the book through which we have so painfully toiled, than we are with that of the three which we have not looked into. "It is not that Mr. Keats (if that be his real name, for we almost doubt that any man in his senses would put his real name to such a rhapsody),—it is not, we say, that the author has not powers of language, rays of fancy, and gleams of genius; he has all these; but he is unhappily a disciple of the new school of what has been somewhere called Cockney poetry, which may be defined to consist of the most incongruous ideas in the most uncouth language. Of this school Mr. Leigh Hunt, as we observed in a former number, aspires to be the hierophant. Our readers will recollect the pleasant recipes for harmonious and sublime poetry which he gave us in his preface to *Rimini*, and the still more facetious instances of his harmony and sublimity in the verses themselves; and they will recollect above all the contempt of Pope, Johnson, and such like poetasters and pseudo-critics, which so forcibly contrasted itself with Mr. Leigh Hunt's self-complacent approbation of

all the things itself had wrote,
Of special merit though of little note.

"This author is a copyist of Mr. Hunt; but he is more unintelligible, almost as rugged, twice as diffuse, and ten times more tiresome and absurd than his prototype, who, though he impudently presumed to seat himself in the chair of criticism and to measure his own poetry by his own standard, yet generally had a meaning. But Mr. Keats has advanced no dogmas which he was bound to support by examples; his nonsense therefore is quite gratuitous; he writes it for its own sake, and, being bitten by Mr. Leigh Hunt's insane criticism, more than rivals the insanity of his poetry. . . .

"Of the story we have been able to make out but little; it seems to be mythological, and probably relates to the loves of Diana and Endymion; but of this, as the scope of the work has altogether escaped us, we cannot speak with any degree of certainty, and must therefore content ourselves with giving some instances of its diction and versification;— and here again we are perplexed and puzzled. At first it appeared to us that Mr. Keats had been amusing himself and wearying his readers with an immeasurable game at *bouts-rimes;* but, if we recollect rightly, it is an indispensable condition at this play that the rhymes when filled up shall have a meaning. He seems to us to write a line at random, and then he follows not the thought excited by this line, but that suggested by the rhyme with which it concludes. There is hardly a complete couplet enclosing a complete idea in the whole book. He wanders from one subject to another, from the association, not of the ideas but of sounds, and the work is composed of hemistichs which, it is quite evident, have forced themselves upon the author by the mere force of the catch-words on which they turn. . . .

"By this time our readers must be pretty well satisfied as to the meaning of his sentences and the structure of his lines; we now present them with some of the new words with which, in imitation of Mr. Leigh Hunt, he adorns our language. We are told that 'turtles *passion* their voices'; that 'an arbour was *nested,*' and a lady's locks '*gordian'd* up'; and, to supply the place of the nouns thus verbalized, Mr. Keats with great fecundity spawns new ones, such as 'men-slugs and human *serpentry,*' the '*honey-feel* of bliss,' 'wives prepare *needments,*' and so forth.

"Then he has formed new verbs by the process of cutting off their natural tails, the adverbs, and affixing them to their foreheads; thus, 'the wine out-sparkled,' the 'multitude up-followed,' and 'night up-took'; 'the wind up-blows,' and the 'hours are down-sunken.' But if he sinks some adverbs in the verbs, he compensates the language with adverbs and adjectives which he separates from the parent stock. Thus a lady 'whispers *pantingly* and close,'

makes '*hushing* signs,' and steers her skiff into a '*ripply* cove'; a shower falls '*refreshfully,*' and a vulture has a '*spreaded* tail.'

"But enough of Mr. Leigh Hunt and his simple neophyte. If any one should be bold enough to purchase this 'Poetic Romance,' and so much more patient than ourselves as to get beyond the first book, and so much more fortunate as to find a meaning, we entreat him to make us acquainted with his success; we shall then return to the task which we now abandon in despair, and endeavour to make all due amends to Mr. Keats and to our readers." (*The Quarterly Review*, April, 1818; written by John Wilson Croker; the April number was held up and actually appeared in the autumn of 1818.)

Page 567.   *From* BOOK I

553. *the zodiac-lion*. The lion is one of the signs of the Zodiac. The line indicates (in spite of the reference to "June" in l. 545) that the time of the episode was midsummer.

555. *ditamy*. The usual spelling is "dittany," —which is a species of mint.

Page 568.

626–7. *sea-born Venus . . . cradle shell*. See a copy of Botticelli's famous painting, "The Birth of Venus," for a pictorial rendering of the myth of Venus, born of the sea foam and wafted ashore on a cradle shell.

777. *Wherein lies happiness*, et seq. See text p. 624, letter IX; and to find a possible explanation of Keats's idea of the importance of this particular passage see text p. 620, col. 2, l. 44 et seq. The passage, taken in its entirety, is a glorification of love and friendship. It begins by showing man joined to nature by the beauty of the earth, to the past of his race by history and legend. He is at once a part of these great things and small beside them. But there is something yet "more self-destroying" (l. 799) which is the true theme of the passage. See also the *Induction* to Book II.

Page 570.   *From* BOOK II

387 et seq. [*Adonis in Slumber*.] See the quotation from Gayley's *Classic Myths* in the introductory material to Shelley's *Adonais*, above. Carrying the myth farther, Gayley goes on to say in his commentary: ". . . The myth derives its origin from the Babylonian worship of Thammuz or Adon, who represents the verdure of spring, and whom his mistress, the goddess of fertility, seeks, after his death, in the lower regions. With their departure all birth and fruitage cease on the earth; but when he has been revived by sprinkling of water, and restored to his mistress and to earth, all nature again rejoices."

Keats's poem relates to the latter part of the myth as Shelley's does to the earlier.

Page 571. *From* BOOK III

142 et seq. [*Address to the Moon.*] "I went up Box hill this evening after the moon," Keats wrote in Nov., 1817, to Reynolds. Amy Lowell's poem *On a Certain Critic* included in her *Pictures of the Floating World* is an interesting comment on that particular trip up the hill and critics in general.

Page 572. *From* BOOK IV

The solution of the "inner meaning" of *Endymion* will be found in the extracts here included. More than one reader has had a distinct sympathy with Peona in the last line of the poem when she "went home through the gloomy wood in wonderment."

Page 576. ISABELLA; OR THE POT OF BASIL

Keats and Reynolds projected a volume of narratives based on tales by Boccaccio. The plan was never carried out, but this poem was the beginning Keats made upon it. Keats's own opinion of the poem after the actual period of composition was not high, and he was persuaded to publish it only by the very active urgency of his friends. To Woodhouse he wrote (in a letter quoted in Amy Lowell's *John Keats*, II, 337): "I will give you a few reasons why I shall persist in not publishing The Pot of Basil. It is too smokeable. . . . There is too much inexperience of line and simplicity of knowledge in it—which might do very well after one's death, but not while one is alive. . . . I intend to use more finesse with the Public. It is possible to write fine things which cannot be laugh'd at in any way. Isabella is what I should call were I a reviewer 'A weak-sided Poem' with an amusing sobersadness about it."

Page 583. LINES ON THE MERMAID TAVERN

It was at the Mermaid that many of the Elizabethan poets and dramatists gathered to drink and jest.
14. *Mine host's sign-board*. The modern system of locating an address by street and number developed late. In Elizabethan days one searched for a pictorial sign: "The Swan"; "The Saracen's Head"; "The Mermaid," etc.

MEG MERRILIES

Keats sent this poem in a letter from Scotland to his small sister Fanny (see text p. 630, col. 1, l. 35). Meg Merrilies figured in Scott's *Guy Mannering*, a popular novel of 1815.

Page 584. BRIGHT STAR, WOULD I WERE STEDFAST AS THOU ART—

Colvin gives as the date of composition February 25, 1819; Amy Lowell says mid-April of the same year—a dispute of no great consequence. For a long time this was believed to have been Keats's "last sonnet," written in Severn's copy of Shakespeare in September, 1820, one night while their ship, delayed by storms, was still hovering off the English coast. The final version was copied into the Shakespeare volume on this occasion, but the 1819 composition date is correct.

The beauty of certain lines of the octave in this sonnet is especially to be noted.

Page 585. WHY DID I LAUGH TO-NIGHT?

See text p. 640, col. 2, l. 14 for Keats's comment on this sonnet in the letter in which he enclosed it to George and Georgiana.

ON THE SONNET

See text p. 642, col. 2, l. 50 for Keats's comment on the "pouncing rhymes" of the sonnet form and notice the rhyme scheme he develops here.
2. *Andromeda*. A beautiful maiden who was chained to a rock to appease a ravening seamonster. The hero Perseus, coming on the scene at a critical moment, disapproved of the whole procedure so completely that he killed the monster and married Andromeda.

Page 586. THE EVE OF ST. AGNES

Keats's lavishness of treatment is his own; the superstition concerning St. Agnes's Eve (Jan., 21) is old: "But for all there be so many bad days in this month I can tell you of one day which is lucky, and many young men and maids have a deal of heart's ease on that day, or the day after shall let you understand; it is the 21st. called St. Agnes' day. This St. Agnes has a favour for young men and maids and will bring to their bedsides their sweethearts if they follow my rules, on this day you must be sure to *keep fast*, and neither eat nor drink all that day, nor night, neither let man, woman or child kiss thee that day; and thou must be sure when thou goest to bed to put on a *clean shift* and the best thou hast, and clean clothes on thy head; for St. Agnes loves to see all clean when she comes. When thou liest down lie as *straight as thou canst*, lay thy hands under thy head and say

> Now St. Agnes play thy part,
> And send to me my own sweetheart
> And show me such a *happy bliss*,
> This night of him to have a kiss.

And be sure to fall asleep as soon as you can and before you awake out of your first sleep you shall see him come before you." (*Mother Bunches Closet newly broke open* (no date), quoted by M. R. Ridley, *Keats' Craftsmanship*, pp. 109–10.)

105. *Gossip*. Godmother; there is no unfriendly connotation to this use of the word.

170–1. *Never on such a night . . . Since Merlin paid his Demon*. The stormy night may refer to the tempest which swept over Broceliande the night after the magician Merlin (the child of a demon) was enchanted by the sorceress Vivian.

218. *gules*. Red.

241. *Clasp'd like a missal where swart Paynims pray*. A Christian book of devotions in a pagan land would have been guarded and cherished.

292. '*La belle dame sans merci*.' The title of a French poem by Alain Chartier (?1390–?1439) which had fallen into Keats's hands. It means: "The lovely lady without pity."

349. *Rhenish*. Rhine wine.

377. *aves told*. Ave stands for *Ave Maria* (Hail Mary), a prayer in Latin. "Told" means counted, on the beads of a rosary.

Page 591.   THE EVE OF ST. MARK

A superstition connected with the Eve of St. Mark is that a person who concealed himself in the church porch at late twilight would see enter the church the apparitions of persons who were to be ill that year. The length of time the apparition remained within the church indicated the length and severity of the illness. If the apparition did not come out again, the death of the person concerned was signified. Keats considered the poem a study in atmosphere. He wrote as follows concerning it to George and Georgiana Keats, September 20, 1819: ". . . The great beauty of poetry is that it makes everything in every place interesting. The palatine Venice and the abbotine Winchester are equally interesting. Some time since I began a poem called *The Eve of St. Mark*, quite in the spirit of town quietude. I think I will give you the sensation of walking about an old country town in a coolish evening. I know not whether I shall ever finish it; I will give it as far as I have gone. *Ut tibi placeat*." Keats never gave any indication of what use he intended to make of his legendary material. Amy Lowell, to express the spirit in which this poem was written, quotes from one of Keats's letters (text p. 650, col. 2, ll. 19–31). That this passage had a connection in Keats's own mind with this poem is indicated by the fact that a line or two later in the letter Keats quoted "Kepen in solitarinesse" (l. 106).

Page. 592.   LA BELLE DAME SANS MERCI

"It would be impertinence to praise this poem, which charms alike old and young: and it stands above the reach of criticism." (Robert Bridges.)

The poem was not included in the 1820 volume but first appeared in Leigh Hunt's new magazine, *The Indicator*, May 10, 1820. Hunt says the title was suggested by a poem by Alain Chartier, a translation of which Keats found in a volume of Chaucer, attributed to Chaucer. The title means "the lovely lady without pity."

There are two versions of the poem, that which Hunt printed and that which Keats copied into his long journal letter (Feb., May, 1819) to George and Georgiana Keats. The latter is superior.

Page 593.   ODE TO PSYCHE

See text p. 642, col. 2, l. 30 for Keats's own comment on this poem. The story of Cupid and Psyche is most beautifully told in the twenty-second chapter of *The Golden Asse* of Apuleius—the story of the young god's love for the mortal princess, the jealousy of Venus, and of how Jupiter finally gave her the cup of immortality to drink so that the lovers could be together forever. But Psyche was a latecomer on Olympus and it is this idea which Keats develops.

4. *soft-conched*. Shell-shaped.

14. *Tyrian*. Purple.

Page 594.   ODE ON A GRECIAN URN

40. *Why thou art desolate*. "Where else does his imagination give us a picture with such economy of detail as in his lines about the little town? What a lightning stroke of genius to depict it only to empty it, leaving it solitary in the morning sun, and, by a swift transition from gay to grave, evoking its eternal desolation. Gay and grave, that is it—Keats tuned to his highest pitch of evocative creation, burning with so clear and white an emotion that all his sense, all his thoughts and beliefs, fuse together into a presentation which is at once firm and infinitely moving, just, but wistfully disillusioned, cordially frank, yet very nearly perfectly concealed. The poem is a magnificent example of joy through resignation, for Keats had looked with ecstasy and anguish at life, at love, at art, and had learnt to submit to immutable law, to grant the necessity of his school of Soul-making, perchance, indeed, to find it good." (Amy Lowell, *John Keats*, II, 243.)

41. *Attic shape*. It was in Attica that Greek civilization found its purest expression.

45. *Cold Pastoral*. The pastoral was a literary form—cold, in this case, because done in marble.

49. "*Beauty is truth*," et seq. There is a traditional and an heretical interpretation of these

lines. The traditional maintains that Keats, faced with the fever and transiency of the senses, found consolation in the enduring beauty of art. The heretical interpretation maintains that the final two lines must be read as a part of the poem as a whole and that Keats had a specific "beauty" in mind when he wrote them.

"... The beauty that he has definitely in mind may be that of the figures on the urn. It is the urn which gives us a message ('thou sayst' are Keats's words). To be grotesquely literal for a moment—does the urn contract its marble lips and labialize the statement, 'Beauty is truth'? Hardly. Or do the scenes upon the urn convey a certain idea? They do. And it is these scenes, not the urn *qua* permanent marble, which make the point on which Keats ends. This is so obvious as scarcely to deserve mention, and yet the equally obvious consequences seem not to have been noticed. The word 'urn' is never once mentioned in the text, its shape, its proportion are unknown; even its material, marble, is unmentioned until the fifth strophe, when we learn that the *figures* on it are marble. It is the beauty of these figures which is 'all Ye know on earth, and all ye need to know,' and the beauty of these figures is the beauty of pipes and timbrels and wild ecstasy.
"Read in its context, Keats is abandoning the problem as insoluble, not advancing a theory of aesthetic." (Royall Snow, "Heresy Concerning Keats," *P.M.L.A.*, XLIII, 1144.)

Page 595.   ODE ON MELANCHOLY

1. *Lethe.* See note on l. 4, *Ode to a Nightingale.*
4. *Proserpine.* Daughter of Ceres, carried off by Pluto to be Queen of Hell. At the prayer of Ceres he relented and allowed her to return to earth each year in the spring for six months. The winter months she returned to the underworld.
6-7. *nor the death-moth be Your mournful Psyche.* In greek, Psyche means both "soul" and "butterfly" or "moth." She also was the heroine of a love story. See introductory material to the *Ode to Psyche.*

ODE TO A NIGHTINGALE

This poem was written at Hampstead while Keats was living with Brown. Twenty years later Brown described the circumstances of its composition: "In the spring of 1819 a nightingale had built her nest near my house. Keats felt a tranquil and continual joy in her song; and one morning he took his chair from the breakfast table to the grass-plot under a plum-tree, where he sat for two or three hours. When he came into the house, I perceived he had some scraps of paper in his hand, and these he was quietly thrusting behind the books. On inquiry, I found those scraps, four or five in number, contained his poetic feeling on the song of our nightingale."
4. *Lethe-wards.* The river Lethe flowed past the Elysian Fields, and those souls which were to be born again into other bodies drank of its waters oblivion of their former lives.
14. *Provençal song.* Provence is a district in the south of France.
32. *Bacchus and his pards.* Bacchus was the god of wine. Tigers or panthers drew his car. Keats represents the car as drawn by leopards (pards).
66. *the sad heart of Ruth.* See Ruth 2.

Page 597.   TO AUTUMN

On September 22, 1819, Keats wrote as follows to Reynolds and enclosed a copy of this poem: "How beautiful the season is now—How fine the air. A temperate sharpness about it. Really, without joking, chaste weather—Dian skies— I never liked stubble-fields so much as now— Aye better than the chilly green of the Spring. Somehow, a stubble-field looks warm—in the same way that some pictures look warm. This struck me so much in my Sunday's walk that I composed upon it."

Page 598.   LAMIA

Lamia, according to the earlier legends, was a queen of Libya with whom Zeus fell in love. Hera in revenge transformed her into a vampire feeding on the blood of young children. Later the name came to cover a whole class of sinister figures, half serpent and half woman, with powers of sorcery and a tendency toward vampirism. Folklore and myth contain many such types, naturally rather vaguely defined. Keats makes clear his conception early in the poem. He took the idea from the following passage in Burton's *Anatomy of Melancholy*:
"Philostratos, in his fourth book *de Vita Apollonii*, hath a memorable instance in this kind, which I may not omit, of one Menippus Lycius, a young man twenty-five years of age that, going betwixt Cenchreas and Corinth, met such a phantasm in the habit of a fair gentlewoman, which, taking him by the hand, carried him home to her house, in the suburbs of Corinth, and told him she was a Phœnician by birth, and if he would tarry with her, he should hear her sing and play, and drink such wine as never any drank, and no man should molest him; but she, being fair and lovely would die with him, that was fair and lovely to behold. The young man, a philosopher, otherwise staid and discreet, able to moderate his passions, thought not this of love, tarried

with her awhile to his great content, and at last married her, to whose wedding, amongst other guests, came Apollonius; who, by some probable conjectures, found her out to be a serpent, a lamia; and that all her furniture was, like Tantulus' gold, described by Homer, no substance, but mere illusions. When she saw herself descried, she wept, and desired Apollonius to be silent, but he would not be moved, and thereupon she, plate, house, and all that was in it, vanished in an instant; many thousands took notice of this fact, for it was done in the midst of Greece." (Part III, sect. 2, memb. I, subs. I.)

The poem was written in the summer of 1819. In mid-July he felt he had "proceeded pretty well" with it, and it was finished in August. Keats thought it had "that sort of fire in it which must take hold of people in some way—" pleasant or unpleasant.

Those students interested in problems of poetical technique will find *Lamia*, coming from Keats, a rather surprising technical performance. The sense of firmness of texture which it gives in the handling of the couplet (as opposed to the sense of laxness in his earlier use of the form) and Keats's use of the triplet and Alexandrine for variation, have struck commentators from the beginning. Keats had been reading Dryden before he began *Lamia* and the traditional explanation for something approaching a century has been that the style of *Lamia* was borrowed from Dryden. Mr. M. R. Ridley has recently examined the explanation with surprising results. There are two obvious points of discussion. There is the matter of the end-stopped line as opposed to the run-on line. Mr. Ridley's figures show that in the couplet poems of the 1817 volume 32.2% are run-on lines and that *Lamia* shows exactly the same percentage. This percentage is between two and one half and three times what Dryden allowed himself. Here, where the technical influence of Dryden might be expected to be most clear, it seems to be nil. Mr. Ridley, however, divides the types of run-on lines into four, and notes an increase in Keats's use of the fourth class until in *Lamia* he is using it ten times as frequently as did Dryden. The second point of discussion is that of feminine rhymes. Mr. Ridley shows that 20% of the rhymes in the 1817 volume were feminine. In *Lamia* there is only one single case—and that doubtful. Just exactly what Keats did and did not learn from Dryden, Mr. Ridley sums up admirably: ". . . There is no doubt that Keats had studied Dryden; no one can read *Lamia* with the least degree of attention and fail to be convinced of that. What I am trying to show is that his study did not lead him along the easy path of lazy imitation, as has

been supposed, but that rather he selected from Dryden, and learned to use, what he wanted for his own purposes, without allowing himself to be lured into a thoughtless copying of what he did not want. He learned two things from Dryden. In the first place he learned how to use the end-stopped couplet when he wanted it, though as we have seen he seldom did want it, and the use of it after the manner of Dryden would have destroyed the effect at which Keats was aiming. But there are a few isolated passages, and effective passages, in *Lamia* when for eight or ten lines there is a run of thoroughly Drydenian couplets. But the chief lesson that he learned from Dryden was the use of the Alexandrine and the triplet, particularly the former. In the 1817 poems there are a few triplets. In *Endymion* there are none. And even his study of Dryden does not seem to have made Keats much fonder of this technical trick, since even in *Lamia* the proportion is considerably less than half that in the *Fables*. But he learned from his study of Dryden to admire the right use of the Alexandrine. Neither in the 1817 poems nor in *Endymion* are there any Alexandrines at all. But in *Lamia* there is a very considerable number (between 5 and 6 per cent of the total number of lines), and indeed a considerably higher proportion than in the *Fables* themselves. Keats saw that the Alexandrine was going to give him something that he particularly needed. The effect of the Alexandrine is much more specific than that of a merely pleasant variation. The end of the ordinary closed heroic couplet is simply a dead stop with no particular expectation of anything to follow. The end of the Alexandrine is just as definite a pause, but with this difference, that it is an expectant pause. It has much the effect of a *ritardando* in music. The ear is waiting for the resumption of the ordinary beat of the rhythm; and therefore, which is the important point, the attention is also waiting for the continuation of the train of thought. The Alexandrine gives a firm articulation, avoiding a shapeless fluency on the one hand and the disjointedness of too heavy end-stopping on the other." (M. R. Ridley, *Keats's Craftsmanship*, pp. 248–9.)

Page 606. HYPERION

The theme of *Hyperion* had been in Keats's mind even before George left England in June, but he worked on the first two books in the autumn and winter of 1818, according to Mr. Middleton Murry, put them aside for a time, and then worked on the third book intermittently from January until April, 1819. How Keats might have continued the poem is conjectural. Woodhouse states: "The poem, if completed, would have treated of the dethronement of Hyperion, the former God of the Sun, by Apollo,—and incidentally of those of Oceanus by Neptune, of Saturn by Jupiter, etc., and of the war of the giants for Saturn's re-establishment—with other events, of which we have but very dark hints in the mythological poets of Greece and Rome. In fact the incidents would have been pure creations of the poet's brain."

There were two wars in ancient Heaven, that in which the younger gods headed by Jupiter overthrew the Titans and a later revolt of the Giants. Keats's poem begins after the first war with a picture of the dethroned Saturn (Cronus) and moves into a debate among the Titans as to whether they shall raise revolt. The speech of Oceanus (II, 181 et seq.) should be noted. The third book leaves the Titans and deals with Apollo, who was ultimately to dethrone Hyperion—a Titan who, after the first war, had retained his power as the sun god.

The stateliness and grandeur of the Titans has often been commented on. Certainly none of the victorious Olympians could have been more god-like in stature than the defeated Saturn, and here was one of the problems which must have confronted Keats had he chosen to go on. The Olympians had to be grander still, or he would have been writing the epic of the defeat of the great by the small. The possible Miltonic comparisons have of course struck critics from the first and struck Keats before they did the critics. In a letter to Reynolds (Sept. 22, 1819) he wrote: ". . . I have given up Hyperion—there were too many Miltonic inversions in it—Miltonic verse cannot be written but in an artful, or, rather, artist's humour. I wish to give myself up to other sensations. English ought to be kept up. It may be interesting to you to pick out some lines from Hyperion, and put a mark x to the false beauty proceeding from art, and one || to the true voice of feeling. Upon my soul 'twas imagination—I cannot make the distinction—Every now and then there is a Miltonic intonation—But I cannot make the division properly. . . ."

Some students may be interested in considering Mr. Middleton Murry's contention that Hyperion is not a fragment but is complete, and, because it is really the poem of Apollo, finishes properly where it does. See his Keats and Shakespeare, especially Chapter VII.

BOOK I

20-1. the Earth, His ancient mother. Gæa, the Earth, was wife of Uranus, the Heavens. The Titans were their children, and Saturn (Cronus) succeeded Uranus.

23. came one. Thea, a female Titan, married to Hyperion, sister and wife.

146-7. Found way unto Olympus, and made quake The rebel three. In the war of the Gods and Titans, Jupiter had made the high Mount Olympus his headquarters and it remained so afterwards. The "rebel three" are Jupiter, Pluto, and Neptune, the three sons of Saturn who had revolted and overthrown him.

166. Blazing Hyperion. Keats's whole imagery in the following passage is based upon the fact that Hyperion was sun-god still.

Page 611.   BOOK II

19. Cœus, and Gyges, and Briareüs. The history of the various Giants and Titans mentioned in the following passage is of little significance to the main thread of Keats's poem. These figures had suffered various punishments after the war; Keats is making Miltonic music of their names and fury, as Milton did before him with other names.

66. Shadow'd Enceladus. One of the leaders of the revolt of the Giants. In l. 70 is a reference to "that second war" which was the revolt of the Giants. See also introductory material on the wars of Gods, Titans, and Giants.

167-8. God of the Sea, Sophist and sage. Oceanus, the Titan sea-god, who had failed to support Saturn in the war and had maintained a precarious position in the seas, although Neptune was one of the conquering "rebel three." There is a very striking comparison, in the debate which follows, in the arguments advanced against war by Keats's Oceanus and by Milton's Belial and Mammon (Paradise Lost, II, 109–298).

181. We fall by course of Nature's law. According to Colvin the story was symbolical and represented "the dethronement of an older and ruder worship by one more advanced and humane." One may question whether the idea of "worship" in its various stages ever entered Keats's mind. Advance very definitely was in his mind and this passage is of great importance.

Page 615.   BOOK III

29. Giant of the Sun. Hyperion.

46. an awful Goddess came. Mnemosyne. She was the mother of the Muses, Jupiter being their father.

63. a lyre all golden. Apollo has, apparently, not yet understood his control of the instrument which the Muse left beside him in his dream. There came a time when, on those occasions when Jupiter summoned all the gods to drink nectar on Olympus, Apollo struck his lyre for the very gods, himself a god among them.

135. *Apollo shriek'd;—and lo! from all his limbs Celestial* . . . Mr. Middleton Murry (*Keats and Shakespeare*, p. 230) quotes from the Woodhouse transcript:

"and lo from all his limbs
Celestial glory dawned: he was a god!"

adding that the addition was "probably a subsequent amendment." Mr. Murry sees in Apollo the symbol of the growing Keats, and the convulsion of Apollo is Keats's own black autumn of 1818 (see introduction to Keats: text pp. 551–4) as he grows into his greatness as a poet.

Page 617.   THE LETTERS OF JOHN KEATS

John Hamilton Reynolds (1796–1852). To Reynolds, Keats wrote more fully perhaps than to any correspondent outside his family. Keats met him through Hunt about 1816 and Hunt in an article in the *Examiner* named Reynolds, Shelley, and Keats as the three most promising young poets in England—which shows his position in the circle. Keats and Reynolds at one time projected a volume of narrative poems taken from Boccaccio, Keats's *Isabella, or the Pot of Basil* having been intended for the volume. In 1818 Reynolds entered a solicitor's office and law gradually cramped literature in his life. It is said that his wit, always somewhat sarcastic, became cynical in later life as he realized that he had failed to accomplish all he had hoped. Even so he published a considerable amount of poetry.

Page 618.

618a, l. 31. *Does Shelley go on telling strange stories of the deaths of kings?* Into a stage coach in which Shelley was riding there entered a countrywoman laden down with baskets of vegetables of the garlic variety. Shelley stood the situation as long as he could and then took his own peculiar revenge. Suddenly, and with great intensity, he began to recite from *Richard II:*

"For God's sake, let us sit upon the ground
And tell sad stories of the death of kings:
How some have been deposed, some slain in war,
Some haunted by the ghosts they have deposed,
Some poison'd by their wives, some sleeping killed;
All murdered!"

It has been reported that this outburst caused great consternation in the proposed victim.

Benjamin Bailey (1791–?1852). Bailey was one of Keats's most important correspondents, especially in the earlier years of his career. Bailey was an Oxford man, reading for the Church, when Keats knew him, and Keats visited him at Oxford in the summer of 1817, writing there the third book of *Endymion*. Bailey was somewhat volatile in his affections toward women and Keats for a time resented what he thought was Bailey's mistreatment of Marianne Reynolds. Rejected by Marianne, Bailey had gone off, apparently with a broken heart, and promptly married someone else. He later became Bishop of Colombo (Ceylon).

618b, ll. 37–8. *Apollo . . . Mockery . . . at Hunt's.* Woodhouse gives an account of the episode referred to: "As Keats and Leigh Hunt were taking their wine together after dinner, at the house of the latter, the whim seized them (probably at Hunt's instigation) to crown themselves with laurel after the fashion of the elder bards. While they were thus attired, two of Hunt's friends happened to call upon him. Just before their entrance Hunt removed the wreath from his own brow, and suggested to Keats that he might as well do the same. Keats, however, in his mad enthusiastic way, vowed that he would not take off his crown for any human being; and he accordingly wore it, without any explanation, as long as the visit lasted. He mentioned the circumstance afterwards to some of his friends, along with his sense of the folly (and, I believe, presumption) of his conduct. And he said he was determined to record it by an apologetic ode to Apollo on the occasion. He shortly after wrote this fragment."

Page 620.

620a, l. 2. *I will speak of something else.* Some unexplained rebuff to Bailey had aroused Keats's anger. The preceding part of this letter is in Maurice Buxton Forman's edition of the *Letters,* I, 63.
620b, l. 3. *poor Cripps.* Haydon in some way had failed to keep some promises toward Cripps whom he had promised to take as a pupil. Bailey was interested in the young man.

Page 621.

621a, l. 11. *Adam's dream.* See the account of the creation of Eve in *Paradise Lost*, VIII, 449–89.
621b, l. 4. *the philosophic Mind.* A reference to Wordsworth's *Ode: Intimations of Immortality.*

Page 622.

622a, l. 41. *Wells.* Charles Wells, author of *Joseph and His Brethren.* Wells later played an unkind trick on Tom Keats for which John never forgave him.
622a, l. 43. *West.* Benjamin West, a pupil of Gilbert Stuart's. He was aged 79 in 1817.

622b, l. 43. *Shelley's poem. Laon and Cythna,* which was immediately withdrawn by the publishers and converted into *The Revolt of Islam,* which appeared the following January.

Page 623.

623a, l. 20. *Ritchie.* Joseph Ritchie, who died in Africa.

623a, ll. 26–7. *Lamb . . . blew up Kingston.* Haydon has left an amusing account of this famous dinner at his studio: "On December 28th the immortal dinner came off in my painting-room, with Jerusalem towering up behind us as a background. Wordsworth was in fine cue, and we had a glorious set-to,—on Homer, Shakespeare, Milton and Virgil. Lamb got exceedingly merry, and exquisitely witty; and his fun in the midst of Wordsworth's solemn intonations of oratory was like the sarcasm and wit of the fool in the intervals of Lear's passion. He made a speech and voted me absent, and made them drink my health. 'Now,' said Lamb, 'you old lake poet, you rascally poet, why do you call Voltaire dull?' We all defended Wordsworth, and affirmed there was a state of mind when Voltaire would be dull. 'Well,' said Lamb, 'here's Voltaire—the Messiah of the French nation, and a very proper one too.'

"He then, in a strain of humour beyond description, abused me for putting Newton's head into my picture,—'a fellow,' said he, 'who believed nothing unless it was as clear as the three sides of a triangle.' And then he and Keats agreed he had destroyed all the poetry of the rainbow by reducing it to the prismatic colours. It was impossible to resist him, and we all drank 'Newton's health, and confusion to mathematics.' It was delightful to see the good-humour of Wordsworth in giving in to all our frolics without affectation and laughing as heartily as the best of us.

"By this time other friends joined, amongst them poor Ritchie who was going to penetrate by Fezzan to Timbuctoo. I introduced him to all as 'a gentleman going to Africa.' Lamb seemed to take no notice; but all of a sudden he roared out, 'Which is the gentleman we are going to lose?' We then drank the victim's health, in which Ritchie joined.

"In the morning of this delightful day, a gentleman, a perfect stranger, had called on me. He said he knew my friends, had an enthusiasm for Wordsworth and begged I would procure him the happiness of an introduction. He told me he was a comptroller of stamps, and often had correspondence with the poet. I thought it a liberty; but still, as he seemed a gentleman, I told him he might come.

"When we retired to tea we found the comptroller. In introducing him to Wordsworth I forgot to say who he was. After a little time the comptroller looked down, looked up and said to Wordsworth, 'Don't you think, sir, Milton was a great genius?' Keats looked at me, Wordsworth looked at the comptroller. Lamb who was dozing by the fire turned round and said, 'Pray, sir, did you say Milton was a great genius?' 'No, sir; I asked Mr. Wordsworth if he were not.' 'Oh,' said Lamb, 'then you are a silly fellow.' 'Charles! my dear Charles!' said Wordsworth; but Lamb, perfectly innocent of the confusion he had created, was off again by the fire.

"After an awful pause the comptroller said, 'Don't you think Newton a great genius?' I could not stand it any longer. Keats put his head into my books. Ritchie squeezed in a laugh. Wordsworth seemed asking himself, 'Who is this?' Lamb got up, and taking a candle, said, 'Sir, will you allow me to look at your phrenological development?' He then turned his back on the poor man, and at every question of the comptroller he chaunted—

'Diddle diddle dumpling, my son John
Went to bed with his breeches on.'

The man in office, finding Wordsworth did not know who he was, said in a spasmodic and half-chuckling anticipation of assured victory, 'I have had the honour of some correspondence with you, Mr. Wordsworth.' 'With me, sir?' said Wordsworth, 'not that I remember.' 'Don't you, sir? I am a comptroller of stamps.' There was a dead silence;—the comptroller evidently thinking that was enough. While we were waiting for Wordsworth's reply, Lamb sung out

'Hey diddle diddle,
The cat and the fiddle.'

'My dear Charles!' said Wordsworth,—

'Diddle diddle dumpling, my son John,'

chaunted Lamb, and then rising, exclaimed, 'Do let me have another look at that gentleman's organs.' Keats and I hurried Lamb into the painting-room, shut the door and gave way to inextinguishable laughter. Monkhouse followed and tried to get Lamb away. We went back, but the comptroller was irreconcilable. We soothed and smiled and asked him to supper. He stayed though his dignity was sorely affected. However, being a good-natured man, we parted all in good-humour, and no ill effects followed.

"All the while, until Monkhouse succeeded, we could hear Lamb struggling in the painting-room and calling at intervals, 'Who is that fellow? Allow me to see his organs once more.' It was indeed an immortal evening. Wordsworth's fine intonation as he quoted Milton and Virgil, Keats' eager inspired look, Lamb's quaint sparkle of lambent humour, so speeded the stream of conversation, that in my life I never passed a more delightful time." (Tom Taylor, *Life of Benjamin Robert Haydon*, as quoted by E. V. Lucas in *The Letters of Charles and Mary Lamb*.)

Page 624.

John Taylor (1781–1864). Taylor, the senior member of Keats's publishing house, Taylor and Hessey, was a critic of no mean ability. His pamphlet, *A Discovery of the Author of the Letters of Junius* (1813), was the first to identify the mysterious Junius with Sir Philip Francis. When his firm took over the *London Magazine*, Taylor himself edited it from 1821 to 1824. Many of the leading men of letters of the time were his friends.

624b, l. 17. *dish of Filberts*. Reynolds's sonnets on Robin Hood.

624b, l. 46. *Sancho*. The prosaic and plump squire of Don Quixote.

Page 625.

625a, ll. 18–19. *Why . . . be of the tribe of Manasseh*, etc. Moses gave to the tribe of Manasseh "the land with the cities thereof" (Numbers 32:33); Esau was "a cunning hunter, a man of the field." (Genesis 25:27). The opposition is between city and field, and is particularly directed against the urbanite Hunt.

625a, ll. 23–4. *nice-eyed wagtails . . . Cherub Contemplation*. The wagtails are from Hunt's *The Nymphs* (ii, 170) and the Cherub from Milton's *Il Penseroso* (54).

625a, ll. 25–6. *Matthew . . . Jacques*. Matthew is from Wordsworth's *The Two April Mornings* (and other poems) and Jacques from *As You Like It*, II, i, 31.

Lord Houghton suggests that some of Keats's irritation with Wordsworth may have been occasioned by an episode which occurred at Haydon's. Keats recited the "Hymn to Pan" from *Endymion*, and Wordsworth patronizingly approved it as "a pretty piece of paganism."

625a, l. 50. *the Mermaid lines*. See *Lines on the Mermaid Tavern*, text p. 583.

625b, l. 45. *O for a Muse of Fire. Henry V*, Prologue, ll. 1–2:

"O for a muse of fire, that would ascend
   The brightest heaven of invention."

Page 626.

Benjamin Robert Haydon (1786–1846). Haydon, the historical painter, was consumed with the idea of his own genius. He struggled through a stormy artistic life with a ferocity and endurance which approached the maniacal. There was a time in his career when visiting Grand Dukes from Russia called at his studio to see

his unfinished paintings and there was a time when he was imprisoned for debt. His last exhibition in 1846 was a failure and he had the mortification of seeing Tom Thumb, the dwarf, who was giving shows in another room of the same building, drawing crowds. He committed suicide, leaving a bitter journal in twenty-six "ledger-like" folios.

Haydon was one of the first to see the merit of the Elgin Marbles and waged a campaign for their purchase. It has been said that his article "On the Judgement of Connoisseurs being preferred to that of Professional Men" saved the marbles for the nation but ruined Haydon, because of the enmities it aroused. At the time of Keats's association with Haydon he was already heavily in debt and he sponged on Keats as on every one else. He was engaged on his "Christ's Entry into Jerusalem" which he worked on for six years and which his creditors seized when he exhibited it in 1822.

626a, l. 44. *Dentatus*. One of Haydon's pictures.

Page 627.

627b, l. 40. *Get learning*. "Get wisdom, get understanding: forget it not; neither decline from the words of my mouth." (Proverbs 4:5.)

Page 628.

628a, l. 30. *Burden of the Mystery*. Cf. Wordsworth's *Tintern Abbey*, a poem to which Keats frequently referred.

628b, ll. 40–1. *Knowledge is sorrow*. Misquoted from *Manfred*. See text p. 274, ll. 9–12.

Page 629.

Fanny Keats. Frances Mary Keats, Keats's only sister, was a girl of fifteen at the time of this letter. After Keats's death she married (in 1826) a Spaniard, Señor Valentin Llanos, a member of the Spanish diplomatic service.

Page 630.

630a, l. 33. *Meg Merrilies*. See text p. 583.

Page 631.

631b, ll. 19–20. *you and Frank Fladgate in the office*. Reynolds was articled to a solicitor named Fladgate, and Frank Fladgate was also in the office, articled to his father.

631b, l. 39. *like to employ Caliph Vathek*. In a scene in William Beckford's *Vathek* the Caliph became so enraged that he attacked the carcasses of his dead bodyguards "and kicked them till evening without intermission."

Page 632.

James Augustus Hessey (1785–1870). Hessey's partnership with Taylor was dissolved in 1825, prior to which time he had attended to the retail business.

632a, l. 14. *letters from the Chronicle.* On Oct. 3, 1818, a letter signed J. S. was printed in the *Chronicle* defending Keats against the *Quarterly* attack on *Endymion* (see Introductory material to that poem, above) which J. S. considered a "gross injustice." On Oct. 8 appeared another letter signed R. B., supporting the stand of J. S. Neither writer has been identified though John Scott has been suggested as the author of the first letter.

632a, ll. 31–2. *J. S. . . . slip-shod.* J. S., in his vigorous defense, had admitted "that there are also many, very many passages indicating haste and carelessness, I will not deny; I will go further, and assert that a real friend of the author would have dissuaded him from an immediate publication."

Page 634.

634a, ll. 33–4. *Tragedy with sceptred pall.*

"Sometime let gorgeous Tragedy
In sceptred pall come sweeping by."
(*Il Penseroso*, 97–8.)

634a, ll. 38–9. *I wander like a lost Soul.*

"No, Pandarus; I stalk about her door
Like a strange soul upon the Stygian banks
Staying for waftage."
(*Troilus and Cressida*, III, ii, 8–10.)

Richard Woodhouse (?1788–1834). Woodhouse was a young barrister who was also in some way a literary advisor to Taylor and Hessey. He was a deep admirer of Keats and in his commonplace books he preserved a great deal of valuable information upon which scholars later drew heavily.

Page 635.

635b, l. 45. *noise of Bentley's Children.* Keats lodged with Bentley in Well Walk. The Bentley progeny seem to have been chiefly remarkable for their noisiness of which Keats often complains.

Page 636.

636a, ll. 30–31. *embroidered round my Calves.* In 1818 men still wore knee-breeches and the calves would be a showy place for the list.

636b, l. 2. *G. Minor.* Georgiana: the "little George" of p. 637b, l. 1.

Page 637.

637a, l. 31. *the thing Kingston.* The unfortunate commissioner baited by Lamb at Haydon's dinner party. See note above on p. 623a, ll. 26–7.

637a, ll. 45–6. *Mrs. Tighe and Beattie.* James Beattie was the author of *The Minstrel.* Mrs.

Mary Tighe's influence on Keats is studied at some length by E. V. Weller in *P.M.L.A.*, XLII, 963–86.

Page 640.

640b, l. 6. *How charming*, etc. *Comus,* ll. 476–8.

640b, l. 30. For the sonnet omitted, see text p. 585.

640b, l. 49. *conversation with Coleridge.* Coleridge's account of this celebrated encounter occurs in *Table Talk* (Aug. 14, 1832) and reads as follows: "A loose, slack, not well-dressed youth met Mr. —— and myself in a lane near Highgate. —— knew him, and spoke. It was Keats. He was introduced to me, and staid a minute or so. After he had left us a little way, he came back and said: 'Let me carry away the memory, Coleridge, of having pressed your hand!'—'There is death in that hand,' I said to ——, when Keats was gone; yet this was, I believe, before the consumption showed itself distinctly."

Page 643.

643a, l. 6. *If by Dull Rhymes.* See text p. 585.

643a, ll. 27–8. *to Abbey's and to the Lawyers.* Keats was trying to raise money to assist Haydon.

643b, l. 23. *I thought I had it in my hand.* This is a reply to a petulant letter from Haydon. Keats had informed Haydon that he was unable to raise money for him. Haydon grumbled: "Why did you hold out such delusive hopes every letter on such slight foundations?—You have led me on step by step, day by day, etc." To do Haydon justice, he was in desperate straits and the failure of funds to come from a source where he had confidently expected to find them added to his difficulties.

Page 646.

646a, l. 9. *pray to your star*, etc. Keats had written his "Bright Star" sonnet earlier in the same year and there may be a reminiscence of it here.

Charles Wentworth Dilke (1789–1864). Dilke at an early age entered the Navy Pay Office where he remained until 1836. Inspired by Lamb's *Specimens* he read in the older dramatists and later brought out a continuation of Dodsley's *Old Plays.* His interests were primarily literary in spite of his Pay Office position, and from 1830 on for some years he was editor of the *Athenaeum.* It was under his guidance that the *Athenaeum* attained its great prestige.

646a, l. 47. *the Tragedy. Otho the Great,* on which Keats and Brown collaborated.

646b, l. 36. *Charles.* Dilke's son, who was at Westminster school.

646b, ll. 41–2. *Lift him from the Tribe of Manasseh*. Gideon, who was poor in Manasseh, after his victory over the Midianites became ruler of Israel. (Judges 6:15; 8:22.)

Page 647.

647a, l. 3. *Reynolds's Piece. One, Two, Three, Four, Five: by Advertisement*—a one-act entertainment.

Page 648.

648a, l. 46. *Mr. Audubon a dishonest man.* Audubon sold George some merchandise knowing, it is said, at the time of the sale that boat and merchandise were already at the bottom of the river.

Page 650.

Charles Armitage Brown (?1797–?1842). At the age of 18, Brown went to Petrograd to conduct his brother's business there. He returned in 1810, completely ruined, and for a few years he was put to it to make a living. Another brother left him a small income and he devoted himself to literary work. He was one of the closest of Keats's friends in the late years. They collaborated on *Otho the Great;* it was Brown who went with Keats on the fatal walking trip of 1818; and they kept house together at Hampstead on their return. Brown's papers were much used by Lord Houghton in his *Life of Keats*.

Page 651.

651a, l. 14. *I may maintain myself decently.* Keats's plan was to take rooms away from his friends and write for the Reviews. Brown was distressed but saw no way to interfere and Keats, on his return to London, took rooms in Westminster. He did not remain there long.

Page 652.

652a, l. 21. *Swiftean . . . Tom-Crib-ean . . . Shandean.* The first and third refer to Jonathan Swift and to Sterne's *Tristram Shandy;* the second probably to Moore's *Tom Crib's Memorial to Congress, with a Preface, Notes, and an Appendix by one of the Fancy*.

James Rice. Rice was trained for the Law but little is known of him except that he died before 1833. References to his ill health occur frequently in Keats's letters. He was a favorite in the circle for his wit, his wisdom, and his generosity. The affection he won from such varied types of men testifies to his character. 652b, l. 18. *Like poor Falstaff.* See *Henry V*, II, iii, 9–28.

Page 655.

655a, l. 3. *I do not write this till the last.* Maurice Buxton Forman suggests that these two lines refer to the heading of the letter—"My dearest girl." Afraid that someone might chance to see it, Keats wrote the letter through and then turned back to add the greeting. It seems probable that this was the last letter he ever wrote to Fanny Brawne as, according to Severn, he was unable to write to her on the voyage or in Italy.

655b, l. 14. *Never seeing any more Dilke or Brown.* Keats, writing with the exasperated nerves of a dying and desperate man, is unjust to his friends in this letter.

655b, l. 26. *in the strain of the letter beside me.* See text p. 543 for Shelley's letter.

655b, l. 39. *my poor poem.* The reference is to *Endymion*.

Page 656.

To Brown. Keats's ship had been held in quarantine at Naples and Keats had suffered severely from the confinement. After his release he wrote Brown (Nov. 1) a letter which was a cry of anguish with the name of Fanny Brawne ringing through it. "Everything . . . that reminds me of her goes through me like a spear." In Rome, more tranquil—perhaps from exhaustion—Keats wrote this, a sad enough letter and the last he ever wrote, which adds to the poignancy of the last line.

THOMAS LOVELL BEDDOES
BIBLIOGRAPHY

I. WORKS

Poetical Works, ed. by Edmund Gosse. 2 vols. (Macmillan: New York, 1890.) The authoritative edition, including a memoir by the editor (which, with some minor additions, had appeared in his *Critical Kit Kats*, 1903); a feature of this work is the series of etchings by Herbert Railton.

The Complete Works of Thomas Lovell Beddoes, ed. by Edmund Gosse. 2 vols. (Fanfrolico Press: London, 1928.) A sumptuous complete edition, with an introduction expressing the editor's final estimate of the poet, (he retreats from the explicit statement of 1890 that Beddoes died of kurari poisoning to the vague statement that he died of "poisoning"); decorated by a complete set of Holbein's *Dance of Death*.

Poems, 2 vols. (Pickering: London, 1851.) The first (and practically complete) edition of the poems and plays, prefaced by an excellent memoir by Thomas F. Kelsall.

Thomas Lovell Beddoes: An Anthology, chosen by F. L. Lucas. Poets in Brief series. (Macmillan: New York, 1932.) A valuable re-presentation of the poems and letters; the introduction comments on the personality of the poet, his imagery, and style.

Poems, ed. by Ramsay Colles. The Muses' Library. (Dutton: New York, 1907.) A convenient edition; includes an introduction by the editor.

Letters, ed. by Edmund Gosse. (Macmillan: New York, 1894.) The editor has supplied useful notes. This edition has long been out of print.

II. BIOGRAPHY AND CRITICISM

Pierce, F. E. "Beddoes and Continental Romanticists," *Philological Quarterly*, VI, 123–32 (Apr., 1927). Traces German influence from the poet's residence on the continent after 1849; cites many parallel passages.

Rickwood, Edgell. "Thomas Lovell Beddoes," *London Mercury*, IX, 162–74 (Dec., 1923). Provides an adequate biographical sketch; points out the poet's sardonic grotesqueness in style and subject-matter.

Snow, Royall H. *Thomas Lovell Beddoes, Eccentric and Poet*. (Covici: New York, 1928.) The fullest biographical and critical study so far published; challenges, with the support of documentary evidence, Gosse's melodramatic statement that Beddoes died of poisoning by kurari.

Stoddard, R. H. "Thomas Lovell Beddoes," in *Under the Evening Lamp*. (Scribner: New York, 1892.) Points to the poet as a man of great promise but of small performance; finally concludes regretfully that he was mad.

Strachey, Lytton. "The Last Elizabethan," in *Books and Characters*. (Chatto: London, 1922.) Sees Beddoes as a reincarnation rather than as a reviver of the Elizabethan genius; remarks the power of his blank verse, admitting his weakness in narrative.

Symons, Arthur. "Thomas Lovell Beddoes," in *Figures of Several Centuries*. (Constable: London, 1916.) Disclaims the poet's claim to be considered a genius or even an effective dramatist; admits that he was astonishing at times, but most effective in the lyric.

NOTES

Page 658.

HOW MANY TIMES DO I LOVE THEE, DEAR?

The opening of the scene is given so that the reader may understand the setting of one of Beddoes' best known lyrics. There is charm and delicacy in the lyric, but not often did he write in the *genre*.

Page 659.

For a discussion of the general character of such lyrics as *Old Adam*, *The Carrion Crow* and *We Do Lie beneath the Grass*, see note below on *The Phantom Wooer*.

SCENE FROM "DEATH'S JEST BOOK"

This play is one of the oddities of nineteenth century literature. It combines a fury and

vigor of expression which suggests the good days of Elizabeth with streaks of sentiment which suggest the days of Victoria. The heroine of this scene is on the Victorian side. A murder had been committed over her—an exiled duke having murdered his most faithful supporter for her sake. Sibylla, without really understanding what it is all about, feels a vague sense of loss at the disappearance of her lover. By an accident, the murdering duke conjures up on earth again the murdered man, and so it is that Wolfram, taking on disguises, is able to appear to Sibylla. This is an extraordinary love scene and the next scene is more so, but also more Elizabethan.

The brother of the murdered Wolfram had been taking steps for revenge, and he had brought the sons of the duke to a quarrel over another woman—with the hope of throwing in the crime of Cain on top of the crime of murder. The climax of this counterplot takes place in the scene immediately following that given in the text. The unsuccessful son of the duke takes poison as he hears the bridal serenade of his successful brother and lies out in the garden, writhing and cursing. It is a false poison and he recovers. He manages to stab the successful brother and then from the garden darkness makes love to his brother's bride. Two very strange scenes, but illustrative of the strange quality of the play.

Page 663.   THE PHANTOM WOOER

"It is Death who lurks always in the luminous fringes of Beddoes' mind: not a powerful and imperious death, not even a slow but inexorable Death. Death in the poems is rather timorous, sceptical of the extent of its own as yet unmeasured powers. Its approaches are subtle and persuasive, have something of the craintive friendliness of a pawnbroker with his eye on a precious jewel—afraid of bartering, escape. It whispers, touches delicately the flashing facets of the beauty it desires—and there is poison in the gentle timidity of its voice. Those who listen rise and follow with misted eyes.

'Young soul, put off your flesh, and come
With me into the quiet tomb,
   Our bed is lovely, dark, and sweet;
The earth will swing us, as she goes,
Beneath our coverlid of snows,
   And the warm leaden sheet.
Dear and dear is their poisoned note,
The little snakes of silver throat,
In mossy skulls that nest and lie,
Ever singing "die, oh! die."'

Delicately, insinuatingly voluptuous: the warmth and sweet privacy, the softness and fragrance of wet moss, the curve of silver throats and the sound of music! But it is snakes who sing and the moss feathers over a skull. So dainty, so persuasive—and the ultimate lovers are skeletons and the bridesmaids are worms.

"It is this haunting evasiveness which is Beddoes' peculiar power, a quality he shares with no one. Hoffman lived among the spectres of his insane imagination. Poe feared death, was hypnotized by the intangible power of those whose open doorway to the world is a closed grave. He portrayed the living in the grip of their vampiric advances. But Beddoes speaks for the dead, finds for them the subtle instinct of those who plead caressingly:

'It is midnight, my wedded;
 Let us lie under
The tempest bright undreaded,
 In the warm thunder:
(Tremble and weep not! What can you fear?)'

No poet but Beddoes could have found that adjective 'warm' for the wild thunder gathering over a murder, nor have given to a spectre that soothing, 'Tremble and weep not!' Herein is the fundamental difference between Beddoes and the other poets of death. There have been advocates of the grave as a place of quiet after tumult, or of death as a gateway to communion with the saints. No other has made the grave an earthly bridal bed, and given to the lips of spectres the music of lovers.

"It is perversely beautiful poetry with its roots deep in the morbid, blending the iron chill of horror with the silken warmth of the sensuous. And such alien elements are fused perfectly, reinforcing one another. What is to be noted, is both Beddoes' economy of means and the complete lack of the physical in the effect of horror he achieves. There is not a superfluous stroke in the two poems which most perfectly represent this type of work in Beddoes. They are short. They are sharp in outline. And upon a sensitive reader they have a sharp impact. There is nothing of the lavishness of physical detail which the young poet employed so unsuccessfully in *The Improvisatore*. Reticence is substituted, that he may obtain a shudder of the soul rather than gooseflesh of the skin. Particularly in *The Phantom Wooer* the horrible is thrust into the background that it may be only the more effective, is disguised in a honey sweetness that it may carry the more suggestion. The ultimate effect is that which all complete poetry must obtain —that it gives one a cerebral chill. It is upon this emotional test, even in an intellectual age, that the last judgment of poetry must be based. "It is this insinuating and miasmatic perfume of wheedling death which hangs over so much of Beddoes' lyrical work and gives it its flavour. It is only in a very few poems that the idea finds its complete and explicit expression. But

having once heard the little snakes of silver throat singing 'Die, oh! die' one can never forget them, however Beddoes may vary his treatment of the theme. His Death can be inexorable, or cruelly decisive. *Old Adam the Carrion Crow*, sung as it is at a drunken carousal, is yet nothing but a lyrical version of the old sermon on the inevitable dust. Hamlet philosophized over the skull of the gay Yorick, and here crows nest in the skull of the great Cleopatra. And that very spectre in 'The Ghosts' Moonshine' who bids his mistress to the 'warm thunder' has come for murder, and to bear her to the bed of the grave. Beddoes' work runs the accustomed gamut of the poetry of death: it adds the accent of persuasiveness." (Royall H. Snow, *Thomas Lovell Beddoes*, pp. 134-7.)

SONG OF THE STYGIAN NAIADES

The Naiads were nymphs of fresh, free-flowing water. None, before Beddoes, had been reported in the Styx—one of the four rivers of hell.
Proserpine, of course, was the daughter of Ceres, ravished off to the underworld by Pluto, its king. Beëlzebub in his most important appearance in English literature is the chief lieutenant of Milton's Satan.

Page 664. STANZAS FROM THE IVORY GATE

In March, 1837, Beddoes wrote home to England from the continent that he was "preparing for the press . . . a volume of prosaic poetry and poetical prose"—a volume which was to be called "The Ivory Gate." It was never published and apparently was never completed.

THOMAS CAMPBELL
BIBLIOGRAPHY

I. WORKS

Complete Poetical Works, ed. by J. Logie Robertson. (Oxford University Press: 1907.) The standard edition, supplied with complete notes.
Selected Poems, ed. by Lewis Campbell. Golden Treasury series. (Macmillan: London, 1904.) The best abridgment of the poetry.

II. BIOGRAPHY AND CRITICISM

Beattie, William. *Life and Letters of Thomas Campbell*. 2 vols. (Harper: New York, 1850.) In many respects a very satisfactory biography: scholarly and complete.
Bierstadt, A. M. "Unacknowledged Poems by Campbell," *Modern Language Notes*, XXXVII, 343-5 (June, 1922). Analyzes eleven "C" poems appearing in the *New Monthly Magazine*, 1821-30, during Campbell's editorship.

Bierstadt, A. M. "*Gertrude of Wyoming*," *Journal of English and Germanic Philology*, XX, 491–501 (Oct., 1922). Attempts to show in the poem the influence of Chateaubriand; somewhat overstressed.

Forsythe, R. S. "Freedom's Shriek," *Notes and Queries*, CL, 23–4 (Jan., 1926). Points out borrowings from Coleridge in *The Pleasures of Hope*.

Graham, Walter. "Byron and Campbell," *Notes and Queries*, X, 45–6 (Jan., 1922). Indicates borrowings from *Childe Harold* in *Lines on the View from St. Leonard's*.

Hadden, J. C. *Thomas Campbell*. (Anderson: Edinburgh, 1899.) Divides with Beattie's Life the claim to being the best biography, but unexpectedly stinting in its praise.

Saintsbury, George. "The English War Songs," in *Essays in English Literature*, Second Series. (Scribner: New York, 1895.) Names Campbell "our chief writer of war songs," which are ranked as his finest achievement, *Hohenlinden* being put first.

Shumway, D. B. "Thomas Campbell and Germany," in *Schelling Anniversary Papers*. (Century: New York, 1923.) Provides an account of the poet's visits; judiciously estimates slender traces of influence on his writings.

Symons, Arthur. "Thomas Campbell," in *The Romantic Movement in English Literature*. (Dutton: New York, 1909.) Brackets the poet with Longfellow; points out the success of his "pathetic ballads" and the *Battle of the Baltic*, —elsewhere "he is never visited by any poetic inspiration."

Turner, A. M. "Wordsworth's Influence on Campbell," *Publications of the Modern Language Association*, XXXVIII, 253–66 (June, 1923). Traces earliest borrowings from 1824, with dominance after 1832; finds most evidence in Campbell's nature scenes and his efforts at simplicity of diction.

NOTES

Page 666. THE HARPER

"Campbell shares with Longfellow the position of favorite poet in elementary schools, where verse is learnt by heart as an exercise. There his good poems and his bad poems are equally appreciated: 'Lord Ullin's Daughter' neither more nor less than 'Hohenlinden,' and 'The Harper' than the 'Battle of the Baltic' . . . There is emotion in them [pathetic ballads, like 'The Harper'], but the emotion, when it is not childish, is genteel." (Arthur Symons, in *The Romantic Movement in English Poetry*.)

YE MARINERS OF ENGLAND

Campbell's "love of England was . . . brought to poetic heat by a love of the sea, and by a curiously vivid appreciation of the life and beauty of warships. In a controversy [which arose out of the Rev. W. L. Bowles's *Strictures on the Life and Writings of Pope*] as to the place of nature and of art in poetry, his most effective argument was drawn from a warship. 'Those who have ever witnessed the spectacle of the launching of a ship of the line will perhaps forgive me for adding this to the examples of the sublime objects of artificial life. Of that spectacle I can never forget the impression, and of having witnessed it reflected from the faces of ten thousand spectators . . . It was not a vulgar joy, but an affecting national solemnity.' Something of this 'mental transport,' as he describes it, this sense of the beauty and grandeur of the actual circumstances of sea-fighting, came, along with the patriotic fervor, into his two naval odes, 'Ye Mariners of England,' and 'The Battle of the Baltic,' his two really great poems." (Symons, *op. cit.*) For the position of Byron, who was prominent in the Bowles-Campbell controversy referred to above, see Byron's letter, "On Artificiality and Pope," text p. 370.

This "naval ode" may owe some of its patriotic enthusiasm to the fact that it was composed abroad (in Germany). Two recent naval victories over the French—Cape St. Vincent, 1797, and the Nile, 1798—may also have heightened the poet's spirit. When the poem was first published in the *Morning Chronicle* in 1801, it was signed "Amator Patriæ" and bore an explanatory note saying that it was "composed on the prospect of a Russian War."

15. *Where Blake and mighty Nelson*. Robert Blake, a famous English admiral under the Commonwealth, died in Plymouth Harbour in 1657 on his return from an expedition against the Spanish. Horatio Nelson, first of English admirals, "fell" at the battle of Copenhagen in April, 1801; but he was wounded, not slain. In 1805 he was killed at Trafalgar, and in that year Campbell made this line read as given in the present text. In the *Morning Chronicle* edition the line was, "Where Granvill, boast of freedom, fell," a reference to Sir Richard Grenville of the "Revenge." (See Tennyson's *The Revenge*.)

HOHENLINDEN

Hohenlinden, an Upper Bavarian village about twenty miles east of Munich, was the scene of the defeat of the Austrians (Huns) by the French (Franks) in December, 1800. Campbell is said to have held this poem in contempt. He called it a "damned drum and trumpet thing" and printed it only to please Scott. Arthur Symons says of the poem: "In 'Hohenlinden' some wandering spark has alighted; the wind has carried it, and one knows not from whence; only, a whole beacon is ablaze."

Page 668.

27. *Munich*. Munich had been taken by General Moreau, leader of the French, some five months before Hohenlinden.

LOCHIEL'S WARNING

In July, 1745, Charles Stuart, the Young Pretender, landed on the west coast of Invernessshire and asked the highland chiefs, who were his loyal and chivalrous supporters, to help him gain the English throne. The undertaking seemed very rash to them, and they advised young Charles to return to France. Stung by the taunt that he would hear of his prince's victories from the newspapers, Donald Cameron of Lochiel, chief of the Camerons, replied, "I will share the fate of my Prince and so shall every man over whom nature or fortune hath given me any power." The Prince won a number of victories with his highland army, but in April, 1746, "proud Cumberland" and his English army defeated Charles at Culloden and punished his followers so brutally that Cumberland was nicknamed "the Butcher." Cameron, who was wounded in this battle, fled to France, where he died two years later. In *Lochiel's Warning* the Wizard is warning Cameron of the disaster which is to befall him at Culloden.

See *Childe Harold's Pilgrimage*, Canto III, text p. 252, ll. 226–7.

15. *Albin.* Gaelic name for Scotland.

Page 669.   BATTLE OF THE BALTIC

See note above to *Ye Mariners of England.*
Of this poem, Campbell wrote: "It is an attempt to write an English ballad on the Battle of Copenhagen, as much as possible in that plain, strong style peculiar to our old ballads which tell us the when, where, and how the events happened—without gaud or ornament but what the subject essentially and easily affords."

In 1801 Paul I, the half-mad emperor of Russia, stirred up the northern powers—Sweden, Denmark, and Russia conspicuously—to form an armed neutrality against England. The powers forming the neutrality did not declare war against England, but announced that they would not be bound by the claims of the English to search neutral vessels for the purpose of finding French goods. First in command of the fleet sent by England to the Baltic against this new foe was a "commonplace" admiral, Sir Hyde Parker, who owed his place over Nelson to some foolish rule of seniority. The English attacked the Danish fleet and batteries in the battle of Copenhagen, April 2, 1801, and so obstinately did the Danes resist that the frightened Parker signaled Nelson to retire. Nelson, who was said to have "looked" for the signal of his superior by putting his blind eye to his telescope, declared he did not see it, ordered his fleet on, and gained a brilliant victory.

Page 670.

53. *the fires of funeral light.* The burning ships.
63. *Elsinore!* The town (Helsingör) on the Danish side of the sound, the scene of Shakespeare's *Hamlet.*
67. *Riou.* Captain Riou, of the *Amazon*, who commanded a squadron of seven vessels of the English line, was killed in the battle.

LORD ULLIN'S DAUGHTER

The scene of *Lord Ullin's Daughter* is the west coast of Scotland. Ulva is an isle on the outer side of Mull, one of the Hebrides, where Campbell planned the poem.

See note to *The Harper* above.
Pointing to this poem as typical of Campbell's romantic ballads, Symons says that it and the rest of them are written "with a methodical building up of circumstantial emotion which in the end becomes ludicrous, from its 'more than usual order.'"

Page 672.   TO MARY SINCLAIR, WITH A
VOLUME OF HIS POEMS

July 5, 1829, Campbell wrote the following from Ramsgate, whither, after a period of depression, he had gone for a change of scene: "After a day or two of Pythagorean silence at our meals, my fellow-boarders and I began to get acquainted. I found that out of the halfdozen, there were three very amiable and estimable individuals. I was also fortunate in the arrival of Alexander Sinclair and his wife [a native of the Cape], who is a very original and agreeable woman—though, as she says, 'a Hottentot by birth.' Their daughter, though only my third cousin, is as like me as a goodlooking girl can be to an ill-looking old man. She is a very interesting girl, and, like her third cousin the *poet*, is a very excellent person!"

It was to Mary Sinclair, the "good-looking girl so like himself," that Campbell playfully wrote this parody.

THE DEAD EAGLE

Oran is in Algeria, northern Africa.
18. *Turms.* An archaic word meaning *turmae.* The *turma* was a subdivision of the cavalry complement of a legion of ancient Rome—originally thirty men, later thirty-two.
22. *The carred aeronaut.* The person who makes a balloon ascension.

Page 673.

67. *A palsy stroke of nature shook Oran.* In 1790 Oran was destroyed by an earthquake, and the next year it was abandoned. In 1831 the French took possession of what remained of it, and it grew into an important city.

JOHN CLARE

BIBLIOGRAPHY

I. WORKS

Poems, ed. by J. W. Tibble. 2 vols. (Dent: London, 1935.) The standard edition, adding over 300 pieces hitherto unpublished; the editor provides a scholarly introduction.

The Poems of John Clare, ed. by Edmund Blunden and Alan Porter. (Cobden: London, 1920.) Compiled chiefly from MSS and other material hitherto unedited; also furnishes a capable introduction.

Poems, ed. by Arthur Symons. (Frowde: London, 1908.) A good one-volume edition, provided with an introduction by the editor.

Madrigals and Chronicles, ed. by Edmund Blunden. (Beaumont Press: London, 1924.) A fine collection, based upon research among the Clare MSS in the Peterborough Museum; 55 new pieces are included.

Sketches in the Life of John Clare, Written by Himself, ed. by Edmund Blunden. (Cobden: London, 1931.) The first publication of the poet's efforts at autobiography; the editor provides a valuable introduction, together with a final essay, "Clare on the Londoners."

II. BIOGRAPHY AND CRITICISM

Drinkwater, John. "John Clare in 1830," in *A Book for Bookmen*. (Doran: New York, 1927.) Includes two sonnets and a letter from Clare to his publisher, John Taylor, which pathetically reveals his ill health and despondency.

Murry, J. M. "The Poetry of John Clare," in *Countries of the Mind*. (Collins: London, 1922.) Draws comparisons between Clare and Keats and Wordsworth; commends Clare for his keen eye for natural objects, calling him "the love poet of nature."

Stoddard, R. H. "John Clare," in *Under the Evening Lamp*. (Scribner: New York, 1892.) Reviews sympathetically the poet's poverty-hounded life; praises his artless simplicity.

Symons, Arthur. "John Clare," in *The Romantic Movement in English Poetry*. (Dutton: New York, 1909.) Provides glimpses of the harassed life of the peasant-poet; compares him with Burns and Bloomfield.

Tibble, J. W. and Annie. *John Clare, A Life*. (Cobden: London, 1932.) The standard biography; furnishes an excellent review of the social set-up against which Clare was in revolt; provides good critiques of his poems in *Rural Life and Scenery* and his *Rural Muse*.

NOTES

"The magazine poetry of . . . Clare . . . is marked by a sincere and childlike simplicity. . . . Obvious but beautiful thoughts and emotions gleam through [his] limpid, childlike language like pebbles through his own rural brooks. . . . [His] inspiration . . . came to him mainly from his rural surroundings. [He]

found the poems in the fields,
And only wrote them down.

As far as he was consciously the disciple of a literary tradition, it was that of the nature poets, Burns, Cowper, Wordsworth, and Crabbe, all of whose poems formed part of his scanty library. . . . Few men have been more poetical in their moods than Clare, though his work is a mournful proof that moods alone, without strength of character and commanding intellect, cannot become supremely great." (F. E. Pierce, in *Currents and Eddies in the English Romantic Generation*.)

Of this poet who "seems to have lived on the same level of existence as the spiked thistle, the firetail, the hare, the white-nosed and the grandfather bee," and hence did not humanize them, Mr. J. Middleton Murry writes: "Into a generation of poets who flirt with nature suddenly descends a true nature-poet, one whose intimate and self-forgetful knowledge of the ways of birds and beasts and flowers rises like the scent of open fields from every page . . . the emotional quality [of his verse] is so assured and individual, the language so simple and inevitable, the posture of mind so unassuming and winning, that one is tempted for a moment to believe that while Wordsworth was engaged in putting the poetry of nature wrong by linking it to a doubtful metaphysic, John Clare was engaged in putting it right. . . . As a poet of nature Clare was truer, more thoroughly subdued to that in which he worked than Wordsworth. . . . Clare's music was a natural music; as with Shelley's skylark, his art was unpremeditated and his strains profuse . . . he whistles [his tune] over and over again. The note is so pure, the tune so full of delight that we can never be tired. . . . The eternity of song was in his blood." (Murry, in *Countries of the Mind*.)

HARTLEY COLERIDGE

BIBLIOGRAPHY

I. WORKS

Complete Poetical Works, ed. by Ramsay Colles. The Muses' Library. (Dutton: New York, 1908.) The standard edition, offering a critical introduction; contains all of the important 1851 edition with about ten additional pieces.

Poetical Works, ed. by William Tirebuck. Canterbury Poets. (Scott: London, 1887.) Contains a fairly comprehensive selection, furnished with a biographical introduction. (Includes the poems of Bowles and Lamb.)

Poems, ed. by Derwent Coleridge. (Moxon:

London, 1851.) The second edition of the earliest collection of the poetry; provided with a memoir by the editor.

Essays, ed. by John Drinkwater. (Blackwell: Oxford, 1925.) The essays are "Parties in Poetry" and "The Character of Hamlet." An introduction calls attention to the critic's sound judgment and his memorable means of expressing it.

II. BIOGRAPHY AND CRITICISM

Griggs, E. L. *Hartley Coleridge, His Life and Work.* (University of London Press: 1929.) Owing some of its information to hitherto unpublished family documents, this study is a thorough and interesting biographical survey, as well as a guide to purposive reading in Coleridge's poetry, which is discussed in the first section of chapter XII.

Hartman, H. W. *Hartley Coleridge: Poet's Son and Poet.* (Oxford University Press: 1931.) In the enforced absence of a definitive biography, this is "no more than a documented narrative" of the poet's life, which intersected at many points the careers of more famous men; treats sympathetically his vagaries; founds his fame upon his sonnets.

Pomeroy, Mary J. *The Poetry of Hartley Coleridge.* (Catholic University of America Press: 1927.) Points out the influence of the Lake School, notably of Wordsworth; names the sonnet as Coleridge's favorite form; discusses his lyrics under four heads: self-delineation, childhood, nature, and religion.

Towle, Eleanor A. *A Poet's Children, Hartley and Sara Coleridge.* (Methuen: London, 1912.) A survey of the careers of two of the most gifted members of the Coleridge family; Sara's quiet purposefulness is contrasted with her brother's vagrant genius, which in many ways resembled the temperament of his father.

III. ARTICLES FROM BOOKS AND PERIODICALS

Bagehot, Walter. "Hartley Coleridge," in *Literary Studies*, I. (Longmans: London, 1898.) Provides an interesting biographical sketch; points out in the poet's work resemblances to his father's style, but finds in the son a truer eye for certain natural aspects.

Drinkwater, John. "Hartley Coleridge," in *A Book for Bookmen.* (Doran: New York, 1927.) Furnishes a cursory review of the poet's life, adding that "his poetry is not a leading example of anything in particular, but has the great merit of being very readable."

Griggs, E L "Hartley Coleridge's Unpublished Correspondence," *London Mercury*, XXIV, 146–51 (June, 1931). Reprints with comments some of the poet's engaging letters, now in possession of the Coleridge family.

Griggs, E. L. "Coleridge and His Son," *Studies in Philology*, XXVII, 634–47 (Oct., 1930). An interesting review of the poet's relations with his children, especially his favorite, Hartley.

Pierce, F. E. "Some Literary Echoes," *Modern Language Notes*, XLII, 28–9 (Jan., 1927). A brief note, showing a borrowing from Byron.

Rea, J. D. "Hartley Coleridge and Wordsworth's 'Lucy,'" *Studies in Philology*, XXVIII, 118–35 (Jan., 1931). Finds the source of the paternal tone of the Lucy poems in Coleridge's affection for Hartley.

Stoddard, R. H. "Hartley Coleridge," in *Under the Evening Lamp.* (Scribner: New York, 1892.) Provides a brief anecdotal biography of the poet, finding in him the cause of his own outward failure.

Turner, A. M. "Wordsworth and Hartley Coleridge," *Journal of English and Germanic Philology*, XXII, 538–57 (1923). Reviews the younger poet's praise of Wordsworth; indicates echoes and borrowings, similar habits of mind and narrative methods.

NOTES

"He spoke of himself as 'one of the small poets,' and he was right; his verse was just such poetry as can be improvised by genuinely poetical natures in which the soil is thin. His was always 'a young lamb's heart among the full-grown flocks,' as it was said by Wordsworth. . . . There are splendid single lines and passages in his sonnets. . . . The sonnets are full of poetical thought, and are as pleasant for their substance as for their easy, gracious forms." (Arthur Symons, in *The Romantic Movement in English Poetry.*)

"His poems are full of graceful beauty, but almost all fall below the level of high poetry. They are not sufficiently powerful for vivid remembrance, and are much too good for oblivion." (Richard Garnett, in *Dictionary of National Biography.*)

Page 683.   MULTUM DILEXIT

For the incident in the New Testament upon which this sonnet is based see Luke 7: 37–50.

ALLAN CUNNINGHAM

BIBLIOGRAPHY

I. WORKS

Songs and Poems, ed. by P. Cunningham. (Murray: London, 1875.) The only inclusive edition, but now out of print; furnishes a biographical introduction.

II. BIOGRAPHY AND CRITICISM

Littell's Living Age, VI, 69–72 (July, 1845); XIII, 469–70 (May, 1847). The first article is a contemporary sketch; reviews the events of the poet's life, compares him with Burns. The second article is a review of his *Poems and Songs*.

Prescott, W. H. "Scottish Song," in *Biographical and Critical Miscellanies.* (Lippincott: Philadelphia, 1882.) A review of the poet's collection,

The Songs of Scotland; provides a discussion of the poet's literary taste and the background of his poetry.

Wilson, J. G., ed. "Allan Cunningham," in *The Poets and Poetry of Scotland*, II. (Harper: New York, 1876.) Provides an outline of the life of the poet, followed by some selections from his poetry.

NOTES

Scott, who called Cunningham a man of genius and "a leal and true Scotsman of the old cast," wrote in his diary that Cunningham "required the tact of knowing when and where to stop"; and in a letter to the poet he said: "Here and there I would pluck a flower from your posy to give what remains an effect of greater simplicity."

Page 684. A WET SHEET AND A FLOWING SEA

Scott said that this English sea-ballad was "among the best songs going," and Mr. C. B. Wheeler considers it of especial interest as the work of a poet who was a confirmed landsman.

ROBERT STEPHEN HAWKER

BIBLIOGRAPHY

I. WORKS

Poetical Works, ed. by Alfred Wallis. (Lane: London, 1899.) The best edition of the poems, based upon the original MSS and annotated copies; furnishes an excellent prefatory notice and a bibliography of Hawker's writings.

Twenty Poems, ed. by John Drinkwater. (Blackwell: Oxford, 1925.) A selection intended to enlarge the range of the average reader, who knows little more of Hawker than the Trelawney ballad; the introduction gives the main facts of the poet's life.

Cornish Ballads and Other Poems, ed. by C. E. Byles. (Lane: London, 1904.) A fine illustrated edition: includes practically all of the two important earlier editions; contains the later version of the "Quest for the Sangraal."

II. BIOGRAPHY AND CRITICISM

Baring-Gould, Sabine. *The Vicar of Morwenstow.* (Methuen: London, 1899.) A pseudo-Boswellian effort to present a detailed biography; fails to leave a well-defined portrait of Hawker amid the details.

Burrows, Margaret F. *Robert Stephen Hawker: A Study of His Thought and Poetry.* (Blackwell: Oxford, 1926.) Interesting for the full light shed on the eccentric central figure, as well as for its insight into certain later 19th-century movements: the return to medievalism, the Oxford movement, Tennyson's pantheism, etc.

Byles, C. E. *Life and Letters of Robert Stephen Hawker.* (Lane: New York, 1905.) The authori-tative biography, by the poet's son-in-law; collected from many sources, consisting largely of letters and other MSS preserved by the poet's friends; contains many illustrations, including lithographs, reproductions from portraits, etc.

III. ARTICLES FROM BOOKS AND PERIODICALS

Drinkwater, John. "Robert Stephen Hawker," in *A Book for Bookmen.* (Doran: New York, 1927.) Offers an interesting review of the life of the eccentric poet; lists his publications, and prints one poem here appearing for the first time.

More, P. E. "The Vicar of Morwenstow," in *Shelburne Essays*, Fourth Series. (Putnam: New York, 1906.) Draws a picture of the surroundings of the poet's home; reviews some scattered biographical facts; points out a "certain fine sonorousness" in Hawker's verse.

Noble, J. A. "Hawker of Morwenstow," in *The Sonnet in England and Other Essays.* (Mathews: London, 1893.) Presents an adequate biographical review; refers to the poet's excellence in ballad and song; reminds us of his "rich humanity."

Pillsbury, R. L. "A Morwenstow Pilgrimage," *Bookman*, XX, 36–41 (Sept., 1904). Filled with interesting photographs, this article provides pen-pictures of Hawker's home and local associations.

NOTES

"The most striking of [the] purely literary qualities [of Hawker's verse] are simplicity and inartificiality . . . [He] had a style—that is, he had a mode of expression which was the natural outcome of an opulent and strongly individualized nature . . . especially at home in the ballad and in the pure lyric, the two poetical forms to the perfection of which this spontaneous simplicity and directness are most absolutely essential—in which self-conscious elaboration is not merely nothing but less than nothing. . . . Though Hawker was quick to discern the one poetic side of a prosaic subject which a thousand men would have missed, he was naturally drawn towards themes, the poetical suggestiveness of which was obvious and unmistakable. In Cornish legendary lore, and especially in that portion of it which dealt with Christian history, or could be made subservient to a mystical Christian use, was a poetic treasure which had been, as it were, 'hid in a field,' waiting for a finder who would know how to prize and use it. Hawker had a claim to the treasure that lay deeper than mere taste. . . . In the region in which the things of sense still remain, but are seen through a luminous mist of spiritual symbolism and association, Hawker was peculiarly at home. He never went on a deliberate search after hidden meanings or morals. . . . Half, or more than half, of the charm of Hawker's verse is to be found in its rich humanity. It is verse through which warm blood circulates, in which a strong pulse beats—verse which moves us as we are moved by a human voice of tenderness in time of sorrow, by the ringing accent of courage in time of fear." (James Ashcroft Noble, in *The Sonnet in England and Other Essays*.)

Page 685.   THE SONG OF THE WESTERN MEN

In a note Hawker wrote to this poem when he revised it for the *Cornish Ballads* in 1869 he said: "With the exception of the choral lines,

> 'And shall Trelawny die?
> Here's twenty thousand Cornish men
> Will know the reason why!'

and which have been, ever since the imprisonment by James the Second of the seven bishops —one of them Sir Jonathan Trelawny—a popular proverb throughout Cornwall, the whole of this song was composed by me in the year 1825. I wrote it under a stag-horned oak in Sir Beville's Walk in Stowe Wood. It was sent by me anonymously to a Plymouth paper, and there it attracted the notice of Mr. Davies Gilbert, who reprinted it at his private press at Eastbourne under the avowed impression that it was the original ballad. It had the good fortune to win the eulogy of Sir Walter Scott, who also deemed it to be the ancient song. It was praised under the same persuasion by Lord Macaulay and by Mr. Dickens, who inserted it at first as of genuine antiquity in his *Household Words*, but who afterwards acknowledged its actual paternity in the same publication."

The refrain that Hawker says he revised was formerly,

> "Here's twenty thousand Cornish men
> Will see the reason why!"

On April 1, 1688, James II, who had ordered the Anglican clergy to read the Declaration of Indulgences in their churches, threw into the Tower seven bishops, among them Trelawny, for refusing to obey his order. A few months later the bishops were tried and acquitted.
11. *Michael's hold*. This is St. Michael's Mount, a high pyramidal rock off the coast of Cornwall.
13. *Tamar*. The Tamar and the Severn (l. 14) are English rivers. For much of its course, the Tamar forms the boundary between Cornwall and Devonshire.
Hawker spoke somewhat bitterly of the tremendous success of this poem "while I have lived on among these far-away rocks unprofited, unpraised, and unknown. This is an epitome of my whole life. Others have drawn profit from my brain, while I have been coolly relinquished to obscurity and unrequital and neglect."

FELICIA DOROTHEA HEMANS

BIBLIOGRAPHY

I. WORKS

Works of Mrs. Hemans. 7 vols. (Blackwood: London, 1844–6.) Almost all of Vol. I is devoted to a memoir by the sister of the poet, Mrs. Hughes, wherein many letters are quoted, together with notes from Mrs. Hemans's diary.
Poetical Works. (Oxford University Press: 1914.) The most accessible edition, intended to supply the place of many previous collections, long out of print.
Poetical Works. (Mason: New York, 1873.) A complete edition, based upon the last London edition; contains a memoir by Mrs. L. H. Sigourney.
Poetical Works. (Crowell: New York, 1892.) A recommended edition, provided with a memoir by W. M. Rossetti.
Poems, ed. by Rufus W. Griswold. (Leavitt: New York, 1852.) A convenient edition, containing an introductory essay by H. T. Tuckerman.

II. BIOGRAPHY AND CRITICISM

Courtney, Mrs. W. S. "Lesser Literary Lights: Nineteenth-Century Poetesses," *North American Review*, CCXI, 793–804 (June, 1920). Provides a brief biographical review; suggests the influence of Longfellow; praises Mrs. Hemans's letters.
Walford, Mrs. Lucy B. "Felicia Dorothea Hemans," in *Twelve English Authoresses.* (Longmans: London, 1892.) Offers an interesting summary of the life of the poet, who exceeded all of her contemporaries in album-inscriptions.

NOTES

"Her poems are stamped with feminine qualities; they have singular grace and tenderness, and exhibit an ardent sympathy with chivalry in every form. In her own day Lord Jeffrey, Byron, the Countess of Blessington, and Christopher North were among her admiring critics or readers. But her poetry lacks deep thought or subtle emotion, and although it had immense popularity in its day, its sweetness and fluency have long palled upon the taste of thoughtful readers." (Charles William Sutton, in *Dictionary of National Biography*.)

THOMAS HOOD

BIBLIOGRAPHY

I. WORKS

Complete Works, ed. by his son and daughter. 11 vols. (Ward: London, 1882–4.) The most complete collection, containing many of the original illustrations of the single volumes.

Complete Poetical Works, ed. by W. C. Jerrold. (Oxford University Press: 1911.) The recommended student's edition.

Poems, ed. by Alfred Ainger. 2 vols. (Macmillan: New York, 1897.) The introduction is outstanding for its readability and completeness.

Poetical Works, ed. by W. M. Rossetti. (Ward: London, 1880.) A satisfactory edition, providing a brief introduction.

Thomas Hood and Charles Lamb, ed. by W. C. Jerrold. (Benn: London, 1930.) In these "Literary Reminiscences of Thomas Hood" we are given an illuminating insight into the friendship of the two writers; the editor supplies notes to each chapter.

II. BIOGRAPHY AND CRITICISM

Eden, Helen P. "Thomas Hood," *Catholic World*, CXXIII, 731–8 (Sept., 1926). Briefly gives the facts of the poet's harassed career; points out the difficulty of identifying the authentic verse among much accredited to him.

Henley, W. E. "Hood," in *Views and Reviews*. (Macmillan: London, 1921.) Agrees with Thackeray that the intellectual element in Hood is predominant, especially in the best of his humor, and that "mere comicalities" were the waste of his genius.

Hudson, W. H. "Tom Hood: the Man, the Wit, and the Poet," in *A Quiet Corner in a Library*. (Rand: Chicago, 1915.) A sympathetic study of the writer's life and genius, bringing out some of the tragic elements, which give an added sharpness to our appreciation of his humor.

Jerrold, W. C. *Thomas Hood: His Life and Times*. (Lane: New York, 1909.) Based upon new material, unused in the earlier *Memorials* by the poet's children; provides a thorough review of the biographical material, with a minimum of literary criticism.

More, P. E. "Hood," in *Shelburne Essays*, Seventh Series. (Putnam: New York, 1910.) Names Hood the "master of the pun in all its shades of excellence"; gives examples from his work to illustrate his humor most effectively.

Saintsbury, George. "Thomas Hood," in *Essays in English Literature*, Second Series. (Scribner: New York, 1895.) A severe review of the edition of the poet's works by his children; sees Hood's claim to fame as resting on his serious poetry, as well as on his comic muse; suggests a small golden treasury of the poet.

NOTES

"There were two sides to Hood's poetical character, either of which would have given him distinction; but his great and unique reputation rests upon the performances in which they appeared in combination. As a poet in the more conventional and restricted sense he was graceful, delicate, and tender, but not very powerful. As a humorist he was exuberant and endowed with a perfectly exceptional faculty of playing upon words. As a poet he is no unworthy disciple of Lamb and Hunt; as a humorist he resembles Barham with less affluence of grotesque invention, but with a pathos to which Barham was a stranger. In his two most famous poems, *The Song of the Shirt* and *The Bridge of Sighs*, this pathos is almost detached from the humorous element in which it is commonly embedded, and the result is two of the rarest achievements of contemporary verse—pieces equally attractive to the highest and the humblest, genuine *Volkslieder* of the nineteenth century. He is, however, most truly himself when the serious and the comic are inextricably combined, as in those masterpieces *Miss Kilmansegg and the Epistle to Rae Wilson*." Here he stands alone even though the association of poetry and humor is the general note of his literary work. As a man he was highly estimable; and the tragic necessity laid upon him of jesting for a livelihood while in the very grasp of death imparts a painful interest to his biography." (Richard Garnett, in *Dictionary of National Biography*.)

Page 688.   THE LAST MAN

This poem, which was published in the first *Whims and Oddities*, was probably suggested to the author by a poem of the same title by Campbell, and by Coleridge's *Ancient Mariner*. "It shows much of the same tragic intensity," says Alfred Ainger, "blended with its grim humor, that belongs to *Eugene Aram* and the serious portions of *Miss Kilmansegg*."

15. *orts.* Scraps; bits; morsels.

Page 690.   FAITHLESS SALLY BROWN

Mr. W. H. Hudson, after commenting upon Hood's talent—with Hood it *was* talent—as a punster, and listing a number of surprisingly apt puns, selects this poem to illustrate the poet's adroitness with the pun. Hudson calls himself a Cockney and apologizes for what he considers "one dreadful cockney pun" in the poem—that about "eye-water" (line 28)—but insists that, this one barred, the poem bristles with puns that are "absolute models in their kind." Punning is out of date now, Hudson admits, but he believes that the reader of understanding and feeling must respond to the cleverness of Hood's puns even if he no longer believes in the fashion. "It is in feats" [of the kind that are in this poem], Hudson concludes, "in feats characterized by an almost boundless prodigality in quibble and equivocation, and at best, as in the marvelous last stanza, . . . by absolute perfection of attainment, that Hood is . . . unsurpassed." With Hood the habit was incurable. With death only a few hours away, he said: "I am dying to please the undertaker, who wishes to earn (urn) a lively Hood (livelihood)."

63-4. *he chew'd His pigtail*. Note the pun. A pigtail is a braid of hair, but also a thin roll or twist of tobacco.

Page 691. THE MERMAID OF MARGATE

Hudibras, the poem from which the motto is taken, was written by Samuel Butler (1612–1680).

1. *Margate beach*. Margate is a watering place in Kent county, England.

7. *Sadler's Wells*. A well-known place of public amusement between the New River Head and St. John Street Road, Islington. The fact that a surveyor by the name of Sadler discovered a spring of mineral water there accounts for the name. In his autobiography John Britton, who lived close by the Wells, writes: "The New River flowed past the theatre and means were taken to introduce 'a large body of water from it to a tank beneath the floor of the stage.' This floor being taken up, a broad sheet of water was displayed to the audience, and rendered very effective in naval spectacles, pantomimes, and burlettas, which were written and adapted to exhibit aquatic scenes."

28. *Goodwin Sand*. A shoal ten miles long in the northern port of Dover Strait, southeast coast of England.

44. *Miss Biffen*. Sarah Biffen (or Biffin) (1784–1850) was a celebrated miniature painter who was born without arms or legs. She taught herself to draw and paint by holding a pencil or brush in her mouth, and in 1812 was exhibited in the principal towns of England by her teacher. Dickens speaks of her in *Nicholas Nickleby* and *Martin Chuzzlewit*.

96. *Or an anker where Hope might lean!* An anker is an old Dutch and German liquid measure, especially for spirits. Note the pun, which involves the four words, "spirits," "anker," "anchor," and "Hope."

103. *Hoy*. (1) A small coasting vessel or (2) a heavy barge.

120. *Deal*. A seaport in Kent. Note the pun, involving Deal (deal) and oak.

Page 694.   FAITHLESS NELLY GRAY

This poem, like *Faithless Sally Brown*, is an excellent example of what Mr. W. H. Hudson called Hood's "almost boundless prodigality in quibble and equivocation."

11-12. *there's as wooden members . . . represent my legs*. A jibe at members of Parliament.

36. *In Badajos's breaches*. Badajos, a fortress in Spain near the Portuguese border, was stormed by Wellington in 1812.

65. *A dozen men sat on his corpse*. A jury assembled to investigate the cause of his death.

68. *A stake in his inside*. According to an old custom a person who had committed suicide was generally buried at a crossroads, and a stake was driven through the body.

Page 695.   *From* HERO AND LEANDER

In Greek legend Hero, a priestess of Aphrodite at Sestos on the Hellespont, and Leander, who lived at Abydos, were lovers. Leander swam the strait nightly to visit her, Hero guiding him in his course by holding up a lighted torch. One tempestuous night Leander was drowned, and Hero, overwhelmed by grief, threw herself into the sea. In the verses here given Hero, weeping over the drowned Leander, is pleading with Death that he may come to her.

FAIR INES

Mr. W. H. Hudson places this poem in the list of Hood's poems "in which the divine accent is most clearly heard," and Mr. Frederick Pierce finds in it "a lingering touch of medieval pageantry." Poe said it had for him "an inexpressible charm."

ODE: AUTUMN

Hood came to be a disciple of Keats through John Hamilton Reynolds, who was the confidant and adviser of Keats, and whose sister in 1825 became Mrs. Hood. The genius and brilliance of Keats made a marked impression on the younger poet, and there are certain of his poems, as this *Ode*, which show a richness of phrase that is unmistakably Keatsian. Hood was in no sense a servile imitator—he was too original an artist to be that—but something there is in the rich fancy and "sensuous beauty" of this ode to Autumn, standing "shadowless like Silence," that inevitably reminds the reader of the languorous Lady "drows'd with the fume of poppies" who symbolizes Autumn in the greater ode of the young master himself.

21. *tearful Proserpine*. Proserpine—or Persephone—daughter of Zeus and Demeter, while gathering flowers in a meadow in Sicily, was seized by Pluto and carried to his underworld kingdom, where he made her his wife and queen.

27. *Dryads' immortality*. The dryads were wood-nymphs.

Page 697.   RUTH

This little idyll is based on the Bible story of *Ruth*.

I REMEMBER, I REMEMBER

This poem, Mr. W. H. Hudson thinks, "will stand secure among far-reaching changes of taste, when many a more pretentious effort will have passed into oblivion." Mr. Hudson admits these verses to a place in his treasure-volume of things he "should most regret to lose from the accumulated wealth of the world's poetry. . . . This apparently slight and incidental poem deserves . . . to be ranked among our 'possessions forever' by reason of the finality with which it expresses through a bit of highly personal recollection, a well-nigh universal emotion. Who does not, . . . in an hour of quiet self-communion, catch himself looking wistfully backward into that dim past whose every detail memory touches with . . . romance; who does not love . . . to dwell upon the thoughts of the lost freshness and bloom of those days when life was so different from all it has since become, and the promise of it so bright and golden in comparison with the after-reality; . . . who does not feel something of the keen, searching sadness, which none the less is hardly pain, with which the recognition of this contrast gradually fills the contemplative mind?" For all such Hood is "the interpreter of this mood of regret and yearning," speaking for them, better than they could have done it for themselves, the heart's own language.

Of the last five lines of the poem Mr. Alfred Ainger says: "This is unquestionably witty, but it is also unquestionably beautiful; for in this instance the wit is subordinate to the deeper human interest, and is felt to be so by the reader."

SILENCE

Mr. William Sharp ranked "the great sonnet" *Silence* "among the twelve finest sonnets in the language."

Page 698. THE DREAM OF EUGENE ARAM, THE MURDERER

Introducing "the superb 'Dream of Eugene Aram,' in which the workings of a crime-tortured soul are laid bare with remorseless power," Hood wrote the following: "The remarkable name of Eugene Aram [1704–1759], belonging to a man of unusual talents and acquirements, is unhappily associated with a deed of blood as extraordinary in its details as any recorded in our calendar of crime. In the year 1745, being then an usher, and deeply engaged in the study of Chaldee, Hebrew, Arabic, and the Celtic dialects, for the formation of a lexicon, he abruptly turned over a still darker page in human knowledge, and the brow that learning might have made illustrious was stamped ignominious for ever with the brand of Cain. To obtain a trifling property he concerted with an accomplice, and with his own hand effected the violent death of one Daniel Clarke, a shoemaker, of Knaresborough, in Yorkshire. For fourteen years nearly the secret slept with the victim in the earth of St. Robert's Cave, and the manner of its dis-

covery would appear a striking example of the divine justice, even amongst those marvels narrated in that curious old volume alluded to in the *Fortunes of Nigel*, under its quaint title of 'God's Revenge against Murther.'

"The accidental digging up of a skeleton, and the unwary and emphatic declaration of Aram's accomplice that it could not be that of Clarke, betraying a guilty knowledge of the true bones, he was wrought to a confession of their deposit. The learned homicide was seized and arraigned; and a trial of uncommon interest was wound up by a defence as memorable as the tragedy itself for eloquence and ingenuity—too ingenious for innocence, and eloquent enough to do credit even to that long premeditation which the interval between the deed and its discovery had afforded. That this dreary period had not passed without paroxysms of remorse may be inferred from a fact of affecting interest. The late Admiral Burney was a scholar at the school at Lynn in Norfolk where Aram was an usher, subsequent to his crime. The Admiral stated that Aram was beloved by the boys, and that he used to discourse to them of murder, not occasionally, as I have written elsewhere, but constantly, and in somewhat of the spirit ascribed to him in the poem.

"For the more imaginative part of the version I must refer back to one of those unaccountable visions which come upon us like frightful monsters thrown up by storms from the great black deeps of slumber. A lifeless body, in love and relationship the nearest and dearest, was imposed upon my back, with an overwhelming sense of obligation—not of filial piety merely, but some awful responsibility, equally vague and intense, and involving, as it seemed, inexpiable sin, horrors unutterable, torments intolerable—to bury my dead, like Abraham, out of my sight. In vain I attempted, again and again, to obey the mysterious mandate—by some dreadful process the burthen was replaced with a more stupendous weight of injunction, and an appalling conviction of the impossibility of its fulfilment. My mental anguish was indescribable;—the mighty agonies of souls tortured on the supernatural racks of sleep are not to be penned—and if in sketching those that belong to blood-guiltiness I have been at all successful, I owe it mainly to the uninvoked inspiration of that terrible dream."

12. *Lynn.* A seaport in Norfolkshire.

204. *Like Cranmer's.* Thomas Cranmer, an English Protestant divine and reformer, was burned at the stake by Queen Mary I, in 1556.

Page 701. SALLY SIMPKIN'S LAMENT

Bryan and Perenne, from which the two lines of the motto are taken, is a West Indian ballad, founded on a real occurrence.

EPICUREAN REMINISCENCES OF A SENTIMENTALIST

16. *trifle*. A light confection of sponge-cake, or the like, flavored with wine or spirit, and served with custard and whipped cream.

20. *pottle of pines*. Basket of pineapples.

28. *prawns*. Marine crustaceans (larger than shrimps), common off the coasts of Great Britain, and used as food.

31. *"grass."* Slang for green vegetables.

36. *brawn*. Chopped cooked edible parts of pig's head, feet, and legs.

40. *turbot*. A large flat fish, found on the European coasts and much esteemed as food.

56. *ate my first natives alone!* Natives are oysters "altogether or partially reared in British waters."

60. *sprats*. Small herrings.

FRENCH AND ENGLISH

In the second stanza the French words with which Hood plays are as follows: *chaise* (chair), *billet* (letter), *mère* (mother), *fille* (daughter), and *cuir* (leather). His spellings, of course, are attempts at representing the French pronunciation. In the fifth stanza, *hog* is English slang for shilling. *Sows* is a play on the French *sous*, which, to make the pun, Hood pronounces like English *sows*.

24. *"beef and bully."* Bully beef is pickled or tinned beef.

Page 703.   PAIR'D, *NOT* MATCH'D

27. *Souchong*. A kind of black tea of fine quality.

THE SONG OF THE SHIRT

"Only one poem in our language can be mentioned in the same breath with *The Song of the Shirt*—Mrs. Browning's *Cry of the Children*—and even that, in my judgment, lags a long way behind. In each case a voice was found for despair hitherto inarticulate, in each case those who could not speak for themselves found one to speak for them with all the eloquence of sympathy; and the world was forced to give heed." (William Henry Hudson, in *A Quiet Corner in a Library*.)

The Times of October 26, 1843, contained an account of the trial of a woman charged with having pawned clothing belonging to her employer. The trial brought out that the "culprit," a widow, was earning sevenpence a pair for making men's trousers, and representatives of her employer loftily asserted that by working steadily she could earn seven shillings a week, which they insisted "was a very good living." Other similar cases had occurred, and *The Times* of the 27th "had an eloquent and indignant leader on the subject," which aroused general sympathy for underpaid needlewomen. The public was deeply stirred by the discovery of these outrageous conditions, and when *The Song of the Shirt* appeared in the Christmas number of *Punch*, it at once became very popular and Hood leaped into high place in public esteem.

On the memorial, which was erected by public subscription over Hood's grave in Kensal Green Cemetery, is inscribed, in fulfillment of his wish, the simple epitaph: "He sang the 'Song of the Shirt.'" Two remarkable bas-reliefs on the memorial represent scenes from *The Bridge of Sighs* and *The Dream of Eugene Aram*.

Page 704.   THE BRIDGE OF SIGHS

Hood takes his title from the Bridge of Sighs, which is the covered passageway connecting the palace of the Doge in Venice with the state prisons. Prisoners were taken over this bridge to and from the hall of judgment. In writing the poem he is said to have had in mind the Waterloo Bridge over the Thames in London. This bridge, since it was a toll bridge until 1878 and hence not greatly used, was frequently selected by unhappy or desperate persons as a place of suicide.

Of this poem Poe wrote that its "vigor . . . is no less remarkable than its pathos. The versification, although carrying the fanciful to the very verge of the fantastic, is nevertheless admirably adapted to the wild insanity which is the thesis of the poem."

Page 706.   THE LAY OF THE LABOURER

This poem was founded on the incident of Gifford White, an eighteen-year-old laborer who, in 1844, was indicted for writing letters to the farmers of his district, threatening to burn their ricks and to visit them with other forms of violence if they would not give him employment. The boy was found guilty and sentenced to transportation for life. Hood's poem, "pervaded by a nobly human spirit," was written as a plea for the boy's pardon or, at the least, for a lightening of his sentence.

97. *New Bastille*. Probably Hood uses this word to indicate a state prison as contrasted with "Gaol" (l. 98), which suggests a local prison.

98. *Spital*. A hospital.

Page 707.   STANZAS

This, Hood's last poem, was written on his deathbed, probably in January, 1845.

LEIGH HUNT

BIBLIOGRAPHY

I. WORKS

Poetical Works, ed. by H. S. Milford. (Oxford University Press: 1923.) This recent edition is noteworthy for its biographical and critical introduction; the appendix contains the most complete chronological bibliography of Hunt.

Essays and Poems, ed. by R. B. Johnson. 2 vols. Temple Library. (Dent: London, 1891.) The most convenient selection, including all of the important verse and a considerable volume of the essays, etc.

Leigh Hunt as Poet and Essayist, ed. by W. C. Kent. (Warne: London, 1888.) An anthology of "choicest passages," furnishing also a short biographical introduction.

Prefaces by Leigh Hunt, ed. by R. B. Johnson. (Oxford University Press: 1927.) A gathering of reprints from periodicals, covering a period of nearly fifty years, showing Hunt's literary and journalistic tastes.

Autobiography, ed. by Edmund Blunden. World's Classics. (Oxford University Press: 1928.) The best edition, equipped with an introduction by Hunt's most recent biographer; supersedes the two-volume edition by Ingpen (1903).

II. BIOGRAPHY AND CRITICISM

Blunden, Edmund. *Leigh Hunt and His Circle*. (Harper: New York, 1930.) Bids fair to be accepted as the standard biography; provides a wealth of new material, drawn largely from unpublished MSS; contains many references to Shelley, Keats, and Byron.

Johnson, R. B. *Leigh Hunt*. (Macmillan: New York, 1896.) A recommended Life, particularly for information on Hunt's journalistic and political activity.

Miller, Barnette. *Leigh Hunt's Relations with Byron, Shelley, and Keats*. (Columbia University Press: 1910.) A detailed and scholarly study; should be read in connection with the important paper by Walter Graham, in which some errors are corrected.

Monkhouse, Cosmo. *Life of Leigh Hunt*. Great Writers series. (Scott: London, 1893.) One of the earliest complete Lives and still the accepted source for matters of fact, even though its tone is somewhat unsympathetic.

III. ARTICLES FROM BOOKS AND PERIODICALS

Blunden, Edmund. "Leigh Hunt: An Annotation," *London Mercury*, III, 618–26 (Apr., 1921). Commends the *Autobiography;* Hunt's political courage is praised, and attention drawn to his best poetry.

Forman, M. B. "Leigh Hunt: Some Unfamiliar Apologists," *London Mercury*, XIV, 180–5 (June, 1926). Laments Dickens's caricature, which may be corrected in part by Hunt's own *Autobiography* and a late-found self-portrait in his *Lord Byron;* also mentions comments from Thornton Hunt and Carlyle.

Gosse, Edmund. "Leigh Hunt," in *More Books on the Table*. (Scribner: New York, 1923.) A brief essay on the man's place in his age, his influence upon Keats, his political satire.

Graham, Walter. "Shelley's Debt to Leigh Hunt and *The Examiner*," *Publications of the Modern Language Association*, XL, 185–92 (Mar., 1925). Shows Hunt's service as a reviewer in pointing out Shelley's social philosophy.

Ingpen, Roger. "Leigh Hunt as a Prose Writer," *Living Age*, CCCXVII, 361–3 (May, 1923). Laments Hunt's journalistic pressure, his necessary facility, but selects a small group of essays that establish his fame; praises the *Autobiography*.

Pierce, F. E. "The Eddy around Leigh Hunt," in *Currents and Eddies in the English Romantic Generation*. (Yale University Press: 1918.) Gives an excellent brief review of Hunt's contacts with the famous men of his day, particularly those of the "Cockney school": shows the political nature of the attacks leveled against Hunt and his friends.

Saintsbury, George. "Leigh Hunt," in *Essays in English Literature*, First Series. (Scribner: New York, 1896.) Provides a brief biographical sketch; laments Hunt's vulgarity but praises a few of his sonnets; sees the foundation of his enduring fame in his associations with greater poets.

Saintsbury, George. "The Landors, Leigh Hunt, De Quincey," in *Cambridge History of English Literature*, XII, 226–56. (Putnam: New York, 1916.) Calls attention to Hunt's influence on other contemporary writers.

Symons, Arthur. "Leigh Hunt," in *The Romantic Movement in English Poetry*. (Dutton: New York, 1909.) Remarks Hunt's share in emancipating the diction and metre of poetry; commends his short narratives and a few of his sonnets.

NOTES

"As a poet Leigh Hunt showed much tenderness, a delicate and vivid fancy, and an entire freedom from any morbid strain of introspection. His verses never lack the sense and expression of quick, keen delight in all things naturally and wholesomely delightful. But an occasional mannerism, bordering on affectation, detracts somewhat from the merits of the poetry." (Alexander Ireland, in *Dictionary of National Biography*.)

". . . Poetry was his first, his last, his most constant love; and if by prose he had to win the meat and the raiment of life, it was poetry that to him was life itself. . . . Even among poets who are poets beyond all doubt, we recognise some as specially poetical poets, and Hunt is one of these. He is never supreme in the way that some poets are supreme, and even on his own level, he is at one time less felicitous than at another; but there is one thing in which he never fails—that imaginative glow and warmth which takes us into another world than the prosaic life of every day, and enables us to forget the dulnesses and the meannesses of the actual. . . ." (James Ashcroft Noble, in *The Sonnet in England and Other Essays*.)

Page 708.   THE STORY OF RIMINI

The Story of Rimini, which was dedicated to Lord Byron, has for its subject the love story and tragedy of Paolo and Francesca, an episode occurring late in the thirteenth century. Paolo was the handsome brother of Giovanni Malatesta of Rimini, a brave but hateful and deformed man to whom, for his military prowess, Francesca's father, Count of Ravenna, gave his daughter in marriage. Francesca and Paolo fell in love, and when their adulterous relations were discovered they were put to death by Giovanni.

"The following story is founded on a passage in Dante, the substance of which is contained in the concluding paragraph of the second [fifth] canto. For the rest of the incidents, generally speaking, the praise or blame remains with myself. The passage in question—the episode of Paolo and Francesca—has long been admired by the readers of Italian poetry, and is indeed the most cordial and refreshing one in the whole of that singular poem, the *Inferno*, which some call a satire, and some an epic, and which, I confess, has always appeared to me a kind of sublime nightmare. We even lose sight of the place, in which the saturnine poet, according to his summary way of disposing both of friends and enemies, has thought proper to put the sufferers; and see the whole melancholy absurdity of his theology, in spite of itself, falling to nothing before one genuine impulse of the affections.
"The interest of the passage is greatly increased by its being founded on acknowledged matter of fact. Even the particular circumstance which Dante describes as having hastened the fall of the lovers,—the perusal of *Launcelot of the Lake*,—is most likely a true anecdote; for he himself, not long after the event, was living at the court of Guido Novella da Polenta, the heroine's father; and indeed the very circumstance of his having related it at all, considering its nature, is a warrant of its authenticity. . . .
"There are no notes to the present poem. I have done my best, as every writer should, to be true to costume and manners, to time and place; and if the reader understands me as he goes, and feels touched where I am most ambitious he should be, I can be content that he shall miss an occasional nicety or so in other matters, and not be quite sensible of the mighty extent of my information. If the poem reach posterity, curiosity may find com-

mentators enough for it, and the sanction of time give interest to whatever they may trace after me. If the case be otherwise, to write notes is only to show to how little purpose has been one's reading. . . .
". . . All the merit I claim is that of having made an attempt to describe natural things in a language becoming to them, and to do something towards a revival of what appears to me a proper English versification. There are narrative poets now living who have fine eyes for the truth of things, and it remains with them perhaps to perfect what I may suggest. If I have succeeded at all, the lovers of nature have still to judge in what proportion the success may be; but let me take them with me a while, whether in doors or out of doors, whether in the room or the green fields,—let my verses, in short, come under the perusal of ingenuous eyes, and be felt a little by the hearts that look out of them, and I am satisfied." (Hunt, Preface to *The Story of Rimini*.)

Four years before his death Hunt wrote of this poem that, except for a few fine lines, it was "conventional, not rich and aromatic, and tending to prose."
See in the text the postscript to Byron's letter to Leigh Hunt (p. 386) and ll. 26 ff. of Shelley's letter to Leigh Hunt (p. 539).
371. *cicale.* The cicada.
401. "*Launcelot of the Lake.*" A famous medieval romance. King Ban, King Arthur, Queen Geneura, all mentioned in this extract, are characters in this romance.

Page 710.   THE POETS

Bryan Waller Procter tells us that Hunt "liked Milton more, and Spenser far more, than Shakespeare," and that over the door of his study he had a line from *The Faerie Queene*.
3. *Pulci.* Luigi Pulci, a Florentine poet (1432–1484).

Page 712.

TO THE GRASSHOPPER AND THE CRICKET

Shelley and Keats went frequently together to Hunt's cottage in December of 1816, a month of much unrest and wretchedness for Shelley. Frequently the three entered into poetical competitions, one of Hunt's favorite pastimes; but on December 30, the day on which Hunt and Keats engaged in friendly poetical rivalry over the cricket and the grasshopper, Shelley could not take part—that was the day of his marriage to Mary Godwin, with whom he had eloped to the continent in July, 1814. Keats thought this impromptu sonnet of Hunt's was excellent, and Hunt thought the same of Keats's impromptu. For Keats's sonnet, see *On the Grasshopper and Cricket* (text p. 559).

THE PRAYER IN THE BOWER

4. *Priapus.* Son of Aphrodite by Dionysus. Hera caused him to be such an ugly child that Aphrodite put him away from her in disgust. He was the god of the creative power of nature in man, beast, and plant.

16. *Psamathe.* Daughter of Crotopus of Argos, and mother of a son, Linus, whose father was Apollo. Linus was torn to pieces by dogs, and Psamathe was buried alive by her father, who refused to believe that Apollo was the father of Linus. Enraged at this, the god sent a monster to destroy the children of the land. He was finally appeased when a shrine was erected between Argos and Delphi to which the Argive women went every year to celebrate the festival of Linus, singing songs of mourning for both Psamathe and her son.

ABOU BEN ADHEM

In this poem, founded on an incident set down in D'Herbelot's *Bibliothèque Orientale* (1697), the "genial enthusiasm of humanity which informs every line that came from Hunt's pen . . . found its most memorable and perfect expression."

"Out of Mrs. Hall's album first appears one of those lucky poems which are instantly household words—'Abou Ben Adhem.' It was one of the many apologues which Hunt's passion for the literature of the Near East, so far as he could get at it in translation, bade him renovate in English verse; and indeed it is not one of the most sensuously poetic. But its touch of glory, like a sacred flame on a clear and graceful altar, has captured the succeeding generations; 'Ben Adhem's name led all the rest.'" (Edmund Blunden, in *Leigh Hunt and His Circle.*)

The line, "Write me as one that loves his fellow-men," is inscribed over Hunt's grave.

Page 714. RONDEAU

Mrs. Carlyle, who was the heroine of this poem, tells with a little touch of malice the following story of Hunt's behavior at a tea which she attended at his house in October, 1835. The unnamed lady in Mrs. Carlyle's story is probably Harriet Martineau. "He sang, talked like a pen-gun, even to ——, who drank it all in like nectar, while my mother looked cross enough, and I had to listen to the whispered confidences of Mrs. Hunt. But for me, who was declared to be grown 'quite prim and elderly,' I believe they would have communicated their mutual experiences in a retired window-seat till morning. 'God bless you, Miss ——,' was repeated by Hunt three several times in tones of ever-increasing pathos and

tenderness, as he handed her downstairs behind me. ——, for once in her life, seemed past speech. At the bottom of the stairs a demur took place. I saw nothing; but I heard, with my wonted glegness—what think you?—a couple of handsome smacks! and then an almost inaudibly soft, 'God bless you, Miss ——!' Now just remember what sort of looking woman is —— ——; and figure their transaction! If he had kissed me, it would have been intelligible, but —— ——, of all people!'" The usual explanation of Mrs. Carlyle's kiss, which so enraptured the poet, is that she was moved to give it in a burst of joy over Hunt's announcement that a publisher had accepted her husband's *Frederick the Great.*

ON THE DEATH OF HIS SON VINCENT

Vincent, Hunt's youngest son, "a willing and sweet-tempered young man," had seldom been separated from his father in all the years since his birth in 1823. In the summer of 1851 he became dangerously ill, but he rallied in September and Hunt, acting upon medical advice, took him to Ewell, "one of the prettiest villages in all the county of Surrey." By December he seemed better, and father and son returned to Hammersmith. The recovery was not real, however, and by July, 1852, Hunt was frantically turning, now here, now there, in search of anything that might stay the dread march of disease. But no help was to be found and the doomed boy died in October of the same year. Of the morning of Vincent's death, Hunt wrote: "It was a colder break of dawn than usual, but equally beautiful, as if, in both respects, it came to take him away, when my son died. His last words were poetry itself. A glass of water had been given him at his request; and on feeling the refreshment of it, he said, 'I drink the morning.'"

CHARLES LAMB
BIBLIOGRAPHY

I. WORKS

Works of Charles and Mary Lamb, ed. by E. V. Lucas. 6 vols. (Macmillan: New York, 1913.) The authoritative edition; the contents of each volume are arranged generally in order of publication. Annotations are somewhat condensed from the original 1903–5 edition, and the portraits (except frontispieces) are omitted; vol. IV contains the poems and plays.

Works, ed. by Alfred Ainger. 7 vols. (Macmillan: London, 1885–8.) In many respects the most desirable edition: the introductions and notes are thorough; the final volume contains the editor's *Life of Lamb.*

Works of Charles and Mary Lamb, ed. by Thomas Hutchinson. 2 vols. (Oxford University Press: 1924.) The recommended edition for student use; Vol. II contains the poetry.

Poetical Works, ed. by William Tirebuck. Canterbury Poets. (Scott: London, 1887.) Includes all of Lamb's worthwhile poetry; prefaced by his whimsical *Autobiography* and a brief Life by the editor. (Includes the poems of Bowles and Hartley Coleridge.)

Thomas Hood and Charles Lamb, ed. by W. C. Jerrold. (Benn: London, 1930.) These "Literary Reminiscences of Thomas Hood" provide a delightful survey of the personal relationships of the two writers; the editor adds notes and corrections to each chapter.

II. BIOGRAPHY AND CRITICISM

Ainger, Alfred. *Lamb*. English Men of Letters series. (Harper: New York, 1894.) A good brief biography, with judicious critical analyses.

Blunden, Edmund. *Charles Lamb and His Contemporaries*. (Cambridge University Press: 1933.) The Clark Lectures, delivered at Trinity College, Cambridge; valuable for the criticism of Lamb's poetry and characterization of the circle of his friends.

Dobell, Bertram. *Sidelights on Charles Lamb*. (Scribner: New York, 1903.) A study chiefly of Lamb's connections with the *London Magazine* and its editors; includes much hitherto unused material.

Jerrold, W. C. *Charles Lamb*. (Bell: London, 1905.) A useful introduction to Lamb's life and writings.

Lucas, E. V. *The Life of Charles Lamb*. 2 vols. (Putnam: New York, 1921.) The standard Life, now in its fifth edition, which omits the illustrations and four appendices, adding a few new passages; the basis of the work is an exhaustive compilation of contemporary records, with editorial comment.

Martin, B. E. *In the Footprints of Charles Lamb*. (Scribner: New York, 1894.) This "topographical biography" reconstructs Lamb's life from reminiscent notations about the houses and places in which he lived and labored; much of the narrative is in his own words, drawn from his essays and letters.

May, J. L. *Charles Lamb: A Study*. (Bles: London, 1934.) Throwing aside bookish attitudes, this study attempts a personal revelation of Lamb, considered in all of his many aspects.

Morley, F. V. *Lamb before Elia*. (Cape: London, 1932.) Takes issue with the accepted theories that Lamb was a natural recluse; finds the causes of his stoical seclusion in his estrangement from Coleridge and Mary Lamb's insanity.

Ward, A. C. *The Frolic and the Gentle*. (Methuen: London, 1934.) Summarizes the biographical facts; seems to lament Lamb's decline in the present day.

Wherry, George. *Cambridge and Charles Lamb*. (Cambridge University Press: 1925.) With Lamb's visits to Cambridge as a background, this volume records the six Lamb dinners celebrated in that city, 1909–1914; especially valuable is E. V. Lucas's essay.

Williams, Orlo. *Charles Lamb*. (Duckworth: London, 1934.) Comments on the friendship of Coleridge; sees Lamb's "childlikeness" as the result of his associations with Mary.

III. ARTICLES FROM BOOKS AND PERIODICALS

Blunden, Edmund. "New Sidelights on Keats, Lamb, and Others, from Letters to J. Clare," *London Mercury*, IV, 141–9 (June, 1921). Quotes letters from Keats's publisher Taylor, concluding with an account of Lamb's death.

French, J. M. "Lamb and Milton," *Studies in Philology*, XXXI, 92–103 (Jan., 1934). Provides a comprehensive survey of Lamb's interest in Milton, based on the *Letters*, etc.; the Lucas edition of Lamb has been used as reference for annotations.

More, P. E. "Charles Lamb Again," in *Shelburne Essays*, Fourth Series. (Putnam: New York, 1906.) Lays down the conditions under which Lamb's poetry may be read with most enjoyment; comments on his critical insight and his droll humor.

Pater, Walter. "Charles Lamb," in *Appreciations*. (Macmillan: New York, 1911.) Provides a sympathetic review of the main facts of Lamb's life, with a survey of his best divinations as expressed chiefly in his original prose and his editorial work.

Thompson, A. H. "Lamb," in *The Cambridge History of English Literature*, XII. (Putnam: New York, 1916.) A brief sympathetic essay, with emphasis on the biographical side.

Woodberry, G. E. "Charles Lamb; or Elia," in *Makers of Literature*. (Macmillan: New York, 1900.) Concerned chiefly with the writer's prose, but offering also an analysis of his character and literary reputation.

NOTES

"No one can judge the verse of Lamb without remembering the circumstances under which it was composed. Gradgrind routine and domestic calamity had clutched him as between the jaws of a trap and would have crushed the sublimely evanescent vision in any one. His period of comparative leisure came late in life when many men can write good prose but few good poetry, and so he became a great essayist, only a minor poet . . . the wonder is that he accomplished what he did. Out of the bitterness of broken friendships . . . he distilled at least one undying poem, 'The Old Familiar Faces.'" (Frederick E. Pierce, in *Currents and Eddies in the English Romantic Generation*.)

Page 717. THE OLD FAMILIAR FACES

This "is scarcely a poem at all; the metre halts, stumbles, there is no touch of magic in it; but it is speech, naked human speech, such as rarely gets through the lovely disguise of verse. It has the raw humanity of Walt Whitman, and almost hurts us by a kind of dumb helplessness in it. A really articulate poet could never have written it; here, the emotion of the poet masters him as he speaks; and you feel, with a strange thrill, that catch in his breath which he cannot help betraying." (Arthur Symons, in *The Romantic Movement in English Poetry.*)

8. *fairest among women.* This was Ann Simmonds, or Simmons, who appears in Lamb's essays as Alice W—n. In *Dream Children* we learn that she married a Mr. Bartrum.

11. *I have a friend.* This was Charles Lloyd (1775-1839), of whom Lamb wrote: "I had well-nigh quarreled with Charles Lloyd, and for no other reason I believe, than that the good creature did all he could to make me happy."

17. *Friend of my bosom.* Coleridge.

21. *And some are taken from me.* This statement, meaningfully italicized by the poet, refers to Mary Lamb's return to the asylum.

Page 718. HESTER

The subject of this poem was Hester Savary, a young Quakeress, with whom Lamb fell in love in 1800. She died in 1803.

WALTER SAVAGE LANDOR

BIBLIOGRAPHY

I. WORKS

Complete Works, ed. by T. E. Welby. 16 vols. (Chapman: London, 1927——.) Of this definitive edition fourteen volumes have thus far appeared; it promises to supersede the editions by Crump and Forster, although already some voices have been raised against it: see *The Times Literary Supplement* (London) for May 15, May 29, and June 19, 1930. Volumes XIII and XIV (the poetry) have been edited by Stephen Wheeler.

Works, ed. by C. G. Crump. 10 vols. (Dent: London, 1893.) An improvement upon the Forster edition, but now being superseded by the definitive edition in preparation under the direction of T. E. Welby; a cheap and convenient collection.

Works, ed. by John Forster. 8 vols. (Chapman: London, 1876.) The first effort at a complete collection; rather unwieldy and now hard to obtain; Vol. I is an abridgment of the editor's two-volume *Life* of 1869.

Selections, ed. by Sidney Colvin. Golden Treasury series. (Macmillan: New York, 1895.) The best abridgment; contains both prose and poetry, with a brief critical introduction.

Last Days, Letters, and Conversations, ed. by H. C. Minchin. (Methuen: London, 1934.) Adds two new *Imaginary Conversations;* sheds much light on the poet's later relations with his family.

Imaginary Conversations and Poems, ed. by Havelock Ellis. (Dutton: New York, 1933.) A recommended inexpensive edition; the editor provides a brief introduction.

Imaginary Conversations, ed. by Ernest de Sélincourt. (Oxford University Press: 1931.) The most satisfactory abridgment of this prose field, with an introduction by the editor.

Letters Private and Public, ed. by S. Wheeler. (Duckworth: London, 1899.) Most interesting are those to Rose Aylmer, a niece and namesake of the woman immortalized in Landor's poetry.

II. BIOGRAPHY AND CRITICISM

Bradley, William. *The Early Poems of Walter Savage Landor.* (Bradbury: London, 1914.) Studies the course of Landor's development as a poet; points out the increasing influence of Milton, notably in the *Gebir* and *Chrysaor.*

Colvin, Sidney. *Landor.* English Men of Letters series. (Harper: New York, 1887.) A satisfactory short biography, offering sound literary comment.

Evans, E. W., Jr. *Walter Savage Landor: A Critical Study.* (Putnam: New York, 1892.) Agrees with Dowden on the prevailing features of Landor's work; accepts the paradox of his eccentric personality expressing itself in an effort to achieve classical perfection of form.

Goldmark, Mrs. Ruth I. *The Influence of Greek Literature on Walter Savage Landor.* (Columbia University Press: 1918.) This thoughtful study (appearing in the series *Influence of the Classics on English Literature*) shows that Landor's Hellenism was probably more sincere and deeply grounded than that of any of his contemporaries in England or in Germany.

III. ARTICLES FROM BOOKS

Bailey, J. C. "Some Notes on the Unpopularity of Landor," in *Essays by Divers Hands.* (Oxford University Press: 1925.) A discussion of the qualities which make Landor the "most neglected of the English classics"; some of the causes which repel the average reader are Landor's immense erudition, his formalism, and his remoteness.

De Vere, Aubrey. "Landor's Poetry," in *Essays Chiefly on Poetry,* II. (Macmillan: New York, 1887.) Points out the inadequacy of extracts from Landor's longer pieces, comments on weakness of plot in his dramatic poems, lays his lack of popularity to his devotion to the ideals of classical literature.

Dowden, Edward. "Walter Savage Landor," in *Studies in Literature.* (Paul: London, 1882.) Presents the since widely heeded opinion that Landor is a classicist, with a personality that forbade attention to form.

Drinkwater, John. "Landor's *Dry Sticks Fagoted,*" in *A Book for Bookmen.* (Doran: New York, 1927.) A publication of and commentary on 38 letters from Landor to his printer, James Nichol, written while Landor's book was going through the press.

Henley, W. E. "Landor," in *Views and Reviews.* (Macmillan: London, 1921.) A curt dismissal of Landor's claim to poetic capability; finds in his classic dramas nothing Greek "except the absence of stage-directions."

Saintsbury, George. "Walter Savage Landor," in *Essays in English Literature,* Second Series.

(Scribner: New York, 1895.) Aims at a middle-of-the-road critical viewpoint; eccentricities and personal weaknesses in Landor are arraigned and literary excellencies fairly commended; compares him with Morris.

Saintsbury, George. "The Landors, Leigh Hunt, De Quincey," in *The Cambridge History of English Literature*, XII. (Putnam: New York, 1916.) A masterly brief discussion, with emphasis on Landor's better poetry.

Scudder, H. E. "Landor as a Classic," in *Men and Letters*. (Houghton: Boston, 1887.) A brief study of the art exhibited in the *Imaginary Conversations*, showing Landor to possess all the elements essential to a classic, but so limited in his appeal as to remain a "literary man's author."

Stephen, Leslie. "Landor's *Imaginary Conversations*," in *Hours in a Library*, III. (Smith: London, 1879.) Sets forth the widely accepted theory that Landor had no well-grounded purpose in his writings, that his reputation must rest on his style alone.

Swinburne, A. C. "Landor," in *Miscellanies*. (Scribner: New York, 1911.) A frank eulogy: "as a poet he may be said on the whole to stand midway between Byron and Shelley."

Symons, Arthur. "Walter Savage Landor," in *The Romantic Movement in English Poetry*. (Dutton: New York, 1909.) Reveals the writer as a master of prose, working occasionally in verse; suggests strong influences from Pindar and Catullus.

Woodberry, G. E. "Landor," in *Literary Essays*. (Harcourt: New York, 1920.) Points out Landor's chief works, interpreting them as beautiful, but lacking depth and permanence.

IV. ARTICLES FROM PERIODICALS

Ashley-Montague, M. F. "Three Unpublished *Imaginary Conversations*," *Nineteenth Century*, CVII, 836–45 (June, 1930). Gives the text of the three pieces, included in papers in possession of Landor's granddaughter; the conversations are between Andrew Marvell and Henry Marten, Diogenes and a Citizen, Solon and Pisistratos.

Field, Kate. "Last Days of Landor," *Atlantic Monthly*, XVII, 385–95; 540–51; 684–705 (Apr., May, June, 1866). A useful detailed record of the last six years of Landor's life in Italy, quoting many letters and conversations, with frequent reference to earlier periods of his life.

Spender, Constance. "Walter Savage Landor," *Contemporary Review*, CXIII, 70–5 (Jan., 1918). A sketch of the poet's life, viewed in its more bellicose and picturesque aspects.

Wheeler, S. "Landor: The Man and the Poet," *Nineteenth Century*, XCI, 236–47 (Feb., 1922). Quoting freely from Landor's letters, the article discusses his theories of art, religious views, his contemporary popularity—all in connection with his lyrics and dramas.

Wheeler, S. "Landor's Llanthony," *Nineteenth Century*, LXXXIX, 445–56 (Mar., 1921). Gives a fairly complete account of Landor's home and his residence there; takes exception to some of Forster's accounts of Landor's quarrels with his Welsh tenants.

Williams, S. T. "The Story of *Gebir*," *Publications of the Modern Language Association*, XXXVI, 615–31 (Dec., 1921). Traces the genesis of the plot of the poem to vague Biblical stories, noting also Clara Reeves's *History of Charoba, Queen of Egypt* as Landor's immediate source; comments on the popularity of the poem.

Williams, S. T. "Landor as Critic of Literature," *Publications of the Modern Language Association*, XXXVIII, 906–28 (Dec., 1923). Takes a high stand, while admitting inconstancy in Landor's application of his ideals; points out his capricious preferences (excepting Dante and Milton) especially among the classics; finds Landor's power chiefly in epigram.

Williams, S. T. "Landor's Criticism in Poetry," *Modern Language Notes*, XL, 413–8 (Nov., 1925). Points to Landor's *Hellenics* and the *Heroic Idylls* as containing the most critical material, with Dante frequently mentioned; Landor's interest in 19th-century literature is here clearly demonstrated.

NOTES

"As a poet, he [Landor] may be said on the whole to stand midway between Byron and Shelley,—about as far above the former as below the latter. If we except Catullus and Simonides, it might be hard to match and it would be impossible to overmatch the flawless and blameless yet living and breathing beauty of his most perfect elegies, epigrams, or epitaphs. As truly as prettily was he likened by Leigh Hunt to 'a stormy mountain pine which should produce lilies.' His passionate compassion, his bitter and burning pity for all wrongs endured in all the world, found only their natural and inevitable outlet in his lifelong defence or advocacy of tyrannicide as the last resource of baffled justice, the last discharge of heroic duty. His tender and ardent love of children, of animals, and of flowers, makes fragrant alike the pages of his writing and the records of his life." (A. C. Swinburne, in *Miscellanies*.)

"One must notice, too, the excellence of Landor, or even his supremacy in one particular form, the epigram. No one has ever used this ancient classic form in English literature so delicately as Landor. . . . He abhorred the facile, the commonplace, and the sensational. He proclaimed by precept and by the example of his own poetry that the desirable qualities of poetry were restraint in form and feeling; dignity of manner; and a kind of austere emotion. His models were, of course, though he himself is often more like the Romans, Greek. His poetry was moulded upon an instinctive ideal of τὸ καλόν [the essence of beauty] in literature. . . . In the poetry is Landor's severity of mood towards life as a whole, but also his tenderness for youth, for children, for flowers. And every line of this poetry is written with that high dignity which Landor thought inseparable from true poetry." (Stanley T. Williams, in *Studies in Victorian Literature*.)

Page 719.   ROSE AYLMER

Rose Aylmer, she of "the fairest form, the sweetest breath," was the daughter of Lord Aylmer, with whose family Landor began a warm friendship after he left Oxford in 1794 and went to Wales. It was she who put him in touch with Clara Reeves's *Progress of Romance*, from which he got the suggestion for his *Gebir*, the poem which so fascinated Shelley. Upon the second marriage of her mother Miss Aylmer was sent to an aunt [in Calcutta, India, where she died in 1800. The news of her death led Landor to write this beautiful little elegy.

REGENERATION

Mr. W. B. D. Henderson, who finds Landor "a child of the political idea of the eighteenth century—a child who never grew up," quotes the following from Sir Sidney Colvin: "In the sphere of politics and government, it must be allowed that he [Landor] never got beyond the elementary principles of love of freedom and hatred of tyranny; . . . of the complexity of political organisms and political problems he had no conception, and practical as he believed and intended much of his writing on politics to be, it is usually so much high-minded declamation and no more."
This, Mr. Henderson believes, is true also of Landor's poetry [assailing tyranny and exalting freedom], as well as of his political prose. Even so he finds that "the highness of the poet's mind and the greatness of his style" sometimes secure for "even half-truths an enviable immortality"; and he quotes as an illustration "a single glorious passage," the first eight lines of this poem.
In this passage, Mr. Henderson concludes, the poet is "led to establish the benefits of free nature under free governments, and to disestablish them because of a political condition." With freedom he associated all good, with tyranny all evil. "He 'panted to be present' on the day of resurgent nations, especially of resurgent Italy and Greece."

19. *Tarentine and Hydruntine mole.* Tarentum was a Greek city in ancient Italy. Hydruntum (now Otranto) was a city of old Italy.
25. *Albion.* England.
37. *Hermus and Melena's brow.* Hermus, a river in western Asia Minor (now Gedis or Sarabat). *Melena,* a high promontory of Ionia, forming the northwestern part of the peninsula. It commands a magnificent view of the Gulf of Smyrna and the islands of Samos and Chios.
41. *old bard of Chios.* Homer. Chios (now Scio) was one of the "seven towns [that] contend[ed] for Homer dead, through which the living Homer begged his bread."

48. *Twice twenty self-devoted Greeks.* The reference is to the War of Greek Independence, an uprising against Ottoman domination which ran from 1821 to 1829. In the first period of the war—1821 to 1824—the maritime communities of the Greek archipelago revolted, thus assuring the insurgents of the command of the sea, a thing very important for the success of the uprising. The Turkish fleet, "adrift in the Archipelago," though greatly superior in tonnage and weight of metal, and in number of men, was in no sense a match for the Greek brigs with their highly trained, if not disciplined, crews. Landor may have had in mind the exploit of Constantine Kanaris, who in the night of June 18–19, 1822, steered a fire ship into the Turkish fleet off Scio and burned its flagship. All Europe, which had aided Greece with numerous volunteers, rejoiced over this exploit. Greece was not free as a result of this act, however. Turkey enlisted the aid of Egypt in the struggle, a movement which led to the intervention of the European powers for Greece, and in 1827 the allied British, French, and Russian fleet defeated the Egyptian and Turkish vessels at Navarino. Greece finally became "free" with the two campaigns of the Russo-Turkish War of 1828–29. For the part of Lord Byron, greatest of the English philhellenes, in the Greek revolt, see text pp. 236–37.
52. *Elis.* A district in the northwestern part of the Peloponnesus. Olympia, seat of the Olympian games, was in this district.
54. *The Marathonian columns never told.* The columns of Greek soldiers at Marathon.
55. *Salamis.* Scene of the great naval battle (480 B.C.) in which the Greeks, under Themistocles and Eurybiades, defeated a large Persian fleet, part of Xerxes's forces.
57. *Platea, nor Anthela.* Platea (Platæa), a city in Boeotia, Greece, the scene of a Greek victory over the Persians in 479 B.C. *Anthelé* (Landor's Anthela) was a small town of Thessaly in the interval between the river Phoenix and the Straits of Thermopylae, near the spot where the Aesopus flows into the sea. In the immediate vicinity were the temples of Demeter (Ceres) Amphictyonia, that of Amphictyon, and the seats of the Amphictyons. It was one of the two places where the Amphictyonic Council met, the other being Delphi. Amphictyon, the son of Deucalion and Pyrrha, was reputed to have been the founder of the Amphictyonic Council. Ceres, looking from her mount, could see the Amphictyon (l. 59), i.e., any "delegate" to the Amphictyonic Council, "dip his weary foot"—go bathing, in short—in the strait.
58. *Benignant Ceres.* Ceres was the goddess of sowing and reaping, of harvest festivals, and of agriculture in general.
63. *Perfidious Ilion, parricidal Thebes.* Ilion,

ancient Troy. Thebes, an ancient Bœotian city, called "parricidal" because of the slaying of its king, Laïus, by his son Oedipus.

67. *Enna's mead.* The Sicilian vale in which Proserpine, daughter of Ceres (Demeter), was gathering flowers when Pluto carried her off to Hades and made her queen of Hell. The grief-stricken Demeter wandered over the earth seeking her.

82. *immortal Spartan.* Leonidas, the hero of the pass of Thermopylae, who repulsed even the "Ten Thousand Immortals" of Xerxes, but who was finally defeated by the treachery of a Greek from Malis.

86. *twin-star of glory.* Archimedes, a Greek mathematician, native of Syracuse, Sicily. Syracuse was founded by colonists from Corinth, one of the most notable of ancient Grecian cities. Corinth lay between two gulfs (the *double sea* of l. 87), the Saronic, and the Corinthian (*Achaian*). Archimedes was slain (212 B.C.) by a spear-thrust given him by a Roman soldier.

Page 722.   FIESOLAN IDYL

". . . When he [Landor] had a story to tell, he chose the idyl; and his work in this kind is no less perfect in form than are his quatrains. Indeed, on the idyls his poetic fame will mainly rest. They are very remote from modern life, but the best of them are very beautiful, and in the highest rank of poetry that appeals to the artistic sense. Those who are able still to hold fast to the truth of Greek mythology to the imagination will not willingly let them die. To read them is like looking at the youths and maidens of an ancient bas-relief. The cultivated will never tire of them; the people will never care for them." (George Edward Woodberry, in *Makers of Literature.*)

Landor has nowhere more beautifully expressed his love for flowers than in this poem. In a letter to H. C. Robinson he said: "I like white flowers better than any others; they resemble fair women. Lily, tuberose, orange, and the truly English syringa are my heart's delight. I do not mean to say that they supplant the rose and violet in my affections, for these are our first loves, before we grew too fond of considering and too fond of displaying our acquaintance with others of sounding titles."

TO CORINTH

1. *Queen of the double sea.* Corinth, at the southern extremity of the Isthmus of Corinth, lay between two gulfs, on each of which it had a fine harbor. "Two parallel walls connected the city with its harbor on the west, and a chain of fortifications" with the east harbor. A tram-road by which vessels could be hauled from one harbor to the other was built across the isthmus.

4-5. *Theseus . . . bones of Sciron.* Sciron was a mythical robber who compelled travelers in his haunt, a narrow and precipitous path overhanging the sea near Megara, to kneel and wash his feet. As they did this he would kick them over the cliff into the sea. Theseus, on his way to Athens, met Sciron on his narrow path and slew him.

9. *Isthmian games.* These games, consisting of contests in bodily strength and agility—chariot-racing, running, jumping, wrestling, throwing the quoit, hurling the javelin, boxing, etc.—were celebrated on the Corinthian isthmus. At the celebration there were also contests in music, poetry, and eloquence. The games therefore gave poets, musicians, authors—all artists, in short—an opportunity to present their work to the public. The victors were highly acclaimed, and their fame was spread far and wide. Other celebrated national games were the Olympic, most distinguished of all, held at Olympia; the Pythian, in the vicinity of Delphi; and the Nemean, at Nemea, Argolis.

Page 723.

17-35. *The Colchian babes,* et seq. A reference to one of the episodes in the story of Jason and Medea. Medea, daughter of a king of Colchis, fell in love with Jason when he came seeking the Golden Fleece. She aided him in escaping from her father with the Fleece and fled with him to the land of the Phæacians, where she married him. Driven out of Iolcus for the murder of Pelias, Jason and Medea went to Corinth, where for ten years they lived together happily. Jason finally deserted Medea for the purpose of marrying Glauce, or Creüsa, daughter of King Creon. Medea frustrated Jason's plan of marrying, however, by burning his bride to death with a poisoned robe which he gave her as a wedding gift, and overwhelmed him with sorrow by murdering the two children that had been born to him and to herself. She then fled in a winged chariot ("fiery car") to Athens. The Eumenides (l. 20) are the Furies.

36-39. *To give the inertest masses,* et seq. The Corinthians were famous for their skill in bronze and clay, the Corinthian clay vase, with its fantastic decorations, perhaps surpassing all other vases in beauty. The Corinthian column, too, is a form of great beauty fashioned from "inertest masses of earth." See Keats's *Ode on a Grecian Urn*, text p. 594.

40. *thy citadel.* "The city was built . . . at the foot of a hill 1886 feet high, a natural citadel, called Acrocorinth, more imposing than the famous Acropolis at Athens."

THE DEATH OF ARTEMIDORA

Pericles and Aspasia, one of Landor's longer prose works, consists of imaginary letters, some of them containing verse, that passed between Aspasia, Pericles, Cleone, and other famous persons of the time of Pericles, among them Anaxagoras and Alcibiades. They both disclose the intimate feelings of Aspasia and Cleone and discuss those subjects which one thinks of as highly esteemed in classic Greece—art, literature, religion, philosophy, and statecraft. They are marked by the unmistakable brand of beauty and culture. Athens touched the summit of her power in the administration of Pericles, which began in 460 B.C. and ended with his death thirty-one years later. Aspasia was a beautiful and cultured courtesan who left her native city, Miletus, went to Athens, and entered upon a companionship with Pericles which lasted till his death. Cleone was a maid of Miletus, a friend from whom Aspasia separated when she went to Athens, and what hurt Cleone felt at the separation one needs but to glance at her letter below to discover.

In her letter to Aspasia Cleone tells the following touching story and then, as she says, "transcribes" the poem for her: "Artemidora of Ephesus was betrothed to Elpenor, and their nuptials . . . were at hand. How gladly would Artemidora have survived Elpenor. I pitied her almost as much as if she had. I must ever love true lovers on the eve of separation. These indeed were little known to me until a short time before. We became friends when our fates had made us relatives. On these occasions there are always many verses, but not always so true in feeling and in fact as those which I shall now transcribe for you."

The version of the poem given here is not that of the first published form but a later form, that of the *Hellenics* of 1847. The present text omits the three lines which closed the poem in the *Pericles and Aspasia* text:

"With her that old boat incorruptible,
  Unwearied, undiverted in its course,
  Had plash'd the water up the farther strand."

In commenting upon this omission Mr. T. Earle Welby, editor of Landor's *Complete Works*, says: "As reprinted in the *Hellenics* this poem is advantageously deprived of its last three lines."

HELLENICS

The *Hellenics*, which were Landor's most important and beautiful work in his third and last period of literary production, are in their ease and grace, in their "classical charm of imagery and narrative and sentiment," highly Greek in tone. They arose out of the wish of Lady Blessington, at whose home in London Landor and other literary men were frequent guests, that he would translate certain of his Latin *Idyllia Heroica* into English. He granted the lady's wish and in addition included in the *Hellenics* some poems on classical subjects which he had written in English.

Mr. W. B. Shubrick Clymer, in his *Selections from Landor* (p. xxx) writes: "He [Landor] was Greek in a sense in which . . . Keats, who is sometimes called so, was not. His method is to present the object undraped; Keats, whose love of beauty, though essentially different, was not more disinterested than his, presents the object clad in the drapery of modern association and personal feeling. The effect of the one method is totally unlike that of the other, as Keats's *Hyperion* and Landor's *Hellenics* sufficiently show. The greater popularity of Keats's method is explained by Landor in the line, 'Most have an eye for colour, few for form.' The classic form of the *Hellenics* is, however, no reason why they should not throb and glow with vitality to as high a degree as *Hyperion:* surely nothing is more classic and nothing more alive with emotion than Greek sculpture and Greek drama. Yet that vitality one does not find in the *Hellenics*. One finds in them classic workmanship, and the beauty resulting from the exercise of that workmanship on subjects of captivating grace and lasting charm—beauty of high order, but not deeply moving."

ON THE HELLENICS

4. *Simois.* A small river near ancient Troy.
6–8. *Aphroditè from Athenè won*, et seq. A reference to the contest of the three goddesses before Paris, son of Priam of Troy, for the prize of beauty. By the Judgment of Paris, Aphrodite, goddess of beauty, won the golden apple from Athene, goddess of wisdom, and from Here, queen of the gods and the special divinity of women. Ares, god of war, is happy because he knows the Judgment of Paris will precipitate the Trojan War.

IPHIGENEIA AND AGAMEMNON

The fleet which Agamemnon had assembled at Aulis for the expedition against Troy could not sail because Artemis, goddess of the chase, wrathful at his slaying a stag that was sacred to her, had "laid the winds" and would not bid them rise. Calchas, a soothsayer, prophesied that the fleet could not sail unless Agamemnon sacrificed his daughter, Iphigeneia, to appease the goddess. Convinced of the truth of the prophecy, Agamemnon prepares for the sacrifice. The dramatic moment when Iphigeneia, left alone with her father, pleads with him that her life be spared, is the subject of Landor's poem.

Page 724.   THE HAMADRYAD

Hamadryads, or Hamadryades, are wood-nymphs. Each tree is the home of a nymph, or dryad, whose life begins and ends with that of her tree. She is the protectress of the tree and rejoices with it in its strength and beauty, and suffers with it when for any reason it languishes or is attacked by man. Dryads sport and dance with the immortals and may be wooed both by gods and men.

The Hamadryad is one of the *Hellenics* group that was originally written in English, not translated from the Latin.

1. *Rhaicos*. In the original Greek story, which goes back to the fifth century, this name appears as Rhoecus. James Russell Lowell tells the same story in his *Rhœcus*.

2. *Gnidos*. An ancient city of Caria. *Caria*. An ancient division of Asia Minor bordering on the Aegean sea.

7. *Pandion*. A king of ancient Athens.

17. *Dis*. Pluto, god of the lower world.

20. *Styx*. The principal river of Hades. Charon ferried all the dead across it to the region of the dead.

22. *Enna's dell*. See note to *Regeneration*, above.

94. *Cydonian bow*. Cydonia was an ancient city of Crete. The Cretans were noted archers.

Page 728.   LYRICS AND EPIGRAMS

"The advantage, to such a poet [as Landor], of shorter and, in some cases, definitely limited forms can hardly be overestimated; and it is enhanced not merely by [a] blend of [the] classic and [the] romantic . . . but by a further blend—to some extent consequential—of eighteenth and nineteenth century touch which is more noticeable in Landor than in almost any of his companions. They, for the most part—even Wordsworth, even Scott—grew out of one strain into the other; Landor kept the mixture. He is thus able, in his best so-called epigrams and elsewhere, to observe the neatness and clear outline of eighteenth century occasional pieces, while suffusing it with the later colour and diffusing over it the later atmosphere. . . . This combination . . . has much to do with the extraordinary charm of the two little masterpieces, *Rose Aylmer* and *Dirce*. But, through all these mote-like poems and poemlets, the total number of which comes not so very far short of a thousand, though there may be triviality, false wit, dulness, and other faults here and there, there is always the chance of coming across that flash and glow of the opal which Landor has in a special manner and measure, which is the dearest of delights

to true lovers of poetry and over which he retained command, in these short pieces, almost to his death." (George Saintsbury, in *Cambridge History of English Literature*.) The quatrain, *Dirce*, which Mr. Saintsbury couples with *Rose Aylmer* as a "little masterpiece," is as follows:

"Stand close around, ye Stygian set,
   With Dirce in one boat convey'd,
 Or Charon, seeing, may forget
   That he is old, and she a shade."

(For Swinburne's high tribute to *Dirce* see *Victorian and Later Poets*, p. 795, letter IX, to E. C. Stedman.)

Page 731.   TO ROBERT BROWNING

In a letter to John Forster, in 1845, Landor called Browning "a great poet, a very great poet indeed, as the world will have to agree with us in thinking. . . . God grant that he may live to be much greater than he is, high as he stands above most of the living: *latis humeris et toto vertice* [head and shoulders above the crowd]."

Pages 732–4.

Of Landor's poems on old age and death (such as those numbered XIX, XXII, XXV, and XXVI) Mr. W. B. Shubrick Clymer says: "Neither Mrs. Barbauld's 'Life! I know not what thou art,' Browning's *Prospice* or his *Epilogue to Asolando*, Tennyson's *Crossing the Bar*, nor Stevenson's *Requiem* expresses a more natural feeling with regard to meeting death than Landor's unstudied verses."

JAMES (CLARENCE) MANGAN

BIBLIOGRAPHY

I. WORKS

Poems, ed. by D. J. O'Donoghue. (O'Donoghue: Dublin, 1903.) The centenary edition, provided with a preface and illuminating notes; there is a biographical introduction by John Mitchel.

Selected Poems. (Wolfe: Boston, 1897.) Contains the best of the poetry; an essay by Louise I. Guiney forms the preface.

Prose Writings, ed. by D. J. O'Donoghue. (O'Donoghue: Dublin, 1904.) The best collection of the prose, furnished with an essay by Lionel Johnson.

II. BIOGRAPHY AND CRITICISM

Boyd, E. A. "James Clarence Mangan," in *Ireland's Literary Renaissance*. (Knopf: New York, 1922.) A passage in chapter I reveals the poet's dependence on ancient Gaelic legend and comments on the spasmodic nature of his work.

Graves, A. P. "James Clarence Mangan," *Cornhill Magazine*, LXXVII, 328–39 (Mar., 1898).

Finds in the poet's work some superficial likenesses to Moore's; discusses Mangan's translations and adaptations, selects a small golden treasury of his lyrics.

Guiney, Louise I. "James Clarence Mangan," *Atlantic Monthly*, LXVIII, 641–59 (Nov., 1891). A fine biographical and critical discussion; explodes the idea of his skill as a translator, compares him with Poe.

Monahan, Michael. "James Clarence Mangan," *Forum*, XLVIII, 565–76 (Nov., 1912). A highly "patriotic" account of the poet; points to his use of native source-material; suggests likenesses to Poe.

Nevinson, H. W. "The Dark Rosaleen," *North American Review*, CLXXIX, 252–62 (Aug., 1904). Provides a history of the composition of the poem, discussing it as a representation of Mangan's spirit of revolt.

O'Donoghue, D. J. *The Life and Writings of James Clarence Mangan.* (Fitzpatrick: Chicago, 1897.) Written in the belief that Mangan is "probably the greatest poet Ireland has ever produced"; wherever possible he is allowed to tell his own story through his letters, poems, etc.

Sillard, P. A. "Clarence Mangan and His Poetry," *Westminster Review*, CXLIX, 648–54 (June, 1898). Provides a brief sketch of the poet's life, commenting on his translations from German poetry; insists upon the need of judging his poetry from a knowledge of the whole of it.

Williams, A. M. "James Clarence Mangan," in *The Poets and Poetry of Ireland.* (Osgood: Boston, 1881.) Offers a brief sketch commenting on the poems, followed by four selections.

NOTES

"His work, at its worst, has the faults inseparable from the conditions under which it was wrought: it is stumbling, pert, diffuse, distraught. He had in full that racial luxuriance and fluency which, wonderful to see in its happier action, tend always to carry a poet off his feet, and wash him into the deep seas of slovenliness. . . . At his best he is astonishingly original and modern; and he is cosmopolitan, after the manner of the Irish, who have the wit to be, at call,

'like almost anything,
Or a yellow albatross!'

His mind is liberal and impassioned, full of the willful strength which repels discipline. His wild excellence looks best confronted with the sweet and adroit lays of his townsman and contemporary, Thomas Moore: these two stand asunder at the poles of the lyric world." (Louise Imogen Guiney, in *Atlantic Monthly*, November, 1891.)

Page 735. DARK ROSALEEN

"*Dark Rosaleen*" says Lionel Johnson, "ranks with the great lyrics of the world; it is one of the fairest and fiercest in its perfection of imagery and rhythm: here is the chivalry of a nation's faith, struck of a sudden into the immortality of music."

Miss Louise Imogen Guiney says of this poem: "Mangan's happiest witchwork is in *My Dark Rosaleen*. This was written by a worthy contemporary of Shakespeare's, an unknown minstrel of the Tyrconnel chief, Hugh the Red O'Donnell, who put on the lips of his lord, as addressed to Ireland, the love-name of Roisin Dubh, the Black-haired Little Rose. More exact versions of this symbolical masterpiece have since been made, but the stormy beauty of Mangan's lines does away with consideration of law and order."

17. *Erne.* The name of a river and two lakes in Ireland.

Page 737.

O'HUSSEY'S ODE TO THE MAGUIRE

In this poem Eochadh O'Hussey, last hereditary bard of the Maguires and one of the most distinguished poets of his time [he died about 1630], laments the disastrous Munster campaign conducted in the war at the end of Queen Elizabeth's reign by Hugh Maguire, Lord of Fermanagh. Dr. Hyde, in his *Literary History of Ireland*, says: "When it is remembered that O'Hussey composed this poem in the most difficult and artificial of metres . . . it will be seen how much Mangan has gained by his free and untrammelled metre, and what technical difficulties fettered O'Hussey's art, and lent glory to his triumph over them." This "Ode," writes Lionel Johnson, "burns with a noble ferocity in lines of the highest Homeric simplicity and grandeur. Here is the true Mangan of greatness and of grandeur."

Page 741. SHAPES AND SIGNS

12. *the red cup drowns.* "Born to unhappiness, dowered with a melancholy temperament and a drifting will . . . [Mangan] found joys . . . in alcohol and opium."

THOMAS MOORE

BIBLIOGRAPHY

I. WORKS

Complete Poetical Works. 2 vols. (Crowell: New York, 1895.) A reprint of the collection made by the poet himself; includes a biographical sketch by N. H. Dole.

Poetical Works, ed. by A. D. Godley. (Oxford University Press: 1910.) This edition is recommended for its very capable introduction.

Selected Poems, ed. by C. L. Falkiner. Golden Treasury series. (Macmillan: New York, 1903.) The best book of selections from the poetry.

Irish Melodies and Songs, ed. by S. L. Gwynn. The Muses' Library. (Dutton: New York, 1908.) The most convenient edition of this important material.

Tom Moore's Diary, ed. by J. B. Priestley. (Cambridge University Press: 1925.) A selection which provides a fairly comprehensive account of Moore's thirty years of ramblings; includes an introduction giving the biographical setting.

II. BIOGRAPHY AND CRITICISM

Gunning, J. P. *Moore: Poet and Patriot*. (Gill: Dublin, 1900.) A eulogistic study of Moore's life, emphasizing his service to Ireland in giving voice to her national aspirations; his public career is seen as an attempt to carry out the ideals set forth in his writings.

Gwynn, S. L. *Thomas Moore*. English Men of Letters series. (Macmillan: New York, 1924.) A good brief biography, centering upon the facts of the poet's life, with little critical comment: to be read with the Life by Symington.

Symington, A. J. *Thomas Moore, His Life and Works*. (Harper: New York, 1880.) A recommended biography, stressing the poet's works; complementary with the Life by Gwynn.

III. ARTICLES FROM BOOKS AND PERIODICALS

Garnett, Richard. "Thomas Moore," in *Essays of an Ex-Librarian*. (Dodd: New York, 1901.) Endeavors to redeem Moore from his current neglect by calling attention to his brilliant versatility; shows that Moore, among many greater contemporaries, best illustrates the taste and spirit of his own generation.

Gosse, Edmund. "Tom Moore in Wiltshire," in *Leaves and Fruit*. (Scribner: New York, 1927.) Comments on the poet's great contemporary following; reviews the merits of Priestley's edition of the *Diary*.

Mortimer, Raymond. "Thomas Moore," *London Mercury*, V, 476–86 (Mar., 1922). Calls attention to the great reputation Moore enjoyed in his day, briefly reviewing his life, with a glance at his unlucky participation in Irish politics.

Saintsbury, George. "Moore," in *Essays in English Literature*, First Series. (Scribner: New York, 1890.) After a brief biographical notice this study evaluates *Lalla Rookh* as a "very respectable poem of the second rank"; praises the shorter lyrics, which best reveal Moore's sensitive ear.

Strahan, J. A. "Byron's Biographer," *Blackwood's*, CCXV, 574–82 (Apr., 1924). A favorable review of Moore's *Life of Byron*, with a backward glance at the associations of the two men.

Vincent, L. H. "A Regency Satirist," in *Dandies and Men of Letters*. (Houghton: Boston, 1913.) Reminds us of the wit of the *Two-Penny Post-Bag* and *The Fudge Family in Paris*.

NOTES

"It is to the Cavalier Lyrics, no doubt, that Moore at his best comes nearest; never within recognisable distance of any Elizabethan work, and never near enough to the good work of the Restoration for the comparison to be seriously made. He has their fluency, but none of their gentlemanly restraint; touches of their crudity, but none of their straightforwardness; and of their fine taste, nothing, and nothing of the quality of mind which lurks under all their disguises. In Moore's songs there is no 'fundamental brain-work'; they have no base in serious idea or in fine emotion. The sensations they render are trivial in themselves, or become so in the rendering; there is a continual effervescence, but no meditation and no ecstasy. Between this faint local heat of the senses and the true lyric rapture there is a great gulf. Moore brims over with feeling, and his feeling is quick, honest, and generous. But he never broods over his feeling until he has found his way down to its roots; the song strikes off from the surface like the spurt of a match; there is no deep fire or steady flame. He never realised the dignity of song or of the passions. In his verse he was amorous, but a foolish lover; shrewd, but without wisdom; honest, but without nobility; a breeder of easy tears and quick laughter. He sang for his evening, not his day; and he had his reward, but must go without the day's wages." (Arthur Symons, in *The Romantic Movement in English Poetry*.)

For Wordsworth's comment on Moore see text page 139. Byron and Leigh Hunt did not share Wordsworth's opinion. Byron dedicated *The Corsair* to Moore as "the poet of all circles and the idol of his own," and Hunt, in his *Feast of the Poets*, admitted him, along with Campbell, Scott, and Southey, as worthy to dine with Apollo.

Page 741.   IRISH MELODIES

"All the depths which, though shallow enough, existed in his [Moore's] nature, were stirred by this work [the *Irish Melodies*], and among the songs he wrote to Ireland's music his best poetry lies—the only poetry of his which will continue to justly please mankind. 'It was,' he says, 'in working the rich mines of my country's melodies that my humble labours as a poet have derived their sole lustre and value.' These songs have variety; they touch both tragedy and comedy. They drink, they dance and sing; they march to battle, they mourn over the dead; they follow the patriot to the scaffold and to exile; they sing the scenery, the legends, the sorrows, and the mirth of Ireland. . . . He did more for Ireland than we think. He made her music charm the world. He brought by his singing of the Melodies . . . the wrongs and sorrows of Ireland into the ears and consideration of that class in society which had not listened to or cared for them before."

(Stopford A. Brooke, in *A Treasury of Irish Poetry*.)

"The Celtic strain in Moore may be adulterated and artificialized; but there is enough of the genuine mood to make parts of the 'Irish Melodies' great poetry. How could we expect compelling sincerity in narrative verse or satire from the man who wrote: 'Music—the only art for which, in my opinion, I was born with a real natural love; my poetry, such as it is, having sprung out of my deep feeling for music.' . . . It may be that his Irish patriotism loved the sound of the harp better than that of the bullet; but the great musician is heard in his lyrics even if the great man is not, and the witchery of song is there." (Frederick E. Pierce, in *English Romantic Generation*.)

Page 742. OH, BREATHE NOT HIS NAME

The subject of this poem was Robert Emmet (1778–1803), an Irish patriot who had been a student companion of Moore's at Trinity College, Dublin. Following his years at Trinity, Emmet tried to enlist the aid or at least the sympathy of Napoleon and Talleyrand in his effort to free Ireland from English rule. Failing in this, he returned to Ireland and led a revolt against the English viceroy in Dublin castle. His forces repulsed, Emmet fled to the Wicklow mountains. He lay in concealment there for a few days and then ventured forth to visit his fiancée, Sarah Curran. He was arrested, condemned, and hanged. A speech which he made just before his execution is often pointed out as a brilliant example of fiery patriotism. See Southey's *The Speech of Robert Emmet*, text p. 785. The subject of Moore's song, *She Is Far from the Land* (text p. 744), was Emmet's Irish sweetheart, Sarah Curran.

THE HARP THAT ONCE THROUGH
TARA'S HALLS

Tara, in county Meath, northwest of Dublin, was an ancient capital of Irish monarchs and hence a center of romantic tradition.

RICH AND RARE WERE THE GEMS SHE WORE

This ballad is said to have been suggested to Moore by the following passage from Warner's *History of Ireland:* "The people were inspired with such a spirit of honour, virtue, and religion, by the great example of Brien, and by his excellent administration that, as a proof of it, we are informed that a young lady of great beauty, adorned with jewels and a costly dress, undertook a journey alone, from one end of the kingdom to the other, with a wand only in her hand, at the top of which was a ring of exceeding great value; and such an impression had the laws and government of this

Monarch made on the minds of all the people that no attempt was made upon her honour, nor was she robbed of her clothes or her jewels."

Brien, of "the great example," was the famous monarch, Brien Borombe, known as "Brien the Brave," who was slain in the battle of Clontarf early in the eleventh century. Before he was finally killed he had won twenty-five victories from the Danes.

Page 743. THE MEETING OF THE WATERS

In the summer of 1807 Moore visited the place of "the meeting of the waters," a beautiful vale between Rathdrum and Arklow, in county Wicklow. The "bright waters" that meet there are the rivers Avon and Avoca.

LET ERIN REMEMBER THE DAYS OF OLD

3. *Malachi.* In an encounter with the Danes, Malachi, an Irish king of the tenth century, slew two Danish champions. As trophies of his victory he took from one of the warriors his sword and from the other a collar of gold.

6. *Led the Red-Branch Knights.* "Military orders of knights existed very early in Ireland. According to the Irish historian, O'Hallaran, an hereditary order of Chivalry, known as the Knights of the Red Branch, was established in Ulster long before the birth of Christ.

9–12. *On Lough Neagh's bank*, et seq. According to old tradition Lough Neagh, a lake in county Antrim, had been originally a fountain. It suddenly overflowed and inundated a region some seventeen miles long, burying the round, ecclesiastical towers, deep under its waters.

THE SONG OF FIONNUALA

Fionnuala and her brothers, the "Children of Lir," were turned into swans by the enchantments of Aoife, their stepmother. For centuries they dwelt on Irish waters, awaiting the sound of St. Patrick's bell (announcing the coming of Christianity), which alone could break the enchantment. When the bell finally rang, they resumed human shape, but they were so old and feeble that they immediately died. The Moyle, one of the waters on which they dwelt, is a channel between Scotland and the northeast corner of Ireland.

In Gaelic mythology Lir was the god of the sea. He is probably to be identified with Llyr, the sea god of the ancient Britons, whose name survives in Shakespeare's *King Lear*.

Page 744. BELIEVE ME, IF ALL THOSE ENDEARING YOUNG CHARMS

When lovers of song say that Moore is famous for the large number of "old favorites" which he wrote, they have in mind such melodies as this poem, *'Tis the Last Rose of Summer* (p.

744), and *Oft, in the Stilly Night* (p. 746). Whatever charge of sentimentality critics may bring against such songs and melodies, it is likely that they will continue to rank high, as generations come and go, among the "old favorites" of the people.

SHE IS FAR FROM THE LAND

See note above to *Oh, Breathe Not His Name.*

Page 746. I WISH I WAS BY THAT DIM LAKE

Dr. Campbell, in his *Strictures on the Ecclesiastical and Literary History of Ireland* writes of "that dim lake": "In the midst of the gloomy regions of Donegal lay a lake which was to become the mystic theatre of this fabled and intermediate state. In the lake were several islands; but one of them was dignified with that called the Mouth of Purgatory, which, during the dark ages, attracted the notice of all Christendom, and was the resort of penitents and pilgrims from almost every country in Europe.

"It was one of the most dismal and dreary spots in the north, almost inaccessible, through deep glens and rugged mountains, frightful with impending rocks, and the hollow murmurs of the western winds in dark caverns, peopled only with such fantastic beings as the mind however gay, is, from strange association, wont to appropriate to such gloomy scenes."

NATIONAL AIRS

In the Advertisement with which Moore introduced his *National Airs* he said: "It is Cicero, I believe, who says *natura ad modos ducimur* [by nature we are led to melody]: and the abundance of wild, indigenous airs, which almost every country, except England, possesses, sufficiently proves the truth of his assertion. The lovers of this simple, but interesting kind of music, are here presented with the first number of a collection, which, I trust, their contributions will enable us to continue. A pretty air without words resembles one of those *half* creatures of Plato, which are described as wandering in search of the remainder of themselves through the world. To supply this other half, by uniting with congenial words the many fugitive melodies which have hitherto had none,—or only such as are unintelligible to the generality of their hearers,—is the object and ambition of the present work. Neither is it our intention to confine ourselves to what are strictly called National Melodies, but, wherever we meet with any wandering and beautiful air, to which poetry has not yet assigned a worthy home, we shall venture to claim it as an *estray* swan, and enrich our humble Hippocrene with its song."

HARK! THE VESPER HYMN IS STEALING

5. *Jubilate.* "Be ye joyful."

Page 747.   CHILD'S SONG

9. *Aden's land.* Aden is a variant of Eden.

WILLIAM MOTHERWELL

BIBLIOGRAPHY

WORKS AND CRITICISM

Poetical Works, ed. by J. M'Conechy. (Miller: New York, 1877.) The best available edition for student use, prefaced by an introduction.

Minstrelsy, Ancient and Modern, Edited by William Motherwell. (Gardner: Paisley, 1873.) A preface reviews the work of earlier collectors; provides some variant readings and tunes; includes 72 pieces.

Stoddard, R. H. "William Motherwell," in *Under the Evening Lamp.* (Scribner: New York, 1892.) Undertakes a brief biography of the poet, concluding with judicious criticism of his poetry.

NOTES

BONNIE GEORGE CAMPBELL

However real the poetic ability of Motherwell may have been, his contribution to romantic poetry was very slight in so far as his own original work is concerned. This little lament of an early century, according to Professor F. B. Gummere, is the product of Motherwell's combination of several ballad versions—perhaps as many as six—of the warrior Campbell's tragic story. Motherwell said that the poem was "probably a lament for one of the adherents of the house of Argyle, who fell in the battle of Glenlivat, stricken on Thursday, the third day of October, 1594 years." The work in which he printed his exquisite shaping of the scattered versions was *Minstrelsy Ancient and Modern*, "a judicious collection of ballads," published in 1827.

15. *Toom.* Empty.
19. *Big.* Build.

THOMAS LOVE PEACOCK

BIBLIOGRAPHY

I. WORKS

Works, ed. by H. F. B. Brett-Smith and C. E. Jones. 10 vols. Halliford Edition. (Wells: New York, 1928.) Undoubtedly the authoritative edition of the complete works; Vols. VI and VII contain the poems and plays.

Works, ed. by Henry Cole. 3 vols. (Bentley: Lon-

don, 1888.) Includes a preface by Lord Houghton and a brief biography by Edith Nicolls
(granddaughter of Peacock): Vol. III contains
the poetry.

Poems, ed. by R. B. Johnson. The Muses' Library.
(Dutton: New York, 1906.) The most easily
available edition of the poetry; the editor supplies a biographical preface.

Selections, ed. by H. F. B. Brett-Smith. (Methuen:
London, 1928.) An excellent introduction provides a biographical review, followed by a judicious appraisal of Peacock's work in prose
and verse.

Selections, ed. by W. H. Helm. Regent Library.
(Herbert: London, 1911.) The aim of this edition is to illustrate Peacock's powers as a satirist
and to show the perfection of his style; includes
an introductory sketch of his life, together with
brief descriptive and critical comments on each
selection.

The Four Ages of Poetry, ed. by H. F. B. Brett-
Smith. Percy Reprints. (Blackwell: Oxford,
1923.) Gives Peacock's celebrated outline of the
development of poetry; includes also Shelley's
reply *A Defence of Poetry* and Browning's
Essay on Shelley.

Letters to Edward Hookham and Percy B. Shelley,
ed. by Richard Garnett. (Bibliographic Society:
Boston, 1910.) Includes also fragments of unpublished MSS.

II. BIOGRAPHY AND CRITICISM

Able, A. H., 3rd. *George Meredith and Thomas Love
Peacock*. (University of Pennsylvania Press:
1933.) A methodical survey of the generally admitted influences, which are found to be most
abundant in Peacock's effect upon Meredith's
prose, although scattered poetical borrowings
are also noted.

Freeman, A. M. *Thomas Love Peacock: A Critical
Survey*. (Kennerley: New York, 1911.) Devotes
a liberal amount of space to Peacock's relations
with Shelley; chapter II discusses the earlier
poems.

Priestley, J. B. *Thomas Love Peacock*. English Men
of Letters series. (Macmillan: New York, 1927.)
An able brief biography, assembling all of the
accepted facts, with a good chapter on the
poetry, which is paradoxically held to be
achieved only when Peacock "ceased to be a
poet."

Van Doren, C. C. *Life of Thomas Love Peacock*.
(Dutton: New York, 1911.) The first, and
probably most reliable, biography, now out of
print; satire and sensitiveness are shown to be
the dual forces in Peacock's life; chapters II,
VI, and X are useful in the study of the poetry.

III. ARTICLES FROM BOOKS AND PERIODICALS

(Anonymous). "The Complete Satirist," *Littell's
Living Age*, CCLXXXIII, 440–4 (Nov., 1914).
Chiefly a review of the novels, with some refer-
ence to the poems contained therein.

Burdett, Osbert. "Thomas Love Peacock, 1785–
1866," *London Mercury*, VIII, 21–32 (May,
1923). Reviews the biographical data; names
"In the Days of Old" (in *Crotchet Castle*) as
Peacock's "one true poem."

Burdett, Osbert. "Peacock the Epicurean," in
Critical Essays. (Faber: London, 1925.) Analyzes
the qualities for which we prize Peacock: his
wit, humor, and (above all) his sanity; shows his
singular position in English letters as a counter-
poise between the intensity of the romantics
and the materialism of Macaulay and the Ben-
thamite school.

Draper, J. W. "The Social Satires of Thomas Love
Peacock," *Modern Language Notes*, XXXIII,
456–63; XXXIV, 23–8 (Dec., 1918; Jan., 1919).
Discusses the intellectual pessimism of Peacock's prose.

Garnett, Richard. "Thomas Love Peacock," in
Essays of an Ex-Librarian. (Dodd: New York,
1901.) Able and well-balanced, this essay is
easily one of the best short accounts of Peacock's life, considered from all sides—personal,
public, and literary.

Saintsbury, George. "Peacock," in *Essays in
English Literature*, First Series. (Scribner: New
York, 1890.) Provides a sketch of the biographical data; comments chiefly on the novels, but
quotes with praise many of the songs they
contain.

Stoddard, R. H. "Thomas Love Peacock," in
Under the Evening Lamp. (Scribner: New York,
1892.) While admitting that the poet will never
be popular, insists upon his sure lyrical touch
and his prevailing sense of humor.

Vincent, L. H. "Thomas Love Peacock," in *Dandies and Men of Letters*. (Houghton: Boston,
1913.) Gives a racy biographical review, the
literary comment touching chiefly on the novels.

Wright, Herbert. "The Associations of Thomas
Love Peacock with Wales," in *Studies of the
English Association*, XII. (Oxford University
Press: 1926.) Shows influence of walking tours,
beginning in 1810, upon Peacock's early verse
and the lyrics in the novels.

NOTES

"He possessed a fine lyrical gift both sad and
joyous, and—what is perhaps even more rare—
a positive genius for writing ballads. The
greater number of these were introduced into
his delightful novels, and have been seldom
detached from their context though a few of
the best appeared with other verse. . . . In
lyrics and ballads Peacock entirely escaped the
pernicious influences of the school which apparently directed his more serious attempts in
verse. Though still impervious to current influences, he wrote from an obviously spontaneous and personal inspiration with original
genius. Lyrical excellence eludes definition;
but Peacock exhibited its essential qualities
by the tuneful expression of single ideas or
moods in simple language. He sings of love or
grief with deep and genuine feeling or natural
gaiety: he never obscures or weakens his effect
by involved metaphor or over-subtlety. The
vigour, restraint, and directness of style per-
fects a form dictated by pure emotion. His
ballads, whether satirical or merely narrative,

are entirely free from the spurious archaisms and conscious simplicity of most modern examples. Their racy vigour betrays neither pose nor effort, but clearly arises from natural energy of thought and fluency. . . . The lyrics and ballads of Thomas Love Peacock must always save his memory from oblivion. . . ." (R. Brimley Johnson, in *The Poems of Thomas Love Peacock*.)

Page 748.   THE GRAVE OF LOVE

Although the date of composition of this poem is given in most texts as 1806, there seems to be some doubt as to the exact year. Mr. Brimley Johnson, in his edition of Peacock's *Poems*, lists the poem with those that are dated 1806, but says that it was written *after* that year. The character of the poem is such that it seems to belong in a group—others of which are *Newark Abbey*, *Remember Me*, and *Al Mio Primiero Amore*—which were inspired by the poet's memory of the "beautiful [unnamed] young lady" to whom he became engaged when he was still a very young man, and from whom he was separated in 1807 "by underhand interference of a third person." The "beautiful young lady" speedily married another man after the breaking off of her engagement with Peacock and soon thereafter died. Peacock's married life with Jane Gryffydh, of Welsh ancestry (need it be remarked?), was long and happy, but apparently he never forgot his early passion. The heroines of much of his fiction are "commonly adumbrations of his early love," and, as has been said above, there is a group of poems of which she is the subject. He "always wore a locket with her hair in it," and for some weeks before his death, which occurred more than sixty years after their separation, she was a figure in his dreams.

FOR THE SLENDER BEECH AND THE
SAPLING OAK

Of Peacock's novels, from one of which—*Maid Marian*—this and the following song are taken, Richard Garnett says: "They owe much of their charm to the simple and melodious lyrics with which they are interspersed, a striking contrast to the frigid artificiality of Peacock's more ambitious attempts in poetry."
The Slender Beech and the Sapling Oak is recited to Sir Ralph by Brother Michael at the end of chapter II. Brother Michael has just been telling Sir Ralph that the Lady Matilda and her lover are incurably sylvan; that "they will now never hear matins but those of the lark, nor reverence vaulted aisle but that of the greenwood canopy."
A Gray, Gray Friar, from chapter IV, is sung mainly by "a catch-singing" friar, "warm with canary, and in his singing vein." After the first

stanza the Lady Matilda chimes in with the friar, and the two go rollicking through the song together.

THE WAR-SONG OF DINAS VAWR

The Misfortunes of Elphin, from which this song is taken, is a parody of the Arthurian legends. In chapter XI, Taliesin, a young bard who is on his way to visit King Arthur at Caer Lleon, has arrived at the castle of Dinas Vawr, which Melvas, a king from beyond the Severn, has taken by force. Taliesin is entertained by the heroes of Melvas who, Peacock writes, "were celebrating their own exploits in sundry choruses, especially in that which follows (*The War-Song of Dinas Vawr*), which is here put upon record as being the quintessence of all the war songs that ever were written, and the sum and substance of all the appetencies, tendencies, and consequences of military glory."
Mr. J. B. Priestley, in *Thomas Love Peacock*, says: "All the other verses in the book pale before this chorus, whose mingled brevity and droll heartiness point the satire. . . . This 'war song' gives the key to the whole story, which displays the same mingling of drollery and irony."
9. *Dyfed's richest valley*. Dyfed was the British name for southwest Wales.
37. *Ednyfed*. Probably this monarch never lived.

WINTHROP MACKWORTH PRAED

BIBLIOGRAPHY

I. WORKS

Poems, ed. by F. Greenslet. (Houghton: Boston, 1909.) Contains the best selections for student use; includes a brief introduction.
Poems. 2 vols. (Moxon: London, 1864.) A matter-of-fact memoir by Rev. Derwent Coleridge provides an introduction.
Select Poems, ed. by A. D. Godley. (Frowde: London, 1909.) A recommended book of selections, supplied with an introduction by the editor.
Poems, ed. by F. Cooper. Canterbury Poets. (Scott: London, 1888.) A convenient book of the more popular poems; includes an introductory notice by the editor.
Political and Occasional Poems, ed. by G. Young. (Ward: London, 1889.) Includes a brief introduction.

II. BIOGRAPHY AND CRITICISM

Hewlett, H. G. "Poets of Society," *Contemporary Review*, XX, 238–68 (July, 1872). Remarks unsuccessful imitations of Byron's style; dwells upon Praed's connection with *The Brazen Head* and other fleeting periodicals.

Smith, G. B. "English Fugitive Poets," in *Poets and Novelists*. (Appleton: New York, 1876.) Incidentally discusses Praed as one in the long tradition of society-verse, which began with Horace and Anacreon.

Saintsbury, George. "Praed," in *Essays in English Literature*, First Series. (Scribner: New York, 1890.) Sketches the biographical data, finds the best of the poet in his light verse, "playing with literature and with life."

NOTES

"Within its limits, the art with which . . . [Praed] has clothed them [his satirical sketches] is perfect. The portraiture of character is as delicate, the representation of movement as graphic, the dialogue as natural, the style as racy, and the versification as smooth as can be desired. The observation of life is quite superficial, but it pretends to be no more; and where thought and feeling would have been out of place, their absence is not remarked. As a piece of compendious word-painting it would be difficult to match the following [from *Good Night to the Season*]:

'Good night to the season!—the dances,
  The fillings of hot little rooms,
The glancings of rapturous glances,
  The fancyings of fancy costumes;
The pleasures which fashion makes duties,
  The praisings of fiddles and flutes,
The luxury of looking at beauties,
  The tedium of talking to mutes;
The female diplomatists, planners
  Of matches for Laura and Jane;
The ice of her ladyship's answers,
  The ice of his lordship's champagne.'"

(Henry G. Hewlett, in *The Contemporary Review*, July, 1872.)

Page 751.   TO ——

39. *Burgundy*. Any of the red and white wines made within the former Duchy of Burgundy, France.

LOVE AT A ROUT

20. *crooks*. Crooks may be pot hooks or, what is more likely, the hinges of a gate or door.
34. *Petrarch*. Francesco Petrarca (1304–1374) was an Italian poet.
60. *In Ettrick, than in Portman Square*. Ettrick, in Scotland, was formerly a forest and hunting ground. It is now a pastoral tract. Portman Square is between Orchard, Oxford, and Baker streets, London.
62. *Sherwood, as in Piccadilly*. Sherwood was an ancient royal forest, chiefly in Nottinghamshire, England. Remains of it may be seen in Mansfield, Rotherham, and vicinity. Picca-

dilly is a London street of shops and fashionable dwelling-houses—running east and west—extending from the top of the Haymarket to Hyde Park Corner.

Page 753.   THE VICAR

3, 6. *Darnel Park was Darnel Waste . . . St. Mary's Hill . . . Sandy Thicket*. Apparently these names are so limited in their application or the places which they signify are so little known and unimportant that they have escaped the vigilance of the usually accepted authorities on place names.
18. *winsome marrow*. Cheerful and merry companion; here the wife.
20. *ponderous Barrow*. Isaac Barrow (1630–1677) was one of the greatest of the Anglican preachers of the Caroline period. His sermons reached inordinate lengths.
22. *Pundit*. A Brahman versed in the laws and religion of the Hindus.
46. *Deist*. One who believes that God is neither immanent in nature nor revealed in history or religious experience.
47. *Levite*. Literally, one of the tribe or family of Levi. Here one of the Jewish faith.
52. *From Jerome, or from Athanasius*. Jerome (340?–420) was a Latin father of the church. Athanasius (296?–373) was a Greek father of the church.
64. *nothings for Sylvanus Urban*. Sylvanus Urban, Gent., was the fictitious name under which the *Gentleman's Magazine* (London) was edited to indicate that it was concerned with town and country affairs.
83. *the rule of three*. The rule for finding the fourth term of a proportion when three are given.
84. *Cat's cradle*, et seq. Various games.
88. *Augustine*. St. Augustine (354–430), bishop of Hippo.
103–4. *Hic jacet*, etc. "Here lies William Brown, a man to whom some honor is due." Or, if one wishes to translate it in something of the jingle of the poem:

"Here lies the body of William Brown,
  A man entitled to some renown."

Page 754.

THE BELLE OF THE BALL-ROOM

MOTTO. *Il faut juger*, etc. "Women should be judged from their shoes and stockings to their hats exclusively: just as one measures a fish between the tail and the head."
4. *Chitty*. Joseph Chitty (1776–1841), an English jurist and legal writer.
31. *Locke*. John Locke (1632–1704), an English philosopher, author of *Essay Concerning Human Understanding*.
32. *Little*. A pseudonym of Thomas Moore.

56. *Baron Rothschild.* Nathaniel Meyer de Rothschild (1777–1836), a London financier.

61. *Handel.* Georg Friedrich Handel (1685–1759), a German musical composer.

62. *Catalani.* Angelica Catalani (1779–1849) was an Italian singer.

70. *Fierce odes.* This may be an allusion to Coleridge's *Fire, Famine, and Slaughter.*

71. *Prince Leboo.* Jean Louis Joseph Lebeau, a distinguished Belgian diplomat, who in 1830–31 carried on important negotiations in England.

Page 755. THE TALENTED MAN

9. *Brazen Nose College.* One of the colleges at Oxford University.

24. *Chez nous.* "With us."

28. *Trevelyan.* Raleigh Trevelyan (1781–1865), an English writer of slight importance.

58. *Entre nous.* "Between us."

Vincent, L. H. "A Giver of Breakfasts," in *Dandies and Men of Letters.* (Houghton: Boston, 1913.) A chatty review of the last 52 years of Rogers's life, with passing comments on his popularity, literary and culinary.

NOTES

Page 757.

"Rogers's rank in English poetry is lower than that of any of his contemporaries. . . . He has one peculiar distinction, that of exemplifying beyond almost any other poet what a moderate poetic endowment can effect when prompted by ardent ambition and guided by refined taste. . . . His inspiration was genuine as far as it went, and it emanated from a store of sweetness and tenderness actually existing in the poet's nature." (Richard Garnett, in *Dictionary of National Biography.*)

SAMUEL ROGERS

BIBLIOGRAPHY

I. WORKS

Poetical Works, ed. by Edward Bell. (Macmillan: New York, 1892.) The most satisfactory edition, including a prefatory memoir.

Reminiscences and Table-Talk, collected by G. H. Powell. (Johnson: London, 1903.) Provides a wealth of chitchat about Rogers and his literary and convivial acquaintances.

II. BIOGRAPHY AND CRITICISM

Clayden, P. W. *Rogers and His Contemporaries.* 2 vols. (Smith: London, 1889.) Vol. I of this work was originally issued (1887) as *The Early Life of Samuel Rogers;* Vol. II covers the St. James Place period, beginning with the poet's fortieth year.

Hayward, Abraham. "Samuel Rogers," in *Biographical and Critical Essays,* I. (Longmans: London, 1858.) Reviews *Table-Talk,* summarizes the poet's literary career; the critical comments reflect favorably on his contemporary fame, some of his works being compared with Spenser's and Wordsworth's.

Mason, E. T. "Rogers," in *Personal Traits of British Authors,* I. (Scribner: New York, 1885.) A collection of numerous brief contemporary and later sketches.

Roberts, R. E. *Samuel Rogers and His Circle.* (Dutton: New York, 1910.) A wholly satisfactory assembly of the biographical facts, with many references to significant background events and characters.

Symons, Arthur. "Samuel Rogers," in *The Romantic Movement in English Poetry.* (Dutton: New York, 1909.) Denies to Rogers the name of poet, calling him "a pleasantly old-fashioned writer of verse"; names *Italy* his best work, points to his wide literary associations.

SIR WALTER SCOTT

BIBLIOGRAPHY

I. WORKS

Poems and Ballads, ed. by Andrew Lang. 6 vols. (Estes: Boston, 1902.) This limited edition is recommended for its excellent notes and introductory material, supplied by the editor.

Poetical Works. 4 vols. (Lippincott: Philadelphia, 1900.) A reprint of the Edinburgh edition (Oliphant: 1898), containing the poet's introductions and notes, together with further annotations by his son-in-law, J. G. Lockhart.

Complete Poetical Works, ed. by H. E. Scudder. Cambridge Edition. (Houghton: Boston, 1900.) A good one-volume edition, providing a biographical introduction.

Poems and Plays. 2 vols. (Dutton: New York, 1927.) A recommended cheap edition, equipped with a brief introduction by Andrew Lang; some notes are provided for each volume.

The Heart of Scott's Poetry, ed. by John H. Holmes. (Oxford University Press: 1932.) The best book of selections.

Minstrelsy of the Scottish Border, ed. by T. F. Henderson. 4 vols. (Blackwood: Edinburgh, 1902.) The best collection for student use; Vol. I has a fine critical introduction by Alfred Noyes who is also the editor of a one-volume abridgment (Stokes: New York, 1913).

Journal, 1825–32, ed. by David Douglas. 2 vols. (Harper: New York, 1900.) Invaluable as a guide to the intimate study of the man during the period of his greatest activity.

Private Letter-Books: Selections from the Abbotsford MSS, ed. by Wilfred Partington. (Hodder: London, 1930.) A book of unique usefulness to the student of Scott's life, impressing the fact of the writer's wide range of interests, his manliness and generosity; includes a letter from Hugh Walpole, the present owner of the MSS.

II. BIOGRAPHY AND CRITICISM

Baikie, James. *The Charm of the Scott Country.* (Black: London, 1927.) An attractive, finely illustrated volume, which does full justice to the Border country, the scene of much of Scott's best poetry; rich in legend and ballad-lore.

Ball, Margaret. *Sir Walter Scott as a Critic of Literature.* (Columbia University Press: 1907.) A scholarly survey of an important phase of Scott's work, hitherto (and later) neglected: his successes and shortcomings are discussed in connection with the following fields: Ballad, Romance, Drama, the 17th century, and the 18th century. The appendix includes an annotated bibliography of Scott's writings.

Brewer, J. W. *Shakespere's Influence on Sir Walter Scott.* (Cornhill: Boston, 1925.) Shakespeare is here read as an important factor in much of Scott's work; the evidence is abundantly produced, but the deductions seem to bear toward exaggeration.

Buchan, John. *Sir Walter Scott.* (Cassell: London, 1932.) This (the fifth) edition is an inexpensive form of one of the best recent estimates of Scott's work and influence; the criticism of the poetry is unoriginal but reliable.

Cecil, Lord David. *Sir Walter Scott.* (Constable: London, 1933.) Beginning with the admission that Scott's influence is declining, this study attempts to re-appraise his work and worth—largely in the field of his prose.

Crockett, W. S. *The Scott Country.* (Macmillan: New York, 1911.) Filled with appropriate illustrations, this literary guide provides the background for the study of Scott's life and work.

Grierson, H. J. C., ed. *Sir Walter Scott Today.* (Constable: London, 1932.) A centenary collection of six essays, including "Scott and Goethe" by Friedrich Gundolf: the two writers are represented as having a deep respect for each other's work, but without showing any actual literary indebtedness.

Hudson, W. H. *Sir Walter Scott.* (Sands: London, 1901.) A study of the life and poetry, valuable in giving a just estimate of Scott's place in the English romantic movement.

Hutton, R. H. *Sir Walter Scott.* English Men of Letters series. (Harper: New York, 1902.) A satisfactory brief biography: two chapters are devoted to sound criticism of Scott's poetry.

Lang, Andrew. *Sir Walter Scott.* Literary Lives series. (Scribner: New York, 1906.) A judicious short biography of Scott as poet and *prosateur:* an avowed abridgment of Lockhart's Life, but often outdoing its original in novelty and interest.

Lang, Andrew. *Sir Walter Scott and the Border Minstrelsy.* (Longmans: New York, 1910.) Attempts to prove that there is no ground for the suspicion of forgery in connection with the ballads, particularly *Auld Maitland*, which Scott obtained from Hogg and published in the sincere belief that they were genuine.

Lockhart, J. G. *Memoirs of the Life of Sir Walter Scott, Baronet.* 10 vols. (Black: Edinburgh, 1882.) Immediately recognized as the authoritative Life (original ed. 1839), this work has been frequently reprinted and abridged (Houghton: Boston, 1901, is recommended.)

Macintosh, W. *Scott and Goethe: German Influence on the Writings of Sir Walter Scott.* (Walker: Galashiels, 1925.) A rather uncritical survey of Scott's interest in German legend and folklore, which Scott never deeply absorbed; his translations and borrowings from Goethe are shown to be influential in his prose as well as in his poetry.

Pope-Hennessey, Una. *The Laird of Abbotsford.* (Putnam: New York, 1932.) Provides a picturesque personal history of Scott from the first attempts at poetry, but dwells upon the Abbotsford period and its disastrous conclusion.

Saintsbury, George. *Sir Walter Scott.* Famous Scots series. (Scribner: New York, 1897.) Not only a capable introduction to Scott, but an interesting and useful book to seasoned readers of his poetry and prose.

Stalker, Archibald. *The Intimate Life of Sir Walter Scott.* (Black: London, 1921.) A picture of the "joyous personal life" of Scott the man, drawn from many sources not available to earlier biographers; much is made of Scott's "first love"—an episode neglected by Lockhart.

Yonge, C. D. *Life of Sir Walter Scott.* Great Writers series. (Scott: London, 1888.) An interesting short biography.

III. ARTICLES FROM BOOKS

Brooke, Stopford A. "Sir Walter Scott," in *Studies in Poetry.* (Duckworth: London, 1920.) Discusses the contemporary effect of Scott's poetry and its relation to the older Scottish verse; finds his best verse in scattered lyrics.

Croce, Benedetto. "Walter Scott," in *European Literature in the Nineteenth Century.* (Knopf: New York, 1924.) Arraigns Scott's superficial taste in poetry; states that his "modest poetry" is found only in his novels.

Henderson, T. F. "Sir Walter Scott," in *The Cambridge History of English Literature*, XII. (Putnam: New York, 1916.) Recommended as a brief comprehensive survey of Scott as a poet and novelist.

Parrott, T. M. "The Last Minstrel," in *Studies of a Booklover.* (Pott: New York, 1904.) Reviews Scott's poetic career, remarking his interest in contemporary events; names him the "golden link that binds us to the middle ages."

Pierce, F. E. "The Popular Supremacy of Scott," in *Currents and Eddies in the English Romantic Generation.* (Yale University Press: 1918.) Traces Scott's career "from folk ballad to original ballad, from this to ballad narrative"; ascribes his popularity to his virile themes and his narrative ability.

Quiller-Couch, A. T. "Scott and Burns," in *Adventures in Criticism.* (Putnam: New York, 1925.) Admitting that Burns is "honored at the feast," maintains that Scott is "read by the fireside": agrees that Scott is inferior in depicting emotions.

Shairp, J. C. "The Homeric Spirit in Walter Scott," in *Aspects of Poetry.* (Houghton: Boston, 1891.) Surveying the growth of epics, maintains that Scott's poetic stimulus and growth were of a kind analogous to epic development: *Marmion* is taken as the best example.

Stevenson, R. L. "A Gossip on Romance," in

Memories and Portraits. (Scribner: New York, 1887.) Contains wholehearted praise by one of Scott's most distinguished literary followers.

Symons, Arthur. "Sir Walter Scott," in *The Romantic Movement in English Poetry.* (Dutton: New York, 1909.) Questions the poet's merit as a writer of war-songs; denominates him an "improviser in rhyme"—except for the song "Proud Maisie."

Woodberry, G. E. "Scott," in *Literary Essays.* (Harcourt: New York, 1920.) An enthusiastic appraisal of the work of Scott; claims for his poetry the merit of novelty and force; rebukes the sneer that Scott "pleases boys."

Wyndham, George. "Sir Walter Scott," in *Essays in Romantic Literature.* (Macmillan: London, 1919.) A reprint of a speech proposing the toast of honor at the fourteenth annual dinner of the Edinburgh Sir Walter Scott Club, Nov. 29, 1907. The tone and contents may be imagined.

IV. ARTICLES FROM PERIODICALS

Cook, Davidson, "Lockhart's Treatment of Scott's Letters," *Nineteenth Century,* CII, 382–98 (Sept., 1927). Accuses Lockhart of tampering with the text of the letters printed in his *Life;* the evidence is produced from the original MSS.

Emerson, O. F. "The Early Literary Life of Sir Walter Scott," *Journal of English and Germanic Philology,* XXIII, 29–62; 241–69; 389–417 (Jan., Apr., July, 1924). A scholarly review of Lockhart's account of the years 1796–1810: a number of errors are corrected (e.g., that it was in London, not Malta, that Stoddart heard Coleridge give the recitation from *Christabel,* from which Scott took an idea for his *Lay of the Last Minstrel*).

Haber, T. B. "The Chapter-Tags in the Waverley Novels," *Publications of the Modern Language Association,* XLV, 1140–9 (Dec., 1930). A comprehensive catalog of the chapter-tags, identifying some "Anonymous" verses; shows the beginning and significance of the "Old Play" and "Old Song" verses.

NOTES

Page 761.   THE LAY OF THE LAST MINSTREL

As a preface for the first edition of *The Lay of the Last Minstrel,* the "first considerable poem of his own composition," Scott wrote as follows: "The Poem, . . . is intended to illustrate the customs and manners which anciently prevailed on the Borders of England and Scotland. The inhabitants living in a state partly pastoral and partly warlike, and combining habits of constant depredation with the influence of a rude spirit of chivalry, were often engaged in scenes highly susceptible of poetical ornament. As the description of scenery and manners was more the object of the Author than a combined and regular narrative, the plan of the ancient Metrical Romance was adopted, which allows greater latitude, in this respect, than would be consistent with the dignity of a regular Poem. The same model offered other facilities, as it permits an occasional alteration of measure, which, in some degree, authorizes the change of rhythm in the text. The machinery, also adopted from popular belief, would have seemed puerile in a Poem which did not partake of the rudeness of the old Ballad, or Metrical Romance.

"For these reasons, the Poem was put into the mouth of an ancient Minstrel, the last of the race, who, as he is supposed to have survived the Revolution, might have caught somewhat of the refinement of modern poetry, without losing the simplicity of his original mode. The date of the Tale itself is about the middle of the sixteenth century, when most of the personages actually flourished. The time occupied by the action is Three Nights and Three Days."

The poem, which is based on an old border legend of the goblin page, Gilpin Horner, was written in honor of the Duchess of Buccleuch, of Branksome Hall on the River Teviot in Roxburghshire. The minstrel is singing in the presence of the Duchess and her ladies. Lockhart, Scott's son-in-law and biographer, said that there is a veiled autobiographic element in the poem—a distinct reference to a secret attachment which Scott cherished "from almost the dawn of the passion. This . . . was the early and innocent affection to which we owe the tenderest pages, not only of *Redgauntlet,* but of *The Lay of the Last Minstrel,* and of *Rokeby,* and which found its first expression in the little poem *The Violet.* In all of these works the heroine has certain distinctive features, drawn from one and the same haunting dream of his manly adolescence."

The original of these heroines of "certain distinctive features" was Williamina Stuart, whom Scott loved for many years. She married Sir William Forbes in 1799, and her death occurred in 1810. In November, 1827, after visiting Lady Jane Stuart, the aged mother of Miss Stuart, Scott wrote in his Journal: "I went to make another visit, and fairly softened myself like an old fool, with recalling old stories, till I was fit for nothing but shedding tears and repeating verses for the whole night." (For a detailed account of Scott and Miss Stuart see the eighth chapter of Lockhart's *Life of Scott* and Miss F. M. F. Skene's "Sir Walter Scott's First Love," in the *Century Magazine* for July, 1899.)

Page 761.   SWEET TEVIOT

2. *bale-fires.* Signal fires.
8. *Tweed.* A river in Scotland flowing east into the North Sea.
20. *great Dundee.* John Graham, of Claver-

house, Viscount of Dundee, was slain in the battle of Killiecrankie, 1689.

BREATHES THERE THE MAN

17. *Caledonia.* The ancient Latin name for Scotland, used poetically.
30. *Yarrow's streams.* See note to Words-worth's *Yarrow Unvisited,* above.
32. *Ettrick.* The Ettrick flows into the Tweed. The Teviot (l. 34) also flows into the Tweed.

Page 762. SONG OF ALBERT GRÆME

2. *The sun . . . wall.* This refrain is from an old Scottish song. Evidently the "English ladye bright" lived in Cumberland, a border county, where she would easily have come to know the "Scottish knight."

HAROLD'S SONG

7. *Castle Ravensheuch.* This castle was on the Firth of Forth, Fifeshire, Scotland. James III of England gave it to William St. Clair in 1471.
18. *Roslin.* The family seat of the St. Clairs in the county of Edinburgh, Scotland.
21. *the ring they ride.* A sport in which mounted riders, galloping at full speed, strive to drive their lances through rings suspended over the course on which they are riding.
32. *cavern'd Hawthornden.* A town in the county of Edinburgh, famous for its caves.

Page 763. MARMION

The poem, in six cantos, has to do with Marmion, a famous English knight—fictitious—whom Henry VIII sent to the Scottish court to discover the reason for James IV's preparation for war. A mysterious palmer acts as his guide from Norham Castle, on the Border, to Edinburgh. Before Marmion had been sent on King Henry's mission he had tired of Constance, a nun with whom he had had a love affair, and had made a base accusation against Sir Ralph de Wilton, the lover of Lady Clare, to whom his vagrant affections had turned after they left Constance. He had even fought with de Wilton in the lists and left him on the field for dead. The embassy to the Scottish court fails, Scotland declares war against England, and Marmion, his perfidy disclosed by his palmer guide, who turns out to be de Wilton, is slain in the battle of Flodden Field (1513).
The poem is significant for its beautiful introductions to the cantos, its moving songs, its "rich scenes of medieval pageantry," and for the "tumultuous battle-piece" with which it closes.
Scott wrote of the poem that his design was to apprise his readers, at the outset, of the date of his story, and to prepare them for the man-

ners of the age in which it was laid. He hoped, he said, that an attempt to point the manners of the feudal times upon a broader scale than that of *The Lay of the Last Minstrel* and in the course of a more interesting story, would not be unacceptable to the public.

THE SHEPHERD

104. *Arcadia's golden creed.* Arcadia was a mountainous and picturesque district of Greece, celebrated as the abode of a simple, pastoral people, dwelling in rural happiness.

LOCHINVAR

This ballad, the song of Lady Heron, is founded, in some slight degree, on a ballad called *Katharine Janfarie,* first published by Scott with the title *The Laird of Laminton,* in *The Minstrelsy of the Scottish Border* (1802). The names of the border families in the poem are traditional.
8. *Eske.* A river in Scotland near the border.
20. *Solway.* An inlet of the Irish Sea, between England and Scotland. Its tides rise swiftly.
32. *Galliard.* A gay, lively dance.
45. *Cannobie Lee* is on the Eske, in Dumfries-shire.

Page 764. CHRISTMAS

33. *stoled priest.* The priest wearing the vestment used in sacred functions.
56. *lusty brawn.* Flesh of the boar. Sometimes used for any kind of flesh used as food.
74. *Who lists may in their mumming see.* "It seems certain that the Mummers of England who (in Northumberland at least) used to go about in disguise to the neighboring houses, bearing the then useless ploughshare; and the *Guisards* of Scotland, not yet in total disuse, present, in some indistinct degree, a shadow of the old mysteries, which were the origin of the English drama. In Scotland (*me ipso teste*) [I myself have witnessed it], we were wont, during my boyhood, to take the characters of the apostles, at least of Peter, Paul, and Judas Iscariot, which last carried the bag in which the dole of our neighbor's plumcake was deposited. One played a Champion, and recited some traditional rhymes; another was

'Alexander, king of Macedon,
Who conquered all the world but Scotland alone;
When he came to Scotland his courage grew cold,
To see a little nation courageous and bold.'

These, and many such verses, were repeated, but by rote, and unconnectedly. There was also occasionally, I believe, a Saint George. In all there was a confused resemblance of the ancient mysteries, in which the characters of

Scripture, the Nine Worthies, and other popular personages were usually exhibited." (Scott's note.)

Page 765.   THE BATTLE

Scott is at his best as a storyteller in stirring battle scenes like this of Flodden Field.

628. *Lord Surrey's o'er the Till!* The Earl of Surrey was the leader of the English army that defeated the Scotch at Flodden Field. "The deep and broad river Till protected James's right flank" on the battlefield.

700. *Berwick.* A town in Northumberland, England, on the Tweed.

716. *vaward post.* Vaward is an archaic form for vanguard.

851. *"Is Wilton there?"* Lady Clare's first thought is of Sir Ralph de Wilton, her true love, whom Marmion had accused of treason and whom he thought he had slain in the lists. As a matter of fact de Wilton was with the English and he and Lady Clare were finally reunited.

945. *died at Holy Isle.* For her part in the affair of love and perfidy, Constance "was betrayed to her convent and walled up alive."

999-1004. *O, for a blast of that dread horn. . . . On Roncesvalles died!* A reference to the legend of Roland (Rowland), a celebrated hero of French romances of chivalry, the nephew of Charlemagne. When Charlemagne was fighting the Saracens in Spain, Roland was defeated and killed at Roncesvalles. His friend Olivier (Oliver) had urged him to blow a blast upon his horn and so bring the main force of Charlemagne to his aid. This he had steadfastly refused to do, but finally he yielded and with his last breath sounded the call which brought the great Charles—too late to save him indeed, but not too late to overthrow the Saracens. The story is told in *The Song of Roland*, which dates from the eleventh century.

Page 770.   THE LADY OF THE LAKE

Lockhart writes of this poem: "I do not recollect that any of all the author's works was ever looked for with more intense anxiety, or that any of them excited a more extraordinary sensation when it did appear. The whole country rang with the praises of the poet—crowds set off to view the scenery of Loch Katrine, till then comparatively unknown; and as the book came out just before the season for excursions, every house and inn in the neighborhood was crammed with a constant succession of visitors."

In reply to Lady Abercorn, who had asked him whether he had ever been in love, Scott made the following comment on *The Lady of the Lake:* "I have tried . . . to make 'a knight of love who never broke a vow.' But welladay, though I have succeeded tolerably well with the damsel, my lover, spite of my best exertions, is like to turn out what the players call a *walking gentleman*. It is incredible the pains it has given me to give him a little dignity. Notwithstanding this, I have had in my time melancholy cause to paint from experience, for I gained no advantage from three years' constancy, except the . . . experience and some advantage to my conversation and manners. Mrs. Scott's match and mine was of our own making, and proceeded from the most sincere affection on both sides, which has rather increased than diminished during twelve years' marriage. But it was something short of love in all its forms, which I suspect people only feel once in their lives."

The lady who gave the poet "melancholy cause to paint from experience" was, of course, Williamina Stuart whom he wooed for some years after 1790. Some of the tenderest passages in *The Lady of the Lake* were inspired by the author's love for her.

In 1812 Scott wrote: "The force in the *Lay* is thrown on style; in *Marmion*, on description; and in *The Lady of the Lake*, on incident."

HARP OF THE NORTH

The Lady of the Lake begins with this invocation to ancient Scottish minstrelsy, symbolized by the harp, which was the national musical instrument of Scotland and therefore used, of course, to accompany the songs of the ancient wandering minstrels.

2. *Saint Fillan's spring.* The spring of St. Fillan's is on a hilltop near Loch Earn, a few miles northeast of the scene of the poem. St. Fillan was the favorite saint of the Scottish hero, Robert Bruce.

SOLDIER, REST

At the close of the evening which Fitz-James spends on the island Ellen sings this song to the music of an unseen harp.

THE FIERY CROSS

The following sketch of the Fiery Cross incident is in substance what Francis Jeffrey wrote in the *Edinburgh Review* of August, 1810: The summoning of the clan is accomplished by the consecration of a small wooden cross, which, with its points scorched and dipped in blood, is carried with incredible celerity through the whole territory of the chieftain. The eager fidelity with which this fatal signal is carried on, is represented with great spirit. A youth starts from the side of his father's coffin to bear it forward, and, having run his stage, delivers it to a young bridegroom returning from church who instantly binds his plaid around him, and rushes onward.

201. *Inch-Cailliach.* An island in Loch Lomond, used as a burial-place for several neigh-

boring clans, the chief of which were the descendants of King Alpine. The meaning of the name is "Isle of Nuns" or "Isle of Old Women."

229. *Ben-an's gray scalp*. Ben-an is a mountain north of the Trossachs, a picturesque wooded valley in Perthshire.

263. *Coir-Uriskin, thy goblin cave!* This cave and the "gray pass" Beala-nam-bo were on the side of Ben Venue, a mountain near Loch Katrine.

296. *Lanrick mead*. A meadow on the road from Loch Vennachar to the Trossachs.

351. *Achray*. A lake in western Perthshire.

359. *Duncraggan's huts*. Duncraggan is a village between Loch Achray and Loch Vennachar.

Page 772. CORONACH

Scott wrote that "the *coronach* of the Highlanders, like the *ululatus* of the Romans, and the *ululoo* of the Irish, was a wild expression of lamentation, poured forth by the mourners over the body of a departed friend."

Page 773.

THE HEATH THIS NIGHT MUST BE MY BED

This song is sung by the bridegroom who, as he comes from the church with his bride, receives the fiery cross and, instantly leaving her, rushes on to summon the clan. See note to "The Fiery Cross," above.

THE TOILS ARE PITCHED

This song is sung by Blanche of Devan, a crazed Lowland maid, whose husband, a forester, had been slain "on the morn she was a bride."

ROKEBY

The advertisement which introduced this poem said: "The scene . . . is laid at Rokeby, near Greta Bridge, in Yorkshire, and shifts to the adjacent fortress of Barnard Castle, and to other places in the vicinity.

"The date of the supposed events is immediately subsequent to the great Battle of Marston Moor, 3d July, 1644."

In a letter to his publisher Scott said of the poem: "I hope the thing will do, chiefly because the world will not expect from me a poem of which the interest turns upon character."

". . . In none of his previous poetic tales did he direct special attention to the portrayal of character. With the exception of Lord Marmion, who, at least, is an artistic, if not psychological, failure, his personalities are rather loosely sketched; in *Rokeby* there is a much more elaborate indication of idiosyncrasies. It thus possesses a more pungent human interest than any of the three previous poems; the story, also, is better constructed and it abounds in thrilling and dramatic situations, all well devised and admirably elaborated; on the other hand, it is rather overburdened with mere sordidness and deficient in the finer elements of romance; it has neither the antique charm of *The Lay*, nor the national appeal of *Marmion*, nor the captivating singularity of *The Lady of the Lake*." (T. F. Henderson, in *Cambridge History of English Literature*.)

BRIGNALL BANKS

The singer of this song is Edmund, a young and daring outlaw.

While *Rokeby* was in process of composition Scott wrote as follows to Mr. John B. S. Morritt, to whom he dedicated the poem and in whose "beautiful demesne of Rokeby" the scene of the poem is laid: "There are two or three songs, and particularly one in praise of Brignall Banks, which I trust you will like— because, *entre nous*, I like them myself. One of them is a little dashing banditti song, called and entitled Allen-a-Dale."

Brignall Banks are in Rokeby Park on the Greta river in Yorkshire. Dalton is four miles southeast of the village Brignall.

Page 775. ALLEN-A-DALE

This also is sung by the outlaw who sings *Brignall Banks*. The bold Allen-a-Dale, the subject of the song, was one of the companions of Robin Hood.

12. *Lord Dacre*. An English nobleman who participated in a poaching escapade in which a keeper was killed. Lord Dacre was tried for the crime and given a death sentence.

THE CYPRESS WREATH

This song is sung by Wycliffe at the bidding of Matilda a short hour or two before Edmund's men drive her from her ancestral seat, Rokeby Castle, and leave it a burning ruin.

Page 776. BALLAD

This ballad is sung by the treacherous Edmund who, disguised as a wandering minstrel, has been admitted to Rokeby Castle in order to prepare for the entrance of his followers, lying concealed in the castle grounds. The ballad is said to be based on the story of "the horrible murder of an infant by Wild Dayrell" (Darrell).

WILLIAM AND HELEN

In 1796 Scott's first publication appeared, a translation or imitation of two ballads, the work of G. A. Bürger, a distinguished German poet of the eighteenth century. Scott probably first came to know of the ballads from a copy of Bürger which was given to him by the daughter of the Saxon ambassador at St. James', a kinswoman of his by marriage. This lady was interested in Scott's study of German and helped him perfect his versions of the ballads. Perhaps a more direct spur to his writing the ballads was the reading, by Mrs. Anna L. Barbauld, at the Dugald Stewart home in Edinburgh, of a translation of Bürger's *Lenore* by William Taylor. Scott was not at the party at which Mrs. Barbauld read, but a report of her reading given to him by a friend who summarized the story and repeated the chorus,

"Tramp! tramp! across the land they speede,
  Splash! splash! across the sea;
  Hurrah! the dead can ride apace!
  Dost fear to ride with me?"

so fired him for composition that he began his version—*William and Helen*—after supper and did not go to bed till he had finished it.

Page 779. THE MAID OF NEIDPATH

Scott gave the following explanation of this poem: "There is a tradition in Tweeddale that, when Neidpath Castle, near Peebles, was inhabited by the Earls of March, a mutual passion subsisted between a daughter of that noble family and a son of the Laird of Tushielaw, in Ettrick Forest. As the alliance was thought unsuitable by her parents, the young man went abroad. During his absence the lady fell into a consumption; and at length, as the only means of saving her life, her father consented that her lover should be recalled. On the day when he was expected to pass through Peebles, on the road to Tushielaw, the young lady, though much exhausted, caused herself to be carried to the balcony of a house in Peebles belonging to the family, that she might see him as he rode past. Her anxiety and eagerness gave such force to her organs that she is said to have distinguished the horse's footsteps at an incredible distance. But Tushielaw, unprepared for the change in her appearance, and not expecting to see her in that place, rode on without recognizing her, or even slackening his pace. The lady was unable to support the shock; and, after a short struggle, died in the arms of her attendants."

Page 780. JOCK OF HAZELDEAN

The first stanza of this poem is taken from an old Scotch ballad, *Jock of Hazel Green.*

SOUND THE CLARION

Mr. Tom B. Haber, writing in the *Publications of the Modern Language Association* for December, 1930, on the subject of "The Chapter Tags in the Waverley Novels," quotes Scott as

follows: "The scraps of poetry which have been in most cases tacked to the beginning of chapters in these novels are sometimes quoted either from reading or from memory, but in the general case are pure invention. . . . I drew on my memory as long as I could, and when that failed, eked it out with invention. I believe that, in some cases, where actual names are affixed to the supposed quotations, it would be to little purpose to seek them in the works of the authors referred to. In some cases I have been entertained when Dr. Watts and other graver authors have been ransacked in vain for stanzas for which the novelist alone was responsible."

"But if 'Dr. Watts,'" Mr. Haber writes, "'and other graver authors' were wrongly suspected of writing lines for which the novelist was himself responsible, still other authors may accuse Sir Walter of borrowing their lines and signing them, for example, 'Anonymous.' An instance of this kind was brought to light ten years ago by Mr. James Rankin, of Galashiels, who discovered the true authorship of the 'anonymous' quatrain prefixed to chapter XXXIV of *Old Mortality*, hitherto supposed to be the product of Scott's best poetic vein. [Here Mr. Haber quotes *Sound the Clarion.*] Among those thus deceived was W. E. Henley, who credited the verses to Scott on the title page of his *Lyra Heroica*. Mr. Rankin found this stanza in a poem of fourteen quatrains contributed to the Edinburgh *Bee* of October 12, 1791, by one Major Mordaunt, who wrote it 'during the last German war'—probably the Seven Years' War, 1756–63. The stanza used by Scott is the only one worth quoting, as a comparison with the preceding quatrain will show:

'But stop, my Clio, wanton muse,
  Indulge not this unmanly strain:
  Beat, beat the drum, my ardour rouse,
  And call the soldier back again.'"

The editors and anthologists of Scott, almost if not quite to a man, have been, like W. E. Henley, "among those thus deceived." In this large company are the editors of the present volume.

PROUD MAISIE

This lyric, found in chapter XL of *The Heart of Midlothian*, is sung by Madge Wildfire just before her death.

Page 781. BONNY DUNDEE

This song, from the second scene of Act II of the drama, *The Doom of Devorgoil,* is sung by Leonard, a forest ranger.

Bonny Dundee was John Graham of Claverhouse, Viscount Dundee, a stout supporter in Scotland of Charles II and James II of England. After James's flight to France, Claverhouse stood strongly for him against William III, even defying the Scotch Convention, which had accepted William. Unable to persuade the Duke of Gordon to defend Edinburgh Castle for James, Dundee and his Highland army fought and defeated William's troops at Killiecrankie (1689), but Dundee was slain in the moment of victory.

10. *The bells are rung backward.* It was sometimes the custom to sound alarms by striking the chimes in reverse order.

11. *the Provost, douce man.* The sedate or prudent chief magistrate.

14. *the sanctified bends of the Bow.* The windings of Bow street, called sanctified because in it were the homes of many Covenanters.

15. *Ilk carline was flyting and shaking her pow.* Each old woman was scolding and shaking her head.

16. *couthie and slee.* Loving and sly.

19. *Grass-market.* The place of execution in Edinburgh before 1784.

24. *These cowls of Kilmarnock had spits.* The cowls of Kilmarnock were Presbyterians, so called because they wore hooded garments (cowls) made at Kilmarnock, an old manufacturing town in Ayrshire. Their spits were their swords.

25. *lang-hafted gullies.* Long-handled knives.

26. *close-heads.* The upper ends of narrow passages leading from a street to a court and the houses within.

29. *Castle rock.* The site of Edinburgh Castle.

31. *Mons Meg.* The nickname of a cannon, believed to have been made in Mons, Belgium. *Marrows* are mates, or companions.

35. *the shade of Montrose.* James Graham, Marquis of Montrose, hoping to win Scotland for King Charles II without the Covenant, led a small army into that country in 1650. He was quickly captured and hanged as an outlaw.

39. *Pentland.* A range of Scottish hills. *Forth* is the great firth or bay on the east coast of Scotland.

41. *Duniewassals.* Highland gentlemen, especially those of secondary rank.

44. *the target of barken'd bull-hide.* A shield made of hide tanned with bark.

ROBERT SOUTHEY

BIBLIOGRAPHY

I. WORKS

Poetical Works, ed. by H. T. Tuckerman. 5 vols. Riverside Edition. (Houghton: Boston, 1884.) The most nearly complete edition, though not easily available; the editor supplies a memoir.

Poems, ed. by M. H. Fitzgerald. (Oxford University Press: 1909.) A convenient edition, containing many of the longer poems and several of the early pieces desirable for a history of Southey's poetical development.

Poems, ed. by Edward Dowden. Golden Treasury series. (Macmillan: New York, 1895.) The best edition for student use.

Letters, ed. by M. H. Fitzgerald. World's Classics. (Oxford University Press: 1912.) The best abridged collection of Southey's correspondence, in which the man is intimately revealed.

II. BIOGRAPHY AND CRITICISM

Dowden, Edward. *Southey.* English Men of Letters series. (Harper: New York, 1880.) A scholarly brief biography, one of the earliest studies of Southey and still an accepted authority.

Haller, William. *The Early Life of Southey.* (Columbia University Press: 1917.) The most detailed survey of the period: the time covered is 1774–1803; valuable for the list of Southey's works given in the appendix.

Southey, C. C. *Life and Correspondence of Robert Southey.* (Harper: New York, 1855.) The standard biography, by Southey's son.

III. ARTICLES FROM BOOKS AND PERIODICALS

Dowden, Edward. "The Early Revolutionary Group and Antagonists," in *The French Revolution and English Literature.* (Scribner: New York, 1908.) Contains an interesting account of young Southey and his colleagues.

Feiling, Keith. "Southey and Wordsworth," in *Sketches in Nineteenth Century Biography.* (Longmans: London, 1930.) Riddles Southey's political tenets, while admitting his conscientiousness; compares his political cycle with Wordsworth's.

Graham, Walter. "Robert Southey as a Tory Reviewer," *Philological Quarterly,* II, 97–111 (Apr., 1923). Points out the extreme conservatism of Southey's political opinions, revealed during thirty years' connection with the *Quarterly Review.*

Haller, William. "Southey's Later Radicalism," *Publications of the Modern Language Association,* XXXVII, 281–92 (Mar., 1922). A valuable sequel to Haller's *Early Life of Southey;* shows Southey's reactions against the machine-age, his hatred of the *laissez-faire* policy, and his plea for the union of church, state, and education.

Kaufman, Paul. "The Reading of Southey and Coleridge," *Modern Philology,* XXI, 317–20 (Feb., 1924). The record of their borrowings from the Bristol Library, 1793–98.

Knowlton, E. C. "Southey's Eclogues," *Philological Quarterly,* VII, 231–41 (July, 1928). Upholds Southey's claims to novelty; traces the relationships with dramatic monologues and idyls of the 19th century, Southey occupying an important transitional position.

Saintsbury, George. "Lesser Poets of the Later Eighteenth Century," in *The Cambridge History of English Literature,* XI. (Putnam: New York, 1914.) An attempt to "place" Southey as a poet and prose-writer, stressing the history of his reputation.

Saintsbury, George. "Robert Southey," in *Essays*

in English Literature. Second Series. (Scribner: New York, 1895.) Provides a concise biographical outline; discusses the decline of a large part of Southey's work, praising *Roderick;* insists upon the need of reading widely in the poet in order to appreciate him.

Stephen, Leslie. "Southey's Letters," in *Studies of a Biographer*, IV. (Putnam: New York, 1902.) Concerned chiefly with Dowden's pronouncement on Southey, this study points out excessive praise of the poet.

Symons, Arthur. "Robert Southey," in *The Romantic Movement in English Poetry*. (Dutton: New York, 1909.) Subjects Southey's verse to severe criticism; questions whether any of it "might not as well have been written in prose."

NOTES

"Competent critics were wont to class Southey during his lifetime with Coleridge and Wordsworth. Since then, however, his fame has singularly waned. Today he is the least read of the Lake poets. Almost the whole of his work is touched with the blight. It has lost its vitality, and there is no reason to expect that it will ever regain it. . . .

"Southey . . . wished to acquire a pure and unadorned style; and in this he had achieved a fair measure of success. He aims at a simple sobriety of expression, at the moving appeal of elementary emotions. But he has not the powerful concentration of Wordsworth, the radiant force of his spiritual lyricism, nor Coleridge's thrill of the supernatural. . . .

"The shorter poems, of occasional or official character, fall too often into a painful mediocrity, which nothing relieves, not even an adventurous and interesting error. The best are those which have demanded least effort, and where rapid inspiration has been most directly expressed. Special mention must be made . . . of the ballads and tales in verse, where he displays an unsuspected gift of forcefulness and humor. Whether the vein be one of imaginative terror or of popular joviality, the language here shows a nervous strength which at times recalls Burns. These short pieces, by their themes as by their familiar and robust art, are related to the whole movement whose outcome is the *Lyrical Ballads*. . . . Widely quoted in anthologies, these ballads probably represent the only living part of his poetical output." (Louis Cazamian, in *A History of English Literature* by Émile Legouis and Louis Cazamian.)

"Wordsworth when alone, speaking of Southey, said, 'He is one of the cleverest men that is now living.' At the same time he justly denied him ideality in his words. 'He never enquires,' says Wordsworth, 'on what idea his poem is to be wrought; what feeling or passion is to be excited; but he determines on a subject, and then reads a great deal, and combines and connects industriously, but he does not give anything which impresses the mind strongly and is recollected in solitude." (Crabb Robinson, *Diary*, May 13, 1812.)

Page 783. THE BATTLE OF BLENHEIM

John Churchill, Duke of Marlborough, commanded the English, Dutch, Austrian, Prussian, Danish, and Hanoverian troops sent into the field by the European league to check Louis XIV in his efforts to establish a French universal monarchy. Marlborough's army won a "famous victory" over the Franco-Bavarian army at Blindheim (called Blenheim by the English), a village on the north bank of the Danube, near Höckstadt, August 13, 1704. This, the first great victory won against Louis in the open field, dealt a heavy blow to his dream of universal monarchy. As a result of it Austria was saved and Bavaria forced to make peace, and the French were driven over the Danube.

Mr. E. A. G. Lamborn, writing of this poem, says: "The irony of Southey's eighth and ninth stanzas, so gentle that it has burnt to the bone almost before its touch is felt, is very rare in English poetry."

23. *For many thousand men.* The French and Bavarian losses were not far from 40,000, the allied more than 11,000.

Page 785. THE SPEECH OF ROBERT EMMET

See the note to Moore's *Oh, Breathe Not His Name.*

This poem is a good example of Southey's "occasional" poems which, Mr. Cazamian charges, "fall too often into a painful mediocrity."

Page 786.

MY DAYS AMONG THE DEAD ARE PAST

Mr. Frederick E. Pierce calls this poem one of the noblest Southey ever wrote. In his lonely life at Keswick, Southey fell "back more and more upon books as his only companions. His library at his death comprised some 14,000 volumes, many of them rare and costly." In a letter to Coleridge, Southey wrote: "Talk of the happiness of getting a great prize in the lottery? What is that to the opening of a box of books! The joy upon lifting up the cover must be something like that we shall feel when Peter the Porter opens the door upstairs, and says 'Please to walk in, sir.' . . . It will be a great delight to me in the next world, to take a fly and visit these old worthies, who are my only society here, and to tell them what excellent company I found them here at the

Lakes of Cumberland, two centuries after they had been dead and turned to dust. In plain truth, I exist more among the dead than the living, and think more about them, and, perhaps, feel more about them."

Wordsworth said of Southey's passion for books: "It is painful to see how completely dead Southey is become to all but books"; and Dr. Arnold said: [It] "*alarmed* me. I could not help saying to myself, 'Am I in danger of becoming like him? Shall I ever lose my interest in things, and retain an interest only in books?'"

Page 787.   PRELUDE

This is the prelude to *The Pilgrim to Compostella*, a Christmas tale described as "being the legend of a cock and a hen, to the honor of Santiago." It is the story of a young pilgrim who, because he had refused to make love to an innkeeper's daughter, was accused of theft by her, tried, and sentenced to be hanged. The "execution" took place, but some months after the event the young man was found to be hanging in happiness on the gibbet, Santiago having miraculously saved him from suffering and death.

THE ABSOLVERS

In *A Vision of Judgement* Southey makes George III come from his tomb and seek entrance to the gates of Heaven. The Devil—and Wilkes—appear to arraign him, but, failing, withdraw discomfited. Washington comes and praises the king and pleads for him with the result that he is admitted to Heaven. Here he is received by earlier rulers of England, by various English worthies, and finally by his family.

Southey wrote a preface for the poem in which he attacked the poetry of Byron for its "monstrous combinations of horrors and mockery, lewdness and impiety," and spoke of him and his kind as having set up a school which "may properly be called the Satanic School." Byron replied with his *The Vision of Judgment*, in which he held up Southey—the laureate—to derision, and treated the incident of George III's appearance before the tribunal of Heaven in a humorous but most disrespectful manner.

22. *Fabius, Aristides, and Solon, and Epaminondas.* Fabius, a Roman general, opponent of Hannibal. Aristides, an Athenian statesman and general. Solon, an Athenian sage and lawgiver. Epaminondas, a Theban statesman and general.

HENRY KIRKE WHITE
BIBLIOGRAPHY

I. WORKS

Poems, Letters, and Prose Fragments, ed. by John Drinkwater. Muses' Library. (Dutton: New York, 1907.) The most accessible edition; the editor provides a brief biographical sketch, followed by a critical introduction, naming White "a poet, earnest, vital, and lovable."

Works. (Leavitt: New York, 1853.) An anonymous Life forms a brief introduction; includes White's preface to the first edition of his poems and twelve prose sketches.

Poetical Works, ed. by H. K. Swann. (Scott: London, 1897.) The editor provides notes and a brief memoir, quoting a number of letters.

Poetical Works and Remains. (Crowell: New York, 1884.) Prefaced by a Life by Southey, which quotes many of the poems; illustrated by Birket Foster.

II. BIOGRAPHY AND CRITICISM

Dale, T. P. "Henry Kirke White," in *A Life's Motto*. (Virtue: New York, n.d.) Discusses the poet's brief life, his first literary ventures; laments his unlucky efforts to win the Cambridge scholarship.

Morley, Christopher. "A Poet of Sad Vigils," in *Shandygaff*. (Doubleday: New York, 1918.) A review of the poet's disappointments in the publication of his poems and in his college career.

NOTES

"Set aside the thin gruel of Kirke White, and put to your lips the pure Greek wine of Keats." (R. H. Horne, in *New Spirit of the Age*.)

"White's poetry is marked by a melancholy and sadness, noble in unfaltering faith and in absolute lack of fear. . . . Love for Nature was in White a very vital thing, no mere poetical pose or formula. . . . Most of his Nature poetry is simple . . . never gorgeous, but always sincere. . . . He is never able, as are the great poets, to see in all the workings of the natural world the symbols of eternal laws and universal harmony, but to the phases of nature in themselves, to her beauty, her comfort and her terror, he is keenly alive, and expresses his emotions in musical verse that is often of great tenderness. . . . In workmanship White maintains a very high level, and his verse, if never quite magical, is always harmonious and easy, and sometimes full-voiced and masterful." (John Drinkwater, in *Poems, Letters and Prose Fragments of Kirke White*.)

Page 790. DESCRIPTION OF A SUMMER'S EVE

14. *Nails the dead kite to the wall.* The kite, a bird of the hawk family, is nailed to the barn as a grim warning to other kites that it is

dangerous for them to hunt their prey among the farmyard fowls.

CHARLES WOLFE

BIBLIOGRAPHY

WORKS AND CRITICISM

The Burial of Sir John Moore and Other Poems, ed. by C. L. Falkiner. (Sidgwick: London, 1909.) Contains all the worthwhile poetry; includes also an introductory memoir.

Remains, ed. by J. A. Russell. (Hamilton: London, 1836.) Consists of a memoir, with Wolfe's poems interspersed; his sermons, with some additional poems, are given in the appendix.

Williams, A. M. "Charles Wolfe," in *The Poets and Poetry of Ireland*. (Osgood: Boston, 1881.) Contains a biographical preface, followed by three poems.

NOTES

Page 791. THE BURIAL OF SIR JOHN MOORE AT CORUNNA

Sir John Moore was an English general in command of the operations against France in Spain, 1808. After the capture of Madrid by Napoleon, Moore, who was in command of a portion of Wellington's army, was forced to retreat and was killed at Corunna while attempting to embark his troops.

The poem is an accurate description of the event as it was reported in the Edinburgh *Annual Register*, 1808. The *Register's* item was as follows: "Sir John Moore had often said that if he was killed in battle he wished to be buried where he fell. The body was removed at midnight to the citadel of Corunna. A grave was dug for him on the rampart there, by a party of the 9th Regiment, the Aides-de-Camp attending by turns. No coffin could be procured, and the officers of his staff wrapped his body, dressed as it was, in a military cloak and blankets. The interment was hastened: for, about eight in the morning, some firing was heard, and the officers feared that if a serious attack was made, they should be ordered away and not suffered to pay him their last duty. The officers of his regiment bore him to his grave; the funeral service was read by the chaplain; and the corpse was covered with earth."

Byron called this poem "the most perfect ode in the language."

APPENDIX III

INDEX OF AUTHORS, TITLES, AND FIRST LINES OF POETRY

Authors' names are set in black face type, titles are set in italics, and first lines of poetry are set in roman type. When a part or all of the first line of a poem is used as the title, the entry is by first line only.

A chieftain, to the Highlands bound 670
A flock of sheep that leisurely pass by . . . 70
A ghost, that loved a lady fair 663
A good sword and a trusty hand 685
A green and silent spot, amid the hills . . . 176
A Poet!—He hath put his heart to school 81
A provident and wakeful fear 732
A Sensitive Plant in a garden grew 428
A simple Child 16
A slumber did my spirit seal 29
A spade! a rake! a hoe! 706
A sunny shaft did I behold 190
A thing of beauty is a joy for ever 566
A wet sheet and a flowing sea 684
A whirl-blast from behind the hill 14
Abou Ben Adhem (may his tribe increase!) 712
Absolvers, The 787
Address to the Moon 571
Addressed to Haydon 558
Adonais 497
Adonis in Slumber 570
Affliction of Margaret ——, The 50
After a thousand mazes overgone 570
After the Battle 744
After the dark vapours have oppress'd our plains 559
Ah what avails the sceptred race 719
Alas, how soon the hours are over 731
"Alas," said he, "were I but always borne" 574
Alastor, or the Spirit of Solitude 444
All how silent and how still 674
All Nature seems at work. Slugs leave their lair 191
All thoughts, all passions, all delights . . . 183
Allen-a-Dale has no fagot for burning . . 775

And is this Yarrow?—This the Stream . . 74
And so he groan'd, as one by beauty slain 572
And thou art dead, as young and fair . . . 239
And well our Christian sires of old 764
And whither would you lead me then? . . 776
Animal Tranquillity and Decay 15
Answer to a Child's Question 187
Approach to Spring 674
Ariel to Miranda:—Take 441
Artemidora! Gods invisible 723
As the black storm upon the mountain-top 91
As mad sexton's bell, tolling 663
At midnight by the stream I roved 175
At the Grave of Burns, 1803 61
Autumn 695
Ave Maria 349
Away! the moor is dark beneath the moon 514

Ballad (Hood) 696
Ballad (Scott) 776
Ballad of the Dark Ladié, The 181
Bards of Passion and of Mirth 584
Battle, The 765
Battle of Blenheim, The 783
Battle of the Baltic 669
Beautiful Night, A 661
Beddoes, Thomas Lovell 657–665
Behold her, single in the field 60
Believe me, if all those endearing young charms 744
Belle of the Ball-Room, The 754
Ben Battle was a soldier bold 694
Beneath these fruit-tree boughs that shed 59
Beneath yon birch with silver bark 181
Best and brightest, come away 441
Biographia Literaria 193

Bitter Meditation 269

Bob Southey! You're a poet—Poet-
laureate 292

Bonnie George Campbell 747

Bonny Dundee 781

Books 90

Breathes there the man, with soul so
dead 761

Bridge of Sighs, The 704

Bright be the place of thy soul 238

Bright Flower! whose home is everywhere 54

Bright star, would I were stedfast as thou
art 584

Brignall Banks 773

Brook and road | Were fellow travellers
in this gloomy Pass 35

Brothers, The 38

*Burial of Sir John Moore at Corunna,
The* 791

But indignation works where hope is
not 93

Byron, George Gordon, Lord ...   233–408

Cambridge and the Alps 91

Campbell, Thomas 665–673

Can it then be, that the earth loved some
city 661

Character of the Happy Warrior 67

Childe Harold's Pilgrimage 247

Child's Song 747

Christabel 164

Christmas 764

Churchyard among the Mountains, The .. 99

Clare, John 673–682

Cloud, The 432

Clouds, lingering yet, extend in solid
bars 74

Coleridge, Hartley 683

Coleridge, Samuel Taylor 141–232

Come, Anna! come, the morning dawns 790

Come back, ye wandering Muses, come
back home 723

Come hither, all sweet maidens soberly 560

Come, rest in this bosom, my own
stricken deer 745

Come then, a song; a winding, gentle
song 658

Come to me, gentle sleep! 686

*Composed by the Sea-side, near Calais,
August, 1802* 59

Composed by the Side of Grasmere Lake .. 74

*Composed in the Valley near Dover, on the
Day of Landing* 58

*Composed upon an Evening of Extraordi-
nary Splendour and Beauty* 79

*Composed upon Westminster Bridge, Sep-
tember 3, 1802* 57

Conclusion 95

Conclusion: the Decision of the Gods 575

Coronach 772

Credo 566

Cunningham, Allan 684

Cypress Wreath, The 775

Dark Rosaleen 735

Dead Eagle, The 672

Dear Alice! you'll laugh when you
know it 755

Dear Child of Nature, let them rail 67

Dear Harp of my Country! in darkness
I found thee 745

Death of Artemidora, The 723

Death stands above me, whispering low 732

Death's Jest-Book 658, 659

Deep in the shady sadness of a vale 606

Defence of Poetry, A 515

Dejection, an Ode 184

Description of a Summer's Eve 790

Despondency Corrected 99

Destruction of Sennacherib, The 242

Diary of Lord Byron, A 363

Dirge (Beddoes) 663

Dirge, A (Shelley) 442

Dirge for an Infant 714

Dirge for a Young Maiden 663

*Domestic Asides; or, Truth in Paren-
theses* 700

Don Juan 292

Down the sultry arc of day 790

Do you ask what the birds say? The
Sparrow, the Dove 187

Dream of Dying 661

Dream of Eugene Aram, the Murderer ... 698

Dream-Pedlary 662

Dull is my verse: not even thou 728

Dying Child, The 682

Earth has not anything to show more
fair 57

Earth, ocean, air, belovèd brotherhood 444

*Elegiac Stanzas Suggested by a Picture of
Peele Castle* 69

Encounter with Sleep 573
Endymion 566
Endymion Chooses Mortal Love 574
Endymion's Vision 567
Eolian Harp, The 145
Epicurean Reminiscences of a Sentimen-
  talist 701
Epistle to Augusta 244
Epitaph 193
Ere on my bed my limbs I lay 188
Ere yet the bands met Marmion's eye ... 765
Ethereal minstrel! pilgrim of the sky 80
Evening Song of the Weary 687
Eve of St. Agnes, The 586
Eve of St. Mark, The 591
Exchange, The 188
Excursion, The 96
Expostulation and Reply 18

Fair Ines 695
Fair Isabel, poor simple Isabel! 576
Fair Star of evening, Splendour of the
  west 59
Faithless Nelly Gray 694
Faithless Sally Brown 690
Fallen as he is, this king of birds still
  seems 672
Fame, like a wayward Girl, will still be
  coy 585
Fare thee well! and if for ever 242
Farewell, Life! My senses swim 707
Father of heaven and earth! 687
Fears in Solitude 176
Feelings of the Tyrolese 74
Fiery Cross, The 770
Fiesolan Idyl 722
Five years have past; five summers, with
  the length 24
For the slender beech and the sapling oak 748
Fountain, The 31
Fragment 791
Fragment: to Music, A 417
Fragment: "When Soft Winds and
  Sunny Skies" 440
Fragments Intended for the Dramas 661
France 93
France, an Ode 174
French and English 702
French Revolution 66
Friend of the wise! and Teacher of the
  Good 188

From heavy dreams fair Helen rose 776
From Nature doth emotion come, and
  moods 95
From Stirling castle we had seen 62
From the forests and highlands 435
Frost at Midnight 173
Full facing their swift flight, from ebon
  streak 574

Glory and loveliness have pass'd away .. 559
Glycine's Song 190
Go, simple Book of Ballads, go 672
Go, Valentine, and tell that lovely Maid 783
God scatters beauty as he scatters flowers 732
Grave of Love, The 748
Great spirits now on earth are sojourn-
  ing 558
Green Linnet, The 59
Green little vaulter in the sunny grass ... 712

Had this effulgence disappeared 79
Hail to thee, blithe Spirit! 433
Hamadryad, The 724
Happy in England! I could be content .. 558
Happy is he who lives to understand ... 99
Hark! the vesper hymn is stealing 746
Harold's Song 762
Harp of the North! that mouldering long
  hast hung 770
Harper, The 666
Hast thou a charm to stay the morning-
  star 186
Hawker, Robert Stephen 684–685
He could not die when trees were green 682
He is dead and gone—a flower 714
He is gone to the mountain 772
He saw not the two maidens, nor their
  smiles 575
Hellas 440
Hellenics 723
Hemans, Felicia Dorothea 685–687
Here, on our native soil, we breathe once
  more 58
Here, where precipitate Spring, with one
  light bound 722
Hero and Leander 695
Hester 718
Hie upon Hielands 747
High in the breathless Hall the Minstrel
  sate 71
His thoughts are so much higher than
  his state 661

Ho! he exclaim'd, King George of England standeth in judgment! 787
Hohenlinden 666
Holly-Tree, The 785
Hood, Thomas 687–707
How am I like her?—for no trace ... 752
How dear to me the hour when daylight dies 743
How fever'd is the man, who cannot look 585
How lovely is the heaven of this night .. 661
How many bards gild the lapses of time 557
How Many Times Do I Love Thee, Dear? 658
Hunt, Leigh 707–714
Hushed be sighing, near the string 663
Hymn before Sun-rise, in the Vale of Chamouni 186
Hymn of Pan 435
Hymn to Intellectual Beauty 415
Hyperion 606

I am not One who much or oft delight .. 70
I arise from dreams of thee 427
I bring fresh showers for the thirsting flowers 432
I cannot tell, not I, why she 730
I cry your mercy—pity—love!—aye, love! 585
I dug, beneath the cypress shade 748
I fear thy kisses, gentle maiden 435
I have a garden of my own 747
I heard a thousand blended notes 14
I know not whether I am proud 731
I love at early morn, from new mown swath 681
I met a traveller from an antique land ... 417
I pant for music which is divine 439
I really take it very kind 700
I remember, I remember 697
I revolved | How much the destiny of man had still 92
I saw an aged Beggar in my walk 25
I saw old Autumn in the misty morn ... 695
I see black dragons mount the sky 741
I shiver, Spirit fierce and bold 61
I stood in Venice on the Bridge of Sighs 266
I stood tip-toe upon a little hill 561
I strove with none, for none was worth my strife 732
I think it was Spring—but not certain I am 701

I travelled among unknown men 28
I wandered lonely as a cloud 66
I was thy neighbor once, thou rugged Pile 69
I weep for Adonais—he is dead 497
I will ease my breast | Of secret grief, here in this bowery nest 567
I wish I was by that dim Lake 746
I would to heaven that I were so much clay 292
Idiot Boy, The 18
If by dull rhymes our English must be chain'd 585
If from the public way you turn your steps 44
If Nature, for a favourite child 30
If there were dreams to sell 662
If thou wilt ease thine heart 658
Imagination and Taste, How Impaired and Restored 93, 95
Imagination—here the Power so called 91
Imitated from the Persian 787
Imitation of Spenser 557
In a drear-nighted December 576
In Clementina's artless mien 728
In Seville, when the feast was long 752
In Siberia's wastes 740
In the sweet shire of Cardigan 15
In Xanadu did Kubla Khan ...'...... 182
In youth from rock to rock I went 52
Indian Maid, The 572
Indian Serenade, The 427
Induction 570
Inland, within a hollow vale, I stood 59
Insignificance of the World 661
Introduction—Childhood and School-Time 81
Iphigeneia and Agamemnon 723
Iphigeneia, when she heard her doom 723
Irish Melodies 742
Is thy face like thy mother's, my fair child! 247
Isabella; or the Pot of Basil 576
It is a beauteous evening, calm and free 57
It is an ancient Mariner 149
It is not to be thought of that the Flood 58
It is the first mild day of March 15
It keeps eternal whisperings around 559
It seems a day | (I speak of one from many singled out) 29
It was a summer evening 783

It was an April morning: fresh and clear   36
It was an English ladye bright   762
It waved not through an Eastern sky . . .   686

Jenny kissed me when we met   714
Jock of Hazeldean   780
Just as the even-bell rang, we set out . . .   675

Kathleen Ny-Houlahan   740
Keats, John   551–656
Keen, fitful gusts are whisp'ring here
    and there   558
Knight's Tomb, The   190
Kubla Khan   182

La Belle Dame sans Merci   592
Lady of the Lake, The   770
Lamb, Charles   714–718
Lament, A   439
Lamia   598
Landing of the Pilgrim Fathers in New
    England, The   685
Landor, Walter Savage   718–734
Laodamia   75
Last Man, The   688
Latin Hymn to the Virgin   756
Lay of the Labourer, The   706
Lay of the Last Minstrel, The   761
Let Erin remember the days of old   743
Let no man write my epitaph; let my
    grave   785
Letters: from Byron, 372; from Keats,
    617; from Shelley, 531; from Words-
    worth, 112
Lewti   175
Lift not the painted veil which those who
    live   426
Like the ghost of a dear friend dead   436
Limbo   190
Lines Composed a Few Miles above Tin-
    tern Abbey   24
Lines Left upon a Seat in a Yew Tree   7
Lines on the Mermaid Tavern   583
Lines to a Lady Weeping   240
Lines: "When the Lamp Is Shattered" . .   440
Lines Written among the Euganean Hills   421
Lines Written at Geneva; July, 1824   664
Lines Written in Early Spring   14
Little you think, my lovely friend   728
Lo! I must tell a tale of chivalry   560
Lochiel! Lochiel! beware of the day   668
Lochiel's Warning   668

Lochinvar   763
London, 1802   58
Long they pine in weary woe—the
    nobles of your land   740
Long time a child, and still a child, when
    years   683
Long Past, The   436
Lord Ullin's Daughter   670
Lord! who art merciful as well as just . . .   787
Loss of the Mortal Maiden   574
Love   183
Love at a Rout   751
Lovely was the death | Of Him whose
    life was Love! Holy with power   147
Love's Philosophy   428
Lucy Gray, or Solitude   35
Lullaby of an Infant Chief   780
Lyrical Fragments   664
Lyrics and Epigrams   728

Maid of Athens, ere we part   239
Maid of Neidpath, The   779
Manfred: A Dramatic Poem   274
Mangan, James (Clarence)   734–741
Many a green isle needs must be   421
Many are the notes | Which, in his tune-
    ful course, the wind draws forth   99
Margaret: or the Ruined Cottage   7
Marmion   763
Matthew   30
Meeting of the Waters, The   743
Meg Merrilies   583
Men of England, wherefore plough   426
Mermaid of Margate, The   691
Michael   44
Mild is the parting year, and sweet   728
Milton! thou shouldst be living at this
    hour   58
Mine be a cot beside the hill   759
Minstrel Boy, The   745
Monarch of Gods, and Dæmons, and
    all Spirits   454
Moore, Thomas   741–747
Most sweet it is with unuplifted eyes   80
Mother, I cannot mind my wheel   730
Motherwell, William   747
Much have I travell'd in the realms of
    gold   558
"Multum Dilexit"   683
Music   439
Music, when soft voices die   438

Mutability 439
My boat is on the shore 246
My days among the dead are past 786
My heart aches, and a drowsy numbness
    pains 595
My heart has thank'd thee, Bowles! for
    those soft strains 145
My heart leaps up when I behold 51
My pensive Sara! thy soft cheek reclined 145
My sister! my sweet sister! if a name 244
My spirit is too weak—mortality 559

National Airs 746
Nay, Traveller! rest. This lonely yew
    tree stands 7
Never go to France 702
Newly-Wedded, The 756
Night clos'd around the conqueror's way 744
Nightingale, The 179
No cloud, no relique of the sunken day 179
No, no, go not to Lethe, neither twist .. 595
No sunny ray, no silver night 665
Noon 674
Nor should this, perchance | Pass unre-
    corded, that I still had loved 89
Not a drum was heard, not a funeral note 791
Now as even's warning bell 677
Now Morning from her orient chamber
    came 557
Now the rite is duly done 756
Nuns fret not at their convent's narrow
    room 70
Nutting 29
Nymph of the downward smile and side-
    long glance 558

O blithe new-comer! I have heard 54
O, Brignall banks are wild and fair 773
O dearer far than light and life are dear .. 79
O Friend! I know not which way I must
    look 57
O Goddess! hear these tuneless numbers,
    wrung 593
O hush thee, my babie, thy sire was a
    knight 780
O, Lady, twine no wreath for me 775
O listen, listen, ladies gay! 762
O lovers' eyes are sharp to see 779
O pale thou art, my lamp, and faint 791
O poesy! for thee I grasp my pen 564
O poppy death!—sweet poisoner of sleep 695
O Reader! hast thou ever stood to see .. 785

O saw you not fair Ines 695
O Solitude! if I must with thee dwell ... 557
O Soul of Nature! excellent and fair 93
O sovereign power of love! O grief!
    O balm! 570
O thou, who plumed with strong desire 435
O what can ail thee, knight at arms 592
O wild West Wind, thou breath of
    Autumn's being 426
O world! O life! O time! 439
O, young Lochinvar is come out of the
    west 763
Ocean, The 272
Ode ("Bards of Passion and of Mirth") .. 584
*Ode: Intimations of Immortality from
    Recollections of Early Childhood* 63
Ode on a Grecian Urn 594
Ode on Melancholy 595
Ode to a Nightingale 595
Ode to Duty 68
Ode to Psyche 593
Ode to the West Wind 426
Of Nelson and the North 669
Of wedded bliss 703
Oft I had heard of Lucy Gray 35
Oft, in the stilly night 746
Oh, breathe not his name, let it sleep in
    the shade 742
Oh Love! no habitant of earth thou art .. 269
Oh! my dark Rosaleen 735
Oh! pleasant exercise of hope and joy ... 66
Oh Rome! my country! city of the soul! 268
Oh! snatch'd away in beauty's bloom ... 240
Oh, sweet it is, in academic groves ... 92
Oh, talk not to me of a name great in
    story 246
Oh! that the Desert were my dwelling-
    place 272
Oh there is blessing in this gentle breeze 81
Oh those were happy days, heaped up
    with wine-skins 662
Oh! what is that comes gliding in 701
O'Hussey's Ode to the Maguire 737
Old Adam, the carrion crow 659
Old Cumberland Beggar, The 25
Old Familiar Faces, The 717
Old Meg, she was a Gypsy 583
On a Picture of Leander 560
On Artificiality and Pope 370
On Fame 585
On First Looking into Chapman's Homer 558

On Linden, when the sun was low   666
On Man, on Nature, and on Human
   Life   96
On Margate beach, where the sick one
   roams   691
On Rome   268
On Seeing the Elgin Marbles   559
On the Death of His Son Vincent   714
On the Extinction of the Venetian Re-
   public   58
On the Grasshopper and Cricket   559
On the green banks of Shannon, when
   Sheelah was nigh   666
On the Hellenics   723
On the Sea   559
On the Sonnet   585
On This Day I Complete My Thirty-
   sixth Year   247
Once did She hold the gorgeous east in
   fee   58
One day,—'twas on a gentle, autumn
   noon   708
One more Unfortunate   704
One word is too often profaned   439
One year ago my path was green   730
Our walk was far among the ancient
   trees   36
Ozymandias   417

Pains of Sleep, The   188
Pair'd, not Match'd   703
Palm Tree, The   686
Pansies, lilies, kingcups, daisies   52
Parsonage, The   100
Pastoral Song, A   790
Peace Be Thine   751
Peacock, Thomas Love   747–750
Peona! ever have I longed to slake   569
Personal Talk   70
Phantom-Wooer, The   663
Poet of Nature, thou hast wept to know   415
Poets, The   710
Praed, Winthrop Mackworth . . .   750–757
Prayer in the Bower, The   712
Preface to Lyrical Ballads   101
Prelude (Southey)   787
Prelude, The (Wordsworth)   81
Prometheus Unbound   453
Proserpine may pull her flowers   663
Prospectus   96
Proud Maisie is in the wood   780

Proud word you never spoke, but you
   will speak   728
Pursuits! alas, I now have none   728

Queen of the double sea, beloved of him   723

Rafael! It must be he; we only miss   712
Rarely, rarely, comest thou   438
Recollections after an Evening Walk   675
Refuge in Venice   266
Regeneration   719
Religious Musings   147
Remember Me   752
Residence in France   92
Resolution and Independence   55
Retrospect—Love of Nature Leading to
   Love of Man   92
Revolt of Islam, The   417
Rhaicos was born amid the hills where-
   from   724
Rich and rare were the gems she wore . .   742
Rime of the Ancient Mariner, The   149
Rogers, Samuel   757–759
Rokeby   773
Rondeau   714
Rose Aylmer   719
Rough wind, that moanest loud   442
Ruth (Hood)   697
Ruth (Wordsworth)   32

Saint Peter sat by the celestial gate   350
Sally Simpkin's Lament   701
School-Time   89
Scorn not the Sonnet; Critic, you have
   frowned   80
Scott, Sir Walter   759–782
Season of mists and mellow fruitfulness   597
Sensitive Plant, The   428
September, 1802, near Dover . . . . :   59
Serving no haughty muse, my hands
   have here   81
Shapes and Signs   741
She dwelt among the untrodden ways . .   28
She is far from the land where her young
   hero sleeps   744
She is not fair to outward view   683
She sat and wept beside His feet; the
   weight   683
She stood breast-high amid the corn . . .   697
She walks in beauty, like the night   240
She was a Phantom of delight   67
Shelley, Percy Bysshe   409–549

Shepherd, The 763

Shivering in fever, weak and parched to
    sand............................ 661

Siberia 740

Silence 697

Silent, O Moyle, be the roar of thy water 743

Silenus in Proteus 662

Silver key of the fountain of tears 417

Simon Lee 15

Simplon Pass, The 35

Sleep and Poetry 564

So now my summer task is ended, Mary 417

So then, I feel not deeply! if I did 732

So, we'll go no more a roving 246

Soldier, rest! thy warfare o'er 770

Solitary, The 99

Solitary Reaper, The 60

Solitude 677

Some years ago, ere time and taste 753

Song (Coleridge) 191

Song (Hood) 697

Song (Shelley) 438

Song at the Feast of Brougham Castle ... 71

Song, ex Improviso 193

Song of Albert Græme 762

Song of Fionnuala, The 743

Song of the Shirt, The 703

Song of the Stygian Naiades 663

Song of the Western Men, The 685

Song on the Water 663

Song to the Evening Star 671

Song to the Men of England 426

Song Translated from the German of
    Walther von der Vogelweide 662

Sonnet (Shelley) 426

Sonnet (Southey) 783

Soul-cheering Light, most bountiful of
    things 99

Souls of Poets dead and gone 583

Sound, sound the clarion, fill the fife! ... 780

Southey, Robert................ 782–789

Specimen of an Induction to a Poem 560

Spring it is cheery 696

St. Agnes' Eve—Ah, bitter chill it was!. 586

Stanzas (Hood) 707

Stanzas (Keats) 576

Stanzas—April, 1814 514

Stanzas for Music 238, 242

Stanzas from the Ivory Gate 664

Stanzas to Augusta 243, 244

Stanzas Written in Dejection, near Naples 425

Stanzas Written on the Road between
    Florence and Pisa 246

Star that bringest home the bee 671

Stay near me—do not take thy flight ... 51

Stepping Westward 63

Stern Daughter of the Voice of God ... 68

Stop, Christian passer-by!—Stop, child
    of God 193

Story of Rimini, The 708

Strange fits of passion have I known 28

Strew not earth with empty stars 658

Subterranean City 661

Summer Images 681

Summer Vacation 90

Surprised by joy—impatient as the
    Wind 74

Swallow, The 681

Sweet are the omens of approaching
    Spring.......................... 674

Sweet Highland Girl, a very shower ... 60

Sweet Teviot! on thy silver tide 761

Swift as a spirit hastening to his task 506

Swift goes the sooty swallow o'er the
    heath 681

Swiftly walk o'er the western wave 436

Tables Turned, The 18

Talented Man, The 755

Tell me, thou Star, whose wings of light 436

Tell us a story, old Robin Gray! 787

The Assyrian came down like a wolf on
    the fold 242

The awful shadow of some unseen
    Power 415

The breaking waves dashed high 685

The cockchafer hums down the rut-
    rifted lane 682

The day returns, my natal day 730

The flower that smiles to-day 439

The fountains mingle with the river 428

The Frost performs its secret ministry .. 173

The harp that once through Tara's halls 742

The heath this night must be my bed .. 773

The hour is starry, and the airs that stray 664

The isles of Greece, the isles of Greece!. 348

The lamp must be replenish'd, but even
    then 274

The Land we from our fathers had in
    trust 74

The little hedgerow birds 15

The maid I love ne'er thought of me ... 730

The mighty thought of an old world ... 664
The Minstrel Boy to the war is gone 745
The Moon hung naked in a firmament .. 95
The mountain sheep are sweeter 748
The poetry of earth is never dead 559
The stars are with the voyager 697
The sun is warm, the sky is clear 425
The swallow leaves her nest 658
The time I've lost in wooing 745
The toils are pitch'd and the stakes are set 773
The Two Spirits: an Allegory 435
The world is too much with us; late and soon 70
The world's great age begins anew 440
Then no one hears me. O! the world's too loud 659
There be none of Beauty's daughters ... 242
There is a silence where hath been no sound 697
There is a sleepy dusk, an odorous shade 573
There is a yew-tree, pride of Lorton Vale 61
There is an Eminence,—of these our hills 37
There is delight in singing, tho' no one hears 731
There is not in the wide world a valley so sweet 743
There was a Boy: ye knew him well, ye cliffs 17
There was a roaring in the wind all night 55
There was a time when meadow, grove, and stream 63
These Tourists, heaven preserve us! needs must live 38
This Lime-Tree Bower My Prison 147
Thou still unravish'd bride of quietness 594
Though I be now a gray, gray friar 748
Though the day of my destiny's over ... 244
Though veiled in spires of myrtle-wreath 191
Three years she grew in sun and shower 28
Threnody 665
Thus to be lost and thus to sink and die 416
Time Long Past 436
'Tis a strange place, this Limbo!—not a Place 190
'Tis eight o'clock,—a clear March night 18
'Tis not the lily-brow I prize 193
'Tis the last rose of summer 744

'Tis the middle of night by the castle clock 164
'Tis time this heart should be unmoved 247
To —— (Shelley) 435, 438, 439
To —— (Praed) 751
To —— (Wordsworth) 79
To a Butterfly 51
To a Highland Girl 60
To a Skylark (Shelley) 433
To a Skylark (Wordsworth) 80
To a Young Lady 67
To Age 734
To Autumn 597
To Constantia, Singing 416
To Corinth 722
To Fanny 585
To G. A. W. 558
To her couch of evening rest 663
To Jane: The Invitation 441
To Leigh Hunt, Esq. 559
To M. H. 36
To Mary Sinclair, with a Volume of His Poems 672
To my ninth decade I have tottered on .. 734
To My Sister 15
To Night 436
To one who has been long in city pent .. 557
To Robert Browning 731
To Sleep 70
To the Cuckoo 54
To the Daisy 52, 54
To the Grasshopper and the Cricket 712
To the Lords of Convention 'twas Claver'se who spoke 781
To the Rainbow 671
To the Rev. W. L. Bowles 145
To the Same Flower 53
To the Small Celandine 52
To Thomas Moore 246
To Toussaint L'Ouverture 58
T'our tale.—The feast was over, the slaves gone 349
To William Wordsworth (Coleridge) ... 188
To Wordsworth (Shelley) 415
To Youth 732
Toussaint, the most unhappy man of men! 58
Triumph of Life, The 506
Triumphal arch, that fill'st the sky 671
Turning down, goatherd, by the oaks, you'll see........................ 712

Two April Mornings, The   30
'Twas all prepared;—and from the rock   770
'Twas in the prime of summer time   698
'Twas in the year two thousand and one   688
'Twas summer and the sun had mounted
   high   7
Twenty years hence my eyes may grow   730
Two Voices are there; one is of the sea ..   73

Under the lime-tree, on the daisied
   ground   662
Up! up! my Friend, and quit your books   18
Upon a Sabbath-day it fell   591
Upon a time, before the faery broods ...   598

Verse, a breeze mid blossoms straying ..   191
Verses   790
Vicar, The   753
Virgin Mother, thou hast known   756
Vision of Judgment, A (Southey)   787
Vision of Judgment, The (Byron)   350

Waking at morn, with the accustomed
   sigh   714
War-Song of Dinas Vawr, The   748
We Are Seven   16
We are what suns and winds and waters
   make us   719
We do lie beneath the grass   659
We met but in one giddy dance   751
We pledged our hearts, my love and I ..   188
We talked with open heart and tongue ..   31
We walked along, while bright and red   30
Weep, daughter of a royal line   240
Welcome, old friend! These many years   734
Welcome, red and roundy sun   676
Well! If the Bard was weather-wise, who
   made   184
Well, they are gone, and here must I
   remain...........................   147
Well! thou art happy, and I feel   238
Were I to name, out of the times gone by   710
What is there in thee, Moon! that thou
   shouldst move   571
"What, you are stepping westward?"—
   "Yea."   63
When all around grew drear and dark ..   243
When coldness wraps this suffering clay   240
When Contemplation, like the night-
   calm felt   90

When first I made | Once more the cir-
   cuit of our little lake   90
When from the Wanderer's lips these
   words had fallen   100
When I have fears that I may cease to be   584
When maidens such as Hester die   718
When passion's trance is overpast   439
When pride and envy, and the scorn ...   790
When red hath set the beamless sun   763
When Ruth was left half desolate   32
When soft winds and sunny skies   440
When some mad bard sits down to muse   751
When Sorrow moves with silent tread ..   751
When the lamp is shattered   440
When, to the attractions of the busy
   world   37
When we two parted   238
Where are they gone, the old familiar
   faces?   717
Where art thou gone, light-ankled
   Youth?   732
Where art thou, my beloved Son   50
Where is my Chief, my Master, this
   bleak night, mavrone!   737
Where is the grave of Sir Arthur
   O'Kellyn?   190
Where lies the Land to which yon Ship
   must go?   57
Wherein Lies Happiness   569
White, Henry Kirke   789–791
Who is the happy Warrior? Who is he ..   67
Why art thou silent? Is thy love a plant   80
Why did I laugh to-night? No voice
   will tell   585
Why weep ye by the tide, ladie?   780
Why what's the world and time? a
   fleeting thought...................   661
Why, why repine, my pensive friend ...   731
Why, William, on that old grey stone ..   18
William and Helen   776
Wish, A   759
With a Guitar, to Jane   441
With fingers weary and worn   703
With how sad steps, O Moon, thou
   climb'st the sky   57
With little here to do or see   53
With sacrifice before the rising morn ...   75
Wolfe, Charles   791–792
Wood-Cutter's Night Song, The   676
Wordsworth, William   1–140
Work without Hope   191

World's Wanderers, The   436
Written Immediately after Reading the
    Speech of Robert Emmet   785
Written in London, September, 1802   57
Written under the Engraving of a Portrait
    of Rafael   712

Yarrow Unvisited   62
Yarrow Visited   74
Ye Clouds! that far above me float and
    pause   174

Ye little household gods, that make   731
Ye mariners of England   666
Years—years ago—ere yet my dreams . .   754
Yes: I write verses now and then   730
Yes, it was the mountain Echo   71
Yet, hail to you | Moors, mountains,
    headlands, and ye hollow vales   92
Yew-Trees   61
Young Ben he was a nice young man . . .   690
Young Jenny   682
Youth and Age   191